SERENITY FOR EVERY DAY

Presented to

_____

By

_____

Date

_____

Philippians 4:6, 7

SERENITY FOR EVERY DAY

Complete with
New Testament
Psalms & Proverbs

Dr. Robert Hemfelt
and
Dr. Richard Fowler

THOMAS NELSON PUBLISHERS
Nashville

1 2 3 4 5 6 7 8 9 10 11 12 13 14 15 16 17 18 19 20—94 93 92

About the Authors

Dr. Robert Hemfelt is a psychologist and specializes in the treatment of codependency, addictions, and adult-children-of-abuse issues.

Dr. Richard Fowler has a diversified background in education, counseling, and administration, and is presently serving as the director of a Christian counseling clinic in Dallas, Texas.

A Note of Appreciation

The publisher is grateful to A.A. World Services, Inc., for permission to quote briefly from the following sources:

Alcoholics Anonymous Comes of Age: A Brief History of A.A. Copyright ©1957, 1985 by Alcoholics Anonymous Publishing, Inc. (now known as A.A. World Services, Inc.).

Alcoholics Anonymous, Third Edition. Copyright ©1939, 1955, 1976 by Alcoholics Anonymous World Services, Inc.

THE TWELVE STEPS
OF ALCOHOLICS ANONYMOUS*

1. We admitted we were powerless over alcohol—that our lives had become unmanageable.
2. Came to believe that a Power greater than ourselves could restore us to sanity.
3. Made a decision to turn our will and our lives over to the care of God *as we understood Him*.
4. Made a searching and fearless moral inventory of ourselves.
5. Admitted to God, to ourselves, and to another human being the exact nature of our wrongs.
6. Were entirely ready to have God remove all these defects of character.
7. Humbly asked Him to remove our shortcomings.
8. Made a list of all persons we had harmed, and became willing to make amends to them all.
9. Made direct amends to such people wherever possible, except when to do so would injure them or others.
10. Continued to take personal inventory and when we were wrong promptly admitted it.
11. Sought through prayer and meditation to improve our conscious contact with God *as we understood Him*, praying only for knowledge of His will for us and the power to carry that out.
12. Having had a spiritual awakening as the result of these steps, we tried to carry this message to alcoholics, and to practice these principles in all our affairs.

Contents

Books of the New Testament, Psalms, And Proverbs with Their Abbreviations

Publisher's Preface

What are the gods in your life? What is most important to you? Is it your sexuality, money, work, power, alcohol or other drugs, relationships, or activities? Do any of these areas dominate your thinking, your emotions, or your actions? If so, they may represent addictions or dependencies. These dependencies must be addressed, because they hold the potential to shift your life dangerously out of balance. *Serenity for Every Day* can assist you in restoring these addictive and compulsive areas of your life to proper balance and perspective.

Have you come from a difficult or painful family background? A dysfunctional family's emotional legacy is often the foundation of adult addictive personalities. *Serenity for Every Day* may serve as a special guide to you in the recognition and resolution of these old emotional wounds.

You will find within the pages of *Serenity for Every Day* an introduction to the Twelve Steps of recovery, which describes the principles embodied in each step and integrates the Twelve Steps with Scripture. With each step is a listing of recovery meditations and related recovery scriptures, highlighted in the text for easy reference. Of these nearly five hundred related Bible passages, we have focused on three hundred sixty-five, a year's worth of Step-related meditations. Please note that the Step 4 personal inventory (page 38) will be particularly helpful to you as you strive to identify your own areas of addiction, dependency, or codependency.

An additional special feature of *Serenity for Every Day* is a Bible-reading plan called "Daily Encouragement," which suggests a way of reading through the New Testament, Psalms, and Proverbs in a year. Each day's reading is highlighted with a brief "Thought for the New Day." An index to "Daily Encouragement" follows this Preface (page 8).

It is our sincere hope that in reading and meditating on *Serenity for Every Day*, you will begin to see how the God of the Bible speaks directly to your every need. He can liberate you from debilitating addictions and restore you to wholeness, stability, and a perfect relationship with Him.

Daily Encouragement Readings

Following is a plan for reading through the New Testament, Psalms, and Proverbs in a year. Each day's reading features a brief "Thought for the New Day" to encourage you in your spiritual growth.

Where to Go for Additional Help

Serenity for Every Day contains a wealth of material that you will find useful for your spiritual healing and growth, but we recognize that there are other avenues you may also wish to pursue. You may want to explore professional psychotherapy, pastoral counseling, or membership in a Twelve Step program. Following is a list of some of the many groups available to you. You may obtain a more complete listing through a large church in your area, by checking the white pages of your telephone directory, or by working through your library's reference specialists.

Alcoholics Anonymous
P.O. Box 459
Grand Central Station
New York, NY 10163
(212) 686-1100

Al-Anon/Alateen Family Group
  Headquarters, Inc.
P.O. Box 182
Madison Square Station
New York, NY 10159
1-800-356-9996
(212) 302-7240

Debtors Anonymous
314 W. 53rd St.
New York, NY 10019
(212) 969-0710

Incest Survivors Anonymous
P.O. Box 5613
Long Beach, CA 90800

Overcomers Outreach
2290 W. Whittier Blvd.
Suite D
La Habra, CA 90631
(213) 697-3994
    (Alcoholics and Adult Children
    Claiming Christ's
    Promises and Accepting His
    Healing)

Adult Children of Alcoholics,
  Central Service Board
P.O. Box 35623
Los Angeles, CA 90035
(213) 464-4423

National Clearinghouse for
  Alcohol Information
P.O. Box 1908
Rockville, MD 20850

Gamblers Anonymous
P.O. Box 17173
Los Angeles, CA 90017
(213) 386-8789

Narcotics Anonymous,
World Service Office
16155 Wyandotte St.
Van Nuys, CA 91406
(818) 780-3951

National Association for
Children of Alcoholics
31582 Coast Highway
Suite B
South Laguna, CA 92677
(714) 499-3889

Emotions Anonymous
P.O. Box 4245
St. Paul, MN 55104
(612) 647-9712
(international)
(612) 738-9099 (Twin Cities)

Overeaters Anonymous,
World Service Office
2190 190th St.
Torrance, CA 90504
(213) 542-8363

The following organizations exist also. You may wish to seek them out locally.

Adult Children
Anonymous
Al-Atot
Alcoholics Victorious
(Christian recovery
support group)
Bulimics/Anorexics
Anonymous
Child Abusers Anonymous
Cocaine Anonymous
Codependents of Sex
Addicts

Parents Anonymous
Pills Anonymous
Sex Addicts Anonymous
Sexaholics Anonymous
Sex and Love Addicts
Anonymous
Shoplifters Anonymous
Smokers Anonymous
Spenders Anonymous
Victims of Incest Can
Emerge
Workaholics Anonymous

For additional reading in the area of recovery, see these books available from Thomas Nelson Publishers:

The Path to Serenity: The Book of Spiritual Growth and Personal Change Through Twelve-Step Recovery. A walk through the Twelve Steps of recovery that puts Jesus Christ back into the center of the process.

Imperative People: Those Who Must Be in Control. A self-evaluation process for determining your level of imperativeness, with specific ways to overcome imperative behavior.

The Lies We Believe. How to break down the barriers that are keeping you from the truth and defeat the lies that you've learned from others.

The Truths We Must Believe. Provides twelve timeless principles that will maximize your emotional health, happiness, confidence, peace, and joy.

Love Is a Choice: Recovery for Codependent Relationships. The successful ten-stage process to recovery from codependency, introducing a new dimension: the important stage of seeing God's unconditional love as the answer to your hunger for love.

Love Is a Choice Workbook. Based on the recovery principles from *Love Is a Choice.*

Love Hunger: Recovery from Food Addiction. Combines the experience of psychiatrists, counselors, and dietitians in the first book for compulsive overeaters, with a ten-stage life plan for your body, mind, and soul.

Love Hunger Weight-Loss Workbook. A twelve-week life plan for body, mind, and soul.

The Blessing. We all need "the blessing"—the knowledge that someone in this world loves and accepts us unconditionally. This book teaches in a step-by-step manner how to *be* a blessing and how to pass that life-changing blessing on to your parents, spouse, children, and friends.

Serenity Meditation™ Series:

Day by Day Love Is a Choice: Daily Devotions for Codependents.

Food for the Hungry Heart: Daily Devotions for Overeaters.

A Walk with the Serenity Prayer: Daily Devotions for People in Recovery.

Setting New Boundaries: Daily Devotions for Those in Recovery.

Serenity for Every Day
An Introduction

That you have picked up *Serenity for Every Day* probably means that you or someone you love is already involved in or considering joining a Twelve Step program of recovery. We embark on recovery as a means of seeking freedom from any one or more of a number of addictive agents. Addictive agents are those persons or things on which we form an excessive dependency. The catalog of addictive agents includes:

1) Alcohol or drugs
2) Work, achievement, and success
3) Money addictions, such as overspending, gambling, hoarding
4) Control addictions, especially if they surface in personal, sexual, family, and business relationships
5) Food addictions
6) Sexual addictions
7) Approval dependency (the need to please people)
8) Rescuing patterns toward other persons
9) Dependency on toxic relationships (relationships that are damaging and hurtful)
10) Physical illness (hypochondria)
11) Exercise and physical conditioning
12) Cosmetics, clothes, cosmetic surgery, trying to look good on the outside
13) Academic pursuits and excessive intellectualizing
14) Religiosity or religious legalism (preoccupation with the form and the rules and regulations of religion, rather than benefiting from the real spiritual message)
15) General perfectionism
16) Cleaning and avoiding contamination and other obsessive-compulsive symptoms
17) Organizing, structuring (the need always to have everything in its place)
18) Materialism

Most of us can see ourselves somewhere in this list. And all of us can benefit from the truths that emerge from Twelve Step recovery, because all of us are, to some degree, codependent. What does that mean? We define codependency as being an effort to control interior feelings by manipulating people, things, and events on the outside. Much of the need to do this arises from our own childhoods—from the experiences we have had in our own families of origin. Perhaps our most basic needs for love and nurturing were not met in those early family encounters. Or we may have been smothered by overzealous caretakers who did not allow us to mature emotionally, spiritually, and mentally. Such dysfunctional families, whether they involved open or veiled abuse, may be the original source of our codependent pain. This early codependent vacuum becomes the root of our later adult addictions.

Our loss of closeness within our own families may extend to a feeling of alienation from a second important family—the spiritual family. We may not feel comfortable with God as Father and may feel a lack of acceptance from those who should be our brothers and sisters in God's family. After all, if we cannot experience healthy, loving relationships within our own families, why should God or people on the outside love and care for us?

Therefore, our healing must progress across several dimensions:

1) We have to heal our human relationships, and that means healing both the past painful memories from the dysfunctional family of origin and our contemporary relationships as well.

2) We must choose a recovery family. This can be a support group, a Twelve Step group, or a church community, but we need a new, healthy chosen family.

3) We need to rejoin and grow closer to God in the spiritual family. Both the church and recovery groups, such as Alcoholics Anonymous, Overeaters Anonymous, and Emotions Anonymous, support us in this growth.

It is critical that we heal our dependencies, not only for ourselves but also for the sake of our children. Psychologists believe that codependency is a love hunger that can be transmitted from generation to generation. Emotionally dysfunctional families beget codependent adult children, who then create their own dysfunctional families and beget more dysfunctional children.

There are healing solutions to this love hunger. Both the Twelve Steps and the Bible speak to the human hunger and neediness that result from codependency— hunger that is emotional and spiritual in nature. To appreciate the biblical foundations of the Twelve Steps, review with us the history of this approach to healing.

History of the Twelve Steps

Twelve Step programs were born in the mid-1930s with the establishment of the first program, Alcoholics Anonymous. Alcoholics Anonymous was adapted from a Christian revival organization referred to as the Oxford Group. Let us take a moment to trace the spiritual lineage of the Oxford Group and A.A.

All of the movements of the church beginning with Peter and Paul and the other apostles had as their goal a spiritual awakening or renewal. This was true through the various monastic movements, the Protestant Reformation, and the Oxford Movement of the early 1800s. It was true, also, of the Oxford Group (originally called "A First Century Christian Fellowship"), an evangelistic movement in the 1900s, out of which the Twelve Steps grew. Both the Oxford Group and the Twelve Steps have at their hearts the desire to take a healing message to people caught in unwholesome life-styles.

Dr. Frank Buchman, a Lutheran minister of Pennsylvania Dutch stock, was the founder of the Oxford Group. This was the parent group of Alcoholics Anonymous, which, in turn, is the source of the Twelve Step recovery process.

While attending the 1908 Keswick Convention in England, Buchman had an experience that changed his life. Bearing resentments and feelings of ill will toward the official board of a hospice he had established and from which he had been compelled to resign because of differences with those board members, he entered a little church in Cumberland. His pride and anger had prevented his serving as a Christian minister should. Suddenly, in that church, through a woman's talk about the Power of Christ's redemption, he envisioned the suffering face of the crucified Christ. In that moment, he realized what a distance his resentments had placed between himself and God's unconditional love. Spiritually transformed, he was filled with an intense feeling of life as he surrendered his will and willfulness to God. The Oxford principles of surrender, restitution, and sharing were founded on his personal experience of spiritual conversion.

Later, Dr. Buchman worked with the YMCA in Pennsylvania and conducted evangelistic work in China. He gained some following through a series of revivals at Princeton, Yale, Harvard, Williams, Smith, and Vassar, and kindred groups arose in Oxford and in other schools in England. Although Dr. Buchman and his following were later banned from Princeton and some of the other campuses, the Group continued to reach out to the suffering through house meetings, which included testimonies, personal witness, Bible study, and informal talks. Members were encouraged to find and work with persons who suffered from problems similar to their own; for example, recovering alcoholics were encouraged to minister to others who suffered from alcohol dependencies. The use of attention-getting, easy-to-remember, easy-to-repeat slogans also became common in Group circles.

Bill Wilson, the founder of Alcoholics Anonymous, traced his journey to sobriety through the Oxford Group. In November 1934, while he was still a practicing alcoholic, Bill was visited by an old friend, Ebby Thatcher, who had been restored to sobriety through the Oxford Group. One month later, while in a hospital undergoing treatment for alcoholism, Bill was again visited by Mr. Thatcher, at which time the principles of the Group were explained. Twenty years later, Bill Wilson described his conversion experience that night in this way:

My depression deepened unbearably and finally it seemed to me as though I were at the very bottom of the pit. I still gagged badly at the notion of a Power greater than myself, but finally, just for the moment, the last vestige of my proud obstinacy was crushed. All at once I found myself crying out, "If there is a God, let Him show Himself! I am ready to do anything, anything!"

Suddenly, the room lit up with a great white light. I was caught up into an ecstasy which there are no words to describe. It seemed to me, in the mind's eye, that I was on a mountain and that a wind not of air but of spirit was blowing. And then it burst upon me that I was a free man. Slowly the ecstasy subsided. I lay on the bed, but now for a time I was in another world, a new world of consciousness. All about me and through me there was a wonderful feeling of Presence, and I thought to myself, "So this is the God of the preachers!" A great peace stole over me and I thought, "No matter how wrong things seem to be, they are still all right. Things are all right with God and His world."

> (*Alcoholics Anonymous Comes of Age: A Brief History of A.A.*, p. 63)

For the next three years, Bill Wilson pursued his recovery through the Oxford Group, which emphasized the following:

1) Complete deflation (of false pride)

2) Dependence and guidance from a Higher Power

3) Moral inventory

4) Confession

5) Restitution

6) Continued work with other suffering persons

In the meantime, during a business trip to Akron, Ohio, Bill experienced a strong urge to drink. Fearing he was going to relapse, he began calling churches and asking if there was an alcoholic in that town with whom he could talk. He knew, as a principle of his Oxford Group activity, that he could only retain his recovery if he were actively involved in helping others like himself. The man with whom he was finally linked was Dr. Bob Smith, an alcoholic surgeon. They first met in May 1935, and Bill shared his own life story and his newfound spiritual realization that if he persisted in his drinking, he would either go mad or die. They talked night after night. Dr. Bob finally began to share frankly with his new friend. After ten days of sobriety that ended in one final binge, Dr. Bob had his last drink on June 10 of that same year. Many people point to this date as the actual founding of Alcoholics Anonymous, although it would not be known by that name for another four years.

In August of 1937, Wilson broke away from the Oxford Group because certain alcoholics had trouble with its rather aggressive evangelism. A large percentage of them were Catholics and were prohibited by Canon Law from becoming affiliated with religious movements outside the church. Also, Frank Buchman had assumed a controversial political stance, from which Wilson wanted to distance himself.

Despite this organizational break, the Oxford Group and the Scriptures remained the foundation for much of Alcoholics Anonymous and the Twelve Steps used in recovery programs today. For example, the tradition of sharing and story-telling that was common in the house meetings of the Oxford Group is perpetuated in A.A. and other recovery group meetings today. Also, no Oxford Group member was ever allowed to appear alone or represent the group as a whole. Likewise in A.A., there is no leader, no president, no representative for the group.

Today tens of millions of Americans suffer from dependency problems, ranging from chemical addiction to sexual compulsivity; and additionally, over 100 million live in families with or are codependently related to these dependent individuals. Recovery is possible. Approximately 15 million persons are actively involved in 500,000 recovery groups, such as Alcoholics Anonymous, Al-Anon, Emotions Anonymous, and Overeaters Anonymous.

For more insight into each of the Twelve Steps that have helped millions battle their addictions, continue reading. You'll discover, too, where to find recovery meditations and related passages, highlighted throughout the Bible text.

*We admitted we were powerless over our
dependencies—that our lives had become unmanageable.*

Admitting powerlessness runs contrary to many of our cultural
messages that say, "Be strong! Be the master of your own destiny!" The
admission of powerlessness also conflicts with the addictive message,
because the addiction itself will tell us, "You have a high tolerance!
Use more of me! You can handle it!"

Nevertheless, the central paradox of Step 1 is that the admission
of complete defeat permits a life-transforming victory through
recovery. The admission of powerlessness over an addiction actually
becomes the foundation for the strength to eventually overcome the
dependency.

Admitting powerlessness is absolutely essential to breaking the
addiction cycle, which is made up of five points:

1) Pain

2) Reaching out to an addictive agent, such as work,
   food, sex, alcohol, or dependent relationships to
   salve our pain

3) Temporary anaesthesia

4) Negative consequences

5) Shame and guilt, which result in more pain or low
   self-esteem

For example, the workaholic who has low self-esteem (pain)
begins to overwork (addictive agent), which results in praise, success,
and achievement (relief). However, as a rule, family relationships and

his personal relationship with God suffer terribly because of preoccupation with work (negative consequences). The result is an even greater sense of shame and guilt because of inadequacies, both real and imagined, which brings him back to point 1 in the addiction cycle. Now the workaholic feels compelled to work even harder to overcome his guilt.

Understanding the addiction cycle is important because it helps explain why for both the Oxford Group and for Bill Wilson (see "Serenity for Every Day: An Introduction"), the admission of powerlessness is the first step to recovery. Otherwise, we remain caught. If we rely on willpower alone, then the only thing we know to do is to escalate our addiction to get out of the pain. Step 1 calls us to do less—to yield, to surrender, to let go.

Two factors that keep the addiction cycle spinning are 1) the fear of withdrawal and 2) denial.

First, in order to take Step 1, we have to move beyond the fear of stepping off the addiction cycle. We may fear withdrawal and the pain that goes with it. Doctors historically thought that withdrawal in drug addiction was mainly biochemical and physical. It is true that when the heroin addict stops taking heroin, for example, the mind and body literally rebel as they struggle to restore balance. However, addictionologists now believe that the emotional and spiritual components of withdrawal from any addiction are of far greater significance than the physiological dimensions. The workaholic, for example, goes through withdrawal when he tries to scale back work activities. The real fear in this case is probably the emotional fear of losing control. The paradox of Step 1 is that the act of surrendering addictive control will actually bring us back into a state of healthy control.

Second, we have to break out of denial about our addictions. Denial is a cloak of self-deception that blinds us and shields us from an honest assessment of our own dependencies. Some of the common denial messages with which we may delude ourselves are: "I can stop any time I want to." "Things aren't that bad." "I only practice my addiction because I want to." "When things get better (or worse!), I'll stop my addiction." We may even project blame onto someone else, saying, "You make me do what I do!" All of these messages deny the force the addictions impose on our lives.

Breaking out of denial often requires a painful encounter with the consequences of our addictions, called "hitting bottom." "Hitting bottom" forces us to admit our powerlessness over our addictive lifestyles. The three major "bottoms" we may hit are:

1) A physical bottom

2) An emotional bottom

3) A spiritual bottom

Common specific examples of "bottoms" that precipitate recovery include:

1) A marital crisis

2) A physical health crisis (as in the case of the workaholic who suffers a heart attack)

3) Confrontation by a family member or loved one

4) Vocational or life-purpose crisis (a pink slip that forces one to look at one's addiction)

5) A financial crisis

6) A spiritual crisis, a feeling of alienation from God

The addiction cycle, as a rule, cannot be broken without yielding to a Power outside ourselves. We may have to surrender again and again, as we admit our powerlessness over, not only the primary addiction, but over various other aspects of our lives. We must recognize when we are powerless over people, places, and situations and learn to let those things go. For example, when we are caught in freeway traffic, instead of allowing anxiety and anger to build, we need to admit that we cannot alter our situation. In even the most trivial issues we face, we must learn to become flexible. We may also find ourselves switching addictions or transferring obsessions, and we will need to apply the first step to these new dependencies as well.

For codependents, control or the lack of it, is central to every aspect of life. As we admit our powerlessness, we embark upon the antidote for our control addiction, an addiction characterized by extremes of both overcontrol and undercontrol. For example, the workaholic may overcontrol efforts to achieve and accomplish. What tends to be undercontrolled is the quality of spiritual life and the investment of time and emotional intimacy with family members. By admitting powerlessness, he opens the door to allow God to create a healthy, new balance in which he can lessen the compulsive control exercised in the work arena. He can then begin to experience greater positive control over his contribution to family relationships and his creation of quality private time.

We should not be fearful that powerlessness will result in passivity. On the contrary, to admit powerlessness is to subordinate our human wills to God's will so that we can become the most effective and potent instruments we were created to be.

STEP 1
Recovery Meditations

To help you understand what the Scriptures say about
admitting the unmanageability of our lives,
see the recovery meditations on the following passages:

Related Recovery Scriptures Highlighted in the Text

Came to believe that a Power greater than ourselves
could restore us to sanity.

The Step 2 phrase "came to believe" suggests a process and a progression of faith that evolves over time. A portion of A.A.'s oral tradition defines this as a three-part unfolding: First, *we came*, that is, we showed up and stumbled in the door. Second, *we came to*, that is, we sobered up, came to our senses, and began to experience emotional sobriety. Third, *we came to believe*. We began our real recovery process and our spiritual growth. This style of spiritual growth closely parallels the strong Christian tradition that each person must come to an individual knowledge of God.

Step 2 is a logical outgrowth of Step 1 because, if in Step 1, we have admitted our own powerlessness, then the next step is to seek a new source of strength or power to take charge for us and to make us sane (well and whole). For some people, spiritual conversion is dramatic as it was for the apostle Paul on the road to Damascus (Acts 9). For most, however, it is very gradual. As one grows and matures emotionally, one also grows spiritually.

Before we can welcome in a new Power to restore us to wellness, we will probably have to engage in some emotional and spiritual "housecleaning":

1) We must bring into abstinence or balance all the addictive agents through which we have sought to meet our deepest needs. Money, sex, career, chemicals, anything and everything about which we have become excessive, must be put into proper perspective—not lifted onto a pedestal to be worshiped.

2) We must transcend the god of reason if we have been worshiping God through an exclusively intellectual approach.

3) We must renounce the tendency to play God ourselves. We must grow beyond selfishness, narcissism, and grandiosity.

4) We must also renounce putting other people or human institutions in the roles of gods.

Not only must we be rid of false gods, if we are looking to the Judeo-Christian God as our higher Power, but we may also need to overcome old sources of bitterness toward Him:

1) We may have identified God with an abusive parent.

2) We may have had negative experiences with the church (hypocrisy, bigotry, condemnation).

3) We may be struggling with a sense that God has failed us—that He has allowed us to become codependent.

4) We may be angry that God has not instantaneously healed us of our addictive illnesses.

As we commit ourselves to a lifetime of recovery, our starting point may be our recovery literature. And that literature makes a valuable contribution toward the opening of spiritual doors. But if we really want to fill the void, if we really want to break down the barriers hindering our progress, we need to turn to the ultimate source of God's Word and discover what the Scriptures have to tell us. By exploring the Bible, we will learn more about God, we will draw closer to Him, and we will discover more about His will for us.

STEP 2
Recovery Meditations

To help you understand what the Scriptures say about
God's power to restore us to wholeness,
see the recovery meditations on the
following passages:

Related Recovery Scriptures Highlighted in the Text

STEP 3

*Made a decision to turn our will and our lives
over to the care of God **as we understood Him.***

Step 3 culminates a process begun in Steps 1 and 2. In Step 1, we
admitted our lives were out of control and that we were powerless to
change things through our own power. In Step 2, we renounced every
old god we had been worshiping as powerless to save us and looked to
a higher Power to restore us to wholeness. In Step 3, we recognize God
as that higher Power and ask Him to assume control over and care of
every aspect of our lives.

A common recovery phrase used in Twelve Step groups is "Turn it
over." For the recovering person, that means turning over to God's
care not only the major, conspicuous addictions like alcoholism. It
means turning over every aspect of life, even the small frustrations
involved in handling children or trying to make a faulty appliance
work or dealing with congested freeway traffic. In the face of these irritations,
the recovering person will say time and time again, "Turn it over; turn it
over; turn it over."

A Step 3 recovery paradox is that codependent or addictive
personalities are often quite willful and egocentric, and yet that
egocentricity often camouflages a deep sense of insecurity. In A.A.'s
oral tradition, an alcoholic or codependent is defined as being "an
egomaniac with an inferiority complex." Step 3 invites us to get out of
the center of our universe and hand that place back to God. As we
move into any addiction or dependency, we tend to become more self-
centered, self-absorbed, and self-preoccupied in trying to address the
pain driving the addiction. Paradoxically, this self-preoccupation only
draws us more deeply into the addiction. We become more self-
centered and self-preoccupied as we seek to address the pain, yet self-
preoccupation itself creates more pain, loneliness, and isolation. The
addiction pulls us more deeply into its pain cycle. In order to
surmount the pain cycle, ultimately we must step out of ourselves and
look beyond ourselves.

Breaking out of this bondage of self does not mean we ignore or deny our needs. In fact, quite the reverse is true. If we can discover healthy, God-directed ways to meet our emotional and physical needs, then we become less needy, less selfish, less self-preoccupied individuals. This is another recovery paradox. Discovering what our needs are and asking to have those needs met may be one of the most *unselfish* things we do. All of us have needs, and all of us have choices as to how those needs are to be met. Addictions, compulsions, and codependencies are counterfeit means of trying to meet our most basic physical, emotional, and spiritual hungers. With God's help we can find genuine ways of satisfying them.

We want to turn ourselves over to God, but how? How do we get out of the driver's seat? The key is *willingness*. If we crack the door just a little bit, then God will direct us in the process. Revelation 3:20 says: "Behold, I stand at the door and knock. If anyone hears My voice and opens the door, I will come in to him and dine with him, and he with Me."

A.A.'s Third Step Prayer is an excellent way to formalize our commitment to this new willingness:

> God, I offer myself to Thee—to build with me and to do with me as Thou wilt. Relieve me of the bondage of self, that I may better do Thy will. Take away my difficulties, that victory over them may bear witness to those I would help of Thy power, Thy love, and Thy way of life. May I do Thy will always!
> (*Alcoholics Anonymous*, p. 63)

STEP 3
Recovery Meditations

To help you understand what the Scriptures
say about surrendering your will and life to God,
see the recovery meditations on the
following passages:

Related Recovery Scriptures Highlighted in the Text

STEP 4

Made a searching and fearless moral inventory of ourselves.

A personal inventory is crucial to understanding the new direction of our spiritual growth. What aspects of our character do we need to retain and emphasize, and what should be modified or discarded? Six components that might go into such an inventory are described in the following paragraphs.

First, we may need to "tell our stories." This can be accomplished by journaling, that is, by writing out our stories, and by sharing them with others in recovery meetings or private dialogue. In John 4, there is a beautiful passage on "The Woman at the Well." When the Samaritan woman encountered Jesus, she was amazed, first of all, that He had anything to do with her. Jews generally had no dealings with Samaritans. Second, He told her that He knew everything about her—the full story of her life—that she had had five husbands and that she was then living with a man who was not her husband. The fact that Jesus, with full knowledge of her life story, accepted her and loved her unconditionally was a life-transforming experience.

Preparing our stories allows us to assess the major events of our lives. Knowing the steps of our past journey helps us to evaluate honestly our present situations. Sharing our stories may enable others to better understand us and may open new avenues through which they can touch and heal our lives.

A second component in our inventory is discovering the roots of our addictions and codependencies. In most cases, this means we have to examine our childhoods. What needs were not met there? What negative experiences or messages about ourselves did we absorb in the dysfunctional family of origin? There are six types of family of origin dysfunction that can generate or create a later adult addiction or codependency:

1) *Active abuse*. A parent's pain or frustration is discharged against or projected onto the child. Any form of direct physical, verbal, or sexual abuse can be classified as active abuse.

2) *Passive abuse*. Passive abuse occurs when key elements are missing within the family. A child growing up needs fifteen to twenty years of steady, consistent loving from two sane, sober, relatively happy parents. A child requires time, attention, and affection. Anything, such as workaholism, that hinders or limits the parents' ability to give these things can result in passive abuse.

3) *Emotional incest*. Typically, in families where one or both parents are in some way emotionally or physically disabled, a young child will begin to assume parental or spousal responsibilities toward the parent. For example, if seven-year-old Suzie's mother is alcoholic, Suzie may begin getting herself up for school, fixing her own breakfast, and urging her mother out of bed in the afternoon to keep peace with Daddy. Suzie is becoming a mother to her own mother.

4) *Unfinished business*. If parents have not made peace with the disillusionments, defects, or limitations in their own lives, the child may pick up their unfinished business. A father who is frustrated and unsuccessful in his work may push his sons and daughters to be compulsive, perfectionistic, and workaholic in order to compensate for his own limitations.

5) *Negative messages about who and what the child is*. These are spoken and experienced messages that destroy feelings of self-worth and become part of the child's personality. Examples of spoken messages are: "You'll never amount to anything." "Can't you do anything right?" "Don't you realize how unhappy you have made me?" An experienced message is felt by the child whose father spends an excessive amount of time with his work and little or no time with the child.

6) *Split-off feelings or needs*. In dysfunctional families, members

deny their feelings and bury their needs. These needs will later try to assert themselves, but may do so in very damaging ways. For example, a wife who assumes a passive role and buries her needs to be assertive in marriage may eventually become passive-aggressive and take out her anger by abusing credit cards and overspending.

Learning what was damaged or missing in our childhoods is not an attempt to blame the previous generation. Rather, it is a genuine effort to understand the deepest root causes that underlie our compulsive adult behaviors.

Third, we must confront and assess the full extent of our dependencies. Doing so, we will learn more about the severity of our primary addictions, and we may uncover other peripheral addictions we had not previously recognized. We should inventory and identify all of these codependent symptoms and addictions, which have manifested themselves in our adolescent and adult lives. As we perform our fourth step inventory, we must be certain to identify all of the possible addictions affecting our lives. (See page 17, "Serenity for Every Day: An Introduction," for a listing of possible addictions.)

Fourth, we need to look back at our relationship history with the people who have been significant in our lives—parents, teachers, mentors, friends, romantic interests. We need to inventory all the ways we have hurt them and hurt ourselves by practicing our adult addictions and codependencies. This is a step toward ridding our lives of resentments and guilt.

Resentments, which arise out of fear and insecurity, may lie behind much of the hurt we have inflicted on others and on ourselves. As part of this fourth inventory component, we must first acknowledge our resentments and then identify the fears and insecurities that underlie them. Only in this manner can we deal effectively with these resentments that will otherwise fester like emotional cancers.

Fifth, we must address our guilt feelings. We realize that most addictions are shame-based and shame-propelled. To move beyond this shame-base, we need to distinguish between two major forms of guilt:

1) *False shame, or carried shame*. This is undeserved blame that we have taken upon ourselves for people or situations over which we may have had no control. Adult children of dysfunctional families often carry an enormous residue of false guilt for their parents' dysfunctions.

2) *Authentic guilt*. As adults and sinners, we have probably hurt many people in many ways. We have caused this hurt through things we have said, through things we have done, and through things we have left undone.

We need to distinguish between these two types of guilt, handing back the false shame and recognizing those areas of authentic guilt for which we do need to ask forgiveness.

Sixth, we must "look for the good." An important counterbalancing dimension is that a Step 4 inventory should include the positive, as well as the negative, things about us. 1) What positive legacies have we derived from our childhood and adolescence? 2) What positive survival mechanisms have emerged from our struggles to cope? For example, the compulsive, overachieving student may possess the positive legacies of being a good academician with strong job skills. 3) What are our skills, talents, gifts, and attributes? 4) What positive permissions have we granted to ourselves (permission to live, permission to be healthy, permission to recover, permission to experience relative happiness in adult life)? 5) What positive recovery steps and changes are currently being implemented in our lives?

NOTE: Perhaps, in taking our inventories, we have now uncovered certain addictions or dependencies we did not previously recognize. If so, we may need to return to Step 1 to address these.

STEP 4
Recovery Meditations

To help you understand what the Scriptures say
about the personal inventorying of our lives,
see the recovery meditations on the
following passages:

Related Recovery Scriptures Highlighted in the Text

STEP 5

*Admitted to God, to ourselves, and to another human being
the exact nature of our wrongs.*

This may be one of the most challenging steps we face in our recovery process, but it can also be one of the most fulfilling in terms of removing us from our isolation. In order to accomplish Step 5, the three-part sharing it endorses must take place. That is, all of what we discovered about ourselves in our Step 4 inventory is to be freely admitted to God, to ourselves, and to another human being.

There are basically five types of wrongs we should share:

1) We need to acknowledge all of our addictions.

2) We need to acknowledge what went wrong in our families of origin to initiate our codependent love hungers.

3) We need to acknowledge the multi-generational wrongs that may have led to our family of origin situations. We need to understand and be compassionate toward the families our parents emerged from.

4) We need to acknowledge the wrongs that have occurred in all major relationships in our lives.

5) We need to acknowledge the specific ways in which we have wronged others by the practice of our addictions.

Because these areas are so sensitive and so very personal, it is important to exercise care in choosing the person or persons with whom we formally share our fifth step. Such individuals should be trustworthy and somewhat detached from the situations about which we will share. For example, one would not usually call on a spouse or immediate family member to hear this confession. In fact, it is quite common to choose a therapist or pastoral counselor for this purpose. Also, such individuals should be compassionate, not condemning.

Four very positive things happen in Step 5 sharing:

1) Our shame is reduced through confession. We know that confession is an ancient tradition in Christianity and that it is an indispensable ingredient in the healing and renewal process.

44

2) Step 5 sharing allows us to express our grief—to expel the resentments, the anger, the fears that eat away at us and keep us from living life to the fullest.

3) We take a major step toward honesty. Perhaps the single greatest barrier to recovery is the inability to be honest. In Step 5 sharing, maybe for the first time in our lives, we open our deepest, darkest secrets and most private hurts to another human being.

4) Addictions, by their very nature, isolate us from other people and from God. Step 5 sharing breaks down the barriers we have erected through our addictions.

Step 5 sharing is the beginning of the end of our isolation.

STEP 5
Recovery Meditations

To help you understand what the Scriptures
say about confession's role in our recovery,
see the recovery meditations on the
following passages:

Related Recovery Scriptures Highlighted in the Text

*Were entirely ready to have God
remove all these defects of character.*

A major question that arises at this point is, <u>Are we genuinely *willing*
to ask God to remove *all* of our addictions and dependencies</u>? We may
be forced into recovery by the sheer pain of a primary addiction, such
as alcoholism, and we may genuinely desire freedom from that
addiction. However, we may have other more subtle dependencies
that, in a way, we still enjoy and want to cling to. For example, an
alcoholic may ask God to remove his addiction to alcohol, but remain
in denial about his compulsive overeating. Perhaps his eating has not
yet cast him into much trouble, and so he is reluctant to surrender that
compulsion. In fact, he may lean on it even more heavily in the
absence of the alcohol. So this is the real struggle in Step 6: Are we
entirely ready to ask God to remove *all* of our defects, even the ones to
which we cling tenaciously?

It is important to realize that we may be blind to some of our flaws.
The ones that have forced us into recovery are probably obvious, but
we may have to search to recognize others. Therefore, we must be
sensitive to God's guidance and to feedback from significant people
around us. Are they seeing certain patterns in our lives that we cannot
see?

Looking back at the relationship inventory we conducted in Step
4 for *recurrent patterns* may be helpful in identifying these character
defects. For example, when we review our relationship history, do we
realize that in every important, intimate relationship, we "had to" be
the passive, subservient partner? A pattern that surfaces over and over
again hints at a character defect. This defect may be either or both of
the relationship extremes of passivity or aggression. We should also
examine the boundaries we set between ourselves and other persons.
Are the boundaries too fragile? Can people spill into our lives in
destructive ways? Or are our boundaries too thick? Are we too well

defended? Do we keep people too far away? Finally, do we see and respect the boundaries of others?

We must be *specific* in our identification of *individual* defects of character, and we must be specific about the changes required to recover from them. One cure does not fit all! The approach for addressing one addiction may not work at all for another. For instance, the rageaholic may need to reduce anger expression. Conversely, the anger phobic person, who has no permission to feel or experience anger, may need to mobilize anger expression and assertiveness. The treatment has to be very specifically tailored to the defect and to the person.

As a rule, most defects of character involve some imbalance in the expression of and the experience of our most basic human needs. For example, sexuality and ambition are not bad unless our experiences of those drives are imbalanced or codependent. If we are addicted to sex or driven by ambition to the point of workaholism, these expressions have become defects we must address. Our sixth step prayers would not be "Make me asexual" or "Take away my ambition." Rather, we might pray, "Grant me a healthy expression of my sexuality" or "Channel my ambition into enhancing my private life as well as my work life."

As we hold known defects of character up to God, we must avoid self-shaming and self-condemnation. The goal here is spiritual release, not spiritual self-punishment. For most of us, this process is ongoing. We will not be healed and sent forward immediately; rather, recovery will be a daily effort to evaluate, balance, and adjust the healthy expression of all of our God-given needs.

STEP 6
Recovery Meditations

To help you understand what the Scriptures
say about willingness to yield our character
defects to God, see the recovery meditations
on the following passages:

Related Recovery Scriptures Highlighted in the Text

Humbly asked Him to remove our shortcomings.

Steps 6 and 7 overlap in emphasizing the significance of God's intervention in addressing our character defects. While Step 6 focuses on our *willingness* to yield these flaws to God, Step 7 centers on the *humility* with which we should approach Him. It is very important that we not confuse *humility* with *humiliation*. God does not want to mortify us. He does want us to submit to Him.

We need humility for three reasons:

1) *So that we can recognize the severity of our character defects.* One aspect of our addictions is that we tend to deny and minimize the pain they inflict. Therefore, as we try to assess our character defects, we may, unless we take a very humble approach, underestimate their severity.

2) *So that we can acknowledge the limits of human power in addressing these character defects.* We cannot do it on our own. We cannot do it by sheer willpower. We cannot do it by our own intellect and reasoning.

3) *So that we can appreciate the enormity of God's power to transform lives.*

The invitation to humility is not an invitation to low self-esteem or a negative self-image. In fact, quite the reverse is true. Poor self-esteem may be camouflaged by a superficial sense of false pride and by a resistance to God's intervention. In contrast, if we have healthy self-esteem, we are freed to come out from behind our haughty masks and to receive and appreciate God's greatness. When our self-esteem has been restored to a proper state of balance, we are able to comfortably humble ourselves before Him.

In order for us to experience life-changing humility, however, we must be aware that 1) what we accomplish, amass, or achieve materially will never bring us true contentment or the satisfaction of our innermost spiritual hunger; and 2) surrender to God's leadership cannot occur until we acknowledge our own limitations and need for His guidance. We must surrender the leadership role to God.

Although Step 7 is the shortest step in terms of wording and is perhaps the least discussed in recovery groups, it is probably the most potent of the twelve. It embodies the miracle of transformation as we turn over to God our broken, defective personalities in order that He might mold them into healthy, effective instruments of His will. A.A.'s Seventh Step Prayer words this commitment as follows:

> My Creator, I am now willing that you should have all of me, good and bad. I pray that you now remove from me every single defect of character which stands in the way of my usefulness to you and my fellows. Grant me strength, as I go out from here, to do your bidding. Amen.

(*Alcoholics Anonymous*, p. 76)

STEP 7
Recovery Meditations

To help you understand what the Scriptures say
about the importance of asking God to
remove our shortcomings, see the recovery
meditations on the following passages:

Related Recovery Scriptures Highlighted in the Text

*Made a list of all persons we had harmed,
and became willing to make amends to them all.*

Step 8 is the more specific person-to-person application of the shame-reduction that was begun in Steps 4 and 5. The making of amends was a very strong tradition among the members of the Oxford Group, which is the parent of all modern Twelve Step organizations. (For more history on the Oxford Group, see "Serenity for Every Day: An Introduction.")

A question we might ask is, Who should be on the list of persons to whom we make amends? Here are four suggestions:

1) We need to include all persons who may have been victims of our addictions.

2) We need to review all of the persons included in our Step 4 relationship history. As a rule, we probably owe some amends to most of the people on that list.

3) We need to include members of the next generation (especially our own children) who have been impacted by our addictions and compulsions.

4) We need to consider whether we need to make amends to the following general "family" groups:

a) All members of our families of origin, living and dead. (We may even owe amends to a highly abusive parent. Making amends does not mean that we ignore, excuse, or condone the abuse, but that we take back any negativity we may have fed into such a relationship.)

b) Our families of procreation, that is, the families we make by marriage.

c) Our work families.

d) Our community families.

e) Our church families.

f) The family of man. (Have we been prejudiced
against and intolerant toward other political, religious, or
racial groups?)

Implicit in both Steps 8 and 9 is the assumption that we carry a
toxic residue of shame from virtually every incident in which we have
hurt, rejected, or ignored others. Steps 8 and 9 provide us with the
opportunity to reduce this guilt by setting things right again. We
should be cautioned, though, that we need to work through and grieve
out our underlying resentment, hurt, anger, and pain before trying to
make amends with those who have also offended us. Otherwise, we are
putting a bandage on a festering, cancerous sore, because the toxicity is
still there. Only after it has been excised can we release our
resentments with a high degree of emotional integrity.

STEP 8
Recovery Meditations

To help you understand what the Scriptures
say about the importance of our willingness
to make amends to the people we have harmed,
see the recovery meditations on the
following passages:

Related Recovery Scriptures Highlighted in the Text

STEP 9

*Made direct amends to such people wherever possible,
except when to do so would injure them or others.*

The making of amends needs to be approached cautiously by
codependent people. There are three things amends are or can be.
There is one thing they definitely should not be.

Amends can be these things:

1) Sincere efforts to offer apology for past harm.

2) Wonderful bridge-builders for more positive future
relationships.

3) Effective agents for removing the tremendous weight of guilt,
shame, and remorse.

The one thing amends should never be, though, are installment
payments on false guilt or false shame. To treat them in that way is to
drift into a kind of legalism and perfectionism that believes if we can
do enough or apologize enough, we can somehow earn our own
redemption and salvation. This is a particular danger for codependent
persons who already tend to assume guilt for people and situations over
which they have no real control.

The second half of this step is very important in that it identifies a
group to which we should not offer amends, that is, to those who
would be more hurt than helped by our action.

There are four categories of persons to whom we may consider
making amends. Notice how this contrasts with what we did in Step 8.
There we included *everyone* to whom we were *willing* to make amends.
In Step 9, however, as we prepare to execute the step, we use a high
degree of discretion regarding *to whom* we will make amends and *when*
this should happen. The four categories to consider as we think about
making amends are these:

1) Those to whom we may turn immediately, such as spouses or
close family members.

2) Those to whom only partial disclosure can be made, because to do more would cause harm to others. For example, if we have taken part in unethical business dealings, we may want to make limited disclosure concerning our involvement, because full disclosure may jeopardize other persons who were in conspiracy with us. We need always to consider the risks to other individuals' security, privacy, and confidentiality.

3) Those to whom amends should be deferred until a later date. Perhaps the hurts are so fresh that our presence would only trigger rage on their part. Maybe we also need to work through some anger and resentments of our own.

4) Those whom we should never contact, because doing so would only open up old relationship doors that need to stay closed. This may be true, for example, in the case of a sex addict who wants to make amends to former partners.

By its very nature, the amends process of Step 9 is one-sided. The people to whom we extend amends may not reciprocate by forgiving us for hurts we have done to them or by asking our forgiveness if they have hurt us. Nevertheless, from the spiritual perspective, casting off old bitternesses and tendering amends can be both freeing and healing.

STEP 9

Recovery Meditations

To help you understand what the Scriptures say
about how to reconcile with people we
have harmed, see the recovery meditations
on the following passages:

Related Recovery Scriptures Highlighted in the Text

STEP 10

*Continued to take personal inventory
and when we were wrong promptly admitted it.*

Steps 10, 11, and 12 are sometimes called the maintenance steps. They repeat many of the points outlined in previous steps, but they emphasize the value of continuing to "work the steps" on a day-to-day basis.

Step 10 encourages the taking of a personal inventory, which, for recovering persons, should be a daily process. Here are five components of this ongoing inventory:

1) What are our needs? These include basic needs, such as the need for love, acceptance, and security. Do we recognize those needs? Are they being met in some reasonable fashion?

2) What are our feelings? Especially we need to allow grief feelings to surface and be expressed. We also need to watch out for deep feelings of resentment, because resentment covers anger, anger covers hurt, hurt usually covers fear, and again, the deepest fear is that our basic human needs are not going to be met. In relationships we fear being rejected or abandoned.

3) What counterfeit, codependent, addictive means are we using in trying to meet our needs? Are we manipulating others? Are we overcontrolling others? Are we being perfectionistic or compulsive with ourselves or others? Are we attempting to win acceptance by playing the martyr or the victim role in relationships? Are we compulsively rescuing or enabling others? All of these are trigger questions to help us assess whether we are using bogus means to meet our needs.

4) What is our relationship with our own boundaries and with the boundaries of others? It is very important to know we can set appropriate interpersonal boundaries that are neither too

rigid nor too fragile. Can we keep people out as we need to? Can we allow people in as we need to? Are we capable of saying yes to other persons, and are we capable of saying no as necessary? Also, do we respect the boundaries of others? Do we hear and honor the yeses and noes they give us regarding their boundaries?

5) If we are aware of violating our own boundaries or the boundaries of others, are we able to reestablish new, proper boundaries? Are we able to make amends to those who have been harmed by our violation of their boundaries?

6) Do we admit our wrongs promptly? Unless we admit them promptly, we will store these wrongs, which can be rationalized into "wrongs against us." They may then become resentments, which sabotage our recovery.

Our daily inventory certainly also needs to assess the status of our relationship with God. Are we still yielding our wills to Him? Bill Wilson emphasized how crucial this evaluation is, especially for addictive personalities, which tend to be willful. Our need to surrender ourselves to God on a daily basis will go on throughout our lives, and we shall explore the means of that continuing spiritual surrender in Step 11.

STEP 10

Recovery Meditations

To help you understand what the Scriptures say
about the need for an ongoing inventory
of our lives, see the recovery meditations
on the following passages:

Related Recovery Scriptures Highlighted in the Text

STEP 11

*Sought through prayer and meditation to improve
our conscious contact with God **as we understood Him,**
praying only for knowledge of His will for us
and the power to carry that out.*

Step 11 provides daily spiritual maintenance. As recovering persons, we may use our support groups and recovery literature as springboards toward spiritual and emotional growth. We will probably reach a level, though, at which we hunger for an even deeper contact and communication with God. This is where the organized church, the Bible, other Christian literature, and prayer and meditation become indispensable tools for lasting spiritual growth. Bill Wilson, for example, found great peace and encouragement through Christian literature and the Bible. In fact, one of the books he came back to again and again was Oswald Chambers' *My Utmost for His Highest.* In Step 11, we slow down, take ourselves out of the driver's seat, and set a specific time to seek God's will through prayer and meditating on His Word.

Studying the Bible helps us to know God better and to find out what He wants for our lives. *Serenity for Every Day* gives specific examples of how God's Word relates to the recovery issues we are facing. We see this in the meditations on the Twelve Steps and in the related recovery scriptures highlighted throughout the text. As we practice Step 11, we may want to use *Serenity for Every Day* as a part of the special time we spend with God.

If we have had little or no experience with prayer, we should probably begin in a simple fashion. That means putting aside perfectionistic concerns about praying "the right way." We should pray simply and forthrightly to God as a loving Father, not worrying about what we should and should not say.

Over time, as we become comfortable with God, we will talk with Him as with a trusted friend. He will be the Person with whom we can conduct our daily inventories of grief and confession issues. And we will begin to sense His answers to our prayers. These may not be cast in stone or echoed from a burning bush; but as we talk with God, we will intuit His direction coming back to us.

As we examine Step 12, we shall explore how this growing spiritual wisdom is to be carried to others and practiced in our own lives.

STEP 11
Recovery Meditations

To help you understand what the Scriptures say
about the value of prayer and meditation
in seeking God's will and power for our lives,
see the recovery meditations on the
following passages:

Related Recovery Scriptures Highlighted in the Text

STEP
12

Having had a spiritual awakening as the result of these steps,
we tried to carry this message to others,
and to practice these principles in all our affairs.

Although we enter recovery to heal a particular affliction, we find
that, in the end, we have received far more than a specific healing of
an addiction; we have received the gift of a profound spiritual
awakening. In a sense, the addiction, the pain, the healing of the
addiction, have only been stepping-stones to spiritual transformation
and renewal. There is a phrase from the oral tradition of A.A. and
other Twelve Step groups, by which people in meetings introduce
themselves: "Hi, I'm _____, and I'm a grateful recovering
alcoholic." What they mean is that there is an element of gratitude for
their addiction or dependency since it has served as the key to a
spiritual awakening.

The second phrase in Step 12 reads: "we tried to carry this
message to others." Twelve Step programs place great emphasis on
outreach to those who still suffer. Another oral tradition says, "You
can't keep it unless you give it away." Having received healing and
spiritual renewal, we can retain them only as we offer them to others.
This evangelism aspect of Twelve Step recovery provides a bridge
between recovery programs and the Christian church, which has a
two thousand-year history of evangelism.

On a practical level, psychologists have long believed that there is
a special capacity for empathy between persons who have shared the
same addictions. That is why Bill Wilson encouraged alcoholics to
help other alcoholics, and it is also why we now have such a
proliferation of recovery support groups for different dependencies.
Again, the premise is that people who have suffered from an addiction
and have found spiritual healing from it are in better positions to
understand and help others with similar problems.

The final phrase in Step 12 emphasizes practicing the Twelve Step principles "in all our affairs." This means that if we have been spiritually transformed, people will begin to observe it in our financial lives, in our relationships, in our community lives, in our sexual conduct, and the list goes on and on. Our transformation will be apparent in all arenas of our lives.

Healing our addictions or codependencies is not the only goal of recovery. Rather, it is the starting place. Certainly we have to cap our addictions and put them in a state of balance or abstinence. But then begins the real journey of spiritual growth. Can our lives be remade?

We must remember that this growth is a process with one of the growth directions being toward God. Bill Wilson left the door open, saying, "It's God as I understand Him," but he was very explicit about who his God was. He was the God of our fathers and of the Lord Jesus Christ. We may start as agnostics. We may then come to view the group or recovery process as our higher power, looking to other people for strength. Gradually we accept a vague notion of god, which grows to a more specific monotheistic god. We may even begin to pray to and dialogue with this god. Eventually, we come to know the one true God.

If you are growing and searching for the true God, may we suggest the God of the Scriptures. Spending time reading *Serenity for Every Day* and meditating on it can help you come to know this caring, loving, and merciful Father.

STEP 12
Recovery Meditations

To help you understand what the Scriptures say
about sharing our spiritual awakening with
others through message and example, see the
recovery meditations on the following passages:

Related Recovery Scriptures Highlighted in the Text

THE
NEW TESTAMENT
of
OUR LORD AND SAVIOR
JESUS CHRIST

THE GOSPEL ACCORDING TO
MATTHEW

THE book of the genealogy of Jesus Christ, the Son of David, the Son of Abraham:

2 Abraham begot Isaac, Isaac begot Jacob, and Jacob begot Judah and his brothers.

3 Judah begot Perez and Zerah by Tamar, Perez begot Hezron, and Hezron begot Ram.

4 Ram begot Amminadab, Amminadab begot Nahshon, and Nahshon begot Salmon.

5 Salmon begot Boaz by Rahab, Boaz begot Obed by Ruth, Obed begot Jesse,

6 and Jesse begot David the king.

David the king begot Solomon by her *who had been the wife* of Uriah.

7 Solomon begot Rehoboam, Rehoboam begot Abijah, and Abijah begot Asa.

8 Asa begot Jehoshaphat, Jehoshaphat begot Joram, and Joram begot Uzziah.

9 Uzziah begot Jotham, Jotham begot Ahaz, and Ahaz begot Hezekiah.

10 Hezekiah begot Manasseh, Manasseh begot Amon, and Amon begot Josiah.

11 Josiah begot Jeconiah and his brothers about the time they were carried away to Babylon.

12 And after they were brought to Babylon, Jeconiah begot Shealtiel, and Shealtiel begot Zerubbabel.

13 Zerubbabel begot Abiud, Abiud begot Eliakim, and Eliakim begot Azor.

14 Azor begot Zadok, Zadok begot Achim, and Achim begot Eliud.

15 Eliud begot Eleazar, Eleazar begot Matthan, and Matthan begot Jacob.

16 And Jacob begot Joseph the husband of Mary, of whom was born Jesus who is called Christ.

17 So all the generations from Abraham to David *are* fourteen generations, from David until the captivity in Babylon *are* fourteen generations, and from the captivity in Babylon until the Christ *are* fourteen generations.

18 Now the birth of Jesus Christ was as follows: After His mother Mary was betrothed to Joseph, before they came together, she was found with child of the Holy Spirit.

19 Then Joseph her husband, being a just *man,* and not wanting to make her a public example, was minded to put her away secretly.

20 But while he thought about these things, behold, an angel of the Lord appeared to him in a dream, saying, "Joseph, son of David, do not be afraid to take to you Mary your wife, for that which is conceived in her is of the Holy Spirit.

21 "And she will bring forth a Son, and you shall call His name JESUS, for He will save His people from their sins."

22 Now all this was done that it might be fulfilled which was spoken by the Lord through the prophet, saying:

23 *"Behold, a virgin shall be with child, and bear a Son, and they shall call His name Immanuel,"* which is translated, "God with us."

24 Then Joseph, being aroused from sleep, did as the angel of the Lord commanded him and took to him his wife,

25 and did not know her till she had brought forth her firstborn Son. And he called His name JESUS.

2 Now after Jesus was born in Bethlehem of Judea in the days of Herod the king, behold, wise men from the East came to Jerusalem,

2 saying, "Where is He who has been born King of the Jews? For

we have seen His star in the East and have come to worship Him."

3 When Herod the king heard *these things,* he was troubled, and all Jerusalem with him.

4 And when he had gathered all the chief priests and scribes of the people together, he inquired of them where the Christ was to be born.

5 So they said to him, "In Bethlehem of Judea, for thus it is written by the prophet:

6 'But you, Bethlehem, in the
    land of Judah,
    Are not the least among the
      rulers of Judah;
    For out of you shall come a
      Ruler
    Who will shepherd My people
      Israel.' "

7 Then Herod, when he had secretly called the wise men, determined from them what time the star appeared.

8 And he sent them to Bethlehem and said, "Go and search diligently for the young Child, and when you have found *Him,* bring back word to me, that I may come and worship Him also."

9 When they heard the king, they departed; and behold, the star which they had seen in the East went before them, till it came and stood over where the young Child was.

10 When they saw the star, they rejoiced with exceedingly great joy.

11 And when they had come into the house, they saw the young Child with Mary His mother, and fell down and worshiped Him. And when they had opened their treasures, they presented gifts to Him: gold, frankincense, and myrrh.

12 Then, being divinely warned in a dream that they should not return to Herod, they departed for their own country another way.

13 Now when they had departed, behold, an angel of the Lord appeared to Joseph in a dream, saying, "Arise, take the young Child and His mother, flee to Egypt, and stay there until I bring you word; for Herod will seek the young Child to destroy Him."

14 When he arose, he took the young Child and His mother by night and departed for Egypt,

15 and was there until the death of Herod, that it might be fulfilled which was spoken by the Lord through the prophet, saying, *"Out of Egypt I called My Son."*

16 Then Herod, when he saw that he was deceived by the wise men, was exceedingly angry; and he sent forth and put to death all the male children who were in Bethlehem and in all its districts, from two years old and under, according to the time which he had determined from the wise men.

STEP 2

17 Then was fulfilled what was spoken by Jeremiah the prophet, saying:

18 *"A voice was heard in Ramah,*
    Lamentation, weeping,
      and great mourning,
    Rachel weeping for her
      children,
    Refusing to be comforted,
      because they were no more."

19 But when Herod was dead, behold, an angel of the Lord appeared in a dream to Joseph in Egypt,

20 saying, "Arise, take the young Child and His mother, and go to the land of Israel, for those who sought the young Child's life are dead."

21 Then he arose, took the young Child and His mother, and came into the land of Israel.

22 But when he heard that Archelaus was reigning over Judea instead of his father Herod, he was afraid to go there. And being

STEP 2

*Came to believe that a Power greater than
ourselves could restore us to sanity.*

Matthew 2:16

King Herod was a man out of step and out of tune with God's loving plan for people through Christ. Herod was addicted to power. When the wise men labeled the Christ child "King of the Jews" (v. 2), Herod's panic gave way to lying, manipulation, and even slaughter. Like all power addicts, Herod dealt with any perceived threat to that power with all means at his disposal. In the end, he lost all human decency as he mercilessly destroyed the babies of Bethlehem. If Herod had been willing to accept the truth that God alone is all-powerful and had yielded to His authority, the name "Herod" might have been associated with honor instead of ignominy.

Today, we each still face the question Herod faced: Are we willing to acknowledge Jesus as King in our lives, or will we continue in our delusion of self-determination?

When we put our trust in the Lord Jesus, we will discover that His mighty power is more than sufficient for every need in our lives.

For further reading on Step 2, turn to page 17.

Daily Encouragement

DAY 1 READING: MATTHEW 1:1—2:23

A Thought for the New Day: No wonder the wise men were glad (2:10, 11). They had found the goal of their quest. Perhaps you have traveled a long and difficult road in search of the wisdom that never fails. God's Spirit is the invisible star that guides your steps until, at last, you stumble upon the real Wisdom of life—the Christ who became a little Child that all might see His innocent beauty and harmlessness. It is your highest wisdom to worship Him. (*Turn to page 5.*)

warned by God in a dream, he turned aside into the region of Galilee.

23 And he came and dwelt in a city called Nazareth, that it might be fulfilled which was spoken by the prophets, "He shall be called a Nazarene."

3 In those days John the Baptist came preaching in the wilderness of Judea,

2 and saying, "Repent, for the kingdom of heaven is at hand!"

3 For this is he who was spoken of by the prophet Isaiah, saying:

"The voice of one crying
in the wilderness:
'Prepare the way of the LORD,
Make His paths straight.' "

4 And John himself was clothed in camel's hair, with a leather belt around his waist; and his food was locusts and wild honey.

5 Then Jerusalem, all Judea, and all the region around the Jordan went out to him

6 and were baptized by him in the Jordan, confessing their sins.

7 But when he saw many of the Pharisees and Sadducees coming to his baptism, he said to them, "Brood of vipers! Who has warned you to flee from the wrath to come?

8 "Therefore bear fruits worthy of repentance,

9 "and do not think to say to yourselves, 'We have Abraham as *our* father.' For I say to you that God is able to raise up children to Abraham from these stones.

10 "And even now the ax is laid to the root of the trees. Therefore every tree which does not bear good fruit is cut down and thrown into the fire.

11 "I indeed baptize you with water unto repentance, but He who is coming after me is mightier than I, whose sandals I am not worthy to carry. He will baptize you with the Holy Spirit and fire.

12 "His winnowing fan *is* in His hand, and He will thoroughly purge His threshing floor, and gather His wheat into the barn; but He will burn up the chaff with unquenchable fire."

13 Then Jesus came from Galilee to John at the Jordan to be baptized by him.

14 And John *tried to* prevent Him, saying, "I have need to be baptized by You, and are You coming to me?"

15 But Jesus answered and said to him, "Permit *it to be so* now, for thus it is fitting for us to fulfill all righteousness." Then he allowed Him.

16 Then Jesus, when He had been baptized, came up immediately from the water; and behold, the heavens were opened to Him, and He saw the Spirit of God descending like a dove and alighting upon Him.

17 And suddenly a voice *came* from heaven, saying, "This is My beloved Son, in whom I am well pleased."

4 Then Jesus was led up by the Spirit into the wilderness to be tempted by the devil.

2 And when He had fasted forty days and forty nights, afterward He was hungry.

3 Now when the tempter came to Him, he said, "If You are the Son of God, command that these stones become bread."

4 But He answered and said, "It is written, *'Man shall not live by bread alone, but by every word that proceeds from the mouth of God.'*"

5 Then the devil took Him up into the holy city, set Him on the pinnacle of the temple,

6 and said to Him, "If You are the Son of God, throw Yourself down. For it is written:

STEP
6

*Were entirely ready to have God
remove all these defects of character.*

Matthew 3:8

John the Baptist was a straight-talking man. He was serious about his mission in life. He had been chosen to prepare human hearts to follow Jesus.

John's baptism and preaching were becoming well known. In fact, you might even say they had become "the place to be and the thing to do." People who had earlier called John a lunatic now decided it would be prudent to join him and thus show how devout they were.

John minces no words with this crowd. He calls them a "brood of vipers." Why? Because they only cared about looking righteous and good instead of truly repenting. The word "repent" simply means "to turn about" or undergo a true change of mind.

In Step 5, we became willing to admit our problems and short-comings. But Step 6 asks for a deeper commitment. We now must truly desire to turn about—to leave the life-style and habits that have bound us and become ready for a new life of freedom and fruitfulness.

For further reading on Step 6, turn to page 31.

Daily Encouragement

DAY 2 READING: MATTHEW 3:1—4:11

A Thought for the New Day: Most of us enjoy a good meal, and having a good appetite is a blessing. But we enjoy an even greater blessing when we learn that the best things of this life cannot completely satisfy (4:4). God made us that way. Can you see that you were made for greater things than working and eating and playing? There is an empty place in all of us that only God Himself can fill. When we let Him fill that emptiness every day—that is fulfillment! (*Turn to page 7.*)

*'He shall give His angels charge
   concerning you,'*

and,

*'In their hands they shall bear
   you up,
Lest you dash your foot
   against a stone.'"*

7 Jesus said to him, "It is written
again, *'You shall not tempt the
Lord your God.'"*
8 Again, the devil took Him up on
an exceedingly high mountain, and
showed Him all the kingdoms of
the world and their glory.
9 And he said to Him, "All these
things I will give You if You will
fall down and worship me."
10 Then Jesus said to him, "Away
with you, Satan! For it is written,
'You shall worship the Lord *your
God, and Him only you shall
serve.'"*
11 Then the devil left Him, and
behold, angels came and ministered to Him.
12 Now when Jesus heard that
John had been put in prison, He
departed to Galilee.
13 And leaving Nazareth, He came
and dwelt in Capernaum, which is
by the sea, in the regions of Zebulun and Naphtali,
14 that it might be fulfilled which
was spoken by Isaiah the prophet,
saying:

15 *"The land of Zebulun and the
   land of Naphtali,
The way of the sea, beyond the
   Jordan,
Galilee of the Gentiles:*
16 *The people who sat in darkness
   saw a great light,
And upon those who sat in the
   region and shadow of death
Light has dawned."*

17 From that time Jesus began to
preach and to say, "Repent, for the
kingdom of heaven is at hand."
18 Now Jesus, walking by the Sea

of Galilee, saw two brothers, Simon called Peter, and Andrew his
brother, casting a net into the sea;
for they were fishermen.
19 And He said to them, "Follow
Me, and I will make you fishers of
men."
20 Then they immediately left *their*
nets and followed Him.
21 And going on from there, He
saw two other brothers, James *the
son* of Zebedee, and John his
brother, in the boat with Zebedee
their father, mending their nets.
And He called them,
22 and immediately they left the
boat and their father, and followed
Him.
23 Now Jesus went about all Galilee, teaching in their synagogues,
preaching the gospel of the kingdom, and healing all kinds of sickness and all kinds of disease
among the people.
24 Then His fame went throughout
all Syria; and they brought to Him
all sick people who were afflicted
with various diseases and torments, and those who were demon-possessed, epileptics, and
paralytics; and He healed them.
25 And great multitudes followed
Him—from Galilee, and *from* Decapolis, Jerusalem, Judea, and beyond the Jordan.
5 And seeing the multitudes, He
went up on a mountain, and
when He was seated His disciples
came to Him.
2 Then He opened His mouth and
taught them, saying:

3 "Blessed *are* the poor in spirit,
   For theirs is the kingdom of
    heaven.
4 Blessed *are* those who mourn,
   For they shall be comforted.
5 Blessed *are* the meek,
   For they shall inherit the
    earth.
6 Blessed *are* those who hunger
   and thirst for righteousness,
   For they shall be filled.

STEP 12

STEP 6

STEP 11

STEP 12

*Having had a spiritual awakening as the result
of these steps, we tried to carry this message to others,
and to practice these principles in all our affairs.*

Matthew 4:19–22

Peter, Andrew, James, and John were fishermen as their fathers had been before them. Their station and goals in life were, to a large extent, limited by the situation they had been born into. Then they met Jesus and everything changed. They began to discover truth, to be filled with new purpose, and to reap abundant blessings as they followed Him.

What a powerful analogy this is to our own lives! Because of our environment and life experiences, we at one time felt limited—unable to change our situation for the better. But then we, too, met Jesus. Now each day as we trust and follow Him our lives are filled with His blessing, and our opportunities seem infinite.

One of our greatest joys can be to share with those around us what God has done in our lives. Step 12 encourages us to carry this message to others.

For further reading on Step 12, turn to page 57.

Daily Encouragement

DAY 3 READING: MATTHEW 4:12–25

A Thought for the New Day: We who want to be disciples of Jesus are called to draw others to Him. Just as in ordinary fishing, so fishing in the service of Christ is an art that requires patience, gentleness, and great care. Reading the New Testament, we find that these qualities were very apparent in Jesus' life. As we follow the example He has set for us, we, too, can become effective "fishers of men" (v. 19). *(Turn to page 9.)*

7 Blessed *are* the merciful,
For they shall obtain mercy.

STEP 10
STEP 9

8 Blessed *are* the pure in heart,
For they shall see God.
9 Blessed *are* the peacemakers,
For they shall be called sons
of God.
10 Blessed are those who are
persecuted for righ-
teousness' sake,
For theirs is the kingdom of
heaven.

11 "Blessed are you when they revile and persecute you, and say all
kinds of evil against you falsely for
My sake.
12 "Rejoice and be exceedingly
glad, for great *is* your reward in
heaven, for so they persecuted the
prophets who were before you.
13 "You are the salt of the earth;
but if the salt loses its flavor, how
shall it be seasoned? It is then good
for nothing but to be thrown out
and trampled under foot by men.
14 "You are the light of the world.
A city that is set on a hill cannot
be hidden.
15 "Nor do they light a lamp and
put it under a basket, but on a
lampstand, and it gives light to all
who are in the house.

STEP 12

16 "Let your light so shine before
men, that they may see your good
works and glorify your Father in
heaven.
17 "Do not think that I came to
destroy the Law or the Prophets. I
did not come to destroy but to
fulfill.
18 "For assuredly, I say to you, till
heaven and earth pass away, one
jot or one tittle will by no means
pass from the law till all is fulfilled.
19 "Whoever therefore breaks one
of the least of these commandments, and teaches men so, shall
be called least in the kingdom of
heaven; but whoever does and
teaches *them,* he shall be called
great in the kingdom of heaven.
20 "For I say to you, that unless

your righteousness exceeds *the
righteousness* of the scribes and
Pharisees, you will by no means
enter the kingdom of heaven.
21 "You have heard that it was
said to those of old, *'You shall not
murder,'* and whoever murders
will be in danger of the judgment.
22 "But I say to you that whoever
is angry with his brother without a
cause shall be in danger of the
judgment. And whoever says to his
brother, 'Raca!' shall be in danger
of the council. But whoever says,
'You fool!' shall be in danger of hell
fire.
23 "Therefore if you bring your gift **STEP 9**
to the altar, and there remember
that your brother has something
against you,
24 "leave your gift there before the
altar, and go your way. First be
reconciled to your brother, and
then come and offer your gift.
25 "Agree with your adversary
quickly, while you are on the way
with him, lest your adversary deliver you to the judge, the judge
hand you over to the officer, and
you be thrown into prison.
26 "Assuredly, I say to you, you
will by no means get out of there
till you have paid the last penny.
27 "You have heard that it was **STEP 4**
said to those of old, *'You shall not
commit adultery.'*
28 "But I say to you that whoever
looks at a woman to lust for her
has already committed adultery
with her in his heart.
29 "And if your right eye causes
you to sin, pluck it out and cast *it*
from you; for it is more profitable
for you that one of your members
perish, than for your whole body
to be cast into hell.
30 "And if your right hand causes
you to sin, cut it off and cast *it*
from you; for it is more profitable
for you that one of your members
perish, than for your whole body
to be cast into hell.
31 "Furthermore it has been said,

STEP 9

*Made direct amends to such people wherever possible,
except when to do so would injure them or others.*

Matthew 5:9

Most people want peace in their lives, but many will never know the complete peace that is available to them, because they are not willing to be true peacemakers. We may simply want to put the past behind us, or at least sweep it under the rug, and get on with our lives. That is the "easy" way, the dysfunctional way of doing things.

We can have the courage and wisdom to be peacemakers because of God's love working in and through us. First John 3:1 says, "Behold what manner of love the Father has bestowed on us, that we should be called children of God!" Not only do we have God's love to guide us in our peacemaking; John 14:27 tells us that we have the promise of God's own peace resting upon our lives, which frees us from fear.

With our hearts full of God's love and peace, we can extend forgiveness and make appropriate amends where needed.

For further reading on Step 9, turn to page 255.

Daily Encouragement

DAY 4 READING: MATTHEW 5:1–37

A Thought for the New Day: The "blessed" sayings of Jesus tell us something very important that He wants for us, that is, to be happy. "Blessed" really means "happy." In these sayings, called the Beatitudes (5:1–10), Jesus shows that there are various conditions in which we can be happy. Be assured that such happiness is His ultimate desire for you. Think about it—who could be unhappy with Jesus for a friend? *(Turn to page 11.)*

'Whoever divorces his wife, let him give her a certificate of divorce.'

32 "But I say to you that whoever divorces his wife for any reason except sexual immorality causes her to commit adultery; and whoever marries a woman who is divorced commits adultery.

33 "Again you have heard that it was said to those of old, 'You shall not swear falsely, but shall perform your oaths to the Lord.'

34 "But I say to you, do not swear at all: neither by heaven, for it is God's throne;

35 "nor by the earth, for it is His footstool; nor by Jerusalem, for it is the city of the great King.

36 "Nor shall you swear by your head, because you cannot make one hair white or black.

37 "But let your 'Yes' be 'Yes,' and your 'No,' 'No.' For whatever is more than these is from the evil one.

38 "You have heard that it was said, *'An eye for an eye and a tooth for a tooth.'*

39 "But I tell you not to resist an evil person. But whoever slaps you on your right cheek, turn the other to him also.

40 "If anyone wants to sue you and take away your tunic, let him have *your* cloak also.

41 "And whoever compels you to go one mile, go with him two.

42 "Give to him who asks you, and from him who wants to borrow from you do not turn away.

43 "You have heard that it was said, 'You shall love your neighbor and hate your enemy.'

44 "But I say to you, love your enemies, bless those who curse you, do good to those who hate you, and pray for those who spitefully use you and persecute you,

45 "that you may be sons of your Father in heaven; for He makes His sun rise on the evil and on the good, and sends rain on the just and on the unjust.

46 "For if you love those who love you, what reward have you? Do not even the tax collectors do the same?

47 "And if you greet your brethren only, what do you do more *than others?* Do not even the tax collectors do so?

48 "Therefore you shall be perfect, just as your Father in heaven is perfect.

6 "Take heed that you do not do your charitable deeds before men, to be seen by them. Otherwise you have no reward from your Father in heaven.

2 "Therefore, when you do a charitable deed, do not sound a trumpet before you as the hypocrites do in the synagogues and in the streets, that they may have glory from men. Assuredly, I say to you, they have their reward.

3 "But when you do a charitable deed, do not let your left hand know what your right hand is doing,

4 "that your charitable deed may be in secret; and your Father who sees in secret will Himself reward you openly.

5 "And when you pray, you shall not be like the hypocrites. For they love to pray standing in the synagogues and on the corners of the streets, that they may be seen by men. Assuredly, I say to you, they have their reward.

6 "But you, when you pray, go into your room, and when you have shut your door, pray to your Father who *is* in the secret *place;* and your Father who sees in secret will reward you openly.

7 "But when you pray, do not use vain repetitions as the heathen *do.* For they think that they will be heard for their many words.

8 "Therefore do not be like them. For your Father knows the things you have need of before you ask Him.

9 "In this manner, therefore, pray:

*Made a list of all persons we had harmed,
and became willing to make amends to them all.*

Matthew 5:43–48

After Corrie Ten Boom had spoken one evening, a burly man came humbly down the aisle toward her. She recognized him immediately as one of the more inhumane prison guards in the Nazi concentration camp where she had been imprisoned for her faith during World War II. All his atrocities flashed into her mind. She had every right to demand payment for those acts. Instead she forgave him and accepted him in Jesus' name.

Corrie's response was a natural outgrowth of her faith. God's love makes natural what is humanly unnatural. It is natural for us to love our friends and hate our enemies. But when we begin to mature spiritually (this is the meaning of the word "perfect"), we "grow up" into Jesus' power and love. That wonderful God-given love makes us able to walk in the steps of Jesus Himself, who prayed for those who coldly crucified Him. It also makes natural the humble, honest entreaty of the prison guard whose spiritual eyes had been opened and who sought to make amends.

For further reading on Step 8, turn to page 35.

Daily Encouragement

DAY 5 READING: MATTHEW 5:38—6:23

A Thought for the New Day: Prayer is our lifeline to God (6:9–13). Across that channel come all the supplies for your daily support. As you offer up your praise and adoration to Him, the Father also bestows upon you the joys of citizenship in His kingdom—His direction of your life, your physical needs, His forgiveness, and His protection from Satan's attacks. Prayer is the first priority of your day and the constant breath of life that is eternal. (*Turn to page 13.*)

Our Father in heaven,
Hallowed be Your name.
10 Your kingdom come.
Your will be done
On earth as *it is* in heaven.
11 Give us this day our daily
bread.
12 And forgive us our debts,
As we forgive our debtors.
13 And do not lead us into
temptation,
But deliver us from the evil
one.
For Yours is the kingdom and
the power and the glory
forever. Amen.

STEP 8

14 "For if you forgive men their
trespasses, your heavenly Father
will also forgive you.
15 "But if you do not forgive men
their trespasses, neither will your
Father forgive your trespasses.
16 "Moreover, when you fast, do
not be like the hypocrites, with a
sad countenance. For they disfig-
ure their faces that they may appear to men to be fasting. Assuredly, I say to you, they have
their reward.
17 "But you, when you fast, anoint
your head and wash your face,
18 "so that you do not appear to
men to be fasting, but to your Father who *is* in the secret *place;* and
your Father who sees in secret will
reward you openly.
19 "Do not lay up for yourselves
treasures on earth, where moth
and rust destroy and where thieves
break in and steal;
20 "but lay up for yourselves treasures in heaven, where neither
moth nor rust destroys and where
thieves do not break in and steal.
21 "For where your treasure is,
there your heart will be also.
22 "The lamp of the body is the
eye. If therefore your eye is good,
your whole body will be full of
light.
23 "But if your eye is bad, your

whole body will be full of darkness.
If therefore the light that is in you
is darkness, how great *is* that darkness!
24 "No one can serve two masters;
for either he will hate the one and
love the other, or else he will be
loyal to the one and despise the
other. You cannot serve God and
mammon.
25 "Therefore I say to you, do not
worry about your life, what you
will eat or what you will drink; nor
about your body, what you will put
on. Is not life more than food and
the body more than clothing?
26 "Look at the birds of the air, for
they neither sow nor reap nor
gather into barns; yet your heavenly Father feeds them. Are you
not of more value than they?
27 "Which of you by worrying can
add one cubit to his stature?
28 "So why do you worry about
clothing? Consider the lilies of the
field, how they grow: they neither
toil nor spin;
29 "and yet I say to you that even
Solomon in all his glory was not
arrayed like one of these.
30 "Now if God so clothes the
grass of the field, which today is,
and tomorrow is thrown into the
oven, *will He* not much more
clothe you, O you of little faith?
31 "Therefore do not worry, saying, 'What shall we eat?' or 'What
shall we drink?' or 'What shall we
wear?'
32 "For after all these things the
Gentiles seek. For your heavenly
Father knows that you need all
these things.
33 "But seek first the kingdom of
God and His righteousness, and all
these things shall be added to you.
34 "Therefore do not worry about
tomorrow, for tomorrow will
worry about its own things. Sufficient for the day *is* its own trouble.

STEP 3

7 "Judge not, that you be not
judged.
2 "For with what judgment you

STEP 8

STEP 3

*Made a decision to turn our will and our lives over to the care of God **as we understood Him.***

Matthew 6:31–34

Watching out for ourselves first is a mind-set that leads us into a faulty and ultimately disastrous set of values. Our self-centeredness drives us to look for fulfillment in all the wrong places—to seek immediate gratification of our wants and needs. Jesus tells us in Matthew 6:32 that this is typical of the way most people think. But in Step 3 we make a decision to reject the world's attitude and to turn every part of our lives over to the Lord Jesus' saving power. We can do this because our Heavenly Father knows all that we need. And since He loved us enough to send Jesus to die for us, He loves us enough to supply every need that we have each day. Verse 33 is a beautiful promise from that loving, wise, and powerful Heavenly Father. As we become willing to turn our lives completely over to Him (which is the essence of seeking His Kingdom), He will supply all our needs.

For further reading on Step 3, turn to page 23.

Daily Encouragement

DAY 6 READING: MATTHEW 6:24—7:29

A Thought for the New Day: Have you ever said, "I wish I hadn't worried about that problem; God took care of it perfectly"? Of course! And He always does. Knowing that fact sets us free to seek what will last forever—the kingdom of God (6:33). God reigns now in His kingdom, and reigning in you He also reigns over all your circumstances. *Father, set me free from self-concern so that, filled with Your concerns, I may bring Your kingdom near to those around me.* *(Turn to page 17.)*

judge, you will be judged; and with the *same* measure you use, it will be measured back to you.

3 "And why do you look at the speck in your brother's eye, but do not consider the plank in your own eye?

4 "Or how can you say to your brother, 'Let me remove the speck out of your eye'; and look, a plank *is* in your own eye?

5 "Hypocrite! First remove the plank from your own eye, and then you will see clearly to remove the speck out of your brother's eye.

6 "Do not give what is holy to the dogs; nor cast your pearls before swine, lest they trample them under their feet, and turn and tear you in pieces.

7 "Ask, and it will be given to you; seek, and you will find; knock, and it will be opened to you.

8 "For everyone who asks receives, and he who seeks finds, and to him who knocks it will be opened.

9 "Or what man is there among you who, if his son asks for bread, will give him a stone?

10 "Or if he asks for a fish, will he give him a serpent?

11 "If you then, being evil, know how to give good gifts to your children, how much more will your Father who is in heaven give good things to those who ask Him!

12 "Therefore, whatever you want men to do to you, do also to them, for this is the Law and the Prophets.

13 "Enter by the narrow gate; for wide *is* the gate and broad *is* the way that leads to destruction, and there are many who go in by it.

14 "Because narrow *is* the gate and difficult *is* the way which leads to life, and there are few who find it.

15 "Beware of false prophets, who come to you in sheep's clothing, but inwardly they are ravenous wolves.

16 "You will know them by their fruits. Do men gather grapes from thornbushes or figs from thistles?

17 "Even so, every good tree bears good fruit, but a bad tree bears bad fruit.

18 "A good tree cannot bear bad fruit, nor *can* a bad tree bear good fruit.

19 "Every tree that does not bear good fruit is cut down and thrown into the fire.

20 "Therefore by their fruits you will know them.

21 "Not everyone who says to Me, 'Lord, Lord,' shall enter the kingdom of heaven, but he who does the will of My Father in heaven.

22 "Many will say to Me in that day, 'Lord, Lord, have we not prophesied in Your name, cast out demons in Your name, and done many wonders in Your name?'

23 "And then I will declare to them, 'I never knew you; depart from Me, you who practice lawlessness!'

24 "Therefore whoever hears these sayings of Mine, and does them, I will liken him to a wise man who built his house on the rock:

25 "and the rain descended, the floods came, and the winds blew and beat on that house; and it did not fall, for it was founded on the rock.

26 "Now everyone who hears these sayings of Mine, and does not do them, will be like a foolish man who built his house on the sand:

27 "and the rain descended, the floods came, and the winds blew and beat on that house; and it fell. And great was its fall."

28 And so it was, when Jesus had ended these sayings, that the people were astonished at His teaching,

29 for He taught them as one having authority, and not as the scribes.

8 When He had come down from the mountain, great multitudes followed Him.

2 And behold, a leper came and worshiped Him, saying, "Lord, if You are willing, You can make me clean."

3 Then Jesus put out *His* hand and touched him, saying, "I am willing; be cleansed." And immediately his leprosy was cleansed.

4 And Jesus said to him, "See that you tell no one; but go your way, show yourself to the priest, and offer the gift that Moses commanded, as a testimony to them."

5 Now when Jesus had entered Capernaum, a centurion came to Him, pleading with Him,

6 saying, "Lord, my servant is lying at home paralyzed, dreadfully tormented."

7 And Jesus said to him, "I will come and heal him."

8 The centurion answered and said, "Lord, I am not worthy that You should come under my roof. But only speak a word, and my servant will be healed.

9 "For I also am a man under authority, having soldiers under me. And I say to this *one,* 'Go,' and he goes; and to another, 'Come,' and he comes; and to my servant, 'Do this,' and he does *it.*"

10 When Jesus heard *it,* He marveled, and said to those who followed, "Assuredly, I say to you, I have not found such great faith, not even in Israel!

11 "And I say to you that many will come from east and west, and sit down with Abraham, Isaac, and Jacob in the kingdom of heaven.

12 "But the sons of the kingdom will be cast out into outer darkness. There will be weeping and gnashing of teeth."

13 Then Jesus said to the centurion, "Go your way; and as you have believed, *so* let it be done for you." And his servant was healed that same hour.

14 Now when Jesus had come into Peter's house, He saw his wife's mother lying sick with a fever.

15 And He touched her hand, and the fever left her. Then she arose and served them.

16 When evening had come, they brought to Him many who were demon-possessed. And He cast out the spirits with a word, and healed all who were sick,

17 that it might be fulfilled which was spoken by Isaiah the prophet, saying:

*"He Himself took our infirmities
And bore our sicknesses."*

18 Now when Jesus saw great multitudes about Him, He gave a command to depart to the other side.

19 Then a certain scribe came and said to Him, "Teacher, I will follow You wherever You go."

20 And Jesus said to him, "Foxes have holes and birds of the air *have* nests, but the Son of Man has nowhere to lay *His* head."

21 Then another of His disciples said to Him, "Lord, let me first go and bury my father."

22 But Jesus said to him, "Follow Me, and let the dead bury their own dead."

23 Now when He got into a boat, His disciples followed Him.

24 And suddenly a great tempest arose on the sea, so that the boat was covered with the waves. But He was asleep.

25 Then His disciples came to *Him* and awoke Him, saying, "Lord, save us! We are perishing!"

26 But He said to them, "Why are you fearful, O you of little faith?" Then He arose and rebuked the winds and the sea. And there was a great calm.

27 And the men marveled, saying, "Who can this be, that even the winds and the sea obey Him?"

28 When He had come to the other side, to the country of the Gergesenes, there met Him two demon-possessed *men,* coming out of the tombs, exceedingly fierce, so that no one could pass that way.

29 And suddenly they cried out, saying, "What have we to do with You, Jesus, You Son of God? Have You come here to torment us before the time?"

30 Now a good way off from them there was a herd of many swine feeding.

31 So the demons begged Him, saying, "If You cast us out, permit us to go away into the herd of swine."

32 And He said to them, "Go." So when they had come out, they went into the herd of swine. And suddenly the whole herd of swine ran violently down the steep place into the sea, and perished in the water.

33 Then those who kept *them* fled; and they went away into the city and told everything, including what *had happened* to the demon-possessed *men.*

34 And behold, the whole city came out to meet Jesus. And when they saw Him, they begged *Him* to depart from their region.

9 So He got into a boat, crossed over, and came to His own city.

2 And behold, they brought to Him a paralytic lying on a bed. And Jesus, seeing their faith, said to the paralytic, "Son, be of good cheer; your sins are forgiven you."

3 And at once some of the scribes said within themselves, "This *Man* blasphemes!"

4 But Jesus, knowing their thoughts, said, "Why do you think evil in your hearts?

5 "For which is easier, to say, '*Your* sins are forgiven you,' or to say, 'Arise and walk'?

6 "But that you may know that the Son of Man has power on earth to forgive sins"—then He said to the paralytic, "Arise, take up your bed, and go to your house."

7 And he arose and departed to his house.

8 Now when the multitudes saw *it,* they marveled and glorified God, who had given such power to men.

9 Then as Jesus passed on from there, He saw a man named Matthew sitting at the tax office. And He said to him, "Follow Me." And he arose and followed Him.

10 And so it was, as Jesus sat at the table in the house, *that* behold, many tax collectors and sinners came and sat down with Him and His disciples.

11 And when the Pharisees saw *it,* they said to His disciples, "Why does your Teacher eat with tax collectors and sinners?"

12 But when Jesus heard *that,* He said to them, "Those who are well have no need of a physician, but those who are sick.

13 "But go and learn what *this* means: '*I desire mercy and not sacrifice.*' For I did not come to call the righteous, but sinners, to repentance."

STEP 2

14 Then the disciples of John came to Him, saying, "Why do we and the Pharisees fast often, but Your disciples do not fast?"

15 And Jesus said to them, "Can the friends of the bridegroom mourn as long as the bridegroom is with them? But the days will come when the bridegroom will be taken away from them, and then they will fast.

16 "No one puts a piece of unshrunk cloth on an old garment; for the patch pulls away from the garment, and the tear is made worse.

17 "Nor do *people* put new wine into old wineskins, or else the wineskins break, the wine is spilled, and the wineskins are ruined. But they put new wine into new wineskins, and both are preserved."

18 While He spoke these things to them, behold, a ruler came and worshiped Him, saying, "My daughter has just died, but come

STEP 2

*Came to believe that a Power greater than ourselves
could restore us to sanity.*

Matthew 9:12, 13

The Pharisees of Jesus' day felt good about themselves and secure in their beliefs and position. Their self-righteous attitude made people who needed help embarrassed to ask for it. But Jesus is never like that. Just as He tenderly reached out to the paralytic, healing him in mind and body, so He reaches out to each of us, paralyzed by addictions and dependencies. His power to heal is as great as are His mercy to forgive and His compassion to understand.

Most of us will not be healed instantly, as the paralytic man was. The road to recovery may be uphill at times. But the power of God is more than able to restore us as we believe and trust in our merciful, loving Lord.

For further reading on Step 2, turn to page 25.

Daily Encouragement

DAY 7 READING: MATTHEW 8:1—9:17

A Thought for the New Day: Why was the Roman centurion's faith so great (8:8–10)? Although he had been an "outsider" to the religious community, the centurion saw clearly that Jesus could be trusted. However, this man's faith also was great on another account: he only needed Jesus to "speak a word" and it would be done. May we, too, not demand spectacular things. It is enough that Jesus gives His promise: we can be sure it will be done. (*Turn to page 19.*)

and lay Your hand on her and she will live."

19 So Jesus arose and followed him, and so *did* His disciples.

20 And suddenly, a woman who had a flow of blood for twelve years came from behind and touched the hem of His garment;

21 for she said to herself, "If only I may touch His garment, I shall be made well."

22 But Jesus turned around, and when He saw her He said, "Be of good cheer, daughter; your faith has made you well." And the woman was made well from that hour.

23 And when Jesus came into the ruler's house, and saw the flute players and the noisy crowd wailing,

24 He said to them, "Make room, for the girl is not dead, but sleeping." And they laughed Him to scorn.

25 But when the crowd was put outside, He went in and took her by the hand, and the girl arose.

26 And the report of this went out into all that land.

27 When Jesus departed from there, two blind men followed Him, crying out and saying, "Son of David, have mercy on us!"

28 And when He had come into the house, the blind men came to Him. And Jesus said to them, "Do you believe that I am able to do this?" They said to Him, "Yes, Lord."

29 Then He touched their eyes, saying, "According to your faith let it be to you."

30 And their eyes were opened. And Jesus sternly warned them, saying, "See *that* no one knows *it.*"

31 But when they had departed, they spread the news about Him in all that country.

32 As they went out, behold, they brought to Him a man, mute and demon-possessed.

33 And when the demon was cast out, the mute spoke. And the mul-

titudes marveled, saying, "It was never seen like this in Israel!"

34 But the Pharisees said, "He casts out demons by the ruler of the demons."

35 And Jesus went about all the cities and villages, teaching in their synagogues, preaching the gospel of the kingdom, and healing every sickness and every disease among the people.

36 But when He saw the multitudes, He was moved with compassion for them, because they were weary and scattered, like sheep having no shepherd.

37 Then He said to His disciples, "The harvest truly *is* plentiful, but the laborers *are* few.

38 "Therefore pray the Lord of the harvest to send out laborers into His harvest."

10 And when He had called His twelve disciples to *Him,* He gave them power *over* unclean spirits, to cast them out, and to heal all kinds of sickness and all kinds of disease.

2 Now the names of the twelve apostles are these: first, Simon, who is called Peter, and Andrew his brother; James the *son* of Zebedee, and John his brother;

3 Philip and Bartholomew; Thomas and Matthew the tax collector; James the *son* of Alphaeus, and Lebbaeus, whose surname was Thaddaeus;

4 Simon the Canaanite, and Judas Iscariot, who also betrayed Him.

5 These twelve Jesus sent out and commanded them, saying: "Do not go into the way of the Gentiles, and do not enter a city of the Samaritans.

6 "But go rather to the lost sheep of the house of Israel.

7 "And as you go, preach, saying, 'The kingdom of heaven is at hand.'

8 "Heal the sick, cleanse the lepers, raise the dead, cast out de-

*We admitted we were powerless over our dependencies—
that our lives had become unmanageable.*

Matthew 9:36

Step 1 asks us to confront the chaos and the unmanageability of our dependent life-styles. The paradox of every addiction is that the more we try to compulsively control ourselves and others through the practice of the addiction, the more out of control our lives spin.

In what counterfeit ways do we seek for interior security through codependent manipulation of the outside world? We may struggle desperately through our perfectionism or workaholism to win the praise and approval of our fellows. We may become preoccupied through hypochondria with health and bodily functions in pursuit of a kind of physical immortality and invincibility. We may strive to shore up our own fragile self-esteem by allowing a love partner to become the only source of affirmation for our worth.

In the depths of our dependency, we are like sheep, "weary and scattered." Scripture assures us that the True Shepherd, Jesus Christ, views this human discord and fragmentation with deep compassion. Twelve Step recovery allows us to confront compassionately but firmly our own human unmanageabilty.

For further reading on Step 1, turn to page 43.

Daily Encouragement

DAY 8 READING: MATTHEW 9:18—10:42

A Thought for the New Day: Our Bibles tell us that death is our "last enemy." But however strong that foe may seem to us, to Jesus death was only a paper tiger. He spoke, and the enemy fled away. There will always be sorrow because of the division death brings, but that sorrow is swallowed up in victory as we look to Jesus, the Master of life and death (9:24, 25). Because He lives, we live—and shall live with Him forevermore. (*Turn to page 23.*)

mons. Freely you have received, freely give.

9 "Provide neither gold nor silver nor copper in your moneybelts,

10 "nor bag for *your* journey, nor two tunics, nor sandals, nor staffs; for a worker is worthy of his food.

11 "Now whatever city or town you enter, inquire who in it is worthy, and stay there till you go out.

12 "And when you go into a household, greet it.

13 "If the household is worthy, let your peace come upon it. But if it is not worthy, let your peace return to you.

14 "And whoever will not receive you nor hear your words, when you depart from that house or city, shake off the dust from your feet.

15 "Assuredly, I say to you, it will be more tolerable for the land of Sodom and Gomorrah in the day of judgment than for that city!

16 "Behold, I send you out as sheep in the midst of wolves. Therefore be wise as serpents and harmless as doves.

17 "But beware of men, for they will deliver you up to councils and scourge you in their synagogues.

18 "And you will be brought before governors and kings for My sake, as a testimony to them and to the Gentiles.

19 "But when they deliver you up, do not worry about how or what you should speak. For it will be given to you in that hour what you should speak;

20 "for it is not you who speak, but the Spirit of your Father who speaks in you.

21 "Now brother will deliver up brother to death, and a father *his* child; and children will rise up against parents and cause them to be put to death.

22 "And you will be hated by all for My name's sake. But he who endures to the end will be saved.

23 "But when they persecute you in this city, flee to another. For assuredly, I say to you, you will not have gone through the cities of Israel before the Son of Man comes.

24 "A disciple is not above *his* teacher, nor a servant above his master.

25 "It is enough for a disciple that he be like his teacher, and a servant like his master. If they have called the master of the house Beelzebub, how much more *will they call* those of his household!

26 "Therefore do not fear them. For there is nothing covered that will not be revealed, and hidden that will not be known.

27 "Whatever I tell you in the dark, speak in the light; and what you hear in the ear, preach on the housetops.

28 "And do not fear those who kill the body but cannot kill the soul. But rather fear Him who is able to destroy both soul and body in hell.

29 "Are not two sparrows sold for a copper coin? And not one of them falls to the ground apart from your Father's will.

30 "But the very hairs of your head are all numbered.

31 "Do not fear therefore; you are of more value than many sparrows.

32 "Therefore whoever confesses Me before men, him I will also confess before My Father who is in heaven.

33 "But whoever denies Me before men, him I will also deny before My Father who is in heaven.

34 "Do not think that I came to bring peace on earth. I did not come to bring peace but a sword.

35 "For I have come to *'set a man against his father, a daughter against her mother, and a daughter-in-law against her mother-in-law.'*

36 "And *'a man's foes will be those of his own household.'*

37 "He who loves father or mother more than Me is not worthy of Me.

STEP 3

20

And he who loves son or daughter more than Me is not worthy of Me.

38 "And he who does not take his cross and follow after Me is not worthy of Me.

39 "He who finds his life will lose it, and he who loses his life for My sake will find it.

40 "He who receives you receives Me, and he who receives Me receives Him who sent Me.

41 "He who receives a prophet in the name of a prophet shall receive a prophet's reward. And he who receives a righteous man in the name of a righteous man shall receive a righteous man's reward.

42 "And whoever gives one of these little ones only a cup of cold *water* in the name of a disciple, assuredly, I say to you, he shall by no means lose his reward."

11 Now it came to pass, when Jesus finished commanding His twelve disciples, that He departed from there to teach and to preach in their cities.

2 And when John had heard in prison about the works of Christ, he sent two of his disciples

3 and said to Him, "Are You the Coming One, or do we look for another?"

4 Jesus answered and said to them, "Go and tell John the things which you hear and see:

5 "*The* blind receive their sight and *the* lame walk; *the* lepers are cleansed and *the* deaf hear; *the* dead are raised up and *the* poor have the gospel preached to them.

6 "And blessed is he who is not offended because of Me."

7 As they departed, Jesus began to say to the multitudes concerning John: "What did you go out into the wilderness to see? A reed shaken by the wind?

8 "But what did you go out to see? A man clothed in soft garments? Indeed, those who wear soft *clothing* are in kings' houses.

9 "But what did you go out to

see? A prophet? Yes, I say to you, and more than a prophet.

10 "For this is *he* of whom it is written:

'Behold, I send My messenger
  before Your face,
Who will prepare Your way
  before You.'

11 "Assuredly, I say to you, among those born of women there has not risen one greater than John the Baptist; but he who is least in the kingdom of heaven is greater than he.

12 "And from the days of John the Baptist until now the kingdom of heaven suffers violence, and the violent take it by force.

13 "For all the prophets and the law prophesied until John.

14 "And if you are willing to receive *it*, he is Elijah who is to come.

15 "He who has ears to hear, let him hear!

16 "But to what shall I liken this generation? It is like children sitting in the marketplaces and calling to their companions,

17 "and saying:

'We played the flute for you,
  And you did not dance;
We mourned to you,
  And you did not lament.'

18 "For John came neither eating nor drinking, and they say, 'He has a demon.'

19 "The Son of Man came eating and drinking, and they say, 'Look, a gluttonous man and a winebibber, a friend of tax collectors and sinners!' But wisdom is justified by her children."

20 Then He began to upbraid the cities in which most of His mighty works had been done, because they did not repent:

21 "Woe to you, Chorazin! Woe to

you, Bethsaida! For if the mighty works which were done in you had been done in Tyre and Sidon, they would have repented long ago in sackcloth and ashes.

22 "But I say to you, it will be more tolerable for Tyre and Sidon in the day of judgment than for you.

23 "And you, Capernaum, who are exalted to heaven, will be brought down to Hades; for if the mighty works which were done in you had been done in Sodom, it would have remained until this day.

24 "But I say to you that it shall be more tolerable for the land of Sodom in the day of judgment than for you."

25 At that time Jesus answered and said, "I thank You, Father, Lord of heaven and earth, because You have hidden these things from the wise and prudent and have revealed them to babes.

26 "Even so, Father, for so it seemed good in Your sight.

27 "All things have been delivered to Me by My Father, and no one knows the Son except the Father. Nor does anyone know the Father except the Son, and *he* to whom the Son wills to reveal *Him*.

28 "Come to Me, all *you* who labor and are heavy laden, and I will give you rest.

29 "Take My yoke upon you and learn from Me, for I am gentle and lowly in heart, and you will find rest for your souls.

30 "For My yoke *is* easy and My burden is light."

12 At that time Jesus went through the grainfields on the Sabbath. And His disciples were hungry, and began to pluck heads of grain and to eat.

2 But when the Pharisees saw *it,* they said to Him, "Look, Your disciples are doing what is not lawful to do on the Sabbath!"

3 Then He said to them, "Have you not read what David did when he was hungry, he and those who were with him:

4 "how he entered the house of God and ate the showbread which was not lawful for him to eat, nor for those who were with him, but only for the priests?

5 "Or have you not read in the law that on the Sabbath the priests in the temple profane the Sabbath, and are blameless?

6 "But I say to you that in this place there is *One* greater than the temple.

7 "But if you had known what *this* means, *'I desire mercy and not sacrifice,'* you would not have condemned the guiltless.

8 "For the Son of Man is Lord even of the Sabbath."

9 Now when He had departed from there, He went into their synagogue.

10 And behold, there was a man who had a withered hand. And they asked Him, saying, "Is it lawful to heal on the Sabbath?"—that they might accuse Him.

11 Then He said to them, "What man is there among you who has one sheep, and if it falls into a pit on the Sabbath, will not lay hold of it and lift *it* out?

12 "Of how much more value then is a man than a sheep? Therefore it is lawful to do good on the Sabbath."

13 Then He said to the man, "Stretch out your hand." And he stretched *it* out, and it was restored as whole as the other.

14 Then the Pharisees went out and took counsel against Him, how they might destroy Him.

15 But when Jesus knew *it,* He withdrew from there; and great multitudes followed Him, and He healed them all.

16 And He warned them not to make Him known,

17 that it might be fulfilled which was spoken by Isaiah the prophet, saying:

STEP 3

*Made a decision to turn our will and our lives
over to the care of God **as we understood Him.***

Matthew 11:28–30

Some of us have been bowed down with burdens of guilt, shame, bitterness, fear, and discouragement since childhood. We are tired of trying to stand, let alone walk under such a heavy load. As we allow God's healing love to infuse our lives, for the first time we may experience true rest.

Yet, just when we have first come to know rest, Jesus tells us to take His yoke upon us and learn from Him. Why? In biblical times, a farmer would yoke a young ox with an older, capable ox so that the young one could learn to plow correctly. Jesus is saying we no longer have to try to pull the plow by ourselves. He will be in the yoke with us; and we will be His disciples, learning from Him. As we walk with Him, the burden of His yoke of discipleship upon our necks will be light indeed compared with the painful burdens we tried to carry before we laid them at His feet.

For further reading on Step 3, turn to page 37.

Daily Encouragement

DAY 9 READING: MATTHEW 11:1–30

A Thought for the New Day: Some of us carry burdens we should never have picked up. Others of us carry loads that must be borne, as when a loving mother bears the burden of a wayward child. To all who feel the weight of life Jesus says, "Come to Me." Let us resolve not to be crushed under our loads anymore, but to join ourselves with Jesus. When we are yoked together with Him, He helps us pull the weight (vv. 28–30). *(Turn to page 25.)*

STEP
2

18 *"Behold, My Servant whom I
have chosen,
My Beloved in whom My soul
is well pleased;
I will put My Spirit upon Him,
And He will declare justice
to the Gentiles.*

19 *He will not quarrel nor cry out,
Nor will anyone hear His voice
in the streets.*

20 *A bruised reed He will not
break,
And smoking flax He will not
quench,
Till He sends forth justice to
victory.*

21 *And in His name Gentiles will
trust."*

22 Then one was brought to Him who was demon-possessed, blind and mute; and He healed him, so that the blind and mute man both spoke and saw.

23 And all the multitudes were amazed and said, "Could this be the Son of David?"

24 But when the Pharisees heard *it* they said, "This *fellow* does not cast out demons except by Beelzebub, the ruler of the demons."

25 But Jesus knew their thoughts, and said to them: "Every kingdom divided against itself is brought to desolation, and every city or house divided against itself will not stand.

26 "And if Satan casts out Satan, he is divided against himself. How then will his kingdom stand?

27 "And if I cast out demons by Beelzebub, by whom do your sons cast *them* out? Therefore they shall be your judges.

28 "But if I cast out demons by the Spirit of God, surely the kingdom of God has come upon you.

29 "Or *else* how can one enter a strong man's house and plunder his goods, unless he first binds the strong man? And then he will plunder his house.

30 "He who is not with Me is against Me, and he who does not gather with Me scatters abroad.

31 "Therefore I say to you, every sin and blasphemy will be forgiven men, but the blasphemy *against* the Spirit will not be forgiven men.

32 "Anyone who speaks a word against the Son of Man, it will be forgiven him; but whoever speaks against the Holy Spirit, it will not be forgiven him, either in this age or in the *age* to come.

33 "Either make the tree good and its fruit good, or else make the tree bad and its fruit bad; for a tree is known by *its* fruit.

34 "Brood of vipers! How can you, being evil, speak good things? For out of the abundance of the heart the mouth speaks.

35 "A good man out of the good treasure of his heart brings forth good things, and an evil man out of the evil treasure brings forth evil things.

STEP
9

36 "But I say to you that for every idle word men may speak, they will give account of it in the day of judgment.

37 "For by your words you will be justified, and by your words you will be condemned."

38 Then some of the scribes and Pharisees answered, saying, "Teacher, we want to see a sign from You."

39 But He answered and said to them, "An evil and adulterous generation seeks after a sign, and no sign will be given to it except the sign of the prophet Jonah.

40 "For as Jonah was three days and three nights in the belly of the great fish, so will the Son of Man be three days and three nights in the heart of the earth.

41 "The men of Nineveh will rise in the judgment with this generation and condemn it, because they repented at the preaching of Jonah; and indeed a greater than Jonah *is* here.

42 "The queen of the South will

*Came to believe that a Power greater than ourselves
could restore us to sanity.*

Matthew 12:18–21

What a beautiful picture of God's gentleness and power are these verses quoted from Isaiah!

Jesus, the Beloved Servant, was God in the flesh. His actions and life while He was on earth show us clearly God's character and concerns. He was so compassionate toward the downtrodden that Isaiah describes Him as careful not to break a battered reed. He would not extinguish a wick struggling to stay lit. He proved again and again His compassion for saint and sinner alike. But that gentleness was underscored by His great and awesome power. The very Savior who could speak kind and encouraging words to a woman caught in adultery could as easily raise the dead, drive out demons, and control the very forces of nature.

The power that resurrected Jesus from the dead is the same power that He offers to resurrect us from the living death of our dependencies and to alter the course of our lives.

For further reading on Step 2, turn to page 29.

Daily Encouragement

DAY 10 READING: MATTHEW 12:1–50

A Thought for the New Day: Jesus is not in the business of crushing burdened people with more problems: "A bruised reed He will not break" (v. 20). Part of His work is to heal the hurts and lift the burdens that are too great for us to bear. The religious leaders of Jesus' time loaded people with heavy duties, while the leaders themselves would not touch any of those loads. Is your heart heavy with cares that no one else seems able to help? Jesus will not turn you away. (*Turn to page 29.*)

rise up in the judgment with this generation and condemn it, for she came from the ends of the earth to hear the wisdom of Solomon; and indeed a greater than Solomon *is* here.

43 "When an unclean spirit goes out of a man, he goes through dry places, seeking rest, and finds none.

44 "Then he says, 'I will return to my house from which I came.' And when he comes, he finds it empty, swept, and put in order.

45 "Then he goes and takes with him seven other spirits more wicked than himself, and they enter and dwell there; and the last *state* of that man is worse than the first. So shall it also be with this wicked generation."

46 While He was still talking to the multitudes, behold, His mother and brothers stood outside, seeking to speak with Him.

47 Then one said to Him, "Look, Your mother and Your brothers are standing outside, seeking to speak with You."

48 But He answered and said to the one who told Him, "Who is My mother and who are My brothers?"

49 And He stretched out His hand toward His disciples and said, "Here are My mother and My brothers!

50 "For whoever does the will of My Father in heaven is My brother and sister and mother."

13 On the same day Jesus went out of the house and sat by the sea.

2 And great multitudes were gathered together to Him, so that He got into a boat and sat; and the whole multitude stood on the shore.

3 Then He spoke many things to them in parables, saying: "Behold, a sower went out to sow.

4 "And as he sowed, some *seed* fell by the wayside; and the birds came and devoured them.

5 "Some fell on stony places, where they did not have much earth; and they immediately sprang up because they had no depth of earth.

6 "But when the sun was up they were scorched, and because they had no root they withered away.

7 "And some fell among thorns, and the thorns sprang up and choked them.

8 "But others fell on good ground and yielded a crop: some a hundredfold, some sixty, some thirty.

9 "He who has ears to hear, let him hear!"

10 And the disciples came and said to Him, "Why do You speak to them in parables?"

11 He answered and said to them, "Because it has been given to you to know the mysteries of the kingdom of heaven, but to them it has not been given.

12 "For whoever has, to him more will be given, and he will have abundance; but whoever does not have, even what he has will be taken away from him.

13 "Therefore I speak to them in parables, because seeing they do not see, and hearing they do not hear, nor do they understand.

14 "And in them the prophecy of Isaiah is fulfilled, which says:

'Hearing you will hear
  and shall not understand,
And seeing you will see
  and not perceive;
15 For the heart of this people
  has grown dull.
Their ears are hard of hearing,
And their eyes they have
  closed,
Lest they should see with their
  eyes and hear with their ears,
Lest they should understand
  with their heart and turn,
So that I should heal them.'

16 "But blessed *are* your eyes for

they see, and your ears for they hear;

17 "for assuredly, I say to you that many prophets and righteous *men* desired to see what you see, and did not see *it*, and to hear what you hear, and did not hear *it*.

18 "Therefore hear the parable of the sower:

19 "When anyone hears the word of the kingdom, and does not understand *it*, then the wicked *one* comes and snatches away what was sown in his heart. This is he who received seed by the wayside.

20 "But he who received the seed on stony places, this is he who hears the word and immediately receives it with joy;

21 "yet he has no root in himself, but endures only for a while. For when tribulation or persecution arises because of the word, immediately he stumbles.

22 "Now he who received seed among the thorns is he who hears the word, and the cares of this world and the deceitfulness of riches choke the word, and he becomes unfruitful.

23 "But he who received seed on the good ground is he who hears the word and understands *it*, who indeed bears fruit and produces: some a hundredfold, some sixty, some thirty."

24 Another parable He put forth to them, saying: "The kingdom of heaven is like a man who sowed good seed in his field;

25 "but while men slept, his enemy came and sowed tares among the wheat and went his way.

26 "But when the grain had sprouted and produced a crop, then the tares also appeared.

27 "So the servants of the owner came and said to him, 'Sir, did you not sow good seed in your field? How then does it have tares?'

28 "He said to them, 'An enemy has done this.' The servants said to him, 'Do you want us then to go and gather them up?'

29 "But he said, 'No, lest while you gather up the tares you also uproot the wheat with them.

30 'Let both grow together until the harvest, and at the time of harvest I will say to the reapers, "First gather together the tares and bind them in bundles to burn them, but gather the wheat into my barn." ' "

31 Another parable He put forth to them, saying: "The kingdom of heaven is like a mustard seed, which a man took and sowed in his field,

32 "which indeed is the least of all the seeds; but when it is grown it is greater than the herbs and becomes a tree, so that the birds of the air come and nest in its branches."

33 Another parable He spoke to them: "The kingdom of heaven is like leaven, which a woman took and hid in three measures of meal till it was all leavened."

34 All these things Jesus spoke to the multitude in parables; and without a parable He did not speak to them,

35 that it might be fulfilled which was spoken by the prophet, saying:

"I will open My mouth in
*   parables;*
I will utter things which have
*   been kept secret from the*
*   foundation of the world."*

36 Then Jesus sent the multitude away and went into the house. And His disciples came to Him, saying, "Explain to us the parable of the tares of the field."

37 He answered and said to them: "He who sows the good seed is the Son of Man.

38 "The field is the world, the good seeds are the sons of the kingdom, but the tares are the sons of the wicked *one*.

39 "The enemy who sowed them is the devil, the harvest is the end of the age, and the reapers are the angels.

40 "Therefore as the tares are gathered and burned in the fire, so it will be at the end of this age.

41 "The Son of Man will send out His angels, and they will gather out of His kingdom all things that offend, and those who practice lawlessness,

42 "and will cast them into the furnace of fire. There will be wailing and gnashing of teeth.

43 "Then the righteous will shine forth as the sun in the kingdom of their Father. He who has ears to hear, let him hear!

44 "Again, the kingdom of heaven is like treasure hidden in a field, which a man found and hid; and for joy over it he goes and sells all that he has and buys that field.

45 "Again, the kingdom of heaven is like a merchant seeking beautiful pearls,

46 "who, when he had found one pearl of great price, went and sold all that he had and bought it.

47 "Again, the kingdom of heaven is like a dragnet that was cast into the sea and gathered some of every kind,

48 "which, when it was full, they drew to shore; and they sat down and gathered the good into vessels, but threw the bad away.

49 "So it will be at the end of the age. The angels will come forth, separate the wicked from among the just,

50 "and cast them into the furnace of fire. There will be wailing and gnashing of teeth."

51 Jesus said to them, "Have you understood all these things?" They said to Him, "Yes, Lord."

52 Then He said to them, "Therefore every scribe instructed concerning the kingdom of heaven is like a householder who brings out of his treasure *things* new and old."

53 Now it came to pass, when Jesus had finished these parables, that He departed from there.

54 And when He had come to His own country, He taught them in their synagogue, so that they were astonished and said, "Where did this *Man* get this wisdom and *these* mighty works?

55 "Is this not the carpenter's son? Is not His mother called Mary? And His brothers James, Joses, Simon, and Judas?

56 "And His sisters, are they not all with us? Where then did this *Man* get all these things?"

57 So they were offended at Him. But Jesus said to them, "A prophet is not without honor except in his own country and in his own house."

58 And He did not do many mighty works there because of their unbelief.

STEP 2

14 At that time Herod the tetrarch heard the report about Jesus

2 and said to his servants, "This is John the Baptist; he is risen from the dead, and therefore these powers are at work in him."

3 For Herod had laid hold of John and bound him, and put *him* in prison for the sake of Herodias, his brother Philip's wife.

4 For John had said to him, "It is not lawful for you to have her."

5 And although he wanted to put him to death, he feared the multitude, because they counted him as a prophet.

6 But when Herod's birthday was celebrated, the daughter of Herodias danced before them and pleased Herod.

7 Therefore he promised with an oath to give her whatever she might ask.

8 So she, having been prompted by her mother, said, "Give me

STEP 2

Came to believe that a Power greater than ourselves
could restore us to sanity.

Matthew 13:58

A good many people who struggle with dependencies experience that hopeless, helpless feeling of Step 1. Anyone who truly wants to overcome a problem must come to a place where he or she admits powerlessness over pain, addiction, or negative relationships. But to stop here can lead only to depression or suicide. The faith in God, upon which Step 2 is based, is the power that begins our healing process. Without this faith, the sad commentary of verse 58 might apply to us, as well. If we are truly hungry for mighty works of healing to begin in our lives, we must reach out to God in faith, believing that He is Creator of all and the Savior and Healer for those who turn in faith to Him.

For further reading on Step 2, turn to page 47.

Daily Encouragement

DAY 11 READING: MATTHEW 13:1–58

A Thought for the New Day: Many of us are bored because we have found nothing really worth living for. We would give anything just to find one thing we could spend our lives on, but we cannot seem to find it. Jesus compared His kingdom to a pearl more valuable than all others, so that a man sold everything to possess it (vv. 45, 46). That was a happy man. He had found the one thing he could live zestfully for. You, too, can have that joy of life. (*Turn to page 31.*)

John the Baptist's head here on a platter."

9 And the king was sorry; nevertheless, because of the oaths and because of those who sat with him at the table, he commanded *it* to be given to her.

10 So he sent and had John beheaded in prison.

11 And his head was brought on a platter and given to the girl, and she brought *it* to her mother.

12 Then his disciples came and took away the body and buried it, and went and told Jesus.

13 When Jesus heard *it,* He departed from there by boat to a deserted place by Himself. But when the multitudes heard it, they followed Him on foot from the cities.

14 And when Jesus went out He saw a great multitude; and He was moved with compassion for them, and healed their sick.

15 When it was evening, His disciples came to Him, saying, "This is a deserted place, and the hour is already late. Send the multitudes away, that they may go into the villages and buy themselves food."

16 But Jesus said to them, "They do not need to go away. You give them something to eat."

17 And they said to Him, "We have here only five loaves and two fish."

18 He said, "Bring them here to Me."

19 Then He commanded the multitudes to sit down on the grass. And He took the five loaves and the two fish, and looking up to heaven, He blessed and broke and gave the loaves to the disciples; and the disciples gave to the multitudes.

20 So they all ate and were filled, and they took up twelve baskets full of the fragments that remained.

21 Now those who had eaten were about five thousand men, besides women and children.

22 Immediately Jesus made His disciples get into the boat and go before Him to the other side, while He sent the multitudes away.

23 And when He had sent the multitudes away, He went up on a mountain by Himself to pray. And when evening had come, He was alone there.

24 But the boat was now in the middle of the sea, tossed by the waves, for the wind was contrary.

25 Now in the fourth watch of the night Jesus went to them, walking on the sea.

26 And when the disciples saw Him walking on the sea, they were troubled, saying, "It is a ghost!" And they cried out for fear.

27 But immediately Jesus spoke to them, saying, "Be of good cheer! It is I; do not be afraid."

28 And Peter answered Him and said, "Lord, if it is You, command me to come to You on the water."

29 So He said, "Come." And when Peter had come down out of the boat, he walked on the water to go to Jesus.

30 But when he saw that the wind *was* boisterous, he was afraid; and beginning to sink he cried out, saying, "Lord, save me!"

31 And immediately Jesus stretched out *His* hand and caught him, and said to him, "O you of little faith, why did you doubt?"

32 And when they got into the boat, the wind ceased.

33 Then those who were in the boat came and worshiped Him, saying, "Truly You are the Son of God."

34 When they had crossed over, they came to the land of Gennesaret.

35 And when the men of that place recognized Him, they sent out into all that surrounding region, brought to Him all who were sick,

36 and begged Him that they might only touch the hem of His garment. And as many as touched it were made perfectly well.

STEP 6

STEP 6

*Were entirely ready to have God
remove all these defects of character.*

Matthew 14:28–31

Most of us can identify with the apostle Peter, because even though he had committed his life to Jesus, he still had lots of rough edges sticking out. In verses 28–31 we get a glimpse of these rough edges. When the disciples saw Jesus walking on water, Peter enthusiastically decided that he, also, wanted to be part of the miracle. He discovered all too quickly, however, that enthusiasm alone could not carry him through.

As Jesus stretched out His hand to help Peter, He reminded the disciple that faith is the key to victory. At this moment many of us find ourselves on the verge of a similar miracle. To rid our lives of our negative habits, dependencies, and shortcomings seems as incredible as walking on water. By ourselves, such a task is ridiculously impossible. But Jesus stretches out His strong hand and says, "Come." Put your faith in His mighty power today and become ready for the exciting new life God has in store for you.

For further reading on Step 6, turn to page 96.

Daily Encouragement

DAY 12 READING: MATTHEW 14:1–36

A Thought for the New Day: You need a good reason to trust someone. Peter had every reason to trust Jesus in the storm: he had seen Him walking on the water. However, when the wind blew, Peter sank! The important thing is, Jesus did not let Peter drown (vv. 30, 31). Neither does He abandon us in the storms of life. Wouldn't it be better for us, though, if we could learn to walk calmly through life, just because we know Jesus can be trusted? (*Turn to page 33.*)

15 Then the scribes and Pharisees who were from Jerusalem came to Jesus, saying,

2 "Why do Your disciples transgress the tradition of the elders? For they do not wash their hands when they eat bread."

3 But He answered and said to them, "Why do you also transgress the commandment of God because of your tradition?

4 "For God commanded, saying, *'Honor your father and your mother'*; and, *'He who curses father or mother, let him be put to death.'*

5 "But you say, 'Whoever says to *his* father or mother, "Whatever profit you might have received from me has been dedicated *to the temple"*—

6 *'is released from* honoring his father or mother.' Thus you have made the commandment of God of no effect by your tradition.

7 "Hypocrites! Well did Isaiah prophesy about you, saying:

8 *'These people draw near to Me
   with their mouth,
   And honor Me with their lips,
   But their heart is far from Me.*
9 *And in vain they worship Me,
   Teaching as doctrines the
      commandments of men.'"*

10 Then He called the multitude and said to them, "Hear and understand:

11 "Not what goes into the mouth defiles a man; but what comes out of the mouth, this defiles a man."

12 Then His disciples came and said to Him, "Do You know that the Pharisees were offended when they heard this saying?"

13 But He answered and said, "Every plant which My heavenly Father has not planted will be uprooted.

14 "Let them alone. They are blind leaders of the blind. And if the blind leads the blind, both will fall into a ditch."

15 Then Peter answered and said to Him, "Explain this parable to us."

16 So Jesus said, "Are you also still without understanding?

17 "Do you not yet understand that whatever enters the mouth goes into the stomach and is eliminated?

18 "But those things which proceed out of the mouth come from the heart, and they defile a man.

19 "For out of the heart proceed evil thoughts, murders, adulteries, fornications, thefts, false witness, blasphemies.

20 "These are *the things* which defile a man, but to eat with unwashed hands does not defile a man."

21 Then Jesus went out from there and departed to the region of Tyre and Sidon.

22 And behold, a woman of Canaan came from that region and cried out to Him, saying, "Have mercy on me, O Lord, Son of David! My daughter is severely demon-possessed."

23 But He answered her not a word. And His disciples came and urged Him, saying, "Send her away, for she cries out after us."

24 But He answered and said, "I was not sent except to the lost sheep of the house of Israel."

25 Then she came and worshiped Him, saying, "Lord, help me!"

26 But He answered and said, "It is not good to take the children's bread and throw *it* to the little dogs."

27 And she said, "True, Lord, yet even the little dogs eat the crumbs which fall from their masters' table."

28 Then Jesus answered and said to her, "O woman, great *is* your faith! Let it be to you as you desire." And her daughter was healed from that very hour.

STEP
7

STEP
7

Humbly asked Him to remove our shortcomings.
Matthew 15:22–28

Humility unquestioningly accepts what Jesus tells us in John 15:5: "Without Me you can do nothing." Beyond that, humility acknowledges that all of us, as sinful human beings, deserve nothing other than eternal separation from God. As soon as we develop a heartfelt recognition of these two truths, we discover ourselves to be in the path of blessing and transformation.

In God's wise plan, Jesus spent His earthly time and energy evangelizing and discipling the nation of Israel. God had ordained that the disciples would later carry His message to the Gentile nations. This is the reason Jesus responded to the woman of Canaan as He did. But her humility and faith moved His heart and unleashed His mighty healing power for her need. In Step 7, we come to God with the same humility, knowing that the same mighty power is there to support us in our struggles and our need.

For further reading on Step 7, turn to page 39.

Daily
Encouragement

DAY 13 READING: MATTHEW 15:1–28

A Thought for the New Day: The Pharisees were more concerned with what looked good than with real goodness (vv. 17–20). Real goodness comes from inside us; it is not something we can put on like a nice dress or suit. While it is good to be clean on the outside, it is absolutely necessary to be clean on the inside. Then the outside takes care of itself, because what is in our hearts comes out for all to see at last. (*Turn to page 35.*)

29 And Jesus departed from there, skirted the Sea of Galilee, and went up on the mountain and sat down there.

30 Then great multitudes came to Him, having with them *those who were* lame, blind, mute, maimed, and many others; and they laid them down at Jesus' feet, and He healed them.

31 So the multitude marveled when they saw *the* mute speaking, *the* maimed made whole, *the* lame walking, and *the* blind seeing; and they glorified the God of Israel.

32 Then Jesus called His disciples *to Him* and said, "I have compassion on the multitude, because they have now continued with Me three days and have nothing to eat. And I do not want to send them away hungry, lest they faint on the way."

33 Then His disciples said to Him, "Where could we get enough bread in the wilderness to fill such a great multitude?"

34 Jesus said to them, "How many loaves do you have?" And they said, "Seven, and a few little fish."

35 And He commanded the multitude to sit down on the ground.

36 And He took the seven loaves and the fish and gave thanks, broke *them* and gave *them* to His disciples; and the disciples *gave* to the multitude.

37 So they all ate and were filled, and they took up seven large baskets full of the fragments that were left.

38 Now those who ate were four thousand men, besides women and children.

39 And He sent away the multitude, got into the boat, and came to the region of Magdala.

16 Then the Pharisees and Sadducees came, and testing Him asked that He would show them a sign from heaven.

2 He answered and said to them,

"When it is evening you say, '*It will be* fair weather, for the sky is red';

3 "and in the morning, '*It will be* foul weather today, for the sky is red and threatening.' Hypocrites! You know how to discern the face of the sky, but you cannot *discern* the signs of the times.

4 "A wicked and adulterous generation seeks after a sign, and no sign shall be given to it except the sign of the prophet Jonah." And He left them and departed.

5 And when His disciples had come to the other side, they had forgotten to take bread.

6 Then Jesus said to them, "Take heed and beware of the leaven of the Pharisees and the Sadducees."

7 And they reasoned among themselves, saying, "*It is* because we have taken no bread."

8 But when Jesus perceived it, He said to them, "O you of little faith, why do you reason among yourselves because you have brought no bread?

9 "Do you not yet understand, or remember the five loaves of the five thousand and how many baskets you took up?

10 "Nor the seven loaves of the four thousand and how many large baskets you took up?

11 "How is it you do not understand that I did not speak to you concerning bread?—but you should beware of the leaven of the Pharisees and Sadducees."

12 Then they understood that He did not tell *them* to beware of the leaven of bread, but of the doctrine of the Pharisees and Sadducees.

13 When Jesus came into the region of Caesarea Philippi, He asked His disciples, saying, "Who do men say that I, the Son of Man, am?"

14 So they said, "Some *say* John the Baptist, some Elijah, and others Jeremiah or one of the prophets."

STEP 8

*Made a list of all persons we had harmed,
and became willing to make amends to them all.*

Matthew 15:32–38

The disciples were overwhelmed by Jesus' suggestion that they feed the vast multitude surrounding them. With barely enough to sustain their own lives, how could Jesus make such an incredible demand of them? As we work through Step 8, we may have similar thoughts. Perhaps we have rationalized, *I'm barely keeping my head above water, and now I suddenly have to be concerned about those around me, as well? It's too much!* To feel this way, it is probably natural, but it is definitely not correct thinking.

This account of Jesus' power tells us that God not only completely covers our needs, but He can give us the wisdom, strength, and courage to make amends to those around us.

For further reading on Step 8, turn to page 41.

Daily Encouragement

DAY 14 READING: MATTHEW 15:29—16:4

A Thought for the New Day: Jesus did not perform the wonders He did in order to amaze the crowds who came to Him. Rather He had compassion (v. 32) on the people, and so He spent Himself to help them. Jesus will perform wonders like this for you, too. Quietly, gently, He alters the conditions, restores relationships, and strengthens our confidence to face every new day. (*Turn to page 37.*)

15 He said to them, "But who do you say that I am?"

16 And Simon Peter answered and said, "You are the Christ, the Son of the living God."

17 Jesus answered and said to him, "Blessed are you, Simon Bar-Jonah, for flesh and blood has not revealed *this* to you, but My Father who is in heaven.

18 "And I also say to you that you are Peter, and on this rock I will build My church, and the gates of Hades shall not prevail against it.

19 "And I will give you the keys of the kingdom of heaven, and whatever you bind on earth will be bound in heaven, and whatever you loose on earth will be loosed in heaven."

20 Then He commanded His disciples that they should tell no one that He was Jesus the Christ.

STEP 3
21 From that time Jesus began to show to His disciples that He must go to Jerusalem, and suffer many things from the elders and chief priests and scribes, and be killed, and be raised again the third day.

22 Then Peter took Him aside and began to rebuke Him, saying, "Far be it from You, Lord; this shall not happen to You!"

23 But He turned and said to Peter, "Get behind Me, Satan! You are an offense to Me, for you are not mindful of the things of God, but the things of men."

24 Then Jesus said to His disciples, "If anyone desires to come after Me, let him deny himself, and take up his cross, and follow Me.

25 "For whoever desires to save his life will lose it, and whoever loses his life for My sake will find it.

26 "For what is a man profited if he gains the whole world, and loses his own soul? Or what will a man give in exchange for his soul?

27 "For the Son of Man will come in the glory of His Father with His angels, and then He will reward each according to his works.

28 "Assuredly, I say to you, there are some standing here who shall not taste death till they see the Son of Man coming in His kingdom."

17 Now after six days Jesus took Peter, James, and John his brother, brought them up on a high mountain by themselves,

2 and was transfigured before them. His face shone like the sun, and His clothes became as white as the light.

3 And behold, Moses and Elijah appeared to them, talking with Him.

4 Then Peter answered and said to Jesus, "Lord, it is good for us to be here; if You wish, let us make here three tabernacles: one for You, one for Moses, and one for Elijah."

5 While he was still speaking, behold, a bright cloud overshadowed them; and suddenly a voice came out of the cloud, saying, "This is My beloved Son, in whom I am well pleased. Hear Him!"

6 And when the disciples heard *it,* they fell on their faces and were greatly afraid.

7 But Jesus came and touched them and said, "Arise, and do not be afraid."

8 And when they had lifted up their eyes, they saw no one but Jesus only.

9 Now as they came down from the mountain, Jesus commanded them, saying, "Tell the vision to no one until the Son of Man is risen from the dead."

10 And His disciples asked Him, saying, "Why then do the scribes say that Elijah must come first?"

11 Then Jesus answered and said to them, "Elijah truly is coming first and will restore all things.

12 "But I say to you that Elijah has come already, and they did not know him but did to him whatever they wished. Likewise the Son of

STEP 3

*Made a decision to turn our will and our lives
over to the care of God **as we understood Him.***

Matthew 16:21–26

The process of recovery involves several important paradoxes. One is that we must give up in order to win. Jesus voices this central paradox when He says, "For whoever desires to save his life will lose it, and whoever loses his life for My sake will find it" (v. 25).

Yielding our human will is not an easy matter. Often, from our limited human perspective, we may even question and challenge the wisdom of God's apparent will for us. Jesus' trusted disciple Peter implored his Lord to avoid the fate of persecution and death. Jesus sternly rebuked Peter, reminding him that he was "not mindful of the things of God, but the things of men" (v. 23).

Spiritual growth demands that we give our lives to God without reservation or restraint. Recovery literature exhorts us in this commitment with the following familiar words: "Half measures availed us nothing. We stood at the turning point. We asked His protection and care with complete abandon" (*Alcoholics Anonymous*, p. 59).

For further reading on Step 3, turn to page 61.

Daily Encouragement

DAY 15 READING: MATTHEW 16:5–28

A Thought for the New Day: Jesus must have had it backwards when He said: "Deny yourself!" (vv. 24, 25). How can giving up our rights be better than demanding them? Jesus said that those who lose themselves for His cause will gain far more than they lose. It is the law of life: Only seeds that are buried flourish at last. Only by losing our lives for Jesus will we find overflowing life. (*Turn to page 39.*)

Man is also about to suffer at their hands."

13 Then the disciples understood that He spoke to them of John the Baptist.

14 And when they had come to the multitude, a man came to Him, kneeling down to Him and saying,

15 "Lord, have mercy on my son, for he is an epileptic and suffers severely; for he often falls into the fire and often into the water.

16 "So I brought him to Your disciples, but they could not cure him."

17 Then Jesus answered and said, "O faithless and perverse generation, how long shall I be with you? How long shall I bear with you? Bring him here to Me."

18 And Jesus rebuked the demon, and he came out of him; and the child was cured from that very hour.

19 Then the disciples came to Jesus privately and said, "Why could we not cast him out?"

20 So Jesus said to them, "Because of your unbelief; for assuredly, I say to you, if you have faith as a mustard seed, you will say to this mountain, 'Move from here to there,' and it will move; and nothing will be impossible for you.

21 "However, this kind does not go out except by prayer and fasting."

22 Now while they were staying in Galilee, Jesus said to them, "The Son of Man is about to be betrayed into the hands of men,

23 "and they will kill Him, and the third day He will be raised up." And they were exceedingly sorrowful.

24 And when they had come to Capernaum, those who received the *temple* tax came to Peter and said, "Does your Teacher not pay the *temple* tax?"

25 He said, "Yes." And when he had come into the house, Jesus anticipated him, saying, "What do you think, Simon? From whom do the kings of the earth take customs or taxes, from their *own* sons or from strangers?"

26 Peter said to Him, "From strangers." Jesus said to him, "Then the sons are free.

27 "Nevertheless, lest we offend them, go to the sea, cast in a hook, and take the fish that comes up first. And when you have opened its mouth, you will find a piece of money; take that and give it to them for Me and you."

18 At that time the disciples came to Jesus, saying, "Who then is greatest in the kingdom of heaven?"

2 And Jesus called a little child to Him, set him in the midst of them,

3 and said, "Assuredly, I say to you, unless you are converted and become as little children, you will by no means enter the kingdom of heaven.

4 "Therefore whoever humbles himself as this little child is the greatest in the kingdom of heaven.

5 "And whoever receives one little child like this in My name receives Me.

6 "But whoever causes one of these little ones who believe in Me to sin, it would be better for him if a millstone were hung around his neck, and he were drowned in the depth of the sea.

7 "Woe to the world because of offenses! For offenses must come, but woe to that man by whom the offense comes!

8 "And if your hand or foot causes you to sin, cut it off and cast *it* from you. It is better for you to enter into life lame or maimed, rather than having two hands or two feet, to be cast into the everlasting fire.

9 "And if your eye causes you to sin, pluck it out and cast *it* from you. It is better for you to enter into life with one eye, rather than having two eyes, to be cast into hell fire.

10 "Take heed that you do not de-

Humbly asked Him to remove our shortcomings.
Matthew 18:4

Childhood is a time of special innocence. Not yet acquiring adult defense mechanisms and emotional shields, children respond to their world with delightful honesty and spontaneity. Unfortunately, their openness also leaves them vulnerable to abuse from the outside, and often the most damaging abuses are inflicted by other family members. Therefore, when Jesus tells us we must become as little children in order to enter the kingdom of heaven (a new spiritual way of living), some of us may find this very difficult. In fact, those earliest violations may be the root of many of our present shortcomings and defects of character. It takes both humility and courage for adult children of abuse to take the first step of trust.

Yet, if we will embark on this walk of faith, coming humbly before God as His children, He is faithful to take away our shortcomings and to begin to build the kingdom of heaven within us.

For further reading on Step 7, turn to page 101.

Daily Encouragement

DAY 16 READING: MATTHEW 17:1—18:9

A Thought for the New Day: Most of us are never given a miraculous vision, but each of us needs an inner vision to carry us through the temptations and trials that are common to people everywhere. Peter, James, and John never forgot the sight of Jesus on the mountain (17:2–9). It was a vision that spurred them to unusual achievements throughout their lives. Likewise, as you come to the hard places, the very thought of Jesus in His beauty makes you triumph. *(Turn to page 41.)*

spise one of these little ones, for I say to you that in heaven their angels always see the face of My Father who is in heaven.

11 "For the Son of Man has come to save that which was lost.

12 "What do you think? If a man has a hundred sheep, and one of them goes astray, does he not leave the ninety-nine and go to the mountains to seek the one that is straying?

13 "And if he should find it, assuredly, I say to you, he rejoices more over that *sheep* than over the ninety-nine that did not go astray.

14 "Even so it is not the will of your Father who is in heaven that one of these little ones should perish.

15 "Moreover if your brother sins against you, go and tell him his fault between you and him alone. If he hears you, you have gained your brother.

16 "But if he will not hear *you*, take with you one or two more, that *'by the mouth of two or three witnesses every word may be established.'*

17 "And if he refuses to hear them, tell *it* to the church. But if he refuses even to hear the church, let him be to you like a heathen and a tax collector.

18 "Assuredly, I say to you, whatever you bind on earth will be bound in heaven, and whatever you loose on earth will be loosed in heaven.

19 "Again I say to you that if two of you agree on earth concerning anything that they ask, it will be done for them by My Father in heaven.

20 "For where two or three are gathered together in My name, I am there in the midst of them."

21 Then Peter came to Him and said, "Lord, how often shall my brother sin against me, and I forgive him? Up to seven times?"

22 Jesus said to him, "I do not say to you, up to seven times, but up to seventy times seven.

23 "Therefore the kingdom of heaven is like a certain king who wanted to settle accounts with his servants.

24 "And when he had begun to settle accounts, one was brought to him who owed him ten thousand talents.

25 "But as he was not able to pay, his master commanded that he be sold, with his wife and children and all that he had, and that payment be made.

26 "The servant therefore fell down before him, saying, 'Master, have patience with me, and I will pay you all.'

27 "Then the master of that servant was moved with compassion, released him, and forgave him the debt.

28 "But that servant went out and found one of his fellow servants who owed him a hundred denarii; and he laid hands on him and took *him* by the throat, saying, 'Pay me what you owe!'

29 "So his fellow servant fell down at his feet and begged him, saying, 'Have patience with me, and I will pay you all.'

30 "And he would not, but went and threw him into prison till he should pay the debt.

31 "So when his fellow servants saw what had been done, they were very grieved, and came and told their master all that had been done.

32 "Then his master, after he had called him, said to him, 'You wicked servant! I forgave you all that debt because you begged me.

33 'Should you not also have had compassion on your fellow servant, just as I had pity on you?'

34 "And his master was angry, and delivered him to the torturers until he should pay all that was due to him.

STEP 8

40

STEP 8

Made a list of all persons we had harmed,
and became willing to make amends to them all.

Matthew 18:21–35

Step 8 encourages us to admit our own responsibility in problem situations and relationships.

The story Jesus tells the apostle Peter is a good springboard to Step 8 whether we are the forgiver or the one asking forgiveness. Peter, Jesus said, should not be like the servant, who, after being forgiven for his huge debt, then refused to show mercy and compassion toward the person who owed him a much smaller debt.

God, in His mercy, forgave us and saved us even in the depths of our addictive illness. Now we must become willing "from the heart" (v. 35) to forgive and be reconciled with others.

If, on the other hand, we are in the position of needing to make amends for wrongs we have done, the underlying attitude must still be "from the heart." When God sees such a heart—totally willing to obey regardless of the outcome—He will move and work and bless far above our ability to ask or even think.

For further reading on Step 8, turn to page 51.

Daily Encouragement

DAY 17 READING: MATTHEW 18:10–35

A Thought for the New Day: Do you ever fear getting lost in the crowd? No one seems to know or care that you exist. Jesus cares about lost people—people who cannot seem to find their way in the world anymore (v. 12). Everything is too overwhelming for them. Such people He seeks along the streets and highways of life. As He calls out to you, turn and let Him find you. (*Turn to page 43.*)

35 "So My heavenly Father also will do to you if each of you, from his heart, does not forgive his brother his trespasses."

19 Now it came to pass, when Jesus had finished these sayings, *that* He departed from Galilee and came to the region of Judea beyond the Jordan.

2 And great multitudes followed Him, and He healed them there.

3 The Pharisees also came to Him, testing Him, and saying to Him, "Is it lawful for a man to divorce his wife for *just* any reason?"

4 And He answered and said to them, "Have you not read that He who made *them* at the beginning *'made them male and female,'*

5 "and said, *'For this reason a man shall leave his father and mother and be joined to his wife, and the two shall become one flesh'*?

6 "So then, they are no longer two but one flesh. Therefore what God has joined together, let not man separate."

7 They said to Him, "Why then did Moses command to give a certificate of divorce, and to put her away?"

8 He said to them, "Moses, because of the hardness of your hearts, permitted you to divorce your wives, but from the beginning it was not so.

9 "And I say to you, whoever divorces his wife, except for sexual immorality, and marries another, commits adultery; and whoever marries her who is divorced commits adultery."

10 His disciples said to Him, "If such is the case of the man with *his* wife, it is better not to marry."

11 But He said to them, "All cannot accept this saying, but only *those* to whom it has been given:

12 "For there are eunuchs who were born thus from *their* mother's womb, and there are eunuchs who were made eunuchs by men, and there are eunuchs who have made themselves eunuchs for the kingdom of heaven's sake. He who is able to accept *it*, let him accept *it*."

13 Then little children were brought to Him that He might put *His* hands on them and pray, but the disciples rebuked them.

14 But Jesus said, "Let the little children come to Me, and do not forbid them; for of such is the kingdom of heaven."

STEP 1

15 And He laid *His* hands on them and departed from there.

16 Now behold, one came and said to Him, "Good Teacher, what good thing shall I do that I may have eternal life?"

17 So He said to him, "Why do you call Me good? No one *is* good but One, *that is*, God. But if you want to enter into life, keep the commandments."

18 He said to Him, "Which ones?" Jesus said, *"'You shall not murder,' 'You shall not commit adultery,' 'You shall not steal,' 'You shall not bear false witness,'*

19 *'Honor your father and your mother,'* and, *'You shall love your neighbor as yourself.'"*

20 The young man said to Him, "All these things I have kept from my youth. What do I still lack?"

21 Jesus said to him, "If you want to be perfect, go, sell what you have and give to the poor, and you will have treasure in heaven; and come, follow Me."

22 But when the young man heard that saying, he went away sorrowful, for he had great possessions.

23 Then Jesus said to His disciples, "Assuredly, I say to you that it is hard for a rich man to enter the kingdom of heaven.

24 "And again I say to you, it is easier for a camel to go through the eye of a needle than for a rich man to enter the kingdom of God."

25 When His disciples heard *it*, they were exceedingly amazed, saying, "Who then can be saved?"

STEP 1

*We admitted we were powerless over our dependencies—
that our lives had become unmanageable.*

Matthew 19:13, 14

Jesus' response to children was a wide departure from the normal mind-set of His day. In those times children were not very important, and for a teacher or rabbi to be interrupted by them was really unthinkable. But Jesus put primary importance on each child brought to Him. Why? Jesus Himself gave us the answer when He said, "Of such is the kingdom of heaven." In other words, there is something in a child that makes it easy for him or her to belong to God's kingdom.

Small children are totally dependent on others to meet their needs. This is exactly the place each of us must reach if we are to begin our restoration. We must admit that we are helpless and powerless over the addictions and pain in our lives. To come to this point of childlike dependency is to open the door to the incredible power of our Almighty Creator.

For further reading on Step 1, turn to page 81.

Daily Encouragement

DAY 18 READING: MATTHEW 19:1–22

A Thought for the New Day: Wealth can be used, as many use it, to bring blessing to those who have little; but wealth, like anything else, can be overemphasized. Then it will hurt rather than heal. The young man in Matthew's story valued his wealth so highly that he lost the greatest wealth of all—the friendship of Jesus (vv. 21, 22). Let us make up our minds not to be possessed by our possessions. (*Turn to page 45.*)

26 But Jesus looked at *them* and said to them, "With men this is impossible, but with God all things are possible."

27 Then Peter answered and said to Him, "See, we have left all and followed You. Therefore what shall we have?"

28 So Jesus said to them, "Assuredly I say to you, that in the regeneration, when the Son of Man sits on the throne of His glory, you who have followed Me will also sit on twelve thrones, judging the twelve tribes of Israel.

29 "And everyone who has left houses or brothers or sisters or father or mother or wife or children or lands, for My name's sake, shall receive a hundredfold, and inherit everlasting life.

30 "But many *who are* first will be last, and the last first.

STEP 10

20 "For the kingdom of heaven is like a landowner who went out early in the morning to hire laborers for his vineyard.

2 "Now when he had agreed with the laborers for a denarius a day, he sent them into his vineyard.

3 "And he went out about the third hour and saw others standing idle in the marketplace,

4 "and said to them, 'You also go into the vineyard, and whatever is right I will give you.' And they went.

5 "Again he went out about the sixth and the ninth hour, and did likewise.

6 "And about the eleventh hour he went out and found others standing idle, and said to them, 'Why have you been standing here idle all day?'

7 "They said to him, 'Because no one hired us.' He said to them, 'You also go into the vineyard, and whatever is right you will receive.'

8 "So when evening had come, the owner of the vineyard said to his steward, 'Call the laborers and give them *their* wages, beginning with the last to the first.'

9 "And when those came who *were hired* about the eleventh hour, they each received a denarius.

10 "But when the first came, they supposed that they would receive more; and they likewise received each a denarius.

11 "And when they had received *it*, they murmured against the landowner,

12 "saying, 'These last *men* have worked *only* one hour, and you made them equal to us who have borne the burden and the heat of the day.'

13 "But he answered one of them and said, 'Friend, I am doing you no wrong. Did you not agree with me for a denarius?

14 'Take *what is* yours and go your way. I wish to give to this last man *the same* as to you.

15 'Is it not lawful for me to do what I wish with my own things? Or is your eye evil because I am good?'

16 "So the last will be first, and the first last. For many are called, but few chosen."

17 Then Jesus, going up to Jerusalem, took the twelve disciples aside on the road and said to them,

18 "Behold, we are going up to Jerusalem, and the Son of Man will be betrayed to the chief priests and to the scribes; and they will condemn Him to death,

19 "and deliver Him to the Gentiles to mock and to scourge and to crucify. And the third day He will rise again."

20 Then the mother of Zebedee's sons came to Him with her sons, kneeling down and asking something from Him.

21 And He said to her, "What do you wish?" She said to Him, "Grant that these two sons of mine may sit, one on Your right hand

STEP 10

*Continued to take personal inventory
and when we were wrong promptly admitted it.*

Matthew 20:1–16

As those who are recovering from dysfunctional family situations, we need to be quick to recognize and root out the common "That's not fair" syndrome from our lives. We should also take care to avoid smugness about our gains in recovery. We rejoice in the blessing of God in our own lives, but it may irk us more than we want to admit when someone whom we feel does not deserve good things from God seems to get them.

Jesus' parable is a word of warning: Not one of us has the right to tell Almighty God what to do. Even though God may choose to be exceedingly gracious in the life of someone we feel does not deserve His graciousness, we must always remember He has never been unfair to us. When we humbly remember the vast difference between what we actually deserve as sinners and the magnificent gift God has given us instead, our hearts will have no room for envy.

For further reading on Step 10, turn to page 65.

Daily Encouragement

DAY 19 READING: MATTHEW 19:23—20:19

A Thought for the New Day: Death is not the end of all, and it was not the end for Jesus. Although He came to die, as He told His followers He would, He died only in order to live again (20:18, 19). Yes, the Good Shepherd not only went about doing good, but He also died for His sheep—for you and me—that we might live with Him. (*Turn to page 47.*)

and the other on the left, in Your kingdom."

22 But Jesus answered and said, "You do not know what you ask. Are you able to drink the cup that I am about to drink, and be baptized with the baptism that I am baptized with?" They said to Him, "We are able."

23 So He said to them, "You will indeed drink My cup, and be baptized with the baptism that I am baptized with; but to sit on My right hand and on My left is not Mine to give, but *it is for those* for whom it is prepared by My Father."

24 And when the ten heard *it,* they were moved with indignation against the two brothers.

25 But Jesus called them *to Himself* and said, "You know that the rulers of the Gentiles lord it over them, and those who are great exercise authority over them.

26 "Yet it shall not be so among you; but whoever desires to become great among you, let him be your servant.

27 "And whoever desires to be first among you, let him be your slave—

28 "just as the Son of Man did not come to be served, but to serve, and to give His life a ransom for many."

STEP
2
29 Now as they departed from Jericho, a great multitude followed Him.

30 And behold, two blind men sitting by the road, when they heard that Jesus was passing by, cried out, saying, "Have mercy on us, O Lord, Son of David!"

31 Then the multitude warned them that they should be quiet; but they cried out all the more, saying, "Have mercy on us, O Lord, Son of David!"

32 So Jesus stood still and called them, and said, "What do you want Me to do for you?"

33 They said to Him, "Lord, that our eyes may be opened."

34 So Jesus had compassion and touched their eyes. And immediately their eyes received sight, and they followed Him.

21 Now when they drew near to Jerusalem, and came to Bethphage, at the Mount of Olives, then Jesus sent two disciples,

2 saying to them, "Go into the village opposite you, and immediately you will find a donkey tied, and a colt with her. Loose *them* and bring *them* to Me.

3 "And if anyone says anything to you, you shall say, 'The Lord has need of them,' and immediately he will send them."

4 All this was done that it might be fulfilled which was spoken by the prophet, saying:

5 *"Tell the daughter of Zion,*
  'Behold, your King is coming to
    you,
  Lowly, and sitting on a donkey,
  A colt, the foal of a donkey.' "

6 So the disciples went and did as Jesus commanded them.

7 They brought the donkey and the colt, laid their clothes on them, and set *Him* on them.

8 And a very great multitude spread their garments on the road; others cut down branches from the trees and spread *them* on the road.

9 Then the multitudes who went before and those who followed cried out, saying:

"Hosanna to the Son of David!
'*Blessed is He who comes*
  in the name of the Lord!'
Hosanna in the highest!"

10 And when He had come into Jerusalem, all the city was moved, saying, "Who is this?"

11 So the multitudes said, "This is Jesus, the prophet from Nazareth of Galilee."

STEP 2

Came to believe that a Power greater than ourselves could restore us to sanity.

Matthew 20:29–34

Picture the ragged, blind men of these verses. Unable to be useful to society, they were forced to sit beside a road, begging for alms. Then one day a crowd, accompanied by great commotion, passed by. With difficulty, the blind men discerned that the Great Healer, Jesus, was the reason for the excitement. They were quick to recognize that Jesus was their only hope, and they were determined to grasp that hope, no matter what. Even though some in the crowd tried to discourage their efforts, they cried out to Jesus.

Jesus brought all other activity to a halt and focused His attention and compassion on these men. He reached out to touch each one, bringing the healing and restoration that nothing and no one else could give. You can be touched by Jesus today. Call out to Him alone. He promises us in Jeremiah 33:3, "Call to Me, and I will answer you, and show you great and mighty things, which you do not know."

For further reading on Step 2, turn to page 91.

Daily Encouragement

DAY 20 READING: MATTHEW 20:20—21:44

A Thought for the New Day: God's way "up" is "down." That seems strange in a world where being "Number One" is the goal of the game of life. Yet Jesus recommends the "servant" way (20:25, 26). After all, He who was King of all kings became the servant of everyone. If we have His promise of reigning with Him, what do we have to lose by following His example? In fact, we have His promise of heaven to win! *(Turn to page 51.)*

12 Then Jesus went into the temple of God and drove out all those who bought and sold in the temple, and overturned the tables of the moneychangers and the seats of those who sold doves.

13 And He said to them, "It is written, *'My house shall be called a house of prayer,'* but you have made it a *'den of thieves.'"*

14 Then *the* blind and *the* lame came to Him in the temple, and He healed them.

15 But when the chief priests and scribes saw the wonderful things that He did, and the children crying out in the temple and saying, "Hosanna to the Son of David!" they were indignant

16 and said to Him, "Do You hear what these are saying?" And Jesus said to them, "Yes. Have you never read, *'Out of the mouth of babes and nursing infants You have perfected praise'?* "

17 Then He left them and went out of the city to Bethany, and He lodged there.

18 Now in the morning, as He returned to the city, He was hungry.

19 And seeing a fig tree by the road, He came to it and found nothing on it but leaves, and said to it, "Let no fruit grow on you ever again." And immediately the fig tree withered away.

20 Now when the disciples saw *it*, they marveled, saying, "How did the fig tree wither away so soon?"

STEP 7

21 So Jesus answered and said to them, "Assuredly, I say to you, if you have faith and do not doubt, you will not only do what was done to the fig tree, but also if you say to this mountain, 'Be removed and be cast into the sea,' it will be done.

22 "And all things, whatever you ask in prayer, believing, you will receive."

23 Now when He came into the temple, the chief priests and the elders of the people confronted Him as He was teaching, and said, "By what authority are You doing these things? And who gave You this authority?"

24 But Jesus answered and said to them, "I also will ask you one thing, which if you tell Me, I likewise will tell you by what authority I do these things:

25 "The baptism of John, where was it from? From heaven or from men?" And they reasoned among themselves, saying, "If we say, 'From heaven,' He will say to us, 'Why then did you not believe him?'

26 "But if we say, 'From men,' we fear the multitude, for all count John as a prophet."

27 So they answered Jesus and said, "We do not know." And He said to them, "Neither will I tell you by what authority I do these things.

28 "But what do you think? A man had two sons, and he came to the first and said, 'Son, go, work today in my vineyard.'

29 "He answered and said, 'I will not,' but afterward he regretted it and went.

30 "Then he came to the second and said likewise. And he answered and said, 'I go, sir,' but he did not go.

31 "Which of the two did the will of *his* father?" They said to Him, "The first." Jesus said to them, "Assuredly, I say to you that tax collectors and harlots enter the kingdom of God before you.

32 "For John came to you in the way of righteousness, and you did not believe him; but tax collectors and harlots believed him; and when you saw *it*, you did not afterward relent and believe him.

33 "Hear another parable: There was a certain landowner who planted a vineyard and set a hedge around it, dug a winepress in it and built a tower. And he leased it to

vinedressers and went into a far country.

34 "Now when vintage-time drew near, he sent his servants to the vinedressers, that they might receive its fruit.

35 "And the vinedressers took his servants, beat one, killed one, and stoned another.

36 "Again he sent other servants, more than the first, and they did likewise to them.

37 "Then last of all he sent his son to them, saying, 'They will respect my son.'

38 "But when the vinedressers saw the son, they said among themselves, 'This is the heir. Come, let us kill him and seize his inheritance.'

39 "And they caught him, and cast *him* out of the vineyard, and killed *him.*

40 "Therefore, when the owner of the vineyard comes, what will he do to those vinedressers?"

41 They said to Him, "He will destroy those wicked men miserably, and lease *his* vineyard to other vinedressers who will render to him the fruits in their seasons."

42 Jesus said to them, "Did you never read in the Scriptures:

'The stone which the builders rejected
Has become the chief cornerstone.
This was the LORD's *doing,*
And it is marvelous in our eyes'?

43 "Therefore I say to you, the kingdom of God will be taken from you and given to a nation bearing the fruits of it.

44 "And whoever falls on this stone will be broken; but on whomever it falls, it will grind him to powder."

45 Now when the chief priests and Pharisees heard His parables, they perceived that He was speaking of them.

46 But when they sought to lay hands on Him, they feared the multitudes, because they took Him for a prophet.

22 And Jesus answered and spoke to them again by parables and said:

2 "The kingdom of heaven is like a certain king who arranged a marriage for his son,

3 "and sent out his servants to call those who were invited to the wedding; and they were not willing to come.

4 "Again, he sent out other servants, saying, 'Tell those who are invited, "See, I have prepared my dinner; my oxen and fatted cattle *are* killed, and all things *are* ready. Come to the wedding." '

5 "But they made light of it and went their ways, one to his own farm, another to his business.

6 "And the rest seized his servants, treated *them* spitefully, and killed *them.*

7 "But when the king heard *about it,* he was furious. And he sent out his armies, destroyed those murderers, and burned up their city.

8 "Then he said to his servants, 'The wedding is ready, but those who were invited were not worthy.

9 'Therefore go into the highways, and as many as you find, invite to the wedding.'

10 "So those servants went out into the highways and gathered together all whom they found, both bad and good. And the wedding *hall* was filled with guests.

11 "But when the king came in to see the guests, he saw a man there who did not have on a wedding garment.

12 "So he said to him, 'Friend, how did you come in here without a wedding garment?' And he was speechless.

13 "Then the king said to the servants, 'Bind him hand and foot,

take him away, and cast *him* into outer darkness; there will be weeping and gnashing of teeth.'

14 "For many are called, but few *are* chosen."

15 Then the Pharisees went and plotted how they might entangle Him in *His* talk.

16 And they sent to Him their disciples with the Herodians, saying, "Teacher, we know that You are true, and teach the way of God in truth; nor do You care about anyone, for You do not regard the person of men.

17 "Tell us, therefore, what do You think? Is it lawful to pay taxes to Caesar, or not?"

18 But Jesus perceived their wickedness, and said, "Why do you test Me, *you* hypocrites?

19 "Show Me the tax money." So they brought Him a denarius.

20 And He said to them, "Whose image and inscription *is* this?"

21 They said to Him, "Caesar's." And He said to them, "Render therefore to Caesar the things that are Caesar's, and to God the things that are God's."

22 When they had heard *these words*, they marveled, and left Him and went their way.

23 The same day the Sadducees, who say there is no resurrection, came to Him and asked Him,

24 saying: "Teacher, Moses said that if a man dies, having no children, his brother shall marry his wife and raise up offspring for his brother.

25 "Now there were with us seven brothers. The first died after he had married, and having no offspring, left his wife to his brother.

26 "Likewise the second also, and the third, even to the seventh.

27 "And last of all the woman died also.

28 "Therefore, in the resurrection, whose wife of the seven will she be? For they all had her."

29 Jesus answered and said to them, "You are mistaken, not knowing the Scriptures nor the power of God.

30 "For in the resurrection they neither marry nor are given in marriage, but are like angels of God in heaven.

31 "But concerning the resurrection of the dead, have you not read what was spoken to you by God, saying,

32 *'I am the God of Abraham, the God of Isaac, and the God of Jacob'*? God is not the God of the dead, but of the living."

33 And when the multitudes heard *this*, they were astonished at His teaching.

34 But when the Pharisees heard that He had silenced the Sadducees, they gathered together.

35 Then one of them, a lawyer, asked *Him a question*, testing Him, and saying,

36 "Teacher, which *is* the great commandment in the law?"

37 Jesus said to him, "'*You shall love the* LORD *your God with all your heart, with all your soul, and with all your mind.'*

38 "This is *the* first and great commandment.

39 "And *the* second *is* like it: *'You shall love your neighbor as yourself.'*

40 "On these two commandments hang all the Law and the Prophets."

41 While the Pharisees were gathered together, Jesus asked them,

42 saying, "What do you think about the Christ? Whose Son is He?" They said to Him, "The Son of David."

43 He said to them, "How then does David in the Spirit call Him *'Lord'*, saying:

44 *'The* LORD *said to my Lord,*
"*Sit at My right hand,*
Till I make Your enemies
Your footstool"'?

STE
8

STEP 8

*Made a list of all persons we had harmed,
and became willing to make amends to them all.*

Matthew 22:36–40

When Jesus tells us the commandment to love our neighbor as we love ourselves is like the first commandment concerning love for God, He gives it a very high priority. So should we. This is why Step 8 is so important. Making amends to the people in our world also increases our own opportunity for abundant life. While we should not simply ignore or excuse those who have offended us, the key to truly abundant life is in the phrase "You shall love your neighbor as you love yourself." When we have offended others, we want them to forgive us and release the negative feelings they have toward us. (Jesus intended the words "your neighbor" to mean anyone besides yourself). And since we are all sinners, perhaps this is love in the best sense of the word. Let us be willing to reach out to all who have had a part in our lives.

For further reading on Step 8, turn to page 103.

Daily Encouragement

DAY 21 READING: MATTHEW 21:45—22:46

A Thought for the New Day: Jesus really gave us no new commands (22:37–39): even Moses taught us that we should love one another (Lev. 19:18). This is not surprising because God Himself is Love. We cannot fully understand that with our minds, except to say that the sum of God's character adds up to LOVE. Truly, to know Him is to love Him, and our daily prayer must be to appropriate that love that Jesus came to show us in Himself. (*Turn to page 53.*)

45 "If David then calls Him *'Lord'*, how is He his Son?"

46 And no one was able to answer Him a word, nor from that day on did anyone dare question Him anymore.

23 Then Jesus spoke to the multitudes and to His disciples,

2 saying: "The scribes and the Pharisees sit in Moses' seat.

3 "Therefore whatever they tell you to observe, *that* observe and do, but do not do according to their works; for they say, and do not do.

4 "For they bind heavy burdens, hard to bear, and lay *them* on men's shoulders; but they *themselves* will not move them with one of their fingers.

5 "But all their works they do to be seen by men. They make their phylacteries broad and enlarge the borders of their garments.

6 "They love the best places at feasts, the best seats in the synagogues,

7 "greetings in the marketplaces, and to be called by men, 'Rabbi, Rabbi.'

8 "But you, do not be called 'Rabbi'; for One is your Teacher, the Christ, and you are all brethren.

9 "Do not call anyone on earth your father; for One is your Father, He who is in heaven.

10 "And do not be called teachers; for One is your Teacher, the Christ.

11 "But he who is greatest among you shall be your servant.

STEP 5

12 "And whoever exalts himself will be abased, and he who humbles himself will be exalted.

13 "But woe to you, scribes and Pharisees, hypocrites! For you shut up the kingdom of heaven against men; for you neither go in *yourselves*, nor do you allow those who are entering to go in.

14 "Woe to you, scribes and Pharisees, hypocrites! For you devour widows' houses, and for a pretense make long prayers. Therefore you will receive greater condemnation.

15 "Woe to you, scribes and Pharisees, hypocrites! For you travel land and sea to win one proselyte, and when he is won, you make him twice as much a son of hell as yourselves.

16 "Woe to you, blind guides, who say, 'Whoever swears by the temple, it is nothing; but whoever swears by the gold of the temple, he is obliged *to perform it*.'

17 "Fools and blind! For which is greater, the gold or the temple that sanctifies the gold?

18 "And, 'Whoever swears by the altar, it is nothing; but whoever swears by the gift that is on it, he is obliged *to perform it*.'

19 "Fools and blind! For which is greater, the gift or the altar that sanctifies the gift?

20 "Therefore he who swears by the altar, swears by it and by all things on it.

21 "He who swears by the temple, swears by it and by Him who dwells in it.

22 "And he who swears by heaven, swears by the throne of God and by Him who sits on it.

23 "Woe to you, scribes and Pharisees, hypocrites! For you pay tithe of mint and anise and cummin, and have neglected the weightier *matters* of the law: justice and mercy and faith. These you ought to have done, without leaving the others undone.

STEP 4

24 "Blind guides, who strain out a gnat and swallow a camel!

25 "Woe to you, scribes and Pharisees, hypocrites! For you cleanse the outside of the cup and dish, but inside they are full of extortion and self-indulgence.

26 "Blind Pharisee, first cleanse the inside of the cup and dish, that the outside of them may be clean also.

27 "Woe to you, scribes and Pharisees, hypocrites! For you are like

STEP 4

Made a searching and fearless moral inventory of ourselves.

Matthew 23:23–28

Modern understandings of addiction suggest that all addictions and compulsions are fundamentally shame-based. Whether our profound shame feelings come from early family situations that we witnessed and experienced, or whether they arise from the practice of our own current dependencies, robust recovery can occur only when this shame is cleansed away. Scripture cautions that this cleansing must work from the inside out, and Twelve Step recovery suggests the tool of a "searching and fearless moral inventory" as a means of accomplishing this cleansing.

Effective inventory work requires that we find the sources of both false and authentic shame. We may carry false guilt about the childhood experience of sexual violation or the impact of parental chemical abuse. Or we may carry authentic feelings of guilt about the damage we have inflicted on others through the practice of our dependent behaviors.

Step 4 is a special opportunity to bring those dark recesses of our lives before the cleansing light of God's Spirit.

For further reading on Step 4, turn to page 75.

Daily Encouragement

DAY 22 READING: MATTHEW 23:1–39

A Thought for the New Day: Although every culture defines beauty in different ways, we are overwhelmed by it when we see it. Personal beauty is a quality that comes from the mind, expressing itself in a look, a word, or a gesture of caring or compassion (v. 27). To witness this beauty is to glimpse the face of God Himself. *Lord, let this beauty be seen in each of us, so that the world may see Jesus.* (*Turn to page 57.*)

whitewashed tombs which indeed appear beautiful outwardly, but inside are full of dead *men's* bones and all uncleanness.

28 "Even so you also outwardly appear righteous to men, but inside you are full of hypocrisy and lawlessness.

29 "Woe to you, scribes and Pharisees, hypocrites! Because you build the tombs of the prophets and adorn the monuments of the righteous,

30 "and say, 'If we had lived in the days of our fathers, we would not have been partakers with them in the blood of the prophets.'

31 "Therefore you are witnesses against yourselves that you are sons of those who murdered the prophets.

32 "Fill up, then, the measure of your fathers' *guilt*.

33 "Serpents, brood of vipers! How can you escape the condemnation of hell?

34 "Therefore, indeed, I send you prophets, wise men, and scribes: *some* of them you will kill and crucify, and *some* of them you will scourge in your synagogues and persecute from city to city,

35 "that on you may come all the righteous blood shed on the earth, from the blood of righteous Abel to the blood of Zechariah, son of Berechiah, whom you murdered between the temple and the altar.

36 "Assuredly, I say to you, all these things will come upon this generation.

37 "O Jerusalem, Jerusalem, the one who kills the prophets and stones those who are sent to her! How often I wanted to gather your children together, as a hen gathers her chicks under *her* wings, but you were not willing!

38 "See! Your house is left to you desolate;

39 "for I say to you, you shall see Me no more till you say, 'Blessed is He who comes in the name of the LORD!'"

24 Then Jesus went out and departed from the temple, and His disciples came to *Him* to show Him the buildings of the temple.

2 And Jesus said to them, "Do you not see all these things? Assuredly, I say to you, not one stone shall be left here upon another, that shall not be thrown down."

3 Now as He sat on the Mount of Olives, the disciples came to Him privately, saying, "Tell us, when will these things be? And what *will be* the sign of Your coming, and of the end of the age?"

4 And Jesus answered and said to them: "Take heed that no one deceives you.

5 "For many will come in My name, saying, 'I am the Christ,' and will deceive many.

6 "And you will hear of wars and rumors of wars. See that you are not troubled; for all *these things* must come to pass, but the end is not yet.

7 "For nation will rise against nation, and kingdom against kingdom. And there will be famines, pestilences, and earthquakes in various places.

8 "All these *are* the beginning of sorrows.

9 "Then they will deliver you up to tribulation and kill you, and you will be hated by all nations for My name's sake.

10 "And then many will be offended, will betray one another, and will hate one another.

11 "Then many false prophets will rise up and deceive many.

12 "And because lawlessness will abound, the love of many will grow cold.

13 "But he who endures to the end shall be saved.

14 "And this gospel of the kingdom will be preached in all the world as a witness to all the nations, and then the end will come.

15 "Therefore when you see the 'abomination of desolation,' spoken of by Daniel the prophet, standing in the holy place" (whoever reads, let him understand),

16 "then let those who are in Judea flee to the mountains.

17 "Let him who is on the housetop not come down to take anything out of his house.

18 "And let him who is in the field not go back to get his clothes.

19 "But woe to those who are pregnant and to those with nursing babies in those days!

20 "And pray that your flight may not be in winter or on the Sabbath.

21 "For then there will be great tribulation, such as has not been since the beginning of the world until this time, no, nor ever shall be.

22 "And unless those days were shortened, no flesh would be saved; but for the elect's sake those days will be shortened.

23 "Then if anyone says to you, 'Look, here *is* the Christ!' or 'There!' do not believe *it.*

24 "For false christs and false prophets will arise and show great signs and wonders, so as to deceive, if possible, even the elect.

25 "See, I have told you beforehand.

26 "Therefore if they say to you, 'Look, He is in the desert!' do not go out; *or* 'Look, *He is* in the inner rooms!' do not believe *it.*

27 "For as the lightning comes from the east and flashes to the west, so also will the coming of the Son of Man be.

28 "For wherever the carcass is, there the eagles will be gathered together.

29 "Immediately after the tribulation of those days the sun will be darkened, and the moon will not give its light; the stars will fall from heaven, and the powers of the heavens will be shaken.

30 "Then the sign of the Son of Man will appear in heaven, and then all the tribes of the earth will mourn, and they will see the Son of Man coming on the clouds of heaven with power and great glory.

31 "And He will send His angels with a great sound of a trumpet, and they will gather together His elect from the four winds, from one end of heaven to the other.

32 "Now learn this parable from the fig tree: When its branch has already become tender and puts forth leaves, you know that summer *is* near.

33 "So you also, when you see all these things, know that it is near, at the *very* doors.

34 "Assuredly, I say to you, this generation will by no means pass away till all these things are fulfilled.

35 "Heaven and earth will pass away, but My words will by no means pass away.

36 "But of that day and hour no one knows, no, not even the angels of heaven, but My Father only.

37 "But as the days of Noah *were,* so also will the coming of the Son of Man be.

38 "For as in the days before the flood, they were eating and drinking, marrying and giving in marriage, until the day that Noah entered the ark,

39 "and did not know until the flood came and took them all away, so also will the coming of the Son of Man be.

40 "Then two *men* will be in the field: one will be taken and the other left.

41 "Two *women will be* grinding at the mill: one will be taken and the other left.

42 "Watch therefore, for you do not know what hour your Lord is coming.

43 "But know this, that if the master of the house had known what hour the thief would come, he

would have watched and not allowed his house to be broken into.

44 "Therefore you also be ready, for the Son of Man is coming at an hour when you do not expect *Him.*

STEP 12

45 "Who then is a faithful and wise servant, whom his master made ruler over his household, to give them food in due season?

46 "Blessed *is* that servant whom his master, when he comes, will find so doing.

47 "Assuredly, I say to you that he will make him ruler over all his goods.

48 "But if that evil servant says in his heart, 'My master is delaying his coming,'

49 "and begins to beat *his* fellow servants, and to eat and drink with the drunkards,

50 "the master of that servant will come on a day when he is not looking for *him* and at an hour that he is not aware of,

51 "and will cut him in two and appoint *him* his portion with the hypocrites. There shall be weeping and gnashing of teeth.

25 "Then the kingdom of heaven shall be likened to ten virgins who took their lamps and went out to meet the bridegroom.

2 "Now five of them were wise, and five *were* foolish.

3 "Those who *were* foolish took their lamps and took no oil with them,

4 "but the wise took oil in their vessels with their lamps.

5 "But while the bridegroom was delayed, they all slumbered and slept.

6 "And at midnight a cry was *heard:* 'Behold, the bridegroom is coming; go out to meet him!'

7 "Then all those virgins arose and trimmed their lamps.

8 "And the foolish said to the wise, 'Give us *some* of your oil, for our lamps are going out.'

9 "But the wise answered, saying,

'No, lest there should not be enough for us and you; but go rather to those who sell, and buy for yourselves.'

10 "And while they went to buy, the bridegroom came, and those who were ready went in with him to the wedding; and the door was shut.

11 "Afterward the other virgins came also, saying, 'Lord, Lord, open to us!'

12 "But he answered and said, 'Assuredly, I say to you, I do not know you.'

13 "Watch therefore, for you know neither the day nor the hour in which the Son of Man is coming.

14 "For *the kingdom of heaven is* like a man traveling to a far country, *who* called his own servants and delivered his goods to them.

15 "And to one he gave five talents, to another two, and to another one, to each according to his own ability; and immediately he went on a journey.

16 "Then he who had received the five talents went and traded with them, and made another five talents.

17 "And likewise he who *had received* two gained two more also.

18 "But he who had received one went and dug in the ground, and hid his lord's money.

19 "After a long time the lord of those servants came and settled accounts with them.

20 "So he who had received five talents came and brought five other talents, saying, 'Lord, you delivered to me five talents; look, I have gained five more talents besides them.'

21 "His lord said to him, 'Well *done,* good and faithful servant; you were faithful over a few things, I will make you ruler over many things. Enter into the joy of your lord.'

22 "He also who had received two talents came and said, 'Lord, you

*Having had a spiritual awakening as the result
of these steps, we tried to carry this message to others,
and to practice these principles in all our affairs.*

Matthew 24:45–51

Faithfulness and wisdom should be the main qualities we are seeking to build into our character as we practice Step 12. Because of the things accomplished in our lives by the power of God, we now have both a position and a mission. Others may be looking to us to lead them into wholeness. Just as the servant who was made ruler of his master's house, we have responsibilities to others, as well as privileges now. If we are faithful to maintain a close walk with God, living wisely ourselves and using the wisdom God has given us to help others, God promises to us abundant blessing both now and for eternity.

For further reading on Step 12, turn to page 69.

Daily Encouragement

DAY 23 READING: MATTHEW 24:1–51

A Thought for the New Day: After we have lived a while, we come to realize that even the things we treasure most slip from our grasp at last (v. 2). An earthquake destroyed a poor man's house, but as he searched through the rubble the poor man made a discovery: the quake had turned up a chest of gold! Our losses are painful until we understand that God only means to give us something far better—if we will let Him. (*Turn to page 59.*)

delivered to me two talents; look, I have gained two more talents besides them.'

23 "His lord said to him, 'Well *done*, good and faithful servant; you have been faithful over a few things, I will make you ruler over many things. Enter into the joy of your lord.'

24 "Then he who had received the one talent came and said, 'Lord, I knew you to be a hard man, reaping where you have not sown, and gathering where you have not scattered seed.

25 'And I was afraid, and went and hid your talent in the ground. Look, *there* you have *what is* yours.'

26 "But his lord answered and said to him, 'You wicked and lazy servant, you knew that I reap where I have not sown, and gather where I have not scattered seed.

27 'Therefore you ought to have deposited my money with the bankers, and at my coming I would have received back my own with interest.

28 'Therefore take the talent from him, and give *it* to him who has ten talents.

29 'For to everyone who has, more will be given, and he will have abundance; but from him who does not have, even what he has will be taken away.

30 'And cast the unprofitable servant into the outer darkness. There will be weeping and gnashing of teeth.'

31 "When the Son of Man comes in His glory, and all the holy angels with Him, then He will sit on the throne of His glory.

32 "All the nations will be gathered before Him, and He will separate them one from another, as a shepherd divides *his* sheep from the goats.

33 "And He will set the sheep on His right hand, but the goats on the left.

34 "Then the King will say to those on His right hand, 'Come, you blessed of My Father, inherit the kingdom prepared for you from the foundation of the world:

35 'for I was hungry and you gave Me food; I was thirsty and you gave Me drink; I was a stranger and you took Me in;

36 'I *was* naked and you clothed Me; I was sick and you visited Me; I was in prison and you came to Me.'

37 "Then the righteous will answer Him, saying, 'Lord, when did we see You hungry and feed *You*, or thirsty and give *You* drink?

38 'When did we see You a stranger and take *You* in, or naked and clothe *You*?

39 'Or when did we see You sick, or in prison, and come to You?'

40 "And the King will answer and say to them, 'Assuredly, I say to you, inasmuch as you did *it* to one of the least of these My brethren, you did *it* to Me.'

41 "Then He will also say to those on the left hand, 'Depart from Me, you cursed, into the everlasting fire prepared for the devil and his angels:

42 'for I was hungry and you gave Me no food; I was thirsty and you gave Me no drink;

43 'I was a stranger and you did not take Me in, naked and you did not clothe Me, sick and in prison and you did not visit Me.'

44 "Then they also will answer Him, saying, 'Lord, when did we see You hungry or thirsty or a stranger or naked or sick or in prison, and did not minister to You?'

45 "Then He will answer them, saying, 'Assuredly, I say to you, inasmuch as you did not do *it* to one of the least of these, you did not do *it* to Me.'

46 "And these will go away into everlasting punishment, but the righteous into eternal life."

STEP 11

*Sought through prayer and meditation to improve our conscious contact with God **as we understood Him,** praying only for knowledge of His will for us and the power to carry that out.*

Matthew 25:31–40

Our everyday lives are full of small opportunities for kindness, helpfulness, patience, and love. As we interact with our coworkers, our spouses, our children, and even casual acquaintances, the Holy Spirit is giving us manifold occasions to reveal His fruit in our lives. When we do, we encourage and lift up those around us and glorify our Heavenly Father.

Sometimes we get sidetracked into thinking that only big projects count with God, or that we have little to offer our Lord. This was exactly the thinking of the steward who received the one talent (see vv. 14–30). But what seems small to us can be multiplied many times over if we are faithful and available to the opportunities which come our way daily—opportunities to serve, to encourage, to help, and to show God's love. Remember Jesus' words: "Inasmuch as you did *it* to one of the least of these My brethren, you did *it* to Me."

For further reading on Step 11, turn to page 63.

Daily Encouragement

DAY 24 READING: MATTHEW 25:1–46

A Thought for the New Day: "What is that in your hand?" God asked Moses. It was only a stick, but with that staff of wood God made Moses able to do wonders. What do you have in *your* hand? "Nothing very much," you say? Whatever it is, God wants to use it to bring His kingdom near to those around you (v. 27). Give what you have to Him, and see the wonders He will perform. *(Turn to page 61.)*

26 Now it came to pass, when Jesus had finished all these sayings, *that* He said to His disciples,

2 "You know that after two days is the Passover, and the Son of Man will be delivered up to be crucified."

3 Then the chief priests, the scribes, and the elders of the people assembled at the palace of the high priest, who was called Caiaphas,

4 and plotted to take Jesus by trickery and kill *Him.*

5 But they said, "Not during the feast, lest there be an uproar among the people."

6 And when Jesus was in Bethany at the house of Simon the leper,

7 a woman came to Him having an alabaster flask of very costly fragrant oil, and she poured it on His head as He sat *at the table.*

8 But when His disciples saw *it,* they were indignant, saying, "To what purpose *is* this waste?

9 "For this fragrant oil might have been sold for much and given to *the* poor."

10 But when Jesus was aware of *it,* He said to them, "Why do you trouble the woman? For she has done a good work for Me.

11 "For you have the poor with you always, but Me you do not have always.

12 "For in pouring this fragrant oil on My body, she did *it* for My burial.

13 "Assuredly, I say to you, wherever this gospel is preached in the whole world, what this woman has done will also be told as a memorial to her."

14 Then one of the twelve, called Judas Iscariot, went to the chief priests

15 and said, "What are you willing to give me if I deliver Him to you?" And they counted out to him thirty pieces of silver.

16 So from that time he sought opportunity to betray Him.

17 Now on the first *day* of the *Feast of* the Unleavened Bread the disciples came to Jesus, saying to Him, "Where do You want us to prepare for You to eat the Passover?"

18 And He said, "Go into the city to a certain man, and say to him, 'The Teacher says, "My time is at hand; I will keep the Passover at your house with My disciples." ' "

19 So the disciples did as Jesus had directed them; and they prepared the Passover.

20 Now when evening had come, He sat down with the twelve.

21 Now as they were eating, He said, "Assuredly, I say to you, one of you will betray Me."

22 And they were exceedingly sorrowful, and each of them began to say to Him, "Lord, is it I?"

23 Then He answered and said, "He who dipped *his* hand with Me in the dish will betray Me.

24 "The Son of Man goes as it is written of Him, but woe to that man by whom the Son of Man is betrayed! It would have been good for that man if he had not been born."

25 Then Judas, who was betraying Him, answered and said, "Rabbi, is it I?" He said to him, "You have said it."

26 And as they were eating, Jesus took bread, blessed *it* and broke *it,* and gave *it* to the disciples and said, "Take, eat; this is My body." | STEP 3 |

27 Then He took the cup, and gave thanks, and gave *it* to them, saying, "Drink from it, all of you.

28 "For this is My blood of the new covenant, which is shed for many for the remission of sins.

29 "But I say to you, I will not drink of this fruit of the vine from now on until that day when I drink it new with you in My Father's kingdom."

30 And when they had sung a

STEP 3

*Made a decision to turn our will and our lives
over to the care of God **as we understood Him.***

Matthew 26:26–28

To many of us, the Christian tradition of Communion has never been anything more than simply that—tradition. But we have come to a point in our lives where we want more than beautiful, but empty tradition. We are ready to connect with God Himself and to entrust ourselves to Him. We are ready to accept His control over our lives.

In essence this is exactly what communion means. The dictionary defines "communion" as intimate fellowship. As Jesus gave the bread and the cup to His disciples, he declared it to be His body and blood given for them and for all who accept and trust in the sacrifice He made on the cross.

Receiving that precious sacrifice means receiving God into our lives. Communion, of course, does not save us. But it is a testimony of our trust in Jesus' sacrifice on the cross. When we receive that sacrifice, we receive the transforming power of God Himself into our lives.

For further reading on Step 3, turn to page 77.

Daily Encouragement

DAY 25 READING: MATTHEW 26:1–29

A Thought for the New Day: No one else understood, but Jesus did (v. 7). The woman's act seemed so pointless, yet it was the only way she knew to express her deep love for Him. Sometimes people may be embarrassed by your simple words and deeds for your Lord. Be glad all the same. Jesus understands, and your gift is not wasted. Jesus sees your heart of love, and that is what really matters. (*Turn to page 63.*)

hymn, they went out to the Mount of Olives.

31 Then Jesus said to them, "All of you will be made to stumble because of Me this night, for it is written:

'I will strike the Shepherd,
And the sheep of the flock
   will be scattered.'

32 "But after I have been raised, I will go before you to Galilee."

33 Peter answered and said to Him, "Even if all are made to stumble because of You, I will never be made to stumble."

34 Jesus said to him, "Assuredly, I say to you that this night, before the rooster crows, you will deny Me three times."

35 Peter said to Him, "Even if I have to die with You, I will not deny You!" And so said all the disciples.

36 Then Jesus came with them to a place called Gethsemane, and said to the disciples, "Sit here while I go and pray over there."

37 And He took with Him Peter and the two sons of Zebedee, and He began to be sorrowful and deeply distressed.

38 Then He said to them, "My soul is exceedingly sorrowful, even to death. Stay here and watch with Me."

39 He went a little farther and fell on His face, and prayed, saying, "O My Father, if it is possible, let this cup pass from Me; nevertheless, not as I will, but as You *will.*"

40 Then He came to the disciples and found them asleep, and said to Peter, "What, could you not watch with Me one hour?

41 "Watch and pray, lest you enter into temptation. The spirit indeed *is* willing, but the flesh *is* weak."

42 He went away again a second time and prayed, saying, "O My Father, if this cup cannot pass

away from Me unless I drink it, Your will be done."

43 And He came and found them asleep again, for their eyes were heavy.

44 So He left them, went away again, and prayed the third time, saying the same words.

45 Then He came to His disciples and said to them, "Are *you* still sleeping and resting? Behold, the hour is at hand, and the Son of Man is being betrayed into the hands of sinners.

46 "Rise, let us be going. See, he who betrays Me is at hand."

47 And while He was still speaking, behold, Judas, one of the twelve, with a great multitude with swords and clubs, came from the chief priests and elders of the people.

48 Now His betrayer had given them a sign, saying, "Whomever I kiss, He is the One; seize Him."

49 Then immediately he went up to Jesus and said, "Greetings, Rabbi!" and kissed Him.

50 And Jesus said to him, "Friend, why have you come?" Then they came and laid hands on Jesus and took Him.

51 And suddenly, one of those *who were* with Jesus stretched out *his* hand and drew his sword, struck the servant of the high priest, and cut off his ear.

52 Then Jesus said to him, "Put your sword in its place, for all who take the sword will perish by the sword.

53 "Or do you think that I cannot now pray to My Father, and He will provide Me with more than twelve legions of angels?

54 "How then could the Scriptures be fulfilled, that it must happen thus?"

55 In that hour Jesus said to the multitudes, "Have you come out, as against a robber, with swords and clubs to take Me? I sat daily with you, teaching in the temple, and you did not seize Me.

*Sought through prayer and meditation to improve our conscious contact with God **as we understood Him,** praying only for knowledge of His will for us and the power to carry that out.*

Matthew 26:39–42

What is the key to knowing God's will? So many people struggle with this question, but the answer is not reserved for a chosen few. Anyone who says with all his or her mind and soul and being, "nevertheless not as I will, but as You *will*" cannot fail to discover the will of God. This is because God is always seeking us more than we are seeking Him. When we surrender completely all that we have and are to God, to do with as He pleases, we will be astonished at the abundant life He unfolds for us. While there may be some pain involved in God's will for us, never doubt for a moment that the blessing and joy and adventure of walking with our Father will make the pain seem small by comparison. And God's transforming power will be continually strengthening us in the hard places.

For further reading on Step 11, turn to page 73.

Daily
Encouragement

DAY 26 READING: MATTHEW 26:30–46

A Thought for the New Day: People who have been touched by God are people with a song, whether the music be on their lips or in their hearts (v. 30). We are thankful for this little window that looks into the life of Jesus and His early followers. Before the Lord went out to be arrested and killed He was able to sing with His friends. Some songs make us brave for facing life's trials. It is good to commit their words to memory. (*Turn to page 65.*)

56 "But all this was done that the Scriptures of the prophets might be fulfilled." Then all the disciples forsook Him and fled.

57 And those who had laid hold of Jesus led *Him* away to Caiaphas the high priest, where the scribes and the elders were assembled.

58 But Peter followed Him at a distance to the high priest's courtyard. And he went in and sat with the servants to see the end.

59 Now the chief priests, the elders, and all the council sought false testimony against Jesus to put Him to death,

60 but found none. Even though many false witnesses came forward, they found none. But at last two false witnesses came forward

61 and said, "This *fellow* said, 'I am able to destroy the temple of God and to build it in three days.' "

62 And the high priest arose and said to Him, "Do You answer nothing? What *is it that* these men testify against You?"

63 But Jesus kept silent. And the high priest answered and said to Him, "I adjure You by the living God that You tell us if You are the Christ, the Son of God."

64 Jesus said to him, "*It is as* you said. Nevertheless, I say to you, hereafter you will see the Son of Man sitting at the right hand of the Power, and coming on the clouds of heaven."

65 Then the high priest tore his clothes, saying, "He has spoken blasphemy! What further need do we have of witnesses? Look, now you have heard His blasphemy!

66 "What do you think?" They answered and said, "He is deserving of death."

67 Then they spat in His face and beat Him; and others struck *Him* with the palms of their hands,

68 saying, "Prophesy to us, Christ! Who is the one who struck You?"

69 Now Peter sat outside in the courtyard. And a servant girl came to him, saying, "You also were with Jesus of Galilee."

70 But he denied it before *them* all, saying, "I do not know what you are saying."

71 And when he had gone out to the gateway, another *girl* saw him and said to those *who were* there, "This *fellow* also was with Jesus of Nazareth."

72 But again he denied with an oath, "I do not know the Man!"

73 And after a while those who stood by came to *him* and said to Peter, "Surely you also are *one* of them, because your speech betrays you."

74 Then he began to curse and swear, *saying,* "I do not know the Man!" And immediately a rooster crowed.

75 And Peter remembered the word of Jesus who had said to him, "Before the rooster crows, you will deny Me three times." Then he went out and wept bitterly.

27 When morning came, all the chief priests and elders of the people took counsel against Jesus to put Him to death.

2 And when they had bound Him, they led Him away and delivered Him to Pontius Pilate the governor.

3 Then Judas, His betrayer, seeing that He had been condemned, was remorseful and brought back the thirty pieces of silver to the chief priests and elders,

4 saying, "I have sinned by betraying innocent blood." And they said, "What *is that* to us? You see *to it!*"

5 Then he threw down the pieces of silver in the temple and departed, and went and hanged himself.

6 But the chief priests took the silver pieces and said, "It is not lawful to put them into the treasury, because they are the price of blood."

7 And they took counsel and

STEP 10

STEP 10

*Continued to take personal inventory
and when we were wrong promptly admitted it.*

Matthew 26:71–75

Jesus had just told His disciples that all of them would desert Him that very night (verses 31, 32). Confusion and panic were about to reign. Peter should have known by then that when Jesus said something, His words should be given credence. While the other disciples were solemnly digesting this information, Peter brashly declared how much braver and more spiritually mature he was than the rest. When Jesus quietly set him straight, he plunged headlong once more into the arms of egocentric proclamation, encouraging the others to join in. We shake our heads and think how blind Peter was, but we must all "watch and pray, lest we enter into temptation."

A key thought in Step 10 is "promptly admitting a wrong." In order to make this step a valuable part of our lives, we need to regularly scrutinize our motives, words, and actions. And when, through Scripture reading, prayer, or the teaching of others, we see a problem in our lives, quick and humble admission of that problem will help us get back on the right track.

For further reading on Step 10, turn to page 85.

Daily Encouragement

DAY 27 READING: MATTHEW 26:47—27:61

A Thought for the New Day: Death comes to everyone. Even Jesus died (27:50), but in His death something different happened. His death became for us the death of death itself. The so-called grim specter can terrify us no more. Death worked in us, but life reigned in Him. To you and me He now imparts that new, abundant life that mocks Satan and the grave. To both of those enemies we can now proclaim, "I know that my Redeemer lives!" (*Turn to page 69.*)

bought with them the potter's field, to bury strangers in.

8 Therefore that field has been called the Field of Blood to this day.

9 Then was fulfilled what was spoken by Jeremiah the prophet, saying, *"And they took the thirty pieces of silver, the value of Him who was priced, whom they of the children of Israel priced,*

10 *"and gave them for the potter's field, as the LORD directed me."*

11 Now Jesus stood before the governor. And the governor asked Him, saying, "Are You the King of the Jews?" So Jesus said to him, *"It is as* you say."

12 And while He was being accused by the chief priests and elders, He answered nothing.

13 Then Pilate said to Him, "Do You not hear how many things they testify against You?"

14 And He answered him not one word, so that the governor marveled greatly.

15 Now at the feast the governor was accustomed to releasing to the multitude one prisoner whom they wished.

16 And they had then a notorious prisoner called Barabbas.

17 Therefore, when they had gathered together, Pilate said to them, "Whom do you want me to release to you? Barabbas, or Jesus who is called Christ?"

18 For he knew that because of envy they had delivered Him.

19 While he was sitting on the judgment seat, his wife sent to him, saying, "Have nothing to do with that just Man, for I have suffered many things today in a dream because of Him."

20 But the chief priests and elders persuaded the multitudes that they should ask for Barabbas and destroy Jesus.

21 The governor answered and said to them, "Which of the two do you want me to release to you?" They said, "Barabbas!"

22 Pilate said to them, "What then shall I do with Jesus who is called Christ?" *They* all said to him, "Let Him be crucified!"

23 Then the governor said, "Why, what evil has He done?" But they cried out all the more, saying, "Let Him be crucified!"

24 When Pilate saw that he could not prevail at all, but rather *that* a tumult was rising, he took water and washed *his* hands before the multitude, saying, "I am innocent of the blood of this just Person. You see *to it.*"

25 And all the people answered and said, "His blood *be* on us and on our children."

26 Then he released Barabbas to them; and when he had scourged Jesus, he delivered *Him* to be crucified.

27 Then the soldiers of the governor took Jesus into the Praetorium and gathered the whole garrison around Him.

28 And they stripped Him and put a scarlet robe on Him.

29 When they had twisted a crown of thorns, they put *it* on His head, and a reed in His right hand. And they bowed the knee before Him and mocked Him, saying, "Hail, King of the Jews!"

30 Then they spat on Him, and took the reed and struck Him on the head.

31 Then when they had mocked Him, they took the robe off Him, put His *own* clothes on Him, and led Him away to be crucified.

32 Now as they came out, they found a man of Cyrene, Simon by name. Him they compelled to bear His cross.

33 And when they had come to a place called Golgotha, that is to say, Place of a Skull,

34 they gave Him sour wine mingled with gall to drink. But when

He had tasted *it*, He would not drink.

35 Then they crucified Him, and divided His garments, casting lots, that it might be fulfilled which was spoken by the prophet:

> "They divided My garments among them,
> And for My clothing they cast lots."

36 Sitting down, they kept watch over Him there.

37 And they put up over His head the accusation written against Him:

THIS IS JESUS
THE KING OF THE JEWS.

38 Then two robbers were crucified with Him, one on the right and another on the left.

39 And those who passed by blasphemed Him, wagging their heads

40 and saying, "You who destroy the temple and build *it* in three days, save Yourself! If You are the Son of God, come down from the cross."

41 Likewise the chief priests, also mocking with the scribes and elders, said,

42 "He saved others; Himself He cannot save. If He is the King of Israel, let Him now come down from the cross, and we will believe Him.

43 "He trusted in God; let Him deliver Him now if He will have Him; for He said, 'I am the Son of God.'"

44 Even the robbers who were crucified with Him reviled Him with the same thing.

45 Now from the sixth hour until the ninth hour there was darkness over all the land.

46 And about the ninth hour Jesus cried out with a loud voice, saying, "Eli, Eli, lama sabachthani?" that is, *"My God, My God, why have You forsaken Me?"*

47 Some of those who stood there, when they heard *that*, said, "This *Man* is calling for Elijah!"

48 Immediately one of them ran and took a sponge, filled *it* with sour wine and put *it* on a reed, and gave it to Him to drink.

49 The rest said, "Let Him alone; let us see if Elijah will come to save Him."

50 Jesus, when He had cried out again with a loud voice, yielded up His spirit.

51 And behold, the veil of the temple was torn in two from top to bottom; and the earth quaked, and the rocks were split,

52 and the graves were opened; and many bodies of the saints who had fallen asleep were raised;

53 and coming out of the graves after His resurrection, they went into the holy city and appeared to many.

54 Now when the centurion and those with him, who were guarding Jesus, saw the earthquake and the things that had happened, they feared greatly, saying, "Truly this was the Son of God!"

55 And many women who followed Jesus from Galilee, ministering to Him, were there looking on from afar,

56 among whom were Mary Magdalene, Mary the mother of James and Joses, and the mother of Zebedee's sons.

57 Now when evening had come, there came a rich man from Arimathea, named Joseph, who himself had also become a disciple of Jesus.

58 This man went to Pilate and asked for the body of Jesus. Then Pilate commanded the body to be given to him.

59 And when Joseph had taken the body, he wrapped it in a clean linen cloth,

60 and laid it in his new tomb which he had hewn out of the

rock; and he rolled a large stone against the door of the tomb, and departed.

61 And Mary Magdalene was there, and the other Mary, sitting opposite the tomb.

62 On the next day, which followed the Day of Preparation, the chief priests and Pharisees gathered together to Pilate,

63 saying, "Sir, we remember, while He was still alive, how that deceiver said, 'After three days I will rise.'

64 "Therefore command that the tomb be made secure until the third day, lest His disciples come by night and steal Him *away*, and say to the people, 'He has risen from the dead.' So the last deception will be worse than the first."

65 Pilate said to them, "You have a guard; go your way, make *it* as secure as you know how."

66 So they went and made the tomb secure, sealing the stone and setting the guard.

28 Now after the Sabbath, as the first *day* of the week began to dawn, Mary Magdalene and the other Mary came to see the tomb.

2 And behold, there was a great earthquake; for an angel of the Lord descended from heaven, and came and rolled back the stone from the door, and sat on it.

3 His countenance was like lightning, and his clothing as white as snow.

4 And the guards shook for fear of him, and became like dead *men*.

5 But the angel answered and said to the women, "Do not be afraid, for I know that you seek Jesus who was crucified.

6 "He is not here; for He is risen, as He said. Come, see the place where the Lord lay.

7 "And go quickly and tell His disciples that He is risen from the dead, and indeed He is going before you into Galilee; there you will see Him. Behold, I have told you."

8 So they departed quickly from the tomb with fear and great joy, and ran to bring His disciples word.

9 And as they went to tell His disciples, behold, Jesus met them, saying, "Rejoice!" And they came and held Him by the feet and worshiped Him.

10 Then Jesus said to them, "Do not be afraid. Go *and* tell My brethren to go to Galilee, and there they will see Me."

11 Now while they were going, behold, some of the guard came into the city and reported to the chief priests all the things that had happened.

12 When they had assembled with the elders and taken counsel, they gave a large sum of money to the soldiers,

13 saying, "Tell them, 'His disciples came at night and stole Him *away* while we slept.'

14 "And if this comes to the governor's ears, we will appease him and make you secure."

15 So they took the money and did as they were instructed; and this saying is commonly reported among the Jews until this day.

16 Then the eleven disciples went away into Galilee, to the mountain which Jesus had appointed for them.

17 And when they saw Him, they worshiped Him; but some doubted.

18 Then Jesus came and spoke to them, saying, "All authority has been given to Me in heaven and on earth.

19 "Go therefore and make disciples of all the nations, baptizing them in the name of the Father and of the Son and of the Holy Spirit,

20 "teaching them to observe all things that I have commanded you; and lo, I am with you always, *even* to the end of the age." Amen.

*Having had a spiritual awakening as the result
of these steps, we tried to carry this message to others,
and to practice these principles in all our affairs.*

Matthew 28:18–20

Sometimes as we read a newspaper or magazine or listen to the news, we are struck by the moral degradation, economic confusion, and physical suffering in our world. It is easy at such times to become fearful and to find ourselves engulfed in feelings of hopelessness. When we begin to struggle with this mind-set, the verses at the end of Matthew's Gospel are a real encouragement. Jesus has lost none of His authority and power. His word and the New Birth He brings to lives are just as powerful today as they were when He said, "All authority has been given to me in heaven and on earth." Just as His disciples had the incredible privilege of carrying that good news to others, we, too, have an awesome privilege and responsibility to share what God has done for us. And even though the world has changed very much since Jesus' day, Jesus' promise is always the same, "Lo, I am with you always, *even* to the end of the age."

For further reading on Step 12, turn to page 83.

Daily Encouragement

DAY 28 READING: MATTHEW 27:62—28:20

A Thought for the New Day: "This is the end—for me, the beginning of life." So spoke Dietrich Bonhoeffer as he calmly mounted the steps to the gallows where he died by Hitler's order in 1945. How could this man, like thousands before him, be so fearless in the face of death? He had lived and walked with the risen Savior (28:6) who says to the martyr, as He also says to you and me, "Because I live, you shall live also." (*Turn to page 71.*)

THE GOSPEL ACCORDING TO
MARK

THE beginning of the gospel of Jesus Christ, the Son of God.

2 As it is written in the Prophets:

"Behold, I send My messenger before Your face,
Who will prepare Your way before You."

3 *"The voice of one crying in the wilderness:*
'Prepare the way of the LORD,
Make His paths straight.' "

STEP 5 4 John came baptizing in the wilderness and preaching a baptism of repentance for the remission of sins.

5 And all the land of Judea, and those from Jerusalem, went out to him and were all baptized by him in the Jordan River, confessing their sins.

6 Now John was clothed with camel's hair and with a leather belt around his waist, and he ate locusts and wild honey.

7 And he preached, saying, "There comes One after me who is mightier than I, whose sandal strap I am not worthy to stoop down and loose.

8 "I indeed baptized you with water, but He will baptize you with the Holy Spirit."

9 It came to pass in those days *that* Jesus came from Nazareth of Galilee, and was baptized by John in the Jordan.

10 And immediately, coming up from the water, He saw the heavens parting and the Spirit descending upon Him like a dove.

11 Then a voice came from heaven, "You are My beloved Son, in whom I am well pleased."

12 And immediately the Spirit drove Him into the wilderness.

13 And He was there in the wilderness forty days, tempted by Satan, and was with the wild beasts; and the angels ministered to Him.

14 Now after John was put in prison, Jesus came to Galilee, preaching the gospel of the kingdom of God,

15 and saying, "The time is fulfilled, and the kingdom of God is at hand. Repent, and believe in the gospel."

16 And as He walked by the Sea of Galilee, He saw Simon and Andrew his brother casting a net into the sea; for they were fishermen.

17 Then Jesus said to them, "Come after Me, and I will make you become fishers of men."

18 And immediately they left their nets and followed Him.

19 When He had gone a little farther from there, He saw James the *son* of Zebedee, and John his brother, who also *were* in the boat mending their nets.

20 And immediately He called them, and they left their father Zebedee in the boat with the hired servants, and went after Him.

21 Then they went into Capernaum, and immediately on the Sabbath He entered the synagogue and taught.

22 And they were astonished at His teaching, for He taught them as one having authority, and not as the scribes.

23 Now there was a man in their synagogue with an unclean spirit. And he cried out,

24 saying, "Let *us* alone! What have we to do with You, Jesus of Nazareth? Did You come to destroy us? I know who You are— the Holy One of God!"

25 But Jesus rebuked him, saying, "Be quiet, and come out of him!"

26 And when the unclean spirit had convulsed him and cried out with a loud voice, he came out of him.

STEP 5

Admitted to God, to ourselves, and to another human being the exact nature of our wrongs.

Mark 1:4, 5

A new work was about to take place in the land of Israel. John the Baptist preached about it and there was an air of expectation among the crowds. God was about to accomplish mighty things among His people. Would this great work begin with trumpets calling the people to all-day meetings at the temple? Or pehaps, God would send fire from heaven as in the days of old. No, neither of these soul-stirring events began God's mighty work in the lives of His people. Instead, the world-changing ministry of Jesus Christ was ushered in by men and women willingly confessing their sins.

Likewise, we can have great expectations for the new work God is doing in our lives today. Willingly and honestly confessing our wrongs to God and to others turns the key in a door that may have been locked for many years. It is the door to God's great work of healing in our lives.

For further reading on Step 5, turn to page 89.

Daily Encouragement

DAY 29 READING: MARK 1:1–28

A Thought for the New Day: When Jesus came, the kingdom of God drew near to us. Where Jesus is present, the kingdom is present. And what a kingdom it is! A kingdom of light and life, a realm where darkness, death, and despair cannot intrude. Today, Jesus knocks at the door of our hearts, saying, "The kingdom of God is at hand" (v. 15). Let us open the door for the King to come in and reign in triumph over all our fears. (*Turn to page 73.*)

27 Then they were all amazed, so that they questioned among themselves, saying, "What is this? What new doctrine *is* this? For with authority He commands even the unclean spirits, and they obey Him."

28 And immediately His fame spread throughout all the region around Galilee.

29 Now as soon as they had come out of the synagogue, they entered the house of Simon and Andrew, with James and John.

30 But Simon's wife's mother lay sick with a fever, and they told Him about her at once.

31 So He came and took her by the hand and lifted her up, and immediately the fever left her. And she served them.

32 Now at evening, when the sun had set, they brought to Him all who were sick and those who were demon-possessed.

33 And the whole city was gathered together at the door.

34 Then He healed many who were sick with various diseases, and cast out many demons; and He did not allow the demons to speak, because they knew Him.

35 Now in the morning, having risen a long while before daylight, He went out and departed to a solitary place; and there He prayed.

36 And Simon and those *who were* with Him searched for Him.

37 When they found Him, they said to Him, "Everyone is looking for You."

38 But He said to them, "Let us go into the next towns, that I may preach there also, because for this purpose I have come forth."

39 And He was preaching in their synagogues throughout all Galilee, and casting out demons.

40 Then a leper came to Him, imploring Him, kneeling down to Him and saying to Him, "If You are willing, You can make me clean."

41 And Jesus, moved with compassion, put out *His* hand and touched him, and said to him, "I am willing; be cleansed."

42 As soon as He had spoken, immediately the leprosy left him, and he was cleansed.

43 And He strictly warned him and sent him away at once.

44 And He said to him, "See that you say nothing to anyone; but go your way, show yourself to the priest, and offer for your cleansing those things which Moses commanded, as a testimony to them."

45 But he went out and began to proclaim *it* freely, and to spread the matter, so that Jesus could no longer openly enter the city, but was outside in deserted places; and they came to Him from every quarter.

2 And again He entered Capernaum after *some* days, and it was heard that He was in the house.

2 Immediately many gathered together, so that there was no longer room to receive *them*, not even near the door. And He preached the word to them.

3 Then they came to Him, bringing a paralytic who was carried by four *men*.

4 And when they could not come near Him because of the crowd, they uncovered the roof where He was. And when they had broken through, they let down the bed on which the paralytic was lying.

5 When Jesus saw their faith, He said to the paralytic, "Son, your sins are forgiven you."

6 But some of the scribes were sitting there and reasoning in their hearts,

7 "Why does this *Man* speak blasphemies like this? Who can forgive sins but God alone?"

8 And immediately, when Jesus perceived in His spirit that they

*Sought through prayer and meditation to improve our conscious contact with God **as we understood Him,** praying only for knowledge of His will for us and the power to carry that out.*

Mark 1:35

Jesus was popular in Peter and Andrew's hometown. In fact, by evening of the day He arrived, "the whole city was gathered together" at the door of Peter's house. It was a busy time for Jesus. Everyone needed His touch or wanted to sit next to Him at the table or needed Him to listen as they shared earnest questions or deep heartache. He was probably the last one into bed that night, and no one would have blamed Him for sleeping in a little. But Jesus needed His Father as much as the people needed Him. This is why we find Him "in a solitary place" long before daylight, communing with the other two members of the Godhead. And it is why we ourselves keep our daily contact with our Lord a top priority. For all the circumstances and events that swirl into our lives daily, we must seek power and wisdom from Almighty God.

For further reading on Step 11, turn to page 111.

Daily Encouragement

DAY 30 READING: MARK 1:29–45

A Thought for the New Day: Why did Jesus perform miracles, such as healing this sick woman? (v. 31). Did He need to prove He was the Son of God? No, although His wonders do show this. Jesus' miracles made it clear that His kingdom was a reign of life-giving power. Sickness and death belong to the dark side of our existence; but when Jesus comes, the Sun of life and healing rises and lights up our lives. (*Turn to page 75.*)

reasoned thus within themselves, He said to them, "Why do you reason about these things in your hearts?

9 "Which is easier, to say to the paralytic, '*Your* sins are forgiven you,' or to say, 'Arise, take up your bed and walk'?

10 "But that you may know that the Son of Man has power on earth to forgive sins"—He said to the paralytic,

11 "I say to you, arise, take up your bed, and go your way to your house."

12 And immediately he arose, took up the bed, and went out in the presence of them all, so that all were amazed and glorified God, saying, "We never saw *anything* like this!"

13 Then He went out again by the sea; and all the multitude came to Him, and He taught them.

14 And as He passed by, He saw Levi the *son* of Alphaeus sitting at the tax office, and said to him, "Follow Me." And he arose and followed Him.

15 Now it happened, as He was dining in *Levi's* house, that many tax collectors and sinners also sat together with Jesus and His disciples; for there were many, and they followed Him.

16 And when the scribes and Pharisees saw Him eating with the tax collectors and sinners, they said to His disciples, "How *is it* that He eats and drinks with tax collectors and sinners?"

17 When Jesus heard *it*, He said to them, "Those who are well have no need of a physician, but those who are sick. I did not come to call *the* righteous, but sinners, to repentance."

18 And the disciples of John and of the Pharisees were fasting. And they came and said to Him, "Why do the disciples of John and of the Pharisees fast, but Your disciples do not fast?"

19 So Jesus said to them, "Can the friends of the bridegroom fast while the bridegroom is with them? As long as they have the bridegroom with them they cannot fast.

20 "But the days will come when the bridegroom will be taken away from them, and then they will fast in those days.

21 "No one sews a piece of unshrunk cloth on an old garment; or else the new piece pulls away from the old, and the tear is made worse.

22 "And no one puts new wine into old wineskins; or else the new wine bursts the wineskins, the wine is spilled, and the wineskins are ruined. But new wine must be put into new wineskins."

23 Now it happened that He went through the grainfields on the Sabbath; and as they went His disciples began to pluck the heads of grain.

24 And the Pharisees said to Him, "Look, why do they do what is not lawful on the Sabbath?"

25 But He said to them, "Have you never read what David did when he was in need and hungry, he and those with him:

26 "how he went into the house of God *in the days* of Abiathar the high priest, and ate the showbread, which is not lawful to eat, except for the priests, and also gave some to those who were with him?"

27 And He said to them, "The Sabbath was made for man, and not man for the Sabbath.

28 "Therefore the Son of Man is also Lord of the Sabbath."

3 And He entered the synagogue again, and a man was there who had a withered hand.

2 And they watched Him closely, whether He would heal him on the Sabbath, so that they might accuse Him.

3 Then He said to the man who

STEP 4

Made a searching and fearless moral inventory of ourselves.

Mark 2:18–28

Jesus' metaphor of the new wine of verse 22 symbolizes the new relationship we can have with God through faith in Jesus. The old wineskins represent the Jewish traditions of the Law.

We may agree that the Pharisees' traditions and laws were cumbersome, harmful, or even downright silly; but many of us who struggle with dependencies have been just as bound by our own unspoken traditions and laws. Perhaps our unspoken law has been denial—denial of our hurt, denial of our addictions, denial of our shame and guilt. Or perhaps we have a family tradition of using physical or verbal abuse.

It is time to be fearlessly honest as we evaluate our past and present. God is beginning a new undertaking of His power and love in our lives. But the wonderful new wine of His grace cannot be poured into the old wineskins of our harmful traditions and unspoken laws.

For further reading on Step 4, turn to page 79.

Daily Encouragement

DAY 31 READING: MARK 2:1–28

A Thought for the New Day: Can you imagine the joy that Jesus' words brought to the paralyzed man? Yes, Jesus would heal the man, although both Jesus and he knew his greatest need—to be forgiven (v. 5). That day was a double joy for the disabled one. He would be able to walk again, but even more important, he would have God's acceptance. We, too, should order our priorities: the friendship of God is the greatest freedom and the highest joy we will ever know. (*Turn to page 77.*)

had the withered hand, "Step forward."

4 And He said to them, "Is it lawful on the Sabbath to do good or to do evil, to save life or to kill?" But they kept silent.

5 So when He had looked around at them with anger, being grieved by the hardness of their hearts, He said to the man, "Stretch out your hand." And he stretched *it* out, and his hand was restored as whole as the other.

6 Then the Pharisees went out and immediately plotted with the Herodians against Him, how they might destroy Him.

7 But Jesus withdrew with His disciples to the sea. And a great multitude from Galilee followed Him, and from Judea

8 and Jerusalem and Idumea and beyond the Jordan; and those from Tyre and Sidon, a great multitude, when they heard how many things He was doing, came to Him.

9 And He told His disciples that a small boat should be kept ready for Him because of the multitude, lest they should crush Him.

10 For He healed many, so that as many as had afflictions pressed about Him to touch Him.

11 And the unclean spirits, whenever they saw Him, fell down before Him and cried out, saying, "You are the Son of God."

12 But He sternly warned them that they should not make Him known.

13 And He went up on the mountain and called *to Him* those He Himself wanted. And they came to Him.

14 Then He appointed twelve, that they might be with Him and that He might send them out to preach,

15 and to have power to heal sicknesses and to cast out demons:

16 Simon, to whom He gave the name Peter;

17 James the *son* of Zebedee and John the brother of James, to whom He gave the name Boanerges, that is, "Sons of Thunder";

18 Andrew, Philip, Bartholomew, Matthew, Thomas, James the *son* of Alphaeus, Thaddaeus, Simon the Canaanite;

19 and Judas Iscariot, who also betrayed Him. And they went into a house.

20 And the multitude came together again, so that they could not so much as eat bread.

21 But when His own people heard *about this*, they went out to lay hold of Him, for they said, "He is out of His mind."

22 And the scribes who came down from Jerusalem said, "He has Beelzebub," and, "By the ruler of the demons He casts out demons."

23 So He called them *to Him* and said to them in parables: "How can Satan cast out Satan?

24 "If a kingdom is divided against itself, that kingdom cannot stand.

25 "And if a house is divided against itself, that house cannot stand.

26 "And if Satan has risen up against himself, and is divided, he cannot stand, but has an end.

27 "No one can enter a strong man's house and plunder his goods, unless he first binds the strong man, and then he will plunder his house.

28 "Assuredly, I say to you, all sins will be forgiven the sons of men, and whatever blasphemies they may utter;

29 "but he who blasphemes against the Holy Spirit never has forgiveness, but is subject to eternal condemnation"—

30 because they said, "He has an unclean spirit."

31 Then His brothers and His mother came, and standing outside they sent to Him, calling Him.

32 And a multitude was sitting around Him; and they said to Him, "Look, Your mother and Your brothers are outside seeking You."

STEP 3

*Made a decision to turn our will and our lives over to the care of God **as we understood Him.***

Mark 3:1–22

Our decision to turn our wills and lives over to the care of God may be met with doubt, confusion, or perhaps even open hostility by those closest to us. We should not be altogether shocked by such reactions. Even Jesus' own family declared Him to be "out of His mind" because He was doing the things God wanted Him to do. Some of the religious leaders of His day hated Jesus for His devotion to God rather than to religious tradition, and so they took great pleasure in declaring He was possessed by Satan. Neither group had the least bit of understanding concerning Jesus' ministry and teaching. You may be feeling alone and unsupported in your choice to turn your life over to the Lord Jesus. But remember, He has walked the same road. He knows what you are feeling. He will give you all the love and encouragement you need to keep going.

For further reading on Step 3, turn to page 99.

Daily Encouragement

DAY 32 READING: MARK 3:1–30

A Thought for the New Day: Be careful to keep a tender heart (v. 5). Jesus sometimes had to speak strongly to hard, unforgiving hearts. The greatest of all human tragedies is the sin of being implacable—unable to be merciful. It is all too easy to consider ourselves superior to others, especially to those who fail. Let us be thankful we have the model of the Savior's compassion for broken lives and broken hearts. *(Turn to page 79.)*

33 But He answered them, saying, "Who is My mother, or My brothers?"

34 And He looked around in a circle at those who sat about Him, and said, "Here are My mother and My brothers!

35 "For whoever does the will of God is My brother and My sister and mother."

4 And again He began to teach by the sea. And a great multitude was gathered to Him, so that He got into a boat and sat *in it* on the sea; and the whole multitude was on the land facing the sea.

2 Then He taught them many things by parables, and said to them in His teaching:

3 "Listen! Behold, a sower went out to sow.

4 "And it happened, as he sowed, *that* some *seed* fell by the wayside; and the birds of the air came and devoured it.

5 "Some fell on stony ground, where it did not have much earth; and immediately it sprang up because it had no depth of earth.

6 "But when the sun was up it was scorched, and because it had no root it withered away.

7 "And some *seed* fell among thorns; and the thorns grew up and choked it, and it yielded no crop.

8 "But other *seed* fell on good ground and yielded a crop that sprang up, increased and produced: some thirtyfold, some sixty, and some a hundred."

9 And He said to them, "He who has ears to hear, let him hear!"

10 But when He was alone, those around Him with the twelve asked Him about the parable.

11 And He said to them, "To you it has been given to know the mystery of the kingdom of God; but to those who are outside, all things come in parables,

12 "so that

'Seeing they may see and not perceive,
And hearing they may hear and not understand;
Lest they should turn,
And their sins be forgiven them.' "

13 And He said to them, "Do you not understand this parable? How then will you understand all the parables?

14 "The sower sows the word.

15 "And these are the ones by the wayside where the word is sown. And when they hear, Satan comes immediately and takes away the word that was sown in their hearts.

16 "These likewise are the ones sown on stony ground who, when they hear the word, immediately receive it with gladness;

17 "and they have no root in themselves, and so endure only for a time. Afterward, when tribulation or persecution arises for the word's sake, immediately they stumble.

18 "Now these are the ones sown among thorns; *they are* the ones who hear the word,

19 "and the cares of this world, the deceitfulness of riches, and the desires for other things entering in choke the word, and it becomes unfruitful.

20 "But these are the ones sown on good ground, those who hear the word, accept *it*, and bear fruit: some thirtyfold, some sixty, and some a hundred."

21 And He said to them, "Is a lamp brought to be put under a basket or under a bed? Is it not to be set on a lampstand?

22 "For there is nothing hidden which will not be revealed, nor has anything been kept secret but that it should come to light.

23 "If anyone has ears to hear, let him hear."

24 And He said to them, "Take heed what you hear. With the

STEP 4

Made a searching and fearless moral inventory of ourselves.

Mark 4:22

As a child, I loved to play hide and seek with my brothers, sisters, and friends. We had a large basement with a laundry area in one corner, and frequently we played down there in the winter. At the start of one of our many games, I decided to hide in the wash tub into which our old washing machine emptied. It turned out to be the perfect hiding place. After all the other children had been "found," everyone started looking for me. As I smirked to myself knowing they would never find me, the washing machine, which had been humming quietly, suddenly emptied hot, soapy water onto me. My shrieks and sputters not only gave away my hiding place, but also made me the object of uproarious laughter.

In Step 4 of our recovery, we must admit that we have had an "emotional hiding place," as well. To remain in our hiding place now is to invite humiliation and possibly disaster. To begin to recognize and admit those hiding places is to take a long step away from potential disaster and toward winning the game of life.

For further reading on Step 4, turn to page 105.

Daily Encouragement

DAY 33 READING: MARK 3:31—4:23

A Thought for the New Day: Jesus compared His Word to seed that grows, but it must find rich soil in the lives of those who will gladly receive that Word, who will treasure and cultivate it (4:20). Foods have value only as they are transformed into healthy flesh, bone, and blood. The Word of Christ is lost and wasted if it only remains on the pages of the Bible. But that same Word, translated into character, brings health and healing to a troubled world. *(Turn to page 81.)*

same measure you use, it will be measured to you; and to you who hear, more will be given.

25 "For whoever has, to him more will be given; but whoever does not have, even what he has will be taken away from him."

26 And He said, "The kingdom of God is as if a man should scatter seed on the ground,

27 "and should sleep by night and rise by day, and the seed should sprout and grow, he himself does not know how.

28 "For the earth yields crops by itself: first the blade, then the head, after that the full grain in the head.

29 "But when the grain ripens, immediately he puts in the sickle, because the harvest has come."

30 And He said, "To what shall we liken the kingdom of God? Or with what parable shall we picture it?

31 "*It is* like a mustard seed which, when it is sown on the ground, is smaller than all the seeds on earth;

32 "but when it is sown, it grows up and becomes greater than all herbs, and shoots out large branches, so that the birds of the air may nest under its shade."

33 And with many such parables He spoke the word to them as they were able to hear *it*.

34 But without a parable He did not speak to them. And when they were alone, He explained all things to His disciples.

35 On the same day, when evening had come, He said to them, "Let us cross over to the other side."

36 Now when they had left the multitude, they took Him along in the boat as He was. And other little boats were also with Him.

37 And a great windstorm arose, and the waves beat into the boat, so that it was already filling.

38 But He was in the stern, asleep on a pillow. And they awoke Him and said to Him, "Teacher, do You not care that we are perishing?"

39 Then He arose and rebuked the wind, and said to the sea, "Peace, be still!" And the wind ceased and there was a great calm.

40 But He said to them, "Why are you so fearful? How *is it* that you have no faith?"

41 And they feared exceedingly, and said to one another, "Who can this be, that even the wind and the sea obey Him!"

5 Then they came to the other side of the sea, to the country of the Gadarenes.

2 And when He had come out of the boat, immediately there met Him out of the tombs a man with an unclean spirit,

3 who had *his* dwelling among the tombs; and no one could bind him, not even with chains,

4 because he had often been bound with shackles and chains. And the chains had been pulled apart by him, and the shackles broken in pieces; neither could anyone tame him.

5 And always, night and day, he was in the mountains and in the tombs, crying out and cutting himself with stones.

6 But when he saw Jesus from afar, he ran and worshiped Him.

7 And he cried out with a loud voice and said, "What have I to do with You, Jesus, Son of the Most High God? I implore You by God that You do not torment me."

8 For He said to him, "Come out of the man, unclean spirit!"

9 Then He asked him, "What *is* your name?" And he answered, saying, "My name *is* Legion; for we are many."

10 And he begged Him earnestly that He would not send them out of the country.

11 Now a large herd of swine was feeding there near the mountains.

12 And all the demons begged Him, saying, "Send us to the swine, that we may enter them."

13 And at once Jesus gave them permission. Then the unclean spir-

STEP 1

*We admitted we were powerless over our dependencies—
that our lives had become unmanageable.*

Mark 4:35–41

If you have ever been unfortunate enough to be caught on stormy seas in a small boat, you can understand completely the great fear that Jesus' friends experienced. Drenching waves spill into the vessel, and the pitching and rocking throw its passengers off balance. Steering is difficult, if not impossible, in the face of fierce winds and rough waters. In such a situation, panic sets in easily, and rational judgment seems difficult.

If this is a picture of your life right now, there is hope. But it is not in straining at the oars and doubling your determination to get to shore yourself. It is, instead, in accepting the fact that your life is out of control on the rough seas of circumstance. To admit this utter powerlessness is to finally let go of our own puny oars, and reach out for the life raft of safety that Jesus offers.

For further reading on Step 1, turn to page 93.

Daily Encouragement

DAY 34 READING: MARK 4:24–41

A Thought for the New Day: Jesus brings peace to troubled lives, just as He calmed the sea storm (v. 39). Sometimes we are driven by the demands and pressures of living in the modern world. Then we do well to look to the Master of Storms. The One who knows the way of the sea also hears our cry and speaks the word that brings settled calm. *(Turn to page 83.)*

its went out and entered the swine (there were about two thousand); and the herd ran violently down the steep place into the sea, and drowned in the sea.

14 Now those who fed the swine fled, and they told *it* in the city and in the country. And they went out to see what it was that had happened.

15 Then they came to Jesus, and saw the one *who had been* demon-possessed and had the legion, sitting and clothed and in his right mind. And they were afraid.

16 And those who saw it told them how it happened to him *who had been* demon-possessed, and about the swine.

17 Then they began to plead with Him to depart from their region.

STEP 12 18 And when He got into the boat, he who had been demon-possessed begged Him that he might be with Him.

19 However, Jesus did not permit him, but said to him, "Go home to your friends, and tell them what great things the Lord has done for you, and how He has had compassion on you."

20 And he departed and began to proclaim in Decapolis all that Jesus had done for him; and all marveled.

21 Now when Jesus had crossed over again by boat to the other side, a great multitude gathered to Him; and He was by the sea.

22 And behold, one of the rulers of the synagogue came, Jairus by name. And when he saw Him, he fell at His feet

23 and begged Him earnestly, saying, "My little daughter lies at the point of death. Come and lay Your hands on her, that she may be healed, and she will live."

24 So *Jesus* went with him, and a great multitude followed Him and thronged Him.

25 Now a certain woman had a flow of blood for twelve years,

26 and had suffered many things from many physicians. She had spent all that she had and was no better, but rather grew worse.

27 When she heard about Jesus, she came behind *Him* in the crowd and touched His garment;

28 for she said, "If only I may touch His clothes, I shall be made well."

29 Immediately the fountain of her blood was dried up, and she felt in *her* body that she was healed of the affliction.

30 And Jesus, immediately knowing in Himself that power had gone out of Him, turned around in the crowd and said, "Who touched My clothes?"

31 But His disciples said to Him, "You see the multitude thronging You, and You say, 'Who touched Me?'"

32 And He looked around to see her who had done this thing.

33 But the woman, fearing and trembling, knowing what had happened to her, came and fell down before Him and told Him the whole truth.

34 And He said to her, "Daughter, your faith has made you well. Go in peace, and be healed of your affliction."

35 While He was still speaking, *some* came from the ruler of the synagogue's *house* who said, "Your daughter is dead. Why trouble the Teacher any further?" STEP 2

36 As soon as Jesus heard the word that was spoken, He said to the ruler of the synagogue, "Do not be afraid; only believe."

37 And He permitted no one to follow Him except Peter, James, and John the brother of James.

38 Then He came to the house of the ruler of the synagogue, and saw a tumult and those who wept and wailed loudly.

39 When He came in, He said to them, "Why make this commotion

STEP 12

*Having had a spiritual awakening as the result
of these steps, we tried to carry this message to others,
and to practice these principles in all our affairs.*

Mark 5:18–20

The man healed of demon-possession sought to remain close to the Lord, the immediate source of his healing. However, Jesus dispatched the man back to his family and community so that knowledge of His healing might be disseminated to a wider audience.

A common recovery saying is that "you must give it away in order to keep it." Step 12 is one of the maintenance steps of our recovery, and a vital aspect of that maintenance is our personal willingness to carry ("give away") the message of recovery to those who still suffer.

How are we to carry the message? Our new life-style, free of the destructive dependencies of the past, is a living witness to recovery. Sharing our life stories and recovery experiences in support group meetings and in personal conversations is a powerful spoken witness. And intervening lovingly, but firmly, on behalf of those trapped in denial about their own dependencies is another way we faithfully carry out Jesus' instruction to tell others what great things God has done for us.

For further reading on Step 12, turn to page 125.

Daily Encouragement

DAY 35 READING: MARK 5:1–43

A Thought for the New Day: Our problems may not be as severe as those of the demented man, but sometimes we are overwhelmed by the decisions we must make. In trying times it is well to know the secret of surrender to the only One who understands our way infinitely better than we can. Then, like the man among the tombs, it will be our great joy to tell our friends "what great things the Lord has done" for us (v. 19). (*Turn to page 85.*)

and weep? The child is not dead, but sleeping."

40 And they laughed Him to scorn. But when He had put them all out, He took the father and the mother of the child, and those *who were* with Him, and entered where the child was lying.

41 Then He took the child by the hand, and said to her, "Talitha, cumi," which is translated, "Little girl, I say to you, arise."

42 Immediately the girl arose and walked, for she was twelve years *of age.* And they were overcome with great amazement.

43 But He commanded them strictly that no one should know it, and said that *something* should be given her to eat.

6 Then He went out from there and came to His own country, and His disciples followed Him.

2 And when the Sabbath had come, He began to teach in the synagogue. And many hearing *Him* were astonished, saying, "Where *did* this *Man get* these things? And what wisdom *is* this which is given to Him, that such mighty works are performed by His hands!

3 "Is this not the carpenter, the Son of Mary, and brother of James, Joses, Judas, and Simon? And are not His sisters here with us?" And they were offended at Him.

4 But Jesus said to them, "A prophet is not without honor except in his own country, among his own relatives, and in his own house."

5 Now He could do no mighty work there, except that He laid His hands on a few sick people and healed *them.*

6 And He marveled because of their unbelief. Then He went about the villages in a circuit, teaching.

7 And He called the twelve *to* Him, and began to send them out two *by* two, and gave them power over unclean spirits.

8 He commanded them to take nothing for the journey except a staff—no bag, no bread, no copper in *their* money belts—

9 but to wear sandals, and not to put on two tunics.

10 Also He said to them, "In whatever place you enter a house, stay there till you depart from that place.

11 "And whoever will not receive you nor hear you, when you depart from there, shake off the dust under your feet as a testimony against them. Assuredly, I say to you, it will be more tolerable for Sodom and Gomorrah in the day of judgment than for that city!"

12 So they went out and preached that *people* should repent.

13 And they cast out many demons, and anointed with oil many who were sick, and healed *them.*

14 Now King Herod heard *of Him,* for His name had become well known. And he said, "John the Baptist is risen from the dead, and therefore these powers are at work in him."

15 Others said, "It is Elijah." And others said, "It is the Prophet, or like one of the prophets."

16 But when Herod heard, he said, "This is John, whom I beheaded; he has been raised from the dead!"

17 For Herod himself had sent and laid hold of John, and bound him in prison for the sake of Herodias, his brother Philip's wife; for he had married her.

18 For John had said to Herod, "It is not lawful for you to have your brother's wife."

19 Therefore Herodias held it against him and wanted to kill him, but she could not;

20 for Herod feared John, knowing that he *was* a just and holy man, and he protected him. And when he heard him, he did many things, and heard him gladly.

21 Then an opportune day came when Herod on his birthday gave a

STEP 10

STEP 10

*Continued to take personal inventory
and when we were wrong promptly admitted it.*

Mark 6:21–29

Have you ever made a rash promise that you wish you could take back? This happened to King Herod on his birthday one year. He had thrown a big party for himself and, having enjoyed the dance of Herodias' daughter, was intending to show how generous he could be to those who pleased him. He offered to give her anything she wanted. But when she requested the death of John the Baptist, he discovered his ego had written a check that was going to be difficult for his heart to cash.

As Step 10 reminds us, a truly wise man admits his mistakes promptly; however, Herod was too proud to be wise. Instead of apologizing and then repeating his offer with appropriate conditions, he plunged ahead "because of those who sat with him" (v. 26). His pride and impulsiveness had caused him not only to speak foolishly, but also to act sinfully. The opposite personality traits—humility and caution—are the graces which Step 10 is building into our lives as we take daily inventory, promptly admitting and correcting our faults.

For further reading on Step 10, turn to page 107.

Daily Encouragement

DAY 36 READING: MARK 6:1–29

A Thought for the New Day: It may be just as well that we do not know where life's path will take us as we begin our journey. John the Baptist surely did not know that one day he would have to lay down his life for his Lord. But he ended his life as he had lived it—as a faithful witness to the truth (vv. 27–29). Each day brings its special opportunity to be at least a signpost for truth before a watching world. (*Turn to page 89.*)

feast for his nobles, the high officers, and the chief *men* of Galilee.
22 And when Herodias' daughter herself came in and danced, and pleased Herod and those who sat with him, the king said to the girl, "Ask me whatever you want, and I will give *it* to you."
23 He also swore to her, "Whatever you ask me, I will give you, up to half of my kingdom."
24 So she went out and said to her mother, "What shall I ask?" And she said, "The head of John the Baptist!"
25 Immediately she came in with haste to the king and asked, saying, "I want you to give me at once the head of John the Baptist on a platter."
26 And the king was exceedingly sorry; *yet,* because of the oaths and because of those who sat with him, he did not want to refuse her.
27 And immediately the king sent an executioner and commanded his head to be brought. And he went and beheaded him in prison,
28 brought his head on a platter, and gave it to the girl; and the girl gave it to her mother.
29 And when his disciples heard *of it,* they came and took away his corpse and laid it in a tomb.
30 Then the apostles gathered to Jesus and told Him all things, both what they had done and what they had taught.
31 And He said to them, "Come aside by yourselves to a deserted place and rest a while." For there were many coming and going, and they did not even have time to eat.
32 So they departed to a deserted place in the boat by themselves.
33 But the multitudes saw them departing, and many knew Him and ran there on foot from all the cities. They arrived before them and came together to Him.
34 And Jesus, when He came out, saw a great multitude and was moved with compassion for them,

because they were like sheep not having a shepherd. So He began to teach them many things.
35 And when the day was now far spent, His disciples came to Him and said, "This is a deserted place, and already the hour *is* late.
36 "Send them away, that they may go into the surrounding country and villages and buy themselves bread; for they have nothing to eat."
37 But He answered and said to them, "You give them something to eat." And they said to Him, "Shall we go and buy two hundred denarii worth of bread and give them *something* to eat?"
38 But He said to them, "How many loaves do you have? Go and see." And when they found out they said, "Five, and two fish."
39 Then He commanded them to make them all sit down in groups on the green grass.
40 So they sat down in ranks, in hundreds and in fifties.
41 And when He had taken the five loaves and the two fish, He looked up to heaven, blessed and broke the loaves, and gave *them* to His disciples to set before them; and the two fish He divided among *them* all.
42 So they all ate and were filled.
43 And they took up twelve baskets full of fragments and of the fish.
44 Now those who had eaten the loaves were about five thousand men.
45 Immediately He made His disciples get into the boat and go before Him to the other side, to Bethsaida, while He sent the multitude away.
46 And when He had sent them away, He departed to the mountain to pray.
47 Now when evening came, the boat was in the middle of the sea; and He *was* alone on the land.
48 Then He saw them straining at rowing, for the wind was against

them. And about the fourth watch of the night He came to them, walking on the sea, and would have passed them by.

49 But when they saw Him walking on the sea, they supposed it was a ghost, and cried out;

50 for they all saw Him and were troubled. And immediately He talked with them and said to them, "Be of good cheer! It is I; do not be afraid."

51 Then He went up into the boat to them, and the wind ceased. And they were greatly amazed in themselves beyond measure, and marveled.

52 For they had not understood about the loaves, because their heart was hardened.

53 When they had crossed over, they came to the land of Gennesaret and anchored there.

54 And when they came out of the boat, immediately the people recognized Him,

55 ran through that whole surrounding region, and began to carry about on beds those who were sick to wherever they heard He was.

56 Wherever He entered, into villages, cities, or the country, they laid the sick in the marketplaces, and begged Him that they might just touch the border of His garment. And as many as touched Him were made well.

7 Then the Pharisees and some of the scribes came together to Him, having come from Jerusalem.

2 Now when they saw some of His disciples eat bread with defiled, that is, with unwashed hands, they found fault.

3 For the Pharisees and all the Jews do not eat unless they wash *their* hands in a special way, holding the tradition of the elders.

4 *When they come* from the marketplace, they do not eat unless they wash. And there are many other things which they have re-

ceived and hold, *like* the washing of cups, pitchers, copper vessels, and couches.

5 Then the Pharisees and scribes asked Him, "Why do Your disciples not walk according to the tradition of the elders, but eat bread with unwashed hands?"

6 He answered and said to them, "Well did Isaiah prophesy of you hypocrites, as it is written:

'This people honors Me with
    their lips,
But their heart is far from Me.
7 And in vain they worship Me,
    Teaching as doctrines the
    commandments of men.'

8 "For laying aside the commandment of God, you hold the tradition of men—the washing of pitchers and cups, and many other such things you do."

9 And He said to them, "*All too* well you reject the commandment of God, that you may keep your tradition.

10 "For Moses said, *'Honor your father and your mother'*; and, *'He who curses father or mother, let him be put to death.'*

11 "But you say, 'If a man says to his father or mother, "Whatever profit you might have received from me *is* Corban"—' " (that is, dedicated *to the temple*);

12 "and you no longer let him do anything for his father or his mother,

13 "making the word of God of no effect through your tradition which you have handed down. And many such things you do."

14 And when He had called all the multitude *to Him*, He said to them, "Hear Me, everyone, and understand:

15 "There is nothing that enters a man from outside which can defile him; but the things which come out of him, those are the things that defile a man.

16 "If anyone has ears to hear, let him hear!"

17 And when He had entered a house away from the crowd, His disciples asked Him concerning the parable.

18 So He said to them, "Are you thus without understanding also? Do you not perceive that whatever enters a man from outside cannot defile him,

19 "because it does not enter his heart but his stomach, and is eliminated, *thus* purifying all foods?"

STEP 5 20 And He said, "What comes out of a man, that defiles a man.

21 "For from within, out of the heart of men, proceed evil thoughts, adulteries, fornications, murders,

22 "thefts, covetousness, wickedness, deceit, licentiousness, an evil eye, blasphemy, pride, foolishness.

23 "All these evil things come from within and defile a man."

24 And from there He arose and went to the region of Tyre and Sidon. And He entered a house and wanted no one to know *it*, but He could not be hidden.

25 For a woman whose young daughter had an unclean spirit heard about Him, and she came and fell at His feet.

26 The woman was a Greek, a Syro-Phoenician by birth, and she kept asking Him to cast the demon out of her daughter.

27 But Jesus said to her, "Let the children be filled first, for it is not good to take the children's bread and throw *it* to the little dogs."

28 And she answered and said to Him, "Yes, Lord, yet even the little dogs under the table eat from the children's crumbs."

29 Then He said to her, "For this saying go your way; the demon has gone out of your daughter."

30 And when she had come to her house, she found the demon gone out, and her daughter lying on the bed.

31 And again, departing from the region of Tyre and Sidon, He came through the midst of the region of Decapolis to the Sea of Galilee.

32 Then they brought to Him one who was deaf and had an impediment in his speech, and they begged Him to put His hand on him.

33 And He took him aside from the multitude, and put His fingers in his ears, and He spat and touched his tongue.

34 Then, looking up to heaven, He sighed, and said to him, "Ephphatha," that is, "Be opened."

35 Immediately his ears were opened, and the impediment of his tongue was loosed, and he spoke plainly.

36 Then He commanded them that they should tell no one; but the more He commanded them, the more widely they proclaimed *it*.

37 And they were astonished beyond measure, saying, "He has done all things well. He makes both the deaf to hear and the mute to speak."

8 In those days, the multitude being very great and having nothing to eat, Jesus called His disciples *to Him* and said to them,

2 "I have compassion on the multitude, because they have now been with Me three days and have nothing to eat.

3 "And if I send them away hungry to their own houses, they will faint on the way; for some of them have come from afar."

4 Then His disciples answered Him, "How can one satisfy these people with bread here in the wilderness?"

5 He asked them, "How many loaves do you have?" And they said, "Seven."

6 And He commanded the multitude to sit down on the ground. And He took the seven loaves and gave thanks, broke *them* and gave *them* to His disciples to set before

STEP 5

*Admitted to God, to ourselves, and to another human being
the exact nature of our wrongs.*

Mark 7:20–23

A true sign of maturity is the ability to recognize that sin is generated from within. Accepting responsibility for our actions, words, and attitudes is absolutely necessary if we are to be whole, capable, and fulfilled human beings. Jeremiah 17:9 tells us that "the heart *is* deceitful above all *things*; and desperately wicked."

In Step 4, we came to understand how deceitful and sick our hearts have been. Now it is time to admit these things to God, to ourselves, and to someone else who can give us understanding and hope. Perhaps members of the group Jesus addressed in Mark 7 had committed some of the very wrongs we must admit.

Remember, God does not stand as judge to those who acknowledge their sin. Instead, He receives us with mercy. Our sins may have isolated us from God and others, but admitting our wrongs breaks down the barriers, leading to restored fellowship.

For further reading on Step 5, turn to page 137.

Daily Encouragement

DAY 37 READING: MARK 6:30—7:23

A Thought for the New Day: It is easy to take the provision of our daily needs for granted, especially if we have never been in want. Elsewhere we are told that the disciples had not fully appreciated the marvelous way (vv. 41–44) in which Jesus fed the crowd. We, too, imagine that our daily food is only what we deserve, unaware that it is a divine hand that governs the apparently endless supply. Thankfulness becomes us and enhances our enjoyment of God's gifts, as we realize His kindness is the source of all our good things. (*Turn to page 91.*)

them; and they set *them* before the multitude.

7 And they had a few small fish; and having blessed them, He said to set them also before *them.*

8 So they ate and were filled, and they took up seven large baskets of leftover fragments.

9 Now those who had eaten were about four thousand. And He sent them away.

10 And immediately He got into the boat with His disciples and came to the region of Dalmanutha.

11 And the Pharisees came out and began to dispute with Him, seeking from Him a sign from heaven, testing Him.

12 But He sighed deeply in His spirit, and said, "Why does this generation seek a sign? Assuredly, I say to you, no sign shall be given to this generation."

13 And He left them, and getting into the boat again, departed to the other side.

14 Now the disciples had forgotten to take bread, and they did not have more than one loaf with them in the boat.

15 Then He charged them, saying, "Take heed, beware of the leaven of the Pharisees and the leaven of Herod."

16 So they reasoned among themselves, saying, *"It is* because we have no bread."

17 And Jesus, being aware of *it,* said to them, "Why do you reason because you have no bread? Do you not yet perceive nor understand? Is your heart still hardened?

18 "Having eyes, do you not see? And having ears, do you not hear? And do you not remember?

19 "When I broke the five loaves for the five thousand, how many baskets full of fragments did you take up?" They said to Him, "Twelve."

20 "And when I broke the seven for the four thousand, how many large baskets full of fragments did

you take up?" And they said, "Seven."

21 So He said to them, "How *is it* you do not understand?"

22 Then He came to Bethsaida; and they brought a blind man to Him, and begged Him to touch him.

23 So He took the blind man by the hand and led him out of the town. And when He had spit on his eyes and put His hands on him, He asked him if he saw anything.

24 And he looked up and said, "I see men like trees, walking."

25 Then He put *His* hands on his eyes again and made him look up. And he was restored and saw everyone clearly.

STEP 2

26 And He sent him away to his house, saying, "Neither go into the town, nor tell anyone in the town."

27 Now Jesus and His disciples went out to the towns of Caesarea Philippi; and on the road He asked His disciples, saying to them, "Who do men say that I am?"

28 And they answered, "John the Baptist; but some *say,* Elijah; and others, one of the prophets."

29 He said to them, "But who do you say that I am?" And Peter answered and said to Him, "You are the Christ."

30 Then He charged them that they should tell no one about Him.

31 And He began to teach them that the Son of Man must suffer many things, and be rejected by the elders and chief priests and scribes, and be killed, and after three days rise again.

32 He spoke this word openly. And Peter took Him aside and began to rebuke Him.

33 But when He had turned around and looked at His disciples, He rebuked Peter, saying, "Get behind Me, Satan! For you are not mindful of the things of God, but the things of men."

34 And when He had called the people *to Him,* with His disciples

STEP 2

*Came to believe that a Power greater than ourselves
could restore us to sanity.*

Mark 8:22–25

Each of us is unique, and is therefore treated uniquely by the Lord. This can be seen quite clearly in the accounts of Jesus' healing miracles. For some, His healing power stretched across the miles, and those He healed never even saw Him personally. Some were healed by simply touching the hem of His garment. Others heard His voice command their illness to depart. Still others He touched in His own special way. In reading the account of this blind man who received his sight, we might be tempted to ask questions, such as, "Why did Jesus have to take him out of town first? Why did He have to spit on his eyes? Why wasn't he healed immediately?" We are not told, but we can rest assured that an all-wise, all-loving, and all-knowing God did exactly what needed to be done to accomplish healing in this manner. And we can rest assured that this same loving, wise, and sovereign God can restore us to wholeness, as well.

For further reading on Step 2, turn to page 95.

Daily Encouragement

DAY 38 READING: MARK 7:24—8:26

A Thought for the New Day: Jesus knew all along that He was going to heal the woman's little daughter. However, He wanted the mother to rightly understand the kindness of God (7:25–30). The healing was no problem, but the mother's heart had to be right before God. Sometimes God postpones the good thing we want until we are able to appreciate the gift and, most of all, appreciate the Giver Himself. (*Turn to page 93.*)

also, He said to them, "Whoever desires to come after Me, let him deny himself, and take up his cross, and follow Me.

35 "For whoever desires to save his life will lose it, but whoever loses his life for My sake and the gospel's will save it.

STEP 1 36 "For what will it profit a man if he gains the whole world, and loses his own soul?

37 "Or what will a man give in exchange for his soul?

38 "For whoever is ashamed of Me and My words in this adulterous and sinful generation, of him the Son of Man also will be ashamed when He comes in the glory of His Father with the holy angels."

9 And He said to them, "Assuredly, I say to you that there are some standing here who will not taste death till they see the kingdom of God present with power."

2 Now after six days Jesus took Peter, James, and John, and led them up on a high mountain apart by themselves; and He was transfigured before them.

3 His clothes became shining, exceedingly white, like snow, such as no launderer on earth can whiten them.

4 And Elijah appeared to them with Moses, and they were talking with Jesus.

5 Then Peter answered and said to Jesus, "Rabbi, it is good for us to be here; and let us make three tabernacles: one for You, one for Moses, and one for Elijah"—

6 because he did not know what to say, for they were greatly afraid.

7 And a cloud came and overshadowed them; and a voice came out of the cloud, saying, "This is My beloved Son. Hear Him!"

8 Suddenly, when they had looked around, they saw no one anymore, but only Jesus with themselves.

9 Now as they came down from the mountain, He commanded them that they should tell no one the things they had seen, till the Son of Man had risen from the dead.

10 So they kept this word to themselves, questioning what the rising from the dead meant.

11 And they asked Him, saying, "Why do the scribes say that Elijah must come first?"

12 Then He answered and told them, "Elijah does come first, and restores all things. And how is it written concerning the Son of Man, that He must suffer many things and be treated with contempt?

13 "But I say to you that Elijah has also come, and they did to him whatever they wished, as it is written of him."

14 And when He came to the disciples, He saw a great multitude around them, and scribes disputing with them.

15 Immediately, when they saw Him, all the people were greatly amazed, and running to *Him*, greeted Him.

16 And He asked the scribes, "What are you discussing with them?"

17 Then one from the multitude answered and said, "Teacher, I brought You my son, who has a mute spirit.

18 "And wherever he seizes him, he throws him down; he foams at the mouth, gnashes his teeth, and becomes rigid. So I spoke to Your disciples, that they should cast him out, but they could not."

19 He answered him and said, "O faithless generation, how long shall I be with you? How long shall I bear with you? Bring him to Me."

20 Then they brought him to Him. And when he saw Him, immediately the spirit convulsed him, and he fell on the ground and wallowed, foaming at the mouth.

21 So He asked his father, "How

STEP 1

*We admitted we were powerless over our dependencies—
that our lives had become unmanageable.*

Mark 8:36, 37

We have developed many different ways to anesthetize emotional pain. Some of us use drugs, others use work, or money, or power, or fame, or thrills. And for a while most of these things work pretty well. But for every person there is a day of reckoning—a day when the ideas expressed in Mark 8:36, 37 push themselves into his or her consciousness and leave a hollow feeling in the stomach. "What is worth giving in exchange for my eternal soul?" If he or she has the courage to be honest, that answer can only be that nothing—nothing, no matter how earthly wonderful, can be worth the sacrifice of my eternal soul.

In fact, these temporal things cannot, in the long run, give us true and lasting satisfaction here on earth. All that people can conjure up, use and abuse, ultimately leaves them empty. Only when we admit this powerlessness, can we take the first step toward eternal fulfillment.

For further reading on Step 1, turn to page 273.

Daily Encouragement

DAY 39 READING: MARK 8:27—9:13

A Thought for the New Day: Self-preservation is a fundamental rule of life. Thus, we even become slaves to ourselves: "What's in it for me?" is the constant question. Then, one day, we are surprised by how foolish and futile it is always to be struggling to hang on to what we are going to lose anyway. As we begin to let go of ourselves and our desires to God's will, our lives can take on new meaning and value in His eternal plan (8:35). (*Turn to page 95.*)

long has this been happening to him?" And he said, "From childhood.

22 "And often he has thrown him both into the fire and into the water to destroy him. But if You can do anything, have compassion on us and help us."

STEP 2
23 Jesus said to him, "If you can believe, all things *are* possible to him who believes."
24 Immediately the father of the child cried out and said with tears, "Lord, I believe; help my unbelief!"

25 When Jesus saw that the people came running together, He rebuked the unclean spirit, saying to him, "*You* deaf and dumb spirit, I command you, come out of him, and enter him no more!"

26 Then *the spirit* cried out, convulsed him greatly, and came out of him. And he became as one dead, so that many said, "He is dead."

27 But Jesus took him by the hand and lifted him up, and he arose.

28 And when He had come into the house, His disciples asked Him privately, "Why could we not cast him out?"

29 So He said to them, "This kind can come out by nothing but prayer and fasting."

30 Then they departed from there and passed through Galilee, and He did not want anyone to know it.

31 For He taught His disciples and said to them, "The Son of Man is being delivered into the hands of men, and they will kill Him. And after He is killed, He will rise the third day."

32 But they did not understand this saying, and were afraid to ask Him.

33 Then He came to Capernaum. And when He was in the house He asked them, "What was it you disputed among yourselves on the road?"

34 But they kept silent, for on the road they had disputed among themselves who *would be the* greatest.

35 And He sat down, called the twelve, and said to them, "If anyone desires to be first, he shall be last of all and servant of all."

36 Then He took a little child and set him in the midst of them. And when He had taken him in His arms, He said to them,

37 "Whoever receives one of these little children in My name receives Me; and whoever receives Me, receives not Me but Him who sent Me."

38 Now John answered Him, saying, "Teacher, we saw someone who does not follow us casting out demons in Your name, and we forbade him because he does not follow us."

39 But Jesus said, "Do not forbid him, for no one who works a miracle in My name can soon afterward speak evil of Me.

40 "For he who is not against us is on our side.

41 "For whoever gives you a cup of water to drink in My name, because you belong to Christ, assuredly, I say to you, he will by no means lose his reward.

42 "And whoever causes one of these little ones who believe in Me to stumble, it would be better for him if a millstone were hung around his neck, and he were thrown into the sea.

STEP 6
43 "And if your hand makes you sin, cut it off. It is better for you to enter into life maimed, than having two hands, to go to hell, into the fire that shall never be quenched—
44 "where *'their worm does not die and the fire is not quenched.'*
45 "And if your foot makes you sin, cut it off. It is better for you to enter life lame, than having two feet, to be cast into hell, into the fire that shall never be quenched—

STEP 2

Came to believe that a Power greater than ourselves could restore us to sanity.

Mark 9:23, 24

When we have been held captive by damaging dependencies or addictive behaviors, it is sometimes hard to believe that we will ever be free of them. The words of Luke 1:37 need to take root deep in our hearts: "For with God nothing will be impossible."

A frightened and doubting father discovered the truth of these words when he brought his precious, demon-possessed son to Jesus for healing. With all hope nearly gone, he pleaded, "If You can do anything, have compassion on us and help us."

Instead of criticizing this man for his lack of faith, Jesus pointed to the importance of the father's trust in God to do what is humanly impossible. The father's cry echoes the cry of each of our hearts, "Lord, I believe; help my unbelief!" He declared his faith but was honest about his weakness.

When we truly want to believe in God's great power to deliver us, He will be there, helping us to release our doubt, to yield our dependencies, and to place trust in Him.

For further reading on Step 2, turn to page 117.

Daily Encouragement

DAY 40 READING: MARK 9:14–37

A Thought for the New Day: Like the distraught father in this passage, we look within ourselves and confess we have so little faith to boast about. Certainly Jesus is *worthy* of our trust, but trusting just is not natural to us. What a relief to know that Jesus understands our weakness and reaches out to our insufficiency! His love is greater than our little faith, and His love triumphs when we come to the end of ourselves. (*Turn to page 96.*)

STEP 6

*Were entirely ready to have God
remove all these defects of character.*

Mark 9:43–48

There are skeptics who have pulled these words of Jesus out of context in order to suggest Christianity is a bloody religion with a God who is highly intolerant of sinners. While it is true that sin saddens and even repulses God, it is also true that He always loves the sinner and desires his good. That is exactly the meaning behind the illustrations Jesus uses here. He is saying that whatever causes us to sin on a continual basis and keeps us from God is not worth the price we pay to keep it. Nothing in our lives is so precious or indispensable that it is worth hanging onto at the expense of our souls.

When our heart comes to grips with the truth Jesus is teaching in these verses, we will be ready for God to cleanse us.

For further reading on Step 6, turn to page 253.

Daily Encouragement

DAY 41 READING: MARK 9:38—10:12

A Thought for the New Day: What is the flavor of a Christian? Like salt (9:50), that individual has a distinct and consistent "taste" to those around him. Read the lives of God's favorite people. Although they were not always popular, they possessed a quality that made them irresistibly attractive to those around them. Jesus was like that, and so are those who follow Him. Dare to be different for Christ's sake, and your life will be exciting beyond imagination. (*Turn to page 99.*)

46 "where *'their worm does not die and the fire is not quenched.'*

47 "And if your eye makes you sin, pluck it out. It is better for you to enter the kingdom of God with one eye, than having two eyes, to be cast into hell fire—

48 "where *'their worm does not die and the fire is not quenched.'*

49 "For everyone will be seasoned with fire, and every sacrifice will be seasoned with salt.

50 "Salt *is* good, but if the salt loses its flavor, how will you season it? Have salt in yourselves, and have peace with one another."

10 Then He arose from there and came to the region of Judea by the other side of the Jordan. And the people gathered to Him again, and as He was accustomed, He taught them again.

2 The Pharisees came and asked Him, "Is it lawful for a man to divorce *his* wife?" testing Him.

3 And He answered and said to them, "What did Moses command you?"

4 They said, "Moses permitted *a man* to write a certificate of divorce, and to dismiss *her*."

5 And Jesus answered and said to them, "Because of the hardness of your heart he wrote you this precept.

6 "But from the beginning of the creation, God *'made them male and female.'*

7 *'For this reason a man shall leave his father and mother and be joined to his wife,*

8 *'and the two shall become one flesh';* so then they are no longer two, but one flesh.

9 "Therefore what God has joined together, let not man separate."

10 And in the house His disciples asked Him again about the same *matter.*

11 So He said to them, "Whoever divorces his wife and marries another commits adultery against her.

12 "And if a woman divorces her husband and marries another, she commits adultery."

13 Then they brought young children to Him, that He might touch them; but the disciples rebuked those who brought *them.*

14 But when Jesus saw *it,* He was greatly displeased and said to them, "Let the little children come to Me, and do not forbid them; for of such is the kingdom of God.

15 "Assuredly, I say to you, whoever does not receive the kingdom of God as a little child will by no means enter it."

16 And He took them up in His arms, put *His* hands on them, and blessed them.

17 Now as He was going out on the road, one came running, knelt before Him, and asked Him, "Good Teacher, what shall I do that I may inherit eternal life?"

18 So Jesus said to him, "Why do you call Me good? No one *is* good but One, *that is,* God.

19 "You know the commandments: *'Do not commit adultery,' 'Do not murder,' 'Do not steal,' 'Do not bear false witness,'* 'Do not defraud,' *'Honor your father and your mother.'*"

20 And he answered and said to Him, "Teacher, all these I have observed from my youth."

21 Then Jesus, looking at him, loved him, and said to him, "One thing you lack: Go your way, sell whatever you have and give to the poor, and you will have treasure in heaven; and come, take up the cross, and follow Me."

22 But he was sad at this word, and went away grieved, for he had great possessions.

23 Then Jesus looked around and said to His disciples, "How hard it is for those who have riches to enter the kingdom of God!"

24 And the disciples were astonished at His words. But Jesus answered again and said to them,

STEP 3

"Children, how hard it is for those who trust in riches to enter the kingdom of God!

25 "It is easier for a camel to go through the eye of a needle than for a rich man to enter the kingdom of God."

26 And they were astonished beyond measure, saying among themselves, "Who then can be saved?"

27 But looking at them, Jesus said, "With men *it is* impossible, but not with God; for with God all things are possible."

28 Then Peter began to say to Him, "See, we have left all and followed You."

29 So Jesus answered and said, "Assuredly, I say to you, there is no one who has left house or brothers or sisters or father or mother or wife or children or lands, for My sake and the gospel's,

30 "who shall not receive a hundredfold now in this time—houses and brothers and sisters and mothers and children and lands, with persecutions—and in the age to come, eternal life.

31 "But many *who are* first will be last, and the last first."

32 Now they were on the road, going up to Jerusalem, and Jesus was going before them; and they were amazed. And as they followed they were afraid. Then He took the twelve aside again and began to tell them the things that would happen to Him:

33 "Behold, we are going up to Jerusalem, and the Son of Man will be delivered to the chief priests and to the scribes, and they will condemn Him to death and deliver Him to the Gentiles;

34 "and they will mock Him, and scourge Him, and spit on Him, and kill Him. And the third day He will rise again."

35 Then James and John, the sons of Zebedee, came to Him, saying,

"Teacher, we want You to do for us whatever we ask."

36 And He said to them, "What do you want Me to do for you?"

37 They said to Him, "Grant us that we may sit, one on Your right hand and the other on Your left, in Your glory."

38 But Jesus said to them, "You do not know what you ask. Can you drink the cup that I drink, and be baptized with the baptism that I am baptized with?"

39 And they said to Him, "We can." And Jesus said to them, "You will indeed drink the cup that I drink, and with the baptism I am baptized with you will be baptized;

40 "but to sit on My right hand and on My left is not Mine to give, but *it is for those* for whom it is prepared."

41 And when the ten heard *it,* they began to be greatly displeased with James and John.

42 But Jesus called them to *Himself* and said to them, "You know that those who are considered rulers over the Gentiles lord it over them, and their great ones exercise authority over them.

43 "Yet it shall not be so among you; but whoever desires to become great among you shall be your servant.

44 "And whoever of you desires to be first shall be slave of all.

45 "For even the Son of Man did not come to be served, but to serve, and to give His life a ransom for many."

46 Then they came to Jericho. And as He went out of Jericho with His disciples and a great multitude, blind Bartimaeus, the son of Timaeus, sat by the road begging.

47 And when he heard that it was Jesus of Nazareth, he began to cry out and say, "Jesus, Son of David, have mercy on me!"

48 Then many warned him to be quiet; but he cried out all the more,

STEP 3

*Made a decision to turn our will and our lives
over to the care of God **as we understood Him**.*

Mark 10:17–27

Jesus perceived that the rich young ruler had a problem with his understanding of how to gain eternal life when the young man asked, "What shall I <u>do</u> that I may inherit eternal life?" He wanted a list of good deeds that would allow him to work his way to heaven. When Jesus asked him instead to sell his possessions, He was showing the young man that he needed to trust and worship God, rather than his money. However, money and possessions had such a stranglehold on his life that he could not extricate himself from their grip. This is the reason Jesus said in verse 24, "How hard it is for those who trust in riches to enter the kingdom of God!"

Whatever we have been worshiping as ruler of our life and trusting in to be the ultimate answer to our needs, we must be willing now to turn over to the Lord Jesus. Only when we are willing to let loose of all things that would take the place of God will God be able to fill us with the bounty of His love and deliverance.

For further reading on Step 3, turn to page 121.

Daily Encouragement

DAY 42 READING: MARK 10:13–45

A Thought for the New Day: To be "grown up" often means worldly sophistication, along with a large dose of skepticism, if not downright cynicism. But the cynical person cannot enter the kingdom of God just as he is (v. 15). Upon discovering Christ, a twentieth-century aristocrat announced, "I have found the meaning of being Christian." Turning his back on his noble heritage, the man went on to impact the lives of thousands for Christ. Can we have that simplicity? *(Turn to page 101.)*

"Son of David, have mercy on me!"

49 So Jesus stood still and commanded him to be called. Then they called the blind man, saying to him, "Be of good cheer. Rise, He is calling you."

50 And throwing aside his garment, he rose and came to Jesus. 51 And Jesus answered and said to him, "What do you want Me to do for you?" The blind man said to Him, "Rabboni, that I may receive my sight."

52 Then Jesus said to him, "Go your way; your faith has made you well." And immediately he received his sight and followed Jesus on the road.

11 Now when they came near Jerusalem, to Bethphage and Bethany, at the Mount of Olives, He sent out two of His disciples; 2 and He said to them, "Go into the village opposite you; and as soon as you have entered it you will find a colt tied, on which no one has sat. Loose it and bring *it.* 3 "And if anyone says to you, 'Why are you doing this?' say, 'The Lord has need of it,' and immediately he will send it here."

4 So they went their way, and found the colt tied by the door outside on the street, and they loosed it.

5 And some of those who stood there said to them, "What are you doing, loosing the colt?"

6 So they spoke to them just as Jesus had commanded. And they let them go.

7 Then they brought the colt to Jesus and threw their garments on it, and He sat on it.

8 And many spread their garments on the road, and others cut down leafy branches from the trees and spread *them* on the road.

9 Then those who went before and those who followed cried out, saying:

"Hosanna!

'Blessed *is* He who comes in the name of the Lord!'

10 Blessed *is* the kingdom of our father David

That comes in the name of the Lord!

Hosanna in the highest!"

11 And Jesus went into Jerusalem and into the temple. So when He had looked around at all things, as the hour was already late, He went out to Bethany with the twelve.

12 Now the next day, when they had come out from Bethany, He was hungry.

13 And seeing from afar a fig tree having leaves, He went to see if perhaps He would find something on it. And when He came to it, He found nothing but leaves, for it was not the season for figs.

14 In response Jesus said to it, "Let no one eat fruit from you ever again." And His disciples heard *it.*

15 So they came to Jerusalem. And Jesus went into the temple and began to drive out those who bought and sold in the temple, and overturned the tables of the moneychangers and the seats of those who sold doves.

16 And He would not allow anyone to carry wares through the temple.

17 Then He taught, saying to them, "Is it not written, 'My house shall be called a house of prayer for all nations'? But you have made it a 'den of thieves.'"

18 And the scribes and chief priests heard it and sought how they might destroy Him; for they feared Him, because all the people were astonished at His teaching.

19 And when evening had come, He went out of the city.

20 Now in the morning, as they passed by, they saw the fig tree dried up from the roots.

21 And Peter, remembering, said to Him, "Rabbi, look! The fig tree

STEP 7

Humbly asked Him to remove our shortcomings.
Mark 10:50–52

Hebrews 11:6 says that "without faith *it is* impossible to please [God]." Faith and humility are closely linked because they both involve a total dependence on God's power and goodness rather than on anything in ourselves. As we now ask God to do a great work in our lives—a miracle as wonderful as the blind man receiving his sight—our faith in God's ability to do this must be without reservation. Although His power is not dependent on our faith, God nevertheless chooses to do His work in response to our faith.

Just a few verses over in Mark 11:22–24 we are told that the person who "does not doubt in his heart, but believes that those things he says will come to pass" will receive them.

God is not only able, but He wants to bring about our healing and remove our shortcomings. He will work in our lives as we trust Him without reservation.

For further reading on Step 7, turn to page 119.

Daily Encouragement

DAY 43 READING: MARK 10:46—11:11

A Thought for the New Day: "See the King of kings riding a donkey!" some of the crowd probably laughed as Jesus rode into Jerusalem (11:7). Jesus did not mind, though. Rather, this hero of the people seemed to make little of Himself for their amusement. Is it not a good-natured, sporting gesture? Jesus, who could command a universe, did not need to look important. Why should we? (*Turn to page 103.*)

which You cursed has withered away."

22 So Jesus answered and said to them, "Have faith in God.

23 "For assuredly, I say to you, whoever says to this mountain, 'Be removed and be cast into the sea,' and does not doubt in his heart, but believes that those things he says will come to pass, he will have whatever he says.

24 "Therefore I say to you, whatever things you ask when you pray, believe that you receive *them*, and you will have *them*.

STEP 8 25 "And whenever you stand praying, if you have anything against anyone, forgive him, that your Father in heaven may also forgive you your trespasses.

26 "But if you do not forgive, neither will your Father in heaven forgive your trespasses."

27 Then they came again to Jerusalem. And as He was walking in the temple, the chief priests, the scribes, and the elders came to Him.

28 And they said to Him, "By what authority are You doing these things? And who gave You this authority to do these things?"

29 But Jesus answered and said to them, "I will also ask you one question; then answer Me, and I will tell you by what authority I do these things:

30 "The baptism of John—was it from heaven or from men? Answer Me."

31 And they reasoned among themselves, saying, "If we say, 'From heaven,' He will say, 'Why then did you not believe him?'

32 "But if we say, 'From men'"— they feared the people, for all counted John to have been a prophet indeed.

33 So they answered and said to Jesus, "We do not know." And Jesus answered and said to them, "Neither will I tell you by what authority I do these things."

12 Then He began to speak to them in parables: "A man planted a vineyard and set a hedge around *it*, dug *a place for* the wine vat and built a tower. And he leased it to vinedressers and went into a far country.

2 "Now at vintage-time he sent a servant to the vinedressers, that he might receive some of the fruit of the vineyard from the vinedressers.

3 "And they took *him* and beat him and sent *him* away empty-handed.

4 "Again he sent them another servant, and at him they threw stones, wounded *him* in the head, and sent *him* away shamefully treated.

5 "And again he sent another, and him they killed; and many others, beating some and killing some.

6 "Therefore still having one son, his beloved, he also sent him to them last, saying, 'They will respect my son.'

7 "But those vinedressers said among themselves, 'This is the heir. Come, let us kill him, and the inheritance will be ours.'

8 "And they took him and killed *him* and cast *him* out of the vineyard.

9 "Therefore what will the owner of the vineyard do? He will come and destroy the vinedressers, and give the vineyard to others.

10 "Have you not read this Scripture:

'The stone which the builders rejected
Has become the chief cornerstone.
11 This was the LORD's doing,
And it is marvelous in our eyes'?"

12 And they sought to lay hold of Him, but feared the multitude, for they knew He had spoken the parable against them. So they left Him and went away.

STEP
8

*Made a list of all persons we had harmed,
and became willing to make amends to them all.*

Mark 11:25

Real forgiveness imitates the heart of God as much or more than any other human virtue. When God became flesh and died for our sins, He took the initiative in restoring us to fellowship with Himself. We had sinned against him, but He still reached out to us in love and reconciliation. That does not give us the right to trample on the grace He extends, but rather to humbly accept His forgiveness. It seems that no matter which end of the relationship we are on, the act of forgiveness requires humility. Philippians tells us that Jesus humbled Himself to come to earth and bring about our forgiveness (see Phil. 2:5–8). And we can only accept that forgiving grace when we humble ourselves as children.

Now as we think about the people we need to forgive, or perhaps those from whom we must ask forgiveness, let us be willing to humbly imitate the heart of our Great Father, who forgave us all so much.

For further reading on Step 8, turn to page 109.

Daily
Encouragement

DAY 44 READING: MARK 11:12–33

A Thought for the New Day: Treasured-up wrongs poison our personalities. A lifetime of not forgiving leads to a bitter old age. And, of course, there is no way we can stand in God's presence when there is someone we cannot (will not) forgive. God will only say, "Forget it! Come back when you have made a friend of your imagined enemy" (v. 25). It costs nothing to forgive— nothing but our foolish pride. *(Turn to page 105.)*

STEP 4

13 Then they sent to Him some of the Pharisees and the Herodians, to catch Him in *His* words.

14 When they had come, they said to Him, "Teacher, we know that You are true, and care about no one; for You do not regard the person of men, but teach the way of God in truth. Is it lawful to pay taxes to Caesar, or not?

15 "Shall we pay, or shall we not pay?" But He, knowing their hypocrisy, said to them, "Why do you test Me? Bring Me a denarius that I may see *it*."

16 So they brought *it*. And He said to them, "Whose image and inscription *is* this?" And they said to Him, "Caesar's."

17 Then Jesus answered and said to them, "Render to Caesar the things that are Caesar's, and to God the things that are God's." And they marveled at Him.

18 Then *some* Sadducees, who say there is no resurrection, came to Him; and they asked Him, saying:

19 "Teacher, Moses wrote to us that if a man's brother dies, and leaves *his* wife behind, and leaves no children, his brother should take his wife and raise up offspring for his brother.

20 "Now there were seven brothers. The first took a wife; and dying, he left no offspring.

21 "And the second took her, and he died; nor did he leave any offspring. And the third likewise.

22 "So the seven had her and left no offspring. Last of all the woman died also.

23 "Therefore, in the resurrection, when they rise, whose wife will she be? For all seven had her as wife."

24 Jesus answered and said to them, "Are you not therefore mistaken, because you do not know the Scriptures nor the power of God?

25 "For when they rise from the dead, they neither marry nor are given in marriage, but are like angels in heaven.

26 "But concerning the dead, that they rise, have you not read in the book of Moses, in the *burning* bush *passage*, how God spoke to him, saying, '*I am the God of Abraham, the God of Isaac, and the God of Jacob*'?

27 "He is not the God of the dead, but the God of the living. You are therefore greatly mistaken."

28 Then one of the scribes came, and having heard them reasoning together, perceiving that He had answered them well, asked Him, "Which is the first commandment of all?"

29 Jesus answered him, "The first of all the commandments *is*: '*Hear, O Israel, the LORD our God, the LORD is one.*

30 '*And you shall love the LORD your God with all your heart, with all your soul, with all your mind, and with all your strength.*' This *is* the first commandment.

31 "And the second, like *it*, *is* this: '*You shall love your neighbor as yourself.*' There is no other commandment greater than these."

32 So the scribe said to Him, "Well *said*, Teacher. You have spoken the truth, for there is one God, and there is no other but He.

33 "And to love Him with all the heart, with all the understanding, with all the soul, and with all the strength, and to love one's neighbor as oneself, is more than all the whole burnt offerings and sacrifices."

34 So when Jesus saw that he answered wisely, He said to him, "You are not far from the kingdom of God." And after that no one dared question Him.

35 Then Jesus answered and said, while He taught in the temple, "How *is it* that the scribes say that the Christ is the Son of David?

36 "For David himself said by the Holy Spirit:

STEP
4

Made a searching and fearless moral inventory of ourselves.

Mark 12:13

The twelfth chapter of Mark is a sad commentary on human blindness—not the physical blindness of a beggar, but rather the spiritual blindness which plagued much of Israel's learned, upper class. Jesus had so easily healed countless people suffering from physical blindness. But these spiritually blind Jewish leaders refused His healing Light. They preferred to stay in their comfortable darkness. Instead of carefully questioning their own motives, they chose instead to question and challenge Jesus. If they had been actually searching for truth, the words and deeds of Jesus would have changed their lives. Many people today still prefer their comfortable darkness. They enjoy questioning and shouting challenges to others, but they are too fearful to honestly question themselves.

Each of us now must make a choice. That choice is to as honestly and fearlessly as we know how, open ourselves to the light of a searching moral inventory.

For further reading on Step 4, turn to page 115.

Daily Encouragement

DAY 45 READING: MARK 12:1–34

A Thought for the New Day: For two thousand years there has been much discussion about what the kingdom of God is. No doubt the kingdom is several things, but the man in this story seems to have satisfied Jesus that he understood the most basic fact about the kingdom of God—that it is love (v. 34). Now that we know this, too, we need to attend to making that kingdom *actually happen* inside and all around us. *(Turn to page 107.)*

'The LORD said to my Lord,
  "Sit at My right hand,
Till I make Your enemies
  Your footstool." '

37 "Therefore David himself calls Him *'Lord';* how is He *then* his Son?" And the common people heard Him gladly.

38 Then He said to them in His teaching, "Beware of the scribes, who desire to go around in long robes, *love* greetings in the marketplaces,

39 "the best seats in the synagogues, and the best places at feasts,

40 "who devour widows' houses, and for a pretense make long prayers. These will receive greater condemnation."

41 Now Jesus sat opposite the treasury and saw how the people put money into the treasury. And many *who were* rich put in much.

42 Then one poor widow came and threw in two mites, which make a quadrans.

43 So He called His disciples *to Him* and said to them, "Assuredly, I say to you that this poor widow has put in more than all those who have given to the treasury;

44 "for they all put in out of their abundance, but she out of her poverty put in all that she had, her whole livelihood."

13 Then as He went out of the temple, one of His disciples said to Him, "Teacher, see what manner of stones and what buildings *are here!*"

2 And Jesus answered and said to him, "Do you see these great buildings? Not *one* stone shall be left upon another, that shall not be thrown down."

3 Now as He sat on the Mount of Olives opposite the temple, Peter, James, John, and Andrew asked Him privately,

4 "Tell us, when will these things be? And what *will be* the sign when all these things will be fulfilled?"

5 And Jesus, answering them, began to say: "Take heed that no one deceives you.

6 "For many will come in My name, saying, 'I am *He*,' and will deceive many.

7 "And when you hear of wars and rumors of wars, do not be troubled; for *such things* must happen, but the end *is* not yet.

8 "For nation will rise against nation, and kingdom against kingdom. And there will be earthquakes in various places, and there will be famines and troubles. These *are* the beginnings of sorrows.

9 "But watch out for yourselves, for they will deliver you up to councils, and you will be beaten in the synagogues. And you will be brought before rulers and kings for My sake, for a testimony to them.

10 "And the gospel must first be preached to all the nations.

11 "But when they arrest *you* and deliver you up, do not worry beforehand, or premeditate what you will speak. But whatever is given you in that hour, speak that; for it is not you who speak, but the Holy Spirit.

12 "Now brother will betray brother to death, and a father *his* child; and children will rise up against parents and cause them to be put to death.

13 "And you will be hated by all *men* for My name's sake. But he who endures to the end shall be saved.

14 "But when you see the *'abomination of desolation,'* spoken of by Daniel the prophet, standing where it ought not" (let the reader understand), "then let those who are in Judea flee to the mountains.

15 "And let him who is on the housetop not go down into the house, nor enter to take anything out of his house.

STEP 10

Continued to take personal inventory
and when we were wrong promptly admitted it.

Mark 13:33–37

Mark 13:33–37 is filled with remarkable predictions, incredible excitement, and heart-stopping terror. Although opinions vary as to just how all Jesus predicted will occur, serious students of Scripture agree that Jesus is coming again and we must be ready. In fact, four times in the last five verses Jesus repeats the command to "watch." How do we "watch" for His appearing? Do we stand gazing at the sky, or perhaps don a white robe and head for the nearest mountain to wait for Him? No, "watching" is an attitude of heart. It is a carefulness to pay attention to the path our life is taking. It is a cautious eye upon our motives, words, and life-style. It is a heart that stays pure and remains in daily communion with the Lord, desiring above all to please Him. It is looking forward to the day when we will hear, "Well done, good and faithful servant."

For further reading on Step 10, turn to page 113.

Daily Encouragement

DAY 46 READING: MARK 12:35—13:37

A Thought for the New Day: God loves common people, and He made that point by living and dying as one among us. It was not mean envy that provoked Jesus' remarks about the religious aristocracy of His time. They were a pretentious group, as anyone could see (12:37–40). We only have to remember that Jesus is continually looking for servants (not masters!) to walk in His steps. (*Turn to page 109.*)

16 "And let him who is in the field not go back to get his garment.

17 "But woe to those who are pregnant and to those with nursing babies in those days!

18 "And pray that your flight may not be in winter.

19 "For *in* those days there will be tribulation, such as has not been from the beginning of creation which God created until this time, nor ever shall be.

20 "And unless the Lord had shortened those days, no flesh would be saved; but for the elect's sake, whom He chose, He shortened the days.

21 "Then if anyone says to you, 'Look, here *is* the Christ!' or, 'Look, He *is* there!' do not believe it.

22 "For false christs and false prophets will rise and show signs and wonders to deceive, if possible, even the elect.

23 "But take heed; see, I have told you all things beforehand.

24 "But in those days, after that tribulation, the sun will be darkened, and the moon will not give its light;

25 "the stars of heaven will fall, and the powers in heaven will be shaken.

26 "Then they will see the Son of Man coming in the clouds with great power and glory.

27 "And then He will send His angels, and gather together His elect from the four winds, from the farthest part of earth to the farthest part of heaven.

28 "Now learn this parable from the fig tree: When its branch has already become tender, and puts forth leaves, you know that summer is near.

29 "So you also, when you see these things happening, know that it is near, at the very doors.

30 "Assuredly, I say to you, this generation will by no means pass away till all these things take place.

31 "Heaven and earth will pass away, but My words will by no means pass away.

32 "But of that day and hour no one knows, neither the angels in heaven, nor the Son, but only the Father.

33 "Take heed, watch and pray; for you do not know when the time is.

34 "*It is* like a man going to a far country, who left his house and gave authority to his servants, and to each his work, and commanded the doorkeeper to watch.

35 "Watch therefore, for you do not know when the master of the house is coming—in the evening, at midnight, at the crowing of the rooster, or in the morning—

36 "lest, coming suddenly, he find you sleeping.

37 "And what I say to you, I say to all: Watch!"

14 After two days it was the Passover and *the Feast* of Unleavened Bread. And the chief priests and the scribes sought how they might take Him by trickery and put *Him* to death.

2 But they said, "Not during the feast, lest there be an uproar of the people."

3 And being in Bethany at the house of Simon the leper, as He sat at the table, a woman came having an alabaster flask of very costly oil of spikenard. And she broke the flask and poured *it* on His head.

4 But there were some who were indignant among themselves, and said, "Why was this fragrant oil wasted?

5 "For it might have been sold for more than three hundred denarii and given to the poor." And they criticized her sharply.

6 But Jesus said, "Let her alone. Why do you trouble her? She has done a good work for Me.

7 "For you have the poor with you always, and whenever you wish you may do them good; but Me you do not have always.

STEP 8

*Made a list of all persons we had harmed,
and became willing to make amends to them all.*

Mark 14:3–9

The habit of criticism is a wet blanket mercilessly smothering the fires of enthusiasm and motivation. Some of Jesus' friends seemed determined to put out the light for everyone, as they criticized this woman's act of beautiful sacrifice and devotion. Probably the disciples were feeling self-righteously correct as they pointed out a far better use for this money. Jesus, however, rebuked their negative narrow-mindedness, and gave praise instead to the thoughtful and devoted attitude of the woman.

Many of us have experienced the wet blanket of criticism in our own lives. If we grew up in an extremely critical home, we may have negative attitudes we need to release toward parents and siblings. Or perhaps we ourselves have been critical and impatient with others and need to ask forgiveness.

Let us be willing to release critical attitudes in ourselves and choose not to be bound by the criticism of others.

For further reading on Step 8, turn to page 141.

Daily Encouragement

DAY 47 READING: MARK 14:1–16

A Thought for the New Day: God's roll of honor includes outstanding Christian leaders, such as the apostles John and Paul, but Jesus has also reserved a place for this sinful woman (v. 9). St. Augustine had been a wild youth, but to Monica his mother it was promised, "The son of so many tears cannot be lost," and her tears will always be remembered along with her famous son's later great works. Let us learn from the fact that, while we weigh reputations, God weighs hearts. (*Turn to page 111.*)

8 "She has done what she could. She has come beforehand to anoint My body for burial.

9 "Assuredly, I say to you, wherever this gospel is preached throughout the whole world, what this woman did will also be spoken of as a memorial to her."

10 Then Judas Iscariot, one of the twelve, went to the chief priests to betray Him to them.

11 So when they heard it, they were glad, and promised to give him money. So he sought how he might conveniently betray Him.

12 Now on the first day of Unleavened Bread, when they killed the Passover *lamb*, His disciples said to Him, "Where do You want us to go and prepare, that You may eat the Passover?"

13 So He sent out two of His disciples and said to them, "Go into the city, and a man will meet you carrying a pitcher of water; follow him.

14 "And wherever he goes in, say to the master of the house, 'The Teacher says, "Where is the guest room in which I may eat the Passover with My disciples?"'

15 "Then he will show you a large upper room, furnished *and* prepared; there make ready for us."

16 And His disciples went out, and came into the city, and found it just as He had said to them; and they prepared the Passover.

17 In the evening He came with the twelve.

18 Now as they sat and ate, Jesus said, "Assuredly, I say to you, one of you who eats with Me will betray Me."

19 And they began to be sorrowful, and to say to Him one by one, "*Is* it I?" And another *said,* "*Is* it I?"

20 Then He answered and said to them, "*It is* one of the twelve, who dips with Me in the dish.

21 "The Son of Man indeed goes just as it is written of Him, but woe to that man by whom the Son of Man is betrayed! It would have been good for that man if he had never been born."

22 And as they were eating, Jesus took bread, blessed *it* and broke *it,* and gave *it* to them and said, "Take, eat; this is My body."

23 Then He took the cup, and when He had given thanks He gave *it* to them, and they all drank from it.

24 And He said to them, "This is My blood of the new covenant, which is shed for many.

25 "Assuredly, I say to you, I will no longer drink of the fruit of the vine until that day when I drink it new in the kingdom of God."

26 And when they had sung a hymn, they went out to the Mount of Olives.

27 Then Jesus said to them, "All of you will be made to stumble because of Me this night, for it is written:

'I will strike the Shepherd,
   And the sheep will be
     scattered.'

28 "But after I have been raised, I will go before you to Galilee."

29 But Peter said to Him, "Even if all are made to stumble, yet I *will* not *be.*"

30 And Jesus said to him, "Assuredly, I say to you that today, *even* this night, before the rooster crows twice, you will deny Me three times."

31 But he spoke more vehemently, "If I have to die with You, I will not deny You!" And they all said likewise.

32 Then they came to a place which was named Gethsemane; and He said to His disciples, "Sit here while I pray."

33 And He took Peter, James, and John with Him, and He began to be troubled and deeply distressed.

34 Then He said to them, "My soul is exceedingly sorrowful, *even* to death. Stay here and watch."

STEP 11

STEP 11

*Sought through prayer and mediation to improve our conscious contact with God **as we understood Him,** praying only for knowledge of His will for us and the power to carry that out.*

Mark 14:24, 25

Sorrow, close-knit fellowship, foreboding, deep love, anticipation—all these emotions filled the Upper Room that night as Jesus took the bread and cup, and gave them to the men He called His friends. Only He knew what was ahead, however. Only He knew the extent of the suffering and humiliation He must face. But Jesus chose to look beyond those grim scenes to the "joy that was set before Him" (Heb. 12:2).

As He lifted the cup, He centered His focus on heaven: the joy ahead was worth the struggle now.

None of us will ever have to face the incredible emotional and physical pain that Jesus faced. But we can look at our own struggles—whatever they are at this point in our lives—and know that as we walk in the obedience and faith, the joy that lies ahead is worth the pain.

For further reading on Step 11, turn to page 127.

Daily Encouragement

DAY 48 READING: MARK 14:17–31

A Thought for the New Day: If we love Jesus, we want to avoid sin, just as Peter did. We are painfully aware that when we do sin, we deny the Savior. This was something Peter was sure he would never do (v. 31), at least not willfully, and yet he did. Peter, and each of us, must learn how weak we are. Then, perhaps, we will put our trust in the One who can make us able to overcome our temptations. (*Turn to page 113.*)

35 He went a little farther, and fell on the ground, and prayed that if it were possible, the hour might pass from Him.

36 And He said, "Abba, Father, all things *are* possible for You. Take this cup away from Me; nevertheless, not what I will, but what You *will*."

37 Then He came and found them sleeping, and said to Peter, "Simon, are you sleeping? Could you not watch one hour?

38 "Watch and pray, lest you enter into temptation. The spirit truly *is* ready, but the flesh *is* weak."

39 Again He went away and prayed, and spoke the same words.

40 And when He returned, He found them asleep again, for their eyes were heavy; and they did not know what to answer Him.

41 Then He came the third time and said to them, "Are you still sleeping and resting? It is enough! The hour has come; behold, the Son of Man is being betrayed into the hands of sinners.

42 "Rise up, let us go. See, My betrayer is at hand."

43 And immediately, while He was still speaking, Judas, one of the twelve, with a great multitude with swords and clubs, came from the chief priests and the scribes and the elders.

44 Now His betrayer had given them a signal, saying, "Whomever I kiss, He is the One; take Him and lead *Him* away safely."

45 And as soon as He had come, immediately he went up to Him and said to Him, "Rabbi, Rabbi!" and kissed Him.

46 Then they laid their hands on Him and took Him.

47 And one of those who stood by drew his sword and struck the servant of the high priest, and cut off his ear.

48 Then Jesus answered and said to them, "Have you come out, as against a robber, with swords and clubs to take Me?

49 "I was daily with you in the temple teaching, and you did not take Me. But the Scriptures must be fulfilled."

50 Then they all forsook Him and fled.

51 Now a certain young man followed Him, having a linen cloth thrown around *his* naked *body.* And the young men laid hold of him,

52 and he left the linen cloth and fled from them naked.

53 And they led Jesus away to the high priest; and with him were assembled all the chief priests, the elders, and the scribes.

54 But Peter followed Him at a distance, right into the courtyard of the high priest. And he sat with the servants and warmed himself at the fire.

55 And the chief priests and all the council sought testimony against Jesus to put Him to death, and found none.

56 For many bore false witness against Him, but their testimonies did not agree.

57 And some rose up and bore false witness against Him, saying,

58 "We heard Him say, 'I will destroy this temple that *is* made with hands, and within three days I will build another made without hands.' "

59 But not even then did their testimony agree.

60 And the high priest stood up in the midst and asked Jesus, saying, "Do You answer nothing? What *is* it these men testify against You?"

61 But He kept silent and answered nothing. Again the high priest asked Him, saying to Him, "Are You the Christ, the Son of the Blessed?"

62 And Jesus said, "I am. And you will see the Son of Man sitting at the right hand of the Power, and coming with the clouds of heaven."

63 Then the high priest tore his

112

STEP 10

*Continued to take personal inventory
and when we were wrong promptly admitted it.*

Mark 14:38

None of us ever reaches the point where our old nature is completely subdued and we will not be tempted by old, codependent patterns of behavior. It is significant that in Mark 14:27 Jesus addresses the apostle Peter as Simon, which was his name before he became a follower of Jesus. Perhaps Jesus was trying to help Peter see how close he was to falling back into his old life-style. Soon after, Peter denied Christ.

When Jesus tells the disciples to "watch," He is exhorting them to be alert to the spiritual dangers around them. And by telling them to pray, He is reminding them to acknowledge continually their dependence upon God rather than themselves. Jesus knew their spirits (their inner desires and intentions) were willing and eager to follow Him. But He also recognized their human inadequacies and how easily they could be overwhelmed by these inadequacies. How important for each of us to remain alert to temptations around us and to pray for strength and wisdom to conquer them!

For further reading on Step 10, turn to page 147.

Daily Encouragement

DAY 49 READING: MARK 14:32–52

A Thought for the New Day: What? Must Jesus—the Son of God—pray just as we must (v. 32)? The dreadful, saving work Jesus had to perform for us was encumbered with real temptation to fail and more suffering than we will ever know. The God who became a Man fought an unthinkable battle for us. But it was a spiritual war for which prayer was His real weapon. Without Gethsemane there could have been no triumph at Calvary. (*Turn to page 115.*)

clothes and said, "What further need do we have of witnesses?
64 "You have heard the blasphemy! What do you think?" And they all condemned Him to be worthy of death.
65 Then some began to spit on Him, and to blindfold Him, and to beat Him, and to say to Him, "Prophesy!" And the officers struck Him with the palms of their hands.
66 Now as Peter was below in the courtyard, one of the servant girls of the high priest came.
67 And when she saw Peter warming himself, she looked at him and said, "You also were with Jesus of Nazareth."
68 But he denied it, saying, "I neither know nor understand what you are saying." And he went out on the porch, and a rooster crowed.
69 And the servant girl saw him again, and began to say to those who stood by, "This is one of them."
70 But he denied it again. And a little later those who stood by said to Peter again, "Surely you are *one* of them; for you are a Galilean, and your speech shows *it*."
71 But he began to curse and swear, "I do not know this Man of whom you speak!"
72 And a second time *the* rooster crowed. And Peter called to mind the word that Jesus had said to him, "Before the rooster crows twice, you will deny Me three times." And when he thought about it, he wept.

15 Immediately, in the morning, the chief priests held a consultation with the elders and scribes and the whole council; and they bound Jesus, led *Him* away, and delivered *Him* to Pilate.
2 Then Pilate asked Him, "Are You the King of the Jews?" And He answered and said to him, "*It is as* you say."

3 And the chief priests accused Him of many things, but He answered nothing.
4 Then Pilate asked Him again, saying, "Do You answer nothing? See how many things they testify against You!"
5 But Jesus still answered nothing, so that Pilate marveled.
6 Now at the feast he was accustomed to releasing one prisoner to them, whomever they requested.
7 And there was one named Barabbas, *who was* chained with his fellow insurrectionists; they had committed murder in the insurrection.
8 Then the multitude, crying aloud, began to ask *him to do* just as he had always done for them.
9 But Pilate answered them, saying, "Do you want me to release to you the King of the Jews?"
10 For he knew that the chief priests had handed Him over because of envy.
11 But the chief priests stirred up the crowd, so that he should rather release Barabbas to them.
12 And Pilate answered and said to them again, "What then do you want me to do *with Him* whom you call the King of the Jews?"
13 So they cried out again, "Crucify Him!"
14 Then Pilate said to them, "Why, what evil has He done?" And they cried out more exceedingly, "Crucify Him!"
15 So Pilate, wanting to gratify the crowd, released Barabbas to them; and he delivered Jesus, after he had scourged *Him*, to be crucified.
16 Then the soldiers led Him away into the hall called Praetorium, and they called together the whole garrison.
17 And they clothed Him with purple; and they twisted a crown of thorns, put it on His *head*,
18 and began to salute Him, "Hail, King of the Jews!"
19 Then they struck Him on the head with a reed and spat on Him;

Made a searching and fearless moral inventory of ourselves.

Mark 15:1–15

Pilate is not alone in losing his conscience to a crowd's demands. Down through the centuries, countless individuals have succumbed to becoming the tool of a mob. Their prestige and the approval of others came to mean more than their own honesty and integrity.

It is an easy trap to get caught in. In school, the trap is called "peer pressure." In the adult world, it is called "climbing the ladder." We may be tempted to belittle Pilate, shaming his cowardly ways, but each of us must take our own inventory. "Wanting to gratify the crowd," have we done and said things we knew to be wrong? Substance abuse often begins with a need to feel the approval of others. Many other problems, as well, can develop from putting too high a price tag on the approval of others. However, when we understand and admit those wrongs, we can begin to free ourselves to walk in emotional integrity.

For further reading on Step 4, turn to page 129.

Daily Encouragement

DAY 50 READING: MARK 14:53—15:20

A Thought for the New Day: The Old Testament preacher wrote, "There is a time to keep silence and a time to speak," and Jesus knew this was a time to keep silent (15:4, 5). Nothing He could say would change the course of coming events. Besides, anything He said now would only be turned against Him. Let us pray that the Christ, who in silence amazed His accusers, will teach us also the wisdom and power of a silent witness that is sometimes appropriate before His enemies. (*Turn to page 117.*)

and bowing the knee, they worshiped Him.

20 And when they had mocked Him, they took the purple off Him, put His own clothes on Him, and led Him out to crucify Him.

21 Now they compelled a certain man, Simon a Cyrenian, the father of Alexander and Rufus, as he was coming out of the country and passing by, to bear His cross.

22 And they brought Him to the place Golgotha, which is translated, Place of a Skull.

23 Then they gave Him wine mingled with myrrh to drink, but He did not take *it*.

24 And when they crucified Him, they divided His garments, casting lots for them to determine what every man should take.

25 Now it was the third hour, and they crucified Him.

26 And the inscription of His accusation was written above:

THE KING OF THE JEWS.

27 With Him they also crucified two robbers, one on His right and the other on His left.

28 So the Scripture was fulfilled which says, *"And He was numbered with the transgressors."*

29 And those who passed by blasphemed Him, wagging their heads and saying, "Aha! *You* who destroy the temple and build *it* in three days,

30 "save Yourself, and come down from the cross!"

31 Likewise the chief priests also, together with the scribes, mocked and said among themselves, "He saved others; Himself He cannot save.

32 "Let the Christ, the King of Israel, descend now from the cross, that we may see and believe." And those who were crucified with Him reviled Him.

33 Now when the sixth hour had come, there was darkness over the whole land until the ninth hour.

34 And at the ninth hour Jesus cried out with a loud voice, saying, "Eloi, Eloi, lama sabachthani?" which is translated, *"My God, My God, why have You forsaken Me?"*

35 Some of those who stood by, when they heard *it*, said, "Look, He is calling for Elijah!"

36 Then someone ran and filled a sponge full of sour wine, put *it* on a reed, and offered *it* to Him to drink, saying, "Let Him alone; let us see if Elijah will come to take Him down."

37 And Jesus cried out with a loud voice, and breathed His last.

38 Then the veil of the temple was torn in two from top to bottom.

39 Now when the centurion, who stood opposite Him, saw that He cried out like this and breathed His last, he said, "Truly this Man was the Son of God!"

40 There were also women looking on from afar, among whom were Mary Magdalene, Mary the mother of James the Less and of Joses, and Salome,

41 who also followed Him and ministered to Him when He was in Galilee; and many other women who came up with Him to Jerusalem.

42 Now when evening had come, because it was the Preparation Day, that is, the day before the Sabbath,

43 Joseph of Arimathea, a prominent council member, who was himself waiting for the kingdom of God, coming and taking courage, went in to Pilate and asked for the body of Jesus.

44 Pilate marveled that He was already dead; and summoning the centurion, he asked him if He had been dead for some time.

45 And when he found out from the centurion, he granted the body to Joseph.

46 Then he bought fine linen, took Him down, and wrapped Him in the linen. And he laid Him in a

STEP 2

*Came to believe that a Power greater than ourselves
could restore us to sanity.*

Mark 15:38

Of all the signs declaring Jesus' power over sin and death, the tearing of the veil recorded in verse 38 is one of the most meaningful. In the Jewish temple a special, singularly woven cloth (or veil) was hung in front of an inner chamber called the Most Holy Place. Only the high priest was allowed to enter this sacred chamber, and he entered very infrequently. This chamber housed the ark of the covenant and contained the mercy seat. God's presence rested there, and the high priest entered only to make atonement for the sins of his people. At the moment of Christ's death when the invisible hand of God tore that veil from the top down, the symbolic meaning was unmistakable. The sacrificial death of Jesus opened the way for every person individually to receive God's power over sin and God's mercy to heal. Because of Jesus' victory over sin and death, we, too, can have victory, as we put our trust in Him.

For further reading on Step 2, turn to page 123.

Daily Encouragement

DAY 51 READING: MARK 15:21–47

A Thought for the New Day: If you have ever been desperate to know the "why" of your position, it may comfort you to know that Jesus also found Himself in that place once. Feelings of helplessness and abandonment prompted this question in His darkest hour (v. 34). We, too, can come near to Him with the very same question and be assured He will not turn us away. He knows all about our loneliness in suffering. *(Turn to page 119.)*

tomb which had been hewn out of the rock, and rolled a stone against the door of the tomb.

47 And Mary Magdalene and Mary *the mother* of Joses observed where He was laid.

STEP 7

16 Now when the Sabbath was past, Mary Magdalene, Mary *the mother* of James, and Salome bought spices, that they might come and anoint Him.

2 Very early in the morning, on the first day of the week, they came to the tomb when the sun had risen.

3 And they said among themselves, "Who will roll away the stone from the door of the tomb for us?"

4 But when they looked up, they saw that the stone had been rolled away—for it was very large.

5 And entering the tomb, they saw a young man clothed in a long white robe sitting on the right side; and they were alarmed.

6 But he said to them, "Do not be alarmed. You seek Jesus of Nazareth, who was crucified. He is risen! He is not here. See the place where they laid Him.

7 "But go *and* tell His disciples—and Peter—that He is going before you into Galilee; there you will see Him, as He said to you."

8 And they went out quickly and fled from the tomb, for they trembled and were amazed. And they said nothing to anyone, for they were afraid.

9 Now when *He* rose early on the first day of the week, He appeared first to Mary Magdalene, out of whom He had cast seven demons.

10 She went and told those who had been with Him, as they mourned and wept.

11 And when they heard that He was alive and had been seen by her, they did not believe.

12 After that, He appeared in another form to two of them as they walked and went into the country.

13 And they went and told *it* to the rest, *but* they did not believe them either.

14 Afterward He appeared to the eleven as they sat at the table; and He rebuked their unbelief and hardness of heart, because they did not believe those who had seen Him after He had risen.

15 And He said to them, "Go into all the world and preach the gospel to every creature.

16 "He who believes and is baptized will be saved; but he who does not believe will be condemned.

17 "And these signs will follow those who believe: In My name they will cast out demons; they will speak with new tongues;

18 "they will take up serpents; and if they drink anything deadly, it will by no means hurt them; they will lay hands on the sick, and they will recover."

19 So then, after the Lord had spoken to them, He was received up into heaven, and sat down at the right hand of God.

20 And they went out and preached everywhere, the Lord working with *them* and confirming the word through the accompanying signs. Amen.

Humbly asked Him to remove our shortcomings.

Mark 16:1–8

Jesus' devoted followers found themselves with much the same problem that we find ourselves with as we undertake Step 8 of our recovery.

The deep desire of the women's hearts was to honor Jesus, and this is also our own desire. However, it cannot be fulfilled because the huge stone of our shortcomings and dependencies hinders us from accomplishing what we earnestly seek. Our sincere question is the same one spoken by the women on Resurrection morning: "Who will roll away the stone?"

But as these verses show us, their anxiety was unnecessary, because what seemed an impossibility to them was entirely accomplished by the power of Almighty God. This same wonderful, powerful Savior will work in our lives, as well. As we admit our inability and rely upon His vast ability, the huge stone of our dependencies, which has so long entombed us, will be rolled away. A new life infused by God's power and grace will begin.

For further reading on Step 7, turn to page 135.

Daily Encouragement

DAY 52 READING: MARK 16:1–20

A Thought for the New Day: Thinking Jesus was dead, His disciples lost hope, and the promise of a new and happier life lay in the dust. They had forgotten, or no longer believed, that Jesus would rise from death (v. 11). However, their despair would soon turn to joy, for they would see Jesus alive again. Are you troubled? Hold out until morning—the true Sun that never fails will rise again as you renew your walk with Jesus. (*Turn to page 121.*)

LUKE

INASMUCH as many have taken in hand to set in order a narrative of those things which are most surely believed among us,

2 just as those who from the beginning were eyewitnesses and ministers of the word delivered them to us,

3 it seemed good to me also, having had perfect understanding of all things from the very first, to write to you an orderly account, most excellent Theophilus,

4 that you may know the certainty of those things in which you were instructed.

STEP 3

5 There was in the days of Herod, the king of Judea, a certain priest named Zacharias, of the division of Abijah. His wife *was* of the daughters of Aaron, and her name *was* Elizabeth.

6 And they were both righteous before God, walking in all the commandments and ordinances of the Lord blameless.

7 But they had no child, because Elizabeth was barren, and they were both well advanced in years.

8 So it was, that while he was serving as priest before God in the order of his division,

9 according to the custom of the priesthood, his lot fell to burn incense when he went into the temple of the Lord.

10 And the whole multitude of the people was praying outside at the hour of incense.

11 Then an angel of the Lord appeared to him, standing on the right side of the altar of incense.

12 And when Zacharias saw *him*, he was troubled, and fear fell upon him.

13 But the angel said to him, "Do not be afraid, Zacharias, for your prayer is heard; and your wife Elizabeth will bear you a son, and you shall call his name John.

14 "And you will have joy and gladness, and many will rejoice at his birth.

15 "For he will be great in the sight of the Lord, and shall drink neither wine nor strong drink. He will also be filled with the Holy Spirit, even from his mother's womb.

16 "And he will turn many of the children of Israel to the Lord their God.

17 "He will also go before Him in the spirit and power of Elijah, *'to turn the hearts of the fathers to the children,'* and the disobedient to the wisdom of the just, to make ready a people prepared for the Lord."

18 And Zacharias said to the angel, "How shall I know this? For I am an old man, and my wife is well advanced in years."

19 And the angel answered and said to him, "I am Gabriel, who stands in the presence of God, and was sent to speak to you and bring you these glad tidings.

20 "But behold, you will be mute and not able to speak until the day these things take place, because you did not believe my words which will be fulfilled in their own time."

21 And the people waited for Zacharias, and marveled that he lingered so long in the temple.

22 But when he came out, he could not speak to them; and they perceived that he had seen a vision in the temple, for he beckoned to them and remained speechless.

23 And so it was, as soon as the days of his service were completed, that he departed to his own house.

24 Now after those days his wife Elizabeth conceived; and she hid herself five months, saying,

25 "Thus the Lord has dealt with me, in the days when He looked on

*Made a decision to turn our will and our lives
over to the care of God **as we understood Him.***

Luke 1:5–20

Even those of us who try to walk closely with God can be temporarily sidelined by lack of faith. Such was the case with
Zacharias. For years this righteous priest had asked God for a child.
Yet when God sent His angel Gabriel with the good news that God
was answering his prayer, Zacharias faltered in doubt and disbelief.

Perhaps today you are struggling to find the faith to believe that
God not only cares about every detail of your life, but also has the
desire and power to make all things work together for your good
and His glory. Perhaps you have concluded that since the struggle
has lasted so long, God must not be listening or does not care, but
He does care and He cares greatly. Continue to trust Him, even
when the way seems long or the answers seem negative. God will
move and answer in His own time and way, and His plan and timing will prove to be wonderful.

For further reading on Step 3, turn to page 151.

Daily Encouragement

DAY 53 READING: LUKE 1:1–25

A Thought for the New Day: Today you may find yourself saying, "I've prayed so long, and nothing happens." Remember,
Zacharias did not believe the angel's promise, but Elizabeth's son
was born just the same (vv. 13, 14). Be sure something will happen—not what you planned, perhaps, but it will be the best of
all you could have dreamed. Yes, we have every reason to trust
God always, but even when we do not He still remains faithful.
(*Turn to page 123.*)

me, to take away my reproach among men."

26 Now in the sixth month the angel Gabriel was sent by God to a city of Galilee named Nazareth,

27 to a virgin betrothed to a man whose name was Joseph, of the house of David. The virgin's name *was* Mary.

28 And having come in, the angel said to her, "Rejoice, highly favored *one*, the Lord *is* with you; blessed *are* you among women!"

29 But when she saw *him*, she was troubled at his saying, and considered what manner of greeting this was.

30 Then the angel said to her, "Do not be afraid, Mary, for you have found favor with God.

31 "And behold, you will conceive in your womb and bring forth a Son, and shall call His name JESUS.

32 "He will be great, and will be called the Son of the Highest; and the Lord God will give Him the throne of His father David.

33 "And He will reign over the house of Jacob forever, and of His kingdom there will be no end."

34 Then Mary said to the angel, "How can this be, since I do not know a man?"

35 And the angel answered and said to her, "*The* Holy Spirit will come upon you, and the power of the Highest will overshadow you; therefore, also, that Holy One who is to be born will be called the Son of God.

36 "Now indeed, Elizabeth your relative has also conceived a son in her old age; and this is now the sixth month for her who was called barren.

STEP 2 37 "For with God nothing will be impossible."

38 Then Mary said, "Behold the maidservant of the Lord! Let it be to me according to your word." And the angel departed from her.

39 Now Mary arose in those days and went into the hill country with haste, to a city of Judah,

40 and entered the house of Zacharias and greeted Elizabeth.

41 And it happened, when Elizabeth heard the greeting of Mary, that the babe leaped in her womb; and Elizabeth was filled with the Holy Spirit.

42 Then she spoke out with a loud voice and said, "Blessed *are* you among women, and blessed *is* the fruit of your womb!

43 "But why *is* this *granted* to me, that the mother of my Lord should come to me?

44 "For indeed, as soon as the voice of your greeting sounded in my ears, the babe leaped in my womb for joy.

45 "Blessed *is* she who believed, for there will be a fulfillment of those things which were told her from the Lord."

46 And Mary said:

"My soul magnifies the Lord,
47 And my spirit has rejoiced
    in God my Savior.
48 For He has regarded the lowly
    state of His maidservant;
For behold, henceforth all
    generations will call me
    blessed.
49 For He who is mighty has done
    great things for me,
And holy *is* His name.
50 And His mercy *is* on those
    who fear Him
From generation to generation.
51 He has shown strength with
    His arm;
He has scattered *the* proud in
    the imagination of their
    hearts.
52 He has put down the mighty
    from *their* thrones,
And exalted *the* lowly.
53 He has filled *the* hungry
    with good things,
And *the* rich He has sent away
    empty.

STEP 2

*Came to believe that a Power greater than ourselves
could restore us to sanity.*

Luke 1:37

Next to "For God so loved the world" these words in verse 37 are
among the most thrilling and life-changing ever written. We finite
beings are so limited in our power and resources and knowledge.
Our physical and emotional strength is quickly depleted in the face
of our overwhelming circumstances. The odds are against us. All
hope is gone until we realize there is Someone who can change us
into winners. He is more than a good coach. He invented the
game. No matter how many points have been scored against us,
God's power is limitless, His resources are vast, and His love for us
is so deep that He has given His very life for us. He is Almighty
God, and with God nothing will be impossible.

For further reading on Step 2, turn to page 133.

Daily Encouragement

DAY 54 READING: LUKE 1:26–56

A Thought for the New Day: As we look carefully into God's
works, we are surprised at how often He prefers to work quietly
and without show. Thus He entered our world—as a helpless
infant, dependent on others for support. Although such divine
behavior baffles us, in all God does in our world and in our lives,
we can trust Him to perform in a divinely perfect way (v. 32).
(*Turn to page 125.*)

54 He has helped His servant
     Israel,
   In remembrance of *His* mercy,
55 As He spoke to our fathers,
   To Abraham and to his seed
     forever."

56 And Mary remained with her about three months, and returned to her house.
57 Now Elizabeth's full time came for her to be delivered, and she brought forth a son.
58 When her neighbors and relatives heard how the Lord had shown great mercy to her, they rejoiced with her.
59 Now so it was, on the eighth day, that they came to circumcise the child; and they would have called him by the name of his father, Zacharias.
60 And his mother answered and said, "No; he shall be called John."
61 But they said to her, "There is no one among your relatives who is called by this name."
62 So they made signs to his father—what he would have him called.
63 And he asked for a writing tablet, and wrote, saying, "His name is John." And they all marveled.
64 Immediately his mouth was opened and his tongue *loosed*, and he spoke, praising God.
65 Then fear came on all who dwelt around them; and all these sayings were discussed throughout all the hill country of Judea.
66 And all those who heard *them* kept *them* in their hearts, saying, "What kind of child will this be?" And the hand of the Lord was with him.
67 Now his father Zacharias was filled with the Holy Spirit, and prophesied, saying:

68"Blessed *is* the Lord God of
     Israel,
   For He has visited and
     redeemed His people,

69 And has raised up a horn of
     salvation for us
   In the house of His servant
     David,
70 As He spoke by the mouth of
     His holy prophets,
   Who *have been* since the world
     began,
71 That we should be saved from
     our enemies
   And from the hand of all who
     hate us,
72 To perform the mercy
     promised to our fathers
   And to remember His holy
     covenant,
73 The oath which He swore to
     our father Abraham:
74 To grant us that we,
   Being delivered from the hand
     of our enemies,
   Might serve Him without fear,
75 In holiness and righteousness
     before Him all the days of
     our life.
76 And you, child, will be called
     the prophet of the Highest;
   For you will go before the face
     of the Lord to prepare His
     ways,
77 To give knowledge of salvation
     to His people
   By the remission of their sins,
78 Through the tender mercy of
     our God,
   With which the Dayspring
     from on high has visited us;
79 To give light to those who sit
     in darkness and the shadow
     of death,
   To guide our feet into the way
     of peace."

STEP
12

80 So the child grew and became strong in spirit, and was in the deserts till the day of his manifestation to Israel.

2 And it came to pass in those days *that* a decree went out from Caesar Augustus that all the world should be registered.
2 This census first took place while Quirinius was governing Syria.

STEP 12

Having had a spiritual awakening as the result
of these steps, we tried to carry this message to others,
and to practice these principles in all our affairs.

Luke 1:76–79

John the Baptist was born to carry a special message. It was his privilege to prepare the way for the earthly ministry of the Lord Jesus. This privilege, however, did not bring with it a life of ease. His desert existence served to toughen him physically and emotionally. He needed that toughness because even though many accepted his message with believing hearts, others persecuted and mocked him.

We, too, carry a special message. Like John, we have been through hard, barren desert experiences. But instead of allowing these experiences to defeat us, through God's grace and strength we have overcome the desert. In His grace now we stand strong. Some people will gladly hear our message. Others will mock us, as they mocked John. This may sadden us, but it need never defeat us. The joy of helping others through the desert of dependency is worth the occasional sandstorm of derision.

For further reading on Step 12, turn to page 165.

Daily Encouragement

DAY 55 READING: LUKE 1:57–80

A Thought for the New Day: The "Dayspring" (v. 78) means the dawn of a new day that Jesus brought into the world. Until He comes we sit in darkness, but Jesus comes like the sun dawning on our hearts, and the darkness of fear, ignorance, and sin passes away forever. Just as the warm sunlight refreshes the earth with new life, so Christ shines into our lives and makes all things new. "In Him was life, and the life was the light of men" (John 1:5). *(Turn to page 127.)*

3 So all went to be registered, everyone to his own city.

4 And Joseph also went up from Galilee, out of the city of Nazareth, into Judea, to the city of David, which is called Bethlehem, because he was of the house and lineage of David,

5 to be registered with Mary, his betrothed wife, who was with child.

6 So it was, that while they were there, the days were completed for her to be delivered.

7 And she brought forth her firstborn Son, and wrapped Him in swaddling cloths, and laid Him in a manger, because there was no room for them in the inn.

STEP 11

8 Now there were in the same country shepherds living out in the fields, keeping watch over their flock by night.

9 And behold, an angel of the Lord stood before them, and the glory of the Lord shone around them, and they were greatly afraid.

10 Then the angel said to them, "Do not be afraid, for behold, I bring you good tidings of great joy which will be to all people.

11 "For there is born to you this day in the city of David a Savior, who is Christ the Lord.

12 "And this *will be* the sign to you: You will find a Babe wrapped in swaddling cloths, lying in a manger."

13 And suddenly there was with the angel a multitude of the heavenly host praising God and saying:

14 "Glory to God in the highest,
    And on earth peace,
      good will toward men!"

15 So it was, when the angels had gone away from them into heaven, that the shepherds said to one another, "Let us now go to Bethlehem and see this thing that has come to pass, which the Lord has made known to us."

16 And they came with haste and found Mary and Joseph, and the Babe lying in a manger.

17 Now when they had seen *Him*, they made widely known the saying which was told them concerning this Child.

18 And all those who heard *it* marveled at those things which were told them by the shepherds.

19 But Mary kept all these things and pondered *them* in her heart.

20 Then the shepherds returned, glorifying and praising God for all the things that they had heard and seen, as it was told them.

21 And when eight days were completed for the circumcision of the Child, His name was called JESUS, the name given by the angel before He was conceived in the womb.

22 Now when the days of her purification according to the law of Moses were completed, they brought Him to Jerusalem to present *Him* to the Lord

23 (as it is written in the law of the Lord, *"Every male who opens the womb shall be called holy to the LORD"*),

24 and to offer a sacrifice according to what is said in the law of the Lord, *"A pair of turtledoves or two young pigeons."*

25 And behold, there was a man in Jerusalem whose name was Simeon, and this man was just and devout, waiting for the Consolation of Israel, and the Holy Spirit was upon him.

26 And it had been revealed to him by the Holy Spirit that he would not see death before he had seen the Lord's Christ.

27 So he came by the Spirit into the temple. And when the parents brought in the Child Jesus, to do for Him according to the custom of the law,

28 he took Him up in his arms and blessed God and said:

29 "Lord, now You are letting Your
    servant depart in peace,
    According to Your word;

STEP 11

*Sought through prayer and meditation to improve our conscious contact with God **as we understood Him,** praying only for knowledge of His will for us and the power to carry that out.*

Luke 2:8–20

What made God choose this group of shepherds to be the ones to see and hear angelic hosts praising His name? Why was this little band given the privilege of seeing the Lord Jesus on the first night of His earthly existence? With schedules to keep, work to be done, places to go, and people to see, perhaps most other people were too busy—far too encumbered with the problems and pleasures around them—to turn their eyes toward the heavens. Some of these others may have looked with disdain upon these lowly men of the fields. But the shepherds' lives contained one beautiful luxury very few others seemed able to afford. It was the magnificent treasure of quiet meditation. Away from the bustling crowds, their eyes turned naturally toward the heavens and their minds more easily contemplated their heavenly Father.

For God to reveal His will to us, for Him to do His work in and through us, we must make ample room in our lives for the treasure of quiet meditation.

For further reading on Step 11, turn to page 139.

Daily Encouragement

DAY 56 READING: LUKE 2:1–21

A Thought for the New Day: "His name was called JESUS," meaning "Deliverer" or "Savior" (v. 21). When we understand how much we need the Savior, then the One who alone can lead us out of the prison of sin also leads us into the freedom of God's children. We may like to think we can be "in charge" of our lives, but all the many problems of living in the world really fall into place when we surrender unconditionally to our Deliverer. (*Turn to page 129.*)

30 For my eyes have seen Your
salvation
31 Which You have prepared
before the face of all peoples,
32 A light to *bring* revelation to
the Gentiles,
And the glory of Your people
Israel."

33 And Joseph and His mother
marveled at those things which
were spoken of Him.
34 Then Simeon blessed them, and
said to Mary His mother, "Behold,
this *Child* is destined for the fall
and rising of many in Israel, and
for a sign which will be spoken
against
35 (yes, a sword will pierce
through your own soul also), that
the thoughts of many hearts may
be revealed."
36 Now there was one, Anna, a
prophetess, the daughter of Pha-
nuel, of the tribe of Asher. She was
of a great age, and had lived with a
husband seven years from her vir-
ginity;
37 and this woman *was* a widow of
about eighty-four years, who did
not depart from the temple, but
served *God* with fastings and prayers night and day.
38 And coming in that instant she
gave thanks to the Lord, and spoke
of Him to all those who looked for
redemption in Jerusalem.
39 So when they had performed all
things according to the law of the
Lord, they returned to Galilee, to
their *own* city, Nazareth.
40 And the Child grew and became
strong in spirit, filled with wisdom;
and the grace of God was upon
Him.
41 His parents went to Jerusalem
every year at the Feast of the Passover.
42 And when He was twelve years
old, they went up to Jerusalem
according to the custom of the
feast.
43 When they had finished the

days, as they returned, the Boy
Jesus lingered behind in Jerusalem.
And Joseph and His mother did not
know *it;*
44 but supposing Him to have been
in the company, they went a day's
journey, and sought Him among
their relatives and acquaintances.
45 So when they did not find Him,
they returned to Jerusalem, seeking Him.
46 Now so it was that after three
days they found Him in the temple,
sitting in the midst of the teachers,
both listening to them and asking
them questions.
47 And all who heard Him were
astonished at His understanding
and answers.
48 So when they saw Him, they
were amazed; and His mother said
to Him, "Son, why have You done
this to us? Look, Your father and I
have sought You anxiously."
49 And He said to them, "Why *is it*
that you sought Me? Did you not
know that I must be about My
Father's business?"
50 But they did not understand the
statement which He spoke to
them.
51 Then He went down with them
and came to Nazareth, and was
subject to them, but His mother
kept all these things in her heart.
52 And Jesus increased in wisdom
and stature, and in favor with God
and men.

3 Now in the fifteenth year of the
reign of Tiberius Caesar, Pontius Pilate being governor of Judea, Herod being tetrarch of Galilee, his brother Philip tetrarch of
Iturea and the region of Trachoni-
tis, and Lysanias tetrarch of Abi-
lene,
2 Annas and Caiaphas being high
priests, the word of God came to
John the son of Zacharias in the
wilderness.
3 And he went into all the region
around the Jordan, preaching a
baptism of repentance for the remission of sins,

STEP
4

STEP
4

Made a searching and fearless moral inventory of ourselves.

Luke 3:1–14

Until John the Baptist began his ministry, no prophet had uttered a message from God in four hundred years. Many people had lost touch with God's Law. They followed vague traditions, but few understood what God wanted of them. Their first question upon hearing John's warning against unrighteousness was, "What shall we do then?"

In verses 10–14, we see that John gave specific advice to each particular group who sincerely hungered to obey God. In the same way now, each of us is searching his or her own life, attempting to evaluate our shortcomings honestly. As these Israelites had determined to listen to God and allow the light of His Word to correct their lives, we, too, are willing to use the principles of God's Word to guide us in our moral inventory.

For further reading on Step 4, turn to page 159.

Daily
Encouragement

DAY 57 READING: LUKE 2:22—3:22

A Thought for the New Day: Our growth in wisdom is modeled by a great example—Jesus also increased in wisdom (2:52). As God, of course, He was all-wise. As a man, He had to grow up in every way. So "growing up," becoming mature, is a divinely arranged occupation. As we come to the stature God has in mind for us, we are then able to carry out the roles in which our lives can honor Him. *(Turn to page 133.)*

4 as it is written in the book of the words of Isaiah the prophet, saying:

"The voice of one crying in the wilderness:
'Prepare the way of the LORD,
Make His paths straight.
5 *Every valley shall be filled*
And every mountain and hill brought low;
And the crooked places shall be made straight
And the rough ways made smooth;
6 *And all flesh shall see the salvation of God.' "*

7 Then he said to the multitudes that came out to be baptized by him, "Brood of vipers! Who warned you to flee from the wrath to come?
8 "Therefore bear fruits worthy of repentance, and do not begin to say to yourselves, 'We have Abraham as our father.' For I say to you that God is able to raise up children to Abraham from these stones.
9 "And even now the ax is laid to the root of the trees. Therefore every tree which does not bear good fruit is cut down and thrown into the fire."
10 So the people asked him, saying, "What shall we do then?"
11 He answered and said to them, "He who has two tunics, let him give to him who has none; and he who has food, let him do likewise."
12 Then tax collectors also came to be baptized, and said to him, "Teacher, what shall we do?"
13 And he said to them, "Collect no more than what is appointed for you."
14 Likewise the soldiers asked him, saying, "And what shall we do?" So he said to them, "Do not intimidate anyone or accuse falsely, and be content with your wages."
15 Now as the people were in ex-

pectation, and all reasoned in their hearts about John, whether he was the Christ or not,
16 John answered, saying to them all, "I indeed baptize you with water; but One mightier than I is coming, whose sandal strap I am not worthy to loose. He will baptize you with the Holy Spirit and with fire.
17 "His winnowing fan is in His hand, and He will thoroughly purge His threshing floor, and gather the wheat into His barn; but the chaff He will burn with unquenchable fire."
18 And with many other exhortations he preached to the people.
19 But Herod the tetrarch, being rebuked by him concerning Herodias, his brother Philip's wife, and for all the evils which Herod had done,
20 also added this, above all, that he shut John up in prison.
21 Now when all the people were baptized, it came to pass that Jesus also was baptized; and while He prayed, the heaven was opened.
22 And the Holy Spirit descended in bodily form like a dove upon Him, and a voice came from heaven which said, "You are My beloved Son; in You I am well pleased."
23 Now Jesus Himself began *His ministry at* about thirty years of age, being (as was supposed) *the* son of Joseph, *the son* of Heli,
24 *the son* of Matthat, *the son* of Levi, *the son* of Melchi, *the son* of Janna, *the son* of Joseph,
25 *the son* of Mattathiah, *the son* of Amos, *the son* of Nahum, *the son* of Esli, *the son* of Naggai,
26 *the son* of Maath, *the son* of Mattathiah, *the son* of Semei, *the son* of Joseph, *the son* of Judah,
27 *the son* of Joannas, *the son* of Rhesa, *the son* of Zerubbabel, *the son* of Shealtiel, *the son* of Neri,
28 *the son* of Melchi, *the son* of Addi, *the son* of Cosam, *the son* of Elmodam, *the son* of Er,

29 *the son* of Jose, *the son* of Elie-
zer, *the son* of Jorim, *the son* of
Matthat, *the son* of Levi,
30 *the son* of Simeon, *the son* of
Judah, *the son* of Joseph, *the son*
of Jonan, *the son* of Eliakim,
31 *the son* of Melea, *the son* of
Menan, *the son* of Mattathah, *the
son* of Nathan, *the son* of David,
32 *the son* of Jesse, *the son* of
Obed, *the son* of Boaz, *the son* of
Salmon, *the son* of Nahshon,
33 *the son* of Amminadab, *the son*
of Ram, *the son* of Hezron, *the son*
of Perez, *the son* of Judah,
34 *the son* of Jacob, *the son* of
Isaac, *the son* of Abraham, *the son*
of Terah, *the son* of Nahor,
35 *the son* of Serug, *the son* of Reu,
the son of Peleg, *the son* of Eber,
the son of Shelah,
36 *the son* of Cainan, *the son* of
Arphaxad, *the son* of Shem, *the
son* of Noah, *the son* of Lamech,
37 *the son* of Methuselah, *the son*
of Enoch, *the son* of Jared, *the son*
of Mahalalel, *the son* of Cainan,
38 *the son* of Enos, *the son* of Seth,
the son of Adam, *the son* of God.

4 Then Jesus, being filled with the
Holy Spirit, returned from the
Jordan and was led by the Spirit
into the wilderness,
2 being tempted for forty days by
the devil. And in those days He ate
nothing, and afterward, when they
had ended, He was hungry.
3 And the devil said to Him, "If
You are the Son of God, command
this stone to become bread."
4 But Jesus answered him, saying,
"It is written, *'Man shall not live
by bread alone, but by every word
of God.'*"
5 Then the devil, taking Him up
on a high mountain, showed Him
all the kingdoms of the world in a
moment of time.
6 And the devil said to Him, "All
this authority I will give You, and
their glory; for *this* has been delivered to me, and I give it to whomever I wish.

7 "Therefore, if You will worship
before me, all will be Yours."
8 And Jesus answered and said to
him, "Get behind Me, Satan! For it
is written, *'You shall worship the
LORD your God, and Him only you
shall serve.'*"
9 Then he brought Him to Jerusalem, set Him on the pinnacle of the
temple, and said to Him, "If You
are the Son of God, throw Yourself
down from here.
10 "For it is written:

*'He shall give His angels charge
over you,
To keep you,'*

11 "and,

*'In their hands they shall bear
you up,
Lest you dash your foot
against a stone.'*"

12 And Jesus answered and said to
him, "It has been said, *'You shall
not tempt the LORD your God.'*"
13 Now when the devil had ended
every temptation, he departed
from Him until an opportune time.
14 Then Jesus returned in the
power of the Spirit to Galilee, and
news of Him went out through all
the surrounding region.
15 And He taught in their synagogues, being glorified by all.
16 So He came to Nazareth, where
He had been brought up. And as
His custom was, He went into the
synagogue on the Sabbath day,
and stood up to read.
17 And He was handed the book of
the prophet Isaiah. And when He
had opened the book, He found the
place where it was written:

18 *"The Spirit of the LORD is upon
Me,
Because He has anointed Me to
preach the gospel to the poor.
He has sent Me to heal the
brokenhearted,*

> To preach deliverance to the
> captives
> And recovery of sight to the
> blind,
> To set at liberty those who are
> oppressed,
> 19 To preach the acceptable year
> of the LORD."

20 Then He closed the book, and gave *it* back to the attendant and sat down. And the eyes of all who were in the synagogue were fixed on Him.

21 And He began to say to them, "Today this Scripture is fulfilled in your hearing."

22 So all bore witness to Him, and marveled at the gracious words which proceeded out of His mouth. And they said, "Is this not Joseph's son?"

23 And He said to them, "You will surely say this proverb to Me, 'Physician, heal yourself! Whatever we have heard done in Capernaum, do also here in Your country.'"

24 Then He said, "Assuredly, I say to you, no prophet is accepted in his own country.

25 "But I tell you truly, many widows were in Israel in the days of Elijah, when the heaven was shut up three years and six months, and there was a great famine throughout all the land;

26 "but to none of them was Elijah sent except to Zarephath, *in the region* of Sidon, to a woman *who was* a widow.

27 "And many lepers were in Israel in the time of Elisha the prophet, and none of them was cleansed except Naaman the Syrian."

28 Then all those in the synagogue, when they heard these things, were filled with wrath,

29 and rose up and thrust Him out of the city; and they led Him to the brow of the hill on which their city was built, that they might throw Him down over the cliff.

30 Then passing through the midst of them, He went His way.

31 Then He went down to Capernaum, a city of Galilee, and was teaching them on the Sabbaths.

32 And they were astonished at His teaching, for His word was with authority.

33 Now in the synagogue there was a man who had a spirit of an unclean demon. And he cried out with a loud voice,

34 saying, "Let *us* alone! What have we to do with You, Jesus of Nazareth? Did You come to destroy us? I know You, who You are—the Holy One of God!"

35 But Jesus rebuked him, saying, "Be quiet, and come out of him!" And when the demon had thrown him in *their* midst, it came out of him and did not hurt him.

36 So they were all amazed and spoke among themselves, saying, "What a word this *is!* For with authority and power He commands the unclean spirits, and they come out."

37 And the report about Him went out into every place in the surrounding region.

38 Now He arose from the synagogue and entered Simon's house. But Simon's wife's mother was sick with a high fever, and they made request of Him concerning her.

39 So He stood over her and rebuked the fever, and it left her. And immediately she arose and served them.

40 Now when the sun was setting, all those who had anyone sick with various diseases brought them to Him; and He laid His hands on every one of them and healed them.

41 And demons also came out of many, crying out and saying, "You are the Christ, the Son of God!" And He, rebuking *them*, did not allow them to speak, for they knew that He was the Christ.

STEP 2

*Came to believe that a Power greater than ourselves
could restore us to sanity.*

Luke 4:16–21

When Jesus came, He came to save all people, but the verses He chose to read that day in Nazareth seem to sum up those who needed Him most. Each phrase is a vivid word picture describing some aspect of the addiction-dependency cycle. "The Spirit of the LORD *is* upon Me, because He has anointed Me to preach the gospel to the poor": Dependencies impoverish us materially, emotionally, and spiritually. "He has sent me to heal the brokenhearted": Other things may soothe our troubled hearts for a time, but only Jesus can heal them. "To preach deliverance to *the* captives": We have been so bound by fear and guilt and pain. Jesus alone has the power to break our chains. "And recovery of sight to *the* blind": Jesus can take the darkest night of confusion and turn it into a day of crystal clear understanding. "To set at liberty those who are oppressed": There is a freedom in surrender to Jesus, which lets our spirits soar. "To preach the acceptable year of the LORD": Now is the time to believe in Him.

For further reading on Step 2, turn to page 143.

Daily Encouragement

DAY 58 READING: LUKE 3:23—4:41

A Thought for the New Day: Everything has a special place in our esteem, and so it should be. We are devoted to our loved ones and our friends in particular ways. Our work also has a unique position among our values. But all things, including our very lives, belong to our Creator to whom we owe highest honor (4:8). When we worship anything less than Him, our lives fall apart; but the service of God brings beauty and order to our existence. (*Turn to page 135.*)

42 Now when it was day, He departed and went into a deserted place. And the crowd sought Him and came to Him, and tried to keep Him from leaving them;

43 but He said to them, "I must preach the kingdom of God to the other cities also, because for this purpose I have been sent."

44 And He was preaching in the synagogues of Galilee.

5 Now so it was, as the multitude pressed about Him to hear the word of God, that He stood by the Lake of Gennesaret,

2 and saw two boats standing by the lake; but the fishermen had gone from them and were washing *their* nets.

STEP
7

3 Then He got into one of the boats, which was Simon's, and asked him to put out a little from the land. And He sat down and taught the multitudes from the boat.

4 Now when He had stopped speaking, He said to Simon, "Launch out into the deep and let down your nets for a catch."

5 But Simon answered and said to Him, "Master, we have toiled all night and caught nothing; nevertheless at Your word I will let down the net."

6 And when they had done this, they caught a great number of fish, and their net was breaking.

7 So they signaled to *their* partners in the other boat to come and help them. And they came and filled both the boats, so that they began to sink.

8 When Simon Peter saw *it*, he fell down at Jesus' knees, saying, "Depart from me, for I am a sinful man, O Lord!"

9 For he and all who were with him were astonished at the catch of fish which they had taken;

10 and so also *were* James and John, the sons of Zebedee, who were partners with Simon. And Jesus said to Simon, "Do not be afraid. From now on you will catch men."

11 So when they had brought their boats to land, they forsook all and followed Him.

12 And it happened when He was in a certain city, that behold, a man who was full of leprosy saw Jesus; and he fell on *his* face and implored Him, saying, "Lord, if You are willing, You can make me clean."

13 Then He put out *His* hand and touched him, saying, "I am willing; be cleansed." And immediately the leprosy left him.

14 And He charged him to tell no one, "But go and show yourself to the priest, and make an offering for your cleansing, as a testimony to them, just as Moses commanded."

15 Then the report went around concerning Him all the more; and great multitudes came together to hear, and to be healed by Him of their infirmities.

16 So He Himself *often* withdrew into the wilderness and prayed.

17 Now it happened on a certain day, as He was teaching, that there were Pharisees and teachers of the law sitting by, who had come out of every town of Galilee, Judea, and Jerusalem. And the power of the Lord was *present* to heal them.

18 Then behold, men brought on a bed a man who was paralyzed. And they sought to bring him in and lay *him* before Him.

19 And when they could not find how they might bring him in, because of the crowd, they went up on the housetop and let him down with *his* bed through the tiling into the midst before Jesus.

20 So when He saw their faith, He said to him, "Man, your sins are forgiven you."

21 And the scribes and the Pharisees began to reason, saying, "Who is this who speaks blasphe-

STEP 7

Humbly asked Him to remove our shortcomings.

Luke 5:3–12

Jesus' words to Simon reflect His desire and command for our own lives at this point in time. Step 7 is indeed a "launch out into the deep." In Step 6, we find ourselves standing on the shore of decision. In Step 7, we step into the boat of commitment. This commitment to the journey of transformation will take us through deep waters. But the reward will be a "net" so full of blessings that those around us will "be astonished at the catch."

When Jesus first told Peter to launch out, Peter replied, "Master, we have toiled all night and caught nothing." What a perfect picture of the undertaking of transformation when it is attempted in our own power instead of God's. We can toil ceaselessly, determined to "turn over a new leaf" and make a fresh start. But our efforts are of little consequence until they are empowered with the wisdom and strength of God.

Today, let us humbly allow God to launch us into the deep waters of transformation and trust Him for the "catch" of a new life.

For further reading on Step 7, turn to page 179.

Daily Encouragement

DAY 59 READING: LUKE 4:42—5:16

A Thought for the New Day: Why should it have made any difference that Peter let down his nets once more (5:4)? Here Jesus was making a point with Peter: catching people, like catching fish, all depended on Peter's following His Lord. However clever we may think we are, we always have to come back to knowing that God's way is the best. In fact, all that we do will be of use only when we follow the Lord's direction. (Turn to page 137.)

mies? Who can forgive sins but God alone?"

22 But when Jesus perceived their thoughts, He answered and said to them, "Why are you reasoning in your hearts?

23 "Which is easier, to say, 'Your sins are forgiven you,' or to say, 'Rise up and walk'?

24 "But that you may know that the Son of Man has power on earth to forgive sins"—He said to the man who was paralyzed, "I say to you, arise, take up your bed, and go to your house."

25 Immediately he rose up before them, took up what he had been lying on, and departed to his own house, glorifying God.

STEP 5

26 And they were all amazed, and they glorified God and were filled with fear, saying, "We have seen strange things today!"

27 After these things He went out and saw a tax collector named Levi, sitting at the tax office. And He said to him, "Follow Me."

28 And he left all, rose up, and followed Him.

29 Then Levi gave Him a great feast in his own house. And there were a great number of tax collectors and others who sat down with them.

30 But their scribes and the Pharisees murmured against His disciples, saying, "Why do You eat and drink with tax collectors and sinners?"

31 And Jesus answered and said to them, "Those who are well do not need a physician, but those who are sick.

32 "I have not come to call *the* righteous, but sinners, to repentance."

33 Then they said to Him, "Why do the disciples of John fast often and make prayers, and likewise those of the Pharisees, but Yours eat and drink?"

34 And He said to them, "Can you make the friends of the bride-groom fast while the bridegroom is with them?

35 "But the days will come when the bridegroom will be taken away from them; then they will fast in those days."

36 Then He spoke a parable to them: "No one puts a piece from a new garment on an old one; otherwise the new makes a tear, and also the piece that was *taken* out of the new does not match the old.

37 "And no one puts new wine into old wineskins; or else the new wine will burst the wineskins and be spilled, and the wineskins will be ruined.

38 "But new wine must be put into new wineskins, and both are preserved.

39 "And no one, having drunk old *wine*, immediately desires new; for he says, 'The old is better.'"

6 Now it happened on the second Sabbath after the first that He went through the grainfields. And His disciples plucked the heads of grain and ate *them*, rubbing *them* in *their* hands.

2 And some of the Pharisees said to them, "Why are you doing what is not lawful to do on the Sabbath?"

3 But Jesus answering them said, "Have you not even read this, what David did when he was hungry, he and those who were with him:

4 "how he went into the house of God, took and ate the showbread, and also gave some to those *who were* with him, which is not lawful for any but the priests to eat?"

5 And He said to them, "The Son of Man is also Lord of the Sabbath."

6 Now it happened on another Sabbath, also, that He entered the synagogue and taught. And a man was there whose right hand was withered.

7 And the scribes and Pharisees watched Him closely, whether He

STEP 5

Admitted to God, to ourselves, and to another human being the exact nature of our wrongs.

Luke 5:26–32

In Luke 5, we read that Jesus called as a disciple a man whose profession as tax collector was looked down upon by Jews and Romans alike. Most men in Levi's profession collected far more than the Roman government required and lined their own pockets with the extra.

However, to those who criticized His action, Jesus responded that those who consider themselves to be well do not have any need for Him. Those who are sick are the ones He has come for.

In Step 4, we took careful inventory of our lives. We have come to grips with our moral and emotional infirmities. We know we need the Great Physician's help. Now we willingly and openly admit these problems to ourselves, to others, and above all to our Great and Loving Physician. We are taking another step down the road to recovery. No one can receive healing until he or she can admit the symptoms of the illness and lay the problem in the hands of Jesus, the Great Physician.

For further reading on Step 5, turn to page 145.

Daily Encouragement

DAY 60 READING: LUKE 5:17—6:5

A Thought for the New Day: Matthew, called Levi (5:27), was the last person in the world you would expect Jesus to invite as His disciple. Everybody hated tax collectors. But Jesus explodes all our ideas of human value. He drew many strange characters into His circle of friends and followers. One was a guerrilla fighter; another had been a prostitute. Wonder of all wonders— there is even room for you and me in that circle. (*Turn to page 139.*)

would heal on the Sabbath, that they might find an accusation against Him.

8 But He knew their thoughts, and said to the man who had the withered hand, "Arise and stand here." And he arose and stood.

9 Then Jesus said to them, "I will ask you one thing: Is it lawful on the Sabbath to do good or to do evil, to save life or to destroy *it?*"

10 And looking around at them all, He said to the man, "Stretch out your hand." And he did so, and his hand was restored as whole as the other.

11 But they were filled with rage, and discussed with one another what they might do to Jesus.

12 Now it came to pass in those days that He went out to the mountain to pray, and continued all night in prayer to God.

13 And when it was day, He called His disciples *to Him;* and from them He chose twelve whom He also named apostles:

14 Simon, whom He also named Peter, and Andrew his brother; James and John; Philip and Bartholomew;

15 Matthew and Thomas; James the *son* of Alphaeus, and Simon called the Zealot;

16 Judas *the son* of James, and Judas Iscariot who also became a traitor.

17 And He came down with them and stood on a level place with a crowd of His disciples and a great multitude of people from all Judea and Jerusalem, and from the seacoast of Tyre and Sidon, who came to hear Him and be healed of their diseases,

18 as well as those who were tormented with unclean spirits. And they were healed.

19 And the whole multitude sought to touch Him, for power went out from Him and healed *them* all.

STEP 11

20 Then He lifted up His eyes toward His disciples, and said:

"Blessed *are you* poor,
    For yours is the kingdom of
        God.

21 Blessed *are you* who hunger
        now,
    For you shall be filled.
    Blessed *are you* who weep
        now,
    For you shall laugh.

22 Blessed are you when men hate
        you,
    And when they exclude you,
    And revile *you*, and cast out
        your name as evil,
    For the Son of Man's sake.

23 Rejoice in that day and leap
        for joy!
    For indeed your reward *is*
        great in heaven,
    For in like manner their
        fathers did to the prophets.

24 "But woe to you who are rich,
    For you have received your
        consolation.

25 Woe to you who are full,
    For you shall hunger.
    Woe to you who laugh now,
    For you shall mourn and
        weep.

26 Woe to you when all men
        speak well of you,
    For so did their fathers
        to the false prophets.

STEP 9

27 "But I say to you who hear: Love your enemies, do good to those who hate you,

28 "bless those who curse you, and pray for those who spitefully use you.

29 "To him who strikes you on the *one* cheek, offer the other also. And from him who takes away your cloak, do not withhold *your* tunic either.

30 "Give to everyone who asks of you. And from him who takes away your goods do not ask *them* back.

31 "And just as you want men to

STEP 11

Sought through prayer and meditation to improve our conscious contact with God **as we understood Him,** *praying only for knowledge of His will for us and the power to carry that out.*

Luke 6:20–26

We cannot read this list of blessings and woes without realizing that what most people think is undesirable God calls blessed. What we generally consider to be good God calls "woe" or sorrow.

Since we have watched God work in our lives through previous steps, it is now a little easier to grasp Jesus' message here. We have come to realize that many things that the world places great value on are truly worthless in the eyes of God and eternity.

There was a time in our own lives when money, physical pleasure, laughter, and popularity were all we cared about. But when we finally realized we were poor and hungry and we truly wept over our condition, then God's abundant blessings could begin to flow.

As we seek to maintain a close walk with our Lord, we must be vigilant not to allow the tinsel of the world to transfix us. We must ask daily for the supreme good of His value system to be our sure foundation.

For further reading on Step 11, turn to page 163.

Daily Encouragement

DAY 61 READING: LUKE 6:6–26

A Thought for the New Day: It is so easy for us to put last things first. Ceremonies are not an end in themselves, and even God's commandments had a larger purpose. The leaders were angry at Jesus because He put love before their twisted ideas of religion. The Lord's Day was made for doing good in ways that we may not take time for on other days (v. 9). May we be careful to have the right priorities. (*Turn to page 141.*)

do to you, you also do to them likewise.

32 "But if you love those who love you, what credit is that to you? For even sinners love those who love them.

33 "And if you do good to those who do good to you, what credit is that to you? For even sinners do the same.

34 "And if you lend *to those* from whom you hope to receive back, what credit is that to you? For even sinners lend to sinners to receive as much back.

35 "But love your enemies, do good, and lend, hoping for nothing in return; and your reward will be great, and you will be sons of the Highest. For He is kind to the unthankful and evil.

36 "Therefore be merciful, just as your Father also is merciful.

STEP 8 37 "Judge not, and you shall not be judged. Condemn not, and you shall not be condemned. Forgive, and you will be forgiven.

38 "Give, and it will be given to you: good measure, pressed down, shaken together, and running over will be put into your bosom. For with the same measure that you use, it will be measured back to you."

39 And He spoke a parable to them: "Can the blind lead the blind? Will they not both fall into the ditch?

40 "A disciple is not above his teacher, but everyone who is perfectly trained will be like his teacher.

STEP 10 41 "And why do you look at the speck in your brother's eye, but do not perceive the plank in your own eye?

42 "Or how can you say to your brother, 'Brother, let me remove the speck that *is* in your eye,' when you yourself do not see the plank that *is* in your own eye? Hypocrite! First remove the plank from your own eye, and then you will see clearly to remove the speck that is in your brother's eye.

43 "For a good tree does not bear bad fruit, nor does a bad tree bear good fruit.

44 "For every tree is known by its own fruit. For *men* do not gather figs from thorns, nor do they gather grapes from a bramble bush.

45 "A good man out of the good treasure of his heart brings forth good; and an evil man out of the evil treasure of his heart brings forth evil. For out of the abundance of the heart his mouth speaks.

46 "But why do you call Me 'Lord, Lord,' and do not do the things which I say? STEP 11

47 "Whoever comes to Me, and hears My sayings and does them, I will show you whom he is like:

48 "He is like a man building a house, who dug deep and laid the foundation on the rock. And when the flood arose, the stream beat vehemently against that house, and could not shake it, for it was founded on the rock.

49 "But he who heard and did nothing is like a man who built a house on the earth without a foundation, against which the stream beat vehemently; and immediately it fell. And the ruin of that house was great."

7 Now when He concluded all His sayings in the hearing of the people, He entered Capernaum.

2 And a certain centurion's servant, who was dear to him, was sick and ready to die.

3 So when he heard about Jesus, he sent elders of the Jews to Him, pleading with Him to come and heal his servant.

4 And when they came to Jesus, they begged Him earnestly, saying that the one for whom He should do this was worthy,

5 "for he loves our nation, and has built us a synagogue."

STEP 8

Made a list of all persons we had harmed,
and became willing to make amends to them all.

Luke 6:37, 38

A motivating and marvelous principle of recovery is that God takes great pleasure in meeting us "more than halfway." For example, He tells us that just a tiny seed of faith will be rewarded by great miracles. And in the same way, as we become willing to make amends to others, and release them and ourselves from the bitterness we have carried, God is there, eager to reward and encourage even our feeble attempts. When we ask the Lord to help us let go of judgment and condemnation, we will soon be aware of remarkable changes taking place within us. The Holy Spirit will begin a wonderful healing work in our lives.

Giving our forgiveness and amends to others allows the principle of verse 38 to be set in motion. Our willingness to forgive those who have harmed us and to ask forgiveness of those whom we have harmed allows us to move on into deeper blessings and growth.

For further reading on Step 8, turn to page 155.

Daily Encouragement

DAY 62 READING: LUKE 6:27–49

A Thought for the New Day: One way of judging success is by how well our work stands up. A builder whose buildings crack and fall down in a few months will not be in business very long. Jesus offers the opportunity to build things that will last forever. Mostly, such building amounts to showing others that God loves them and wants them for His friends. Every life won for Christ is an achievement for eternity. These are monuments to success that never crumble (vv. 47–49). (*Turn to page 143.*)

6 Then Jesus went with them. And when He was already not far from the house, the centurion sent friends to Him, saying to Him, "Lord, do not trouble Yourself, for I am not worthy that You should enter under my roof.

7 "Therefore I did not even think myself worthy to come to You. But say the word, and my servant will be healed.

8 "For I also am a man placed under authority, having soldiers under me. And I say to one, 'Go,' and he goes; and to another, 'Come,' and he comes; and to my servant, 'Do this,' and he does *it*."

9 When Jesus heard these things, He marveled at him, and turned around and said to the crowd that followed Him, "I say to you, I have not found such great faith, not even in Israel!"

10 And those who were sent, returning to the house, found the servant well who had been sick.

STEP 2 11 Now it happened, the day after, *that* He went into a city called Nain; and many of His disciples went with Him, and a large crowd.

12 And when He came near the gate of the city, behold, a dead man was being carried out, the only son of his mother; and she was a widow. And a large crowd from the city was with her.

13 When the Lord saw her, He had compassion on her and said to her, "Do not weep."

14 Then He came and touched the open coffin, and those who carried *him* stood still. And He said, "Young man, I say to you, arise."

15 And he who was dead sat up and began to speak. And He presented him to his mother.

16 Then fear came upon all, and they glorified God, saying, "A great prophet has risen up among us"; and, "God has visited His people."

17 And this report about Him went throughout all Judea and all the surrounding region.

18 Then the disciples of John reported to him concerning all these things.

19 And John, calling two of his disciples to *him*, sent *them* to Jesus, saying, "Are You the Coming One, or do we look for another?"

20 When the men had come to Him, they said, "John the Baptist has sent us to You, saying, 'Are You the Coming One, or do we look for another?' "

21 And that very hour He cured many *people* of *their* infirmities, afflictions, and evil spirits; and to many *who were* blind He gave sight.

22 Then Jesus answered and said to them, "Go and tell John the things you have seen and heard: that *the* blind see, *the* lame walk, *the* lepers are cleansed, *the* deaf hear, *the* dead are raised, *the* poor have the gospel preached to them.

23 "And blessed is *he* who is not offended because of Me."

24 When the messengers of John had departed, He began to speak to the multitudes concerning John: "What did you go out into the wilderness to see? A reed shaken by the wind?

25 "But what did you go out to see? A man clothed in soft garments? Indeed those who are gorgeously appareled and live in luxury are in kings' courts.

26 "But what did you go out to see? A prophet? Yes, I say to you, and more than a prophet.

27 "This is *he* of whom it is written:

'Behold, I send My messenger
  before Your face,
Who will prepare Your way
  before You.'

28 "For I say to you, among those born of women there is not a

*Came to believe that a Power greater than ourselves
could restore us to sanity.*

Luke 7:11–16

At the death of a loved one, feelings of pain, grief, and power-lessness can seem unbearable. In Nain, a widowed mother stumbled along, grieving beside the coffin of her son. Now she was completely alone in the world, for in that day an older woman without a husband or son to care for her was unprotected, truly alone and powerless against society. Or at least she was until Jesus came. As soon as He saw her, He had compassion on her. The word "compassion" could be literally translated, "His heart went out to her." He felt what she was feeling—her grief, her suffering, and her fear. The coffin bearers stood still as He tenderly touched the coffin and then spoke a miracle, "Young man, I say to you, arise." "And he who was dead sat up and began to speak."

Some of us have reckoned ourselves as good as dead. We have felt as powerless against our pain and dependencies as a corpse. Jesus not only has compassion on our pain, but He has the power to give us new life in Himself, as well.

For further reading on Step 2, turn to page 157.

Daily
Encouragement

DAY 63 READING: Luke 7:1–35

A Thought for the New Day: It is normal to value life highly. That is why it is so strange that violence grows among us. Jesus came to bring life—overflowing life. The young man's resurrection (vv. 14, 15) is a picture of Jesus' great concern—that we should live! Life exists originally in Him who is the Author of all life. Let us not settle for less than the eternal life God planned for us. (*Turn to page 145.*)

greater prophet than John the Baptist; but he who is least in the kingdom of God is greater than he."

29 And when all the people heard *Him*, even the tax collectors justified God, having been baptized with the baptism of John.

30 But the Pharisees and lawyers rejected the counsel of God for themselves, not having been baptized by him.

31 And the Lord said, "To what then shall I liken the men of this generation, and what are they like?

32 "They are like children sitting in the marketplace and calling to one another, saying:

'We played the flute for you,
   And you did not dance;
We mourned to you,
   And you did not weep.'

33 "For John the Baptist came neither eating bread nor drinking wine, and you say, 'He has a demon.'

34 "The Son of Man has come eating and drinking, and you say, 'Look, a glutton and a winebibber, a friend of tax collectors and sinners!'

35 "But wisdom is justified by all her children."

36 Then one of the Pharisees asked Him to eat with him. And He went to the Pharisee's house, and sat down to eat.

37 And behold, a woman in the city who was a sinner, when she knew that *Jesus* sat at the table in the Pharisee's house, brought an alabaster flask of fragrant oil,

38 and stood at His feet behind *Him* weeping; and she began to wash His feet with her tears, and wiped *them* with the hair of her head; and she kissed His feet and anointed *them* with the fragrant oil.

39 Now when the Pharisee who had invited Him saw *this*, he spoke to himself, saying, "This man, if He were a prophet, would know who and what manner of woman *this is* who is touching Him, for she is a sinner."

40 And Jesus answered and said to him, "Simon, I have something to say to you." And he said, "Teacher, say it."

41 "There was a certain creditor who had two debtors. One owed five hundred denarii, and the other fifty.

42 "And when they had nothing with which to repay, he freely forgave them both. Tell Me, therefore, which of them will love him more?"

43 Simon answered and said, "I suppose the *one* whom he forgave more." And He said to him, "You have rightly judged."

44 Then He turned to the woman and said to Simon, "Do you see this woman? I entered your house; you gave Me no water for My feet, but she has washed My feet with her tears and wiped *them* with the hair of her head.

45 "You gave Me no kiss, but this woman has not ceased to kiss My feet since the time I came in.

46 "You did not anoint My head with oil, but this woman has anointed My feet with fragrant oil.

47 "Therefore I say to you, her sins, *which are* many, are forgiven, for she loved much. But to whom little is forgiven, *the same* loves little."

48 And He said to her, "Your sins are forgiven."

49 And those who sat at the table with Him began to say to themselves, "Who is this who even forgives sins?"

50 Then He said to the woman, "Your faith has saved you. Go in peace."

8 Now it came to pass, afterward, that He went through every city and village, preaching and

STEP 5

*Admitted to God, to ourselves, and to another human being
the exact nature of our wrongs.*

Luke 7:36–50

Luke's account of the Pharisee and the woman "who was a sinner" teaches us a very important lesson. The kernel of that truth is found in Jesus' short parable (vv. 41, 42) and His question to Simon, the Pharisee. Jesus wanted Simon to see that in God's eyes, all of us are debtors who cannot possibly pay our Great Creditor. We have nothing that is valuable enough and we can never work long enough to repay our debt. Some may owe more than others, but we all owe far more than we can pay.

In Step 4, we began to "take account" of our lives. We may have felt overwhelmed at the "debts incurred." But Jesus is telling us in this passage that the "amount owed" does not matter to Him. He gladly forgives those who love Him and have chosen to turn their lives over to His care. The woman "who was a sinner" could not in that situation verbally recount her sins. But Jesus who knows all things saw in her tears and actions a heart of repentance.

For further reading on Step 5, turn to page 171.

Daily Encouragement

DAY 64 READING: LUKE 7:36—8:3

A Thought for the New Day: Make no mistake about this woman. She was not really as wicked as some of her critics. But her *sense* of sin was great, and when she was forgiven her love knew no limits (7:47). It is being good in our own eyes that makes us incapable of love. We neither need love, nor can we give it. It is truly a glad day when we find out how needy we are. Then we are able to love very much indeed. (*Turn to page 147.*)

bringing the glad tidings of the kingdom of God. And the twelve *were* with Him,

2 and certain women who had been healed of evil spirits and infirmities—Mary called Magdalene, out of whom had come seven demons,

3 and Joanna the wife of Chuza, Herod's steward, and Susanna, and many others who provided for Him from their substance.

STEP 10

4 And when a great multitude had gathered, and *others* had come to Him from every city, He spoke by a parable:

5 "A sower went out to sow his seed. And as he sowed, some fell by the wayside; and it was trampled down, and the birds of the air devoured it.

6 "Some fell on rock; and as soon as it sprang up, it withered away because it lacked moisture.

7 "And some fell among thorns, and the thorns sprang up with it and choked it.

8 "But others fell on good ground, sprang up, and yielded a crop a hundredfold." When He had said these things He cried, "He who has ears to hear, let him hear!"

9 Then His disciples asked Him, saying, "What does this parable mean?"

10 And He said, "To you it has been given to know the mysteries of the kingdom of God, but to the rest *it is given* in parables, that

> 'Seeing they may not see,
> And hearing they may not
>   understand.'

11 "Now the parable is this: The seed is the word of God.

12 "Those by the wayside are the ones who hear; then the devil comes and takes away the word out of their hearts, lest they should believe and be saved.

13 "But the ones on the rock *are* those who, when they hear, receive the word with joy; and these have no root, who believe for a while and in time of temptation fall away.

14 "And the ones *that* fell among thorns are those who, when they have heard, go out and are choked with cares, riches, and pleasures of life, and bring no fruit to maturity.

15 "But the ones *that* fell on the good ground are those who, having heard the word with a noble and good heart, keep *it* and bear fruit with patience.

16 "No one, when he has lit a lamp, covers it with a vessel or puts *it* under a bed, but sets *it* on a lampstand, that those who enter may see the light.

17 "For nothing is secret that will not be revealed, nor *anything* hidden that will not be known and come to light.

18 "Therefore take heed how you hear. For whoever has, to him *more* will be given; and whoever does not have, even what he seems to have will be taken from him."

19 Then His mother and brothers came to Him, and could not approach Him because of the crowd.

20 And it was told Him *by some,* who said, "Your mother and Your brothers are standing outside, desiring to see You."

21 But He answered and said to them, "My mother and My brothers are these who hear the word of God and do it."

22 Now it happened, on a certain day, that He got into a boat with His disciples. And He said to them, "Let us go over to the other side of the lake." And they launched out.

23 But as they sailed He fell asleep. And a windstorm came down on the lake, and they were filling *with water,* and were in jeopardy.

24 And they came to Him and awoke Him, saying, "Master, Master, we are perishing!" Then He arose and rebuked the wind and

STEP 10

*Continued to take personal inventory
and when we were wrong promptly admitted it.*

Luke 8:4–18

The parable of the seed and the sower is a pronouncement, a prophecy, and a promise.

The pronouncement is one of judgment. Those whose hearts are like the hard soil will not receive the Seed of Life. Their doom is sure.

The prophecy is one of warning. Some who hear respond only with impulsive emotion, a spur of the moment caprice. There is no root of commitment and it is only a matter of time until they return to their old life-style.

Finally, however, this parable is a promise for those who receive the Seed of Life and commit everything they are and have to its growth. These "keep *it* [the Seed of Life] and bear fruit with patience" (v. 15). It takes a great deal of patience to carefully, prayerfully, and steadily stay on the course of recovery.

This is why Step 10 is so important for us each day—checking ourselves to see if we are daily keeping the Word of Life and bearing fruit with patience.

For further reading on Step 10, turn to page 169.

Daily Encouragement

DAY 65 READING: LUKE 8:4–56

A Thought for the New Day: We know Jesus loved His mother because of what He said to her when He was dying (John 19:26, 27). But God's work sometimes compels us to leave behind home and loved ones. A Christian family in World War II Germany did not know their son had been martyred until they heard it on a foreign broadcast. Yes, some things are even more important than family (v. 21). However, if God has blessed us with a home, that is where love must begin. *(Turn to page 151.)*

the raging of the water. And they ceased, and there was a calm.

25 But He said to them, "Where is your faith?" And they were afraid, and marveled, saying to one another, "Who can this be? For He commands even the winds and water, and they obey Him!"

26 Then they sailed to the country of the Gadarenes, which is opposite Galilee.

27 And when He stepped out on the land, there met Him a certain man from the city who had demons for a long time. And he wore no clothes, nor did he live in a house but in the tombs.

28 When he saw Jesus, he cried out, fell down before Him, and with a loud voice said, "What have I to do with You, Jesus, Son of the Most High God? I beg You, do not torment me!"

29 For He had commanded the unclean spirit to come out of the man. For it had often seized him, and he was kept under guard, bound with chains and shackles; and he broke the bonds and was driven by the demon into the wilderness.

30 Jesus asked him, saying, "What is your name?" And he said, "Legion," because many demons had entered him.

31 And they begged Him that He would not command them to go out into the abyss.

32 Now a herd of many swine was feeding there on the mountain. And they begged Him that He would permit them to enter them. And He permitted them.

33 Then the demons went out of the man and entered the swine, and the herd ran violently down the steep place into the lake and drowned.

34 When those who fed *them* saw what had happened, they fled and told *it* in the city and in the country.

35 Then they went out to see what had happened, and came to Jesus, and found the man from whom the demons had departed, sitting at the feet of Jesus, clothed and in his right mind. And they were afraid.

36 They also who had seen *it* told them by what means he who had been demon-possessed was healed.

37 Then the whole multitude of the surrounding region of the Gadarenes asked Him to depart from them, for they were seized with great fear. And He got into the boat and returned.

38 Now the man from whom the demons had departed begged Him that he might be with Him. But Jesus sent him away, saying,

39 "Return to your own house, and tell what great things God has done for you." And he went his way and proclaimed throughout the whole city what great things Jesus had done for him.

40 So it was, when Jesus returned, that the multitude welcomed Him, for they were all waiting for Him.

41 And behold, there came a man named Jairus, and he was a ruler of the synagogue. And he fell down at Jesus' feet and begged Him to come to his house,

42 for he had an only daughter about twelve years of age, and she was dying. But as He went, the multitudes thronged Him.

43 Now a woman, having a flow of blood for twelve years, who had spent all her livelihood on physicians and could not be healed by any,

44 came from behind and touched the border of His garment. And immediately her flow of blood stopped.

45 And Jesus said, "Who touched Me?" When all denied it, Peter and those with him said, "Master, the multitudes throng You and press *You*, and You say, 'Who touched Me?' "

46 But Jesus said, "Somebody

touched Me, for I perceived power going out from Me."

47 Now when the woman saw that she was not hidden, she came trembling; and falling down before Him, she declared to Him in the presence of all the people the reason she had touched Him and how she was healed immediately.

48 And He said to her, "Daughter, be of good cheer; your faith has made you well. Go in peace."

49 While He was still speaking, someone came from the ruler of the synagogue's *house*, saying to him, "Your daughter is dead. Do not trouble the Teacher."

50 But when Jesus heard *it*, He answered him, saying, "Do not be afraid; only believe, and she will be made well."

51 When He came into the house, He permitted no one to go in except Peter, James, and John, and the father and mother of the girl.

52 Now all wept and mourned for her; but He said, "Do not weep; she is not dead, but sleeping."

53 And they laughed Him to scorn, knowing that she was dead.

54 But He put them all out, took her by the hand and called, saying, "Little girl, arise."

55 Then her spirit returned, and she arose immediately. And He commanded that she be given *something* to eat.

56 And her parents were astonished, but He charged them to tell no one what had happened.

9 Then He called His twelve disciples together and gave them power and authority over all demons, and to cure diseases.

2 He sent them to preach the kingdom of God and to heal the sick.

3 And He said to them, "Take nothing for the journey, neither staffs nor bag nor bread nor money; and do not have two tunics apiece.

4 "Whatever house you enter, stay there, and from there depart.

5 "And whoever will not receive you, when you go out of that city, shake off the very dust from your feet as a testimony against them."

6 So they departed and went through the towns, preaching the gospel and healing everywhere.

7 Now Herod the tetrarch heard of all that was done by Him; and he was perplexed, because it was said by some that John had risen from the dead,

8 and by some that Elijah had appeared, and by others that one of the old prophets had risen again.

9 And Herod said, "John I have beheaded, but who is this of whom I hear such things?" And he sought to see Him.

10 And the apostles, when they had returned, told Him all that they had done. And He took them and went aside privately into a deserted place belonging to the city called Bethsaida.

11 But when the multitudes knew *it*, they followed Him; and He received them and spoke to them about the kingdom of God, and healed those who had need of healing.

12 When the day began to wear away, the twelve came and said to Him, "Send the multitude away, that they may go into the surrounding towns and country, and lodge and get provisions; for we are in a deserted place here."

13 But He said to them, "You give them something to eat." And they said, "We have no more than five loaves and two fish, unless we go and buy food for all these people."

14 For there were about five thousand men. And He said to His disciples, "Make them sit down in groups of fifty."

15 And they did so, and made them all sit down.

16 Then He took the five loaves and the two fish, and looking up to heaven, He blessed and broke

them, and gave *them* to the disciples to set before the multitude.

17 So they all ate and were filled, and twelve baskets of the leftover fragments were taken up by them.

18 And it happened, as He was alone praying, *that* His disciples joined Him, and He asked them, saying, "Who do the crowds say that I am?"

19 So they answered and said, "John the Baptist, but some *say* Elijah; and others *say* that one of the old prophets has risen again."

20 He said to them, "But who do you say that I am?" Peter answered and said, "The Christ of God."

21 And He strictly warned and commanded them to tell this to no one,

22 saying, "The Son of Man must suffer many things, and be rejected by the elders and chief priests and scribes, and be killed, and be raised the third day."

STEP 3
23 Then He said to *them* all, "If anyone desires to come after Me, let him deny himself, and take up his cross daily, and follow Me.

24 "For whoever desires to save his life will lose it, but whoever loses his life for My sake will save it.

25 "For what advantage is it to a man if he gains the whole world, and is himself destroyed or lost?

26 "For whoever is ashamed of Me and My words, of him the Son of Man will be ashamed when He comes in His *own* glory, and in His Father's, and of the holy angels.

27 "But I tell you truly, there are some standing here who shall not taste death till they see the kingdom of God."

28 And it came to pass, about eight days after these sayings, that He took Peter, John, and James and went up on the mountain to pray.

29 And as He prayed, the appearance of His face was altered, and His robe *became* white *and* glistening.

30 Then behold, two men talked with Him, who were Moses and Elijah,

31 who appeared in glory and spoke of His decease which He was about to accomplish at Jerusalem.

32 But Peter and those with him were heavy with sleep; and when they were fully awake, they saw His glory and the two men who stood with Him.

33 And it happened, as they were parting from Him, *that* Peter said to Jesus, "Master, it is good for us to be here; and let us make three tabernacles: one for You, one for Moses, and one for Elijah"—not knowing what he said.

34 While he was saying this, a cloud came and overshadowed them; and they were fearful as they entered the cloud.

35 Then a voice came out of the cloud, saying, "This is My beloved Son. Hear Him!"

36 And when the voice had ceased, Jesus was found alone. But they kept quiet, and told no one in those days any of the things they had seen.

37 Now it happened on the next day, when they had come down from the mountain, that a great multitude met Him.

38 Suddenly a man from the multitude cried out, saying, "Teacher, I implore You, look on my son, for he is my only child.

39 "And behold, a spirit seizes him, and he suddenly cries out; it convulses him so that he foams *at the mouth*, and bruising him, it departs from him with great difficulty.

40 "So I implored Your disciples to cast it out, but they could not."

41 Then Jesus answered and said, "O faithless and perverse generation, how long shall I be with you and bear with you? Bring your son here."

42 And as he was still coming, the demon threw him down and convulsed *him*. Then Jesus rebuked

STEP 3

*Made a decision to turn our will and our lives over to the care of God **as we understood Him.***

Luke 9:23–25

When we come to understand that the cleansing and healing of our hearts and lives can only occur when we willingly turn our lives over to God, we will understand the depths of verse 24.

Losing our lives, denying ourselves, taking up our cross to follow Jesus may sound scary at first. We may envision ourselves in monk's clothing in a third world country, preaching on a street corner. While many people have chosen to do this work for Jesus, that is not the specific meaning of verses 23–25.

Instead, Jesus is telling us not to be motivated by our own selfish desires any longer. Instead, we are to turn our lives over to God to accept His leading and will in our lives. We are to begin looking for ways to glorify God rather than self. And finally, as the cross lifted Jesus up and set Him apart, taking up our cross daily means that we daily choose to separate ourselves from our old life-styles and be lifted up to obey and honor our Lord.

For further reading on Step 3, turn to page 153.

Daily Encouragement

DAY 66 READING: LUKE 9:1–36

A Thought for the New Day: You and I have a larger world to reach than did the disciples of Jesus' day (v. 6). But to each of us is assigned a small space in which to work every day. That is the place where we are commissioned to draw others to know Christ and find relief from their hopeless and stressful lives. Each person we meet on our way is infinitely significant as an immortal life journeying into eternity. (*Turn to page 153.*)

the unclean spirit, healed the child, and gave him back to his father.
43 And they were all amazed at the majesty of God. But while everyone marveled at all the things which Jesus did, He said to His disciples,
44 "Let these words sink down into your ears, for the Son of Man is about to be delivered into the hands of men."
45 But they did not understand this saying, and it was hidden from them so that they did not perceive it; and they were afraid to ask Him about this saying.
46 Then a dispute arose among them as to which of them would be greatest.
47 And Jesus, perceiving the thought of their heart, took a little child and set him by Him,
48 and said to them, "Whoever receives this little child in My name receives Me; and whoever receives Me receives Him who sent Me. For he who is least among you all will be great."
49 Then John answered and said, "Master, we saw someone casting out demons in Your name, and we forbade him because he does not follow with us."
50 But Jesus said to him, "Do not forbid *him*, for he who is not against us is for us."
51 Now it came to pass, when the time had come for Him to be received up, that He steadfastly set His face to go to Jerusalem,
52 and sent messengers before His face. And as they went, they entered a village of the Samaritans, to prepare for Him.
53 But they did not receive Him, because His face was *set* for the journey to Jerusalem.
54 And when His disciples James and John saw *this*, they said, "Lord, do You want us to command fire to come down from heaven and consume them, just as Elijah did?"

55 But He turned and rebuked them, and said, "You do not know what manner of spirit you are of.
56 "For the Son of Man did not come to destroy men's lives but to save *them*." And they went to another village.

57 Now it happened as they journeyed on the road, *that* someone said to Him, "Lord, I will follow You wherever You go."
58 And Jesus said to him, "Foxes have holes and birds of the air *have* nests, but the Son of Man has nowhere to lay *His* head."
59 Then He said to another, "Follow Me." But he said, "Lord, let me first go and bury my father."
60 Jesus said to him, "Let the dead bury their own dead, but you go and preach the kingdom of God."
61 And another also said, "Lord, I will follow You, but let me first go *and* bid them farewell who are at my house."
62 But Jesus said to him, "No one, having put his hand to the plow, and looking back, is fit for the kingdom of God."

10 After these things the Lord appointed seventy others also, and sent them two by two before His face into every city and place where He Himself was about to go.
2 Then He said to them, "The harvest truly *is* great, but the laborers *are* few; therefore pray the Lord of the harvest to send out laborers into His harvest.
3 "Go your way; behold, I send you out as lambs among wolves.
4 "Carry neither money bag, sack, nor sandals; and greet no one along the road.
5 "But whatever house you enter, first say, 'Peace to this house.'
6 "And if a son of peace is there, your peace will rest on it; if not, it will return to you.
7 "And remain in the same house, eating and drinking such things as they give, for the laborer is worthy

*Made a decision to turn our will and our lives
over to the care of God **as we understood Him.***

Luke 9:57–62

Jesus was gaining a great deal of popularity at this point in His earthly ministry. Lots of people wanted to "be on His team." But Jesus knew each heart. His remarks to these three would-be disciples are short and yet probe to the core of each one's particular problem.

The first exuberant volunteer is reminded that material things must be of secondary importance. The second, whom Jesus calls to follow Him, seems to want to accept that call, but not just yet. The son declares that when his father is dead and buried, then the time will be right to become a follower of Jesus. Jesus answers that those who are dead spiritually can take care of these matters. To put off our commitment is to risk losing out completely.

Jesus' last response teaches us that no friendship or relationship should come before our love and commitment to Him.

When we truly understand what the Lord Jesus gave when He suffered and died for us on the cross, then we can willingly yield all that we are and have to Him.

For further reading on Step 3, turn to page 186.

Daily Encouragement

DAY 67 READING: LUKE 9:37–62

A Thought for the New Day: The young disciples were suffering from a malady known as "sectarianism," the belief that only one's own group is qualified to serve Christ. Jesus had to set them straight (vv. 49, 50). All who truly confess Him are on the long road to heavenly perfection. Be willing to let others mature in their way, and pray that they may give us room to grow also. (*Turn to page 155.*)

of his wages. Do not go from house to house.

8 "Whatever city you enter, and they receive you, eat such things as are set before you.

9 "And heal the sick *who are* there, and say to them, 'The kingdom of God has come near to you.'

10 "But whatever city you enter, and they do not receive you, go out into its streets and say,

11 'The very dust of your city which clings to us we wipe off against you. Nevertheless know this, that the kingdom of God has come near you.'

12 "But I say to you that it will be more tolerable in that Day for Sodom than for that city.

13 "Woe to you, Chorazin! Woe to you, Bethsaida! For if the mighty works which were done in you had been done in Tyre and Sidon, they would have repented a great while ago, sitting in sackcloth and ashes.

14 "But it will be more tolerable for Tyre and Sidon at the judgment than for you.

15 "And you, Capernaum, who are exalted to heaven, will be thrust down to Hades.

16 "He who hears you hears Me, he who rejects you rejects Me, and he who rejects Me rejects Him who sent Me."

17 Then the seventy returned with joy, saying, "Lord, even the demons are subject to us in Your name."

18 And He said to them, "I saw Satan fall like lightning from heaven.

19 "Behold, I give you the authority to trample on serpents and scorpions, and over all the power of the enemy, and nothing shall by any means hurt you.

20 "Nevertheless do not rejoice in this, that the spirits are subject to you, but rather rejoice because your names are written in heaven."

21 In that hour Jesus rejoiced in the Spirit and said, "I praise You, Father, Lord of heaven and earth, that You have hidden these things from *the* wise and prudent and revealed them to babes. Even so, Father, for so it seemed good in Your sight.

22 "All things have been delivered to Me by My Father, and no one knows who the Son is but the Father, and who the Father is but the Son, and *the one* to whom the Son wills to reveal *Him*."

23 And He turned to *His* disciples and said privately, "Blessed *are* the eyes which see the things you see;

24 "for I tell you that many prophets and kings have desired to see what you see, and have not seen *it*, and to hear what you hear, and have not heard *it*."

25 And behold, a certain lawyer stood up and tested Him, saying, "Teacher, what shall I do to inherit eternal life?"

26 He said to him, "What is written in the law? What is your reading *of it?*"

27 So he answered and said, " 'You shall love the LORD your God with all your heart, with all your soul, with all your strength, and with all your mind,' and 'your neighbor as yourself.' "

28 And He said to him, "You have answered rightly; do this and you will live."

29 But he, wanting to justify himself, said to Jesus, "And who is my neighbor?"

30 Then Jesus answered and said: "A certain *man* went down from Jerusalem to Jericho, and fell among thieves, who stripped him of his clothing, wounded *him*, and departed, leaving *him* half dead.

31 "Now by chance a certain priest came down that road. And when he saw him, he passed by on the other side.

32 "Likewise a Levite, when he arrived at the place, came and

STEP 8

STEP 8

*Made a list of all persons we had harmed,
and became willing to make amends to them all.*

Luke 10:25–37

"But he, wanting to justify himself, said to Jesus, 'And who is my neighbor?'" There are very few of us who do not seek to justify ourselves.

There may be people in our past or present whom we feel are not worthy to be treated with love. They may have caused us emotional or physical pain. The Samaritans and Jews were good at inflicting such pain on each other. The Jews especially despised the Samaritans, calling them names like "half-breed" and "dog," and declaring that the people of Samaria did not worship God properly. Yet it was the Samaritan who best understood and practiced one of God's most important commandments. Instead of turning away from the wounded traveler, he went out of his way to care for him. He could have justified his disregard as the others had, but instead the Samaritan chose to show mercy. Let us also yield our grudges and negative attitudes to God, and ask Him to fill our hearts with His love.

For further reading on Step 8, turn to page 183.

Daily Encouragement

DAY 68 READING: LUKE 10:1–42

A Thought for the New Day: In verse 21 is a pronouncement whose meaning may escape us, unless we think long about it. The mental giant is the object of the world's admiration. But Jesus did not invite the most brilliant to be His ambassadors to the world. He initially chose very ordinary—even unlikely—people. Pride in academic ability does not get us anywhere in serving the King of the universe. In Him alone are hidden all the treasures of wisdom. (*Turn to page 157.*)

looked, and passed by on the other side.

33 "But a certain Samaritan, as he journeyed, came where he was. And when he saw him, he had compassion *on him,*

34 "and went to *him* and bandaged his wounds, pouring on oil and wine; and he set him on his own animal, brought him to an inn, and took care of him.

35 "On the next day, when he departed, he took out two denarii, gave *them* to the innkeeper, and said to him, 'Take care of him; and whatever more you spend, when I come again, I will repay you.'

36 "So which of these three do you think was neighbor to him who fell among the thieves?"

37 And he said, "He who showed mercy on him." Then Jesus said to him, "Go and do likewise."

38 Now it happened as they went that He entered a certain village; and a certain woman named Martha welcomed Him into her house.

39 And she had a sister called Mary, who also sat at Jesus' feet and heard His word.

40 But Martha was distracted with much serving, and she approached Him and said, "Lord, do You not care that my sister has left me to serve alone? Therefore tell her to help me."

41 And Jesus answered and said to her, "Martha, Martha, you are worried and troubled about many things.

42 "But one thing is needed, and Mary has chosen that good part, which will not be taken away from her."

11 And it came to pass, as He was praying in a certain place, when He ceased, *that* one of His disciples said to Him, "Lord, teach us to pray, as John also taught his disciples."

2 So He said to them, "When you pray, say:

STEP 3

Our Father in heaven,
Hallowed be Your name.
Your kingdom come.
Your will be done
On earth as *it is* in heaven.
3 Give us day by day our daily bread.
4 And forgive us our sins,
For we also forgive everyone who is indebted to us.
And do not lead us into temptation,
But deliver us from the evil one."

STEP 2

5 And He said to them, "Which of you shall have a friend, and go to him at midnight and say to him, 'Friend, lend me three loaves;

6 'for a friend of mine has come to me on his journey, and I have nothing to set before him';

7 "and he will answer from within and say, 'Do not trouble me; the door is now shut, and my children are with me in bed; I cannot rise and give to you'?

8 "I say to you, though he will not rise and give to him because he is his friend, yet because of his persistence he will rise and give him as many as he needs.

9 "And I say to you, ask, and it will be given to you; seek, and you will find; knock, and it will be opened to you.

10 "For everyone who asks receives, and he who seeks finds, and to him who knocks it will be opened.

11 "If a son asks for bread from any father among you, will he give him a stone? Or if *he asks* for a fish, will he give him a serpent instead of a fish?

12 "Or if he asks for an egg, will he offer him a scorpion?

13 "If you then, being evil, know how to give good gifts to your children, how much more will *your*

STEP
2

*Came to believe that a Power greater than ourselves
could restore us to sanity.*

Luke 11:5–13

The Lord Jesus gave us two very different word pictures here to describe the act of petitioning. They are connected by the key verses 9 and 10. The first picture is of a friend needing desperately to borrow food. The point is that persistence pays off. Even though the neighbor was already in bed, his friend's persistence kept him sleepless and he finally gave what was needed. The second set of verses describes the love of a father and his natural desire to give his child the good things he asks for.

Verses 5–8 portray how we should seek God. In Step 1, we came to know we were powerless to help ourselves. In Step 2, we discover that God is the friend who has what we need. Verse 9 tells us what to do about our discovery: "Ask, and it will be given to you; seek, and you will find; knock, and it will be opened to you." Verses 10–13 give us the assurance of God's love and His desire to meet our every need through giving us the Holy Spirit.

For further reading on Step 2, turn to page 167.

Daily Encouragement

DAY 69 READING: LUKE 11:1–13

A Thought for the New Day: Notice the careful order of things in our Lord's brief, model prayer (vv. 2–4). Here is a blueprint for true worship. Not primarily our self-perceived wants, but an appreciation for God *Himself*, is always the right starting point. Once we see our relationship to God in perspective, all other matters fall into their true place of importance: We may even blush at some things we thought were important at all! (*Turn to page 159.*)

heavenly Father give the Holy Spirit to those who ask Him!"

14 And He was casting out a demon, and it was mute. So it was, when the demon had gone out, that the mute spoke; and the multitudes marveled.

15 But some of them said, "He casts out demons by Beelzebub, the ruler of the demons."

16 And others, testing *Him*, sought from Him a sign from heaven.

17 But He, knowing their thoughts, said to them: "Every kingdom divided against itself is brought to desolation, and a house *divided* against a house falls.

18 "If Satan also is divided against himself, how will his kingdom stand? Because you say I cast out demons by Beelzebub.

19 "And if I cast out demons by Beelzebub, by whom do your sons cast *them* out? Therefore they will be your judges.

20 "But if I cast out demons with the finger of God, surely the kingdom of God has come upon you.

21 "When a strong man, fully armed, guards his own palace, his goods are in peace.

22 "But when a stronger than he comes upon him and overcomes him, he takes from him all his armor in which he trusted, and divides his spoils.

23 "He who is not with Me is against Me, and he who does not gather with Me scatters.

24 "When an unclean spirit goes out of a man, he goes through dry places, seeking rest; and finding none, he says, 'I will return to my house from which I came.'

25 "And when he comes, he finds *it* swept and put in order.

26 "Then he goes and takes with *him* seven other spirits more wicked than himself, and they enter and dwell there; and the last *state* of that man is worse than the first."

27 And it happened, as He spoke

these things, that a certain woman from the crowd raised her voice and said to Him, "Blessed *is* the womb that bore You, and *the* breasts which nursed You!"

28 But He said, "More than that, blessed *are* those who hear the word of God and keep it!"

29 And while the crowds were thickly gathered together, He began to say, "This is an evil generation. It seeks a sign, and no sign will be given to it except the sign of Jonah the prophet.

30 "For as Jonah became a sign to the Ninevites, so also the Son of Man will be to this generation.

31 "The queen of the South will rise up in the judgment with the men of this generation and condemn them, for she came from the ends of the earth to hear the wisdom of Solomon; and indeed a greater than Solomon *is* here.

32 "The men of Nineveh will rise up in the judgment with this generation and condemn it, for they repented at the preaching of Jonah; and indeed a greater than Jonah *is* here.

33 "No one, when he has lit a lamp, puts *it* in a secret place or under a basket, but on a lampstand, that those who come in may see the light.

34 "The lamp of the body is the eye. Therefore, when your eye is good, your whole body also is full of light. But when *your eye* is bad, your body also *is* full of darkness.

35 "Therefore take heed that the light which is in you is not darkness.

36 "If then your whole body *is* full of light, having no part dark, *the* whole *body* will be full of light, as when the bright shining of a lamp gives you light."

37 And as He spoke, a certain Pharisee asked Him to dine with him. So He went in and sat down to eat.

38 And when the Pharisee saw *it*,

STEP
4

STEP 4

Made a searching and fearless moral inventory of ourselves.

Luke 11:33–36

Jesus, the Light of the world, has lit the beautiful lamp of His presence within our souls. We have His power glowing within us. Finally the dark specters of our past will no longer hold us captive. Now in Step 4 we allow the light of Jesus' words to illumine the hidden closets and corners of our lives. Our broom of honesty begins to sweep away the cobwebs of dependency and the dust of resentment and guilt.

Scripture is our guide in our moral inventory because it is the true light, giving us clear spiritual insight.

And when we have completed our search and finished our inventory, then, "*the* whole body will be full of light, as when the bright shining of a lamp gives you light."

For further reading on Step 4, turn to page 161.

Daily Encouragement

DAY 70 READING: LUKE 11:14–36

A Thought for the New Day: You can usually measure evil by the bad sense it makes. If you think about the social sins of our time, you can see they do not make good sense because of the misery they bring. The false theologians of Jesus' time even imagined He was in league with the Devil (v. 15)—as if the Devil could possibly be in the business of doing the works Jesus did! (*Turn to page 161.*)

he marveled that He had not first washed before dinner.

39 But the Lord said to him, "Now you Pharisees make the outside of the cup and dish clean, but your inward part is full of greed and wickedness.

40 "Foolish ones! Did not He who made the outside make the inside also?

41 "But rather give alms of such things as you have; then indeed all things are clean to you.

42 "But woe to you Pharisees! For you tithe mint and rue and all manner of herbs, and pass by justice and the love of God. These you ought to have done, without leaving the others undone.

43 "Woe to you Pharisees! For you love the best seats in the synagogues and greetings in the marketplaces.

44 "Woe to you, scribes and Pharisees, hypocrites! For you are like graves which are not seen, and the men who walk over *them* are not aware *of them.*"

45 Then one of the lawyers answered and said to Him, "Teacher, by saying these things You reproach us also."

46 And He said, "Woe to you also, *you* lawyers! For you load men with burdens hard to bear, and you yourselves do not touch the burdens with one of your fingers.

47 "Woe to you! For you build the tombs of the prophets, and your fathers killed them.

48 "In fact, you bear witness that you approve the deeds of your fathers; for they indeed killed them, and you build their tombs.

49 "Therefore the wisdom of God also said, 'I will send them prophets and apostles, and *some* of them they will kill and persecute,'

50 "that the blood of all the prophets which was shed from the foundation of the world may be required of this generation,

51 "from the blood of Abel to the blood of Zechariah who perished between the altar and the temple. Yes, I say to you, it shall be required of this generation.

52 "Woe to you lawyers! For you have taken away the key of knowledge. You did not enter in yourselves, and those who were entering in you hindered."

53 And as He said these things to them, the scribes and the Pharisees began to assail *Him* vehemently, and to cross-examine Him about many things,

54 lying in wait for Him, and seeking to catch Him in something He might say, that they might accuse Him.

12 In the meantime, when an innumerable multitude of people had gathered together, so that they trampled one another, He began to say to His disciples first *of all*, "Beware of the leaven of the Pharisees, which is hypocrisy.

STEP 4

2 "For there is nothing covered that will not be revealed, nor hidden that will not be known.

3 "Therefore whatever you have spoken in the dark will be heard in the light, and what you have spoken in the ear in inner rooms will be proclaimed on the housetops.

4 "And I say to you, My friends, do not be afraid of those who kill the body, and after that have no more that they can do.

5 "But I will show you whom you should fear: Fear Him who, after He has killed, has power to cast into hell; yes, I say to you, fear Him!

6 "Are not five sparrows sold for two copper coins? And not one of them is forgotten before God.

7 "But the very hairs of your head are all numbered. Do not fear therefore; you are of more value than many sparrows.

8 "Also I say to you, whoever confesses Me before men, him the Son of Man also will confess before the angels of God.

STEP 4

Made a searching and fearless moral inventory of ourselves.

Luke 12:1–6

In Luke 12:1, Jesus warns His disciples against hypocrisy, pretending to be something one is not. Step 4 encourages us to thoroughly evaluate our lives and to fearlessly accept the truth of our personal history. As we embark on this inventory, we may want to be mindful of the following guidelines:

1) God already knows everything about us anyway (vv. 2, 3). There is nothing to hide.

2) We must face and acknowledge our fears in order to move beyond them. Otherwise, we will be so wrought up emotionally that we cannot deal with the most important issue in our lives—our relationship with God (vv. 4, 5).

3) God cares about us very deeply (vv. 6, 7). The inventory process becomes a special opportunity to feel that personal care as we experience the grace of His acceptance and forgiveness.

Now that we have put our trust in God, He is present with us to help in the process of uncovering our real selves.

For further reading on Step 4, turn to page 175.

Daily Encouragement

DAY 71 READING: LUKE 11:37—12:12

A Thought for the New Day: When we realize all that Christ has done for us, it becomes a privilege to confess Him (12:8). We can never say or do enough to spread His fame in the world. There are so many ways to confess Christ. Even "a cup of water" given for His sake is treasured in heaven (Mark 9:41). A life beautifully lived in the world praises Him more than many pompous speeches. (*Turn to page 163.*)

9 "But he who denies Me before men will be denied before the angels of God.

10 "And anyone who speaks a word against the Son of Man, it will be forgiven him; but to him who blasphemes against the Holy Spirit, it will not be forgiven.

11 "Now when they bring you to the synagogues and magistrates and authorities, do not worry about how or what you should answer, or what you should say.

12 "For the Holy Spirit will teach you in that very hour what you ought to say."

13 Then one from the crowd said to Him, "Teacher, tell my brother to divide the inheritance with me."

14 But He said to him, "Man, who made Me a judge or an arbitrator over you?"

STEP 4

15 And He said to them, "Take heed and beware of covetousness, for one's life does not consist in the abundance of the things he possesses."

16 Then He spoke a parable to them, saying: "The ground of a certain rich man yielded plentifully.

17 "And he thought within himself, saying, 'What shall I do, since I have no room to store my crops?'

18 "So he said, 'I will do this: I will pull down my barns and build greater, and there I will store all my crops and my goods.

19 'And I will say to my soul, "Soul, you have many goods laid up for many years; take your ease; eat, drink, *and* be merry."'

20 "But God said to him, '*You* fool! This night your soul will be required of you; then whose will those things be which you have provided?'

21 "So *is* he who lays up treasure for himself, and is not rich toward God."

22 And He said to His disciples, "Therefore I say to you, do not worry about your life, what you will eat; nor about the body, what you will put on.

23 "Life is more than food, and the body *is more* than clothing.

24 "Consider the ravens, for they neither sow nor reap, which have neither storehouse nor barn; and God feeds them. Of how much more value are you than the birds?

25 "And which of you by worrying can add one cubit to his stature?

26 "If you then are not able to do *the* least, why are you anxious for the rest?

27 "Consider the lilies, how they grow: they neither toil nor spin; and yet I say to you, even Solomon in all his glory was not arrayed like one of these.

STEP 11

28 "If then God so clothes the grass, which today is in the field and tomorrow is thrown into the oven, how much more *will He clothe* you, O *you* of little faith?

29 "And do not seek what you should eat or what you should drink, nor have an anxious mind.

30 "For all these things the nations of the world seek after, and your Father knows that you need these things.

31 "But seek the kingdom of God, and all these things shall be added to you.

32 "Do not fear, little flock, for it is your Father's good pleasure to give you the kingdom.

33 "Sell what you have and give alms; provide yourselves money bags which do not grow old, a treasure in the heavens that does not fail, where no thief approaches nor moth destroys.

34 "For where your treasure is, there your heart will be also.

35 "Let your waist be girded and *your* lamps burning;

STEP 12

36 "and you yourselves be like men who wait for their master, when he will return from the wedding, that when he comes and knocks they may open to him immediately.

37 "Blessed *are* those servants

*Sought through prayer and meditation to improve our conscious contact with God **as we understood Him,** praying only for knowledge of His will for us and the power to carry that out.*

Luke 12:27–34

The way we handle our possessions says much about our concept of God. Selfish attitudes about material blessings and overprotection of inanimate objects indicates that our God is small. Or perhaps, more correctly put, our faith is small. Jesus tells us that those who do not believe fill their days being concerned about earthly cares and possessions. But believers should not. Why? Because we do not need to worry about such things. God knows exactly what we need. He is powerful enough to supply us with every need we have and loving enough to give us far more than we ever could ask for. In fact, He has chosen to give us the treasures of His vast and marvelous kingdom, as we seek to honor Him.

When we walk according to this truth, we will have plenty to share with others, plenty to supply our own needs, and treasure untold in heaven.

For further reading on Step 11, turn to page 177.

Daily Encouragement

DAY 72 READING: LUKE 12:13–34

A Thought for the New Day: You often hear that it is the quality of life that matters, not its quantity. An ancient wise man wrote, "A life well lived makes every yesterday a dream of happiness, and every tomorrow a vision of new hope." We do well to take stock of how we invest our few years on earth. Running after the toys of time leaves us empty, but Jesus gives us days of heaven on earth (v. 15). (*Turn to page 165.*)

whom the master, when he comes, will find watching. Assuredly, I say to you that he will gird himself and have them sit down *to eat,* and will come and serve them.

38 "And if he should come in the second watch, or come in the third watch, and find *them* so, blessed are those servants.

39 "But know this, that if the master of the house had known what hour the thief would come, he would have watched and not allowed his house to be broken into.

40 "Therefore you also be ready, for the Son of Man is coming at an hour you do not expect."

41 Then Peter said to Him, "Lord, do You speak this parable *only* to us, or to all *people?* "

42 And the Lord said, "Who then is that faithful and wise steward, whom *his* master will make ruler over his household, to give *them their* portion of food in due season?

43 "Blessed *is* that servant whom his master will find so doing when he comes.

44 "Truly, I say to you that he will make him ruler over all that he has.

45 "But if that servant says in his heart, 'My master is delaying his coming,' and begins to beat the menservants and maidservants, and to eat and drink and be drunk,

46 "the master of that servant will come on a day when he is not looking for *him,* and at an hour when he is not aware, and will cut him in two and appoint *him* his portion with the unbelievers.

47 "And that servant who knew his master's will, and did not prepare *himself* or do according to his will, shall be beaten with many *stripes.*

48 "But he who did not know, yet committed things worthy of stripes, shall be beaten with few. For everyone to whom much is given, from him much will be required; and to whom much has

been committed, of him they will ask the more.

49 "I came to send fire on the earth, and how I wish it were already kindled!

50 "But I have a baptism to be baptized with, and how distressed I am till it is accomplished!

51 "Do *you* suppose that I came to give peace on earth? I tell you, not at all, but rather division.

52 "For from now on five in one house will be divided: three against two, and two against three.

53 "Father will be divided against son and son against father, mother against daughter and daughter against mother, mother-in-law against her daughter-in-law and daughter-in-law against her mother-in-law."

54 Then He also said to the multitudes, "When *you see* a cloud rising out of the west, immediately you say, 'A shower is coming'; and so it is.

55 "And when you see the south wind blow, you say, 'There will be hot weather'; and there is.

56 "Hypocrites! You can discern the face of the sky and of the earth, but how *is it* you do not discern this time?

57 "Yes, and why, even of yourselves, do you not judge what is right?

58 "When you go with your adversary to the magistrate, make every effort along the way to settle with him, lest he drag you to the judge, the judge deliver you to the officer, and the officer throw you into prison.

59 "I tell you, you shall not depart from there till you have paid the very last mite."

13 There were present at that season some who told Him about the Galileans whose blood Pilate had mingled with their sacrifices.

2 And Jesus answered and said to them, "Do you suppose that these

STEP 12

*Having had a spiritual awakening as the result
of these steps, we tried to carry this message to others,
and to practice these principles in all our affairs.*

Luke 12:35–40

The encouragement in these verses is a comfort to us as we daily seek to be servants of the Lord Jesus. Steadfast obedience and trust, we are told, will bring great reward when Jesus returns. The specific picture Jesus paints here is of the faithful servant sitting down at the banquet table while his Master serves him.

But the word of exhortation is also clear. Jesus warns us that it will be easy to become complacent about our commitment to Him. The allure of the world can make us lazy, unwatchful, and unconcerned. We can allow the locks of steadfastness to rust and weaken. Our fortress of obedience, trust, and hard-fought victories can be ransacked before we are even aware of the intruder.

Perhaps at this moment in time we are in the "second watch," eternally speaking. Perhaps we are already far into the third watch and Jesus will be returning on the golden streamers of soon-coming dawn. "Blessed are those servants whom the Master finds watching."

For further reading on Step 12, turn to page 207.

Daily Encouragement

DAY 73 READING: LUKE 12:35–59

A Thought for the New Day: Winning an argument often does not really matter except to our pride. Most of our disputes are about things we later wonder why we even bothered with. Let the angry man have his way, especially if it costs you nothing of importance (v. 58). Quarreling shortens your life, but a peaceable temperament is of great worth in terms of the lifetime of tranquillity and well-being it brings. (*Turn to page 167.*)

Galileans were worse sinners than all *other* Galileans, because they suffered such things?

3 "I tell you, no; but unless you repent you will all likewise perish.

4 "Or those eighteen on whom the tower in Siloam fell and killed them, do you think that they were worse sinners than all *other* men who dwelt in Jerusalem?

5 "I tell you, no; but unless you repent you will all likewise perish."

6 He also spoke this parable: "A certain *man* had a fig tree planted in his vineyard, and he came seeking fruit on it and found none.

7 "Then he said to the keeper of his vineyard, 'Look, for three years I have come seeking fruit on this fig tree and find none. Cut it down; why does it use up the ground?'

8 "But he answered and said to him, 'Sir, let it alone this year also, until I dig around it and fertilize *it.*

9 'And if it bears fruit, *well.* But if not, after that you can cut it down.' "

10 Now He was teaching in one of the synagogues on the Sabbath.

11 And behold, there was a woman who had a spirit of infirmity eighteen years, and was bent over and could in no way raise *herself* up.

12 But when Jesus saw her, He called *her* to *Him* and said to her, "Woman, you are loosed from your infirmity."

13 And He laid *His* hands on her, and immediately she was made straight, and glorified God.

14 But the ruler of the synagogue answered with indignation, because Jesus had healed on the Sabbath; and he said to the crowd, "There are six days on which men ought to work; therefore come and be healed on them, and not on the Sabbath day."

15 The Lord then answered him and said, "Hypocrite! Does not each one of you on the Sabbath loose his ox or *his* donkey from the stall, and lead *it* away to water it?

16 "So ought not this woman, being a daughter of Abraham, whom Satan has bound—think of it—for eighteen years, be loosed from this bond on the Sabbath?"

17 And when He said these things, all His adversaries were put to shame; and all the multitude rejoiced for all the glorious things that were done by Him.

18 Then He said, "What is the kingdom of God like? And to what shall I compare it?

19 "It is like a mustard seed, which a man took and put in his garden; and it grew and became a large tree, and the birds of the air nested in its branches."

20 And again He said, "To what shall I liken the kingdom of God?

21 "It is like leaven, which a woman took and hid in three measures of meal till it was all leavened."

22 And He went through the cities and villages, teaching, and journeying toward Jerusalem.

23 Then one said to Him, "Lord, are there few who are saved?" And He said to them,

24 "Strive to enter through the narrow gate, for many, I say to you, will seek to enter and will not be able.

25 "When once the Master of the house has risen up and shut the door, and you begin to stand outside the door, and knock at the door, saying, 'Lord, Lord, open for us,' and He will answer and say to you, 'I do not know you, where you are from,'

26 "then you will begin to say, 'We ate and drank in Your presence, and You taught in our streets.'

27 "But He will say, 'I tell you I do not know you, where you are from. Depart from Me, all you workers of iniquity.'

28 "There will be weeping and gnashing of teeth, when you see Abraham and Isaac and Jacob and all the prophets in the kingdom of God, and yourselves thrust out.

STEP 2

Came to believe that a Power greater than ourselves
could restore us to sanity.

Luke 13:10–13

The New Testament is filled with accounts of God's healing as transmitted by Jesus' touch upon the sick and infirm. For those of us seeking recovery, we bring the emotional infirmities of anxiety and depression to the altar of a restoring God.

The history of recovery movements in our modern culture is built upon innumerable stories of persons who have been delivered miraculously from obsessions, chemical and otherwise. The style of these healings from God varies. Some have experienced instantaneous and dramatic deliverance from old compulsions or dependencies. For others, recovery has been a gradual process of transformation. Whatever the style, when God's help was earnestly sought, the resultant healing impact was unmistakable.

While healings are significant in their own right, they are even more important as stepping-stones toward a higher purpose. That purpose is the discovery of a deeper and more meaningful relationship with God.

For further reading on Step 2, turn to page 181.

Daily Encouragement

DAY 74 READING: LUKE 13:1–21

A Thought for the New Day: God does spectacular things sometimes. Creation was one of them. However, some of His most special works begin and go forward in amazingly quiet ways (vv. 18, 19). Jesus reminds us more than once that His kingdom is not now a dramatic movement in the world. It began in a small way and is not widely hailed in media and press, but His eternal work grows continually. One day it will burst forth in full bloom. (*Turn to page 169.*)

29 "They will come from the east and the west, from the north and the south, and sit down in the kingdom of God.

30 "And indeed there are last who will be first, and there are first who will be last."

31 On that very day some Pharisees came, saying to Him, "Get out and depart from here, for Herod wants to kill You."

32 And He said to them, "Go, tell that fox, 'Behold, I cast out demons and perform cures today and tomorrow, and the third *day* I shall be perfected.'

33 "Nevertheless I must journey today, tomorrow, and the *day* following; for it cannot be that a prophet should perish outside of Jerusalem.

34 "O Jerusalem, Jerusalem, the one who kills the prophets and stones those who are sent to her! How often I wanted to gather your children together, as a hen *gathers* her brood under *her* wings, but you were not willing!

35 "See! Your house is left to you desolate; and assuredly, I say to you, you shall not see Me until *the time* comes when you say, *'Blessed is He who comes in the name of the LORD!'*"

14 Now it happened, as He went into the house of one of the rulers of the Pharisees to eat bread on the Sabbath, that they watched Him closely.

2 And behold, there was a certain man before Him who had dropsy.

3 And Jesus, answering, spoke to the lawyers and Pharisees, saying, "Is it lawful to heal on the Sabbath?"

4 But they kept silent. And He took *him* and healed him, and let him go.

5 Then He answered them, saying, "Which of you, having a donkey or an ox that has fallen into a pit, will not immediately pull him out on the Sabbath day?"

6 And they could not answer Him regarding these things.

7 So He told a parable to those who were invited, when He noted how they chose the best places, saying to them:

8 "When you are invited by anyone to a wedding feast, do not sit down in the best place, lest one more honorable than you be invited by him;

9 "and he who invited you and him come and say to you, 'Give place to this man,' and then you begin with shame to take the lowest place.

10 "But when you are invited, go and sit down in the lowest place, so that when he who invited you comes he may say to you, 'Friend, go up higher.' Then you will have glory in the presence of those who sit at the table with you.

11 "For whoever exalts himself will be abased, and he who humbles himself will be exalted."

12 Then He also said to him who invited Him, "When you give a dinner or a supper, do not ask your friends, your brothers, your relatives, nor *your* rich neighbors, lest they also invite you back, and you be repaid.

13 "But when you give a feast, invite *the* poor, *the* maimed, *the* lame, *the* blind.

14 "And you will be blessed, because they cannot repay you; for you shall be repaid at the resurrection of the just."

15 Now when one of those who sat at the table with Him heard these things, he said to Him, "Blessed *is* he who shall eat bread in the kingdom of God!"

16 Then He said to him, "A certain man gave a great supper and invited many,

17 "and sent his servant at supper time to say to those who were invited, 'Come, for all things are now ready.'

18 "But they all with one *accord*

STEP 10

*Continued to take personal inventory
and when we were wrong promptly admitted it.*

Luke 14:7–14

As Jesus watched the invited guests choose the best seats at the table, He responded to them. In Jesus' day, the seats farthest away from the host were for the least honored guests. How much better, Jesus noted, to slip into a lowly seat and be invited higher, rather than endure the embarrassment of having a higher place taken away. The moral of the story, of course, is verse 11. Humility, in the end, always lifts us up. God has so ordered it. True humility does not take away our self-confidence, but simply allows us to think of others first. This is why Jesus goes on to tell the dinner guests that they will be happiest when they invite to dinner those who can never hope to repay.

Exalting oneself (pride) is the easiest of all sins to commit when we are seeing real growth and victory in our lives. It is good to remind ourselves that God treasures a humble heart.

For further reading on Step 10, turn to page 195.

Daily Encouragement

DAY 75 READING: LUKE 13:22—14:15

A Thought for the New Day: We hear much cynicism about humility, like, "Nice guys finish last!" And so it often seems, but not if you take the long view. People who bite and scratch their way to "the top" also often end up with ulcers or cardiac arrest. They discover the trip was not worth the ticket after all. On the other hand, the one who quietly accepts his place, finding satisfaction in a job well done, receives immeasurable reward at last (14:10). *(Turn to page 171.)*

began to make excuses. The first said to him, 'I have bought a piece of ground, and I must go and see it. I ask you to have me excused.'

19 "And another said, 'I have bought five yoke of oxen, and I am going to test them. I ask you to have me excused.'

20 "Still another said, 'I have married a wife, and therefore I cannot come.'

21 "So that servant came and reported these things to his master. Then the master of the house, being angry, said to his servant, 'Go out quickly into the streets and lanes of the city, and bring in here *the* poor and *the* maimed and *the* lame and *the* blind.'

22 "And the servant said, 'Master, it is done as you commanded, and still there is room.'

23 "Then the master said to the servant, 'Go out into the highways and hedges, and compel *them* to come in, that my house may be filled.

24 'For I say to you that none of those men who were invited shall taste my supper.' "

25 And great multitudes went with Him. And He turned and said to them,

26 "If anyone comes to Me and does not hate his father and mother, wife and children, brothers and sisters, yes, and his own life also, he cannot be My disciple.

27 "And whoever does not bear his cross and come after Me cannot be My disciple.

28 "For which of you, intending to build a tower, does not sit down first and count the cost, whether he has *enough* to finish *it*—

29 "lest, after he has laid the foundation, and is not able to finish *it*, all who see *it* begin to mock him,

30 "saying, 'This man began to build and was not able to finish.'

31 "Or what king, going to make war against another king, does not sit down first and consider whether he is able with ten thousand to meet him who comes against him with twenty thousand?

32 "Or else, while the other is still a great way off, he sends a delegation and asks conditions of peace.

33 "So likewise, whoever of you does not forsake all that he has cannot be My disciple.

34 "Salt *is* good; but if the salt has lost its flavor, how shall it be seasoned?

35 "It is neither fit for the land nor for the dunghill, *but* men throw it out. He who has ears to hear, let him hear!"

15 Then all the tax collectors and the sinners drew near to Him to hear Him.

2 And the Pharisees and scribes murmured, saying, "This man receives sinners and eats with them."

3 So He spoke this parable to them, saying:

4 "What man of you, having a hundred sheep, if he loses one of them, does not leave the ninety-nine in the wilderness, and go after the one which is lost until he finds it?

5 "And when he has found *it*, he lays *it* on his shoulders, rejoicing.

6 "And when he comes home, he calls together *his* friends and neighbors, saying to them, 'Rejoice with me, for I have found my sheep which was lost!'

7 "I say to you that likewise there will be more joy in heaven over one sinner who repents than over ninety-nine just persons who need no repentance.

8 "Or what woman, having ten silver coins, if she loses one coin, does not light a lamp, sweep the house, and seek diligently until she finds *it*?

9 "And when she has found *it*, she calls *her* friends and neighbors together, saying, 'Rejoice with me,

STEP 5

Admitted to God, to ourselves, and to another human being the exact nature of our wrongs.

Luke 15:4–7

The whole fifteenth chapter of Luke is God's song of invitation. In all these verses we feel His great heart yearning after His wayward, struggling children. The chapter opens with a picture of outcast and needy people huddled around Jesus listening to His voice. The raised eyebrows, murmurs, and pointed fingers of the Pharisees, do not influence the Lord.

Instead He pictures Himself as a shepherd, searching for His precious, lost sheep. When that sheep is found, the Good Shepherd cradles it securely and gently over His shoulders, calling out with great joy that His sheep has been found. That precious sheep is a picture of each of us who has turned to God to rescue and heal us.

Verse 7 makes us realize what is happening as we move through Step 5 of our recovery. Angels in heaven rejoice as we become able to admit our wrongs to God, to ourselves, and to others.

For further reading on Step 5, turn to page 173.

Daily Encouragement

DAY 76 READING: LUKE 14:16—15:10

A Thought for the New Day: Do you feel alone in the crowd? Has life lost its meaning? Someone cares very much about your loneliness. That Someone is Jesus. No one is lonely when he or she is found by Christ, the Great Shepherd (15:4). He is the One who makes your life significant, full of value, beauty, and zest. There is no way you can ever be lost again when you return to the care of Him who made you for Himself. (*Turn to page 173.*)

for I have found the piece which I lost!'

10 "Likewise, I say to you, there is joy in the presence of the angels of God over one sinner who repents."

11 Then He said: "A certain man had two sons.

12 "And the younger of them said to *his* father, 'Father, give me the portion of goods that falls *to me.*' So he divided to them *his* livelihood.

13 "And not many days after, the younger son gathered all together, journeyed to a far country, and there wasted his possessions with prodigal living.

14 "But when he had spent all, there arose a severe famine in that land, and he began to be in want.

15 "Then he went and joined himself to a citizen of that country, and he sent him into his fields to feed swine.

16 "And he would gladly have filled his stomach with the pods that the swine ate, and no one gave him *anything.*

17 "But when he came to himself, he said, 'How many of my father's hired servants have bread enough and to spare, and I perish with hunger!

18 'I will arise and go to my father, and will say to him, "Father, I have sinned against heaven and before you,

19 and I am no longer worthy to be called your son. Make me like one of your hired servants."'

20 "And he arose and came to his father. But when he was still a great way off, his father saw him and had compassion, and ran and fell on his neck and kissed him.

21 "And the son said to him, 'Father, I have sinned against heaven and in your sight, and am no longer worthy to be called your son.'

22 "But the father said to his servants, 'Bring out the best robe and put *it* on him, and put a ring on his hand and sandals on *his* feet.

23 'And bring the fatted calf here and kill *it*, and let us eat and be merry;

24 'for this my son was dead and is alive again; he was lost and is found.' And they began to be merry.

25 "Now his older son was in the field. And as he came and drew near to the house, he heard music and dancing.

26 "So he called one of the servants and asked what these things meant.

27 "And he said to him, 'Your brother has come, and because he has received him safe and sound, your father has killed the fatted calf.'

28 "But he was angry and would not go in. Therefore his father came out and pleaded with him.

29 "So he answered and said to *his* father, 'Lo, these many years I have been serving you; I never transgressed your commandment at any time; and yet you never gave me a young goat, that I might make merry with my friends.

30 'But as soon as this son of yours came, who has devoured your livelihood with harlots, you killed the fatted calf for him.'

31 "And he said to him, 'Son, you are always with me, and all that I have is yours.

32 'It was right that we should make merry and be glad, for your brother was dead and is alive again, and was lost and is found.'"

16 And He also said to His disciples: "There was a certain rich man who had a steward, and an accusation was brought to him that this man was wasting his goods.

2 "So he called him and said to him, 'What is this I hear about you? Give an account of your stewardship, for you can no longer be steward.'

3 "Then the steward said within himself, 'What shall I do? For my

*Admitted to God, to ourselves, and to another human being
the exact nature of our wrongs.*

Luke 15:17–20

The story of the prodigal son reminds us that confession can be a stepping-stone toward renewed fellowship with God.

The embodiment of so many of our addictive tendencies, the prodigal son had dissipated his own resources and those of his father in a mistaken effort to establish his youthful identity. He returned home filled with shame and confessing in his heart, "Father, I have sinned against heaven and before you, and I am no longer worthy to be called your son" (vv. 18, 19).

The father's response to his errant son is a mirror of God's response to our authentic confession. Although the prodigal son expected rejection and chastisement, he found compassion, acceptance, and renewed kinship. As we seek new relationship to God through the acknowledgment of our wrongs, can we envision a Heavenly Father who greets us as warmly as the father greeted his wayward son? As we confess our brokenness, can we feel a God who reaches out, not to chastise us, but to embrace us and welcome us home to His everlasting family?

For further reading on Step 5, turn to page 271.

Daily Encouragement

DAY 77 READING: LUKE 15:11–32

A Thought for the New Day: What is your picture of God? Is He the angry Judge who can hardly wait to throw you into everlasting torment? But you are saying, "I'm suffering enough now; I sure don't need any more of that!" And you are right. Do not be afraid of God anymore. As Father, He waits to give you His kiss of love and acceptance (v. 20). Will you let Him show you the love He really has for you? (*Turn to page 175.*)

master is taking the stewardship away from me. I cannot dig; I am ashamed to beg.

4 'I have resolved what to do, that when I am put out of the stewardship, they may receive me into their houses.'

5 "So he called every one of his master's debtors to *him*, and said to the first, 'How much do you owe my master?'

6 "And he said, 'A hundred measures of oil.' So he said to him, 'Take your bill, and sit down quickly and write fifty.'

7 "Then he said to another, 'And how much do you owe?' So he said, 'A hundred measures of wheat.' And he said to him, 'Take your bill, and write eighty.'

8 "So the master commended the unjust steward because he had dealt shrewdly. For the sons of this world are more shrewd in their generation than the sons of light.

9 "And I say to you, make friends for yourselves by unrighteous mammon, that when you fail, they may receive you into everlasting habitations.

10 "He who *is* faithful in *what is* least is faithful also in much; and he who is unjust in *what is* least is unjust also in much.

11 "Therefore if you have not been faithful in the unrighteous mammon, who will commit to your trust the true *riches*?

12 "And if you have not been faithful in what is another man's, who will give you what is your own?

13 "No servant can serve two masters; for either he will hate the one and love the other, or else he will be loyal to the one and despise the other. You cannot serve God and mammon."

STEP 4 14 Now the Pharisees, who were lovers of money, also heard all these things, and they derided Him.

15 And He said to them, "You are those who justify yourselves before men, but God knows your hearts. For what is highly esteemed among men is an abomination in the sight of God.

16 "The law and the prophets *were* until John. Since that time the kingdom of God has been preached, and everyone is pressing into it.

17 "And it is easier for heaven and earth to pass away than for one tittle of the law to fail.

18 "Whoever divorces his wife and marries another commits adultery; and whoever marries her who is divorced from *her* husband commits adultery.

19 "There was a certain rich man who was clothed in purple and fine linen and fared sumptuously every day.

20 "But there was a certain beggar named Lazarus, full of sores, who was laid at his gate,

21 "desiring to be fed with the crumbs which fell from the rich man's table. Moreover the dogs came and licked his sores.

22 "So it was that the beggar died, and was carried by the angels to Abraham's bosom. The rich man also died and was buried.

23 "And being in torments in Hades, he lifted up his eyes and saw Abraham afar off, and Lazarus in his bosom.

24 "Then he cried and said, 'Father Abraham, have mercy on me, and send Lazarus that he may dip the tip of his finger in water and cool my tongue; for I am tormented in this flame.'

25 "But Abraham said, 'Son, remember that in your lifetime you received your good things, and likewise Lazarus evil things; but now he is comforted and you are tormented.

26 'And besides all this, between us and you there is a great gulf fixed, so that those who want to pass from here to you cannot, nor can those from there pass to us.'

STEP 4

Made a searching and fearless moral inventory of ourselves.

Luke 16:14, 15

Once upon a time there was a tiny, isolated kingdom where, from an early age, its people were taught that the word "up" meant down, and the word "down" meant up. Then one day a stranger appeared on the scene proclaiming that what had been held as indisputable truth was, in fact, totally wrong. In the greater world outside the little kingdom, the meaning of these words was totally reversed.

This little fairy tale may sound a bit farfetched, but then the Pharisees thought the same about Jesus' words when He declared to them that all the things they considered to be the value and measure of a person meant little or nothing in the eyes of God.

Through the years, because of our family backgrounds, our dependencies, our confusion or shame, we have begun to think of "down" as "up." We have not valued and nurtured the areas of life that have great importance. But now in Step 4 we are ready to acknowledge our problems. We are ready for our little kingdom to know the truth.

For further reading on Step 4, turn to page 217.

Daily Encouragement

DAY 78 READING: LUKE 16:1–31

A Thought for the New Day: Some people in Jesus' day laughed at Him, and others today do, too (v. 14). They are so calloused that they are no longer able to respect anyone, let alone the Son of Glory. Their values are upside down. Let us have hearts that are able to appreciate real worth when we see it. When we respect the Creator for all that He is, then our regard for one human life will also increase a million times. (*Turn to page 177.*)

27 "Then he said, 'I beg you therefore, father, that you would send him to my father's house,

28 'for I have five brothers, that he may testify to them, lest they also come to this place of torment.'

29 "Abraham said to him, 'They have Moses and the prophets; let them hear them.'

30 "And he said, 'No, father Abraham; but if one goes to them from the dead, they will repent.'

31 "But he said to him, 'If they do not hear Moses and the prophets, neither will they be persuaded though one rise from the dead.' "

17 Then He said to the disciples, "It is impossible that no offenses should come, but woe *to him* through whom they do come!

2 "It would be better for him if a millstone were hung around his neck, and he were thrown into the sea, than that he should offend one of these little ones.

STEP 4

3 "Take heed to yourselves. If your brother sins against you, rebuke him; and if he repents, forgive him.

4 "And if he sins against you seven times in a day, and seven times in a day returns to you, saying, 'I repent,' you shall forgive him."

5 And the apostles said to the Lord, "Increase our faith."

6 So the Lord said, "If you have faith as a mustard seed, you can say to this mulberry tree, 'Be pulled up by the roots and be planted in the sea,' and it would obey you.

STEP 11

7 "And which of you, having a servant plowing or tending sheep, will say to him when he has come in from the field, 'Come at once and sit down to eat'?

8 "But will he not rather say to him, 'Prepare something for my supper, and gird yourself and serve me till I have eaten and drunk, and afterward you will eat and drink'?

9 "Does he thank that servant because he did the things that were commanded him? I think not.

10 "So likewise you, when you have done all those things which you are commanded, say, 'We are unprofitable servants. We have done what was our duty to do.' "

11 Now it happened as He went to Jerusalem that He passed through the midst of Samaria and Galilee.

12 Then as He entered a certain village, there met Him ten men who were lepers, who stood afar off.

13 And they lifted up *their* voices and said, "Jesus, Master, have mercy on us!"

14 So when He saw *them*, He said to them, "Go, show yourselves to the priests." And so it was that as they went, they were cleansed.

15 Now one of them, when he saw that he was healed, returned, and with a loud voice glorified God,

16 and fell down on *his* face at His feet, giving Him thanks. And he was a Samaritan.

17 So Jesus answered and said, "Were there not ten cleansed? But where *are* the nine?

18 "Were there not any found who returned to give glory to God except this foreigner?"

19 And He said to him, "Arise, go your way. Your faith has made you well."

20 Now when He was asked by the Pharisees when the kingdom of God would come, He answered them and said, "The kingdom of God does not come with observation;

21 "nor will they say, 'See here!' or 'See there!' For indeed, the kingdom of God is within you."

22 Then He said to the disciples, "The days will come when you will desire to see one of the days of the Son of Man, and you will not see *it*.

23 "And they will say to you, 'Look here!' or 'Look there!' Do not go after *them* or follow *them*.

24 "For as the lightning that

*Sought through prayer and meditation to improve our conscious contact with God **as we understood Him,** praying only for knowledge of His will for us and the power to carry that out.*

Luke 17:7–10

Why does the Bible so often emphasize the need of a humble heart? It is because God can do His best work in lives that are humble and receptive to Him. Gratitude, trust, and obedience naturally flow from the spring of humility. And God rejoices to give His best to those who drink deeply and continually from that spring. Humility before God and others gives power to a life that no amount of pride can match. It is the power of the blessing and favor of the almighty God.

For further reading on Step 11, turn to page 191.

Daily Encouragement

DAY 79 READING: LUKE 17:1–19

A Thought for the New Day: A thankful heart is a tender heart (vv. 15, 16). Its possessor is filled with the joy of living. Of what value is a gift if we cannot appreciate it? Life for the ungrateful individual must be a bleak and sorry affair. By contrast, to have your eyes open to all the beauty and goodness the Creator affords is to know boundless ecstasy. *(Turn to page 179.)*

flashes out of one *part* under heaven shines to the other *part* under heaven, so also the Son of Man will be in His day.

25 "But first He must suffer many things and be rejected by this generation.

26 "And as it was in the days of Noah, so it will be also in the days of the Son of Man:

27 "They ate, they drank, they married wives, they were given in marriage, until the day that Noah entered the ark, and the flood came and destroyed them all.

28 "Likewise as it was also in the days of Lot: They ate, they drank, they bought, they sold, they planted, they built;

29 "but on the day that Lot went out of Sodom it rained fire and brimstone from heaven and destroyed *them* all.

30 "Even so will it be in the day when the Son of Man is revealed.

31 "In that day, he who is on the housetop, and his goods *are* in the house, let him not come down to take them away. And likewise the one who is in the field, let him not turn back.

32 "Remember Lot's wife.

33 "Whoever seeks to save his life will lose it, and whoever loses his life will preserve it.

34 "I tell you, in that night there will be two *men* in one bed: the one will be taken and the other will be left.

35 "Two *women* will be grinding together: the one will be taken and the other left.

36 "Two *men* will be in the field: the one will be taken and the other left."

37 And they answered and said to Him, "Where, Lord?" So He said to them, "Wherever the body is, there the eagles will be gathered together."

18 Then He spoke a parable to them, that men always ought to pray and not lose heart,

2 saying: "There was in a certain city a judge who did not fear God nor regard man.

3 "Now there was a widow in that city; and she came to him, saying, 'Avenge me of my adversary.'

4 "And he would not for a while; but afterward he said within himself, 'Though I do not fear God nor regard man,

5 'yet because this widow troubles me I will avenge her, lest by her continual coming she weary me.' "

6 Then the Lord said, "Hear what the unjust judge said.

7 "And shall God not avenge His own elect who cry out day and night to Him, though He bears long with them?

8 "I tell you that He will avenge them speedily. Nevertheless, when the Son of Man comes, will He really find faith on the earth?"

9 Also He spoke this parable to some who trusted in themselves that they were righteous, and despised others:

10 "Two men went up to the temple to pray, one a Pharisee and the other a tax collector.

11 "The Pharisee stood and prayed thus with himself, 'God, I thank You that I am not like other men—extortioners, unjust, adulterers, or even as this tax collector.

12 'I fast twice a week; I give tithes of all that I possess.'

13 "And the tax collector, standing afar off, would not so much as raise *his* eyes to heaven, but beat his breast, saying, 'God be merciful to me a sinner!'

14 "I tell you, this man went down to his house justified *rather* than the other; for everyone who exalts himself will be abased, and he who humbles himself will be exalted."

15 Then they also brought infants to Him that He might touch them; but when *His* disciples saw *it*, they rebuked them.

16 But Jesus called them to *Him*

STEP 7

Humbly asked Him to remove our shortcomings.

Luke 18:9–14

Realizing that we have offended God and others by our actions is a painful realization. But it is also a blessing. It is a blessing the Pharisees knew nothing about. In their self-righteous state, they could never know the grace, mercy, and transforming power of God. However, the tax collector, who could not bring himself even to "raise *his* eyes to heaven," recognized the enormity of his needs and thus experienced the enormity of God's power to cleanse and justify.

As we humbly ask God to remove our shortcomings, let us rejoice that we can experience the greatness of His mercy and power.

For further reading on Step 7, turn to page 263.

Daily Encouragement

DAY 80 READING: LUKE 17:20—18:14

A Thought for the New Day: Are you dissatisfied with yourself? Join the crowd! If we are honest, we have to admit there is much about ourselves to be unhappy with. We just have to get it through our heads that God loves self-dissatisfied people (18:13, 14). The self-satisfied has gone as far as he can go, which is not very far. When we know and are sorry for our failings, we can grow to great stature, and we have heaven to gain. (*Turn to page 181.*)

and said, "Let the little children come to Me, and do not forbid them; for of such is the kingdom of God.

17 "Assuredly, I say to you, whoever does not receive the kingdom of God as a little child will by no means enter it."

18 Now a certain ruler asked Him, saying, "Good Teacher, what shall I do to inherit eternal life?"

19 So Jesus said to him, "Why do you call Me good? No one *is* good but One, *that is,* God.

20 "You know the commandments: *'Do not commit adultery,' 'Do not murder,' 'Do not steal,' 'Do not bear false witness,' 'Honor your father and your mother.'*"

21 And he said, "All these I have kept from my youth."

22 So when Jesus heard these things, He said to him, "You still lack one thing. Sell all that you have and distribute to the poor, and you will have treasure in heaven; and come, follow Me."

23 But when he heard this, he became very sorrowful, for he was very rich.

24 And when Jesus saw that he became very sorrowful, He said, "How hard it is for those who have riches to enter the kingdom of God!

25 "For it is easier for a camel to go through a needle's eye than for a rich man to enter the kingdom of God."

26 And those who heard it said, "Who then can be saved?"

STEP 2 27 But He said, "The things which are impossible with men are possible with God."

28 Then Peter said, "See, we have left all and followed You."

29 So He said to them, "Assuredly, I say to you, there is no one who has left house or parents or brothers or wife or children, for the sake of the kingdom of God,

30 "who shall not receive many times more in this present time, and in the age to come everlasting life."

31 Then He took the twelve aside and said to them, "Behold, we are going up to Jerusalem, and all things that are written by the prophets concerning the Son of Man will be accomplished.

32 "For He will be delivered to the Gentiles and will be mocked and insulted and spit upon.

33 "And they will scourge *Him* and put Him to death. And the third day He will rise again."

34 But they understood none of these things; this saying was hidden from them, and they did not know the things which were spoken.

35 Then it happened, that as He was coming near Jericho, that a certain blind man sat by the road begging. **STEP 2**

36 And hearing a multitude passing by, he asked what it meant.

37 So they told him that Jesus of Nazareth was passing by.

38 And he cried out, saying, "Jesus, Son of David, have mercy on me!"

39 Then those who went before warned him that he should be quiet; but he cried out all the more, "Son of David, have mercy on me!"

40 So Jesus stood still and commanded him to be brought to Him. And when he had come near, He asked him,

41 saying, "What do you want Me to do for you?" And he said, "Lord, that I may receive my sight."

42 Then Jesus said to him, "Receive your sight; your faith has saved you."

43 And immediately he received his sight, and followed Him, glorifying God. And all the people, when they saw *it,* gave praise to God.

19 Then *Jesus* entered and passed through Jericho.

2 Now behold, *there was* a man

STEP 2

Came to believe that a Power greater than ourselves could restore us to sanity.

Luke 18:27

"Impossible" is a word that begins to loom larger and larger in our minds as we sink into the pit of dependency. What we first thought to be just a few potholes in the road of life has become a deep mire from which we cannot escape. The more we have tried, the deeper we have sunk. Our situation seems impossible.

But this verse trumpets hope for us. It is a promise that has proven true for millions of people down through the centuries. The same God who sent manna to feed His people, tumbled the walls of Jericho, closed the lions' mouths, walked on water, and raised the dead is the God who loves us and wants to help us. Nothing is impossible for Him. His power is limitless, and His love is boundless. There is nothing too hard for Him.

For further reading on Step 2, turn to page 215.

Daily Encouragement

DAY 81 READING: LUKE 18:15–43

A Thought for the New Day: Why didn't Jesus' followers understand Him (v. 34)? He certainly spoke plainly enough. The truth is that their values were so mixed up that they were unable to think straight. Like us, they valued their lives above all else. On the other hand, Jesus knew that dying to one's most urgent desire was the real way to life. Later, the disciples would understand this truth. As St. Francis said, "It is in dying that we are born to eternal life." (*Turn to page 183.*)

named Zacchaeus who was a chief tax collector, and he was rich.

3 And he sought to see who Jesus was, but could not because of the crowd, for he was of short stature.

4 So he ran ahead and climbed up into a sycamore tree to see Him, for He was going to pass that *way.*

5 And when Jesus came to the place, He looked up and saw him, and said to him, "Zacchaeus, make haste and come down, for today I must stay at your house."

6 So he made haste and came down, and received Him joyfully.

7 But when they saw *it,* they all murmured, saying, "He has gone to be a guest with a man who is a sinner."

STEP 8

8 Then Zacchaeus stood and said to the Lord, "Look, Lord, I give half of my goods to the poor; and if I have taken anything from anyone by false accusation, I restore fourfold."

9 And Jesus said to him, "Today salvation has come to this house, because he also is a son of Abraham;

10 "for the Son of Man has come to seek and to save that which was lost."

11 Now as they heard these things, He spoke another parable, because He was near Jerusalem and because they thought the kingdom of God would appear immediately.

12 Therefore He said: "A certain nobleman went into a far country to receive for himself a kingdom and to return.

13 "So he called ten of his servants, delivered to them ten minas, and said to them, 'Do business till I come.'

14 "But his citizens hated him, and sent a delegation after him, saying, 'We will not have this *man* to reign over us.'

15 "And so it was that when he returned, having received the kingdom, he then commanded these servants, to whom he had given the money, to be called to

him, that he might know how much every man had gained by trading.

16 "Then came the first, saying, 'Master, your mina has earned ten minas.'

17 "And he said to him, 'Well *done,* good servant; because you were faithful in a very little, have authority over ten cities.'

18 "And the second came, saying, 'Master, your mina has earned five minas.'

19 "Likewise he said to him, 'You also be over five cities.'

20 "And another came, saying, 'Master, here is your mina, which I have kept put away in a handkerchief.

21 'For I feared you, because you are an austere man. You collect what you did not deposit, and reap what you did not sow.'

22 "And he said to him, 'Out of your own mouth I will judge you, *you* wicked servant. You knew that I was an austere man, collecting what I did not deposit and reaping what I did not sow.

23 'Why then did you not put my money in the bank, that at my coming I might have collected it with interest?'

24 "And he said to those who stood by, 'Take the mina from him, and give *it* to him who has ten minas.'

25 ("But they said to him, 'Master, he has ten minas.')

26 'For I say to you, that to everyone who has will be given; and from him who does not have, even what he has will be taken away from him.

27 'But bring here those enemies of mine, who did not want me to reign over them, and slay *them* before me.' "

28 When He had said this, He went on ahead, going up to Jerusalem.

29 And it came to pass, when He came near to Bethphage and Bethany, at the mountain called Olivet, *that* He sent two of His disciples,

30 saying, "Go into the village op-

STEP 8

*Made a list of all persons we had harmed,
and became willing to make amends to them all.*

Luke 19:8

Step 8 is based on the principle that we can only be restored to newness of being as we acknowledge and make restitution for the emotional damage of the past.

The gospel tells us that Zacchaeus, a tax collector, became willing to make financial reparations to all those he had abused. Likewise, we must become willing to review the history of a lifetime of relationships and make amends to those persons whom we have harmed by our codependent manipulations.

If we have wounded others, it is vitally important that we begin to offer appropriate amends for the healing of those wounds. If we have been wounded by others, especially in childhood, it is important that we discover how to engage in the necessary self-nurturing and reparenting activities as means of healing the wounded child we carry within us.

For further reading on Step 8, turn to page 237.

Daily Encouragement

DAY 82 READING: LUKE 19:1–48

A Thought for the New Day: Why Zacchaeus of all people (vv. 1–6)? A chief tax collector! He must have been one of the loneliest men in the world. Everybody hated him, it seemed—everybody but Jesus. The case of Zacchaeus is a window that looks into the heart of God. Zacchaeus was a man weary of his load of loneliness and, yes, his sin. He could hardly wait to surrender to Jesus. Such people are made welcome in God's family. *(Turn to page 186.)*

posite *you,* where as you enter you will find a colt tied, on which no one has ever sat. Loose him and bring *him* here.

31 "And if anyone asks you, 'Why are you loosing *him?*' thus you shall say to him, 'Because the Lord has need of him.' "

32 So those who were sent departed and found *it* just as He had said to them.

33 But as they were loosing the colt, the owners of it said to them, "Why are you loosing the colt?"

34 And they said, "The Lord has need of him."

35 Then they brought him to Jesus. And they threw their own garments on the colt, and they set Jesus on him.

36 And as He went, they spread their clothes on the road.

37 Then, as He was now drawing near the descent of the Mount of Olives, the whole multitude of the disciples began to rejoice and praise God with a loud voice for all the mighty works they had seen, 38 saying:

" 'Blessed is the King who comes
   in the name of the LORD!'
Peace in heaven and glory in
   the highest!"

39 And some of the Pharisees called to Him from the crowd, "Teacher, rebuke Your disciples."

40 But He answered and said to them, "I tell you that if these should keep silent, the stones would immediately cry out."

41 Now as He drew near, He saw the city and wept over it,

42 saying, "If you had known, even you, especially in this your day, the things *that make* for your peace! But now they are hidden from your eyes.

43 "For *the* days will come upon you when your enemies will build an embankment around you, surround you and close you in on every side,

44 "and level you, and your children within you, to the ground; and they will not leave in you one stone upon another, because you did not know the time of your visitation."

45 Then He went into the temple and began to drive out those who bought and sold in it,

46 saying to them, "It is written, *'My house is a house of prayer,'* but you have made it a *'den of thieves.'*"

47 And He was teaching daily in the temple. But the chief priests, the scribes, and the leaders of the people sought to destroy Him,

48 and were unable to do anything; for all the people were very attentive to hear Him.

20 Now it happened on one of those days, as He taught the people in the temple and preached the gospel, *that* the chief priests and the scribes, together with the elders, confronted *Him*

2 and spoke to Him, saying, "Tell us, by what authority are You doing these things? Or who is he who gave You this authority?"

3 But He answered and said to them, "I will also ask you one thing, and answer Me:

4 "The baptism of John—was it from heaven or from men?"

5 And they reasoned among themselves, saying, "If we say, 'From heaven,' He will say, 'Why then did you not believe him?'

6 "But if we say, 'From men,' all the people will stone us, for they are persuaded that John was a prophet."

7 So they answered that they did not know where *it was* from.

8 And Jesus said to them, "Neither will I tell you by what authority I do these things."

9 Then He began to tell the people this parable: "A certain man planted a vineyard, leased it to

vinedressers, and went into a far country for a long time.

10 "Now at vintage-time he sent a servant to the vinedressers, that they might give him some of the fruit of the vineyard. But the vinedressers beat him and sent *him* away empty-handed.

11 "Again he sent another servant; and they beat him also, treated *him* shamefully, and sent *him* away empty-handed.

12 "And again he sent a third; and they wounded him also and cast *him* out.

13 "Then the owner of the vineyard said, 'What shall I do? I will send my beloved son. Probably they will respect *him* when they see him.'

14 "But when the vinedressers saw him, they reasoned among themselves, saying, 'This is the heir. Come, let us kill him, that the inheritance may be ours.'

15 "So they cast him out of the vineyard and killed *him*. Therefore what will the owner of the vineyard do to them?

16 "He will come and destroy those vinedressers and give the vineyard to others." And when they heard *it* they said, "Certainly not!"

17 And He looked at them and said, "What then is this that is written:

> 'The stone which the builders rejected
> Has become the chief cornerstone'?

18 "Whoever falls on that stone will be broken; but on whomever it falls, it will grind him to powder."

19 And the chief priests and the scribes that very hour sought to lay hands on Him, but they feared the people—for they knew that He had spoken this parable against them.

20 So they watched *Him*, and sent spies who pretended to be righ-

teous, that they might seize on His words, in order to deliver Him to the power and the authority of the governor.

21 And they asked Him, saying, "Teacher, we know that You say and teach rightly, and You do not show personal favoritism, but teach the way of God truly:

22 "Is it lawful for us to pay taxes to Caesar or not?"

23 But He perceived their craftiness, and said to them, "Why do you test Me?

24 "Show Me a denarius. Whose image and inscription does it have?" They answered and said, "Caesar's."

25 And He said to them, "Render therefore to Caesar the things that are Caesar's, and to God the things that are God's."

26 But they could not catch Him in His words in the presence of the people. And they marveled at His answer and kept silent.

27 Then some of the Sadducees, who deny that there is a resurrection, came to *Him* and asked Him,

28 saying: "Teacher, Moses wrote to us *that* if a man's brother dies, having a wife, and he dies without children, his brother should take his wife and raise up offspring for his brother.

29 "Now there were seven brothers. And the first took a wife, and died without children.

30 "And the second took her as wife, and he died childless.

31 "Then the third took her, and in like manner the seven also; and they left no children, and died.

32 "Last of all the woman died also.

33 "Therefore, in the resurrection, whose wife does she become? For all seven had her as wife."

34 And Jesus answered and said to them, "The sons of this age marry and are given in marriage.

35 "But those who are counted worthy to attain that age, and the

STEP 3

*Made a decision to turn our will and our lives
over to the care of God **as we understood Him.***

Luke 20:17, 18

There are only two kinds of people in the world—those who will
be broken and those who will be crushed. This does not sound like
a message of hope, but it is. The stone that either breaks or crushes
is the Lord Jesus. Those of us who fall before Him seeking His forgiveness and healing must first endure brokenness of spirit. We
must accept the fact that we are powerless to help ourselves and
that we have sinned against God and others. The humility required
to yield our lives to God and make amends for our wrongs calls for
a spirit of brokenness before the Lord. There is no room for pride.
But the reward is abundant life and eternal salvation.

Those who choose to retain their pride and reject Jesus as their
Rock have a bleak future indeed. Each of us must decide whether
Jesus will be our Rock of Refuge and Hope or the Rock of Remorse.

For further reading on Step 3, turn to page 197.

Daily Encouragement

DAY 83 READING: LUKE 20:1—21:38

A Thought for the New Day: Some people say Jesus never
laughed. But He must have had a broad grin sometimes. Can't
you see Jesus walking away from those scribes and elders as they
stood scratching their heads? They had fallen into their own
foolish trap (20:7, 8). Can you also see that it is wise not to play
games with God? (*Turn to page 191.*)

resurrection from the dead, neither marry nor are given in marriage;
36 "nor can they die anymore, for they are equal to the angels and are sons of God, being sons of the resurrection.

37 "Now even Moses showed in the *burning* bush *passage* that the dead are raised, when he called the Lord *'the God of Abraham, the God of Isaac, and the God of Jacob.'*

38 "For He is not the God of the dead but of the living, for all live to Him."

39 Then some of the scribes answered and said, "Teacher, You have spoken well."

40 But after that they dared not question Him anymore.

41 And He said to them, "How can they say that the Christ is David's Son?

42 "Now David himself said in the Book of Psalms,

'The LORD said to my Lord,
"Sit at My right hand,
43 Till I make Your enemies
    Your footstool." '

44 "David therefore calls Him *'Lord'*; how is He then his Son?"

45 Then, in the hearing of all the people, He said to His disciples,

46 "Beware of the scribes, who desire to walk in long robes, love greetings in the marketplaces, the best seats in the synagogues, and the best places at feasts,

47 "who devour widows' houses, and for a pretense make long prayers. These will receive greater condemnation."

21 Then He looked up and saw the rich putting their gifts into the treasury,

2 and He saw also a certain poor widow putting in two mites.

3 So He said, "Truly I say to you that this poor widow has put in more than all;

4 "for all these out of their abun-

dance have put in offerings for God, but she out of her poverty has put in all the livelihood that she had."

5 Then, as some spoke of the temple, how it was adorned with beautiful stones and donations, He said,

6 "As for these things which you see, the days will come in which not one stone shall be left upon another that shall not be thrown down."

7 And they asked Him, saying, "Teacher, but when will these things be? And what sign *will there be* when these things are about to take place?"

8 And He said: "Take heed that you not be deceived. For many will come in My name, saying, 'I am He,' and, 'The time has drawn near.' Therefore do not go after them.

9 "But when you hear of wars and commotions, do not be terrified; for these things must come to pass first, but the end *will not come* immediately."

10 Then He said to them, "Nation will rise against nation, and kingdom against kingdom.

11 "And there will be great earthquakes in various places, and famines and pestilences; and there will be fearful sights and great signs from heaven.

12 "But before all these things, they will lay their hands on you and persecute *you*, delivering *you* up to the synagogues and prisons, and you will be brought before kings and rulers for My name's sake.

13 "But it will turn out for you as an occasion for testimony.

14 "Therefore settle *it* in your hearts not to meditate beforehand on what you will answer;

15 "for I will give you a mouth and wisdom which all your adversaries will not be able to contradict or resist.

16 "You will be betrayed even by parents and brothers, relatives and friends; and they will send *some* of you to *your* death.

17 "And you will be hated by all for My name's sake.

18 "But not a hair of your head shall be lost.

19 "In your patience possess your souls.

20 "But when you see Jerusalem surrounded by armies, then know that its desolation is near.

21 "Then let those in Judea flee to the mountains, let those who are in the midst of her depart, and let not those who are in the country enter her.

22 "For these are the days of vengeance, that all things which are written may be fulfilled.

23 "But woe to those who are pregnant and to those who are nursing babies in those days! For there will be great distress in the land and wrath upon this people.

24 "And they will fall by the edge of the sword, and be led away captive into all nations. And Jerusalem will be trampled by Gentiles until the times of the Gentiles are fulfilled.

25 "And there will be signs in the sun, in the moon, and in the stars; and on the earth distress of nations, with perplexity, the sea and the waves roaring;

26 "men's hearts failing them from fear and the expectation of those things which are coming on the earth, for the powers of heaven will be shaken.

27 "Then they will see the Son of Man coming in a cloud with power and great glory.

28 "Now when these things begin to happen, look up and lift up your heads, because your redemption draws near."

29 And He spoke to them a parable: "Look at the fig tree, and all the trees.

30 "When they are already budding, you see and know for yourselves that summer is now near.

31 "So you, likewise, when you see these things happening, know that the kingdom of God is near.

32 "Assuredly, I say to you, this generation will by no means pass away till all things are fulfilled.

33 "Heaven and earth will pass away, but My words will by no means pass away.

34 "But take heed to yourselves, lest your hearts be weighed down with carousing, drunkenness, and cares of this life, and that Day come on you unexpectedly.

35 "For it will come as a snare on all those who dwell on the face of the whole earth.

36 "Watch therefore, and pray always that you may be counted worthy to escape all these things that will come to pass, and to stand before the Son of Man."

37 And in the daytime He was teaching in the temple, but at night He went out and stayed on the mountain called Olivet.

38 Then early in the morning all the people came to Him in the temple to hear Him.

22 Now the Feast of Unleavened Bread drew near, which is called Passover.

2 And the chief priests and the scribes sought how they might kill Him, for they feared the people.

3 Then Satan entered Judas, surnamed Iscariot, who was numbered among the twelve.

4 So he went his way and conferred with the chief priests and captains, how he might betray Him to them.

5 And they were glad, and agreed to give him money.

6 Then he promised and sought opportunity to betray Him to them in the absence of the multitude.

7 Then came the Day of Unleavened Bread, when the Passover must be killed.

8 And He sent Peter and John,

saying, "Go and prepare the Passover for us, that we may eat."

9 So they said to Him, "Where do You want us to prepare?"

10 And He said to them, "Behold, when you have entered the city, a man will meet you carrying a pitcher of water; follow him into the house which he enters.

11 "Then you shall say to the master of the house, 'The Teacher says to you, "Where is the guest room in which I may eat the Passover with My disciples?" '

12 "Then he will show you a large, furnished upper room; there make ready."

13 So they went and found it as He had said to them, and they prepared the Passover.

14 And when the hour had come, He sat down, and the twelve apostles with Him.

15 Then He said to them, "With *fervent* desire I have desired to eat this Passover with you before I suffer;

16 "for I say to you, I will no longer eat of it until it is fulfilled in the kingdom of God."

17 Then He took the cup, and gave thanks, and said, "Take this and divide *it* among yourselves;

18 "for I say to you, I will not drink of the fruit of the vine until the kingdom of God comes."

19 And He took bread, gave thanks and broke *it*, and gave *it* to them, saying, "This is My body which is given for you; do this in remembrance of Me."

20 Likewise He also *took* the cup after supper, saying, "This cup *is* the new covenant in My blood, which is shed for you.

21 "But behold, the hand of My betrayer *is* with Me on the table.

22 "And truly the Son of Man goes as it has been determined, but woe to that man by whom He is betrayed!"

23 Then they began to question among themselves, which of them it was who would do this thing.

24 But there was also rivalry among them, as to which of them should be considered the greatest.

25 And He said to them, "The kings of the Gentiles exercise lordship over them, and those who exercise authority over them are called 'benefactors.'

26 "But not so *among* you; on the contrary, he who is greatest among you, let him be as the younger, and he who governs as he who serves.

27 "For who *is* greater, he who sits at the table, or he who serves? *Is* it not he who sits at the table? Yet I am among you as the One who serves.

28 "But you are those who have continued with Me in My trials.

29 "And I bestow upon you a kingdom, just as My Father bestowed *one* upon Me,

30 "that you may eat and drink at My table in My kingdom, and sit on thrones judging the twelve tribes of Israel."

31 And the Lord said, "Simon, Simon! Indeed, Satan has asked for you, that he may sift *you* as wheat.

32 "But I have prayed for you, that your faith should not fail; and when you have returned to *Me*, strengthen your brethren."

33 But he said to Him, "Lord, I am ready to go with You, both to prison and to death."

34 Then He said, "I tell you, Peter, the rooster will not crow this day before you will deny three times that you know Me."

35 And He said to them, "When I sent you without money bag, sack, and sandals, did you lack anything?" So they said, "Nothing."

36 Then He said to them, "But now, he who has a money bag, let him take *it*, and likewise a sack; and he who has no sword, let him sell his garment and buy one.

37 "For I say to you that this

which is written must still be accomplished in Me: *'And He was numbered with the transgressors.'* For the things concerning Me have an end."

38 Then they said, "Lord, look, here *are* two swords." And He said to them, "It is enough."

39 And coming out, He went to the Mount of Olives, as He was accustomed, and His disciples also followed Him.

40 When He came to the place, He said to them, "Pray that you may not enter into temptation."

41 And He was withdrawn from them about a stone's throw, and He knelt down and prayed,

42 saying, "Father, if it is Your will, remove this cup from Me; nevertheless not My will, but Yours, be done."

43 Then an angel appeared to Him from heaven, strengthening Him.

44 And being in agony, He prayed more earnestly. And His sweat became like great drops of blood falling down to the ground.

45 When He rose up from prayer, and had come to His disciples, He found them sleeping from sorrow.

46 Then He said to them, "Why do you sleep? Rise and pray, lest you enter into temptation."

47 And while He was still speaking, behold, a multitude; and he who was called Judas, one of the twelve, went before them and drew near to Jesus to kiss Him.

48 But Jesus said to him, "Judas, are you betraying the Son of Man with a kiss?"

49 When those around Him saw what was going to happen, they said to Him, "Lord, shall we strike with the sword?"

50 And one of them struck the servant of the high priest and cut off his right ear.

51 But Jesus answered and said, "Permit even this." And He touched his ear and healed him.

52 Then Jesus said to the chief priests, captains of the temple, and the elders who had come to Him, "Have you come out, as against a robber, with swords and clubs?

53 "When I was with you daily in the temple, you did not try to seize Me. But this is your hour, and the power of darkness."

54 Then, having arrested Him, they led *Him* and brought Him into the high priest's house. And Peter followed at a distance.

55 Now when they had kindled a fire in the midst of the courtyard and sat down together, Peter sat among them.

56 And a certain servant girl, seeing him as he sat by the fire, looked intently at him and said, "This man was also with Him."

57 But he denied Him, saying, "Woman, I do not know Him."

58 And after a little while another saw him and said, "You also are of them." But Peter said, "Man, I am not!"

59 Then after about an hour had passed, another confidently affirmed, saying, "Surely this *fellow* also was with Him, for he is a Galilean."

60 But Peter said, "Man, I do not know what you are saying!" And immediately, while he was still speaking, the rooster crowed.

61 And the Lord turned and looked at Peter. And Peter remembered the word of the Lord, how He had said to him, "Before the rooster crows, you will deny Me three times."

62 Then Peter went out and wept bitterly.

63 Now the men who held Jesus mocked Him and beat Him.

64 And having blindfolded Him, they struck Him on the face and asked Him, saying, "Prophesy! Who is it that struck You?"

65 And many other things they blasphemously spoke against Him.

66 As soon as it was day, the elders of the people, both chief priests

STEP 11

STEP 11

*Sought through prayer and meditation to improve our conscious contact with God **as we understood Him,** praying only for knowledge of His will for us and the power to carry that out.*

Luke 22:42

"Not my will, but Yours, be done."

What makes us able to say these words and mean them with all our heart? We must know God intimately. Determination alone will never cause such complete surrender of heart, mind, and will. But hourly, daily, monthly, as we read God's Word and bow before Him in prayer, we will discover that our lives are changing. The more we know God the more we will trust Him. We will see how He loves us. We will discover how wise He is. We will stand in awe of His ability to work in circumstances and people. We will see how He can bring great blessings out of hard, unhappy situations. And, as we grow up into His love, we will find that our mind and heart and will agree "Your will be done."

For further reading on Step 11, turn to page 203.

Daily Encouragement

DAY 84 READING: LUKE 22:1—23:49

A Thought for the New Day: In instituting the Lord's Supper, Jesus pointed forward to a happy banquet in the coming kingdom (22:16). We should follow Jesus' direction and be forward-looking. The new Day will dawn, and we will sing the New Song in a feast that the emperors of Rome could never imagine. The King will be there in His beauty, and our joy will be boundless. Come, glad day of Coronation! *(Turn to page 195.)*

and scribes, came together and led Him into their council, saying,

67 "If You are the Christ, tell us." But He said to them, "If I tell you, you will by no means believe.

68 "And if I also ask *you*, you will by no means answer Me or let *Me* go.

69 "Hereafter the Son of Man will sit on the right hand of the power of God."

70 Then they all said, "Are You then the Son of God?" And He said to them, "You *rightly* say that I am."

71 And they said, "What further testimony do we need? For we have heard it ourselves from His own mouth."

23 Then the whole multitude of them arose and led Him to Pilate.

2 And they began to accuse Him, saying, "We found this *fellow* perverting the nation, and forbidding to pay taxes to Caesar, saying that He Himself is Christ, a King."

3 So Pilate asked Him, saying, "Are You the King of the Jews?" And He answered him and said, "*It is as* you say."

4 Then Pilate said to the chief priests and the crowd, "I find no fault in this Man."

5 But they were the more fierce, saying, "He stirs up the people, teaching throughout all Judea, beginning from Galilee to this place."

6 When Pilate heard of Galilee, he asked if the Man were a Galilean.

7 And as soon as he knew that He belonged to Herod's jurisdiction, he sent Him to Herod, who was also in Jerusalem at that time.

8 Now when Herod saw Jesus, he was exceedingly glad; for he had desired for a long *time* to see Him, because he had heard many things about Him, and he hoped to see some miracle done by Him.

9 Then he questioned Him with many words, but He answered him nothing.

10 And the chief priests and scribes stood and vehemently accused Him.

11 Then Herod, with his men of war, treated Him with contempt and mocked *Him*, arrayed Him in a gorgeous robe, and sent Him back to Pilate.

12 That very day Pilate and Herod became friends with each other, for before *that* they had been at enmity with each other.

13 Then Pilate, when he had called together the chief priests, the rulers, and the people,

14 said to them, "You have brought this Man to me, as one who misleads the people. And indeed, having examined *Him* in your presence, I have found no fault in this Man concerning those things of which you accuse Him;

15 "no, neither did Herod, for I sent you back to him; and indeed nothing worthy of death has been done by Him.

16 "I will therefore chastise Him and release *Him*"

17 (for it was necessary for him to release one to them at the feast).

18 And they all cried out at once, saying, "Away with this *Man*, and release to us Barabbas"—

19 who had been thrown into prison for a certain insurrection made in the city, and for murder.

20 Pilate, therefore, wishing to release Jesus, again called out to them.

21 But they shouted, saying, "Crucify *Him*, crucify Him!"

22 And he said to them the third time, "Why, what evil has He done? I have found no reason for death in Him. I will therefore chastise Him and let *Him* go."

23 But they were insistent, demanding with loud voices that He be crucified. And the voices of these men and of the chief priests prevailed.

24 So Pilate gave sentence that it should be as they requested.

25 And he released to them the one they requested, who for insurrection and murder had been thrown into prison; but he delivered Jesus to their will.

26 Now as they led Him away, they laid hold of a certain man, Simon a Cyrenian, who was coming from the country, and on him they laid the cross that he might bear *it* after Jesus.

27 And a great multitude of the people followed Him, and women who also mourned and lamented Him.

28 But Jesus, turning to them, said, "Daughters of Jerusalem, do not weep for Me, but weep for yourselves and for your children.

29 "For indeed the days are coming in which they will say, 'Blessed *are* the barren, *the* wombs that never bore, and *the* breasts which never nursed!'

30 "Then they will begin *'to say to the mountains, "Fall on us!" and to the hills, "Cover us!"' '*

31 "For if they do these things in the green wood, what will be done in the dry?"

32 There were also two others, criminals, led with Him to be put to death.

33 And when they had come to the place called Calvary, there they crucified Him, and the criminals, one on the right hand and the other on the left.

34 Then Jesus said, "Father, forgive them, for they do not know what they do." And they divided His garments and cast lots.

35 And the people stood looking on. But even the rulers with them sneered, saying, "He saved others; let Him save Himself if He is the Christ, the chosen of God."

36 And the soldiers also mocked Him, coming and offering Him sour wine,

37 and saying, "If You are the King of the Jews, save Yourself."

38 And an inscription also was written over Him in letters of Greek, Latin, and Hebrew:

THIS IS
THE KING OF THE JEWS.

39 Then one of the criminals who were hanged blasphemed Him, saying, "If You are the Christ, save Yourself and us."

40 But the other, answering, rebuked him, saying, "Do you not even fear God, seeing you are under the same condemnation?

41 "And we indeed justly, for we receive the due reward of our deeds; but this Man has done nothing wrong."

42 Then he said to Jesus, "Lord, remember me when You come into Your kingdom."

43 And Jesus said to him, "Assuredly, I say to you, today you will be with Me in Paradise."

44 And it was about the sixth hour, and there was darkness over all the earth until the ninth hour.

45 Then the sun was darkened, and the veil of the temple was torn in two.

46 And when Jesus had cried out with a loud voice, He said, "Father, *'into Your hands I commend My spirit.'*" And having said this, He breathed His last.

47 Now when the centurion saw what had happened, he glorified God, saying, "Certainly this was a righteous Man!"

48 And the whole crowd who came together to that sight, seeing what had been done, beat their breasts and returned.

49 But all His acquaintances, and the women who followed Him from Galilee, stood at a distance, watching these things.

50 And behold, *there was* a man named Joseph, a council member, a good and just man.

51 He had not consented to their counsel and deed. *He was* from Arimathea, a city of the Jews, who himself was also waiting for the kingdom of God.

52 This *man* went to Pilate and asked for the body of Jesus.

53 Then he took it down, wrapped it in linen, and laid it in a tomb *that was* hewn out of the rock, where no one had ever lain before.

54 That day was the Preparation, and the Sabbath drew near.

55 And the women who had come with Him from Galilee followed after, and they observed the tomb and how His body was laid.

56 Then they returned and prepared spices and fragrant oils. And they rested on the Sabbath according to the commandment.

STEP 10

24 Now on the first *day* of the week, very early in the morning, they, and certain *other women* with them, came to the tomb bringing the spices which they had prepared.

2 But they found the stone rolled away from the tomb.

3 Then they went in and did not find the body of the Lord Jesus.

4 And it happened, as they were greatly perplexed about this, that behold, two men stood by them in shining garments.

5 Then, as they were afraid and bowed *their* faces to the earth, they said to them, "Why do you seek the living among the dead?

6 "He is not here, but is risen! Remember how He spoke to you when He was still in Galilee,

7 "saying, 'The Son of Man must be delivered into the hands of sinful men, and be crucified, and the third day rise again.'"

8 And they remembered His words.

9 Then they returned from the tomb and told all these things to the eleven and to all the rest.

10 It was Mary Magdalene, Joanna, Mary *the mother* of James, and the other *women* with them, who told these things to the apostles.

11 And their words seemed to them like idle tales, and they did not believe them.

12 But Peter arose and ran to the tomb; and stooping down, he saw the linen cloths lying by themselves; and he departed, marveling to himself at what had happened.

13 Now behold, two of them were traveling that same day to a village called Emmaus, which was *about* seven miles from Jerusalem.

14 And they talked together of all these things which had happened.

15 So it was, while they conversed and reasoned, that Jesus Himself drew near and went with them.

16 But their eyes were restrained, so that they did not know Him.

17 And He said to them, "What kind of conversation *is* this that you have with one another as you walk and are sad?"

18 Then the one whose name was Cleopas answered and said to Him, "Are You the only stranger in Jerusalem, and have You not known the things which happened there in these days?"

19 And He said to them, "What things?" And they said to Him, "The things concerning Jesus of Nazareth, who was a Prophet mighty in deed and word before God and all the people,

20 "and how the chief priests and our rulers delivered Him to be condemned to death, and crucified Him.

21 "But we were hoping that it was He who was going to redeem Israel. Indeed, besides all this, today is the third day since these things happened.

22 "Yes, and certain women of our company, who arrived at the tomb early, astonished us.

23 "When they did not find His body, they came saying that they had also seen a vision of angels who said He was alive.

24 "And certain of those *who were* with us went to the tomb and found *it* just as the women had said; but Him they did not see."

25 Then He said to them, "O fool-

STEP 10

*Continued to take personal inventory
and when we were wrong promptly admitted it.*

Luke 24:1–35

In the three years that Jesus and the disciples were together, Christ told them pointedly on numerous occasions that He would have to suffer and die and then be raised again. Moreover, these men knew the Old Testament and were aware of prophecies concerning the suffering of the Messiah. How is it then that they became so frightened and confused when these prophecies were fulfilled? The answer is simple. They were blinded to spiritual truth because they had their own agenda for their Messiah. As verse 21 tells us, "We were hoping that it was He who was going to redeem Israel." The disciples' idea of redeeming Israel was to make Jesus an earthly king with an earthly kingdom. Likewise, we all want God to fit our agenda, but God has His own ways and His own timetable for His work. Sometimes He may ask us to simply wait and pray. Sometimes we will need His wisdom to see the truth of a situation. We must depend on Him and not on ourselves.

For further reading on Step 10, turn to page 211.

Daily Encouragement

DAY 85 READING: LUKE 23:50—24:35

A Thought for the New Day: The Savior had died earlier, and the hearts of the two men were heavy as they walked the seven-mile journey. Then Jesus came alongside, and as He walked with them their hearts "burned," although they did not recognize Him (24:32). In the pressing duties of life we may not always perceive Jesus' nearness, but let us store up His words so that our hearts also may be warmed along the way by His risen life in us. (*Turn to page 197.*)

ish ones, and slow of heart to believe in all that the prophets have spoken!

26 "Ought not the Christ to have suffered these things and to enter into His glory?"

27 And beginning at Moses and all the Prophets, He expounded to them in all the Scriptures the things concerning Himself.

28 Then they drew near to the village where they were going, and He indicated that He would have gone farther.

29 But they constrained Him, saying, "Abide with us, for it is toward evening, and the day is far spent." And He went in to stay with them.

30 Now it came to pass, as He sat at the table with them, that He took bread, blessed and broke *it*, and gave it to them.

31 Then their eyes were opened and they knew Him; and He vanished from their sight.

32 And they said to one another, "Did not our heart burn within us while He talked with us on the road, and while He opened the Scriptures to us?"

33 So they rose up that very hour and returned to Jerusalem, and found the eleven and those *who were* with them gathered together,

34 saying, "The Lord is risen indeed, and has appeared to Simon!"

35 And they told about the things *that had happened* on the road, and how He was known to them in the breaking of bread.

36 Now as they said these things, Jesus Himself stood in the midst of them, and said to them, "Peace to you."

37 But they were terrified and frightened, and supposed they had seen a spirit.

38 And He said to them, "Why are you troubled? And why do doubts arise in your hearts?

39 "Behold My hands and My feet, that it is I Myself. Handle Me and see, for a spirit does not have flesh and bones as you see I have."

40 When He had said this, He showed them His hands and His feet.

41 But while they still did not believe for joy, and marveled, He said to them, "Have you any food here?"

42 So they gave Him a piece of a broiled fish and some honeycomb.

43 And He took *it* and ate in their presence.

44 Then He said to them, "These *are* the words which I spoke to you while I was still with you, that all things must be fulfilled which were written in the Law of Moses and *the* Prophets and *the* Psalms concerning Me."

45 And He opened their understanding, that they might comprehend the Scriptures.

46 Then He said to them, "Thus it is written, and thus it was necessary for the Christ to suffer and to rise from the dead the third day,

47 "and that repentance and remission of sins should be preached in His name to all nations, beginning at Jerusalem.

48 "And you are witnesses of these things.

49 "Behold, I send the Promise of My Father upon you; but tarry in the city of Jerusalem until you are endued with power from on high."

50 And He led them out as far as Bethany, and He lifted up His hands and blessed them.

51 Now it came to pass, while He blessed them, that He was parted from them and carried up into heaven.

52 And they worshiped Him, and returned to Jerusalem with great joy,

53 and were continually in the temple praising and blessing God. Amen.

STEP 3

STEP 3

*Made a decision to turn our will and our lives
over to the care of God **as we understood Him.***

Luke 24:46, 47

Somewhere between Step 2 and Step 3 a person sincerely seeking God makes a wonderful discovery. God has paid the price for our sin. When Jesus allowed Himself to be sacrificed on the cross, His blood atoned for every sin we have ever committed or will commit. As soon as we experience repentance, we are given remission. "Repentance" means we agree with God's assessment of our situation: we are sinners who need a Savior. "Remission" is a big word for forgiveness or pardon: God will not demand payment from us because the debt has been paid by Jesus. But there is more good news! Christ's death gave us pardon, and now Christ's resurrection gives us power. The same mighty power that raised Jesus from the dead can be ours as we make the decision to allow God to have control of our lives.

For further reading on Step 3, turn to page 199.

Daily Encouragement

DAY 86 READING: LUKE 24:36–53

A Thought for the New Day: Jesus is no ghost (v. 39). His resurrection was a guarantee of our own risen bodies that, like His, will one day be full of endless life and health. God did not contrive a partial salvation, but a renewal of the whole universe to be as He dreamed it and peopled with those who would share His Son's triumph in every way. Yes, we will be like Him and see Him as He is. (*Turn to page 199.*)

IN the beginning was the Word, and the Word was with God, and the Word was God.

2 He was in the beginning with God.

3 All things were made through Him, and without Him nothing was made that was made.

4 In Him was life, and the life was the light of men.

5 And the light shines in the darkness, and the darkness did not comprehend it.

6 There was a man sent from God, whose name *was* John.

7 This man came for a witness, to bear witness of the Light, that all through him might believe.

8 He was not that Light, but *was sent* to bear witness of that Light.

9 *That was* the true Light which gives light to every man who comes into the world.

10 He was in the world, and the world was made through Him, and the world did not know Him.

11 He came to His own, and His own did not receive Him.

12 But as many as received Him, to them He gave the right to become children of God, *even* to those who believe in His name:

13 who were born, not of blood, nor of the will of the flesh, nor of the will of man, but of God.

14 And the Word became flesh and dwelt among us, and we beheld His glory, the glory as of the only begotten of the Father, full of grace and truth.

15 John bore witness of Him and cried out, saying, "This was He of whom I said, 'He who comes after me is preferred before me, for He was before me.'"

16 And of His fullness we have all received, and grace for grace.

17 For the law was given through Moses, *but* grace and truth came through Jesus Christ.

18 No one has seen God at any time. The only begotten Son, who is in the bosom of the Father, He has declared *Him.*

19 Now this is the testimony of John, when the Jews sent priests and Levites from Jerusalem to ask him, "Who are you?"

20 He confessed, and did not deny, but confessed, "I am not the Christ."

21 And they asked him, "What then? Are you Elijah?" He said, "I am not." "Are you the Prophet?" And he answered, "No."

22 Then they said to him, "Who are you, that we may give an answer to those who sent us? What do you say about yourself?"

23 He said: "I *am*

'The voice of one crying in the wilderness:
"Make straight the way of the LORD,"'

as the prophet Isaiah said."

24 Now those who were sent were from the Pharisees.

25 And they asked him, saying, "Why then do you baptize if you are not the Christ, nor Elijah, nor the Prophet?"

26 John answered them, saying, "I baptize with water, but there stands One among you whom you do not know.

27 "It is He who, coming after me, is preferred before me, whose sandal strap I am not worthy to loose."

28 These things were done in Bethabara beyond the Jordan, where John was baptizing.

29 The next day John saw Jesus coming toward him, and said, "Behold! The Lamb of God who takes away the sin of the world!

30 "This is He of whom I said, 'After me comes a Man who is pre-

STEP 3

*Made a decision to turn our will and our lives
over to the care of God **as we understood Him.***

John 1:12, 13

People devise theories and carry out programs. Theories and programs are good at helping us "turn over a new leaf." They are good at giving us incentive and education, which can help us change our minds or broaden our understanding. But they can go no farther. Only God can change a heart. When a heart weighed down by sorrow, sin, and suffering receives Jesus as Savior and "believes in His name," there is total, eternal transformation. The person to whom that heart belongs has become a child of God. The spiritual part of that person, which was dead because of sin, has now come to life. This cannot happen by being born into the right family or by simply determining to make it happen. God alone creates in us the desire to know Him and believe in Him.

For further reading on Step 3, turn to page 209.

Daily Encouragement

DAY 87 READING: JOHN 1:1—2:25

A Thought for the New Day: Wherever He is, Jesus brings joy, and a wedding was the ideal occasion on which to do so (2:10). After all, this is the real desire that God had for each of us—that in every aspect and circumstance of life "[our] joy may be full." Jesus has brought supreme happiness to millions, and this is a grand purpose for you and me, also. (*Turn to page 203.*)

ferred before me, for He was before me.'

31 "I did not know Him; but that He should be revealed to Israel, therefore I came baptizing with water."

32 And John bore witness, saying, "I saw the Spirit descending from heaven like a dove, and He remained upon Him.

33 "I did not know Him, but He who sent me to baptize with water said to me, 'Upon whom you see the Spirit descending, and remaining on Him, this is He who baptizes with the Holy Spirit.'

34 "And I have seen and testified that this is the Son of God."

35 Again, the next day, John stood with two of his disciples.

36 And looking at Jesus as He walked, he said, "Behold the Lamb of God!"

37 The two disciples heard him speak, and they followed Jesus.

38 Then Jesus turned, and seeing them following, said to them, "What do you seek?" They said to Him, "Rabbi" (which is to say, when translated, Teacher), "where are You staying?"

39 He said to them, "Come and see." They came and saw where He was staying, and remained with Him that day (now it was about the tenth hour).

40 One of the two who heard John *speak*, and followed Him, was Andrew, Simon Peter's brother.

41 He first found his own brother Simon, and said to him, "We have found the Messiah" (which is translated, the Christ).

42 And he brought him to Jesus. Now when Jesus looked at him, He said, "You are Simon the son of Jonah. You shall be called Cephas" (which is translated, A Stone).

43 The following day Jesus wanted to go to Galilee, and He found Philip and said to him, "Follow Me."

44 Now Philip was from Bethsaida, the city of Andrew and Peter.

45 Philip found Nathanael and said to him, "We have found Him of whom Moses in the law, and also the prophets, wrote—Jesus of Nazareth, the son of Joseph."

46 And Nathanael said to him, "Can anything good come out of Nazareth?" Philip said to him, "Come and see."

47 Jesus saw Nathanael coming toward Him, and said of him, "Behold, an Israelite indeed, in whom is no guile!"

48 Nathanael said to Him, "How do You know me?" Jesus answered and said to him, "Before Philip called you, when you were under the fig tree, I saw you."

49 Nathanael answered and said to Him, "Rabbi, You are the Son of God! You are the King of Israel!"

50 Jesus answered and said to him, "Because I said to you, 'I saw you under the fig tree,' do you believe? You will see greater things than these."

51 And He said to him, "Most assuredly, I say to you, hereafter you shall see heaven open, and the angels of God ascending and descending upon the Son of Man."

2 On the third day there was a wedding in Cana of Galilee, and the mother of Jesus was there.

2 Now both Jesus and His disciples were invited to the wedding.

3 And when they ran out of wine, the mother of Jesus said to Him, "They have no wine."

4 Jesus said to her, "Woman, what does your concern have to do with Me? My hour has not yet come."

5 His mother said to the servants, "Whatever He says to you, do *it*."

6 Now there were set there six waterpots of stone, according to the manner of purification of the Jews, containing twenty or thirty gallons apiece.

7 Jesus said to them, "Fill the waterpots with water." And they filled them up to the brim.

8 And He said to them, "Draw

some out now, and take *it* to the master of the feast." And they took *it*.

9 When the master of the feast had tasted the water that was made wine, and did not know where it came from (but the servants who had drawn the water knew), the master of the feast called the bridegroom.

10 And he said to him, "Every man at the beginning sets out the good wine, and when the *guests* have well drunk, then that *which is* inferior; *but* you have kept the good wine until now."

11 This beginning of signs Jesus did in Cana of Galilee, and manifested His glory; and His disciples believed in Him.

12 After this He went down to Capernaum, He, His mother, His brothers, and His disciples; and they did not stay there many days.

13 Now the Passover of the Jews was at hand, and Jesus went up to Jerusalem.

14 And He found in the temple those who sold oxen and sheep and doves, and the moneychangers doing business.

15 When He had made a whip of cords, He drove them all out of the temple, with the sheep and the oxen, and poured out the changers' money and overturned the tables.

16 And He said to those who sold doves, "Take these things away! Do not make My Father's house a house of merchandise!"

17 Then His disciples remembered that it was written, *"Zeal for Your house has eaten Me up."*

18 So the Jews answered and said to Him, "What sign do You show to us, since You do these things?"

19 Jesus answered and said to them, "Destroy this temple, and in three days I will raise it up."

20 Then the Jews said, "It has taken forty-six years to build this temple, and will You raise it up in three days?"

21 But He was speaking of the temple of His body.

22 Therefore, when He had risen from the dead, His disciples remembered that He had said this to them; and they believed the Scripture and the word which Jesus had said.

23 Now when He was in Jerusalem at the Passover, during the feast, many believed in His name when they saw the signs which He did.

24 But Jesus did not commit Himself to them, because He knew all *men,*

25 and had no need that anyone should testify of man, for He knew what was in man.

3 There was a man of the Pharisees named Nicodemus, a ruler of the Jews.

2 This man came to Jesus by night and said to Him, "Rabbi, we know that You are a teacher come from God; for no one can do these signs that You do unless God is with him."

3 Jesus answered and said to him, "Most assuredly, I say to you, unless one is born again, he cannot see the kingdom of God."

4 Nicodemus said to Him, "How can a man be born when he is old? Can he enter a second time into his mother's womb and be born?"

5 Jesus answered, "Most assuredly, I say to you, unless one is born of water and the Spirit, he cannot enter the kingdom of God.

6 "That which is born of the flesh is flesh, and that which is born of the Spirit is spirit.

7 "Do not marvel that I said to you, 'You must be born again.'

8 "The wind blows where it wishes, and you hear the sound of it, but cannot tell where it comes from and where it goes. So is everyone who is born of the Spirit."

9 Nicodemus answered and said to Him, "How can these things be?"

10 Jesus answered and said to him,

"Are you the teacher of Israel, and do not know these things?

11 "Most assuredly, I say to you, We speak what We know and testify what We have seen, and you do not receive Our witness.

12 "If I have told you earthly things and you do not believe, how will you believe if I tell you heavenly things?

13 "No one has ascended to heaven but He who came down from heaven, *that is,* the Son of Man who is in heaven.

STEP 2

14 "And as Moses lifted up the serpent in the wilderness, even so must the Son of Man be lifted up,

15 "that whoever believes in Him should not perish but have eternal life.

16 "For God so loved the world that He gave His only begotten Son, that whoever believes in Him should not perish but have everlasting life.

17 "For God did not send His Son into the world to condemn the world, but that the world through Him might be saved.

18 "He who believes in Him is not condemned; but he who does not believe is condemned already, because he has not believed in the name of the only begotten Son of God.

19 "And this is the condemnation, that the light has come into the world, and men loved darkness rather than light, because their deeds were evil.

20 "For everyone practicing evil hates the light and does not come to the light, lest his deeds should be exposed.

21 "But he who does the truth comes to the light, that his deeds may be clearly seen, that they have been done in God."

22 After these things Jesus and His disciples came into the land of Judea, and there He remained with them and baptized.

23 Now John also was baptizing in Aenon near Salim, because there was much water there. And they came and were baptized.

24 For John had not yet been thrown into prison.

25 Then there arose a dispute between *some* of John's disciples and the Jews about purification.

26 And they came to John and said to him, "Rabbi, He who was with you beyond the Jordan, to whom you have testified—behold, He is baptizing, and all are coming to Him!"

27 John answered and said, "A man can receive nothing unless it has been given to him from heaven.

28 "You yourselves bear me witness, that I said, 'I am not the Christ,' but, 'I have been sent before Him.'

29 "He who has the bride is the bridegroom; but the friend of the bridegroom, who stands and hears him, rejoices greatly because of the bridegroom's voice. Therefore this joy of mine is fulfilled.

30 "He must increase, but I *must* decrease.

STEP 11

31 "He who comes from above is above all; he who is of the earth is earthly and speaks of the earth. He who comes from heaven is above all.

32 "And what He has seen and heard, that He testifies; and no one receives His testimony.

33 "He who has received His testimony has certified that God is true.

34 "For He whom God has sent speaks the words of God, for God does not give the Spirit by measure.

35 "The Father loves the Son, and has given all things into His hand.

36 "He who believes in the Son has everlasting life; and he who does not believe the Son shall not see life, but the wrath of God abides on him."

STEP
11

*Sought through prayer and meditation to improve our conscious contact with God **as we understood Him,** praying only for knowledge of His will for us and the power to carry that out.*

John 3:30

John the Baptist was feared by the Pharisees, beloved by the common people, and respected by a devoted group of disciples. In the job of prophet he was doing pretty well. But John knew from the beginning that his main calling in life was to prepare the way for Someone greater. To that end, John's message and attitude were always the same: he pointed people to Jesus. He was not looking for acclaim for himself and even encouraged disciples who were following him to follow Jesus instead (John 1:35–37).

John's attitude should be ours, as well. Because we have come so far in our recovery, there may be people who truly look up to us and seem to set us on a pedestal. We must take every opportunity to point these people to the Lamb of God. As we daily seek to glorify and honor the Lord Jesus through our words, attitudes, and actions, our self-centeredness will decrease and His power in our lives will increase.

For further reading on Step 11, turn to page 205.

Daily
Encouragement

DAY 88 READING: JOHN 3:1–36

A Thought for the New Day: A "Pollyanna" is a dreamer who sees nothing but good everywhere. However, you do not need to be a Pollyanna to see, above all, that God loves His world—and you—very much. What more could He do to convince you of this than to send His very best-loved One to bear all your sins and sorrows? (v. 16). Turn away from dark thoughts, and let His love fill you today. *(Turn to page 205.)*

4 Therefore, when the Lord knew that the Pharisees had heard that Jesus made and baptized more disciples than John

2 (though Jesus Himself did not baptize, but His disciples),

3 He left Judea and departed again to Galilee.

4 But He needed to go through Samaria.

5 So He came to a city of Samaria which is called Sychar, near the plot of ground that Jacob gave to his son Joseph.

6 Now Jacob's well was there. Jesus therefore, being wearied from *His* journey, sat thus by the well. It was about the sixth hour.

7 A woman of Samaria came to draw water. Jesus said to her, "Give Me a drink."

8 For His disciples had gone away into the city to buy food.

9 Then the woman of Samaria said to Him, "How is it that You, being a Jew, ask a drink from me, a Samaritan woman?" For Jews have no dealings with Samaritans.

10 Jesus answered and said to her, "If you knew the gift of God, and who it is who says to you, 'Give Me a drink,' you would have asked Him, and He would have given you living water."

11 The woman said to Him, "Sir, You have nothing to draw with, and the well is deep. Where then do You get that living water?

12 "Are You greater than our father Jacob, who gave us the well, and drank from it himself, as well as his sons and his livestock?"

STEP 11 13 Jesus answered and said to her, "Whoever drinks of this water will thirst again,

14 "but whoever drinks of the water that I shall give him will never thirst. But the water that I shall give him will become in him a fountain of water springing up into everlasting life."

15 The woman said to Him, "Sir, give me this water, that I may not thirst, nor come here to draw."

16 Jesus said to her, "Go, call your husband, and come here."

17 The woman answered and said, "I have no husband." Jesus said to her, "You have well said, 'I have no husband,'

18 "for you have had five husbands, and the one whom you now have is not your husband; in that you spoke truly."

19 The woman said to Him, "Sir, I perceive that You are a prophet.

20 "Our fathers worshiped on this mountain, and you *Jews* say that in Jerusalem is the place where one ought to worship."

21 Jesus said to her, "Woman, believe Me, the hour is coming when you will neither on this mountain, nor in Jerusalem, worship the Father.

22 "You worship what you do not know; we know what we worship, for salvation is of the Jews.

23 "But the hour is coming, and now is, when the true worshipers will worship the Father in spirit and truth; for the Father is seeking such to worship Him.

24 "God *is* Spirit, and those who worship Him must worship in spirit and truth."

25 The woman said to Him, "I know that Messiah is coming" (who is called Christ). "When He comes, He will tell us all things."

26 Jesus said to her, "I who speak to you am *He*."

27 And at this *point* His disciples came, and they marveled that He talked with a woman; yet no one said, "What do You seek?" or, "Why are You talking with her?"

28 The woman then left her waterpot, went her way into the city, and said to the men,

29 "Come, see a Man who told me all things that I ever did. Could this be the Christ?"

30 Then they went out of the city and came to Him.

31 In the meantime His disciples urged Him, saying, "Rabbi, eat."

32 But He said to them, "I have

*Sought through prayer and meditation to improve our conscious contact with God **as we understood Him,** praying only for knowledge of His will for us and the power to carry that out.*

John 4:13, 14

For most of us, life has been a thirsty experience. We have thirsted for love, security, self-worth, and peace. Many of us have tried to quench that thirst through excessive control, addictions, and other inappropriate behavior patterns. But finally we have come to know the One who can satisfy the deepest thirst of every human spirit. We have put our trust in Jesus Christ who gives to us, as He did to the woman at the well, the fountain of water springing up into everlasting life.

How do we participate in the joy and peace of everlasting life right now? The Lord speaking through Paul in Ephesians 5:26 connects water with the Word of God. Just as water is essential to our physical lives for quenching our thirst and cleansing us, so the Word of God satisfies and purifies our spiritual lives. Through it, we come to a better knowledge of God and His will for us, and our relationship with Him is nourished and enriched.

For further reading on Step 11, turn to page 239.

Daily Encouragement

DAY 89 READING: JOHN 4:1–30

A Thought for the New Day: The woman was a Samaritan, and Samaritans were hated by the Jews. But Jesus had a surprise for the woman: He accepted her (vv. 25, 26). He would be her Messiah, too. Some people have been so rejected by everyone else that they cannot imagine the Savior reaching out to them. Jesus wants to surprise them with the greatest of all Christmas gifts: He wants to claim them as His friends forever. (*Turn to page 207.*)

food to eat of which you do not know."

33 Therefore the disciples said to one another, "Has anyone brought Him *anything* to eat?"

STEP 12 34 Jesus said to them, "My food is to do the will of Him who sent Me, and to finish His work.

35 "Do you not say, 'There are still four months and *then* comes the harvest'? Behold, I say to you, lift up your eyes and look at the fields, for they are already white for harvest!

36 "And he who reaps receives wages, and gathers fruit for eternal life, that both he who sows and he who reaps may rejoice together.

37 "For in this the saying is true: 'One sows and another reaps.'

38 "I sent you to reap that for which you have not labored; others have labored, and you have entered into their labors."

39 And many of the Samaritans of that city believed in Him because of the word of the woman who testified, "He told me all that I *ever* did."

40 So when the Samaritans had come to Him, they urged Him to stay with them; and He stayed there two days.

41 And many more believed because of His own word.

42 Then they said to the woman, "Now we believe, not because of what you said, for we have heard for ourselves and know that this is indeed the Christ, the Savior of the world."

43 Now after the two days He departed from there and went to Galilee.

44 For Jesus Himself testified that a prophet has no honor in his own country.

45 So when He came to Galilee, the Galileans received Him, having seen all the things He did in Jerusalem at the feast; for they also had gone to the feast.

46 So Jesus came again to Cana of Galilee where He had made the water wine. And there was a certain nobleman whose son was sick at Capernaum.

47 When he heard that Jesus had come out of Judea into Galilee, he went to Him and implored Him to come down and heal his son, for he was at the point of death.

48 Then Jesus said to him, "Unless you *people* see signs and wonders, you will by no means believe."

49 The nobleman said to Him, "Sir, come down before my child dies!"

50 Jesus said to him, "Go your way; your son lives." So the man believed the word that Jesus spoke to him, and he went his way.

51 And as he was now going down, his servants met him and told *him*, saying, "Your son lives!"

52 Then he inquired of them the hour when he got better. And they said to him, "Yesterday at the seventh hour the fever left him."

53 So the father knew that *it was* at the same hour in which Jesus said to him, "Your son lives." And he himself believed, and his whole household.

54 This again *is* the second sign *that* Jesus did when He had come out of Judea into Galilee.

5 After this there was a feast of the Jews, and Jesus went up to Jerusalem.

2 Now there is in Jerusalem by the Sheep *Gate* a pool, which is called in Hebrew, Bethesda, having five porches.

3 In these lay a great multitude of sick people, blind, lame, paralyzed, waiting for the moving of the water.

4 For an angel went down at a certain time into the pool and stirred up the water; then whoever stepped in first, after the stirring of the water, was made well of whatever disease he had.

5 Now a certain man was there who had an infirmity thirty-eight years.

STEP 12

*Having had a spiritual awakening as the result
of these steps, we tried to carry this message to others,
and to practice these principles in all our affairs.*

John 4:34–36

Our pain and resulting struggle with dependencies has taught us many things. Although we may not have expressed it quite this way, most of us have discovered that "the fields . . . are already white for harvest." Jesus uses this metaphor to show us that everywhere we go, we will find hungry, receptive hearts—hearts just ready and waiting to be harvested with the wonderful message of Hope that we carry. This in itself is cause for joy. But there is a promise here, as well. Whether we simply sow the Seed of Life or actually have the privilege of reaping precious souls for eternity, we are promised rewards (wages) given to us by God Himself. These rewards mean earthly blessings now and blessings in heaven, too. Ask God today to open your eyes and ears and heart to those who are ready to hear His message.

For further reading on Step 12, turn to page 231.

Daily Encouragement

DAY 90 READING: JOHN 4:31–54

A Thought for the New Day: The Samaritan woman did not scare people with compulsive or fanatical behavior. She was so filled with gladness at having met her Messiah that all who knew her could see the beautiful, new quality of life she possessed (v. 39). This kind of "true religion" is contagious. Just cultivating the Savior's friendship produces the same infectious quality in each of us. (*Turn to page 209.*)

6 When Jesus saw him lying there, and knew that he already had been *in that condition* a long time, He said to him, "Do you want to be made well?"

7 The sick man answered Him, "Sir, I have no man to put me into the pool when the water is stirred up; but while I am coming, another steps down before me."

8 Jesus said to him, "Rise, take up your bed and walk."

9 And immediately the man was made well, took up his bed, and walked. And that day was the Sabbath.

10 The Jews therefore said to him who was cured, "It is the Sabbath; it is not lawful for you to carry *your* bed."

11 He answered them, "He who made me well said to me, 'Take up your bed and walk.'"

12 Then they asked him, "Who is the Man who said to you, 'Take up your bed and walk'?"

13 But the one who was healed did not know who it was, for Jesus had withdrawn, a multitude being in *that* place.

14 Afterward Jesus found him in the temple, and said to him, "See, you have been made well. Sin no more, lest a worse thing come upon you."

15 The man departed and told the Jews that it was Jesus who had made him well.

16 For this reason the Jews persecuted Jesus, and sought to kill Him, because He had done these things on the Sabbath.

17 But Jesus answered them, "My Father has been working until now, and I have been working."

18 Therefore the Jews sought all the more to kill Him, because He not only broke the Sabbath, but also said that God was His Father, making Himself equal with God.

19 Then Jesus answered and said to them, "Most assuredly, I say to you, the Son can do nothing of Himself, but what He sees the Father do; for whatever He does, the Son also does in like manner.

20 "For the Father loves the Son, and shows Him all things that He Himself does; and He will show Him greater works than these, that you may marvel.

21 "For as the Father raises the dead and gives life to *them*, even so the Son gives life to whom He will.

22 "For the Father judges no one, but has committed all judgment to the Son,

23 "that all should honor the Son just as they honor the Father. He who does not honor the Son does not honor the Father who sent Him.

24 "Most assuredly, I say to you, he who hears My word and believes in Him who sent Me has everlasting life, and shall not come into judgment, but has passed from death into life.

25 "Most assuredly, I say to you, the hour is coming, and now is, when the dead will hear the voice of the Son of God; and those who hear will live.

26 "For as the Father has life in Himself, so He has granted the Son to have life in Himself,

27 "and has given Him authority to execute judgment also, because He is the Son of Man.

28 "Do not marvel at this; for the hour is coming in which all who are in the graves will hear His voice

29 "and come forth—those who have done good, to the resurrection of life, and those who have done evil, to the resurrection of condemnation.

30 "I can of Myself do nothing. As I hear, I judge; and My judgment is righteous, because I do not seek My own will but the will of the Father who sent Me.

31 "If I bear witness of Myself, My witness is not true.

STEP 3

*Made a decision to turn our will and our lives
over to the care of God **as we understood Him.***

John 5:24

When we accepted Jesus as Savior, we "passed from death into life." Before we came to trust Him, we were totally powerless against the pain in our lives, our dependencies, our shame, anger, and depression. We could find ways to temporarily ease the pain, but we had no power to overcome it. We were what the Bible calls "dead in trespasses and sins" (Eph. 2:1). Physically we were alive, but spiritually (in our souls) we were dead, and dead people have no power. However, when we believed in Jesus, the Holy Spirit of God breathed His Eternal Life into our souls. People who are alive spiritually have the power of God's Spirit indwelling them. We no longer need to be slaves to our problems. Our guilt and shame are gone because God no longer judges us for our sins. Real life is now ours.

For further reading on Step 3, turn to page 213.

Daily Encouragement

DAY 91 READING: JOHN 5:1–47

A Thought for the New Day: Who doesn't want "eternal life"? But such life is not merely an infinitely long existence. If it were, it could soon become boring and even downright miserable after ten thousand years or so. Jesus offers us something better that He uniquely possesses—life that is infinitely sublime. The best part is that this "peace of God, which surpasses all understanding" (Phil. 4:7) begins here and now in a living relationship with Him. (*Turn to page 211.*)

32 "There is another who bears witness of Me, and I know that the witness which He witnesses of Me is true.

33 "You have sent to John, and he has borne witness to the truth.

34 "Yet I do not receive testimony from man, but I say these things that you may be saved.

35 "He was the burning and shining lamp, and you were willing for a time to rejoice in his light.

36 "But I have a greater witness than John's; for the works which the Father has given Me to finish—the very works that I do—bear witness of Me, that the Father has sent Me.

37 "And the Father Himself, who sent Me, has testified of Me. You have neither heard His voice at any time, nor seen His form.

38 "But you do not have His word abiding in you, because whom He sent, Him you do not believe.

39 "You search the Scriptures, for in them you think you have eternal life; and these are they which testify of Me.

40 "But you are not willing to come to Me that you may have life.

41 "I do not receive honor from men.

42 "But I know you, that you do not have the love of God in you.

43 "I have come in My Father's name, and you do not receive Me; if another comes in his own name, him you will receive.

44 "How can you believe, who receive honor from one another, and do not seek the honor that *comes* from the only God?

45 "Do not think that I shall accuse you to the Father; there is *one* who accuses you—Moses, in whom you trust.

46 "For if you believed Moses, you would believe Me; for he wrote about Me.

47 "But if you do not believe his writings, how will you believe My words?"

6 After these things Jesus went over the Sea of Galilee, which is *the Sea* of Tiberias.

2 Then a great multitude followed Him, because they saw His signs which He performed on those who were diseased.

3 And Jesus went up on a mountain, and there He sat with His disciples.

4 Now the Passover, a feast of the Jews, was near.

5 Then Jesus lifted up *His* eyes, and seeing a great multitude coming toward Him, He said to Philip, "Where shall we buy bread, that these may eat?"

6 But this He said to test him, for He Himself knew what He would do.

7 Philip answered Him, "Two hundred denarii worth of bread is not sufficient for them, that every one of them may have a little."

8 One of His disciples, Andrew, Simon Peter's brother, said to Him,

9 "There is a lad here who has five barley loaves and two small fish, but what are they among so many?"

10 Then Jesus said, "Make the people sit down." Now there was much grass in the place. So the men sat down, in number about five thousand.

11 And Jesus took the loaves, and when He had given thanks He distributed *them* to the disciples, and the disciples to those sitting down; and likewise of the fish, as much as they wanted.

12 So when they were filled, He said to His disciples, "Gather up the fragments that remain, so that nothing is lost."

13 Therefore they gathered *them* up, and filled twelve baskets with the fragments of the five barley loaves which were left over by those who had eaten.

14 Then those men, when they had seen the sign that Jesus did, said, "This is truly the Prophet who is to come into the world."

STEP 10

*Continued to take personal inventory
and when we were wrong promptly admitted it.*

John 6:15–20

The disciples made a big mistake. They started off without Jesus. We are not told why they were in such a hurry to get to Capernaum. Maybe they figured that since this would be such a quick trip they need not bother waiting for Jesus. Maybe they figured they would be back before He even missed them. What they did not count on was the storm. The sky had not looked so ominous when they had started out. Who would have guessed? These are the famous last words of many believers who find themselves suddenly swamped by the winds of temptation and the waves of trial. Their lives were floating along so smoothly, they figured they did not need to bother Jesus about things. If spending time in prayer and Bible study has slipped down on your priority scale, correct the situation now before the seas of trouble find you unprepared.

For further reading on Step 10, turn to page 227.

Daily Encouragement

DAY 92 READING: JOHN 6:1–21

A Thought for the New Day: Sometimes our environment seems to threaten us and the foundations beneath us. Our health breaks down or financial distress pursues us. In such times we can take courage in knowing that the Master of circumstances walks beside us (v. 20). Then fear loses its grip as we begin to enjoy the settled confidence that God is in charge of our every environment. (*Turn to page 213.*)

STEP 10

15 Therefore when Jesus perceived that they were about to come and take Him by force to make Him king, He departed again to a mountain by Himself alone.

16 And when evening came, His disciples went down to the sea,

17 got into the boat, and went over the sea toward Capernaum. And it was now dark, and Jesus had not come to them.

18 Then the sea arose because a great wind was blowing.

19 So when they had rowed about three or four miles, they saw Jesus walking on the sea and drawing near the boat; and they were afraid.

20 But He said to them, "It is I; do not be afraid."

21 Then they willingly received Him into the boat, and immediately the boat was at the land where they were going.

22 On the following day, when the people who were standing on the other side of the sea saw that there was no other boat there, except that one which His disciples had entered, and that Jesus had not entered the boat with His disciples, but His disciples had gone away alone—

23 however, other boats came from Tiberias, near the place where they ate bread after the Lord had given thanks—

24 when the people therefore saw that Jesus was not there, nor His disciples, they also got into boats and came to Capernaum, seeking Jesus.

25 And when they found Him on the other side of the sea, they said to Him, "Rabbi, when did You come here?"

26 Jesus answered them and said, "Most assuredly, I say to you, you seek Me, not because you saw the signs, but because you ate of the loaves and were filled.

27 "Do not labor for the food which perishes, but for the food which endures to everlasting life, which the Son of Man will give you, because God the Father has set His seal on Him."

STEP 2

28 Then they said to Him, "What shall we do, that we may work the works of God?"

29 Jesus answered and said to them, "This is the work of God, that you believe in Him whom He sent."

30 Therefore they said to Him, "What sign will You perform then, that we may see it and believe You? What work will You do?

31 "Our fathers ate the manna in the desert; as it is written, *'He gave them bread from heaven to eat.'*"

32 Then Jesus said to them, "Most assuredly, I say to you, Moses did not give you the bread from heaven, but My Father gives you the true bread from heaven.

33 "For the bread of God is He who comes down from heaven and gives life to the world."

34 Then they said to Him, "Lord, give us this bread always."

STEP 3

35 And Jesus said to them, "I am the bread of life. He who comes to Me shall never hunger, and he who believes in Me shall never thirst.

36 "But I said to you that you have seen Me and yet do not believe.

37 "All that the Father gives Me will come to Me, and the one who comes to Me I will by no means cast out.

38 "For I have come down from heaven, not to do My own will, but the will of Him who sent Me.

39 "This is the will of the Father who sent Me, that of all He has given Me I should lose nothing, but should raise it up at the last day.

40 "And this is the will of Him who sent Me, that everyone who sees the Son and believes in Him may have everlasting life; and I will raise him up at the last day."

41 The Jews then murmured against Him, because He said, "I

*Made a decision to turn our will and our lives
over to the care of God **as we understood Him.***

John 6:35–40

Addictions are attempts to fill unmet needs in our lives. Many of
us have developed these problems because we experienced rejection from someone who was extremely important to us. We substituted addictive behaviors to fill the void in our lives. Now we may
be fearful of relationships because we have been hurt in the past.
But here in verse 37, God promises us the security and joy of an
everlasting and unconditional relationship. Jesus truly is the Bread
of Life who can fill every need we have. When we come to Him,
putting our trust in Him alone, He says, "I will by no means cast
out." There will never come a time when Jesus rejects us or comes
to care less about us. We may need to know His discipline from
time to time, but it will be the perfect, loving discipline of an all-
wise Father who never stops loving us unconditionally. In giving
ourselves to Him we find the freedom to become the best we can
be.

For further reading on Step 3, turn to page 219.

Daily Encouragement

DAY 93 READING: JOHN 6:22–51

A Thought for the New Day: When He taught us to pray, Jesus
included our "daily bread." Food is essential for survival, and
Jesus understood that fact. But more necessary is a day-by-day
relationship with Christ, who calls Himself "the bread of life"
(v. 48). The life that Jesus refers to is that which transcends
mere survival in the world. The One who called the universe
into existence has residing in Himself totally fulfilling eternal
life, and He offers it to us. (*Turn to page 215.*)

am the bread which came down from heaven."

42 And they said, "Is not this Jesus, the son of Joseph, whose father and mother we know? How is it then that He says, 'I have come down from heaven'?"

43 Jesus therefore answered and said to them, "Do not murmur among yourselves.

44 "No one can come to Me unless the Father who sent Me draws him; and I will raise him up at the last day.

45 "It is written in the prophets, *'And they shall all be taught by God.'* Therefore everyone who has heard and learned from the Father comes to Me.

46 "Not that anyone has seen the Father, except He who is from God; He has seen the Father.

47 "Most assuredly, I say to you, he who believes in Me has everlasting life.

48 "I am the bread of life.

49 "Your fathers ate the manna in the wilderness, and are dead.

50 "This is the bread which comes down from heaven, that one may eat of it and not die.

51 "I am the living bread which came down from heaven. If anyone eats of this bread, he will live forever; and the bread that I shall give is My flesh, which I shall give for the life of the world."

52 The Jews therefore quarreled among themselves, saying, "How can this *Man* give us *His* flesh to eat?"

53 Then Jesus said to them, "Most assuredly, I say to you, unless you eat the flesh of the Son of Man and drink His blood, you have no life in you.

54 "Whoever eats My flesh and drinks My blood has eternal life, and I will raise him up at the last day.

55 "For My flesh is food indeed, and My blood is drink indeed.

56 "He who eats My flesh and

drinks My blood abides in Me, and I in him.

57 "As the living Father sent Me, and I live because of the Father, so he who feeds on Me will live because of Me.

58 "This is the bread which came down from heaven—not as your fathers ate the manna, and are dead. He who eats this bread will live forever."

59 These things He said in the synagogue as He taught in Capernaum.

60 Therefore many of His disciples, when they heard *this*, said, "This is a hard saying; who can understand it?"

61 When Jesus knew in Himself that His disciples murmured about this, He said to them, "Does this offend you?

62 "*What* then if you should see the Son of Man ascend where He was before?

63 "It is the Spirit who gives life; the flesh profits nothing. The words that I speak to you are spirit, and *they* are life.

STEP 2

64 "But there are some of you who do not believe." For Jesus knew from the beginning who they were who did not believe, and who would betray Him.

65 And He said, "Therefore I have said to you that no one can come to Me unless it has been granted to him by My Father."

66 From that *time* many of His disciples went back and walked with Him no more.

67 Then Jesus said to the twelve, "Do you also want to go away?"

68 Then Simon Peter answered Him, "Lord, to whom shall we go? You have the words of eternal life.

STEP 2

69 "Also we have come to believe and know that You are the Christ, the Son of the living God."

70 Jesus answered them, "Did I not choose you, the twelve, and one of you is a devil?"

71 He spoke of Judas Iscariot, *the*

STEP 2

Came to believe that a Power greater than ourselves could restore us to sanity.

John 6:63

Addiction and codependency are often defined as an unhealthy reliance on the control of exterior things in order to fill interior needs. Scripture cautions against this manipulation of the material and physical realms, the flesh, as a means of satisfying our deepest spiritual and emotional hungers. The belief that these hungers can be addressed on a physical, material, or financial level alone is its own special form of insanity.

Step 2 promises that we shall be restored to sanity as we turn away from codependent engagement with the flesh and turn toward the revitalizing life source of the Spirit. Indeed, we shall experience nothing less than a rebirth.

Our recovery literature describes this rebirth and infilling of the Holy Spirit in the following way: "As we felt new power flow in, as we enjoyed peace of mind, as we discovered we could face life successfully, as we became conscious of His presence, we began to lose our fear of today, tomorrow or the hereafter. We were reborn" (*Alcoholics Anonymous*, p. 63).

For further reading on Step 2, turn to page 221.

Daily Encouragement

DAY 94 READING: JOHN 6:52–71

A Thought for the New Day: You do not need to spend much time thinking about Jesus' words before you begin to realize that no one has ever spoken as He has. Even self-willed, impulsive Peter understood, having heard Jesus speak, that there was nowhere else to go for "the words of eternal life" that Jesus spoke (v. 68). God speaks with unique effect, and, when we allow Him, His word penetrates all our defenses. Then we become His willing captives. (*Turn to page 217.*)

son of Simon, for it was he who would betray Him, being one of the twelve.

7 After these things Jesus walked in Galilee; for He did not want to walk in Judea, because the Jews sought to kill Him.

2 Now the Jews' Feast of Tabernacles was at hand.

3 His brothers therefore said to Him, "Depart from here and go into Judea, that Your disciples also may see the works that You are doing.

4 "For no one does anything in secret while he himself seeks to be known openly. If You do these things, show Yourself to the world."

5 For even His brothers did not believe in Him.

6 Then Jesus said to them, "My time has not yet come, but your time is always ready.

7 "The world cannot hate you, but it hates Me because I testify of it that its works are evil.

8 "You go up to this feast. I am not yet going up to this feast, for My time has not yet fully come."

9 When He had said these things to them, He remained in Galilee.

10 But when His brothers had gone up, then He also went up to the feast, not openly, but as it were in secret.

11 Then the Jews sought Him at the feast, and said, "Where is He?"

12 And there was much murmuring among the people concerning Him. Some said, "He is good"; others said, "No, on the contrary, He deceives the people."

13 However, no one spoke openly of Him for fear of the Jews.

14 Now about the middle of the feast Jesus went up into the temple and taught.

15 And the Jews marveled, saying, "How does this Man know letters, having never studied?"

16 Jesus answered them and said, "My doctrine is not Mine, but His who sent Me.

17 "If anyone wants to do His will, he shall know concerning the doctrine, whether it is from God or *whether* I speak on My own *authority*.

18 "He who speaks from himself seeks his own glory; but He who seeks the glory of the One who sent Him is true, and no unrighteousness is in Him.

19 "Did not Moses give you the law, and *yet* none of you keeps the law? Why do you seek to kill Me?"

20 The people answered and said, "You have a demon. Who is seeking to kill You?"

21 Jesus answered and said to them, "I did one work, and you all marvel.

22 "Moses therefore gave you circumcision (not that it is from Moses, but from the fathers), and you circumcise a man on the Sabbath.

23 "If a man receives circumcision on the Sabbath, so that the law of Moses should not be broken, are you angry with Me because I made a man completely well on the Sabbath?

24 "Do not judge according to appearance, but judge with righteous judgment."   STEP 4

25 Then some of them from Jerusalem said, "Is this not He whom they seek to kill?

26 "But look! He speaks boldly, and they say nothing to Him. Do the rulers know indeed that this is truly the Christ?

27 "However, we know where this Man is from; but when the Christ comes, no one knows where He is from."

28 Then Jesus cried out, as He taught in the temple, saying, "You both know Me, and you know where I am from; and I have not come of Myself, but He who sent Me is true, whom you do not know.

29 "But I know Him, for I am from Him, and He sent Me."

30 Then they sought to take Him; but no one laid a hand on Him,

STEP 4

Made a searching and fearless moral inventory of ourselves.

John 7:24

Much of our energy until now has been focused on "keeping up appearances." We have worked hard to hide not only our addictions, but the results of those addictions, as well. We have tricked ourselves into believing that if we can look "right" and act "right" and talk "right," we will be accepted. We are not alone. Most of the world bases its judgment on appearances. But now Jesus asks us to take off our masks of denial and pretense and to evaluate ourselves by His true judgment. He asks us to gaze beneath the surface and be willing to acknowledge honestly what we see there.

For further reading on Step 4, turn to page 248.

Daily Encouragement

DAY 95 READING: JOHN 7:1–31

A Thought for the New Day: How can I understand what God is saying to me? Much of what He says has always been so out of step with the common view of life and the world. Jesus gives me the key: I must *want* "to do His will" (v. 17). Are you seeking the vision to see real values? Then you will surely understand God's words, and you will never part with them for anything. (*Turn to page 219.*)

because His hour had not yet come.

31 And many of the people believed in Him, and said, "When the Christ comes, will He do more signs than these which this *Man* has done?"

32 The Pharisees heard the crowd murmuring these things concerning Him, and the Pharisees and the chief priests sent officers to take Him.

33 Then Jesus said to them, "I shall be with you a little while longer, and *then* I go to Him who sent Me.

34 "You will seek Me and not find *Me*, and where I am you cannot come."

35 Then the Jews said among themselves, "Where does He intend to go that we shall not find Him? Does He intend to go to the Dispersion among the Greeks and teach the Greeks?

36 "What is this thing that He said, 'You will seek Me and not find Me, and where I am you cannot come'?"

STEP 2

37 On the last day, that great *day* of the feast, Jesus stood and cried out, saying, "If anyone thirsts, let him come to Me and drink.

38 "He who believes in Me, as the Scripture has said, out of his heart will flow rivers of living water."

39 But this He spoke concerning the Spirit, whom those believing in Him would receive; for the Holy Spirit was not yet *given*, because Jesus was not yet glorified.

40 Therefore many from the crowd, when they heard this saying, said, "Truly this is the Prophet."

41 Others said, "This is the Christ," but some said, "Will the Christ come out of Galilee?

42 "Has not the Scripture said that the Christ comes from the seed of David and from the town of Bethlehem, where David was?"

43 So there was a division among the people because of Him.

44 Now some of them wanted to take Him, but no one laid hands on Him.

45 Then the officers came to the chief priests and Pharisees, who said to them, "Why have you not brought Him?"

46 The officers answered, "No man ever spoke like this Man!"

47 Then the Pharisees answered them, "Are you also deceived?

48 "Have any of the rulers or the Pharisees believed in Him?

49 "But this crowd that does not know the law is accursed."

50 Nicodemus (he who came to Jesus by night, being one of them) said to them,

51 "Does our law judge a man before it hears him and knows what he is doing?"

52 They answered and said to him, "Are you also from Galilee? Search and look, for no prophet has arisen out of Galilee."

53 And everyone went to his *own* house.

8 But Jesus went to the Mount of Olives.

STEP 3

2 But early in the morning He came again into the temple, and all the people came to Him; and He sat down and taught them.

3 Then the scribes and Pharisees brought to Him a woman caught in adultery. And when they had set her in the midst,

4 they said to Him, "Teacher, this woman was caught in adultery, in the very act.

5 "Now Moses, in the law, commanded us that such should be stoned. But what do You say?"

6 This they said, testing Him, that they might have *something* of which to accuse Him. But Jesus stooped down and wrote on the ground with *His* finger, as though He did not hear.

7 So when they continued asking Him, He raised Himself up and said to them, "He who is without sin among you, let him throw a stone at her first."

STEP 3

*Made a decision to turn our will and our lives over to the care of God **as we understood Him.***

John 8:1–11

When we have struggled with dependencies, we are very aware of condemnation. We know the bitterness of self-condemnation, and we go to great lengths to make our lives appear to be other than what they are in order to avoid the condemnation of others. The woman taken in adultery knew the pain and humiliation that accompanied the icy stare of condemnation. But she learned a wonderful truth. God does not deal in condemnation. His commodities are mercy, love, and grace, which He bestows freely upon any soul who comes to Him. As long as we live on this earth, we will never hear His voice of condemnation. We will only hear His call to walk righteously with Him by faith.

For further reading on Step 3, turn to page 233.

Daily Encouragement

DAY 96 READING: JOHN 7:32—8:11

A Thought for the New Day: Thirsty people come to Jesus (7:37). They are not thirsty for water but for inner satisfaction and peace. Such people find these qualities fully in Him. In a parched and arid world, He is the very Water of Life. Not only that, says Jesus, but out of our hearts will flow "rivers of living water" that refresh the lives of other thirsty people as well. (*Turn to page 221.*)

8 And again He stooped down and wrote on the ground.

9 Then those who heard *it*, being convicted by *their* conscience, went out one by one, beginning with the oldest *even* to the last. And Jesus was left alone, and the woman standing in the midst.

10 When Jesus had raised Himself up and saw no one but the woman, He said to her, "Woman, where are those accusers of yours? Has no one condemned you?"

11 She said, "No one, Lord." And Jesus said to her, "Neither do I condemn you; go and sin no more."

STEP 2

12 Then Jesus spoke to them again, saying, "I am the light of the world. He who follows Me shall not walk in darkness, but have the light of life."

13 The Pharisees therefore said to Him, "You bear witness of Yourself; Your witness is not true."

14 Jesus answered and said to them, "Even if I bear witness of Myself, My witness is true, for I know where I came from and where I am going; but you do not know where I come from and where I am going.

15 "You judge according to the flesh; I judge no one.

16 "And yet if I do judge, My judgment is true; for I am not alone, but I *am* with the Father who sent Me.

17 "It is also written in your law that the testimony of two men is true.

18 "I am One who bears witness of Myself, and the Father who sent Me bears witness of Me."

19 Then they said to Him, "Where is Your Father?" Jesus answered, "You know neither Me nor My Father. If you had known Me, you would have known My Father also."

20 These words Jesus spoke in the treasury, as He taught in the temple; and no one laid hands on Him, for His hour had not yet come.

21 Then Jesus said to them again, "I am going away, and you will seek Me, and will die in your sin. Where I go you cannot come."

22 So the Jews said, "Will He kill Himself, because He says, 'Where I go you cannot come'?"

23 And He said to them, "You are from beneath; I am from above. You are of this world; I am not of this world.

24 "Therefore I said to you that you will die in your sins; for if you do not believe that I am *He*, you will die in your sins."

25 Then they said to Him, "Who are You?" And Jesus said to them, "Just what I have been saying to you from the beginning.

26 "I have many things to say and to judge concerning you, but He who sent Me is true; and I speak to the world those things which I heard from Him."

27 They did not understand that He spoke to them of the Father.

28 Then Jesus said to them, "When you lift up the Son of Man, then you will know that I am *He*, and *that* I do nothing of Myself; but as My Father taught Me, I speak these things.

29 "And He who sent Me is with Me. The Father has not left Me alone, for I always do those things that please Him."

30 As He spoke these words, many believed in Him.

STEP 11

31 Then Jesus said to those Jews who believed Him, "If you abide in My word, you are My disciples indeed.

32 "And you shall know the truth, and the truth shall make you free."

33 They answered Him, "We are Abraham's descendants, and have never been in bondage to anyone. How *can* you say, 'You will be made free'?"

34 Jesus answered them, "Most assuredly, I say to you, whoever commits sin is a slave of sin.

35 "And a slave does not abide in

STEP 2

*Came to believe that a Power greater than ourselves
could restore us to sanity.*

John 8:12

For centuries people have looked for ways to illuminate the darkness. The true, total darkness of night can be a terrifying thing. Caught out in it unprepared, we find ourselves stumbling over ruts or rocks; noises unnerve us because we cannot locate their source; and the chill of the air quickly penetrates our bodies. Perhaps Jesus was thinking of these things when He promised that the soul who followed Him would not walk in darkness. He realizes that our minds and hearts can falter while searching for the right path. He is aware that we tend to live in fear of unnamed and unseen things. And He knows how we shiver in the darkness of cold, unhappy relationships.

If this describes your experience until now, you only need to respond to Jesus' call to see the first rays of dawn. When we turn in faith to Him, we will have the light of life.

For further reading on Step 2, turn to page 225.

Daily Encouragement

DAY 97 READING: JOHN 8:12—9:41

A Thought for the New Day: Many bound in dark prisons are nevertheless free because they have finished with the slavery of falsehood. Christ, who is Himself the Truth, stands in their midst to remind them that they are not alone in their privations. Their freedom consists in the infallible knowledge that God will not desert them nor His cause (8:32). *Lord, whatever our place in life, grant us Your presence continually that we may be faithful to the truth.* (Turn to page 225.)

the house forever, *but* a son abides forever.

36 "Therefore if the Son makes you free, you shall be free indeed.

37 "I know that you are Abraham's descendants, but you seek to kill Me, because My word has no place in you.

38 "I speak what I have seen with My Father, and you do what you have seen with your father."

39 They answered and said to Him, "Abraham is our father." Jesus said to them, "If you were Abraham's children, you would do the works of Abraham.

40 "But now you seek to kill Me, a Man who has told you the truth which I heard from God. Abraham did not do this.

41 "You do the deeds of your father." Then they said to Him, "We were not born of fornication; we have one Father—God."

42 Jesus said to them, "If God were your Father, you would love Me, for I proceeded forth and came from God; nor have I come of Myself, but He sent Me.

43 "Why do you not understand My speech? Because you are not able to listen to My word.

44 "You are of *your* father the devil, and the desires of your father you want to do. He was a murderer from the beginning, and *does not* stand in the truth, because there is no truth in him. When he speaks a lie, he speaks from his own *resources*, for he is a liar and the father of it.

45 "But because I tell the truth, you do not believe Me.

46 "Which of you convicts Me of sin? And if I tell the truth, why do you not believe Me?

47 "He who is of God hears God's words; therefore you do not hear, because you are not of God."

48 Then the Jews answered and said to Him, "Do we not say rightly that You are a Samaritan and have a demon?"

49 Jesus answered, "I do not have a demon; but I honor My Father, and you dishonor Me.

50 "And I do not seek My *own* glory; there is One who seeks and judges.

51 "Most assuredly, I say to you, if anyone keeps My word he shall never see death."

52 Then the Jews said to Him, "Now we know that You have a demon! Abraham is dead, and the prophets; and You say, 'If anyone keeps My word he shall never taste death.'

53 "Are You greater than our father Abraham, who is dead? And the prophets are dead. Who do You make Yourself out to be?"

54 Jesus answered, "If I honor Myself, My honor is nothing. It is My Father who honors Me, of whom you say that He is your God.

55 "Yet you have not known Him, but I know Him. And if I say, 'I do not know Him,' I shall be a liar like you; but I do know Him and keep His word.

56 "Your father Abraham rejoiced to see My day, and he saw *it* and was glad."

57 Then the Jews said to Him, "You are not yet fifty years old, and have You seen Abraham?"

58 Jesus said to them, "Most assuredly, I say to you, before Abraham was, I AM."

59 Then they took up stones to throw at Him; but Jesus hid Himself and went out of the temple, going through the midst of them, and so passed by.

9 Now as *Jesus* passed by, He saw a man who was blind from birth.

2 And His disciples asked Him, saying, "Rabbi, who sinned, this man or his parents, that he was born blind?"

3 Jesus answered, "Neither this man nor his parents sinned, but that the works of God should be revealed in him.

4 "I must work the works of Him who sent Me while it is day; *the* night is coming when no one can work.

5 "As long as I am in the world, I am the light of the world."

6 When He had said these things, He spat on the ground and made clay with the saliva; and He anointed the eyes of the blind man with the clay.

7 And He said to him, "Go, wash in the pool of Siloam" (which is translated, Sent). So he went and washed, and came back seeing.

8 Therefore the neighbors and those who previously had seen that he was blind said, "Is not this he who sat and begged?"

9 Some said, "This is he." Others said, "He is like him." He said, "I am *he*."

10 Therefore they said to him, "How were your eyes opened?"

11 He answered and said, "A Man called Jesus made clay and anointed my eyes and said to me, 'Go to the pool of Siloam and wash.' So I went and washed, and I received sight."

12 Then they said to him, "Where is He?" He said, "I do not know."

13 They brought him who formerly was blind to the Pharisees.

14 Now it was a Sabbath when Jesus made the clay and opened his eyes.

15 Then the Pharisees also asked him again how he had received his sight. He said to them, "He put clay on my eyes, and I washed, and I see."

16 Therefore some of the Pharisees said, "This Man is not from God, because He does not keep the Sabbath." Others said, "How can a man who is a sinner do such signs?" And there was a division among them.

17 They said to the blind man again, "What do you say about Him because He opened your eyes?" He said, "He is a prophet."

18 But the Jews did not believe concerning him, that he had been blind and received his sight, until they called the parents of him who had received his sight.

19 And they asked them, saying, "Is this your son, who you say was born blind? How then does he now see?"

20 His parents answered them and said, "We know that this is our son, and that he was born blind;

21 "but by what means he now sees we do not know, or who opened his eyes we do not know. He is of age; ask him. He will speak for himself."

22 His parents said these *things* because they feared the Jews, for the Jews had agreed already that if anyone confessed *that* He *was* Christ, he would be put out of the synagogue.

23 Therefore his parents said, "He is of age; ask him."

24 So they again called the man who was blind, and said to him, "Give God the glory! We know that this Man is a sinner."

25 He answered and said, "Whether He is a sinner *or not* I do not know. One thing I know: that though I was blind, now I see."

26 Then they said to him again, "What did He do to you? How did He open your eyes?"

27 He answered them, "I told you already, and you did not listen. Why do you want to hear *it* again? Do you also want to become His disciples?"

28 Then they reviled him and said, "You are His disciple, but we are Moses' disciples.

29 "We know that God spoke to Moses; *as for* this *fellow*, we do not know where He is from."

30 The man answered and said to them, "Why, this is a marvelous thing, that you do not know where He is from, and *yet* He has opened my eyes!

31 "Now we know that God does

not hear sinners; but if anyone is a worshiper of God and does His will, He hears him.

32 "Since the world began it has been unheard of that anyone opened the eyes of one who was born blind.

33 "If this Man were not from God, He could do nothing."

34 They answered and said to him, "You were completely born in sins, and are you teaching us?" And they cast him out.

35 Jesus heard that they had cast him out; and when He had found him, He said to him, "Do you believe in the Son of God?"

36 He answered and said, "Who is He, Lord, that I may believe in Him?"

37 And Jesus said to him, "You have both seen Him and it is He who is talking with you."

38 Then he said, "Lord, I believe!" And he worshiped Him.

39 And Jesus said, "For judgment I have come into this world, that those who do not see may see, and that those who see may be made blind."

40 Then *some* of the Pharisees who were with Him heard these words, and said to Him, "Are we blind also?"

41 Jesus said to them, "If you were blind, you would have no sin; but now you say, 'We see.' Therefore your sin remains.

10 "Most assuredly, I say to you, he who does not enter the sheepfold by the door, but climbs up some other way, the same is a thief and a robber.

2 "But he who enters by the door is the shepherd of the sheep.

3 "To him the doorkeeper opens, and the sheep hear his voice; and he calls his own sheep by name and leads them out.

4 "And when he brings out his own sheep, he goes before them; and the sheep follow him, for they know his voice.

5 "Yet they will by no means follow a stranger, but will flee from him, for they do not know the voice of strangers."

6 Jesus used this illustration, but they did not understand the things which He spoke to them.

7 Then Jesus said to them again, "Most assuredly, I say to you, I am the door of the sheep.

8 "All who *ever* came before Me are thieves and robbers, but the sheep did not hear them.

9 "I am the door. If anyone enters by Me, he will be saved, and will go in and out and find pasture.

10 "The thief does not come except to steal, and to kill, and to destroy. I have come that they may have life, and that they may have *it* more abundantly.

STEP 2

11 "I am the good shepherd. The good shepherd gives His life for the sheep.

12 "But *he who is* a hireling and not the shepherd, one who does not own the sheep, sees the wolf coming and leaves the sheep and flees; and the wolf catches the sheep and scatters them.

13 "The hireling flees because he is a hireling and does not care about the sheep.

14 "I am the good shepherd; and I know My *sheep*, and am known by My own.

15 "As the Father knows Me, even so I know the Father; and I lay down My life for the sheep.

16 "And other sheep I have which are not of this fold; them also I must bring, and they will hear My voice; and there will be one flock *and* one shepherd.

17 "Therefore My Father loves Me, because I lay down My life that I may take it again.

18 "No one takes it from Me, but I lay it down of Myself. I have power to lay it down, and I have power to take it again. This command I have received from My Father."

19 Therefore there was a division

STEP 2

Came to believe that a Power greater than ourselves could restore us to sanity.

John 10:9, 10

Often the Bible likens human beings to sheep. There are many similarities here, some of which are not too flattering. Sheep, for example, are not very self-sufficient. To thrive, they need a benevolent master. We human beings want to believe that we are self-sufficient, but the truth is that we, too, are lost without the Master. We have discovered that the dependency or addiction that we have allowed to control us is actually a thief, which can only steal and kill and destroy. To remain with the thief is to die, because his pasture is poisoned and his water nothing but a mirage. But the Good Shepherd calls to us, opening the door to abundant pastures and cool, refreshing waters. To believe in Him is to step through that door and into the safety and blessing of His fold.

For further reading on Step 2, turn to page 229.

Daily Encouragement

DAY 98 READING: JOHN 10:1–18

A Thought for the New Day: Jesus was no religious quack who callously deceived His followers by clever words and empty promises. Had Jesus been anyone other than the Son of God He might have shirked the responsibility His Father had given Him to lay down His life for us. However, throughout His career He stayed on the path that led to the Cross (v. 11). Doesn't His pure conduct nerve you, also, for the battle of life? (*Turn to page 227.*)

again among the Jews because of these sayings.

20 And many of them said, "He has a demon and is mad. Why do you listen to Him?"

21 Others said, "These are not the words of one who has a demon. Can a demon open the eyes of the blind?"

22 Now it was the Feast of Dedication in Jerusalem, and it was winter.

23 And Jesus walked in the temple, in Solomon's porch.

24 Then the Jews surrounded Him and said to Him, "How long do You keep us in doubt? If You are the Christ, tell us plainly."

25 Jesus answered them, "I told you, and you do not believe. The works that I do in My Father's name, they bear witness of Me.

26 "But you do not believe, because you are not of My sheep, as I said to you.

STEP 10
27 "My sheep hear My voice, and I know them, and they follow Me.

28 "And I give them eternal life, and they shall never perish; neither shall anyone snatch them out of My hand.

29 "My Father, who has given *them* to Me, is greater than all; and no one is able to snatch *them* out of My Father's hand.

30 "I and *My* Father are one."

31 Then the Jews took up stones again to stone Him.

32 Jesus answered them, "Many good works I have shown you from My Father. For which of those works do you stone Me?"

33 The Jews answered Him, saying, "For a good work we do not stone You, but for blasphemy, and because You, being a Man, make Yourself God."

34 Jesus answered them, "Is it not written in your law, *'I said, "You are gods"'*?

35 "If He called them gods, to whom the word of God came (and the Scripture cannot be broken),

36 "do you say of Him whom the Father sanctified and sent into the world, 'You are blaspheming,' because I said, 'I am the Son of God'?

37 "If I do not do the works of My Father, do not believe Me;

38 "but if I do, though you do not believe Me, believe the works, that you may know and believe that the Father *is* in Me, and I in Him."

39 Therefore they sought again to seize Him, but He escaped out of their hand.

40 And He went away again beyond the Jordan to the place where John was baptizing at first, and there He stayed.

41 Then many came to Him and said, "John performed no sign, but all the things that John spoke about this Man were true."

42 And many believed in Him there.

11 Now a certain *man* was sick, Lazarus of Bethany, the town of Mary and her sister Martha.

2 It was *that* Mary who anointed the Lord with fragrant oil and wiped His feet with her hair, whose brother Lazarus was sick.

3 Therefore the sisters sent to Him, saying, "Lord, behold, he whom You love is sick."

4 When Jesus heard *that*, He said, "This sickness is not unto death, but for the glory of God, that the Son of God may be glorified through it."

5 Now Jesus loved Martha and her sister and Lazarus.

6 So, when He heard that he was sick, He stayed two more days in the place where He was.

7 Then after this He said to *the* disciples, "Let us go to Judea again."

8 *The* disciples said to Him, "Rabbi, lately the Jews sought to stone You, and are You going there again?"

9 Jesus answered, "Are there not twelve hours in the day? If anyone

STEP 10

*Continued to take personal inventory
and when we were wrong promptly admitted it.*

John 10:27–30

Fear of rejection is a cruel taskmaster. When we trust in Jesus as our Savior and Shepherd, the death knell for that fear is sounded. It can no longer bind us. It may try to haunt us from time to time, but as we continue to walk with our precious Shepherd, our communion with Him will empower us to erase those apparitions. The more we hear His voice and realize His limitless love for us, the more trust will replace fear. We have an eternal, unchanging place of safety and security. We are ever held in the hand of the All-Powerful Good Shepherd.

If the ghost fears of rejection begin to bother us, the promises of these verses can help to reprogram our minds and hearts. Once we belong to God, He will never reject us. He will faithfully, loyally love us and hold us in the palm of His almighty hand.

For further reading on Step 10, turn to page 245.

Daily Encouragement

DAY 99 READING: JOHN 10:19–42

A Thought for the New Day: We belong to Jesus forever. No one can alter the arrangement that has been made between you and the Savior: "Neither shall anyone snatch them out of My hand" (vv. 27–29). What confidence this promise should give you in your journey through life! Sheep sometimes wander away from their shepherd, but a good shepherd takes great pains to find them and bring them back from the dark places where they were lost. Jesus is that Good Shepherd to us. (*Turn to page 229.*)

walks in the day, he does not stumble, because he sees the light of this world.

10 "But if one walks in the night, he stumbles, because the light is not in him."

11 These things He said, and after that He said to them, "Our friend Lazarus sleeps, but I go that I may wake him up."

12 Then His disciples said, "Lord, if he sleeps he will get well."

13 However, Jesus spoke of his death, but they thought that He was speaking about taking rest in sleep.

14 Then Jesus said to them plainly, "Lazarus is dead.

15 "And I am glad for your sakes that I was not there, that you may believe. Nevertheless let us go to him."

16 Then Thomas, who is called Didymus, said to his fellow disciples, "Let us also go, that we may die with Him."

17 So when Jesus came, He found that he had already been in the tomb four days.

18 Now Bethany was near Jerusalem, about two miles away.

19 And many of the Jews had joined the women around Martha and Mary, to comfort them concerning their brother.

20 Then Martha, as soon as she heard that Jesus was coming, went and met Him, but Mary was sitting in the house.

21 Then Martha said to Jesus, "Lord, if You had been here, my brother would not have died.

22 "But even now I know that whatever You ask of God, God will give You."

23 Jesus said to her, "Your brother will rise again."

24 Martha said to Him, "I know that he will rise again in the resurrection at the last day."

25 Jesus said to her, "I am the resurrection and the life. He who believes in Me, though he may die, he shall live.

26 "And whoever lives and believes in Me shall never die. Do you believe this?"

27 She said to Him, "Yes, Lord, I believe that You are the Christ, the Son of God, who is to come into the world."

28 And when she had said these things, she went her way and secretly called Mary her sister, saying, "The Teacher has come and is calling for you."

29 As soon as she heard *that*, she arose quickly and came to Him.

30 Now Jesus had not yet come into the town, but was in the place where Martha met Him.

31 Then the Jews who were with her in the house, and comforting her, when they saw that Mary rose up quickly and went out, followed her, saying, "She is going to the tomb to weep there."

32 Then, when Mary came where Jesus was, and saw Him, she fell down at His feet, saying to Him, "Lord, if You had been here, my brother would not have died."

33 Therefore, when Jesus saw her weeping, and the Jews who came with her weeping, He groaned in the spirit and was troubled.

34 And He said, "Where have you laid him?" They said to Him, "Lord, come and see."

35 Jesus wept.

36 Then the Jews said, "See how He loved him!"

37 And some of them said, "Could not this Man, who opened the eyes of the blind, also have kept this man from dying?"

38 Then Jesus, again groaning in Himself, came to the tomb. It was a cave, and a stone lay against it.

39 Jesus said, "Take away the stone." Martha, the sister of him who was dead, said to Him, "Lord, by this time there is a stench, for he has been *dead* four days."

40 Jesus said to her, "Did I not say to you that if you would believe you would see the glory of God?"

41 Then they took away the stone

*Came to believe that a Power greater than ourselves
could restore us to sanity.*

John 11:25, 26

"Out of death issues life." Is this just a phrase meant to comfort the bereaved at funerals? No, it is infinitely more. It is the hinge upon which the door of Scripture swings. Indeed, to die is to live when we believe what Jesus said concerning Himself here. Jesus' claims are obvious and absolute. He claims to be the God who has power over death itself. He overcame death by rising physically from the grave, and He promises to everyone who believes in Him eternal life, also. But this is only part of the reason we have for rejoicing. The great message is that all that He is for our future, He is now, as well. The power that will resurrect those who believe is also the power that can give new life now on this earth.

Are you tired of the endless cycle of pain, dependency, and guilt? Are you ready for Jesus to change your heart and renew your mind? Trust in Him today and discover His power.

For further reading on Step 2, turn to page 235.

Daily Encouragement

DAY 100 READING: JOHN 11:1–44

A Thought for the New Day: Like many others of her time Martha probably did not fully understand the mission of Jesus. Although she believed in a future resurrection, she had failed to see that her hope of new life was embodied in the very Person of Jesus. Does it seem a riddle to us that Jesus says, "Whoever lives and believes in Me shall never die"? (vv. 25, 26). Christ has conquered our last enemy. If you are living in Him, you shall never taste death, but only pass into *life*. (*Turn to page 231.*)

from the place where the dead man was lying. And Jesus lifted up *His* eyes and said, "Father, I thank You that You have heard Me.

42 "And I know that You always hear Me, but because of the people who are standing by I said *this*, that they may believe that You sent Me."

43 Now when He had said these things, He cried with a loud voice, "Lazarus, come forth!"

44 And he who had died came out bound hand and foot with grave-clothes, and his face was wrapped with a cloth. Jesus said to them, "Loose him, and let him go."

45 Then many of the Jews who had come to Mary, and had seen the things Jesus did, believed in Him.

46 But some of them went away to the Pharisees and told them the things Jesus did.

47 Then the chief priests and the Pharisees gathered a council and said, "What shall we do? For this Man works many signs.

48 "If we let Him alone like this, everyone will believe in Him, and the Romans will come and take away both our place and nation."

49 And one of them, Caiaphas, being high priest that year, said to them, "You know nothing at all,

50 "nor do you consider that it is expedient for us that one man should die for the people, and not that the whole nation should perish."

51 Now this he did not say on his own *authority;* but being high priest that year he prophesied that Jesus would die for the nation,

52 and not for that nation only, but also that He would gather together in one the children of God who were scattered abroad.

53 Then from that day on they plotted to put Him to death.

54 Therefore Jesus no longer walked openly among the Jews, but went from there into the country near the wilderness, to a city called Ephraim, and there remained with His disciples.

55 And the Passover of the Jews was near, and many went from the country up to Jerusalem before the Passover, to purify themselves.

56 Then they sought Jesus, and spoke among themselves as they stood in the temple, "What do you think—that He will not come to the feast?"

57 Now both the chief priests and the Pharisees had given a command, that if anyone knew where He was, he should report *it*, that they might seize Him.

12 Then, six days before the Passover, Jesus came to Bethany, where Lazarus was who had been dead, whom He had raised from the dead.

2 There they made Him a supper; and Martha served, but Lazarus was one of those who sat at the table with Him.

3 Then Mary took a pound of very costly oil of spikenard, anointed the feet of Jesus, and wiped His feet with her hair. And the house was filled with the fragrance of the oil.

4 Then one of His disciples, Judas Iscariot, Simon's *son,* who would betray Him, said,

5 "Why was this fragrant oil not sold for three hundred denarii and given to the poor?"

6 This he said, not that he cared for the poor, but because he was a thief, and had the money box; and he used to take what was put in it.

7 Then Jesus said, "Let her alone; she has kept this for the day of My burial.

8 "For the poor you have with you always, but Me you do not have always."

9 Then a great many of the Jews knew that He was there; and they came, not for Jesus' sake only, but that they might also see Lazarus, whom He had raised from the dead.

STEP 12

STEP 12

Having had a spiritual awakening as the result
of these steps, we tried to carry this message to others,
and to practice these principles in all our affairs.

John 12:9–11

Benjamin still found the whole affair a bit incredible. His neighbor Lazarus had died and had actually been entombed, when the Teacher called Jesus arrived in town and used His amazing power to bring him back to life. Benjamin would not have paid much attention to this Jesus ordinarily. After all, life was so busy. But to see the power of God so clearly demonstrated in Lazarus' life made him take notice. He was suddenly interested in what Jesus was saying.

There may be people like Benjamin in your circle of friends and acquaintances who have been aware of your struggle with addictions. When Jesus begins to change your life, energizing you to live a life of victory and power, these people will begin to notice. They may say nothing at first, but be aware: your new life in Jesus is speaking volumes to them. And just as "many of the Jews went away and believed in Jesus" on account of Lazarus, your changed life can be the catalyst of a friend's salvation.

For further reading on Step 12, turn to page 243.

Daily Encouragement

DAY 101 READING: JOHN 11:45—12:11

A Thought for the New Day: Caiaphas (11:49, 50) was no friend of Jesus. In fact, had he understood what he was saying, he would have bitten his lip, for what he described was the divine plan itself: "that one man should die for the people." We would not die, but live, because Jesus died in our place. This is the greatest of all good news. God has not abandoned us, but has opened a way to life through the death of His Son. (*Turn to page 233.*)

10 But the chief priests took counsel that they might also put Lazarus to death,

11 because on account of him many of the Jews went away and believed in Jesus.

12 The next day a great multitude that had come to the feast, when they heard that Jesus was coming to Jerusalem,

13 took branches of palm trees and went out to meet Him, and cried out:

"Hosanna!
'Blessed is He who comes
in the name of the LORD!'
The King of Israel!"

14 Then Jesus, when He had found a young donkey, sat on it; as it is written:

15 "Fear not, daughter of Zion;
Behold, your King is coming,
Sitting on a donkey's colt."

16 His disciples did not understand these things at first; but when Jesus was glorified, then they remembered that these things were written about Him and *that* they had done these things to Him.

17 Therefore the people, who were with Him when He called Lazarus out of his tomb and raised him from the dead, bore witness.

18 For this reason the people also met Him, because they heard that He had done this sign.

19 The Pharisees therefore said among themselves, "You see that you are accomplishing nothing. Look, the world has gone after Him!"

20 Now there were certain Greeks among those who came up to worship at the feast.

21 Then they came to Philip, who was from Bethsaida of Galilee, and asked him, saying, "Sir, we wish to see Jesus."

22 Philip came and told Andrew, and in turn Andrew and Philip told Jesus.

23 But Jesus answered them, saying, "The hour has come that the Son of Man should be glorified.

24 "Most assuredly, I say to you, unless a grain of wheat falls into the ground and dies, it remains alone; but if it dies, it produces much grain.

25 "He who loves his life will lose it, and he who hates his life in this world will keep it for eternal life.

26 "If anyone serves Me, let him follow Me; and where I am, there My servant will be also. If anyone serves Me, him *My* Father will honor.

STEP 3

27 "Now My soul is troubled, and what shall I say? 'Father, save Me from this hour'? But for this purpose I came to this hour.

28 "Father, glorify Your name." Then a voice came from heaven, *saying*, "I have both glorified *it* and will glorify *it* again."

29 Therefore the people who stood by and heard *it* said that it had thundered. Others said, "An angel has spoken to Him."

30 Jesus answered and said, "This voice did not come because of Me, but for your sake.

31 "Now is the judgment of this world; now the ruler of this world will be cast out.

32 "And I, if I am lifted up from the earth, will draw all *peoples* to Myself."

33 This He said, signifying by what death He would die.

34 The people answered Him, "We have heard from the law that the Christ remains forever; and how *can* You say, 'The Son of Man must be lifted up'? Who is this Son of Man?"

35 Then Jesus said to them, "A little while longer the light is with you. Walk while you have the light, lest darkness overtake you; he who walks in darkness does not know where he is going.

*Made a decision to turn our will and our lives
over to the care of God **as we understood Him.***

John 12:26

When we turn our lives over to the care of God, we receive from Him infinitely more than we give to Him. Yes, following Jesus involves accepting His principles to live by and His will to obey. But if this makes us begin to feel somehow hindered in our enjoyment of life, we are not understanding the Christian life correctly. Jesus makes two wonderful promises in this verse, which underscore the meaning of abundant life in Christ. First, our place in heaven is assured. Fear of death need never fetter us again. Jesus' second promise is energizing, but also humbling. He tells us that God delights in honoring those who serve Him. We do not deserve that honor, but it is wonderful to experience the smile of God's approval on our lives.

For further reading on Step 3, turn to page 259.

Daily Encouragement

DAY 102 READING: JOHN 12:12–41

A Thought for the New Day: Probably most people in Jesus' time were sure their Messiah would visit them as a great king and lead them in conquering the nations. The idea was right, but their timing was off. They had no room in their minds for a Suffering Servant (v. 34). We should be careful about closing our minds too quickly or too tightly. Rather, we should trust God to do His own perfect work, in His own perfect way, in His own perfect time. *(Turn to page 235.)*

36 "While you have the light, believe in the light, that you may become sons of light." These things Jesus spoke, and departed, and was hidden from them.
37 But although He had done so many signs before them, they did not believe in Him,
38 that the word of Isaiah the prophet might be fulfilled, which he spoke:

"Lord, who has believed our
report?
And to whom has the arm
of the LORD been revealed?"

39 Therefore they could not believe, because Isaiah said again:

40 "He has blinded their eyes and
hardened their heart,
Lest they should see with
their eyes
And understand with their
heart,
Lest they should turn,
so that I should heal them."

41 These things Isaiah said when he saw His glory and spoke of Him.
42 Nevertheless even among the rulers many believed in Him, but because of the Pharisees they did not confess *Him*, lest they should be put out of the synagogue;
43 for they loved the praise of men more than the praise of God.
44 Then Jesus cried out and said, "He who believes in Me, believes not in Me but in Him who sent Me.
45 "And he who sees Me sees Him who sent Me.
46 "I have come *as* a light into the world, that whoever believes in Me should not abide in darkness.
47 "And if anyone hears My words and does not believe, I do not judge him; for I did not come to judge the world but to save the world.
48 "He who rejects Me, and does not receive My words, has that which judges him—the word that I have spoken will judge him in the last day.
49 "For I have not spoken on My own *authority;* but the Father who sent Me gave Me a command, what I should say and what I should speak.
50 "And I know that His command is everlasting life. Therefore, whatever I speak, just as the Father has told Me, so I speak."

13 Now before the feast of the Passover, when Jesus knew that His hour had come that He should depart from this world to the Father, having loved His own who were in the world, He loved them to the end.
2 And supper being ended, the devil having already put it into the heart of Judas Iscariot, Simon's *son,* to betray Him,
3 Jesus, knowing that the Father had given all things into His hands, and that He had come from God and was going to God,
4 rose from supper and laid aside His garments, took a towel and girded Himself.
5 After that, He poured water into a basin and began to wash the disciples' feet, and to wipe *them* with the towel with which He was girded.
6 Then He came to Simon Peter. And *Peter* said to Him, "Lord, are You washing my feet?"
7 Jesus answered and said to him, "What I am doing you do not understand now, but you will know after this."
8 Peter said to Him, "You shall never wash my feet!" Jesus answered him, "If I do not wash you, you have no part with Me."
9 Simon Peter said to Him, "Lord, not my feet only, but also *my* hands and *my* head!"
10 Jesus said to him, "He who is bathed needs only to wash *his* feet, but is completely clean; and you are clean, but not all of you."

STEP 2

Came to believe that a Power greater than ourselves could restore us to sanity.

John 12:46

If, as a child, you had been hidden away in the dark recesses of a cave, it is possible that you could have grown to maturity never having seen the light or observed yourself in that light. Because you had always dwelt in darkness, the light and what it revealed would be foreign and incomprehensible.

In somewhat the same sense, those of us who have struggled with disabling conditions since childhood, may actually be totally unaware of the extent of our problems. Because of our traumatic childhood experiences, we may be defiant, resentful, self-deluded, or overcontrolling without ever realizing it.

When we come to the light of God's Power and Love, we no longer have to abide in that crippling darkness. In the light of His Love we can accept ourselves as we truly are, and then in the light of His Power we can walk out of the darkness for eternity.

For further reading on Step 2, turn to page 261.

Daily Encouragement

DAY 103 READING: JOHN 12:42–50

A Thought for the New Day: Are you still a secret believer? Has it become clear to you at last that Jesus really is the Christ after all? No one should judge you if you are not ready to share what you believe; indeed, forced efforts to confess Him openly might come off awkwardly. Seek the friendship and encouragement of other Christians, and in due time God will open the right doors for you to show others what Jesus means to you. (*Turn to page 237.*)

11 For He knew who would betray Him; therefore He said, "You are not all clean."

12 So when He had washed their feet, taken His garments, and sat down again, He said to them, "Do you know what I have done to you?

13 "You call Me Teacher and Lord, and you say well, for *so* I am.

14 "If I then, *your* Lord and Teacher, have washed your feet, you also ought to wash one another's feet.

15 "For I have given you an example, that you should do as I have done to you.

16 "Most assuredly, I say to you, a servant is not greater than his master; nor is he who is sent greater than he who sent him.

17 "If you know these things, happy are you if you do them.

18 "I do not speak concerning all of you. I know whom I have chosen; but that the Scripture may be fulfilled, *'He who eats bread with Me has lifted up his heel against Me.'*

19 "Now I tell you before it comes, that when it does come to pass, you may believe that I am *He*.

20 "Most assuredly, I say to you, he who receives whomever I send receives Me; and he who receives Me receives Him who sent Me."

21 When Jesus had said these things, He was troubled in spirit, and testified and said, "Most assuredly, I say to you, one of you will betray Me."

22 Then the disciples looked at one another, perplexed about whom He spoke.

23 Now there was leaning on Jesus' bosom one of His disciples, whom Jesus loved.

24 Simon Peter therefore motioned to him to ask who it was of whom He spoke.

25 Then, leaning back on Jesus' breast, he said to Him, "Lord, who is it?"

26 Jesus answered, "It is he to whom I shall give a piece of bread when I have dipped *it*." And having dipped the bread, He gave *it* to Judas Iscariot, *the son* of Simon.

27 Now after the piece of bread, Satan entered him. Then Jesus said to him, "What you do, do quickly."

28 But no one at the table knew for what reason He said this to him.

29 For some thought, because Judas had the money box, that Jesus had said to him, "Buy *those things* we need for the feast," or that he should give something to the poor.

30 Having received the piece of bread, he then went out immediately. And it was night.

31 So, when he had gone out, Jesus said, "Now the Son of Man is glorified, and God is glorified in Him.

32 "If God is glorified in Him, God will also glorify Him in Himself, and glorify Him immediately.

33 "Little children, I shall be with you a little while longer. You will seek Me; and as I said to the Jews, 'Where I am going, you cannot come,' so now I say to you.

34 "A new commandment I give to you, that you love one another; as I have loved you, that you also love one another.

35 "By this all will know that you are My disciples, if you have love for one another."

STEP 8

36 Simon Peter said to Him, "Lord, where are You going?" Jesus answered him, "Where I am going you cannot follow Me now, but you shall follow Me afterward."

37 Peter said to Him, "Lord, why can I not follow You now? I will lay down my life for Your sake."

38 Jesus answered him, "Will you lay down your life for My sake? Most assuredly, I say to you, the rooster shall not crow till you have denied Me three times.

14 "Let not your heart be troubled; you believe in God, believe also in Me.

2 "In My Father's house are many

STEP 8

*Made a list of all persons we had harmed,
and became willing to make amends to them all.*

John 13:34, 35

How do we love one another as Jesus commands?

It is impossible to give away what we do not possess. If our inventory of past relationships reveals that love was missing, marginal, or intermingled with pain in our earliest childhood experiences, we must grieve that loss and seek new sources of healthy reparenting. If our inventory of contemporary relationships indicates that we are exploiting or tightly possessing others in order to fill our own emptiness, we must make healing amends in two ways. First, we must acknowledge and apologize for the ways we have hurt others by those patterns. Second, we must set healthy relationship boundaries for ourselves and allow these boundaries to become a form of "living amends."

The gospel reminds us that we are to be known by our capacity for love. The source of this love is God's love. As we discover this source of unconditional love, we become more effective in all of our ongoing relationships.

For further reading on Step 8, turn to page 319.

Daily Encouragement

DAY 104 READING: JOHN 13:1–35

A Thought for the New Day: What was "new" about Jesus' commandment (vv. 34, 35)? Nothing essentially. From very ancient times God had commanded His people to love. But Jesus had just given an object lesson in what He specifically meant. He had washed His followers' feet. He thus conveys to us what is perhaps hardest to accept as members of His community. Taking the low road, that is, the road of humble service, toward one another is the test of true discipleship. (*Turn to page 239.*)

mansions; if *it were* not *so,* I would have told you. I go to prepare a place for you.

3 "And if I go and prepare a place for you, I will come again and receive you to Myself; that where I am, *there* you may be also.

4 "And where I go you know, and the way you know."

5 Thomas said to Him, "Lord, we do not know where You are going, and how can we know the way?"

6 Jesus said to him, "I am the way, the truth, and the life. No one comes to the Father except through Me.

7 "If you had known Me, you would have known My Father also; and from now on you know Him and have seen Him."

8 Philip said to Him, "Lord, show us the Father, and it is sufficient for us."

9 Jesus said to him, "Have I been with you so long, and yet you have not known Me, Philip? He who has seen Me has seen the Father; so how can you say, 'Show us the Father'?

10 "Do you not believe that I am in the Father, and the Father in Me? The words that I speak to you I do not speak on My own *authority;* but the Father who dwells in Me does the works.

11 "Believe Me that I *am* in the Father and the Father in Me, or else believe Me for the sake of the works themselves.

STEP 11

12 "Most assuredly, I say to you, he who believes in Me, the works that I do he will do also; and greater *works* than these he will do, because I go to My Father.

13 "And whatever you ask in My name, that I will do, that the Father may be glorified in the Son.

14 "If you ask anything in My name, I will do *it.*

15 "If you love Me, keep My commandments.

16 "And I will pray the Father, and He will give you another Helper, that He may abide with you forever,

17 "*even* the Spirit of truth, whom the world cannot receive, because it neither sees Him nor knows Him; but you know Him, for He dwells with you and will be in you.

18 "I will not leave you orphans; I will come to you.

19 "A little while longer and the world will see Me no more, but you will see Me. Because I live, you will live also.

20 "At that day you will know that I *am* in My Father, and you in Me, and I in you.

21 "He who has My commandments and keeps them, it is he who loves Me. And he who loves Me will be loved by My Father, and I will love him and manifest Myself to him."

22 Judas (not Iscariot) said to Him, "Lord, how is it that You will manifest Yourself to us, and not to the world?"

23 Jesus answered and said to him, "If anyone loves Me, he will keep My word; and My Father will love him, and We will come to him and make Our home with him.

24 "He who does not love Me does not keep My words; and the word which you hear is not Mine but the Father's who sent Me.

25 "These things I have spoken to you while being present with you.

26 "But the Helper, the Holy Spirit, whom the Father will send in My name, He will teach you all things, and bring to your remembrance all things that I said to you.

27 "Peace I leave with you, My peace I give to you; not as the world gives do I give to you. Let not your heart be troubled, neither let it be afraid.

28 "You have heard Me say to you, 'I am going away and coming *back* to you.' If you loved Me, you would rejoice because I said, 'I am going to the Father,' for My Father is greater than I.

STEP 11

*Sought through prayer and meditation to improve our conscious contact with God **as we understood Him,** praying only for knowledge of His will for us and the power to carry that out.*

John 14:12–21

Love, of course, means more than sweet sentiments. It means sacrifice and perseverance in the real world. It is not always fun. Jesus knew how easy it is for us to speak one way and yet act another. He also knew how easily we can fool ourselves into believing that because we can say "I love you, Lord," that is the same as truly loving Him.

Real love always demands total commitment. For a believer, really loving Jesus means being totally committed to live by His Word. This is the reason that twice in these verses Jesus declares that if we truly love Him we will keep His commandments. But we cannot keep what we do not know. This is why we must daily make reading and memorizing God's Word a top priority in our lives.

For further reading on Step 11, turn to page 241.

Daily Encouragement

DAY 105 READING: JOHN 13:36—14:31

A Thought for the New Day: We do not worship an absentee God (14:16, 26). Although He is beyond the universe, God also fills heaven and earth with His near presence. To know His nearness we have only to unlock the doors of our hearts and let Him in. The Spirit of God Himself desires to live in us and communicate to us all the good things that Jesus died and lives again to obtain for us. Friendship with God is life's greatest gift. (*Turn to page 241.*)

29 "And now I have told you before it comes, that when it does come to pass, you may believe.

30 "I will no longer talk much with you, for the ruler of this world is coming, and he has nothing in Me.

31 "But that the world may know that I love the Father, and as the Father gave Me commandment, so I do. Arise, let us go from here.

15 "I am the true vine, and My Father is the vinedresser.

2 "Every branch in Me that does not bear fruit He takes away; and every *branch* that bears fruit He prunes, that it may bear more fruit.

3 "You are already clean because of the word which I have spoken to you.

4 "Abide in Me, and I in you. As the branch cannot bear fruit of itself, unless it abides in the vine, neither can you, unless you abide in Me.

5 "I am the vine, you *are* the branches. He who abides in Me, and I in him, bears much fruit; for without Me you can do nothing.

6 "If anyone does not abide in Me, he is cast out as a branch and is withered; and they gather them and throw *them* into the fire, and they are burned.

7 "If you abide in Me, and My words abide in you, you will ask what you desire, and it shall be done for you.

8 "By this My Father is glorified, that you bear much fruit; so you will be My disciples.

9 "As the Father loved Me, I also have loved you; abide in My love.

10 "If you keep My commandments, you will abide in My love, just as I have kept My Father's commandments and abide in His love.

11 "These things I have spoken to you, that My joy may remain in you, and that your joy may be full.

12 "This is My commandment, that you love one another as I have loved you.

13 "Greater love has no one than this, than to lay down one's life for his friends.

14 "You are My friends if you do whatever I command you.

15 "No longer do I call you servants, for a servant does not know what his master is doing; but I have called you friends, for all things that I heard from My Father I have made known to you.

16 "You did not choose Me, but I chose you and appointed you that you should go and bear fruit, and *that* your fruit should remain, that whatever you ask the Father in My name He may give you.

17 "These things I command you, that you love one another.

18 "If the world hates you, you know that it hated Me before *it hated* you.

19 "If you were of the world, the world would love its own. Yet because you are not of the world, but I chose you out of the world, therefore the world hates you.

20 "Remember the word that I said to you, 'A servant is not greater than his master.' If they persecuted Me, they will also persecute you. If they kept My word, they will keep yours also.

21 "But all these things they will do to you for My name's sake, because they do not know Him who sent Me.

22 "If I had not come and spoken to them, they would have no sin, but now they have no excuse for their sin.

23 "He who hates Me hates My Father also.

24 "If I had not done among them the works which no one else did, they would have no sin; but now they have seen and also hated both Me and My Father.

25 "But *this happened* that the word might be fulfilled which is written in their law, 'They hated Me without a cause.'

26 "But when the Helper comes,

STEP 11

STEP 11

*Sought through prayer and meditation to improve our conscious contact with God **as we understood Him,** praying only for knowledge of His will for us and the power to carry that out.*

John 15:4–11

These words of Jesus contain God's own prescription for joy. The main ingredient of that prescription is repeated ten times in eight verses. Undoubtedly then, there can be no joy without that special element—*abiding*. Today we do not use this word much, but in old English it meant "to remain with continually." We cannot love someone we do not know, nor can we serve when we do not know what is expected of us. Jesus says, "Come, stay with Me." His call to abide in Him carries a much deeper commitment than saying a quick prayer and reading a few verses of Scripture each day. Jesus wants quality time with us. When we give priority to meditating on His Word, as well as memorizing it, that is abiding. When we can sit before Him and listen to His voice, as well as lay out all our requests, that is abiding. Abiding takes time and work, but as we see our lives producing the fruit of the Spirit, our joy will be full.

For further reading on Step 11, turn to page 257.

Daily Encouragement

DAY 106 READING: JOHN 15:1–27

A Thought for the New Day: What could make more sense than Jesus' words in verses 4–8? Imagine a branch of a vine or a fruit tree producing any fruit apart from the parent stock. Likewise, we cannot produce anything of eternal value by ourselves. It is the life of Jesus *in us* that yields beautiful results that last forever. You, like a good branch in Christ, can bear fruit that brings infinite happiness to others. (*Turn to page 243.*)

whom I shall send to you from the Father, the Spirit of truth who proceeds from the Father, He will testify of Me.

27 "And you also will bear witness, because you have been with Me from the beginning.

16 "These things I have spoken to you, that you should not be made to stumble.

2 "They will put you out of the synagogues; yes, the time is coming that whoever kills you will think that he offers God service.

3 "And these things they will do to you because they have not known the Father nor Me.

4 "But these things I have told you, that when the time comes, you may remember that I told you of them. And these things I did not say to you at the beginning, because I was with you.

5 "But now I go away to Him who sent Me, and none of you asks Me, 'Where are You going?'

6 "But because I have said these things to you, sorrow has filled your heart.

7 "Nevertheless I tell you the truth. It is to your advantage that I go away; for if I do not go away, the Helper will not come to you; but if I depart, I will send Him to you.

8 "And when He has come, He will convict the world of sin, and of righteousness, and of judgment:

9 "of sin, because they do not believe in Me;

10 "of righteousness, because I go to My Father and you see Me no more;

11 "of judgment, because the ruler of this world is judged.

12 "I still have many things to say to you, but you cannot bear *them* now.

13 "However, when He, the Spirit of truth, has come, He will guide you into all truth; for He will not speak on His own *authority*, but whatever He hears He will speak;

and He will tell you things to come.

14 "He will glorify Me, for He will take of what is Mine and declare *it* to you.

15 "All things that the Father has are Mine. Therefore I said that He will take of Mine and declare *it* to you.

16 "A little while, and you will not see Me; and again a little while, and you will see Me, because I go to the Father."

17 Then *some* of His disciples said among themselves, "What is this that He says to us, 'A little while, and you will not see Me; and again a little while, and you will see Me'; and, 'because I go to the Father'?"

18 They said therefore, "What is this that He says, 'A little while'? We do not know what He is saying."

19 Now Jesus knew that they desired to ask Him, and He said to them, "Are you inquiring among yourselves about what I said, 'A little while, and you will not see Me; and again a little while, and you will see Me'?

20 "Most assuredly, I say to you that you will weep and lament, but the world will rejoice; and you will be sorrowful, but your sorrow will be turned into joy.

21 "A woman, when she is in labor, has sorrow because her hour has come; but as soon as she has given birth to the child, she no longer remembers the anguish, for joy that a human being has been born into the world.

22 "Therefore you now have sorrow; but I will see you again and your heart will rejoice, and your joy no one will take from you.

23 "And in that day you will ask Me nothing. Most assuredly, I say to you, whatever you ask the Father in My name He will give you.

24 "Until now you have asked nothing in My name. Ask, and you

STEP 11

STEP 12

*Having had a spiritual awakening as the result
of these steps, we tried to carry this message to others,
and to practice these principles in all our affairs.*

John 16:33

Perhaps when we were in the early stages of our program, we looked ahead to Step 12 longingly, believing that trouble would be far behind us when we had attained that level. But on this earth our lives will never be totally free of struggle. Sometimes we are misunderstood, tempted, sorrowful, or frustrated. The world can still be a hard place in which to live. But Jesus makes the difference. As we practice His teachings and spend time with Him we come to know a peace that the world absolutely cannot comprehend. For those who do not know God, peace is an absence of trouble. That is why most people experience so little of it. However, believers discover that trusting Jesus and faithfully obeying Him brings peace even in the midst of tribulation. We have learned that no problem is too big for God to handle. We can by our lips and lives proclaim to others, "Jesus has overcome the world."

For further reading on Step 12, turn to page 267.

Daily Encouragement

DAY 107 READING: JOHN 16:1–33

A Thought for the New Day: You have known and talked to people whose genuine warmth and friendship brought you an experience of peace that was uncommon. Jesus was like that in the superlative degree. He made His friends feel that they "belonged" and that He would stand by them through all their difficulties and disappointments. He had "overcome" the world with all its oppressive hostility, and now He can also give us the peace that never fades. (*Turn to page 245.*)

will receive, that your joy may be full.

25 "These things I have spoken to you in figurative language; but the time is coming when I will no longer speak to you in figurative language, but I will tell you plainly about the Father.

26 "In that day you will ask in My name, and I do not say to you that I shall pray the Father for you;

27 "for the Father Himself loves you, because you have loved Me, and have believed that I came forth from God.

28 "I came forth from the Father and have come into the world. Again, I leave the world and go to the Father."

29 His disciples said to Him, "See, now You are speaking plainly, and using no figure of speech!

30 "Now we are sure that You know all things, and have no need that anyone should question You. By this we believe that You came forth from God."

31 Jesus answered them, "Do you now believe?

32 "Indeed the hour is coming, yes, has now come, that you will be scattered, each to his own, and will leave Me alone. And yet I am not alone, because the Father is with Me.

STEP 12

33 "These things I have spoken to you, that in Me you may have peace. In the world you will have tribulation; but be of good cheer, I have overcome the world."

17 Jesus spoke these words, lifted up His eyes to heaven, and said: "Father, the hour has come. Glorify Your Son, that Your Son also may glorify You,

2 "as You have given Him authority over all flesh, that He should give eternal life to as many as You have given Him.

STEP 3

3 "And this is eternal life, that they may know You, the only true God, and Jesus Christ whom You have sent.

4 "I have glorified You on the earth. I have finished the work which You have given Me to do.

5 "And now, O Father, glorify Me together with Yourself, with the glory which I had with You before the world was.

6 "I have manifested Your name to the men whom You have given Me out of the world. They were Yours, You gave them to Me, and they have kept Your word.

7 "Now they have known that all things which You have given Me are from You.

8 "For I have given to them the words which You have given Me; and they have received *them*, and have known surely that I came forth from You; and they have believed that You sent Me.

9 "I pray for them. I do not pray for the world but for those whom You have given Me, for they are Yours.

10 "And all Mine are Yours, and Yours are Mine, and I am glorified in them.

11 "Now I am no longer in the world, but these are in the world, and I come to You. Holy Father, keep through Your name those whom You have given Me, that they may be one as We *are*.

12 "While I was with them in the world, I kept them in Your name. Those whom You gave Me I have kept; and none of them is lost except the son of perdition, that the Scripture might be fulfilled.

13 "But now I come to You, and these things I speak in the world, that they may have My joy fulfilled in themselves.

14 "I have given them Your word; and the world has hated them because they are not of the world, just as I am not of the world.

15 "I do not pray that You should take them out of the world, but that You should keep them from the evil *one*.

STEP 10

16 "They are not of the world, just as I am not of the world.

STEP 10

*Continued to take personal inventory
and when we were wrong promptly admitted it.*

John 17:15–17

Sometimes it seems like it would be a lot better if Jesus would just take us to heaven as soon as we come to trust Him. There would be no more struggle or sadness or pain or fear. But our all-wise and all-loving Father knows that this is not best. Our souls would never grow to maturity and strength. So our challenges here on earth are actually designed to prepare us for the great privileges that will be ours in heaven, where our true citizenship now lies.

Since we are no longer part of this world's system, we must be careful not to be captivated by its tinsel and glitter. The world is very good at making what is only a vaporous mirage appear solid and desirable, but Jesus is interceding before the Father on our behalf. He is praying that we will immerse ourselves in the true riches of Scripture. Doing so, the bangles and baubles of the world will begin to look less and less appealing.

For further reading on Step 10, turn to page 295.

Daily Encouragement

DAY 108 READING: JOHN 17:1–26

A Thought for the New Day: Our prayers are never perfect: sometimes we ask for inappropriate things, or else we have the wrong motives. But we can count on Jesus' prayers. It is more than a good idea to review the requests that Jesus made on our behalf—that we will have oneness together in Him, that He will dwell in us, and that we will be with Him where He is and see His glory (vv. 20–26). These are prayers that cannot fail. (*Turn to page 248.*)

17 "Sanctify them by Your truth. Your word is truth.

18 "As You sent Me into the world, I also have sent them into the world.

19 "And for their sakes I sanctify Myself, that they also may be sanctified by the truth.

20 "I do not pray for these alone, but also for those who will believe in Me through their word;

21 "that they all may be one, as You, Father, *are* in Me, and I in You; that they also may be one in Us, that the world may believe that You sent Me.

22 "And the glory which You gave Me I have given them, that they may be one just as We are one:

23 "I in them, and You in Me; that they may be made perfect in one, and that the world may know that You have sent Me, and have loved them as You have loved Me.

24 "Father, I desire that they also whom You gave Me may be with Me where I am, that they may behold My glory which You have given Me; for You loved Me before the foundation of the world.

25 "O righteous Father! The world has not known You, but I have known You; and these have known that You sent Me.

26 "And I have declared to them Your name, and will declare *it*, that the love with which You loved Me may be in them, and I in them."

18 When Jesus had spoken these words, He went out with His disciples over the Brook Kidron, where there was a garden, which He and His disciples entered.

2 And Judas, who betrayed Him, also knew the place; for Jesus often met there with His disciples.

3 Then Judas, having received a detachment *of troops*, and officers from the chief priests and Pharisees, came there with lanterns, torches, and weapons.

4 Jesus therefore, knowing all things that would come upon Him, went forward and said to them, "Whom are you seeking?"

5 They answered Him, "Jesus of Nazareth." Jesus said to them, "I am *He*." And Judas, who betrayed Him, also stood with them.

6 Then—when He said to them, "I am *He*,"—they drew back and fell to the ground.

7 Then He asked them again, "Whom are you seeking?" And they said, "Jesus of Nazareth."

8 Jesus answered, "I have told you that I am *He*. Therefore, if you seek Me, let these go their way,"

9 that the saying might be fulfilled which He spoke, "Of those whom You gave Me I have lost none."

10 Then Simon Peter, having a sword, drew it and struck the high priest's servant, and cut off his right ear. The servant's name was Malchus.

11 Then Jesus said to Peter, "Put your sword into the sheath. Shall I not drink the cup which My Father has given Me?"

12 Then the detachment *of troops* and the captain and the officers of the Jews arrested Jesus and bound Him.

13 And they led Him away to Annas first, for he was the father-in-law of Caiaphas who was high priest that year.

14 Now it was Caiaphas who gave counsel to the Jews that it was expedient that one man should die for the people.

15 And Simon Peter followed Jesus, and so *did* another disciple. Now that disciple was known to the high priest, and went with Jesus into the courtyard of the high priest.

16 But Peter stood at the door outside. Then the other disciple, who was known to the high priest, went out and spoke to her who kept the door, and brought Peter in.

17 Then the servant girl who kept the door said to Peter, "You are not also *one* of this Man's disciples, are you?" He said, "I am not."

18 And the servants and officers who had made a fire of coals stood there, for it was cold, and they warmed themselves. And Peter stood with them and warmed himself.

19 The high priest then asked Jesus about His disciples and His doctrine.

20 Jesus answered him, "I spoke openly to the world. I always taught in synagogues and in the temple, where the Jews always meet, and in secret I have said nothing.

21 "Why do you ask Me? Ask those who have heard Me what I said to them. Indeed they know what I said."

22 And when He had said these things, one of the officers who stood by struck Jesus with the palm of his hand, saying, "Do You answer the high priest like that?"

23 Jesus answered him, "If I have spoken evil, bear witness of the evil; but if well, why do you strike Me?"

24 Then Annas sent Him bound to Caiaphas the high priest.

25 Now Simon Peter stood and warmed himself. Therefore they said to him, "You are not also *one* of His disciples, are you?" He denied *it* and said, "I am not!"

26 One of the servants of the high priest, a relative *of him* whose ear Peter cut off, said, "Did I not see you in the garden with Him?"

27 Peter then denied again; and immediately a rooster crowed.

28 Then they led Jesus from Caiaphas to the Praetorium, and it was early morning. But they themselves did not go into the Praetorium, lest they should be defiled, but that they might eat the Passover.

29 Pilate then went out to them and said, "What accusation do you bring against this Man?"

30 They answered and said to him, "If He were not an evildoer, we would not have delivered Him up to you."

31 Then Pilate said to them, "You take Him and judge Him according to your law." Therefore the Jews said to him, "It is not lawful for us to put anyone to death,"

32 that the saying of Jesus might be fulfilled which He spoke, signifying by what death He would die.

33 Then Pilate entered the Praetorium again, called Jesus, and said to Him, "Are You the King of the Jews?"

34 Jesus answered him, "Are you speaking for yourself on this, or did others tell you this about Me?"

35 Pilate answered, "Am I a Jew? Your own nation and the chief priests have delivered You to me. What have You done?"

36 Jesus answered, "My kingdom is not of this world. If My kingdom were of this world, My servants would fight, so that I should not be delivered to the Jews; but now My kingdom is not from here."

37 Pilate therefore said to Him, "Are You a king then?" Jesus answered, "You say *rightly* that I am a king. For this cause I was born, and for this cause I have come into the world, that I should bear witness to the truth. Everyone who is of the truth hears My voice."

38 Pilate said to Him, "What is truth?" And when he had said this, he went out again to the Jews, and said to them, "I find no fault in Him *at all.*

39 "But you have a custom that I should release someone to you at the Passover. Do you therefore want me to release to you the King of the Jews?"

40 Then they all cried again, saying, "Not this Man, but Barabbas!" Now Barabbas was a robber.

STEP 4

Made a searching and fearless moral inventory of ourselves.

John 18:37, 38

The prophet Isaiah wrote: "Let grace be shown to the wicked, *yet* he will not learn righteousness; in the land of uprightness he will deal unjustly, and will not behold the majesty of the LORD" (Is. 26:10).

If we inserted Pilate's name into these verses, they would fit his character all too well. Pilate could have made remarkable and life-changing discoveries, if he had listened to what Jesus was saying. Having asked Jesus one of life's most important questions, he did not even wait for an answer! He wanted to know the truth, but not enough to spend time or energy seeking it. As a result, he failed to "behold the majesty of the LORD" who stood in front of him.

For those in recovery, investing time and energy seeking the truth is vital, since so much time has been spent previously in denying or evading truth. And when we come face-to-face with the truth, we must accept it and allow it to impact our hearts and our lives.

For further reading on Step 4, turn to page 345.

Daily Encouragement

DAY 109 READING: JOHN 18:1—19:37

A Thought for the New Day: It was natural for Pilate to say what he said (19:10). He represented the greatest power on earth, but what Jesus replied (19:11) seems to have shaken up that Roman governor. Pilate began to understand that he was, after all, only a chessman in the exercise of God's sovereign power over him. As a result, Pilate sought to release Jesus, but the Cross was the divine design of salvation for us. (*Turn to page 253.*)

19 So then Pilate took Jesus and scourged *Him*.

2 And the soldiers twisted a crown of thorns and put *it* on His head, and they put on Him a purple robe.

3 Then they said, "Hail, King of the Jews!" And they struck Him with their hands.

4 Pilate then went out again, and said to them, "Behold, I am bringing Him out to you, that you may know that I find no fault in Him."

5 Then Jesus came out, wearing the crown of thorns and the purple robe. And *Pilate* said to them, "Behold the Man!"

6 Therefore, when the chief priests and officers saw Him, they cried out, saying, "Crucify *Him*, crucify *Him!*" Pilate said to them, "You take Him and crucify *Him*, for I find no fault in Him."

7 The Jews answered him, "We have a law, and according to our law He ought to die, because He made Himself the Son of God."

8 Therefore, when Pilate heard that saying, he was the more afraid,

9 and went again into the Praetorium, and said to Jesus, "Where are You from?" But Jesus gave him no answer.

10 Then Pilate said to Him, "Are You not speaking to me? Do You not know that I have power to crucify You, and power to release You?"

11 Jesus answered, "You could have no power *at all* against Me unless it had been given you from above. Therefore the one who delivered Me to you has the greater sin."

12 From then on Pilate sought to release Him, but the Jews cried out, saying, "If you let this Man go, you are not Caesar's friend. Whoever makes himself a king speaks against Caesar."

13 When Pilate therefore heard that saying, he brought Jesus out and sat down in the judgment seat in a place that is called *The* Pavement, but in Hebrew, Gabbatha.

14 Now it was the Preparation Day of the Passover, and about the sixth hour. And he said to the Jews, "Behold your King!"

15 But they cried out, "Away with *Him*, away with *Him!* Crucify Him!" Pilate said to them, "Shall I crucify your King?" The chief priests answered, "We have no king but Caesar!"

16 So he delivered Him to them to be crucified. So they took Jesus and led *Him* away.

17 And He, bearing His cross, went out to a place called *the Place* of a Skull, which is called in Hebrew, Golgotha,

18 where they crucified Him, and two others with Him, one on either side, and Jesus in the center.

19 Now Pilate wrote a title and put *it* on the cross. And the writing was:

JESUS OF NAZARETH,
THE KING OF THE JEWS.

20 Then many of the Jews read this title, for the place where Jesus was crucified was near the city; and it was written in Hebrew, Greek, *and* Latin.

21 Then the chief priests of the Jews said to Pilate, "Do not write, 'The King of the Jews,' but, 'He said, "I am the King of the Jews." '"

22 Pilate answered, "What I have written, I have written."

23 Then the soldiers, when they had crucified Jesus, took His garments and made four parts, to each soldier a part, and also the tunic. Now the tunic was without seam, woven from the top in one piece.

24 They said therefore among themselves, "Let us not tear it, but cast lots for it, whose it shall be," that the Scripture might be fulfilled which says:

*"They divided My garments
     among them,
And for My clothing they cast
     lots."*

Therefore the soldiers did these things.

25 Now there stood by the cross of Jesus His mother, and His mother's sister, Mary the *wife* of Clopas, and Mary Magdalene.

26 When Jesus therefore saw His mother, and the disciple whom He loved standing by, He said to His mother, "Woman, behold your son!"

27 Then He said to the disciple, "Behold your mother!" And from that hour that disciple took her to his own *home.*

28 After this, Jesus, knowing that all things were now accomplished, that the Scripture might be fulfilled, said, "I thirst!"

29 Now a vessel full of sour wine was sitting there; and they filled a sponge with sour wine, put *it* on hyssop, and put *it* to His mouth.

30 So when Jesus had received the sour wine, He said, "It is finished!" And bowing His head, He gave up His spirit.

31 Therefore, because it was the Preparation *Day,* that the bodies should not remain on the cross on the Sabbath (for that Sabbath was a high day), the Jews asked Pilate that their legs might be broken, and *that* they might be taken away.

32 Then the soldiers came and broke the legs of the first and of the other who was crucified with Him.

33 But when they came to Jesus and saw that He was already dead, they did not break His legs.

34 But one of the soldiers pierced His side with a spear, and immediately blood and water came out.

35 And he who has seen has testified, and his testimony is true; and he knows that he is telling the truth, so that you may believe.

36 For these things were done that the Scripture should be fulfilled, *"Not one of His bones shall be broken."*

37 And again another Scripture says, *"They shall look on Him whom they pierced."*

38 After this, Joseph of Arimathea, being a disciple of Jesus, but secretly, for fear of the Jews, asked Pilate that he might take away the body of Jesus; and Pilate gave *him* permission. So he came and took the body of Jesus.

39 And Nicodemus, who at first came to Jesus by night, also came, bringing a mixture of myrrh and aloes, about a hundred pounds.

40 Then they took the body of Jesus, and bound it in strips of linen with the spices, as the custom of the Jews is to bury.

41 Now in the place where He was crucified there was a garden, and in the garden a new tomb in which no one had yet been laid.

42 So there they laid Jesus, because of the Jews' Preparation *Day,* for the tomb was nearby.

20 On the first *day* of the week Mary Magdalene came to the tomb early, while it was still dark, and saw *that* the stone had been taken away from the tomb.

2 Then she ran and came to Simon Peter, and to the other disciple, whom Jesus loved, and said to them, "They have taken away the Lord out of the tomb, and we do not know where they have laid Him."

3 Peter therefore went out, and the other disciple, and were going to the tomb.

4 So they both ran together, and the other disciple outran Peter and came to the tomb first.

5 And he, stooping down and looking in, saw the linen cloths lying *there;* yet he did not go in.

6 Then Simon Peter came, following him, and went into the tomb; and he saw the linen cloths lying *there,*

7 and the handkerchief that had been around His head, not lying with the linen cloths, but folded together in a place by itself.

8 Then the other disciple, who came to the tomb first, went in also; and he saw and believed.

9 For as yet they did not know the Scripture, that He must rise again from the dead.

10 Then the disciples went away again to their own homes.

11 But Mary stood outside by the tomb weeping, and as she wept she stooped down *and looked* into the tomb.

12 And she saw two angels in white sitting, one at the head and the other at the feet, where the body of Jesus had lain.

13 Then they said to her, "Woman, why are you weeping?" She said to them, "Because they have taken away my Lord, and I do not know where they have laid Him."

14 Now when she had said this, she turned around and saw Jesus standing *there*, and did not know that it was Jesus.

15 Jesus said to her, "Woman, why are you weeping? Whom are you seeking?" She, supposing Him to be the gardener, said to Him, "Sir, if You have carried Him away, tell me where You have laid Him, and I will take Him away."

16 Jesus said to her, "Mary!" She turned and said to Him, "Rabboni!" (which is to say, Teacher).

17 Jesus said to her, "Do not cling to Me, for I have not yet ascended to My Father; but go to My brethren and say to them, 'I am ascending to My Father and your Father, and *to* My God and your God.' "

18 Mary Magdalene came and told the disciples that she had seen the Lord, and *that* He had spoken these things to her.

19 Then, the same day at evening, being the first *day* of the week, when the doors were shut where the disciples were assembled, for fear of the Jews, Jesus came and stood in the midst, and said to them, "Peace *be* with you."

20 Now when He had said this, He showed them *His* hands and His side. Then the disciples were glad when they saw the Lord.

21 Then Jesus said to them again, "Peace to you! As the Father has sent Me, I also send you."

22 And when He had said this, He breathed on *them*, and said to them, "Receive the Holy Spirit.

23 "If you forgive the sins of any, they are forgiven them; if you retain the *sins* of any, they are retained."

24 But Thomas, called Didymus, one of the twelve, was not with them when Jesus came.

25 The other disciples therefore said to him, "We have seen the Lord." But he said to them, "Unless I see in His hands the print of the nails, and put my finger into the print of the nails, and put my hand into His side, I will not believe."

26 And after eight days His disciples were again inside, and Thomas with them. Jesus came, the doors being shut, and stood in the midst, and said, "Peace to you!"

27 Then He said to Thomas, "Reach your finger here, and look at My hands; and reach your hand *here*, and put *it* into My side. Do not be unbelieving, but believing."

28 And Thomas answered and said to Him, "My Lord and my God!"

29 Jesus said to him, "Thomas, because you have seen Me, you have believed. Blessed *are* those who have not seen and *yet* have believed."

30 And truly Jesus did many other signs in the presence of His disciples, which are not written in this book;

31 but these are written that you may believe that Jesus is the Christ, the Son of God, and that

believing you may have life in His name.

STEP 6

21 After these things Jesus showed Himself again to the disciples at the Sea of Tiberias, and in this way He showed *Himself:*

2 Simon Peter, Thomas called Didymus, Nathanael of Cana in Galilee, the *sons* of Zebedee, and two others of His disciples were together.

3 Simon Peter said to them, "I am going fishing." They said to him, "We are going with you also." They went out and immediately got into the boat, and that night they caught nothing.

4 But when the morning had now come, Jesus stood on the shore; yet the disciples did not know that it was Jesus.

5 Then Jesus said to them, "Children, have you any food?" They answered Him, "No."

6 And He said to them, "Cast the net on the right side of the boat, and you will find *some.*" So they cast, and now they were not able to draw it in because of the multitude of fish.

7 Therefore that disciple whom Jesus loved said to Peter, "It is the Lord!" Now when Simon Peter heard that it was the Lord, he put on *his* outer garment (for he had removed it), and plunged into the sea.

8 But the other disciples came in the little boat (for they were not far from land, but about two hundred cubits), dragging the net with fish.

9 Then, as soon as they had come to land, they saw a fire of coals there, and fish laid on it, and bread.

10 Jesus said to them, "Bring some of the fish which you have just caught."

11 Simon Peter went up and dragged the net to land, full of large fish, one hundred and fifty-three; and although there were so many, the net was not broken.

12 Jesus said to them, "Come *and* eat breakfast." Yet none of the disciples dared ask Him, "Who are You?"—knowing that it was the Lord.

13 Jesus then came and took the bread and gave it to them, and likewise the fish.

14 This *is* now the third time Jesus showed Himself to His disciples after He was raised from the dead.

15 So when they had eaten breakfast, Jesus said to Simon Peter, "Simon, *son* of Jonah, do you love Me more than these?" He said to Him, "Yes, Lord; You know that I love You." He said to him, "Feed My lambs."

16 He said to him again a second time, "Simon, *son* of Jonah, do you love Me?" He said to Him, "Yes, Lord; You know that I love You." He said to him, "Tend My sheep."

17 He said to him the third time, "Simon, *son* of Jonah, do you love Me?" Peter was grieved because He said to him the third time, "Do you love Me?" And he said to Him, "Lord, You know all things; You know that I love You." Jesus said to him, "Feed My sheep.

18 "Most assuredly, I say to you, when you were younger, you girded yourself and walked where you wished; but when you are old, you will stretch out your hands, and another will gird you and carry *you* where you do not wish."

19 This He spoke, signifying by what death he would glorify God. And when He had spoken this, He said to him, "Follow Me."

20 Then Peter, turning around, saw the disciple whom Jesus loved following, who also had leaned on His breast at the supper, and said, "Lord, who is the one who betrays You?"

21 Peter, seeing him, said to Jesus, "But Lord, what *about* this man?"

22 Jesus said to him, "If I will that he remain till I come, what *is that* to you? You follow Me."

STEP 6

*Were entirely ready to have God
remove all these defects of character.*

John 21:1–17

In one of His post-Resurrection appearances, Jesus sat with His disciples around a fire. As they talked, Jesus began to ask Peter some probing questions. He knew Peter was, for the first time, ready to allow God to mold him into a truly great servant-leader.

Earlier Peter had wanted to lead in his own way, clinging to character traits that were damaging to himself and others. But as Peter declared his love for the Lord, he was on the threshold of change. He was no longer the swaggering know-it-all. He was no longer a tough guy. When Jesus asked him, "Do you love Me more than these?" the word "these" referred to the other disciples. Peter had bragged that although all others might desert Jesus, he would not. The night before Jesus' crucifixion he was forced to face the bitter truth about himself. He was in reality far weaker than he had imagined himself to be. Here, as he answered Jesus, he humbly acknowledged God's wisdom instead of his own. He was ready for great things.

For further reading on Step 6, turn to page 327.

Daily Encouragement

DAY 110 READING: JOHN 19:38—21:25

A Thought for the New Day: Unlike Thomas and the others (20:29), we have never seen or touched Jesus. So how can we know Him and know that He is alive? The Holy Spirit convinces us, in a way that surpasses all other proof, that Christ lives and dwells in us; and we thus enjoy His unique, resurrection life day-by-day. This revelation is called "the internal testimony of the Holy Spirit." It is a privilege that belongs to you as you trust in Jesus as your Lord and Savior. (*Turn to page 255.*)

23 Then this saying went out among the brethren that this disciple would not die. Yet Jesus did not say to him that he would not die, but, "If I will that he remain till I come, what *is that* to you?" 24 This is the disciple who testifies of these things, and wrote these things; and we know that his testimony is true. 25 And there are also many other things that Jesus did, which if they were written one by one, I suppose that even the world itself could not contain the books that would be written. Amen.

THE ACTS

OF THE APOSTLES

THE former account I made, O Theophilus, of all that Jesus began both to do and teach, 2 until the day in which He was taken up, after He through the Holy Spirit had given commandments to the apostles whom He had chosen, 3 to whom He also presented Himself alive after His suffering by many infallible proofs, being seen by them during forty days and speaking of the things pertaining to the kingdom of God. 4 And being assembled together with *them*, He commanded them not to depart from Jerusalem, but to wait for the Promise of the Father, "which," *He said*, "you have heard from Me; 5 "for John truly baptized with water, but you shall be baptized with the Holy Spirit not many days from now."

6 Therefore, when they had come together, they asked Him, saying, "Lord, will You at this time restore the kingdom to Israel?"

7 And He said to them, "It is not for you to know times or seasons which the Father has put in His own authority.

8 "But you shall receive power when the Holy Spirit has come upon you; and you shall be witnesses to Me in Jerusalem, and in all Judea and Samaria, and to the end of the earth."

9 Now when He had spoken these things, while they watched, He was taken up, and a cloud received Him out of their sight. 10 And while they looked steadfastly toward heaven as He went up, behold, two men stood by them in white apparel, 11 who also said, "Men of Galilee, why do you stand gazing up into heaven? This *same* Jesus, who was taken up from you into heaven, will so come in like manner as you saw Him go into heaven."

12 Then they returned to Jerusalem from the Mount called Olivet, which is near Jerusalem, a Sabbath day's journey. 13 And when they had entered, they went up into the upper room where they were staying: Peter, James, John, and Andrew; Philip and Thomas; Bartholomew and Matthew; James *the son* of Alphaeus and Simon the Zealot; and Judas *the son* of James.

14 These all continued with one accord in prayer and supplication, with the women and Mary the mother of Jesus, and with His brothers.

15 And in those days Peter stood up in the midst of the disciples (altogether the number of names

STEP 9

*Made direct amends to such people wherever possible,
except when to do so would injure them or others.*

Acts 1:14

Undoubtedly, at one time, there had been animosity between
Jesus' brothers and His disciples. Jesus' family had tried to take custody of Him, declaring He was insane (Mark 3:21). His brothers
had mocked Him, refusing to believe that He was who He claimed
to be (John 7:3–5). Jesus Himself had declared that His disciples
were more of a family to Him than His own brothers, because the
disciples were doing God's will. Yes, it sounds like some hard words
had been spoken and an obvious rift had occurred.

Yet sometime after Jesus' resurrection and return to heaven,
apologies had been made and received, and fresh relationships
begun. The disciples and Jesus' family united as brothers in Him.

The joys of reconciliation are worth the effort it takes to overcome our fears and doubts. It is a wonderful thing to lose a foe and
gain a brother.

For further reading on Step 9, turn to page 277.

Daily Encouragement

DAY 111 READING: ACTS 1:1–14

A Thought for the New Day: Jesus was seen alive by a great
many people after He arose from death (v. 3). Paul the apostle
says that the risen Christ was witnessed by over five hundred
people at one time. The men Jesus had chosen as apostles dedicated their entire lives to telling the world the story of a risen
Savior, and all but one of them accepted violent death rather
than renounce their witness to the risen Savior. Be assured: Jesus
is alive! (*Turn to page 257.*)

was about a hundred and twenty), and said,

16 "Men *and* brethren, this Scripture had to be fulfilled, which the Holy Spirit spoke before by the mouth of David concerning Judas, who became a guide to those who arrested Jesus;

17 "for he was numbered with us and obtained a part in this ministry."

18 (Now this man purchased a field with the wages of iniquity; and falling headlong, he burst open in the middle and all his entrails gushed out.

19 And it became known to all those dwelling in Jerusalem; so that field is called in their own language, Akel Dama, that is, Field of Blood.)

20 "For it is written in the book of Psalms:

'Let his habitation be desolate,
And let no one live in it';

and,

'Let another take his office.'

21 "Therefore, of these men who have accompanied us all the time that the Lord Jesus went in and out among us,

22 "beginning from the baptism of John to that day when He was taken up from us, one of these must become a witness with us of His resurrection."

23 And they proposed two: Joseph called Barsabas, who was surnamed Justus, and Matthias.

24 And they prayed and said, "You, O Lord, who know the hearts of all, show which of these two You have chosen

25 "to take part in this ministry and apostleship from which Judas by transgression fell, that he might go to his own place."

26 And they cast their lots, and the lot fell on Matthias. And he was numbered with the eleven apostles.

2 Now when the Day of Pentecost had fully come, they were all with one accord in one place.

2 And suddenly there came a sound from heaven, as of a rushing mighty wind, and it filled the whole house where they were sitting.

3 Then there appeared to them divided tongues, as of fire, and *one* sat upon each of them.

4 And they were all filled with the Holy Spirit and began to speak with other tongues, as the Spirit gave them utterance.

5 Now there were dwelling in Jerusalem Jews, devout men, from every nation under heaven.

6 And when this sound occurred, the multitude came together, and were confused, because everyone heard them speak in his own language.

7 Then they were all amazed and marveled, saying to one another, "Look, are not all these who speak Galileans?

8 "And how *is it that* we hear, each in our own language in which we were born?

9 "Parthians and Medes and Elamites, those dwelling in Mesopotamia, Judea and Cappadocia, Pontus and Asia,

10 "Phrygia and Pamphylia, Egypt and the parts of Libya adjoining Cyrene, visitors from Rome, both Jews and proselytes,

11 "Cretans and Arabs—we hear them speaking in our own tongues the wonderful works of God."

12 So they were all amazed and perplexed, saying to one another, "Whatever could this mean?"

13 Others mocking said, "They are full of new wine."

14 But Peter, standing up with the eleven, raised his voice and said to them, "Men of Judea and all who dwell in Jerusalem, let this be known to you, and heed my words.

15 "For these are not drunk, as you

STEP 11

STEP 11

*Sought through prayer and meditation to improve our conscious contact with God **as we understood Him**, praying only for knowledge of His will for us and the power to carry that out.*

Acts 2:1–4

The coming of the Holy Spirit on Pentecost must have been an awesome and unforgettable experience for the little band of 120 believers. Their lives were forever changed as He actually came to indwell and empower each of them. What a difference His presence has made! He is the believer's Comforter, Teacher, and Guide.

Because that same precious Holy Spirit indwells us today, we have all the guidance and wisdom and strength to do God's will that we will ever need. We do not need to make random guesses about our future. Our Comforter and Guide is waiting to be asked—wanting us to seek His guidance in finding the path we should follow. He speaks through Scripture, circumstances, and the still, quiet inclination of our hearts as we commune with God in prayer. Anyone who truly desires to obey Him will be aware of the Holy Spirit's leading.

For further reading on Step 11, turn to page 285.

Daily Encouragement

DAY 112 READING: ACTS 1:15—2:13

A Thought for the New Day: What did it mean (2:12)? These Christians were behaving in a very unusual way. However, hadn't Jesus said that "the wind blows where it wishes . . . So is everyone who is born of the Spirit"? (John 3:8). Although we cannot see God with our natural eyes, we can experience His action in and around us. The Spirit of God moves like the invisible wind; and, when He does, we receive new life and strength to do new things for God. (*Turn to page 259.*)

suppose, since it is *only* the third hour of the day.

16 "But this is what was spoken by the prophet Joel:

17 '*And it shall come to pass in the last days, says God,*
That I will pour out of My Spirit on all flesh;
Your sons and your daughters shall prophesy,
Your young men shall see visions,
Your old men shall dream dreams.

18 *And on My menservants and on My maidservants*
I will pour out My Spirit in those days;
And they shall prophesy.

19 *I will show wonders in heaven above*
And signs in the earth beneath:
Blood and fire and vapor of smoke.

20 *The sun shall be turned into darkness,*
And the moon into blood,
Before the coming of the great and notable day of the LORD.

21 *And it shall come to pass that whoever calls on the name of the LORD shall be saved.'*

22 "Men of Israel, hear these words: Jesus of Nazareth, a Man attested by God to you by miracles, wonders, and signs which God did through Him in your midst, as you yourselves also know—

23 "Him, being delivered by the determined counsel and foreknowledge of God, you have taken by lawless hands, have crucified, and put to death;

24 "whom God raised up, having loosed the pains of death, because it was not possible that He should be held by it.

25 "For David says concerning Him:

'*I foresaw the LORD always before my face,*
For He is at my right hand, that I may not be shaken;

26 *Therefore my heart rejoiced, and my tongue was glad;*
Moreover my flesh will also rest in hope,

27 *Because You will not leave my soul in Hades,*
Nor will You allow Your Holy One to see corruption.

28 *You have made known to me the ways of life;*
You will make me full of joy in Your presence.'

29 "Men *and* brethren, let *me* speak freely to you of the patriarch David, that he is both dead and buried, and his tomb is with us to this day.

30 "Therefore, being a prophet, and knowing that God had sworn with an oath to him that of the fruit of his body, according to the flesh, He would raise up the Christ to sit on his throne,

31 "he, foreseeing this, spoke concerning the resurrection of the Christ, that His soul was not left in Hades, nor did His flesh see corruption.

32 "This Jesus God has raised up, of which we are all witnesses.

33 "Therefore being exalted to the right hand of God, and having received from the Father the promise of the Holy Spirit, He poured out this which you now see and hear.

34 "For David did not ascend into the heavens, but he says himself:

'*The LORD said to my Lord,*
"*Sit at My right hand,*

35 *Till I make Your enemies Your footstool.*" '

36 "Therefore let all the house of Israel know assuredly that God has made this Jesus, whom you crucified, both Lord and Christ."

STEP 3

Made a decision to turn our will and our lives
*over to the care of God **as we understood Him**.*

Acts 2:21

In the three years of Jesus' public ministry on earth, thousands felt His healing touch, heard His claims and His teaching, and even ate the food He miraculously provided. Still, by the time of Pentecost, only 120 of His followers were courageous enough and committed enough to own Him as Lord.

Where were all the others He had helped? A less patient God might have decided that these people did not deserve any more chances or any more miracles. But our God is gracious, longsuffering, and compassionate.

The Holy Spirit's evidence at Pentecost and Peter's message of hope were yet another call from God to wandering souls. God longs after us. This means He desires greatly for us to bring Him our lives. We have longed after many unworthy things in the past. Now a great blessing awaits us as we begin to long for Him.

For further reading on Step 3, turn to page 306.

Daily Encouragement

DAY 113 READING: ACTS 2:14–47

A Thought for the New Day: What is the visible quality you most desire in others? It comes by many names: friendliness, agreeableness, cooperativeness, the forsaking of one's personal interests for the good of others. This is how the early Christians are described, and they had "favor with all the people" (vv. 46, 47). The attainment of this reputation is an ideal that could be more often achieved. We must pray for that reputation, then *be* what we pray to be made. (*Turn to page 261.*)

37 Now when they heard *this*, they were cut to the heart, and said to Peter and the rest of the apostles, "Men *and* brethren, what shall we do?"

38 Then Peter said to them, "Repent, and let every one of you be baptized in the name of Jesus Christ for the remission of sins; and you shall receive the gift of the Holy Spirit.

39 "For the promise is to you and to your children, and to all who are afar off, as many as the Lord our God will call."

40 And with many other words he testified and exhorted them, saying, "Be saved from this perverse generation."

41 Then those who gladly received his word were baptized; and that day about three thousand souls were added *to them*.

42 And they continued steadfastly in the apostles' doctrine and fellowship, in the breaking of bread, and in prayers.

43 Then fear came upon every soul, and many wonders and signs were done through the apostles.

44 Now all who believed were together, and had all things in common,

45 and sold their possessions and goods, and divided them among all, as anyone had need.

46 So continuing daily with one accord in the temple, and breaking bread from house to house, they ate their food with gladness and simplicity of heart,

47 praising God and having favor with all the people. And the Lord added to the church daily those who were being saved.

3 Now Peter and John went up together to the temple at the hour of prayer, the ninth *hour*.

2 And a certain man lame from his mother's womb was carried, whom they laid daily at the gate of the temple which is called Beautiful, to ask alms from those who entered the temple;

3 who, seeing Peter and John about to go into the temple, asked for alms.

4 And fixing his eyes on him, with John, Peter said, "Look at us."

5 So he gave them his attention, expecting to receive something from them.

6 Then Peter said, "Silver and gold I do not have, but what I do have I give you: In the name of Jesus Christ of Nazareth, rise up and walk."

7 And he took him by the right hand and lifted *him* up, and immediately his feet and ankle bones received strength.

8 So he, leaping up, stood and walked and entered the temple with them—walking, leaping, and praising God.

9 And all the people saw him walking and praising God.

10 Then they knew that it was he who sat begging alms at the Beautiful Gate of the temple; and they were filled with wonder and amazement at what had happened to him.

11 Now as the lame man who was healed held on to Peter and John, all the people ran together to them in the porch which is called Solomon's, greatly amazed.

12 So when Peter saw *it*, he responded to the people: "Men of Israel, why do you marvel at this? Or why look so intently at us, as though by our own power or godliness we had made this man walk?

13 "The God of Abraham, Isaac, and Jacob, the God of our fathers, glorified His Servant Jesus, whom you delivered up and denied in the presence of Pilate, when he was determined to let *Him* go.

14 "But you denied the Holy One and the Just, and asked for a murderer to be granted to you,

15 "and killed the Prince of life, whom God raised from the dead, of which we are witnesses.

16 "And His name, through faith in

STEP 2

STEP 2

Came to believe that a Power greater than ourselves could restore us to sanity.

Acts 3:16

Expectations—most of us have lived life having them shattered. Our hopes and dreams have been dashed. The things we expected would bring us happiness and peace have instead brought pain and disillusionment. Our strength is gone, and we feel emotionally and spiritually crippled.

So we can understand to a certain extent how the lame man at the temple felt as Peter spoke to him. As soon as the words "Silver and gold I do not have" fell from Peter's lips, we may have expected the lame man to turn away, complaining bitterly about more failed expectations. Yes, his bitterness and preconceived ideas about what he ought to be receiving could have kept him from the greatest blessing of his life. However, this man, crippled and helpless as he was, still had the courage and faith to believe in the name of Jesus, and to experience the power and healing of God in his life. Faith in the power of Jesus' name will bring us healing as well.

For further reading on Step 2, turn to page 283.

Daily Encouragement

DAY 114 READING: ACTS 3:1–18

A Thought for the New Day: Peter was not wealthy, but he gave what he had (v. 6). He gave the love of Christ, in this case expressed in healing the lame man. Our gift may not be riches or brilliance or worldly power, but we can be blessed possessors of the grace of Jesus that is expressed in many ways that bring God near to people's needs. What is my near neighbor's need? Let me share "what I do have" with that one. (*Turn to page 263.*)

His name, has made this man strong, whom you see and know. Yes, the faith which *comes* through Him has given him this perfect soundness in the presence of you all.

17 "Yet now, brethren, I know that you did *it* in ignorance, as *did* also your rulers.

18 "But those things which God foretold by the mouth of all His prophets, that the Christ would suffer, He has thus fulfilled.

STEP 7

19 "Repent therefore and be converted, that your sins may be blotted out, so that times of refreshing may come from the presence of the Lord,

20 "and that He may send Jesus Christ, who was preached to you before,

21 "whom heaven must receive until the times of restoration of all things, which God has spoken by the mouth of all His holy prophets since the world began.

22 "For Moses truly said to the fathers, *'The Lord your God will raise up for you a Prophet like me from your brethren. Him you shall hear in all things, whatever He says to you.*

23 *'And it shall come to pass that every soul who will not hear that Prophet shall be utterly destroyed from among the people.'*

24 "Yes, and all the prophets, from Samuel and those who follow, as many as have spoken, have also foretold these days.

25 "You are sons of the prophets, and of the covenant which God made with our fathers, saying to Abraham, *'And in your seed all the families of the earth shall be blessed.'*

26 "To you first, God, having raised up His Servant Jesus, sent Him to bless you, in turning away every one *of you* from your iniquities."

4 Now as they spoke to the people, the priests, the captain of the temple, and the Sadducees came upon them,

2 being greatly disturbed that they taught the people and preached in Jesus the resurrection from the dead.

3 And they laid hands on them, and put *them* in custody until the next day, for it was already evening.

4 However, many of those who heard the word believed; and the number of the men came to be about five thousand.

5 And it came to pass, on the next day, that their rulers, elders, and scribes,

6 as well as Annas the high priest, Caiaphas, John, and Alexander, and as many as were of the family of the high priest, were gathered together at Jerusalem.

7 And when they had set them in the midst, they asked, "By what power or by what name have you done this?"

8 Then Peter, filled with the Holy Spirit, said to them, "Rulers of the people and elders of Israel:

9 "If we this day are judged for a good deed *done* to *the* helpless man, by what means he has been made well,

10 "let it be known to you all, and to all the people of Israel, that by the name of Jesus Christ of Nazareth, whom you crucified, whom God raised from the dead, by Him this man stands here before you whole.

11 "This is the *'stone which was rejected by you builders, which has become the chief cornerstone.'*

12 "Nor is there salvation in any other, for there is no other name under heaven given among men by which we must be saved."

STEP 2

13 Now when they saw the boldness of Peter and John, and perceived that they were uneducated and untrained men, they marveled. And they realized that they had been with Jesus.

Humbly asked Him to remove our shortcomings.

Acts 3:19

Step 7 embodies God's mysterious power to rebuild our very character and leads us toward the miracle of transformation and conversion.

Alcoholics Anonymous (p. 76) offers the following prayer for seventh step conversions: "My Creator, I am now willing that you should have all of me, good and bad. I pray that you now remove from me every single defect of character which stands in the way of my usefulness to you and my fellows. Grant me strength, as I go out from here, to do your bidding. Amen."

What is entailed in this conversion! We admit and yield every character distortion to God's transforming touch. We open our every relationship to His guidance. We surrender to His care and discipline all addictive and compulsive behavior patterns. We ask without restraint that He be the God of our lives.

If we approach this act of repentance with a sincere heart, we emerge with a refreshed spirit that comes "from the presence of the Lord."

For further reading on Step 7, turn to page 485.

Daily Encouragement

DAY 115 READING: ACTS 3:19—4:37

A Thought for the New Day: Although we may not come face-to-face with every kind of suffering, we are aware it exists all around us. We know, too, that we cannot escape our own share of suffering. Even great faith will not spare us, but faith does give us the steel to endure, even thankfully, all the sorrows that come our way. The unpleasant and unjust happenings of our experience also strengthen us to live more vitally and effectively during the better times. (*Turn to page 267.*)

14 And seeing the man who had been healed standing with them, they could say nothing against it.

15 But when they had commanded them to go aside out of the council, they conferred among themselves,

16 saying, "What shall we do to these men? For, indeed, that a notable miracle has been done through them is evident to all who dwell in Jerusalem, and we cannot deny it.

17 "But so that it spreads no further among the people, let us severely threaten them, that from now on they speak to no man in this name."

18 And they called them and commanded them not to speak at all nor teach in the name of Jesus.

19 But Peter and John answered and said to them, "Whether it is right in the sight of God to listen to you more than to God, you judge.

20 "For we cannot but speak the things which we have seen and heard."

21 So when they had further threatened them, they let them go, finding no way of punishing them, because of the people, since they all glorified God for what had been done.

22 For the man was over forty years old on whom this miracle of healing had been performed.

23 And being let go, they went to their own *companions* and reported all that the chief priests and elders had said to them.

24 So when they heard that, they raised their voice to God with one accord and said: "Lord, You *are* God, who made heaven and earth and the sea, and all that is in them,

25 "who by the mouth of Your servant David have said:

'Why did the nations rage,
And the people plot vain
    things?

26 The kings of the earth took
    their stand,

And the rulers were gathered
    together
Against the Lord and against
    His Christ.'

27 "For truly against Your holy Servant Jesus, whom You anointed, both Herod and Pontius Pilate, with the Gentiles and the people of Israel, were gathered together

28 "to do whatever Your hand and Your purpose determined before to be done.

29 "Now, Lord, look on their threats, and grant to Your servants that with all boldness they may speak Your word,

30 "by stretching out Your hand to heal, and that signs and wonders may be done through the name of Your holy Servant Jesus."

31 And when they had prayed, the place where they were assembled together was shaken; and they were all filled with the Holy Spirit, and they spoke the word of God with boldness.

32 Now the multitude of those who believed were of one heart and one soul; neither did anyone say that any of the things he possessed was his own, but they had all things in common.

33 And with great power the apostles gave witness to the resurrection of the Lord Jesus. And great grace was upon them all.

34 Nor was there anyone among them who lacked; for all who were possessors of lands or houses sold them, and brought the proceeds of the things that were sold,

35 and laid *them* at the apostles' feet; and they distributed to each as anyone had need.

36 And Joses, who was also named Barnabas by the apostles (which is translated Son of Encouragement), a Levite of the country of Cyprus,

37 having land, sold *it,* and brought the money and laid *it* at the apostles' feet.

5 But a certain man named Ananias, with Sapphira his wife, sold a possession.

2 And he kept back *part* of the proceeds, his wife also being aware *of it*, and brought a certain part and laid *it* at the apostles' feet.

3 But Peter said, "Ananias, why has Satan filled your heart to lie to the Holy Spirit and keep back *part* of the price of the land for yourself?

4 "While it remained, was it not your own? And after it was sold, was it not in your own control? Why have you conceived this thing in your heart? You have not lied to men but to God."

5 Then Ananias, hearing these words, fell down and breathed his last. So great fear came upon all those who heard these things.

6 And the young men arose and wrapped him up, carried *him* out, and buried *him*.

7 Now it was about three hours later when his wife came in, not knowing what had happened.

8 And Peter answered her, "Tell me whether you sold the land for so much?" And she said, "Yes, for so much."

9 Then Peter said to her, "How is it that you have agreed together to test the Spirit of the Lord? Look, the feet of those who have buried your husband *are* at the door, and they will carry you out."

10 Then immediately she fell down at his feet and breathed her last. And the young men came in and found her dead, and carrying *her* out, buried *her* by her husband.

11 So great fear came upon all the church and upon all who heard these things.

12 And through the hands of the apostles many signs and wonders were done among the people. And they were all with one accord in Solomon's Porch.

13 Yet none of the rest dared join them, but the people esteemed them highly.

14 And believers were increasingly added to the Lord, multitudes of both men and women,

15 so that they brought the sick out into the streets and laid *them* on beds and couches, that at least the shadow of Peter passing by might fall on some of them.

16 Also a multitude gathered from the surrounding cities to Jerusalem, bringing sick people and those who were tormented by unclean spirits, and they were all healed.

17 Then the high priest rose up, and all those who *were* with him (which is the sect of the Sadducees), and they were filled with indignation,

18 and laid their hands on the apostles and put them in the common prison.

19 But at night an angel of the Lord opened the prison doors and brought them out, and said,

20 "Go, stand in the temple and speak to the people all the words of this life."

21 And when they heard *that*, they entered the temple early in the morning and taught. But the high priest and those with him came and called the council together, with all the elders of the children of Israel, and sent to the prison to have them brought.

22 But when the officers came and did not find them in the prison, they returned and reported,

23 saying, "Indeed we found the prison shut securely, and the guards standing outside before the doors; but when we opened them, we found no one inside!"

24 Now when the high priest, the captain of the temple, and the chief priests heard these things, they wondered what the outcome would be.

25 Then one came and told them, saying, "Look, the men whom you put in prison are standing in the temple and teaching the people!"

26 Then the captain went with the officers and brought them without

violence, for they feared the people, lest they should be stoned.

27 And when they had brought them, they set *them* before the council. And the high priest asked them,

28 saying, "Did we not strictly command you not to teach in this name? And look, you have filled Jerusalem with your doctrine, and intend to bring this Man's blood on us!"

29 Then Peter and the *other* apostles answered and said: "We ought to obey God rather than men.

30 "The God of our fathers raised up Jesus whom you murdered by hanging on a tree.

31 "Him God has exalted to His right hand *to be* Prince and Savior, to give repentance to Israel and forgiveness of sins.

32 "And we are His witnesses to these things, and *so* also *is* the Holy Spirit whom God has given to those who obey Him."

33 When they heard *this*, they were furious and took counsel to kill them.

34 Then one in the council stood up, a Pharisee named Gamaliel, a teacher of the law held in respect by all the people, and commanded them to put the apostles outside for a little while.

35 And he said to them: "Men of Israel, take heed to yourselves what you intend to do regarding these men.

36 "For some time ago Theudas rose up, claiming to be somebody. A number of men, about four hundred, joined him. He was slain, and all who obeyed him were scattered and came to nothing.

37 "After this man, Judas of Galilee rose up in the days of the census, and drew away many people after him. He also perished, and all who obeyed him were dispersed.

38 "And now I say to you, keep away from these men and let them alone; for if this plan or this work is of men, it will come to nothing;

39 "but if it is of God, you cannot overthrow it—lest you even be found to fight against God."

40 And they agreed with him, and when they had called for the apostles and beaten *them*, they commanded that they should not speak in the name of Jesus, and let them go.

41 So they departed from the presence of the council, rejoicing that they were counted worthy to suffer shame for His name.

42 And daily in the temple, and in every house, they did not cease teaching and preaching Jesus *as* the Christ.

6 Now in those days, when *the number of* the disciples was multiplying, there arose a murmuring against the Hebrews by the Hellenists, because their widows were neglected in the daily distribution.

2 Then the twelve summoned the multitude of the disciples and said, "It is not desirable that we should leave the word of God and serve tables.

3 "Therefore, brethren, seek out from among you seven men of *good* reputation, full of the Holy Spirit and wisdom, whom we may appoint over this business;

4 "but we will give ourselves continually to prayer and to the ministry of the word."

5 And the saying pleased the whole multitude. And they chose Stephen, a man full of faith and the Holy Spirit, and Philip, Prochorus, Nicanor, Timon, Parmenas, and Nicolas, a proselyte from Antioch,

6 whom they set before the apostles; and when they had prayed, they laid hands on them.

7 And the word of God spread, and the number of the disciples multiplied greatly in Jerusalem, and a great many of the priests were obedient to the faith.

8 And Stephen, full of faith and

STEP 12

*Having had a spiritual awakening as the result
of these steps, we tried to carry this message to others,
and to practice these principles in all our affairs.*

Acts 5:34–42

The Pharisee named Gamaliel inadvertently declared salvation
through faith in Jesus Christ to be the work of Almighty God.
Although he did not intend to give credence to the disciples' faith,
the sands of time have shown the truth of all he said. The plans
and work of human beings eventually burn themselves out. But
God's work can never be extinguished. Down through the centuries
people have sought to destroy or discredit the simple message of salvation through faith in Jesus' death and resurrection. They have
mounted huge campaigns to eradicate God's Word from existence.
But God's work is protected by God Himself. We are now a part of
that great work. Our message may be mocked or discredited from
time to time, but it cannot be destroyed because the power behind
the message we carry is not our own. God Himself is causing our
witness to bear fruit.

For further reading on Step 12, turn to page 299.

Daily Encouragement

DAY 116 READING: ACTS 5:1—6:7

A Thought for the New Day: We know little about Gamaliel,
other than that he had been a principal teacher of the apostle
Paul before the latter's conversion to Christ. Although we may
be disturbed by Gamaliel's "fence-sitting" position on the
Christian matter (5:38, 39), he showed wisdom in not rushing
into judgment. Likewise, we do well to be cautious in our own
judgments. (*Turn to page 271.*)

power, did great wonders and signs among the people.

9 Then there arose some from what is called the Synagogue of the Freedmen (Cyrenians, Alexandrians, and those from Cilicia and Asia), disputing with Stephen.

10 And they were not able to resist the wisdom and the Spirit by which he spoke.

11 Then they secretly induced men to say, "We have heard him speak blasphemous words against Moses and God."

12 And they stirred up the people, the elders, and the scribes; and they came upon *him*, seized him, and brought *him* to the council.

13 They also set up false witnesses who said, "This man does not cease to speak blasphemous words against this holy place and the law;

14 "for we have heard him say that this Jesus of Nazareth will destroy this place and change the customs which Moses delivered to us."

15 And all who sat in the council, looking steadfastly at him, saw his face as the face of an angel.

7 Then the high priest said, "Are these things so?"

2 And he said, "Men and brethren and fathers, listen: The God of glory appeared to our father Abraham when he was in Mesopotamia, before he dwelt in Haran,

3 "and said to him, *'Get out of your country and from your relatives, and come to a land that I will show you.'*

4 "Then he came out of the land of the Chaldeans and dwelt in Haran. And from there, when his father was dead, He moved him to this land in which you now dwell.

5 "And *God* gave him no inheritance in it, not even *enough* to set his foot on. But even when *Abraham* had no child, He promised to give it to him for a possession, and to his descendants after him.

6 "But God spoke in this way: that his descendants would sojourn in a foreign land, and that

they would bring them into bondage and oppress *them* four hundred years.

7 *'And the nation to whom they will be in bondage I will judge,'* said God, *'and after that they shall come out and serve Me in this place.'*

8 "Then He gave him the covenant of circumcision; and so *Abraham* begot Isaac and circumcised him on the eighth day; and Isaac *begot* Jacob, and Jacob *begot* the twelve patriarchs.

9 "And the patriarchs, becoming envious, sold Joseph into Egypt. But God was with him

10 "and delivered him out of all his troubles, and gave him favor and wisdom in the presence of Pharaoh, king of Egypt; and he made him governor over Egypt and all his house.

11 "Now a famine and great trouble came over all the land of Egypt and Canaan, and our fathers found no sustenance.

12 "But when Jacob heard that there was grain in Egypt, he sent out our fathers first.

13 "And the second *time* Joseph was made known to his brothers, and Joseph's family became known to the Pharaoh.

14 "Then Joseph sent and called his father Jacob and all his relatives to *him*, seventy-five people.

15 "So Jacob went down to Egypt; and he died, he and our fathers.

16 "And they were carried back to Shechem and laid in the tomb that Abraham bought for a sum of money from the sons of Hamor, *the father* of Shechem.

17 "But when the time of the promise drew near which God had sworn to Abraham, the people grew and multiplied in Egypt

18 "till another king arose who did not know Joseph.

19 "This man dealt treacherously with our people, and oppressed our forefathers, making them expose

their babies, so that they might not live.

20 "At this time Moses was born, and was well pleasing to God; and he was brought up in his father's house for three months.

21 "But when he was set out, Pharaoh's daughter took him away and brought him up as her own son.

22 "And Moses was learned in all the wisdom of the Egyptians, and was mighty in words and deeds.

23 "But when he was forty years old, it came into his heart to visit his brethren, the children of Israel.

24 "And seeing one of *them* suffer wrong, he defended and avenged him who was oppressed, and struck down the Egyptian.

25 "For he supposed that his brethren would have understood that God would deliver them by his hand, but they did not understand.

26 "And the next day he appeared to two of them as they were fighting, and *tried to* reconcile them, saying, 'Men, you are brethren; why do you wrong one another?'

27 "But he who did his neighbor wrong pushed him away, saying, *'Who made you a ruler and a judge over us?*

28 *Do you want to kill me as you did the Egyptian yesterday?'*

29 "Then, at this saying, Moses fled and became a sojourner in the land of Midian, where he had two sons.

30 "And when forty years had passed, an Angel of the Lord appeared to him in a flame of fire in a bush, in the wilderness of Mount Sinai.

31 "When Moses saw *it,* he marveled at the sight; and as he drew near to observe, the voice of the Lord came to him,

32 "saying, *'I am the God of your fathers—the God of Abraham, the God of Isaac, and the God of Jacob.'* And Moses trembled and dared not look.

33 *'Then the LORD said to him,* "Take your sandals off your feet,

for the place where you stand is holy ground.

34 "*I have certainly seen the oppression of My people who are in Egypt; I have heard their groaning and have come down to deliver them. And now come, I will send you to Egypt."* '

35 "This Moses whom they rejected, saying, *'Who made you a ruler and a judge?'* is the one God sent *to be* a ruler and a deliverer by the hand of the Angel who appeared to him in the bush.

36 "He brought them out, after he had shown wonders and signs in the land of Egypt, and in the Red Sea, and in the wilderness forty years.

37 "This is that Moses who said to the children of Israel, *'The LORD your God will raise up for you a Prophet like me from your brethren. Him you shall hear.'*

38 "This is he who was in the congregation in the wilderness with the Angel who spoke to him on Mount Sinai, and *with* our fathers, the one who received the living oracles to give to us,

39 "whom our fathers would not obey, but rejected. And in their hearts they turned back to Egypt,

40 "saying to Aaron, *'Make us gods to go before us; as for this Moses who brought us out of the land of Egypt, we do not know what has become of him.'*

41 "And they made a calf in those days, offered sacrifices to the idol, and rejoiced in the works of their own hands.

42 "Then God turned and gave them up to worship the host of heaven, as it is written in the book of the Prophets:

'Did you offer Me slaughtered animals and sacrifices during forty years in the wilderness, O house of Israel?

43 *Yes, you took up the tabernacle of Moloch,*

And the star of your god
　Remphan,
Images which you made to
　worship;
And I will carry you away
　beyond Babylon.'

44 "Our fathers had the tabernacle of witness in the wilderness, as He appointed, instructing Moses to make it according to the pattern that he had seen,

45 "which our fathers, having received it in turn, also brought with Joshua into the land possessed by the Gentiles, whom God drove out before the face of our fathers until the days of David,

46 "who found favor before God and asked to find a dwelling for the God of Jacob.

47 "But Solomon built Him a house.

48 "However, the Most High does not dwell in temples made with hands, as the prophet says:

49 'Heaven is My throne,
　And earth is My footstool.
　What house will you build for
　　Me? says the LORD,
　Or what is the place of My
　　rest?
50 Has My hand not made all
　these things?'

51 "You stiff-necked and uncircumcised in heart and ears! You always resist the Holy Spirit; as your fathers did, so do you.

52 "Which of the prophets did your fathers not persecute? And they killed those who foretold the coming of the Just One, of whom you now have become the betrayers and murderers,

53 "who have received the law by the direction of angels and have not kept it."

54 When they heard these things they were cut to the heart, and they gnashed at him with their teeth.

55 But he, being full of the Holy Spirit, gazed into heaven and saw the glory of God, and Jesus standing at the right hand of God,

56 and said, "Look! I see the heavens opened and the Son of Man standing at the right hand of God!"

57 Then they cried out with a loud voice, stopped their ears, and ran at him with one accord;

58 and they cast him out of the city and stoned him. And the witnesses laid down their clothes at the feet of a young man named Saul.

59 And they stoned Stephen as he was calling on God and saying, "Lord Jesus, receive my spirit."

60 Then he knelt down and cried out with a loud voice, "Lord, do not charge them with this sin." And when he had said this, he fell asleep.

8 Now Saul was consenting to his death. At that time a great persecution arose against the church which was at Jerusalem; and they were all scattered throughout the regions of Judea and Samaria, except the apostles.

2 And devout men carried Stephen to his burial, and made great lamentation over him.

3 As for Saul, he made havoc of the church, entering every house, and dragging off men and women, committing them to prison.

4 Therefore those who were scattered went everywhere preaching the word.

5 Then Philip went down to the city of Samaria and preached Christ to them.

6 And the multitudes with one accord heeded the things spoken by Philip, hearing and seeing the miracles which he did.

7 For unclean spirits, crying with a loud voice, came out of many who were possessed; and many who were paralyzed and lame were healed.

8 And there was great joy in that city.

STEP 5

*Admitted to God, to ourselves, and to another human being
the exact nature of our wrongs.*

Acts 7:51–60

The Jewish leaders living during apostolic times wanted to reassure themselves that they had learned from the mistakes of their ancestors. This is why they were so angry at Stephen's indictment against them. They proudly voiced their rejection of their forefathers' persecution of the prophets, when they themselves had just finished crucifying Jesus.

Indeed, nothing upsets us more than when we are forced to see in ourselves the very traits we have vehemently rejected in our parents. If we have grown up in a home where emotional or physical abuse occurred, we have undoubtedly promised ourselves that our own homes would be free of it. If we had to watch a parent struggle with addictions, we have probably assured ourselves that we would never fall prey to those weaknesses. Sadly, statistics reveal otherwise. But there is hope, and that hope is found in a reaction quite the opposite of the Jewish council's. The cycle of sin is broken when we acknowledge what is wrong. Then and only then can God begin to make it right.

For further reading on Step 5, turn to page 297.

Daily Encouragement

DAY 117 READING: ACTS 6:8—8:3

A Thought for the New Day: A set routine is valuable for the healthy growth of a child, but when we are grown, we exchange the routine for an adult decision process. Many of Stephen's time wanted to defend and maintain their familiar customs against all innovation (6:14). Their customs were like a security blanket. We must be able to grow up and change our customs, not for the mere sake of change or novelty, but for effective communication. (*Turn to page 273.*)

STEP
1

9 But there was a certain man called Simon, who previously practiced sorcery in the city and astonished the people of Samaria, claiming that he was someone great,

10 to whom they all gave heed, from the least to the greatest, saying, "This man is the great power of God."

11 And they heeded him because he had astonished them with his sorceries for a long time.

12 But when they believed Philip as he preached the things concerning the kingdom of God and the name of Jesus Christ, both men and women were baptized.

13 Then Simon himself also believed; and when he was baptized he continued with Philip, and was amazed, seeing the miracles and signs which were done.

14 Now when the apostles who were at Jerusalem heard that Samaria had received the word of God, they sent Peter and John to them,

15 who, when they had come down, prayed for them that they might receive the Holy Spirit.

16 For as yet He had fallen upon none of them. They had only been baptized in the name of the Lord Jesus.

17 Then they laid hands on them, and they received the Holy Spirit.

18 Now when Simon saw that through the laying on of the apostles' hands the Holy Spirit was given, he offered them money,

19 saying, "Give me this power also, that anyone on whom I lay hands may receive the Holy Spirit."

20 But Peter said to him, "Your money perish with you, because you thought that the gift of God could be purchased with money!

21 "You have neither part nor portion in this matter, for your heart is not right in the sight of God.

22 "Repent therefore of this your wickedness, and pray God if per-

haps the thought of your heart may be forgiven you.

23 "For I see that you are poisoned by bitterness and bound by iniquity."

24 Then Simon answered and said, "Pray to the Lord for me, that none of the things which you have spoken may come upon me."

25 So when they had testified and preached the word of the Lord, they returned to Jerusalem, preaching the gospel in many villages of the Samaritans.

26 Now an angel of the Lord spoke to Philip, saying, "Arise and go toward the south along the road which goes down from Jerusalem to Gaza." This is desert.

27 So he arose and went. And behold, a man of Ethiopia, a eunuch of great authority under Candace the queen of the Ethiopians, who had charge of all her treasury, and had come to Jerusalem to worship,

28 was returning. And sitting in his chariot, he was reading Isaiah the prophet.

29 Then the Spirit said to Philip, "Go near and overtake this chariot."

30 So Philip ran to him, and heard him reading the prophet Isaiah, and said, "Do you understand what you are reading?"

31 And he said, "How can I, unless someone guides me?" And he asked Philip to come up and sit with him.

32 The place in the Scripture which he read was this:

"He was led as a sheep to the
   slaughter;
And like a lamb silent before
   its shearer,
So He opened not His mouth.
33 In His humiliation His justice
   was taken away.
And who will declare His
   generation?
For His life is taken from the
   earth."

STEP 1

*We admitted we were powerless over our dependencies—
that our lives had become unmanageable.*

Acts 8:9–23

Simon wanted power and influence. He wanted it so badly, he was even willing to use demons and to be used by them. This is what the Bible means when it calls Simon a sorcerer. Verse 9 gives us a pretty good picture of Simon's motives and goals. He is described as "claiming that he was someone great." Then along came a man named Philip, who could perform miracles more amazing than Simon's, but he never made any claims about himself. Rather, he preached Jesus, and many people responded to his message. Even Simon was impressed, but instead of beginning to care about the things of God, he continued to be consumed by his self-centered desire for power.

Simon failed to recognize that God's power will only be given to those who are willing to admit that in themselves they are powerless. And the bonds of iniquity will only fall when our hearts respond in trust to what our minds know to be true.

For further reading on Step 1, turn to page 321.

Daily Encouragement

DAY 118 READING: ACTS 8:4—9:31

A Thought for the New Day: Many experiences in life become doorways to heaven, but faith is the key to all of these doors. The story of the African man (8:29–39) is typical. Sometimes we, too, seem at the end of ourselves. Then, one day, we receive a new insight from the Bible or through prayer; and sharing our discovery with another, a whole world of possibility opens to us. We face life with new hope and expectation. That threat of a broken family will be averted. That job change will work out. (*Turn to page 277.*)

34 So the eunuch answered Philip and said, "I ask you, of whom does the prophet say this, of himself or of some other man?"

35 Then Philip opened his mouth, and beginning at this Scripture, preached Jesus to him.

36 Now as they went down the road, they came to some water. And the eunuch said, "See, *here is* water. What hinders me from being baptized?"

37 Then Philip said, "If you believe with all your heart, you may." And he answered and said, "I believe that Jesus Christ is the Son of God."

38 So he commanded the chariot to stand still. And both Philip and the eunuch went down into the water, and he baptized him.

39 Now when they came up out of the water, the Spirit of the Lord caught Philip away, so that the eunuch saw him no more; and he went on his way rejoicing.

40 But Philip was found at Azotus. And passing through, he preached in all the cities till he came to Caesarea.

9 Then Saul, still breathing threats and murder against the disciples of the Lord, went to the high priest

2 and asked letters from him to the synagogues of Damascus, so that if he found any who were of the Way, whether men or women, he might bring them bound to Jerusalem.

3 And as he journeyed he came near Damascus, and suddenly a light shone around him from heaven.

4 Then he fell to the ground, and heard a voice saying to him, "Saul, Saul, why are you persecuting Me?"

5 And he said, "Who are You, Lord?" And the Lord said, "I am Jesus, whom you are persecuting. *It is* hard for you to kick against the goads."

6 So he, trembling and aston- ished, said, "Lord, what do You want me to do?" And the Lord *said* to him, "Arise and go into the city, and you will be told what you must do."

7 And the men who journeyed with him stood speechless, hearing a voice but seeing no one.

8 Then Saul arose from the ground, and when his eyes were opened he saw no one. But they led him by the hand and brought *him* into Damascus.

9 And he was three days without sight, and neither ate nor drank.

10 Now there was a certain disciple at Damascus named Ananias; and to him the Lord said in a vision, "Ananias." And he said, "Here I am, Lord."

11 So the Lord *said* to him, "Arise and go to the street called Straight, and inquire at the house of Judas for *one* called Saul of Tarsus, for behold, he is praying.

12 "And in a vision he has seen a man named Ananias coming in and putting *his* hand on him, so that he might receive his sight."

13 Then Ananias answered, "Lord, I have heard from many about this man, how much harm he has done to Your saints in Jerusalem.

14 "And here he has authority from the chief priests to bind all who call on Your name."

15 But the Lord said to him, "Go, for he is a chosen vessel of Mine to bear My name before Gentiles, kings, and the children of Israel.

16 "For I will show him how many things he must suffer for My name's sake."

17 And Ananias went his way and entered the house; and laying his hands on him he said, "Brother Saul, the Lord Jesus, who appeared to you on the road as you came, has sent me that you may receive your sight and be filled with the Holy Spirit."

18 Immediately there fell from his eyes *something* like scales, and he

received his sight at once; and he arose and was baptized.

19 And when he had received food, he was strengthened. Then Saul spent some days with the disciples at Damascus.

20 Immediately he preached the Christ in the synagogues, that He is the Son of God.

21 Then all who heard were amazed, and said, "Is this not he who destroyed those who called on this name in Jerusalem, and has come here for that purpose, so that he might bring them bound to the chief priests?"

22 But Saul increased all the more in strength, and confounded the Jews who dwelt in Damascus, proving that this *Jesus* is the Christ.

23 Now after many days were past, the Jews plotted to kill him.

24 But their plot became known to Saul. And they watched the gates day and night, to kill him.

25 Then the disciples took him by night and let *him* down through the wall in a large basket.

26 And when Saul had come to Jerusalem, he tried to join the disciples; but they were all afraid of him, and did not believe that he was a disciple.

27 But Barnabas took him and brought *him* to the apostles. And he declared to them how he had seen the Lord on the road, and that He had spoken to him, and how he had preached boldly at Damascus in the name of Jesus.

28 So he was with them at Jerusalem, coming in and going out.

29 And he spoke boldly in the name of the Lord Jesus and disputed against the Hellenists, but they attempted to kill him.

30 When the brethren found out, they brought him down to Caesarea and sent him out to Tarsus.

31 Then the churches throughout all Judea, Galilee, and Samaria had peace and were edified. And walk-

ing in the fear of the Lord and in the comfort of the Holy Spirit, they were multiplied.

32 Now it came to pass, as Peter went through all *parts of the country*, that he also came down to the saints who dwelt in Lydda.

33 There he found a certain man named Aeneas, who had been bedridden eight years and was paralyzed.

34 And Peter said to him, "Aeneas, Jesus the Christ heals you. Arise and make your bed." Then he arose immediately.

35 So all who dwelt at Lydda and Sharon saw him and turned to the Lord.

36 At Joppa there was a certain disciple named Tabitha, which is translated Dorcas. This woman was full of good works and charitable deeds which she did.

37 But it happened in those days that she became sick and died. When they had washed her, they laid *her* in an upper room.

38 And since Lydda was near Joppa, and the disciples had heard that Peter was there, they sent two men to him, imploring *him* not to delay in coming to them.

39 Then Peter arose and went with them. When he had come, they brought *him* to the upper room. And all the widows stood by him weeping, showing the tunics and garments which Dorcas had made while she was with them.

40 But Peter put them all out, and knelt down and prayed. And turning to the body he said, "Tabitha, arise." And she opened her eyes, and when she saw Peter she sat up.

41 Then he gave her *his* hand and lifted her up; and when he had called the saints and widows, he presented her alive.

42 And it became known throughout all Joppa, and many believed on the Lord.

43 So it was that he stayed many days in Joppa with Simon, a tanner.

10 There was a certain man in Caesarea called Cornelius, a centurion of what was called the Italian Regiment,

2 a devout *man* and one who feared God with all his household, who gave alms generously to the people, and prayed to God always.

3 About the ninth hour of the day he saw clearly in a vision an angel of God coming in and saying to him, "Cornelius!"

4 And when he observed him, he was afraid, and said, "What is it, lord?" So he said to him, "Your prayers and your alms have come up for a memorial before God.

5 "Now send men to Joppa, and send for Simon whose surname is Peter.

6 "He is lodging with Simon, a tanner, whose house is by the sea. He will tell you what you must do."

7 And when the angel who spoke to him had departed, Cornelius called two of his household servants and a devout soldier from among those who waited on him continually.

8 So when he had explained all *these* things to them, he sent them to Joppa.

STEP 9

9 The next day, as they went on their journey and drew near the city, Peter went up on the housetop to pray, about the sixth hour.

10 Then he became very hungry and wanted to eat; but while they made ready, he fell into a trance

11 and saw heaven opened and an object like a great sheet bound at the four corners, descending to him and let down to the earth.

12 In it were all kinds of four-footed animals of the earth, wild beasts, creeping things, and birds of the air.

13 And a voice came to him, "Rise, Peter; kill and eat."

14 But Peter said, "Not so, Lord! For I have never eaten anything common or unclean."

15 And a voice *spoke* to him again the second time, "What God has cleansed you must not call common."

16 This was done three times. And the object was taken up into heaven again.

17 Now while Peter wondered within himself what this vision which he had seen meant, behold, the men who had been sent from Cornelius had made inquiry for Simon's house, and stood before the gate.

18 And they called and asked whether Simon, whose surname was Peter, was lodging there.

19 While Peter thought about the vision, the Spirit said to him, "Behold, three men are seeking you.

20 "Arise therefore, go down and go with them, doubting nothing; for I have sent them."

21 Then Peter went down to the men who had been sent to him from Cornelius, and said, "Yes, I am he whom you seek. For what reason have you come?"

22 And they said, "Cornelius *the* centurion, a just man, one who fears God and has a good reputation among all the nation of the Jews, was divinely instructed by a holy angel to summon you to his house, and to hear words from you."

23 Then he invited them in and lodged *them*. On the next day Peter went away with them, and some brethren from Joppa accompanied him.

24 And the following day they entered Caesarea. Now Cornelius was waiting for them, and had called together his relatives and close friends.

25 As Peter was coming in, Cornelius met him and fell down at his feet and worshiped *him*.

26 But Peter lifted him up, saying, "Stand up; I myself am also a man."

27 And as he talked with him, he

STEP 9

Made direct amends to such people wherever possible,
except when to do so would injure them or others.

Acts 10:9–28

When we experience a new relationship with God, changes in our human relationships are bound to follow. For centuries there had been separation and animosity between the Jews and Gentiles (all non-Jews). But when Jesus truly transforms a life, every aspect of relating changes. This is exactly what God was showing Peter in the vision on the rooftop. Our preconceived ideas of who is worthy of love, grace, and forgiveness must bow to God's outstretched arms of acceptance. When we are willing to yield our ingrained negative attitudes to God, He can bring about amazing and exciting results. Our willingness to build bridges of trust and friendship may actually result in souls being saved, and lead others to follow our examples, as well.

For further reading on Step 9, turn to page 347.

Daily Encouragement

DAY 119 READING: ACTS 9:32—11:30

A Thought for the New Day: Times change. There was a time when Jews were intolerant of Gentiles. More recently it has been the other way round. But God made it clear that racism was no part of His great plan (10:28). The distinctions and discriminations we make among people are often very unjust. All of us equally need God's kindness and forgiveness. It is our place, if we understand the gospel, to reflect God's attitude to everyone around us. (*Turn to page 283.*)

went in and found many who had come together.

28 Then he said to them, "You know how unlawful it is for a Jewish man to keep company with or go to one of another nation. But God has shown me that I should not call any man common or unclean.

29 "Therefore I came without objection as soon as I was sent for. I ask, then, for what reason have you sent for me?"

30 And Cornelius said, "Four days ago I was fasting until this hour; and at the ninth hour I prayed in my house, and behold, a man stood before me in bright clothing,

31 "and said, 'Cornelius, your prayer has been heard, and your alms are remembered in the sight of God.

32 'Send therefore to Joppa and call Simon here, whose surname is Peter. He is lodging in the house of Simon, a tanner, by the sea. When he comes, he will speak to you.'

33 "So I sent to you immediately, and you have done well to come. Now therefore, we are all present before God, to hear all the things commanded you by God."

34 Then Peter opened *his* mouth and said: "In truth I perceive that God shows no partiality.

35 "But in every nation whoever fears Him and works righteousness is accepted by Him.

36 "The word which *God* sent to the children of Israel, preaching peace through Jesus Christ—He is Lord of all—

37 "that word you know, which was proclaimed throughout all Judea, and began from Galilee after the baptism which John preached:

38 "how God anointed Jesus of Nazareth with the Holy Spirit and with power, who went about doing good and healing all who were oppressed by the devil, for God was with Him.

39 "And we are witnesses of all things which He did both in the land of the Jews and in Jerusalem, whom they killed by hanging on a tree.

40 "Him God raised up on the third day, and showed Him openly,

41 "not to all the people, but to witnesses chosen before by God, *even* to us who ate and drank with Him after He arose from the dead.

42 "And He commanded us to preach to the people, and to testify that it is He who was ordained by God *to be* Judge of the living and the dead.

43 "To Him all the prophets witness that, through His name, whoever believes in Him will receive remission of sins."

44 While Peter was still speaking these words, the Holy Spirit fell upon all those who heard the word.

45 And those of the circumcision who believed were astonished, as many as came with Peter, because the gift of the Holy Spirit had been poured out on the Gentiles also.

46 For they heard them speak with tongues and magnify God. Then Peter answered,

47 "Can anyone forbid water, that these should not be baptized who have received the Holy Spirit just as we *have*?"

48 And he commanded them to be baptized in the name of the Lord. Then they asked him to stay a few days.

11 Now the apostles and brethren who were in Judea heard that the Gentiles had also received the word of God.

2 And when Peter came up to Jerusalem, those of the circumcision contended with him,

3 saying, "You went in to uncircumcised men and ate with them!"

4 But Peter explained *it* to them in order from the beginning, saying:

5 "I was in the city of Joppa praying; and in a trance I saw a vision, an object descending like a great

sheet, let down from heaven by four corners; and it came to me.

6 "When I observed it intently and considered, I saw four-footed animals of the earth, wild beasts, creeping things, and birds of the air.

7 "And I heard a voice saying to me, 'Rise, Peter; kill and eat.'

8 "But I said, 'Not so, Lord! For nothing common or unclean has at any time entered my mouth.'

9 "But the voice answered me again from heaven, 'What God has cleansed you must not call common.'

10 "Now this was done three times, and all were drawn up again into heaven.

11 "At that very moment, three men stood before the house where I was, having been sent to me from Caesarea.

12 "Then the Spirit told me to go with them, doubting nothing. Moreover these six brethren accompanied me, and we entered the man's house.

13 "And he told us how he had seen an angel standing in his house, who said to him, 'Send men to Joppa, and call for Simon whose surname is Peter,

14 'who will tell you words by which you and all your household will be saved.'

15 "And as I began to speak, the Holy Spirit fell upon them, as upon us at the beginning.

16 "Then I remembered the word of the Lord, how He said, 'John indeed baptized with water, but you shall be baptized with the Holy Spirit.'

17 "If therefore God gave them the same gift as *He gave* us when we believed on the Lord Jesus Christ, who was I that I could withstand God?"

18 When they heard these things they became silent; and they glorified God, saying, "Then God has also granted to the Gentiles repentance to life."

19 Now those who were scattered after the persecution that arose over Stephen traveled as far as Phoenicia, Cyprus, and Antioch, preaching the word to no one but the Jews only.

20 But some of them were men from Cyprus and Cyrene, who, when they had come to Antioch, spoke to the Hellenists, preaching the Lord Jesus.

21 And the hand of the Lord was with them, and a great number believed and turned to the Lord.

22 Then news of these things came to the ears of the church in Jerusalem, and they sent out Barnabas to go as far as Antioch.

23 When he came and had seen the grace of God, he was glad, and encouraged them all that with purpose of heart they should continue with the Lord.

24 For he was a good man, full of the Holy Spirit and of faith. And a great many people were added to the Lord.

25 Then Barnabas departed for Tarsus to seek Saul.

26 And when he had found him, he brought him to Antioch. So it was that for a whole year they assembled with the church and taught a great many people. And the disciples were first called Christians in Antioch.

27 And in these days prophets came from Jerusalem to Antioch.

28 Then one of them, named Agabus, stood up and showed by the Spirit that there was going to be a great famine throughout all the world, which also happened in the days of Claudius Caesar.

29 Then the disciples, each according to his ability, determined to send relief to the brethren dwelling in Judea.

30 This they also did, and sent it to the elders by the hands of Barnabas and Saul.

12 Now about that time Herod the king stretched out *his*

hand to harass some from the church.

2 Then he killed James the brother of John with the sword.

3 And because he saw that it pleased the Jews, he proceeded further to seize Peter also. Now it was *during* the Days of Unleavened Bread.

4 So when he had apprehended him, he put *him* in prison, and delivered *him* to four squads of soldiers to keep him, intending to bring him before the people after Passover.

5 Peter was therefore kept in prison, but constant prayer was offered to God for him by the church.

6 And when Herod was about to bring him out, that night Peter was sleeping, bound with two chains between two soldiers; and the guards before the door were keeping the prison.

7 Now behold, an angel of the Lord stood by *him*, and a light shone in the prison; and he struck Peter on the side and raised him up, saying, "Arise quickly!" And his chains fell off *his* hands.

8 Then the angel said to him, "Gird yourself and tie on your sandals"; and so he did. And he said to him, "Put on your garment and follow me."

9 So he went out and followed him, and did not know that what was done by the angel was real, but thought he was seeing a vision.

10 When they were past the first and the second guard posts, they came to the iron gate that leads to the city, which opened to them of its own accord; and they went out and went down one street, and immediately the angel departed from him.

11 And when Peter had come to himself, he said, "Now I know for certain that the Lord has sent His angel, and has delivered me from the hand of Herod and *from* all the expectation of the Jewish people."

12 So, when he had considered *this*, he came to the house of Mary, the mother of John whose surname was Mark, where many were gathered together praying.

13 And as Peter knocked at the door of the gate, a girl named Rhoda came to answer.

14 When she recognized Peter's voice, because of *her* gladness she did not open the gate, but ran in and announced that Peter stood before the gate.

15 But they said to her, "You are beside yourself!" Yet she kept insisting that it was so. So they said, "It is his angel."

16 Now Peter continued knocking; and when they opened *the door* and saw him, they were astonished.

17 But motioning to them with his hand to keep silent, he declared to them how the Lord had brought him out of the prison. And he said, "Go, tell these things to James and to the brethren." And he departed and went to another place.

18 Then, as soon as it was day, there was no small stir among the soldiers about what had become of Peter.

19 But when Herod had searched for him and not found him, he examined the guards and commanded that *they* should be put to death. And he went down from Judea to Caesarea, and stayed *there*.

20 Now Herod had been very angry with the people of Tyre and Sidon; but they came to him with one accord, and having made Blastus the king's chamberlain their friend, they asked for peace, because their country was supplied with food by the king's *country*.

21 So on a set day Herod, arrayed in royal apparel, sat on his throne and gave an oration to them.

22 And the people kept shouting, "The voice of a god and not of a man!"

23 Then immediately an angel of the Lord struck him, because he did not give glory to God. And he was eaten by worms and died.

24 But the word of God grew and multiplied.

25 And Barnabas and Saul returned from Jerusalem when they had fulfilled *their* ministry, and they also took with them John whose surname was Mark.

13 Now in the church that was at Antioch there were certain prophets and teachers: Barnabas, Simeon who was called Niger, Lucius of Cyrene, Manaen who had been brought up with Herod the tetrarch, and Saul.

2 As they ministered to the Lord and fasted, the Holy Spirit said, "Now separate to Me Barnabas and Saul for the work to which I have called them."

3 Then, having fasted and prayed, and laid hands on them, they sent *them* away.

4 So, being sent out by the Holy Spirit, they went down to Seleucia, and from there they sailed to Cyprus.

5 And when they arrived in Salamis, they preached the word of God in the synagogues of the Jews. They also had John as *their* assistant.

6 Now when they had gone through the island to Paphos, they found a certain sorcerer, a false prophet, a Jew whose name *was* Bar-Jesus,

7 who was with the proconsul, Sergius Paulus, an intelligent man. This man called for Barnabas and Saul and sought to hear the word of God.

8 But Elymas the sorcerer (for so his name is translated) withstood them, seeking to turn the proconsul away from the faith.

9 Then Saul, who also *is called* Paul, filled with the Holy Spirit, looked intently at him

10 and said, "O full of all deceit and all fraud, *you* son of the devil, *you* enemy of all righteousness, will you not cease perverting the straight ways of the Lord?

11 "And now, indeed, the hand of the Lord *is* upon you, and you shall be blind, not seeing the sun for a time." And immediately a dark mist fell on him, and he went around seeking someone to lead him by the hand.

12 Then the proconsul believed, when he saw what had been done, being astonished at the teaching of the Lord.

13 Now when Paul and his party set sail from Paphos, they came to Perga in Pamphylia; and John, departing from them, returned to Jerusalem.

14 But when they departed from Perga, they came to Antioch in Pisidia, and went into the synagogue on the Sabbath day and sat down.

15 And after the reading of the Law and the Prophets, the rulers of the synagogue sent to them, saying, "Men *and* brethren, if you have any word of exhortation for the people, say on."

16 Then Paul stood up, and motioning with *his* hand said, "Men of Israel, and you who fear God, listen:

17 "The God of this people Israel chose our fathers, and exalted the people when they dwelt as strangers in the land of Egypt, and with an uplifted arm He brought them out of it.

18 "Now for a time of about forty years He put up with their ways in the wilderness.

19 "And when He had destroyed seven nations in the land of Canaan, He distributed their land to them by allotment.

20 "After that He gave *them* judges for about four hundred and fifty years, until Samuel the prophet.

21 "And afterward they asked for a king; so God gave them Saul the

son of Kish, a man of the tribe of Benjamin, for forty years.

22 "And when He had removed him, He raised up for them David as king, to whom also He gave testimony and said, '*I have found David the son of Jesse, a man after My own heart,* who will do all My will.'

23 "From this man's seed, according to *the* promise, God raised up for Israel a Savior—Jesus—

24 "after John had first preached, before His coming, the baptism of repentance to all the people of Israel.

25 "And as John was finishing his course, he said, 'Who do you think I am? I am not *He.* But behold, there comes One after me, the sandals of whose feet I am not worthy to loose.'

26 "Men *and* brethren, sons of the family of Abraham, and those among you who fear God, to you the word of this salvation has been sent.

27 "For those who dwell in Jerusalem, and their rulers, because they did not know Him, nor even the voices of the Prophets which are read every Sabbath, have fulfilled *them* in condemning *Him.*

28 "And though they found no cause for death *in Him,* they asked Pilate that He should be put to death.

29 "Now when they had fulfilled all that was written concerning Him, they took *Him* down from the tree and laid *Him* in a tomb.

30 "But God raised Him from the dead.

31 "He was seen for many days by those who came up with Him from Galilee to Jerusalem, who are His witnesses to the people.

32 "And we declare to you glad tidings—that promise which was made to the fathers.

33 "God has fulfilled this for us their children, in that He has raised up Jesus. As it is also written in the second Psalm:

'You are My Son,
Today I have begotten You.'

34 "And that He raised Him from the dead, no more to return to corruption, He has spoken thus:

'I will give you the sure mercies of David.'

35 "Therefore He also says in another *Psalm:*

'You will not allow Your Holy One to see corruption.'

36 "For David, after he had served his own generation by the will of God, fell asleep, was buried with his fathers, and saw corruption;

37 "but He whom God raised up saw no corruption.

38 "Therefore let it be known to you, brethren, that through this Man is preached to you the forgiveness of sins;

39 "and by Him everyone who believes is justified from all things from which you could not be justified by the law of Moses.

40 "Beware therefore, lest what has been spoken in the prophets come upon you:

41 '*Behold, you despisers,
Marvel and perish;
For I work a work in your days,
A work which you will by no means believe,
Though one were to declare it to you.*'"

42 And when the Jews went out of the synagogue, the Gentiles begged that these words might be preached to them the next Sabbath.

43 Now when the congregation had broken up, many of the Jews and devout proselytes followed Paul and Barnabas, who, speaking to them, persuaded them to continue in the grace of God.

STEP 2

Came to believe that a Power greater than ourselves
could restore us to sanity.

Acts 13:38, 39

"Fix it, Daddy! Make it right." This is the typical cry of a child looking at a precious possession inadvertently broken. But fixing what has broken is not always an easy task. Whether that which is broken is a toy, a reputation, a relationship, or a life, making it right again may be humanly impossible. However, nothing is too difficult for God to make right. "By Him everyone who believes is justified." "Justified" means "made right." At one time, when people sinned, they followed the Law of Moses, offering the prescribed sacrifice to show God they were sorry for that sin. The Law could patch and repair lives, but it could never cleanse and transform a person's heart. Only trusting in Jesus' power can accomplish such a miracle. Because He is Creator God, He can do far more than repair our old life. He can create for us a whole new life in Him.

For further reading on Step 2, turn to page 291.

Daily Encouragement

DAY 120 READING: ACTS 12:1—13:43

A Thought for the New Day: No doubt, Peter's imprisonment was high on his friends' priorities for prayer. Yet, when the freed Peter arrived at their door (12:12), they could hardly believe their eyes! God is more ready to answer than we are to ask, but we fail to trust Him in asking. When we do pray, often we only half expect to be heard. God loves His children: He wants you to come with your requests and will fully satisfy all your needs. *(Turn to page 285.)*

44 And the next Sabbath almost the whole city came together to hear the word of God.

45 But when the Jews saw the multitudes, they were filled with envy; and contradicting and blaspheming, they opposed the things spoken by Paul.

46 Then Paul and Barnabas grew bold and said, "It was necessary that the word of God should be spoken to you first; but since you reject it, and judge yourselves unworthy of everlasting life, behold, we turn to the Gentiles.

47 "For so the Lord has commanded us:

'I have set you to be a light
to the Gentiles,
That you should be for
salvation to the ends of the
earth.' "

48 Now when the Gentiles heard this, they were glad and glorified the word of the Lord. And as many as had been appointed to eternal life believed.

49 And the word of the Lord was being spread throughout all the region.

50 But the Jews stirred up the devout and prominent women and the chief men of the city, raised up persecution against Paul and Barnabas, and expelled them from their region.

51 But they shook off the dust from their feet against them, and came to Iconium.

52 And the disciples were filled with joy and with the Holy Spirit.

14 Now it happened in Iconium that they went together to the synagogue of the Jews, and so spoke that a great multitude both of the Jews and of the Greeks believed.

2 But the unbelieving Jews stirred up the Gentiles and poisoned their minds against the brethren.

3 Therefore they stayed there a long time, speaking boldly in the Lord, who was bearing witness to the word of His grace, granting signs and wonders to be done by their hands.

4 But the multitude of the city was divided: part sided with the Jews, and part with the apostles.

5 And when a violent attempt was made by both the Gentiles and Jews, with their rulers, to abuse and stone them,

6 they became aware of it and fled to Lystra and Derbe, cities of Lycaonia, and to the surrounding region.

7 And they were preaching the gospel there.

8 And in Lystra a certain man without strength in his feet was sitting, a cripple from his mother's womb, who had never walked.

9 *This* man heard Paul speaking. Paul, observing him intently and seeing that he had faith to be healed,

10 said with a loud voice, "Stand up straight on your feet!" And he leaped and walked.

11 Now when the people saw what Paul had done, they raised their voices, saying in the Lycaonian *language,* "The gods have come down to us in the likeness of men!"

12 And Barnabas they called Zeus, and Paul, Hermes, because he was the chief speaker.

13 Then the priest of Zeus, whose temple was in front of their city, brought oxen and garlands to the gates, intending to sacrifice with the multitudes.

14 But when the apostles Barnabas and Paul heard this, they tore their clothes and ran in among the multitude, crying out

15 and saying, "Men, why are you doing these things? We also are men with the same nature as you, and preach to you that you should turn from these vain things to the living God, who made the heaven,

STEP 11

*Sought through prayer and meditation to improve our conscious contact with God **as we understood Him,** praying only for knowledge of His will for us and the power to carry that out.*

Acts 14

"We must through many tribulations enter the kingdom of God," the apostle Paul warned (v. 22). These are not words we enjoy keeping in the forefront of our thinking. It is much more pleasant to dwell on God's faithfulness, love, and provision for us. But a servant is not greater than his master. Jesus experienced hardship and suffering, and we will, too, if we are earnestly following Him. Believers who are willing to take a stand for Jesus can expect a reaction from the world. Some may want to harm us, as those in Iconium who attempted to stone Paul. We may be dumbfounded the way Paul was, at the unexpected hero worship of others. But whatever reaction we receive, we must be careful not to allow it to change our goal of serving the Lord Jesus and exalting Him alone.

For further reading on Step 11, turn to page 287.

Daily Encouragement

DAY 121 READING: ACTS 13:44—14:28

A Thought for the New Day: Notice the occasion of the apostles' joy (13:52). The fact that many people had believed the gospel was surely good reason for their jubilation. However, more recently, the apostles had been persecuted and put out of the city. Nevertheless, they were "filled with joy and with the Holy Spirit." It is in the reversals of life that we most need— and will receive—the joy that God gives. (*Turn to page 287.*)

Conflict over Circumcision

the earth, the sea, and all things that are in them,

16 "who in bygone generations allowed all nations to walk in their own ways.

17 "Nevertheless He did not leave Himself without witness, in that He did good, gave us rain from heaven and fruitful seasons, filling our hearts with food and gladness."

18 And with these sayings they could scarcely restrain the multitudes from sacrificing to them.

19 Then Jews from Antioch and Iconium came there; and having persuaded the multitudes, they stoned Paul *and* dragged *him* out of the city, supposing him to be dead.

20 However, when the disciples gathered around him, he rose up and went into the city. And the next day he departed with Barnabas to Derbe.

21 And when they had preached the gospel to that city and made many disciples, they returned to Lystra, Iconium, and Antioch,

22 strengthening the souls of the disciples, exhorting *them* to continue in the faith, and *saying*, "We must through many tribulations enter the kingdom of God."

23 So when they had appointed elders in every church, and prayed with fasting, they commended them to the Lord in whom they had believed.

24 And after they had passed through Pisidia, they came to Pamphylia.

25 Now when they had preached the word in Perga, they went down to Attalia.

26 From there they sailed to Antioch, where they had been commended to the grace of God for the work which they had completed.

27 And when they had come and gathered the church together, they reported all that God had done with them, and that He had

opened the door of faith to the Gentiles.

28 So they stayed there a long time with the disciples.

15 And certain *men* came down from Judea and taught the brethren, "Unless you are circumcised according to the custom of Moses, you cannot be saved."

2 Therefore, when Paul and Barnabas had no small dissension and dispute with them, they determined that Paul and Barnabas and certain others of them should go up to Jerusalem, to the apostles and elders, about this question.

3 So, being sent on their way by the church, they passed through Phoenicia and Samaria, describing the conversion of the Gentiles; and they caused great joy to all the brethren.

4 And when they had come to Jerusalem, they were received by the church and the apostles and the elders; and they reported all things that God had done with them.

5 But some of the sect of the Pharisees who believed rose up, saying, "It is necessary to circumcise them, and to command *them* to keep the law of Moses."

6 So the apostles and elders came together to consider this matter.

7 And when there had been much dispute, Peter rose up and said to them: "Men and brethren, you know that a good while ago God chose among us, that by my mouth the Gentiles should hear the word of the gospel and believe.

8 "So God, who knows the heart, acknowledged them, by giving them the Holy Spirit just as *He did* to us,

9 "and made no distinction between us and them, purifying their hearts by faith.

10 "Now therefore, why do you test God by putting a yoke on the neck of the disciples which neither our fathers nor we were able to bear?

STEP 11

STEP 11

*Sought through prayer and meditation to improve our conscious contact with God **as we understood Him,** praying only for knowledge of His will for us and the power to carry that out.*

Acts 15:1, 2

Disagreement—to some it is an evil to be avoided at all costs. Others apparently enjoy it so much, they take every opportunity to argue. Neither of these viewpoints is biblical or even emotionally healthy. In Acts 15, we see the apostle Paul involved twice in disagreements, but he went on to take special precautions against confrontation (Acts 16). Is there reason behind Paul's actions, or did it just depend on how he happened to feel on a given day?

When the outcome of an issue was absolutely vital to integrity and spread of the gospel, Paul stood his ground. He refused to compromise the message of salvation by grace (15:11), nor would he compromise his ability to preach unencumbered by superficial concerns (15:38).

However, when it was within his ability to appease, he willingly did so. God wants to give us the same wise discernment when faced with conflict, so that whatever we say and do will exalt Him.

For further reading on Step 11, turn to page 301.

Daily Encouragement

DAY 122 READING: ACTS 15:1—16:10

A Thought for the New Day: John Mark was a young man, and there were great things ahead for him to do, but first he had to learn to be responsible (15:37, 38). In a tender way, Paul remarks in one of his later letters that Mark was now "profitable" to him in the ministry. God gives us all the time we need to grow up in Christ. Mark became the writer of the Gospel under his name, and he was a valuable assistant to Peter at Rome. *(Turn to page 291.)*

11 "But we believe that through the grace of the Lord Jesus Christ we shall be saved in the same manner as they."

12 Then all the multitude kept silent and listened to Barnabas and Paul declaring how many miracles and wonders God had worked through them among the Gentiles.

13 And after they had become silent, James answered, saying, "Men *and* brethren, listen to me:

14 "Simon has declared how God at the first visited the Gentiles to take out of them a people for His name.

15 "And with this the words of the prophets agree, just as it is written:

16 '*After this I will return*
And will rebuild the tabernacle
of David which has fallen
down.
I will rebuild its ruins,
And I will set it up,
17 *So that the rest of mankind*
may seek the LORD,
Even all the Gentiles who are
called by My name,
Says the LORD who does all
these things.'

18 "Known to God from eternity are all His works.

19 "Therefore I judge that we should not trouble those from among the Gentiles who are turning to God,

20 "but that we write to them to abstain from things polluted by idols, *from* sexual immorality, *from* things strangled, and *from* blood.

21 "For Moses has had throughout many generations those who preach him in every city, being read in the synagogues every Sabbath."

22 Then it pleased the apostles and elders, with the whole church, to send chosen men of their own company to Antioch with Paul and Barnabas, *namely*, Judas who was also named Barsabas, and Silas, leading men among the brethren.

23 They wrote this *letter* by them:

The apostles, the elders, and the brethren,
To the brethren who are of the Gentiles in Antioch, Syria, and Cilicia:
Greetings.

24 Since we have heard that some who went out from us have troubled you with words, unsettling your souls, saying, '*You must* be circumcised and keep the law'—to whom we gave no *such* commandment—

25 it seemed good to us, being assembled with one accord, to send chosen men to you with our beloved Barnabas and Paul,

26 men who have risked their lives for the name of our Lord Jesus Christ.

27 We have therefore sent Judas and Silas, who will also report the same things by word of mouth.

28 For it seemed good to the Holy Spirit, and to us, to lay upon you no greater burden than these necessary things:

29 that you abstain from things offered to idols, from blood, from things strangled, and from sexual immorality. If you keep yourselves from these, you will do well.
Farewell.

30 So when they were sent off, they came to Antioch; and when they had gathered the multitude together, they delivered the letter.

31 When they had read it, they rejoiced over its encouragement.

32 Now Judas and Silas, themselves being prophets also, exhorted the brethren with many words and strengthened *them.*

33 And after they had stayed *there* for a time, they were sent back with greetings from the brethren to the apostles.

34 However, it seemed good to Silas to remain there.

35 Paul and Barnabas also remained in Antioch, teaching and preaching the word of the Lord, with many others also.

36 Then after some days Paul said to Barnabas, "Let us now go back and visit our brethren in every city where we have preached the word of the Lord, *and see* how they are doing."

37 Now Barnabas was determined to take with them John called Mark.

38 But Paul insisted that they should not take with them the one who had departed from them in Pamphylia, and had not gone with them to the work.

39 Then the contention became so sharp that they parted from one another. And so Barnabas took Mark and sailed to Cyprus;

40 but Paul chose Silas and departed, being commended by the brethren to the grace of God.

41 And he went through Syria and Cilicia, strengthening the churches.

16 Then he came to Derbe and Lystra. And behold, a certain disciple was there, named Timothy, *the* son of a certain Jewish woman who believed, but his father *was* Greek.

2 He was well spoken of by the brethren who were at Lystra and Iconium.

3 Paul wanted to have him go on with him. And he took *him* and circumcised him because of the Jews who were in that region, for they all knew that his father was Greek.

4 And as they went through the cities, they delivered to them the decrees to keep, which were determined by the apostles and elders at Jerusalem.

5 So the churches were strengthened in the faith, and increased in number daily.

6 Now when they had gone through Phrygia and the region of Galatia, they were forbidden by the Holy Spirit to preach the word in Asia.

7 After they had come to Mysia, they tried to go into Bithynia, but the Spirit did not permit them.

8 So passing by Mysia, they came down to Troas.

9 And a vision appeared to Paul in the night. A man of Macedonia stood and pleaded with him, saying, "Come over to Macedonia and help us."

10 Now after he had seen the vision, immediately we sought to go to Macedonia, concluding that the Lord had called us to preach the gospel to them.

11 Therefore, sailing from Troas, we ran a straight course to Samothrace, and the next *day* came to Neapolis,

12 and from there to Philippi, which is the foremost city of that part of Macedonia, a colony. And we were staying in that city for some days.

13 And on the Sabbath day we went out of the city to the riverside, where prayer was customarily made; and we sat down and spoke to the women who met *there.*

14 Now a certain woman named Lydia heard *us.* She was a seller of purple from the city of Thyatira, who worshiped God. The Lord opened her heart to heed the things spoken by Paul.

15 And when she and her household were baptized, she begged *us,* saying, "If you have judged me to be faithful to the Lord, come to my house and stay." And she constrained us.

16 Now it happened, as we went to prayer, that a certain slave girl possessed with a spirit of divination met us, who brought her masters much profit by fortune-telling.

17 This girl followed Paul and us, and cried out, saying, "These men are the servants of the Most High God, who proclaim to us the way of salvation."

18 And this she did for many days. But Paul, greatly annoyed, turned and said to the spirit, "I command you in the name of Jesus Christ to come out of her." And he came out that very hour.

19 But when her masters saw that their hope of profit was gone, they seized Paul and Silas and dragged *them* into the marketplace to the authorities.

20 And they brought them to the magistrates, and said, "These men, being Jews, exceedingly trouble our city;

21 "and they teach customs which are not lawful for us, being Romans, to receive or observe."

22 Then the multitude rose up together against them; and the magistrates tore off their clothes and commanded *them* to be beaten with rods.

23 And when they had laid many stripes on them, they threw *them* into prison, commanding the jailer to keep them securely.

24 Having received such a charge, he put them into the inner prison and fastened their feet in the stocks.

25 But at midnight Paul and Silas were praying and singing hymns to God, and the prisoners were listening to them.

26 Suddenly there was a great earthquake, so that the foundations of the prison were shaken; and immediately all the doors were opened and everyone's chains were loosed.

27 And the keeper of the prison, awaking from sleep and seeing the prison doors open, supposing the prisoners had fled, drew his sword and was about to kill himself.

28 But Paul called with a loud voice, saying, "Do yourself no harm, for we are all here."

29 Then he called for a light, ran in, and fell down trembling before Paul and Silas.

30 And he brought them out and said, "Sirs, what must I do to be saved?"

31 So they said, "Believe on the Lord Jesus Christ, and you will be saved, you and your household." STEP 2

32 Then they spoke the word of the Lord to him and to all who were in his house.

33 And he took them the same hour of the night and washed *their* stripes. And immediately he and all his family were baptized.

34 Now when he had brought them into his house, he set food before them; and he rejoiced, having believed in God with all his household.

35 And when it was day, the magistrates sent the officers, saying, "Let those men go."

36 So the keeper of the prison reported these words to Paul, saying, "The magistrates have sent to let you go. Now therefore depart, and go in peace."

37 But Paul said to them, "They have beaten us openly, uncondemned Romans, *and* have thrown *us* into prison. And now do they put us out secretly? No indeed! Let them come themselves and get us out."

38 And the officers told these words to the magistrates, and they were afraid when they heard that they were Romans.

39 Then they came and pleaded with them and brought *them* out, and asked *them* to depart from the city.

40 So they went out of the prison and entered *the house of* Lydia; and when they had seen the brethren, they encouraged them and departed.

17 Now when they had passed through Amphipolis and Apollonia, they came to Thessalonica, where there was a synagogue of the Jews.

2 Then Paul, as his custom was, went in to them, and for three Sabbaths reasoned with them from the Scriptures,

STEP 2

*Came to believe that a Power greater than ourselves
could restore us to sanity.*

Acts 16:31

For the Philippian jailer, suicide seemed the only alternative
(v. 27). In those days, a jailer who lost his prisoners was severely
punished by the Roman government.

When Paul called out, "Do yourself no harm, for we are all here,"
the astonished jailer realized that no earthly power had caused this
earthquake. And certainly no human power could have kept all the
prisoners from bolting for freedom. The wonder, fear, and hope
within his mind and heart collided as he fell at the feet of Paul and
Silas and asked the most important question that lips can ever
speak: "Sirs, what must I do to be saved?" Paul's answer is the hope
of the hopeless, "Believe on the Lord Jesus Christ, and you will be
saved, you and your household."

Though we may feel nothing but despair over our situation, God
does not despair, His arms are always stretched out in love, offering
His power and healing to all who will believe.

For further reading on Step 2, turn to page 335.

Daily Encouragement

DAY 123 READING: ACTS 16:11—17:15

A Thought for the New Day: You can never be sure what con-
venience God will use to help you in your cause. It was a fact
that Paul and Silas were privileged Roman citizens. Yet they had
been abused by the authorities as if they were disenfranchised
barbarians (16:37, 38). This was not the last time Paul was able
to appeal to his legal status as a Roman. Yes, "all things" work
together for our good when we follow Jesus (see Rom. 8:28).
(*Turn to page 295.*)

3 explaining and demonstrating that the Christ had to suffer and rise again from the dead, and *saying*, "This Jesus whom I preach to you is the Christ."

4 And some of them were persuaded; and a great multitude of the devout Greeks, and not a few of the leading women, joined Paul and Silas.

5 But the Jews who were not persuaded, becoming envious, took some of the evil men from the marketplace, and gathering a mob, set all the city in an uproar and attacked the house of Jason, and sought to bring them out to the people.

6 But when they did not find them, they dragged Jason and some brethren to the rulers of the city, crying out, "These who have turned the world upside down have come here too.

7 "Jason has harbored them, and these are all acting contrary to the decrees of Caesar, saying there is another king—Jesus."

8 And they troubled the crowd and the rulers of the city when they heard these things.

9 So when they had taken security from Jason and the rest, they let them go.

10 Then the brethren immediately sent Paul and Silas away by night to Berea. When they arrived, they went into the synagogue of the Jews.

11 These were more fair-minded than those in Thessalonica, in that they received the word with all readiness, and searched the Scriptures daily *to find out* whether these things were so.

12 Therefore many of them believed, and also not a few of the Greeks, prominent women as well as men.

13 But when the Jews from Thessalonica learned that the word of God was preached by Paul at Berea, they came there also and stirred up the crowds.

14 Then immediately the brethren sent Paul away, to go to the sea; but both Silas and Timothy remained there.

15 So those who conducted Paul brought him to Athens; and receiving a command for Silas and Timothy to come to him with all speed, they departed.

16 Now while Paul waited for them at Athens, his spirit was provoked within him when he saw that the city was given over to idols.

17 Therefore he reasoned in the synagogue with the Jews and with the *Gentile* worshipers, and in the marketplace daily with those who happened to be there.

18 Then certain Epicurean and Stoic philosophers encountered him. And some said, "What does this babbler want to say?" Others said, "He seems to be a proclaimer of foreign gods," because he preached to them Jesus and the resurrection.

19 And they took him and brought him to the Areopagus, saying, "May we know what this new doctrine *is* of which you speak?

20 "For you are bringing some strange things to our ears. Therefore we want to know what these things mean."

21 For all the Athenians and the foreigners who were there spent their time in nothing else but either to tell or to hear some new thing.

22 Then Paul stood in the midst of the Areopagus and said, "Men of Athens, I perceive that in all things you are very religious;

23 "for as I was passing through and considering the objects of your worship, I even found an altar with this inscription:

TO THE UNKNOWN GOD.

Therefore, the One whom you worship without knowing, Him I proclaim to you:

24 "God, who made the world and everything in it, since He is Lord of

heaven and earth, does not dwell in temples made with hands.

25 "Nor is He worshiped with men's hands, as though He needed anything, since He gives to all life, breath, and all things.

26 "And He has made from one blood every nation of men to dwell on all the face of the earth, and has determined their preappointed times and the boundaries of their habitation,

27 "so that they should seek the Lord, in the hope that they might grope for Him and find Him, though He is not far from each one of us;

28 "for in Him we live and move and have our being, as also some of your own poets have said, 'For we are also His offspring.'

29 "Therefore, since we are the offspring of God, we ought not to think that the Divine Nature is like gold or silver or stone, something shaped by art and man's devising.

30 "Truly, these times of ignorance God overlooked, but now commands all men everywhere to repent,

31 "because He has appointed a day on which He will judge the world in righteousness by the Man whom He has ordained. He has given assurance of this to all by raising Him from the dead."

32 And when they heard of the resurrection of the dead, some mocked, while others said, "We will hear you again on this *matter.*"

33 So Paul departed from among them.

34 However, some men joined him and believed, among them Dionysius the Areopagite, a woman named Damaris, and others with them.

18 After these things Paul departed from Athens and went to Corinth.

2 And he found a certain Jew named Aquila, born in Pontus, who had recently come from Italy with his wife Priscilla (because Claudius had commanded all the Jews to depart from Rome); and he came to them.

3 So, because he was of the same trade, he stayed with them and worked; for by occupation they were tentmakers.

4 And he reasoned in the synagogue every Sabbath, and persuaded both Jews and Greeks.

5 When Silas and Timothy had come from Macedonia, Paul was constrained by the Spirit, and testified to the Jews *that* Jesus *is* the Christ.

6 But when they opposed him and blasphemed, he shook *his* garments and said to them, "Your blood *be* upon your *own* heads; I *am* clean. From now on I will go to the Gentiles."

7 And he departed from there and entered the house of a certain *man* named Justus, *one* who worshiped God, whose house was next door to the synagogue.

8 Then Crispus, the ruler of the synagogue, believed on the Lord with all his household. And many of the Corinthians, hearing, believed and were baptized.

9 Now the Lord spoke to Paul in the night by a vision, "Do not be afraid, but speak, and do not keep silent;

10 "for I am with you, and no one will attack you to hurt you; for I have many people in this city."

11 And he continued *there* a year and six months, teaching the word of God among them.

12 Now when Gallio was proconsul of Achaia, the Jews with one accord rose up against Paul and brought him to the judgment seat,

13 saying, "This *fellow* persuades men to worship God contrary to the law."

14 And when Paul was about to open *his* mouth, Gallio said to the Jews, "If it were a matter of

wrongdoing or wicked crimes, O Jews, there would be reason why I should bear with you.

15 "But if it is a question of words and names and your own law, look *to it* yourselves; for I do not want to be a judge of such *matters*."

16 And he drove them from the judgment seat.

17 Then all the Greeks took Sosthenes, the ruler of the synagogue, and beat *him* before the judgment seat. But Gallio took no notice of these things.

18 So Paul still remained a good while. Then he took leave of the brethren and sailed for Syria, and Priscilla and Aquila *were* with him. He had *his* hair cut off at Cenchrea, for he had taken a vow.

19 And he came to Ephesus, and left them there; but he himself entered the synagogue and reasoned with the Jews.

20 When they asked *him* to stay a longer time with them, he did not consent;

21 but took leave of them, saying, "I must by all means keep this coming feast in Jerusalem; but I will return again to you, God willing." And he sailed from Ephesus.

22 And when he had landed at Caesarea, and gone up and greeted the church, he went down to Antioch.

23 After he had spent some time *there*, he departed and went over *all* the region of Galatia and Phrygia in order, strengthening all the disciples.

STEP 10

24 Now a certain Jew named Apollos, born at Alexandria, an eloquent man *and* mighty in the Scriptures, came to Ephesus.

25 This man had been instructed in the way of the Lord; and being fervent in spirit, he spoke and taught accurately the things of the Lord, though he knew only the baptism of John.

26 So he began to speak boldly in the synagogue. When Aquila and Priscilla heard him, they took him aside and explained to him the way of God more accurately.

27 And when he desired to cross to Achaia, the brethren wrote, exhorting the disciples to receive him; and when he arrived, he greatly helped those who had believed through grace;

28 for he vigorously refuted the Jews publicly, showing from the Scriptures that Jesus is the Christ.

19 And it happened, while Apollos was at Corinth, that Paul, having passed through the upper regions, came to Ephesus. And finding some disciples

2 he said to them, "Did you receive the Holy Spirit when you believed?" And they said to him, "We have not so much as heard whether there is a Holy Spirit."

3 And he said to them, "Into what then were you baptized?" So they said, "Into John's baptism."

4 Then Paul said, "John indeed baptized with a baptism of repentance, saying to the people that they should believe on Him who would come after him, that is, on Christ Jesus."

5 When they heard *this*, they were baptized in the name of the Lord Jesus.

6 And when Paul had laid hands on them, the Holy Spirit came upon them, and they spoke with tongues and prophesied.

7 Now the men were about twelve in all.

8 And he went into the synagogue and spoke boldly for three months, reasoning and persuading concerning the things of the kingdom of God.

9 But when some were hardened and did not believe, but spoke evil of the Way before the multitude, he departed from them and withdrew the disciples, reasoning daily in the school of Tyrannus.

10 And this continued for two years, so that all who dwelt in Asia heard the word of the Lord Jesus, both Jews and Greeks.

STEP 10

*Continued to take personal inventory
and when we were wrong promptly admitted it.*

Acts 18:24—19:7

One of the greatest joys and responsibilities in the Christian life is to continue to gain a deeper understanding of who God is and what He expects of us.

In Acts 18:24—19:7, we meet people who loved God deeply. They sincerely tried to live to please Him. But their understanding was imperfect because they were only aware of the baptism of John. As soon as these disciples were introduced to the deeper truths of Jesus' deity, death, and resurrection they accepted Him as Savior and moved on to greater maturity. This could never have occurred if their hearts had not been humble before God and truly seeking insight, even if it meant leaving behind old ways of thinking.

As we daily search the Scriptures, may we be humble enough to allow God's Holy Spirit to change any imperfect ideas and attitudes we have, bringing us to full maturity in Christ.

For further reading on Step 10, turn to page 339.

Daily Encouragement

DAY 124 READING: ACTS 17:16—19:10

A Thought for the New Day: What is God like? Is He a big man in the sky somewhere? Or is God a mass of energy out in space? God cannot be either of these things, because, if He is to be God, He must be infinite; and, as such, we can never completely comprehend Him. Nevertheless, He is with us in a real and personal way every moment: we have our very existence *in Him* (17:28). He is totally in charge of all that happens to us, and He wants to be our Father. (*Turn to page 297.*)

11 Now God worked unusual miracles by the hands of Paul,

12 so that even handkerchiefs or aprons were brought from his body to the sick, and the diseases left them and the evil spirits went out of them.

13 Then some of the itinerant Jewish exorcists took it upon themselves to call the name of the Lord Jesus over those who had evil spirits, saying, "We adjure you by the Jesus whom Paul preaches."

14 Also there were seven sons of Sceva, a Jewish chief priest, who did so.

15 And the evil spirit answered and said, "Jesus I know, and Paul I know; but who are you?"

16 Then the man in whom the evil spirit was leaped on them, overpowered them, and prevailed against them, so that tney fled out of that house naked and wounded.

17 This became known both to all Jews and Greeks dwelling in Ephesus; and fear fell on them all, and the name of the Lord Jesus was magnified.

STEP 5

18 And many who had believed came confessing and telling their deeds.

19 Also, many of those who had practiced magic brought their books together and burned *them* in the sight of all. And they counted up the value of them, and *it* totaled fifty thousand *pieces* of silver.

20 So the word of the Lord grew mightily and prevailed.

21 When these things were accomplished, Paul purposed in the Spirit, when he had passed through Macedonia and Achaia, to go to Jerusalem, saying, "After I have been there, I must also see Rome."

22 So he sent into Macedonia two of those who ministered to him, Timothy and Erastus, but he himself stayed in Asia for a time.

23 And about that time there arose a great commotion about the Way.

24 For a certain man named Demetrius, a silversmith, who made silver shrines of Diana, brought no small profit to the craftsmen.

25 He called them together with the workers of similar occupation, and said: "Men, you know that we have our prosperity by this trade.

26 "Moreover you see and hear that not only at Ephesus, but throughout almost all Asia, this Paul has persuaded and turned away many people, saying that they are not gods which are made with hands.

27 "So not only is this trade of ours in danger of falling into disrepute, but also the temple of the great goddess Diana may be despised and her magnificence destroyed, whom all Asia and the world worship."

28 And when they heard *this*, they were full of wrath and cried out, saying, "Great *is* Diana of the Ephesians!"

29 So the whole city was filled with confusion, and rushed into the theater with one accord, having seized Gaius and Aristarchus, Macedonians, Paul's travel companions.

30 And when Paul wanted to go in to the people, the disciples would not allow him.

31 Then some of the officials of Asia, who were his friends, sent to him pleading that he would not venture into the theater.

32 Some therefore cried one thing and some another, for the assembly was confused, and most of them did not know why they had come together.

33 And they drew Alexander out of the multitude, the Jews putting him forward. And Alexander motioned with his hand, and wanted to make his defense to the people.

34 But when they found out that he was a Jew, all with one voice cried out for about two hours, "Great *is* Diana of the Ephesians!"

STEP 5

*Admitted to God, to ourselves, and to another human being
the exact nature of our wrongs.*

Acts 19:18

Almost as soon as a child can talk, we discover that this precious
bundle of energy and joy can also lie. Some children are born risk-
takers. Because of this personality trait, parents find themselves
having to discipline such children frequently. Sometimes it might
seem easier just to believe the little lies they tell to avoid the discipline. And yet we learn that once the truth is admitted, even if discipline has to follow, our children feel cleansed and relieved.

This same principle held true for the believers at Ephesus; and it
does in our own lives as well. When we come confessing and telling
our deeds, we will be amazed at the cleansing and release that the
Holy Spirit will impart to us. Even though it may seem easier to
continue to deny or excuse our behavior, in the long run the relief
and cleansing are worth the momentary pain.

For further reading on Step 5, turn to page 311.

Daily Encouragement

DAY 125 READING: ACTS 19:11–41

A Thought for the New Day: Peace is an intermittent experience in this world, alternating with violence and unrest. Even
Jesus said He would not bring peace. Why? Because, generally
speaking, few people agree with Him (vv. 28, 29). Our outward
calm is often broken by people with violent intentions, and we
do well to expect this. In spite of this, God gives us His inward
peace that no one can take away (John 14:27). (*Turn to page
299.*)

35 And when the city clerk had quieted the crowd, he said: "Men of Ephesus, what man is there who does not know that the city of the Ephesians is temple guardian of the great goddess Diana, and of the *image* which fell down from Zeus?

36 "Therefore, since these things cannot be denied, you ought to be quiet and do nothing rashly.

37 "For you have brought these men here who are neither robbers of temples nor blasphemers of your goddess.

38 "Therefore, if Demetrius and his fellow craftsmen have a case against anyone, the courts are open and there are proconsuls. Let them bring charges against one another.

39 "But if you have any other inquiry to make, it shall be determined in the lawful assembly.

40 "For we are in danger of being called in question for today's uproar, there being no reason which we may give to account for this disorderly gathering."

41 And when he had said these things, he dismissed the assembly.

STEP 12

20 After the uproar had ceased, Paul called the disciples to *him*, embraced *them*, and departed to go to Macedonia.

2 Now when he had gone over that region and encouraged them with many words, he came to Greece

3 and stayed three months. And when the Jews plotted against him as he was about to sail to Syria, he decided to return through Macedonia.

4 And Sopater of Berea accompanied him to Asia—also Aristarchus and Secundus of the Thessalonians, and Gaius of Derbe, and Timothy, and Tychicus and Trophimus of Asia.

5 These men, going ahead, waited for us at Troas.

6 But we sailed away from Philippi after the Days of Unleavened Bread, and in five days joined them at Troas, where we stayed seven days.

7 Now on the first *day* of the week, when the disciples came together to break bread, Paul, ready to depart the next day, spoke to them and continued his message until midnight.

8 There were many lamps in the upper room where they were gathered together.

9 And in a window sat a certain young man named Eutychus, who was sinking into a deep sleep. He was overcome by sleep; and as Paul continued speaking, he fell down from the third story and was taken up dead.

10 But Paul went down, fell on him, and embracing *him* said, "Do not trouble yourselves, for his life is in him."

11 Now when he had come up, had broken bread and eaten, and talked a long while, even till daybreak, he departed.

12 And they brought the young man in alive, and they were not a little comforted.

13 Then we went ahead to the ship and sailed to Assos, there intending to take Paul on board; for so he had given orders, intending himself to go on foot.

14 And when he met us at Assos, we took him on board and came to Mitylene.

15 We sailed from there, and the next *day* came opposite Chios; the following *day* we arrived at Samos and stayed at Trogyllium; the next *day* we came to Miletus.

16 For Paul had decided to sail past Ephesus, so that he would not have to spend time in Asia; for he was hurrying to be at Jerusalem, if possible, on the Day of Pentecost.

17 From Miletus he sent to Ephesus and called for the elders of the church.

18 And when they had come to

STEP 12

*Having had a spiritual awakening as the result
of these steps, we tried to carry this message to others,
and to practice these principles in all our affairs.*

Acts 20:1–15

If our personality happens to be that of a people-pleaser, we may sometimes struggle with the first part of Step 12. We may end up experiencing what psychologists call an approach-avoidance conflict. That is, because we care about others, we want to share our message of hope, but our fear of a negative response tends to keep us tongue-tied.

The apostle Paul understood the extent to which a negative response could be carried. He underwent the pain of flogging and faced attempts on his life because he dared to share what God had done for him. And even though Paul was no longer a young man, his enthusiasm and determination never wavered, no matter the circumstances or the time of day!

We may not all have Paul's dynamic and tireless personality, but with God's help and strength each of us can be a faithful witness to His power to change lives. The task ahead of us is never as great as the Power behind us.

For further reading on Step 12, turn to page 317.

Daily Encouragement

DAY 126 READING: ACTS 20:1–15

A Thought for the New Day: Paul was no wild-eyed fanatic who gloried in the possibility of his dying at the hands of persecutors (v. 3). Someday this would be necessary, but until then he would stay alive as long as he could to proclaim his wonderful Good News about Christ. Therefore, let us also keep our eye on the goal: not suffering, not luxuriating, but by all means holding up our vital message of a risen Savior who makes us alive with Him. *(Turn to page 301.)*

him, he said to them: "You know, from the first day that I came to Asia, in what manner I always lived among you,

19 "serving the Lord with all humility, with many tears and trials which happened to me by the plotting of the Jews;

20 "*and* how I kept back nothing that was helpful, but proclaimed it to you, and taught you publicly and from house to house,

21 "testifying to Jews, and also to Greeks, repentance toward God and faith toward our Lord Jesus Christ.

22 "And see, now I go bound in the spirit to Jerusalem, not knowing the things that will happen to me there,

23 "except that the Holy Spirit testifies in every city, saying that chains and tribulations await me.

24 "But none of these things move me; nor do I count my life dear to myself, so that I may finish my race with joy, and the ministry which I received from the Lord Jesus, to testify to the gospel of the grace of God.

25 "And indeed, now I know that you all, among whom I have gone preaching the kingdom of God, will see my face no more.

26 "Therefore I testify to you this day that I *am* innocent of the blood of all *men*.

27 "For I have not shunned to declare to you the whole counsel of God.

STEP 11 28 "Therefore take heed to yourselves and to all the flock, among which the Holy Spirit has made you overseers, to shepherd the church of God which He purchased with His own blood.

29 "For I know this, that after my departure savage wolves will come in among you, not sparing the flock.

30 "Also from among yourselves men will rise up, speaking perverse things, to draw away the disciples after themselves.

31 "Therefore watch, and remember that for three years I did not cease to warn everyone night and day with tears.

32 "And now, brethren, I commend you to God and to the word of His grace, which is able to build you up and give you an inheritance among all those who are sanctified.

33 "I have coveted no one's silver or gold or apparel.

34 "Yes, you yourselves know that these hands have provided for my necessities, and for those who were with me.

35 "I have shown you in every way, by laboring like this, that you must support the weak. And remember the words of the Lord Jesus, that He said, 'It is more blessed to give than to receive.' "

36 And when he had said these things, he knelt down and prayed with them all.

37 Then they all wept freely, and fell on Paul's neck and kissed him,

38 sorrowing most of all for the words which he spoke, that they would see his face no more. And they accompanied him to the ship.

21 Now it came to pass, that when we had departed from them and set sail, running a straight course we came to Cos, the following *day* to Rhodes, and from there to Patara.

2 And finding a ship sailing over to Phoenicia, we went aboard and set sail.

3 When we had sighted Cyprus, we passed it on the left, sailed to Syria, and landed at Tyre; for there the ship was to unload her cargo.

4 And finding disciples, we stayed there seven days. They told Paul through the Spirit not to go up to Jerusalem.

5 When we had come to the end of those days, we departed and went on our way; and they all ac-

STEP 11

*Sought through prayer and meditation to improve our conscious contact with God **as we understood Him,** praying only for knowledge of His will for us and the power to carry that out.*

Acts 20:28–32

"Take care of each other, watch out for false teachers, stay in the Word." This is the essence of Paul's parting words to his dear friends at Ephesus, whom he knew he would see no more on earth. His admonitions are just as pertinent and necessary to us today.

Believers must stay in close fellowship with one another, allowing for mutual edification and accountability. We must love enough to admonish one another and feel comfortable enough to share our lives with one another.

Paul's warning concerning false teachers is also vital today. The world is full of those who claim to be God's spokespersons, but who instead distort His Word and care only for personal gain.

Paul's third charge to his dear friends should be the central focus of our lives. Stay in the Word. Read it. Pray it. Sing it. Memorize it. Listen to it as it is preached. It is the Word of God, which is "able to build you up and give you an inheritance among all those who are sanctified."

For further reading on Step 11, turn to page 325.

Daily Encouragement

DAY 127 READING: ACTS 20:16—21:14

A Thought for the New Day: Paul's prudent act of self-preservation in Greece (see Day 126) was a temporary measure enabling him to achieve his goals in this life. Having accomplished these goals, his life or death mattered little to him (20:23, 24). It is good to remember that we will not be here forever. We can begin now to cultivate the promised full life we can expect with Christ in the new world He is preparing for us. (*Turn to page 306.*)

Paul Urged to Make Peace

companied us, with wives and children, till *we were* out of the city. And we knelt down on the shore and prayed.

6 When we had taken our leave of one another, we boarded the ship, and they returned home.

7 And when we had finished *our* voyage from Tyre, we came to Ptolemais, greeted the brethren, and stayed with them one day.

8 On the next *day* we who were Paul's companions departed and came to Caesarea, and entered the house of Philip the evangelist, who was *one* of the seven, and stayed with him.

9 Now this man had four virgin daughters who prophesied.

10 And as we stayed many days, a certain prophet named Agabus came down from Judea.

11 When he had come to us, he took Paul's belt, bound his *own* hands and feet, and said, "Thus says the Holy Spirit, 'So shall the Jews at Jerusalem bind the man who owns this belt, and deliver *him* into the hands of the Gentiles.' "

12 And when we heard these things, both we and those from that place pleaded with him not to go up to Jerusalem.

13 Then Paul answered, "What do you mean by weeping and breaking my heart? For I am ready not only to be bound, but also to die at Jerusalem for the name of the Lord Jesus."

14 So when he would not be persuaded, we ceased, saying, "The will of the Lord be done."

15 And after those days we packed and went up to Jerusalem.

16 Also some of the disciples from Caesarea went with us and brought with them one, Mnason of Cyprus, an early disciple, with whom we were to lodge.

17 And when we had come to Jerusalem, the brethren received us gladly.

18 On the following *day* Paul went in with us to James, and all the elders were present.

19 When he had greeted them, he told in detail those things which God had done among the Gentiles through his ministry.

20 And when they heard *it*, they glorified the Lord. And they said to him, "You see, brother, how many myriads of Jews there are who have believed, and they are all zealous for the law;

21 "but they have been informed about you that you teach all the Jews who are among the Gentiles to forsake Moses, saying that they ought not to circumcise *their* children nor to walk according to the customs.

22 "What then? The assembly must certainly meet, for they will hear that you have come.

23 "Therefore do what we tell you: We have four men who have taken a vow.

24 "Take them and be purified with them, and pay their expenses so that they may shave *their* heads, and that all may know that those things of which they were informed concerning you are nothing, but *that* you yourself also walk orderly and keep the law.

25 "But concerning the Gentiles who believe, we have written *and* decided that they should observe no such thing, except that they should keep themselves from *things* offered to idols, from blood, from things strangled, and from sexual immorality."

26 Then Paul took the men, and the next day, having been purified with them, entered the temple to announce the expiration of the days of purification, at which time an offering should be made for each one of them.

27 And when the seven days were almost ended, the Jews from Asia, seeing him in the temple, stirred up the whole crowd and laid hands on him,

28 crying out, "Men of Israel, help! This is the man who teaches all *men* everywhere against the people, the law, and this place; and furthermore he also brought Greeks into the temple and has defiled this holy place."

29 (For they had previously seen Trophimus the Ephesian with him in the city, whom they supposed that Paul had brought into the temple.)

30 And all the city was disturbed; and the people ran together, seized Paul, and dragged him out of the temple; and immediately the doors were shut.

31 Now as they were seeking to kill him, news came to the commander of the garrison that all Jerusalem was in an uproar.

32 He immediately took soldiers and centurions, and ran down to them. And when they saw the commander and the soldiers, they stopped beating Paul.

33 Then the commander came near and took him, and commanded *him* to be bound with two chains; and he asked who he was and what he had done.

34 And some among the multitude cried one thing and some another. And when he could not ascertain the truth because of the tumult, he commanded him to be taken into the barracks.

35 And when he reached the stairs, he had to be carried by the soldiers because of the violence of the mob.

36 For the multitude of the people followed after, crying out, "Away with him!"

37 And as Paul was about to be led into the barracks, he said to the commander, "May I speak to you?" He replied, "Can you speak Greek?

38 "Are you not the Egyptian who some time ago raised an insurrection and led the four thousand assassins out into the wilderness?"

39 But Paul said, "I am a Jew from Tarsus, in Cilicia, a citizen of no mean city; and I implore you, permit me to speak to the people."

40 So when he had given him permission, Paul stood on the stairs and motioned with his hand to the people. And when there was a great silence, he spoke to *them* in the Hebrew language, saying,

22 "Men, brethren, and fathers, hear my defense before you now."

2 And when they heard that he spoke to them in the Hebrew language, they kept all the more silent. Then he said:

3 "I am indeed a Jew, born in Tarsus of Cilicia, but brought up in this city at the feet of Gamaliel, taught according to the strictness of our fathers' law, and was zealous toward God as you all are today.

4 "I persecuted this Way to the death, binding and delivering into prisons both men and women,

5 "as also the high priest bears me witness, and all the council of the elders, from whom I also received letters to the brethren, and went to Damascus to bring in chains even those who were there to Jerusalem to be punished.

6 "Now it happened, as I journeyed and came near Damascus at about noon, suddenly a great light from heaven shone around me.

7 "And I fell to the ground and heard a voice saying to me, 'Saul, Saul, why are you persecuting Me?'

8 "So I answered, 'Who are You, Lord?' And He said to me, 'I am Jesus of Nazareth, whom you are persecuting.'

9 "Now those who were with me indeed saw the light and were afraid, but they did not hear the voice of Him who spoke to me.

10 "So I said, 'What shall I do, Lord?' And the Lord said to me, 'Arise and go into Damascus, and there you will be told all things which are appointed for you to do.'

11 "And since I could not see for

the glory of that light, being led by the hand of those who were with me, I came into Damascus.

12 "Then one, Ananias, a devout man according to the law, having a good testimony with all the Jews who dwelt *there,*

13 "came to me; and he stood and said to me, 'Brother Saul, receive your sight.' And at that same hour I looked up at him.

14 "Then he said, 'The God of our fathers has chosen you that you should know His will, and see the Just One, and hear the voice of His mouth.

15 'For you will be His witness to all men of what you have seen and heard.

16 'And now why are you waiting? Arise and be baptized, and wash away your sins, calling on the name of the Lord.'

17 "Then it happened, when I returned to Jerusalem and was praying in the temple, that I was in a trance

18 "and saw Him saying to me, 'Make haste and get out of Jerusalem quickly, for they will not receive your testimony concerning Me.'

19 "So I said, 'Lord, they know that in every synagogue I imprisoned and beat those who believe on You.

20 'And when the blood of Your martyr Stephen was shed, I also was standing by consenting to his death, and guarding the clothes of those who were killing him.'

21 "Then He said to me, 'Depart, for I will send you far from here to the Gentiles.' "

22 And they listened to him until this word, and *then* they raised their voices and said, "Away with such a *fellow* from the earth, for he is not fit to live!"

23 Then, as they cried out and tore off *their* clothes and threw dust into the air,

24 the commander ordered him to be brought into the barracks, and said that he should be examined under scourging, so that he might know why they shouted so against him.

25 And as they bound him with thongs, Paul said to the centurion who stood by, "Is it lawful for you to scourge a man who is a Roman, and uncondemned?"

26 When the centurion heard *that,* he went and told the commander, saying, "Take care what you do, for this man is a Roman."

27 Then the commander came and said to him, "Tell me, are you a Roman?" He said, "Yes."

28 And the commander answered, "With a large sum I obtained this citizenship." And Paul said, "But I was born *a citizen.*"

29 Then immediately those who were about to examine him withdrew from him; and the commander was also afraid after he found out that he was a Roman, and because he had bound him.

30 The next day, because he wanted to know for certain why he was accused by the Jews, he released him from *his* bonds, and commanded the chief priests and all their council to appear, and brought Paul down and set him before them.

23 Then Paul, looking earnestly at the council, said, "Men *and* brethren, I have lived in all good conscience before God until this day."

2 And the high priest Ananias commanded those who stood by him to strike him on the mouth.

3 Then Paul said to him, "God will strike you, *you* whitewashed wall! For you sit to judge me according to the law, and do you command me to be struck contrary to the law?"

4 And those who stood by said, "Do you revile God's high priest?"

5 Then Paul said, "I did not know, brethren, that he was the high

priest; for it is written, *'You shall not speak evil of the ruler of your people.'"*

6 But when Paul perceived that one part were Sadducees and the other Pharisees, he cried out in the council, "Men *and* brethren, I am a Pharisee, the son of a Pharisee; concerning the hope and resurrection of the dead I am being judged!"

7 And when he had said this, a dissension arose between the Pharisees and the Sadducees; and the assembly was divided.

8 For *the* Sadducees say that there is no resurrection—and no angel or spirit; but the Pharisees confess both.

9 Then there arose a loud outcry. And the scribes *who were* of the Pharisees' party arose and protested, saying, "We find no evil in this man; but if a spirit or an angel has spoken to him, let us not fight against God."

10 And when there arose a great dissension, the commander, fearing lest Paul might be pulled to pieces by them, commanded the soldiers to go down and take him by force from among them, and bring *him* into the barracks.

11 But the following night the Lord stood by him and said, "Be of good cheer, Paul; for as you have testified for Me in Jerusalem, so you must also bear witness at Rome."

12 And when it was day, some of the Jews banded together and bound themselves under an oath, saying that they would neither eat nor drink till they had killed Paul.

13 Now there were more than forty who had formed this conspiracy.

14 They came to the chief priests and elders, and said, "We have bound ourselves under a great oath that we will eat nothing until we have killed Paul.

15 "Now you, therefore, together with the council, suggest to the commander that he be brought down to you tomorrow, as though you were going to make further inquiries concerning him; but we are ready to kill him before he comes near."

16 And when Paul's sister's son heard of their ambush, he went and entered the barracks and told Paul.

17 Then Paul called one of the centurions to *him* and said, "Take this young man to the commander, for he has something to tell him."

18 So he took him and brought *him* to the commander and said, "Paul the prisoner called me to *him* and asked *me* to bring this young man to you. He has something to say to you."

19 Then the commander took him by the hand, went aside and asked *him* privately, "What is it that you have to tell me?"

20 And he said, "The Jews have agreed to ask that you bring Paul down to the council tomorrow, as though they were going to inquire more fully about him.

21 "But do not yield to them, for more than forty of them lie in wait for him, men who have bound themselves by an oath that they will neither eat nor drink till they have killed him; and now they are ready, waiting for the promise from you."

22 So the commander let the young man depart, and commanded *him*, "Tell no one that you have revealed these things to me."

23 And he called for two centurions, saying, "Prepare two hundred soldiers, seventy horsemen, and two hundred spearmen to go to Caesarea at the third hour of the night;

24 "and provide mounts to set Paul on, and bring *him* safely to Felix the governor."

25 He wrote a letter in the following manner:

STEP 3

*Made a decision to turn our will and our lives
over to the care of God **as we understood Him.***

Acts 23:11

Paul was born a Jew and trained as a Pharisee under the leading
rabbi. Thus he could most effectively reason with the Pharisees on
their own level. But God also ordained that he be born into a
household that held coveted Roman citizenship. Paul used that
leverage on more than one occasion. In Acts 23, we discover that
Paul happened to have a sister living in Jerusalem, who happened
to have a son, who happened to overhear the plot on Paul's life.
With God, of course, there are no accidents. He is able to make
every particular of our lives bring glory to Himself and blessing to
us. We may not always understand at first how God can use the
sadness of a dysfunctional family, or the sorrow of a deep loss, or the
pain of addiction. But do not doubt it. When we are willing to turn
all the events and hurt and happenstance over to Him, He will use
each part to create a beautiful and powerful masterpiece.

For further reading on Step 3, turn to page 313.

Daily Encouragement

DAY 128 READING: ACTS 21:15—23:35

A Thought for the New Day: The high priest had hardly acted
in a manner that would cause anyone to recognize that he was
God's representative. Nevertheless, in spite of the high priest's
disgraceful behavior, Paul bowed before the man's authority
(23:5). What a lesson in the respect we owe authority figures—
even those leaders we consider to be unworthy. Our profession
of Christ is adorned by respectfulness toward all. (*Turn to page
311.*)

26 Claudius Lysias,
To the most excellent governor Felix:
Greetings.
27 This man was seized by the Jews and was about to be killed by them. Coming with the troops I rescued him, having learned that he was a Roman.
28 And when I wanted to know the reason they accused him, I brought him before their council.
29 I found out that he was accused concerning questions of their law, but had nothing charged against him worthy of death or chains.
30 And when it was told me that the Jews lay in wait for the man, I sent him immediately to you, and also commanded his accusers to state before you the charges against him. Farewell.

31 Then the soldiers, as they were commanded, took Paul and brought *him* by night to Antipatris.
32 The next day they left the horsemen to go on with him, and returned to the barracks.
33 When they came to Caesarea and had delivered the letter to the governor, they also presented Paul to him.
34 And when the governor had read *it*, he asked what province he was from. And when he understood that *he was* from Cilicia,
35 he said, "I will hear you when your accusers also have come." And he commanded him to be kept in Herod's Praetorium.

24 Now after five days Ananias the high priest came down with the elders and a certain orator *named* Tertullus. These gave evidence to the governor against Paul.
2 And when he was called upon, Tertullus began his accusation, saying: "Seeing that through you

we enjoy great peace, and prosperity is being brought to this nation by your foresight,
3 "we accept *it* always and in all places, most noble Felix, with all thankfulness.
4 "Nevertheless, not to be tedious to you any further, I beg you to hear, by your courtesy, a few words from us.
5 "For we have found this man *a* plague, a creator of dissension among all the Jews throughout the world, and a ringleader of the sect of the Nazarenes.
6 "He even tried to profane the temple, and we seized him, and wanted to judge him according to our law.
7 "But the commander Lysias came by and with great violence took *him* out of our hands,
8 "commanding his accusers to come to you. By examining him yourself you may ascertain all these things of which we accuse him."
9 And the Jews also assented, maintaining that these things were so.
10 Then Paul, after the governor had nodded to him to speak, answered: "Inasmuch as I know that you have been for many years a judge of this nation, I do the more cheerfully answer for myself,
11 "because you may ascertain that it is no more than twelve days since I went up to Jerusalem to worship.
12 "And they neither found me in the temple disputing with anyone nor inciting the crowd, either in the synagogues or in the city.
13 "Nor can they prove the things of which they now accuse me.
14 "But this I confess to you, that according to the Way which they call a sect, so I worship the God of my fathers, believing all things which are written in the Law and in the Prophets.
15 "I have hope in God, which they themselves also accept, that there

will be a resurrection of *the* dead, both of *the* just and *the* unjust.

16 "This *being* so, I myself always strive to have a conscience without offense toward God and men.

17 "Now after many years I came to bring alms and offerings to my nation,

18 "in the midst of which some Jews from Asia found me purified in the temple, neither with a multitude nor with tumult.

19 "They ought to have been here before you to object if they had anything against me.

20 "Or else let those who are *here* themselves say if they found any wrongdoing in me while I stood before the council,

21 "unless *it is* for this one statement which I cried out, standing among them, 'Concerning the resurrection of the dead I am being judged by you this day.'"

22 But when Felix heard these things, having more accurate knowledge of *the* Way, he adjourned the proceedings and said, "When Lysias the commander comes down, I will make a decision on your case."

23 So he commanded the centurion to keep Paul and to let *him* have liberty, and told him not to forbid any of his friends to provide for or visit him.

24 And after some days, when Felix came with his wife Drusilla, who was Jewish, he sent for Paul and heard him concerning the faith in Christ.

25 Now as he reasoned about righteousness, self-control, and the judgment to come, Felix was afraid and answered, "Go away for now; when I have a convenient time I will call for you."

26 Meanwhile he also hoped that money would be given him by Paul, that he might release him. Therefore he sent for him more often and conversed with him.

27 But after two years Porcius Festus succeeded Felix; and Felix,

wanting to do the Jews a favor, left Paul bound.

25 Now when Festus had come to the province, after three days he went up from Caesarea to Jerusalem.

2 Then the high priest and the chief men of the Jews informed him against Paul; and they petitioned him,

3 asking a favor against him, that he would summon him to Jerusalem—while *they* lay in ambush along the road to kill him.

4 But Festus answered that Paul should be kept at Caesarea, and that he himself was going *there* shortly.

5 "Therefore," he said, "let those who have authority among you go down with *me* and accuse this man, to see if there is any fault in him."

6 And when he had remained among them more than ten days, he went down to Caesarea. And the next day, sitting on the judgment seat, he commanded Paul to be brought.

7 When he had come, the Jews who had come down from Jerusalem stood about and laid many serious complaints against Paul, which they could not prove,

8 while he answered for himself, "Neither against the law of the Jews, nor against the temple, nor against Caesar have I offended in anything at all."

9 But Festus, wanting to do the Jews a favor, answered Paul and said, "Are you willing to go up to Jerusalem and there be judged before me concerning these things?"

10 Then Paul said, "I stand at Caesar's judgment seat, where I ought to be judged. To the Jews I have done no wrong, as you very well know.

11 "For if I am an offender, or have committed anything worthy of death, I do not object to dying; but if there is nothing in these things of which these men accuse me, no

one can deliver me to them. I appeal to Caesar."

12 Then Festus, when he had conferred with the council, answered, "You have appealed to Caesar? To Caesar you shall go!"

13 And after some days King Agrippa and Bernice came to Caesarea to greet Festus.

14 When they had been there many days, Festus laid Paul's case before the king, saying: "There is a certain man left a prisoner by Felix,

15 "about whom the chief priests and the elders of the Jews informed *me*, when I was in Jerusalem, asking for a judgment against him.

16 "To them I answered, 'It is not the custom of the Romans to deliver any man to destruction before the accused meets the accusers face to face, and has opportunity to answer for himself concerning the charge against him.'

17 "Therefore when they had come together, without any delay, the next day I sat on the judgment seat and commanded the man to be brought in.

18 "When the accusers stood up, they brought no accusation against him of such things as I supposed,

19 "but had some questions against him about their own religion and about one, Jesus, who had died, whom Paul affirmed to be alive.

20 "And because I was uncertain of such questions, I asked whether he was willing to go to Jerusalem and there be judged concerning these matters.

21 "But when Paul appealed to be reserved for the decision of Augustus, I commanded him to be kept till I could send him to Caesar."

22 Then Agrippa said to Festus, "I also would like to hear the man myself." "Tomorrow," he said, "you shall hear him."

23 So the next day, when Agrippa and Bernice had come with great pomp, and had entered the auditorium with the commanders and the prominent men of the city, at Festus' command Paul was brought in.

24 And Festus said: "King Agrippa and all the men who are here present with us, you see this man about whom the whole assembly of the Jews petitioned me, both at Jerusalem and here, crying out that he was not fit to live any longer.

25 "But when I found that he had committed nothing worthy of death, and that he himself had appealed to Augustus, I decided to send him.

26 "I have nothing certain to write to my lord concerning him. Therefore I have brought him out before you, and especially before you, King Agrippa, so that after the examination has taken place I may have something to write.

27 "For it seems to me unreasonable to send a prisoner and not to specify the charges against him."

26 Then Agrippa said to Paul, "You are permitted to speak for yourself." So Paul stretched out his hand and answered for himself:

2 "I think myself happy, King Agrippa, because today I shall answer for myself before you concerning all the things of which I am accused by the Jews,

3 "especially because you are expert in all customs and questions which have to do with the Jews. Therefore I beg you to hear me patiently.

4 "My manner of life from my youth, which was spent from the beginning among my own nation at Jerusalem, all the Jews know.

5 "They knew me from the first, if they were willing to testify, that according to the strictest sect of our religion I lived a Pharisee.

6 "And now I stand and am

judged for the hope of the promise made by God to our fathers.

7 "To this *promise* our twelve tribes, earnestly serving *God* night and day, hope to attain. For this hope's sake, King Agrippa, I am accused by the Jews.

8 "Why should it be thought incredible by you that God raises the dead?

STEP 5

9 "Indeed, I myself thought I must do many things contrary to the name of Jesus of Nazareth.

10 "This I also did in Jerusalem, and many of the saints I shut up in prison, having received authority from the chief priests; and when they were put to death, I cast my vote against *them.*

11 "And I punished them often in every synagogue and compelled *them* to blaspheme; and being exceedingly enraged against them, I persecuted *them* even to foreign cities.

12 "While thus occupied, as I journeyed to Damascus with authority and commission from the chief priests,

13 "at midday, O king, along the road I saw a light from heaven, brighter than the sun, shining around me and those who journeyed with me.

14 "And when we all had fallen to the ground, I heard a voice speaking to me and saying in the Hebrew language, 'Saul, Saul, why are you persecuting Me? *It is* hard for you to kick against the goads.'

15 "So I said, 'Who are You, Lord?' And He said, 'I am Jesus, whom you are persecuting.

16 'But rise and stand on your feet; for I have appeared to you for this purpose, to make you a minister and a witness both of the things which you have seen and of the things which I will yet reveal to you.

17 'I will deliver you from the *Jewish* people, as well as *from* the Gentiles, to whom I now send you,

18 'to open their eyes *and* to turn them from darkness to light, and *from* the power of Satan to God, that they may receive forgiveness of sins and an inheritance among those who are sanctified by faith in Me.'

19 "Therefore, King Agrippa, I was not disobedient to the heavenly vision,

20 "but declared first to those in Damascus and in Jerusalem, and throughout all the region of Judea, and *then* to the Gentiles, that they should repent, turn to God, and do works befitting repentance.

21 "For these reasons the Jews seized me in the temple and tried to kill *me.*

22 "Therefore, having obtained help from God, to this day I stand, witnessing both to small and great, saying no other things than those which the prophets and Moses said would come—

23 "that the Christ would suffer, that He would be the first to rise from the dead, and would proclaim light to the *Jewish* people and to the Gentiles."

24 Now as he thus made his defense, Festus said with a loud voice, "Paul, you are beside yourself! Much learning is driving you mad!"

25 But he said, "I am not mad, most noble Festus, but speak the words of truth and reason.

26 "For the king, before whom I also speak freely, knows these things; for I am convinced that none of these things escapes his attention, since this thing was not done in a corner.

27 "King Agrippa, do you believe the prophets? I know that you do believe."

28 Then Agrippa said to Paul, "You almost persuade me to become a Christian."

29 And Paul said, "I would to God that not only you, but also all who hear me today, might become both almost and altogether such as I am, except for these chains."

*Admitted to God, to ourselves, and to another human being
the exact nature of our wrongs.*

Acts 26:9–11

When we think about the apostle Paul's devotion to Christ, few of us feel able to measure up to his determination, godliness, motivation, and wisdom. But even Paul had to acknowledge that he carried painful memories of a time in his life when he was in constant rebellion against God. When he told of those days and the hatred and violence he had displayed against people he now loved, he probably winced and shook his head in sadness and regret. Yet, although it was painful to remember and admit such things, there were benefits to be gained.

Paul could rejoice in a God who had loved him and sought him even in the midst of his sin. As he shared his background with others, they could identify with him and better understand who he was and what motivated him. And Paul could remind himself anew of the cleansing power of Christ who promises forgiveness of sins and an inheritance among those set apart by faith in Him (see Acts 26:18).

For further reading on Step 5, turn to page 371.

Daily Encouragement

DAY 129 READING: ACTS 24:1—26:32

A Thought for the New Day: In light of all that followed, it may seem foolish that Paul appealed to Caesar (25:11). Had he not done so, he could have been released on the spot. However, Paul had a greater goal in view: with free passage to Italy, he would increase his opportunities to spread the gospel—perhaps even to Spain. Thus, for several years Paul continued his work unhindered. We always need to keep our own minds open to the best options available. (*Turn to page 313.*)

30 When he had said these things, the king stood up, as well as the governor and Bernice and those who sat with them;

31 and when they had gone aside, they talked among themselves, saying, "This man is doing nothing worthy of death or chains."

32 Then Agrippa said to Festus, "This man might have been set free if he had not appealed to Caesar."

27 And when it was decided that we should sail to Italy, they delivered Paul and some other prisoners to *one* named Julius, a centurion of the Augustan Regiment.

2 So, entering a ship of Adramyttium, we put to sea, meaning to sail along the coasts of Asia. Aristarchus, a Macedonian of Thessalonica, was with us.

3 And the next *day* we landed at Sidon. And Julius treated Paul kindly and gave *him* liberty to go to his friends and receive care.

4 When we had put to sea from there, we sailed under *the shelter of* Cyprus, because the winds were contrary.

5 And when we had sailed over the sea which is off Cilicia and Pamphylia, we came to Myra, *a city* of Lycia.

6 There the centurion found an Alexandrian ship sailing to Italy, and he put us on board.

7 And when we had sailed slowly many days, and arrived with difficulty off Cnidus, the wind not permitting us to proceed, we sailed under *the* shelter of Crete off Salmone.

8 Passing it with difficulty, we came to a place called Fair Havens, near the city *of* Lasea.

9 Now when much time had been spent, and sailing was now dangerous because the Fast was already over, Paul advised them,

10 saying, "Men, I perceive that this voyage will end with disaster and much loss, not only of the cargo and ship, but also our lives."

11 Nevertheless the centurion was more persuaded by the helmsman and the owner of the ship than by the things spoken by Paul.

12 And because the harbor was not suitable to winter in, the majority advised to set sail from there also, if by any means they could reach Phoenix, a harbor of Crete opening toward the southwest and northwest, *and* winter *there.*

13 When the south wind blew softly, supposing that they had obtained *their* purpose, putting out to sea, they sailed close by Crete.

14 But not long after, a tempestuous head wind arose, called Euroclydon.

15 So when the ship was caught, and could not head into the wind, we let *her* drive.

16 And running under *the shelter of* an island called Clauda, we secured the skiff with difficulty.

17 When they had taken it on board, they used cables to undergird the ship; and fearing lest they should run aground on the Syrtis *Sands,* they struck sail and so were driven.

18 And because we were exceedingly tempest-tossed, the next *day* they lightened the ship.

19 On the third *day* we threw the ship's tackle overboard with our own hands.

20 Now when neither sun nor stars appeared for many days, and no small tempest beat on *us,* all hope that we would be saved was finally given up.

21 But after long abstinence from food, then Paul stood in the midst of them and said, "Men, you should have listened to me, and not have sailed from Crete and incurred this disaster and loss.

22 "And now I urge you to take heart, for there will be no loss of life among you, but only of the ship.

STEP 3

STEP 3

Made a decision to turn our will and our lives
*over to the care of God **as we understood Him.***

Acts 27:21–25

If God loves me, why did this terrible problem have to happen in my life? Most of us have had such thoughts from time to time. The Lord Jesus called Paul His "chosen vessel," but if Paul ever thought that would mean a life of ease and privilege, he found out otherwise very quickly. Beaten, mobbed, shipwrecked, plotted against, and imprisoned—Paul's life was anything but peaceful and easy. God does not promise us a rose garden, but He does promise us His peace in the midst of trial and His presence in the midst of uncertainty. This is why Paul was the one encouraging and cheering the passengers of the doomed ship. Others who had put their trust in good weather or a strong ship or ample supplies were experiencing disappointment and fear. Paul's anchor of trust, however, was the Lord Jesus. And when our faith is anchored firmly in Him alone, the storms of life may batter us, but they can never sink us.

For further reading on Step 3, turn to page 323.

Daily Encouragement

DAY 130 READING: ACTS 27:1—28:31

A Thought for the New Day: Do you sometimes feel that your life has little or no effect (28:25, 26)? Do not try to measure what God will do with your life by present results. Jesus said that His kingdom is like a tree that grows from the smallest seed, and such growth takes time. God is most concerned with the final achievement of His goals, and our business is to spend our lives in doing all the great and little things that please Him and bless others. (*Turn to page 317.*)

23 "For there stood by me this night an angel of the God to whom I belong and whom I serve,

24 "saying, 'Do not be afraid, Paul; you must be brought before Caesar; and indeed God has granted you all those who sail with you.'

25 "Therefore take heart, men, for I believe God that it will be just as it was told me.

26 "However, we must run aground on a certain island."

27 But when the fourteenth night had come, as we were driven up and down in the Adriatic *Sea*, about midnight the sailors sensed that they were drawing near some land.

28 And they took soundings and found *it* to be twenty fathoms; and when they had gone a little farther, they took soundings again and found *it* to be fifteen fathoms.

29 Then, fearing lest we should run aground on the rocks, they dropped four anchors from the stern, and prayed for day to come.

30 And as the sailors were seeking to escape from the ship, when they had let down the skiff into the sea, under pretense of putting out anchors from the prow,

31 Paul said to the centurion and the soldiers, "Unless these men stay in the ship, you cannot be saved."

32 Then the soldiers cut away the ropes of the skiff and let it fall off.

33 And as day was about to dawn, Paul implored *them* all to take food, saying, "Today is the fourteenth day you have waited and continued without food, and eaten nothing.

34 "Therefore I urge you to take nourishment, for this is for your survival, since not a hair will fall from the head of any of you."

35 And when he had said these things, he took bread and gave thanks to God in the presence of them all; and when he had broken *it* he began to eat.

36 Then they were all encouraged, and also took food themselves.

37 And in all we were two hundred and seventy-six persons on the ship.

38 So when they had eaten enough, they lightened the ship and threw out the wheat into the sea.

39 Now when it was day, they did not recognize the land; but they observed a bay with a beach, onto which they planned to run the ship if possible.

40 And they let go the anchors and left *them* in the sea, meanwhile loosing the rudder ropes; and they hoisted the mainsail to the wind and made for shore.

41 But striking a place where two seas met, they ran the ship aground; and the prow stuck fast and remained immovable, but the stern was being broken up by the violence of the waves.

42 Now the soldiers' plan was to kill the prisoners, lest any of them should swim away and escape.

43 But the centurion, wanting to save Paul, kept them from *their* purpose, and commanded that those who could swim should jump *overboard* first and get to land,

44 and the rest, some on boards and some on *broken pieces* of the ship. And so it was that they all escaped safely to land.

28 Now when they had escaped, they then found out that the island was called Malta.

2 And the natives showed us unusual kindness; for they kindled a fire and made us all welcome, because of the rain that was falling and because of the cold.

3 But when Paul had gathered a bundle of sticks and laid *them* on the fire, a viper came out because of the heat, and fastened on his hand.

4 So when the natives saw the creature hanging from his hand, they said to one another, "No

doubt this man is a murderer, whom, though he has escaped the sea, yet justice does not allow to live."

5 But he shook off the creature into the fire and suffered no harm. 6 However, they were expecting that he would swell up or suddenly fall down dead; but after they had looked for a long time and saw no harm come to him, they changed their minds and said that he was a god.

7 Now in that region there was an estate of the leading citizen of the island, whose name was Publius, who received us and entertained us courteously for three days. 8 And it happened that the father of Publius lay sick of a fever and dysentery. Paul went in to him and prayed, and he laid his hands on him and healed him. 9 So when this was done, the rest of those on the island who had diseases also came and were healed. 10 They also honored us in many ways; and when we departed, they provided such things as were necessary.

11 After three months we sailed in an Alexandrian ship whose figurehead was the Twin Brothers, which had wintered at the island. 12 And landing at Syracuse, we stayed three days. 13 From there we circled round and reached Rhegium. And after one day the south wind blew; and the next day we came to Puteoli, 14 where we found brethren, and were invited to stay with them seven days. And so we went toward Rome. 15 And from there, when the brethren heard about us, they came to meet us as far as Appii Forum and Three Inns. When Paul saw them, he thanked God and took courage.

16 Now when we came to Rome, the centurion delivered the prisoners to the captain of the guard; but Paul was permitted to dwell by himself with the soldier who guarded him.

17 And it came to pass after three days that Paul called the leaders of the Jews together. So when they had come together, he said to them: "Men *and* brethren, though I have done nothing against our people or the customs of our fathers, yet I was delivered as a prisoner from Jerusalem into the hands of the Romans, 18 "who, when they had examined me, wanted to let *me* go, because there was no cause for putting me to death. 19 "But when the Jews spoke against *it*, I was compelled to appeal to Caesar, not that I had anything of which to accuse my nation. 20 "For this reason therefore I have called for you, to see *you* and speak with *you*, because for the hope of Israel I am bound with this chain."

21 And they said to him, "We neither received letters from Judea concerning you, nor have any of the brethren who came reported or spoken any evil of you. 22 "But we desire to hear from you what you think; for concerning this sect, we know that it is spoken against everywhere."

23 So when they had appointed him a day, many came to him at *his* lodging, to whom he explained and solemnly testified of the kingdom of God, persuading them concerning Jesus from both the Law of Moses and the Prophets, from morning till evening. 24 And some were persuaded by the things which were spoken, and some disbelieved.

25 So when they did not agree among themselves, they departed after Paul had said one word: "The Holy Spirit spoke rightly through Isaiah the prophet to our fathers, 26 "saying,

'Go to this people and say:
"Hearing you will hear,
   and shall not understand;
And seeing you will see,
   and not perceive;
27 For the heart of this people
   has grown dull.
Their ears are hard of hearing,
And their eyes they have
   closed,
Lest they should see with their
   eyes and hear with their ears,
Lest they should understand
   with their heart and turn,
So that I should heal them." ' "

28 "Therefore let it be known to you that the salvation of God has been sent to the Gentiles, and they will hear it!"

29 And when he had said these words, the Jews departed and had a great dispute among themselves.

30 Then Paul dwelt two whole years in his own rented house, and received all who came to him,

31 preaching the kingdom of God and teaching the things which concern the Lord Jesus Christ with all confidence, no one forbidding him.

THE EPISTLE OF PAUL THE APOSTLE TO THE
ROMANS

PAUL, a servant of Jesus Christ, called *to be* an apostle, separated to the gospel of God

2 which He promised before through His prophets in the Holy Scriptures,

3 concerning His Son Jesus Christ our Lord, who was born of the seed of David according to the flesh,

4 and declared *to be* the Son of God with power, according to the Spirit of holiness, by the resurrection from the dead,

5 through whom we have received grace and apostleship for obedience to the faith among all nations for His name,

6 among whom you also are the called of Jesus Christ;

7 To all who are in Rome, beloved of God, called *to be* saints:

Grace to you and peace from God our Father and the Lord Jesus Christ.

8 First, I thank my God through Jesus Christ for you all, that your faith is spoken of throughout the whole world.

9 For God is my witness, whom I serve with my spirit in the gospel of His Son, that without ceasing I make mention of you always in my prayers,

10 making request if, by some means, now at last I may find a way in the will of God to come to you.

11 For I long to see you, that I may impart to you some spiritual gift, so that you may be established—

12 that is, that I may be encouraged together with you by the mutual faith both of you and me.

13 Now I do not want you to be unaware, brethren, that I often planned to come to you (but was hindered until now), that I might have some fruit among you also, just as among the other Gentiles.

14 I am a debtor both to Greeks and to barbarians, both to wise and to unwise.

15 So, as much as is in me, *I am* ready to preach the gospel to you who are in Rome also.

16 For I am not ashamed of the gospel of Christ, for it is the power of God to salvation for everyone

STEP 12

*Having had a spiritual awakening as the result
of these steps, we tried to carry this message to others,
and to practice these principles in all our affairs.*

Romans 1:14–17

If there was ever a center of earthly power, Rome was the place. Its emperors were worshiped as gods, and its military might had conquered the world. Romans related to power. So when Paul declared that the good news he brought was the "power of God," he had undoubtedly caught the attention of the people to whom he wrote. Paul was well aware that the proof of the gospel resided in this remarkable dynamic to transform lives. And he was also aware that any life could experience the infinite resources of the gospel's power, because its method of appropriation is the same, regardless of status or education. Faith from first to last (v. 17) is the key, not only for salvation, but for experiencing the transforming power of God in our lives. Our message of hope is salvation through faith. The power to practice our new life hinges on daily trust in the Lord Jesus. "The just shall live by faith."

For further reading on Step 12, turn to page 337. *For further reading on Step 12, turn to page 337.*

Daily Encouragement

DAY 131 READING: ROMANS 1:1–32

A Thought for the New Day: It has been said that "righteousness is its own reward." But what is righteousness? It is the essential character of God Himself (v. 17); and if we are to possess it, that righteousness must be His very own gift. This is the Christian's joy—that he or she is a blessed possessor of the gift of God's righteousness. We ask God for that gift, and He gives it to us from Christ's inexhaustible treasury. *(Turn to page 319.)*

who believes, for the Jew first and also for the Greek.

17 For in it the righteousness of God is revealed from faith to faith; as it is written, *"The just shall live by faith."*

18 For the wrath of God is revealed from heaven against all ungodliness and unrighteousness of men, who suppress the truth in unrighteousness,

19 because what may be known of God is manifest in them, for God has shown *it* to them.

20 For since the creation of the world His invisible *attributes* are clearly seen, being understood by the things that are made, *even* His eternal power and Godhead, so that they are without excuse,

21 because, although they knew God, they did not glorify *Him* as God, nor were thankful, but became futile in their thoughts, and their foolish hearts were darkened.

22 Professing to be wise, they became fools,

23 and changed the glory of the incorruptible God into an image made like corruptible man—and birds and four-footed beasts and creeping things.

24 Therefore God also gave them up to uncleanness, in the lusts of their hearts, to dishonor their bodies among themselves,

25 who exchanged the truth of God for the lie, and worshiped and served the creature rather than the Creator, who is blessed forever. Amen.

26 For this reason God gave them up to vile passions. For even their women exchanged the natural use for what is against nature.

27 Likewise also the men, leaving the natural use of the woman, burned in their lust for one another, men with men committing what is shameful, and receiving in themselves the penalty of their error which was due.

28 And even as they did not like to retain God in *their* knowledge, God gave them over to a debased mind, to do those things which are not fitting;

29 being filled with all unrighteousness, sexual immorality, wickedness, covetousness, maliciousness; full of envy, murder, strife, deceit, evil-mindedness; *they are* whisperers,

30 backbiters, haters of God, violent, proud, boasters, inventors of evil things, disobedient to parents,

31 undiscerning, untrustworthy, unloving, unforgiving, unmerciful;

32 who, knowing the righteous judgment of God, that those who practice such things are worthy of death, not only do the same but also approve of those who practice them.

2 Therefore you are inexcusable, O man, whoever you are who judge, for in whatever you judge another you condemn yourself; for you who judge practice the same things.

2 But we know that the judgment of God is according to truth against those who practice such things.

3 And do you think this, O man, you who judge those practicing such things, and doing the same, that you will escape the judgment of God?

4 Or do you despise the riches of His goodness, forbearance, and longsuffering, not knowing that the goodness of God leads you to repentance?

5 But in accordance with your hardness and your impenitent heart you are treasuring up for yourself wrath in the day of wrath and revelation of the righteous judgment of God,

6 who *"will render to each one according to his deeds":*

7 eternal life to those who by patient continuance in doing good seek for glory, honor, and immortality;

8 but to those who are self-seeking and do not obey the truth, but

STEP 8

STEP 8

*Made a list of all persons we had harmed,
and became willing to make amends to them all.*

Romans 2:1–4

In this passage, Paul tells us that we are not justified in blaming our own behavior on the actions and attitudes of others. He also gives us a biblical principle, which has become well accepted by psychologists when he states, "you who judge, practice the same things." Therapists agree that people have a tendency to imprint their own attitudes over the actions of others. For example, if no one seems trustworthy to us, perhaps it is because we ourselves are untrustworthy. On the other hand, if those around us seem kind and loving, it may be because we are kind and loving.

Judgment of others is God's department (v. 2). Our department is acceptance and reconciliation wherever possible. God's goodness, forbearance, and longsuffering brought us to repentance. As we allow these beautiful qualities of God to be reflected in our own lives, we can experience harmony with others we never thought possible.

For further reading on Step 8, turn to page 373.

Daily Encouragement

DAY 132 READING: ROMANS 2:1–16

A Thought for the New Day: Some people suppose their own worth is proved to the extent that they can uncover the faults of others, but the practice of continually judging and condemning those around us eats away at our own souls. Instead, cultivate the habit that Paul advocates in Philippians 4:8: "whatever things *are* lovely . . . if *there is* any virtue and if *there is* anything praiseworthy—meditate on these things." (*Turn to page 321.*)

Circumcision of No Avail

obey unrighteousness—indignation and wrath,

9 tribulation and anguish, on every soul of man who does evil, of the Jew first and also of the Greek;

10 but glory, honor, and peace to everyone who works what is good, to the Jew first and also to the Greek.

11 For there is no partiality with God.

12 For as many as have sinned without law will also perish without law, and as many as have sinned in the law will be judged by the law

13 (for not the hearers of the law *are* just in the sight of God, but the doers of the law will be justified;

14 for when Gentiles, who do not have the law, by nature do the things *contained* in the law, these, although not having the law, are a law to themselves,

15 who show the work of the law written in their hearts, their conscience also bearing witness, and between themselves *their* thoughts accusing or else excusing *them*)

16 in the day when God will judge the secrets of men by Jesus Christ, according to my gospel.

17 Indeed you are called a Jew, and rest on the law, and make your boast in God,

18 and know *His* will, and approve the things that are excellent, being instructed out of the law,

19 and are confident that you yourself are a guide to the blind, a light to those who are in darkness,

20 an instructor of the foolish, a teacher of babes, having the form of knowledge and truth in the law.

21 You, therefore, who teach another, do you not teach yourself? You who preach that a man should not steal, do you steal?

22 You who say, "Do not commit adultery," do you commit adultery? You who abhor idols, do you rob temples?

23 You who make your boast in the law, do you dishonor God through breaking the law?

24 For *"The name of God is blasphemed among the Gentiles because of you,"* as it is written.

25 For circumcision is indeed profitable if you keep the law; but if you are a breaker of the law, your circumcision has become uncircumcision.

26 Therefore, if an uncircumcised man keeps the righteous requirements of the law, will not his uncircumcision be counted as circumcision?

27 And will not the physically uncircumcised, if he fulfills the law, judge you who, *even* with *your* written *code* and circumcision, *are* a transgressor of the law?

28 For he is not a Jew who *is one* outwardly, nor *is* that circumcision *which is* outward in the flesh;

29 but *he is* a Jew who *is one* inwardly, and circumcision *is that* of the heart, in the Spirit, *and* not in the letter; whose praise *is* not from men but from God.

3 What advantage then has the Jew, or what *is* the profit of circumcision?

2 Much in every way! Chiefly because to them were committed the oracles of God.

3 For what if some did not believe? Will their unbelief make the faithfulness of God without effect?

4 Certainly not! Indeed, let God be true but every man a liar. As it is written:

> *"That You may be justified*
> *in Your words,*
> *And may overcome when*
> *You are judged."*

5 But if our unrighteousness demonstrates the righteousness of God, what shall we say? *Is* God unjust who inflicts wrath? (I speak as a man.)

6 Certainly not! For then how will God judge the world?

7 For if the truth of God has in-

STEP 1

We admitted we were powerless over our dependencies—
that our lives had become unmanageable.

Romans 3:1–20

There is the mistaken notion that the world is divided into two groups of people—the worthy and the unworthy, the sinners and the nonsinners. But such a world view does not agree with God's Word. Scripture tells us that no person ever has had or will have the power to be good or righteous or worthy. In ourselves, we do not have the power to obey God or to be worthy of His goodness. Those who go through life falsely believing in their own ability to be good persons whom God will ultimately accept into heaven are the big losers both now and eternally. However, those of us who come to the end of ourselves and realize that we are totally powerless to be what we want to be are fortunate indeed. Even though we may come to that realization through pain and anguish and deep frustration, we have taken the first step down the road to true peace and goodness. We have agreed with our Maker.

For further reading on Step 1, turn to page 331.

Daily Encouragement

DAY 133 READING: ROMANS 2:17—3:20

A Thought for the New Day: Elsewhere Paul says, "The law is good," and it is—for its intended purpose. The law is meant to preserve outward and civil order, but it cannot make us good on the *inside* (3:20). Only God can do that. Therefore, we do well to realize all the time just how much we depend on the Lord to make us what He wants us to be. (*Turn to page 323.*)

creased through my lie to His glory, why am I also still judged as a sinner?

8 And *why* not *say,* "Let us do evil that good may come"?—as we are slanderously reported and as some affirm that we say. Their condemnation is just.

9 What then? Are we better *than they?* Not at all. For we have previously charged both Jews and Greeks that they are all under sin.

10 As it is written:

    "There is none righteous, no,
       not one;
11 There is none who
      understands;
    There is none who seeks after
      God.
12 They have all gone out of the
      way;
    They have together become
      unprofitable;
    There is none who does good,
      no, not one."
13 "Their throat is an open tomb;
    With their tongues they have
      practiced deceit";
  "The poison of asps is under
      their lips";
14 "Whose mouth is full of cursing
    and bitterness."
15 "Their feet are swift to shed
    blood;
16 Destruction and misery are in
    their ways;
17 And the way of peace they
    have not known."
18 "There is no fear of God before
    their eyes."

19 Now we know that whatever the law says, it says to those who are under the law, that every mouth may be stopped, and all the world may become guilty before God.

20 Therefore by the deeds of the law no flesh will be justified in His sight, for by the law *is* the knowledge of sin.

21 But now the righteousness of God apart from the law is revealed, being witnessed by the Law and the Prophets,

22 even the righteousness of God *which is* through faith in Jesus Christ to all and on all who believe. For there is no difference;

23 for all have sinned and fall short of the glory of God,

24 being justified freely by His grace through the redemption that is in Christ Jesus,

25 whom God set forth *to be* a propitiation by His blood, through faith, to demonstrate His righteousness, because in His forbearance God had passed over the sins that were previously committed,

26 to demonstrate at the present time His righteousness, that He might be just and the justifier of the one who has faith in Jesus.

27 Where *is* boasting then? It is excluded. By what law? Of works? No, but by the law of faith.

28 Therefore we conclude that a man is justified by faith apart from the deeds of the law.

29 Or *is He* the God of the Jews only? *Is He* not also the God of the Gentiles? Yes, of the Gentiles also,

30 since *there is* one God who will justify the circumcised by faith and the uncircumcised through faith.

31 Do we then make void the law through faith? Certainly not! On the contrary, we establish the law.

4 What then shall we say that Abraham our father has found according to the flesh?

2 For if Abraham was justified by works, he has *something of which* to boast, but not before God.

3 For what does the Scripture say? *"Abraham believed God, and it was accounted to him for righteousness."*

4 Now to him who works, the wages are not counted as grace but as debt.

5 But to him who does not work but believes on Him who justifies the ungodly, his faith is accounted for righteousness,

STEP 3

*Made a decision to turn our will and our lives over to the care of God **as we understood Him.***

Romans 3:21–24

The Law and the Prophets both pointed to salvation through faith in Jesus. The Jewish people were given the law to teach them what true righteousness was. No one could ever keep that law perfectly, but there was always a sacrifice they could bring to the priest to atone for sin. That sacrifice pointed to and stood for the perfect Lamb of God, Christ Jesus, who would one day atone for sin once and for all. The prophets foretold the coming of this Chosen One of God, whose enabling power of grace is freely given to all who choose to yield their lives to Him. But what about the wrongs we have committed?

A just judge demands punishment for sin. God, the Just Judge willingly suffered a humiliating death upon the cross so that the punishment for sin could be paid. When you turn your life over to Him by faith, God looks at your faith in Jesus' sacrifice and declares you "not guilty."

For further reading on Step 3, turn to page 393.

Daily Encouragement

DAY 134 READING: ROMANS 3:21—4:8

A Thought for the New Day: Just what is "the righteousness of God . . . through faith in Jesus Christ" (3:22)? Faith recognizes what should be self-evident—that true righteousness is an infinitely high mountain that we can never climb. However, if we let God take charge of our lives, then all the strain of "being righteous" is taken away. The blood of His Son cleanses me from all unrighteousness. *(Turn to page 325.)*

6 just as David also describes the blessedness of the man to whom God imputes righteousness apart from works:

7 *"Blessed are those whose
      lawless deeds are forgiven,
      And whose sins are covered;*
8 *Blessed is the man to whom
      the* LORD *shall not impute
      sin."*

9 *Does* this blessedness then *come* upon the circumcised *only*, or upon the uncircumcised also? For we say that faith was accounted to Abraham for righteousness.
10 How then was it accounted? While he was circumcised, or uncircumcised? Not while circumcised, but while uncircumcised.
11 And he received the sign of circumcision, a seal of the righteousness of the faith which *he had while still* uncircumcised, that he might be the father of all those who believe, though they are uncircumcised, that righteousness might be imputed to them also,
12 and the father of circumcision to those who not only *are* of the circumcision, but who also walk in the steps of the faith which our father Abraham *had while still* uncircumcised.
13 For the promise that he would be the heir of the world *was* not to Abraham or to his seed through the law, but through the righteousness of faith.
14 For if those who are of the law *are* heirs, faith is made void and the promise made of no effect,
15 because the law brings about wrath; for where there is no law *there is* no transgression.
16 Therefore *it is* of faith that *it might be* according to grace, so that the promise might be sure to all the seed, not only to those who are of the law, but also to those who are of the faith of Abraham, who is the father of us all

17 (as it is written, *"I have made you a father of many nations"*) in the presence of Him whom he believed, *even* God, who gives life to the dead and calls those things which do not exist as though they did;
18 who, contrary to hope, in hope believed, so that he became the father of many nations, according to what was spoken, *"So shall your descendants be."*
19 And not being weak in faith, he did not consider his own body, already dead (since he was about a hundred years old), and the deadness of Sarah's womb.
20 He did not waver at the promise of God through unbelief, but was strengthened in faith, giving glory to God,

STEP 3

21 and being fully convinced that what He had promised He was also able to perform.
22 And therefore *"it was accounted to him for righteousness."*
23 Now it was not written for his sake alone that it was imputed to him,
24 but also for us. It shall be imputed to us who believe in Him who raised up Jesus our Lord from the dead,
25 who was delivered up because of our offenses, and was raised because of our justification.

5 Therefore, having been justified by faith, we have peace with God through our Lord Jesus Christ,

STEP 3

2 through whom also we have access by faith into this grace in which we stand, and rejoice in hope of the glory of God.
3 And not only *that*, but we also glory in tribulations, knowing that tribulation produces perseverance;

STEP 11

4 and perseverance, character; and character, hope.
5 Now hope does not disappoint, because the love of God has been poured out in our hearts by the Holy Spirit who was given to us.
6 For when we were still without

STEP 11

*Sought through prayer and meditation to improve our conscious contact with God **as we understood Him,** praying only for knowledge of His will for us and the power to carry that out.*

Romans 5:3–5

Our goal in Step 11 is to get to know God. It is possible to know about God and even to have been saved for some time, yet not know God deeply. There is, however, a price to pay if we want to know God deeply: that price is suffering. Although we should not seek out trouble, when the tribulations (that is, distresses and pressures) of life do come our way, our reaction to those problems will lead us closer to God or farther away from Him. If we look to God and ask His help to respond as we should, there will be marked and precious growth in our lives. God wants us to glory, or rejoice, in and because of our troubles. In the same way that Paul and Silas sang praises to God in the Philippian jail, we can praise God for our suffering because we know that our trials bring forth perseverance, strong character, and the precious, sure hope of God's overcoming and overwhelming love.

For further reading on Step 11, turn to page 333.

Daily Encouragement

DAY 135 READING: ROMANS 4:9—5:11

A Thought for the New Day: We all wish we could do away with suffering, but we realize that wishing will not end it. Even in the midst of suffering and "tribulation," though, God's peace gives us a gateway to hope (5:3, 4). Such hope has no "natural" explanation; rather, it results "because the love of God has been poured out in our hearts by the Holy Spirit who was given to us" (5:5). (*Turn to page 327.*)

strength, in due time Christ died for the ungodly.

7 For scarcely for a righteous man will one die; yet perhaps for a good man someone would even dare to die.

STEP 3
8 But God demonstrates His own love toward us, in that while we were still sinners, Christ died for us.

9 Much more then, having now been justified by His blood, we shall be saved from wrath through Him.

10 For if when we were enemies we were reconciled to God through the death of His Son, much more, having been reconciled, we shall be saved by His life.

11 And not only *that,* but we also rejoice in God through our Lord Jesus Christ, through whom we have now received the reconciliation.

12 Therefore, just as through one man sin entered the world, and death through sin, and thus death spread to all men, because all sinned—

13 (For until the law sin was in the world, but sin is not imputed when there is no law.

14 Nevertheless death reigned from Adam to Moses, even over those who had not sinned according to the likeness of the transgression of Adam, who is a type of Him who was to come.

15 But the free gift *is* not like the offense. For if by the one man's offense many died, much more the grace of God and the gift by the grace of the one Man, Jesus Christ, abounded to many.

16 And the gift *is* not like *that which came* through the one who sinned. For the judgment *which came* from one *offense resulted* in condemnation, but the free gift *which came* from many offenses *resulted* in justification.

17 For if by the one man's offense death reigned through the one,

much more those who receive abundance of grace and of the gift of righteousness will reign in life through the One, Jesus Christ.)

18 Therefore, as through one man's offense *judgment* came to all men, resulting in condemnation, even so through one Man's righteous act *the free gift came* to all men, resulting in justification of life.

19 For as by one man's disobedience many were made sinners, so also by one Man's obedience many will be made righteous.

20 Moreover the law entered that the offense might abound. But where sin abounded, grace abounded much more,

21 so that as sin reigned in death, even so grace might reign through righteousness to eternal life through Jesus Christ our Lord.

STEP 6
6 What shall we say then? Shall we continue in sin that grace may abound?

2 Certainly not! How shall we who died to sin live any longer in it?

3 Or do you not know that as many of us as were baptized into Christ Jesus were baptized into His death?

4 Therefore we were buried with Him through baptism into death, that just as Christ was raised from the dead by the glory of the Father, even so we also should walk in newness of life.

5 For if we have been united together in the likeness of His death, certainly we also shall be *in the likeness* of *His* resurrection,

6 knowing this, that our old man was crucified with *Him,* that the body of sin might be done away with, that we should no longer be slaves of sin.

7 For he who has died has been freed from sin.

8 Now if we died with Christ, we believe that we shall also live with Him,

9 knowing that Christ, having

STEP 6

*Were entirely ready to have God
remove all these defects of character.*

Romans 6:1–4

It is time to die. We have come to God and accepted the forgiveness and love He offers us in Christ Jesus. We have admitted our resentments and guilt and addictions. We have faced the truth about ourselves and our family of origin. Now we are ready to begin a new life in the power of God's Holy Spirit. But we cannot embark upon our voyage unless we are willing to leave behind the old, broken "furniture" of the past. Even though it was never beautiful, we have become comfortable with its lumps and bumps and sags. The prospect of a new habitat is both exciting and frightening to us. Becoming willing and ready for God to remove our defects is much like burning the old couches and mattresses. We have made the decision that we do not want this stained and ragged furniture of the past. We have chosen to die to all that would hinder our ability to prosper on our voyage of transformation. We are ready to "walk in newness of life."

For further reading on Step 6, turn to page 329.

Daily Encouragement

DAY 136 READING: ROMANS 5:12—6:7

A Thought for the New Day: Unrighteousness is a condition from which spring the thousands of problems that torment us in life. However, the gift of God's righteousness is "much more" than our unrighteousness. Righteousness is not only a free gift, but it is even the greatest of all gifts. God's righteousness rolls back the problem of sin and sets us free to live in His light. (*Turn to page 329.*)

been raised from the dead, dies no more. Death no longer has dominion over Him.

10 For *the death* that He died, He died to sin once for all; but *the life* that He lives, He lives to God.

STEP 6

11 Likewise you also, reckon yourselves to be dead indeed to sin, but alive to God in Christ Jesus our Lord.

12 Therefore do not let sin reign in your mortal body, that you should obey it in its lusts.

13 And do not present your members *as* instruments of unrighteousness to sin, but present yourselves to God as being alive from the dead, and your members *as* instruments of righteousness to God.

14 For sin shall not have dominion over you, for you are not under law but under grace.

15 What then? Shall we sin because we are not under law but under grace? Certainly not!

16 Do you not know that to whom you present yourselves slaves to obey, you are that one's slaves whom you obey, whether of sin to death, or of obedience to righteousness?

17 But God be thanked that *though* you were slaves of sin, yet you obeyed from the heart that form of doctrine to which you were delivered.

18 And having been set free from sin, you became slaves of righteousness.

19 I speak in human *terms* because of the weakness of your flesh. For just as you presented your members *as* slaves of uncleanness, and of lawlessness *leading* to *more* lawlessness, so now present your members *as* slaves *of* righteousness for holiness.

20 For when you were slaves of sin, you were free in regard to righteousness.

21 What fruit did you have then in the things of which you are now ashamed? For the end of those things *is* death.

22 But now having been set free from sin, and having become slaves of God, you have your fruit to holiness, and the end, everlasting life.

23 For the wages of sin *is* death, but the gift of God *is* eternal life in Christ Jesus our Lord.

7 Or do you not know, brethren (for I speak to those who know the law), that the law has dominion over a man as long as he lives?

2 For the woman who has a husband is bound by the law to *her* husband as long as he lives. But if the husband dies, she is released from the law of *her* husband.

3 So then if, while *her* husband lives, she marries another man, she will be called an adulteress; but if her husband dies, she is free from that law, so that she is no adulteress, though she has married another man.

4 Therefore, my brethren, you also have become dead to the law through the body of Christ, that you may be married to another, *even* to Him who was raised from the dead, that we should bear fruit to God.

5 For when we were in the flesh, the passions of sins which were aroused by the law were at work in our members to bear fruit to death.

6 But now we have been delivered from the law, having died to what we were held by, so that we should serve in the newness of the Spirit and not *in* the oldness of the letter.

7 What shall we say then? *Is* the law sin? Certainly not! On the contrary, I would not have known sin except through the law. For I would not have known covetousness unless the law had said, *"You shall not covet."*

8 But sin, taking opportunity by the commandment, produced in me all *manner of evil* desire. For apart from the law sin *was* dead.

STEP 6

*Were entirely ready to have God
remove all these defects of character.*

Romans 6:11, 12

The recovery process is a series of deaths and rebirths. We die time and again to the old reliance on our carnal dependencies. We continually give birth to new life that is spiritually oriented and infilled with the love of God.

In Step 6, we ask God to remove defects of character, and this removal requires that we die to old ways of being and acting. We must die to a false reliance on possessive and jealous human relationships. We must die to a narrow preoccupation with material wealth, power, or authority. We must die to our dependency on mood-altering chemicals or food as means of satiating spiritual needs. The expression of the Holy Spirit within us can only be alive to the extent that we have died to our old ways. We seek to be thorough in this invocation of God's help, for "half measures availed us nothing" (*Alcoholics Anonymous*, p. 59).

For further reading on Step 6, turn to page 341.

Daily Encouragement

DAY 137 READING: ROMANS 6:8—7:12

A Thought for the New Day: How are we made free to live in God's light? Jesus has broken the power of disobedience that worked against us. He did this by putting our sins to death with His own death on the cross. Furthermore, He received a new life at His resurrection that He now shares with us (6:8–11). Our destructive life-styles can no longer control us. As we let Him, Christ now lives out His new life through us. (*Turn to page 331.*)

9 I was alive once without the law, but when the commandment came, sin revived and I died.

10 And the commandment, which *was* to *bring* life, I found to *bring* death.

11 For sin, taking occasion by the commandment, deceived me, and by it killed *me.*

12 Therefore the law *is* holy, and the commandment holy and just and good.

13 Has then what is good become death to me? Certainly not! But sin, that it might appear sin, was producing death in me through what is good, so that sin through the commandment might become exceedingly sinful.

14 For we know that the law is spiritual, but I am carnal, sold under sin.

STEP 4 15 For what I am doing, I do not understand. For what I will to do, that I do not practice; but what I hate, that I do.

16 If, then, I do what I will not to do, I agree with the law that *it is* good.

17 But now, *it is* no longer I who do it, but sin that dwells in me.

STEP 1 18 For I know that in me (that is, in my flesh) nothing good dwells; for to will is present with me, but *how* to perform what is good I do not find.

19 For the good that I will *to do,* I do not do; but the evil I will not *to do,* that I practice.

20 Now if I do what I will not *to do,* it is no longer I who do it, but sin that dwells in me.

21 I find then a law, that evil is present with me, the one who wills to do good.

22 For I delight in the law of God according to the inward man.

23 But I see another law in my members, warring against the law of my mind, and bringing me into captivity to the law of sin which is in my members.

24 O wretched man that I am! Who will deliver me from this body of death?

25 I thank God—through Jesus Christ our Lord! So then, with the mind I myself serve the law of God, but with the flesh the law of sin.

8 *There is* therefore now no condemnation to those who are in Christ Jesus, who do not walk according to the flesh, but according to the Spirit. STEP 3

2 For the law of the Spirit of life in Christ Jesus has made me free from the law of sin and death.

3 For what the law could not do in that it was weak through the flesh, God *did* by sending His own Son in the likeness of sinful flesh, on account of sin: He condemned sin in the flesh,

4 that the righteous requirement of the law might be fulfilled in us who do not walk according to the flesh but according to the Spirit.

5 For those who live according to the flesh set their minds on the things of the flesh, but those *who* live according to the Spirit, the things of the Spirit.

6 For to be carnally minded *is* death, but to be spiritually minded *is* life and peace.

7 Because the carnal mind *is* enmity against God; for it is not subject to the law of God, nor indeed can be.

8 So then, those who are in the flesh cannot please God.

9 But you are not in the flesh but in the Spirit, if indeed the Spirit of God dwells in you. Now if anyone does not have the Spirit of Christ, he is not His.

10 And if Christ *is* in you, the body *is* dead because of sin, but the Spirit *is* life because of righteousness.

11 But if the Spirit of Him who raised Jesus from the dead dwells in you, He who raised Christ from the dead will also give life to your

STEP 1

We admitted we were powerless over our dependencies—
that our lives had become unmanageable.

Romans 7:18–20

Two indicators of addiction are the gradual loss of identity and the progressive violation of one's own values in the practice of the addiction. The gospel describes these addiction symptoms in the following terms: "It is no longer I who do it, but sin that dwells in me" (v. 20).

In assessing the presence of addictions and codependencies, we frequently ask the following simple diagnostic question: Is the dog wagging the tail, or is the tail wagging the dog? For example, the conscientious workaholic may have strong values concerning the primacy of home and family life. However, as the workaholism progresses, the workaholic does violence to those values by diverting increasing amounts of time and energy into work pursuits. The tail is now wagging the dog.

A universal warning sign of all addictions is the frightening recognition that I have begun to "do what I will not *to do*." This recognition is the beginning of the awareness of powerlessness and can be used by God as the beginning of the end of the addiction.

For further reading on Step 1, turn to page 511.

Daily Encouragement

DAY 138 READING: ROMANS 7:13—8:11

A Thought for the New Day: Sometimes we feel sick about wrongs committed against others from whom we can no longer seek forgiveness. A right or wrong feeling of guilt can drive people even to suicide. No doubt about it—we are guilty! But God is willing to free us from that load of guilt, because of the sacrifice His Son made in dying for us. God judges us no longer (8:1). Let us accept His great forgiveness. (*Turn to page 333.*)

mortal bodies through His Spirit who dwells in you.

12 Therefore, brethren, we are debtors—not to the flesh, to live according to the flesh.

13 For if you live according to the flesh you will die; but if by the Spirit you put to death the deeds of the body, you will live.

14 For as many as are led by the Spirit of God, these are sons of God.

15 For you did not receive the spirit of bondage again to fear, but you received the Spirit of adoption by whom we cry out, "Abba, Father."

16 The Spirit Himself bears witness with our spirit that we are children of God,

17 and if children, then heirs—heirs of God and joint heirs with Christ, if indeed we suffer with *Him*, that we may also be glorified together.

18 For I consider that the sufferings of this present time are not worthy *to be compared* with the glory which shall be revealed in us.

19 For the earnest expectation of the creation eagerly waits for the revealing of the sons of God.

20 For the creation was subjected to futility, not willingly, but because of Him who subjected *it* in hope;

21 because the creation itself also will be delivered from the bondage of corruption into the glorious liberty of the children of God.

22 For we know that the whole creation groans and labors with birth pangs together until now.

23 And not only *they*, but we also who have the firstfruits of the Spirit, even we ourselves groan within ourselves, eagerly waiting for the adoption, the redemption of our body.

24 For we were saved in this hope, but hope that is seen is not hope; for why does one still hope for what he sees?

25 But if we hope for what we do not see, *then* we eagerly wait for *it* with perseverance.

26 Likewise the Spirit also helps in our weaknesses. For we do not know what we should pray for as we ought, but the Spirit Himself makes intercession for us with groanings which cannot be uttered.

27 Now He who searches the hearts knows what the mind of the Spirit *is*, because He makes intercession for the saints according to *the will of* God.

28 And we know that all things work together for good to those who love God, to those who are the called according to *His* purpose.

29 For whom He foreknew, He also predestined *to be* conformed to the image of His Son, that He might be the firstborn among many brethren.

30 Moreover whom He predestined, these He also called; whom He called, these He also justified; and whom He justified, these He also glorified.

31 What then shall we say to these things? If God *is* for us, who *can be* against us?

32 He who did not spare His own Son, but delivered Him up for us all, how shall He not with Him also freely give us all things?

33 Who shall bring a charge against God's elect? *It is* God who justifies.

34 Who *is* he who condemns? *It is* Christ who died, and furthermore is also risen, who is even at the right hand of God, who also makes intercession for us.

35 Who shall separate us from the love of Christ? *Shall* tribulation, or distress, or persecution, or famine, or nakedness, or peril, or sword?

36 As it is written:

"For Your sake we are killed
  all day long;
We are accounted as sheep
  for the slaughter."

STEP 11

*Sought through prayer and meditation to improve our conscious contact with God **as we understood Him,** praying only for knowledge of His will for us and the power to carry that out.*

Romans 8:26–28

Step 11 reminds us that just as the quality of our emotional recovery is dependent upon the maintenance of our spiritual condition, so is the quality of our spiritual condition dependent upon the maintenance of close communication with God. Prayer is to be the channel of our contact with Him, but we may doubt our own capacity to approach God in this way.

However, Romans 8:26, 27 assures us that we have divine assistance from and through the Holy Spirit as we seek to commune with God. Indeed, He intercedes on our behalf to express prayer needs that escape our own awareness or that exceed the language of our human vocabulary (v. 26). Furthermore, we may be confident that the Holy Spirit's prayers on our behalf are "according to *the will* of God" (v. 27). Therefore, as we pray with His aid, we are indeed "praying only for knowledge of [God's] will for us."

For further reading on Step 11, turn to page 349.

Daily Encouragement

DAY 139 READING: ROMANS 8:12–30

A Thought for the New Day: Perhaps the most glaring need in our growing society is the individual's need to belong somewhere. Family relationships unhappily grow less and less important so that we feel orphaned in the world. Lonely people become broken, aimless, and even violent. If we could recapture the understanding of God's fatherly interest in us (v. 16), we would never spend another lonely day, and then we could share our Father's love with others. (*Turn to page 335.*)

37 Yet in all these things we are more than conquerors through Him who loved us.

STEP 2

38 For I am persuaded that neither death nor life, nor angels nor principalities nor powers, nor things present nor things to come,

39 nor height nor depth, nor any other created thing, shall be able to separate us from the love of God which is in Christ Jesus our Lord.

9 I tell the truth in Christ, I am not lying, my conscience also bearing me witness in the Holy Spirit,

2 that I have great sorrow and continual grief in my heart.

3 For I could wish that I myself were accursed from Christ for my brethren, my kinsmen according to the flesh,

4 who are Israelites, to whom *pertain* the adoption, the glory, the covenants, the giving of the law, the service *of God*, and the promises;

5 of whom *are* the fathers and from whom, according to the flesh, Christ *came*, who is over all, *the* eternally blessed God. Amen.

6 But it is not that the word of God has taken no effect. For they *are* not all Israel who *are* of Israel,

7 nor *are they* all children because they are the seed of Abraham; but, *"In Isaac your seed shall be called."*

8 That is, those who *are* the children of the flesh, these *are* not the children of God; but the children of the promise are counted as the seed.

9 For this *is* the word of promise: *"At this time I will come and Sarah shall have a son."*

10 And not only *this*, but when Rebecca also had conceived by one man, *even* by our father Isaac

11 (for *the children* not yet being born, nor having done any good or evil, that the purpose of God according to election might stand, not of works but of Him who calls),

12 it was said to her, *"The older shall serve the younger."*

13 As it is written, *"Jacob I have loved, but Esau I have hated."*

14 What shall we say then? *Is there* unrighteousness with God? Certainly not!

15 For He says to Moses, *"I will have mercy on whomever I will have mercy, and I will have compassion on whomever I will have compassion."*

16 So then *it is* not of him who wills, nor of him who runs, but of God who shows mercy.

17 For the Scripture says to Pharaoh, *"Even for this same purpose I have raised you up, that I might show My power in you, and that My name might be declared in all the earth."*

18 Therefore He has mercy on whom He wills, and whom He wills He hardens.

19 You will say to me then, "Why does He still find fault? For who has resisted His will?"

20 But indeed, O man, who are you to reply against God? Will the thing formed say to him who formed *it*, "Why have you made me like this?"

21 Does not the potter have power over the clay, from the same lump to make one vessel for honor and another for dishonor?

22 *What* if God, wanting to show His wrath and to make His power known, endured with much longsuffering the vessels of wrath prepared for destruction,

23 and that He might make known the riches of His glory on the vessels of mercy, which He had prepared beforehand for glory,

24 *even* us whom He called, not of the Jews only, but also of the Gentiles?

25 As He says also in Hosea:

"I will call them My people,
who were not My people,
And her beloved,
who was not beloved."

*Came to believe that a Power greater than ourselves
could restore us to sanity.*

Romans 8:38, 39

To the wayward nation of Israel God said through the prophet Jeremiah, "Yes, I have loved you with an everlasting love; therefore with lovingkindness I have drawn you" (Jer. 31:3). No matter how monumental their sin, Israel could not erase God's love for them, nor can we. Human beings may desert us, fears may overwhelm us, addictions may encumber us, but none of these things can ever separate us from God's love.

His love made Him willing to leave the splendor and joy of heaven. It made Him willing to accept physical and emotional suffering we cannot fully imagine or comprehend.

In the past, we may have scorned, denied, or ignored His love; but the heart of God is greater than our rejection. The love that sent Him to the cross and the power that resurrected Him from the grave still call. They call to each one whose ears are ready to hear and whose heart is ready to reach out and accept His strong love.

For further reading on Step 2, turn to page 353.

Daily Encouragement

DAY 140 READING: ROMANS 8:31—9:29

A Thought for the New Day: Here is your iron supplement for everyday living: If God is for you, no one can stand against you—however hard they may try (8:31). God wants you to find out that He is much greater than the adverse conditions you face on your job or in your home. Even monetary setbacks will turn out in the end to be the very circumstances that were working in your favor. (*Turn to page 337.*)

26 *"And it shall come to pass in*
the place where it was said to
them,
'You are not My people,'
There they will be called sons
of the living God."

27 Isaiah also cries out concerning
Israel:

"Though the number of the
children of Israel be as the
sand of the sea,
The remnant will be saved.
28 *For He will finish the work*
and cut it short in
righteousness,
Because the LORD will make a
short work upon the earth."

29 And as Isaiah said before:

"Unless the LORD of Sabaoth
had left us a seed,
We would have become like
Sodom,
And we would have been made
like Gomorrah."

30 What shall we say then? That
Gentiles, who did not pursue righteousness, have attained to righteousness, even the righteousness
of faith;
31 but Israel, pursuing the law of
righteousness, has not attained to
the law of righteousness.
32 Why? Because *they* did not *seek*
it by faith, but as it were, by the
works of the law. For they stumbled at that stumbling stone.
33 As it is written:

"Behold, I lay in Zion a
stumbling stone and rock of
offense,
And whoever believes on Him
will not be put to shame."

10 Brethren, my heart's desire
and prayer to God for Israel
is that they may be saved.
2 For I bear them witness that

they have a zeal for God, but not
according to knowledge.
3 For they being ignorant of
God's righteousness, and seeking
to establish their own righteousness, have not submitted to the
righteousness of God.
4 For Christ *is* the end of the law
for righteousness to everyone who
believes.
5 For Moses writes about the
righteousness which is of the law,
"The man who does those things
shall live by them."
6 But the righteousness of faith
speaks in this way, *"Do not say in*
your heart, 'Who will ascend into
heaven?' " (that is, to bring Christ
down *from above*)
7 or, *" 'Who will descend into the*
abyss?' " (that is, to bring Christ
up from the dead).
8 But what does it say? *"The*
word is near you, even in your
mouth and in your heart" (that is,
the word of faith which we
preach):
9 that if you confess with your
mouth the Lord Jesus and believe
in your heart that God has raised
Him from the dead, you will be
saved. [STEP 3]
10 For with the heart one believes
to righteousness, and with the
mouth confession is made to salvation.
11 For the Scripture says, *"Who-*
ever believes on Him will not be
put to shame."
12 For there is no distinction between Jew and Greek, for the same
Lord over all is rich to all who call
upon Him.
13 For *"whoever calls upon the*
name of the LORD shall be saved."
14 How then shall they call on Him [STEP 12]
in whom they have not believed?
And how shall they believe in Him
of whom they have not heard? And
how shall they hear without a
preacher?
15 And how shall they preach unless they are sent? As it is written:

STEP 12

*Having had a spiritual awakening as the result
of these steps, we tried to carry this message to others,
and to practice these principles in all our affairs.*

Romans 10:14, 15

"Let the preacher do it," is one of the favorite attitudes of
Christians today. It is the preacher's "job," we believe, to preach
the gospel, visit the sick, and counsel the troubled. Yes, all those
things are part of the pastor's job, but they are definitely not the
exclusive domain of pastors. God's Word teaches that each of us
will be called on to preach and counsel and visit as part of our service to the Lord Jesus. Step 12 emphasizes this scriptural principle,
because it exhorts us to share with others the valuable lessons we
have learned about God's love and power and forgiveness.

There will be people who will listen carefully to what we have to
say simply because they will be able to identify with us. These people may be very unwilling to go to church and listen to a preacher,
but they will allow us to share what God has done in our lives.
They cannot believe unless they hear. "And how shall they hear
without a preacher?"

For further reading on Step 12, turn to page 367.

Daily Encouragement

DAY 141 READING: ROMANS 9:30—10:21

A Thought for the New Day: How can faith grow strong? The
more we listen to what God is saying in His Word, the better listeners we become (10:17). That is, we become listeners who
really *hear* what God wants to say to us. We must not let Bible
study become a mechanical exercise. As we read, we must take
care to listen. Our faith will grow as God's thoughts more and
more become our own thoughts about everything in life. (*Turn
to page 339.*)

> *"How beautiful are the feet of*
> *those who preach the gospel*
> *of peace,*
> *Who bring glad tidings of good*
> *things!"*

16 But they have not all obeyed the gospel. For Isaiah says, *"Lord, who has believed our report?"*
17 So then faith *comes* by hearing, and hearing by the word of God.
18 But I say, have they not heard? Yes indeed:

> *"Their sound has gone out*
> *to all the earth,*
> *And their words to the ends*
> *of the world."*

19 But I say, did Israel not know? First Moses says:

> *"I will provoke you to jealousy*
> *by those who are not a*
> *nation,*
> *I will anger you by a foolish*
> *nation."*

20 But Isaiah is very bold and says:

> *"I was found by those*
> *who did not seek Me;*
> *I was made manifest to those*
> *who did not ask for Me."*

21 But to Israel he says:

> *"All day long I have stretched*
> *out My hands*
> *To a disobedient and contrary*
> *people."*

STEP 10

11 I say then, has God cast away His people? Certainly not! For I also am an Israelite, of the seed of Abraham, *of* the tribe of Benjamin.
2 God has not cast away His people whom He foreknew. Or do you not know what the Scripture says of Elijah, how he pleads with God against Israel, saying,
3 *"LORD, they have killed Your*

prophets and torn down Your altars, and I alone am left, and they seek my life"?
4 But what does the divine response say to him? *"I have reserved for Myself seven thousand men who have not bowed the knee to Baal."*
5 Even so then, at this present time there is a remnant according to the election of grace.
6 And if by grace, then *it is* no longer of works; otherwise grace is no longer grace. But if *it is* of works, it is no longer grace; otherwise work is no longer work.
7 What then? Israel has not obtained what it seeks; but the elect have obtained it, and the rest were hardened.
8 Just as it is written:

> *"God has given them a spirit of*
> *stupor,*
> *Eyes that they should not see*
> *And ears that they should not*
> *hear,*
> *To this very day."*

9 And David says:

> *"Let their table become a snare*
> *and a trap,*
> *A stumbling block and*
> *a recompense to them;*
> 10 *Let their eyes be darkened,*
> *that they may not see,*
> *And bow down their back*
> *always."*

11 I say then, have they stumbled that they should fall? Certainly not! But through their fall, to provoke them to jealousy, salvation *has come* to the Gentiles.
12 Now if their fall *is* riches for the world, and their failure riches for the Gentiles, how much more their fullness!
13 For I speak to you Gentiles; inasmuch as I am an apostle to the Gentiles, I magnify my ministry,
14 if by any means I may provoke

STEP 10

*Continued to take personal inventory
and when we were wrong promptly admitted it.*

Romans 11:1–5

The great prophet Elijah complained to God that he alone was left to serve the Lord. Many churches today seem to be led entirely by a small group of people suffering from Elijah complex. This is not God's design for His church; and in the long run, these sincere, well-meaning people can do more harm than good.

Our God is big enough to carry on His work apart from any one person. And any work that is truly of God will be protected by Him. When we discover that we are becoming exhausted, negative, complaining people because the work of God is a burden instead of a privilege, it is time to take personal inventory. Is this our work or God's? Is His glory or our own at stake? Are we trying to meet needs in the wrong way? If honest answers point to an Elijah complex in our lives, we must give God's work back to God so that He can do what He wants in the way that He chooses.

For further reading on Step 10, turn to page 351.

Daily Encouragement

DAY 142 READING: ROMANS 11:1–10

A Thought for the New Day: When Elijah the prophet grew pessimistic, he needed encouragement, and so do we (vv. 2–4). Sometimes we feel that God's work is very poorly represented in the world, and at times it may be. However, the Lord is never without human resources. Although we do not see it every day, from time to time we are encouraged by the realization that God does have a great army of servants working to build a kingdom that will last forever. *(Turn to page 341.)*

to jealousy *those who are* my flesh and save some of them.

15 For if their being cast away *is* the reconciling of the world, what *will* their acceptance *be* but life from the dead?

16 For if the firstfruit *is* holy, the lump *is* also *holy*; and if the root *is* holy, so *are* the branches.

17 And if some of the branches were broken off, and you, being a wild olive tree, were grafted in among them, and with them became a partaker of the root and fatness of the olive tree,

18 do not boast against the branches. But if you boast, *remember that* you do not support the root, but the root supports you.

19 You will say then, "Branches were broken off that I might be grafted in."

20 Well *said*. Because of unbelief they were broken off, and you stand by faith. Do not be haughty, but fear.

21 For if God did not spare the natural branches, He may not spare you either.

22 Therefore consider the goodness and severity of God: on those who fell, severity; but toward you, goodness, if you continue in *His* goodness. Otherwise you also will be cut off.

23 And they also, if they do not continue in unbelief, will be grafted in, for God is able to graft them in again.

24 For if you were cut out of the olive tree which is wild by nature, and were grafted contrary to nature into a good olive tree, how much more will these, who *are the* natural *branches*, be grafted into their own olive tree?

25 For I do not desire, brethren, that you should be ignorant of this mystery, lest you should be wise in your own opinion, that hardening in part has happened to Israel until the fullness of the Gentiles has come in.

26 And so all Israel will be saved, as it is written:

> "The Deliverer will come out of Zion,
> And He will turn away ungodliness from Jacob;

27 For this is My covenant with them,
> When I take away their sins."

28 Concerning the gospel *they are* enemies for your sake, but concerning the election *they are* beloved for the sake of the fathers.

29 For the gifts and the calling of God *are* irrevocable.

30 For as you were once disobedient to God, yet have now obtained mercy through their disobedience,

31 even so these also have now been disobedient, that through the mercy shown you they also may obtain mercy.

32 For God has committed them all to disobedience, that He might have mercy on all.

33 Oh, the depth of the riches both of the wisdom and knowledge of God! How unsearchable *are* His judgments and His ways past finding out!

34 "For who has known the mind of the Lᴏʀᴅ?
> Or who has become His counselor?"

35 "Or who has first given to Him
> And it shall be repaid to him?"

36 For of Him and through Him and to Him *are* all things, to whom *be* glory forever. Amen.

12 I beseech you therefore, brethren, by the mercies of God, that you present your bodies a living sacrifice, holy, acceptable to God, *which is* your reasonable service.

2 And do not be conformed to this world, but be transformed by the renewing of your mind, that you may prove what *is* that good and acceptable and perfect will of God.

*Were entirely ready to have God
remove all these defects of character.*

Romans 12:2

In this passage, Paul tells his brothers and sisters in Christ not to conform to the world around them. He exhorts us instead to make the most of our New Birth in Christ Jesus, by living a transformed life with a renewed mind. The English word derived from the Greek rendering here is "metamorphosis." It means literally "a total change from the inside out."

Truly, there is no other way we can be delivered from our destructive life-style. This total change comes only through a mind that is continuously being made new by the power of God's Word, praying, and Christian fellowship.

The idea of changing our lives so drastically may be a little unsettling to some of us. But God's promise should put our hearts at rest. He tells us in the end of verse 2 that as our minds are renewed we will come to recognize God's will for our lives and will discover, not only that His will is good for us, but that it is perfect in every way.

For further reading on Step 6, turn to page 379.

Daily
Encouragement

DAY 143 READING: ROMANS 11:11—12:2

A Thought for the New Day: The word "worship" has some very dull associations for some people. Unfortunately worship has often come to suggest a meaningless routine of singing, praying, and preaching. That is not the main idea of worship at all. "Reasonable service" (or "worship") calls us to use our entire lives as sacrifices of praise to God. Then all we do is, in some way, true spiritual worship: church worship will then mean more, too. *(Turn to page 343.)*

STEP 10

3 For I say, through the grace given to me, to everyone who is among you, not to think *of himself* more highly than he ought to think, but to think soberly, as God has dealt to each one a measure of faith.

4 For as we have many members in one body, but all the members do not have the same function,

5 so we, *being* many, are one body in Christ, and individually members of one another.

6 Having then gifts differing according to the grace that is given to us, *let us use them:* if prophecy, *let us prophesy* in proportion to our faith;

7 or ministry, *let us use it* in *our* ministering; he who teaches, in teaching;

8 he who exhorts, in exhortation; he who gives, with liberality; he who leads, with diligence; he who shows mercy, with cheerfulness.

STEP 8

9 *Let* love *be* without hypocrisy. Abhor what is evil. Cling to what is good.

STEP 11

10 *Be* kindly affectionate to one another with brotherly love, in honor giving preference to one another;

11 not lagging in diligence, fervent in spirit, serving the Lord;

12 rejoicing in hope, patient in tribulation, continuing steadfastly in prayer;

13 distributing to the needs of the saints, given to hospitality.

STEP 8

14 Bless those who persecute you; bless and do not curse.

15 Rejoice with those who rejoice, and weep with those who weep.

STEP 10

16 Be of the same mind toward one another. Do not set your mind on high things, but associate with the humble. Do not be wise in your own opinion.

STEP 8

17 Repay no one evil for evil. Have regard for good things in the sight of all men.

STEP 9

18 If it is possible, as much as depends on you, live peaceably with all men.

19 Beloved, do not avenge yourselves, but *rather* give place to wrath; for it is written, *"Vengeance is Mine, I will repay,"* says the Lord.

20 *"Therefore if your enemy hungers, feed him;*
If he thirsts, give him a drink;
For in so doing you will heap coals of fire on his head."

21 Do not be overcome by evil, but overcome evil with good.

13 Let every soul be subject to the governing authorities. For there is no authority except from God, and the authorities that exist are appointed by God.

2 Therefore whoever resists the authority resists the ordinance of God, and those who resist will bring judgment on themselves.

3 For rulers are not a terror to good works, but to evil. Do you want to be unafraid of the authority? Do what is good, and you will have praise from the same.

4 For he is God's minister to you for good. But if you do evil, be afraid; for he does not bear the sword in vain; for he is God's minister, an avenger to *execute* wrath on him who practices evil.

5 Therefore *you* must be subject, not only because of wrath but also for conscience' sake.

6 For because of this you also pay taxes, for they are God's ministers attending continually to this very thing.

7 Render therefore to all their due: taxes to whom taxes *are due,* customs to whom customs, fear to whom fear, honor to whom honor.

STEP 8

8 Owe no one anything except to love one another, for he who loves another has fulfilled the law.

9 For the commandments, *"You shall not commit adultery," "You shall not murder," "You shall not steal," "You shall not bear false witness," "You shall not covet,"* and if *there is* any other command-

STEP 10

*Continued to take personal inventory
and when we were wrong promptly admitted it.*

Romans 12:3

When we begin to experience success in turning our lives around, we may believe that these accomplishments have resulted from our own human power. The apostle Paul warns against that prideful attitude.

On the other hand, neither should we become hypercritical or overjudgmental when we do make mistakes or slip back into past patterns of behavior. Paul warns us "to think soberly," which simply means to have sound thinking about ourselves. This is why Step 10 is so important to our spiritual and emotional well-being.

Our daily and weekly inventory is exactly what we need to keep us "thinking soberly." Have we had success in breaking old dependencies? We should praise God and continue to acknowledge our need of his help. Have we failed in our attempt to handle a problem? We can honestly admit our error and ask God's help to correct the situation. Our personal inventory helps us remain focused on who we are and the direction God wants for our lives.

For further reading on Step 10, turn to page 351.

Daily Encouragement

DAY 144 READING: ROMANS 12:3–21

A Thought for the New Day: Peace with others is one of those goals that everyone would like to have, but not everyone is willing to pay the price for it (v. 18). Is "making your point" the most important thing in a discussion? We can be very, very right about something, but with the wrong attitude. Let us have more concern for individuals and be less defensive about their opinions. (*Turn to page 345.*)

ment, are *all* summed up in this saying, namely, *"You shall love your neighbor as yourself."*

10 Love does no harm to a neighbor; therefore love *is* the fulfillment of the law.

11 And *do* this, knowing the time, that now *it is* high time to awake out of sleep; for now our salvation *is* nearer than when we *first* believed.

12 The night is far spent, the day is at hand. Therefore let us cast off the works of darkness, and let us put on the armor of light.

13 Let us walk properly, as in the day, not in revelry and drunkenness, not in licentiousness and lewdness, not in strife and envy.

14 But put on the Lord Jesus Christ, and make no provision for the flesh, to *fulfill its* lusts.

14 Receive one who is weak in the faith, *but* not to disputes over doubtful things.

2 For one believes he may eat all things, but he who is weak eats *only* vegetables.

3 Let not him who eats despise him who does not eat, and let not him who does not eat judge him who eats; for God has received him.

4 Who are you to judge another's servant? To his own master he stands or falls. Indeed, he will be made to stand, for God is able to make him stand.

5 One person esteems *one* day above another; another esteems every day *alike*. Let each be fully convinced in his own mind.

6 He who observes the day, observes *it* to the Lord; and he who does not observe the day, to the Lord he does not observe *it*. He who eats, eats to the Lord, for he gives God thanks; and he who does not eat, to the Lord he does not eat, and gives God thanks.

7 For none of us lives to himself, and no one dies to himself.

8 For if we live, we live to the Lord; and if we die, we die to the

Lord. Therefore, whether we live or die, we are the Lord's.

9 For to this end Christ died and rose and lived again, that He might be Lord of both the dead and the living.

10 But why do you judge your brother? Or why do you show contempt for your brother? For we shall all stand before the judgment seat of Christ.

11 For it is written:

> "As I live, says the LORD,
> Every knee shall bow to Me,
> And every tongue shall confess
>   to God."

12 So then each of us shall give account of himself to God.

13 Therefore let us not judge one another anymore, but rather resolve this, not to put a stumbling block or a cause to fall in *our* brother's way.

14 I know and am convinced by the Lord Jesus that *there is* nothing unclean of itself; but to him who considers anything to be unclean, to him *it is* unclean.

15 Yet if your brother is grieved because of *your* food, you are no longer walking in love. Do not destroy with your food the one for whom Christ died.

16 Therefore do not let your good be spoken of as evil;

17 for the kingdom of God is not food and drink, but righteousness and peace and joy in the Holy Spirit.

18 For he who serves Christ in these things *is* acceptable to God and approved by men.

19 Therefore let us pursue the things *which make* for peace and the things by which one may edify another.

20 Do not destroy the work of God for the sake of food. All things indeed *are* pure, but *it is* evil for the man who eats with offense.

21 *It is* good neither to eat meat

STEP 4

Made a searching and fearless moral inventory of ourselves.

Romans 13:11–14

Just as Romans 13:11 calls us to awaken out of sleep, so Step 4 of our recovery process calls for a similar response. We probably have been unaware of the deepest reasons for our attitudes and actions. We were a bit like sleepwalkers moving through scenes and events, yet unconscious of how we did so. God calls us now to awaken. The night of our emotional imprisonment is ending. The day of our recovery is at hand. But we cannot cast off the "works of darkness" (v. 12) until we are completely aware of what those inventory issues are. Basically, the apostle Paul is asking us to accept reality. Instead of denying or excusing or becoming angry or fearful, we consciously choose to allow the light of God's scrutiny to fall upon us.

On the positive side, Paul tells us in verse 14 to "put on the Lord Jesus Christ." We do this by drawing on His strength, aligning our thoughts with His Word, and yielding our wills to Him.

For further reading on Step 4, turn to page 355.

Daily Encouragement

DAY 145 READING: ROMANS 13:1—14:13

A Thought for the New Day: A feeling of moral superiority to others does not achieve the highest goal we are capable of. It is very helpful, when we are tempted to feel we are better than others, to remember Paul's warning that we will all someday stand before God (14:10, 11). Despite our imperfections, God does not condemn us out of hand. He reasons with us and begs us to remember that He became a servant for us—to the death! (*Turn to page 347.*)

nor drink wine nor *do anything* by which your brother stumbles or is offended or is made weak.

STEP 5

22 Do you have faith? Have *it* to yourself before God. Happy *is* he who does not condemn himself in what he approves.

23 But he who doubts is condemned if he eats, because *he does* not *eat* from faith; for whatever *is* not from faith is sin.

15 We then who are strong ought to bear with the scruples of the weak, and not to please ourselves.

STEP 9

2 Let each of us please *his* neighbor for *his* good, leading to edification.

3 For even Christ did not please Himself; but as it is written, *"The reproaches of those who reproached You fell on Me."*

4 For whatever things were written before were written for our learning, that we through the patience and comfort of the Scriptures might have hope.

STEP 9

5 Now may the God of patience and comfort grant you to be likeminded toward one another, according to Christ Jesus,

6 that you may with one mind *and* one mouth glorify the God and Father of our Lord Jesus Christ.

7 Therefore receive one another, just as Christ also received us, to the glory of God.

8 Now I say that Jesus Christ has become a servant to the circumcision for the truth of God, to confirm the promises *made* to the fathers,

9 and that the Gentiles might glorify God for *His* mercy, as it is written:

"For this reason I will confess
    to You among the Gentiles,
And sing to Your name."

10 And again he says:

"Rejoice, O Gentiles, with His
    people!"

11 And again:

"Praise the LORD, all you
    Gentiles!
Laud Him, all you peoples!"

12 And again, Isaiah says:

"There shall be a root of Jesse;
And He who shall rise to reign
    over the Gentiles,
In Him the Gentiles shall
    hope."

13 Now may the God of hope fill you with all joy and peace in believing, that you may abound in hope by the power of the Holy Spirit.

14 Now I myself am confident concerning you, my brethren, that you also are full of goodness, filled with all knowledge, able also to admonish one another.

15 Nevertheless, brethren, I have written more boldly to you on *some* points, as reminding you, because of the grace given to me by God,

16 that I might be a minister of Jesus Christ to the Gentiles, ministering the gospel of God, that the offering of the Gentiles might be acceptable, sanctified by the Holy Spirit.

17 Therefore I have reason to glory in Christ Jesus in the things *which pertain* to God.

18 For I will not dare to speak of any of those things which Christ has not accomplished through me, in word and deed, to make the Gentiles obedient—

19 in mighty signs and wonders, by the power of the Spirit of God, so that from Jerusalem and round about to Illyricum I have fully preached the gospel of Christ.

20 And so I have made it my aim to preach the gospel, not where Christ was named, lest I should build on another man's foundation,

21 but as it is written:

*Made direct amends to such people wherever possible,
except when to do so would injure them or others.*

Romans 15:2

Steps 8 and 9 are bridges to the restoration of healthy relationships in our lives. We know that our actions for good or ill have enormous impact on those around us. Romans 15:2 calls us to be sacrificial in putting aside the selfishness of our old behaviors.

Second only in importance to our relationship with God Himself, the establishment of balanced interpersonal relationships is the highest priority for recovery. If we are not at peace with our fellows, we will not be at peace with ourselves. And if we are not at peace with ourselves, we are susceptible to being ravaged by our old dependencies and our addictions.

The establishment of good human relationships requires a delicate balance between giving and receiving, between meeting the needs of others and finding healthful ways to meet our own needs. Step 9 emphasizes the giving of amends to others as a corrective balance against the self-centeredness of our old relationship patterns.

For further reading on Step 9, turn to page 363.

Daily Encouragement

DAY 146 READING: ROMANS 14:14—15:13

A Thought for the New Day: "To the pure all things are pure," Paul later wrote (Titus 1:15). If there is any fault in the things we see around us—or what we do—it is our own. May we resolve to stop being faultfinders. Each of us can remember special people who never seemed able to think any evil. Shall we meditate on their secret, and pray to be like them? (*Turn to page 349.*)

*"To whom He was not
announced, they shall see;
And those who have not heard
shall understand."*

22 For this reason I also have been
much hindered from coming to
you.
23 But now no longer having a
place in these parts, and having a
great desire these many years to
come to you,
24 whenever I journey to Spain, I
shall come to you. For I hope to
see you on my journey, and to be
helped on my way there by you, if
first I may enjoy your *company* for
a while.
25 But now I am going to Jerusalem to minister to the saints.
26 For it pleased those from Macedonia and Achaia to make a certain contribution for the poor
among the saints who are in Jerusalem.
27 It pleased them indeed, and
they are their debtors. For if the
Gentiles have been partakers of
their spiritual things, their duty is
also to minister to them in material
things.
28 Therefore, when I have performed this and have sealed to
them this fruit, I shall go by way of
you to Spain.
29 But I know that when I come to
you, I shall come in the fullness of
the blessing of the gospel of Christ.

30 Now I beg you, brethren,
through the Lord Jesus Christ, and
through the love of the Spirit, that
you strive together with me in
your prayers to God for me,
31 that I may be delivered from
those in Judea who do not believe,
and that my service for Jerusalem
may be acceptable to the saints,
32 that I may come to you with joy
by the will of God, and may be
refreshed together with you.
33 Now the God of peace *be* with
you all. Amen.

16 I commend to you Phoebe
our sister, who is a servant of
the church in Cenchrea,
2 that you may receive her in the
Lord in a manner worthy of the
saints, and assist her in whatever
business she has need of you; for
indeed she has been a helper of
many and of myself also.
3 Greet Priscilla and Aquila, my
fellow workers in Christ Jesus,
4 who risked their own necks for
my life, to whom not only I give
thanks, but also all the churches of
the Gentiles.
5 Likewise *greet* the church that
is in their house. Greet my beloved
Epaenetus, who is the firstfruits of
Achaia to Christ.
6 Greet Mary, who labored much
for us.
7 Greet Andronicus and Junia,
my kinsmen and my fellow prisoners, who are of note among the
apostles, who also were in Christ
before me.
8 Greet Amplias, my beloved in
the Lord.
9 Greet Urbanus, our fellow
worker in Christ, and Stachys, my
beloved.
10 Greet Apelles, approved in
Christ. Greet those who are of the
household of Aristobulus.
11 Greet Herodion, my kinsman.
Greet those who are of the *household* of Narcissus who are in the
Lord.
12 Greet Tryphena and Tryphosa,
who have labored in the Lord.
Greet the beloved Persis, who labored much in the Lord.
13 Greet Rufus, chosen in the
Lord, and his mother and mine.
14 Greet Asyncritus, Phlegon, Her-
mas, Patrobas, Hermes, and the
brethren who are with them.
15 Greet Philologus and Julia, Ne-
reus and his sister, and Olympas,
and all the saints who are with
them.
16 Greet one another with a holy
kiss. The churches of Christ greet
you.

STEP
11

*Sought through prayer and meditation to improve our conscious contact with God **as we understood Him,** praying only for knowledge of His will for us and the power to carry that out.*

Romans 15:30–33

Paul knew the power that prayer held to transform both situations and people. Prayer does not aid the work of God. Prayer *is* the work of God. So when we hear someone say, "I couldn't do anything but pray," we realize that person does not know much about the activity he or she is engaging in. The greatest heroes of the faith have considered prayer to be the most important aspect of their lives. The Protestant Reformation leader Martin Luther commented that since he had so much business to accomplish, he could not "get on without spending three hours daily in prayer."

Looking at the prayer lives of such great men we may feel inadequate to the point of despair. But God, the great and loving Father, does not demand. Instead He meets us where we are with grace and love and the encouragement to move on to greater victories in prayer.

For further reading on Step 11, turn to page 365.

Daily Encouragement

DAY 147 READING: ROMANS 15:14—16:16

A Thought for the New Day: Paul was quick to praise, not only His Lord, but those with whom he served. He seems to have been a generous man who enjoyed building up others. We are thankful, after all these centuries, for the life of Phoebe, who counted it a privilege to serve, and Paul was not willing to let her go unnoticed. Let us learn from his example and look for opportunities to praise. (*Turn to page 351.*)

17 Now I urge you, brethren, note those who cause divisions and offenses, contrary to the doctrine which you learned, and avoid them.

18 For those who are such do not serve our Lord Jesus Christ, but their own belly, and by smooth words and flattering speech deceive the hearts of the simple.

STEP 10

19 For your obedience has become known to all. Therefore I am glad on your behalf; but I want you to be wise in what is good, and simple concerning evil.

20 And the God of peace will crush Satan under your feet shortly. The grace of our Lord Jesus Christ *be* with you. Amen.

21 Timothy, my fellow worker, and Lucius, Jason, and Sosipater, my kinsmen, greet you.

22 I, Tertius, who wrote *this* epistle, greet you in the Lord.

23 Gaius, my host and *the host* of the whole church, greets you. Erastus, the treasurer of the city, greets you, and Quartus, a brother.

24 The grace of our Lord Jesus Christ *be* with you all. Amen.

25 Now to Him who is able to establish you according to my gospel and the preaching of Jesus Christ, according to the revelation of the mystery *which was* kept secret since the world began

26 but now has been made manifest, and by the prophetic Scriptures has been made known to all nations, according to the commandment of the everlasting God, for obedience to the faith—

27 to God, alone wise, *be* glory through Jesus Christ forever. Amen.

THE FIRST EPISTLE OF PAUL THE APOSTLE TO THE
CORINTHIANS

PAUL, called *to be* an apostle of Jesus Christ through the will of God, and Sosthenes *our* brother,

2 To the church of God which is at Corinth, to those who are sanctified in Christ Jesus, called *to be* saints, with all who in every place call on the name of Jesus Christ our Lord, both theirs and ours:

3 Grace to you and peace from God our Father and the Lord Jesus Christ.

4 I thank my God always concerning you for the grace of God which was given to you by Christ Jesus,

5 that you were enriched in everything by Him in all utterance and all knowledge,

6 even as the testimony of Christ was confirmed in you,

7 so that you come short in no gift, eagerly waiting for the revelation of our Lord Jesus Christ,

8 who will also confirm you to the end, *that you may be* blameless in the day of our Lord Jesus Christ.

9 God *is* faithful, by whom you were called into the fellowship of His Son, Jesus Christ our Lord.

10 Now I plead with you, brethren, by the name of our Lord Jesus Christ, that you all speak the same thing, and *that* there be no divisions among you, but *that* you be perfectly joined together in the same mind and in the same judgment.

11 For it has been declared to me concerning you, my brethren, by those of Chloe's *household*, that there are contentions among you.

STEP 10

*Continued to take personal inventory
and when we were wrong promptly admitted it.*

Romans 16:19, 20

By the time we reach Step 10 of the recovery program, people around us will have begun to notice our obedience to God's Word. Many will rejoice over this growth and change in our lives, but a few will try in subtle or obvious ways to cause us to stumble. Paul knew the Roman believers faced similar situations, and his exhortation for them was twofold.

First, he reminded them "to be wise in what is good." Wisdom always involves caution, foresight, and prudence; the word "good" means "integrity of a moral nature." Taking time to allow the Holy Spirit to clear and direct our minds brings actions and attitudes that honor God and keep us at peace.

Second, we are to be "simple concerning evil." "Simple" here means "unmixed or unweakened." This is why we routinely take inventory of our lives. In the same way that a cold can turn into pneumonia if it goes unchecked, seemingly insignificant sins can weaken our spiritual lives. Honest appraisal and decisive correction when our lives need it will pay great dividends for us in every way.

For further reading on Step 10, turn to page 359.

Daily Encouragement

DAY 148 READING: ROMANS 16:17–27

A Thought for the New Day: Sometimes the world seems to shake around us, and we think we may not make it to the end of the day. In those times, we can be encouraged by Paul's words: "Him who is able to establish you" (v. 25). Such reminders of God's sovereign control over our circumstances merit our careful meditation. We all live and move and have our being in the One whose very glance turns the tide of nations. (*Turn to page 353.*)

12 Now I say this, that each of you says, "I am of Paul," or "I am of Apollos," or "I am of Cephas," or "I am of Christ."

13 Is Christ divided? Was Paul crucified for you? Or were you baptized in the name of Paul?

14 I thank God that I baptized none of you except Crispus and Gaius,

15 lest anyone should say that I had baptized in my own name.

16 Yes, I also baptized the household of Stephanas. Besides, I do not know whether I baptized any other.

17 For Christ did not send me to baptize, but to preach the gospel, not with wisdom of words, lest the cross of Christ should be made of no effect.

 18 For the message of the cross is foolishness to those who are perishing, but to us who are being saved it is the power of God.

19 For it is written:

> "I will destroy the wisdom of the wise,
> And bring to nothing the understanding of the prudent."

20 Where *is* the wise? Where *is* the scribe? Where *is* the disputer of this age? Has not God made foolish the wisdom of this world?

21 For since, in the wisdom of God, the world through wisdom did not know God, it pleased God through the foolishness of the message preached to save those who believe.

22 For Jews request a sign, and Greeks seek after wisdom;

23 but we preach Christ crucified, to the Jews a stumbling block and to the Greeks foolishness,

24 but to those who are called, both Jews and Greeks, Christ the power of God and the wisdom of God.

25 Because the foolishness of God is wiser than men, and the weakness of God is stronger than men.

26 For you see your calling, brethren, that not many wise according to the flesh, not many mighty, not many noble, *are called.*

27 But God has chosen the foolish things of the world to put to shame the wise, and God has chosen the weak things of the world to put to shame the things which are mighty;

28 and the base things of the world and the things which are despised God has chosen, and the things which are not, to bring to nothing the things that are,

29 that no flesh should glory in His presence.

30 But of Him you are in Christ Jesus, who became for us wisdom from God—and righteousness and sanctification and redemption—

31 that, as it is written, *"He who glories, let him glory in the LORD."*

2 And I, brethren, when I came to you, did not come with excellence of speech or of wisdom declaring to you the testimony of God.

2 For I determined not to know anything among you except Jesus Christ and Him crucified.

3 I was with you in weakness, in fear, and in much trembling.

4 And my speech and my preaching *were* not with persuasive words of human wisdom, but in demonstration of the Spirit and of power,

5 that your faith should not be in the wisdom of men but in the power of God.

6 However, we speak wisdom among those who are mature, yet not the wisdom of this age, nor of the rulers of this age, who are coming to nothing.

7 But we speak the wisdom of God in a mystery, the hidden *wisdom* which God ordained before the ages for our glory,

8 which none of the rulers of this

STEP 2

*Came to believe that a Power greater than ourselves
could restore us to sanity.*

1 Corinthians 1:18–25

In the days past, when we still believed in the power of our addictions or reason or self, we may have scoffed at the idea that the true God would die on a cross for us. But those days are gone and our eyes and hearts have been opened to experience the real power of the almighty God. Why did God ordain that salvation would come to people by their believing that He Himself would choose to suffer on a Roman cross, die, and be resurrected from the grave? Why does salvation not come instead through reason or works? The wisdom of God saw the great weakness and problems both these alternatives would create. If the Cross is foolish, it is still a far wiser means than any human being ever devised to attain salvation. If the Cross reveals weakness, it is still imbued with more power than any who has ever lived could muster. Almighty God can satisfy the void in our hearts and fill our lives with His power.

For further reading on Step 2, turn to page 381.

Daily Encouragement

DAY 149 READING: 1 CORINTHIANS 1:1–31

A Thought for the New Day: Evidently our notion of wisdom is not God's notion (vv. 26–31). The common mark of wisdom is the worldly savvy that enables one person to beat another in a deal. James, another Christian leader, wrote, "The wisdom that is from above is pure, then peaceable, gentle, willing to yield" (James 3:17). Winning the hard way can be losing, but those who lose themselves in a good cause are wise and receive rewards the world never sees. (*Turn to page 355.*)

age knew; for had they known, they would not have crucified the Lord of glory.

9 But as it is written:

> "Eye has not seen, nor ear heard,
> Nor have entered into the heart of man
> The things which God has prepared for those who love Him."

10 But God has revealed *them* to us through His Spirit. For the Spirit searches all things, yes, the deep things of God.

11 For what man knows the things of a man except the spirit of the man which is in him? Even so no one knows the things of God except the Spirit of God.

12 Now we have received, not the spirit of the world, but the Spirit who is from God, that we might know the things that have been freely given to us by God.

13 These things we also speak, not in words which man's wisdom teaches but which the Holy Spirit teaches, comparing spiritual things with spiritual.

14 But the natural man does not receive the things of the Spirit of God, for they are foolishness to him; nor can he know *them*, because they are spiritually discerned.

15 But he who is spiritual judges all things, yet he himself is *rightly* judged by no one.

16 For "Who has known the mind of the LORD that he may instruct Him?" But we have the mind of Christ.

STEP 4 **3** And I, brethren, could not speak to you as to spiritual *people* but as to carnal, as to babes in Christ.

2 I fed you with milk and not with solid food; for until now you were not able *to receive it*, and even now you are still not able;

3 for you are still carnal. For where *there are* envy, strife, and divisions among you, are you not carnal and behaving like *mere* men?

4 For when one says, "I am of Paul," and another, "I *am* of Apollos," are you not carnal?

5 Who then is Paul, and who *is* Apollos, but ministers through whom you believed, as the Lord gave to each one?

6 I planted, Apollos watered, but God gave the increase.

7 So then neither he who plants is anything, nor he who waters, but God who gives the increase.

8 Now he who plants and he who waters are one, and each one will receive his own reward according to his own labor.

9 For we are God's fellow workers; you are God's field, *you are* God's building.

10 According to the grace of God which was given to me, as a wise master builder I have laid the foundation, and another builds on it. But let each one take heed how he builds on it.

11 For no other foundation can anyone lay than that which is laid, which is Jesus Christ. STEP 10

12 Now if anyone builds on this foundation *with* gold, silver, precious stones, wood, hay, straw,

13 each one's work will become manifest; for the Day will declare it, because it will be revealed by fire; and the fire will test each one's work, of what sort it is.

14 If anyone's work which he has built on *it* endures, he will receive a reward.

15 If anyone's work is burned, he will suffer loss; but he himself will be saved, yet so as through fire.

16 Do you not know that you are the temple of God and *that* the Spirit of God dwells in you?

17 If anyone defiles the temple of God, God will destroy him. For the temple of God is holy, which *temple* you are.

18 Let no one deceive himself. If

Made a searching and fearless moral inventory of ourselves.

1 Corinthians 3:1–3

Many of us, when we reach Step 4, are baby Christians, having only recently trusted Jesus to be our Savior and Protector. But some of us have been believers in Jesus a lot longer. We may even hold positions in the church. Yet, for some reason we have not been able to grow effectively. There is an area of our lives that Scripture and prayer cannot seem to penetrate. Step 4 goes to the root of that problem. By honestly and carefully evaluating our lives and childhoods, we may begin to uncover the reasons that deeper growth and greater victory have not occurred.

For those of us who have only been saved a short time, the focus of our inventory may be a little different, but the results will hopefully be the same. We want to be more than justified before God by faith in Jesus. We want now to begin to be transformed into strong, mature believers who can be nourished by the solid food of God's Word.

For further reading on Step 4, turn to page 357.

Daily Encouragement

DAY 150 READING: 1 CORINTHIANS 2:1—3:17

A Thought for the New Day: Striving to build things that last forever is a tall order (3:14). Not only the man-made monuments, but even the mountains, will pass away. So what does last forever? A family patiently and graciously raised in the love of God. A life that inspires all around and lights the way for fellow travelers. Such will endure, although everything else dissolves. *Lord, let us work together with You in building for eternity.* *(Turn to page 357.)*

anyone among you seems to be wise in this age, let him become a fool that he may become wise.

19 For the wisdom of this world is foolishness with God. For it is written, *"He catches the wise in their own craftiness";*

20 and again, *"The* LORD *knows the thoughts of the wise, that they are futile."*

21 Therefore let no one glory in men. For all things are yours:

22 whether Paul or Apollos or Cephas, or the world or life or death, or things present or things to come—all are yours.

23 And you *are* Christ's, and Christ *is* God's.

4 Let a man so consider us, as servants of Christ and stewards of the mysteries of God.

2 Moreover it is required in stewards that one be found faithful.

3 But with me it is a very small thing that I should be judged by you or by a human court. In fact, I do not even judge myself.

4 For I know nothing against myself, yet I am not justified by this; but He who judges me is the Lord.

5 Therefore judge nothing before the time, until the Lord comes, who will both bring to light the hidden things of darkness and reveal the counsels of the hearts; and then each one's praise will come from God.

6 Now these things, brethren, I have figuratively transferred to myself and Apollos for your sakes, that you may learn in us not to think beyond what is written, that none of you may be puffed up on behalf of one against the other.

7 For who makes you differ *from another?* And what do you have that you did not receive? Now if you did indeed receive *it,* why do you glory as if you had not received *it?*

8 You are already full! You are already rich! You have reigned as kings without us—and indeed I could wish you did reign, that we also might reign with you!

9 For I think that God has displayed us, the apostles, last, as men condemned to death; for we have been made a spectacle to the world, both to angels and to men.

10 We *are* fools for Christ's sake, but you *are* wise in Christ! We *are* weak, but you *are* strong! You *are* distinguished, but we *are* dishonored!

11 *Even* to the present hour we both hunger and thirst, and we are poorly clothed, and beaten, and homeless.

12 And we labor, working with our own hands. Being reviled, we bless; being persecuted, we endure *it;*

13 being defamed, we entreat. We have been made as the filth of the world, the offscouring of all things until now.

14 I do not write these things to shame you, but as my beloved children I warn *you.*

15 For though you might have ten thousand instructors in Christ, yet *you do* not *have* many fathers; for in Christ Jesus I have begotten you through the gospel.

16 Therefore I urge you, imitate me.

17 For this reason I have sent Timothy to you, who is my beloved and faithful son in the Lord, who will remind you of my ways in Christ, as I teach everywhere in every church.

18 Now some are puffed up, as though I were not coming to you.

19 But I will come to you shortly, if the Lord wills, and I will know, not the word of those who are puffed up, but the power.

20 For the kingdom of God *is* not in word but in power.

21 What do you want? Shall I come to you with a rod, or in love and a spirit of gentleness?

5 It is actually reported *that there is* sexual immorality among you, and such sexual im-

Made a searching and fearless moral inventory of ourselves.

1 Corinthians 4:19, 20

Denial acts to prevent our completion of a thorough fourth step inventory. Our hearts may know profound areas of pain that need to be acknowledged and grieved for. However, our "puffed up" words will tend to minimize and discount the gravity of both the wrongs we have committed against others and the wrongs we have suffered at the hands of others.

How do we deceive ourselves with "puffed up" words? The adult child of workaholism may minimize the pain of an absentee parent. The abuser of prescription drugs may discount the growing addiction, because "the doctor ordered it." The relationship addict or sex addict may rationalize countless violations of the boundaries of others by saying these things are done in the name of love.

A.A. literature warns that recovery is within the reach of all except those "who are constitutionally incapable of being honest with themselves" (*Alcoholics Anonymous*, p. 58). The kingdom of God is attainable to those who will utilize the power of confession.

For further reading on Step 4, turn to page 361.

Daily Encouragement

DAY 151 READING: 1 CORINTHIANS 3:18—4:21

A Thought for the New Day: Thankfulness is not hard for us when we realize that all we possess, in the way of natural or spiritual endowments, is not of our own doing (4:7). We have received these things as gifts from God so that, with them, we may serve others. Therefore, even pride in our attainments is inappropriate. (*Turn to page 359.*)

morality as is not even named among the Gentiles—that a man has his father's wife!

2 And you are puffed up, and have not rather mourned, that he who has done this deed might be taken away from among you.

3 For I indeed, as absent in body but present in spirit, have already judged, as though I were present, *concerning* him who has so done this deed.

4 In the name of our Lord Jesus Christ, when you are gathered together, along with my spirit, with the power of our Lord Jesus Christ,

5 deliver such a one to Satan for the destruction of the flesh, that his spirit may be saved in the day of the Lord Jesus.

6 Your glorying *is* not good. Do you not know that a little leaven leavens the whole lump?

7 Therefore purge out the old leaven, that you may be a new lump, since you truly are unleavened. For indeed Christ, our Passover, was sacrificed for us.

8 Therefore let us keep the feast, not with old leaven, nor with the leaven of malice and wickedness, but with the unleavened *bread* of sincerity and truth.

9 I wrote to you in my epistle not to keep company with sexually immoral people.

10 Yet *I* certainly *did* not *mean* with the sexually immoral people of this world, or with the covetous, or extortioners, or idolaters, since then you would need to go out of the world.

11 But now I have written to you not to keep company with anyone named a brother, who is a fornicator, or covetous, or an idolater, or a reviler, or a drunkard, or an extortioner—not even to eat with such a person.

12 For what *have* I *to do* with judging those also who are outside? Do you not judge those who are inside?

13 But those who are outside God judges. Therefore *"put away from yourselves that wicked person."*

6 Dare any of you, having a matter against another, go to law before the unrighteous, and not before the saints?

2 Do you not know that the saints will judge the world? And if the world will be judged by you, are you unworthy to judge the smallest matters?

3 Do you not know that we shall judge angels? How much more, things that pertain to this life?

4 If then you have judgments concerning things pertaining to this life, do you appoint those who are least esteemed by the church to judge?

5 I say this to your shame. Is it so, that there is not a wise man among you, not even one, who will be able to judge between his brethren?

6 But brother goes to law against brother, and that before unbelievers!

7 Now therefore, it is already an utter failure for you that you go to law against one another. Why do you not rather accept wrong? Why do you not rather *let yourselves* be defrauded?

8 No, you yourselves do wrong and defraud, and *you do* these things *to your* brethren!

9 Do you not know that the unrighteous will not inherit the kingdom of God? Do not be deceived. Neither fornicators, nor idolaters, nor adulterers, nor homosexuals, nor sodomites,

10 nor thieves, nor covetous, nor drunkards, nor revilers, nor extortioners will inherit the kingdom of God.

11 And such were some of you. But you were washed, but you were sanctified, but you were justified in the name of the Lord Jesus and by the Spirit of our God.

12 All things are lawful for me, but all things are not helpful. All things are lawful for me, but I will

STEP 10

STEP 10

*Continued to take personal inventory
and when we were wrong promptly admitted it.*

1 Corinthians 6:12

There is a wonderful freedom in Jesus Christ. There is freedom from shame, freedom from legalism, and freedom from slavery to sin. But all these freedoms in Jesus depend on a constant, close fellowship with Him. Sometimes we may wonder if a particular activity is acceptable for us to participate in. If in our hearts we are truly seeking to honor and glorify our Lord, the Holy Spirit will enlighten us as to whether what we are considering would be "helpful," as Paul puts it. And if we are in constant fellowship with our Lord through genuine prayer and study of His Word, we will have the strength and wisdom to keep away from those things that could begin to have power over us. We will remain free to serve Jesus and rejoice in the good life He has given us.

For further reading on Step 10, turn to page 369.

Daily Encouragement

DAY 152 READING: 1 CORINTHIANS 5:1—6:20

A Thought for the New Day: Paul realized that all created things are "good." Fully aware of this fact, he went on to say that not everything has equal value for everyone (6:12). Collecting scrap iron may be useful for some people, but for others it would be a waste of energy. We need to decide—even make a list—of what is truly important for us right now, and live in a way that has greatest benefit for those around us. (*Turn to page 361.*)

not be brought under the power of any.

13 Foods for the stomach and the stomach for foods, but God will destroy both it and them. Now the body *is* not for sexual immorality but for the Lord, and the Lord for the body.

14 And God both raised up the Lord and will also raise us up by His power.

15 Do you not know that your bodies are members of Christ? Shall I then take the members of Christ and make *them* members of a harlot? Certainly not!

16 Or do you not know that he who is joined to a harlot is one body *with her*? For *"The two,"* He says, *"shall become one flesh."*

17 But he who is joined to the Lord is one spirit *with Him*.

18 Flee sexual immorality. Every sin that a man does is outside the body, but he who commits sexual immorality sins against his own body.

19 Or do you not know that your body is the temple of the Holy Spirit *who is* in you, whom you have from God, and you are not your own?

20 For you were bought at a price; therefore glorify God in your body and in your spirit, which are God's.

7 Now concerning the things of which you wrote to me: *It is* good for a man not to touch a woman.

2 Nevertheless, because of sexual immorality, let each man have his own wife, and let each woman have her own husband.

3 Let the husband render to his wife the affection due her, and likewise also the wife to her husband.

4 The wife does not have authority over her own body, but the husband *does*. And likewise the husband does not have authority over his own body, but the wife *does*.

5 Do not deprive one another ex-

cept with consent for a time, that you may give yourselves to fasting and prayer; and come together again so that Satan does not tempt you because of your lack of self-control.

6 But I say this as a concession, not as a commandment.

7 For I wish that all men were even as I myself. But each one has his own gift from God, one in this manner and another in that.

8 But I say to the unmarried and to the widows: It is good for them if they remain even as I am;

9 but if they cannot exercise self-control, let them marry. For it is better to marry than to burn *with passion*.

10 Now to the married I command, *yet* not I but the Lord: A wife is not to depart from *her* husband.

11 But even if she does depart, let her remain unmarried or be reconciled to *her* husband. And a husband is not to divorce *his* wife.

12 But to the rest I, not the Lord, say: If any brother has a wife who does not believe, and she is willing to live with him, let him not divorce her.

13 And a woman who has a husband who does not believe, if he is willing to live with her, let her not divorce him.

14 For the unbelieving husband is sanctified by the wife, and the unbelieving wife is sanctified by the husband; otherwise your children would be unclean, but now they are holy.

15 But if the unbeliever departs, let him depart; a brother or a sister is not under bondage in such *cases*. But God has called us to peace.

16 For how do you know, O wife, whether you will save *your* husband? Or how do you know, O husband, whether you will save *your* wife?

17 But as God has distributed to each one, as the Lord has called each one, so let him walk. And so I ordain in all the churches.

STEP
4

STEP 4

Made a searching and fearless moral inventory of ourselves.

1 Corinthians 7:3–16

No institution of life is under more pressure today than the institution of marriage. The "I have my rights" generation has spawned prenuptial agreements, easy divorce, and acceptance of couples living together outside marriage. Western society becomes highly offended or even dumbfounded when it is suggested that we give up our rights for the good of our children, our spouse, or the kingdom of God. Yet this passage in 1 Corinthians definitely teaches that this is God's way.

For those of us who have already been divorced, we must realize that God offers us healing, forgiveness, and usefulness in His Kingdom. But Step 4 is a careful, honest evaluation of what has gone wrong with our past. Some of us may require the courage to admit that we worshiped the god of self and allowed it to destroy a sacrament ordained by God. Though we can never erase the scars of divorce, we can with God's help discover the roots of our problems and be assured of brighter tomorrows.

For further reading on Step 4, turn to page 401.

Daily Encouragement

DAY 153 READING: 1 CORINTHIANS 7:1–24

A Thought for the New Day: Jumping impetuously from one career to another throws you for a loss because you will always find yourself at the bottom of the ladder. God's idea for us is to cultivate the gifts He gives us in the place of our greatest potential (v. 24). We may experience trials as we learn and develop in the fields to which we are called. However, traveling this road leads to a sense of fulfillment. (*Turn to page 363.*)

18 Was anyone called while circumcised? Let him not become uncircumcised. Was anyone called while uncircumcised? Let him not be circumcised.

19 Circumcision is nothing and uncircumcision is nothing, but keeping the commandments of God *is what matters.*

20 Let each one remain in the same calling in which he was called.

21 Were you called *while* a slave? Do not be concerned about it; but if you can be made free, rather use *it.*

22 For he who is called in the Lord *while* a slave is the Lord's freedman. Likewise he who is called *while* free is Christ's slave.

23 You were bought at a price; do not become slaves of men.

24 Brethren, let each one remain with God in that *calling* in which he was called.

25 Now concerning virgins: I have no commandment from the Lord; yet I give judgment as one whom the Lord in His mercy *has made* trustworthy.

26 I suppose therefore that this is good because of the present distress—that *it is* good for a man to remain as he is:

27 Are you bound to a wife? Do not seek to be loosed. Are you loosed from a wife? Do not seek a wife.

28 But even if you do marry, you have not sinned; and if a virgin marries, she has not sinned. Nevertheless such will have trouble in the flesh, but I would spare you.

29 But this I say, brethren, the time *is* short, so that from now on even those who have wives should be as though they had none,

30 those who weep as though they did not weep, those who rejoice as though they did not rejoice, those who buy as though they did not possess,

31 and those who use this world as not misusing *it.* For the form of this world is passing away.

32 But I want you to be without care. He who is unmarried cares for the things *that belong* to the Lord—how he may please the Lord.

33 But he who is married cares about the things of the world—how he may please *his* wife.

34 There is a difference between a wife and a virgin. The unmarried woman cares about the things of the Lord, that she may be holy both in body and in spirit. But she who is married cares about the things of the world—how she may please *her* husband.

35 And this I say for your own profit, not that I may put a leash on you, but for what is proper, and that you may serve the Lord without distraction.

36 But if any man thinks he is behaving improperly toward his virgin, if she is past the flower of *her* youth, and thus it must be, let him do what he wishes; he does not sin; let them marry.

37 Nevertheless he who stands steadfast in his heart, having no necessity, but has power over his own will, and has so determined in his heart that he will keep his virgin, does well.

38 So then he who gives *her* in marriage does well, but he who does not give *her* in marriage does better.

39 A wife is bound by law as long as her husband lives; but if her husband dies, she is at liberty to be married to whom she wishes, only in the Lord.

40 But she is happier if she remains as she is, according to my judgment—and I think I also have the Spirit of God.

8 Now concerning things offered to idols: We know that we all have knowledge. Knowledge puffs up, but love edifies.

2 And if anyone thinks that he

STEP
9

STEP 9

*Made direct amends to such people wherever possible,
except when to do so would injure them or others.*

1 Corinthians 8:1–3

We can never know another person completely. We can see character traits, actions, abilities, and weakness, but we cannot see the inner motivation and spirit of a person. God alone sees and understands the deep part of each mind and heart.

When we make blanket judgments about anyone, we simply reveal how little we actually know. We do have the right to declare certain actions as right or wrong, appropriate or inappropriate. But we must admit our limitations beyond this point. Our knowledge can point out problems, but solutions require love. Love edifies. God reached out over the gulf of our sin and confusion and bridged that chasm with the love and forgiveness of the Cross. We now have that same opportunity. We can reach across a gulf of hurt and build the bridge of love in the name of Jesus.

For further reading on Step 9, turn to page 425.

Daily Encouragement

DAY 154 READING: 1 CORINTHIANS 7:25—8:13

A Thought for the New Day: What is harmless to you may be dangerous for someone else (8:13). It is probably safe for you to drive a car if you have been trained to do it, but driving is suicide for the inexperienced person. We need to be interested in the well-being of those around us, to the extent that we do not mislead them by our example, even in our enjoyment of good things. (*Turn to page 365.*)

knows anything, he knows nothing yet as he ought to know.

3 But if anyone loves God, this one is known by Him.

4 Therefore concerning the eating of things offered to idols, we know that an idol *is* nothing in the world, and that *there is* no other God but one.

5 For even if there are so-called gods, whether in heaven or on earth (as there are many gods and many lords),

6 yet for us *there is only* one God, the Father, of whom *are* all things, and we for Him; and one Lord Jesus Christ, through whom *are* all things, and through whom we *live.*

7 However, *there is* not in everyone that knowledge; for some, with consciousness of the idol, until now eat *it* as a thing offered to an idol; and their conscience, being weak, is defiled.

8 But food does not commend us to God; for neither if we eat are we the better, nor if we do not eat are we the worse.

9 But beware lest somehow this liberty of yours become a stumbling block to those who are weak.

10 For if anyone sees you who have knowledge eating in an idol's temple, will not the conscience of him who is weak be emboldened to eat those things offered to idols?

11 And because of your knowledge shall the weak brother perish, for whom Christ died?

12 But when you thus sin against the brethren, and wound their weak conscience, you sin against Christ.

13 Therefore, if food makes my brother stumble, I will never again eat meat, lest I make my brother stumble.

9 Am I not an apostle? Am I not free? Have I not seen Jesus Christ our Lord? Are you not my work in the Lord?

2 If I am not an apostle to others, yet doubtless I am to you. For you are the seal of my apostleship in the Lord.

3 My defense to those who examine me is this:

4 Do we have no right to eat and drink?

5 Do we have no right to take along a believing wife, as *do* also the other apostles, the brothers of the Lord, and Cephas?

6 Or *is it* only Barnabas and I *who* have no right to refrain from working?

7 Who ever goes to war at his own expense? Who plants a vineyard and does not eat of its fruit? Or who tends a flock and does not drink of the milk of the flock?

8 Do I say these things as a *mere* man? Or does not the law say the same also?

9 For it is written in the law of Moses, *"You shall not muzzle an ox while it treads out the grain."* Is it oxen God is concerned about?

10 Or does He say *it* altogether for our sakes? For our sakes, no doubt, *this* is written, that he who plows should plow in hope, and he who threshes in hope should be partaker of his hope.

11 If we have sown spiritual things for you, *is it* a great thing if we reap your material things?

12 If others are partakers of *this* right over you, *are* we not even more? Nevertheless we have not used this right, but endure all things lest we hinder the gospel of Christ.

STEP 11

13 Do you not know that those who minister the holy things eat *of the things* of the temple, and those who serve at the altar partake of *the offerings of* the altar?

14 Even so the Lord has commanded that those who preach the gospel should live from the gospel.

15 But I have used none of these things, nor have I written these things that it should be done so to me; for it *would be* better for me to die than that anyone should make my boasting void.

STEP 11

*Sought through prayer and meditation to improve our conscious contact with God **as we understood Him,** praying only for knowledge of His will for us and the power to carry that out.*

1 Corinthians 9:12

It is amazing what some people willingly choose to endure. For a well-conditioned body there are those who will endure hours of weight lifting and strenuous exercise. For a beautiful face and perfect curves, others gladly endure the pains of surgery. The goals of all this time and pain (not to mention money) are generally self-seeking and transitory.

Paul was willing to endure much, as well. But the goal of his endurance was building the kingdom of God and seeking souls saved for eternity. For the gospel of Christ he endured "all things." Paul's remarkable energy and motivation had found a worthy devotion.

To what do we devote ourselves? What consumes our thoughts and fills our extra hours? What are our financial priorities and commitments? What have we chosen to endure for Christ and His kingdom?

For further reading on Step 11, turn to page 399.

Daily Encouragement

DAY 155 READING: 1 CORINTHIANS 9:1–18

A Thought for the New Day: Paul had not charged anyone for listening to his preaching of the gospel (v. 18). However, he reminded the Corinthians that he did have physical needs. We handle, not only heavenly and spiritual values, but also material goods that come to us from God's generous hand. He wants us to share what we have with those in need—and especially if they are in His service. *(Turn to page 367.)*

16 For if I preach the gospel, I have nothing to boast of, for necessity is laid upon me; yes, woe is me if I do not preach the gospel!
17 For if I do this willingly, I have a reward; but if against my will, I have been entrusted with a stewardship.
18 What is my reward then? That when I preach the gospel, I may present the gospel of Christ without charge, that I may not abuse my authority in the gospel.
19 For though I am free from all *men*, I have made myself a servant to all, that I might win the more;
20 and to the Jews I became as a Jew, that I might win Jews; to those *who are* under the law, as under the law, that I might win those *who are* under the law;
21 to those *who are* without law, as without law (not being without law toward God, but under law toward Christ), that I might win those *who are* without law;

STEP 12
22 to the weak I became as weak, that I might win the weak. I have become all things to all *men*, that I might by all means save some.
23 Now this I do for the gospel's sake, that I may be partaker of it with *you*.
24 Do you not know that those who run in a race all run, but one receives the prize? Run in such a way that you may obtain *it*.
25 And everyone who competes *for the prize* is temperate in all things. Now they *do it* to obtain a perishable crown, but we *for* an imperishable *crown*.
26 Therefore I run thus: not with uncertainty. Thus I fight: not as one *who* beats the air.
27 But I discipline my body and bring *it* into subjection, lest, when I have preached to others, I myself should become disqualified.

10 Moreover, brethren, I do not want you to be unaware that all our fathers were under the cloud, all passed through the sea,

2 all were baptized into Moses in the cloud and in the sea,
3 all ate the same spiritual food,
4 and all drank the same spiritual drink. For they drank of that spiritual Rock that followed them, and that Rock was Christ.
5 But with most of them God was not well pleased, for *their bodies* were scattered in the wilderness.
6 Now these things became our examples, to the intent that we should not lust after evil things as they also lusted. STEP 10
7 And do not become idolaters as *were* some of them. As it is written, *"The people sat down to eat and drink, and rose up to play."*
8 Nor let us commit sexual immorality, as some of them did, and in one day twenty-three thousand fell;
9 nor let us tempt Christ, as some of them also tempted, and were destroyed by serpents;
10 nor murmur, as some of them also murmured, and were destroyed by the destroyer.
11 Now all these things happened to them as examples, and they were written for our admonition, on whom the ends of the ages have come.
12 Therefore let him who thinks he stands take heed lest he fall.
13 No temptation has overtaken you except such as is common to man; but God *is* faithful, who will not allow you to be tempted beyond what you are able, but with the temptation will also make the way of escape, that you may be able to bear *it*.
14 Therefore, my beloved, flee from idolatry.
15 I speak as to wise men; judge for yourselves what I say.
16 The cup of blessing which we bless, is it not the communion of the blood of Christ? The bread which we break, is it not the communion of the body of Christ?
17 For we, *being* many, are one

*Having had a spiritual awakening as the result
of these steps, we tried to carry this message to others,
and to practice these principles in all our affairs.*

1 Corinthians 9:22–27

One of the seeming paradoxes of Christianity is that believers
are free people who are servants. Since we have been freed from sin
and self-preoccupation, this very freedom has allowed us to become
the servants of Christ. Because we belong to God, we are free from
other people's control and power over our lives. Now we can freely
choose to do whatever it takes to share the message of God's love
and regeneration with them. This is the apostle Paul's mind-set in
verses 22 and 23. As we continually commit ourselves to recovery
and spiritual growth, we will be asking God to keep us ever alert for
ways in which to share our experiences with others.

The last part of this passage can be summed up in one word—
"vigilance." The need for spiritual self-discipline never ceases. This
is why Step 12 urges us to "practice these principles in all our
affairs." Doing this will minimize our slips and hold us close to the
presence of God, covered with the peace and serenity of His grace.

For further reading on Step 12, turn to page 377.

Daily Encouragement

DAY 156 READING: 1 CORINTHIANS 9:19—10:13

A Thought for the New Day: Paul was not content to sit in an
ivory tower and watch the world go by. He truly walked along
the road as a friend to those around him. In his own words, he
became "all things to all *men*" (9:22). *Lord, teach me the divine art
of having "the common touch" that makes people feel at home, so that
I may show them Your lovingkindness.* (Turn to page 369.)

bread *and* one body; for we all partake of that one bread.

18 Observe Israel after the flesh: Are not those who eat of the sacrifices partakers of the altar?

19 What am I saying then? That an idol is anything, or what is offered to idols is anything?

20 But *I* say that the things which the Gentiles sacrifice they sacrifice to demons and not to God, and I do not want you to have fellowship with demons.

21 You cannot drink the cup of the Lord and the cup of demons; you cannot partake of the Lord's table and of the table of demons.

22 Or do we provoke the Lord to jealousy? Are we stronger than He?

STEP 10   23 All things are lawful for me, but all things are not helpful; all things are lawful for me, but all things do not edify.

24 Let no one seek his own, but each one the other's *well-being*.

25 Eat whatever is sold in the meat market, asking no questions for conscience' sake;

26 for *"The earth is the LORD's, and all its fullness."*

27 If any of those who do not believe invites you *to dinner*, and you desire to go, eat whatever is set before you, asking no question for conscience' sake.

28 But if anyone says to you, "This was offered to idols," do not eat it for the sake of the one who told you, and for conscience' sake; for *"The earth is the LORD's, and all its fullness."*

29 Conscience, I say, not your own, but that of the other. For why is my liberty judged by another *man's* conscience?

30 But if I partake with thanks, why am I evil spoken of for *the food* over which I give thanks?

STEP 11   31 Therefore, whether you eat or drink, or whatever you do, do all to the glory of God.

32 Give no offense, either to the Jews or to the Greeks or to the church of God,

33 just as I also please all *men* in all *things*, not seeking my own profit, but the *profit* of many, that they may be saved.

11 Imitate me, just as I also *imitate* Christ.

2 Now I praise you, brethren, that you remember me in all things and keep the traditions as I delivered *them* to you.

3 But I want you to know that the head of every man is Christ, the head of woman *is* man, and the head of Christ *is* God.

4 Every man praying or prophesying, having *his* head covered, dishonors his head.

5 But every woman who prays or prophesies with *her* head uncovered dishonors her head, for that is one and the same as if her head were shaved.

6 For if a woman is not covered, let her also be shorn. But if it is shameful for a woman to be shorn or shaved, let her be covered.

7 For a man indeed ought not to cover *his* head, since he is the image and glory of God; but woman is the glory of man.

8 For man is not from woman, but woman from man.

9 Nor was man created for the woman, but woman for the man.

10 For this reason the woman ought to have *a symbol of* authority on *her* head, because of the angels.

11 Nevertheless, neither *is* man independent of woman, nor woman independent of man, in the Lord.

12 For as the woman *was* from the man, even so the man also *is* through the woman; but all things are from God.

13 Judge among yourselves. Is it proper for a woman to pray to God with her head uncovered?

14 Does not even nature itself teach you that if a man has long hair, it is a dishonor to him?

STEP 10

*Continued to take personal inventory
and when we were wrong promptly admitted it.*

1 Corinthians 10:23, 24

Soon after our daughter got her driver's license, she took the car out alone for the first time, rejoicing in her new sense of freedom. We reminded her, however, that with her freedom came two major responsibilities—to keep herself safe, and to be a courteous and careful driver so that other people would not be hurt.

Paul emphasized the same points each time he reminded the Corinthians of their freedom in Jesus. Although no longer bound by legalism and all its trappings, if they exercised freedom without wisdom and concern for the welfare of others, the result would be selfish indulgence.

Like the Corinthians, we should daily take thought for the things we do and say, lest our "careless driving" frighten or anger others onto dangerous detours as they journey toward heaven. How sad it would be to arrive at heaven's portals only to take a peek in the rearview mirror and suddenly realize the destruction we had left in our wake!

For further reading on Step 10, turn to page 397.

Daily Encouragement

DAY 157 READING: 1 CORINTHIANS 10:14–33

A Thought for the New Day: Benevolence involves attitude. A benevolent spirit is not only generous but also sweet in its giving. If we can convey to those we serve that we are genuinely interested in benefiting them rather than contradicting them or quarreling with them, then they will be more open to our approach. *(Turn to page 371.)*

15 But if a woman has long hair, it is a glory to her; for *her* hair is given to her for a covering.

16 But if anyone seems to be contentious, we have no such custom, nor *do* the churches of God.

17 Now in giving these instructions I do not praise *you*, since you come together not for the better but for the worse.

18 But first of all, when you come together as a church, I hear that there are divisions among you, and in part I believe it.

19 For there must also be factions among you, that those who are approved may be recognized among you.

20 Therefore when you come together in one place, it is not to eat the Lord's Supper.

21 For in eating, each one takes his own supper ahead of *others;* and one is hungry and another is drunk.

22 What! Do you not have houses to eat and drink in? Or do you despise the church of God and shame those who have nothing? What shall I say to you? Shall I praise you in this? I do not praise *you.*

23 For I received from the Lord that which I also delivered to you: that the Lord Jesus on the *same* night in which He was betrayed took bread;

24 and when He had given thanks, He broke *it* and said, "Take, eat; this is My body which is broken for you; do this in remembrance of Me."

25 In the same manner *He* also *took* the cup after supper, saying, "This cup is the new covenant in My blood. This do, as often as you drink *it*, in remembrance of Me."

26 For as often as you eat this bread and drink this cup, you proclaim the Lord's death till He comes.

STEP
5

27 Therefore whoever eats this bread or drinks *this* cup of the Lord in an unworthy manner will be guilty of the body and blood of the Lord.

28 But let a man examine himself, and so let him eat of *that* bread and drink of *that* cup.

29 For he who eats and drinks in an unworthy manner eats and drinks judgment to himself, not discerning the Lord's body.

30 For this reason many *are* weak and sick among you, and many sleep.

31 For if we would judge ourselves, we would not be judged.

32 But when we are judged, we are chastened by the Lord, that we may not be condemned with the world.

33 Therefore, my brethren, when you come together to eat, wait for one another.

34 But if anyone is hungry, let him eat at home, lest you come together for judgment. And the rest I will set in order when I come.

12 Now concerning spiritual *gifts*, brethren, I do not want you to be ignorant:

2 You know that you were Gentiles, carried away to these dumb idols, however you were led.

3 Therefore I make known to you that no one speaking by the Spirit of God calls Jesus accursed, and no one can say that Jesus is Lord except by the Holy Spirit.

4 Now there are diversities of gifts, but the same Spirit.

5 There are differences of ministries, but the same Lord.

6 And there are diversities of activities, but it is the same God who works all in all.

7 But the manifestation of the Spirit is given to each one for the profit *of all:*

8 for to one is given the word of wisdom through the Spirit, to another the word of knowledge through the same Spirit,

9 to another faith by the same

*Admitted to God, to ourselves, and to another human being
the exact nature of our wrongs.*

1 Corinthians 11:27–32

A major problem of the church at Corinth was the lack of unity and devotion to all the members of the assembly. Dissension was rampant and factions arose. Even during the most sacred time—the Communion feast—some members were inconsiderate toward others in the body of Christ. By their gluttony, drunkenness, and unkind behavior, they were actually incurring guilt and the judgment of God as they partook of the Lord's Supper.

This is why the willingness, not only to scrutinize our behavior, but also to admit problems and to seek to correct them is so important. We have two choices: we can examine our lives and acknowledge our wrongs, or we can close our eyes to our harmful behavior and open ourselves to the judgment and chastening of the Lord.

Too many people choose plan B because it seems the easy way out at first. But even though self-examination is harder in the beginning, the end is joy and peace instead of judgment.

For further reading on Step 5, turn to page 395.

Daily
Encouragement

DAY 158 READING: 1 CORINTHIANS 11:1–34

A Thought for the New Day: One of the greatest helps toward a strong and healthy character is the habit of periodic self-examination. So much social upheaval in our world occurs because we allow our impulses to be obeyed unchecked and unscrutinized. An inward search of our motives is a sound practice having a divine origin (v. 28). Our first need is to open our hearts before God: "Search me, O God . . . Try me . . . and lead me in the way everlasting" (Ps. 139:23, 24). (*Turn to page 373.*)

Spirit, to another gifts of healings by the same Spirit,

10 to another the working of miracles, to another prophecy, to another discerning of spirits, to another *different* kinds of tongues, to another the interpretation of tongues.

11 But one and the same Spirit works all these things, distributing to each one individually as He wills.

12 For as the body is one and has many members, but all the members of that one body, being many, are one body, so also *is* Christ.

13 For by one Spirit we were all baptized into one body—whether Jews or Greeks, whether slaves or free—and have all been made to drink into one Spirit.

14 For in fact the body is not one member but many.

15 If the foot should say, "Because I am not a hand, I am not of the body," is it therefore not of the body?

16 And if the ear should say, "Because I am not an eye, I am not of the body," is it therefore not of the body?

17 If the whole body *were* an eye, where *would be* the hearing? If the whole *were* hearing, where *would be* the smelling?

18 But now God has set the members, each one of them, in the body just as He pleased.

19 And if they *were* all one member, where *would* the body *be?*

20 But now indeed *there are* many members, yet one body.

21 And the eye cannot say to the hand, "I have no need of you"; nor again the head to the feet, "I have no need of you."

22 No, much rather, those members of the body which seem to be weaker are necessary.

23 And those *members* of the body which we think to be less honorable, on these we bestow greater honor; and our unpresentable *parts* have greater modesty,

24 but our presentable *parts* have no need. But God composed the body, having given greater honor to that *part* which lacks it,

25 that there should be no schism in the body, but *that* the members should have the same care for one another.

26 And if one member suffers, all the members suffer with *it;* or if one member is honored, all the members rejoice with *it.*

27 Now you are the body of Christ, and members individually.

28 And God has appointed these in the church: first apostles, second prophets, third teachers, after that miracles, then gifts of healings, helps, administrations, varieties of tongues.

29 *Are* all apostles? *Are* all prophets? *Are* all teachers? *Are* all workers of miracles?

30 Do all have gifts of healings? Do all speak with tongues? Do all interpret?

31 But earnestly desire the best gifts. And yet I show you a more excellent way.

13 Though I speak with the tongues of men and of angels, but have not love, I have become *as* sounding brass or a clanging cymbal.

2 And though I have *the gift of* prophecy, and understand all mysteries and all knowledge, and though I have all faith, so that I could remove mountains, but have not love, I am nothing.

3 And though I bestow all my goods to feed *the poor,* and though I give my body to be burned, but have not love, it profits me nothing.

4 Love suffers long *and* is kind; love does not envy; love does not parade itself, is not puffed up;

5 does not behave rudely, does not seek its own, is not provoked, thinks no evil;

6 does not rejoice in iniquity, but rejoices in the truth;

7 bears all things, believes all

STEP 8

Made a list of all persons we had harmed,
and became willing to make amends to them all.

1 Corinthians 13

In the first two verses of 1 Corinthians 13, Paul tells the worldly wise Corinthians that no matter how talented, smart, and determined they are, if they do not have real love—God's kind of love for others (and themselves)—they are nothing. This message is relevant for our society, as well.

Then in verse 3 we find that Paul addresses the issue of codependency long before twentieth-century psychiatrists had given it a name. He identifies the personality type that sacrifices itself completely and unsparingly for others and yet has misplaced motivation and focus for those seemingly altruistic deeds.

In Step 8, as we work to replace the codependent feelings we have had about others and ourselves with feelings of true love and compassion, each verse of this powerful chapter can speak to us and move us toward the willing heart God wants us to have.

For further reading on Step 8, turn to page 427.

Daily Encouragement

DAY 159 READING: 1 CORINTHIANS 12:1—14:40

A Thought for the New Day: First Corinthians 13 is one of the loveliest passages in the Bible—beautiful enough to be a poem. But more beautiful still are those people who live out the characteristics of love described in these verses. We meet such individuals from time to time, and we are drawn to them. They are truly unforgettable and impact our lives for the good. (*Turn to page 377.*)

things, hopes all things, endures all things.

8 Love never fails. But whether *there are* prophecies, they will fail; whether *there are* tongues, they will cease; whether *there is* knowledge, it will vanish away.

9 For we know in part and we prophesy in part.

10 But when that which is perfect has come, then that which is in part will be done away.

11 When I was a child, I spoke as a child, I understood as a child, I thought as a child; but when I became a man, I put away childish things.

12 For now we see in a mirror, dimly, but then face to face. Now I know in part, but then I shall know just as I also am known.

13 And now abide faith, hope, love, these three; but the greatest of these *is* love.

14 Pursue love, and desire spiritual *gifts*, but especially that you may prophesy.

2 For he who speaks in a tongue does not speak to men but to God, for no one understands *him;* however, in the spirit he speaks mysteries.

3 But he who prophesies speaks edification and exhortation and comfort to men.

4 He who speaks in a tongue edifies himself, but he who prophesies edifies the church.

5 I wish you all spoke with tongues, but even more that you prophesied; for he who prophesies *is* greater than he who speaks with tongues, unless indeed he interprets, that the church may receive edification.

6 But now, brethren, if I come to you speaking with tongues, what shall I profit you unless I speak to you either by revelation, by knowledge, by prophesying, or by teaching?

7 Even things without life, whether flute or harp, when they make a sound, unless they make a distinction in the sounds, how will it be known what is piped or played?

8 For if the trumpet makes an uncertain sound, who will prepare himself for battle?

9 So likewise you, unless you utter by the tongue words easy to understand, how will it be known what is spoken? For you will be speaking into the air.

10 There are, it may be, so many kinds of languages in the world, and none of them *is* without significance.

11 Therefore, if I do not know the meaning of the language, I shall be a foreigner to him who speaks, and he who speaks *will be* a foreigner to me.

12 Even so you, since you are zealous for spiritual *gifts, let it be* for the edification of the church *that* you seek to excel.

13 Therefore let him who speaks in a tongue pray that he may interpret.

14 For if I pray in a tongue, my spirit prays, but my understanding is unfruitful.

15 What is *the result* then? I will pray with the spirit, and I will also pray with the understanding. I will sing with the spirit, and I will also sing with the understanding.

16 Otherwise, if you bless with the spirit, how will he who occupies the place of the uninformed say "Amen" at your giving of thanks, since he does not understand what you say?

17 For you indeed give thanks well, but the other is not edified.

18 I thank my God I speak with tongues more than you all;

19 yet in the church I would rather speak five words with my understanding, that I may teach others also, than ten thousand words in a tongue.

20 Brethren, do not be children in understanding; however, in malice be babes, but in understanding be mature.

STEP 11

374

21 In the law it is written:

> "With men of other tongues
> and other lips
> I will speak to this people;
> And yet, for all that,
> they will not hear Me,"

says the Lord.

22 Therefore tongues are for a sign, not to those who believe but to unbelievers; but prophesying is not for unbelievers but for those who believe.

23 Therefore if the whole church comes together in one place, and all speak with tongues, and there come in *those who are* uninformed or unbelievers, will they not say that you are out of your mind?

24 But if all prophesy, and an unbeliever or an uninformed person comes in, he is convinced by all, he is judged by all.

25 And thus the secrets of his heart are revealed; and so, falling down on *his* face, he will worship God and report that God is truly among you.

26 How is it then, brethren? Whenever you come together, each of you has a psalm, has a teaching, has a tongue, has a revelation, has an interpretation. Let all things be done for edification.

27 If anyone speaks in a tongue, *let there be* two or at the most three, *each* in turn, and let one interpret.

28 But if there is no interpreter, let him keep silent in church, and let him speak to himself and to God.

29 Let two or three prophets speak, and let the others judge.

30 But if *anything* is revealed to another who sits by, let the first keep silent.

31 For you can all prophesy one by one, that all may learn and all may be encouraged.

32 And the spirits of the prophets are subject to the prophets.

33 For God is not *the author* of confusion but of peace, as in all the churches of the saints.

34 Let your women keep silent in the churches, for they are not permitted to speak; but *they are* to be submissive, as the law also says.

35 And if they want to learn something, let them ask their own husbands at home; for it is shameful for women to speak in church.

36 Or did the word of God come *originally* from you? Or *was it* you only that it reached?

37 If anyone thinks himself to be a prophet or spiritual, let him acknowledge that the things which I write to you are the commandments of the Lord.

38 But if anyone is ignorant, let him be ignorant.

39 Therefore, brethren, desire earnestly to prophesy, and do not forbid to speak with tongues.

40 Let all things be done decently and in order.

15 Moreover, brethren, I declare to you the gospel which I preached to you, which also you received and in which you stand,

2 by which also you are saved, if you hold fast that word which I preached to you—unless you believed in vain.

3 For I delivered to you first of all that which I also received: that Christ died for our sins according to the Scriptures,

4 and that He was buried, and that He rose again the third day according to the Scriptures,

5 and that He was seen by Cephas, then by the twelve.

6 After that He was seen by over five hundred brethren at once, of whom the greater part remain to the present, but some have fallen asleep.

7 After that He was seen by James, then by all the apostles.

8 Then last of all He was seen by me also, as by one born out of due time.

9 For I am the least of the apostles, who am not worthy to be called an apostle, because I persecuted the church of God.

STEP
12

10 But by the grace of God I am what I am, and His grace toward me was not in vain; but I labored more abundantly than they all, yet not I, but the grace of God *which was* with me.

11 Therefore, whether *it was* I or they, so we preach and so you believed.

12 Now if Christ is preached that He has been raised from the dead, how do some among you say that there is no resurrection of the dead?

13 But if there is no resurrection of the dead, then Christ is not risen.

14 And if Christ is not risen, then our preaching *is* vain and your faith *is* also vain.

15 Yes, and we are found false witnesses of God, because we have testified of God that He raised up Christ, whom He did not raise up—if in fact the dead do not rise.

16 For if *the* dead do not rise, then Christ is not risen.

17 And if Christ is not risen, your faith *is* futile; you are still in your sins!

18 Then also those who have fallen asleep in Christ have perished.

19 If in this life only we have hope in Christ, we are of all men the most pitiable.

STEP
2

20 But now Christ is risen from the dead, *and* has become the firstfruits of those who have fallen asleep.

21 For since by man *came* death, by Man also *came* the resurrection of the dead.

22 For as in Adam all die, even so in Christ all shall be made alive.

23 But each one in his own order: Christ the firstfruits, afterward those *who are* Christ's at His coming.

24 Then *comes* the end, when He delivers the kingdom to God the Father, when He puts an end to all rule and all authority and power.

25 For He must reign till He has put all enemies under His feet.

26 The last enemy *that* will be destroyed *is* death.

27 For "*He has put all things under His feet.*" But when He says "all things are put under *Him,*" *it is* evident that He who put all things under Him is excepted.

28 Now when all things are made subject to Him, then the Son Himself will also be subject to Him who put all things under Him, that God may be all in all.

29 Otherwise, what will they do who are baptized for the dead, if the dead do not rise at all? Why then are they baptized for the dead?

30 And why do we stand in jeopardy every hour?

31 I affirm, by the boasting in you which I have in Christ Jesus our Lord, I die daily.

32 If, in the manner of men, I have fought with beasts at Ephesus, what advantage *is it* to me? If *the* dead do not rise, *"Let us eat and drink, for tomorrow we die."*

33 Do not be deceived: "Evil company corrupts good habits."

STEP
4

34 Awake to righteousness, and do not sin; for some do not have the knowledge of God. I speak *this* to your shame.

35 But someone will say, "How are the dead raised up? And with what body do they come?"

36 Foolish one, what you sow is not made alive unless it dies.

37 And what you sow, you do not sow that body that shall be, but mere grain—perhaps wheat or some other *grain.*

38 But God gives it a body as He pleases, and to each seed its own body.

39 All flesh *is* not the same flesh, but *there is* one *kind of* flesh of men, another flesh of beasts, another of fish, *and* another of birds.

40 *There are* also celestial bodies and terrestrial bodies; but the glory of the celestial *is* one, and the *glory* of the terrestrial *is* another.

41 *There is* one glory of the sun,

STEP 12

*Having had a spiritual awakening as the result
of these steps, we tried to carry this message to others,
and to practice these principles in all our affairs.*

1 Corinthians 15:10

One of our favorite recovery slogans is "But for the grace of God." This phrase has multiple meanings for recovering persons. But for the grace of God, we might not have broken out of denial and recognized the gravity of our dependencies. But for the grace of God, we might not have found support groups, Twelve Step recovery organizations, and the church community, which have ministered to our areas of dependency. But for the grace of God, we might not have "hit bottom" as a crossroads to propel our lives into a radically new direction. But for the grace of God, we might not have found God and then been reborn to Him.

Step 12 is a grace-filled step. Having been ushered into a spiritual awakening, we are charged to radiate God's grace to those around us. As we diligently seek to practice these principles in all of our affairs, we become living testimonies to Paul's words that God's grace was "not in vain" and that "by the grace of God I am what I am."

For further reading on Step 12, turn to page 383.

Daily Encouragement

DAY 160 READING: 1 CORINTHIANS 15:1–49

A Thought for the New Day: Some time ago the author dreamed of a boyhood friend he had not seen in many years. In the dream his friend was young again—smiling and glowing with health, not feeble with pain as he had, in fact, become. A few days later we learned that our friend had died, but we knew better. We knew that he had entered into the special life of our risen Savior (v. 49). (*Turn to page 379.*)

another glory of the moon, and another glory of the stars; for *one* star differs from *another* star in glory.

42 So also *is* the resurrection of the dead. *The body* is sown in corruption, it is raised in incorruption.

43 It is sown in dishonor, it is raised in glory. It is sown in weakness, it is raised in power.

44 It is sown a natural body, it is raised a spiritual body. There is a natural body, and there is a spiritual body.

45 And so it is written, *"The first man Adam became a living being."* The last Adam *became* a life-giving spirit.

46 However, the spiritual is not first, but the natural, and afterward the spiritual.

47 The first man *was* of the earth, *made* of dust; the second Man *is* the Lord from heaven.

48 As *was* the *man* of dust, so also *are* those *who are made* of dust; and as *is* the heavenly *Man*, so also *are* those *who are* heavenly.

49 And as we have borne the image of the *man* of dust, we shall also bear the image of the heavenly *Man*.

50 Now this I say, brethren, that flesh and blood cannot inherit the kingdom of God; nor does corruption inherit incorruption.

51 Behold, I tell you a mystery: We shall not all sleep, but we shall all be changed—

52 in a moment, in the twinkling of an eye, at the last trumpet. For the trumpet will sound, and the dead will be raised incorruptible, and we shall be changed.

53 For this corruptible must put on incorruption, and this mortal *must* put on immortality.

54 So when this corruptible has put on incorruption, and this mortal has put on immortality, then shall be brought to pass the saying that is written: *"Death is swallowed up in victory."*

55 *"O Death, where is your sting? O Hades, where is your victory?"*

56 The sting of death *is* sin, and the strength of sin *is* the law.

57 But thanks *be* to God, who gives us the victory through our Lord Jesus Christ.

58 Therefore, my beloved brethren, be steadfast, immovable, always abounding in the work of the Lord, knowing that your labor is not in vain in the Lord.

16 Now concerning the collection for the saints, as I have given orders to the churches of Galatia, so you must do also:

2 On the first *day* of the week let each one of you lay something aside, storing up as he may prosper, that there be no collections when I come.

3 And when I come, whomever you approve by *your* letters I will send to bear your gift to Jerusalem.

4 But if it is fitting that I go also, they will go with me.

5 Now I will come to you when I pass through Macedonia (for I am passing through Macedonia).

6 But it may be that I will remain, or even spend the winter with you, that you may send me on my journey, wherever I go.

7 For I do not wish to see you now on the way; but I hope to stay a while with you, if the Lord permits.

8 But I will tarry in Ephesus until Pentecost.

9 For a great and effective door has opened to me, and *there are* many adversaries.

10 Now if Timothy comes, see that he may be with you without fear; for he does the work of the Lord, as I also *do*.

11 Therefore let no one despise him. But send him on his journey in peace, that he may come to me; for I am waiting for him with the brethren.

STEP 6

*Were entirely ready to have God
remove all these defects of character.*

1 Corinthians 15:57

Recovery without Jesus can never be a full or completed work. We may learn to cope with our dependencies, but we can never be emancipated from them. We may be able to endure life, but to deeply enjoy life we need to do more than give up our addictions. We need to fill the inner void that gave rise to those problems. Only Jesus can fill our emptiness. He alone can satisfy the deepest longings of our souls and keep us satisfied every day of our lives. This is exactly what He meant when He called Himself the Bread of Life and the Living Water. Because His love and power can heal the most crucial areas of life, we have everything we need in Him. As we become ready to let go of the past and reach out in trust to Jesus, we have power enough to do more than cope. We have love enough to do more than endure. We have victory in Jesus.

For further reading on Step 6, turn to page 389.

Daily Encouragement

DAY 161 READING: 1 CORINTHIANS 15:50—16:24

A Thought for the New Day: Most of the world's history is the record of a dreary, long night of pain and sadness. Although we must face up to that reality, there is a bright and happy episode in the midst of that history: it is the episode of the empty tomb. We can and will be victors over all that breaks our hearts now. Because Jesus lives, we shall live, also. (*Turn to page 381.*)

12 Now concerning *our* brother Apollos, I strongly urged him to come to you with the brethren, but he was quite unwilling to come at this time; however, he will come when he has a convenient time.

STEP 11

13 Watch, stand fast in the faith, be brave, be strong. **14** Let all *that* you *do* be done with love.

15 I urge you, brethren—you know the household of Stephanas, that it is the firstfruits of Achaia, and *that* they have devoted themselves to the ministry of the saints—

16 that you also submit to such, and to everyone who works and labors with *us*.

17 I am glad about the coming of Stephanas, Fortunatus, and Achaicus, for what was lacking on your part they supplied.

18 For they refreshed my spirit and yours; therefore acknowledge such men.

19 The churches of Asia greet you. Aquila and Priscilla greet you heartily in the Lord, with the church that is in their house.

20 All the brethren greet you. Greet one another with a holy kiss.

21 The salutation with my own hand—Paul.

22 If anyone does not love the Lord Jesus Christ, let him be accursed. O Lord, come!

23 The grace of our Lord Jesus Christ *be* with you.

24 My love *be* with you all in Christ Jesus. Amen.

THE SECOND EPISTLE OF PAUL THE APOSTLE TO THE

CORINTHIANS

PAUL, an apostle of Jesus Christ by the will of God, and Timothy *our* brother,

To the church of God which is at Corinth, with all the saints who are in all Achaia:

2 Grace to you and peace from God our Father and the Lord Jesus Christ.

STEP 12

3 Blessed *be* the God and Father of our Lord Jesus Christ, the Father of mercies and God of all comfort,

4 who comforts us in all our tribulation, that we may be able to comfort those who are in any trouble, with the comfort with which we ourselves are comforted by God.

5 For as the sufferings of Christ abound in us, so our consolation also abounds through Christ.

6 Now if we are afflicted, *it is* for your consolation and salvation, which is effective for enduring the same sufferings which we also suffer. Or if we are comforted, *it is* for your consolation and salvation.

7 And our hope for you *is* steadfast, because we know that as you are partakers of the sufferings, so also *you will partake* of the consolation.

8 For we do not want you to be ignorant, brethren, of our trouble which came to us in Asia: that we were burdened beyond measure, above strength, so that we despaired even of life.

9 Yes, we had the sentence of death in ourselves, that we should not trust in ourselves but in God who raises the dead,

10 who delivered us from so great a death, and does deliver us; in

STEP 2

*Came to believe that a Power greater than ourselves
could restore us to sanity.*

2 Corinthians 1:8–10

Paul was no stranger to suffering. He knew what it meant to be
burdened beyond his strength, almost to the point of despair. In an
outlying province of Asia, Paul's religious opponents had beaten
him severely; but his suffering never caused him to lose hope. His
pain turned his eyes from himself to God. God's power, he knew,
was sufficient even in the worst possible circumstances. In verses 9
and 10, Paul declared that he should have been dead, without
God's delivering him in a miraculous manner.

The God of the Bible is a God of power and compassion. When
we are "burdened beyond measure, above strength, so that we
despair even of life" (v. 8), our answer is close at hand. "We should
not trust in ourselves but in God who raises the dead" (v. 9). God is
able and waiting to deliver us.

For further reading on Step 2, turn to page 403.

Daily Encouragement

DAY 162 READING: 2 CORINTHIANS 1:1–24

A Thought for the New Day: It is hard to comfort others who
are suffering when suffering is all we know. When we find comfort, though, we are so glad for it that we want to share that
comfort with others, too. Has God comforted you in some hard
place in your life (vv. 3, 4)? (He wants to.) Then do not miss the
doubled joy of sharing that happy relief with someone else.
(*Turn to page 383.*)

whom we trust that He will still deliver *us*,

11 you also helping together in prayer for us, that thanks may be given by many persons on our behalf for the gift *granted* to us through many.

12 For our boasting is this: the testimony of our conscience that we conducted ourselves in the world in simplicity and godly sincerity, not with fleshly wisdom but by the grace of God, and more abundantly toward you.

13 For we are not writing any other things to you than what you read or understand. Now I trust you will understand, even to the end

14 (as also you have understood us in part), that we are your boast as you also *are* ours, in the day of the Lord Jesus.

15 And in this confidence I intended to come to you before, that you might have a second benefit—

16 to pass by way of you to Macedonia, to come again from Macedonia to you, and be helped by you on my way to Judea.

17 Therefore, when I was planning this, did I do it lightly? Or the things I plan, do I plan according to the flesh, that with me there should be Yes, Yes, and No, No?

18 But *as* God *is* faithful, our word to you was not Yes and No.

19 For the Son of God, Jesus Christ, who was preached among you by us—by me, Silvanus, and Timothy—was not Yes and No, but in Him was Yes.

20 For all the promises of God in Him *are* Yes, and in Him Amen, to the glory of God through us.

21 Now He who establishes us with you in Christ and has anointed us *is* God,

22 who also has sealed us and given us the Spirit in our hearts as a deposit.

23 Moreover I call God as witness against my soul, that to spare you I came no more to Corinth.

24 Not that we have dominion over your faith, but are fellow workers for your joy; for by faith you stand.

2 But I determined this within myself, that I would not come again to you in sorrow.

2 For if I make you sorrowful, then who is he who makes me glad but the one who is made sorrowful by me?

3 And I wrote this very thing to you, lest, when I came, I should have sorrow over those from whom I ought to have joy, having confidence in you all that my joy is *the joy* of you all.

4 For out of much affliction and anguish of heart I wrote to you, with many tears, not that you should be grieved, but that you might know the love which I have so abundantly for you.

5 But if anyone has caused grief, he has not grieved me, but all of you to some extent—not to be too severe.

6 This punishment which *was inflicted* by the majority *is* sufficient for such a man,

7 so that, on the contrary, you *ought* rather to forgive and comfort *him*, lest perhaps such a one be swallowed up with too much sorrow.

8 Therefore I urge you to reaffirm *your* love to him.

9 For to this end I also wrote, that I might put you to the test, whether you are obedient in all things.

10 Now whom you forgive anything, I also *forgive*. For if indeed I have forgiven anything, I have forgiven that one for your sakes in the presence of Christ,

11 lest Satan should take advantage of us; for we are not ignorant of his devices.

12 Furthermore, when I came to Troas to *preach* Christ's gospel, and a door was opened to me by the Lord,

13 I had no rest in my spirit, because I did not find Titus my

STEP 12

*Having had a spiritual awakening as the result
of these steps, we tried to carry this message to others,
and to practice these principles in all our affairs.*

2 Corinthians 2:12–17

In Paul's day, when an army had achieved a great victory, the conquering general was given a parade of triumph. Often the treasures and prisoners of war were displayed in such a march. Paul had this picture in mind as he rejoiced in being part of Christ's triumphant parade, taken captive by His great love.

Paul continued his analogy with the idea of aroma or incense. It was common to burn incense during the triumphal procession. Those on the conquering side came to associate that aroma with life and joy. But to the defeated, it meant death.

Our lives, Paul wrote, produce a similar response. Our words, actions, and life-styles are the sweet fragrance of salvation and joy for those who hear God's call. But to those who reject God's message of hope and love, our lives are like the stench of death. Sadly, they are smelling their own destruction.

Still, it is not for us to worry over others' reactions. Our part is to be faithful and sincere stewards of the message of Christ.

For further reading on Step 12, turn to page 385.

Daily Encouragement

DAY 163 READING: 2 CORINTHIANS 2:1–17

A Thought for the New Day: How could Paul speak so optimistically? This same Paul had been stoned in Lystra, beaten many times, and even shipwrecked. Yet he still declared that God led him *in triumph*. Is this more than you can grasp? You have only to reach out and accept God's word that He is as much your God as He was Paul's. He waits to show you in every crisis of life that Paul's song of victory can be yours, too. (*Turn to page 385.*)

brother; but taking my leave of them, I departed for Macedonia.

14 Now thanks *be* to God who always leads us in triumph in Christ, and through us diffuses the fragrance of His knowledge in every place.

15 For we are to God the fragrance of Christ among those who are being saved and among those who are perishing.

16 To the one *we are* the aroma of death to death, and to the other the aroma of life to life. And who *is* sufficient for these things?

17 For we are not, as so many, peddling the word of God; but as of sincerity, but as from God, we speak in the sight of God in Christ.

3 Do we begin again to commend ourselves? Or do we need, as some *others*, epistles of commendation to you or *letters* of commendation from you?

2 You are our epistle written in our hearts, known and read by all men;

3 *you are* manifestly an epistle of Christ, ministered by us, written not with ink but by the Spirit of the living God, not on tablets of stone but on tablets of flesh, *that is*, of the heart.

4 And we have such trust through Christ toward God.

5 Not that we are sufficient of ourselves to think of anything as *being* from ourselves, but our sufficiency *is* from God,

6 who also made us sufficient as ministers of the new covenant, not of the letter but of the Spirit; for the letter kills, but the Spirit gives life.

7 But if the ministry of death, written *and* engraved on stones, was glorious, so that the children of Israel could not look steadily at the face of Moses because of the glory of his countenance, which *glory* was passing away,

8 how will the ministry of the Spirit not be more glorious?

9 For if the ministry of condemnation *had* glory, the ministry of righteousness exceeds much more in glory.

10 For even what was made glorious had no glory in this respect, because of the glory that excels.

11 For if what is passing away *was* glorious, what remains *is* much more glorious.

12 Therefore, since we have such hope, we use great boldness of speech—

13 unlike Moses, *who* put a veil over his face so that the children of Israel could not look steadily at the end of what was passing away.

14 But their minds were hardened. For until this day the same veil remains unlifted in the reading of the Old Testament, because the *veil* is taken away in Christ.

15 But even to this day, when Moses is read, a veil lies on their heart.

16 Nevertheless when one turns to the Lord, the veil is taken away.

17 Now the Lord is the Spirit; and where the Spirit of the Lord *is*, there *is* liberty.

18 But we all, with unveiled face, beholding as in a mirror the glory of the Lord, are being transformed into the same image from glory to glory, just as by the Spirit of the Lord.

4 Therefore, since we have this ministry, as we have received mercy, we do not lose heart.

2 But we have renounced the hidden things of shame, not walking in craftiness nor handling the word of God deceitfully, but by manifestation of the truth commending ourselves to every man's conscience in the sight of God.

3 But even if our gospel is veiled, it is veiled to those who are perishing,

4 whose minds the god of this age has blinded, who do not believe, lest the light of the gospel of the glory of Christ, who is the image of God, should shine on them.

STEP 12

*Having had a spiritual awakening as the result
of these steps, we tried to carry this message to others,
and to practice these principles in all our affairs.*

2 Corinthians 4:1, 2

In some ways, Paul's life parallels the lives of people in recovery. He had a past that he was not proud of, but God had saved him and allowed him to make amends to many believers he had harmed. Then God had given him a ministry—carrying the good news of freedom in Jesus to other people. In Step 12, we come to realize that we, too, have a ministry of sharing the emotional and spiritual healing Jesus offers. Just as Paul had renounced the shame of his past and put it behind him, we do the same. Now our daily walk and talk are constantly being transformed by the principles we have learned and incorporated into our lives. We are able to "be a manifestation of the truth." More simply put, we no longer have to hide behind masks of denial and pretense. We can be genuine toward every person we encounter. Our lives can be an open book, declaring God's love, faithfulness, and righteousness to a needy world.

For further reading on Step 12, turn to page 387.

Daily Encouragement

DAY 164 READING: 2 CORINTHIANS 3:1—4:15

A Thought for the New Day: Death and life are extreme opposites in our common culture, but Paul did not always look at them in that way. For him death was essential to the experience of real life. The Greek word *bios* has to do with biological existence, but the word *zoe* is about life that is indestructible and eternal. The Christian's goal is to nourish the second kind of life—the life that comes from God—even though our outward lives pass away. (*Turn to page 387.*)

STEP 11

5 For we do not preach ourselves, but Christ Jesus the Lord, and ourselves your servants for Jesus' sake.

6 For it is the God who commanded light to shine out of darkness who has shone in our hearts to *give* the light of the knowledge of the glory of God in the face of Jesus Christ.

7 But we have this treasure in earthen vessels, that the excellence of the power may be of God and not of us.

8 *We are* hard pressed on every side, yet not crushed; *we are* perplexed, but not in despair;

9 persecuted, but not forsaken; struck down, but not destroyed—

10 always carrying about in the body the dying of the Lord Jesus, that the life of Jesus also may be manifested in our body.

11 For we who live are always delivered to death for Jesus' sake, that the life of Jesus also may be manifested in our mortal flesh.

12 So then death is working in us, but life in you.

13 But since we have the same spirit of faith, according to what is written, *"I believed and therefore I spoke,"* we also believe and therefore speak,

14 knowing that He who raised up the Lord Jesus will also raise us up with Jesus, and will present *us* with you.

15 For all things *are* for your sakes, that grace, having spread through the many, may cause thanksgiving to abound to the glory of God.

16 Therefore we do not lose heart. Even though our outward man is perishing, yet the inward *man* is being renewed day by day.

17 For our light affliction, which is but for a moment, is working for us a far more exceeding *and* eternal weight of glory,

18 while we do not look at the things which are seen, but at the things which are not seen. For the things which are seen *are* tem-

porary, but the things which are not seen *are* eternal.

5 For we know that if our earthly house, *this* tent, is destroyed, we have a building from God, a house not made with hands, eternal in the heavens.

2 For in this we groan, earnestly desiring to be clothed with our habitation which is from heaven,

3 if indeed, having been clothed, we shall not be found naked.

4 For we who are in *this* tent groan, being burdened, not because we want to be unclothed, but further clothed, that mortality may be swallowed up by life.

5 Now He who has prepared us for this very thing *is* God, who also has given us the Spirit as a guarantee.

6 Therefore *we are* always confident, knowing that while we are at home in the body we are absent from the Lord.

7 For we walk by faith, not by sight.

8 We are confident, yes, well pleased rather to be absent from the body and to be present with the Lord.

9 Therefore we make it our aim, whether present or absent, to be well pleasing to Him.

10 For we must all appear before the judgment seat of Christ, that each one may receive the things *done* in the body, according to what he has done, whether good or bad.

11 Knowing, therefore, the terror of the Lord, we persuade men; but we are well known to God, and I also trust are well known in your consciences.

12 For we do not commend ourselves again to you, but give you opportunity to glory on our behalf, that you may have *something to answer* those who glory in appearance and not in heart.

13 For if we are beside ourselves, *it is* for God; or if we are of sound mind, *it is* for you.

STEP 12

Having had a spiritual awakening as the result
of these steps, we tried to carry this message to others,
and to practice these principles in all our affairs.

2 Corinthians 5:10, 11

A final test can be a scary thing if we have failed to study and listen in class. It pays to prepare. God gives a final test, too. It is called the Judgment Seat, and every believer graduating from Earth 101 takes it. The Judgment Seat of Christ does not decide whether we enter heaven. That was decided when we accepted Jesus as Savior. God uses the Judgment Seat to reward us according to what we have done with our knowledge of Jesus.

By the time we reach Step 12, we have begun to learn much about our God and ourselves. Now it is time to begin sharing those lessons with others in need. We do this for two reasons. First, we want to be received as good and faithful servants when we stand at the Lord's Judgment Seat. Second, we know the "terror of the Lord": we know that those who do not accept Jesus as Savior are headed for eternal condemnation. These certainties motivate us continually to "persuade men."

For further reading on Step 12, turn to page 433.

Daily Encouragement

DAY 165 READING: 2 CORINTHIANS 4:16—5:11

A Thought for the New Day: How can we have the same confidence Paul has about life and death (5:5)? Surely not by wishful thinking. Yet we have a present reality that convinces us that our goal is "to be present with the Lord" (5:8). Paul calls this inward reality the "guarantee" of the Holy Spirit. For us there is no evidence of eternal life so great as the evidence of the Spirit of God Himself living in us. (*Turn to page 389.*)

STEP 11 14 For the love of Christ constrains us, because we judge thus: that if One died for all, then all died; 15 and He died for all, that those who live should live no longer for themselves, but for Him who died for them and rose again.

16 Therefore, from now on, we regard no one according to the flesh. Even though we have known Christ according to the flesh, yet now we know *Him thus* no longer.

STEP 6 17 Therefore, if anyone *is* in Christ, *he is* a new creation; old things have passed away; behold, all things have become new.

STEP 12 18 Now all things *are* of God, who has reconciled us to Himself through Jesus Christ, and has given us the ministry of reconciliation,

19 that is, that God was in Christ reconciling the world to Himself, not imputing their trespasses to them, and has committed to us the word of reconciliation.

20 Therefore we are ambassadors for Christ, as though God were pleading through us: we implore *you* on Christ's behalf, be reconciled to God.

STEP 2 21 For He made Him who knew no sin *to be* sin for us, that we might become the righteousness of God in Him.

6 We then, *as* workers together *with Him* also plead with *you* not to receive the grace of God in vain.

2 For He says:

    "In an acceptable time I have
       heard you,
    And in the day of salvation I
       have helped you."

Behold, now *is* the accepted time; behold, now *is* the day of salvation. 3 We give no offense in anything, that our ministry may not be blamed.

4 But in all *things* we commend ourselves as ministers of God: in much patience, in tribulations, in needs, in distresses,

5 in stripes, in imprisonments, in tumults, in labors, in sleeplessness, in fastings;

6 by purity, by knowledge, by longsuffering, by kindness, by the Holy Spirit, by sincere love,

7 by the word of truth, by the power of God, by the armor of righteousness on the right hand and on the left,

8 by honor and dishonor, by evil report and good report; as deceivers, and *yet* true;

9 as unknown, and *yet* well known; as dying, and behold we live; as chastened, and *yet* not killed;

10 as sorrowful, yet always rejoicing; as poor, yet making many rich; as having nothing, and *yet* possessing all things.

11 O Corinthians! We have spoken openly to you, our heart is wide open.

12 You are not restricted by us, but you are restricted by your *own* affections.

13 Now in return for the same (I speak as to children), you also be open.

14 Do not be unequally yoked together with unbelievers. For what fellowship has righteousness with lawlessness? And what communion has light with darkness? **STEP 4**

15 And what accord has Christ with Belial? Or what part has a believer with an unbeliever?

16 And what agreement has the temple of God with idols? For you are the temple of the living God. As God has said:

    "I will dwell in them
    And walk among them.
    I will be their God,
    And they shall be My people."

17 Therefore

    "Come out from among them

STEP
6

*Were entirely ready to have God
remove all these defects of character.*

2 Corinthians 5:17

For much of our time on earth we have crawled about like caterpillars, limited to the ground and the few leaves within our reach. The scars of our childhood, our dependencies, and our sin have kept us earthbound. Wrong mind-sets and bad habits have conspired to dwarf our legs and slow our progress. To remain a caterpillar is to fall easy prey to the crows of despair and indifference. But this is not God's desire or plan for us. Breathtaking vistas and glorious heights await those who are humbly willing to accept the chrysalis of God's total control over their lives. The metamorphosis probably will not be instantaneous. At times, we may feel uncomfortably cramped or shaky and uncertain in our slender, midair suspension. However, in God's perfect timing, the exquisite butterfly of His grace will emerge. "Behold, all things have become new."

For further reading on Step 6, turn to page 391.

Daily
Encouragement

DAY 166 READING: 2 CORINTHIANS 5:12—6:10

A Thought for the New Day: When we have Paul's inward vision of joy that lies beyond the present scene, then temporary setbacks, stresses, and needs cannot destroy us. Suffering is never pleasant, but we can accept it when it comes, safe in the assurance that our faithful God is behind the scenes. Although this physical life with both its joys and its pains ends, we are secure in the knowledge of our salvation. (*Turn to page 391.*)

*And be separate, says the Lord.
Do not touch what is unclean,
And I will receive you."*
18 *"I will be a Father to you,
And you shall be My sons
and daughters,
Says the LORD Almighty."*

7 Therefore, having these promises, beloved, let us cleanse ourselves from all filthiness of the flesh and spirit, perfecting holiness in the fear of God.

2 Open *your hearts* to us. We have wronged no one, we have corrupted no one, we have defrauded no one.

3 I do not say *this* to condemn; for I have said before that you are in our hearts, to die together and to live together.

4 Great *is* my boldness of speech toward you, great *is* my boasting on your behalf. I am filled with comfort. I am exceedingly joyful in all our tribulation.

5 For indeed, when we came to Macedonia, our flesh had no rest, but we were troubled on every side. Outside *were* conflicts, inside *were* fears.

6 Nevertheless God, who comforts the downcast, comforted us by the coming of Titus,

7 and not only by his coming, but also by the consolation with which he was comforted in you, when he told us of your earnest desire, your mourning, your zeal for me, so that I rejoiced even more.

8 For even if I made you sorry with my letter, I do not regret it; though I did regret it. For I perceive that the same epistle made you sorry, though only for a while.

9 Now I rejoice, not that you were made sorry, but that your sorrow led to repentance. For you were made sorry in a godly manner, that you might suffer loss from us in nothing.

10 For godly sorrow produces repentance to salvation, not to be regretted; but the sorrow of the world produces death.

11 For observe this very thing, that you sorrowed in a godly manner: What diligence it produced in you, *what* clearing *of yourselves, what* indignation, *what* fear, *what* vehement desire, *what* zeal, *what* vindication! In all *things* you proved yourselves to be clear in this matter.

12 Therefore, although I wrote to you, *I* did not *do it* for the sake of him who had done the wrong, nor for the sake of him who suffered wrong, but that our care for you in the sight of God might appear to you.

13 Therefore we have been comforted in your comfort. And we rejoiced exceedingly more for the joy of Titus, because his spirit has been refreshed by you all.

14 For if in anything I have boasted to him about you, I am not ashamed. But as we spoke all things to you in truth, even so our boasting to Titus was found true.

15 And his affections are greater for you as he remembers the obedience of you all, how with fear and trembling you received him.

16 Therefore I rejoice that I have confidence in you in everything.

8 Moreover, brethren, we make known to you the grace of God bestowed on the churches of Macedonia:

2 that in a great trial of affliction the abundance of their joy and their deep poverty abounded in the riches of their liberality.

3 For I bear witness that according to *their* ability, yes, and beyond *their* ability, *they were* freely willing,

4 imploring us with much urgency that we would receive the gift and the fellowship of the ministering to the saints.

5 And *this they did*, not as we had

STEP
6

*Were entirely ready to have God
remove all these defects of character.*

2 Corinthians 7:9, 10

"The sorrow of the world produces death." Very, very few people
are without sorrow if they have lived long under the cloud of
dependency. Sorrow seems to be the unwelcome, but constant companion of most. We feel sorrow over our own condition and sometimes sorrow for what our problems have caused others to endure.
Sorrow can only lead in two directions. If we choose to let the
world dictate the road sorrow leads us down, we will pass through
the villages of Remorse, Repetition, Intensification, and Despair.
The end of this sad road is death.

But sorrow can take us by the hand and lead us down a far better
road. On this road, Repentance is the first stop. Repentance means
not only to agree with God about our problems, but to desire to
change and walk with God. When we become willing for God to
change us, the journey to Peace and Joy and Abundant Life begins.

For further reading on Step 6, turn to page 419.

Daily Encouragement

DAY 167 READING: 2 CORINTHIANS 6:11—7:16

A Thought for the New Day: All of us feel low at times, and
Paul apparently was no exception. Even so, he showed us where
to go for comfort. If you only reach out to God, He will not disappoint you, and you will find consolation beyond imagining.
Falling victim to circumstances is not a necessary state for us: we
can rise above unhappy conditions when we see them from
God's point of view. (*Turn to page 393.*)

hoped, but first gave themselves to the Lord, and *then* to us by the will of God.

6 So we urged Titus, that as he had begun, so he would also complete this grace in you as well.

7 But as you abound in everything—in faith, in speech, in knowledge, in all diligence, and in your love for us—*see* that you abound in this grace also.

8 I speak not by commandment, but I am testing the sincerity of your love by the diligence of others.

STEP 3 9 For you know the grace of our Lord Jesus Christ, that though He was rich, yet for your sakes He became poor, that you through His poverty might become rich.

10 And in this I give *my* advice: It is to your advantage not only to be doing what you began and were desiring to do a year ago;

11 but now you also must complete the doing *of it;* that as *there was* a readiness to desire *it,* so *there* also *may be* a completion out of what *you* have.

12 For if there is first a willing mind, *it is* accepted according to what one has, *and* not according to what he does not have.

13 For *I do* not *mean* that others should be eased and you burdened;

14 but by an equality, *that* now at this time your abundance may *supply* their lack, that their abundance also may *supply* your lack—that there may be equality.

15 As it is written, *"He who gathered much had nothing left over, and he who gathered little had no lack."*

16 But thanks *be* to God who puts the same earnest care for you into the heart of Titus.

17 For he not only accepted the exhortation, but being more diligent, he went to you of his own accord.

18 And we have sent with him the brother whose praise *is* in the gospel throughout all the churches,

19 and not only *that,* but who was also chosen by the churches to travel with us with this gift, which is administered by us to the glory of the Lord Himself and *to show* your ready mind,

20 avoiding this: that anyone should blame us in this lavish gift which is administered by us—

21 providing honorable things, not only in the sight of the Lord, but also in the sight of men.

22 And we have sent with them our brother whom we have often proved diligent in many things, but now much more diligent, because of the great confidence which *we have* in you.

23 If *anyone inquires* about Titus, *he is* my partner and fellow worker concerning you. Or if our brethren *are inquired about, they are* messengers of the churches, the glory of Christ.

24 Therefore show to them, and before the churches, the proof of your love and of our boasting on your behalf.

9 Now concerning the ministering to the saints, it is superfluous for me to write to you;

2 for I know your willingness, about which I boast of you to the Macedonians, that Achaia was ready a year ago; and your zeal has stirred up the majority.

3 Yet I have sent the brethren, lest our boasting of you should be in vain in this respect, that, as I said, you may be ready;

4 lest if *some* Macedonians come with me and find you unprepared, we (not to mention you!) should be ashamed of this confident boasting.

5 Therefore I thought it necessary to exhort the brethren to go to you ahead of time, and prepare your bountiful gift beforehand, which *you had* previously promised, that it may be ready as *a matter of* generosity and not as a grudging obligation.

*Made a decision to turn our will and our lives
over to the care of God **as we understood Him.***

2 Corinthians 8:9

We would have no concept of goodness, kindness, mercy, generosity, wisdom, patience, or compassion except for the fact that we are made in the image of God. To the extent that any of us shows these attributes we show forth God. But because of our sinful, fallen natures, our ability to achieve these virtues is limited at best.

God's goodness, on the other hand, has no limit. Evidence of His goodness fills our world everywhere, and the Bible teaches us that God loves to give His children good gifts. God's best good gift of all was the Lord Jesus—God in the flesh—who left heaven to die for our sin and who rose from the dead to give us eternal life.

The riches, power, and majesty of God cannot even begin to be described. But God's good and gracious heart willingly left it all for suffering, scorn, and poverty. Turning our lives over to the goodness of His control will bring us the true riches of His love and grace.

For further reading on Step 3, turn to page 409.

Daily
Encouragement

DAY 168 READING: 2 CORINTHIANS 8:1–24

A Thought for the New Day: Have you ever considered all that it cost Jesus to win heaven for you and me (v. 9)? The very thought bewilders us, but He is the One who inhabited eternity when time did not exist. Jesus Christ left glory to become our servant—even allowing Himself to be treated and executed as a criminal. He became poor for us, so that we could share His wealth throughout eternity. (*Turn to page 395.*)

STEP 11

6 But this *I say:* He who sows sparingly will also reap sparingly, and he who sows bountifully will also reap bountifully.

7 *So let* each one *give* as he purposes in his heart, not grudgingly or of necessity; for God loves a cheerful giver.

8 And God *is* able to make all grace abound toward you, that you, always having all sufficiency in all *things,* have an abundance for every good work.

9 As it is written:

> "He has dispersed abroad,
> He has given to the poor;
> His righteousness remains
> forever."

10 Now may He who supplies seed to the sower, and bread for food, supply and multiply the seed you have *sown* and increase the fruits of your righteousness,

11 while *you are* enriched in everything for all liberality, which causes thanksgiving through us to God.

12 For the administration of this service not only supplies the needs of the saints, but also is abounding through many thanksgivings to God,

13 while, through the proof of this ministry, they glorify God for the obedience of your confession to the gospel of Christ, and for *your* liberal sharing with them and all *men,*

14 and by their prayer for you, who long for you because of the exceeding grace of God in you.

15 Thanks *be* to God for His indescribable gift!

10 Now I, Paul, myself am pleading with you by the meekness and gentleness of Christ—who in presence *am* lowly among you, but being absent am bold toward you.

2 But I beg *you* that when I am present I may not be bold with that confidence by which I intend to be bold against some, who think of us as if we walked according to the flesh.

3 For though we walk in the flesh, we do not war according to the flesh.

STEP 5

4 For the weapons of our warfare *are* not carnal but mighty in God for pulling down strongholds,

5 casting down arguments and every high thing that exalts itself against the knowledge of God, bringing every thought into captivity to the obedience of Christ,

6 and being ready to punish all disobedience when your obedience is fulfilled.

7 Do you look at things according to the outward appearance? If anyone is convinced in himself that he is Christ's, let him again consider this in himself, that just as he *is* Christ's, even so we *are* Christ's.

8 For even if I should boast somewhat more about our authority, which the Lord gave us for edification and not for your destruction, I shall not be ashamed—

9 lest I seem to terrify you by letters.

10 "For *his* letters," they say, "*are* weighty and powerful, but *his* bodily presence *is* weak, and *his* speech contemptible."

11 Let such a person consider this, that what we are in word by letters when we are absent, such *we will* also *be* in deed when we are present.

12 For we dare not class ourselves or compare ourselves with those who commend themselves. But they, measuring themselves by themselves, and comparing themselves among themselves, are not wise.

STEP 4

13 We, however, will not boast beyond measure, but within the limits of the sphere which God appointed us—a sphere which especially includes you.

14 For we are not extending our-

STEP 5

Admitted to God, to ourselves, and to another human being the exact nature of our wrongs.

2 Corinthians 10:3–5

The ultimate goal of all recovery is the experience of a profound spiritual awakening and renewal. Scripture reminds us that "though we walk in the flesh, we do not war according to the flesh" (v. 3). Although fifth step sharing may include the acknowledgment of many sins of the flesh, we eventually come to the realization that the true recovery battle is not on the physical level at all. It is a spiritual struggle.

This realization that all issues are ultimately spiritual issues gives rise to an important recovery irony. In the early stages of recovery, we may feel that we are human beings passing through a temporary spiritual experience. As recovery matures, we reverse that perspective and begin to see ourselves as spiritual beings, children of a loving God, passing through temporary and transitory human experiences and trials. From this new perspective, we see that indeed the "weapons of our warfare are not carnal but mighty in God" (v. 4) and that through God's grace we are able to bring "every thought into captivity to the obedience of Christ" (v. 5).

For further reading on Step 5, turn to page 473.

Daily Encouragement

DAY 169 READING: 2 CORINTHIANS 9:1—10:6

A Thought for the New Day: We find happiness in many things, but a special joy results when we give to supply the needs of others (9:7). Just knowing that we have brought relief to an elderly person's hardship, or seeing the smile on a grateful child's face, is an immeasurable reward. To give from the heart is to give cheerfully. (*Turn to page 397.*)

selves beyond *our sphere* (thus not reaching you), for it was to you that we came with the gospel of Christ;

15 not boasting of things beyond measure, *that is,* in other men's labors, but having hope, *that* as your faith is increased, we shall be greatly enlarged by you in our sphere,

16 to preach the gospel in the *regions* beyond you, *and* not to boast in another man's sphere of accomplishment.

STEP 10 17 But *"He who glories, let him glory in the Lord."*
18 For not he who commends himself is approved, but whom the Lord commends.

11 Oh, that you would bear with me in a little folly—and indeed you do bear with me.

2 For I am jealous for you with godly jealousy. For I have betrothed you to one husband, that I may present *you as* a chaste virgin to Christ.

3 But I fear, lest somehow, as the serpent deceived Eve by his craftiness, so your minds may be corrupted from the simplicity that is in Christ.

4 For if he who comes preaches another Jesus whom we have not preached, or *if* you receive a different spirit which you have not received, or a different gospel which you have not accepted, you may well put up with it.

5 For I consider that I am not at all inferior to the most eminent apostles.

6 Even though *I am* untrained in speech, yet *I am* not in knowledge. But we have been thoroughly made manifest among you in all things.

7 Did I commit sin in abasing myself that you might be exalted, because I preached the gospel of God to you free of charge?

8 I robbed other churches, taking wages *from them* to minister to you.

9 And when I was present with you, and in need, I was a burden to no one, for what was lacking to me the brethren who came from Macedonia supplied. And in everything I kept myself from being burdensome to you, and so I will keep *myself.*

10 As the truth of Christ is in me, no one shall stop me from this boasting in the regions of Achaia.

11 Why? Because I do not love you? God knows!

12 But what I do, I will also continue to do, that I may cut off the opportunity from those who desire an opportunity to be regarded just as we are in the things of which they boast.

13 For such *are* false apostles, deceitful workers, transforming themselves into apostles of Christ.

14 And no wonder! For Satan himself transforms himself into an angel of light.

15 Therefore *it is* no great thing if his ministers also transform themselves into ministers of righteousness, whose end will be according to their works.

16 I say again, let no one think me a fool. If otherwise, at least receive me as a fool, that I also may boast a little.

17 What I speak, I speak not according to the Lord, but as it were, foolishly, in this confidence of boasting.

18 Seeing that many boast according to the flesh, I also will boast.

19 For you put up with fools gladly, since you *yourselves* are wise!

20 For you put up with it if one brings you into bondage, if one devours *you,* if one takes *from you,* if one exalts himself, if one strikes you on the face.

21 To *our* shame, I say that we were too weak for that! But in whatever anyone is bold—I speak foolishly—I am bold also.

22 Are they Hebrews? So *am* I. Are

STEP 10

*Continued to take personal inventory
and when we were wrong promptly admitted it.*

2 Corinthians 10:17, 18

The right attitude is nine-tenths of the battle. This is true in many areas of life, but it is especially true for those of us seeking to maintain the spiritual, emotional, and physical gains we have experienced in recovery. Feeling genuinely good about ourselves and our lives, we should express our gratitude. As we look about us and see how far we have come, we may be tempted to pat ourselves on the back or let the praise and admiration of others "go to our heads" a little. But let us remember who brought us to this point in our recovery. The Lord Jesus is the One who has saved us and empowered us with the Holy Spirit. God's Word has brought us comfort, motivation, and hope. He is both the source and the completion of our recovery. We have every right to rejoice in our new abilities and strengths. If we do so with hearts full of gratitude and thankfulness to our wonderful Lord, His approving smile will continue to light and direct our lives.

For further reading on Step 10, turn to page 407.

Daily Encouragement

DAY 170 READING: 2 CORINTHIANS 10:7—11:15

A Thought for the New Day: Paul had committed the social error of being an unpaid missionary (11:7). His worldly beneficiaries therefore concluded that his services must be worth just what he charged—nothing. Such evaluations are common. Yet the Corinthians owed Paul their lives, and more! We need to pray for tender hearts so that we may always be aware of and grateful for God's kindness to us. (*Turn to page 399.*)

they Israelites? So *am* I. Are they the seed of Abraham? So *am* I.

23 Are they ministers of Christ?—I speak as a fool—I *am* more: in labors more abundant, in stripes above measure, in prisons more frequently, in deaths often.

24 From the Jews five times I received forty *stripes* minus one.

25 Three times I was beaten with rods; once I was stoned; three times I was shipwrecked; a night and a day I have been in the deep;

26 *in* journeys often, *in* perils of waters, *in* perils of robbers, *in* perils of *my own* countrymen, *in* perils of the Gentiles, *in* perils in the city, *in* perils in the wilderness, *in* perils in the sea, *in* perils among false brethren;

27 in weariness and toil, in sleeplessness often, in hunger and thirst, in fastings often, in cold and nakedness—

28 besides the other things, what comes upon me daily: my deep concern for all the churches.

29 Who is weak, and I am not weak? Who is made to stumble, and I do not burn with indignation?

30 If I must boast, I will boast in the things which concern my infirmity.

31 The God and Father of our Lord Jesus Christ, who is blessed forever, knows that I am not lying.

32 In Damascus the governor, under Aretas the king, was guarding the city of the Damascenes with a garrison, desiring to apprehend me;

33 but I was let down in a basket through a window in the wall, and escaped from his hands.

12 It is doubtless not profitable for me to boast. I will come to visions and revelations of the Lord:

2 I know a man in Christ who fourteen years ago—whether in the body I do not know, or whether out of the body I do not

know, God knows—such a one was caught up to the third heaven.

3 And I know such a man— whether in the body or out of the body I do not know, God knows—

4 how he was caught up into Paradise and heard inexpressible words, which it is not lawful for a man to utter.

5 Of such a one I will boast; yet of myself I will not boast, except in my infirmities.

6 For though I might desire to boast, I will not be a fool; for I will speak the truth. But I forbear, lest anyone should think of me above what he sees me *to be* or hears from me.

7 And lest I should be exalted above measure by the abundance of the revelations, a thorn in the flesh was given to me, a messenger of Satan to buffet me, lest I be exalted above measure.

8 Concerning this thing I pleaded with the Lord three times that it might depart from me.

9 And He said to me, "My grace is sufficient for you, for My strength is made perfect in weakness." Therefore most gladly I will rather boast in my infirmities, that the power of Christ may rest upon me.

10 Therefore I take pleasure in infirmities, in reproaches, in needs, in persecutions, in distresses, for Christ's sake. For when I am weak, then I am strong.

11 I have become a fool in boasting; you have compelled me. For I ought to have been commended by you; for in nothing was I behind the most eminent apostles, though I am nothing.

12 Truly the signs of an apostle were accomplished among you with all perseverance, in signs and wonders and mighty deeds.

13 For what is it in which you were inferior to other churches, except that I myself was not burdensome to you? Forgive me this wrong!

14 Now *for* the third time I am

STEP 11

STEP 11

*Sought through prayer and meditation to improve our conscious contact with God **as we understood Him,** praying only for knowledge of His will for us and the power to carry that out.*

2 Corinthians 12:7–10

Although we may chuckle at the mythologies of some earlier cultures, we have bowed to a mythology of our own making—the chief of which is the myth of self-sufficiency. The main virtues taught by this myth are determination, shrewdness, and pride. Believe it or not, many Christians are found among its devotees.

The great apostle Paul, however, found his strength in an attitude and philosophy diametrically opposed to the myth of self-sufficiency. Only those who walk with God and have experienced His power can plumb the depths of God's words to Paul, "My grace is sufficient for you, for My strength is made perfect in weakness." Paul knew that the less he tried to do in his own power, the more God's perfect and miraculous power was able to work and move.

Each of us experiences the power of God in our lives today to the extent that we are willing to rejoice in our struggles and problems, admitting our inability and trusting in His total ability.

For further reading on Step 11, turn to page 405.

Daily Encouragement

DAY 171 READING: 2 CORINTHIANS 11:16—12:13

A Thought for the New Day: Paul was only too aware of his weakness and realized that he could do nothing about it by himself. At that point, Paul learned something new—that our weakness is just the opportunity for God's strength to take over (12:9). That is what God meant by "My grace." God's supernatural power goes to work when all our own resources are exhausted. We can avoid many such crises if we learn to lean on the arms that never fail. (*Turn to page 401.*)

ready to come to you. And I will not be burdensome to you; for I do not seek yours, but you. For the children ought not to lay up for the parents, but the parents for the children.

15 And I will very gladly spend and be spent for your souls; though the more abundantly I love you, the less I am loved.

16 But be that *as it may*, I did not burden you. Nevertheless, being crafty, I caught you with guile!

17 Did I take advantage of you by any of those whom I sent to you?

18 I urged Titus, and sent our brother with *him*. Did Titus take advantage of you? Did we not walk in the same spirit? Did *we* not *walk* in the same steps?

19 Again, do you think that we excuse ourselves to you? We speak before God in Christ. But *we do* all things, beloved, for your edification.

20 For I fear lest, when I come, I shall not find you such as I wish, and *that* I shall be found by you such as you do not wish; lest *there be* contentions, jealousies, outbursts of wrath, selfish ambitions, backbitings, whisperings, conceits, tumults;

21 *and* lest, when I come again, my God will humble me among you, and I shall mourn for many who have sinned before and have not repented of the uncleanness, fornication, and licentiousness which they have practiced.

13 This *will be* the third *time* I am coming to you. *"By the mouth of two or three witnesses every word shall be established."*

2 I have told you before, and foretell as if I were present the second time, and now being absent I write to those who have sinned before,

and to all the rest, that if I come again I will not spare—

3 since you seek a proof of Christ speaking in me, who is not weak toward you, but mighty in you.

4 For though He was crucified in weakness, yet He lives by the power of God. For we also are weak in Him, but we shall live with Him by the power of God toward you.

5 Examine yourselves *as to* whether you are in the faith. Prove yourselves. Do you not know yourselves, that Jesus Christ is in you?—unless indeed you are disqualified. **STEP 4**

6 But I trust that you will know that we are not disqualified.

7 Now I pray to God that you do no evil, not that we should appear approved, but that you should do what is honorable, though we may seem disqualified.

8 For we can do nothing against the truth, but for the truth.

9 For we are glad when we are weak and you are strong. And this also we pray, that you may be made complete.

10 Therefore I write these things being absent, lest being present I should use sharpness, according to the authority which the Lord has given me for edification and not for destruction.

11 Finally, brethren, farewell. Become complete. Be of good comfort, be of one mind, live in peace; and the God of love and peace will be with you.

12 Greet one another with a holy kiss.

13 All the saints greet you.

14 The grace of the Lord Jesus Christ, and the love of God, and the communion of the Holy Spirit *be* with you all. Amen.

STEP 4

Made a searching and fearless moral inventory of ourselves.

2 Corinthians 13:5

Throughout the letter of 2 Corinthians, Paul had willingly submitted his ministry to the scrutiny of others. He had answered questions concerning his credentials and his motivation for preaching the gospel. Here he told the church at Corinth to examine themselves regarding whether their lives demonstrated that they were willing to obey God.

This is also the emphasis of our work in Step 4. Self-examination is seldom joyous. It may be terrifying or tedious or troublesome, but it is absolutely necessary if we intend to prove the sincerity of our commitment to recovery.

A doctor cannot diagnose a patient's illness merely by looking at his outward appearance, nor can we begin to recover before we understand the causes and depth of our sickness. Careful examination takes time and possibly includes some painful probing. Our willingness to endure its hardships is a manifestation of the new life we have begun to lead in Christ Jesus.

For further reading on Step 4, turn to page 411.

Daily Encouragement

DAY 172 READING: 2 CORINTHIANS 12:14—13:14

A Thought for the New Day: Communion is a state of mutually sympathetic relations between persons. All parties in communion have one mind. This relationship is also called "fellowship." Paul prayed that we might have that kind of communion with the Holy Spirit—that is, with God Himself (13:14). We need no longer be orphans in the world, but we can have the real presence of God Himself to walk beside us and lead us through our days. (*Turn to page 403.*)

THE EPISTLE OF PAUL THE APOSTLE TO THE
GALATIANS

PAUL, an apostle (not from men nor through man, but through Jesus Christ and God the Father who raised Him from the dead),

2 and all the brethren who are with me,

To the churches of Galatia:

3 Grace to you and peace from God the Father and our Lord Jesus Christ,

STEP 2
4 who gave Himself for our sins, that He might deliver us from this present evil age, according to the will of our God and Father,

5 to whom *be* glory forever and ever. Amen.

6 I marvel that you are turning away so soon from Him who called you in the grace of Christ, to a different gospel,

7 which is not another; but there are some who trouble you and want to pervert the gospel of Christ.

8 But even if we, or an angel from heaven, preach any other gospel to you than what we have preached to you, let him be accursed.

9 As we have said before, so now I say again, if anyone preaches any other gospel to you than what you have received, let him be accursed.

10 For do I now persuade men, or God? Or do I seek to please men? For if I still pleased men, I would not be a servant of Christ.

11 But I make known to you, brethren, that the gospel which was preached by me is not according to man.

12 For I neither received it from man, nor was I taught *it*, but *it came* through the revelation of Jesus Christ.

13 For you have heard of my former conduct in Judaism, how I persecuted the church of God beyond measure and *tried to* destroy it.

14 And I advanced in Judaism beyond many of my contemporaries in my own nation, being more exceedingly zealous for the traditions of my fathers.

15 But when it pleased God, who separated me from my mother's womb and called *me* through His grace,

16 to reveal His Son in me, that I might preach Him among the Gentiles, I did not immediately confer with flesh and blood,

17 nor did I go up to Jerusalem to those *who were* apostles before me; but I went to Arabia, and returned again to Damascus.

18 Then after three years I went up to Jerusalem to see Peter, and remained with him fifteen days.

19 But I saw none of the other apostles except James, the Lord's brother.

20 (Now *concerning* the things which I write to you, indeed, before God, I do not lie.)

21 Afterward I went into the regions of Syria and Cilicia;

22 and I was unknown by face to the churches of Judea which *were* in Christ.

23 But they were hearing only, "He who formerly persecuted us now preaches the faith which he once *tried to* destroy."

24 And they glorified God in me.

2 Then after fourteen years I went up again to Jerusalem with Barnabas, and also took Titus with *me*.

2 And I went up by revelation, and communicated to them that gospel which I preach among the Gentiles, but privately to those who were of reputation, lest by any means I might run, or had run, in vain.

3 Yet not even Titus who *was* with me, being a Greek, was compelled to be circumcised.

STEP 2

Came to believe that a Power greater than ourselves could restore us to sanity.

Galatians 1:4

Our meditation verse for today could be considered the core of Step 2. It addresses every need and part of our lives at this beginning stage of recovery. The verse includes three important points, each crucial to our understanding.

First, we see that Christ voluntarily died for us. Even though we have felt unlovable and unworthy, God gazed across the centuries and loved you and me enough to choose to die for us.

Second, because He died for us and rose from the dead, He now has the power "to deliver us from this present evil age." The world around us is controlled and manipulated by Satan to cause us continual temptation, struggle, and harm. But the power of Christ can deliver us from the bondage of harmful addictions and behaviors.

Third, Christ's power is not only able to provide deliverance, but God the Father deeply desires this for each of us. God loves us and wills to save us. All that remains is for us to believe Him.

For further reading on Step 2, turn to page 435.

Daily Encouragement

DAY 173 READING: GALATIANS 1:1–24

A Thought for the New Day: Why didn't Paul immediately want to discuss his newfound faith with others? Why go to Arabia of all places (v. 17)? All his life Paul had followed human counsel that had led him astray, but now he wanted to meet with God alone. There, in the desert of Arabia, Paul thought and prayed about all that happened to him. We need to make sure to have our own private Arabias, where we can meet with God away from all distractions. (*Turn to page 405.*)

4 But *this occurred* because of false brethren secretly brought in (who came in by stealth to spy out our liberty which we have in Christ Jesus, that they might bring us into bondage),

5 to whom we did not yield submission even for an hour, that the truth of the gospel might continue with you.

6 But from those who seemed to be something—whatever they were, it makes no difference to me; God shows personal favoritism to no man—for those who seemed to *be something* added nothing to me.

7 But on the contrary, when they saw that the gospel for the uncircumcised had been committed to me, as *the gospel* for the circumcised *was* to Peter

8 (for He who worked effectively in Peter for the apostleship to the circumcised also worked effectively in me toward the Gentiles),

9 and when James, Cephas, and John, who seemed to be pillars, perceived the grace that had been given to me, they gave me and Barnabas the right hand of fellowship, that we *should go* to the Gentiles and they to the circumcised.

10 *They desired* only that we should remember the poor, the very thing which I also was eager to do.

11 But when Peter had come to Antioch, I withstood him to his face, because he was to be blamed;

12 for before certain men came from James, he would eat with the Gentiles; but when they came, he withdrew and separated himself, fearing those who were of the circumcision.

13 And the rest of the Jews also played the hypocrite with him, so that even Barnabas was carried away with their hypocrisy.

14 But when I saw that they were not straightforward about the truth of the gospel, I said to Peter before *them* all, "If you, being a Jew, live in the manner of Gentiles and not as the Jews, why do you compel Gentiles to live as Jews?

15 "We *who are* Jews by nature, and not sinners of the Gentiles,

16 "knowing that a man is not justified by the works of the law but by faith in Jesus Christ, even we have believed in Christ Jesus, that we might be justified by faith in Christ and not by the works of the law; for by the works of the law no flesh shall be justified.

17 "But if, while we seek to be justified by Christ, we ourselves also are found sinners, *is* Christ therefore a minister of sin? Certainly not!

18 "For if I build again those things which I destroyed, I make myself a transgressor.

19 "For I through the law died to the law that I might live to God.

20 "I have been crucified with Christ; it is no longer I who live, but Christ lives in me; and the *life* which I now live in the flesh I live by faith in the Son of God, who loved me and gave Himself for me. STEP 11

21 "I do not set aside the grace of God; for if righteousness *comes* through the law, then Christ died in vain."

3 O foolish Galatians! Who has bewitched you that you should not obey the truth, before whose eyes Jesus Christ was clearly portrayed among you as crucified? 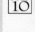 STEP 10

2 This only I want to learn from you: Did you receive the Spirit by the works of the law, or by the hearing of faith?

3 Are you so foolish? Having begun in the Spirit, are you now being made perfect by the flesh?

4 Have you suffered so many things in vain—if indeed *it was* in vain?

5 Therefore He who supplies the Spirit to you and works miracles among you, *does He do it* by the works of the law, or by the hearing of faith?—

*Sought through prayer and meditation to improve our conscious contact with God **as we understood Him,** praying only for knowledge of His will for us and the power to carry that out.*

Galatians 2:20

One of our most fundamental recovery principles is captured in the simple admonition: "Let go, and let God." We let go of our compulsive need to be at centerstage or even at the center of our own universe. We let go of desperate efforts to function as our own higher power. We have indeed "been crucified with Christ," and we have died to and let go of excessive codependent reliance upon people and things.

Through spiritual rebirth and awakening, we let God resume His rightful position as the centerpiece of our lives. As we seek spiritual solutions to the old dependent hungers of the flesh, we discover that "we will intuitively know how to handle situations which used to baffle us. We will suddenly realize that God is doing for us what we could not do for ourselves" (*Alcoholics Anonymous*, p. 84).

For further reading on Step 11, turn to page 413.

Daily Encouragement

DAY 174 READING: GALATIANS 2:1–21

A Thought for the New Day: Galatians 2:20 is one of the most fabulous statements in the Bible. Paul said he had died, and yet he lived! Were these the words of a madman? No, Paul put his finger on the nerve of the New Testament faith. Christians have really died to their former reasons for living. Their new life consists in the real power of Christ in them, enabling them to perform works of eternal value. Christ is our life, and we desire no life apart from Him. (*Turn to page 407.*)

6 just as Abraham *"believed God, and it was accounted to him for righteousness."*

7 Therefore know that *only* those who are of faith are sons of Abraham.

8 And the Scripture, foreseeing that God would justify the nations by faith, preached the gospel to Abraham beforehand, *saying, "In you all the nations shall be blessed."*

9 So then those who *are* of faith are blessed with believing Abraham.

10 For as many as are of the works of the law are under the curse; for it is written, *"Cursed is everyone who does not continue in all things which are written in the book of the law, to do them."*

11 But that no one is justified by the law in the sight of God *is* evident, for *"The just shall live by faith."*

12 Yet the law is not of faith, but *"The man who does them shall live by them."*

13 Christ has redeemed us from the curse of the law, having become a curse for us (for it is written, *"Cursed is everyone who hangs on a tree"*),

14 that the blessing of Abraham might come upon the Gentiles in Christ Jesus, that we might receive the promise of the Spirit through faith.

15 Brethren, I speak in the manner of men: Though *it is* only a man's covenant, yet *if it is* confirmed, no one annuls or adds to it.

16 Now to Abraham and his Seed were the promises made. He does not say, "And to seeds," as of many, but as of one, *"And to your Seed,"* who is Christ.

17 And this I say, *that* the law, which was four hundred and thirty years later, cannot annul the covenant that was confirmed before by God in Christ, that it should make the promise of no effect.

18 For if the inheritance *is* of the law, *it is* no longer of promise; but God gave *it* to Abraham by promise.

19 What purpose then *does* the law *serve?* It was added because of transgressions, till the Seed should come to whom the promise was made; *and it was* appointed through angels by the hand of a mediator.

20 Now a mediator does not *mediate* for one *only,* but God is one.

21 *Is* the law then against the promises of God? Certainly not! For if there had been a law given which could have given life, truly righteousness would have been by the law.

22 But the Scripture has confined all under sin, that the promise by faith in Jesus Christ might be given to those who believe.

23 But before faith came, we were kept under guard by the law, kept for the faith which would afterward be revealed.

24 Therefore the law was our tutor *to bring us* to Christ, that we might be justified by faith.

25 But after faith has come, we are no longer under a tutor.

26 For you are all sons of God through faith in Christ Jesus.

27 For as many of you as were baptized into Christ have put on Christ.

28 There is neither Jew nor Greek, there is neither slave nor free, there is neither male nor female; for you are all one in Christ Jesus.

29 And if you *are* Christ's, then you are Abraham's seed, and heirs according to the promise.

4 Now I say *that* the heir, as long as he is a child, does not differ at all from a slave, though he is master of all,

2 but is under guardians and stewards until the time appointed by the father.

3 Even so we, when we were children, were in bondage under the elements of the world.

STEP 10

*Continued to take personal inventory
and when we were wrong promptly admitted it.*

Galatians 3:1–9

Every believer discovers that it is possible to fall prey to the "Galatian Syndrome." Daily, hourly we are making a choice: Do I trust in and depend on the power of the Holy Spirit, or do I attempt to do God's will in my own strength? The Galatian church had sadly chosen the latter. They had trusted in Christ to save them and had received the Holy Spirit's power to live for God. But soon they began to ignore the voice and leading of the Holy Spirit and instead trusted in certain works or Jewish rituals to make them righteous.

If we find ourselves developing a list of dos and don'ts that goes beyond Scripture in order to feel accepted by God, we have slipped into the same trap of legalism and performance. The faith that saved us is the faith that will keep us walking with God and knowing His blessing. His power and wisdom are ours for the asking as we continue to abide in Him.

For further reading on Step 10, turn to page 445.

Daily Encouragement

DAY 175 READING: GALATIANS 3:1–29

A Thought for the New Day: Did Paul actually say Christians ought never to obey rules (v.11)? Of course not! But we cannot please God by merely following the rule book. People may obey laws for reasons other than love for God or others. What gladdens the heart of God is the same as what delights a good parent—when His children *want* to live for Him rather than feel they *have* to. Such living springs from faith that sees the supreme necessity of Christ for life that counts. (*Turn to page 409.*)

4 But when the fullness of the time had come, God sent forth His Son, born of a woman, born under the law,

STEP 3 **5** to redeem those who were under the law, that we might receive the adoption as sons.

6 And because you are sons, God has sent forth the Spirit of His Son into your hearts, crying out, "Abba, Father!"

7 Therefore you are no longer a slave but a son, and if a son, then an heir of God through Christ.

8 But then, indeed, when you did not know God, you served those which by nature are not gods.

STEP 10 **9** But now after you have known God, or rather are known by God, how *is it that* you turn again to the weak and beggarly elements, to which you desire again to be in bondage?

10 You observe days and months and seasons and years.

11 I am afraid for you, lest I have labored for you in vain.

12 Brethren, I urge you to become as I *am*, for I *am* as you *are*. You have not injured me at all.

13 You know that because of physical infirmity I preached the gospel to you at the first.

14 And my trial which was in my flesh you did not despise or reject, but you received me as an angel of God, *even* as Christ Jesus.

15 What then was the blessing you *enjoyed*? For I bear you witness that, if possible, you would have plucked out your own eyes and given them to me.

16 Have I therefore become your enemy because I tell you the truth?

17 They zealously court you, *but* for no good; yes, they want to exclude you, that you may be zealous for them.

18 But it is good to be zealous in a good thing always, and not only when I am present with you.

19 My little children, for whom I labor in birth again until Christ is formed in you,

20 I would like to be present with you now and to change my tone; for I have doubts about you.

21 Tell me, you who desire to be under the law, do you not hear the law?

22 For it is written that Abraham had two sons: the one by a bondwoman, the other by a freewoman.

23 But he *who was* of the bondwoman was born according to the flesh, and he of the freewoman through promise,

24 which things are symbolic. For these are the two covenants: the one from Mount Sinai which gives birth to bondage, which is Hagar—

25 for this Hagar is Mount Sinai in Arabia, and corresponds to Jerusalem which now is, and is in bondage with her children—

26 but the Jerusalem above is free, which is the mother of us all.

27 For it is written:

"Rejoice, O barren,
You who do not bear!
Break forth and shout,
You who do not travail!
For the desolate has
  many more children
Than she who has a husband."

28 Now we, brethren, as Isaac *was*, are children of promise.

29 But, as he who was born according to the flesh then persecuted him *who was born* according to the Spirit, even so *it is* now.

30 Nevertheless what does the Scripture say? *"Cast out the bondwoman and her son, for the son of the bondwoman shall not be heir with the son of the freewoman."*

31 So then, brethren, we are not children of the bondwoman but of the free.

5 Stand fast therefore in the liberty by which Christ has made us free, and do not be entangled again with a yoke of bondage. STEP 10

STEP 3

*Made a decision to turn our will and our lives
over to the care of God **as we understood Him.***

Galatians 4:5, 6

The children of India have a special form of address that they use for their earthly fathers. It can be roughly translated "Daddy, Sir." Their word for *daddy* shows the inherent trust of a child toward a wise and loving parent. Their word for *sir* denotes respect for the power and authority of the father over the life of his child.

In Step 3 of our recovery program and in our reading for today, we come to understand the same concept. In fact, the words "Abba, Father" convey a similar concept in themselves. "Abba" is a word that shows simple trust and dependence. We have come to trust God and to depend upon His power to help us. Now we are ready to acknowledge the second part of the phrase—"Father." As children of God, we have the wonderful privileges of His grace, but we also acknowledge His authority and power. Our lives belong to Him, and we willingly yield them to His wise and loving control.

For further reading on Step 3, turn to page 415.

Daily Encouragement

DAY 176 READING: GALATIANS 4:1–20

A Thought for the New Day: We worship what we value most. Some people may practice formal religious rituals, although they really worship wealth, power, or just themselves. But now we have been set free to worship God Himself, as He truly is (vv. 7–9). St. Augustine wrote, "You have made us for Yourself, O God, and our hearts are restless, nor can they rest, until they find their rest in You." Serving God is our highest privilege. *(Turn to page 411.)*

2 Indeed I, Paul, say to you that if you become circumcised, Christ will profit you nothing.

3 And I testify again to every man who becomes circumcised that he is a debtor to keep the whole law.

4 You have become estranged from Christ, you who *attempt to* be justified by law; you have fallen from grace.

5 For we through the Spirit eagerly wait for the hope of righteousness by faith.

6 For in Christ Jesus neither circumcision nor uncircumcision avails anything, but faith working through love.

7 You ran well. Who hindered you from obeying the truth?

8 This persuasion does not *come* from Him who calls you.

9 A little leaven leavens the whole lump.

10 I have confidence in you, in the Lord, that you will have no other mind; but he who troubles you shall bear his judgment, whoever he is.

11 And I, brethren, if I still preach circumcision, why do I still suffer persecution? Then the offense of the cross has ceased.

12 I could wish that those who trouble you would even cut themselves off!

STEP 10

13 For you, brethren, have been called to liberty; only do not *use* liberty as an opportunity for the flesh, but through love serve one another.

14 For all the law is fulfilled in one word, *even* in this: *"You shall love your neighbor as yourself."*

15 But if you bite and devour one another, beware lest you be consumed by one another!

STEP 6

16 I say then: Walk in the Spirit, and you shall not fulfill the lust of the flesh.

17 For the flesh lusts against the Spirit, and the Spirit against the flesh; and these are contrary to one another, so that you do not do the things that you wish.

18 But if you are led by the Spirit, you are not under the law.

STEP 4

19 Now the works of the flesh are evident, which are: adultery, fornication, uncleanness, licentiousness,

20 idolatry, sorcery, hatred, contentions, jealousies, outbursts of wrath, selfish ambitions, dissensions, heresies,

21 envy, murders, drunkenness, revelries, and the like; of which I tell you beforehand, just as I also told *you* in time past, that those who practice such things will not inherit the kingdom of God.

STEP 11

22 But the fruit of the Spirit is love, joy, peace, longsuffering, kindness, goodness, faithfulness,

23 gentleness, self-control. Against such there is no law.

24 And those *who are* Christ's have crucified the flesh with its passions and desires.

25 If we live in the Spirit, let us also walk in the Spirit.

26 Let us not become conceited, provoking one another, envying one another.

STEP 12

6 Brethren, if a man is overtaken in any trespass, you who *are* spiritual restore such a one in a spirit of gentleness, considering yourself lest you also be tempted.

2 Bear one another's burdens, and so fulfill the law of Christ.

STEP 4

3 For if anyone thinks himself to be something, when he is nothing, he deceives himself.

4 But let each one examine his own work, and then he will have rejoicing in himself alone, and not in another.

5 For each one shall bear his own load.

6 Let him who is taught the word share in all good things with him who teaches.

7 Do not be deceived, God is not mocked; for whatever a man sows, that he will also reap.

8 For he who sows to his flesh will of the flesh reap corruption, but he

Made a searching and fearless moral inventory of ourselves.

Galatians 6:3–5

One of the paradoxes of recovery is that chronically low self-esteem often results in an exaggerated sense of self-preoccupation and self-importance. The taking of a personal inventory serves to put everything back into proper balance.

What is this balance that we are seeking? On the one hand, scripture asks that we not pretend to be something we are not. It asks that we deflate our false grandiosity. On the other hand, scripture also urges that we take credit for and rejoice in our legitimate accomplishments.

This balanced perspective gained through the execution of a Step 4 inventory is important for two reasons. First, it spares us from the extremes of either grandiosity or self-condemnation. Second, this new plateau of self-honesty and self-examination lifts us away from a destructive dependence on the approval of others. We are enabled to move toward a healthy, new sense of responsibility as each of us begins to "bear his own load" (v. 5).

For further reading on Step 4, turn to page 421.

Daily Encouragement

DAY 177 READING: GALATIANS 4:21—6:5

A Thought for the New Day: In Galatians 6:2, Paul focused, not on helping one another with heavy jobs, but on how we should treat one another's failings. Fixing others' faults can be a demanding task, because it is so easy to be misunderstood. Harsh criticism, resentment, and a critical attitude never do any good. Instead, we need to help one another in the same careful way a physician sets a broken bone. That requires extreme gentleness, and we must pray for that quality. *(Turn to page 413.)*

who sows to the Spirit will of the Spirit reap everlasting life.

9 And let us not grow weary while doing good, for in due season we shall reap if we do not lose heart.

10 Therefore, as we have opportunity, let us do good to all, especially to those who are of the household of faith.

11 See with what large letters I have written to you with my own hand!

12 As many as desire to make a good showing in the flesh, these *try to* compel you to be circumcised, only that they may not suffer persecution for the cross of Christ.

13 For not even those who are circumcised keep the law, but they desire to have you circumcised that they may glory in your flesh.

14 But God forbid that I should glory except in the cross of our Lord Jesus Christ, by whom the world has been crucified to me, and I to the world.

15 For in Christ Jesus neither circumcision nor uncircumcision avails anything, but a new creation.

16 And as many as walk according to this rule, peace and mercy *be* upon them, and upon the Israel of God.

17 From now on let no one trouble me, for I bear in my body the marks of the Lord Jesus.

18 Brethren, the grace of our Lord Jesus Christ *be* with your spirit. Amen.

THE EPISTLE OF PAUL THE APOSTLE TO THE
EPHESIANS

PAUL, an apostle of Jesus Christ by the will of God,

To the saints who are in Ephesus, and faithful in Christ Jesus:

2 Grace to you and peace from God our Father and the Lord Jesus Christ.

3 Blessed *be* the God and Father of our Lord Jesus Christ, who has blessed us with every spiritual blessing in the heavenly *places* in Christ,

4 just as He chose us in Him before the foundation of the world, that we should be holy and without blame before Him in love,

5 having predestined us to adoption as sons by Jesus Christ to Himself, according to the good pleasure of His will,

6 to the praise of the glory of His grace, by which He has made us accepted in the Beloved.

7 In Him we have redemption through His blood, the forgiveness of sins, according to the riches of His grace

8 which He made to abound toward us in all wisdom and prudence,

9 having made known to us the mystery of His will, according to His good pleasure which He purposed in Himself,

10 that in the dispensation of the fullness of the times He might gather together in one all things in Christ, both which are in heaven and which are on earth—in Him,

11 in whom also we have obtained an inheritance, being predestined according to the purpose of Him who works all things according to the counsel of His will,

STEP 11

*Sought through prayer and meditation to improve our conscious contact with God **as we understood Him,** praying only for knowledge of His will for us and the power to carry that out.*

Galatians 6:14

Have you ever witnessed a sports team, overly confident and boasting about its leads in a game? Every coach knows this can spell disaster. Once pride takes the place of preparedness and prudence, a team may end up beating itself.

Paul knew the only safe place for pride and boasting was "in the cross of our Lord Jesus Christ." He gloried in the love and power, the forgiveness and hope of the Cross. The longer we abide in Jesus, the more our lives will reflect Paul's sentiment. We will begin to realize that every recovery gain, every good relationship, every blessing we have comes from our association with the Cross. The allurements, displays, and accepted norms of the world will mean less and less to us. In fact, we will discover that we have about as much appetite for the indulgences of the past as a dead man might. Instead, we will hunger to know our Lord deeply; and feeding on His Word, we will be fulfilled and blessed.

For further reading on Step 11, turn to page 417.

Daily Encouragement

DAY 178 READING: GALATIANS 6:6–18

A Thought for the New Day: As beneficiaries of God's great love, we have plenty of reasons for sharing His kindness with those around us. Indeed, we should expect that kindness to flow from us like an endless river of generous deeds, remembering God's great generosity to us: We are especially to keep in mind our brothers and sisters in the faith, for they are often in greatest need of our consideration (v. 10). *(Turn to page 415.)*

12 that we who first trusted in Christ should be to the praise of His glory.

13 In Him you also *trusted*, after you heard the word of truth, the gospel of your salvation; in whom also, having believed, you were sealed with the Holy Spirit of promise,

14 who is the guarantee of our inheritance until the redemption of the purchased possession, to the praise of His glory.

15 Therefore I also, after I heard of your faith in the Lord Jesus and your love for all the saints,

16 do not cease to give thanks for you, making mention of you in my prayers:

STEP 11 17 that the God of our Lord Jesus Christ, the Father of glory, may give to you the spirit of wisdom and revelation in the knowledge of Him,

18 the eyes of your understanding being enlightened; that you may know what is the hope of His calling, what are the riches of the glory of His inheritance in the saints,

19 and what *is* the exceeding greatness of His power toward us who believe, according to the working of His mighty power

20 which He worked in Christ when He raised Him from the dead and seated *Him* at His right hand in the heavenly *places*,

21 far above all principality and power and might and dominion, and every name that is named, not only in this age but also in that which is to come.

22 And He put all *things* under His feet, and gave Him *to be* head over all *things* to the church,

23 which is His body, the fullness of Him who fills all in all.

STEP 1 **2** And you *He made alive*, who were dead in trespasses and sins,

2 in which you once walked according to the course of this world,

according to the prince of the power of the air, the spirit who now works in the sons of disobedience,

3 among whom also we all once conducted ourselves in the lusts of our flesh, fulfilling the desires of the flesh and of the mind, and were by nature children of wrath, just as the others.

4 But God, who is rich in mercy, because of His great love with which He loved us, STEP 2

5 even when we were dead in trespasses, made us alive together with Christ (by grace you have been saved),

6 and raised *us* up together, and made *us* sit together in the heavenly *places* in Christ Jesus,

7 that in the ages to come He might show the exceeding riches of His grace in *His* kindness toward us in Christ Jesus.

8 For by grace you have been saved through faith, and that not of yourselves; *it is* the gift of God, STEP 3

9 not of works, lest anyone should boast.

10 For we are His workmanship, created in Christ Jesus for good works, which God prepared beforehand that we should walk in them. STEP 12

11 Therefore remember that you, once Gentiles in the flesh—who are called Uncircumcision by what is called the Circumcision made in the flesh by hands—

12 that at that time you were without Christ, being aliens from the commonwealth of Israel and strangers from the covenants of promise, having no hope and without God in the world.

13 But now in Christ Jesus you who once were far off have been made near by the blood of Christ.

14 For He Himself is our peace, who has made both one, and has broken down the middle wall of division *between us*,

15 having abolished in His flesh the

STEP 3

Made a decision to turn our will and our lives
*over to the care of God **as we understood Him.***

Ephesians 2:8, 9

A recovery slogan that may sound somewhat cryptic to the new-comer is the dangling statement, "But for the grace of God. . . ." What does it mean? For some, it means that but for the grace of God, they might never have reached an emotional, spiritual, or physical "bottom"; and they might not have begun the upward journey of recovery growth.

"But for the grace of God" also means that the miracle of our recovery is not paid for through some ledger of good works or good behavior. Our old perfectionism may boast that our redemption can be purchased through the refining of ourselves or our physical environment. In contrast, the gospel cautions against this boasting because our salvation is not to be earned; it is a gift from God.

In recovery we surrender this false god of human perfection, and we embrace the merciful grace of God. We surrender the need to be perfect craftsmen; and, instead, we accept the creation He has made us to be, "His workmanship, created in Christ Jesus" (v. 10).

For further reading on Step 3, turn to page 559.

Daily Encouragement

DAY 179 READING: EPHESIANS 1:1—2:13

A Thought for the New Day: God used to seem far off, but now we have been brought near, just as we feel near to a special friend (2:13). A great Old Testament saint, Abraham, was called "the friend of God," and Jesus called His early followers His "friends." God wants us to be His friends, too, and He has opened the way for us through the life and death of His Son. (*Turn to page 417.*)

enmity, *that is*, the law of commandments *contained* in ordinances, so as to create in Himself one new man *from* the two, *thus* making peace,

16 and that He might reconcile them both to God in one body through the cross, thereby putting to death the enmity.

17 And He came and preached peace to you who were afar off and to those who were near.

18 For through Him we both have access by one Spirit to the Father.

19 Now, therefore, you are no longer strangers and foreigners, but fellow citizens with the saints and members of the household of God,

20 having been built on the foundation of the apostles and prophets, Jesus Christ Himself being the chief corner*stone*,

21 in whom the whole building, being joined together, grows into a holy temple in the Lord,

22 in whom you also are being built together for a habitation of God in the Spirit.

3 For this reason I, Paul, the prisoner of Jesus Christ for you Gentiles—

2 if indeed you have heard of the dispensation of the grace of God which was given to me for you,

3 how that by revelation He made known to me the mystery (as I wrote before in a few words,

4 by which, when you read, you may understand my knowledge in the mystery of Christ),

5 which in other ages was not made known to the sons of men, as it has now been revealed by the Spirit to His holy apostles and prophets:

6 that the Gentiles should be fellow heirs, of the same body, and partakers of His promise in Christ through the gospel,

7 of which I became a minister according to the gift of the grace of God given to me by the effective working of His power.

8 To me, who am less than the least of all the saints, this grace was given, that I should preach among the Gentiles the unsearchable riches of Christ,

9 and to make all *people* see what *is* the fellowship of the mystery, which from the beginning of the ages has been hidden in God who created all things through Jesus Christ;

10 to the intent that now the manifold wisdom of God might be made known by the church to the principalities and powers in the heavenly *places*,

11 according to the eternal purpose which He accomplished in Christ Jesus our Lord,

12 in whom we have boldness and access with confidence through faith in Him.

13 Therefore I ask that you do not lose heart at my tribulations for you, which is your glory.

14 For this reason I bow my knees to the Father of our Lord Jesus Christ,

15 from whom the whole family in heaven and earth is named,

16 that He would grant you, according to the riches of His glory, to be strengthened with might through His Spirit in the inner man,

17 that Christ may dwell in your hearts through faith; that you, being rooted and grounded in love,

18 may be able to comprehend with all the saints what *is* the width and length and depth and height—

19 to know the love of Christ which passes knowledge; that you may be filled with all the fullness of God.

20 Now to Him who is able to do exceedingly abundantly above all that we ask or think, according to the power that works in us,

21 to Him *be* glory in the church by Christ Jesus throughout all ages, world without end. Amen.

*Sought through prayer and meditation to improve our conscious contact with God **as we understood Him,** praying only for knowledge of His will for us and the power to carry that out.*

Ephesians 3:14–20

In this prayer, Paul makes three petitions for the believer.

The first asks for inner strength through the Holy Spirit. The inner man is the part of us that includes our mind, will, and emotions. Step 11 of our recovery process emphasizes this area of life. Our inner man has experienced rebirth. Now that part of us needs daily strengthening by the Holy Spirit if we are to be all that we are capable of being.

Next, Paul prays for the indwelling of Christ—for His preeminence in our thoughts, actions, and life-styles.

Finally, when we have been strengthened by the Holy Spirit and indwelt fully by Christ, we are able to begin to understand both intellectually and experientially, the love of Christ. Christ's love is so great toward each of us that it infinitely stretches above, beneath, and around us. Nothing is too difficult for His powerful love.

For further reading on Step 11, turn to page 431.

Daily Encouragement

DAY 180 READING: EPHESIANS 2:14—3:21

A Thought for the New Day: Peace is what we experience when all the problems in our personal world seem to be under control. Fear is gone; only tranquillity remains. Such peace can be permanent when we know that Jesus is "our peace" (2:14). He will take charge of all our troubles and lead us through the circumstances of life. (*Turn to page 419.*)

4 I, therefore, the prisoner of the Lord, beseech you to have a walk worthy of the calling with which you were called,

2 with all lowliness and gentleness, with longsuffering, bearing with one another in love,

3 endeavoring to keep the unity of the Spirit in the bond of peace.

4 *There is* one body and one Spirit, just as you were called in one hope of your calling;

5 one Lord, one faith, one baptism;

6 one God and Father of all, who *is* above all, and through all, and in you all.

7 But to each one of us grace was given according to the measure of Christ's gift.

8 Therefore He says:

"When He ascended on high,
He led captivity captive,
And gave gifts to men."

9 (Now this, *"He ascended"*— what does it mean but that He also first descended into the lower parts of the earth?

10 He who descended is also the One who ascended far above all the heavens, that He might fill all things.)

11 And He Himself gave some *to be* apostles, some prophets, some evangelists, and some pastors and teachers,

12 for the equipping of the saints for the work of ministry, for the edifying of the body of Christ,

13 till we all come to the unity of the faith and the knowledge of the Son of God, to a perfect man, to the measure of the stature of the fullness of Christ;

 14 that we should no longer be children, tossed to and fro and carried about with every wind of doctrine, by the trickery of men, in the cunning craftiness by which they lie in wait to deceive,

15 but, speaking the truth in love, may grow up in all things into Him who is the head—Christ—

16 from whom the whole body, joined and knit together by what every joint supplies, according to the effective working by which every part does its share, causes growth of the body for the edifying of itself in love.

17 This I say, therefore, and testify in the Lord, that you should no longer walk as the rest of the Gentiles walk, in the futility of their mind,

18 having their understanding darkened, being alienated from the life of God, because of the ignorance that is in them, because of the hardening of their heart;

19 who, being past feeling, have given themselves over to licentiousness, to work all uncleanness with greediness.

20 But you have not so learned Christ,

21 if indeed you have heard Him and have been taught by Him, as the truth is in Jesus:

22 that you put off, concerning your former conduct, the old man which grows corrupt according to the deceitful lusts,

23 and be renewed in the spirit of your mind,

24 and that you put on the new man which was created according to God, in righteousness and true holiness.

25 Therefore, putting away lying, each one speak truth with his neighbor, for we are members of one another.

26 *"Be angry, and do not sin":* do not let the sun go down on your wrath,

27 nor give place to the devil.

28 Let him who stole steal no longer, but rather let him labor, working with *his* hands what is good, that he may have something to give him who has need.

29 Let no corrupt communication proceed out of your mouth, but

STEP 6

STEP 5

STEP 10

STEP 5

STEP 6

*Were entirely ready to have God
remove all these defects of character.*

Ephesians 4:17–23

Letting go of old dependencies is easier said than done. Each of us must come to the point where we are truly committed to making that break with our past, no matter how painful the process.

This struggle is like the one faced by Linus in the Charlie Brown comic strip. Sometimes, with seemingly great resolve, Linus will fling his tattered, dirty blanket behind him, determined never again to pick it up. After all, it is an embarrassment, it is dirty, and it gets in the way! Yet, in a moment of weakness, he runs for the comfort and security it seems to offer.

In Ephesians 4, the apostle Paul encourages Christians at Ephesus to determine once and for all with God's help to throw away their dirty, dark blankets of character defects and to desire to be completely "renewed in the spirit" of their minds (v. 23). Such renewal can take place only when we have become totally willing and ready for God to work radically in our lives.

For further reading on Step 6, turn to page 437.

Daily Encouragement

DAY 181 READING: EPHESIANS 4:1–32

A Thought for the New Day: The purpose Jesus had when He died and rose again is that we should be renewed or "regenerated." Our old natures that gave us and others so much trouble would be "put off," and the new nature that Jesus obtained for us—a nature that pleased God—would be "put on" (vv. 22–24). May we learn to clothe ourselves each morning with the new person God has provided for us in His Son. *(Turn to page 421.)*

what is good for necessary edification, that it may impart grace to the hearers.

30 And do not grieve the Holy Spirit of God, by whom you were sealed for the day of redemption.

31 Let all bitterness, wrath, anger, clamor, and evil speaking be put away from you, with all malice.

32 And be kind to one another, tenderhearted, forgiving one another, just as God in Christ also forgave you.

5 Therefore be followers of God as dear children.

2 And walk in love, as Christ also has loved us and given Himself for us, an offering and a sacrifice to God for a sweet-smelling aroma.

3 But fornication and all uncleanness or covetousness, let it not even be named among you, as is fitting for saints;

4 neither filthiness, nor foolish talking, nor coarse jesting, which are not fitting, but rather giving of thanks.

5 For this you know, that no fornicator, unclean person, nor covetous man, who is an idolater, has any inheritance in the kingdom of Christ and God.

6 Let no one deceive you with empty words, for because of these things the wrath of God comes upon the sons of disobedience.

7 Therefore do not be partakers with them.

8 For you were once darkness, but now *you are* light in the Lord. Walk as children of light

9 (for the fruit of the Spirit *is* in all goodness, righteousness, and truth),

10 proving what is acceptable to the Lord.

11 And have no fellowship with the unfruitful works of darkness, but rather expose *them*.

12 For it is shameful even to speak of those things which are done by them in secret.

13 But all things that are exposed are made manifest by the light, for whatever makes manifest is light.

14 Therefore He says:

"Awake, you who sleep,
Arise from the dead,
And Christ will give you light."

15 See then that you walk circumspectly, not as fools but as wise,

16 redeeming the time, because the days are evil.

17 Therefore do not be unwise, but understand what the will of the Lord *is*.

18 And do not be drunk with wine, in which is dissipation; but be filled with the Spirit,

19 speaking to one another in psalms and hymns and spiritual songs, singing and making melody in your heart to the Lord,

20 giving thanks always for all things to God the Father in the name of our Lord Jesus Christ,

21 submitting to one another in the fear of God.

22 Wives, submit to your own husbands, as to the Lord.

23 For the husband is head of the wife, as also Christ is head of the church; and He is the Savior of the body.

24 Therefore, just as the church is subject to Christ, so *let* the wives *be* to their own husbands in everything.

25 Husbands, love your wives, just as Christ also loved the church and gave Himself for it,

26 that He might sanctify and cleanse it with the washing of water by the word,

27 that He might present it to Himself a glorious church, not having spot or wrinkle or any such thing, but that it should be holy and without blemish.

28 So husbands ought to love their own wives as their own bodies; he who loves his wife loves himself.

29 For no one ever hated his own flesh, but nourishes and cherishes

STEP 4

Made a searching and fearless moral inventory of ourselves.

Ephesians 5:18

In Step 4, we are searching for the things that control our actions and attitudes. Many of us will have to name obvious addicting or controlling substances, such as drugs, food, or alcohol. Paul used drunkenness as an example of excessive behavior, which creates a wasted life. But attitudes ingrained in childhood can destroy sound logic and reasoning, just as overindulging in alcohol can. They, too, can control us to the point that our lives seem dissipated, wasted, and meaningless. Step 4 helps uncover those hidden chains that have bound us. Identifying them is crucial to freeing ourselves from their control.

Our ultimate goal or desire then is found in the second part of verse 18. We determine to break the bonds of all that has negatively impacted our lives and seek instead the power and peace that the Holy Spirit's control can give us.

For further reading on Step 4, turn to page 423.

Daily Encouragement

DAY 182 READING: EPHESIANS 5:1–33

A Thought for the New Day: It is easy to love those who live far away from us. Not seeing them often, the personality "warts" (that we all have) do not come into view. However, love that sees beyond and rises above these faults, poured out especially on those closest to us, is the greater proof of love. Our world becomes a more beautiful place as family members love, honor, and care for each other (v. 33). (*Turn to page 423.*)

it, just as the Lord *does* the church.

30 For we are members of His body, of His flesh and of His bones.

31 *"For this reason a man shall leave his father and mother and be joined to his wife, and the two shall become one flesh."*

32 This is a great mystery, but I speak concerning Christ and the church.

33 Nevertheless let each one of you in particular so love his own wife as himself, and let the wife *see* that she respects *her* husband.

STEP 4
6 Children, obey your parents in the Lord, for this is right.

2 *"Honor your father and mother,"* which is the first commandment with promise:

3 *"that it may be well with you and you may live long on the earth."*

4 And you, fathers, do not provoke your children to wrath, but bring them up in the training and admonition of the Lord.

5 Servants, be obedient to those who are your masters according to the flesh, with fear and trembling, in sincerity of heart, as to Christ;

6 not with eyeservice, as menpleasers, but as servants of Christ, doing the will of God from the heart,

7 with good will doing service, as to the Lord, and not to men,

8 knowing that whatever good anyone does, he will receive the same from the Lord, whether *he is* a slave or free.

9 And you, masters, do the same things to them, giving up threatening, knowing that your own Master also is in heaven, and there is no partiality with Him.

STEP 11
10 Finally, my brethren, be strong in the Lord and in the power of His might.

11 Put on the whole armor of God, that you may be able to stand against the wiles of the devil.

12 For we do not wrestle against flesh and blood, but against principalities, against powers, against the rulers of the darkness of this age, against spiritual *hosts* of wickedness in the heavenly *places*.

13 Therefore take up the whole armor of God, that you may be able to withstand in the evil day, and having done all, to stand.

14 Stand therefore, having girded your waist with truth, having put on the breastplate of righteousness,

15 and having shod your feet with the preparation of the gospel of peace;

16 above all, taking the shield of faith with which you will be able to quench all the fiery darts of the wicked one.

17 And take the helmet of salvation, and the sword of the Spirit, which is the word of God;

18 praying always with all prayer and supplication in the Spirit, being watchful to this end with all perseverance and supplication for all the saints—

19 and for me, that utterance may be given to me, that I may open my mouth boldly to make known the mystery of the gospel,

20 for which I am an ambassador in chains; that in it I may speak boldly, as I ought to speak.

21 But that you also may know my affairs *and* how I am doing, Tychicus, a beloved brother and faithful minister in the Lord, will make all things known to you;

22 whom I have sent to you for this very purpose, that you may know our affairs, and *that* he may comfort your hearts.

23 Peace to the brethren, and love with faith, from God the Father and the Lord Jesus Christ.

24 Grace *be* with all those who love our Lord Jesus Christ in sincerity. Amen.

STEP 4

Made a searching and fearless moral inventory of ourselves.

Ephesians 6:1–4

The word "family" conjures up almost as many meanings and feelings as there are people in the world. Few things can be dearer, sadder, more frustrating, or more fulfilling.

What God ordained the family to be may be very different from your actual experience as a child or a parent. Families can inflict untold hurt and trauma when individuals do not function as God intended they should. On the other hand, they can be the foundation of a healthy and fulfilling life when each member honors God and one another.

In Step 4, we are not seeking to lay blame or denigrate. We are simply seeking to understand. We need to take the model God gives us here in Ephesians and hold our relationships up to its light. Where there has been deviance from God's plan, we must realize and understand the problems that deviance caused. Then we can begin to establish positive patterns of thought and behavior.

For further reading on Step 4, turn to page 454.

Daily Encouragement

DAY 183 READING: EPHESIANS 6:1–24

A Thought for the New Day: Life is filled with struggles on every plane—physical, emotional, mental, and spiritual. Many people go down to defeat in the battle of life because they fight all alone, relying on their own limited resources. God does not ask us to win the war on our own. Rather, He provides us with the means to win every day (vv. 10–12). "Thanks *be* to God, who gives us the victory, through our Lord Jesus Christ" (1 Cor. 15:57). (*Turn to page 425.*)

THE EPISTLE OF PAUL THE APOSTLE TO THE
PHILIPPIANS

PAUL and Timothy, servants of Jesus Christ,

To all the saints in Christ Jesus who are in Philippi, with the bishops and deacons:

2 Grace to you and peace from God our Father and the Lord Jesus Christ.

3 I thank my God upon every remembrance of you,

4 always in every prayer of mine making request for you all with joy,

5 for your fellowship in the gospel from the first day until now,

STEP 12
6 being confident of this very thing, that He who has begun a good work in you will complete *it* until the day of Jesus Christ;

7 just as it is right for me to think this of you all, because I have you in my heart, inasmuch as both in my chains and in the defense and confirmation of the gospel, you all are partakers with me of grace.

8 For God is my witness, how greatly I long for you all with the affection of Jesus Christ.

STEP 9
9 And this I pray, that your love may abound still more and more in knowledge and all discernment,

10 that you may approve the things that are excellent, that you may be sincere and without offense till the day of Christ,

11 being filled with the fruits of righteousness which *are* by Jesus Christ, to the glory and praise of God.

12 But I want you to know, brethren, that the things *which happened* to me have actually turned out for the furtherance of the gospel,

13 so that it has become evident to the whole palace guard, and to all the rest, that my chains are in Christ;

14 and most of the brethren in the Lord, having become confident by my chains, are much more bold to speak the word without fear.

15 Some indeed preach Christ even from envy and strife, and some also from good will:

16 The former preach Christ from selfish ambition, not sincerely, supposing to add affliction to my chains;

17 but the latter out of love, knowing that I am appointed for the defense of the gospel.

18 What then? Only *that* in every way, whether in pretense or in truth, Christ is preached; and in this I rejoice, yes, and will rejoice.

19 For I know that this will turn out for my salvation through your prayer and the supply of the Spirit of Jesus Christ,

STEP 11
20 according to my earnest expectation and hope that in nothing I shall be ashamed, but *that* with all boldness, as always, so now also Christ will be magnified in my body, whether by life or by death.

21 For to me, to live *is* Christ, and to die *is* gain.

22 But if *I* live on in the flesh, this *will mean* fruit from *my* labor; yet what I shall choose I cannot tell.

23 For I am hard pressed between the two, having a desire to depart and be with Christ, *which is* far better.

24 Nevertheless to remain in the flesh *is* more needful for you.

25 And being confident of this, I know that I shall remain and continue with you all for your progress and joy of faith,

26 that your rejoicing for me may be more abundant in Jesus Christ by my coming to you again.

STEP 11
27 Only let your conduct be worthy of the gospel of Christ, so that whether I come and see you or am absent, I may hear of your affairs, that you stand fast in one spirit,

STEP 9

Made direct amends to such people wherever possible,
except when to do so would injure them or others.

Philippians 1:9–11

As we carry out Step 9, we are attempting to disclose ourselves to others in a very special and sensitive manner. We may feel overwhelmed by the challenge of discerning what needs to be said, to whom it should be said, and how to say it with sincerity and without offense.

If we rely solely on our own human resources to formulate the making of the amends, the challenge may indeed surpass our capabilities. Remember, however, that we have invited God's Spirit to accompany and guide us on the journey. Scripture offers the strong reassurance that, as we grow in communion with God's love, we will also "abound still more and more in knowledge and all discernment" (v. 9). We can expect with confidence that as we speak our words of amends, we are not speaking on our own power, but rather, God is speaking through us to others. He will empower us to "approve the things that are excellent" and to "be sincere and without offense" (v. 10).

For further reading on Step 9, turn to page 429.

Daily Encouragement

DAY 184 READING: PHILIPPIANS 1:1–30

A Thought for the New Day: Are you ever anxious that you will not make it to the end? Many people do make shipwreck of their lives. But take stock of yourself. Who was it that changed your life and started you down the new road that leads to God's city? Certainly not yourself. No, you are God's own work, and He never gives up on any work He begins (v. 6). He will see your through. God could not disgrace Himself by abandoning you before you reach your goal. (*Turn to page 427.*)

with one mind striving together for the faith of the gospel,

28 and not in any way terrified by your adversaries, which is to them a proof of perdition, but to you of salvation, and that from God.

29 For to you it has been granted on behalf of Christ, not only to believe in Him, but also to suffer for His sake,

30 having the same conflict which you saw in me and now hear *is* in me.

2 Therefore if *there is* any consolation in Christ, if any comfort of love, if any fellowship of the Spirit, if any affection and mercy,

2 fulfill my joy by being likeminded, having the same love, *being* of one accord, of one mind.

3 *Let* nothing *be done* through selfish ambition or conceit, but in lowliness of mind let each esteem others better than himself.

4 Let each of you look out not only for his own interests, but also for the interests of others.

5 Let this mind be in you which was also in Christ Jesus,

6 who, being in the form of God, did not consider it robbery to be equal with God,

7 but made Himself of no reputation, taking the form of a servant, *and* coming in the likeness of men.

8 And being found in appearance as a man, He humbled Himself and became obedient to *the point of* death, even the death of the cross.

9 Therefore God also has highly exalted Him and given Him the name which is above every name,

10 that at the name of Jesus every knee should bow, of those in heaven, and of those on earth, and of those under the earth,

11 and *that* every tongue should confess that Jesus Christ *is* Lord, to the glory of God the Father.

12 Therefore, my beloved, as you have always obeyed, not as in my presence only, but now much more in my absence, work out your own

salvation with fear and trembling;

13 for it is God who works in you both to will and to do for *His* good pleasure.

14 Do all things without murmuring and disputing,

15 that you may become blameless and harmless, children of God without fault in the midst of a crooked and perverse generation, among whom you shine as lights in the world,

16 holding fast the word of life, so that I may rejoice in the day of Christ that I have not run in vain or labored in vain.

17 Yes, and if I am being poured out *as a drink offering* on the sacrifice and service of your faith, I am glad and rejoice with you all.

18 For the same reason you also be glad and rejoice with me.

19 But I trust in the Lord Jesus to send Timothy to you shortly, that I also may be encouraged when I know your state.

20 For I have no one like-minded, who will sincerely care for your state.

21 For all seek their own, not the things which are of Christ Jesus.

22 But you know his proven character, that as a son with *his* father he served with me in the gospel.

23 Therefore I hope to send him at once, as soon as I see how it goes with me.

24 But I trust in the Lord that I myself shall also come shortly.

25 Yet I considered it necessary to send to you Epaphroditus, my brother, fellow worker, and fellow soldier, but your messenger and the one who ministered to my need;

26 since he was longing for you all, and was distressed because you had heard that he was sick.

27 For indeed he was sick almost unto death; but God had mercy on him, and not only on him but on me also, lest I should have sorrow upon sorrow.

STEP 8

*Made a list of all persons we had harmed,
and became willing to make amends to them all.*

Philippians 2:3, 4

When we love and are concerned only for those who can meet our own personal needs, our love is immature and self-seeking. The Holy Spirit, however, can give us a true love and concern for others. This is the focus of our attention and effort in Step 8.

In order to accomplish all that this Step asks of us, we need the "lowliness of mind" of which Paul speaks. This is not the groveling or pathetic attitude some people may conjure up at these words. Rather, it is simply a peaceful state of mind that desires to submit to God's authority and does not imprudently exalt itself. Asking God for this mind-set in our lives is the prerequisite to successfully laying hold of Step 8. Having true concern for other people and a desire to make amends to those we have hurt will be a natural outgrowth of this attitude.

For further reading on Step 8, turn to page 443.

Daily Encouragement

DAY 185 READING: PHILIPPIANS 2:1–30

A Thought for the New Day: Humility is not popular these days. It never really was. Anyone willing to take a back seat is viewed by many as a loser. If that is true, Jesus was a loser, because He "made Himself of no reputation" (v. 7). Yet we know He won His fight against evil. Prizes won by putting others down cannot long be relished because they are tainted with someone else's suffering. (*Turn to page 429.*)

28 Therefore I sent him the more eagerly, that when you see him again you may rejoice, and I may be less sorrowful.

29 Receive him therefore in the Lord with all gladness, and hold such men in esteem;

30 because for the work of Christ he came close to death, not regarding his life, to supply what was lacking in your service toward me.

3 Finally, my brethren, rejoice in the Lord. For me to write the same things to you *is* not tedious, but for you *it is* safe.

2 Beware of dogs, beware of evil workers, beware of the mutilation!

3 For we are the circumcision, who worship God in the Spirit, rejoice in Christ Jesus, and have no confidence in the flesh,

4 though I also might have confidence in the flesh. If anyone else thinks he may have confidence in the flesh, I more so:

5 circumcised the eighth day, of the stock of Israel, *of* the tribe of Benjamin, a Hebrew of the Hebrews; concerning the law, a Pharisee;

6 concerning zeal, persecuting the church; concerning the righteousness which is in the law, blameless.

STEP 11

7 But what things were gain to me, these I have counted loss for Christ.

8 But indeed I also count all things loss for the excellence of the knowledge of Christ Jesus my Lord, for whom I have suffered the loss of all things, and count them as rubbish, that I may gain Christ

9 and be found in Him, not having my own righteousness, which *is* from the law, but that which *is* through faith in Christ, the righteousness which is from God by faith;

10 that I may know Him and the power of His resurrection, and the fellowship of His sufferings, being conformed to His death,

11 if, by any means, I may attain to the resurrection from the dead.

12 Not that I have already attained, or am already perfected; but I press on, that I may lay hold of that for which Christ Jesus has also laid hold of me.

13 Brethren, I do not count myself to have apprehended; but one thing *I do*, forgetting those things which are behind and reaching forward to those things which are ahead,

14 I press toward the goal for the prize of the upward call of God in Christ Jesus.

15 Therefore let us, as many as are mature, have this mind; and if in anything you think otherwise, God will reveal even this to you.

16 Nevertheless, to *the degree* that we have already attained, let us walk by the same rule, let us be of the same mind.

17 Brethren, join in following my example, and note those who so walk, as you have us for a pattern.

18 For many walk, of whom I have told you often, and now tell you even weeping, *that they are* the enemies of the cross of Christ:

19 whose end *is* destruction, whose god *is their* belly, and *whose* glory *is* in their shame—who set their mind on earthly things.

20 For our citizenship is in heaven, from which we also eagerly wait for the Savior, the Lord Jesus Christ,

21 who will transform our lowly body that it may be conformed to His glorious body, according to the working by which He is able even to subdue all things to Himself.

4 Therefore, my beloved and longed-for brethren, my joy and crown, so stand fast in the Lord, beloved.

2 I implore Euodia and I implore Syntyche to be of the same mind in the Lord.

3 And I urge you also, true companion, help these women who la-

STEP 9

STEP 9

*Made direct amends to such people wherever possible,
except when to do so would injure them or others.*

Philippians 4:2, 3

Euodia and Syntyche were not just a couple of fussy, old women who enjoyed keeping the cauldron stirred up. In verse 2, Paul called these women fellow-laborers who had both worked hard to share the gospel. Each had been born again by faith in Jesus. Yet, angry words and hurt feelings had passed between them. Perhaps they had even dragged others into their disagreement, causing people to take sides and resulting in greater dissension in the church.

Paul told them that this was the time for apologies. This was the time to seek common ground and to build the bridges of trust and friendship. Not only would this apology and reunion benefit them. Obviously, the whole church would be strengthened and the name of Jesus Christ would receive honor instead of reproach.

Today God calls us to similar action. For our own good, as well as for the good of many others, let us determine to do our part to bring about reconciliation where it is needed.

For further reading on Step 9, turn to page 439.

Daily Encouragement

DAY 186 READING: PHILIPPIANS 3:1—4:3

A Thought for the New Day: One of the keys to success in business is long-range goals. We read of Old Testament saints who are described as seeking a better country than is found in the Palestine of this world. With their compass set for that heavenly country, those men and women achieved some great feats on this planet as well. We are better citizens here when we are good citizens of heaven (3:20). *(Turn to page 431.)*

bored with me in the gospel, with Clement also, and the rest of my fellow workers, whose names *are* in the Book of Life.

4 Rejoice in the Lord always. Again I will say, rejoice!

5 Let your gentleness be known to all men. The Lord *is* at hand.

6 Be anxious for nothing, but in everything by prayer and supplication, with thanksgiving, let your requests be made known to God;

7 and the peace of God, which surpasses all understanding, will guard your hearts and minds through Christ Jesus.

8 Finally, brethren, whatever things are true, whatever things *are* noble, whatever things *are* just, whatever things *are* pure, whatever things *are* lovely, whatever things *are* of good report, if *there is* any virtue and if *there is* anything praiseworthy—meditate on these things.

9 The things which you learned and received and heard and saw in me, these do, and the God of peace will be with you.

10 But I rejoiced in the Lord greatly that now at last your care for me has flourished again; though you surely did care, but you lacked opportunity.

11 Not that I speak in regard to need, for I have learned in whatever state I am, to be content:

12 I know how to be abased, and I know how to abound. Everywhere and in all things I have learned both to be full and to be hungry, both to abound and to suffer need.

13 I can do all things through Christ who strengthens me.

14 Nevertheless you have done well that you shared in my distress.

15 Now you Philippians know also that in the beginning of the gospel, when I departed from Macedonia, no church shared with me concerning giving and receiving but you only.

16 For even in Thessalonica you sent *aid* once and again for my necessities.

17 Not that I seek the gift, but I seek the fruit that abounds to your account.

18 Indeed I have all and abound. I am full, having received from Epaphroditus the things *which were sent* from you, a sweet-smelling aroma, an acceptable sacrifice, well pleasing to God.

19 And my God shall supply all your need according to His riches in glory by Christ Jesus.

20 Now to our God and Father *be* glory forever and ever. Amen.

21 Greet every saint in Christ Jesus. The brethren who are with me greet you.

22 All the saints greet you, but especially those who are of Caesar's household.

23 The grace of our Lord Jesus Christ be with you all. Amen.

STEP 11

*Sought through prayer and meditation to improve our conscious contact with God **as we understood Him,** praying only for knowledge of His will for us and the power to carry that out.*

Philippians 4:6–9

Step 11 urges us to seek intimate and meaningful contact with God through the spiritual channels of prayer and meditation. How are we to exercise these important disciplines in our lives?

The apostle Paul offers five ingredients for prayerful communion with God: First, we are to quiet our anxieties. We are to be still and know that God is God (Ps. 46:10), and He is in control. Second, we are to thank Him for the many good things in our lives. Third, we are to candidly lay before Him all of our sincere needs. Fourth, our time of meditation should also be a time to receive the infilling of the peace of God, a peace that transcends human understanding or comprehension. And fifth, we are to meditate on those things that are of highest value: "whatever things are true, whatever things *are* noble, whatever things *are* just, whatever things *are* pure, whatever things *are* lovely, whatever things *are* of good report" (v. 8).

For further reading on Step 11, turn to page 447.

Daily Encouragement

DAY 187 READING: PHILIPPIANS 4:4–23

A Thought for the New Day: Most, if not all, our failures are due to failure to pray "in everything" (v. 6). Matters inevitably go right when we put them in God's hands and then attend to our business of doing those things we should in order to achieve our goals. God is always willing to help us sort out our tangled affairs. We only discover the full joy of answered prayer when we make prayer a practice as constant as breathing. (*Turn to page 433.*)

THE EPISTLE OF PAUL THE APOSTLE TO THE

COLOSSIANS

PAUL, an apostle of Jesus Christ by the will of God, and Timothy our brother,

2 To the saints and faithful brethren in Christ *who are* in Colosse:

Grace to you and peace from God our Father and the Lord Jesus Christ.

3 We give thanks to the God and Father of our Lord Jesus Christ, praying always for you,

4 since we heard of your faith in Christ Jesus and of your love for all the saints;

5 because of the hope which is laid up for you in heaven, of which you heard before in the word of the truth of the gospel,

6 which has come to you, as *it has* also in all the world, and is bringing forth fruit, as *it is* also among you since the day you heard and knew the grace of God in truth;

7 as you also learned from Epaphras, our dear fellow servant, who is a faithful minister of Christ on your behalf,

8 who also declared to us your love in the Spirit.

 9 For this reason we also, since the day we heard it, do not cease to pray for you, and to ask that you may be filled with the knowledge of His will in all wisdom and spiritual understanding;

10 that you may have a walk worthy of the Lord, fully pleasing *Him,* being fruitful in every good work and increasing in the knowledge of God;

11 strengthened with all might, according to His glorious power, for all patience and longsuffering with joy;

12 giving thanks to the Father who has qualified us to be partakers of the inheritance of the saints in the light.

13 He has delivered us from the power of darkness and translated *us* into the kingdom of the Son of His love,

14 in whom we have redemption through His blood, the forgiveness of sins.

15 He is the image of the invisible God, the firstborn over all creation.

16 For by Him all things were created that are in heaven and that are on earth, visible and invisible, whether thrones or dominions or principalities or powers. All things were created through Him and for Him.

17 And He is before all things, and in Him all things consist.

18 And He is the head of the body, the church, who is the beginning, the firstborn from the dead, that in all things He may have the preeminence.

19 For it pleased *the Father that* in Him all the fullness should dwell,

20 and by Him to reconcile all things to Himself, by Him, whether things on earth or things in heaven, having made peace through the blood of His cross.

21 And you, who once were alienated and enemies in your mind by wicked works, yet now He has reconciled

22 in the body of His flesh through death, to present you holy, and blameless, and irreproachable in His sight—

23 if indeed you continue in the faith, grounded and steadfast, and are not moved away from the hope of the gospel which you heard, which was preached to every creature under heaven, of which I, Paul, became a minister.

24 I now rejoice in my sufferings for you, and fill up in my flesh what is lacking in the afflictions of Christ, for the sake of His body, which is the church,

25 of which I became a minister

STEP 12

*Having had a spiritual awakening as the result
of these steps, we tried to carry this message to others,
and to practice these principles in all our affairs.*

Colossians 1:9–13

In this passage, the apostle Paul asked for a full and deep understanding of God's will. Such knowledge cannot come from a mind saturated with the world's thinking and values. Rather, it comes from a mind and heart enlightened by the Holy Spirit and the Word of God. When Paul asked for spiritual wisdom, he was asking God to give believers the ability to make good decisions in the various problems of life. Then Paul requested that they be given a "walk worthy of the Lord, fully pleasing *Him*." When we experience this kind of living and thinking, we will be practicing the principles of true recovery in all our affairs.

But Paul also asked that believers be fruit-bearing and able to be patient, longsuffering, and full of joy. These qualities will enable us to reach out to those around us who need to hear our message. It will also make these needy souls hungry for what we have to offer.

For further reading on Step 12, turn to page 441.

Daily Encouragement

DAY 188 READING: COLOSSIANS 1:1–23

A Thought for the New Day: Do you think of the Creator as Someone you could never possibly know? How could mere human beings like us appreciate the One who brought the vast universe into existence by His command? God has made it easy for us. He came into the world as a Man just so we could see what He is like. This is the Creator, the infinitely high but lowly Christ, who breathed the breath of life into all things (v. 16). (*Turn to page 435.*)

according to the stewardship from God which was given to me for you, to fulfill the word of God,

26 the mystery which has been hidden from ages and from generations, but now has been revealed to His saints.

STEP 12

27 To them God willed to make known what are the riches of the glory of this mystery among the Gentiles: which is Christ in you, the hope of glory.

28 Him we preach, warning every man and teaching every man in all wisdom, that we may present every man perfect in Christ Jesus.

29 To this *end* I also labor, striving according to His working which works in me mightily.

2 For I want you to know what a great conflict I have for you and those in Laodicea, and *for* as many as have not seen my face in the flesh,

2 that their hearts may be encouraged, being knit together in love, and *attaining* to all riches of the full assurance of understanding, to the knowledge of the mystery of God, both of the Father and of Christ,

3 in whom are hidden all the treasures of wisdom and knowledge.

4 Now this I say lest anyone should deceive you with persuasive words.

5 For though I am absent in the flesh, yet I am with you in spirit, rejoicing to see your *good* order and the steadfastness of your faith in Christ.

STEP 11

6 As you have therefore received Christ Jesus the Lord, so walk in Him,

7 rooted and built up in Him and established in the faith, as you have been taught, abounding in it with thanksgiving.

8 Beware lest anyone cheat you through philosophy and empty deceit, according to the tradition of men, according to the basic principles of the world, and not according to Christ.

9 For in Him dwells all the fullness of the Godhead bodily;

10 and you are complete in Him, who is the head of all principality and power.

11 In Him you were also circumcised with the circumcision made without hands, by putting off the body of the sins of the flesh, by the circumcision of Christ,

12 buried with Him in baptism, in which you also were raised with *Him* through faith in the working of God, who raised Him from the dead.

13 And you, being dead in your trespasses and the uncircumcision of your flesh, He has made alive together with Him, having forgiven you all trespasses,

STEP 2

14 having wiped out the handwriting of requirements that was against us, which was contrary to us. And He has taken it out of the way, having nailed it to the cross.

15 Having disarmed principalities and powers, He made a public spectacle of them, triumphing over them in it.

16 Therefore let no one judge you in food or in drink, or regarding a festival or a new moon or sabbaths,

17 which are a shadow of things to come, but the substance is of Christ.

18 Let no one defraud you of your reward, taking delight in *false* humility and worship of angels, intruding into those things which he has not seen, vainly puffed up by his fleshly mind,

19 and not holding fast to the Head, from whom all the body, nourished and knit together by joints and ligaments, grows with the increase *which is* from God.

20 Therefore, if you died with Christ from the basic principles of the world, why, as *though* living in the world, do you subject yourselves to regulations—

21 "Do not touch, do not taste, do not handle,"

STEP 2

*Came to believe that a Power greater than ourselves
could restore us to sanity.*

Colossians 2:13, 14

Through Step 1 we came to grips with the first part of Colossians 2:13. We realized that we had as much power to get rid of our trespasses as a dead man had to make himself alive. Because of "the uncircumcision of the flesh," that is, our carnal, worldly state of mind, we were prompted to do and think wrong things. But Step 2 falls into place right in the middle of this verse. Coming to believe that the Lord Jesus is the One who has the power to heal causes God to make us "alive together with Him, having forgiven [us] all trespasses."

Just as Jesus arose in mighty power from the tyranny of the grave, our faith in Him gives us new life and power to fight and win our battles in life. We are no longer under sin's condemnation. Our guilt and shame have been taken away. And new freedom to recover from its domination becomes ours in Jesus.

For further reading on Step 2, turn to page 477.

Daily Encouragement

DAY 189 READING: COLOSSIANS 1:24—2:23

A Thought for the New Day: What is the greatest news of all? Not only did Jesus die and rise again and ascend into heaven, but much more. The ultimate result of all His work is that the very Christ of eternity, who died and is alive, now actually comes to live in those who receive Him for who He is (1:27). So Jesus is not separated from us by the centuries or by the pages of the Bible, but He is closer to us than even our own breath! (*Turn to page 437.*)

22 which all concern things which perish with the using—according to the commandments and doctrines of men?

23 These things indeed have an appearance of wisdom in self-imposed religion, *false* humility, and neglect of the body, *but are* of no value against the indulgence of the flesh.

STEP 10 **3** If then you were raised with Christ, seek those things which are above, where Christ is, sitting at the right hand of God.

2 Set your mind on things above, not on things on the earth.

3 For you died, and your life is hidden with Christ in God.

4 When Christ *who is* our life appears, then you also will appear with Him in glory.

STEP 6 5 Therefore put to death your members which are on the earth: fornication, uncleanness, passion, evil desire, and covetousness, which is idolatry.

6 Because of these things the wrath of God is coming upon the sons of disobedience,

7 in which you also once walked when you lived in them.

8 But now you must also put off all these: anger, wrath, malice, blasphemy, filthy language out of your mouth.

STEP 5 9 Do not lie to one another, since you have put off the old man with his deeds,

10 and have put on the new *man* who is renewed in knowledge according to the image of Him who created him,

11 where there is neither Greek nor Jew, circumcised nor uncircumcised, barbarian, Scythian, slave *nor* free, but Christ *is* all and in all.

STEP 9 12 Therefore, as *the* elect of God, holy and beloved, put on tender mercies, kindness, humbleness of mind, meekness, longsuffering;

13 bearing with one another, and forgiving one another, if anyone has a complaint against another; even as Christ forgave you, so you also *must do*.

14 But above all these things put on love, which is the bond of perfection. STEP 11

15 And let the peace of God rule in your hearts, to which also you were called in one body; and be thankful.

16 Let the word of Christ dwell in you richly in all wisdom, teaching and admonishing one another in psalms and hymns and spiritual songs, singing with grace in your hearts to the Lord.

17 And *whatever* you do in word or deed, *do* all in the name of the Lord Jesus, giving thanks to God the Father through Him.

18 Wives, submit to your own husbands, as is fitting in the Lord. STEP 9

19 Husbands, love your wives and do not be bitter toward them.

20 Children, obey your parents in all things, for this is well pleasing to the Lord.

21 Fathers, do not provoke your children, lest they become discouraged.

22 Servants, obey in all things your masters according to the flesh, not with eyeservice, as men-pleasers, but in sincerity of heart, fearing God.

23 And whatever you do, do it heartily, as to the Lord and not to men, STEP 11

24 knowing that from the Lord you will receive the reward of the inheritance; for you serve the Lord Christ.

25 But he who does wrong will be repaid for *the wrong* which he has done, and there is no partiality.

4 Masters, give your servants what is just and fair, knowing that you also have a Master in heaven.

2 Continue earnestly in prayer, being vigilant in it with thanksgiving;

3 meanwhile praying also for us,

STEP 6

*Were entirely ready to have God
remove all these defects of character.*

Colossians 3:5–8

One of the greatest challenges of our human experience is to find a proper balance in the expression and the fulfillment of our God-given needs for love, security, and acceptance. Our addictive personalities may propel us toward radical distortions of these needs.

In the search for this balance, we want to avoid two extremes: 1) the tendency to deny or suppress the existence of our God-ordained needs and 2) the tendency to overexpress or overfulfill these same needs.

Our improper fulfillment of these human appetites brings only greater frustration. In the heart of our dependency, we discover that there is never enough of the addictive agent to satisfy our codependent hungers. Lacking a true sense of God's ability to fill our needs, we establish such things as sexuality, money, and power as false gods or idols in our lives. Scripture warns us to "put to death" these false gods. We ask God to remove these defects of character in order that we may more fully embrace Him.

For further reading on Step 6, turn to page 475.

Daily Encouragement

DAY 190 READING: COLOSSIANS 3:1–25

A Thought for the New Day: Singing is one of the chief delights of the soul, and especially when God is the subject and object of our songs and hymns (v. 16). No doubt this was one of the ways that early believers committed God's Word to memory. When the Bible is translated in a way that accentuates its natural rhythm and music, singing the Word becomes easier. (*Turn to page 439.*)

that God would open to us a door for the word, to speak the mystery of Christ, for which I am also in chains,

4 that I may make it manifest, as I ought to speak.

 5 Walk in wisdom toward those *who are* outside, redeeming the time.

6 *Let* your speech always *be* with grace, seasoned with salt, that you may know how you ought to answer each one.

7 Tychicus, *who is* a beloved brother, a faithful minister, and a fellow servant in the Lord, will tell you all the news about me.

8 I am sending him to you for this very purpose, that he may know your circumstances and comfort your hearts,

9 with Onesimus, a faithful and beloved brother, who is *one* of you. They will make known to you all things which *are happening* here.

10 Aristarchus my fellow prisoner greets you, with Mark the cousin of Barnabas (about whom you received instructions: if he comes to you, welcome him),

11 and Jesus who is called Justus. These *are my* only fellow workers for the kingdom of God who are of the circumcision; they have proved to be a comfort to me.

12 Epaphras, who is *one* of you, a servant of Christ, greets you, always laboring fervently for you in prayers, that you may stand perfect and complete in all the will of God.

13 For I bear him witness that he has a great zeal for you, and those who are in Laodicea, and those in Hierapolis.

14 Luke the beloved physician and Demas greet you.

15 Greet the brethren who are in Laodicea, and Nymphas and the church that *is* in his house.

16 Now when this epistle is read among you, see that it is read also in the church of the Laodiceans, and that you likewise read the epistle from Laodicea.

17 And say to Archippus, "Take heed to the ministry which you have received in the Lord, that you may fulfill it."

18 This salutation by my own hand—Paul. Remember my chains. Grace *be* with you. Amen.

THE FIRST EPISTLE OF PAUL THE APOSTLE TO THE
THESSALONIANS

PAUL, Silvanus, and Timothy,

To the church of the Thessalonians in God the Father and the Lord Jesus Christ:

Grace to you and peace from God our Father and the Lord Jesus Christ.

2 We give thanks to God always for you all, making mention of you in our prayers,

3. remembering without ceasing your work of faith, labor of love, and patience of hope in our Lord Jesus Christ in the sight of our God and Father,

4 knowing, beloved brethren, your election by God.

5 For our gospel did not come to you in word only, but also in power, and in the Holy Spirit and in much assurance, as you know what kind of men we were among you for your sake.

6 And you became followers of us and of the Lord, having received the word in much affliction, with joy of the Holy Spirit,

Made direct amends to such people wherever possible,
except when to do so would injure them or others.

Colossians 4:5, 6

Steps 8 and 9 are steps toward reconciliation. With whom are we to be reconciled?

First, we are to be reconciled with our own conscience. We must put to rest lingering remnants of guilt and remorse, which have kept us divided from ourselves.

Second, we must reconcile with other persons. Step 9 provides us with a concrete tool to stretch back through years of broken relationships to make new amends.

Third, and perhaps most importantly, as we have reconciled with ourselves and others, we are now prepared to reconcile with God. Step 9 allows us to reach out to God without the encumbrance of weighty feelings of regret and guilt.

What is to be the language of these amends? It is to be the language of grace and compassion. As we seek to reconcile with our own conscience and as we seek to reunite with those who appear to be on the "outside," our words must always be words of harmony and peace.

For further reading on Step 9, turn to page 465.

Daily
Encouragement

DAY 191 READING: COLOSSIANS 4:1–18

A Thought for the New Day: Do you ever stop to ask yourself how your speech sounds to others? Some of us have an abrupt, hurried manner of speaking that makes people feel ill at ease. Let us teach ourselves, whenever we must speak, to do so graciously and kindly, never with animosity or sarcasm (v. 6). Of course, the guarantee of right speech is a right heart, or inner life, which is the source of all our actions. (*Turn to page 441.*)

7 so that you became examples to all in Macedonia and Achaia who believe.

8 For from you the word of the Lord has sounded forth, not only in Macedonia and Achaia, but also in every place. Your faith toward God has gone out, so that we do not need to say anything.

9 For they themselves declare concerning us what manner of entry we had to you, and how you turned to God from idols to serve the living and true God,

10 and to wait for His Son from heaven, whom He raised from the dead, *even* Jesus who delivers us from the wrath to come.

2 For you yourselves know, brethren, that our coming to you was not in vain.

2 But even after we had suffered before and were spitefully treated at Philippi, as you know, we were bold in our God to speak to you the gospel of God in much conflict.

| STEP |
| 12 |

3 For our exhortation *did* not come from deceit or uncleanness, nor *was it* in guile.

4 But as we have been approved by God to be entrusted with the gospel, even so we speak, not as pleasing men, but God who tests our hearts.

5 For neither at any time did we use flattering words, as you know, nor a cloak for covetousness—God *is* witness.

6 Nor did we seek glory from men, either from you or from others, when we might have made demands as apostles of Christ.

7 But we were gentle among you, just as a nursing *mother* cherishes her own children.

8 So, affectionately longing for you, we were well pleased to impart to you not only the gospel of God, but also our own lives, because you had become dear to us.

9 For you remember, brethren, our labor and toil; for laboring night and day, that we might not

be a burden to any of you, we preached to you the gospel of God.

10 You *are* witnesses, and God *also,* how devoutly and justly and blamelessly we behaved ourselves among you who believe;

11 as you know how we exhorted, and comforted, and charged every one of you, as a father *does* his own children,

12 that you would have a walk worthy of God who calls you into His own kingdom and glory.

13 For this reason we also thank God without ceasing, because when you received the word of God which you heard from us, you welcomed *it* not *as* the word of men, but as it is in truth, the word of God, which also effectively works in you who believe.

14 For you, brethren, became imitators of the churches of God which are in Judea in Christ Jesus. For you also suffered the same things from your own countrymen, just as they *did* from the Jews,

15 who killed both the Lord Jesus and their own prophets, and have persecuted us; and they do not please God and are contrary to all men,

16 forbidding us to speak to the Gentiles that they may be saved, so as always to fill up *the measure of* their sins; but wrath has come upon them to the uttermost.

17 But we, brethren, having been taken away from you for a short time in presence, not in heart, endeavored more eagerly to see your face with great desire.

18 Therefore we wanted to come to you—even I, Paul, time and again—but Satan hindered us.

19 For what *is* our hope, or joy, or crown of rejoicing? *Is it* not even you in the presence of our Lord Jesus Christ at His coming?

20 For you are our glory and joy.

3 Therefore, when we could no longer endure it, we thought it good to be left in Athens alone,

STEP 12

*Having had a spiritual awakening as the result
of these steps, we tried to carry this message to others,
and to practice these principles in all our affairs.*

1 Thessalonians 2:3, 4

Honesty is one of the greatest lessons we have learned during our recovery. We have learned not to hide behind generalizations, clichés, and masks. We have learned to be genuine with other people, to "speak the truth in love." We have also learned to be honest with ourselves, coming to understand and be aware of our innermost feelings and motivations. We are working daily at approaching the world and ourselves without deceit, uncleanness, or guile" (v. 3).

This is exactly the reason that we, too, have been approved by God to be entrusted with the gospel. Because we ourselves know the deep despair and pain of dependency, we are acutely aware of those in need around us. When we learned to trust in Jesus instead of ourselves, we experienced both the power and the humility that characterize God's true servants. And because we are servants of a faithful and loving God, our primary motive should always be that of pleasing Him.

For further reading on Step 12, turn to page 451.

Daily Encouragement

DAY 192 READING: 1 THESSALONIANS 1:1—2:16

A Thought for the New Day: "Words, words, words," complained one of Shakespeare's characters. Words alone do not accomplish God's work or change lives. The words must be mixed with heavenly power, imparted by the Spirit of God Himself. Of course we cannot invent or simply work up that life-transforming power. But if we know we need to speak for Christ, then we must allow God to strengthen us. He will gladly use our efforts. (*Turn to page 443.*)

2 and sent Timothy, our brother and minister of God, and our fellow laborer in the gospel of Christ, to establish you and encourage you concerning your faith,

3 that no one should be shaken by these afflictions; for you yourselves know that we are appointed to this.

4 For, in fact, we told you before when we were with you that we would suffer tribulation, just as it happened, and you know.

5 For this reason, when I could no longer endure it, I sent to know your faith, lest by some means the tempter had tempted you, and our labor might be in vain.

6 But now that Timothy has come to us from you, and brought us good news of your faith and love, and that you always have good remembrance of us, greatly desiring to see us, as we also *to see* you—

7 therefore, brethren, in all our affliction and distress we were comforted concerning you by your faith.

8 For now we live, if you stand fast in the Lord.

9 For what thanks can we render to God for you, for all the joy with which we rejoice for your sake before our God,

10 night and day praying exceedingly that we may see your face and perfect what is lacking in your faith?

11 Now may our God and Father Himself, and our Lord Jesus Christ, direct our way to you.

12 And may the Lord make you increase and abound in love to one another and to all, just as we *do* to you,

13 so that He may establish your hearts blameless in holiness before our God and Father at the coming of our Lord Jesus Christ with all His saints.

4 Finally then, brethren, we urge and exhort in the Lord Jesus that you should abound more and

more, just as you received from us how you ought to walk and to please God;

2 for you know what commandments we gave you through the Lord Jesus.

3 For this is the will of God, your sanctification: that you should abstain from sexual immorality;

4 that each of you should know how to possess his own vessel in sanctification and honor,

5 not in passion of lust, like the Gentiles who do not know God;

6 that no one should take advantage of and defraud his brother in this matter, because the Lord *is* the avenger of all such, as we also forewarned you and testified.

7 For God did not call us to uncleanness, but in holiness.

8 Therefore he who rejects *this* does not reject man, but God, who has also given us His Holy Spirit.

9 But concerning brotherly love you have no need that I should write to you, for you yourselves are taught by God to love one another;

10 and indeed you do so toward all the brethren who are in all Macedonia. But we urge you, brethren, that you increase more and more;

11 that you also aspire to lead a quiet life, to mind your own business, and to work with your own hands, as we commanded you,

12 that you may walk properly toward those who are outside, and *that* you may lack nothing.

13 But I do not want you to be ignorant, brethren, concerning those who have fallen asleep, lest you sorrow as others who have no hope.

14 For if we believe that Jesus died and rose again, even so God will bring with Him those who sleep in Jesus.

15 For this we say to you by the word of the Lord, that we who are alive *and* remain until the coming of the Lord will by no means precede those who are asleep.

STEP 6

STEP 11

STEP 8

STEP 8

*Made a list of all persons we had harmed,
and became willing to make amends to them all.*

1 Thessalonians 3:12, 13

A cup overflowing with love—that would be the picture in your mind if you were an early Christian reading Paul's letter in the Greek language. Paul encouraged the Thessalonian Christians, not only to love one another, but to extend their love "to all." As was true for the Thessalonians, if this is to become reality in our lives, God's grace must first fill us. When we are willing to open our hearts to His purifying and motivating grace, the circumstances of our past will become secondary. Our hearts will begin to bubble forth with the type of love that seeks to rebuild relationships and remove obstacles.

Then we can experience the joy of a heart that is blameless before God. Blameless is different from sinless, of course. Blameless means that sin has been dealt with as God requires and that the heart is free of any charges against it. Step 8 is a step toward this wonderful freedom.

For further reading on Step 8, turn to page 457.

Daily Encouragement

DAY 193 READING: 1 THESSALONIANS 2:17—4:18

A Thought for the New Day: Paul tells us to comfort one another with the words in 4:16–18. Why are they a comfort? Although life's earthly end is never a beautiful thing *in itself*, living in us there is special, joyful expectation that reaches beyond what we see. It is God's living promise of better things than earth, at its best, affords. It is eternal life in the presence of our risen Savior. That is heaven! (*Turn to page 445.*)

16 For the Lord Himself will descend from heaven with a shout, with the voice of an archangel, and with the trumpet of God. And the dead in Christ will rise first.

17 Then we who are alive *and* remain shall be caught up together with them in the clouds to meet the Lord in the air. And thus we shall always be with the Lord.

18 Therefore comfort one another with these words.

5 But concerning the times and the seasons, brethren, you have no need that I should write to you.

2 For you yourselves know perfectly that the day of the Lord so comes as a thief in the night.

3 For when they say, "Peace and safety!" then sudden destruction comes upon them, as labor pains upon a pregnant woman. And they shall not escape.

4 But you, brethren, are not in darkness, so that this Day should overtake you as a thief.

5 You are all sons of light and sons of the day. We are not of the night nor of darkness.

6 Therefore let us not sleep, as others *do,* but let us watch and be sober.

7 For those who sleep, sleep at night, and those who get drunk are drunk at night.

8 But let us who are of the day be sober, putting on the breastplate of faith and love, and *as* a helmet the hope of salvation.

9 For God did not appoint us to wrath, but to obtain salvation through our Lord Jesus Christ,

10 who died for us, that whether we wake or sleep, we should live together with Him.

11 Therefore comfort each other and edify one another, just as you also are doing.

12 And we urge you, brethren, to recognize those who labor among you, and are over you in the Lord and admonish you,

13 and to esteem them very highly in love for their work's sake. Be at peace among yourselves.

14 Now we exhort you, brethren, warn those who are unruly, comfort the fainthearted, uphold the weak, be patient with all.

15 See that no one renders evil for evil to anyone, but always pursue what is good both for yourselves and for all.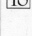

16 Rejoice always,

17 pray without ceasing,

18 in everything give thanks; for this is the will of God in Christ Jesus for you.

19 Do not quench the Spirit.

20 Do not despise prophecies.

21 Test all things; hold fast what is good.

22 Abstain from every form of evil.

23 Now may the God of peace Himself sanctify you completely; and may your whole spirit, soul, and body be preserved blameless at the coming of our Lord Jesus Christ.

24 He who calls you *is* faithful, who also will do *it.*

25 Brethren, pray for us.

26 Greet all the brethren with a holy kiss.

27 I charge you by the Lord that this epistle be read to all the holy brethren.

28 The grace of our Lord Jesus Christ *be* with you. Amen.

STEP 10

*Continued to take personal inventory
and when we were wrong promptly admitted it.*

1 Thessalonians 5:17–22

Steps 10, 11, and 12 are often referred to as the maintenance steps of recovery. Recovery literature describes the first nine steps as preparatory to new life. With Step 10 begins the adventure of living what we are learning. In practical terms, how are we to conduct a daily personal inventory? This passage from Thessalonians offers five recommendations for the components of a daily inventory:

1) We are to pray constantly.

2) We are to praise and be thankful. In recovery we frequently refer to the compilation of a "gratitude list."

3) We are to invite God's Spirit into our hearts daily.

4) We are to search for God's direction and will for all of our future activities.

5) We are to engage in a regular and consistent evaluation of both our assets and liabilities. We are indeed called to hold fast to that which is good and to abstain from every manifestation and symptom of our old character defects.

For further reading on Step 10, turn to page 449.

Daily Encouragement

DAY 194 READING: 1 THESSALONIANS 5:1–28

A Thought for the New Day: It is easy to be thankful for the pleasant things of life. But what of the unpleasant? How is it possible to be grateful for that financial failure, a disabling sickness, or a lost job? It just does not seem reasonable. That is why we need to get the bird's eye view of life, or—more truly—God's view of our needs. He never allows anything that does not meet His highest purpose for us. As we discover that fact, we are thankful (v. 18). (*Turn to page 447.*)

THE SECOND EPISTLE OF PAUL THE APOSTLE TO THE

THESSALONIANS

PAUL, Silvanus, and Timothy,

To the church of the Thessalonians in God our Father and the Lord Jesus Christ:

2 Grace to you and peace from God our Father and the Lord Jesus Christ.

3 We are bound to thank God always for you, brethren, as it is fitting, because your faith grows exceedingly, and the love of every one of you all abounds toward each other,

4 so that we ourselves boast of you among the churches of God for your patience and faith in all your persecutions and tribulations that you endure,

5 *which is* manifest evidence of the righteous judgment of God, that you may be counted worthy of the kingdom of God, for which you also suffer;

6 since *it is* a righteous thing with God to repay with tribulation those who trouble you,

7 and to *give* you who are troubled rest with us when the Lord Jesus is revealed from heaven with His mighty angels, .

8 in flaming fire taking vengeance on those who do not know God, and on those who do not obey the gospel of our Lord Jesus Christ.

9 These shall be punished with everlasting destruction from the presence of the Lord and from the glory of His power,

10 when He comes, in that Day, to be glorified in His saints and to be admired among all those who believe, because our testimony among you was believed.

11 Therefore we also pray always for you that our God would count you worthy of *this* calling, and fulfill all the good pleasure of *His* goodness and the work of faith with power,

12 that the name of our Lord Jesus Christ may be glorified in you, and you in Him, according to the grace of our God and the Lord Jesus Christ.

2 Now, brethren, concerning the coming of our Lord Jesus Christ and our gathering together to Him, we ask you,

2 not to be soon shaken in mind or troubled, either by spirit or by word or by letter, as if from us, as though the day of Christ had come.

3 Let no one deceive you by any means; for *that Day will not come* unless the falling away comes first, and the man of sin is revealed, the son of perdition,

4 who opposes and exalts himself above all that is called God or that is worshiped, so that he sits as God in the temple of God, showing himself that he is God.

5 Do you not remember that when I was still with you I told you these things?

6 And now you know what is restraining, that he may be revealed in his own time.

7 For the mystery of lawlessness is already at work; only He who now restrains *will do so* until He is taken out of the way.

8 And then the lawless one will be revealed, whom the Lord will consume with the breath of His mouth and destroy with the brightness of His coming.

9 The coming of the *lawless one* is according to the working of Satan, with all power, signs, and lying wonders,

10 and with all unrighteous deception among those who perish, because they did not receive the love of the truth, that they might be saved.

STEP 11

*Sought through prayer and meditation to improve our conscious contact with God **as we understood Him,** praying only for knowledge of His will for us and the power to carry that out.*

2 Thessalonians 2:16, 17

God's desire for His growing believers is comfort and establishment. He wants those of us who know Him to feel secure, encouraged, and cared for. This happens naturally when we meditate on and experience His great love for us. "Everlasting consolation" has also been given to us. Through prayer and praise, we can tap into this unending flow of encouragement from the Holy Spirit Himself. Finally we have the good, sure hope of eternity with Jesus. When we take time daily to remember and respond to these wonderful gifts, our hearts are comforted and established. The word "established" means that our lives become stable and strong in the love and power of God. Then our words and our work will be a reflection of all that we are and have in the Lord Jesus.

For further reading on Step 11, turn to page 463.

Daily Encouragement

DAY 195 READING: 2 THESSALONIANS 1:1—2:17

A Thought for the New Day: There is a right time for everything, and that is God's time. When Christ comes again, the time will be ripe, it will be the climax of many catastrophic events, and those who are awaiting Him will know that His appearing is near at hand (2:1, 2). What a day of rejoicing that will be! All the ageless ills that have tormented humanity will pass away, and Christ's glad reign will begin. *(Turn to page 449.)*

11 And for this reason God will send them strong delusion, that they should believe the lie,

12 that they all may be condemned who did not believe the truth but had pleasure in unrighteousness.

13 But we are bound to give thanks to God always for you, brethren beloved by the Lord, because God from the beginning chose you for salvation through sanctification by the Spirit and belief in the truth,

14 to which He called you by our gospel, for the obtaining of the glory of our Lord Jesus Christ.

15 Therefore, brethren, stand fast and hold the traditions which you were taught, whether by word or our epistle.

16 Now may our Lord Jesus Christ Himself, and our God and Father, who has loved us and given *us* everlasting consolation and good hope by grace,

17 comfort your hearts and establish you in every good word and work.

3 Finally, brethren, pray for us, that the word of the Lord may have *free* course and be glorified, just as *it is* with you,

2 and that we may be delivered from unreasonable and wicked men; for not all have faith.

3 But the Lord is faithful, who will establish you and guard *you* from the evil one.

4 And we have confidence in the Lord concerning you, both that you do and will do the things we command you.

5 Now may the Lord direct your hearts into the love of God and into the patience of Christ.

6 But we command you, brethren, in the name of our Lord Jesus Christ, that you withdraw from every brother who walks disorderly and not according to the tradition which he received from us.

7 For you yourselves know how you ought to follow us, for we were not disorderly among you;

8 nor did we eat anyone's bread free of charge, but worked with labor and toil night and day, that we might not be a burden to any of you,

9 not because we do not have authority, but to make ourselves an example of how you should follow us.

10 For even when we were with you, we commanded you this: If anyone will not work, neither shall he eat.

11 For we hear that there are some who walk among you in a disorderly manner, not working at all, but are busybodies.

12 Now those who are such we command and exhort through our Lord Jesus Christ that they work in quietness and eat their own bread.

13 But *as for* you, brethren, do not grow weary *in* doing good.

14 And if anyone does not obey our word in this epistle, note that person and do not keep company with him, that he may be ashamed.

15 Yet do not count *him* as an enemy, but admonish *him* as a brother.

16 Now may the Lord of peace Himself give you peace always in every way. The Lord *be* with you all.

17 The salutation of Paul with my own hand, which is a sign in every epistle; so I write.

18 The grace of our Lord Jesus Christ *be* with you all. Amen.

STEP 10

Continued to take personal inventory
and when we were wrong promptly admitted it.

2 Thessalonians 3:3–5

Fear can impoverish and paralyze us. If we believe that we alone are responsible for keeping ourselves on the recovery track, we will have doubts about our ability to maintain emotional health. We may even become overly introspective—too cautious with our words and actions, constantly afraid of slipping back into our old habits and thinking patterns. God expects us to be aware and watchful, but He does not want us to be fearful to the point of paralysis.

As 2 Thessalonians 3:3–5 reminds us, God is faithful. He cares about us and knows exactly what we need to keep growing in Him. His deep desire is that we be firm and stable in Him like a strong tree deeply rooted beside a nourishing stream. He also knows that Satan will try to sabotage our recovery with doubts and discouragement. This is why the Holy Spirit will be there with us continually to guard our hearts, to lift us up, and to lead us.

For further reading on Step 10, turn to page 459.

Daily Encouragement

DAY 196 READING: 2 THESSALONIANS 3:1–18

A Thought for the New Day: Not everyone possesses the faith that you may have, and this fact should not be a source of frustration—certainly not of pride (v. 2). We need to learn not to have an expectation of others that is too high or impossible for them. On the other hand, we should expect greater things of ourselves. If we have been blessed with an intimate knowledge of the Savior, let us seize every opportunity to show His love to a lonely world. (*Turn to page 451.*)

THE FIRST EPISTLE OF PAUL THE APOSTLE TO
TIMOTHY

PAUL, an apostle of Jesus Christ, by the commandment of God our Savior and the Lord Jesus Christ, our hope,

2 To Timothy, *my* true son in the faith:

Grace, mercy, *and* peace from God our Father and Jesus Christ our Lord.

3 As I urged you when I went into Macedonia—remain in Ephesus that you may charge some that they teach no other doctrine,

4 nor give heed to fables and endless genealogies, which cause disputes rather than godly edification which is in faith.

STEP 12 5 Now the purpose of the commandment is love from a pure heart, *from* a good conscience, and *from* sincere faith,

6 from which some, having strayed, have turned aside to idle talk,

7 desiring to be teachers of the law, understanding neither what they say nor the things which they affirm.

8 But we know that the law *is* good if one uses it lawfully,

9 knowing this: that the law is not made for a righteous person, but for *the* lawless and insubordinate, for *the* ungodly and for sinners, for *the* unholy and profane, for murderers of fathers and murderers of mothers, for manslayers,

10 for fornicators, for sodomites, for kidnappers, for liars, for perjurers, and if there is any other thing that is contrary to sound doctrine,

11 according to the glorious gospel of the blessed God which was committed to my trust.

STEP 12 12 And I thank Christ Jesus our Lord who has enabled me, because He counted me faithful, putting *me* into the ministry,

13 although I was formerly a blasphemer, a persecutor, and an insolent man; but I obtained mercy because I did *it* ignorantly in unbelief.

14 And the grace of our Lord was exceedingly abundant, with faith and love which are in Christ Jesus.

15 This *is* a faithful saying and worthy of all acceptance, that Christ Jesus came into the world to save sinners, of whom I am chief.

16 However, for this reason I obtained mercy, that in me first Jesus Christ might show all longsuffering, as a pattern to those who are going to believe on Him for everlasting life.

17 Now to the King eternal, immortal, invisible, to God who alone is wise, *be* honor and glory forever and ever. Amen.

18 This charge I commit to you, son Timothy, according to the prophecies previously made concerning you, that by them you may wage the good warfare,

19 having faith and a good conscience, which some having rejected, concerning the faith have suffered shipwreck,

20 of whom are Hymenaeus and Alexander, whom I delivered to Satan that they may learn not to blaspheme.

2 Therefore I exhort first of all that supplications, prayers, intercessions, *and* giving of thanks be made for all men,

2 for kings and all who are in authority, that we may lead a quiet and peaceable life in all godliness and reverence.

3 For this *is* good and acceptable in the sight of God our Savior,

4 who desires all men to be saved and to come to the knowledge of the truth.

5 For *there is* one God and one Mediator between God and men, *the* Man Christ Jesus,

STEP 12

Having had spiritual awakening as the result of these steps,
we tried to carry this message to others,
and to practice these principles in all our affairs.

1 Timothy 1:12–16

The apostle Paul never concealed his past. In sharing his former life as "a blasphemer, a persecutor, and an insolent man," he was able to show others just how merciful, gracious, and patient God is.

Paul's attitude is a good one for each of us to emulate. God wants to use our triumphs over our past to glorify Himself. If we are listening carefully to His voice, we will find that He is placing before us opportunities to share how we have been changed.

Many people agonize through life because they believe they are not good enough for God to love or to save. Sharing the recovery stories of how our lives have been transformed may become the key that opens the door of God's love to a struggling friend.

As we continue to practice and apply each of the Twelve Steps, our daily lives can be "a pattern to those who are going to believe on Him."

For further reading on Step 12, turn to page 481.

Daily Encouragement

DAY 197 READING: 1 TIMOTHY 1:1—3:16

A Thought for the New Day: To honor someone is to regard that person with unusual respect. Above all, let us never for a moment fail to hold God in highest honor (1:17). So doing, we prove we are true members of His family and develop a corresponding self-respect as those whom He has "honored" to be included in that family. Then we love all things that please Him. (*Turn to page 454.*)

6 who gave Himself a ransom for all, to be testified in due time,

7 for which I was appointed a preacher and an apostle—I am speaking the truth in Christ *and* not lying—a teacher of the Gentiles in faith and truth.

8 Therefore I desire that the men pray everywhere, lifting up holy hands, without wrath and doubting;

9 in like manner also, that the women adorn themselves in modest apparel, with propriety and moderation, not with braided hair or gold or pearls or costly clothing,

10 but, which is proper for women professing godliness, with good works.

11 Let a woman learn in silence with all submission.

12 And I do not permit a woman to teach or to have authority over a man, but to be in silence.

13 For Adam was formed first, then Eve.

14 And Adam was not deceived, but the woman being deceived, fell into transgression.

15 Nevertheless she will be saved in childbearing if they continue in faith, love, and holiness, with self-control.

3 This *is* a faithful saying: If a man desires the position of a bishop, he desires a good work.

2 A bishop then must be blameless, the husband of one wife, temperate, sober-minded, of good behavior, hospitable, able to teach;

3 not given to wine, not violent, not greedy for money, but gentle, not quarrelsome, not covetous;

4 one who rules his own house well, having *his* children in submission with all reverence

5 (for if a man does not know how to rule his own house, how will he take care of the church of God?);

6 not a novice, lest being puffed up with pride he fall into the *same* condemnation as the devil.

7 Moreover he must have a good testimony among those who are outside, lest he fall into reproach and the snare of the devil.

8 Likewise deacons *must be* reverent, not double-tongued, not given to much wine, not greedy for money,

9 holding the mystery of the faith with a pure conscience.

10 But let these also first be proved; then let them serve as deacons, being *found* blameless.

11 Likewise *their* wives *must be* reverent, not slanderers, temperate, faithful in all things.

12 Let deacons be the husbands of one wife, ruling *their* children and their own houses well.

13 For those who have served well as deacons obtain for themselves a good standing and great boldness in the faith which is in Christ Jesus.

14 These things I write to you, though I hope to come to you shortly;

15 but if I am delayed, *I write* so that you may know how you ought to conduct yourself in the house of God, which is the church of the living God, the pillar and ground of the truth.

16 And without controversy great is the mystery of godliness:

> God was manifested in the flesh,
> Justified in the Spirit,
> Seen by angels,
> Preached among the Gentiles,
> Believed on in the world,
> Received up in glory.

4 Now the Spirit expressly says that in latter times some will depart from the faith, giving heed to deceiving spirits and doctrines of demons,

2 speaking lies in hypocrisy, having their own conscience seared with a hot iron,

3 forbidding to marry, *and commanding* to abstain from foods

which God created to be received with thanksgiving by those who believe and know the truth.

4 For every creature of God *is* good, and nothing is to be refused if it is received with thanksgiving; 5 for it is sanctified by the word of God and prayer.

6 If you instruct the brethren in these things, you will be a good minister of Jesus Christ, nourished in the words of faith and of the good doctrine which you have carefully followed.

7 But reject profane and old wives' fables, and exercise yourself *rather* to godliness.

8 For bodily exercise profits a little, but godliness is profitable for all things, having promise of the life that now is and of that which is to come.

9 This *is* a faithful saying and worthy of all acceptance.

10 For to this *end* we both labor and suffer reproach, because we trust in the living God, who is *the* Savior of all men, especially of those who believe.

11 These things command and teach.

12 Let no one despise your youth, but be an example to the believers in word, in conduct, in love, in spirit, in faith, in purity.

13 Till I come, give attention to reading, to exhortation, to doctrine.

14 Do not neglect the gift that is in you, which was given to you by prophecy with the laying on of the hands of the presbytery.

15 Meditate on these things; give yourself entirely to them, that your progress may be evident to all.

16 Take heed to yourself and to the doctrine. Continue in them, for in doing this you will save both yourself and those who hear you.

5 Do not rebuke an older man, but exhort *him* as a father, *the* younger men as brothers,

2 *the* older women as mothers, *the* younger as sisters, with all purity.

3 Honor widows who are really widows.

4 But if any widow has children or grandchildren, let them first learn to show piety at home and to repay their parents; for this is good and acceptable before God.

5 Now she who is really a widow, and left alone, trusts in God and continues in supplications and prayers night and day.

6 But she who lives in pleasure is dead while she lives.

7 And these things command, that they may be blameless.

8 But if anyone does not provide for his own, and especially for those of his household, he has denied the faith and is worse than an unbeliever.

9 Do not let a widow under sixty years old be taken into the number, *and not unless* she has been the wife of one man,

10 well reported for good works: if she has brought up children, if she has lodged strangers, if she has washed the saints' feet, if she has relieved the afflicted, if she has diligently followed every good work.

11 But refuse *the* younger widows; for when they have begun to grow wanton against Christ, they desire to marry,

12 having condemnation because they have cast off their first faith.

13 And besides they learn *to be* idle, wandering about from house to house, and not only idle but also gossips and busybodies, saying things which they ought not.

14 Therefore I desire that *the* younger *widows* marry, bear children, manage the house, give no opportunity to the adversary to speak reproachfully.

15 For some have already turned aside after Satan.

16 If any believing man or woman has widows, let them relieve them,

STEP 4

453

STEP 4

Made a searching and fearless moral inventory of ourselves.

1 Timothy 5:8

The phrase "provide for his own" can carry many levels of meaning. When Paul wrote the verse, he had in mind those men who were heads of households, and thus financially responsible for the members within their homes. Yet a person can be fed, clothed, and sheltered and still be neglected or even abandoned. Jesus knew this and spoke often about it. Each child born also needs love, attention, guidance, and acceptance. When parents do not or cannot provide these things, the soul is cold although the body is covered.

As we take time to think back on our own childhoods, we need to understand what needs were not provided for (perhaps simply out of ignorance or inability). Then if we ourselves have become parents, we must also take stock of the way we have provided for our families. As God opens our understanding in this area, it is important that we not blame, but rather take steps to confront and assess our dependencies.

For further reading on Step 4, turn to page 493.

Daily Encouragement

DAY 198 READING: 1 TIMOTHY 4:1—6:21

A Thought for the New Day: Here is a wonderful saying: "Godliness with contentment is great gain" (6:6). The two are inseparable. God is not like a slot machine that rewards a few coins with a candy bar. Fortunately He does not give us everything we want. The lover of God is a contented person, however, because he has found the source of the only real and abiding satisfaction—in God Himself. *(Turn to page 457.)*

and do not let the church be burdened, that it may relieve those who are really widows.

17 Let the elders who rule well be counted worthy of double honor, especially those who labor in the word and doctrine.

18 For the Scripture says, *"You shall not muzzle an ox while it treads out the grain,"* and, "The laborer *is* worthy of his wages."

19 Do not receive an accusation against an elder except from two or three witnesses.

20 Those who are sinning rebuke in the presence of all, that the rest also may fear.

21 I charge *you* before God and the Lord Jesus Christ and the elect angels that you observe these things without prejudice, doing nothing with partiality.

22 Do not lay hands on anyone hastily, nor share in other people's sins; keep yourself pure.

23 No longer drink only water, but use a little wine for your stomach's sake and your frequent infirmities.

24 Some men's sins are clearly evident, preceding *them* to judgment, but those of some *men* follow later.

25 Likewise, the good works *of some* are clearly evident, and those that are otherwise cannot be hidden.

6 Let as many servants as are under the yoke count their own masters worthy of all honor, so that the name of God and *His* doctrine may not be blasphemed.

2 And those who have believing masters, let them not despise *them* because they are brethren, but rather serve *them* because those who are benefited are believers and beloved. Teach and exhort these things.

3 If anyone teaches otherwise and does not consent to wholesome words, *even* the words of our Lord Jesus Christ, and to the doctrine which is according to godliness,

4 he is proud, knowing nothing, but is obsessed with disputes and arguments over words, from which come envy, strife, reviling, evil suspicions,

5 useless wranglings of men of corrupt minds and destitute of the truth, who suppose that godliness is a *means of* gain. From such withdraw yourself.

6 But godliness with contentment is great gain.

7 For we brought nothing into *this* world, *and it is* certain we can carry nothing out.

8 And having food and clothing, with these we shall be content.

9 But those who desire to be rich fall into temptation and a snare, and *into* many foolish and harmful lusts which drown men in destruction and perdition.

10 For the love of money is a root of all *kinds of* evil, for which some have strayed from the faith in their greediness, and pierced themselves through with many sorrows.

11 But you, O man of God, flee these things and pursue righteousness, godliness, faith, love, patience, gentleness.

12 Fight the good fight of faith, lay hold on eternal life, to which you were also called and have confessed the good confession in the presence of many witnesses.

13 I urge you in the sight of God who gives life to all things, and *before* Christ Jesus who witnessed the good confession before Pontius Pilate,

14 that you keep *this* commandment without spot, blameless until our Lord Jesus Christ's appearing,

15 which He will manifest in His own time, *He who is* the blessed and only Potentate, the King of kings and Lord of lords,

16 who alone has immortality, dwelling in unapproachable light, whom no man has seen or can see, to whom *be* honor and everlasting power. Amen.

17 Command those who are rich in this present age not to be haughty, nor to trust in uncertain riches but in the living God, who gives us richly all things to enjoy.

18 *Let them* do good, that they be rich in good works, ready to give, willing to share,

19 storing up for themselves a good foundation for the time to come, that they may lay hold on eternal life.

20 O Timothy! Guard what was committed to your trust, avoiding the profane *and* vain babblings and contradictions of what is falsely called knowledge—

21 by professing it, some have strayed concerning the faith. Grace *be* with you. Amen.

THE SECOND EPISTLE OF PAUL THE APOSTLE TO
TIMOTHY

PAUL, an apostle of Jesus Christ by the will of God, according to the promise of life which is in Christ Jesus,

2 To Timothy, *my* beloved son:

Grace, mercy, *and* peace from God the Father and Christ Jesus our Lord.

3 I thank God, whom I serve with a pure conscience, as *my* forefathers *did*, as without ceasing I remember you in my prayers night and day,

4 greatly desiring to see you, being mindful of your tears, that I may be filled with joy,

5 when I call to remembrance the genuine faith that is in you, which dwelt first in your grandmother Lois and your mother Eunice, and I am persuaded is in you also.

6 Therefore I remind you to stir up the gift of God which is in you through the laying on of my hands.

 7 For God has not given us a spirit of fear, but of power and of love and of a sound mind.

8 Therefore do not be ashamed of the testimony of our Lord, nor of me His prisoner, but share with me in the sufferings for the gospel according to the power of God,

9 who has saved us and called *us* with a holy calling, not according to our works, but according to His own purpose and grace which was given to us in Christ Jesus before time began,

10 but has now been revealed by the appearing of our Savior Jesus Christ, *who* has abolished death and brought life and immortality to light through the gospel,

11 to which I was appointed a preacher, an apostle, and a teacher of the Gentiles.

12 For this reason I also suffer these things; nevertheless I am not ashamed, for I know whom I have believed and am persuaded that He is able to keep what I have committed to Him until that Day.

13 Hold fast the pattern of sound words which you have heard from me, in faith and love which are in Christ Jesus.

14 That good thing which was committed to you, keep by the Holy Spirit who dwells in us.

15 This you know, that all those in Asia have turned away from me, among whom are Phygellus and Hermogenes.

16 The Lord grant mercy to the household of Onesiphorus, for he often refreshed me, and was not ashamed of my chain;

STEP 11

STEP 8

STEP 8

*Made a list of all persons we had harmed,
and became willing to make amends to them all.*

2 Timothy 1:7

For the great majority of people, the thought of facing another person and speaking honestly of hurts, regrets, bitterness, or hard feelings is one of the most frightening scenarios they can imagine.

Perhaps the sensitive, young pastor Timothy faced this same fear. Timothy was like a son to the apostle Paul, who wrote the advice and encouragement given in 2 Timothy 1:7. Paul reminds Timothy that instead of being fearful, he should release the three wonderful gifts that God has given him: "a spirit of power and of love and of a sound mind."

As we work through Step 8, this verse can be a great encouragement to us as well. Because of the Holy Spirit's power in our lives, we are able to do what is right by forgiving and asking to be forgiven. We have God's love inspiring us to offer these amends; and we have the sound mind of God's wisdom leading us in the timing and method of these amends.

For further reading on Step 8, turn to page 495.

Daily Encouragement

DAY 199 READING: 2 TIMOTHY 1:1–18

A Thought for the New Day: Think of the days, hours, and years Lois and Eunice must have jointly invested in planting the Word of God in young Timothy's heart and mind (v. 5). Paul does not mention Timothy's father, who was Greek. Apparently the Jewish mother and grandmother provided the boy's education. Let us pray there will always be caring parents carrying on this most vital of all work, even in the presence of uncooperative family members. (*Turn to page 459.*)

17 but when he arrived in Rome, he sought me out very diligently and found *me.*

18 The Lord grant to him that he may find mercy from the Lord in that Day—and you know very well how many ways he ministered to me at Ephesus.

2 You therefore, my son, be strong in the grace that is in Christ Jesus.

2 And the things that you have heard from me among many witnesses, commit these to faithful men who will be able to teach others also.

3 You therefore must endure hardship as a good soldier of Jesus Christ.

STEP 10
4 No one engaged in warfare entangles himself with the affairs of *this* life, that he may please him who enlisted him as a soldier.

5 And also if anyone competes in athletics, he is not crowned unless he competes according to the rules.

6 The hard-working farmer must be first to partake of the crops.

7 Consider what I say, and may the Lord give you understanding in all things.

8 Remember that Jesus Christ, of the seed of David, was raised from the dead according to my gospel,

9 for which I suffer trouble as an evildoer, *even* to the point of chains; but the word of God is not chained.

10 Therefore I endure all things for the sake of the elect, that they also may obtain the salvation which is in Christ Jesus with eternal glory.

11 *This is* a faithful saying:

For if we died with *Him,*
    We shall also live with *Him.*
12 If we endure,
    We shall also reign with *Him.*
If we deny *Him,*
    He also will deny us.
13 If we are faithless,
    He remains faithful;
    He cannot deny Himself.

14 Remind *them* of these things, charging *them* before the Lord not to strive about words to no profit, to the ruin of the hearers.

15 Be diligent to present yourself approved to God, a worker who does not need to be ashamed, rightly dividing the word of truth.
STEP 11

16 But shun profane *and* vain babblings, for they will increase to more ungodliness.

17 And their message will spread like cancer. Hymenaeus and Philetus are of this sort,

18 who have strayed concerning the truth, saying that the resurrection is already past; and they overthrow the faith of some.

19 Nevertheless the solid foundation of God stands, having this seal: "The Lord knows those who are His," and, "Let everyone who names the name of Christ depart from iniquity."

20 But in a great house there are not only vessels of gold and silver, but also of wood and clay, some for honor and some for dishonor.
STEP 10

21 Therefore if anyone cleanses himself from the latter, he will be a vessel for honor, sanctified and useful for the Master, prepared for every good work.

22 Flee also youthful lusts; but pursue righteousness, faith, love, peace with those who call on the Lord out of a pure heart.

23 But avoid foolish and ignorant disputes, knowing that they generate strife.

24 And a servant of the Lord must not quarrel but be gentle to all, able to teach, patient,

25 in humility correcting those who are in opposition, if God perhaps will grant them repentance, so that they may know the truth,

26 and *that* they may come to their senses *and escape* the snare of the devil, having been taken captive by him to *do* his will.

3 But know this, that in the last days perilous times will come:
2 For men will be lovers of them-

STEP 10

*Continued to take personal inventory
and when we were wrong promptly admitted it.*

2 Timothy 2:4–7

When a diligent soldier knows the approval of his commander, there is encouragement. When a diligent athlete gains the winner's crown, there is joy. When a diligent farmer partakes of the food he has grown, there is satisfaction.

Each of these metaphors illumines and explains our walk as believers. God wants us to be industrious in our Christian lives. As good soldiers of the Cross, we should pay attention to with what and with whom we become involved. Are the hours in our day filled with worthy activities? As runners in the Heavenly Marathon, are we keeping God's commands so that we can win the prize? And as farmers in the King's Garden, are we sowing the seeds that will yield the fruit of the Spirit (love, joy, peace, longsuffering, kindness, goodness, faithfulness, gentleness, and self-control) in our lives?

Paul tells his young friend Timothy to consider these things. They are a worthy meditation for us all.

For further reading on Step 10, turn to page 469.

Daily Encouragement

DAY 200 READING: 2 TIMOTHY 2:1—4:22

A Thought for the New Day: How we marvel at this miracle of Paul's confidence in his heavenly destiny! Picture this wasted man in the Mamertine dungeon at Rome. A man of small frame to begin with, he had been beaten and stoned so often that his form and face were repulsive. Still he had unspeakable joy in his great hope of the glorious life that awaited him beyond the executioner's sword (4:8). Yet Paul is not unique. He declared the hope we are all heirs to when Christ is our great treasure. (*Turn to page 463.*)

selves, lovers of money, boasters, proud, blasphemers, disobedient to parents, unthankful, unholy,

3 unloving, unforgiving, slanderers, without self-control, brutal, despisers of good,

4 traitors, headstrong, haughty, lovers of pleasure rather than lovers of God,

5 having a form of godliness but denying its power. And from such people turn away!

6 For of this sort are those who creep into households and make captives of gullible women loaded down with sins, led away by various lusts,

7 always learning and never able to come to the knowledge of the truth.

8 Now as Jannes and Jambres resisted Moses, so do these also resist the truth: men of corrupt minds, disapproved concerning the faith;

9 but they will progress no further, for their folly will be manifest to all, as theirs also was.

10 But you have carefully followed my doctrine, manner of life, purpose, faith, longsuffering, love, perseverance,

11 persecutions, afflictions, which happened to me at Antioch, at Iconium, at Lystra—what persecutions I endured. And out of *them* all the Lord delivered me.

12 Yes, and all who desire to live godly in Christ Jesus will suffer persecution.

13 But evil men and impostors will grow worse and worse, deceiving and being deceived.

14 But *as for* you, continue in the things which you have learned and been assured of, knowing from whom you have learned *them,*

15 and that from childhood you have known the Holy Scriptures, which are able to make you wise for salvation through faith which is in Christ Jesus.

16 All Scripture *is* given by inspiration of God, and *is* profitable for doctrine, for reproof, for correction, for instruction in righteousness,

17 that the man of God may be complete, thoroughly equipped for every good work.

4 I charge *you* therefore before God and the Lord Jesus Christ, who will judge the living and the dead at His appearing and His kingdom:

2 Preach the word! Be ready in season *and* out of season. Convince, rebuke, exhort, with all longsuffering and teaching.

3 For the time will come when they will not endure sound doctrine, but according to their own desires, *because* they have itching ears, they will heap up for themselves teachers;

4 and they will turn *their* ears away from the truth, and be turned aside to fables.

5 But you be watchful in all things, endure afflictions, do the work of an evangelist, fulfill your ministry.

6 For I am already being poured out *as a drink offering,* and the time of my departure is at hand.

7 I have fought the good fight, I have finished the race, I have kept the faith.

8 Finally, there is laid up for me the crown of righteousness, which the Lord, the righteous Judge, will give to me on that Day, and not to me only but also to all who have loved His appearing.

9 Be diligent to come to me quickly;

10 for Demas has forsaken me, having loved this present world, and has departed for Thessalonica—Crescens for Galatia, Titus for Dalmatia.

11 Only Luke is with me. Get Mark and bring him with you, for he is useful to me for ministry.

12 And Tychicus I have sent to Ephesus.

13 Bring the cloak that I left with Carpus at Troas when you come—

and the books, especially the parchments.

14 Alexander the coppersmith did me much harm. May the Lord repay him according to his works.

15 You also must beware of him, for he has greatly resisted our words.

16 At my first defense no one stood with me, but all forsook me. May it not be charged against them.

17 But the Lord stood with me and strengthened me, so that the message might be preached fully through me, and *that* all the Gentiles might hear. And I was delivered out of the mouth of the lion.

18 And the Lord will deliver me from every evil work and preserve *me* for His heavenly kingdom. To Him *be* glory forever and ever. Amen!

19 Greet Prisca and Aquila, and the household of Onesiphorus.

20 Erastus stayed in Corinth, but Trophimus I have left in Miletus sick.

21 Do your utmost to come before winter. Eubulus greets you, as well as Pudens, Linus, Claudia, and all the brethren.

22 The Lord Jesus Christ be with your spirit. Grace be with you. Amen.

THE EPISTLE OF PAUL THE APOSTLE TO

TITUS

PAUL, a servant of God and an apostle of Jesus Christ, according to the faith of God's elect and the acknowledgment of the truth which is according to godliness,

2 in hope of eternal life which God, who cannot lie, promised before time began,

3 but has in due time manifested His word through preaching, which was committed to me according to the commandment of God our Savior;

4 To Titus, *my* true son in *our* common faith:

Grace, mercy, *and* peace from God the Father and the Lord Jesus Christ our Savior.

5 For this reason I left you in. Crete, that you should set in order the things that are lacking, and appoint elders in every city as I commanded you—

6 if a man is blameless, the husband of one wife, having faithful children not accused of dissipation or insubordination.

7 For a bishop must be blameless, as a steward of God, not self-willed, not quick-tempered, not given to wine, not violent, not greedy for money,

8 but hospitable, a lover of what is good, sober-minded, just, holy, self-controlled,

9 holding fast the faithful word as he has been taught, that he may be able, by sound doctrine, both to exhort and convict those who contradict.

10 For there are many insubordinate, both idle talkers and deceivers, especially those of the circumcision,

11 whose mouths must be stopped, who subvert whole households, teaching things which they ought not, for the sake of dishonest gain.

12 One of them, a prophet of their own, said, "Cretans *are* always liars, evil beasts, lazy gluttons."

13 This testimony is true. There-

fore rebuke them sharply, that they may be sound in the faith,

14 not giving heed to Jewish fables and commandments of men who turn from the truth.

15 To the pure all things are pure, but to those who are defiled and unbelieving nothing is pure; but even their mind and conscience are defiled.

16 They profess to know God, but in works they deny Him, being abominable, disobedient, and disqualified for every good work.

2 But as for you, speak the things which are proper for sound doctrine:

2 that the older men be sober, reverent, temperate, sound in faith, in love, in patience;

3 the older women likewise, that they be reverent in behavior, not slanderers, not given to much wine, teachers of good things—

4 that they admonish the young women to love their husbands, to love their children,

5 to be discreet, chaste, homemakers, good, obedient to their own husbands, that the word of God may not be blasphemed.

6 Likewise exhort the young men to be sober-minded,

STEP 12 7 in all things showing yourself *to be* a pattern of good works; in doctrine *showing* integrity, reverence, incorruptibility,

8 sound speech that cannot be condemned, that one who is an opponent may be ashamed, having nothing evil to say of you.

9 *Exhort* servants to be obedient to their own masters, to be well pleasing in all *things*, not answering back,

10 not pilfering, but showing all good fidelity, that they may adorn the doctrine of God our Savior in all things.

STEP 6 11 For the grace of God that brings salvation has appeared to all men,

12 teaching us that, denying un-

godliness and worldly lusts, we should live soberly, righteously, and godly in the present age,

13 looking for the blessed hope and glorious appearing of our great God and Savior Jesus Christ,

14 who gave Himself for us, that He might redeem us from every lawless deed and purify for Himself *His* own special people, zealous for good works.

15 Speak these things, exhort, and rebuke with all authority. Let no one despise you.

3 Remind them to be subject to rulers and authorities, to obey, to be ready for every good work, STEP 11

2 to speak evil of no one, to be peaceable, gentle, showing all humility to all men.

3 For we ourselves were also once foolish, disobedient, deceived, serving various lusts and pleasures, living in malice and envy, hateful and hating one another.

4 But when the kindness and the love of God our Savior toward man appeared,

5 not by works of righteousness which we have done, but according to His mercy He saved us, through the washing of regeneration and renewing of the Holy Spirit,

6 whom He poured out on us abundantly through Jesus Christ our Savior,

7 that having been justified by His grace we should become heirs according to the hope of eternal life.

8 This is a faithful saying, and these things I want you to affirm constantly, that those who have believed in God should be careful to maintain good works. These things are good and profitable to men.

9 But avoid foolish disputes, genealogies, contentions, and strivings about the law; for they are unprofitable and useless.

*Sought through prayer and meditation to improve our conscious contact with God **as we understood Him,** praying only for knowledge of His will for us and the power to carry that out.*

Titus 3:1–7

Our compulsive nature frequently tempts us with the illusion that we can somehow "work our way to Heaven." Ashamed by our sense of inadequacy, we seek to redeem ourselves through self-achievement, self-sacrifice, or self-fulfillment.

We know without question our need for redemption, because, prior to recovery, we were "foolish, disobedient, deceived, serving various lusts and pleasures, living in malice and envy, hateful and hating one another" (v. 3).

The miracle of salvation is that we do not have to function as our own codependent redeemer. We do not have to attempt to win, buy, or barter our salvation "by works of righteousness" (v. 5). Our redemption comes as a gift from God, "through the washing of regeneration and renewing of the Holy Spirit, whom He poured out on us abundantly through Jesus Christ our Savior" (vv. 5, 6).

For further reading on Step 11, turn to page 467.

Daily Encouragement

DAY 201 READING: TITUS 1:1—3:15

A Thought for the New Day: Have you thought very long about God's kindness? Unhappily, we are all very self-righteous people, and it too often appears that we treat God as our debtor (3:4, 5). We feel that we deserve His very best. Yet, throughout all our lives we are inclined to live as if He were not there or did not matter. Let us stop and consider the infinitely good things God showers us with daily—and the better things He will yet do for us if only we will let Him! (*Turn to page 465.*)

10 Reject a divisive man after the first and second admonition,

11 knowing that such a person is warped and sinning, being self-condemned.

12 When I send Artemas to you, or Tychicus, be diligent to come to me at Nicopolis, for I have decided to spend the winter there.

13 Send Zenas the lawyer and Apollos on their journey with haste, that they may lack nothing.

14 And let our *people* also learn to maintain good works, to *meet* urgent needs, that they may not be unfruitful.

15 All who *are* with me greet you. Greet those who love us in the faith. Grace *be* with you all. Amen.

THE EPISTLE OF PAUL THE APOSTLE TO
PHILEMON

PAUL, a prisoner of Christ Jesus, and Timothy *our* brother,

To Philemon our beloved *friend* and fellow laborer,

2 to the beloved Apphia, Archippus our fellow soldier, and to the church in your house:

3 Grace to you and peace from God our Father and the Lord Jesus Christ.

4 I thank my God, making mention of you always in my prayers,

5 hearing of your love and faith which you have toward the Lord Jesus and toward all the saints,

6 that the sharing of your faith may become effective by the acknowledgment of every good thing which is in you in Christ Jesus.

7 For we have great joy and consolation in your love, because the hearts of the saints have been refreshed by you, brother.

8 Therefore, though I might be very bold in Christ to command you what is fitting,

9 yet for love's sake I rather appeal to you—being such a one as Paul, the aged, and now also a prisoner of Jesus Christ—

10 I appeal to you for my son Onesimus, whom I have begotten *while* in my chains,

11 who once was unprofitable to you, but now is profitable to you and to me.

12 I am sending him back. You therefore receive him, that is, my own heart,

13 whom I wished to keep with me, that on your behalf he might minister to me in my chains for the gospel.

14 But without your consent I wanted to do nothing, that your good deed might not be by compulsion, as it were, but voluntary.

15 For perhaps he departed for a while for this *purpose*, that you might receive him forever,

16 no longer as a slave but more than a slave, *as* a beloved brother, especially to me but how much more to you, both in the flesh and in the Lord.

17 If then you count me as a partner, receive him as *you would* me.

18 But if he has wronged you or owes *you* anything, put that on my account.

19 I, Paul, am writing with my own hand. I will repay—not to mention to you that you owe me even your own self besides.

20 Yes, brother, let me have joy

STEP 9

*Made direct amends to such people wherever possible,
except when to do so would injure them or others.*

Philemon 8–17

One of the most insidious results of our addictions is their corrosive effect on our sense of responsibility. A major factor determining the quality and the success of our recovery is our willingness to assume new, healthy self-responsibility.

In the apostle Paul's letter to Philemon, we hear an extraordinary message of responsibility. In this epistle, Paul urges that old resentments be set aside and that a follower of Christ be welcomed home and unconditionally reunited with his former church.

A similar spirit is required in our execution of Step 9. In Step 9, we extend the hand of reconciliation to those who have wronged us and to those we have wronged, regardless of their ability to reciprocate. In this way, God working through us becomes a radiant source of relationship healing, much as Paul was a mediator among members of the fragmented early church.

For further reading on Step 9, turn to page 487.

Daily Encouragement

DAY 202 READING: PHILEMON 1–25

A Thought for the New Day: In this most beautiful of all Paul's letters we see the apostle's ability to put the best interpretation on a bad situation. Philemon had lost his servant "for a while," but he now received him back "forever" as a new person in Christ (v. 15). Now Philemon and Onesimus would be bound together, no longer as slave and master, but as eternal friends. Nothing would ever separate the young man from Christ's love—or from Philemon's. (*Turn to page 467.*)

from you in the Lord; refresh my heart in the Lord.

21 Having confidence in your obedience, I write to you, knowing that you will do even more than I say.

22 But, meanwhile, also prepare a guest room for me, for I trust that through your prayers I shall be granted to you.

23 Epaphras, my fellow prisoner in Christ Jesus, greets you,

24 *as do* Mark, Aristarchus, Demas, Luke, my fellow laborers.

25 The grace of our Lord Jesus Christ *be* with your spirit. Amen.

THE EPISTLE TO THE
HEBREWS

GOD, who at various times and in different ways spoke in time past to the fathers by the prophets,

2 has in these last days spoken to us by *His* Son, whom He has appointed heir of all things, through whom also He made the worlds;

3 who being the brightness of *His* glory and the express image of His person, and upholding all things by the word of His power, when He had by Himself purged our sins, sat down at the right hand of the Majesty on high,

4 having become so much better than the angels, as He has by inheritance obtained a more excellent name than they.

5 For to which of the angels did He ever say:

> "You are My Son,
> Today I have begotten You"?

And again:

> "I will be to Him a Father,
> And He shall be to Me a Son"?

6 But when He again brings the firstborn into the world, He says:

> "Let all the angels of God
> worship Him."

7 And of the angels He says:

> "Who makes His angels spirits
> And His ministers a flame of
> fire."

8 But to the Son *He says:*

> "Your throne, O God,
> is forever and ever;
> A scepter of righteousness is
> the scepter of Your Kingdom.
9 You have loved righteousness
> and hated lawlessness;
> Therefore God, Your God,
> has anointed You
> With the oil of gladness more
> than Your companions."

10 And:

> "You, LORD, in the beginning
> laid the foundation of the
> earth,
> And the heavens are the work
> of Your hands;
11 They will perish, but You
> remain;
> And they will all grow old
> like a garment;
12 Like a cloak You will fold them
> up,
> And they will be changed.
> But You are the same,
> And Your years will not fail."

*Sought through prayer and meditation to improve our conscious contact with God **as we understood Him,** praying only for knowledge of His will for us and the power to carry that out.*

Hebrews 1

Right thinking about God is absolutely crucial to true and lasting recovery. This passage helps us understand that Jesus is God. He is not simply chief among the angels in the spirit world; He is the Second Person in a Triune Godhead. He is the Creator and sustainer of all things that exist; and by the power of His sacrifice on the cross, He has purged our sins. He is eternal and unchanging and righteous. When we remove any misconceptions about God, which have clouded our thinking, His Truth will illuminate our path to recovery.

God is not Santa Claus, and God is not an avenging scorekeeper. He is a tender, compassionate, and merciful Father to those who truly seek Him. His power is awesome and all-encompassing, and so is His love toward those who believe.

For further reading on Step 11, turn to page 505.

Daily Encouragement

DAY 203 READING: HEBREWS 1:1–14

A Thought for the New Day: It is right to think of Jesus as the gentle Teacher who went about the land two thousand years ago "doing good." This was the way God wanted us to understand Him—as the One who loved us enough to bring some of the brightness of heaven into our dark world. Lest we forget, however, this gentle Man veiled in His flesh the very Lord of Glory, here addressed as the enthroned God Himself (v. 8). God Himself has visited us in His Son. (*Turn to page 469.*)

13 But to which of the angels has He ever said:

> "Sit at My right hand,
> Till I make Your enemies
>   Your footstool"?

14 Are they not all ministering spirits sent forth to minister for those who will inherit salvation?

STEP 10

2 Therefore we must give the more earnest heed to the things we have heard, lest we drift away. 2 For if the word spoken through angels proved steadfast, and every transgression and disobedience received a just reward, 3 how shall we escape if we neglect so great a salvation, which at the first began to be spoken by the Lord, and was confirmed to us by those who heard *Him,* 4 God also bearing witness both with signs and wonders, with various miracles, and gifts of the Holy Spirit, according to His own will? 5 For He has not put the world to come, of which we speak, in subjection to angels. 6 But one testified in a certain place, saying:

> "What is man that You
>   are mindful of him,
> Or the son of man that You
>   take care of him?
> 7 You made him a little lower
>   than the angels;
> You crowned him with glory
>   and honor,
> And set him over the works
>   of Your hands.
> 8 You have put all things
>   in subjection under his feet."

For in that He put all in subjection under him, He left nothing *that is* not put under him. But now we do not yet see all things put under him. 9 But we see Jesus, who was made a little lower than the angels, for the suffering of death crowned with glory and honor, that He, by the grace of God, might taste death for everyone. 10 For it was fitting for Him, for whom *are* all things and by whom *are* all things, in bringing many sons to glory, to make the author of their salvation perfect through sufferings. 11 For both He who sanctifies and those who are being sanctified *are* all of one, for which reason He is not ashamed to call them brethren, 12 saying:

> "I will declare Your name to My
>   brethren;
> In the midst of the
>   congregation I will sing
>   praise to You."

13 And again:

> "I will put My trust in Him."

And again:

> "Here am I and the children
>   whom God has given Me."

STEP 2

14 Inasmuch then as the children have partaken of flesh and blood, He Himself likewise shared in the same, that through death He might destroy him who had the power of death, that is, the devil, 15 and release those who through fear of death were all their lifetime subject to bondage. 16 For indeed He does not give aid to angels, but He does give aid to the seed of Abraham. 17 Therefore, in all things He had to be made like *His* brethren, that He might be a merciful and faithful High Priest in things *pertaining* to God, to make propitiation for the sins of the people. 18 For in that He Himself has suffered, being tempted, He is able to aid those who are tempted.

3 Therefore, holy brethren, partakers of the heavenly calling, consider the Apostle and High

STEP 10

*Continued to take personal inventory
and when we were wrong promptly admitted it.*

Hebrews 2:1–3

The children were enjoying the sunshine of a warm summer day. They had taken the rowboat out on the lake and had carefully rowed to the end farthest away from the restricted area around the power plant. They swam and played and then rested in the boat, while enjoying the gentle breeze. But their enjoyment turned to fear and dismay upon discovering the current had inch by inch carried them deep into forbidden territory. Fortunately, rescued by a stern but caring patrolman, they learned a valuable lesson that day: "Give heed, lest you drift away."

Likewise, enjoying our new assurance and progress in life, we may drift quite unknowingly to the brink of disaster. We may neglect our recovery program, thinking it no longer important. However, Step 10 warns us, "Take inventory; take heed," lest, in our complacency, we drift toward the sinister power plant of our old character defects.

For further reading on Step 10, turn to page 471.

Daily Encouragement

DAY 204 READING: HEBREWS 2:1–18

A Thought for the New Day: The word "tempted" in verse 18 is more accurately, "tested." Testing takes many forms: sickness, loss of loved ones, financial failure, persecution. Elsewhere we read that God never allows us to be tested beyond our ability to pass the test. You can remain calm and collected when things go wrong and others are giving up, because you have the friendship of that One who was tested and overcame. With His help, you will always pass the test. (*Turn to page 471.*)

Priest of our confession, Christ Jesus,

2 who was faithful to Him who appointed Him, as Moses also *was faithful* in all His house.

3 For this One has been counted worthy of more glory than Moses, inasmuch as He who built the house has more honor than the house.

4 For every house is built by someone, but He who built all things *is* God.

5 And Moses indeed *was* faithful in all His house as a servant, for a testimony of those things which would be spoken *afterward,*

6 but Christ as a Son over His own house, whose house we are if we hold fast the confidence and the rejoicing of the hope firm to the end.

STEP 10

7 Therefore, as the Holy Spirit says:

"Today, if you will hear His
    voice,
8 Do not harden your hearts
    as in the rebellion,
  In the day of trial in the
    wilderness,
9 Where your fathers tested Me,
    proved Me,
  And saw My works forty years.
10 Therefore I was angry with
    that generation,
  And said, 'They always go
    astray in their heart,
  And they have not known My
    ways.'
11 So I swore in My wrath,
  'They shall not enter My rest.'"

12 Beware, brethren, lest there be in any of you an evil heart of unbelief in departing from the living God;

13 but exhort one another daily, while it is called *"Today,"* lest any of you be hardened through the deceitfulness of sin.

14 For we have become partakers of Christ if we hold the beginning of our confidence steadfast to the end,

15 while it is said:

"Today, if you will hear His
    voice,
  Do not harden your hearts as
    in the rebellion."

16 For who, having heard, rebelled? Indeed, *was it* not all who came out of Egypt, *led* by Moses?

17 Now with whom was He angry forty years? *Was it* not with those who sinned, whose corpses fell in the wilderness?

18 And to whom did He swear that they would not enter His rest, but to those who did not obey?

19 So we see that they could not enter in because of unbelief.

STEP 3

4 Therefore, since a promise remains of entering His rest, let us fear lest any of you seem to have come short of it.

2 For indeed the gospel was preached to us as well as to them; but the word which they heard did not profit them, not being mixed with faith in those who heard *it.*

3 For we who have believed do enter that rest, as He has said:

"So I swore in My wrath,
'They shall not enter My rest,'"

although the works were finished from the foundation of the world.

4 For He has spoken in a certain place of the seventh *day* in this way: *"And God rested on the seventh day from all His works";*

5 and again in this *place:* *"They shall not enter My rest."*

6 Since therefore it remains that some *must* enter it, and those to whom it was first preached did not enter because of disobedience,

7 again He designates a certain day, saying in David, *"Today,"* after such a long time, as it has been said:

STEP 10

Continued to take personal inventory
and when we were wrong promptly admitted it.

Hebrews 3:7–13

The first generation of Israelites who left Egypt under Moses' leadership was a source of deep sadness to God. Patiently, constantly God revealed Himself to them. Over and over they observed His power and His miraculous protection. They received His law and His promises. They saw His presence in the cloud and the fiery pillar that led them. Still, when it came time to conquer the Promised Land, they shrank away in unbelief. God forgave them, but this did not erase the consequences of their lack of faith. Because of their unbelief, that generation was not allowed the joy and peace of the Promised Land. They had escaped the bondage of Egypt, but they had also missed the full blessing of God's rest in the Promised Land. We, too, have escaped bondage. Now we must daily exercise our faith in the promises and power of the Lord Jesus. If our heart's desire is to grow in His love and wisdom, we will allow His Word to direct us and to keep us strong in our faith.

For further reading on Step 10, turn to page 483.

Daily Encouragement

DAY 205 READING: HEBREWS 3:1—4:11

A Thought for the New Day: Rest is not just inactivity. Some people are resting even when they are active. Others burn up energy even while they sleep. In a way, rest is a state of mind or attitude that can be present in all circumstances. It comes from an inward calm that arises from the assurance that everything is under control and moving in the most desirable direction. Rest is the peace that comes from knowing God's good purposes cannot fail, and neither will He let you fail (4:9). *(Turn to page 473.)*

"Today, if you will hear His
  voice,
Do not harden your hearts."

8 For if Joshua had given them
rest, then He would not afterward
have spoken of another day.

9 There remains therefore a rest
for the people of God.

10 For he who has entered His rest
has himself also ceased from his
works as God *did* from His.

11 Let us therefore be diligent to
enter that rest, lest anyone fall
after the same example of disobedience.

STEP 5

12 For the word of God *is* living
and powerful, and sharper than
any two-edged sword, piercing
even to the division of soul and
spirit, and of joints and marrow,
and is a discerner of the thoughts
and intents of the heart.

13 And there is no creature hidden
from His sight, but all things *are*
naked and open to the eyes of Him
to whom we *must give* account.

14 Seeing then that we have a
great High Priest who has passed
through the heavens, Jesus the
Son of God, let us hold fast *our*
confession.

15 For we do not have a High
Priest who cannot sympathize
with our weaknesses, but was in
all *points* tempted as *we are, yet*
without sin.

16 Let us therefore come boldly to
the throne of grace, that we may
obtain mercy and find grace to
help in time of need.

5 For every high priest taken
from among men is appointed
for men in things *pertaining* to
God, that he may offer both gifts
and sacrifices for sins.

2 He can have compassion on
those who are ignorant and going
astray, since he himself is also
beset by weakness.

3 Because of this he is required as
for the people, so also for himself,
to offer for sins.

4 And no man takes this honor to
himself, but he who is called by
God, just as Aaron *was*.

5 So also Christ did not glorify
Himself to become High Priest, *but
it* was He who said to Him:

"You are My Son,
Today I have begotten You."

6 As *He* also *says* in another
place:

"You are a priest forever
According to the order of
  Melchizedek";

7 who, in the days of His flesh,
when He had offered up prayers
and supplications, with vehement
cries and tears to Him who was
able to save Him from death, and
was heard because of His godly
fear,

8 though He was a Son, *yet* He
learned obedience by the things
which He suffered.

9 And having been perfected, He
became the author of eternal salvation to all who obey Him,

10 called by God as High Priest
*"according to the order of Melchiz-
edek,"*

11 of whom we have much to say,
and hard to explain, since you
have become dull of hearing.

12 For though by this time you
ought to be teachers, you need
someone to teach you again the
first principles of the oracles of
God; and you have come to need
milk and not solid food.

13 For everyone who partakes *only*
of milk *is* unskilled in the word of
righteousness, for he is a babe.

14 But solid food belongs to those
who are of full age, *that is*, those
who by reason of use have their
senses exercised to discern both
good and evil.

6 Therefore, leaving the discussion of the elementary *principles* of Christ, let us go on to per-

STEP 5

*Admitted to God, to ourselves, and to another human being
the exact nature of our wrongs.*

Hebrews 4:12–16

The sharing of fifth step confessional material is delicate, because, in doing so, we lower psychological defenses and become emotionally vulnerable. We may be pouring out memories of experience and behavior about which we hold deep feelings of shame. We may be disclosing confidences that we have clung to for a lifetime.

Perhaps we have hesitated to engage in the fifth step experience because we feared criticism. Since the fifth step invites us to confess "to God, to ourselves, and to another human being," we may fear condemnation from ourselves, from that other human being, or even from God. The antidote to this fear is to extend compassion to ourselves, to select an understanding person with whom to share this step, and to accept God's merciful intercession for our inventory issues.

What reassurance there is in knowing that as we turn to confess our sins to God, He has provided One who can both emphasize and understand our sins with an infinite capacity for grace!

For further reading on Step 5, turn to page 497.

Daily Encouragement

DAY 206 READING: HEBREWS 4:12—5:14

A Thought for the New Day: God is the constant spectator who observes, not only our actions, but also all our thoughts (4:13). You might say that He has a front seat in the great drama of life. If this fact seems scary, it probably should be. It makes no sense to amble casually through our daily lives, unconscious of the ever-present One. However, God's presence also excites us to more meaningful action: with Him, every moment of our lives is important. (*Turn to page 475.*)

fection, not laying again the foundation of repentance from dead works and of faith toward God,

2 of the doctrine of baptisms, of laying on of hands, of resurrection of the dead, and of eternal judgment.

3 And this we will do if God permits.

4 For *it is* impossible for those who were once enlightened, and have tasted the heavenly gift, and have become partakers of the Holy Spirit,

5 and have tasted the good word of God and the powers of the age to come,

6 if they fall away, to renew them again to repentance, since they crucify again for themselves the Son of God, and put *Him* to an open shame.

7 For the earth which drinks in the rain that often comes upon it, and bears herbs useful for those by whom it is cultivated, receives blessing from God;

8 but if it bears thorns and briars, *it is* rejected and near to being cursed, whose end *is* to be burned.

9 But, beloved, we are confident of better things concerning you, yes, things that accompany salvation, though we speak in this manner.

10 For God *is* not unjust to forget your work and labor of love which you have shown toward His name, *in that* you have ministered to the saints, and do minister.

STEP 6 11 And we desire that each one of you show the same diligence to the full assurance of hope until the end,

12 that you do not become sluggish, but imitate those who through faith and patience inherit the promises.

13 For when God made a promise to Abraham, because He could swear by no one greater, He swore by Himself,

14 saying, *"Surely blessing I will bless you, and multiplying I will multiply you."*

15 And so, after he had patiently endured, he obtained the promise.

16 For men indeed swear by the greater, and an oath for confirmation *is* for them an end of all dispute.

17 Thus God, determining to show more abundantly to the heirs of promise the immutability of His counsel, confirmed *it* by an oath,

18 that by two immutable things, in which it *is* impossible for God to lie, we might have strong consolation, who have fled for refuge to lay hold of the hope set before *us.*

19 This *hope* we have as an anchor of the soul, both sure and steadfast, and which enters the Presence *behind* the veil,

20 where the forerunner has entered for us, *even* Jesus, having become High Priest forever according to the order of Melchizedek.

7 For this Melchizedek, king of Salem, priest of the Most High God, who met Abraham returning from the slaughter of the kings and blessed him,

2 to whom also Abraham gave a tenth part of all, first being translated "king of righteousness," and then also king of Salem, meaning "king of peace,"

3 without father, without mother, without genealogy, having neither beginning of days nor end of life, but made like the Son of God, remains a priest continually.

4 Now consider how great this man *was,* to whom even the patriarch Abraham gave a tenth of the spoils.

5 And indeed those who are of the sons of Levi, who receive the priesthood, have a commandment to receive tithes from the people according to the law, that is, from their brethren, though they have come from the loins of Abraham;

6 but he whose genealogy is not

STEP 6

Were entirely ready to have God
remove all these defects of character.

Hebrews 6:11, 12

The angels of heaven rejoice in the progress each person makes as he or she moves from hopelessness to trust, and then on to insight and admission. We have chosen a good and wise course. Now these verses encourage us to continue that diligent work so that the hope we have for recovery will become a full assurance for us.

We are at another crucial juncture. To admit our problems is important. But admission is meaningless without the desire to do something to change our situation. Now is not the time to "become sluggish." Now is the time for decisive faith and firm patience in order that we may inherit all the blessings God has to offer us. There are possibly some hard places ahead, but that need not deter us. Our confidence is not in ourselves, but in the power of our Lord. Because He is able, we are ready.

For further reading on Step 6, turn to page 491.

Daily Encouragement

DAY 207 READING: HEBREWS 6:1–20

A Thought for the New Day: The hope we have in Christ is compared to an "anchor of the soul" (v. 19). That anchor is the stabilizer of our lives: it holds us steady as an anchor holds a ship steady and firm against every storm that blows. Behind the veil that hides a present view of heaven is our risen Savior who keeps us strong in the face of every trial and disappointment. As we are secured to our heavenly Anchor, we are bound to succeed. (*Turn to page 477.*)

derived from them received tithes from Abraham and blessed him who had the promises.

7 Now beyond all contradiction the lesser is blessed by the better.

8 Here mortal men receive tithes, but there he *receives them*, of whom it is witnessed that he lives.

9 Even Levi, who receives tithes, paid tithes through Abraham, so to speak,

10 for he was still in the loins of his father when Melchizedek met him.

11 Therefore, if perfection were through the Levitical priesthood (for under it the people received the law), what further need *was there* that another priest should rise according to the order of Melchizedek, and not be called according to the order of Aaron?

12 For the priesthood being changed, of necessity there is also a change of the law.

13 For He of whom these things are spoken belongs to another tribe, from which no man has officiated at the altar.

14 For *it is* evident that our Lord arose from Judah, of which tribe Moses spoke nothing concerning priesthood.

15 And it is yet far more evident if, in the likeness of Melchizedek, there arises another priest

16 who has come, not according to the law of a fleshly commandment, but according to the power of an endless life.

17 For He testifies:

"You are a priest forever
   According to the order of
      Melchizedek."

18 For on the one hand there is an annulling of the former commandment because of its weakness and unprofitableness,

19 for the law made nothing perfect; on the other hand, *there is the* bringing in of a better hope, through which we draw near to God.

20 And inasmuch as *He was* not *made priest* without an oath

21 (for they have become priests without an oath, but He with an oath by Him who said to Him:

"The LORD has sworn
   And will not relent,
'You are a priest forever
   According to the order of
      Melchizedek' "),

22 by so much more Jesus has become a surety of a better covenant.

23 And there were many priests, because they were prevented by death from continuing.

24 But He, because He continues forever, has an unchangeable priesthood.

25 Therefore He is also able to save to the uttermost those who come to God through Him, since He ever lives to make intercession for them.

26 For such a High Priest was fitting for us, *who is* holy, harmless, undefiled, separate from sinners, and has become higher than the heavens;

27 who does not need daily, as those high priests, to offer up sacrifices, first for His own sins and then for the people's, for this He did once for all when He offered up Himself.

28 For the law appoints as high priests men who have weakness, but the word of the oath, which came after the law, *appoints* the Son who has been perfected forever.

8 Now *this is* the main point of the things we are saying: We have such a High Priest, who is seated at the right hand of the throne of the Majesty in the heavens,

2 a Minister of the sanctuary and of the true tabernacle which the Lord erected, and not man.

3 For every high priest is appointed to offer both gifts and sac-

STEP
2

*Came to believe that a Power greater than ourselves
could restore us to sanity.*

Hebrews 7:24, 25

Few people would consider taking a difficult journey in a vehicle that was not mechanically dependable. If it is natural and important to want reliability in our worldly possessions, how much more natural and important to feel confident about the Spiritual Entity to which we entrust our eternal souls.

This promise in Hebrews gives us a sure foundation for confidence concerning the Person of Jesus Christ. Completely, entirely, and forevermore, the Lord Jesus is able to save us and make us whole again. When we come in faith to Him, He will "save to the uttermost." There is no trial or difficulty in our lives from which He is unable to deliver us. But that is not all. Jesus "ever lives to make intercession" for us. On earth, He died for us; but now as our Great High Priest, He intervenes on behalf of those who are His children. His power and love will be with us to the very end of the journey.

For further reading on Step 2, turn to page 538.

Daily Encouragement

DAY 208 READING: HEBREWS 7:1–28

A Thought for the New Day: How long does our salvation last? Hebrews 7:25 says that Christ assures us of everlasting or "uttermost" salvation. How can we be assured of Jesus' safekeeping forever? Is it because our prayers are so very effective? Surely our human prayers are not so great after all. However, Jesus, our High Priest in heaven, prays for us continually. His prayers are assurance that we will never be separated from Him. (*Turn to page 481.*)

rifices. Therefore *it is* necessary that this One also have something to offer.

4 For if He were on earth, He would not be a priest, since there are priests who offer the gifts according to the law;

5 who serve the copy and shadow of the heavenly things, as Moses was divinely instructed when he was about to make the tabernacle. For He said, *"See that you make all things according to the pattern shown you on the mountain."*

6 But now He has obtained a more excellent ministry, inasmuch as He is also Mediator of a better covenant, which was established on better promises.

7 For if that first *covenant* had been faultless, then no place would have been sought for a second.

8 Because finding fault with them, He says: *"Behold, the days are coming, says the Lord, when I will make a new covenant with the house of Israel and with the house of Judah—*

9 *"not according to the covenant that I made with their fathers in the day when I took them by the hand to lead them out of the land of Egypt; because they did not continue in My covenant, and I disregarded them, says the Lord.*

10 *"For this is the covenant that I will make with the house of Israel after those days, says the Lord: I will put My laws in their mind and write them on their hearts; and I will be their God, and they shall be My people.*

11 *"None of them shall teach his neighbor, and none his brother, saying, 'Know the Lord,' for all shall know Me, from the least of them to the greatest of them.*

12 *"For I will be merciful to their unrighteousness, and their sins and their lawless deeds I will remember no more."*

13 In that He says, *"A new covenant,"* He has made the first obsolete. Now what is becoming obsolete and growing old is ready to vanish away.

9 Then indeed, even the first *covenant* had ordinances of divine service and the earthly sanctuary.

2 For a tabernacle was prepared: the first *part*, in which *was* the lampstand, the table, and the showbread, which is called the sanctuary;

3 and behind the second veil, the part of the tabernacle which is called the Holiest of All,

4 which had the golden altar of incense and the ark of the covenant overlaid on all sides with gold, in which *were* the golden pot that had the manna, Aaron's rod that budded, and the tablets of the covenant;

5 and above it were the cherubim of glory overshadowing the mercy seat. Of these things we cannot now speak in detail.

6 Now when these things had been thus prepared, the priests always went into the first part of the tabernacle, performing *the services.*

7 But into the second part the high priest *went* alone once a year, not without blood, which he offered for himself and *for* the people's sins *committed* in ignorance;

8 the Holy Spirit indicating this, that the way into the Holiest of All was not yet made manifest while the first tabernacle was still standing.

9 It *was* symbolic for the present time in which both gifts and sacrifices are offered which cannot make him who performed the service perfect in regard to the conscience—

10 *concerned* only with foods and drinks, various washings, and fleshly ordinances imposed until the time of reformation.

11 But Christ came *as* High Priest of the good things to come, with the greater and more perfect tabernacle not made with hands, that is, not of this creation.

12 Not with the blood of goats and calves, but with His own blood He entered the Most Holy Place once for all, having obtained eternal redemption.

13 For if the blood of bulls and goats and the ashes of a heifer, sprinkling the unclean, sanctifies for the purifying of the flesh,

14 how much more shall the blood of Christ, who through the eternal Spirit offered Himself without spot to God, purge your conscience from dead works to serve the living God?

15 And for this reason He is the Mediator of the new covenant, by means of death, for the redemption of the transgressions under the first covenant, that those who are called may receive the promise of the eternal inheritance.

16 For where there *is* a testament, there must also of necessity be the death of the testator.

17 For a testament *is* in force after men are dead, since it has no power at all while the testator lives.

18 Therefore not even the first *covenant* was dedicated without blood.

19 For when Moses had spoken every precept to all the people according to the law, he took the blood of calves and goats, with water, scarlet wool, and hyssop, and sprinkled both the book itself and all the people,

20 saying, *"This is the blood of the covenant which God has commanded you."*

21 Then likewise he sprinkled with blood both the tabernacle and all the vessels of the ministry.

22 And according to the law almost all things are purged with blood, and without shedding of blood there is no remission.

23 Therefore *it was* necessary that the copies of the things in the heavens should be purified with these, but the heavenly things themselves with better sacrifices than these.

24 For Christ has not entered the holy places made with hands, *which are* copies of the true, but into heaven itself, now to appear in the presence of God for us;

25 not that He should offer Himself often, as the high priest enters the Most Holy Place every year with blood of another—

26 He then would have had to suffer often since the foundation of the world; but now, once at the end of the ages, He has appeared to put away sin by the sacrifice of Himself.

27 And as it is appointed for men to die once, but after this the judgment,

28 so Christ was offered once to bear the sins of many. To those who eagerly wait for Him He will appear a second time, apart from sin, for salvation.

10 For the law, having a shadow of the good things to come, *and* not the very image of the things, can never with these same sacrifices, which they offer continually year by year, make those who approach perfect.

2 For then would they not have ceased to be offered? For the worshipers, once purged, would have had no more consciousness of sins.

3 But in those *sacrifices there is* a reminder of sins every year.

4 For *it is* not possible that the blood of bulls and goats could take away sins.

5 Therefore, when He came into the world, He said:

"Sacrifice and offering You did
*   not desire,*
But a body You have prepared
*   for Me.*
6 *In burnt offerings and*
*   sacrifices for sin*
You had no pleasure.
7 *Then I said, 'Behold, I have*
*   come—*

*In the volume of the book
   it is written of Me—
To do Your will, O God.'* "

8 Previously saying, *"Sacrifice
and offering, burnt offerings, and
offerings for sin You did not desire,
nor had pleasure in them"* (which
are offered according to the law),
9 then He said, *"Behold, I have
come to do Your will, O God."* He
takes away the first that He may
establish the second.

10 By that will we have been sanctified through the offering of the
body of Jesus Christ once *for all.*
11 And every priest stands ministering daily and offering repeatedly
the same sacrifices, which can
never take away sins.

12 But this Man, after He had offered one sacrifice for sins forever,
sat down at the right hand of God,
13 from that time waiting till His
enemies are made His footstool.

14 For by one offering He has perfected forever those who are being
sanctified.

15 And the Holy Spirit also witnesses to us; for after He had said
before,

16 *"This is the covenant that I will
make with them after those days,
says the LORD: I will put My laws
into their hearts, and in their
minds I will write them,"*

17 then He adds, *"Their sins and
their lawless deeds I will remember
no more."*

18 Now where there is remission of
these, *there is* no longer an offering for sin.

19 Therefore, brethren, having
boldness to enter the Holiest by
the blood of Jesus,

20 by a new and living way which
He consecrated for us, through the
veil, that is, His flesh,

21 and *having* a High Priest over
the house of God,

22 let us draw near with a true
heart in full assurance of faith,
having our hearts sprinkled from

an evil conscience and our bodies
washed with pure water.

23 Let us hold fast the confession
of *our* hope without wavering, for
He who promised *is* faithful.

24 And let us consider one another
in order to stir up love and good
works,

STEP 12

25 not forsaking the assembling of
ourselves together, as *is* the manner of some, but exhorting *one
another,* and so much the more as
you see the Day approaching.

26 For if we sin willfully after we
have received the knowledge of
the truth, there no longer remains
a sacrifice for sins,

27 but a certain fearful expectation
of judgment, and fiery indignation
which will devour the adversaries.

28 Anyone who has rejected Moses' law dies without mercy on the
testimony of two or three witnesses.

29 Of how much worse punishment, do you suppose, will he be
thought worthy who has trampled
the Son of God underfoot, counted
the blood of the covenant by
which he was sanctified a common
thing, and insulted the Spirit of
grace?

30 For we know Him who said,
"Vengeance is Mine, I will repay,"
says the Lord. And again, *"The
LORD will judge His people."*

31 It is a fearful thing to fall into
the hands of the living God.

32 But recall the former days in
which, after you were illuminated,
you endured a great struggle with
sufferings:

33 partly while you were made a
spectacle both by reproaches and
tribulations, and partly while you
became companions of those who
were so treated;

34 for you had compassion on me
in my chains, and joyfully accepted the plundering of your
goods, knowing that you have a
better and an enduring possession
for yourselves in heaven.

STEP 12

*Having had a spiritual awakening as the result of these steps,
we tried to carry this message to others,
and to practice these principles in all our affairs.*

Hebrews 10:24, 25

Each one of us is either a help or a hindrance to those with
whom we associate. As we abide in Christ and watchfully practice
the concepts we have learned in recovery, our lives encourage and
bless others. We must take care and be diligent to keep in mind the
good of our family, friends, coworkers, and acquaintances. We must
"consider" their struggles and limitations and needs. Then by our
godly example, our unselfish kindness, and our wise words, we must
encourage others to know and walk with Jesus.

Verse 25 emphasizes the importance of continual fellowship and
group worship. Private Bible study is important, but corporate
study, praise, and worship carry blessings and fulfill needs that
nothing else can.

God wants us to be oriented toward others, not only for what we
can give to them, but also because we need others to experience
some of God's best blessings.

For further reading on Step 12, turn to page 525.

Daily Encouragement

DAY 209 READING: HEBREWS 8:1—10:25

A Thought for the New Day: Visible Christianity is love at
work. Such love does not happen automatically, but requires
planned consideration of our partners in life. The idea is
thoughtfulness of one another, as contrasted with careless indifference to each other's concerns and interests. In Christ we have
an inexhaustible store of love. Let us draw constantly on His
infinite resources in order to build up those around us (10:24).
(Turn to page 483.)

35 Therefore do not cast away your confidence, which has great reward.

36 For you have need of endurance, so that after you have done the will of God, you may receive the promise:

37 "For yet a little while,
  And He who is coming will
    come and will not tarry.
38 Now the just shall live by
    faith;
  But if anyone draws back,
  My soul has no pleasure in
    him."

39 But we are not of those who draw back to perdition, but of those who believe to the saving of the soul.

11 Now faith is the substance of things hoped for, the evidence of things not seen.

2 For by it the elders obtained a good testimony.

3 By faith we understand that the worlds were framed by the word of God, so that the things which are seen were not made of things which are visible.

4 By faith Abel offered to God a more excellent sacrifice than Cain, through which he obtained witness that he was righteous, God testifying of his gifts; and through it he being dead still speaks.

5 By faith Enoch was translated so that he did not see death, "and was not found because God had translated him"; for before his translation he had this testimony, that he pleased God.

6 But without faith it is impossible to please Him, for he who comes to God must believe that He is, and that He is a rewarder of those who diligently seek Him.

7 By faith Noah, being divinely warned of things not yet seen, moved with godly fear, prepared an ark for the saving of his household, by which he condemned the world and became heir of the righteousness which is according to faith.

8 By faith Abraham obeyed when he was called to go out to the place which he would afterward receive as an inheritance. And he went out, not knowing where he was going.

9 By faith he sojourned in the land of promise as in a foreign country, dwelling in tents with Isaac and Jacob, the heirs with him of the same promise;

10 for he waited for the city which has foundations, whose builder and maker is God.

11 By faith Sarah herself also received strength to conceive seed, and she bore a child when she was past the age, because she judged Him faithful who had promised.

12 Therefore from one man, and him as good as dead, were born as many as the stars of the sky in multitude—innumerable as the sand which is by the seashore.

13 These all died in faith, not having received the promises, but having seen them afar off were assured of them, embraced them, and confessed that they were strangers and pilgrims on the earth.

14 For those who say such things declare plainly that they seek a homeland.

15 And truly if they had called to mind that country from which they had come out, they would have had opportunity to return.

16 But now they desire a better, that is, a heavenly country. Therefore God is not ashamed to be called their God, for He has prepared a city for them.

17 By faith Abraham, when he was tested, offered up Isaac, and he who had received the promises offered up his only begotten son,

18 of whom it was said, "In Isaac your seed shall be called,"

19 accounting that God was able to raise him up, even from the

STEP 10

Continued to take personal inventory
and when we were wrong promptly admitted it.

Hebrews 10:35–38

What is confidence? It is deep and abiding trust, which circumstances and the vicissitudes of life cannot shake. It is trust that endures in spite of hardship or loss. When we have this kind of confidence in God's love and care and wisdom, we have an anchor that keeps us on track emotionally, mentally, and spiritually. Sometimes we may lapse into old patterns of thinking and reacting, but these do not need to overtake us or control us as they once did. As we take time to evaluate and assess our thinking patterns and relationships, the Holy Spirit will be faithful to show us the areas in which we need adjustment or repentance. But we always can rest confident and assured in the great love of our Heavenly Father and our inestimable value in His sight.

We need never again be enslaved and drawn back into fears of worthlessness, abandonment, or rejection. Our faith rests in the never changing, deep, strong love of our precious Lord.

For further reading on Step 10, turn to page 489.

Daily Encouragement

DAY 210 READING: HEBREWS 10:26—11:40

A Thought for the New Day: When you think about it, Christians are walking miracles. Moses "endured as seeing Him who is invisible" (11:27). Although many people have endured suffering and persecutions in our world, God's saints have done so with an uncanny joy that defies natural human ability or understanding. How? They see Him who is "invisible," and the vision of their Christ in glory empowers them to live, endure, and die triumphantly (see Acts 7:56). (*Turn to page 485.*)

dead, from which he also received him in a figurative sense.

20 By faith Isaac blessed Jacob and Esau concerning things to come.

21 By faith Jacob, when he was dying, blessed each of the sons of Joseph, and worshiped, *leaning* on the top of his staff.

22 By faith Joseph, when he was dying, made mention of the departure of the children of Israel, and gave instructions concerning his bones.

23 By faith Moses, when he was born, was hidden three months by his parents, because they saw *he was* a beautiful child; and they were not afraid of the king's command.

24 By faith Moses, when he became of age, refused to be called the son of Pharaoh's daughter,

25 choosing rather to suffer affliction with the people of God than to enjoy the passing pleasures of sin,

26 esteeming the reproach of Christ greater riches than the treasures in Egypt; for he looked to the reward.

27 By faith he forsook Egypt, not fearing the wrath of the king; for he endured as seeing Him who is invisible.

28 By faith he kept the Passover and the sprinkling of blood, lest he who destroyed the firstborn should touch them.

29 By faith they passed through the Red Sea as by dry *land*, *whereas* the Egyptians, attempting *to do* so, were drowned.

30 By faith the walls of Jericho fell down after they were encircled for seven days.

31 By faith the harlot Rahab did not perish with those who did not believe, when she had received the spies with peace.

32 And what more shall I say? For the time would fail me to tell of Gideon and Barak and Samson and Jephthah, also *of* David and Samuel and the prophets:

33 who through faith subdued kingdoms, worked righteousness, obtained promises, stopped the mouths of lions,

34 quenched the violence of fire, escaped the edge of the sword, out of weakness were made strong, became valiant in battle, turned to flight the armies of the aliens.

35 Women received their dead raised to life again. And others were tortured, not accepting deliverance, that they might obtain a better resurrection.

36 Still others had trial of mockings and scourgings, yes, and of chains and imprisonment.

37 They were stoned, they were sawn in two, were tempted, were slain with the sword. They wandered about in sheepskins and goatskins, being destitute, afflicted, tormented—

38 of whom the world was not worthy. They wandered in deserts and mountains, *in* dens and caves of the earth.

39 And all these, having obtained a good testimony through faith, did not receive the promise,

40 God having provided something better for us, that they should not be made perfect apart from us.

12 Therefore we also, since we are surrounded by so great a cloud of witnesses, let us lay aside every weight, and the sin which so easily ensnares *us*, and let us run with endurance the race that is set before us,

2 looking unto Jesus, the author and finisher of *our* faith, who for the joy that was set before Him endured the cross, despising the shame, and has sat down at the right hand of the throne of God.

3 For consider Him who endured such hostility from sinners against Himself, lest you become weary and discouraged in your souls.

4 You have not yet resisted to bloodshed, striving against sin.

5 And you have forgotten the ex-

STEP 6

STEP 7

484

STEP 7

Humbly asked Him to remove our shortcomings.

Hebrews 12:5–11

Forms of the word *chasten* (meaning "discipline") occur many times in Hebrews 12:5–11, a passage that issues a call to total humility and submission toward God in the life of the believer.

Apparently, these Hebrew Christians were having trouble yielding to the ways God had chosen to work in their lives. The writer reminds them that God is a wise and loving Father. And as a son should humble himself to accept his father's discipline, so believers should willingly and humbly place themselves under the loving hand of their Heavenly Father's infinitely wise discipline.

In Step 7, we are doing just that. We are humbly asking God to remove and discipline out of our lives those things that are damaging to ourselves, to our relationships with others, and to our relationship with Him.

Even though, as verse 11 says, this discipline may be "grievous" in the short term, as we continue to humbly acknowledge God's authority over our lives and submit to His leading, we look forward to the priceless reward of "the peaceful fruit of righteousness."

For further reading on Step 7, turn to page 507.

Daily Encouragement

DAY 211 READING: HEBREWS 12:1–11

A Thought for the New Day: Another translation for "chastening" is "discipline." As soldiers must discipline their bodies to strengthen them for running obstacle courses, Christians must submit themselves to spiritual discipline. Our spiritual resources need to be developed until we are ready to take on whatever task our great Leader assigns to us in the battle of living for Him in the world. (*Turn to page 487.*)

hortation which speaks to you as to sons:

> "My son, do not despise the
>   chastening of the LORD,
> Nor be discouraged when you
>   are rebuked by Him;
> 6 For whom the LORD loves He
>   chastens,
> And scourges every son whom
>   He receives."

7 If you endure chastening, God deals with you as with sons; for what son is there whom a father does not chasten?

8 But if you are without chastening, of which all have become partakers, then you are illegitimate and not sons.

9 Furthermore, we have had human fathers who corrected *us*, and we paid *them* respect. Shall we not much more readily be in subjection to the Father of spirits and live?

10 For they indeed for a few days chastened *us* as seemed *best* to them, but He for *our* profit, that *we* may be partakers of His holiness.

11 Now no chastening seems to be joyful for the present, but grievous; nevertheless, afterward it yields the peaceable fruit of righteousness to those who have been trained by it.

12 Therefore strengthen the hands which hang down, and the feeble knees,

13 and make straight paths for your feet, so that what is lame may not be *dislocated*, but rather be healed.

14 Pursue peace with all *men*, and holiness, without which no one will see the Lord:

15 looking diligently lest anyone fall short of the grace of God; lest any root of bitterness springing up cause trouble, and by this many become defiled;

16 lest there *be* any fornicator or profane person like Esau, who for one morsel of food sold his birthright.

17 For you know that afterward, when he wanted to inherit the blessing, he was rejected, for he found no place for repentance, though he sought it diligently with tears.

18 For you have not come to the mountain that may be touched and that burned with fire, and to blackness and darkness and tempest,

19 and the sound of a trumpet and the voice of words, so that those who heard *it* begged that the word should not be spoken to them anymore.

20 (For they could not endure what was commanded: *"And if so much as a beast touches the mountain, it shall be stoned or thrust through with an arrow."*

21 And so terrifying was the sight *that* Moses said, *"I am exceedingly afraid and trembling."*)

22 But you have come to Mount Zion and to the city of the living God, the heavenly Jerusalem, to an innumerable company of angels,

23 to the general assembly and church of the firstborn *who are* registered in heaven, to God the Judge of all, to the spirits of just men made perfect,

24 to Jesus the Mediator of the new covenant, and to the blood of sprinkling that speaks better things than *that of* Abel.

25 See that you do not refuse Him who speaks. For if they did not escape who refused Him who spoke on earth, much more *shall we not escape* if we turn away from Him who *speaks* from heaven,

26 whose voice then shook the earth; but now He has promised, saying, *"Yet once more I shake not only the earth, but also heaven."*

27 Now this, *"Yet once more,"* indicates the removal of those things

STEP 9

STEP 10

STEP 9

Made direct amends to such people wherever possible, except when to do so would injure them or others.

Hebrews 12:14, 15

Peace with others and holiness before God are inseparably linked. Longing for these fruits of the Spirit, however, will not bring them. We must pursue peace and holiness in order to attain them. The word "pursue" in the Greek means "to chase after in order to lay hold of." Sometimes peace seems to want to elude our grasp. But we must be resolute in our determination to do everything within our power to bring peace between ourselves and others. This is part of true holiness.

Hebrews 12:15 tells us further that if we are careful to pursue peace, then we will not fail (or fall short) in allowing God's grace to fill and control our lives. "Grace" means "enabling power." God has a vast reservoir of enabling power ready to help us make amends to those we have wronged. The same reservoir of grace is sufficient to help us to truly forgive others. Grace destroys the roots of bitterness and plants the beautiful flowers of peace.

For further reading on Step 9, turn to page 626.

Daily Encouragement

DAY 212 READING: HEBREWS 12:12–27

A Thought for the New Day: What is the real goal of life? Is it to go to heaven? Heaven could not be a desirable goal for everyone—at least not the heaven we read about in the Bible. Heaven is a place of holiness, the possession of people who themselves love holiness and "pursue" it (v. 14). To be holy is God-likeness that is also *wholeness.* God made us to be like Him, and nothing less can satisfy us. (*Turn to page 489.*)

that are being shaken, as of things that are made, that the things which cannot be shaken may remain.

STEP 10

28 Therefore, since we are receiving a kingdom which cannot be shaken, let us have grace, by which we may serve God acceptably with reverence and godly fear. 29 For our God is a consuming fire.

STEP 11

13 Let brotherly love continue. 2 Do not forget to entertain strangers, for by so *doing* some have unwittingly entertained angels.

3 Remember the prisoners as if chained with them, *and* those who are mistreated, since you yourselves are in the body also.

4 Marriage *is* honorable among all, and the bed undefiled; but fornicators and adulterers God will judge.

5 *Let your* conduct *be* without covetousness, *and be* content with such things as you have. For He Himself has said, *"I will never leave you nor forsake you."*

6 So we may boldly say:

"The LORD is my helper;
I will not fear.
What can man do to me?"

7 Remember those who rule over you, who have spoken the word of God to you, whose faith follow, considering the outcome of *their* conduct.

8 Jesus Christ *is* the same yesterday, today, and forever.

9 Do not be carried about with various and strange doctrines. For *it is* good that the heart be established by grace, not with foods which have not profited those who have been occupied with them.

10 We have an altar from which those who serve the tabernacle have no right to eat.

11 For the bodies of those beasts, whose blood is brought into the sanctuary by the high priest for sin, are burned outside the camp. 12 Therefore Jesus also, that He might sanctify the people with His own blood, suffered outside the gate.

13 Therefore let us go forth to Him, outside the camp, bearing His reproach.

14 For here we have no continuing city, but we seek the one to come. 15 Therefore by Him let us continually offer the sacrifice of praise to God, that is, the fruit of *our* lips, giving thanks to His name.

16 But do not forget to do good and to share, for with such sacrifices God is well pleased.

17 Obey those who rule over you, and be submissive, for they watch out for your souls, as those who must give account. Let them do so with joy and not with grief, for that would be unprofitable for you. 18 Pray for us; for we are confident that we have a good conscience, in all things desiring to live honorably.

19 But I especially urge *you* to do this, that I may be restored to you the sooner.

20 Now may the God of peace who brought up our Lord Jesus from the dead, that great Shepherd of the sheep, through the blood of the everlasting covenant,

21 make you complete in every good work to do His will, working in you what is well pleasing in His sight, through Jesus Christ, to whom *be* glory forever and ever. Amen.

22 And I appeal to you, brethren, bear with the word of exhortation, for I have written to you in few words.

23 Know that *our* brother Timothy has been set free, with whom I shall see you if he comes shortly. 24 Greet all those who rule over you, and all the saints. Those from Italy greet you.

25 Grace *be* with you all. Amen.

STEP 10

*Continued to take personal inventory
and when we were wrong promptly admitted it.*

Hebrews 12:28

We cannot begin to sound the depths of the wonderful grace of God. When we deserved punishment and death, God's grace bought us freedom and new life in Jesus. We are now children of the Eternal Kingdom. We entered that kingdom by grace, and we will one day inherit its riches the same way. In the meantime, God does not want us to set up a strict list of dos and don'ts in order to work our way into righteousness. He does not want us to begin to put our trust in anything else, no matter how good it seems. He alone is our righteousness. As we daily abide in Him, His Word and His Holy Spirit will guide us and enable us to serve Him in ways that honor Him (reverence Him) and obey His commands (fear Him). This is not only the way to keep our lives acceptable to God; it is also the way to keep our lives healthy emotionally and mentally.

For further reading on Step 10, turn to page 501.

Daily Encouragement

DAY 213 READING: HEBREWS 12:28—13:25

A Thought for the New Day: An Old Testament proverb speaks of a friend who sticks closer than a brother. Jesus is that Friend who never leaves you (13:5). Perhaps real friendship is what we most hunger for—someone who always understands us but loves us enough to tell us the truth about ourselves. What good is a friend who just flatters us to gain our favor? *Lord, help me today and always to realize the great privilege I enjoy in having Your unwavering friendship.* *(Turn to page 491.)*

THE EPISTLE OF
JAMES

JAMES, a servant of God and of the Lord Jesus Christ,

To the twelve tribes which are scattered abroad:

Greetings.

2 My brethren, count it all joy when you fall into various trials,

3 knowing that the testing of your faith produces patience.

4 But let patience have *its* perfect work, that you may be perfect and complete, lacking nothing.

STEP 6
5 If any of you lacks wisdom, let him ask of God, who gives to all liberally and without reproach, and it will be given to him.

6 But let him ask in faith, with no doubting, for he who doubts is like a wave of the sea driven and tossed by the wind.

7 For let not that man suppose that he will receive anything from the Lord;

8 *he is* a double-minded man, unstable in all his ways.

9 Let the lowly brother glory in his exaltation,

10 but the rich in his humiliation, because as a flower of the field he will pass away.

11 For no sooner has the sun risen with a burning heat than it withers the grass; its flower falls, and its beautiful appearance perishes. So the rich man also will fade away in his pursuits.

12 Blessed *is* the man who endures temptation; for when he has been proved, he will receive the crown of life which the Lord has promised to those who love Him.

STEP 10
13 Let no one say when he is tempted, "I am tempted by God"; for God cannot be tempted by evil, nor does He Himself tempt anyone.

14 But each one is tempted when he is drawn away by his own desires and enticed.

15 Then, when desire has conceived, it gives birth to sin; and sin, when it is full-grown, brings forth death.

16 Do not be deceived, my beloved brethren.

STEP 2
17 Every good gift and every perfect gift is from above, and comes down from the Father of lights, with whom there is no variation or shadow of turning.

18 Of His own will He brought us forth by the word of truth, that we might be a kind of firstfruits of His creatures.

STEP 10
19 Therefore, my beloved brethren, let every man be swift to hear, slow to speak, slow to wrath;

20 for the wrath of man does not produce the righteousness of God.

STEP 6
21 Therefore lay aside all filthiness and overflow of wickedness, and receive with meekness the implanted word, which is able to save your souls.

STEP 11
22 But be doers of the word, and not hearers only, deceiving yourselves.

23 For if anyone is a hearer of the word and not a doer, he is like a man observing his natural face in a mirror;

24 for he observes himself, goes away, and immediately forgets what kind of man he was.

25 But he who looks into the perfect law of liberty and continues *in it*, and is not a forgetful hearer but a doer of the work, this one will be blessed in what he does.

26 If anyone among you thinks he is religious, and does not bridle his tongue but deceives his own heart, this one's religion *is* useless.

27 Pure and undefiled religion before God and the Father is this: to visit orphans and widows in their trouble, *and* to keep oneself unspotted from the world.

2 My brethren, do not hold the faith of our Lord Jesus Christ,

STEP 6

*Were entirely ready to have God
remove all these defects of character.*

James 1:5, 6

"Lord, truly I want to be free of my dependencies and my
bondage, but I do not begin to know how to go about it." If you
have overheard your heart speak such thoughts, these verses are a
gold mine of help. James tells us that our loving God is waiting for
us to ask Him. He knows how to rid us of our fears and addictions
and how to set our feet on a new path of freedom and stability. And
even though this wisdom is priceless, He gladly and liberally gives
it to those who ask in faith, believing they will surely receive. So
ask God now to give you everything you need for your journey to
freedom. Trust Him to reveal the deep truths you need to know and
to give you the courage and wisdom to face the bumps and twists
and turns along the way. He earnestly wants to give you all that you
need. Reach out to Him and ask in faith.

For further reading on Step 6, turn to page 499.

Daily Encouragement

DAY 214 READING: JAMES 1:1–27

A Thought for the New Day: Wisdom is a scarce commodity,
and who among us can boast that we have enough wisdom to
face every concern in life? There is great consolation here: All
we have to do is ask, "Lord, show me the right path to take,
guide my steps in the darkness" (v. 5). The answer is never long
in coming. The way ahead is made clear, and our steps are set
firmly in the right path. *(Turn to page 493.)*

the Lord of glory, with partiality.

2 For if there should come into your assembly a man with gold rings, in fine apparel, and there should also come in a poor man in filthy clothes,

3 and you pay attention to the one wearing the fine clothes and say to him, "You sit here in a good place," and say to the poor man, "You stand there," or, "Sit here at my footstool,"

4 have you not shown partiality among yourselves, and become judges with evil thoughts?

5 Listen, my beloved brethren: Has God not chosen the poor of this world *to be* rich in faith and heirs of the kingdom which He promised to those who love Him?

6 But you have dishonored the poor man. Do not the rich oppress you and drag you into the courts?

7 Do they not blaspheme that noble name by which you are called?

8 If you really fulfill *the* royal law according to the Scripture, *"You shall love your neighbor as yourself,"* you do well;

9 but if you show partiality, you commit sin, and are convicted by the law as transgressors.

10 For whoever shall keep the whole law, and yet stumble in one *point*, he is guilty of all.

11 For He who said, *"Do not commit adultery,"* also said, *"Do not murder."* Now if you do not commit adultery, but you do murder, you have become a transgressor of the law.

12 So speak and so do as those who will be judged by the law of liberty.

13 For judgment is without mercy to the one who has shown no mercy. Mercy triumphs over judgment.

14 What *does it* profit, my brethren, if someone says he has faith but does not have works? Can faith save him?

15 If a brother or sister is naked and destitute of daily food,

16 and one of you says to them, "Depart in peace, be warmed and filled," but you do not give them the things which are needed for the body, what *does it* profit?

17 Thus also faith by itself, if it does not have works, is dead.

18 But someone will say, "You have faith, and I have works." Show me your faith without your works, and I will show you my faith by my works.

19 You believe that there is one God. You do well. Even the demons believe—and tremble!

20 But do you want to know, O foolish man, that faith without works is dead?

21 Was not Abraham our father justified by works when he offered Isaac his son on the altar?

22 Do you see that faith was working together with his works, and by works faith was made perfect?

23 And the Scripture was fulfilled which says, *"Abraham believed God, and it was accounted to him for righteousness."* And he was called the friend of God.

24 You see then that a man is justified by works, and not by faith only.

25 Likewise, was not Rahab the harlot also justified by works when she received the messengers and sent *them* out another way?

26 For as the body without the spirit is dead, so faith without works is dead also.

3 My brethren, let not many of you become teachers, knowing that we shall receive a stricter judgment.

2 For we all stumble in many things. If anyone does not stumble in word, he *is* a perfect man, able also to bridle the whole body.

3 Indeed, we put bits in horses' mouths that they may obey us, and we turn their whole body.

4 Look also at ships: although

STEP 4

Made a searching and fearless moral inventory of ourselves.

James 2:2–8

Even in the early church, there were social climbers. In essence, they used wealthy people to identify vicariously with their power and prestige. Since showing kindness and concern for poor people would not boost the image they sought, the poor were ignored or ill-treated. All in all, the social climbers did not really love anyone, including themselves.

This is a soul-searching passage for all of us. Scripture teaches us that each person with whom we come into contact is "our neighbor," and we are to love our neighbors as we love ourselves.

However, if we have a low self-worth, then we have difficulty loving anyone as we should. This is why every part of our lives hinges on knowing the God who loves us. No matter what our situation or background, our worth in God's eyes is beyond measure. When our hearts learn this truth, our relationship with others will change dramatically.

For further reading on Step 4, turn to page 641.

Daily Encouragement

DAY 215 READING: JAMES 2:1–26

A Thought for the New Day: Someone has said, "The faith I like to see is the kind that is wearing out shoe leather." Faith, like ideas, must have legs to be of any value. That is, faith produces works or else it is no faith at all—it is dead because it does no one any good (v. 26). We should expect that the faith we claim to have in Jesus will result in Christ-like actions, just as we expect an apple tree to produce tasty apples. (*Turn to page 495.*)

they are so large and are driven by fierce winds, they are turned by a very small rudder wherever the pilot desires.

5 Even so the tongue is a little member and boasts great things. See how great a forest a little fire kindles!

6 And the tongue *is* a fire, a world of iniquity. The tongue is so set among our members that it defiles the whole body, and sets on fire the course of nature; and it is set on fire by hell.

7 For every kind of beast and bird, of reptile and creature of the sea, is tamed and has been tamed by mankind.

8 But no man can tame the tongue. *It is* an unruly evil, full of deadly poison.

9 With it we bless our God and Father, and with it we curse men, who have been made in the similitude of God.

10 Out of the same mouth proceed blessing and cursing. My brethren, these things ought not to be so.

11 Does a spring send forth fresh *water* and bitter from the same opening?

12 Can a fig tree, my brethren, bear olives, or a grapevine bear figs? Thus no spring *can* yield both salt water and fresh.

13 Who *is* wise and understanding among you? Let him show by good conduct *that* his works *are* done in the meekness of wisdom.

14 But if you have bitter envy and self-seeking in your hearts, do not boast and lie against the truth.

15 This wisdom does not descend from above, but *is* earthly, sensual, demonic.

16 For where envy and self-seeking *exist,* confusion and every evil thing *will be* there.

STEP 9
17 But the wisdom that is from above is first pure, then peaceable, gentle, willing to yield, full of mercy and good fruits, without partiality and without hypocrisy.

18 Now the fruit of righteousness is sown in peace by those who make peace.

4 Where do wars and fights *come* from among you? Do *they* not *come* from your *desires for* pleasure that war in your members?

2 You lust and do not have. You murder and covet and cannot obtain. You fight and war. Yet you do not have because you do not ask.

3 You ask and do not receive, because you ask amiss, that you may spend *it* on your pleasures.

4 Adulterers and adulteresses! Do you not know that friendship with the world is enmity with God? Whoever therefore wants to be a friend of the world makes himself an enemy of God.

5 Or do you think that the Scripture says in vain, "The Spirit who dwells in us yearns jealously"?

6 But He gives more grace. Therefore He says:

STEP 7

    "God resists the proud,
      But gives grace to the
        humble."

7 Therefore submit to God. Resist the devil and he will flee from you.

STEP 5

8 Draw near to God and He will draw near to you. Cleanse *your* hands, *you* sinners; and purify *your* hearts, *you* double-minded.

9 Lament and mourn and weep! Let your laughter be turned to mourning and *your* joy to gloom.

10 Humble yourselves in the sight of the Lord, and He will lift you up.

11 Do not speak evil of one another, brethren. He who speaks evil of a brother and judges his brother, speaks evil of the law and judges the law. But if you judge the law, you are not a doer of the law but a judge.

STEP 8

12 There is one Lawgiver, who is able to save and to destroy. Who are you to judge another?

13 Come now, you who say, "Today or tomorrow we will go to

STEP 8

*Made a list of all persons we had harmed,
and became willing to make amends to them all.*

James 4:11, 12

Both Step 8 and James 4:11, 12 ask us to suspend judgment, bitterness, and resentments toward others. It may be tempting to tell ourselves that we will make amends to others if and when we know that they can reciprocate. The spirit of Step 8, however, requires that we be willing to make such amends unconditionally.

How can we forgive and make amends to those whom we feel have offended us in the past? How can we forgive when the stings of wounds are still fresh and alive in our hearts?

The willingness to forgive can be attained only when we have passed through a series of God-given steps for grieving over these offenses. If we have been violated by others, we must experience the stages of shock, denial, anger, depression, and sadness in order to purify our hearts. Only then will we be ready to approach the final step of the grieving process—forgiveness—without resentment and with emotional integrity.

For further reading on Step 8, turn to page 503.

Daily Encouragement

DAY 216 READING: JAMES 3:1—4:17

A Thought for the New Day: Talk is cheap. Perhaps that is why there is so much of it. In Ecclesiastes 5:2 we read, "Let your words be few." The less we speak, the less likely we are to say foolish things (3:2). It is a happy habit to think long and speak short. "Speak-think" should be replaced by "think-speak," but let us be thinking about speaking words that bring blessing and help to those around us. (*Turn to page 497.*)

such and such a city, spend a year there, buy and sell, and make a profit";

14 whereas you do not know what *will happen* tomorrow. For what *is* your life? It is even a vapor that appears for a little time and then vanishes away.

15 Instead you *ought* to say, "If the Lord wills, we shall live and do this or that."

16 But now you boast in your arrogance. All such boasting is evil.

17 Therefore, to him who knows to do good and does not do *it*, to him it is sin.

5 Come now, *you* rich, weep and howl for your miseries that are coming upon *you!*

2 Your riches are corrupted, and your garments are moth-eaten.

3 Your gold and silver are corroded, and their corrosion will be a witness against you and will eat your flesh like fire. You have heaped up treasure in the last days.

4 Indeed the wages of the laborers who mowed your fields, which you kept back by fraud, cry out; and the cries of the reapers have reached the ears of the Lord of Sabaoth.

5 You have lived on the earth in pleasure and luxury; you have fattened your hearts as in a day of slaughter.

6 You have condemned, you have murdered the just; he does not resist you.

7 Therefore be patient, brethren, until the coming of the Lord. See *how* the farmer waits for the precious fruit of the earth, waiting patiently for it until it receives the early and latter rain.

8 You also be patient. Establish your hearts, for the coming of the Lord is at hand.

STEP 8

9 Do not grumble against one another, brethren, lest you be condemned. Behold, the Judge is standing at the door!

10 My brethren, take the prophets, who spoke in the name of the Lord, as an example of suffering and patience.

11 Indeed we count them blessed who endure. You have heard of the perseverance of Job and seen the end *intended by* the Lord—that the Lord is very compassionate and merciful.

12 But above all, my brethren, do not swear, either by heaven or by earth or with any other oath. But let your "Yes" be "Yes," and *your* "No," "No," lest you fall into judgment.

13 Is anyone among you suffering? Let him pray. Is anyone cheerful? Let him sing psalms.

14 Is anyone among you sick? Let him call for the elders of the church, and let them pray over him, anointing him with oil in the name of the Lord.

15 And the prayer of faith will save the sick, and the Lord will raise him up. And if he has committed sins, he will be forgiven.

16 Confess *your* trespasses to one another, and pray for one another, that you may be healed. The effective, fervent prayer of a righteous man avails much.

STEP 5

17 Elijah was a man with a nature like ours, and he prayed earnestly that it would not rain; and it did not rain on the land for three years and six months.

18 And he prayed again, and the heaven gave rain, and the earth produced its fruit.

19 Brethren, if anyone among you wanders from the truth, and someone turns him back,

STEP 12

20 let him know that he who turns a sinner from the error of his way will save a soul from death and cover a multitude of sins.

STEP 5

Admitted to God, to ourselves, and to another human being the exact nature of our wrongs.

James 5:16

Our isolated, me-centered society has developed a strong repugnance for the word "accountability." We no longer want to be accountable to and for our families, our community, or even ourselves. Although the idea of accountability is out of vogue, the Bible has much to say about it.

God says we are not only accountable to Him, but we are accountable to other Christians as well. And far from being an odious burden, this is, in fact, a major source of joy and healing.

When we find the courage to acknowledge our wrongs to a fellow believer, we open ourselves to a new energy and capacity to change our lives. Our confession actually strengthens our commitment toward spiritual growth since we now have a companion interceding in prayer for us, encouraging and sharing with us. And even though we may have times of weakness when we fall back into our old ways, we will also have the love and support of God and our fellow believers to pick us up and help us back onto the path of life.

For further reading on Step 5, turn to page 513.

Daily Encouragement

DAY 217 READING: JAMES 5:1–20

A Thought for the New Day: A grumbler vents anger by continually complaining about real or imagined problems or faults in others. It is easy to become trapped in this habit. There is always something wrong in the world to grumble about, but giving in to the practice of grumbling only sours our own spirits (v. 9). There are problems in life we may not be able to solve. However, we can carry them to the One who can, and He will. (*Turn to page 499.*)

THE FIRST EPISTLE OF
PETER

PETER, an apostle of Jesus Christ,

To the pilgrims of the Dispersion in Pontus, Galatia, Cappadocia, Asia, and Bithynia,
2 elect according to the foreknowledge of God the Father, in sanctification of the Spirit, for obedience and sprinkling of the blood of Jesus Christ:

Grace to you and peace be multiplied.

STEP 3
3 Blessed *be* the God and Father of our Lord Jesus Christ, who according to His abundant mercy has begotten us again to a living hope through the resurrection of Jesus Christ from the dead,
4 to an inheritance incorruptible and undefiled and that does not fade away, reserved in heaven for you,
5 who are kept by the power of God through faith for salvation ready to be revealed in the last time.
6 In this you greatly rejoice, though now for a little while, if need be, you have been grieved by various trials,
7 that the genuineness of your faith, *being* much more precious than gold that perishes, though it is tested by fire, may be found to praise, honor, and glory at the revelation of Jesus Christ,
8 whom having not seen you love. Though now you do not see *Him,* yet believing, you rejoice with joy inexpressible and full of glory,
9 receiving the end of your faith—the salvation of *your* souls.
10 Of this salvation the prophets have inquired and searched diligently, who prophesied of the grace *that would come* to you,
11 searching what, or what manner of time, the Spirit of Christ who was in them was indicating when He testified beforehand the sufferings of Christ and the glories that would follow.
12 To them it was revealed that, not to themselves, but to us they were ministering the things which now have been reported to you through those who have preached the gospel to you by the Holy Spirit sent from heaven—things which angels desire to look into.

STEP 6
13 Therefore gird up the loins of your mind, be sober, and rest *your* hope fully upon the grace that is to be brought to you at the revelation of Jesus Christ;
14 as obedient children, not conforming yourselves to the former lusts, *as* in your ignorance;
15 but as He who called you *is* holy, you also be holy in all *your* conduct,
16 because it is written, "Be holy, for I am holy."
17 And if you call on the Father, who without partiality judges according to each one's work, conduct yourselves throughout the time of your sojourning *here* in fear;
18 knowing that you were not redeemed with corruptible things, *like* silver or gold, from your aimless conduct *received* by tradition from your fathers,
19 but with the precious blood of Christ, as of a lamb without blemish and without spot.
20 He indeed was foreordained before the foundation of the world, but was manifest in these last times for you
21 who through Him believe in God, who raised Him from the dead and gave Him glory, so that your faith and hope are in God.

STEP 9
22 Since you have purified your souls in obeying the truth through the Spirit in sincere love of the brethren, love one another fervently with a pure heart,

STEP 6

*Were entirely ready to have God
remove all these defects of character.*

1 Peter 1:13–16

In the first five steps of recovery, we have engaged in much looking back and digging, many times painfully, into our pasts. Step 6 is a turning point. Now it is time to prepare for action, to "gird up the loins of [our minds]" (v. 13). The word picture here is of a man of Bible times tucking his long, flowing robes into his wide belt to move them out of the way so he can accompish his work. Peter uses this metaphor to show us that we must prepare to invite God's serious work in our minds. "Be sober" means "be self-controlled." These two phrases, along with "rest your hope upon . . . Jesus Christ," help us know the mind-set necessary to live the holy life commanded in verses 14–16.

Sometimes we think of holiness as a very pious, abnormal way of living. But being holy simply means having a fully integrated personality. God wants us to enjoy and delight as whole persons in the life He has given us.

For further reading on Step 6, turn to page 519.

Daily Encouragement

DAY 218 READING: 1 PETER 1:1–25

A Thought for the New Day: We are creatures of our five senses, and we believe what our senses tell us. So how is it that we so passionately love a Savior we have never seen (v. 8)? His followers, many of them brilliant and highly gifted, spent their lives and died violently for a Christ they said is alive. No natural or psychological phenomenon can account for such love. This can only be a miracle of "Christ in you, the hope of glory" (Col. 1:27). (*Turn to page 501.*)

23 having been born again, not of corruptible seed but incorruptible, through the word of God which lives and abides forever,
24 because

"All flesh is as grass,
  And all the glory of man
    as the flower of the grass.
The grass withers,
  And its flower falls away,
25 But the word of the LORD
    endures forever."

Now this is the word which by the gospel was preached to you.

STEP 6

2 Therefore, laying aside all malice, all guile, hypocrisy, envy, and all evil speaking,
2 as newborn babes, desire the pure milk of the word, that you may grow thereby,
3 if indeed you have tasted that the Lord is gracious.
4 Coming to Him as to a living stone, rejected indeed by men, but chosen by God and precious,
5 you also, as living stones, are being built up a spiritual house, a holy priesthood, to offer up spiritual sacrifices acceptable to God through Jesus Christ.
6 Therefore it is also contained in the Scripture,

"Behold, I lay in Zion
  A chief cornerstone, elect,
    precious,
And he who believes on Him
  will by no means be put to
    shame."

7 Therefore, to you who believe, He is precious; but to those who are disobedient,

"The stone which the builders
    rejected
Has become the chief
    cornerstone,"

8 and

"A stone of stumbling
  And a rock of offense."

They stumble, being disobedient to the word, to which they also were appointed.
9 But you are a chosen generation, a royal priesthood, a holy nation, His own special people, that you may proclaim the praises of Him who called you out of darkness into His marvelous light;

STEP 12

10 who once were not a people but are now the people of God, who had not obtained mercy but now have obtained mercy.
11 Beloved, I beg you as sojourners and pilgrims, abstain from fleshly lusts which war against the soul,

STEP 10

12 having your conduct honorable among the Gentiles, that when they speak against you as evildoers, they may, by your good works which they observe, glorify God in the day of visitation.
13 Therefore submit yourselves to every ordinance of man for the Lord's sake, whether to the king as supreme,
14 or to governors, as to those who are sent by him for the punishment of evildoers and for the praise of those who do good.
15 For this is the will of God, that by doing good you may put to silence the ignorance of foolish men—
16 as free, yet not using your liberty as a cloak for vice, but as servants of God.
17 Honor all people. Love the brotherhood. Fear God. Honor the king.
18 Servants, be submissive to your masters with all fear, not only to the good and gentle, but also to the harsh.
19 For this is commendable, if because of conscience toward God one endures grief, suffering wrongfully.

STEP 8

20 For what credit is it if, when you are beaten for your faults, you take it patiently? But when you do

STEP 10

*Continued to take personal inventory
and when we were wrong promptly admitted it.*

1 Peter 2:11

Our old dependencies and character defects hold a strangely seductive spell over us. Even though countless harsh experiences warn us that the practice of our addictions only brings new pain, we may find ourselves lured back to the false promise these addictions hold out to us. Speaking through the mask of denial, our codependencies may cry out for the misuse of food, sexuality, money, relationships, authority, or chemicals as means to satiate the spiritual hungers that gnaw inside us.

What is the antidote against this temptation to slip into the "fleshly lusts which war against the soul"? The central message of recovery is that these codependent hungers can never be satisfied by human means or on human terms alone. Instead, we turn repeatedly toward the infilling of God's Spirit that we may "grow in the grace and knowledge of our Lord and Savior Jesus Christ" (2 Pet. 3:18).

For further reading on Step 10, turn to page 523.

Daily Encouragement

DAY 219 READING: 1 PETER 2:1–25

A Thought for the New Day: God's church is really built of living stones (v. 5). The stone structures and facades in church buildings symbolize the spiritual edifice that God is putting together with ordinary people like you and me. It is a building that is designed to last forever. The lives of Christians who have gone before us are permanently fitted into that living, eternal structure that is even called "the body of Christ." (*Turn to page 503.*)

good and suffer *for it*, if you take it patiently, this *is* commendable before God.

21 For to this you were called, because Christ also suffered for us, leaving us an example, that you should follow His steps:

22 *"Who committed no sin,*
  Nor was guile found in His
    mouth";

23 who, when He was reviled, did not revile in return; when He suffered, He did not threaten, but committed *Himself* to Him who judges righteously;

STEP 3

24 who Himself bore our sins in His own body on the tree, that we, having died to sins, might live for righteousness—by whose stripes you were healed.

25 For you were like sheep going astray, but have now returned to the Shepherd and Overseer of your souls.

3 Likewise *you* wives, be submissive to your own husbands, that even if some do not obey the word, they, without a word, may be won by the conduct of their wives,

2 when they observe your chaste conduct *accompanied* by fear.

3 Do not let your beauty be that outward *adorning* of arranging the hair, of wearing gold, or of putting on *fine* apparel;

4 but *let it be* the hidden person of the heart, with the incorruptible *ornament* of a gentle and quiet spirit, which is very precious in the sight of God.

5 For in this manner, in former times, the holy women who trusted in God also adorned themselves, being submissive to their own husbands,

6 as Sarah obeyed Abraham, calling him lord, whose daughters you are if you do good and are not afraid with any terror.

7 Likewise *you* husbands, dwell with *them* with understanding,

giving honor to the wife, as to the weaker vessel, and as *being* heirs together of the grace of life, that your prayers may not be hindered.

8 Finally, all of *you be* of one mind, having compassion for one another; love as brothers, *be* tenderhearted, *be* courteous;

STEP 8

9 not returning evil for evil or reviling for reviling, but on the contrary blessing, knowing that you were called to this, that you may inherit a blessing.

10 For

  "He who would love life
    And see good days,
  Let him refrain his tongue
    from evil,
  And his lips from speaking
    guile;

11 *Let him turn away from evil*
    and do good;
  Let him seek peace and pursue
    it.

12 *For the eyes of the* LORD
    are on the righteous,
  And his ears are open to their
    prayers;
  But the face of the LORD *is*
    against those who do evil."

13 And who *is* he who will harm you if you become followers of what is good?

14 But even if you should suffer for righteousness' sake, *you are* blessed. *"And do not be afraid of their threats, nor be troubled."*

15 But sanctify the Lord God in your hearts, and always *be* ready to *give* a defense to everyone who asks you a reason for the hope that is in you, with meekness and fear;

STEP 12

16 having a good conscience, that when they defame you as evildoers, those who revile your good conduct in Christ may be ashamed.

17 For *it is* better, if it is the will of God, to suffer for doing good than for doing evil.

18 For Christ also suffered once for sins, the just for the unjust, that

STEP 8

*Made a list of all persons we had harmed,
and became willing to make amends to them all.*

1 Peter 3:8–12

When God asks us to do something hard, He often gives us a promise of reward as well. For many of us, Steps 8 and 9 will be the most difficult steps of our recovery. They will require humility and determination on our part, but God has rewards in store for those who are willing to obey His Word. This passage describes the qualities of a heart willing to make amends.

First, such a heart has compassion for other people, identifying with their pains and sorrows. As long as we are consumed by our own struggles, we will not be able to be compassionate, so we must ask God to help us forget about ourselves.

Second, it blesses. God tells us that rather than trying to get back at those who hurt us, we should bless (that is, speak well of) them instead.

When we seek peace with others and determine in our hearts to pursue it, God is pleased and places the joy of His blessing on our lives.

For further reading on Step 8, turn to page 515.

Daily Encouragement

DAY 220 READING: 1 PETER 3:1–22

A Thought for the New Day: Unity enforced by dictatorship is undesirable. But the "one mind" that Peter speaks about (v. 8) results when, because of our devotion to the divinely revealed ideal of mutual love, we willingly accommodate the differences among us as a matter of Christian courtesy. This courtesy or "oneness" springs from the respect (love) we owe one another because we are made in God's own image. (*Turn to page 505.*)

He might bring us to God, being put to death in the flesh but made alive by the Spirit,

19 by whom also He went and preached to the spirits in prison,

20 who formerly were disobedient, when once the longsuffering of God waited in the days of Noah, while *the* ark was being prepared, in which a few, that is, eight souls, were saved through water.

21 There is also an antitype which now saves us, *namely* baptism (not the removal of the filth of the flesh, but the answer of a good conscience toward God), through the resurrection of Jesus Christ,

22 who has gone into heaven and is at the right hand of God, angels and authorities and powers having been made subject to Him.

4 Therefore, since Christ suffered for us in the flesh, arm yourselves also with the same mind, for he who has suffered in the flesh has ceased from sin,

2 that he no longer should live the rest of *his* time in the flesh for the lusts of men, but for the will of God.

3 For we *have spent* enough of our past lifetime in doing the will of the Gentiles—when we walked in licentiousness, lusts, drunkenness, revelries, drinking parties, and abominable idolatries.

4 In regard to these, they think it strange that you do not run with *them* in the same flood of dissipation, speaking evil of *you.*

5 They will give an account to Him who is ready to judge the living and the dead.

6 For this reason the gospel was preached also to those who are dead, that they might be judged according to men in the flesh, but live according to God in the spirit.

7 But the end of all things is at hand; therefore be serious and watchful in your prayers.

8 And above all things have fervent love for one another, for *"love will cover a multitude of sins."*

9 *Be* hospitable to one another without grumbling.

10 As each one has received a gift, minister it to one another, as good stewards of the manifold grace of God.

11 If anyone speaks, *let him speak* as the oracles of God. If anyone ministers, *let him do it* as with the ability which God supplies, that in all things God may be glorified through Jesus Christ, to whom belong the glory and the dominion forever and ever. Amen.

12 Beloved, do not think it strange concerning the fiery trial which is to try you, as though some strange thing happened to you;

13 but rejoice to the extent that you partake of Christ's sufferings, that when His glory is revealed, you may also be glad with exceeding joy.

14 If you are reproached for the name of Christ, blessed *are you,* for the Spirit of glory and of God rests upon you. On their part He is blasphemed, but on your part He is glorified.

15 But let none of you suffer as a murderer, a thief, an evildoer, or as a busybody in other people's matters.

16 Yet if *anyone suffers* as a Christian, let him not be ashamed, but let him glorify God in this matter.

17 For the time *has come* for judgment to begin at the house of God; and if *it begins* with us first, what will *be* the end of those who do not obey the gospel of God?

18 Now

"If the righteous one is scarcely saved,
Where will the ungodly and
the sinner appear?"

19 Therefore let those who suffer according to the will of God commit their souls *to Him* in doing good, as to a faithful Creator.

5 The elders who are among you I exhort, I who am a fellow

504

*Sought through prayer and meditation to improve our conscious contact with God **as we understood Him,** praying only for knowledge of His will for us and the power to carry that out.*

1 Peter 4:7–11

Is my desire to glorify Jesus at the center of everything I do? Each of us should ask this question regularly and often. It is easy to become so involved in doing the work of God that we forget what our motivation should be. It is also easy to forget where our ability and strength for service originate. When we received Jesus as Savior, the Holy Spirit gave us a spiritual gift, which God wants us to use to build His Kingdom and bring Him glory (Rom. 12; 1 Cor. 12). However, without the power and love of God operating in our lives, our gift is only a lot of noise.

In our hurried world we may be tempted to rush into the day, depending on our own strength and abilities. But if we want our lives and service to really count for eternity, we will take the time we need to seek God's face and go forth in His power.

For further reading on Step 11, turn to page 509.

Daily Encouragement

DAY 221 READING: 1 PETER 4:1–19

A Thought for the New Day: We are constantly called upon, in this world, to make the best of what is often a bad situation. All of the whistling in the dark cannot hide what the sciences agree is the inevitable end of our present world order. Christians, however, see these things as a prelude to the dawning new world that will burst forth into eternal springtime at Christ's coming (v. 7). We are therefore excited at the first light of that glorious Day. *(Turn to page 507.)*

elder and a witness of the sufferings of Christ, and also a partaker of the glory that will be revealed:

2 Shepherd the flock of God which is among you, serving as overseers, not by constraint but willingly, not for dishonest gain but eagerly;

3 nor as being lords over those entrusted to you, but being examples to the flock;

4 and when the Chief Shepherd appears, you will receive the crown of glory that does not fade away.

5 Likewise you younger people, submit yourselves to *your* elders. Yes, all of *you* be submissive to one another, and be clothed with humility, for

"God resists the proud,
But gives grace to the
   humble."

STEP 7 6 Therefore humble yourselves under the mighty hand of God, that He may exalt you in due time,

7 casting all your care upon Him, for He cares for you.

8 Be sober, be vigilant; because your adversary the devil walks about like a roaring lion, seeking whom he may devour. **STEP 11**

9 Resist him, steadfast in the faith, knowing that the same sufferings are experienced by your brotherhood in the world.

10 But may the God of all grace, who called us to His eternal glory by Christ Jesus, after you have suffered a while, perfect, establish, strengthen, and settle *you*.

11 To Him *be* the glory and the dominion forever and ever. Amen.

12 By Silvanus, our faithful brother as I consider him, I have written to you briefly, exhorting and testifying that this is the true grace of God in which you stand.

13 She who is in Babylon, elect together with *you*, greets you; and *so does* Mark my son.

14 Greet one another with a kiss of love. Peace to you all who are in Christ Jesus. Amen.

THE SECOND EPISTLE OF
PETER

SIMON PETER, a servant and apostle of Jesus Christ,

To those who have obtained like precious faith with us by the righteousness of our God and Savior Jesus Christ:

STEP 11 2 Grace and peace be multiplied to you in the knowledge of God and of Jesus our Lord,

3 as His divine power has given to us all things that *pertain* to life and godliness, through the knowledge of Him who called us by glory and virtue,

4 by which have been given to us exceedingly great and precious promises, that through these you may be partakers of the divine nature, having escaped the corruption *that is* in the world through lust.

5 But also for this very reason, giving all diligence, add to your faith virtue, to virtue knowledge,

6 to knowledge self-control, to self-control perseverance, to perseverance godliness,

7 to godliness brotherly kindness, and to brotherly kindness love.

8 For if these things are yours and abound, *you will be* neither barren

STEP 7

Humbly asked Him to remove our shortcomings.

1 Peter 5:6, 7

As we encounter Step 7, there may be confusion between the distinctly different experiences of humiliation and humility. The practice of our old dependencies may have brought upon us many disparaging experiences of humiliation, and these compounding humiliations may have precipitated our reaching a final emotional "bottom."

The humble approach called for in Step 7 is not to be equated with humiliation. God does not want to mortify us, but He does want us to submit to His leadership. As we humble ourselves before God as His children in need, He lifts us up by filling our innermost hungers. Step 7 is the humble confession that we cannot meet our needs by our own codependent striving. Instead, we must cast our anxieties and burdens into God's care.

For further reading on Step 7, turn to page 517.

Daily Encouragement

DAY 222 READING: 1 PETER 5:1–14

A Thought for the New Day: Carry verse 7 with you everywhere you go. There is no difficulty, no sadness, no pain of yours, that God is oblivious to. In fact, Jesus bore all your pains long ago, and He is therefore intimately familiar with your deepest suffering. He invites you to place your care upon Him in all your circumstances. So doing, you will find He always gives peace and rest in exchange for your heaviest loads. (*Turn to page 509.*)

nor unfruitful in the knowledge of our Lord Jesus Christ.

9 For he who lacks these things is shortsighted, even to blindness, and has forgotten that he was purged from his old sins.

10 Therefore, brethren, be even more diligent to make your calling and election sure, for if you do these things you will never stumble;

11 for so an entrance will be supplied to you abundantly into the everlasting kingdom of our Lord and Savior Jesus Christ.

12 Therefore I will not be negligent to remind you always of these things, though you know *them,* and *are* established in the present truth.

13 Yes, I think it is right, as long as I am in this tent, to stir you up by reminding *you,*

14 knowing that shortly I *must* put off my tent, just as our Lord Jesus Christ showed me.

15 Moreover I will be careful to ensure that you always have a reminder of these things after my decease.

16 For we did not follow cunningly devised fables when we made known to you the power and coming of our Lord Jesus Christ, but were eyewitnesses of His majesty.

17 For He received from God the Father honor and glory when such a voice came to Him from the Excellent Glory: "This is My beloved Son, in whom I am well pleased."

18 And we heard this voice which came from heaven when we were with Him on the holy mountain.

19 We also have the prophetic word made more sure, which you do well to heed as a light that shines in a dark place, until the day dawns and the morning star rises in your hearts;

20 knowing this first, that no prophecy of Scripture is of any private interpretation,

21 for prophecy never came by the will of man, but holy men of God spoke *as they were* moved by the Holy Spirit.

2 But there were also false prophets among the people, even as there will be false teachers among you, who will secretly bring in destructive heresies, even denying the Lord who bought them, *and* bring on themselves swift destruction.

2 And many will follow their destructive ways, because of whom the way of truth will be blasphemed.

3 By covetousness they will exploit you with deceptive words; for a long time their judgment has not been idle, and their destruction does not slumber.

4 For if God did not spare the angels who sinned, but cast *them* down to hell and delivered *them* into chains of darkness, to be reserved for judgment;

5 and did not spare the ancient world, but saved Noah, *one of* eight *people,* a preacher of righteousness, bringing in the flood on the world of the ungodly;

6 and turning the cities of Sodom and Gomorrah into ashes, condemned *them* to destruction, making *them* an example to those who afterward would live ungodly;

7 and delivered righteous Lot, *who was* oppressed with the filthy conduct of the wicked

8 (for that righteous man, dwelling among them, tormented *his* righteous soul from day to day by seeing and hearing *their* lawless deeds)—

9 *then* the Lord knows how to deliver the godly out of temptations and to reserve the unjust under punishment for the day of judgment,

10 and especially those who walk according to the flesh in the lust of uncleanness and despise authority. *They are* presumptuous, selfwilled; they are not afraid to speak evil of dignitaries,

11 whereas angels, who are greater

*Sought through prayer and meditation to improve our conscious contact with God **as we understood Him,** praying only for knowledge of His will for us and the power to carry that out.*

2 Peter 1:2–8

The deep, multiplied grace and peace God wants to give every believer come from a *full knowledge* of the Lord Jesus. *Epignosei* is the Greek word used in verse 2 for knowledge, and it indicates a personal and intimate relationship with Jesus our God.

When we begin to know Him richly and deeply through earnest prayer, Bible study, and meditation, we begin to experience His divine power working for us, in us, and through us. The temptations that once beckoned us so strongly will start to dim and lose their allure. Instead of partaking of old temptations, we will day by day be partaking of God's own divine nature as He guides our thoughts, attitudes, and actions.

Not only will our lives abound with His grace and peace, but they will also abound in fruit for the kingdom of God.

For further reading on Step 11, turn to page 527.

Daily Encouragement

DAY 223 READING: 2 PETER 1:1–21

A Thought for the New Day: The most astounding truth of all is that we human beings can actually be "partakers of the divine nature" (v. 4). No, we never become God, but He plants His own nature in us by means of that great promise He has made to us. That is why we are able to commune with Him as friend with friend, because we share this "family" likeness with Him. (*Turn to page 511.*)

in power and might, do not bring a reviling accusation against them before the Lord.

12 But these, like natural brute beasts made to be caught and destroyed, speak evil of the things they do not understand, and will utterly perish in their own corruption,

13 *and* will receive the wages of unrighteousness, *as* those who count it pleasure to carouse in the daytime. *They are* spots and blemishes, carousing in their own deceptions while they feast with you,

14 having eyes full of adultery and that cannot cease from sin, beguiling unstable souls. *They have* a heart trained in covetous practices, *and are* accursed children.

15 They have forsaken the right way and gone astray, following the way of Balaam the *son* of Beor, who loved the wages of unrighteousness;

16 but he was rebuked for his iniquity: a dumb donkey speaking with a man's voice restrained the madness of the prophet.

17 These are wells without water, clouds carried by a tempest, to whom the gloom of darkness is reserved forever.

18 For when they speak great swelling *words* of emptiness, they allure through the lusts of the flesh, through licentiousness, the ones who have actually escaped from those who live in error.

19 While they promise them liberty, they themselves are slaves of corruption; for by whom a person is overcome, by him also he is brought into bondage.

20 For if, after they have escaped the pollutions of the world through the knowledge of the Lord and Savior Jesus Christ, they are again entangled in them and overcome, the latter end is worse for them than the beginning.

21 For it would have been better for them not to have known the way of righteousness, than having known *it*, to turn from the holy commandment delivered to them.

22 But it has happened to them according to the true proverb: *"A dog returns to his own vomit,"* and, "a sow, having washed, to her wallowing in the mire."

3 Beloved, I now write to you this second epistle (in *both of* which I stir up your pure minds by way of reminder),

2 that you may be mindful of the words which were spoken before by the holy prophets, and of the commandment of us the apostles of the Lord and Savior,

3 knowing this first: that scoffers will come in the last days, walking according to their own lusts,

4 and saying, "Where is the promise of His coming? For since the fathers fell asleep, all things continue as *they were* from the beginning of creation."

5 For this they willfully forget: that by the word of God the heavens were of old, and the earth standing out of water and in the water,

6 by which the world *that* then existed perished, being flooded with water.

7 But the heavens and the earth *which* now *exist* are kept in store by the same word, reserved for fire until the day of judgment and perdition of ungodly men.

8 But, beloved, do not forget this one thing, that with the Lord one day *is* as a thousand years, and a thousand years as one day.

9 The Lord is not slack concerning *His* promise, as some count slackness, but is longsuffering toward us, not willing that any should perish but that all should come to repentance.

10 But the day of the Lord will come as a thief in the night, in which the heavens will pass away with a great noise, and the elements will melt with fervent heat;

STEP 1

We admitted we were powerless over our dependencies—
that our lives had become unmanageable.

2 Peter 2:19

The commercials and ads make it look like so much fun! The people are glamorous, and the product they are using obviously makes them happy and successful in all the important ways.

It makes us want to run right out and buy or drink or smoke or eat the same things. But there is a catch. The products of the world and the slogans that work so hard to influence our thinking may not deliver what is promised. Instead of being captivating, we may become captives. When our lives are filled with deep voids and unexpressed needs, it is easy to fall prey to something that seems to fill that void, even for a little while. And soon what we convince ourselves was temporary or unimportant has totally overcome us and we must finally admit that we are in bondage. To come to such a low point is hard and sorrowful. But our admission is the beginning of real joy and peace.

For further reading on Step 1, turn to page 561.

Daily Encouragement

DAY 224 READING: 2 PETER 2:1—3:18

A Thought for the New Day: It is an axiom that living things grow. When we share in Christ's life, we continually grow to be more like Him (3:18). Sometimes we are discouraged with ourselves because we see so little evidence of this growth, but frustration with ourselves does not help. Spending time in communion with Jesus—this is the water and nutrient that stimulates our growth in eternal things. (*Turn to page 513.*)

both the earth and the works that are in it will be burned up.

11 Therefore, since all these things will be dissolved, what manner *of persons* ought you to be in holy conduct and godliness,

12 looking for and hastening the coming of the day of God, because of which the heavens will be dissolved being on fire, and the elements will melt with fervent heat?

13 Nevertheless we, according to His promise, look for new heavens and a new earth in which righteousness dwells.

14 Therefore, beloved, looking forward to these things, be diligent to be found by Him in peace, without spot and blameless;

15 and account *that* the longsuffer-

ing of our Lord *is* salvation—as also our beloved brother Paul, according to the wisdom given to him, has written to you,

16 as also in all his epistles, speaking in them of these things, in which are some things hard to understand, which those *who are* untaught and unstable twist to their own destruction, as *they do* also the rest of the Scriptures.

17 You therefore, beloved, since you know *these things* beforehand, beware lest you also fall from your own steadfastness, being led away with the error of the wicked;

18 but grow in the grace and knowledge of our Lord and Savior Jesus Christ. To Him *be* the glory both now and forever. Amen.

THE FIRST EPISTLE OF
JOHN

THAT which was from the beginning, which we have heard, which we have seen with our eyes, which we have looked upon, and our hands have handled, concerning the Word of life—

2 the life was manifested, and we have seen, and bear witness, and declare to you that eternal life which was with the Father and was manifested to us—

3 that which we have seen and heard we declare to you, that you also may have fellowship with us; and truly our fellowship *is* with the Father and with His Son Jesus Christ.

4 And these things we write to you that your joy may be full.

5 This is the message which we have heard from Him and declare to you, that God is light and in Him is no darkness at all.

6 If we say that we have fellow-

ship with Him, and walk in darkness, we lie and do not practice the truth.

7 But if we walk in the light as He is in the light, we have fellowship with one another, and the blood of Jesus Christ His Son cleanses us from all sin.

8 If we say that we have no sin, we deceive ourselves, and the truth is not in us.

9 If we confess our sins, He is faithful and just to forgive us *our* sins and to cleanse us from all unrighteousness.

10 If we say that we have not sinned, we make Him a liar, and His word is not in us.

2 My little children, these things I write to you, that you may not sin. And if anyone sins, we have an Advocate with the Father, Jesus Christ the righteous.

STEP 5

Admitted to God, to ourselves, and to another human being the exact nature of our wrongs.

1 John 1:8, 9

In Step 4, we courageously probed our inner selves, perhaps facing the reality of who we are for the first time in our lives. Now we must go a step further. We must openly confess to God, to ourselves, and to another human being all of those things that we have worked for years to conceal. We are able to take this step because we know that God loves us unconditionally. He already knows everything about us; but He asks us to confess our wrongs to Him, because once we acknowledge those wrongs, we are able to begin moving toward a healthier life.

Our confession opens our hearts to receive the love that God is already extending to us. This great love not only makes God faithful to forgive us, but also faithful to cleanse us. Once we are clean we can release all those old "survival skills," which have actually been destroying us; and we can walk into the fresh air of a stronger and more peaceful life.

For further reading on Step 5, turn to page 607.

Daily Encouragement

DAY 225 READING: 1 JOHN 1:1—2:2

A Thought for the New Day: It does no good to ignore our sins in the hope that they will just "go away." Most counselors will tell you that facing the truth is important for mental health. Confessing our sins has the same benefit, only more so, because our friendship with God is restored. He has the power to do what we cannot—take our sins away (1:8, 9). Not hiding from God, but opening ourselves up to Him, is the way to happiness. (*Turn to page 515.*)

2 And He Himself is the propitiation for our sins, and not for ours only but also for the whole world.

3 Now by this we know that we know Him, if we keep His commandments.

4 He who says, "I know Him," and does not keep His commandments, is a liar, and the truth is not in him.

5 But whoever keeps His word, truly the love of God is perfected in him. By this we know that we are in Him.

6 He who says he abides in Him ought himself also to walk just as He walked.

7 Brethren, I write no new commandment to you, but an old commandment which you have had from the beginning. The old commandment is the word which you heard from the beginning.

8 Again, a new commandment I write to you, which thing is true in Him and in you, because the darkness is passing away, and the true light is already shining.

STEP 8

9 He who says he is in the light, and hates his brother, is in darkness until now.

10 He who loves his brother abides in the light, and there is no cause for stumbling in him.

11 But he who hates his brother is in darkness and walks in darkness, and does not know where he is going, because the darkness has blinded his eyes.

12 I write to you, little children,
   Because your sins are forgiven you for His name's sake.

13 I write to you, fathers,
   Because you have known Him *who is* from the beginning.
  I write to you, young men,
   Because you have overcome the wicked one.
  I write to you, little children,
   Because you have known the Father.

14 I have written to you, fathers,
   Because you have known Him *who is* from the beginning.
 I have written to you, young men,
   Because you are strong, and the word of God abides in you,
   And you have overcome the wicked one.

STEP 10

15 Do not love the world or the things in the world. If anyone loves the world, the love of the Father is not in him.

16 For all that *is* in the world—the lust of the flesh, the lust of the eyes, and the pride of life—is not of the Father but is of the world.

17 And the world is passing away, and the lust of it; but he who does the will of God abides forever.

18 Little children, it is the last hour; and as you have heard that the Antichrist is coming, even now many antichrists have come, by which we know that it is the last hour.

19 They went out from us, but they were not of us; for if they had been of us, they would have continued with us; but *they went out* that they might be made manifest, that none of them were of us.

20 But you have an anointing from the Holy One, and you know all things.

21 I have not written to you because you do not know the truth, but because you know it, and that no lie is of the truth.

22 Who is a liar but he who denies that Jesus is the Christ? He is antichrist who denies the Father and the Son.

23 Whoever denies the Son does not have the Father either; he who acknowledges the Son has the Father also.

24 Therefore let that abide in you which you heard from the beginning. If what you heard from the beginning abides in you, you also

STEP 8

Made a list of all persons we had harmed,
and became willing to make amends to them all.

1 John 2:9–11

Hatred is a dark forest, fraught with the unseen pitfalls of pride, the suffocating swamps of self-pity, and the ravenous beast of bitterness. It destroys all who choose to wander in it. The saddest part of this scenario is that people who could walk in the quiet pastures of God's love and peace sometimes choose the forests of hate. God offers every believer His power to forgive. He offers His presence to comfort and the healing balm of His love to heal the wounds of the past. When we choose to walk in God's love, our steps are sure and our lives stay strong and stable. But if we choose to wander into the dark forest of hatred, we go without God's blessing and help.

We do not lose our salvation, but we lose all the peace and joy and blessing of walking in the light.

For further reading on Step 8, turn to page 737.

Daily Encouragement

DAY 226 READING: 1 JOHN 2:3–29

A Thought for the New Day: John seems to say a great deal in these words: "You know all things" (v. 20). Of course he does not want us to think we are omniscient, but we do have the Spirit of God dwelling in us (the "anointing"). God's Spirit reminds us constantly of everything we need to know in order to live pleasingly to Him. This is a very great privilege. We are never left to our own folly, but always God directs our steps. (*Turn to page 517.*)

will abide in the Son and in the Father.

25 And this is the promise that He has promised us—eternal life.

26 These *things* I have written to you concerning those who *try to* deceive you.

27 But the anointing which you have received from Him abides in you, and you do not need that anyone teach you; but as the same anointing teaches you concerning all things, and is true, and is not a lie, and just as it has taught you, you will abide in Him.

STEP 6

28 And now, little children, abide in Him, that when He appears, we may have confidence and not be ashamed before Him at His coming.

29 If you know that He is righteous, you know that everyone who practices righteousness is born of Him.

3 Behold what manner of love the Father has bestowed on us, that we should be called children of God! Therefore the world does not know us, because it did not know Him.

2 Beloved, now we are children of God; and it has not yet been revealed what we shall be, but we know that when He is revealed, we shall be like Him, for we shall see Him as He is.

3 And everyone who has this hope in Him purifies himself, just as He is pure.

STEP 7

4 Whoever commits sin also commits lawlessness, and sin is lawlessness.

5 And you know that He was manifested to take away our sins, and in Him there is no sin.

6 Whoever abides in Him does not sin. Whoever sins has neither seen Him nor known Him.

7 Little children, let no one deceive you. He who practices righteousness is righteous, just as He is righteous.

8 He who sins is of the devil, for the devil has sinned from the be-

ginning. For this purpose the Son of God was manifested, that He might destroy the works of the devil.

9 Whoever has been born of God does not sin, for His seed remains in him; and he cannot sin, because he has been born of God.

10 In this the children of God and the children of the devil are manifest: Whoever does not practice righteousness is not of God, nor *is* he who does not love his brother.

11 For this is the message that you heard from the beginning, that we should love one another,

12 not as Cain *who* was of the wicked one and murdered his brother. And why did he murder him? Because his works were evil and his brother's righteous.

13 Do not marvel, my brethren, if the world hates you.

14 We know that we have passed from death to life, because we love the brethren. He who does not love *his* brother abides in death.

15 Whoever hates his brother is a murderer, and you know that no murderer has eternal life abiding in him.

16 By this we know love, because He laid down His life for us. And we also ought to lay down *our* lives for the brethren.

17 But whoever has this world's goods, and sees his brother in need, and shuts up his heart from him, how does the love of God abide in him?

STEP 9

18 My little children, let us not love in word or in tongue, but in deed and in truth.

19 And by this we know that we are of the truth, and shall assure our hearts before Him.

20 For if our heart condemns us, God is greater than our heart, and knows all things.

21 Beloved, if our heart does not condemn us, we have confidence toward God.

22 And whatever we ask we receive from Him, because we keep

STEP 7

Humbly asked Him to remove our shortcomings.

1 John 3:4–9

God's perfect plan for us is a right relationship with Him. But we cannot be right with God when we cling to sins and dependencies that have characterized our lives. These things of the world—be they obsessions with power or our work, addictions to chemicals, the need to be in control—any of the things by which we find ourselves tightly bound—get in the way of our communion with Him. They represent lawlessness, or sin, which separates us from God and violates His order and balance. And *that* is Satan's perfect plan!

Jesus Christ, the only begotten Son of God, was sent into the world to tear down the Devil's works. He came to free us from our bondage to the things of the world. Only as we admit our weaknesses in the face of God's righteousness do we begin to practice righteousness ourselves and to move forward unencumbered in knowing Him.

For further reading on Step 7, turn to page 521.

Daily Encouragement

DAY 227 READING: 1 JOHN 3:1–24

A Thought for the New Day: Love begins with an attitude toward those around us, but that attitude must find practical expression to be real (v. 18). If faith that does not work is dead, as James said, the same is true of love. Elsewhere we read that "faith that works by love" is the acid test of what we say. The greatest sermon is love at work: this is a message that the world can understand. (*Turn to page 519.*)

His commandments and do those things that are pleasing in His sight.

23 And this is His commandment: that we should believe on the name of His Son Jesus Christ and love one another, as He gave us commandment.

24 Now he who keeps His commandments abides in Him, and He in him. And by this we know that He abides in us, by the Spirit whom He has given us.

4 Beloved, do not believe every spirit, but test the spirits, whether they are of God; because many false prophets have gone out into the world.

2 By this you know the Spirit of God: Every spirit that confesses that Jesus Christ has come in the flesh is of God,

3 and every spirit that does not confess that Jesus Christ has come in the flesh is not of God. And this is the *spirit* of the Antichrist, which you have heard was coming, and is now already in the world.

4 You are of God, little children, and have overcome them, because He who is in you is greater than he who is in the world.

5 They are of the world. Therefore they speak *as* of the world, and the world hears them.

6 We are of God. He who knows God hears us; he who is not of God does not hear us. By this we know the spirit of truth and the spirit of error.

7 Beloved, let us love one another, for love is of God; and everyone who loves is born of God and knows God.

8 He who does not love does not know God, for God is love.

9 In this the love of God was manifested toward us, that God has sent His only begotten Son into the world, that we might live through Him.

STEP 2
10 In this is love, not that we loved God, but that He loved us and sent

His Son *to be* the propitiation for our sins.

11 Beloved, if God so loved us, we also ought to love one another.

12 No one has seen God at any time. If we love one another, God abides in us, and His love has been perfected in us.

13 By this we know that we abide in Him, and He in us, because He has given us of His Spirit.

14 And we have seen and testify that the Father has sent the Son *as* Savior of the world.

15 Whoever confesses that Jesus is the Son of God, God abides in him, and he in God.

16 And we have known and believed the love that God has for us. God is love, and he who abides in love abides in God, and God in him.

17 Love has been perfected among us in this: that we may have boldness in the day of judgment; because as He is, so are we in this world.

18 There is no fear in love; but perfect love casts out fear, because fear involves torment. But he who fears has not been made perfect in love.
STEP 6

19 We love Him because He first loved us.
STEP 8

20 If someone says, "I love God," and hates his brother, he is a liar; for he who does not love his brother whom he has seen, how can he love God whom he has not seen?

21 And this commandment we have from Him: that he who loves God *must* love his brother also.

5 Whoever believes that Jesus is the Christ is born of God, and everyone who loves Him who begot also loves him who is begotten of Him.

2 By this we know that we love the children of God, when we love God and keep His commandments.

3 For this is the love of God, that we keep His commandments. And

*Were entirely ready to have God
remove all these defects of character.*

1 John 4:18

As we work Step 6 of our recovery program, we are much like emotional cripples requiring "surgery" in order to restore us as whole, functioning individuals. Many of us have been bent double by the troubles of our past. Even though our conditions are confining and painful, the thought of allowing the Great Physician to do the much-needed surgery in our lives is still frightening. We are afraid of letting go of the status quo, because, although painful, it is familiar.

However, 1 John 4:18 tells us how to become willing to allow God to straighten our crippled lives into beautiful, strong ones. We simply surrender our compulsive efforts to create our own security, recognizing that the Lord loves us and wants us to experience perfect joy, peace, and fulfillment in our lives. By trusting completely in Him, our fears will fall away. We will be made ready to have Him remove the old dependencies and addictions that have hampered our walk with Him.

For further reading on Step 6, turn to page 531.

Daily Encouragement

DAY 228 READING: 1 JOHN 4:1–21

A Thought for the New Day: A famous philosopher has said that "dread" is a leading religious motivator. Fear has its place—like fear of fire—but it is not the highest ideal for a child of God. When we love God because He first loved us in Christ, then the need for dread or fear becomes obsolete. Fear paralyzes us for positive action, but love displaces fear and enables us to please God as He planned we should (v. 18). *(Turn to page 521.)*

His commandments are not burdensome.

STEP 11 4 For whatever is born of God overcomes the world. And this is the victory that has overcome the world—our faith.

5 Who is he who overcomes the world, but he who believes that Jesus is the Son of God?

6 This is He who came by water and blood—Jesus Christ; not only by water, but by water and blood. And it is the Spirit who bears witness, because the Spirit is truth.

7 For there are three who bear witness in heaven: the Father, the Word, and the Holy Spirit; and these three are one.

8 And there are three that bear witness on earth: the Spirit, the water, and the blood; and these three agree as one.

9 If we receive the witness of men, the witness of God is greater; for this is the witness of God which He has testified of His Son.

10 He who believes in the Son of God has the witness in himself; he who does not believe God has made Him a liar, because he has not believed the testimony that God has given of His Son.

11 And this is the testimony: that God has given us eternal life, and this life is in His Son.

12 He who has the Son has life; he who does not have the Son of God does not have life.

13 These things I have written to you who believe in the name of the Son of God, that you may know that you have eternal life, and that you may *continue to* believe in the name of the Son of God.

14 Now this is the confidence that we have in Him, that if we ask anything according to His will, He hears us.

STEP 7

15 And if we know that He hears us, whatever we ask, we know that we have the petitions that we have asked of Him.

16 If anyone sees his brother sinning a sin *which does* not *lead* to death, he will ask, and He will give him life for those who commit sin not *leading* to death. There is sin *leading* to death. I do not say that he should pray about that.

17 All unrighteousness is sin, and there is sin not *leading* to death.

18 We know that whoever is born of God does not sin; but he who has been born of God keeps himself, and the wicked one does not touch him.

STEP 11

19 We know that we are of God, and the whole world lies *under the sway of* the wicked one.

20 And we know that the Son of God has come and has given us an understanding, that we may know Him who is true; and we are in Him who is true, in His Son Jesus Christ. This is the true God and eternal life.

21 Little children, keep yourselves from idols. Amen.

Humbly asked Him to remove our shortcomings.

1 John 5:14, 15

In John 5:14, the apostle declares we can have great confidence in our prayers "if we ask anything according to [God's] will." And no prayer is of greater delight to our Loving Father than a humble believer's asking Him to do a work of power and grace in his or her life.

We know that Jesus delights in answering this prayer because it is in total alignment with His revealed will for our lives—that we abide in Him and become more Christlike. When His desire for our lives becomes our true longing, Psalm 37:4 will ring true in our lives: "Delight yourself also in the LORD, and He shall give you the desires of your heart."

In Step 7, we have turned from trusting in ourselves to trusting and delighting in the power and strength of God alone. This humility opens to us a new door of blessing as the Lord begins to do His wonderful work of grace in our lives.

For further reading on Step 7, turn to page 567.

Daily Encouragement

DAY 229 READING: 1 JOHN 5:1–21

A Thought for the New Day: Trying to define life is like trying to define infinity. We can describe some of its characteristics, but we still do not understand it. That is because life, like infinity, is an attribute of God, who imparts His quality of "life" in varying degrees to His creation. When we have Christ, we have life at its fullest measure, that is, God-like (or eternal) in quality (vv. 11, 12). We enjoy the life of God, but we can never comprehend that life. *(Turn to page 523.)*

THE SECOND EPISTLE OF
JOHN

THE ELDER,

To the elect lady and her children, whom I love in truth, and not only I, but also all those who have known the truth,

2 because of the truth which abides in us and will be with us forever:

3 Grace, mercy, *and* peace will be with you from God the Father and from the Lord Jesus Christ, the Son of the Father, in truth and love.

4 I rejoiced greatly that I have found *some* of your children walking in truth, as we received commandment from the Father.

5 And now I plead with you, lady, not as though I wrote a new commandment to you, but that which we have had from the beginning: that we love one another.

6 This is love, that we walk according to His commandments. This is the commandment, that as you have heard from the beginning, you should walk in it.

7 For many deceivers have gone out into the world who do not confess Jesus Christ *as* coming in the flesh. This is a deceiver and an antichrist.

8 Look to yourselves, that we do not lose those things we worked for, but *that* we may receive a full reward.

STEP 10

9 Whoever transgresses and does not abide in the doctrine of Christ does not have God. He who abides in the doctrine of Christ has both the Father and the Son.

10 If anyone comes to you and does not bring this doctrine, do not receive him into your house nor greet him;

11 for he who greets him shares in his evil deeds.

12 Having many things to write to you, I did not wish *to do so* with paper and ink; but I hope to come to you and speak face to face, that our joy may be full.

13 The children of your elect sister greet you. Amen.

THE THIRD EPISTLE OF
JOHN

THE ELDER,

To the beloved Gaius, whom I love in truth:

2 Beloved, I pray that you may prosper in all things and be in health, just as your soul prospers.

3 For I rejoiced greatly when brethren came and testified of the truth *that is* in you, just as you walk in the truth.

4 I have no greater joy than to hear that my children walk in truth.

5 Beloved, you do faithfully whatever you do for the brethren and for strangers,

6 who have borne witness of your love before the church. *If* you send them forward on their journey in a manner worthy of God, you will do well,

7 because they went forth for His name's sake, taking nothing from the Gentiles.

522

STEP 10

*Continued to take personal inventory
and when we were wrong promptly admitted it.*

2 John 8

Which is more important—fervent love or right doctrine? If a person does not have God's love for others, he or she is unable to reach beyond self and experience the blessings of sharing, giving, receiving, and comforting with which God's love abounds. Yet, if one is drawn away from the simple, clear truths of Scripture, or becomes side-tracked by overemphasizing one portion of Scripture in relation to another, stunted growth may also result.

The apostle John warns us to look to ourselves, taking time to assess our relationships to God, to His Word, and to others. We must be humble enough to admit that we are capable of error, and without God's help we are prone to it. And when the Holy Spirit reveals to us where we have slipped or become confused, we need to be patient with ourselves, realizing we are only human, but that our gracious God lovingly forgives and guides us back onto the right path.

For further reading on Step 10, turn to page 543.

Daily Encouragement

DAY 230 READING: 2 JOHN—3 JOHN

A Thought for the New Day: The truth is most commonly a statement according to fact. Or it is a code by which we live. Or it is a principle according to which all values are measured. But where can we find an absolute fact, an absolute code, or a principle that is an absolute standard? We find rest and assurance in God's Word as the measure of all that is true, while Jesus Himself, the Living Word, is "the Truth" personified (v. 4). (*Turn to page 525.*)

8 We therefore ought to receive such, that we may become fellow workers for the truth.

9 I wrote to the church, but Diotrephes, who loves to have the preeminence among them, does not receive us.

10 Therefore, if I come, I will call to mind his deeds which he does, prating against us with malicious words. And not content with that, he himself does not receive the brethren, and forbids those who wish to, putting *them* out of the church.

11 Beloved, do not imitate what is evil, but what is good. He who does good is of God, but he who does evil has not seen God.

12 Demetrius has a *good* testimony from all, and from the truth itself. And we also bear witness, and you know that our testimony is true.

13 I had many things to write, but I do not wish to write to you with pen and ink;

14 but I hope to see you shortly, and we shall speak face to face. Peace to you. Our friends greet you. Greet the friends by name.

THE EPISTLE OF
JUDE

JUDE, a servant of Jesus Christ, and brother of James,

To those who are called, sanctified by God the Father, and preserved in Jesus Christ:

2 Mercy, peace, and love be multiplied to you.

3 Beloved, while I was very diligent to write to you concerning our common salvation, I found it necessary to write to you exhorting you to contend earnestly for the faith which was once for all delivered to the saints.

4 For certain men have crept in unnoticed, who long ago were marked out for this condemnation, ungodly men, who turn the grace of our God into licentiousness and deny the only Lord God and our Lord Jesus Christ.

5 But I want to remind you, though you once knew this, that the Lord, having saved the people out of the land of Egypt, afterward destroyed those who did not believe.

6 And the angels who did not keep their proper domain, but left their own habitation, He has reserved in everlasting chains under darkness for the judgment of the great day;

7 as Sodom and Gomorrah, and the cities around them in a similar manner to these, having given themselves over to sexual immorality and gone after strange flesh, are set forth as an example, suffering the vengeance of eternal fire.

8 Likewise also these dreamers defile the flesh, reject authority, and speak evil of dignitaries.

9 Yet Michael the archangel, in contending with the devil, when he disputed about the body of Moses, dared not bring against him a reviling accusation, but said, "The Lord rebuke you!"

10 But these speak evil of whatever they do not know; and whatever they know naturally, like brute beasts, in these things they corrupt themselves.

11 Woe to them! For they have gone in the way of Cain, have run

STEP 12

*Having had a spiritual awakening as the result of these steps,
we tried to carry this message to others,
and to practice these principles in all our affairs.*

Jude 20–25

Jude was inspired by God to warn believers "to earnestly contend for the faith." Surrounded by counterfeit religions, how do we oppose such a force? Jude 20–25 gives us all we need for victory.

First, as we daily practice the things we have learned in God's Word, we will be building ourselves up in our faith. Second, we are to "[pray] in the Holy Spirit." If we are to earnestly contend for the faith, we need a regular time of quiet and complete meditation and interaction with our God. Third, we are to *keep* ourselves in the love of God; that is, we are to conduct our lives in a way that allows God's love to cover and protect us. Then we can carry our message to others.

In whatever situations we may find ourselves, God is able to supply all the wisdom and strength we need to keep us from stumbling and bring us, at last, faultless into His presence.

For further reading on Step 12, turn to page 535.

Daily Encouragement

DAY 231 READING: JUDE 1–25

A Thought for the New Day: One ancient reading of Jude 22 is, "on some have compassion, who are doubting." If we are honest, we all get into hard places that test our faith: at such times it seems our world is about to come apart. It is good to remember our own weakness when we meet people who feel their feet are giving way under them. Instead of criticizing, we should be ready always to sympathize with those in slippery places. Jesus did. (*Turn to page 527.*)

greedily in the error of Balaam for profit, and perished in the rebellion of Korah.

12 These are spots in your love feasts, while they feast with you without fear, serving *only* themselves; *they are* clouds without water, carried about by the winds; late autumn trees without fruit, twice dead, pulled up by the roots; 13 raging waves of the sea, foaming up their own shame; wandering stars for whom is reserved the blackness of darkness forever.

14 Now Enoch, the seventh from Adam, prophesied about these men also, saying, "Behold, the Lord comes with ten thousands of His saints, 15 "to execute judgment on all, to convict all who are ungodly among them of all their ungodly deeds which they have committed in an ungodly way, and of all the harsh things which ungodly sinners have spoken against Him."

16 These are murmurers, complainers, walking according to their own lusts; and they mouth great swelling *words*, flattering people to gain advantage.

17 But you, beloved, remember the words which were spoken before by the apostles of our Lord Jesus Christ:

18 how they told you that there would be mockers in the last time who would walk according to their own ungodly lusts.

19 These are sensual persons, who cause divisions, not having the Spirit.

20 But you, beloved, building yourselves up on your most holy faith, praying in the Holy Spirit, 21 keep yourselves in the love of God, looking for the mercy of our Lord Jesus Christ unto eternal life. 22 And on some have compassion, making a distinction; 23 but others save with fear, pulling *them* out of the fire, hating even the garment defiled by the flesh.

24 Now to Him who is able
    to keep you from stumbling,
And to present *you* faultless
Before the presence of His
    glory with exceeding joy,
25 To God our Savior,
Who alone is wise,
Be glory and majesty,
Dominion and power,
Both now and forever.
Amen.

STEP 12

THE REVELATION

OF JESUS CHRIST

THE Revelation of Jesus Christ, which God gave Him to show His servants—things which must shortly take place. And He sent and signified *it* by His angel to His servant John, 2 who bore witness to the word of God, and to the testimony of Jesus Christ, and to all things that he saw.

STEP 11

3 Blessed *is* he who reads and those who hear the words of this prophecy, and keep those things which are written in it; for the time *is* near.

4 John, to the seven churches which are in Asia:

Grace to you and peace from Him who is and who was and who is to come, and from the seven Spirits who are before His throne, 5 and from Jesus Christ, the faith-

*Sought through prayer and meditation to improve our conscious contact with God **as we understood Him,** praying only for knowledge of His will for us and the power to carry that out.*

Revelation 1:3

During the Dark Ages and long afterward, the Book of Revelation was little read. It was considered too difficult and obscure to understand or gain instruction from. But God Himself urges that we know and love this book. No other scripture receives a special benediction from God just for reading and hearing its words and keeping them. The Holy Spirit knew the visions of the Revelation would appear confusing to some and unsettling to others. Some would shrug it off as unimportant, while others would mock it as science fiction. Yet God says it is true and that it is of utmost importance for us to study and do our best to understand its message. The core of that message is that Jesus Himself is coming back to this earth to rule in righteousness and peace. He wants us to look forward to that day with hope and joy because we love Him and have done our best to live for Him.

For further reading on Step 11, turn to page 547.

Daily Encouragement

DAY 232 READING: REVELATION 1:1–20

A Thought for the New Day: Who is this plain Man we read about in the earlier Gospels, so gentle He would not quench a smoking flax or break a bruised reed, who answered not a word when accused of crimes against humanity and the state? Yes, He is "the First and the Last" and holds the keys of life and death (vv. 17, 18). He was before all things, and by Him all things are held together. What a glorious Savior we have! (*Turn to page 531.*)

ful witness, the firstborn from the dead, and the ruler over the kings of the earth. To Him who loved us and washed us from our sins in His own blood,

6 and has made us kings and priests to His God and Father, to Him *be* glory and dominion forever and ever. Amen.

7 Behold, He is coming with clouds, and every eye will see Him, and they *also* who pierced Him. And all the tribes of the earth will mourn because of Him. Even so, Amen.

8 "I am the Alpha and the Omega, *the* Beginning and *the* End," says the Lord, "who is and who was and who is to come, the Almighty."

9 I, John, both your brother and companion in tribulation, and in the kingdom and patience of Jesus Christ, was on the island that is called Patmos for the word of God and for the testimony of Jesus Christ.

10 I was in the Spirit on the Lord's Day, and I heard behind me a loud voice, as of a trumpet,

11 saying, "I am the Alpha and the Omega, the First and the Last," and, "What you see, write in a book and send *it* to the seven churches which are in Asia: to Ephesus, to Smyrna, to Pergamos, to Thyatira, to Sardis, to Philadelphia, and to Laodicea."

12 Then I turned to see the voice that spoke with me. And having turned I saw seven golden lampstands,

13 and in the midst of the seven lampstands *One* like the Son of Man, clothed with a garment down to the feet and girded about the chest with a golden band.

14 His head and *His* hair *were* white like wool, as white as snow, and His eyes like a flame of fire;

15 His feet *were* like fine brass, as if refined in a furnace, and His voice as the sound of many waters;

16 He had in His right hand seven stars, out of His mouth went a sharp two-edged sword, and His countenance *was* like the sun shining in its strength.

17 And when I saw Him, I fell at His feet as dead. But He laid His right hand on me, saying to me, "Do not be afraid; I am the First and the Last.

18 "I *am* He who lives, and was dead, and behold, I am alive forevermore. Amen. And I have the keys of Hades and of Death.

19 "Write the things which you have seen, and the things which are, and the things which will take place after this.

20 "The mystery of the seven stars which you saw in My right hand, and the seven golden lampstands: The seven stars are the angels of the seven churches, and the seven lampstands which you saw are the seven churches.

2 "To the angel of the church of Ephesus write,

'These things says He who holds the seven stars in His right hand, who walks in the midst of the seven golden lampstands:

2 "I know your works, your labor, your patience, and that you cannot bear those who are evil. And you have tested those who say they are apostles and are not, and have found them liars;

3 "and you have persevered and have patience, and have labored for My name's sake and have not become weary.

4 "Nevertheless I have *this* against you, that you have left your first love.

5 "Remember therefore from where you have fallen; repent and do the first works, or else I will come to you quickly and remove your lampstand from its place—unless you repent.

6 "But this you have, that you hate the deeds of the Nicolaitans, which I also hate.

7 "He who has an ear, let him hear what the Spirit says to the churches. To him who overcomes I

will give to eat from the tree of life, which is in the midst of the Paradise of God." '

8 "And to the angel of the church in Smyrna write,

'These things says the First and the Last, who was dead, and came to life:

9 "I know your works, tribulation, and poverty (but you are rich); and *I know* the blasphemy of those who say they are Jews and are not, but *are* a synagogue of Satan.

10 "Do not fear any of those things which you are about to suffer. Indeed, the devil is about to throw *some* of you into prison, that you may be tested, and you will have tribulation ten days. Be faithful until death, and I will give you the crown of life.

11 "He who has an ear, let him hear what the Spirit says to the churches. He who overcomes shall not be hurt by the second death." '

12 "And to the angel of the church in Pergamos write,

'These things says He who has the sharp two-edged sword:

13 "I know your works, and where you dwell, where Satan's throne *is.* And you hold fast to My name, and did not deny My faith even in the days in which Antipas *was* My faithful martyr, who was killed among you, where Satan dwells.

14 "But I have a few things against you, because you have there those who hold the doctrine of Balaam, who taught Balak to put a stumbling block before the children of Israel, to eat things sacrificed to idols, and to commit sexual immorality.

15 "Thus you also have those who hold the doctrine of the Nicolaitans, which thing I hate.

16 "Repent, or else I will come to you quickly and will fight against them with the sword of My mouth.

17 "He who has an ear, let him hear what the Spirit says to the churches. To him who overcomes I will give some of the hidden manna to eat. And I will give him a white stone, and on the stone a new name written which no one knows except him who receives *it.*' '

18 "And to the angel of the church in Thyatira write,

'These things says the Son of God, who has eyes like a flame of fire, and His feet like fine brass:

19 "I know your works, love, service, faith, and your patience; and *as* for your works, the last *are* more than the first.

20 "Nevertheless I have a few things against you, because you allow that woman Jezebel, who calls herself a prophetess, to teach and beguile My servants to commit sexual immorality and to eat things sacrificed to idols.

21 "And I gave her time to repent of her sexual immorality, and she did not repent.

22 "Indeed I will cast her into a sickbed, and those who commit adultery with her into great tribulation, unless they repent of their deeds.

23 "And I will kill her children with death. And all the churches shall know that I am He who searches the minds and hearts. And I will give to each one of you according to your works.

24 "But to you I say, and to the rest in Thyatira, as many as do not have this doctrine, and who have not known the depths of Satan, as they call *them,* I will put on you no other burden.

25 "But hold fast what you have till I come.

26 "And he who overcomes, and keeps My works until the end, to him I will give power over the nations—

27 'He shall rule them with a rod
    of iron;
   As the potter's vessels
    shall be broken to pieces'—

as I also have received from My Father;

28 "and I will give him the morning star.

29 "He who has an ear, let him hear what the Spirit says to the churches." '

3 "And to the angel of the church in Sardis write,

'These things says He who has the seven Spirits of God and the seven stars: "I know your works, that you have a name that you are alive, but you are dead.

2 "Be watchful, and strengthen the things which remain, that are ready to die, for I have not found your works perfect before God.

3 "Remember therefore how you have received and heard; hold fast and repent. Therefore if you will not watch, I will come upon you as a thief, and you will not know what hour I will come upon you.

4 "You have a few names even in Sardis who have not defiled their garments; and they shall walk with Me in white, for they are worthy.

5 "He who overcomes shall be clothed in white garments, and I will not blot out his name from the Book of Life; but I will confess his name before My Father and before His angels.

6 "He who has an ear, let him hear what the Spirit says to the churches." '

7 "And to the angel of the church in Philadelphia write,

'These things says He who is holy, He who is true, "*He who has the key of David, He who opens and no one shuts, and shuts and no one opens*":

8 "I know your works. See, I have set before you an open door, and no one can shut it; for you have a little strength, have kept My word, and have not denied My name.

9 "Indeed I will make *those* of the synagogue of Satan, who say they are Jews and are not, but lie— indeed I will make them come and worship before your feet, and to know that I have loved you.

10 "Because you have kept My command to persevere, I also will keep you from the hour of trial which shall come upon the whole world, to test those who dwell on the earth.

11 "Behold, I come quickly! Hold fast what you have, that no one may take your crown.

12 "He who overcomes, I will make him a pillar in the temple of My God, and he shall go out no more. And I will write on him the name of My God and the name of the city of My God, the New Jerusalem, which comes down out of heaven from My God. And *I will write on him* My new name.

13 "He who has an ear, let him hear what the Spirit says to the churches." '

14 "And to the angel of the church of the Laodiceans write,

'These things says the Amen, the Faithful and True Witness, the Beginning of the creation of God:

15 "I know your works, that you are neither cold nor hot. I could wish you were cold or hot.

16 "So then, because you are lukewarm, and neither cold nor hot, I will spew you out of My mouth.

17 "Because you say, 'I am rich, have become wealthy, and have need of nothing'—and do not know that you are wretched, miserable, poor, blind, and naked—

18 "I counsel you to buy from Me gold refined in the fire, that you may be rich; and white garments, that you may be clothed, *that* the shame of your nakedness may not be revealed; and anoint your eyes with eye salve, that you may see.

19 "As many as I love, I rebuke and chasten. Therefore be zealous and repent.

20 "Behold, I stand at the door and knock. If anyone hears My voice and opens the door, I will come in to him and dine with him, and he with Me.

STEP 6

*Were entirely ready to have God
remove all these defects of character.*

Revelation 3:19, 20

Strange though it may seem, we may be inclined to mourn the loss of our character defects. It is true that in yielding these we are saying good-bye to old coping mechanisms that have been painful but familiar friends.

God's Word reminds us that the removal of our defects of character is more than a good-bye. It is a life-changing hello. God stands patiently at the door awaiting our return. As we lay down our old, destructive dependencies, we open the door for new discovery of and communion with Him.

How may these new discoveries of God show themselves in our lives? The anger-filled person may display a new mellowness of personality. The chronically anxious person may find a lasting peace and security. The desperately possessive person may begin to take a balanced approach in all human relationships. All of these transformations await the opening of a door as we ask God to remove our defects of character.

For further reading on Step 6, turn to page 579.

Daily Encouragement

DAY 233 READING: REVELATION 2:1—3:22

A Thought for the New Day: It is easy to be faithful when everything is going well for us. At such times we may even pat ourselves on the back, imagining what ideal Christians we are. Tilt! Comes the test, and our blood turns to ice water. For most of us these little tests soon pass, but they remind us of how much we need to rely on our risen Lord for the hard times. Through Him we will be faithful—as others have been—"until death" (2:10). *(Turn to page 535.)*

21 "To him who overcomes I will grant to sit with Me on My throne, as I also overcame and sat down with My Father on His throne.

22 "He who has an ear, let him hear what the Spirit says to the churches." ' "

4 After these things I looked, and behold, a door *standing* open in heaven. And the first voice which I heard *was* like a trumpet speaking with me, saying, "Come up here, and I will show you things which must take place after this."

2 Immediately I was in the Spirit; and behold, a throne set in heaven, and *One* sat on the throne.

3 And He who sat there was like a jasper and a sardius stone in appearance; and *there was* a rainbow around the throne, in appearance like an emerald.

4 Around the throne *were* twenty-four thrones, and on the thrones I saw twenty-four elders sitting, clothed in white robes; and they had crowns of gold on their heads.

5 And from the throne proceeded lightnings, thunderings, and voices. And *there were* seven lamps of fire burning before the throne, which are the seven Spirits of God.

6 Before the throne *there was* a sea of glass, like crystal. And in the midst of the throne, and around the throne, *were* four living creatures full of eyes in front and in back.

7 The first living creature *was* like a lion, the second living creature like a calf, the third living creature had a face like a man, and the fourth living creature *was* like a flying eagle.

8 And *the* four living creatures, each having six wings, were full of eyes around and within. And they do not rest day or night, saying:

"Holy, holy, holy,
Lord God Almighty,

Who was and is and is to come!"

9 Whenever the living creatures give glory and honor and thanks to Him who sits on the throne, who lives forever and ever,

10 the twenty-four elders fall down before Him who sits on the throne and worship Him who lives forever and ever, and cast their crowns before the throne, saying:

11 "You are worthy, O Lord,
To receive glory and honor and power;
For You created all things,
And by Your will they exist and were created."

5 And I saw in the right *hand* of Him who sat on the throne a scroll written inside and on the back, sealed with seven seals.

2 Then I saw a strong angel proclaiming with a loud voice, "Who is worthy to open the scroll and to loose its seals?"

3 And no one in heaven or on the earth or under the earth was able to open the scroll, or to look at it.

4 So I wept much, because no one was found worthy to open and read the scroll, or to look at it.

5 But one of the elders said to me, "Do not weep. Behold, the Lion of the tribe of Judah, the Root of David, has prevailed to open the scroll and to loose its seven seals."

6 And I looked, and behold, in the midst of the throne and of the four living creatures, and in the midst of the elders, stood a Lamb as though it had been slain, having seven horns and seven eyes, which are the seven Spirits of God sent out into all the earth.

7 Then He came and took the scroll out of the right hand of Him who sat on the throne.

8 Now when He had taken the scroll, the four living creatures and the twenty-four elders fell down

before the Lamb, each having a harp, and golden bowls full of incense, which are the prayers of the saints.

9 And they sang a new song, saying:

"You are worthy to take the
  scroll,
And to open its seals;
For You were slain,
And have redeemed us to God
  by Your blood
Out of every tribe and tongue
  and people and nation,
10 And have made us kings and
  priests to our God;
And we shall reign on the
  earth."

11 Then I looked, and I heard the voice of many angels around the throne, the living creatures, and the elders; and the number of them was ten thousand times ten thousand, and thousands of thousands, 12 saying with a loud voice:

"Worthy is the Lamb who was
  slain
To receive power and riches
  and wisdom,
And strength and honor and
  glory and blessing!"

13 And every creature which is in heaven and on the earth and under the earth and such as are in the sea, and all that are in them, I heard saying:

"Blessing and honor and glory
  and power
Be to Him who sits on the
  throne,
And to the Lamb, forever and
  ever!"

14 Then the four living creatures said, "Amen!" And the twenty-four elders fell down and worshiped Him who lives forever and ever.

6 Now I saw when the Lamb opened one of the seals; and I heard one of the four living creatures saying with a voice like thunder, "Come and see."

2 And I looked, and behold, a white horse. And he who sat on it had a bow; and a crown was given to him, and he went out conquering and to conquer.

3 When He opened the second seal, I heard the second living creature saying, "Come and see."

4 And another horse, fiery red, went out. And it was granted to the one who sat on it to take peace from the earth, and that *people* should kill one another; and there was given to him a great sword.

5 When He opened the third seal, I heard the third living creature say, "Come and see." And I looked, and behold, a black horse, and he who sat on it had a pair of scales in his hand.

6 And I heard a voice in the midst of the four living creatures saying, "A quart of wheat for a denarius, and three quarts of barley for a denarius; and do not harm the oil and the wine."

7 When He opened the fourth seal, I heard the voice of the fourth living creature saying, "Come and see."

8 And I looked, and behold, a pale horse. And the name of him who sat on it was Death, and Hades followed with him. And power was given to them over a fourth of the earth, to kill with sword, with hunger, with death, and by the beasts of the earth.

9 When He opened the fifth seal, I saw under the altar the souls of those who had been slain for the word of God and for the testimony which they held.

10 And they cried with a loud voice, saying, "How long, O Lord, holy and true, until You judge and avenge our blood on those who dwell on the earth?"

11 And a white robe was given to each of them; and it was said to

them that they should rest a little
while longer, until both *the number of* their fellow servants and
their brethren, who would be killed
as they *were*, was completed.

12 I looked when He opened the
sixth seal, and behold, there was a
great earthquake; and the sun became black as sackcloth of hair,
and the moon became like blood.

13 And the stars of heaven fell to
the earth, as a fig tree drops its late
figs when it is shaken by a mighty
wind.

14 Then the sky receded as a scroll
when it is rolled up, and every
mountain and island was moved
out of its place.

15 And the kings of the earth, the
great men, the rich men, the commanders, the mighty men, every
slave and every free man, hid
themselves in the caves and in the
rocks of the mountains,

16 and said to the mountains and
rocks, "Fall on us and hide us from
the face of Him who sits on the
throne and from the wrath of the
Lamb!

17 "For the great day of His wrath
has come, and who is able to
stand?"

7 After these things I saw four
angels standing at the four corners of the earth, holding the four
winds of the earth, that the wind
should not blow on the earth, on
the sea, or on any tree.

2 Then I saw another angel ascending from the east, having the
seal of the living God. And he cried
with a loud voice to the four angels
to whom it was granted to harm
the earth and the sea,

3 saying, "Do not harm the earth,
the sea, or the trees till we have
sealed the servants of our God on
their foreheads."

4 And I heard the number of
those who were sealed. One hundred *and* forty-four thousand of all
the tribes of the children of Israel
were sealed:

5 of the tribe of Judah
　twelve thousand *were* sealed;
of the tribe of Reuben
　twelve thousand *were* sealed;
of the tribe of Gad
　twelve thousand *were* sealed;

6 of the tribe of Asher
　twelve thousand *were* sealed;
of the tribe of Naphtali
　twelve thousand *were* sealed;
of the tribe of Manasseh
　twelve thousand *were* sealed;

7 of the tribe of Simeon
　twelve thousand *were* sealed;
of the tribe of Levi
　twelve thousand *were* sealed;
of the tribe of Issachar
　twelve thousand *were* sealed;

8 of the tribe of Zebulun
　twelve thousand *were* sealed;
of the tribe of Joseph
　twelve thousand *were* sealed;
of the tribe of Benjamin
　twelve thousand *were* sealed.

9 After these things I looked, and
behold, a great multitude which no
one could number, of all nations,
tribes, peoples, and tongues, standing before the throne and before
the Lamb, clothed with white
robes, with palm branches in their
hands,

10 and crying out with a loud
voice, saying, "Salvation *belongs*
to our God who sits on the throne,
and to the Lamb!"

11 And all the angels stood around
the throne and the elders and the
four living creatures, and fell on
their faces before the throne and
worshiped God,

12 saying:

"Amen! Blessing and glory
　and wisdom,
Thanksgiving and honor and
　power and might,
Be to our God forever and
　ever.
Amen."

13 Then one of the elders answered, saying to me, "Who are

STEP 12

*Having had a spiritual awakening as the result of these steps,
we tried to carry this message to others,
and to practice these principles in all our affairs.*

Revelation 6:15–17

Between chapters 3 and 4 of Revelation, there is a distinct break in thought and sequence. Many Bible scholars believe that an event we call the Rapture of the church (recorded in 1 Thessalonians 4:13–18) takes place after chapter 3. These verses describe how all believers will be caught up to meet the Lord. The rest of the people living on earth must then face seven years of the most terrible tribulation ever known. After we are allowed a glimpse of the incredible glory and majesty of heaven in chapters 4 and 5, we become spectators of the beginning events of the Tribulation in chapter 6. Anyone who believes God's Word is true must shudder at the prophecies given there. But beyond that comes an urgency to share God's message of hope while there is still time. This is the day of God's grace. His arms of love and forgiveness are extended to anyone who will hear His voice and believe in His work of redemption on the Cross.

For further reading on Step 12, turn to page 659.

Daily Encouragement

DAY 234 READING: REVELATION 4:1—6:17

A Thought for the New Day: John's unglorified eyes could not comprehend what he saw seated on the throne (4:3), but in the best language available the aged apostle described his vision of God. In summary, John was viewing the ultimately Beautiful. How else can we account for the loveliness of all things created, their excellent artistry, their perfect order and symmetry, except that the Author of all beauty is Himself perfectly beautiful? *(Turn to page 538.)*

these arrayed in white robes, and where did they come from?"

14 And I said to him, "Sir, you know." So he said to me, "These are the ones who come out of the great tribulation, and washed their robes and made them white in the blood of the Lamb.

15 "Therefore they are before the throne of God, and serve Him day and night in His temple. And He who sits on the throne will dwell among them.

16 "They shall neither hunger anymore nor thirst anymore; the sun shall not strike them, nor any heat;

17 "for the Lamb who is in the midst of the throne will shepherd them and lead them to living fountains of waters. And God will wipe away every tear from their eyes."

8 When He opened the seventh seal, there was silence in heaven for about half an hour.

2 And I saw the seven angels who stand before God, and to them were given seven trumpets.

3 Then another angel, having a golden censer, came and stood at the altar. And he was given much incense, that he should offer *it* with the prayers of all the saints upon the golden altar which was before the throne.

4 And the smoke of the incense, with the prayers of the saints, ascended before God from the angel's hand.

5 Then the angel took the censer, filled it with fire from the altar, and threw *it* to the earth. And there were noises, thunderings, lightnings, and an earthquake.

6 So the seven angels who had the seven trumpets prepared themselves to sound.

7 The first angel sounded: And hail and fire followed, mingled with blood, and they were thrown to the earth; and a third of the trees were burned up, and all green grass was burned up.

8 Then the second angel sounded:

And *something* like a great mountain burning with fire was thrown into the sea, and a third of the sea became blood;

9 and a third of the living creatures in the sea died, and a third of the ships were destroyed.

10 Then the third angel sounded: And a great star fell from heaven, burning like a torch, and it fell on a third of the rivers and on the springs of water;

11 and the name of the star is Wormwood; and a third of the waters became wormwood; and many men died from the water, because it was made bitter.

12 Then the fourth angel sounded: And a third of the sun was struck, a third of the moon, and a third of the stars, so that a third of them were darkened; and a third of the day did not shine, and likewise the night.

13 And I looked, and I heard an angel flying through the midst of heaven, saying with a loud voice, "Woe, woe, woe to the inhabitants of the earth, because of the remaining blasts of the trumpet of the three angels who are about to sound!"

9 Then the fifth angel sounded: And I saw a star fallen from heaven to the earth. And to him was given the key to the bottomless pit.

2 And he opened the bottomless pit, and smoke arose out of the pit like the smoke of a great furnace. And the sun and the air were darkened because of the smoke of the pit.

3 Then out of the smoke locusts came upon the earth. And to them was given power, as the scorpions of the earth have power.

4 They were commanded not to harm the grass of the earth, or any green thing, or any tree, but only those men who do not have the seal of God on their foreheads.

5 And they were not given *authority* to kill them, but to torment

them *for* five months. And their torment *was* like the torment of a scorpion when it strikes a man.

6 In those days men will seek death and will not find it; they will desire to die, and death will flee from them.

7 And the shape of the locusts was like horses prepared for battle; and on their heads were crowns of something like gold, and their faces *were* like the faces of men.

8 They had hair like women's hair, and their teeth were like lions' *teeth*.

9 And they had breastplates like breastplates of iron, and the sound of their wings *was* like the sound of chariots with many horses running into battle.

10 They had tails like scorpions, and there were stings in their tails. And their power *was* to hurt men five months.

11 And they had as king over them the angel of the bottomless pit, whose name in Hebrew *is* Abaddon, but in Greek he has the name Apollyon.

12 One woe is past. Behold, still two more woes are coming after these things.

13 Then the sixth angel sounded: And I heard a voice from the four horns of the golden altar which is before God,

14 saying to the sixth angel who had the trumpet, "Release the four angels who are bound at the great river Euphrates."

15 So the four angels, who had been prepared for the hour and day and month and year, were released to kill a third of mankind.

16 Now the number of the army of the horsemen *was* two hundred million, and I heard the number of them.

17 And thus I saw the horses in the vision: those who sat on them had breastplates of fiery red, hyacinth blue, and sulfur yellow; and the heads of the horses *were* like the heads of lions; and out of their mouths came fire, smoke, and brimstone.

18 By these three *plagues* a third of mankind was killed—by the fire and the smoke and the brimstone which came out of their mouths.

19 For their power is in their mouth and in their tails; for their tails *are* like serpents, having heads; and with them they do harm.

20 But the rest of mankind, who were not killed by these plagues, did not repent of the works of their hands, that they should not worship demons, and idols of gold, silver, brass, stone, and wood, which can neither see nor hear nor walk;

21 and they did not repent of their murders or their sorceries or their sexual immorality or their thefts.

10 And I saw still another mighty angel coming down from heaven, clothed with a cloud. And a rainbow *was* on his head, his face *was* like the sun, and his feet like pillars of fire.

2 And he had a little book open in his hand. And he set his right foot on the sea and *his* left *foot* on the land,

3 and cried with a loud voice, as *when* a lion roars. And when he cried out, seven thunders uttered their voices.

4 Now when the seven thunders uttered their voices, I was about to write; but I heard a voice from heaven saying to me, "Seal up the things which the seven thunders uttered, and do not write them."

5 And the angel whom I saw standing on the sea and on the land lifted up his hand to heaven

6 and swore by Him who lives forever and ever, who created heaven and the things that are in it, the earth and the things that are in it, and the sea and the things that are in it, that there should be delay no longer,

7 but in the days of the sounding

STEP 2

*Came to believe that a Power greater than ourselves
could restore us to sanity.*

Revelation 9:20, 21

The plagues and horrors of the Tribulation time seem terrible
beyond imagining. It is hard to believe that people who refuse to
repent and call on God for deliverance could somehow live
through such disaster. For such people there is no hope.

But we do not belong to that group of people. We have come to
realize the hopelessness of our situation and our own powerlessness.
We have agreed with God concerning the unbearable condition of
our lives. This is called repentance, and it is the first great step
toward wisdom and deliverance. The second step is to acknowledge
the power of the One who can deliver us—Jesus Christ. Jesus does
not want us to suffer and be in bondage. He wants us to accept His
love and His gift of salvation. When we repent and turn to God for
help, He offers us His forgiveness, His unconditional love, and His
sovereign power.

For further reading on Step 2, turn to page 551.

Daily Encouragement

DAY 235 READING: REVELATION 7:1—11:19

A Thought for the New Day: The temple and the ark of the
covenant (11:19) have always stood for the inexorable demands
of God's holy law. We know we have not met these demands,
and on the basis of sheer justice we all must stand condemned.
Yet this is our story and song—that Jesus has paid our debt to
the Law in full, and we can stand acquitted before Him, heads
bowed only in eternal gratitude for His unspeakable mercy.
(*Turn to page 543.*)

of the seventh angel, when he is about to sound, the mystery of God would be finished, as He declared to His servants the prophets.

8 Then the voice which I heard from heaven spoke to me again and said, "Go, take the little book which is open in the hand of the angel who stands on the sea and on the earth."

9 And I went to the angel and said to him, "Give me the little book." And he said to me, "Take and eat it; and it will make your stomach bitter, but it will be as sweet as honey in your mouth."

10 And I took the little book out of the angel's hand and ate it, and it was as sweet as honey in my mouth. But when I had eaten it, my stomach became bitter.

11 And he said to me, "You must prophesy again about many peoples, nations, tongues, and kings."

11 Then I was given a reed like a measuring rod. And the angel stood, saying, "Rise and measure the temple of God, the altar, and those who worship there.

2 "But leave out the court which is outside the temple, and do not measure it, for it has been given to the Gentiles. And they will tread the holy city under foot *for* forty-two months.

3 "And I will give *power* to my two witnesses, and they will prophesy one thousand two hundred and sixty days, clothed in sackcloth."

4 These are the two olive trees and the two lampstands standing before the God of the earth.

5 And if anyone wants to harm them, fire proceeds from their mouth and devours their enemies. And if anyone wants to harm them, he must be killed in this manner.

6 These have power to shut heaven, so that no rain falls in the days of their prophecy; and they have power over waters to turn them to blood, and to strike the earth with all plagues, as often as they desire.

7 Now when they finish their testimony, the beast that ascends out of the bottomless pit will make war against them, overcome them, and kill them.

8 And their dead bodies *will lie* in the street of the great city which spiritually is called Sodom and Egypt, where also our Lord was crucified.

9 Then *those* from the peoples, tribes, tongues, and nations will see their dead bodies three and a half days, and not allow their dead bodies to be put into graves.

10 And those who dwell on the earth will rejoice over them, make merry, and send gifts to one another, because these two prophets tormented those who dwell on the earth.

11 Now after the three and a half days the breath of life from God entered them, and they stood on their feet, and great fear fell on those who saw them.

12 And they heard a loud voice from heaven saying to them, "Come up here." And they ascended to heaven in a cloud, and their enemies saw them.

13 In the same hour there was a great earthquake, and a tenth of the city fell. In the earthquake seven thousand men were killed, and the rest were afraid and gave glory to the God of heaven.

14 The second woe is past. Behold, the third woe is coming quickly.

15 Then the seventh angel sounded: And there were loud voices in heaven, saying, "The kingdoms of this world have become *the kingdoms* of our Lord and of His Christ, and He shall reign forever and ever!"

16 And the twenty-four elders who sat before God on their thrones fell on their faces and worshiped God,

17 saying:

Satan Thrown Out

"We give You thanks,
    O Lord God Almighty,
The One who is and who was
    and who is to come,
Because You have taken Your
    great power and reigned.
18 The nations were angry,
    and Your wrath has come,
And the time of the dead,
    that they should be judged,
And that You should reward
    Your servants the prophets
    and the saints,
And those who fear Your
    name, small and great,
And should destroy those
    who destroy the earth."

19 Then the temple of God was opened in heaven, and the ark of His covenant was seen in His temple. And there were lightnings, noises, thunderings, an earthquake, and great hail.

12 Now a great sign appeared in heaven: a woman clothed with the sun, with the moon under her feet, and on her head a garland of twelve stars.
2 Then being with child, she cried out in labor and in pain to give birth.
3 And another sign appeared in heaven: behold, a great, fiery red dragon having seven heads and ten horns, and seven diadems on his heads.
4 His tail drew a third of the stars of heaven and threw them to the earth. And the dragon stood before the woman who was ready to give birth, to devour her Child as soon as it was born.
5 And she bore a male Child who was to rule all nations with a rod of iron. And her Child was caught up to God and *to* His throne.
6 Then the woman fled into the wilderness, where she has a place prepared by God, that they should feed her there one thousand two hundred and sixty days.
7 And war broke out in heaven:

Michael and his angels fought against the dragon; and the dragon and his angels fought,
8 but they did not prevail, nor was a place found for them in heaven any longer.
9 So the great dragon was cast out, that serpent of old, called the Devil and Satan, who deceives the whole world; he was cast to the earth, and his angels were cast out with him.
10 Then I heard a loud voice saying in heaven, "Now salvation, and strength, and the kingdom of our God, and the power of His Christ have come, for the accuser of our brethren, who accused them before our God day and night, has been cast down.
11 "And they overcame him by the blood of the Lamb and by the word of their testimony, and they did not love their lives to the death.
12 "Therefore rejoice, O heavens, and you who dwell in them! Woe to the inhabitants of the earth and the sea! For the devil has come down to you, having great wrath, because he knows that he has a short time."
13 Now when the dragon saw that he had been cast to the earth, he persecuted the woman who gave birth to the male *Child*.
14 But the woman was given two wings of a great eagle, that she might fly into the wilderness to her place, where she is nourished for a time and times and half a time, from the presence of the serpent.
15 So the serpent spewed water out of his mouth like a flood after the woman, that he might cause her to be carried away by the flood.
16 But the earth helped the woman, and the earth opened its mouth and swallowed up the flood which the dragon had spewed out of his mouth.
17 And the dragon was enraged with the woman, and he went to make war with the rest of her off-

spring, who keep the commandments of God and have the testimony of Jesus Christ.

13 Then I stood on the sand of the sea. And I saw a beast rising up out of the sea, having seven heads and ten horns, and on his horns ten crowns, and on his heads a blasphemous name.

2 Now the beast which I saw was like a leopard, his feet were like *the feet of* a bear, and his mouth like the mouth of a lion. And the dragon gave him his power, his throne, and great authority.

3 I saw one of his heads as if it had been mortally wounded, and his deadly wound was healed. And all the world marveled and followed the beast.

4 So they worshiped the dragon who gave authority to the beast; and they worshiped the beast, saying, "Who *is* like the beast? Who is able to make war with him?"

5 And he was given a mouth speaking great things and blasphemies, and he was given authority to continue for forty-two months.

6 Then he opened his mouth in blasphemy against God, to blaspheme His name, His tabernacle, and those who dwell in heaven.

7 And it was granted to him to make war with the saints and to overcome them. And authority was given him over every tribe, tongue, and nation.

8 And all who dwell on the earth will worship him, whose names have not been written in the Book of Life of the Lamb slain from the foundation of the world.

9 If anyone has an ear, let him hear.

10 He who leads into captivity shall go into captivity; he who kills with the sword must be killed with the sword. Here is the patience and the faith of the saints.

11 Then I saw another beast coming up out of the earth, and he had two horns like a lamb and spoke like a dragon.

12 And he exercises all the authority of the first beast in his presence, and causes the earth and those who dwell in it to worship the first beast, whose deadly wound was healed.

13 He performs great signs, so that he even makes fire come down from heaven on the earth in the sight of men.

14 And he deceives those who dwell on the earth by those signs which he was granted to do in the sight of the beast, telling those who dwell on the earth to make an image to the beast who was wounded by the sword and lived.

15 He was granted *power* to give breath to the image of the beast, that the image of the beast should both speak and cause as many as would not worship the image of the beast to be killed.

16 And he causes all, both small and great, rich and poor, free and slave, to receive a mark on their right hand or on their foreheads,

17 and that no one may buy or sell except one who has the mark or the name of the beast, or the number of his name.

18 Here is wisdom. Let him who has understanding calculate the number of the beast, for it is the number of a man: His number *is* 666.

14 Then I looked, and behold, a Lamb standing on Mount Zion, and with Him one hundred *and* forty-four thousand, having His Father's name written on their foreheads.

2 And I heard a voice from heaven, like the voice of many waters, and like the voice of loud thunder. And I heard the sound of harpists playing their harps.

3 And they sang as it were a new song before the throne, before the four living creatures, and the elders; and no one could learn that song except the hundred *and* forty-four thousand who were redeemed from the earth.

4 These are the ones who were not defiled with women, for they are virgins. These are the ones who follow the Lamb wherever He goes. These were redeemed from *among* men, *being* firstfruits to God and to the Lamb.

5 And in their mouth was found no guile, for they are without fault before the throne of God.

6 Then I saw another angel flying in the midst of heaven, having the everlasting gospel to preach to those who dwell on the earth—to every nation, tribe, tongue, and people—

7 saying with a loud voice, "Fear God and give glory to Him, for the hour of His judgment has come; and worship Him who made heaven and earth, the sea and springs of water."

8 And another angel followed, saying, "Babylon is fallen, is fallen, that great city, because she has made all nations drink of the wine of the wrath of her fornication."

9 Then a third angel followed them, saying with a loud voice, "If anyone worships the beast and his image, and receives *his* mark on his forehead or on his hand,

10 "he himself shall also drink of the wine of the wrath of God, which is poured out full strength into the cup of His indignation. And he shall be tormented with fire and brimstone in the presence of the holy angels and in the presence of the Lamb.

11 "And the smoke of their torment ascends forever and ever; and they have no rest day or night, who worship the beast and his image, and whoever receives the mark of his name."

12 Here is the patience of the saints; here *are* those who keep the commandments of God and the faith of Jesus.

13 Then I heard a voice from heaven saying to me, "Write: 'Blessed *are* the dead who die in the Lord from now on.'" "Yes,"

says the Spirit, "that they may rest from their labors, and their works follow them."

14 And I looked, and behold, a white cloud, and on the cloud sat *One* like the Son of Man, having on His head a golden crown, and in His hand a sharp sickle.

15 And another angel came out of the temple, crying with a loud voice to Him who sat on the cloud, "Thrust in Your sickle and reap, for the time has come for You to reap, for the harvest of the earth is ripe."

16 So He who sat on the cloud thrust in His sickle on the earth, and the earth was reaped.

17 Then another angel came out of the temple which is in heaven, he also having a sharp sickle.

18 And another angel came out from the altar, who had power over fire, and he cried with a loud cry to him who had the sharp sickle, saying, "Thrust in your sharp sickle and gather the clusters of the vine of the earth, for her grapes are fully ripe."

19 So the angel thrust his sickle into the earth and gathered the vine of the earth, and threw *it* into the great winepress of the wrath of God.

20 And the winepress was trampled outside the city, and blood came out of the winepress, up to the horses' bridles, for one thousand six hundred furlongs.

15 Then I saw another sign in heaven, great and marvelous: seven angels having the seven last plagues, for in them the wrath of God is complete.

2 And I saw *something* like a sea of glass mingled with fire, and those who have the victory over the beast, over his image and over his mark *and* over the number of his name, standing on the sea of glass, having harps of God.

3 And they sing the song of Moses, the servant of God, and the song of the Lamb, saying:

STEP 10

*Continued to take personal inventory
and when we were wrong promptly admitted it.*

Revelation 16:15

As John recounts the great judgment to come upon the earth, God Himself interrupts the vision and speaks to us directly in verse 15. He reminds us to stay prepared for His coming, watchful and aware of what is happening in the world around us, which may point to His return.

Being prepared also means "keeping our garments," or staying dressed in His righteousness. As we daily abide in the Lord Jesus and seek to obey Him and honor Him with our lives, we will be dressed in His righteousness and looking forward to His coming with joy and anticipation. But if we become nonchalant about our relationship with Him and allow ourselves to slip back into old habits, we have much to lose. Taking our eyes off of the Lord Jesus and allowing the idols of the world to fill our thoughts and time risks shame and embarrassment at His coming. Let us heed His own exhortation to us: "Blessed *is* he who watches."

For further reading on Step 10, turn to page 621.

Daily Encouragement

DAY 236 READING: REVELATION 12:1—16:21

A Thought for the New Day: Our hearts are filled with rapture as, at times, we think we hear the tones of that distant song of the overcoming saints (15:2, 3). Not all of us experience the same measure of testing in the world, and therefore our victories are not equally spectacular. But for each of us there is some special trial that we will one day look back on and declare with that heavenly assembly, "Jesus led me all the way!" (*Turn to page 547.*)

"Great and marvelous *are* Your
      works,
   Lord God Almighty!
   Just and true *are* Your ways,
   O King of the saints!
4 Who shall not fear You, O
      Lord, and glorify Your name?
   For *You* alone *are* holy.
   For all nations shall come and
      worship before You,
   For Your judgments have been
      manifested."

5 After these things I looked, and
behold, the temple of the tabernacle of the testimony in heaven was
opened.
6 And out of the temple came the
seven angels having the seven
plagues, clothed in pure bright
linen, and having their chests
girded with golden bands.
7 Then one of the four living creatures gave to the seven angels
seven golden bowls full of the
wrath of God who lives forever
and ever.
8 The temple was filled with
smoke from the glory of God and
from His power, and no one was
able to enter the temple till the
seven plagues of the seven angels
were completed.

16 Then I heard a loud voice
from the temple saying to the
seven angels, "Go and pour out
the bowls of the wrath of God on
the earth."
2 So the first went and poured out
his bowl upon the earth, and a foul
and loathsome sore came upon the
men who had the mark of the
beast and those who worshiped his
image.
3 Then the second angel poured
out his bowl on the sea, and it
became blood as of a dead *man;*
and every living creature in the sea
died.
4 Then the third angel poured out
his bowl on the rivers and springs
of water, and they became blood.
5 And I heard the angel of the
waters saying:

"You are righteous, O Lord,
   The One who is and who was
      and who is to be,
   Because You have judged
      these things.
6 For they have shed the blood
      of saints and prophets,
   And You have given them
      blood to drink.
   For it is their just due."

7 And I heard another from the
altar saying, "Even so, Lord God
Almighty, true and righteous *are*
Your judgments."
8 Then the fourth angel poured
out his bowl on the sun, and power
was given to him to scorch men
with fire.
9 And men were scorched with
great heat, and they blasphemed
the name of God who has power
over these plagues; and they did
not repent and give Him glory.
10 Then the fifth angel poured out
his bowl on the throne of the
beast, and his kingdom became full
of darkness; and they gnawed their
tongues because of the pain.
11 And they blasphemed the God
of heaven because of their pains
and their sores, and did not repent
of their deeds.
12 Then the sixth angel poured out
his bowl on the great river Euphrates, and its water was dried up, so
that the way of the kings from the
east might be prepared.
13 And I saw three unclean spirits
like frogs *coming* out of the mouth
of the dragon, out of the mouth of
the beast, and out of the mouth of
the false prophet.
14 For they are spirits of demons,
performing signs, *which* go out to
the kings of the earth and of the
whole world, to gather them to the
battle of that great day of God
Almighty.
15 "Behold, I am coming as a thief.
Blessed *is* he who watches, and
keeps his garments, lest he walk
naked and they see his shame."

STEP
10

16 And they gathered them together to the place called in Hebrew, Armageddon.

17 Then the seventh angel poured out his bowl into the air, and a loud voice came out of the temple of heaven, from the throne, saying, "It is done!"

18 And there were noises and thunderings and lightnings; and there was a great earthquake, such a mighty and great earthquake as had not occurred since men were on the earth.

19 Now the great city was divided into three parts, and the cities of the nations fell. And great Babylon was remembered before God, to give her the cup of the wine of the fierceness of His wrath.

20 Then every island fled away, and the mountains were not found.

21 And great hail from heaven fell upon men, *every hailstone* about the weight of a talent. And men blasphemed God because of the plague of the hail, since that plague was exceedingly great.

17 Then one of the seven angels who had the seven bowls came and talked with me, saying to me, "Come, I will show you the judgment of the great harlot who sits on many waters,

2 "with whom the kings of the earth committed fornication, and the inhabitants of the earth were made drunk with the wine of her fornication."

3 So he carried me away in the Spirit into the wilderness. And I saw a woman sitting on a scarlet beast *which was* full of names of blasphemy, having seven heads and ten horns.

4 The woman was arrayed in purple and scarlet, and adorned with gold and precious stones and pearls, having in her hand a golden cup full of abominations and the filthiness of her fornication.

5 And on her forehead a name *was* written:

MYSTERY,
BABYLON THE GREAT,
THE MOTHER OF HARLOTS
AND OF THE ABOMINATIONS
OF THE EARTH.

6 And I saw the woman, drunk with the blood of the saints and with the blood of the martyrs of Jesus. And when I saw her, I marveled with great amazement.

7 But the angel said to me, "Why did you marvel? I will tell you the mystery of the woman and of the beast that carries her, which has the seven heads and the ten horns.

8 "The beast that you saw was, and is not, and will ascend out of the bottomless pit and go to perdition. And those who dwell on the earth will marvel, whose names are not written in the Book of Life from the foundation of the world, when they see the beast that was, and is not, and yet is.

9 "Here *is* the mind which has wisdom: The seven heads are seven mountains on which the woman sits.

10 There are also seven kings. Five have fallen, one is, *and* the other has not yet come. And when he comes, he must continue a short time.

11 "And the beast that was, and is not, is himself also the eighth, and is of the seven, and is going to perdition.

12 "And the ten horns which you saw are ten kings who have received no kingdom as yet, but they receive authority for one hour as kings with the beast.

13 "These are of one mind, and they will give their power and authority to the beast.

14 "These will make war with the Lamb, and the Lamb will overcome them, for He is Lord of lords and King of kings; and those *who are* with Him *are* called, chosen, and faithful."

15 And he said to me, "The waters

which you saw, where the harlot sits, are peoples, multitudes, nations, and tongues.

16 "And the ten horns which you saw on the beast, these will hate the harlot, make her desolate and naked, eat her flesh and burn her with fire.

17 "For God has put it into their hearts to fulfill His purpose, to be of one mind, and to give their kingdom to the beast, until the words of God are fulfilled.

18 "And the woman whom you saw is that great city which reigns over the kings of the earth."

18 After these things I saw another angel coming down from heaven, having great authority, and the earth was illuminated with his glory.

2 And he cried mightily with a loud voice, saying, "Babylon the great is fallen, is fallen, and has become a habitation of demons, a prison for every foul spirit, and a cage for every unclean and hated bird!

3 "For all the nations have drunk of the wine of the wrath of her fornication, the kings of the earth have committed fornication with her, and the merchants of the earth have become rich through the abundance of her luxury."

STEP 11

4 And I heard another voice from heaven saying, "Come out of her, my people, lest you share in her sins, and lest you receive of her plagues.

5 "For her sins have reached to heaven, and God has remembered her iniquities.

6 "Render to her just as she rendered to you, and repay her double according to her works; in the cup which she has mixed, mix for her double.

7 "In the measure that she glorified herself and lived luxuriously, in the same measure give her torment and sorrow; for she says in her heart, 'I sit *as* queen, and am

no widow, and will not see sorrow.'

8 "Therefore her plagues will come in one day—death and mourning and famine. And she will be utterly burned with fire, for strong *is* the Lord God who judges her.

9 "And the kings of the earth who committed fornication and lived luxuriously with her will weep and lament for her, when they see the smoke of her burning,

10 "standing at a distance for fear of her torment, saying, 'Alas, alas, that great city Babylon, that mighty city! For in one hour your judgment has come.'

11 "And the merchants of the earth will weep and mourn over her, for no one buys their merchandise anymore:

12 "merchandise of gold and silver, precious stones and pearls, fine linen and purple, silk and scarlet, every kind of citron wood, every kind of object of ivory, every kind of object of most precious wood, bronze, iron, and marble;

13 "and cinnamon and incense, fragrant oil and frankincense, wine and oil, fine flour and wheat, cattle and sheep, horses and chariots, and bodies and souls of men.

14 "And the fruit that your soul longed for has gone from you, and all the things which are rich and splendid have gone from you, and you shall find them no more at all.

15 "The merchants of these things, who became rich by her, will stand at a distance for fear of her torment, weeping and wailing,

16 "and saying, 'Alas, alas, that great city that was clothed in fine linen, purple, and scarlet, and adorned with gold and precious stones and pearls!

17 'For in one hour such great riches came to nothing.' And every shipmaster, all who travel by ship, sailors, and as many as trade on the sea, stood at a distance

18 "and cried out when they saw

*Sought through prayer and meditation to improve our conscious contact with God **as we understood Him,** praying only for knowledge of His will for us and the power to carry that out.*

Revelation 18:4

God's people are meant to be set apart for Him. Because we have been purchased with the blood of the Lamb, Christ Jesus, we no longer belong to this world. Our citizenship is in heaven, and in Revelation 18:4, the Lord Jesus reminds us that His people are to be separate and different from the rest of the world. Bible scholars have several possibilities for the exact identity of the woman who sits upon the beast and the seven mountains. But they all would agree that she represents the love of this present world and what it can bring in the way of riches, honor, fame, power, and pleasure. The woman, whoever she represents, has compromised her standards and beliefs for the sake of worldly gain. When God's judgment falls on her, it is swift and sure and final. This is why God especially calls to His people in verse 4, reminding them to stay true to His Word alone, uncompromised in their love for Him and the purity of His doctrine.

For further reading on Step 11, turn to page 553.

Daily Encouragement

DAY 237 READING: REVELATION 17:1—18:24

A Thought for the New Day: Those who love God and His kingdom cannot help being amazed at the severity of evil that prevails in the world system, the "Babylon" to which John here refers (18:21). Our comfort resides partly in the confidence that these ills are short-lived and must soon come to a violent end. Then our rejoicing will be in a kingdom of righteousness and peace that will never end. (*Turn to page 551.*)

the smoke of her burning, saying, 'What *is* like this great city?'

19 "And they threw dust on their heads and cried out, weeping and wailing, and saying, 'Alas, alas, that great city, in which all who had ships on the sea became rich by her wealth! For in one hour she is made desolate.'

20 "Rejoice over her, O heaven, and *you* holy apostles and prophets, for God has avenged you on her!"

21 Then a mighty angel took up a stone like a great millstone and threw *it* into the sea, saying, "Thus with violence the great city Babylon shall be thrown down, and shall not be found anymore.

22 "The sound of harpists, musicians, flutists, and trumpeters shall not be heard in you anymore. And no craftsman of any craft shall be found in you anymore. And the sound of a millstone shall not be heard in you anymore.

23 "And the light of a lamp shall not shine in you anymore. And the voice of bridegroom and bride shall not be heard in you anymore. For your merchants were the great men of the earth, for by your sorcery all the nations were deceived.

24 "And in her was found the blood of prophets and saints, and of all who were slain on the earth."

19 After these things I heard a loud voice of a great multitude in heaven, saying, "Alleluia! Salvation and glory and honor and power to the Lord our God!

2 "For true and righteous *are* His judgments, because He has judged the great harlot who corrupted the earth with her fornication; and He has avenged on her the blood of His servants *shed* by her."

3 Again they said, "Alleluia! And her smoke rises up forever and ever!"

4 And the twenty-four elders and the four living creatures fell down and worshiped God who sat on the throne, saying, "Amen! Alleluia!"

5 Then a voice came from the throne, saying, "Praise our God, all you His servants and those who fear Him, both small and great!"

6 And I heard, as it were, the voice of a great multitude, as the sound of many waters and as the sound of mighty thunderings, saying, "Alleluia! For the Lord God Omnipotent reigns!

7 "Let us be glad and rejoice and give Him glory, for the marriage of the Lamb has come, and His wife has made herself ready."

8 And to her it was granted to be arrayed in fine linen, clean and bright, for the fine linen is the righteous acts of the saints.

9 Then he said to me, "Write: 'Blessed *are* those who are called to the marriage supper of the Lamb!' " And he said to me, "These are the true sayings of God."

10 And I fell at his feet to worship him. But he said to me, "See *that you* do not *do that!* I am your fellow servant, and of your brethren who have the testimony of Jesus. Worship God! For the testimony of Jesus is the spirit of prophecy."

11 Then I saw heaven opened, and behold, a white horse. And He who sat on him *was* called Faithful and True, and in righteousness He judges and makes war.

12 His eyes *were* like a flame of fire, and on His head *were* many crowns. He had a name written that no one knew except Himself.

13 He *was* clothed with a robe dipped in blood, and His name is called The Word of God.

14 And the armies in heaven, clothed in fine linen, white and clean, followed Him on white horses.

15 Now out of His mouth goes a sharp sword, that with it He should strike the nations. And He Himself will rule them with a rod of iron. He Himself treads the winepress of the fierceness and wrath of Almighty God.

16 And He has on *His* robe and on His thigh a name written:

KING OF KINGS
AND LORD OF LORDS.

17 Then I saw an angel standing in the sun; and he cried with a loud voice, saying to all the birds that fly in the midst of heaven, "Come and gather together for the supper of the great God,

18 "that you may eat the flesh of kings, the flesh of captains, the flesh of mighty men, the flesh of horses and of those who sit on them, and the flesh of all *people,* free and slave, both small and great."

19 And I saw the beast, the kings of the earth, and their armies, gathered together to make war against Him who sat on the horse and against His army.

20 Then the beast was captured, and with him the false prophet who worked signs in his presence, by which he deceived those who received the mark of the beast and those who worshiped his image. These two were cast alive into the lake of fire burning with brimstone.

21 And the rest were killed with the sword which proceeded from the mouth of Him who sat on the horse. And all the birds were filled with their flesh.

20 Then I saw an angel coming down from heaven, having the key to the bottomless pit and a great chain in his hand.

2 He laid hold of the dragon, that serpent of old, who is *the* Devil and Satan, and bound him for a thousand years;

3 and he cast him into the bottomless pit, and shut him up, and set a seal on him, so that he should deceive the nations no more till the thousand years were finished. But after these things he must be released for a little while.

4 And I saw thrones, and they sat on them, and judgment was committed to them. And *I saw* the souls of those who had been beheaded for their witness to Jesus and for the word of God, who had not worshiped the beast or his image, and had not received *his* mark on their foreheads or on their hands. And they lived and reigned with Christ for a thousand years.

5 But the rest of the dead did not live again until the thousand years were finished. This *is* the first resurrection.

6 Blessed and holy *is* he who has part in the first resurrection. Over such the second death has no power, but they shall be priests of God and of Christ, and shall reign with Him a thousand years.

7 Now when the thousand years have expired, Satan will be released from his prison

8 and will go out to deceive the nations which are in the four corners of the earth, Gog and Magog, to gather them together to battle, whose number *is* as the sand of the sea.

9 They went up on the breadth of the earth and surrounded the camp of the saints and the beloved city. And fire came down from God out of heaven and devoured them.

10 And the devil, who deceived them, was cast into the lake of fire and brimstone where the beast and the false prophet *are*. And they will be tormented day and night forever and ever.

11 Then I saw a great white throne and Him who sat on it, from whose face the earth and the heaven fled away. And there was found no place for them.

12 And I saw the dead, small and great, standing before God, and books were opened. And another book was opened, which is *the* Book of Life. And the dead were judged according to their works, by the things which were written in the books.

13 The sea gave up the dead who were in it, and Death and Hades delivered up the dead who were in them. And they were judged, each one according to his works.

14 Then Death and Hades were cast into the lake of fire. This is the second death.

15 And anyone not found written in the Book of Life was cast into the lake of fire.

21 And I saw a new heaven and a new earth, for the first heaven and the first earth had passed away. Also there was no more sea.

2 Then I, John, saw the holy city, New Jerusalem, coming down out of heaven from God, prepared as a bride adorned for her husband.

STEP 2

3 And I heard a loud voice from heaven saying, "Behold, the tabernacle of God *is* with men, and He will dwell with them, and they shall be His people, and God Himself will be with them *and be* their God.

4 "And God will wipe away every tear from their eyes; there shall be no more death, nor sorrow, nor crying; and there shall be no more pain, for the former things have passed away."

5 Then He who sat on the throne said, "Behold, I make all things new." And He said to me, "Write, for these words are true and faithful."

6 And He said to me, "It is done! I am the Alpha and the Omega, the Beginning and the End. I will give of the fountain of the water of life freely to him who thirsts.

7 "He who overcomes shall inherit all things, and I will be his God and he shall be My son.

8 "But the cowardly, unbelieving, abominable, murderers, sexually immoral, sorcerers, idolaters, and all liars shall have their part in the lake which burns with fire and brimstone, which is the second death."

9 Then one of the seven angels who had the seven bowls filled with the seven last plagues came to me and talked with me, saying, "Come, I will show you the bride, the Lamb's wife."

10 And he carried me away in the Spirit to a great and high mountain, and showed me the great city, the holy Jerusalem, descending out of heaven from God,

11 having the glory of God. And her light *was* like a most precious stone, like a jasper stone, clear as crystal.

12 Also she had a great and high wall with twelve gates, and twelve angels at the gates, and names written on them, which are *the names* of the twelve tribes of the children of Israel:

13 three gates on the east, three gates on the north, three gates on the south, and three gates on the west.

14 Now the wall of the city had twelve foundations, and on them were the names of the twelve apostles of the Lamb.

15 And he who talked with me had a gold reed to measure the city, its gates, and its wall.

16 And the city is laid out as a square, and its length is as great as its breadth. And he measured the city with the reed: twelve thousand furlongs. Its length, breadth, and height are equal.

17 Then he measured its wall: one hundred *and* forty-four cubits, *according* to the measure of a man, that is, of an angel.

18 And the construction of its wall was *of* jasper; and the city *was* pure gold, like clear glass.

19 And the foundations of the wall of the city *were* adorned with all kinds of precious stones: the first foundation *was* jasper, the second sapphire, the third chalcedony, the fourth emerald,

20 the fifth sardonyx, the sixth sardius, the seventh chrysolite, the eighth beryl, the ninth topaz, the

STEP 2

Came to believe that a Power greater than ourselves could restore us to sanity.

Revelation 21:3–7

What does a person do to inherit the precious and fantastic blessings we read about here? There are those who would want us to believe we must work to become good enough for God to accept us. There are those who teach that if we give enough money or do enough good deeds or suffer enough we will finally be worthy of the incredible joys described here. But God's Word does not teach such things. The Scriptures declare again and again that everyone who comes to the fountain of the water of life and believes in the God who calls Himself the Alpha and Omega may freely drink (John 7:37, 38). He alone can make all things new. And when we believe in Him, He gives us the power to become overcomers. But beyond this, He declares us to be His own sons and daughters; and He gives us an eternal inheritance, whose glories cannot be described in words. His words are true and faithful. He asks only that we trust in Him.

For further reading on Step 2, turn to page 575.

Daily Encouragement

DAY 238 READING: REVELATION 19:1—21:27

A Thought for the New Day: What a grand assurance: God is going to "make all things new" (21:5). The present creation is growing tired of wars, sickness, death, and sin. Another apostle, Paul, wrote that "the whole creation groans" for the realization of this event, when God will make everything new again, and the former sorrows will pass away forever. Our sadness will be lessened as we concentrate on that coming time. (*Turn to page 553.*)

tenth chrysoprase, the eleventh jacinth, and the twelfth amethyst.
21 And the twelve gates *were* twelve pearls: each individual gate was of one pearl. And the street of the city *was* pure gold, like transparent glass.

22 But I saw no temple in it, for the Lord God Almighty and the Lamb are its temple.

23 And the city had no need of the sun or of the moon to shine in it, for the glory of God illuminated it, and the Lamb *is* its light.

24 And the nations of those who are saved shall walk in its light, and the kings of the earth bring their glory and honor into it.

25 Its gates shall not be shut at all by day (there shall be no night there).

26 And they shall bring the glory and the honor of the nations into it.

27 But there shall by no means enter it anything that defiles, or causes an abomination or a lie, but only those who are written in the Lamb's Book of Life.

22 And he showed me a pure river of water of life, clear as crystal, proceeding from the throne of God and of the Lamb.

2 In the middle of its street, and on either side of the river, *was* the tree of life, which bore twelve fruits, each *tree* yielding its fruit every month. And the leaves of the tree *were* for the healing of the nations.

3 And there shall be no more curse, but the throne of God and of the Lamb shall be in it, and His servants shall serve Him.

4 They shall see His face, and His name *shall be* on their foreheads.

5 And there shall be no night there: They need no lamp nor light of the sun, for the Lord God gives them light. And they shall reign forever and ever.

6 Then he said to me, "These words *are* faithful and true." And the Lord God of the holy prophets

sent His angel to show His servants the things which must shortly take place.

7 "Behold, I am coming quickly! Blessed *is* he who keeps the words of the prophecy of this book."

8 Now I, John, saw and heard these things. And when I heard and saw, I fell down to worship before the feet of the angel who showed me these things.

9 Then he said to me, "See *that you do* not *do that.* For I am your fellow servant, and of your brethren the prophets, and of those who keep the words of this book. Worship God."

10 And he said to me, "Do not seal the words of the prophecy of this book, for the time is at hand.

STEP 11

11 "He who is unjust, let him be unjust still; he who is filthy, let him be filthy still; he who is righteous, let him be righteous still; he who is holy, let him be holy still."

12 "And behold, I am coming quickly, and My reward *is* with Me, to give to every one according to his work.

13 "I am the Alpha and the Omega, *the* Beginning and *the* End, the First and the Last."

14 Blessed *are* those who do His commandments, that they may have the right to the tree of life, and may enter through the gates into the city.

15 But outside *are* dogs and sorcerers and sexually immoral and murderers and idolaters, and whoever loves and practices a lie.

16 "I, Jesus, have sent My angel to testify to you these things in the churches. I am the Root and the Offspring of David, the Bright and Morning Star."

17 And the Spirit and the bride say, "Come!" And let him who hears say, "Come!" And let him who thirsts come. And whoever desires, let him take the water of life freely.

18 For I testify to everyone who hears the words of the prophecy of

STEP 11

*Sought through prayer and meditation to improve our conscious contact with God **as we understood Him,** praying only for knowledge of His will for us and the power to carry that out.*

Revelation 22:10–17

Reading the Book of Revelation, hopefully we have gained a greater fear of the Lord. This kind of godly fear does not debilitate the way human fear does. Instead, it strengthens and motivates us.

Revelation tells us that God is a holy God. He is longsuffering toward sinners and loves them beyond measure, but a day is coming when His patience with humankind will end. A time of inevitable and terrible judgment lies ahead for all those who refuse to accept the work of His Son on the cross as payment for their sin. When we truly comprehend God's power, God's holiness, and God's wrath against sin, we naturally develop the fear of the Lord. This means we have a healthy fear of displeasing God by deliberately sinning, and we care that others understand the consequences of purposely rejecting God's grace. This quality in our lives will not only protect us, but will bring God's honor and blessing upon our lives.

For further reading on Step 11, turn to page 557.

Daily Encouragement

DAY 239 READING: REVELATION 22:1–21

A Thought for the New Day: What makes the prospect of the New Creation so exciting is that the King of Creation Himself is coming to preside over His grand new order. Throughout history we have been seeking the perfect leader whose wisdom would resolve all conflicts. However, only Jesus is endowed with the authority, wisdom, and power to govern all things beautifully and perfectly. Therefore, let John's prayer be your prayer, too: "Come, Lord Jesus" (v. 20). (*Turn to page 557.*)

this book: If anyone adds to these things, God will add to him the plagues that are written in this book;

19 and if anyone takes away from the words of the book of this prophecy, God shall take away his part from the Book of Life, from the holy city, and *from* the things which are written in this book.

20 He who testifies to these things says, "Surely I am coming quickly." Amen. Even so, come, Lord Jesus!

21 The grace of our Lord Jesus Christ *be* with you all. Amen.

The Books

of

PSALMS

and

PROVERBS

THE BOOK OF
PSALMS

BOOK ONE
Psalms 1–41

PSALM 1

BLESSED *is* the man
Who walks not in the
counsel of the ungodly,
Nor stands in the path of
sinners,
Nor sits in the seat of the
scornful;
2 But his delight *is* in the law of
the LORD,
And in His law he meditates
day and night.
3 He shall be like a tree
Planted by the rivers of
water,
That brings forth its fruit in
its season,
Whose leaf also shall not
wither;
And whatever he does shall
prosper.

4 The ungodly *are* not so,
But *are* like the chaff which
the wind drives away.
5 Therefore the ungodly shall
not stand in the
judgment,
Nor sinners in the
congregation of the
righteous.

6 For the LORD knows the way
of the righteous,
But the way of the ungodly
shall perish.

PSALM 2

WHY do the nations rage,
And the people plot a vain
thing?
2 The kings of the earth set
themselves,
And the rulers take counsel
together,

Against the LORD and against
His Anointed, *saying,*
3 "Let us break Their bonds in
pieces
And cast away Their cords
from us."

4 He who sits in the heavens
shall laugh;
The LORD shall hold them in
derision.
5 Then He shall speak to them
in His wrath,
And distress them in His deep
displeasure:
6 "Yet I have set My King
On My holy hill of Zion."

7 "I will declare the decree:
The LORD has said to Me,
You *are* My Son,
Today I have begotten You.
8 Ask of Me, and I will give *You*
The nations *for* Your
inheritance,
And the ends of the earth *for*
Your possession.
9 You shall break them with a
rod of iron;
You shall dash them in pieces
like a potter's vessel.' "

10 Now therefore, be wise, O
kings;
Be instructed, you judges of
the earth.
11 Serve the LORD with fear,
And rejoice with trembling.
12 Kiss the Son, lest He be angry,
And you perish *in* the way,
When His wrath is kindled but
a little.
Blessed *are* all those who put
their trust in Him.

PSALM 3

A Psalm of David when he fled from Absalom
his son.

LORD, how they have increased
who trouble me!

STEP
11

*Sought through prayer and meditation to improve our conscious contact with God **as we understood Him,** praying only for knowledge of His will for us and the power to carry that out.*

Psalm 1:1–3

What does it mean to delight in God's law—to meditate in it day and night? How does this happen? Isn't it a little farfetched to expect such old-fashioned actions in our fast-paced world? No, the admonitions and wisdom in God's Word are still the only basis for true understanding of our Creator, ourselves, our world, and our eternal destiny.

When we accept the fact that Almighty God is seeking to communicate individually with us through His Word, then that Word, the Holy Bible, becomes precious to us. Meditating on what God says about Himself, studying His commands, and memorizing His precious promises becomes an extremely important part of our day. Our life-styles begin to change in accordance with the biblical precepts that have become part of our mind-sets. Verse 3 of Psalm 1 is the result of our love affair with God's Word: spiritual and emotional vitality and an abundance of the fruit of the Holy Spirit will enrich and bless our lives.

For further reading on Step 11, turn to page 619.

Daily Encouragement

DAY 240 READING: PSALMS 1:1—2:12

A Thought for the New Day: Another word for "fruitfulness" might be "prosperity." Some trees never prosper, while others are seasonally loaded down with fruit. There must be good soil into which the tree sends down its roots if it is to be fruitful. We, too, must draw our resources from right thoughts and attitudes that are derived uniquely from God's own thoughts and attitudes unveiled in His Word. Then we will think God's thoughts after Him, and we will become more fruitful (1:3). (*Turn to page 559.*)

Many *are* they who rise up
    against me.
2 Many *are* they who say of me,
  "*There is* no help for him in
    God."   Selah

3 But You, O LORD, *are* a shield
    for me,
  My glory and the One who
    lifts up my head.
4 I cried to the LORD with my
    voice,
  And He heard me from His
    holy hill.   Selah

5 I lay down and slept;
  I awoke, for the LORD
    sustained me.
6 I will not be afraid of ten
    thousands of people
  Who have set *themselves*
    against me all around.

7 Arise, O LORD;
  Save me, O my God!
  For You have struck all my
    enemies on the cheekbone;
  You have broken the teeth of
    the ungodly.
8 Salvation *belongs* to the LORD.
  Your blessing *is* upon Your
    people.   Selah

PSALM 4

To the Chief Musician. With stringed
instruments. A Psalm of David.

HEAR me when I call,
  O God of my righteousness!
You have relieved me *when I
    was* in distress;
Have mercy on me,
  and hear my prayer.

2 How long, O you sons of men,
  Will you turn my glory to
    shame?
  How long will you love
    worthlessness
  And seek falsehood?   Selah
3 But know that the LORD has
    set apart for Himself him
    who is godly;

The LORD will hear when I
    call to Him.

4 Be angry, and do not sin.
  Meditate within your heart on
    your bed, and be still.   Selah
5 Offer the sacrifices of
    righteousness,
  And put your trust in the
    LORD.

6 *There are* many who say,
  "Who will show us *any* good?"
  LORD, lift up the light of Your
    countenance upon us.
7 You have put gladness in my
    heart,
  More than in the season that
    their grain and wine
    increased.
8 I will both lie down in peace,
    and sleep;
  For You alone, O LORD, make
    me dwell in safety.

PSALM 5

To the Chief Musician. With flutes. A Psalm of
David.

GIVE ear to my words, O LORD,
  Consider my meditation.
2 Give heed to the voice of my
    cry,
  My King and my God,
  For to You I will pray.
3 My voice You shall hear in
    the morning, O LORD;
  In the morning I will direct *it*
    to You,
  And I will look up.

4 For You *are* not a God who
    takes pleasure in
    wickedness,
  Nor shall evil dwell with You.
5 The boastful shall not stand in
    Your sight;
  You hate all workers of
    iniquity.
6 You shall destroy those who
    speak falsehood;
  The LORD abhors the
    bloodthirsty and deceitful
    man.

*Made a decision to turn our will and our lives
over to the care of God **as we understood Him.***
Psalm 3:5, 6

In the beginning of Psalm 3, David echoes the doubts of others who taunt, *"There is no help for him in God."*

How often have we been plagued with similar doubts? At how many junctures in our lives have we questioned, Is there a God, and does He know the challenges we face? Does He care that we are lonely and sick and hurting? When we finally realize that we cannot continue to live with our dependencies and yet, seemingly, cannot survive without them, are we afraid that we have reached this point alone, alienated from the God of the universe?

At the spiritual doorway of Step 3, we throw open our hungry hearts to receive a merciful and eternally present God. As David came to rest in God, freed from fears of "ten thousands of people who have set *themselves* against me," we fully surrender our troubles and anxieties to His care. And we rest in Him, confident that His Spirit will likewise protect, empower, and uplift us.

For further reading on Step 3, turn to page 563.

Daily Encouragement

DAY 241 READING: PSALMS 3:1—4:8

A Thought for the New Day: It is a common notion that happiness is the result of pleasing our senses—tasting, smelling, touching, seeing, and hearing pleasant things. While we should not discount the real value of enjoying the good things of earth as we are able, we must realize that happiness will not result from these things alone. Real happiness, contentment, and joy come from an ongoing interaction with the One who is the Author of all good things (4:7). (*Turn to page 561.*)

7 But as for me, I will come into
Your house in the multitude
of Your mercy;
In fear of You I will worship
toward Your holy temple.
8 Lead me, O Lᴏʀᴅ, in Your
righteousness because of
my enemies;
Make Your way straight
before my face.

9 For *there is* no faithfulness in
their mouth;
Their inward part *is*
destruction;
Their throat *is* an open tomb;
They flatter with their tongue.
10 Pronounce them guilty, O
God!
Let them fall by their own
counsels;
Cast them out in the
multitude of their
transgressions,
For they have rebelled against
You.

11 But let all those rejoice who
put their trust in You;
Let them ever shout for joy,
because You defend them;
Let those also who love Your
name
Be joyful in You.
12 For You, O Lᴏʀᴅ, will bless
the righteous;
With favor You will surround
him as *with* a shield.

PSALM 6

To the Chief Musician. With stringed
instruments. On an eight-stringed harp. A
Psalm of David.

O LORD, do not rebuke me in
   Your anger,
Nor chasten me in Your hot
displeasure.

2 Have mercy on me, O Lᴏʀᴅ,
for I *am* weak;
O Lᴏʀᴅ, heal me,
for my bones are troubled.

3 My soul also is greatly
troubled;
But You, O Lᴏʀᴅ—how long?

4 Return, O Lᴏʀᴅ, deliver me!
Oh, save me for Your mercies'
sake!
5 For in death *there is* no
remembrance of You;
In the grave who will give
You thanks?

6 I am weary with my groaning; STEP 1
All night I make my bed
swim;
I drench my couch with my
tears.
7 My eye wastes away because
of grief;
It grows old because of all my
enemies.

8 Depart from me,
all you workers of iniquity;
For the Lᴏʀᴅ has heard the
voice of my weeping.
9 The Lᴏʀᴅ has heard my
supplication;
The Lᴏʀᴅ will receive my
prayer.
10 Let all my enemies be
ashamed and greatly
troubled;
Let them turn back
and be ashamed suddenly.

PSALM 7

A Meditation of David, which he sang to the
Lᴏʀᴅ concerning the words of Cush, a
Benjamite.

O LORD my God,
   in You I put my trust;
Save me from all those who
persecute me;
And deliver me,
2 Lest they tear me like a lion,
Rending *me* in pieces,
while *there is* none to
deliver.

3 O Lᴏʀᴅ my God, if I have
done this:

We admitted we were powerless over our dependencies—
that our lives had become unmanageable.

Psalm 6:2–4

It is human nature to want to be (and to believe that we are) in complete control of our circumstances and our lives. But truly fortunate people come to a point in their lives when they realize this is definitely not possible nor even desirable. These people are the fortunate ones because they have come to the end of themselves just as the psalmist David has come to the end of his physical and emotional resources.

"My bones are troubled" is a Hebrew way of saying "I am racked with pain." David, the valiant warrior, admits his weakness, his emotional collapse. But instead of being defeated by this admission, David has actually placed himself in the strongest position possible. Now he is free to transcend the emptiness of his own resources, free to surrender trying to manage things on his own strength, and free to partake of God's unlimited resources!

For further reading on Step 1, turn to page 569.

Daily Encouragement

DAY 242 READING: PSALMS 5:1—6:10

A Thought for the New Day: When is the best time to pray? Not when your mind is jammed with business problems and decisions. Certainly not when you are worn out from a day's work and your eyes are heavy. Of course, prayer is necessary at various times. But especially valuable is the prayer offered in the morning, after refreshing rest, when we are alert and able to think clearly about the issues of our lives and concentrate on God's great purposes for us (5:3). *(Turn to page 563.)*

If there is iniquity in my
hands,

4 If I have repaid evil to him
who was at peace with me,
Or have plundered my enemy
without cause,

5 Let the enemy pursue me
and overtake *me;*
Yes, let him trample my life to
the earth,
And lay my honor in the dust.
Selah

6 Arise, O LORD, in Your anger;
Lift Yourself up because of
the rage of my enemies,
And awake for me *to* the
judgment You have
commanded!

7 So the congregation of the
peoples shall surround You;
For their sakes, therefore,
return on high.

8 The LORD shall judge the
peoples;
Judge me, O LORD, according
to my righteousness,
And according to my integrity
within me.

9 Oh, let the wickedness of the
wicked come to an end,
But establish the just;
For the righteous God tests
the hearts and minds.

10 My defense *is* of God,
Who saves the upright in
heart.

11 God *is* a just judge,
And God is angry *with the
wicked* every day.

12 If he does not turn back,
He will sharpen His sword;
He bends His bow and makes
it ready.

13 He also prepares for Himself
instruments of death;
He makes His arrows into
fiery shafts.

14 Behold, *the wicked* travails
with iniquity,

Conceives trouble and brings
forth falsehood.

15 He made a pit and dug it out,
And has fallen into the ditch
which he made.

16 His trouble shall return upon
his own head,
And his violent dealing shall
come down on his own
crown.

17 I will praise the LORD
according to His
righteousness,
And will sing praise to the
name of the LORD Most
High.

PSALM 8

To the Chief Musician. On the instrument of
Gath. A Psalm of David.

O LORD, our Lord,
How excellent *is* Your name
in all the earth,
You who set Your glory above
the heavens!

2 Out of the mouth of babes
and infants
You have ordained strength,
Because of Your enemies,
That You may silence the
enemy and the avenger.

3 When I consider Your
heavens, the work of
Your fingers,
The moon and the stars,
which You have ordained,

4 What is man that You are
mindful of him,
And the son of man that You
visit him?

5 For You have made him a
little lower than the angels,
And You have crowned him
with glory and honor.

6 You have made him to have
dominion over the works of
Your hands;
You have put all *things* under
his feet,

STEP
3

*Made a decision to turn our will and our lives over to the care of God **as we understood Him.***

Psalm 8

Many people today have become devotees of the religion of humanism, believing that they can become the masters of their own fates and the controllers of their own destinies. Truly, there is no greater tragedy than for an individual to take up such a philosophy. In it, the real greatness and beauty of humankind becomes debauched and diminished. Only when we bow to the infinite and almighty God who inhabits eternity can we experience fully the glory and extent of our personhood. Even though we are just finite beings on the celestial grain of dust called earth, God has chosen to create each of us in His own image. He has given us intellect and emotion and the ability to communicate with Him through prayer and through His Word. When we listen to His voice and choose to obey and honor Him, we will begin indeed to be "crowned . . . with glory and honor."

For further reading on Step 3, turn to page 565.

Daily Encouragement

DAY 243 READING: PSALMS 7:1—8:9

A Thought for the New Day: Psalm 8:9 is a good-sounding poetic line, but what does it mean? The face value of the words in this case is their deepest meaning. God has indeed written His name "in all the earth." If we have eyes to see, His hand is everywhere and in all things. His works everywhere bear His unique signature. When we observe this reality we are overwhelmed, and cry out, "How excellent!" (*Turn to page 565.*)

7 All sheep and oxen—
Even the beasts of the field,
8 The birds of the air,
And the fish of the sea
That pass through the paths
of the seas.

9 O LORD, our Lord,
How excellent *is* Your name
in all the earth!

PSALM 9

To the Chief Musician. To *the tune of* "Death
of the Son." A Psalm of David.

I WILL praise *You*, O LORD,
with my whole heart;
I will tell of all Your
marvelous works.
2 I will be glad and rejoice in
You;
I will sing praise to Your
name, O Most High.

3 When my enemies turn back,
They shall fall and perish at
Your presence.
4 For You have maintained my
right and my cause;
You sat on the throne judging
in righteousness.
5 You have rebuked the nations,
You have destroyed the
wicked;
You have blotted out their
name forever and ever.

6 O enemy, destructions are
finished forever!
And you have destroyed cities;
Even their memory has
perished.
7 But the LORD shall endure
forever;
He has prepared His throne
for judgment.
8 He shall judge the world in
righteousness,
And He shall administer
judgment for the peoples in
uprightness.

9 The LORD also will be a refuge
for the oppressed,

A refuge in times of trouble.
10 And those who know Your
name will put their trust in
You;
For You, LORD, have not
forsaken those who seek
You.

11 Sing praises to the LORD,
who dwells in Zion!
Declare His deeds among the
people.
12 When He avenges blood,
He remembers them;
He does not forget the cry of
the humble.

13 Have mercy on me, O LORD!
Consider my trouble from
those who hate me,
You who lift me up from the
gates of death,
14 That I may tell of all Your
praise
In the gates of the daughter
of Zion.
I will rejoice in Your
salvation.

15 The nations have sunk down
in the pit *which* they made;
In the net which they hid,
their own foot is caught.
16 The LORD is known *by* the
judgment He executes;
The wicked is snared in the
work of his own hands.
Meditation.   Selah

17 The wicked shall be turned
into hell,
And all the nations that forget
God.
18 For the needy shall not always
be forgotten;
The expectation of the poor
shall *not* perish forever.

19 Arise, O LORD,
Do not let man prevail;
Let the nations be judged in
Your sight.

STEP
3

*Made a decision to turn our will and our lives
over to the care of God **as we understood Him.***

Psalm 9:9, 10

Many of us have known the pain of oppression. We have felt
oppressed by the burdens of our dependencies, our guilt, and our
backgrounds. Life has left us feeling tattered and bruised. If we are
feeling pummeled by relationships, memories, or struggles with
addiction, God has a special promise for us. He says He Himself
will be a refuge for us. David, who wrote this Psalm, knew what it
meant to need refuge. Here the word pictures security and protection in a high, safe retreat. When David had nowhere to turn and
no one to turn to, he made the right choice. He entrusted his life
and will to the Lord.

In Step 2, we began to seek the Lord and to believe in His power
to help us. Now God asks us to turn our lives over to His care and
to let Him be all that He wants to be for us—the security and protection we need—a refuge in times of trouble.

For further reading on Step 3, turn to page 573.

Daily Encouragement

DAY 244 READING: PSALM 9:1–20

A Thought for the New Day: "Judgment" means not only condemnation, or even an assessment of value. The word is used
also in the sense of vindication, as when it is said that "God
judges the poor." God is a defender of those who trust Him.
Often it seems that wrong is winning, and our suffering is completely unnoticed. But not by everyone! The Lord is our cham-
pion, and He fights our battles against everything that threatens
our peace and well-being (9:4). *(Turn to page 567.)*

20 Put them in fear, O LORD,
   That the nations may know
   themselves *to be but* men.
                                    Selah

PSALM 10

WHY do You stand afar off, O
    LORD?
   Why do You hide *Yourself* in
   times of trouble?
2 The wicked in *his* pride
   persecutes the poor;
   Let them be caught in the
   plots which they have
   devised.

3 For the wicked boasts of his
   heart's desire;
   He blesses the greedy
   and renounces the LORD.
4 The wicked in his proud
   countenance does not seek
   God;
   God *is* in none of his
   thoughts.

5 His ways are always
   prospering;
   Your judgments *are* far above,
   out of his sight;
   As for all his enemies,
   he sneers at them.
6 He has said in his heart,
   "I shall not be moved;
   I shall never be in adversity."
7 His mouth is full of cursing
   and deceit and oppression;
   Under his tongue *is* trouble
   and iniquity.

8 He sits in the lurking places of
   the villages;
   In the secret places he
   murders the innocent;
   His eyes are secretly fixed on
   the helpless.
9 He lies in wait secretly,
   as a lion in his den;
   He lies in wait to catch the
   poor;
   He catches the poor when he
   draws him into his net.

10 So he crouches, he lies low,
   That the helpless may fall by
   his strength.
11 He has said in his heart,
   "God has forgotten;
   He hides His face;
   He will never see *it.*"

12 Arise, O LORD!
   O God, lift up Your hand!
   Do not forget the humble.
13 Why do the wicked renounce
   God?
   He has said in his heart,
   "You will not require *an
   account.*"

14 But You have seen *it,*
   for You observe trouble and
   grief,
   To repay *it* by Your hand.
   The helpless commits himself
   to You;
   You are the helper of the
   fatherless.

   STEP 1

15 Break the arm of the wicked
   and the evil *man;*
   Seek out his wickedness *until*
   You find none.

16 The LORD *is* King forever and
   ever;
   The nations have perished out
   of His land.
17 LORD, You have heard the
   desire of the humble;
   You will prepare their heart;
   You will cause Your ear to
   hear,

   STEP 7

18 To do justice to the fatherless
   and the oppressed,
   That the man of the earth
   may oppress no more.

PSALM 11

To the Chief Musician. A Psalm of David.

IN the LORD I put my trust;
   How can you say to my soul,
   "Flee *as* a bird to your
   mountain"?
2 For look! The wicked bend
   their bow,

STEP 7

Humbly asked Him to remove our shortcomings.

Psalm 10:17

There is no greater source of power or peace than that which comes from knowing that God is on our side and that the battle belongs to Him. This is especially true for those of us who, for years, have tried to manipulate, control, and "fix" things in our own strength. When we can finally admit the limitations of our own devices, we are ready to experience the immensity of God's power in our lives and hearts. And we no longer have to figure out how to change ourselves when we come to understand the message of verse 17: "You [God] will prepare their heart."

When we truly desire to allow God to change us, the doors of deliverance are opened. This is a desire that God loves to honor and a prayer that His ear is always open to hear. We will be amazed at the ways and means God will begin to use in our lives to remove the shortcomings that have caused us grief for so many years. An earnest heart, submissive to the work of God, is the perfect soil for sprouting miracles.

For further reading on Step 7, turn to page 587.

Daily Encouragement

DAY 245 READING: PSALMS 10:1—11:7

A Thought for the New Day: It clearly seems at times—and even for a long time—that "the foundations are destroyed" (11:3). The godly foundations seemed completely eroded for over seventy years in what was known as Soviet Russia. Then, almost in a day, the evil system was reversed. How could such a thing happen? The answer is in Psalm 11:4: "The LORD's throne *is* in heaven." God is Ruler, even in the worst of times. (*Turn to page 569.*)

They make ready their arrow
  on the string,
That they may shoot secretly
  at the upright in heart.
3 If the foundations are
  destroyed,
What can the righteous do?

4 The Lord *is* in His holy
  temple,
The Lord's throne *is* in
  heaven;
His eyes behold,
His eyelids test the sons of
  men.
5 The Lord tests the righteous,
But the wicked and the one
  who loves violence His soul
  hates.
6 Upon the wicked He will rain
  coals,
Fire and brimstone and a
  burning wind;
This shall be the portion of
  their cup.

7 For the Lord *is* righteous,
He loves righteousness;
His countenance beholds the
  upright.

PSALM 12

To the Chief Musician. On an eight-stringed
harp. A Psalm of David.

HELP, Lord, for the godly man
  ceases!
For the faithful disappear
  from among the sons of
  men.
2 They speak idly everyone with
  his neighbor;
With flattering lips *and* a
  double heart they speak.

3 May the Lord cut off all
  flattering lips,
And the tongue that speaks
  proud things,
4 Who have said,
"With our tongue we will
  prevail;
Our lips *are* our own;
Who *is* lord over us?"

5 "For the oppression of the
  poor, for the sighing of the
  needy,
Now I will arise," says the
  Lord;
"I will set *him* in the safety for
  which he yearns."

6 The words of the Lord *are*
  pure words,
Like silver tried in a furnace
  of earth,
Purified seven times.
7 You shall keep them, O Lord,
You shall preserve them from
  this generation forever.

8 The wicked prowl on every
  side,
When vileness is exalted
  among the sons of men.

PSALM 13

To the Chief Musician. A Psalm of David.

HOW long, O Lord?
  Will You forget me forever?
How long will You hide Your
  face from me?
2 How long shall I take counsel
  in my soul,
Having sorrow in my heart
  daily?
How long will my enemy be
  exalted over me?

3 Consider *and* hear me,
  O Lord my God;
Enlighten my eyes,
Lest I sleep the *sleep of* death;
4 Lest my enemy say,
"I have prevailed against him";
Lest those who trouble me
  rejoice when I am moved.

5 But I have trusted in Your
  mercy;
My heart shall rejoice in Your
  salvation.
6 I will sing to the Lord,
Because He has dealt
  bountifully with me.

STEP 1

*We admitted we were powerless over our dependencies—
that our lives had become unmanageable.*

Psalm 12:5

Sometimes it is embarrassing or even humiliating to have to apply the words "poor" and "needy" to ourselves. These are expressions we feel more comfortable applying to other people, but all of us must come to a point where we can acknowledge that these words describe us, too. Those who refuse to see this truth can never know God, nor can they ever know true joy and peace and deliverance. As long as we blindly believe that this pitiable condition cannot be applied to us, we will stay in a state of hopelessness and helplessness. But when we realize that we are poor and oppressed and needy in our hearts and lives, an amazing thing happens. Our eyes are finally opened to see that there is hope and help beyond ourselves. There is a God who has been waiting for this understanding to come to us. And now He is ready to act on our behalf.

For further reading on Step 1, turn to page 571.

Daily Encouragement

DAY 246 READING: PSALMS 12:1—13:6

A Thought for the New Day: All events in the world seem to be the products of chance. In such a world, how can we depend on the words contained in Scripture? How can we be sure that God's Word will remain in its integrity? The answer is that it is just because these words are the Word of God: God's entire message will remain intact as His own revealed Truth—even when the heavens and the earth are dissolved (12:6, 7). (*Turn to page 571.*)

Traits of the Righteous

PSALM 14

To the Chief Musician. A Psalm of David.

THE fool has said in his heart,
  "There is no God."
  They are corrupt,
  They have done abominable
    works,
  There is none who does good.

2 The LORD looks down from
    heaven upon the children of
    men,
  To see if there are any who
    understand, who seek God.
3 They have all turned aside,
  They have together become
    corrupt;
  There is none who does good,
  No, not one.

4 Have all the workers of
    iniquity no knowledge,
  Who eat up my people *as* they
    eat bread,
  And do not call on the LORD?
5 There they are in great fear,
  For God *is* with the
    generation of the righteous.
6 You shame the counsel of the
    poor,
  But the LORD *is* his refuge.

7 Oh, that the salvation of Israel
    would come out of Zion!
  When the LORD brings back
    the captivity of His people,
  Let Jacob rejoice *and* Israel be
    glad.

PSALM 15

A Psalm of David.

LORD, who may abide in Your
    tabernacle?
  Who may dwell in Your holy
    hill?

2 He who walks uprightly,
  And works righteousness,
  And speaks the truth in his
    heart;
3 He *who* does not backbite
    with his tongue,

Nor does evil to his
    neighbor,
  Nor does he take up a
    reproach against his
    friend;
4 In whose eyes a vile person is
    despised,
  But he honors those who
    fear the LORD;
  He *who* swears to his own
    hurt and does not change;
5 He *who* does not put out his
    money at usury,
  Nor does he take a bribe
    against the innocent.

He who does these *things*
  shall never be moved.

PSALM 16

A Michtam of David.

PRESERVE me, O God,
  for in You I put my trust.

2 *O my soul,* you have said to
    the LORD,
  "You *are* my Lord,
  My goodness is nothing apart
    from You"—
3 *And* to the saints who *are* on
    the earth,
  "They are the excellent ones,
    in whom is all my delight."

4 Their sorrows shall be
    multiplied who hasten *after*
    another *god;*
  Their drink offerings of blood
    I will not offer,
  Nor take up their names on
    my lips.

5 *You,* O LORD, *are* the portion
    of my inheritance and my
    cup;
  You maintain my lot.
6 The lines have fallen to me in
    pleasant *places;*
  Yes, I have a good
    inheritance.

STEP 1

We admitted we were powerless over our dependencies—
that our lives had become unmanageable.

Psalm 16:4

There are people who like to declare that they do not worship a god. They may proudly call themselves atheistic or agnostic and consider themselves to be avant-garde in their ideas. But anyone who is truly honest and thoughtful knows that everyone worships something. It may be money, a job, a drug, an ideology, fame, or another person, but we all bow down to something. This is because the God who created us designed the human race with an inner need to worship. Although His perfect plan for us is to know and worship Him and enjoy the sweet blessings of His fellowship, He will not make us worship Him. We have the free will to choose what we will give our allegiance to. But we must pay the consequences of that choice. When we go after other "gods," the end result is always the same—sorrow and emptiness. The Creator God who has loved us and died for us is the only One worthy of our devotion and love.

For further reading on Step 1, turn to page 577.

Daily Encouragement

DAY 247 READING: PSALMS 14:1—16:11

A Thought for the New Day: Eternal life is life in God's presence. Along the daily path into that life there are intimations of the joy that awaits us in that Presence "forevermore" (16:11). *Holy Father, lead me on the road that leads to Life, for my limbs grow weary and weak, and my feet easily slip in the way. Grant me Your light for the journey.* *(Turn to page 573.)*

STEP
6

7 I will bless the LORD who has
   given me counsel;
   My heart also instructs me in
     the night seasons.
8 I have set the LORD always
   before me;
   Because *He is* at my right
     hand I shall not be moved.

9 Therefore my heart is glad,
   and my glory rejoices;
   My flesh also will rest in hope.
10 For You will not leave my
    soul in Sheol,
   Nor will You allow Your Holy
    One to see corruption.
11 You will show me the path of
   life;
   In Your presence *is* fullness of
    joy;
   At Your right hand *are*
    pleasures forevermore.

PSALM 17

A Prayer of David.

HEAR a just cause, O LORD,
   Attend to my cry;
   Give ear to my prayer *that is*
    not from deceitful lips.
2 Let my vindication come from
   Your presence;
   Let Your eyes look on the
    things that are upright.

3 You have tested my heart;
   You have visited *me* in the
    night;
   You have tried me
    and have found nothing;
   I have purposed that my
    mouth shall not transgress.
4 Concerning the works of men,
   By the word of Your lips,
   I have kept *myself* from the
    paths of the destroyer.
5 Uphold my steps in Your
   paths,
   That my footsteps may not
    slip.

STEP
3

6 I have called upon You,
   for You will hear me, O
    God;

   Incline Your ear to me, *and*
    hear my speech.
7 Show Your marvelous
   lovingkindness by Your
    right hand,
   O You who save those who
    trust *in You*
   From those who rise up
    against them.
8 Keep me as the apple of Your
   eye;
   Hide me under the shadow of
    Your wings,
9 From the wicked who oppress
   me,
   From my deadly enemies who
    surround me.

10 They have closed up their fat
    hearts;
   With their mouths they speak
    proudly.
11 They have now surrounded us
    in our steps;
   They have set their eyes,
    crouching down to the
    earth,
12 Like a lion *that* is eager to
    tear his prey,
   And as a young lion lurking in
    secret places.

13 Arise, O LORD,
   Confront him, cast him down;
   Deliver my life from the
    wicked with Your sword,
14 With Your hand from men, O
    LORD,
   From men of the world *who
    have* their portion in *this*
    life,
   And whose belly You fill with
    Your hidden treasure.
   They are satisfied with
    children,
   And leave the rest of their
    substance for their babes.

15 As for me, I will see Your face
    in righteousness;
   I shall be satisfied when I
    awake in Your likeness.

STEP 3

*Made a decision to turn our will and our lives over to the care of God **as we understood Him.***

Psalm 17:6–8

As we face Step 3, we realize that even though our enemies may be different, our needs are very similar to those David was experiencing when he wrote this Psalm. David knew that God's power alone could save him, and he had also come to understand something else about God. The almighty God of the Bible is also the God whose very nature is lovingkindness toward His children. "Lovingkindness" is translated from the Hebrew word *hesed*. It means loyal love. God's love for us never falters or changes. When we become His children, we receive a father whose love is perfect, even though we are not. His lovingkindness will always be there for us, it will always know what is best for us, and it will be strong and steady to the end. When we truly begin to understand God's lovingkindness, our natural response will be to turn our lives, our will, and everything that concerns us over to Him. His loyal love for us makes it easy to trust Him completely.

For further reading on Step 3, turn to page 585.

Daily Encouragement

DAY 248 READING: PSALM 17:1–15

A Thought for the New Day: Heaven is described in several ways, and yet our words fall short of the total reality of that happy condition. One thing is clear: the former imperfections that kept us from enjoying the best God had for us will be no more. At last we will be like God. And this was the goal of our lives all along—to be transformed into His image. In addition to beholding God's own beauty, we will bear the divine family "likeness" (v. 15). (*Turn to page 575.*)

PSALM 18

To the Chief Musician. A Psalm of David the servant of the LORD, who spoke to the LORD the words of this song on the day that the LORD delivered him from the hand of all his enemies and from the hand of Saul. And he said:

I WILL love You, O LORD, my strength.

2 The LORD is my rock and my fortress and my deliverer;
My God, my strength,
in whom I will trust;
My shield and the horn of my salvation, my stronghold.

3 I will call upon the LORD,
who is worthy to be praised;
So shall I be saved from my enemies.

4 The pangs of death encompassed me,
And the floods of ungodliness made me afraid.

5 The sorrows of Sheol surrounded me;
The snares of death confronted me.

6 In my distress I called upon the LORD,
And cried out to my God;
He heard my voice from His temple,
And my cry came before Him, *even* to His ears.

7 Then the earth shook and trembled;
The foundations of the hills also quaked and were shaken,
Because He was angry.

8 Smoke went up from His nostrils,
And devouring fire from His mouth;
Coals were kindled by it.

9 He bowed the heavens also, and came down
With darkness under His feet.

10 And He rode upon a cherub, and flew;
He flew upon the wings of the wind.

11 He made darkness His secret place;
His canopy around Him *was* dark waters
And thick clouds of the skies.

12 From the brightness before Him,
His thick clouds passed with hailstones and coals of fire.

13 The LORD also thundered in the heavens,
And the Most High uttered His voice,
Hailstones and coals of fire.

14 He sent out His arrows and scattered the foe,
Lightnings in abundance, and He vanquished them.

15 Then the channels of waters were seen,
And the foundations of the world were uncovered
At Your rebuke, O LORD,
At the blast of the breath of Your nostrils.

16 He sent from above, He took me;
He drew me out of many waters.

17 He delivered me from my strong enemy,
From those who hated me,
For they were too strong for me.

18 They confronted me in the day of my calamity,
But the LORD was my support.

19 He also brought me out into a broad place;
He delivered me because He delighted in me.

20 The LORD rewarded me according to my righteousness;
According to the cleanness of my hands He has recompensed me.

21 For I have kept the ways of the LORD,
And have not wickedly departed from my God.

Came to believe that a Power greater than ourselves could restore us to sanity.

Psalm 18:1–3

Steps 1 and 2 involve what recovery literature describes as ego deflation at depth. Our own efforts at self-control and willpower have proved fruitless against the enemies of compulsivity, drivenness, and neediness.

We find ourselves at a critical crossroads. On the one hand, our old addictions or dependencies beckon to us and tell us that the practice of those dependencies will be the ultimate source of our comfort. On the other hand, we have begun to experience that the promises of our addictions are false promises. We have discovered, along with many other recovering persons, that our addictions have stopped working for us. The alternatives appear bleak.

How shall we be saved from the enemies of our dependencies? The psalmist David celebrates a God who is "my rock and my fortress and my deliverer" (v. 2). Our dependencies brought us to a position of powerlessness. That powerlessness has brought us to the threshold of the God of our fathers who has infinite strength to provide our salvation.

For further reading on Step 2, turn to page 581.

Daily Encouragement

DAY 249 READING: PSALM 18:1–24

A Thought for the New Day: There are times when you feel you just cannot take another step or hold your eyes open a minute longer. Your bones seem to turn to water, but at such times remember that you have Power that will keep you going. It is the strength of the Lord (18:1, 2). *(Turn to page 577.)*

22 For all His judgments *were* before me,
And I did not put away His statutes from me.

23 I was also blameless before Him,
And I kept myself from my iniquity.

24 Therefore the LORD has recompensed me according to my righteousness,
According to the cleanness of my hands in His sight.

25 With the merciful
You will show Yourself merciful;
With a blameless man
You will show Yourself blameless;

26 With the pure You will show Yourself pure;
And with the devious
You will show Yourself shrewd.

STEP
1

27 For You will save the humble people,
But will bring down haughty looks.

28 For You will light my lamp;
The LORD my God will enlighten my darkness.

29 For by You I can run against a troop,
And by my God I can leap over a wall.

30 *As for* God, His way *is* perfect;
The word of the LORD is proven;
He *is* a shield to all who trust in Him.

31 For who *is* God, except the LORD?
And who *is* a rock, except our God?

32 *It is* God who arms me with strength,
And makes my way perfect.

33 He makes my feet like the *feet of* deer,
And sets me on my high places.

34 He teaches my hands to make war,
So that my arms can bend a bow of bronze.

35 You have also given me the shield of Your salvation;
Your right hand has held me up,
Your gentleness has made me great.

36 You enlarged my path under me,
So that my feet did not slip.

37 I have pursued my enemies and overtaken them;
Neither did I turn back again till they were destroyed.

38 I have wounded them,
So that they were not able to rise;
They have fallen under my feet.

39 For You have armed me with strength for the battle;
You have subdued under me those who rose up against me.

40 You have also given me the necks of my enemies,
So that I destroyed those who hated me.

41 They cried out, but *there was* none to save *them,*
Even to the LORD,
but He did not answer them.

42 Then I beat them as fine as the dust before the wind;
I cast them out like dirt in the streets.

43 You have delivered me from the strivings of the people,
You have made me the head of the nations;
A people I have not known shall serve me.

44 As soon as they hear of me they obey me;
The foreigners submit to me.

45 The foreigners fade away,
And come frightened from their hideouts.

We admitted we were powerless over our dependencies—
that our lives had become unmanageable.

Psalm 18:27

We do not like to apply such words as "haughty" to ourselves. We prefer to think of ourselves as self-confident and assured. But as long as we are trusting in ourselves and our own devices, God considers us to be haughty, and as the Bible says, "God resists [sets Himself in battle array against] the proud" (1 Pet. 5:5). However, a person may be totally unhappy with his or her life and determine to "turn over a new leaf" and still be haughty. Sadness alone does not change a person's heart from haughty to humble. Desiring a different life cannot bring about such a change. We must come to the point where we can admit that we are totally powerless to help ourselves or to bring about the changes that are so desperately needed. When we can accept our hopelessness, then we can turn away from ourselves and toward the only One who can help. Our hearts have become humble, and our lives are now finally ready for change.

For further reading on Step 1, turn to page 583.

Daily Encouragement

DAY 250 READING: PSALM 18:25–50

A Thought for the New Day: Living in isolation may result in a kind of purity. However, should one then be forced out of isolation and into an encounter with a virus, one would not have developed resistance to ward off disease. Likewise, spiritual purity must include the ability to meet evil, to identify it, and reject it. Holiness is not naïveté, rather, it is the result of understanding life from God's pure viewpoint. (*Turn to page 579.*)

46 The LORD lives!
Blessed *be* my Rock!
Let the God of my salvation
be exalted.
47 *It is* God who avenges me,
And subdues the peoples
under me;
48 He delivers me from my
enemies.
You also lift me up above
those who rise against me;
You have delivered me from
the violent man.
49 Therefore I will give thanks to
You, O LORD, among the
Gentiles,
And sing praises to Your
name.

50 Great deliverance He gives to
His king,
And shows mercy to His
anointed,
To David and his descendants
forevermore.

PSALM 19

To the Chief Musician. A Psalm of David.

THE heavens declare the glory
of God;
And the firmament shows His
handiwork.
2 Day unto day utters speech,
And night unto night reveals
knowledge.
3 *There is* no speech nor
language
Where their voice is not
heard.
4 Their line has gone out
through all the earth,
And their words to the end of
the world.

In them He has set a
tabernacle for the sun,
5 Which *is* like a bridegroom
coming out of his chamber,
And rejoices like a strong man
to run its race.
6 Its rising *is* from one end of
heaven,

And its circuit to the other
end;
And there is nothing hidden
from its heat.

7 The law of the LORD *is*
perfect, converting the soul;
The testimony of the LORD *is*
sure, making wise the
simple;
8 The statutes of the LORD *are*
right, rejoicing the heart;
The commandment of the
LORD *is* pure, enlightening
the eyes;
9 The fear of the LORD *is* clean,
enduring forever;
The judgments of the LORD
are true *and* righteous
altogether.
10 More to be desired *are they*
than gold,
Yea, than much fine gold;
Sweeter also than honey and
the honeycomb.
11 Moreover by them Your
servant is warned,
And in keeping them *there is*
great reward.

12 Who can understand *his*
errors?
Cleanse me from secret *faults.*
13 Keep back Your servant also
from presumptuous *sins;*
Let them not have dominion
over me.
Then I shall be blameless,
And I shall be innocent of
great transgression.

14 Let the words of my mouth
and the meditation of my
heart
Be acceptable in Your sight,
O LORD, my strength and my
redeemer.

PSALM 20

To the Chief Musician. A Psalm of David.

MAY the LORD answer you in
the day of trouble;

STEP 6

*Were entirely ready to have God
remove all these defects of character.*

Psalm 19:12, 13

David knew we all have blind spots. In Step 4, we did our best to understand the reasons for our behavior, to accept our errors and our secret faults. But quite possibly, there are still facets of our personality and thought patterns that remain hidden from our understanding. What a comfort to know, however, that they are not hidden from God. He understands us completely, and He loves us just as thoroughly. Because He alone knows us so well and loves us so much, we can trust Him to do in our lives the work that needs to be done. We never have to be afraid of His methods nor unsure of His motives. His desire is that we become all that we can be in Him, and He knows how to go about that transformation in the way that is best for us. As we become convinced of these things, we will become totally ready to allow God to remove our defects, known and unknown. We will be ready to be changed from the inside out.

For further reading on Step 6, turn to page 663.

Daily Encouragement

DAY 251 READING: PSALM 19:1–14

A Thought for the New Day: The writer of this psalm is exuberant in his celebration of the qualities of God's Word. To the outside observer, the psalmist's remarks are almost excessive (vv. 8–11). Who ever heard of mere "words" being able to change one's life? "More to be desired than gold"? Really! But the outside observer always misses the gift that is enjoyed by those who *taste and see and find* that God's Word has a unique, transforming, gracious quality that leaves us different than it finds us. (*Turn to page 581.*)

May the name of the God of
Jacob defend you;
2 May He send you help from
the sanctuary,
And strengthen you out of
Zion;
3 May He remember all your
offerings,
And accept your burnt
sacrifice.   Selah

4 May He grant you according
to your heart's *desire,*
And fulfill all your purpose.
5 We will rejoice in your
salvation,
And in the name of our God
we will set up *our* banners!
May the LORD fulfill all your
petitions.

6 Now I know that the LORD
saves His anointed;
He will answer him from His
holy heaven
With the saving strength of
His right hand.

STEP
2

7 Some *trust* in chariots,
and some in horses;
But we will remember the
name of the LORD our God.
8 They have bowed down and
fallen;
But we have risen and stand
upright.

9 Save, LORD!
May the King answer us when
we call.

PSALM 21

To the Chief Musician. A Psalm of David.

THE king shall have joy in Your
strength, O LORD;
And in Your salvation how
greatly shall he rejoice!
2 You have given him his
heart's desire,
And have not withheld the
request of his lips.   Selah

3 For You meet him with the
blessings of goodness;
You set a crown of pure gold
upon his head.
4 He asked life from You,
and You gave *it* to him—
Length of days forever and
ever.
5 His glory *is* great in Your
salvation;
Honor and majesty You have
placed upon him.
6 For You have made him most
blessed forever;
You have made him
exceedingly glad with Your
presence.
7 For the king trusts in the
LORD,
And through the mercy of the
Most High he shall not be
moved.

8 Your hand will find all Your
enemies;
Your right hand will find
those who hate You.
9 You shall make them as a
fiery oven in the time of
Your anger;
The LORD shall swallow them
up in His wrath,
And the fire shall devour
them.
10 Their offspring You shall
destroy from the earth,
And their descendants from
among the sons of men.
11 For they intended evil against
You;
They devised a plot *which*
they are not able *to
perform.*
12 Therefore You will make them
turn their back;
You will make ready *Your
arrows* on Your string
toward their faces.

13 Be exalted, O LORD, in Your
own strength!
We will sing and praise Your
power.

STEP 2

*Came to believe that a Power greater than ourselves
could restore us to sanity.*

Psalm 20:7, 8

Today we might transliterate Psalm 20:7 by saying, "Some trust
in power and some in wealth." The world is full of ideas on what
will save, protect, and prosper. Boldly outright or by subtle implica-
tion, various media preach to us their own special philosophy of
how to find fulfillment and security for our searching souls.

The Bible is clear and emphatic concerning this issue. God alone
is the answer to human need. He is the One, revealed through His
Word, to whom we can turn in order to find security, fulfillment,
and wholeness. He alone can give our lives purpose and strength.

Sooner or later, those who have put their faith and trust in other
things will begin to feel empty and disappointed. But those who
come to understand and believe what God tells us in His Word
about who He is and how much He loves us will find solid ground
at last. They will know the truth and find the Source of Life.

For further reading on Step 2, turn to page 617.

Daily Encouragement

DAY 252 READING: PSALMS 20:1—21:13

A Thought for the New Day: We all put our trust in something (20:7). Most people probably trust in themselves when all
else fails. What do you trust in as your last hope when you see
your world dissolving around you? Our trust in all that is earthly,
including ourselves, will fail the test of durability. However, we
can reach beyond the barriers of time and sense to lay hold on
that eternal Name—"the LORD our God." (*Turn to page 583.*)

PSALM 22

To the Chief Musician. Set to "The Deer of the Dawn." A Psalm of David.

M Y God, My God, why have You forsaken Me?
Why are You so far from helping Me,
And from the words of My groaning?

2 O My God, I cry in the daytime, but You do not hear;
And in the night season, and am not silent.

3 But You *are* holy,
Who inhabit the praises of Israel.

4 Our fathers trusted in You;
They trusted, and You delivered them.

5 They cried to You, and were delivered;
They trusted in You, and were not ashamed.

6 But I *am* a worm, and no man;
A reproach of men, and despised of the people.

7 All those who see Me laugh Me to scorn;
They shoot out the lip, they shake the head, *saying,*

8 "He trusted in the LORD, let Him rescue Him;
Let Him deliver Him, since He delights in Him!"

9 But You *are* He who took Me out of the womb;
You made Me trust *when I was* on My mother's breasts.

10 I was cast upon You from birth.
From My mother's womb You *have been* My God.

11 Be not far from Me,
For trouble *is* near;
For *there is* none to help.

12 Many bulls have surrounded Me;

Strong *bulls* of Bashan have encircled Me.

13 They gape at Me *with* their mouths,
As a raging and roaring lion.

14 I am poured out like water,
And all My bones are out of joint;
My heart is like wax;
It has melted within Me.

15 My strength is dried up like a potsherd,
And My tongue clings to My jaws;
You have brought Me to the dust of death.

16 For dogs have surrounded Me;
The assembly of the wicked has enclosed Me.
They pierced My hands and My feet;

17 I can count all My bones.
They look *and* stare at Me.

18 They divide My garments among them,
And for My clothing they cast lots.

19 But You, O LORD, do not be far from Me;
O My Strength, hasten to help Me!

20 Deliver Me from the sword,
My precious *life* from the power of the dog.

21 Save Me from the lion's mouth
And from the horns of the wild oxen!

You have answered Me.

22 I will declare Your name to My brethren;
In the midst of the congregation I will praise You.

23 You who fear the LORD, praise Him!
All you descendants of Jacob, glorify Him,

STEP 1

*We admitted we were powerless over our dependencies—
that our lives had become unmanageable.*

Psalm 22:1, 2

When our dependencies have brought us to the depths of pain and despondency, we may feel that God has forsaken us. It may seem that even though we cry to Him to help us, that our prayers do not get past the ceiling. We feel abandoned.

Sometimes we must reach such depths before we can begin our journey upward toward healing. As human beings, it is both our glory and our undoing that we tend to cling to any shred of hope, no matter how small. As long as we think there is a way out that does not involve the radical changes we fear, we will not give up our addictions and dependencies. We may even try to bargain with God, promising one thing or another in return for His help. But it is only when we come to the end of ourselves and admit that we have no place to turn and no room to bargain that God will begin to respond to our need.

For further reading on Step 1, turn to page 591.

Daily Encouragement

DAY 253 READING: PSALM 22:1–31

A Thought for the New Day: The words of verse 1 were later spoken by God's beloved Son in His agony. If we can get beyond the theological issues, we will be moved by the realization that the Holy One Himself was not spared even this suffering. Does His cry mean anything at all for your "impossible" situation? Yes, it means that the greatest extremity of trial is not "impossible" after all. The blackness of the Cross gave way to the dawn of the Resurrection. (*Turn to page 585.*)

And fear Him, all you
    offspring of Israel!
24 For He has not despised nor
    abhorred the affliction of
    the afflicted;
    Nor has He hidden His face
    from Him;
    But when He cried to Him, He
    heard.

25 My praise *shall be* of You in
    the great congregation;
    I will pay My vows before
    those who fear Him.
26 The poor shall eat and be
    satisfied;
    Those who seek Him will
    praise the LORD.
    Let your heart live forever!

27 All the ends of the world
    Shall remember and turn to
    the LORD,
    And all the families of the
    nations
    Shall worship before You.
28 For the kingdom *is* the
    LORD'S,
    And He rules over the nations.

29 All the prosperous of the earth
    Shall eat and worship;
    All those who go down to the
    dust
    Shall bow before Him,
    Even he who cannot keep
    himself alive.

30 A posterity shall serve Him.
    It will be recounted of the
    Lord to the *next* generation,
31 They will come and declare
    His righteousness to a
    people who will be born,
    That He has done *this.*

PSALM 23

A Psalm of David.

STEP 3

THE LORD *is* my shepherd;
  I shall not want.
2 He makes me to lie down in
    green pastures;

He leads me beside the still
    waters.
3 He restores my soul;
    He leads me in the paths of
    righteousness
    For His name's sake.

4 Yea, though I walk through
    the valley of the shadow of
    death,
    I will fear no evil;
    For You *are* with me;
    Your rod and Your staff,
    they comfort me.

5 You prepare a table before me
    in the presence of my
    enemies;
    You anoint my head with oil;
    My cup runs over.
6 Surely goodness and mercy
    shall follow me
    All the days of my life;
    And I will dwell in the house
    of the LORD
    Forever.

PSALM 24

A Psalm of David.

THE earth *is* the LORD'S,
  and all its fullness,
    The world and those who
    dwell therein.
2 For He has founded it upon
    the seas,
    And established it upon the
    waters.

STEP 10

3 Who may ascend into the hill
    of the LORD?
    Or who may stand in His holy
    place?
4 He who has clean hands and a
    pure heart,
    Who has not lifted up his soul
    to an idol,
    Nor sworn deceitfully.
5 He shall receive blessing from
    the LORD,
    And righteousness from the
    God of his salvation.

STEP 3

*Made a decision to turn our will and our lives
over to the care of God **as we understood Him.***

Psalm 23

Throughout the Bible God uses the metaphor of the sheep and the shepherd. In John 10:14, Jesus calls Himself "the good shepherd" who gives His life for His sheep. David knew what it felt like to be the beloved sheep of the Good Shepherd. We can know the same restoration and protection and abundance because the Good Shepherd gave His life for us. As we make the commitment to turn our lives over to Him, we become His sheep. As we relinquish our self-will, our dependencies, and our excessive ambitions, we will find peace and restoration.

Becoming the sheep of the Good Shepherd offers a security that nothing else on earth can match. Not only is our Shepherd good to us in the best sense of the word, but He is also totally wise and all-powerful. This is why David feared no evil. He knew that even on the roughest path, the Good Shepherd was leading to comfort and protect him.

For further reading on Step 3, turn to page 635.

Daily Encouragement

DAY 254 READING: PSALMS 23:1—24:10

A Thought for the New Day: King David had once been a shepherd and understood the ways of shepherds with their sheep. David saw himself, also, as having enjoyed the Great Shepherd's tender care all of his life. This led him to the conclusion that what had been would always continue to be (23:6). David was confident that nothing could ever separate him from the care of his Shepherd. His confidence can be yours, too. (*Turn to page 587.*)

6 This *is* Jacob, the generation
    of those who seek Him,
  Who seek Your face.   Selah

7 Lift up your heads, O you
    gates!
  And be lifted up, you
    everlasting doors!
  And the King of glory shall
    come in.
8 Who *is* this King of glory?
  The Lord strong and mighty,
  The Lord mighty in battle.
9 Lift up your heads, O you
    gates!
  And lift *them* up, you
    everlasting doors!
  And the King of glory shall
    come in.
10 Who is this King of glory?
   The Lord of hosts,
   He *is* the King of glory.   Selah

PSALM 25

A Psalm of David.

To You, O Lord, I lift up my
    soul.
2 O my God, I trust in You;
  Let me not be ashamed;
  Let not my enemies triumph
    over me.
3 Indeed, let no one who waits
    on You be ashamed;
  Let those be ashamed who
    deal treacherously without
    cause.

4 Show me Your ways, O Lord;
  Teach me Your paths.
5 Lead me in Your truth and
    teach me,
  For You *are* the God of my
    salvation;
  On You I wait all the day.

6 Remember, O Lord, Your
    tender mercies and Your
    lovingkindnesses,
  For they *have been* from of
    old.
7 Do not remember the sins of
    my youth, nor my
    transgressions;

According to Your mercy
    remember me,
  For Your goodness' sake, O
    Lord.

8 Good and upright *is* the Lord;
  Therefore He teaches sinners
    in the way.
9 The humble He guides in
    justice,
  And the humble He teaches
    His way.
10 All the paths of the Lord *are*
    mercy and truth,
   To such as keep His covenant
    and His testimonies.
11 For Your name's sake, O
    Lord,
   Pardon my iniquity, for it *is*
    great.

12 Who *is* the man that fears the
    Lord?
   Him shall He teach in the way
    He chooses.
13 He himself shall dwell in
    prosperity,
   And his descendants shall
    inherit the earth.
14 The secret of the Lord *is* with
    those who fear Him,
   And He will show them His
    covenant.
15 My eyes *are* ever toward the
    Lord,
   For He shall pluck my feet out
    of the net.

16 Turn Yourself to me,   STEP 1
    and have mercy on me,
   For I *am* desolate and
    afflicted.
17 The troubles of my heart have
    enlarged;
   Oh, bring me out of my
    distresses!
18 Look on my affliction and my
    pain,
   And forgive all my sins.
19 Consider my enemies,
    for they are many;
   And they hate me with cruel
    hatred.

Humbly asked Him to remove our shortcomings.

Psalm 25:8–11

Why does God want to help us? What makes Him care about us and work on our behalf? Because our God is a good God, His heart is truly and naturally benevolent toward all His creatures. And for His dear children, purchased with His own blood, He carries an even deeper desire and purpose for their spiritual and emotional well-being. "Therefore," these verses tell us, He teaches and guides the one whose heart is humble before Him. When we come to God with a heart of dependence and trust in Him alone, ready to submit to His leading, He responds to us because of who He is. The paths He will lead us down as He removes our shortcomings will be specially ordered according to His mercy and truth. And each path will be uniquely carved out to minister to our individual personality and needs.

The more we understand and get to know our wonderful God, the easier it is to come to Him in humble trust.

For further reading on Step 7, turn to page 595.

Daily Encouragement

DAY 255 READING: PSALMS 25:1—28:9

A Thought for the New Day: The "secret of the LORD" and "His covenant" are taken as one and the same in Psalm 25:14. Covenants, or binding agreements, are usually made in writing. Under this covenant, God pays the price of our salvation by the death of His Son. But the covenant is also the "secret" of those who are its beneficiaries—secret in the sense that they have internalized that covenant written on paper. It is their blessed possession forever. (*Turn to page 591.*)

20 Oh, keep my soul, and deliver
    me;
   Let me not be ashamed,
   for I put my trust in You.
21 Let integrity and uprightness
    preserve me,
   For I wait for You.

22 Redeem Israel, O God,
   Out of all their troubles!

PSALM 26

A Psalm of David.

VINDICATE me, O LORD,
   For I have walked in my
    integrity.
   I have also trusted in the
    LORD;
   I shall not slip.
2 Examine me, O LORD, and
    prove me;
   Try my mind and my heart.
3 For Your lovingkindness *is*
    before my eyes,
   And I have walked in Your
    truth.
4 I have not sat with idolatrous
    mortals,
   Nor will I go in with
    hypocrites.
5 I have hated the congregation
    of evildoers,
   And will not sit with the
    wicked.

6 I will wash my hands in
    innocence;
   So I will go about Your altar,
    O LORD,
7 That I may proclaim with the
    voice of thanksgiving,
   And tell of all Your wondrous
    works.
8 LORD, I have loved the
    habitation of Your house,
   And the place where Your
    glory dwells.

9 Do not gather my soul
    together with sinners,
   Nor my life with bloodthirsty
    men,

10 In whose hands *is* a sinister
    scheme,
   And whose right hand is full
    of bribes.

11 But as for me,
    I will walk in my integrity;
   Redeem me and be merciful to
    me.
12 My foot stands in an even
    place;
   In the congregations I will
    bless the LORD.

PSALM 27

A Psalm of David.

THE LORD *is* my light and my
   salvation;
   Whom shall I fear?
   The LORD *is* the strength of
    my life;
   Of whom shall I be afraid?
2 When the wicked came
    against me
   To eat up my flesh,
   My enemies and foes,
   They stumbled and fell.
3 Though an army should
    encamp against me,
   My heart shall not fear;
   Though war should rise
    against me,
   In this I *will be* confident.

4 One *thing* I have desired of
    the LORD,
   That will I seek:
   That I may dwell in the house
    of the LORD
   All the days of my life,
   To behold the beauty of the
    LORD,
   And to inquire in His temple.
5 For in the time of trouble
   He shall hide me in His
    pavilion;
   In the secret place of His
    tabernacle
   He shall hide me;
   He shall set me high upon a
    rock.

6 And now my head shall be
     lifted up above my enemies
     all around me;
  Therefore I will offer sacrifices
     of joy in His tabernacle;
  I will sing, yes, I will sing
     praises to the LORD.

7 Hear, O LORD, *when* I cry
     with my voice!
  Have mercy also upon me,
     and answer me.
8 *When You said,* "Seek My
     face,"
  My heart said to You,
     "Your face, LORD, I will
     seek."
9 Do not hide Your face from
     me;
  Do not turn Your servant
     away in anger;
  You have been my help;
  Do not leave me nor forsake
     me,
  O God of my salvation.
10 When my father and my
     mother forsake me,
   Then the LORD will take care
     of me.

11 Teach me Your way, O LORD,
   And lead me in a smooth
     path, because of my
     enemies.
12 Do not deliver me to the will
     of my adversaries;
   For false witnesses have risen
     against me,
   And such as breathe out
     violence.

13 *I would have lost heart,* unless
     I had believed
   That I would see the goodness
     of the LORD
   In the land of the living.

14 Wait on the LORD;
   Be of good courage,
   And He shall strengthen your
     heart;
   Wait, I say, on the LORD!

PSALM 28

A Psalm of David.

T O You I will cry, O LORD my
     Rock:
  Do not be silent to me,
  Lest, if You *are* silent to me,
  I become like those who go
     down to the pit.
2 Hear the voice of my
     supplications
  When I cry to You,
  When I lift up my hands
     toward Your holy
     sanctuary.

3 Do not take me away with the
     wicked
  And with the workers of
     iniquity,
  Who speak peace to their
     neighbors,
  But evil *is* in their hearts.
4 Give to them according to
     their deeds,
  And according to the
     wickedness of their
     endeavors;
  Give to them according to the
     work of their hands;
  Render to them what they
     deserve.
5 Because they do not regard
     the works of the LORD,
  Nor the operation of His
     hands,
  He shall destroy them
  And not build them up.

6 Blessed *be* the LORD,
  Because He has heard the
     voice of my supplications!
7 The LORD *is* my strength
     and my shield;
  My heart trusted in Him,
     and I am helped;
  Therefore my heart greatly
     rejoices,
  And with my song I will
     praise Him.

8 The LORD *is* their strength,
  And He *is* the saving refuge of
     His anointed.

9 Save Your people,
And bless Your inheritance;
Shepherd them also,
And bear them up forever.

PSALM 29

A Psalm of David.

GIVE unto the LORD,
  O you mighty ones,
Give unto the LORD
  glory and strength.
2 Give unto the LORD
  the glory due to His name;
Worship the LORD
  in the beauty of holiness.

3 The voice of the LORD *is* over
  the waters;
The God of glory thunders;
The LORD *is* over many
  waters.
4 The voice of the LORD *is*
  powerful;
The voice of the LORD *is* full
  of majesty.

5 The voice of the LORD breaks
  the cedars,
Yes, the LORD splinters the
  cedars of Lebanon.
6 He makes them also skip like
  a calf,
Lebanon and Sirion like a
  young wild ox.
7 The voice of the LORD divides
  the flames of fire.

8 The voice of the LORD shakes
  the wilderness;
The LORD shakes the
  Wilderness of Kadesh.
9 The voice of the LORD makes
  the deer give birth,
And strips the forests bare;
And in His temple everyone
  says, "Glory!"

10 The LORD sat *enthroned* at the
  Flood,
And the LORD sits as King
  forever.
11 The LORD will give strength to
  His people;

The LORD will bless His people
  with peace.

PSALM 30

A Psalm. A Song at the dedication of the house
of David.

I WILL extol You, O LORD,
  for You have lifted me up,
And have not let my foes
  rejoice over me.
2 O LORD my God, I cried out to
  You,
And You have healed me.
3 O LORD, You have brought my
  soul up from the grave;
You have kept me alive, that I
  should not go down to the
  pit.

4 Sing praise to the LORD,
  you saints of His,
And give thanks at the
  remembrance of His holy
  name.
5 For His anger *is but for* a
  moment,
His favor *is for* life;
Weeping may endure for a
  night,
But joy *comes* in the morning.

6 Now in my prosperity I said,
  "I shall never be moved."
7 LORD, by Your favor You have
  made my mountain stand
  strong;
You hid Your face, *and* I was
  troubled.

8 I cried out to You, O LORD;
And to the LORD I made
  supplication:
9 "What profit *is there* in my
  blood,
When I go down to the pit?
Will the dust praise You?
Will it declare Your truth?
10 Hear, O LORD, and have mercy
  on me;
LORD, be my helper!"
11 You have turned for me my
  mourning into dancing;

STEP 1

STEP 1

*We admitted we were powerless over our dependencies—
that our lives had become unmanageable.*

Psalm 30:10

Real justice would condemn us all, because all of us are sinners who have willingly transgressed God's laws. But what relief and hope it gives us to come to understand that this is only part of the picture! Although God is completely holy, He is also completely merciful. In fact, it is because of who He is that we as human beings even comprehend or have a word for "mercy."

The word "mercy" carries several shades of meaning as it is used throughout the Bible. Here it means that God is naturally inclined to be gracious. David knew this about God, so he knew he could ask God to show mercy on his behalf. He could ask God to help him even though he might not deserve that help.

We can call out to God now, just as David did. Even though we are undeserving and powerless to correct our situation, we can still look to God and ask for help. Because of who He is, He will answer us.

For further reading on Step 1, turn to page 593.

Daily Encouragement

DAY 256 READING: PSALMS 29:1—30:12

A Thought for the New Day: Worship is discussed more today than it has been for some time, probably because of the varieties of worship that have recently sprung up. It is difficult to legislate a correct form of worship, but the psalmist gives us a key to it: worship occurs wherever God's beauty, or majesty, is recognized in public and in the heart (29:2). Thus, the method is not so important as the attitude. When our hearts are right, all is right. (*Turn to page 593.*)

You have put off my
　　sackcloth and clothed me
　　with gladness,
12　To the end that *my* glory may
　　sing praise to You and not
　　be silent.
　　O LORD my God,
　　I will give thanks to You
　　forever.

PSALM 31

To the Chief Musician. A Psalm of David.

IN You, O LORD, I put my trust;
　Let me never be ashamed;
　Deliver me in Your
　　righteousness.
2　Bow down Your ear to me,
　Deliver me speedily;
　Be my rock of refuge,
　A fortress of defense to save
　　me.

3　For You *are* my rock and my
　　fortress;
　Therefore, for Your name's
　　sake,
　Lead me and guide me.
4　Pull me out of the net which
　　they have secretly laid for
　　me,
　For You *are* my strength.
5　Into Your hand I commit my
　　spirit;
　You have redeemed me,
　　O LORD God of truth.

6　I have hated those who regard
　　vain idols;
　But I trust in the LORD.
7　I will be glad
　　and rejoice in Your mercy,
　For You have considered my
　　trouble;
　You have known my soul in
　　adversities,
8　And have not shut me up into
　　the hand of the enemy;
　You have set my feet in a
　　wide place.

9　Have mercy on me, O LORD,
　　for I am in trouble;

My eye wastes away with
　grief,
Yes, my soul and my body!
10　For my life is spent with grief,
　And my years with sighing;
　My strength fails because of
　　my iniquity,
　And my bones waste away.
11　I am a reproach among all my
　　enemies,
　But especially among my
　　neighbors,
　And *am* repulsive to my
　　acquaintances;
　Those who see me outside flee
　　from me.
12　I am forgotten like a dead
　　man, out of mind;
　I am like a broken vessel.
13　For I hear the slander of
　　many;
　Fear *is* on every side;
　While they take counsel
　　together against me,
　They scheme to take away my
　　life.

14　But as for me, I trust in You,
　　O LORD;
　I say, "You *are* my God."
15　My times *are* in Your hand;
　Deliver me from the hand of
　　my enemies,
　And from those who persecute
　　me.
16　Make Your face shine upon
　　Your servant;
　Save me for Your mercies'
　　sake.
17　Do not let me be ashamed, O
　　LORD, for I have called upon
　　You;
　Let the wicked be ashamed;
　Let them be silent in the
　　grave.
18　Let the lying lips be put to
　　silence,
　Which speak insolent things
　　proudly and contemptuously
　　against the righteous.

19　Oh, how great *is* Your
　　goodness,

STEP 1

STEP 3

STEP 1

We admitted we were powerless over our dependencies—
that our lives had become unmanageable.

Psalm 31:9, 10

David laments, "My life is spent with grief." For those of us who have contended with crippling dependencies, such lamentation is necessary if we are to fully surrender our broken lives to God.

Although we may associate brokenness, or powerlessness, with defeat, in reality this admission is the first building block toward lasting victory over all of our addictions and dependencies. A paradox of our recovery is that we must give up in order to win.

Usually the admission of powerlessness cannot be achieved unless we have first assessed the magnitude and gravity of what our addiction has cost us. We may want to compile a list of the losses that have resulted from the practice of our dependencies. These losses may include such things as diminished vocational achievement, impaired intimacy in our most important relationships, and even a ruptured spiritual relationship with God.

Only as we appreciate the full grief of those losses can we approach the surrender required in Step 1. Grieving as David grieved cleanses our wounds so that the healing can begin.

For further reading on Step 1, turn to page 599.

Daily Encouragement

DAY 257 READING: PSALM 31:1–24

A Thought for the New Day: Our "times" all hinge on God's perfect design (v. 15). Of one thing we can be assured: whatever our plans, God always has better thoughts in mind for us. As we go through life we are surprised, again and again, by the way God turns affairs so that our mistaken notions of how we should go are superseded by entirely perfect—because divine—arrangements. *(Turn to page 595.)*

Which You have laid up for
    those who fear You,
Which You have prepared for
    those who trust in You
In the presence of the sons of
    men!
20 You shall hide them in the
    secret place of Your
    presence
From the plots of man;
You shall keep them secretly
    in a pavilion
From the strife of tongues.

21 Blessed *be* the LORD,
For He has shown me His
    marvelous kindness in a
    strong city!

22 For I said in my haste,
    "I am cut off from before Your
    eyes";
Nevertheless You heard the
    voice of my supplications
When I cried out to You.

23 Oh, love the LORD, all you His
    saints!
For the LORD preserves the
    faithful,
And fully repays the proud
    person.
24 Be of good courage,
And He shall strengthen your
    heart,
All you who hope in the LORD.

PSALM 32

A Psalm of David. A Contemplation.

BLESSED *is he whose*
    transgression *is* forgiven,
Whose sin *is* covered.
2 Blessed *is* the man to whom
    the LORD does not impute
    iniquity,
And in whose spirit *there is*
    no guile.

3 When I kept silent, my bones
    grew old
Through my groaning all the
    day long.
4 For day and night Your hand
    was heavy upon me;

My vitality was turned into
    the drought of summer.
                                    Selah
5 I acknowledged my sin to
    You,
And my iniquity I have not
    hidden.
I said, "I will confess my
    transgressions to the LORD,"
And You forgave the iniquity
    of my sin.   *Selah*

6 For this cause everyone who
    is godly shall pray to You
In a time when You may be
    found;
Surely in a flood of great
    waters
They shall not come near him.
7 You *are* my hiding place;
You shall preserve me from
    trouble;
You shall surround me with
    songs of deliverance.   *Selah*

8 I will instruct you and teach
    you in the way you should
    go;
I will guide you with My eye.
9 Do not be like the horse
    or like the mule,
Which have no understanding,
Which must be harnessed
    with bit and bridle,
Else they will not come near
    you.

10 Many sorrows *shall be* to the
    wicked;
But he who trusts in the
    LORD, mercy shall surround
    him.
11 Be glad in the LORD and
    rejoice, you righteous;
And shout for joy,
    all *you* upright in heart!

PSALM 33

REJOICE in the LORD, O you
    righteous!
For praise from the upright is
    beautiful.

STEP 7

Humbly asked Him to remove our shortcomings.

Psalm 32:6–8

David continually acknowledged his total confidence in God who became to him a Hiding Place and surrounded him with ".songs of deliverance." Just as God delivered David from his foes, He will deliver us from our shortcomings and old behavior patterns. When God sees us humble and trusting before Him, He will bring about changes in our lives, repair the damage of our past, and restore us to wholeness.

God has said: "I will instruct you and teach you in the way you should go; I will guide you with My eye" (v. 8). That is, God takes special, personal interest in each one who belongs to Him. How incredibly wonderful that our God is so loving and caring! We are not just a number or statistic to Him. Rather, His relationship to us is supremely important to Him. And because it is, we can have the faith to humble ourselves before Him and allow Him to transform our lives into beautiful examples of His serenity and love.

For further reading on Step 7, turn to page 597.

Daily Encouragement

DAY 258 READING: PSALM 32:1–11

A Thought for the New Day: Some horses are spirited and must be closely controlled to guide their steps in the desired direction. Others seem to know almost intuitively what their masters want (vv. 8, 9). A mere nudge seems enough to direct them. God wants us to be like the second case: "I will guide you with My eye." May we become so attuned to His wishes that our steps automatically follow in the path He makes for us. *(Turn to page 597.)*

2 Praise the LORD with the harp;
Make melody to Him with an
instrument of ten strings.
3 Sing to Him a new song;
Play skillfully with a shout of
joy.

4 For the word of the LORD *is*
right,
And all His work *is done* in
truth.
5 He loves righteousness and
justice;
The earth is full of the
goodness of the LORD.

6 By the word of the LORD
the heavens were made,
And all the host of them
by the breath of His mouth.
7 He gathers the waters of the
sea together as a heap;
He lays up the deep in
storehouses.

8 Let all the earth fear the
LORD;
Let all the inhabitants of the
world stand in awe of Him.
9 For He spoke, and it was
done;
He commanded, and it stood
fast.

10 The LORD brings the counsel
of the nations to nothing;
He makes the plans of the
peoples of no effect.
11 The counsel of the LORD
stands forever,
The plans of His heart to all
generations.
12 Blessed *is* the nation whose
God *is* the LORD,
And the people *whom* He has
chosen as His own
inheritance.

13 The LORD looks from heaven;
He sees all the sons of men.
14 From the place of His
habitation He looks
On all the inhabitants of the
earth;

15 He fashions their hearts
individually;
He considers all their works.

16 No king *is* saved by the
multitude of an army;
A mighty man is not delivered
by great strength.
17 A horse *is* a vain hope for
safety;
Neither shall it deliver *any*
by its great strength.

18 Behold, the eye of the LORD *is*
on those who fear Him,
On those who hope in His
mercy,   STEP 2
19 To deliver their soul from
death,
And to keep them alive in
famine.

20 Our soul waits for the LORD;
He *is* our help and our shield.
21 For our heart shall rejoice in
Him,
Because we have trusted in
His holy name.
22 Let Your mercy, O LORD, be
upon us,
Just as we hope in You.

PSALM 34

A Psalm of David when he pretended madness
before Abimelech, who drove him away, and he
departed.

I WILL bless the LORD at all
times;
His praise *shall* continually *be*
in my mouth.
2 My soul shall make its boast
in the LORD;
The humble shall hear *of it*
and be glad.
3 Oh, magnify the LORD with
me,
And let us exalt His name
together.

4 I sought the LORD, and He
heard me,

STEP 7

Humbly asked Him to remove our shortcomings.
Psalm 34:4–6

Facing the possibilities and implications of Step 7 may give us goose bumps of excitement and hope, or it may just as easily fill our stomachs with the butterflies of fear. The "what ifs" may be hard to shake even though we are following God as best we know how. Do not be alarmed. Fear is not a sin or even a sign of weakness. It is natural to be uncertain when such big changes are about to occur in our lives, but there is a way to handle such fears. It begins by earnestly seeking God through His Word and in prayer. When we keep our eyes fixed on Jesus Christ and His power to transform us, we will not be embarrassed or ashamed. The same great God who was able to deliver David is waiting to perform miracles in our lives, as well.

For further reading on Step 7, turn to page 603.

Daily Encouragement

DAY 259 READING: PSALMS 33:1—34:7

A Thought for the New Day: We are not sure who the angel of Psalm 34:7 is. Sometimes "the angel of the LORD" refers to the Lord Himself, rather than to one of His messengers. Truly God is the continual Presence surrounding those who revere Him. Awareness of Him, like the awareness of the presence of a cherished friend, leaves nothing to be desired. Not only is God always near to comfort us, but He "delivers" us from our distresses in His own special ways. (*Turn to page 599.*)

And delivered me from all my
fears.

5 They looked to Him and were
radiant,
And their faces were not
ashamed.

6 This poor man cried out,
and the LORD heard *him,*
And saved him out of all his
troubles.

7 The angel of the LORD
encamps all around those
who fear Him,
And delivers them.

8 Oh, taste and see that the
LORD *is* good;
Blessed *is* the man *who* trusts
in Him!

9 Oh, fear the LORD, you His
saints!
There is no want to those who
fear Him.

10 The young lions lack
and suffer hunger;
But those who seek the LORD
shall not lack any good
thing.

11 Come, you children, listen to
me;
I will teach you the fear of
the LORD.

12 Who *is* the man *who* desires
life,
And loves *many* days,
that he may see good?

13 Keep your tongue from evil,
And your lips from speaking
guile.

14 Depart from evil, and do good;
Seek peace, and pursue it.

15 The eyes of the LORD *are* on
the righteous,
And His ears *are open* to their
cry.

16 The face of the LORD *is*
against those who do evil,
To cut off the remembrance of
them from the earth.

17 *The righteous* cry out,
and the LORD hears,

And delivers them out of all
their troubles.

18 The LORD *is* near to those
who have a broken heart,
And saves such as have a
contrite spirit.

19 Many *are* the afflictions of the
righteous,
But the LORD delivers him
out of them all.

20 He guards all his bones;
Not one of them is broken.

21 Evil shall slay the wicked,
And those who hate the
righteous shall be
condemned.

22 The LORD redeems the soul of
His servants,
And none of those who trust
in Him shall be condemned.

PSALM 35

A Psalm of David.

PLEAD *my cause,* O LORD, with
those who strive with me;
Fight against those who fight
against me.

2 Take hold of shield and
buckler,
And stand up for my help.

3 Also draw out the spear,
And stop those who pursue
me.
Say to my soul,
"I *am* your salvation."

4 Let those be put to shame
and brought to dishonor
Who seek after my life;
Let those be turned back
and brought to confusion
Who plot my hurt.

5 Let them be like chaff before
the wind,
And let the angel of the LORD
chase *them.*

6 Let their way be dark and
slippery,
And let the angel of the LORD
pursue them.

STEP 1

We admitted we were powerless over our dependencies—
that our lives had become unmanageable.

Psalm 34:18

What good is a broken heart? Not much if you want to look at it the way most people do. Broken hearts bring along pain and shame as their favorite roommates. They generally leave us feeling useless and exhausted. Many times they even make us feel as if life itself is not worth the struggle.

And yet, believe it or not, good can result from a broken heart. In verse 18, we read that "the LORD *is* near to those who have a broken heart." When we are feeling confident and secure and happy, we generally are not too interested in what God is trying to tell us. But when we come to the end of our rope and experience the pain and hopelessness of a broken heart, then we are more ready to hear God's voice. He knows this and moves near to comfort us when all earthly comfort and hope has gone. He is near to us now, reaching out His arms of love and healing.

For further reading on Step 1, turn to page 605.

Daily Encouragement

DAY 260 READING: PSALMS 34:8—36:12

A Thought for the New Day: It is a good thing to know and commit to memory as much Scripture as you can. Yet it is entirely possible to have a literary knowledge of the Bible and never enter into the enjoyment of all that is described and offered there. We need most urgently to "taste" God for ourselves and find that He is surely "good" (34:8). It is an ultimate goal of life to *enjoy* God, as well as to know what He has said. (*Turn to page 603.*)

7 For without cause they have
hidden their net for me *in* a
pit,
Which they have dug without
cause for my life.
8 Let destruction come upon
him unexpectedly,
And let his net that he has
hidden catch himself;
Into that very destruction let
him fall.

9 And my soul shall be joyful in
the LORD;
It shall rejoice in His
salvation.
10 All my bones shall say,
"LORD, who *is* like You,
Delivering the poor from him
who is too strong for him,
Yes, the poor and the needy
from him who plunders
him?"

11 Fierce witnesses rise up;
They ask me *things* that I do
not know.
12 They reward me evil for good,
To the sorrow of my soul.
13 But as for me, when they
were sick,
My clothing *was* sackcloth;
I humbled myself with fasting;
And my prayer would return
to my own heart.
14 I paced about as though *he*
were my friend *or* brother;
I bowed down heavily, as one
who mourns *for his* mother.

15 But in my adversity they
rejoiced
And gathered together;
Attackers gathered against
me,
And I did not know *it;*
They tore *at me* and did not
cease;
16 With ungodly mockers at
feasts
They gnashed at me with
their teeth.

17 Lord, how long will You look
on?
Rescue me from their
destructions,
My precious *life* from the
lions.
18 I will give You thanks in the
great congregation;
I will praise You among many
people.

19 Let them not rejoice over me
who are wrongfully my
enemies;
Nor let them wink with the
eye who hate me without a
cause.
20 For they do not speak peace,
But they devise deceitful
matters
Against *those who are* quiet in
the land.
21 They also opened their mouth
wide against me,
And said, "Aha, aha!
Our eyes have seen *it."*

22 *This* You have seen, O LORD;
Do not keep silence.
O Lord, do not be far from
me.
23 Stir up Yourself,
and awake to my
vindication,
To my cause, my God and my
Lord.
24 Vindicate me, O LORD my
God, according to Your
righteousness;
And let them not rejoice over
me.
25 Let them not say in their
hearts, "Ah, so we would
have it!"
Let them not say,
"We have swallowed him
up."

26 Let them be ashamed
and brought to mutual
confusion
Who rejoice at my hurt;

Let them be clothed with
  shame and dishonor
Who magnify themselves
  against me.

27 Let them shout for joy and be
  glad,
Who favor my righteous
  cause;
And let them say continually,
"Let the LORD be magnified,
Who has pleasure in the
  prosperity of His servant."
28 And my tongue shall speak of
  Your righteousness
  And of Your praise all the day
  long.

PSALM 36

To the Chief Musician. A Psalm of David the
servant of the LORD.

AN oracle within my heart
  concerning the
  transgression of the wicked:
  There is no fear of God before
  his eyes.
2 For he flatters himself in his
  own eyes,
When he finds out his iniquity
  and when he hates.
3 The words of his mouth *are*
  wickedness and deceit;
He has ceased to be wise *and*
  to do good.
4 He devises wickedness on his
  bed;
He sets himself in a way *that*
  is not good;
He does not abhor evil.

5 Your mercy, O LORD, *is* in the
  heavens,
  And Your faithfulness *reaches*
  to the clouds.
6 Your righteousness *is* like the
  great mountains;
Your judgments *are* a great
  deep;
O LORD, You preserve man
  and beast.

7 How precious *is* Your
  lovingkindness, O God!
Therefore the children of men
  put their trust under the
  shadow of Your wings.
8 They are abundantly satisfied
  with the fullness of Your
  house,
And You give them drink
  from the river of Your
  pleasures.
9 For with You *is* the fountain
  of life;
In Your light we see light.

10 Oh, continue Your
  lovingkindness to those who
  know You,
And Your righteousness
  to the upright in heart.
11 Let not the foot of pride come
  against me,
And let not the hand of the
  wicked drive me away.
12 There the workers of iniquity
  have fallen;
They have been cast down
  and are not able to rise.

PSALM 37

A Psalm of David.

DO not fret because of
  evildoers,
Nor be envious of the workers
  of iniquity.
2 For they shall soon be cut
  down like the grass,
And wither as the green herb.

3 Trust in the LORD, and do
  good;
Dwell in the land, and feed on
  His faithfulness.
4 Delight yourself also in the
  LORD,
And He shall give you the
  desires of your heart.

5 Commit your way to the
  LORD,
Trust also in Him,
And He shall bring *it* to pass.

STEP
7

6 He shall bring forth your
    righteousness as the light,
And your justice as the
    noonday.

7 Rest in the LORD,
    and wait patiently for Him;
Do not fret because of him
    who prospers in his way,
Because of the man who
    brings wicked schemes to
    pass.
8 Cease from anger, and forsake
    wrath;
Do not fret—*it* only *causes*
    harm.

9 For evildoers shall be cut off;
But those who wait on the
    LORD,
They shall inherit the earth.
10 For yet a little while and the
    wicked *shall be* no *more;*
Indeed, you will look
    diligently for his place,
But it *shall be* no *more.*
11 But the meek shall inherit the
    earth,
And shall delight themselves
    in the abundance of peace.

12 The wicked plots against the
    just,
And gnashes at him with his
    teeth.
13 The Lord laughs at him,
For He sees that his day is
    coming.
14 The wicked have drawn the
    sword
And have bent their bow,
To cast down the poor and
    needy,
To slay those who are of
    upright conduct.
15 Their sword shall enter their
    own heart,
And their bows shall be
    broken.

16 A little that a righteous man
    has

Is better than the riches of
    many wicked.
17 For the arms of the wicked
    shall be broken,
But the LORD upholds the
    righteous.

18 The LORD knows the days of
    the upright,
And their inheritance shall be
    forever.
19 They shall not be ashamed in
    the evil time,
And in the days of famine
    they shall be satisfied.
20 But the wicked shall perish;
And the enemies of the LORD,
Like the splendor of the
    meadows, shall vanish.
Into smoke they shall vanish
    away.

21 The wicked borrows
    and does not repay,
But the righteous shows
    mercy and gives.
22 For *those who are* blessed by
    Him shall inherit the earth,
But *those who are* cursed by
    Him shall be cut off.

23 The steps of a *good* man are
    ordered by the LORD,
And He delights in his way.
24 Though he fall, he shall not be
    utterly cast down;
For the LORD upholds *him*
    with His hand.

STEP
7

25 I have been young, and *now*
    am old;
Yet I have not seen the
    righteous forsaken,
Nor his descendants begging
    bread.
26 *He is* ever merciful, and lends;
And his descendants *are*
    blessed.

27 Depart from evil, and do good;
And dwell forevermore.
28 For the LORD loves justice,

Humbly asked Him to remove our shortcomings.

Psalm 37:23, 24

The psalmist David reminds us that "the steps of a good man are ordered by the LORD" (v. 23). In modern recovery language we echo his words when we pray, "Let go, and let God." The orderliness of our steps is determined by our willingness to humbly surrender to God's guidance.

Perhaps the most serious challenge we confront in day-to-day recovery is that long-established pattern of destructive reliance on people and things to function as gods in our lives. Each day we choose who will be Lord of our lives. Will our direction come from the dictates of our old, false dependencies, or will it come from the one true God?

As we seek God's order with a spirit of humility, we encounter not only the elimination of our most conspicuous shortcomings, but also we encounter His sustaining hand, outstretched to uphold us for eternity.

For further reading on Step 7, turn to page 665.

Daily Encouragement

DAY 261 READING: PSALM 37:1–40

A Thought for the New Day: Here is a beautiful alternate translation of verse 5: "Roll off your way onto the Lord." This is the essence of real trust—letting go of the burdens and problems that we can never solve, knowing that they are in good hands with Him. It is a lesson many of us relearn repeatedly: "He shall bring *it* to pass." And still we are surprised that He always does what He promises. (*Turn to page 605.*)

And does not forsake His
saints;
They are preserved forever,
But the descendants of the
wicked shall be cut off.
29 The righteous shall inherit the
land,
And dwell in it forever.

30 The mouth of the righteous
speaks wisdom,
And his tongue talks of
justice.
31 The law of his God *is* in his
heart;
None of his steps shall slide.

32 The wicked watches the
righteous,
And seeks to slay him.
33 The LORD will not leave him
in his hand,
Nor condemn him when he is
judged.

34 Wait on the LORD,
And keep His way,
And He shall exalt you to
inherit the land;
When the wicked are cut off,
you shall see *it*.
35 I have seen the wicked in
great power,
And spreading himself like a
native green tree.
36 Yet he passed away, and
behold, he *was* no *more;*
Indeed I sought him,
but he could not be found.

37 Mark the blameless *man,*
and observe the upright;
For the future of *that* man *is*
peace.
38 But the transgressors shall be
destroyed together;
The future of the wicked shall
be cut off.

39 But the salvation of the
righteous *is* from the LORD;
He is their strength in the
time of trouble.

40 And the LORD shall help them
and deliver them;
He shall deliver them from the
wicked,
And save them,
Because they trust in Him.

PSALM 38

A Psalm of David. To bring to remembrance.

O LORD, do not rebuke me in
Your wrath,
Nor chasten me in Your hot
displeasure!
2 For Your arrows pierce me
deeply,
And Your hand presses me
down.

3 *There is* no soundness in my
flesh
Because of Your anger,
Nor *is there any* health in my
bones
Because of my sin.
4 For my iniquities have gone
over my head;
Like a heavy burden they are
too heavy for me.
5 My wounds are foul *and*
festering
Because of my foolishness.

6 I am troubled,
I am bowed down greatly;
I go mourning all the day
long.
7 For my loins are full of
inflammation,
And *there is* no soundness in
my flesh.
8 I am feeble and severely
broken;
I groan because of the turmoil
of my heart.

9 Lord, all my desire *is* before
You;
And my sighing is not hidden
from You.
10 My heart pants, my strength
fails me;

STEP 1

We admitted we were powerless over our dependencies—
that our lives had become unmanageable.

Psalm 38:1–9

David is called "the man after God's own heart" (see 1 Sam. 13:14; Acts 13:22). We would think that such a person would have a life of peace and serenity. Yet Psalm 38 shows us that David experienced periods in his life when he had to go back to Square One. In this psalm, he mourns over how unmanageable his life has become. He has strayed from allowing God to control his life; and because of this, he admits he has become foolish (v. 5) and crushed by his own behavior (v. 4). David realizes his behavior has caused him great physical and emotional pain. He declares in verse 8, "I am feeble and severely broken." Nevertheless, surrender to God does not come easily, for he still experiences groaning "because of the turmoil of [his] heart" (v. 8).

An ironic aspect of addiction is that letting go of the things that cause us misery is extremely difficult. But with David we can say to God, "My sighing is not hidden from You" (v. 9). God knows our struggles and will give us the power to look to Him for help.

For further reading on Step 1, turn to page 613.

Daily Encouragement

DAY 262 READING: PSALM 38:1–16

A Thought for the New Day: Another good translation of verse 15 is, "I will wait for You, O Lord." The promise of a costly gift shipped from far away is worth waiting for. Waiting is part of trusting—knowing that, if we will give God time to work on His own schedule, everything will work out as it should. And we will be satisfied with His answer. So let us not miss God's best because of our impatience. *(Turn to page 607.)*

Prayer for God's Favor

As for the light of my eyes,
   it also has gone from me.

11 My loved ones and my friends
      stand aloof from my plague,
   And my kinsmen stand afar
      off.
12 Those also who seek my life
      lay snares *for me;*
   Those who seek my hurt
      speak of destruction,
   And plan deception all the day
      long.

13 But I, like a deaf *man,* do not
      hear;
   And *I am* like a mute *who*
      does not open his mouth.
14 Thus I am like a man who
      does not hear,
   And in whose mouth *is* no
      response.

15 For in You, O LORD, I hope;
   You will hear, O Lord my
      God.
16 For I said, *"Hear me,*
      lest they rejoice over me,
   Lest, when my foot slips,
      they magnify *themselves*
      against me."

STEP
5

17 For I *am* ready to fall,
   And my sorrow *is* continually
      before me.
18 For I will declare my iniquity;
   I will be in anguish over my
      sin.
19 But my enemies *are* vigorous,
      and they are strong;
   And those who hate me
      wrongfully have multiplied.
20 Those also who render evil for
      good,
   They are my adversaries,
      because I follow *what is*
      good.

21 Do not forsake me, O LORD;
   O my God, be not far from
      me!
22 Make haste to help me,
   O Lord, my salvation!

PSALM 39

To the Chief Musician. To Jeduthun. A Psalm
of David.

I SAID, "I will guard my ways,
   Lest I sin with my tongue;
   I will restrain my mouth with
      a muzzle,
   While the wicked are before
      me."
2 I was mute with silence,
   I held my peace *even* from
      good;
   And my sorrow was stirred
      up.
3 My heart was hot within me;
   While I was musing, the fire
      burned.
   Then I spoke with my tongue:

4 "LORD, make me to know my
      end,
   And what *is* the measure of
      my days,
   That I may know how frail I
      am.
5 Indeed, You have made my
      days *as* handbreadths,
   And my age *is* as nothing
      before You;
   Certainly every man at his
      best state *is* but vapor.
                           Selah
6 Surely every man walks about
      like a shadow;
   Surely they busy themselves
      in vain;
   He heaps up *riches,*
   And does not know who will
      gather them.

STEP
1

7 "And now, Lord, what do I
      wait for?
   My hope *is* in You.
8 Deliver me from all my
      transgressions;
   Do not make me the reproach
      of the foolish.

STEP
7

9 I was mute, I did not open my
      mouth,
   Because it was You who did
      it.
10 Remove Your plague from me;

STEP 5

Admitted to God, to ourselves, and to another human being the exact nature of our wrongs.

Psalm 38:17, 18

The self-examination and acknowledgment required in Steps 4 and 5 may be a difficult struggle for some of us. David, called "the man after [God's] own heart," seemed to understand that kind of emotional pain.

Several times in his life, David ached with knowledge that he had traveled a road that God had not chosen for him. He also understood that his actions had caused God sorrow.

This awareness led to anguish on David's part, as well. However, instead of trying to hide or excuse or ignore what he had done, David declared openly the sins he had committed and his anguish over those wrongs. Since David was open in acknowledging his wrongs, God never failed to be quick and open in His forgiveness and restoration of David.

As we face this time of admission in our own lives, our hearts can be strengthened by knowing that God does not judge for that admission but instead is anxious to forgive and restore us.

For further reading on Step 5, turn to page 609.

Daily Encouragement

DAY 263 READING: PSALMS 38:17—39:13

A Thought for the New Day: The psalm writer had just been lamenting his weakness and sense of futility. But in Psalm 39:7 he paused to remember that his "hope" or expectation of good was from the Lord. If we are honest with ourselves, none of us has anything to boast about—although we still boast sometimes, even if only to ourselves. In the end, we come back to where David sits, and we see the obvious: from God Himself is our expectation of good. (*Turn to page 609.*)

I am consumed by the blow of
Your hand.
11 When with rebukes You
correct man for iniquity,
You make his beauty melt
away like a moth;
Surely every man *is* vapor.
                              Selah

12 "Hear my prayer, O LORD,
And give ear to my cry;
Do not be silent at my tears;
For I *am* a stranger with You,
A sojourner, as all my fathers
were.
13 Remove Your gaze from me,
that I may regain strength,
Before I go away and am no
more."

PSALM 40

To the Chief Musician. A Psalm of David.

I WAITED patiently for the
LORD;
And He inclined to me,
And heard my cry.
2 He also brought me up out of
a horrible pit,
Out of the miry clay,
And set my feet upon a rock,
And established my steps.
3 He has put a new song in my
mouth—
Praise to our God;
Many will see *it* and fear,
And will trust in the LORD.

4 Blessed *is* that man who
makes the LORD his trust,
And does not respect the
proud, nor such as turn
aside to lies.
5 Many, O LORD my God,
are Your wonderful works
Which You have done;
And Your thoughts *which are*
toward us
Cannot be recounted to You
in order;
If I would declare and speak
of them,

They are more than can be
numbered.

6 Sacrifice and offering
You did not desire;
My ears You have opened;
Burnt offering and sin offering
You did not require.
7 Then I said, "Behold, I come;
In the scroll of the Book *it is*
written of me.
8 I delight to do Your will, O
my God,
And Your law *is* within my
heart."

9 I have proclaimed the good
news of righteousness
In the great congregation;
Indeed, I do not restrain my
lips,
O LORD, You Yourself know.
10 I have not hidden Your
righteousness within my
heart;
I have declared Your
faithfulness and Your
salvation;
I have not concealed Your
lovingkindness and Your
truth
From the great congregation.

11 Do not withhold Your tender
mercies from me, O LORD;
Let Your lovingkindness and
Your truth continually
preserve me.
12 For innumerable evils have
surrounded me;
My iniquities have overtaken
me, so that I am not able to
look up;
They are more than the hairs
of my head;
Therefore my heart fails me.

13 Be pleased, O LORD, to deliver
me;
O LORD, make haste to help
me!

STEP 5

STEP 5

*Admitted to God, to ourselves, and to another human being
the exact nature of our wrongs.*

Psalm 40:11–13

Denial is a favorite comfort zone for those of us with dependencies. We have spent years carefully refusing to see things that were too painful or upsetting to handle. In those years, we very likely began to pile wrong upon wrong. Now as we peel back those layers of character defects, abuses, and wrongs, we may feel indeed that "innumerable evils" have surrounded us and that our iniquities have "overtaken" us. But we need not stay in this pit of sadness and despair.

God's lovingkindness, tender mercy, and truth are always available to us. They are able to meet every need we have. In fact, it is because we can be so sure of God's mercy and love that we are able to admit our problems. We need not fear His rejection. And even if our admissions cause us to be despondent for a time, we can know that God is working in our lives to help us and deliver us.

For further reading on Step 5, turn to page 611.

Daily Encouragement

DAY 264 READING: PSALM 40:1–17

A Thought for the New Day: Singing is the language of the soul. A sad song is the song of a discouraged soul, but God gives us His "new song" (v. 3). In the Book of Revelation, John recorded seeing a large company in heaven singing this new song. It is the song of those who have drunk deeply at the Well of Water of Life, which is Jesus. No need to live in the swamp of despondency! Come to the Fountain of Life, and find new resources every day. (*Turn to page 611.*)

14 Let them be ashamed
    and brought to mutual
    confusion
  Who seek to destroy my life;
  Let them be driven backward
    and brought to dishonor
  Who wish me evil.
15 Let them be appalled because
    of their shame,
  Who say to me, "Aha, aha!"

16 Let all those who seek You
    rejoice and be glad in You;
  Let such as love Your
    salvation say continually,
  "The LORD be magnified!"

17 But I *am* poor and needy;
  Yet the LORD thinks upon me.
  You *are* my help and my
    deliverer;
  Do not delay, O my God.

PSALM 41

To the Chief Musician. A Psalm of David.

BLESSED *is* he who considers
  the poor;
  The LORD will deliver him in
    time of trouble.
2 The LORD will preserve him
    and keep him alive,
  And he will be blessed on the
    earth;
  You will not deliver him to
    the will of his enemies.
3 The LORD will strengthen him
    on his bed of illness;
  You will sustain him on his
    sickbed.

4 I said, "LORD, be merciful to
    me;
  Heal my soul, for I have
    sinned against You."
5 My enemies speak evil of me:
  "When will he die,
    and his name perish?"
6 And if he comes to see *me*,
    he speaks vain *words;*
  His heart gathers iniquity to
    itself;
  When he goes out, he tells *it.*

7 All who hate me whisper
    together against me;
  Against me they devise my
    hurt.
8 "An evil disease," *they say,*
    "clings to him.
  And *now* that he lies down,
    he will rise up no more."
9 Even my own familiar friend
    in whom I trusted,
  Who ate my bread,
  Has lifted up *his* heel against
    me.

10 But You, O LORD, be merciful
    to me, and raise me up,
  That I may repay them.
11 By this I know that You are
    well pleased with me,
  Because my enemy does not
    triumph over me.
12 As for me, You uphold me in
    my integrity,
  And set me before Your face
    forever.

13 Blessed *be* the LORD God of
    Israel
  From everlasting to
    everlasting!
  Amen and Amen.

BOOK TWO

Psalms 42–72

PSALM 42

To the Chief Musician. A Contemplation of the
sons of Korah.

AS the deer pants for the water
  brooks,
  So pants my soul for You, O
    God.
2 My soul thirsts for God,
    for the living God.
  When shall I come and appear
    before God?
3 My tears have been my food
    day and night,
  While they continually say to
    me,
  Where *is* your God?"

STEP 5

Admitted to God, to ourselves, and to another human being the exact nature of our wrongs.

Psalm 41:4

"No pain, no gain" is a favorite slogan of highly motivated athletes. To win on the field of competition generally requires painful hours of exercise and struggle beforehand. In much the same way, Steps 4 and 5 have been a painful exertion for many of us.

The probing and examination of the dark and hidden corners of our lives has been hard work. Such efforts are undeniably emotionally exhausting. In some cases we may even feel physically exhausted. But our hard work is worth the effort. When we have struggled to understand and admit our dependencies and character faults, we have not struggled in vain. God's mercy is available to us, not only to give us endurance in our struggle, but to take us far beyond our present situation. God's power is also working to bring about healing in our lives. Though these days may have been sorely trying, they carry with them the joyous expectation of healing and reward.

For further reading on Step 5, turn to page 625.

Daily Encouragement

DAY 265 READING: PSALM 41:1–13

A Thought for the New Day: Many of the poems we call psalms are really songs of praise to the Lord, whether for His salvation, His kindness, His providence, or His mercy. In verse 13 the psalmist did not seem to praise God for any particular benefit. The writer was in a mood of praise and could not restrain himself from shouting, "Blessed be the LORD!" As we live, may we become so sensitive to God's grand qualities that His praise is our constant state of mind. (*Turn to page 613.*)

4 When I remember these
    things,
I pour out my soul within me.
For I used to go with the
    multitude;
I went with them to the house
    of God,
With the voice of joy and
    praise,
With a multitude that kept a
    pilgrim feast.

5 Why are you cast down, O my
    soul?
And *why* are you disquieted
    within me?
Hope in God,
    for I shall yet praise Him
For the help of His
    countenance.

STEP 1

6 O my God, my soul is cast
    down within me;
Therefore I will remember
    You from the land of the
    Jordan,
And from the heights of
    Hermon,
From the Hill Mizar.
7 Deep calls unto deep at the
    noise of Your waterfalls;
All Your waves and billows
    have gone over me.
8 The LORD will command His
    lovingkindness in the
    daytime,
And in the night His song
    shall be with me—
A prayer to the God of my
    life.

9 I will say to God my Rock,
    Why have You forgotten me?
Why do I go mourning
    because of the oppression of
    the enemy?"
10 *As* with a breaking of my
    bones,
My enemies reproach me,
While they say to me all day
    long,
"Where *is* your God?"

11 Why are you cast down, O my
    soul?
And why are you disquieted
    within me?
Hope in God;
For I shall yet praise Him,
The help of my countenance
    and my God.

PSALM 43

VINDICATE me, O God,
    And plead my cause against
    an ungodly nation;
Oh, deliver me from the
    deceitful and unjust man!
2 For You *are* the God of my
    strength;
Why do You cast me off?
Why do I go mourning
    because of the oppression of
    the enemy?

3 Oh, send out Your light and
    Your truth!
Let them lead me;
Let them bring me to Your
    holy hill
And to Your tabernacle.
4 Then I will go to the altar of
    God,
To God my exceeding joy;
And on the harp I will praise
    You,
O God, my God.

5 Why are you cast down, O my
    soul?
And why are you disquieted
    within me?
Hope in God;
For I shall yet praise Him,
The help of my countenance
    and my God.

PSALM 44

To the Chief Musician. A Contemplation of the
sons of Korah.

WE have heard with our ears,
    O God,
Our fathers have told us,

STEP 1

*We admitted we were powerless over our dependencies—
that our lives had become unmanageable.*

Psalm 42:6–8

In this psalm, the writer declared his deep depression when he spoke of his soul's being downcast. And his distress was figuratively portrayed by the billows and waves that overwhelmed him. He felt swept away and drowned by this waterfall of trouble that had become a flood.

It is interesting that the psalmist considered the waterfall and billows to belong to God, and yet in verse 8 he spoke of God's lovingkindness. It may be hard for us to understand how God could allow a flood of trouble to come into someone's life and yet that person could continue to believe and trust in God's lovingkindness.

Even though it may be hard to accept, it is important to know that troubles can bring about good if they lead us to a knowledge of our own powerlessness. It is then that God can begin to show us His lovingkindness and truth.

For further reading on Step 1, turn to page 615.

Daily Encouragement

DAY 266 READING: PSALMS 42:1—43:5

A Thought for the New Day: Usually others can tell when our spirits are low (42:11). At such times some of them may be inclined to question (although not too charitably) whether our God is real (42:10). This really is one of the hard places of life. However, in another psalm David wrote that "weeping may endure for a night, but joy *comes* in the morning" (30:5). Keep your eye on the morning. It is never far away! (*Turn to page 615.*)

What deeds You did in their
    days,
In days of old:

2 *How* You drove out the
    nations with Your hand,
But them You planted;
How You afflicted the peoples,
    and cast them out.

3 For they did not gain
    possession of the land by
    their own sword,
Nor did their own arm save
    them;
But it was Your right hand,
    Your arm, and the light of
    Your countenance,
Because You favored them.

4 You are my King, O God;
Command victories for Jacob.

5 Through You we will push
    down our enemies;
Through Your name we will
    trample those who rise up
    against us.

6 For I will not trust in my bow,
Nor shall my sword save me.

7 But You have saved us from
    our enemies,
And have put to shame those
    who hated us.

8 In God we boast all day long,
And praise Your name
    forever.   Selah

9 But You have cast *us* off and
    put us to shame,
And You do not go out with
    our armies.

10 You make us turn back from
    the enemy,
And those who hate us have
    taken spoil for themselves.

11 You have given us up like
    sheep *intended* for food,
And have scattered us among
    the nations.

12 You sell Your people for
    naught,
And are not enriched by their
    price.

13 You make us a reproach
    to our neighbors,

A scorn and a derision
    to those all around us.

14 You make us a byword
    among the nations,
A shaking of the head
    among the peoples.

15 My dishonor *is* continually
    before me,
And the shame of my face
    has covered me,

16 Because of the voice of him
    who reproaches and reviles,
Because of the enemy and the
    avenger.

STEP
1

17 All this has come upon us;
But we have not forgotten
    You,
Nor have we dealt falsely with
    Your covenant.

18 Our heart has not turned
    back,
Nor have our steps departed
    from Your way;

19 But You have severely broken
    us in the place of jackals,
And covered us with the
    shadow of death.

20 If we had forgotten the name
    of our God,
Or stretched out our hands to
    a foreign god,

21 Would not God search this
    out?
For He knows the secrets of
    the heart.

22 Yet for Your sake we are
    killed all day long;
We are accounted as sheep for
    the slaughter.

23 Awake! Why do You sleep, O
    Lord?
Arise! Do not cast *us* off
    forever.

24 Why do You hide Your face,
And forget our affliction and
    our oppression?

25 For our soul is bowed down to
    the dust;
Our body clings to the ground.

26 Arise for our help,

STEP 1

*We admitted we were powerless over our dependencies—
that our lives had become unmanageable.*
Psalm 44:15, 16

A sense of shame is one of the most toxic emotions we can experience. Modern medical understanding of addictions and compulsivity tells us that our drivenness is often an effort to escape from or compensate for a profound sense of shame and inadequacy. Thousands of years ago, a psalmist spoke of this phenomenon when he lamented that "the shame of my face has covered me" (v. 15).

What is this shame that can envelop and paralyze us? We may feel shame about our estrangement from God. We may harbor shame feelings about our inability to pull in the reins on addictive or compulsive behaviors. We may regret and feel ashamed for the damage we have inflicted on others through our life-styles. We may carry memories of false shame about the dysfunction of our childhood families.

At Step 1, we face a turning point. Will we allow this flood of guilt to overwhelm us and to drive us back into the practice of our dependencies? Or will we yield this colossal unmanageability over to the care of God's grace? The choice is ours.

For further reading on Step 1, turn to page 629.

Daily Encouragement

DAY 267 READING: PSALM 44:1–26

A Thought for the New Day: When things seem to go wrong, that is the time to remember the good times (v. 1). History has great value in reminding us of how far we have come. The exploits of the great ones of the past are an inspiration for us to realize that we, like they, have the same God—a God who desires to continue working with us to do mighty acts, as He did in the past. Never say, "It's all over." Our God lives! (*Turn to page 617.*)

And redeem us for Your
mercies' sake.

PSALM 45

To the Chief Musician. Set to "The Lilies." A
Contemplation of the sons of Korah. A Song of
Love.

MY heart is overflowing with a
good theme;
I recite my composition
concerning the King;
My tongue *is* the pen of a
ready writer.

2 You are fairer than the sons
of men;
Grace is poured upon Your
lips;
Therefore God has blessed
You forever.

3 Gird Your sword upon *Your*
thigh, O Mighty One,
With Your glory and Your
majesty.

4 And in Your majesty ride
prosperously because of
truth, humility, *and*
righteousness;
And Your right hand shall
teach You awesome things.

5 Your arrows *are* sharp in the
heart of the King's enemies;
The peoples fall under You.

6 Your throne, O God, *is* forever
and ever;
A scepter of righteousness *is*
the scepter of Your
kingdom.

7 You love righteousness
and hate wickedness;
Therefore God, Your God, has
anointed You
With the oil of gladness more
than Your companions.

8 All Your garments are scented
with myrrh and aloes *and*
cassia,
Out of the ivory palaces,
by which they have made
You glad.

9 Kings' daughters *are* among
Your honorable women;

At Your right hand stands the
queen in gold from Ophir.

10 Listen, O daughter,
Consider and incline your ear;
Forget your own people also,
and your father's house;

11 So the King will greatly desire
your beauty;
Because He *is* your Lord,
worship Him.

12 And the daughter of Tyre *will
be there* with a gift;
The rich among the people
will seek your favor.

13 The royal daughter *is* all
glorious within *the palace;*
Her clothing *is* woven with
gold.

14 She shall be brought to the
King in robes of many
colors;
The virgins, her companions
who follow her, shall be
brought to You.

15 With gladness and rejoicing
they shall be brought;
They shall enter the King's
palace.

16 Instead of Your fathers shall
be Your sons,
Whom You shall make princes
in all the earth.

17 I will make Your name to be
remembered in all
generations;
Therefore the people shall
praise You forever and ever.

PSALM 46

To the Chief Musician. A Psalm of the sons of
Korah. A Song for Alamoth.

GOD *is* our refuge and
strength,
A very present help in trouble.

2 Therefore we will not fear,
Though the earth be removed,
And though the mountains be
carried into the midst of the
sea;

STEP
2

STEP 2

Came to believe that a Power greater than ourselves
could restore us to sanity.

Psalm 46:1–3

When the whole world seems to be crumbling around us, there is refuge. When things are changing so fast we feel unable to find stability, there is strength. When the river of life has become a roaring rapids and we cannot see beyond the bends and rocks, there is help. Trouble never takes God by surprise. Though we may feel unprepared and unsure in the small raft of our own abilities, a Strong Hand is reaching toward us, offering the stability and shelter of the Solid Rock. That Rock is Jesus Christ. He knows our needs and struggles and fears better than we know them ourselves. His life offers us peace and fulfillment; His death and resurrection offer us eternal salvation. His hand is stretched out to us now. All that remains is for us to reach up in faith to Him and allow Him to rescue us from the leaky raft of our own devices.

For further reading on Step 2, turn to page 649.

Daily Encouragement

DAY 268 READING: PSALMS 45:1—46:11

A Thought for the New Day: Nothing steadies our nerve like meditation on the eternity of God (45:6). This unique quality of the Lord has many tributary values: being eternal He is not subject to the changes that time brings to our temporary existence. Also, though we are mortal, God imparts this eternal property to us. The writer to the Hebrews refers to the "God" of this text as Christ. Because He lives, we shall live, also. (*Turn to page 619.*)

3 *Though* its waters roar *and* be
    troubled,
Though the mountains shake
    with its swelling.   Selah

4 *There is* a river whose streams
    shall make glad the city of
    God,
The holy *place* of the
    tabernacle of the Most High.
5 God *is* in the midst of her,
    she shall not be moved;
God shall help her,
    just at the break of dawn.
6 The nations raged, the
    kingdoms were moved;
He uttered His voice, the
    earth melted.

7 The LORD of hosts *is* with us;
The God of Jacob *is* our
    refuge.   Selah

8 Come, behold the works of
    the LORD,
Who has made desolations in
    the earth.
9 He makes wars cease to the
    end of the earth;
He breaks the bow
    and cuts the spear in two;
He burns the chariot in the
    fire.

10 Be still, and know that I *am*
    God;
I will be exalted among the
    nations,
I will be exalted in the earth!

11 The LORD of hosts *is* with us;
The God of Jacob *is* our
    refuge.   Selah

PSALM 47

To the Chief Musician. A Psalm of the sons of
Korah.

OH, clap your hands, all you
    peoples!
Shout to God with the voice
    of triumph!
2 For the LORD Most High *is*
    awesome;

He is a great King over all the
    earth.
3 He will subdue the peoples
    under us,
And the nations under our
    feet.
4 He will choose our inheritance
    for us,
The excellence of Jacob whom
    He loves.   Selah

5 God has gone up with a shout,
The LORD with the sound of a
    trumpet.
6 Sing praises to God, sing
    praises!
Sing praises to our King, sing
    praises!
7 For God *is* the King of all the
    earth;
Sing praises with
    understanding.

8 God reigns over the nations;
God sits on His holy throne.
9 The princes of the people have
    gathered together.
The people of the God of
    Abraham.
For the shields of the earth
    belong to God;
He is greatly exalted.

PSALM 48

A Song. A Psalm of the sons of Korah.

GREAT *is* the LORD,
    and greatly to be praised
In the city of our God,
In His holy mountain.
2 Beautiful in elevation,
The joy of the whole earth,
Is Mount Zion *on* the sides of
    the north,
The city of the great King.
3 God *is* in her palaces;
He is known as her refuge.

4 For behold, the kings
    assembled,
They passed by together.
5 They saw *it, and* so they
    marveled;

*Sought through prayer and meditation to improve our conscious contact with God **as we understood Him,** praying only for knowledge of His will for us and the power to carry that out.*

Psalm 47:6–9

Our corporate and private worship of God is centered in our praise to Him. And we are not alone in this thanksgiving and adoration. Indeed Psalm 145:10 declares "All Your works shall praise You, O LORD." The Old and New Testaments are filled with exhortations encouraging us to praise God and examples of praise in the lives of the saints. Praise is a vital ingredient in a strong Christian walk. But negative attitudes and fear can sidetrack us from true praise to God. This is why Psalm 47:7 tells us to sing praises *with understanding.* The whole of Psalm 47 rejoices in who God is. The psalmist exalts in God's awesome power and love. His triumphant and joyful attitude of praise is a direct result of his firsthand knowledge and experience concerning his God.

The deeper and fuller our understanding of God is, the more natural and overflowing our praise will become. Determine to seek God's face in His Word and in prayer.

For further reading on Step 11, turn to page 623.

Daily
Encouragement

DAY 269 READING: PSALMS 47:1—48:14

A Thought for the New Day: Being an aimless wanderer in the world is not a happy condition, but it is the lot of many. "Eat, drink, and be merry" is their only option, because, when life is over, they see only a dead end. Such a life can have no purpose. However, if the Lord is "our God forever and ever" (48:14), we have purpose, and we have confidence that day by day our steps are rightly ordered. Even in death He is still with us. (*Turn to page 621.*)

They were troubled, they
hastened away.
6 Fear took hold of them there,
And pain, as of a woman in
travail,
7 *As when* You break the ships
of Tarshish
With an east wind.

8 As we have heard,
So we have seen
In the city of the LORD of
hosts,
In the city of our God:
God will establish it forever.
                 Selah

9 We have thought, O God, on
Your lovingkindness,
In the midst of Your temple.
10 According to Your name, O
God,
So *is* Your praise to the ends
of the earth;
Your right hand is full of
righteousness.
11 Let Mount Zion rejoice,
Let the daughters of Judah be
glad,
Because of Your judgments.

12 Walk about Zion,
And go all around her.
Count her towers;
13 Mark well her bulwarks;
Consider her palaces;
That you may tell *it*
to the generation following.
14 For this *is* God,
Our God forever and ever;
He will be our guide
Even to death.

PSALM 49

To the Chief Musician. A Psalm of the sons of
Korah.

HEAR this, all *you* peoples;
Give ear, all *you* inhabitants
of the world,
2 Both low and high,
Rich and poor together.
3 My mouth shall speak
wisdom,

And the meditation of my
heart *shall bring*
understanding.
4 I will incline my ear to a
proverb;
I will disclose my dark saying
on the harp.

5 Why should I fear in the days
of evil,
When the iniquity at my heels
surrounds me?
6 Those who trust in their
wealth
And boast in the multitude of
their riches,
7 None *of them* can by any
means redeem *his* brother,
Nor give to God a ransom for
him—
8 For the redemption of their
souls *is* costly,
And it shall cease forever—
9 That he should continue to
live eternally,
And not see the Pit.

10 For he sees *that* wise men die;
Likewise the fool and the
senseless person perish,
And leave their wealth to
others.
11 Their inner thought *is that*
their houses *will continue*
forever,
And their dwelling places to
all generations;
They call *their* lands after
their own names.
12 Nevertheless man, *though* in
honor, does not remain;
He is like the beasts *that*
perish.

13 This is the way of those who
are foolish,
And of their posterity who
approve their sayings. Selah
14 Like sheep they are laid in the
grave;
Death shall feed on them;
The upright shall have
dominion over them in the
morning;

*Continued to take personal inventory
and when we were wrong promptly admitted it.*

Psalm 49

When we have struggled and worked to get our lives back on course spiritually and emotionally, we may find ourselves irritated by people who obviously do not care about God. Seeing someone who is not only wicked, but who seems to prosper in that wickedness, can provoke feelings of jealousy and bitterness, as well as confusion. The author of Psalm 49 had obviously known the same feelings. He shares two basic thoughts for us to remember.

First, no matter how rich one is, wealth cannot prevent death. Each person will die at the time God has appointed for him, whether rich or poor.

Second, God's judgment on sin is as certain as God's rewards for His righteous ones. Through the incredibly vast ages of eternity, God's holy justice will erase the inequities of our short earthly lives.

When we remind ourselves of these truths, bitterness will not be able to take root, but the sweet flowers of joy will grow in abundance.

For further reading on Step 10, turn to page 653.

Daily Encouragement

DAY 270 READING: PSALM 49:1–20

A Thought for the New Day: The surprising declaration of verse 15 should be compared with the one in Psalm 16:10. We do not hear much about life beyond death in the Old Testament. Some skeptics even discount such life as an absent article in the Old Testament faith. However, like Job's shout of triumph in Job 19:25, here the sons of Korah proclaim their faith in the risen life. God created us to live with Him forever. (*Turn to page 623.*)

God the Righteous Judge

And their beauty shall be
consumed in the grave, far
from their dwelling.

15 But God will redeem my soul
from the power of the
grave,
For He shall receive me. Selah

16 Do not be afraid when one
becomes rich,
When the glory of his house is
increased;

17 For when he dies he shall
carry nothing away;
His glory shall not descend
after him.

18 Though while he lives he
blesses himself
(For *men* will praise you when
you do well for yourself),

19 He shall go to the generation
of his fathers;
They shall never see light.

20 Man *who is* in honor,
yet does not understand,
Is like the beasts *that* perish.

PSALM 50

A Psalm of Asaph.

THE Mighty One, God the
LORD,
Has spoken and called the
earth
From the rising of the sun to
its going down.

2 Out of Zion, the perfection of
beauty,
God will shine forth.

3 Our God shall come,
and shall not keep silent;
A fire shall devour before
Him,
And it shall be very
tempestuous all around
Him.

4 He shall call to the heavens
from above,
And to the earth,
that He may judge His
people:

5 "Gather My saints together to
Me,
Those who have made a
covenant with Me by
sacrifice."

6 Let the heavens declare His
righteousness,
For God Himself *is* Judge.
Selah

7 "Hear, O My people, and I will
speak,
O Israel, and I will testify
against you;
I *am* God, your God!

8 I will not reprove you for your
sacrifices
Or your burnt offerings,
Which are continually before
Me.

9 I will not take a bull from
your house,
Nor goats out of your folds.

10 For every beast of the forest *is*
Mine,
And the cattle on a thousand
hills.

11 I know all the birds of the
mountains,
And the wild beasts of the
field *are* Mine.

12 "If I were hungry, I would not
tell you;
For the world *is* Mine,
and all its fullness.

13 Will I eat the flesh of bulls,
Or drink the blood of goats?

14 Offer to God thanksgiving,
And pay your vows to the
Most High.

15 Call upon Me in the day of
trouble;
I will deliver you,
and you shall glorify Me."

STEP
11

16 But to the wicked God says:
"What *right* have you to
declare My statutes,
Or take My covenant in your
mouth,

17 Seeing you hate instruction

622

STEP 11

*Sought through prayer and meditation to improve our conscious contact with God **as we understood Him,** praying only for knowledge of His will for us and the power to carry that out.*

Psalm 50:14, 15

A vow to God is a serious step, but such a vow can bring greater results and breakthroughs in our lives than anything else can do. When we seem continually to come up against a solid wall in our efforts to defeat a habit or correct a situation, God may sometimes lead us to make a vow to Him. Vows are as individual as the people who make them, but their unifying chord is that the person making the vow desires God's will and blessing and is willing to take whatever steps necessary in order to release God's power to move and work and heal. A vow is a promise to God that must not be broken. This is why careful consideration must be the rule before a vow is made.

But when God sees the earnest sincerity of heart that prompts a vow, He releases power we never knew existed and delivers us in mighty and glorious ways that bring honor to Him.

For further reading on Step 11, turn to page 631.

Daily Encouragement

DAY 271 READING: PSALM 50:1–23

A Thought for the New Day: The ancient writer of this poem was telling his contemporaries that God was more interested in the grateful offerings of their hearts than in their religious reforms. We dare not let our worship become thoughtless ritual, although ritual can be helpful in focusing our attention on what is important in worship. Rather, our worship should express the true gratitude of our heart for God's infinite benefits (v. 14). *(Turn to page 625.)*

And cast My words behind
  you?

18 When you saw a thief,
  you consented with him,
  And have been a partaker
  with adulterers.
19 You give your mouth to evil,
  And your tongue frames
  deceit.
20 You sit *and* speak against
  your brother;
  You slander your own
  mother's son.
21 These *things* you have done,
  and I kept silent;
  You thought that I was
  altogether like you;
  But I will reprove you,
  And set *them* in order before
  your eyes.

22 "Now consider this, you who
  forget God,
  Lest I tear *you* in pieces,
  And *there be* none to deliver:
23 Whoever offers praise glorifies
  Me;
  And to him who orders *his*
  conduct *aright*
  I will show the salvation of
  God."

PSALM 51

To the Chief Musician. A Psalm of David when
Nathan the prophet went to him, after he had
gone in to Bathsheba.

HAVE mercy upon me, O God,
  According to Your
  lovingkindness;
  According to the multitude of
  Your tender mercies,
  Blot out my transgressions.
2 Wash me thoroughly from my
  iniquity,
  And cleanse me from my sin.

3 For I acknowledge my
  transgressions,
  And my sin *is* ever before me.
4 Against You, You only, have I
  sinned,
  And done *this* evil in Your
  sight—

That You may be found just
  when You speak,
  And blameless when You
  judge.

5 Behold, I was brought forth in
  iniquity,
  And in sin my mother
  conceived me.
6 Behold, You desire truth in
  the inward parts,
  And in the hidden *part* You
  will make me to know
  wisdom.

7 Purge me with hyssop,
  and I shall be clean;
  Wash me, and I shall be
  whiter than snow.
8 Make me to hear joy and
  gladness,
  That the bones *which* You
  have broken may rejoice.
9 Hide Your face from my sins,
  And blot out all my iniquities.

10 Create in me a clean heart, O
  God,
  And renew a steadfast spirit
  within me.

11 Do not cast me away from
  Your presence,
  And do not take Your Holy
  Spirit from me.

12 Restore to me the joy of Your
  salvation,
  And uphold me *with Your*
  generous Spirit.
13 *Then* I will teach
  transgressors Your ways,
  And sinners shall be converted
  to You.

14 Deliver me from
  bloodguiltiness, O God,
  The God of my salvation,
  And my tongue shall sing
  aloud of Your righteousness.

15 O Lord, open my lips,
  And my mouth shall show
  forth Your praise.

STEP 5

Admitted to God, to ourselves, and to another human being the exact nature of our wrongs.

Psalm 51:3–6

God's blessing is upon us when we become willing and able to accomplish Step 5. God desires "truth in the inward parts." Even though David was aware of this, he still had trouble admitting and confessing his sin until his friend, Nathan the prophet, confronted him. None of us enjoys scrutinizing the deep motives of our lives or admitting that we have sinned and offended God. But we should not feel isolated in that acknowledgment. We are all born sinners, "brought forth in iniquity." When we can accept this truth in general and the specifics of our own wrongs, we take a great step toward wholeness. We also take our first steps toward real wisdom. Wisdom is often characterized as the ability to take what is learned and apply it to specific life situations.

Admitting the truth concerning our inner self makes us ready for God to give us wisdom for inner healing, too.

For further reading on Step 5, turn to page 637.

Daily Encouragement

DAY 272 READING: PSALM 51:1–13

A Thought for the New Day: Our hearts are filled with boundless joy when God first draws us into His family circle. After a while the cares of just being in the world may weigh us down: then that special joy departs. It is a rare individual who does not find himself or herself in this place sometimes. Let us be quick to remember that God stands ready to renew His joy within us (v. 12). (*Turn to page 626.*)

STEP 9

*Made direct amends to such people wherever possible,
except when to do so would injure them or others.*

Psalm 51:14–17

David was the beloved psalmist and shepherd whom God elevated to king of Israel. One important reason David was able to fellowship so closely with God throughout his life was that he was willing to humble himself before God and others. Humility is an attitude that God has been building in us throughout our recovery program, and it is a key ingredient to the successful completion of Step 9.

David's words "broken and contrite" are very close in idea to the attitude underlying Step 9. In the same way David asked God to help him "open his lips," we should depend on God to bring a new power and grace to our lives as we correct past wrongs and achieve healthy ways of relating to the people around us.

As we turn to God for the willingness to make amends, we release ourselves from the power of old resentments, which have held us in bondage.

For further reading on Step 9, turn to page 767.

Daily Encouragement

DAY 273 READING: PSALMS 51:14—53:6

A Thought for the New Day: What is real fulfillment? It is the unique satisfaction that comes in knowing we are working within God's plan for our lives—setting and achieving the goals He wants us to reach. Doing so, we go on, like the "green olive tree" (52:8), bearing fruit every season. God has a special plan in mind for each of us. When that plan has been worked through, we will be all that He has delightedly designed us to be. (*Turn to page 629.*)

16 For You do not desire sacrifice, or else I would give *it;*
You do not delight in burnt
offering.
17 The sacrifices of God *are* a
broken spirit,
A broken and a contrite
heart—
These, O God, You will not
despise.

18 Do good in Your good
pleasure to Zion;
Build the walls of Jerusalem.
19 Then You shall be pleased
with the sacrifices of
righteousness,
With burnt offering and whole
burnt offering;
Then they shall offer bulls on
Your altar.

PSALM 52

To the Chief Musician. A Contemplation of
David when Doeg the Edomite went and told
Saul, and said to him, "David has gone to the
house of Ahimelech."

WHY do you boast in evil,
O mighty man?
The goodness of God *endures*
continually.
2 Your tongue devises
destruction,
Like a sharp razor, working
deceitfully.
3 You love evil more than good,
And lying rather than
speaking righteousness.
Selah
4 You love all devouring words,
You deceitful tongue.

5 God shall likewise destroy you
forever;
He shall take you away, and
pluck you out of *your*
dwelling place,
And uproot you from the land
of the living.   Selah
6 The righteous also shall see
and fear,

And shall laugh at him,
saying,
7 "Here is the man *who* did not
make God his strength,
But trusted in the abundance
of his riches,
And strengthened himself
in his wickedness."

8 But I *am* like a green olive
tree in the house of God;
I trust in the mercy of God
forever and ever.
9 I will praise You forever,
Because You have done *it;*
And in the presence of Your
saints
I will wait on Your name,
for *it is* good.

PSALM 53

To the Chief Musician. Set to "Mahalath." A
Contemplation of David.

THE fool has said in his heart,
"*There is* no God."
They are corrupt,
and have done abominable
iniquity;
There is none who does good.

2 God looks down from heaven
upon the children of men,
To see if there are *any* who
understand, who seek God.
3 Every one of them has turned
aside;
They have together become
corrupt;
There is none who does good,
No, not one.

4 Have the workers of iniquity
no knowledge,
Who eat up my people *as* they
eat bread,
And do not call upon God?
5 There they are in great fear
Where no fear was,
For God has scattered the
bones of him who encamps
against you;
You have put *them* to shame,
Because God has despised
them.

6 Oh, that the salvation of Israel
would come out of Zion!
When God brings back the
captivity of His people,
Let Jacob rejoice *and* Israel be
glad.

PSALM 54

To the Chief Musician. With stringed
instruments. A Contemplation of David when
the Ziphites went and said to Saul, "Is David
not hiding with us?"

S AVE me, O God, by Your
name,
And vindicate me by Your
strength.
2 Hear my prayer, O God;
Give ear to the words of my
mouth.
3 For strangers have risen up
against me,
And oppressors have sought
after my life;
They have not set God before
them.   Selah

4 Behold, God *is* my helper;
The Lord *is* with those who
uphold my life.
5 He will repay my enemies for
their evil.
Cut them off in Your truth.

6 I will freely sacrifice to You;
I will praise Your name, O
LORD, for *it is* good.
7 For He has delivered me out
of all trouble;
And my eye has seen *its*
desire upon my enemies.

PSALM 55

To the Chief Musician. With stringed
instruments. A Contemplation of David.

G IVE ear to my prayer, O God,
And do not hide Yourself
from my supplication.
2 Attend to me, and hear me;
I am restless in my complaint,
and moan noisily,

3 Because of the voice of the
enemy,
Because of the oppression of
the wicked;
For they bring down trouble
upon me,
And in wrath they hate me.

4 My heart is severely pained
within me,
And the terrors of death have
fallen upon me.
5 Fearfulness and trembling
have come upon me,
And horror has overwhelmed
me.
6 And I said, "Oh, that I had
wings like a dove!
For then I would fly away
and be at rest.
7 Indeed, I would wander far
off,
And remain in the wilderness.
Selah
8 I would hasten my escape
From the windy storm *and*
tempest."

9 Destroy, O Lord, *and* divide
their tongues,
For I have seen violence and
strife in the city.
10 Day and night they go around
it on its walls;
Iniquity and trouble *are* also
in the midst of it.
11 Destruction *is* in its midst;
Deceit and guile do not depart
from its streets.

12 For *it is* not an enemy *who*
reproaches me;
Then I could bear *it*.
Nor *is it* one *who* hates me
who has magnified *himself*
against me;
Then I could hide from him.
13 But *it was* you, a man my
equal,
My companion and my
acquaintance.
14 We took sweet counsel
together,

STEP 1

*We admitted we were powerless over our dependencies—
that our lives had become unmanageable.*

Psalm 55:4–8

Escape has been the unspoken motto of life for many of us. Because our relationships or work or inner self often becomes too unbearable, we have developed a favorite way of escape. For some, it is drugs or alcohol; for others, it may be overspending, overeating, or pornography. The ways to escape reality are numerous indeed, but the underlying reason is always the same: our lives are so full of pain and fear that we can no longer cope with them. Our chosen dependency gives us respite for a little while, but then the pain returns. However, when our world is filled with "the windy storm *and* tempest" and the trouble seems unbearable, there *is* a place of mercy, peace, security, and love available to us. That place is not a temporary high but rather an experience of permanence and stability in the arms of God. When we can admit the unbearableness of our lives, we can finally find rest in Him.

For further reading on Step 1, turn to page 647.

Daily Encouragement

DAY 274 READING: PSALMS 54:1—55:8

A Thought for the New Day: Life is not always pleasant. Hard times come, and we find out that even best friends can fail us. But isn't it great to know that we do have a safe hiding place from these storms? David knew this (55:6), and so can we. Perhaps one of the greatest statements of theological truth is that "Jesus Never Fails." He takes us into His own home, heals up our wounds, and wipes away all tears. (*Turn to page 631.*)

Prayer for Relief

And walked to the house of
God in the throng.

15 Let death seize them;
Let them go down alive into
hell,
For wickedness *is* in their
dwellings *and* among them.

16 As for me, I will call upon
God,
And the LORD shall save me.
17 Evening and morning and at
noon
I will pray, and cry aloud,
And He shall hear my voice.
18 He has redeemed my soul in
peace from the battle *which
was* against me,
For there were many against
me.

19 God will hear, and afflict
them.
Even He who abides from of
old.   Selah
Because they do not change,
Therefore they do not fear
God.

20 He has put forth his hands
against those who were at
peace with him;
He has broken his covenant.
21 *The words* of his mouth were
smoother than butter,
But war *was* in his heart;
His words were softer than oil,
Yet they *were* drawn swords.

22 Cast your burden on the
LORD,
And He shall sustain you;
He shall never permit the
righteous to be moved.

23 But You, O God, shall bring
them down to the pit of
destruction;
Bloodthirsty and deceitful men
shall not live out half their
days;
But I will trust in You.

PSALM 56

*To the Chief Musician. Set to "The Silent Dove
in Distant Lands." A Michtam of David when
the Philistines captured him in Gath.*

BE merciful to me, O God,
for man would swallow me
up;
Fighting all day he oppresses
me.
2 My enemies would hound *me*
all day,
For *there are* many who fight
against me, O Most High.

3 Whenever I am afraid,
I will trust in You.
4 In God (I will praise His
word),
In God I have put my trust;
I will not fear.
What can flesh do to me?

5 All day they twist my words;
All their thoughts *are* against
me for evil.
6 They gather together,
They hide, they mark my
steps,
When they lie in wait for my
life.
7 Shall they escape by iniquity?
In anger cast down the
peoples, O God!

8 You number my wanderings;
Put my tears into Your bottle;
Are they not in Your book?
9 When I cry out *to You,*
Then my enemies will turn
back;
This I know, because God *is*
for me.
10 In God (I will praise *His*
word),
In the LORD (I will praise *His*
word),
11 In God I have put my trust;
I will not be afraid.
What can man do to me?

12 Vows *made* to You *are*
binding upon me, O God;
I will render praises to You,

*Sought through prayer and meditation to improve our conscious contact with God **as we understood Him,** praying only for knowledge of His will for us and the power to carry that out.*

Psalm 55:22

Grace, the enabling power of God in our lives, is the believer's ever-present stability and strength. Our lives will never be free of dangers and temptations until we go home to heaven. But God promises us that He will not allow those things to overwhelm us *if* we remember to cast our burdens on Him. Too many times we seek to handle the problems, temptations, and sorrows of life in our own strength and intellect. But in verse 22 we find both a command and a promise. When we quit carrying our burdens ourselves and instead lay them at God's feet, we are obeying His Word. Our obedience and trust are rewarded with God's strength meeting us in our time of need and His wisdom directing our thoughts and actions. He cares deeply about our physical, emotional, and spiritual stability; and as we obey His admonition here, He honors our obedience with peace and confident security in Him.

For further reading on Step 11, turn to page 671.

Daily Encouragement

DAY 275 READING: PSALMS 55:9—57:11

A Thought for the New Day: Everyone is afraid of something sometimes (56:3). What do we do with our fear? A dying lady seemed to be listening to a favorite hymn that was being read to her, and then fell ominously silent. After a long moment, however, her lips parted as she whispered the beloved line: "I am His, and He is mine." Thus fearlessly her earthly life drew beautifully to its close. (*Turn to page 635.*)

13 For You have delivered my
      soul from death.
      Have You not *delivered* my
      feet from falling,
      That I may walk before God
      In the light of the living?

PSALM 57

To the Chief Musician. Set to "Do Not
Destroy." A Michtam of David when he fled
from Saul into the cave.

BE merciful to me, O God,
      be merciful to me!
      For my soul trusts in You;
      And in the shadow of Your
      wings I will make my
      refuge,
      Until *these* calamities have
      passed by.

2 I will cry out to God Most
      High,
      To God who performs *all
      things* for me.
3 He shall send from heaven
      and save me;
      He reproaches the one who
      would swallow me up. Selah
      God shall send forth His
      mercy and His truth.

4 My soul *is* among lions;
      I lie *among* the sons of men
      Who are set on fire,
      Whose teeth *are* spears and
      arrows,
      And their tongue a sharp
      sword.
5 Be exalted, O God, above the
      heavens;
      Let Your glory *be* above all
      the earth.

6 They have prepared a net for
      my steps;
      My soul is bowed down;
      They have dug a pit before
      me;
      Into the midst of it they
      themselves have fallen.
                                          Selah

7 My heart is steadfast, O God,
      my heart is steadfast;
      I will sing and give praise.
8 Awake, my glory!
      Awake, lute and harp!
      I will awaken the dawn.

9 I will praise You, O Lord,
      among the peoples;
      I will sing to You among the
      nations.
10 For Your mercy reaches unto
      the heavens,
      And Your truth unto the
      clouds.

11 Be exalted, O God, above the
      heavens;
      Let Your glory *be* above all
      the earth.

PSALM 58

To the Chief Musician. Set to "Do Not
Destroy." A Michtam of David.

DO you indeed speak
      righteousness,
      you silent ones?
      Do you judge uprightly,
      you sons of men?
2 No, in heart you work
      wickedness;
      You weigh out the violence of
      your hands in the earth.

3 The wicked are estranged
      from the womb;
      They go astray as soon as
      they are born, speaking lies.
4 Their poison *is* like the poison
      of a serpent;
      They are like the deaf cobra
      that stops its ear,
5 Which will not heed the voice
      of charmers,
      Charming ever so skillfully.

6 Break their teeth in their
      mouth, O God!
      Break out the fangs of the
      young lions, O LORD!
7 Let them flow away as waters
      which run continually;

When he bends *his bow*,
Let his arrows be as if cut in
pieces.
8 *Let them be* like a snail which
melts away as it goes,
Like a stillborn child of a
woman, that they may not
see the sun.

9 Before your pots can feel *the
burning* thorns,
He shall take them away as
with a whirlwind,
As in His living and burning
wrath.
10 The righteous shall rejoice
when he sees the
vengeance;
He shall wash his feet in the
blood of the wicked,
11 So that men will say,
"Surely *there is* a reward for
the righteous;
Surely He is God who judges
in the earth."

PSALM 59

To the Chief Musician. Set to "Do Not
Destroy." A Michtam of David when Saul sent
men, and they watched the house in order to
kill him.

DELIVER me from my enemies,
O my God;
Defend me from those who
rise up against me.
2 Deliver me from the workers
of iniquity,
And save me from
bloodthirsty men.

3 For look, they lie in wait for
my life;
The mighty gather against me,
Not *for* my transgression nor
for my sin, O LORD.
4 They run and prepare
themselves through no fault
of *mine*.

Awake to help me, and
behold!

5 You therefore, O LORD God of
hosts, the God of Israel,
Awake to punish all the
nations;
Do not be merciful to any
wicked transgressors.   Selah

6 At evening they return,
They growl like a dog,
And go all around the city.
7 Indeed, they belch out with
their mouth;
Swords *are* in their lips;
For *they say*, "Who hears?"

8 But You, O LORD, shall laugh
at them;
You shall have all the nations
in derision.
9 O *You* his Strength,
I will wait for You.

For God *is* my defense;
10 My merciful God shall come
to meet me;
God shall let me see *my desire*
on my enemies.

11 Do not slay them,
lest my people forget;
Scatter them by Your power,
And bring them down,
O Lord our shield.
12 *For* the sin of their mouth *and*
the words of their lips,
Let them even be taken in
their pride,
And for the cursing and lying
which they speak.
13 Consume *them* in wrath,
consume *them*,
That they *may* not *be;*
And let them know that God
rules in Jacob
To the ends of the earth.
Selah

14 And at evening they return,
They growl like a dog,
And go all around the city.
15 They wander up and down for
food,
And howl if they are not
satisfied.

16 But I will sing of Your power;
Yes, I will sing aloud of Your
mercy in the morning;
For You have been my
defense
And refuge in the day of my
trouble.

17 To You, O my Strength,
I will sing praises;
For God *is* my defense,
The God of my mercy.

PSALM 60

To the Chief Musician. Set to "Lily of the
Testimony." A Michtam of David. For
teaching. When he fought against
Mesopotamia and Syria of Zobah, and Joab
returned and killed twelve thousand Edomites
in the Valley of Salt.

O GOD, You have cast us off;
You have broken us down;
You have been displeased;
Oh, restore us again!

2 You have made the earth
tremble;
You have broken it;
Heal its breaches, for it is
shaking.

3 You have shown Your people
hard things;
You have made us drink the
wine of confusion.

4 You have given a banner to
those who fear You,
That it may be displayed
because of the truth.   Selah

5 That Your beloved may be
delivered,
Save *with* Your right hand,
and hear me.

6 God has spoken in His
holiness:
"I will rejoice;
I will divide Shechem
And measure out the Valley of
Succoth.

7 Gilead *is* Mine, and Manasseh
is Mine;
Ephraim also *is* the helmet for
My head;
Judah *is* My lawgiver.

8 Moab *is* My washpot;
Over Edom I will cast My
shoe;
Philistia, shout in triumph
because of Me."

9 Who will bring me *into* the
strong city?
Who will lead me to Edom?

10 *Is it* not You, O God, *who* cast
us off?
And *You*, O God, *who* did not
go out with our armies?

11 Give us help from trouble,
For vain *is* the help of man.

12 Through God we will do
valiantly,
For *it is* He *who* shall tread
down our enemies.

PSALM 61

To the Chief Musician. On a stringed
instrument. A Psalm of David.

HEAR my cry, O God;
Attend to my prayer.

2 From the end of the earth I
will cry to You,
When my heart is
overwhelmed;
Lead me to the rock that is
higher than I.

3 For You have been a shelter
for me,
And a strong tower from the
enemy.

4 I will abide in Your tabernacle
forever;
I will trust in the shelter of
Your wings.   Selah

5 For You, O God, have heard
my vows;
You have given *me* the
heritage of those who fear
Your name.

6 You will prolong the king's
life,
His years as many
generations.

7 He shall abide before God
forever.

STEP 3

*Made a decision to turn our will and our lives
over to the care of God **as we understood Him.***

Psalm 61:1–4

If you have ever spent any time observing birds, you may have witnessed a powerful instinct given for protection of the young. Whenever danger threatens, a warning call comes from the mother. All the young scurry to the shelter of her wings, which will hide them from the enemy's eyes and claws. There is no hesitation on the part of the chicks when that warning call is sounded, for they instinctively know two things. First, they know they are helpless; and second, they know that under their parent's wings they will be safe and secure.

We have come to the same basic understanding of our own situation. Now it is time to commit our will and our lives to the One who can protect us from all our enemies, within and without.

God is listening to our cries for help. He wants to cover us with His wings of protection and love. But we ourselves must run to those "wings" by committing all that we are to Him.

For further reading on Step 3, turn to page 643.

Daily Encouragement

DAY 276 READING: PSALMS 58:1—61:8

A Thought for the New Day: In these beautiful lines by David we are lifted up to God, "to the rock that is higher than I" (61:1–4). Ideally, prayer should do that very thing for us; otherwise we come away feeling that we have just wasted time. But even in the dry seasons, when we may feel no inner renewal, let us remember that God Himself is not deaf to the cry of our hearts. He understands our "lows" and our "highs," and He is steadfastly faithful. *(Turn to page 637.)*

God Our Salvation

Oh, prepare mercy and truth,
which may preserve him!

8 So I will sing praise to Your
name forever,
That I may daily perform my
vows.

PSALM 62

To the Chief Musician. To Jeduthun. A Psalm
of David.

TRULY my soul silently *waits*
for God;
From Him *comes* my
salvation.
2 He only *is* my rock and my
salvation;
He is my defense;
I shall not be greatly moved.

3 How long will you attack a
man?
You shall be slain, all of you,
Like a leaning wall and a
tottering fence.
4 They only consult to cast *him*
down from his high
position;
They delight in lies;
They bless with their mouth,
But they curse inwardly.
Selah

5 My soul, wait silently for God
alone,
For my expectation *is* from
Him.
6 He only *is* my rock and my
salvation;
He is my defense;
I shall not be moved.
7 In God *is* my salvation and
my glory;
The rock of my strength,
And my refuge, *is* in God.

8 Trust in Him at all times, you
people;
Pour out your heart before
Him;
God *is* a refuge for us.   Selah

9 Surely men of low degree *are*
a vapor,

Men of high degree *are* a lie;
If they are weighed in the
balances,
They *are* altogether *lighter*
than vapor.
10 Do not trust in oppression,
Nor vainly hope in robbery;
If riches increase,
Do not set *your* heart *on*
them.

11 God has spoken once,
Twice I have heard this:
That power *belongs* to God.
12 Also to You, O Lord, *belongs*
mercy;
For You render to each one
according to his work.

PSALM 63

A Psalm of David when he was in the
wilderness of Judah.

O GOD, You *are* my God;
Early will I seek You;
My soul thirsts for You;
My flesh longs for You
In a dry and thirsty land
Where there is no water.
2 So I have looked for You
in the sanctuary,
To see Your power and
Your glory.

3 Because Your lovingkindness
is better than life,
My lips shall praise You.
4 Thus I will bless You while I
live;
I will lift up my hands in Your
name.
5 My soul shall be satisfied as
with marrow and fatness,
And my mouth shall praise
You with joyful lips.

6 When I remember You on my
bed,
I meditate on You in the *night*
watches.
7 Because You have been my
help,
Therefore in the shadow of
Your wings I will rejoice.

STEP 5

Admitted to God, to ourselves, and to another human being the exact nature of our wrongs.

Psalm 62:8

Language can be a frustrating tool at times. When we want to express the deepest thoughts of our hearts, words often fail us. But the mind and compassion of God are not bound by our ability to express ourselves in oral or written form. God knows and sympathizes with the part of us that is so deep that words are inadequate to express it. So when we come before God, finally able to admit what has gone wrong with our past, we need not feel tongue-tied or embarrassed by the depths of emotion we may suddenly feel. God can hear the cries too deep for words alone. He sees the sorrow and pain and regret that cannot fully be expressed in words. When we pour out our hearts before Him, He honors our sincerity, accepts our confession, and bends to comfort us in our pain. He is a Friend we can trust with the deepest secrets of our lives.

For further reading on Step 5, turn to page 645.

Daily Encouragement

DAY 277 READING: PSALMS 62:1—64:10

A Thought for the New Day: Sometimes our times of meditation and prayer just "happen." These are often the richest times. We may be on an airplane, in a slow period at work, or out on a walk. Suddenly we find ourselves being lifted up to heaven with the most amazing thoughts of God and His goodness. This apparently was common for David when he could not sleep (63:6–8). Likewise, our otherwise empty moments can be opportunities for sweet communion with God. (*Turn to page 641.*)

8 My soul follows close behind
   You;
   Your right hand upholds me.

9 But those *who* seek my life,
   to destroy *it*,
   Shall go into the lower parts
   of the earth.
10 They shall fall by the sword;
   They shall be a portion for
   jackals.

11 But the king shall rejoice in
   God;
   Everyone who swears by Him
   shall glory;
   But the mouth of those who
   speak lies shall be stopped.

PSALM 64

To the Chief Musician. A Psalm of David.

HEAR my voice, O God, in my
   meditation;
   Preserve my life from fear of
   the enemy.
2 Hide me from the secret
   counsel of the wicked,
   From the insurrection of the
   workers of iniquity,
3 Who sharpen their tongue like
   a sword,
   And bend *their bows to shoot*
   their arrows—bitter words,
4 That they may shoot in secret
   at the blameless;
   Suddenly they shoot at him
   and do not fear.

5 They encourage themselves *in*
   an evil matter;
   They talk of laying snares
   secretly;
   They say, "Who will see
   them?"
6 They devise iniquities:
   "We have perfected a shrewd
   scheme."
   Both the inward thought and
   the heart of man are deep.

7 But God shall shoot at them
   with an arrow;

Suddenly they shall be
   wounded.
8 So He will make them stumble
   over their own tongue;
   All who see them shall flee
   away.
9 All men shall fear,
   And shall declare the work of
   God;
   For they shall wisely consider
   His doing.

10 The righteous shall be glad in
   the LORD, and trust in Him.
   And all the upright in heart
   shall glory.

PSALM 65

To the Chief Musician. A Psalm of David. A
Song.

PRAISE is awaiting You, O
   God, in Zion;
   And to You the vow shall be
   performed.
2 O You who hear prayer,
   To You all flesh will come.
3 Iniquities prevail against me;
   As for our transgressions,
   You will provide atonement
   for them.

4 Blessed *is the man whom* You
   choose,
   And cause to approach *You,*
   That he may dwell in Your
   courts.
   We shall be satisfied with the
   goodness of Your house,
   Of Your holy temple.

5 *By* awesome deeds in
   righteousness You will
   answer us,
   O God of our salvation,
   You who are the confidence of
   all the ends of the earth,
   And of the far-off seas;
6 Who established the
   mountains by His strength,
   Being clothed with power;
7 You who still the noise of the
   seas,

The noise of their waves,
And the tumult of the peoples.
8 They also who dwell in the
farthest parts are afraid of
Your signs;
You make the outgoings of
the morning and evening
rejoice.

9 You visit the earth and water
it,
You greatly enrich it;
The river of God is full of
water;
You provide their grain,
For so You have prepared it.
10 You water its ridges
abundantly,
You settle its furrows;
You make it soft with
showers,
You bless its growth.

11 You crown the year with
Your goodness,
And Your paths drip *with*
abundance.
12 They drop *on* the pastures of
the wilderness,
And the little hills rejoice on
every side.
13 The pastures are clothed with
flocks;
The valleys also are covered
with grain;
They shout for joy, they also
sing.

PSALM 66

To the Chief Musician. A Song. A Psalm.

MAKE a joyful shout to God,
all the earth!
2 Sing out the honor of His
name;
Make His praise glorious.
3 Say to God,
"How awesome are Your
works!
Through the greatness of
Your power
Your enemies shall submit
themselves to You.

4 All the earth shall worship
You
And sing praises to You;
They shall sing praises *to*
Your name."　　　Selah

5 Come and see the works of
God;
He is awesome *in His* doing
toward the sons of men.
6 He turned the sea into dry
land;
They went through the river
on foot.
There we will rejoice in Him.
7 He rules by His power forever;
His eyes observe the nations;
Do not let the rebellious exalt
themselves.　　　Selah

8 Oh, bless our God, you
peoples!
And make the voice of His
praise to be heard,
9 Who keeps our soul among
the living,
And does not allow our feet to
be moved.
10 For You, O God, have proved
us;
You have refined us as silver
is refined.
11 You brought us into the net;
You laid affliction on our
backs.
12 You have caused men to ride
over our heads;
We went through fire
and through water;
But You brought us out to
rich *fulfillment.*

13 I will go into Your house with
burnt offerings;
I will pay You my vows,
14 Which my lips have uttered
And my mouth has spoken
when I was in trouble.
15 I will offer You burnt
sacrifices of fat animals,
With the sweet aroma of
rams;
I will offer bulls with goats.
　　　　　　　　　Selah

PSALM 66:16

16 Come *and* hear, all you who
  fear God,
  And I will declare what He
  has done for my soul.
17 I cried to Him with my
  mouth,
  And He was extolled with my
  tongue.

STEP 4

18 If I regard iniquity in my
  heart,
  The Lord will not hear.
19 *But* certainly God has heard
  me;
  He has attended to the voice
  of my prayer.

20 Blessed *be* God,
  Who has not turned away my
  prayer,
  Nor His mercy from me!

PSALM 67

To the Chief Musician. On stringed
instruments. A Psalm. A Song.

GOD be merciful to us and
  bless us,
  And cause His face to shine
  upon us,   Selah
2 That Your way may be known
  on earth,
  Your salvation among all
  nations.

3 Let the peoples praise You, O
  God;
  Let all the peoples praise You.
4 Oh, let the nations be glad
  and sing for joy!
  For You shall judge the
  people righteously,
  And govern the nations on
  earth.   Selah

5 Let the peoples praise You, O
  God;
  Let all the peoples praise You.
6 *Then* the earth shall yield her
  increase;
  God, our own God, shall bless
  us.
7 God shall bless us,
  And all the ends of the earth
  shall fear Him.

God's Goodness to Israel

PSALM 68

To the Chief Musician. A Psalm of David. A
Song.

LET God arise,
  Let His enemies be scattered;
  Let those also who hate Him
  flee before Him.
2 As smoke is driven away,
  So drive *them* away;
  As wax melts before the fire,
  So let the wicked perish at the
  presence of God.
3 But let the righteous be glad;
  Let them rejoice before God;
  Yes, let them rejoice
  exceedingly.

4 Sing to God, sing praises to
  His name;
  Extol Him who rides on the
  clouds,
  By His name YAH,
  And rejoice before Him.

5 A father of the fatherless,
  a defender of widows,
  Is God in His holy habitation.
6 God sets the solitary in
  families;
  He brings out those who are
  bound into prosperity;
  But the rebellious dwell in a
  dry *land.*

7 O God, when You went out
  before Your people,
  When You marched through
  the wilderness,   Selah
8 The earth shook;
  The heavens also dropped *rain*
  at the presence of God;
  Sinai itself *was moved* at the
  presence of God, the God of
  Israel.
9 You, O God, sent a plentiful
  rain,
  Whereby You confirmed Your
  inheritance,
  When it was weary.
10 Your congregation dwelt in it;
  You, O God, provided from
  Your goodness for the poor.

STEP 4

Made a searching and fearless moral inventory of ourselves.
Psalm 66:18

Once we have accepted Jesus as our Savior, we quickly become aware of the fact that God wants us to obey the exhortations, commands, and principles of His Word. Most of us try not to rebel openly against God. However, those of us with dependencies are extremely vulnerable to another kind of sin trap. It is the trap of excuses and denial. Many of us have spent our entire lives perfecting these two techniques, and so it is even difficult to realize we are trapped. Furthermore, these devices may have become so much a part of our daily lives that we are unaware of the hold they have on us and the damage they have caused.

This is why it is so important for us to come to Step 4 as honestly and openly as we know how. Whatever our blind spots are, we must be willing to allow the Holy Spirit to shine His light into those dark corners and face the problems uncovered there.

For further reading on Step 4, turn to page 655.

Daily Encouragement

DAY 278 READING: PSALMS 65:1—67:7

A Thought for the New Day: It is a healthy exercise to consider often God's creative works (65:6–8). The mighty mountains speak so loudly of His awesome majesty. The trees, flowers, bubbling brooks, and cloud-decked skies show His glory and beauty. We are too self-centered: "What's in it for me?" But God draws us out of ourselves to honor Him for all that He is. (*Turn to page 643.*)

11 The Lord gave the word;
Great *was* the company of
those who proclaimed *it:*

12 "Kings of armies flee, they flee,
And she who remains at home
divides the spoil.

13 Though you lie down among
the sheepfolds,
Yet you will be like the wings
of a dove covered with
silver,
And her feathers with yellow
gold."

14 When the Almighty scattered
kings in it,
It was *white* as snow in
Zalmon.

15 A mountain of God *is* the
mountain of Bashan;
A mountain *of many* peaks
is the mountain of Bashan.

16 Why do you fume with envy,
you mountains of *many*
peaks?
This is the mountain *which*
God desires to dwell in;
Yes, the LORD will dwell *in it*
forever.

17 The chariots of God *are*
twenty thousand,
Even thousands of thousands;
The Lord is among them *as in*
Sinai, in the Holy *Place.*

18 You have ascended on high,
You have led captivity
captive;
You have received gifts
among men,
Even *among* the rebellious,
That the LORD God might
dwell *there.*

STEP
3

19 Blessed *be* the Lord,
Who daily loads us *with
benefits,*
The God of our salvation!
Selah

20 Our God *is* the God of
salvation;
And to GOD the Lord *belong*
escapes from death.

21 But God will wound the head
of His enemies,
The hairy scalp of the one
who still goes on in His
trespasses.

22 The Lord said, "I will bring
back from Bashan,
I will bring *them* back from
the depths of the sea,

23 That your foot may crush
them in blood,
And the tongues of your dogs
may have their portion from
your enemies."

24 They have seen Your
procession, O God,
The procession of my God, my
King, into the sanctuary.

25 The singers went before, the
players on instruments
followed after;
Among *them were* the
maidens playing timbrels.

26 Bless God in the
congregations,
The Lord, from the fountain
of Israel.

27 There *is* little Benjamin, their
leader,
The princes of Judah *and* their
company,
The princes of Zebulun *and*
the princes of Naphtali.

28 Your God has commanded
your strength;
Strengthen, O God, what You
have done for us.

29 Because of Your temple at
Jerusalem,
Kings will bring presents to
You.

30 Rebuke the beasts of the
reeds,
The herd of bulls with the
calves of the peoples,
Till everyone submits himself
with pieces of silver.
Scatter the peoples *who*
delight in war.

31 Envoys will come out of
Egypt;

STEP 3

*Made a decision to turn our will and our lives over to the care of God **as we understood Him.***

Psalm 68:19, 20

The God of the Bible is infinitely complex and yet deeply knowable. He is awesome beyond comprehension, but still intimate enough with those who trust Him to speak directly to the deepest needs of their individual lives. Those who truly know Him find His loyal love and His absolute holiness in perfect harmony. David, who knew Him very well, tells us that our wonderful Lord "daily loads us *with benefits.*" David could see that God loved to give good gifts to His children. The benefits He loads upon us may be material, but they can also be emotional and spiritual. David also rejoiced in the mighty power of God, who could bring about miraculous escapes from death.

As we take the step that turns our lives and will over to God, we can do so with complete confidence. Our God is a wonderful, loving, and powerful God whom we can trust completely with every detail of our lives.

For further reading on Step 3, turn to page 675.

Daily Encouragement

DAY 279 READING: PSALM 68:1–35

A Thought for the New Day: If we are thankful, we will never be unhappy. David's exuberant thankfulness is a good model for us. As he looked around, he could see only the "load" of benefits that the Lord daily showered on him (v. 19). Life can be pretty tough sometimes, but thankfulness becomes a habit. As we look for reasons to be thankful every day, we will handle the rough times better, too. (*Turn to page 645.*)

Ethiopia will quickly stretch
out her hands to God.

32 Sing to God, you kingdoms of
the earth;
Oh, sing praises to the Lord,
Selah

33 To Him who rides on the
heaven of heavens, *which
were* of old!
Indeed, He sends out His
voice, a mighty voice.

34 Ascribe strength to God;
His excellence *is* over Israel,
And His strength *is* in the
clouds.

35 O God, *You are* more
awesome than Your holy
places.
The God of Israel *is* He who
gives strength and power to
His people.

Blessed *be* God!

PSALM 69

To the Chief Musician. Set to "The Lilies." A
Psalm of David.

STEP 1

SAVE me, O God!
For the waters have come up
to *my* neck.

2 I sink in deep mire,
Where *there is* no standing;
I have come into deep waters,
Where the floods overflow me.

3 I am weary with my crying;
My throat is dry;
My eyes fail while I wait for
my God.

4 Those who hate me without a
cause
Are more than the hairs of my
head;
They are mighty who would
destroy me,
Being my enemies wrongfully;
Though I have stolen nothing,
I *still* must restore *it.*

STEP 5

5 O God, You know my
foolishness;

And my sins are not hidden
from You.

6 Let not those who wait for
You, O Lord G OD of hosts,
be ashamed because of me;
Let not those who seek You
be confounded because of
me, O God of Israel.

7 Because for Your sake I have
borne reproach;
Shame has covered my face.

8 I have become a stranger to
my brothers,
And an alien to my mother's
children;

9 Because zeal for Your house
has eaten me up,
And the reproaches of those
who reproach You have
fallen on me.

10 When I wept *and chastened*
my soul with fasting,
That became my reproach.

11 I also made sackcloth my
garment;
I became a byword to them.

12 Those who sit in the gate
speak against me,
And I *am* the song of the
drunkards.

13 But as for me, my prayer *is* to
You,
O L ORD, *in* the acceptable
time;
O God, in the multitude of
Your mercy,
Hear me in the truth of Your
salvation.

14 Deliver me out of the mire,
And let me not sink;
Let me be delivered from
those who hate me,
And out of the deep waters.

15 Let not the floodwater
overflow me,
Nor let the deep swallow me
up;
And let not the pit shut its
mouth on me.

*Admitted to God, to ourselves, and to another human being
the exact nature of our wrongs.*

Psalm 69:5

If God knows everything about us already, why do we have to go
through the pain and time it takes to enumerate and admit the
wrongs in our lives? Does He just enjoy seeing people struggle? The
answer to the second question is, of course, no. God does not want
us to admit our sins and wrongs because He wants us to suffer. In
fact, quite the reverse is true. From the earliest days of creation,
God has made a way for people to confess sins to Him. Confession
of our own sin delivers us from shame and guilt and restores our
communion with God. Confession of the wrongs in our family of
origin allows us to verbalize our grief, to vent and dispense with the
resentment, anger, and fear that have bound us. Confession also
helps us achieve emotional honesty. It breaks down the walls of
denial and escape, which can easily imprison our souls and minds.
Confession moves us from isolation to communion with God and
with others.

For further reading on Step 5, turn to page 727.

Daily Encouragement

DAY 280 READING: PSALM 69:1–18

A Thought for the New Day: Self-righteousness can have
tragic results. If we store up a long-overdue account of moral
debts—whether we admit their existence or not—we are eventually overwhelmed and crushed by their weight. But openness
and confession are a sure road to right relationship with God (v.
5) and others. It is hard to be angry with someone who sincerely
admits a wrong and asks for acceptance. (*Turn to page 647.*)

16 Hear me, O LORD,
　for Your lovingkindness *is*
　good;
　Turn to me according to the
　multitude of Your tender
　mercies.

17 And do not hide Your face
　from Your servant,
　For I am in trouble;
　Hear me speedily.

18 Draw near to my soul, *and*
　redeem it;
　Deliver me because of my
　enemies.

19 You know my reproach, my
　shame, and my dishonor;
　My adversaries *are* all before
　You.

20 Reproach has broken my
　heart,
　And I am full of heaviness;
　I looked *for someone* to take
　pity, but *there was* none;
　And for comforters, but I
　found none.

21 They also gave me gall for my
　food,
　And for my thirst they gave
　me vinegar to drink.

22 Let their table become a snare
　before them,
　And their well-being a trap.

23 Let their eyes be darkened,
　so that they do not see;
　And make their loins shake
　continually.

24 Pour out Your indignation
　upon them,
　And let Your wrathful anger
　take hold of them.

25 Let their habitation be
　desolate;
　Let no one dwell in their
　tents.

26 For they persecute *him* whom
　You have struck,
　And talk of the grief of those
　You have wounded.

27 Add iniquity to their iniquity,
　And let them not come into
　Your righteousness.

28 Let them be blotted out of the
　book of the living,
　And not be written with the
　righteous.

29 But I *am* poor and sorrowful;
　Let Your salvation, O God, set
　me up on high.

30 I will praise the name of God
　with a song,
　And will magnify Him with
　thanksgiving.

31 *This* also shall please the LORD
　better than an ox *or* bull,
　Which has horns and hooves.

32 The humble shall see *this and*
　be glad;
　And you who seek God,
　your hearts shall live.

33 For the LORD hears the poor,
　And does not despise His
　prisoners.

34 Let heaven and earth praise
　Him,
　The seas and everything that
　moves in them.

35 For God will save Zion
　And build the cities of Judah,
　That they may dwell there
　and possess it.

36 Also, the descendants of His
　servants shall inherit it,
　And those who love His name
　shall dwell in it.

PSALM 70

To the Chief Musician. *A Psalm* of David. To
bring to remembrance.

Make *haste*, O God, to deliver
me!
Make haste to help me, O
LORD!

2 Let them be ashamed and
confounded
Who seek my life;
Let them be turned back and
confused
Who desire my hurt.

3 Let them be turned back
because of their shame,
Who say, "Aha, aha!"

STEP 1

We admitted we were powerless over our dependencies—
that our lives had become unmanageable.

Psalm 69:20

"Isolation" defines what the psalmist was feeling here. The island of isolation is a painful place to live. Though we often praise the rugged individualist and tend to glamorize the tough and uncommunicative type of person, the truth is that feelings of loneliness are among the most difficult for anyone to cope with. Such feelings may have actually been the cause of our initial steps toward dependency. The irony is that usually our dependency has only served to increase the lonely, empty feelings of isolation in our lives. Dependencies have a way of destroying families and shredding the fabric of friendship a thread at a time. But when we come to the point in our lives where the isolation is no longer bearable, then there is hope. When we can admit that the things we have depended upon for happiness and acceptance have let us down, we can begin our search for true fellowship and love.

For further reading on Step 1, turn to page 651.

Daily Encouragement

DAY 281 READING: PSALMS 69:19—70:5

A Thought for the New Day: Seeking God with a long face is bad enough, but worshiping God with a long heart is worse. Although God's presence makes us feel properly inadequate and humble, the goal of His companionship is joy (70:4). Knowing God brings gladness—not flippancy—but delight beyond all earthly comparisons. Do you want to know happiness? Then seek God! (*Turn to page 649.*)

4 Let all those who seek You
    rejoice and be glad in You;
  And let those who love Your
    salvation say continually,
  "Let God be magnified!"

5 But I *am* poor and needy;
  Make haste to me, O God!
  You *are* my help and my
    deliverer;
  O LORD, do not delay.

PSALM 71

I N You, O LORD, I put my trust;
    Let me never be put to shame.
2 Deliver me in Your
    righteousness,
    and cause me to escape;
  Incline Your ear to me, and
    save me.
3 Be my strong habitation,
  To which I may resort
    continually;
  You have given the
    commandment to save me,
  For You *are* my rock and my
    fortress.

4 Deliver me, O my God, out of
    the hand of the wicked,
  Out of the hand of the
    unrighteous and cruel man.
5 For You are my hope, O Lord
    GOD;
  You are my trust from my
    youth.
6 By You I have been upheld
    from *my* birth;
  You are He who took me out
    of my mother's womb.
  My praise *shall be* continually
    of You.

7 I have become as a wonder to
    many,
  But You *are* my strong refuge.
8 Let my mouth be filled *with*
    Your praise
  And with Your glory all the
    day.

9 Do not cast me off in the time
    of old age;
  Do not forsake me when my
    strength fails.
10 For my enemies speak against
    me;
  And those who lie in wait for
    my life take counsel
    together,
11 Saying, "God has forsaken
    him;
  Pursue and take him,
    for *there is* none to deliver
    him."

12 O God, do not be far from me;
  O my God, make haste to help
    me!
13 Let them be confounded *and*
    consumed
  Who are adversaries of my
    life;
  Let them be covered *with*
    reproach and dishonor
  Who seek my hurt.

14 But I will hope continually,
  And will praise You yet more
    and more.
15 My mouth shall tell of Your
    righteousness
  And Your salvation all the
    day,
  For I do not know *their* limits.
16 I will go in the strength of the
    Lord GOD;
  I will make mention of Your
    righteousness, of Yours
    only.

17 O God, You have taught me
    from my youth;
  And to this *day* I declare Your
    wondrous works.
18 Now also when *I am* old and
    grayheaded,
  O God, do not forsake me,
  Until I declare Your strength
    to *this* generation,
  Your power to everyone *who*
    is to come.

STEP 2

Came to believe that a Power greater than ourselves could restore us to sanity.

Psalm 71:1–3

We have learned that we cannot trust in our own abilities to save us or even help us. Rather, we must put our trust in God. Only He can help us to escape the trap of our addictions; only He can deliver us from the bondage of our guilt and pain. When we become convinced of these things, we can leave the battered shack of our own contrivances behind. Nearer to us than we ever imagined is the strong fortress of His love and power. He is inviting us to come and live there. We no longer have to face the hurricane of temptation and trial in such pitiable shelter. We have the key to the fortress on the Rock, which is Jesus Christ. When we come to believe that He died to save us from sin and rose from the grave to give us eternal life, our faith becomes the key that opens the doors to the fortress of His love and power.

For further reading on Step 2, turn to page 667.

Daily Encouragement

DAY 282 READING: PSALM 71:1–24

A Thought for the New Day: A lady who once entertained many with her beautiful voice lay dying. As she contemplated her future with God, this was her text: "My lips shall greatly rejoice when I sing to You" (v. 23). Now the courts of glory resound with her song. And while here below, shall we not imitate the psalm writer: "My tongue shall talk of Your righteousness all the day long" (v. 24). (*Turn to page 651.*)

19 Also Your righteousness, O
   God, *is* very high,
   You who have done great
   things;
   O God, who *is* like You?

20 *You*, who have shown me
   great and severe troubles,
   Shall revive me again,
   And bring me up again from
   the depths of the earth.

21 You shall increase my
   greatness,
   And comfort me on every
   side.

22 Also with the lute I will praise
   You—
   And Your faithfulness, O my
   God!
   To You I will sing with the
   harp,
   O Holy One of Israel.

23 My lips shall greatly rejoice
   when I sing to You,
   And my soul, which You have
   redeemed.

24 My tongue also shall talk of
   Your righteousness all the
   day long;
   For they are confounded,
   For they are brought to shame
   Who seek my hurt.

PSALM 72

A Psalm of Solomon.

GIVE the king Your judgments,
   O God,
   And Your righteousness to the
   king's Son.

2 He will judge Your people
   with righteousness,
   And Your poor with justice.

3 The mountains will bring
   peace to the people,
   And the little hills, by
   righteousness.

4 He will bring justice to the
   poor of the people;
   He will save the children of
   the needy,
   And will break in pieces the
   oppressor.

5 They shall fear You
   As long as the sun and moon
   endure,
   Throughout all generations.

6 He shall come down like rain
   upon the mown grass,
   Like showers *that* water the
   earth.

7 In His days the righteous shall
   flourish,
   And abundance of peace,
   Until the moon is no more.

8 He shall have dominion also
   from sea to sea,
   And from the River to the
   ends of the earth.

9 Those who dwell in the
   wilderness will bow before
   Him,
   And His enemies will lick the
   dust.

10 The kings of Tarshish and of
   the isles
   Will bring presents;
   The kings of Sheba and Seba
   Will offer gifts.

11 Yes, all kings shall fall down
   before Him;
   All nations shall serve Him.

12 For He will deliver the needy
   when he cries,
   The poor also, and *him* who
   has no helper.

13 He will spare the poor and
   needy,
   And will save the souls of the
   needy.

14 He will redeem their life from
   oppression and violence;
   And precious shall be their
   blood in His sight.

15 And He shall live;
   And the gold of Sheba will be
   given to Him;
   Prayer also will be made for
   Him continually,
   And daily He shall be praised.

16 There will be an abundance of
   grain in the earth,

STEP 1

*We admitted we were powerless over our dependencies—
that our lives had become unmanageable.*

Psalm 72:12, 13

Pretending or assuming that we are strong and able and in control prevents our taking even the first step toward physical, emotional, and spiritual healing. Wise King Solomon wrote that God was ready to save any who would humble themselves to cry out to Him for help. Deliverances will come only for those who acknowledge their lives are unmanageable. As long as we are too proud to admit our failures and powerlessness, we will not begin to see God work in our lives.

Even when we begin to acknowledge the unmanageability of our condition, we may find ourselves looking to friends and relatives to rescue us. It is only as we come to grips with the fact that God alone is our ultimate source of healing that we are ready for true liberation.

For further reading on Step 1, turn to page 661.

Daily Encouragement

DAY 283 READING: PSALM 72:1–20

A Thought for the New Day: Solomon wrote this song in honor of the coming Christ, the greater Son of David of whom Solomon himself was only a foreshadowing. Jesus is depicted as a King who will rule "to the ends of the earth" (v. 8). It would be inappropriate not to fear this great King, who has the authority of judgment over all. And so, along with our delight in "the king's Son," we are also in awe and reverence before Him (v. 5). *(Turn to page 653.)*

On the top of the mountains;
Its fruit shall wave like
    Lebanon;
And *those* of the city shall
    flourish like grass of the
    earth.

17 His name shall endure forever;
His name shall continue as
    long as the sun.
And *men* shall be blessed in
    Him;
All nations shall call Him
    blessed.

18 Blessed *be* the LORD God,
    the God of Israel,
Who only does wondrous
    things!

19 And blessed *be* His glorious
    name forever!
And let the whole earth be
    filled *with* His glory.
Amen and Amen.

20 The prayers of David the son
    of Jesse are ended.

BOOK THREE
Psalms 73–89

PSALM 73
A Psalm of Asaph.

TRULY God *is* good to Israel,
    To such as are pure in heart.
2 But as for me, my feet had
    almost stumbled;
My steps had nearly slipped.
3 For I *was* envious of the
    boastful,
When I saw the prosperity of
    the wicked.

4 For *there are* no pangs in
    their death,
But their strength *is* firm.
5 They *are* not in trouble *as
other* men,
Nor are they plagued like
    other men.

6 Therefore pride serves as their
    necklace;
Violence covers them *like a*
    garment.
7 Their eyes bulge with
    abundance;
They have more than heart
    could wish.
8 They scoff and speak wickedly
    concerning oppression;
They speak loftily.
9 They set their mouth
    against the heavens,
And their tongue walks
    through the earth.

10 Therefore his people return
    here,
And waters of a full *cup* are
    drained by them.
11 And they say, "How does God
    know?
And is there knowledge in the
    Most High?"
12 Behold, these *are* the ungodly,
Who are always at ease;
They increase *in* riches.
13 Surely I have cleansed my
    heart *in* vain,
And washed my hands in
    innocence.
14 For all day long I have been
    plagued,
And chastened every morning.

STEP 10

15 If I had said, "I will speak
    thus,"
Behold, I would have been
    untrue to the generation of
    Your children.
16 When I thought *how* to
    understand this,
It *was* too painful for me—
17 Until I went into the
    sanctuary of God;
Then I understood their end.

18 Surely You set them in
    slippery places;
You cast them down to
    destruction.
19 Oh, how they are *brought* to
    desolation, as in a moment!

STEP 10

*Continued to take personal inventory
and when we were wrong promptly admitted it.*

Psalm 73:13, 14

This Psalm shows how a godly man named Asaph fought with his own misconceptions and preconceived ideas about how God should work.

When we have carefully and diligently followed the Lord to the best of our ability, it is easy to slip into the thinking, which says, "I've been good, so I deserve good things from God. I deserve to be rewarded for my efforts." Of course, the truth is that we never can be *worthy* of God's goodness; and furthermore, we are not wise enough to say what is really best for our lives. And so if God has chosen to take us through hard situations, it is not because He does not love us, but because, in fact, He loves us so much. He is altogether wise, and His compassion and lovingkindness toward His children never fail. If you are feeling "chastened" by God today, do not despair. He has your best interest at heart, and He will never take you through any trial that is unnecessary.

For further reading on Step 10, turn to page 673.

Daily Encouragement

DAY 284 READING: PSALM 73:1–17

A Thought for the New Day: Asaph, the author of this psalm, was mistaken in his observation (v. 5). A trouble-free life is a fantasy. Even those around us who seem without trouble, or who are in no trouble at the moment, will experience their own measure of difficulties. In the face of trouble, may we seek consolation in God, and may we show compassion—especially for those who have no God to comfort them. (*Turn to page 655.*)

They are utterly consumed
with terrors.
20 As a dream when *one* awakes,
So, Lord, when You awake,
You shall despise their image.

STEP 4
21 Thus my heart was grieved,
And I was vexed in my mind.
22 I *was* so foolish and ignorant;
I was *like* a beast before You.
23 Nevertheless I *am* continually
with You;
You hold *me* by my right
hand.
24 You will guide me with Your
counsel,
And afterward receive me *to*
glory.

25 Whom have I in heaven *but*
You?
And *there is* none upon earth
that I desire besides You.
26 My flesh and my heart fail;
But God *is* the strength of my
heart and my portion
forever.

27 For indeed, those who are far
from You shall perish;
You have destroyed all those
who desert You for harlotry.
28 But *it is* good for me to draw
near to God;
I have put my trust in the
Lord God,
That I may declare all Your
works.

PSALM 74

A Contemplation of Asaph.

O GOD, why have You cast *us*
off forever?
Why does Your anger smoke
against the sheep of Your
pasture?
2 Remember Your congregation,
which You have purchased
of old,
The tribe of Your inheritance,
which You have
redeemed—

This Mount Zion where You
have dwelt.
3 Lift up Your feet to the
perpetual desolations.
The enemy has damaged
everything in the sanctuary.
4 Your enemies roar in the
midst of Your meeting
place;
They set up their banners *for*
signs.
5 They seem like men who lift
up
Axes among the thick trees.
6 And now they break down its
carved work, all at once,
With axes and hammers.
7 They have set fire to Your
sanctuary;
They have defiled the dwelling
place of Your name to the
ground.
8 They said in their hearts,
"Let us destroy them
altogether."
They have burned up all the
meeting places of God in
the land.

9 We do not see our signs;
There is no longer any
prophet;
Nor *is there* any among us
who knows how long.
10 O God, how long will the
adversary reproach?
Will the enemy blaspheme
Your name forever?
11 Why do You withdraw Your
hand, even Your right hand?
Take it out of Your bosom
and destroy *them.*
12 For God *is* my King from of
old,
Working salvation in the
midst of the earth.
13 You divided the sea by Your
strength;
You broke the heads of the
sea serpents in the waters.
14 You broke the heads of
Leviathan in pieces,

Made a searching and fearless moral inventory of ourselves.
Psalm 73:21–24

As we begin to take a serious inventory of our lives, each of us will experience strong emotions. We may grieve over the abuses and inadequacies in our family background. We may feel that these family problems have caused us to be foolish and ignorant concerning important aspects of our emotional and physical health. We may know the feeling of being vexed (worried, distressed, and harassed) by our dependencies and problems.

Step 4 means accepting some unpleasant facts about ourselves and our family of origin and being willing to come to grips with feelings we have long tried to escape or deny. But we do not have to walk through this alone. God is right here with us, supporting our first steps toward freedom and guiding our thinking. His presence can give us the courage we need to accomplish this very important task.

For further reading on Step 4, turn to page 697.

Daily Encouragement

DAY 285 READING: PSALMS 73:18—75:10

A Thought for the New Day: What is heaven? It is portrayed in many ways as a place of ideal beauty and bliss. But what makes heaven altogether lovely and happy? Is it the golden streets? or the tree of life? or the river of life? None of these things could make heaven an eternally ecstatic existence. But God does! Heaven is where God is (73:25): in fact, its name is "THE LORD IS THERE" (Ezek. 48:35). *(Turn to page 659.)*

And gave him *as* food to the
    people inhabiting the
    wilderness.
15 You broke open the fountain
    and the flood;
    You dried up mighty rivers.
16 The day *is* Yours,
    the night also *is* Yours;
    You have prepared the light
    and the sun.
17 You have set all the borders
    of the earth;
    You have made summer and
    winter.

18 Remember this, *that* the
    enemy has reproached, O
    LORD,
    And *that* a foolish people has
    blasphemed Your name.
19 Oh, do not deliver the life of
    Your turtledove to the wild
    beast!
    Do not forget the life of Your
    poor forever.
20 Have respect to the covenant;
    For the dark places of the
    earth are full of the
    habitations of cruelty.
21 Oh, do not let the oppressed
    return ashamed!
    Let the poor and needy praise
    Your name.

22 Arise, O God, plead Your own
    cause;
    Remember how the foolish
    man reproaches You daily.
23 Do not forget the voice of
    Your enemies;
    The tumult of those who rise
    up against You increases
    continually.

PSALM 75

To the Chief Musician. Set to "Do Not
Destroy." A Psalm of Asaph. A Song.

WE give thanks to You, O
    God, we give thanks!
For Your wondrous works
    declare *that* Your name is
    near.

2 "When I choose the proper
    time,
    I will judge uprightly.
3 The earth and all its
    inhabitants are dissolved;
    I set up its pillars firmly.
                              Selah

4 "I said to the boastful,
    'Do not deal boastfully,'
    And to the wicked,
    'Do not lift up the horn.
5 Do not lift up your horn on
    high;
    Do *not* speak with a stiff
    neck.' "

6 For exaltation *comes* neither
    from the east
    Nor from the west nor from
    the south.
7 But God *is* the Judge:
    He puts down one,
    And exalts another.
8 For in the hand of the LORD
    there is a cup,
    And the wine is red;
    It is fully mixed, and He pours
    it out;
    Surely its dregs shall all the
    wicked of the earth
    Drain *and* drink down.

9 But I will declare forever,
    I will sing praises to the God
    of Jacob.

10 "All the horns of the wicked
    I will also cut off,
    But the horns of the righteous
    shall be exalted."

PSALM 76

To the Chief Musician. On stringed
instruments. A Psalm of Asaph. A Song.

IN Judah God *is* known;
    His name *is* great in Israel.
2 In Salem also is His
    tabernacle,
    And His dwelling place in
    Zion.
3 There He broke the arrows of
    the bow,

The shield and sword of
　　battle.　　　　　Selah

4　You *are* more glorious and
　　excellent
　　Than the mountains of prey.
5　The stouthearted were
　　plundered;
　　They have sunk into their
　　sleep;
　　And none of the mighty men
　　have found the use of their
　　hands.
6　At Your rebuke, O God of
　　Jacob,
　　Both the chariot and horse
　　were cast into a dead sleep.

7　You, Yourself, *are* to be
　　feared;
　　And who may stand in Your
　　presence
　　When once You are angry?
8　You caused judgment to be
　　heard from heaven;
　　The earth feared and was still,
9　When God arose to judgment,
　　To deliver all the oppressed of
　　the earth.　　　　　Selah

10　Surely the wrath of man shall
　　praise You;
　　With the remainder of wrath
　　You shall gird Yourself.

11　Make vows to the LORD your
　　God, and pay *them;*
　　Let all who are around Him
　　bring presents to Him who
　　ought to be feared.
12　He shall cut off the spirit of
　　princes;
　　He is awesome to the kings of
　　the earth.

PSALM 77

To the Chief Musician. To Jeduthun. A Psalm
of Asaph.

I CRIED out to God with my
　　voice—
　　To God with my voice;
　　And He gave ear to me.

2　In the day of my trouble I
　　sought the Lord;
　　My hand was stretched out in
　　the night without ceasing;
　　My soul refused to be
　　comforted.
3　I remembered God, and was
　　troubled;
　　I complained, and my spirit
　　was overwhelmed.　　　Selah

4　You hold my eyelids *open;*
　　I am so troubled that I cannot
　　speak.
5　I have considered the days of
　　old,
　　The years of ancient times.
6　I call to remembrance my
　　song in the night;
　　I meditate within my heart,
　　And my spirit makes diligent
　　search.

7　Will the Lord cast off forever?
　　And will He be favorable no
　　more?
8　Has His mercy ceased forever?
　　Has *His* promise failed
　　forevermore?
9　Has God forgotten to be
　　gracious?
　　Has He in anger shut up His
　　tender mercies?　　　Selah

10　And I said, "This *is* my
　　anguish;
　　But I will remember the years
　　of the right hand of the
　　Most High."
11　I will remember the works of
　　the LORD;
　　Surely I will remember Your
　　wonders of old.
12　I will also meditate on all
　　Your work,
　　And talk of Your deeds.
13　Your way, O God, *is* in the
　　sanctuary;
　　Who *is* so great a God as *our*
　　God?
14　You *are* the God who does
　　wonders;
　　You have declared Your
　　strength among the peoples.

15 You have with *Your* arm
   redeemed Your people,
   The sons of Jacob and Joseph.
                              Selah

16 The waters saw You, O God;
   The waters saw You, they
   were afraid;
   The depths also trembled.
17 The clouds poured out water;
   The skies sent out a sound;
   Your arrows also flashed
   about.
18 The voice of Your thunder
   was in the whirlwind;
   The lightnings lit up the
   world;
   The earth trembled and shook.
19 Your way *was* in the sea,
   Your path in the great waters,
   And Your footsteps were not
   known.
20 You led Your people like a
   flock
   By the hand of Moses and
   Aaron.

PSALM 78

A Contemplation of Asaph.

G IVE ear, O my people, *to* my
   law;
   Incline your ears to the words
   of my mouth.
2 I will open my mouth in a
   parable;
   I will utter dark sayings of
   old,
3 Which we have heard and
   known,
   And our fathers have told us.

4 We will not hide *them* from
   their children,
   Telling to the generation to
   come the praises of the
   LORD,
   And His strength and His
   wonderful works that He
   has done.

5 For He established a
   testimony in Jacob,
   And appointed a law in Israel,

Which He commanded our
   fathers,
   That they should make them
   known to their children;
6 That the generation to come
   might know *them,*
   The children *who* would be
   born,
   That they may arise and
   declare *them* to their
   children,
7 That they may set their hope
   in God,
   And not forget the works of
   God,
   But keep His commandments;
8 And may not be like their
   fathers,
   A stubborn and rebellious
   generation,
   A generation *that* did not set
   its heart aright,
   And whose spirit was not
   faithful to God.

9 The children of Ephraim,
   being armed *and* carrying
   bows,
   Turned back in the day of
   battle.
10 They did not keep the
   covenant of God;
   They refused to walk in His
   law,
11 And forgot His works
   And His wonders that He had
   shown them.

12 Marvelous things He did
   in the sight of their fathers,
   In the land of Egypt,
   in the field of Zoan.
13 He divided the sea
   and caused them to pass
   through;
   And He made the waters
   stand up like a heap.
14 In the daytime also He led
   them with the cloud,
   And all the night with a light
   of fire.
15 He split the rocks in the
   wilderness,

Having had a spiritual awakening as the result of these steps,
we tried to carry this message to others,
and to practice these principles in all our affairs.

Psalm 78:4

My neighbor once told me that she would never admit her wrongs to her son. "He will always use it as ammunition against me," she declared. Actually, nothing is further from the truth. Children are always quite aware that their parents are not perfect. Older persons who can admit that they have struggled with particular problems gain far more credibility than elders who put on a facade of perfection. Likewise, when older friends or parents can share how God has changed them, they usually capture a child's full attention.

We are to be good examples to our children; but this does not mean we are to pretend we are perfect. Instead, we should ask God to help us glorify His name in our attitudes, actions, and words. Praising God for how His strength has helped us to overcome our problems and is changing us day by day will carry a far greater impact for Christ than any veneer of perfectionism ever could.

For further reading on Step 12, turn to page 683.

Daily Encouragement

DAY 286 READING: PSALMS 76:1—78:4

A Thought for the New Day: Charity begins at home, and so does the work of evangelizing the world. Who would be so hard-hearted as to share his earthly goods with strangers, but let his children starve? So our first job as parents is to transmit God's truth to our little ones (78:4). As we do so, we provide them with the lifeline by which the Holy Spirit will draw them to Christ. (*Turn to page 661.*)

And gave *them* drink in
abundance like the depths.

16 He also brought streams out
of the rock,
And caused waters to run
down like rivers.

17 But they sinned even more
against Him
By rebelling against the Most
High in the wilderness.

18 And they tested God in their
heart
By asking for the food of their
fancy.

19 Yes, they spoke against God:
They said, "Can God prepare
a table in the wilderness?

20 Behold, He struck the rock,
So that the waters gushed
out,
And the streams overflowed.
Can He give bread also?
Can He provide meat for His
people?"

21 Therefore the Lord heard *this*
and was furious;
So a fire was kindled against
Jacob,
And anger also came up
against Israel,

22 Because they did not believe
in God,
And did not trust in His
salvation.

23 Yet He had commanded the
clouds above,
And opened the doors of
heaven,

24 Had rained down manna on
them to eat,
And given them of the bread
of heaven.

25 Men ate angels' food;
He sent them food to the full.

26 He caused an east wind to
blow in the heavens;
And by His power He brought
in the south wind.

27 He also rained meat on them
like the dust,

Feathered fowl like the sand
of the seas;

28 And He let *them* fall in the
midst of their camp,
All around their habitations.

29 So they ate and were well
filled,
For He gave them their own
desire.

30 They were not deprived of
their craving;
But while their food *was* still
in their mouths,

31 The wrath of God came
against them,
And slew the stoutest of them,
And struck down the choice
men of Israel.

32 In spite of this they still
sinned,
And did not believe in His
wondrous works.

33 Therefore their days He
consumed in futility,
And their years in fear.

34 When He slew them,
then they sought Him;
And they returned and sought
diligently for God.

35 Then they remembered that
God *was* their rock,
And the Most High God their
redeemer.

36 Nevertheless they flattered
Him with their mouth,
And they lied to Him with
their tongue;

37 For their heart was not
steadfast with Him,
Nor were they faithful in His
covenant.

38 But He, *being* full of
compassion, forgave *their*
iniquity,
And did not destroy *them*.
Yes, many a time He turned
His anger away,
And did not stir up all His
wrath;

39 For He remembered that they
were but flesh,

STEP 1

STEP 1

We admitted we were powerless over our dependencies—
that our lives had become unmanageable.

Psalm 78:38, 39

Psalm 78 recounts the wilderness years of the children of Israel. God's desire was to bring His people into the beautiful land He had promised them—a place of abundance and rest. He carefully protected them on their journey and provided Israel with special food and water. But instead of responding to God with hearts of trust and steadfastness, the Israelites continually broke their promises to Him and refused to trust Him.

We may see parallels to our own lives in these verses. We may be aware that again and again God has called to us and even protected us; but still we have chosen to go our own way. Finally, we have found ourselves at the foot of the mountain called Hopelessness. Even though we have turned our face away from God in the past, He does not respond to us in anger. Instead, He is full of compassion toward us, ready to forgive our iniquity and give us the power we need to reach the promised land of healing and contentment.

For further reading on Step 1, turn to page 676.

Daily Encouragement

DAY 287 READING: PSALM 78:5–39

A Thought for the New Day: It is a sad thing to be unable to be sorry for sin. But to those who can, "I forgive you" are the sweetest words ever spoken. Jesus went about forgiving people. "Man, your sins are forgiven you," were the first words He spoke to one who was paralyzed (Luke 5:20). As we think about God and His many mercies and kindnesses, let us grow sensitive to our need for His forgiveness. He wants us to be His own forever. (*Turn to page 663.*)

A breath that passes away
and does not come again.

STEP
6

40 How often they provoked Him
in the wilderness,
And grieved Him in the
desert!

41 Yes, again and again they
tempted God,
And limited the Holy One of
Israel.

42 They did not remember His
power:
The day when He redeemed
them from the enemy,

43 When He worked His signs in
Egypt,
And His wonders in the field
of Zoan;

44 Turned their rivers into blood,
And their streams,
that they could not drink.

45 He sent swarms of flies among
them, which devoured them,
And frogs, which destroyed
them.

46 He also gave their crops to the
caterpillar,
And their labor to the locust.

47 He destroyed their vines with
hail,
And their sycamore trees with
frost.

48 He also gave up their cattle to
the hail,
And their flocks to fiery
lightning.

49 He cast on them the fierceness
of His anger,
Wrath, indignation, and
trouble,
By sending angels of
destruction *among them.*

50 He made a path for His anger;
He did not spare their soul
from death,
But gave their life over to the
plague,

51 And destroyed all the firstborn
in Egypt,
The first of *their* strength in
the tents of Ham.

52 But He made His own people
go forth like sheep,

And guided them in the
wilderness like a flock;

53 And He led them on safely,
so that they did not fear;
But the sea overwhelmed their
enemies.

54 And He brought them to His
holy border,
This mountain *which* His right
hand had acquired.

55 He also drove out the nations
before them,
Allotted them an inheritance
by survey,
And made the tribes of Israel
dwell in their tents.

56 Yet they tested and provoked
the Most High God,
And did not keep His
testimonies,

57 But turned back and acted
unfaithfully like their
fathers;
They were turned aside like a
deceitful bow.

58 For they provoked Him to
anger with their high places,
And moved Him to jealousy
with their carved images.

59 When God heard *this,* He was
furious,
And greatly abhorred Israel,

60 So that He forsook the
tabernacle of Shiloh,
The tent *which* He had placed
among men,

61 And delivered His strength
into captivity,
And His glory into the
enemy's hand.

62 He also gave His people over
to the sword,
And was furious with His
inheritance.

63 The fire consumed their young
men,
And their maidens were not
given in marriage.

64 Their priests fell by the sword,
And their widows made no
lamentation.

STEP 6

*Were entirely ready to have God
remove all these defects of character.*

Psalm 78:40–42

Our lack of trust will not lessen God's *ability* to work for us and
through us, but the degree to which we are willing to trust is often
the degree to which God is willing to work. When God is leading
us to take specific steps of faith in accord with His Word, we honor
Him by acting in obedience. Our trust and obedience are the cata-
lysts for unleashing His wonderful power.

The seed of trust comes from God Himself, and we honor Him
when we ask, as the disciples did, "Lord, increase our faith." Then,
the water and fertilizer for that precious seed is resident within each
of us. We must daily meditate on God's Word (the promises and
principles recorded there) and on God's power (what God has
accomplished in our own life in the past).

Remembering these things and how He has redeemed us, we will
become ready for God's power to work in us.

For further reading on Step 6, turn to page 685.

Daily Encouragement

DAY 288 READING: PSALM 78:40–72

A Thought for the New Day: Quite often, God's way of thinking and doing are just the opposite of our own. God did not necessarily want the tallest, or the most handsome, or the most brilliant to be His king. He wanted someone who knew first how to
follow, but also how to lead. David learned the first lesson from
being an obedient son; the second he learned from leading sheep
(vv. 70, 71). (*Turn to page 665.*)

65 Then the Lord awoke as *one
     out of* sleep,
   And like a mighty man who
     shouts because of wine.
66 And He beat back His
     enemies;
   He put them to a perpetual
     reproach.

67 Moreover He rejected the tent
     of Joseph,
   And did not choose the tribe
     of Ephraim,
68 But chose the tribe of Judah,
   Mount Zion which He loved.
69 And He built His sanctuary
     like the heights,
   Like the earth which He has
     established forever.
70 He also chose David His
     servant,
   And took him from the
     sheepfolds;
71 From following the ewes that
     had young He brought him,
   To shepherd Jacob His people,
   And Israel His inheritance.
72 So he shepherded them
     according to the integrity of
     his heart,
   And guided them by the
     skillfulness of his hands.

PSALM 79

A Psalm of Asaph.

O GOD, the nations have come
     into Your inheritance;
   Your holy temple they have
     defiled;
   They have laid Jerusalem in
     heaps.
2 The dead bodies of Your
     servants
   They have given *as* food
     for the birds of the heavens,
   The flesh of Your saints
     to the beasts of the earth.
3 Their blood they have shed
     like water all around
     Jerusalem,
   And *there was* no one to bury
     them.

4 We have become a reproach
     to our neighbors,
   A scorn and derision to those
     who are around us.

5 How long, LORD?
   Will You be angry forever?
   Will Your jealousy burn like
     fire?
6 Pour out Your wrath on the
     nations that do not know
     You,
   And on the kingdoms that do
     not call on Your name.
7 For they have devoured Jacob,
   And laid waste his dwelling
     place.

8 Oh, do not remember former
     iniquities against us!
   Let Your tender mercies come
     speedily to meet us,
   For we have been brought
     very low.
9 Help us, O God of our
     salvation,
   For the glory of Your name;
   And deliver us, and provide
     atonement for our sins,
   For Your name's sake!
10 Why should the nations say,
   "Where *is* their God?"
   Let there be known among
     the nations in our sight
   The avenging of the blood of
     Your servants *which has
     been* shed.

11 Let the groaning of the
     prisoner come before You;
   According to the greatness of
     Your power
   Preserve those who are
     appointed to die;
12 And return to our neighbors
     sevenfold into their bosom
   Their reproach with which
     they have reproached You,
   O Lord.

13 So we, Your people and sheep
     of Your pasture,

STEP
7

Humbly asked Him to remove our shortcomings.
Psalm 79:9

The honor of God's name is of great importance to Him. So when we became His children, by faith in Jesus Christ, we received a wonderful gift. We were given His name, and God bestowed on us the privileges of belonging to His own eternal family. Now God longs to see our lives grow and shine forth with His own glory because, as we defeat our spiritual and emotional shortcomings, we are bringing honor to His wonderful name.

When we humbly ask God for the help and power we need to remove our shortcomings, we glorify and honor His name in many ways. Allowing the Lord Jesus to take control of our situation glorifies Him. Our desire to obey brings honor to His name. Acknowledging God's awesome power, which works on our behalf, brings praise to Him. And when those around us watch as God molds us and changes us, they will praise His name, as well.

For further reading on Step 7, turn to page 731.

Daily Encouragement

DAY 289 READING: PSALM 79:1–13

A Thought for the New Day: The general tone of Asaph's song is not very uplifting. We must understand that the prayers of the Old Testament people were not always on the highest level. (The same is true for us today.) Nevertheless, the Holy Spirit saw fit to record their attitudes for our thoughtful meditation. It is at the end of his psalm that Asaph reaches the high point: "We will show forth Your praise" (v. 13). Praise to God always makes sense. (*Turn to page 667.*)

Will give You thanks forever;
We will show forth Your
praise to all generations.

PSALM 80

To the Chief Musician. Set to "The Lilies." A
Testimony of Asaph. A Psalm.

GIVE ear, O Shepherd of Israel,
You who lead Joseph like a
flock;
You who dwell *between* the
cherubim, shine forth!

2 Before Ephraim, Benjamin,
and Manasseh,
Stir up Your strength,
And come *and* save us!

3 Restore us, O God;
Cause Your face to shine,
And we shall be saved!

4 O LORD God of hosts,
How long will You be angry
Against the prayer of Your
people?

5 You have fed them with the
bread of tears,
And given them tears to drink
in great measure.

6 You have made us a strife to
our neighbors,
And our enemies laugh among
themselves.

7 Restore us, O God of hosts;
Cause Your face to shine,
And we shall be saved!

8 You have brought a vine out
of Egypt;
You have cast out the nations,
and planted it.

9 You prepared *room* for it,
And caused it to take deep
root,
And it filled the land.

10 The hills were covered with its
shadow,
And the mighty cedars with
its boughs.

11 She sent out her boughs to
the Sea,
And her branches to the
River.

12 Why have You broken down
her hedges,
So that all who pass by the
way pluck her *fruit?*

13 The boar out of the woods
uproots it,
And the wild beast of the field
devours it.

14 Return, we beseech You,
O God of hosts;
Look down from heaven and
see,
And visit this vine

15 And the vineyard which Your
right hand has planted,
And the branch *that* You
made strong for Yourself.

16 *It is* burned with fire, *it is* cut
down;
They perish at the rebuke of
Your countenance.

17 Let Your hand be upon the
man of Your right hand,
Upon the son of man *whom*
You made strong for
Yourself.

18 Then we will not turn back
from You;
Revive us, and we will call
upon Your name.

19 Restore us, O LORD God of
hosts;
Cause Your face to shine,
And we shall be saved!

PSALM 81

To the Chief Musician. On an instrument of
Gath. A Psalm of Asaph.

SING aloud to God our
strength;
Make a joyful shout to the
God of Jacob.

2 Raise a song and strike the
timbrel,
The pleasant harp with the
lute.

3 Blow the trumpet at the time
of the New Moon,
At the full moon,
on our solemn feast day.

STEP 2

Came to believe that a Power greater than ourselves could restore us to sanity.

Psalm 80:7–13

Even people who have professed faith in Christ sometimes develop dependency problems. This can happen for a variety of reasons, but the solution to the problem is always the same. Such individuals need restoration and healing in much the same way that Israel did in Psalm 80. Israel was the precious vine that God Himself planted (vv. 7–11). But because Israel had made wrong decisions and alliances, the children of God found themselves eating "the bread of tears" (v. 5), broken (v. 12), uprooted, and devoured (v. 13). The answer for Israel's problems is the help we need for our own lives. Israel needed restoration and revival. They needed to reaffirm their helplessness apart from God. They needed to call out in faith, believing that God could and would once again demonstrate His power to save and deliver. Likewise, struggling believers must reaffirm their trust in God's power and desire to deliver them now from the oppression of dependency.

For further reading on Step 2, turn to page 669.

Daily Encouragement

DAY 290 READING: PSALM 80:1–19

A Thought for the New Day: Three times the lines of verse 3 are repeated throughout this song. Whatever the Old Testament people did not understand, they nevertheless clearly knew that their happiness depended on God's kindness toward them. That is a good place to begin when we pray. "If God *is* for us, who can be against us?" Paul wrote in Romans 8:31. Yes, and God will be on our side if only we put our lives in His hands. (*Turn to page 669.*)

4 For this *is* a statute for Israel,
　And a law of the God of
　　Jacob.
5 This He established in Joseph
　for a testimony,
　When He went throughout
　　the land of Egypt,
　Where I heard a language
　that I did not understand.

6 "I removed his shoulder from
　　the burden;
　His hands were freed from the
　　baskets.

STEP 2

7 You called in trouble,
　and I delivered you;
　I answered you in the secret
　　place of thunder;
　I proved you at the waters of
　　Meribah.　　　　　Selah

8 "Hear, O My people,
　and I will admonish you!
　O Israel, if you will listen to
　　Me!
9 There shall be no foreign god
　　among you;
　Nor shall you worship any
　　foreign god.
10 I *am* the LORD your God,
　Who brought you out of the
　　land of Egypt;
　Open your mouth wide,
　　and I will fill it.

11 "But My people would not heed
　　My voice,
　And Israel would *have* none
　　of Me.
12 So I gave them over to their
　　own stubborn heart,
　To walk in their own counsels.

13 "Oh, that My people would
　　listen to Me,
　That Israel would walk in My
　　ways!
14 I would soon subdue their
　　enemies,
　And turn My hand against
　　their adversaries.
15 The haters of the LORD would
　　pretend submission to Him,

But their fate would endure
　forever.
16 He would have fed them also
　with the finest of wheat;
　And with honey from the rock
　I would have satisfied you."

PSALM 82

A Psalm of Asaph.

GOD stands in the
　congregation of the mighty;
He judges among the gods.
2 How long will you judge
　　unjustly,
　And show partiality to the
　　wicked?　　　　　Selah
3 Defend the poor and
　　fatherless;
　Do justice to the afflicted and
　　needy.
4 Deliver the poor and needy;
　Free *them* from the hand of
　　the wicked.

5 They do not know,
　nor do they understand;
　They walk about in darkness;
　All the foundations of the
　　earth are unstable.

6 I said, "You *are* gods,
　And all of you *are* children of
　　the Most High.
7 But you shall die like men,
　And fall like one of the
　　princes."

8 Arise, O God, judge the earth;
　For You shall inherit all
　　nations.

PSALM 83

A Song. A Psalm of Asaph.

DO not keep silent, O God!
　Do not hold Your peace,
And do not be still, O God!
2 For behold, Your enemies
　make a tumult;
　And those who hate You have
　lifted up their head.
3 They have taken crafty
　counsel against Your people,

*Came to believe that a Power greater than ourselves
could restore us to sanity.*

Psalm 81:7–10

The patience and the longsuffering love of God are sometimes more than we can comprehend. Time after time Israel promised to walk with God. Time after time the nation disobeyed, turning toward her own devices and desires. God allowed great trouble to come upon Israel so that His people would come to understand their helplessness apart from Him. But He never disowned or discarded them; rather, He continued to reach out in love and forgiveness. God deals the same way with us today. When we call in faith to Him, He is there to deliver us. When we come to realize that we must worship Him, rather than anything this world has to offer, He responds with power and love that cannot even be measured. He tells us to open our mouths so that He may fill them. He wants to satisfy our deepest hungers. He can and He will when we put our trust in Him alone.

For further reading on Step 2, turn to page 711.

Daily Encouragement

DAY 291 READING: PSALMS 81:1—82:8

A Thought for the New Day: If we are not careful, we may misunderstand the words of Psalm 82:6. Of course, we can never become God, any more than a child becomes its parent, but we are called to be God-like. It has been remarked more than once, and truly, that we ought to be "little Christs" in the world— meaning that we should become enough like Christ that we remind people of Him. This is our amazing privilege when His Spirit indwells us. (*Turn to page 671.*)

And consulted together
  against Your sheltered ones.
4 They have said, "Come, and
  let us cut them off from
  being a nation,
  That the name of Israel may
  be remembered no more."

5 For they have consulted
  together with one *consent;*
  They form a confederacy
  against You:
6 The tents of Edom and the
  Ishmaelites;
  Moab and the Hagarites;
7 Gebal, Ammon, and Amalek;
  Philistia with the inhabitants
  of Tyre;
8 Assyria also has joined with
  them;
  They have helped the children
  of Lot.   Selah

9 Deal with them as *with*
  Midian,
  As *with* Sisera,
  As *with* Jabin at the Brook
  Kishon,
10 Who perished at En Dor,
  Who became *as* refuse on the
  earth.
11 Make their nobles like Oreb
  and like Zeeb,
  Yes, all their princes like
  Zebah and Zalmunna,
12 Who said, "Let us take for
  ourselves
  The pastures of God for a
  possession."

13 O my God, make them like
  the whirling dust,
  Like the chaff before the
  wind!
14 As the fire burns the woods,
  And as the flame sets the
  mountains on fire,
15 So pursue them with Your
  tempest,
  And frighten them with Your
  storm.
16 Fill their faces with shame,
  That they may seek Your
  name, O Lord.

17 Let them be confounded
  and dismayed forever;
  Yes, let them be put to shame
  and perish,
18 That *men* may know that
  You, whose name alone *is*
  the Lord,
  Are the Most High over all the
  earth.

PSALM 84

To the Chief Musician. On an instrument of
Gath. A Psalm of the sons of Korah.

HOW lovely *is* Your tabernacle,
  O Lord of hosts!
2 My soul longs, yes, even faints
  For the courts of the Lord;
  My heart and my flesh cry out
  for the living God.

3 Even the sparrow has found a
  home,
  And the swallow a nest for
  herself,
  Where she may lay her
  young—
  Even Your altars, O Lord of
  hosts,
  My King and my God.
4 Blessed *are* those who dwell in
  Your house;
  They will still be praising You.
                Selah

5 Blessed *is* the man whose
  strength *is* in You,
  Whose heart *is* set on
  pilgrimage.
6 *As they* pass through the
  Valley of Baca,
  They make it a spring;
  The rain also covers it with
  pools.
7 They go from strength to
  strength;
  Every one of them appears
  before God in Zion.

8 O Lord God of hosts, hear my
  prayer;
  Give ear, O God of Jacob!
                Selah

STEP
11

STEP 11

*Sought through prayer and meditation to improve our conscious contact with God **as we understood Him,** praying only for knowledge of His will for us and the power to carry that out.*

Psalm 84:5–12

During Old Testament days, devout Jews made an annual pilgrimage to the temple in Jerusalem for a time of special prayer and worship. When they continued their journey in spite of all obstacles, their strength was increased.

Although we may not make such pilgrimages today, our search to know God more intimately through recovery is in itself a journey. This faith journey may not be easy. Daily we will encounter rough roads of temptation. We may pass through waterless valleys of struggle and discouragement, but if we will persist in trusting and obeying God, He will strengthen us.

The psalmist ends his song by declaring in verse 10 that being a humble servant of God is far better than being one who serves wickedness. God promises to guide and shield those who seek Him and desire to know and obey Him. He will bestow grace, glory, and countless blessings on all who are His children.

For further reading on Step 11, turn to page 689.

Daily Encouragement

DAY 292 READING: PSALMS 83:1—84:12

A Thought for the New Day: "How lovely *is* Your tabernacle!" (84:1). Yes, the house of God is lovely, whether it be a stately cathedral in one of our Western cities or a straw hut in the jungle. Wherever Spirit-filled hearts meet to worship the King in His beauty, there heaven comes down and glory fills that place. The Lord Himself is the real loveliness of His house. (*Turn to page 673.*)

9 O God, behold our shield,
    And look upon the face of
        Your anointed.

10 For a day in Your courts *is*
        better than a thousand.
    I would rather be a
        doorkeeper in the house of
        my God
    Than dwell in the tents of
        wickedness.
11 For the LORD God *is* a sun and
        shield;
    The LORD will give grace and
        glory;
    No good *thing* will He
        withhold
    From those who walk
        uprightly.

12 O LORD of hosts,
    Blessed *is* the man who trusts
        in You!

PSALM 85

To the Chief Musician. A Psalm of the sons of
Korah.

LORD, You have been favorable
    to Your land;
    You have brought back the
        captivity of Jacob.
2 You have forgiven the iniquity
        of Your people;
    You have covered all their sin.
        Selah
3 You have taken away all Your
        wrath;
    You have turned from the
        fierceness of Your anger.

4 Restore us, O God of our
        salvation,
    And cause Your anger toward
        us to cease.
5 Will You be angry with us
        forever?
    Will You prolong Your anger
        to all generations?
6 Will You not revive us again,
        That Your people may rejoice
        in You?
7 Show us Your mercy, O LORD,

And grant us Your salvation.

8 I will hear what God the LORD
        will speak,
    For He will speak peace
    To His people and to His
        saints;
    But let them not turn back to
        folly.
9 Surely His salvation *is* near to
        those who fear Him,
    That glory may dwell in our
        land.

10 Mercy and truth have met
        together;
    Righteousness and peace have
        kissed *each other.*
11 Truth shall spring out of the
        earth,
    And righteousness shall look
        down from heaven.
12 Yes, the LORD will give *what
        is* good;
    And our land will yield its
        increase.
13 Righteousness will go before
        Him,
    And shall make His footsteps
        our pathway.

PSALM 86

A Prayer of David.

BOW down Your ear, O LORD,
    hear me;
    For I *am* poor and needy.
2 Preserve my life, for I *am*
        holy;
    You are my God;
    Save Your servant who trusts
        in You!
3 Be merciful to me, O Lord,
    For I cry to You all day long.
4 Rejoice the soul of Your
        servant,
    For to You, O Lord, I lift up
        my soul.
5 For You, Lord, *are* good,
        and ready to forgive,
    And abundant in mercy to all
        those who call upon You.

STEP 10

*Continued to take personal inventory
and when we were wrong promptly admitted it.*

Psalm 85:8, 9

Our journey through the first nine steps of recovery has been a life-changing experience. However, in the absence of an ongoing inventory, we are liable to lose our course and "turn back to folly" (v. 8).

Without continual self-evaluation, we may fall prey to the old nemesis of denial. We may deny the severity of our addictions and dependencies. We may deny the futility of willpower and intellect alone as tools to combat our dependencies. We may deny the destructive pattern of past codependent relationships. We may question the reality of the spiritual realm and even question God's sovereignty and ability to heal us from our dependencies. We may lapse into old patterns of negative thinking and feelings, including envy, fear, resentment, and self-pity.

Only the rigorous honesty that we bring to the practice of personal inventory and a willingness to "hear what the LORD will speak" provide the antidotes against self-delusion.

For further reading on Step 10, turn to page 691.

Daily Encouragement

DAY 293 READING: PSALM 85:1–13

A Thought for the New Day: It is possible to sit through a beautiful symphony, but not hear it. Yes, there were sounds and voices, but we did not let the beautiful melodies reach into our souls. We may as well have been asleep! God is speaking continually, but do we hear Him? Or have we trained our hearts to tune Him out? Then how much we're missing: "He will speak peace to His people and to His saints" (v. 8). (*Turn to page 675.*)

6 Give ear, O Lord, to my
    prayer;
And attend to the voice of my
    supplications.
7 In the day of my trouble I will
    call upon You,
For You will answer me.

8 Among the gods *there is* none
    like You, O Lord;
Nor *are there any works* like
    Your works.
9 All nations whom You have
    made
Shall come and worship before
    You, O Lord,
And shall glorify Your name.
10 For You *are* great,
    and do wondrous things;
You alone *are* God.

STEP 3

11 Teach me Your way, O Lord;
I will walk in Your truth;
Unite my heart to fear Your
    name.
12 I will praise You, O Lord my
    God, with all my heart,
And I will glorify Your name
    forevermore.
13 For great *is* Your mercy
    toward me,
And You have delivered my
    soul from the depths of
    Sheol.

14 O God, the proud have risen
    against me,
And a mob of violent *men*
    have sought my life,
And have not set You before
    them.
15 But You, O Lord, *are* a God
    full of compassion, and
    gracious,
Longsuffering and abundant
    in mercy and truth.

16 Oh, turn to me,
    and have mercy on me!
Give Your strength to Your
    servant,
And save the son of Your
    maidservant.

17 Show me a sign for good,
That those who hate me may
    see *it* and be ashamed,
Because You, Lord, have
    helped me and comforted
    me.

PSALM 87

A Psalm of the sons of Korah. A Song.

HIS foundation *is* in the holy
    mountains.
2 The Lord loves the gates of
    Zion
More than all the dwellings of
    Jacob.
3 Glorious things are spoken of
    you,
O city of God!   Selah

4 "I will make mention of Rahab
    and Babylon to those who
    know Me;
Behold, O Philistia and Tyre,
    with Ethiopia:
'This *one* was born there.' "

5 And of Zion it will be said,
"This *one* and that *one* were
    born in her;
And the Most High Himself
    shall establish her."
6 The Lord will record,
When He registers the
    peoples:
"This *one* was born there."
      Selah

7 Both the singers and the
    players on instruments *say*,
"All my springs *are* in you."

PSALM 88

A Song. A Psalm of the sons of Korah. To the
Chief Musician. Set to "Mahalath Leannoth." A
Contemplation of Heman the Ezrahite.

O LORD, God of my salvation,
    I have cried out day and
    night before You.
2 Let my prayer come before
    You;
Incline Your ear to my cry.

STEP 1

STEP 3

*Made a decision to turn our will and our lives
over to the care of God **as we understood Him.***

Psalm 86:11–13

David was a man who knew how to make decisions. He had the strength of character to weigh a situation carefully and then stand firmly in the choice he made. Even when David enjoyed great popularity, riches, and military might as king of Israel, he never put his confidence in any of those things. Instead, he made the decision to entrust all that he had and was to God alone. He had considered the possibilities and decided on the best course of action he could take.

Having chosen to walk in God's truth, he asked for God's help in irrevocably sealing that choice. He asked God first, "Teach me Your way"; and then he prayed, "Unite my heart to fear Your name." In other words, David desired to know God's way so that he could devote every area of his life to God's lordship. God always honors the prayer of a heart that is ready to give everything over to His care and leading.

For further reading on Step 3, turn to page 681.

Daily Encouragement

DAY 294 READING: PSALMS 86:1—87:7

A Thought for the New Day: Just as *hearing* music in the right way requires a listening heart, so *making* music calls for deep personal investment. God is not worshiped, nor is He pleased, when we only go through the motions of praising Him. Sometimes we are tired or just feeling off-color, and God understands. But we need to pray for hearts that overflow with praise to Him (87:7). (*Turn to page 676.*)

STEP 1

We admitted we were powerless over our dependencies—
that our lives had become unmanageable.

Psalm 88:1–4

We have come to realize a bitter truth. The very thing or things
we have depended on to bring us happiness, security, and peace
have turned on us and robbed us of all we hold dear. Some of us
have lost families or jobs. Some have depleted financial resources
and lost reputations. Others have lost self-respect and confidence.
And for some, life itself hangs in the balance as our physical and
emotional well-being is drained away by our addiction. It is time to
find a way out, but our way out is not in the way most people imagine. It is not to determine to turn over yet another "new leaf of attitude and action." It is instead to determine that we cannot determine. The way out comes by squarely facing the fact that we
cannot help ourselves. When we can admit that on our own we are
powerless to break the terrible cycle that has entrapped us, we take
our first step toward hope.

For further reading on Step 1, turn to page 693.

Daily Encouragement

DAY 295 READING: PSALMS 88:1—89:52

A Thought for the New Day: A covenant is an agreement; and
God made an agreement, or binding promise, with David that
his throne would last forever (89:3, 4). Of course, David is dead,
but Jesus the Son of David is enthroned forever, and there will
be no end to His kingdom. Even when the whole world seems to
be blowing up in violence, we have the settled confidence that
Jesus is still in charge. *(Turn to page 681.)*

3 For my soul is full of troubles,
   And my life draws near to the
      grave.
4 I am counted with those who
   go down to the pit;
   I am like a man *who has* no
      strength,
5 Adrift among the dead,
   Like the slain who lie in the
      grave,
   Whom You remember no
      more,
   And who are cut off from
      Your hand.

6 You have laid me in the
      lowest pit,
   In darkness, in the depths.
7 Your wrath lies heavy upon
      me,
   And You have afflicted *me*
      with all Your waves.   Selah
8 You have put away my
      acquaintances far from me;
   You have made me an
      abomination to them;
   I am shut up, and I cannot get
      out;
9 My eye wastes away because
      of affliction.

   LORD, I have called daily upon
      You;
   I have stretched out my hands
      to You.
10 Will You work wonders for
      the dead?
   Shall the dead arise *and* praise
      You?   Selah
11 Shall Your lovingkindness be
      declared in the grave?
   Or Your faithfulness
      in the place of destruction?
12 Shall Your wonders be known
      in the dark?
   And Your righteousness
      in the land of forgetfulness?

13 But to You I have cried out, O
      LORD,
   And in the morning my prayer
      comes before You.
14 LORD, why do You cast off my
      soul?

Why do You hide Your face
      from me?
15 I *have been* afflicted and
      ready to die from *my* youth
      up;
   I suffer Your terrors;
   I am distraught.
16 Your fierce wrath has gone
      over me;
   Your terrors have cut me off.
17 They came around me all day
      long like water;
   They engulfed me altogether.
18 Loved one and friend You
      have put far from me,
   And my acquaintances into
      darkness.

PSALM 89

A Contemplation of Ethan the Ezrahite.

I WILL sing of the mercies of
   the LORD forever;
   With my mouth will I make
      known Your faithfulness to
      all generations.
2 For I have said, "Mercy shall
      be built up forever;
   Your faithfulness You shall
      establish in the very
      heavens."

3 "I have made a covenant with
      My chosen,
   I have sworn to My servant
      David:
4 'Your seed I will establish
      forever,
   And build up your throne to
      all generations.' "   Selah

5 And the heavens will praise
      Your wonders, O LORD;
   Your faithfulness also in the
      congregation of the saints.
6 For who in the heavens can
      be compared to the LORD?
   Who among the sons of the
      mighty can be likened to
      the LORD?
7 God is greatly to be feared in
      the assembly of the saints,

And to be held in reverence
   by all *those who are* around
   Him.
8 O LORD God of hosts,
   Who *is* mighty like You, O
   LORD?
   Your faithfulness also
    surrounds You.
9 You rule the raging of the sea;
   When its waves rise, You still
    them.
10 You have broken Rahab in
   pieces, as one who is slain;
   You have scattered Your
    enemies with Your mighty
    arm.

11 The heavens *are* Yours,
   the earth also *is* Yours;
   The world and all its fullness,
    You have founded them.
12 The north and the south,
   You have created them;
   Tabor and Hermon rejoice in
    Your name.
13 You have a mighty arm;
   Strong is Your hand,
    and high is Your right hand.
14 Righteousness and justice *are*
   the foundation of Your
   throne;
   Mercy and truth go before
    Your face.
15 Blessed *are* the people who
   know the joyful sound!
   They walk, O LORD, in the
    light of Your countenance.
16 In Your name they rejoice all
   day long,
   And in Your righteousness
    they are exalted.
17 For You *are* the glory of their
   strength,
   And in Your favor our horn is
    exalted.
18 For our shield *belongs* to the
   LORD,
   And our king to the Holy One
    of Israel.

19 Then You spoke in a vision
   to Your holy one,
   And said: "I have given help
    to *one who is* mighty;

I have exalted one chosen
   from the people.
20 I have found My servant
   David;
   With My holy oil I have
    anointed him,
21 With whom My hand shall be
   established;
   Also My arm shall strengthen
    him.
22 The enemy shall not outwit
   him,
   Nor the son of wickedness
    afflict him.
23 I will beat down his foes
   before his face,
   And plague those who hate
    him.

24 "But My faithfulness and My
   mercy *shall be* with him,
   And in My name his horn
    shall be exalted.
25 Also I will set his hand over
   the sea,
   And his right hand over the
    rivers.
26 He shall cry to Me,
   'You *are* my Father,
   My God, and the rock of my
    salvation.'
27 Also I will make him *My*
   firstborn,
   The highest of the kings of
    the earth.
28 My mercy I will keep for him
   forever,
   And My covenant shall stand
    firm with him.
29 His seed also I will make *to
   endure* forever,
   And his throne as the days of
    heaven.

30 "If his sons forsake My law
   And do not walk in My
    judgments,
31 If they break My statutes
   And do not keep My
    commandments,
32 Then I will visit their
   transgression with the rod,
   And their iniquity with stripes.

33 Nevertheless My lovingkindness I will not utterly
take from him,
Nor allow My faithfulness to
fail.

34 My covenant I will not break,
Nor alter the word that has
gone out of My lips.

35 Once I have sworn by My
holiness;
I will not lie to David:

36 His seed shall endure forever,
And his throne as the sun
before Me;

37 It shall be established forever
like the moon,
Even *like* the faithful witness
in the sky."   Selah

38 But You have cast off and
abhorred,
You have been furious with
Your anointed.

39 You have renounced the
covenant of Your servant;
You have profaned his crown
by casting it to the ground.

40 You have broken down all his
hedges;
You have brought his
strongholds to ruin.

41 All who pass by the way
plunder him;
He is a reproach to his
neighbors.

42 You have exalted the right
hand of his adversaries;
You have made all his
enemies rejoice.

43 You have also turned back
the edge of his sword,
And have not sustained him in
the battle.

44 You have made his glory
cease,
And cast his throne down to
the ground.

45 The days of his youth You
have shortened;
You have covered him with
shame.   Selah

46 How long, LORD?

Will You hide Yourself
forever?
Will Your wrath burn like
fire?

47 Remember how short my time
is;
For what futility have You
created all the children of
men?

48 What man can live and not
see death?
Can he deliver his life from
the power of the grave?
                                  Selah

49 Lord, where *are* Your former
lovingkindnesses,
Which You swore to David in
Your truth?

50 Remember, Lord, the reproach
of Your servants—
How I bear in my bosom *the
reproach of* all the many
peoples,

51 With which Your enemies
have reproached, O LORD,
With which they have
reproached the footsteps of
Your anointed.

52 Blessed *be* the LORD
forevermore!
Amen and Amen.

BOOK FOUR
Psalms 90–106

PSALM 90
A Prayer of Moses the man of God.

LORD, You have been our
dwelling place in all
generations.

2 Before the mountains were
brought forth,
Or ever You had formed the
earth and the world,
Even from everlasting to
everlasting, You *are* God.

3 You turn man to destruction,
And say, "Return, O children
of men."

4 For a thousand years in Your
    sight
  Are like yesterday when it is
    past,
  And *like* a watch in the night.

5 You carry them away *like* a
    flood;
  They are like a sleep.
  In the morning they are like
    grass *which* grows up:

6 In the morning it flourishes
    and grows up;
  In the evening it is cut down
    and withers.

7 For we have been consumed
    by Your anger,
  And by Your wrath we are
    terrified.

8 You have set our iniquities
    before You,
  Our secret *sins* in the light of
    Your countenance.

9 For all our days have passed
    away in Your wrath;
  We finish our years like a
    sigh.

10 The days of our lives *are*
    seventy years;
   And if by reason of strength
    they are eighty years,
   Yet their boast *is* only labor
    and sorrow;
   For it is soon cut off, and we
    fly away.

11 Who knows the power of
    Your anger?
   For as the fear of You,
    so is Your wrath.

12 So teach *us* to number our
    days,
   That we may gain a heart of
    wisdom.

13 Return, O LORD!
   How long?
   And have compassion on Your
    servants.

14 Oh, satisfy us early with Your
    mercy,
   That we may rejoice and be
    glad all our days!

15 Make us glad according to the
    days *in which* You have
    afflicted us,
   And the years *in which* we
    have seen evil.

16 Let Your work appear to Your
    servants,
   And Your glory to their
    children.

17 And let the beauty of the
    LORD our God be upon us,
   And establish the work of our
    hands for us;
   Yes, establish the work of our
    hands.

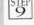

PSALM 91

HE who dwells in the secret
    place of the Most High
  Shall abide under the shadow
    of the Almighty.

2 I will say of the LORD, "*He is*
    my refuge and my fortress;
  My God, in Him I will trust."

3 Surely He shall deliver you
    from the snare of the fowler
  And from the perilous
    pestilence.

4 He shall cover you with His
    feathers,
  And under His wings you shall
    take refuge;
  His truth *shall be your* shield
    and buckler.

5 You shall not be afraid of the
    terror by night,
  Nor of the arrow *that* flies by
    day,

6 *Nor* of the pestilence *that*
    walks in darkness,
  Nor of the destruction *that*
    lays waste at noonday.

7 A thousand may fall at your
    side,
  And ten thousand at your
    right hand;
  But it shall not come near
    you.

8 Only with your eyes shall you
    look,

STEP 3

*Made a decision to turn our will and our lives over to the care of God **as we understood Him.***

Psalm 91:1–4

When we choose to trust God as our Savior and to turn our will and our lives over to Him, we are lifted into "the secret place." Here, the love and protection of our God can continually enfold and support us. The problem comes when we use our "secret place" more like a temporary refuge than a permanent home. The psalmist uses the words "dwells" and "shall abide" for good reason. We cannot know the peace and serenity of God unless we communicate with Him regularly through studying His Word and through praying to Him. As we begin to commune with God, we will be delivered from the snare of our old dependencies and pestilence of our old, negative thinking.

The truth of God's Word will begin to shield our minds from fear and doubt. And knowing how completely we can trust Him will give us confidence and hope for the future.

For further reading on Step 3, turn to page 719.

Daily Encouragement

DAY 296 READING: PSALMS 90:1—91:16

A Thought for the New Day: We should work with an eternal purpose (90:17). Some of the great cathedrals of Europe were built with this idea in mind. Of course, as Isaiah the prophet declared, even "the mountains shall depart" (54:8), but he also said, "the word of our God stands forever" (40:8). Some things, such as truth, are immortal; and we should pray for help to be part of God's business for eternity. (*Turn to page 683.*)

And see the reward of the
    wicked.

9 Because you have made the
    LORD, *who is* my refuge,
    Even the Most High, your
    habitation,
10 No evil shall befall you,
    Nor shall any plague come
    near your dwelling;
11 For He shall give His angels
    charge over you,
    To keep you in all your ways.
12 They shall bear you up in
    their hands,
    Lest you dash your foot
    against a stone.
13 You shall tread upon
    the lion and the cobra,
    The young lion and the
    serpent you shall trample
    underfoot.

14 "Because he has set his love
    upon Me, therefore I will
    deliver him;
    I will set him on high,
    because he has known My
    name.
15 He shall call upon Me,
    and I will answer him;
    I *will be* with him in trouble;
    I will deliver him and honor
    him.
16 With long life I will satisfy
    him,
    And show him My salvation."

PSALM 92

A Psalm. A Song for the Sabbath day.

*I*T is good to give thanks to the
    LORD,
    And to sing praises to Your
    name, O Most High;
2 To declare Your loving-
    kindness in the morning,
    And Your faithfulness every
    night,
3 On an instrument of ten
    strings,
    On the lute,

And on the harp,
    With harmonious sound.
4 For You, LORD, have made me
    glad through Your work;
    I will triumph in the works of
    Your hands.

5 O LORD, how great are Your
    works!
    Your thoughts are very deep.
6 A senseless man does not
    know,
    Nor does a fool understand
    this.
7 When the wicked spring up
    like grass,
    And when all the workers of
    iniquity flourish,
    It is that they may be
    destroyed forever.

8 But You, LORD, *are* on high
    forevermore.
9 For behold, Your enemies, O
    LORD,
    For behold, Your enemies
    shall perish;
    All the workers of iniquity
    shall be scattered.

10 But my horn You have
    exalted like a wild ox;
    I have been anointed with
    fresh oil.
11 My eye also has seen *my
    desire* on my enemies;
    My ears hear *my desire* on the
    wicked
    Who rise up against me.

12 The righteous shall flourish
    like a palm tree,
    He shall grow like a cedar in
    Lebanon.
13 Those who are planted in the
    house of the LORD
    Shall flourish in the courts of
    our God.
14 They shall still bear fruit in
    old age;
    They shall be fresh and
    flourishing,
15 To declare that the LORD is
    upright;

STEP 12

*Having had a spiritual awakening as the result of these steps,
we tried to carry this message to others,
and to practice these principles in all our affairs.*

Psalm 92:1–4

The delightful bounty pointed to by Step 12 is the discovery that all of the sacrifices of the first eleven steps have purchased a gift beyond measure—our spiritual awakening to the God of our understanding. We may have come into recovery merely to save ourselves. We have gained far more than that: we have come to a new and intimate understanding of God. Now we can celebrate with the song of the psalmist, "*It is* good to give thanks to the LORD, and to sing praises to Your name, O Most High" (v. 1).

Furthermore, Step 12 reminds us that this "spiritual awakening" is not a passive, static, or historical event. Rather, it is an ongoing, unfolding experience. Again we echo the psalmist as we pray that we might "carry this message to others." Doing so, we will "declare [God's] lovingkindness in the morning, and [His] faithfulness every night" (v. 2).

For further reading on Step 12, turn to page 687.

Daily Encouragement

DAY 297 READING: PSALMS 92:1—93:5

A Thought for the New Day: If everything depended on my faithfulness, what a sorry state my affairs would be in. But thanks be to God for His infallible faithfulness (92:2). In Psalm 89:3 the Lord declares, "I will not . . . allow My faithfulness to fail." So often we make a mess of things, but God always comes through for us just when we imagine all is lost. How much better to trust in His faithfulness! *Lord, teach us this way of perfect trust.* (*Turn to page 685.*)

He is my rock, and *there is* no
unrighteousness in Him.

PSALM 93

THE LORD reigns,
He is clothed with majesty;
The LORD is clothed,
He has girded Himself with
strength.
Surely the world is
established, so that it
cannot be moved.
2 Your throne *is* established
from of old;
You *are* from everlasting.

3 The floods have lifted up, O
LORD,
The floods have lifted up their
voice;
The floods lift up their waves.
4 The LORD on high *is* mightier
Than the noise of many
waters,
Than the mighty waves of the
sea.

5 Your testimonies are very
sure;
Holiness adorns Your house,
O LORD, forever.

PSALM 94

O LORD God, to whom
vengeance belongs—
O God, to whom vengeance
belongs, shine forth!
2 Rise up, O Judge of the earth;
Render punishment to the
proud.
3 LORD, how long will the
wicked,
How long will the wicked
triumph?

4 They utter speech,
and speak insolent things;
All the workers of iniquity
boast in themselves.
5 They break in pieces Your
people, O LORD,
And afflict Your heritage.

6 They slay the widow and the
stranger,
And murder the fatherless.
7 Yet they say, "The LORD does
not see,
Nor does the God of Jacob
understand."

8 Understand, you senseless
among the people;
And *you* fools, when will you
be wise?
9 He who planted the ear,
shall He not hear?
He who formed the eye,
shall He not see?
10 He who instructs the nations,
shall He not correct,
He who teaches man
knowledge?
11 The LORD knows the thoughts
of man,
That they *are* futile.

12 Blessed *is* the man whom You
instruct, O LORD,
And teach out of Your law,   STEP 6
13 That You may give him rest
from the days of adversity,
Until the pit is dug for the
wicked.
14 For the LORD will not cast off
His people,
Nor will He forsake His
inheritance.
15 But judgment will return to
righteousness,
And all the upright in heart
will follow it.

16 Who will rise up for me
against the evildoers?
Who will stand up for me
against the workers of
iniquity?
17 Unless the LORD *had been* my
help,   STEP 3
My soul would soon have
settled in silence.
18 If I say, "My foot slips,"
Your mercy, O LORD, will hold
me up.
19 In the multitude of my
anxieties within me,

STEP 6

*Were entirely ready to have God
remove all these defects of character.*

Psalm 94:12, 13

The "how" and "why" for Step 6 are contained in Psalm 94:12, 13. We may have wondered if all the work ahead of us is going to be worth the trouble. After all, most of us have begun a Twelve Step Program to leave trouble behind and to finally find contentment and peace. We were looking for rest, not rigor. Believe it or not, there is rest ahead. It is a more perfect and complete rest than most of us have ever known could exist. God wants to give us "rest from the days of adversity." But how? How do we finally make it to that place of contentment? We do so by allowing God to instruct us, teach us, and work in us. We may have had second thoughts about Step 6 because we knew the way ahead might get harder before it became easier. Take courage, friend, and be willing to allow God to show the way over the mountains to the valley of rest.

For further reading on Step 6, turn to page 723.

Daily Encouragement

DAY 298 READING: PSALM 94:1–23

A Thought for the New Day: It is a healthy exercise to practice the presence of God. As human beings, limited in space and time, our knowledge is also very limited. However, it is God's unique quality to be infinitely on hand everywhere at the same time and all times (94:7). His knowledge of us is complete. This is a sobering thought, but also comforting in that we are never alone, and we can tap into God's divinely infinite resources wherever we are. (*Turn to page 687.*)

Your comforts delight my
soul.

20 Shall the throne of iniquity,
which devises evil by law,
Have fellowship with You?
21 They gather together against
the life of the righteous,
And condemn innocent blood.
22 But the LORD has been my
defense,
And my God the rock of my
refuge.
23 He has brought on them their
own iniquity,
And shall cut them off in their
own wickedness;
The LORD our God shall cut
them off.

PSALM 95

OH come, let us sing to the
LORD!
Let us shout joyfully to the
Rock of our salvation.
2 Let us come before His
presence with thanksgiving;
Let us shout joyfully to Him
with psalms.
3 For the LORD *is* the great God,
And the great King above all
gods.
4 In His hand *are* the deep
places of the earth;
The heights of the hills *are*
His also.
5 The sea *is* His, for He made it;
And His hands formed the dry
land.

6 Oh come, let us worship
and bow down;
Let us kneel before the LORD
our Maker.
7 For He *is* our God,
And we *are* the people of His
pasture,
And the sheep of His hand.

Today, if you will hear His
voice:
8 "Do not harden your hearts,
as in the rebellion,

And as *in* the day of trial in
the wilderness,
9 When your fathers tested Me;
They proved Me,
though they saw My work.
10 For forty years I was grieved
with *that* generation,
And said, 'It *is* a people who
go astray in their hearts,
And they do not know My
ways.'
11 So I swore in My wrath,
'They shall not enter My
rest.' "

PSALM 96

OH, sing to the LORD a new
song!
Sing to the LORD, all the
earth.
2 Sing to the LORD, bless His
name;
Proclaim the good news of His
salvation from day to day.
3 Declare His glory among the
nations,
His wonders among all
peoples.

STEP
12

4 For the LORD *is* great
and greatly to be praised;
He *is* to be feared above all
gods.
5 For *all* the gods of the peoples
are idols,
But the LORD made the
heavens.
6 Honor and majesty *are* before
Him;
Strength and beauty *are* in
His sanctuary.

7 Give to the LORD,
O kindreds of the peoples,
Give to the LORD glory and
strength.
8 Give to the LORD the glory
due His name;
Bring an offering,
and come into His courts.
9 Oh, worship the LORD in the
beauty of holiness!

STEP 12

*Having had a spiritual awakening as the result of these steps,
we tried to carry this message to others,
and to practice these principles in all our affairs.*

Psalm 96:1, 2

As our own lives become properly focused, the Lord allows us to become instruments of His healing in the world. What a privilege we have in being able to "proclaim the good news of His salvation from day to day" (v. 2).

This proclaiming happens in two ways. First, as people see our new values and the strength and love God has poured into our lives, the very way we live in the world will show forth His salvation. And second, as we are willing to verbally share our story with others, God will use our message to bring glory to His name. Perhaps we will be a little unsure the first time we feel the Holy Spirit encouraging us to share the message He has given us. But as we explain how God has transformed our lives, our words will not only help others see their need, but will encourage our own spiritual growth, as well.

For further reading on Step 12, turn to page 703.

Daily Encouragement

DAY 299 READING: PSALMS 95:1—96:13

A Thought for the New Day: What is it that moves us to worship God? Mere blind compulsion is not a good motive—for fear He will punish us because we do not worship Him. No, we need to see beyond the veil of outward sight to the One who dwells in the Most Holy Place. There He is displayed in inexpressible beauty, and it is that beauty of His holiness that compels us to fall down before Him in adoration (96:9). *(Turn to page 689.)*

Tremble before Him, all the
earth.

10 Say among the nations,
"The LORD reigns;
The world also is firmly
established,
It shall not be moved;
He shall judge the peoples
righteously."

11 Let the heavens rejoice,
and let the earth be glad;
Let the sea roar, and all its
fullness;
12 Let the field be joyful, and all
that *is* in it.
Then all the trees of the
woods will rejoice before
the LORD.
13 For He is coming, for He is
coming to judge the earth.
He shall judge the world with
righteousness,
And the peoples with His
truth.

PSALM 97

THE LORD reigns;
Let the earth rejoice;
Let the multitude of isles be
glad!

2 Clouds and darkness surround
Him;
Righteousness and justice *are*
the foundation of His
throne.
3 A fire goes before Him,
And burns up His enemies
round about.
4 His lightnings light the world;
The earth sees and trembles.
5 The mountains melt like wax
at the presence of the LORD,
At the presence of the Lord of
the whole earth.
6 The heavens declare His
righteousness,
And all the peoples see His
glory.

7 Let all be put to shame who
serve carved images,
Who boast of idols.
Worship Him, all *you* gods.
8 Zion hears and is glad,
And the daughters of Judah
rejoice
Because of Your judgments, O
LORD.
9 For You, LORD, *are* most high
above all the earth;
You are exalted far above all
gods.

10 You who love the LORD, hate
evil!
He preserves the souls of His
saints;
He delivers them out of the
hand of the wicked.
11 Light is sown for the
righteous,
And gladness for the upright
in heart.
12 Rejoice in the LORD, you
righteous,
And give thanks at the
remembrance of His holy
name.

PSALM 98

A Psalm.

OH, sing to the LORD a new
song!
For He has done marvelous
things;
His right hand and His holy
arm have gained Him the
victory.
2 The LORD has made known
His salvation;
His righteousness He has
openly shown in the sight of
the nations.
3 He has remembered His mercy
and His faithfulness to the
house of Israel;
All the ends of the earth have
seen the salvation of our
God.

4 Shout joyfully to the LORD,
all the earth;

STEP 11

*Sought through prayer and meditation to improve our conscious contact with God **as we understood Him,** praying only for knowledge of His will for us and the power to carry that out.*

Psalm 97:10–12

Hating evil may seem to be a tall order for those of us who have spent much of our lives trying to placate or appease others. We are afraid of how others will respond to the stand we have taken. God knows and understands our insecurities, and He has given us promises to help us step out in the courage of His strength. First, God promises us deliverance from the hand of the wicked. This does not mean that God's soldiers will never suffer. But it does mean that the enemy cannot defeat us spiritually and emotionally, because God "preserves the souls of His saints." God accomplishes this by giving His dear saints *light* and *gladness* (v. 11). The image of light is closely connected with God Himself, and is synonymous with purity, wise understanding, and love. To take a stand against evil may involve hardship, but we can go in His power and we can reap His rich rewards.

For further reading on Step 11, turn to page 699.

Daily Encouragement

DAY 300 READING: PSALMS 97:1—98:9

A Thought for the New Day: The Bible is a difficult book for readers without imagination. The Hebrew writers wrote in word pictures, not in theoretical language. So we have to catch their spirit when they speak about nature clapping its hands and breaking forth into joyful song. Jesus said that the stones would worship Him if people did not (see Luke 19:40). Are you listening for the music in God's world? (*Turn to page 691.*)

Break forth in song, rejoice,
and sing praises.
5 Sing to the LORD with the
harp,
With the harp and the sound
of a psalm,
6 With trumpets and the sound
of a horn;
Shout joyfully before the
LORD, the King.

7 Let the sea roar, and all its
fullness,
The world and those who
dwell in it;
8 Let the rivers clap *their* hands;
Let the hills be joyful together
before the LORD,
9 For He is coming to judge the
earth.
With righteousness He shall
judge the world,
And the peoples with equity.

PSALM 99

THE LORD reigns;
Let the peoples tremble!
He dwells *between* the
cherubim;
Let the earth be moved!
2 The LORD *is* great in Zion,
And He *is* high above all the
peoples.
3 Let them praise Your great
and awesome name—
He *is* holy.

4 The King's strength also loves
justice;
You have established equity;
You have executed justice and
righteousness in Jacob.
5 Exalt the LORD our God,
And worship at His footstool;
For He *is* holy.

6 Moses and Aaron were among
His priests,
And Samuel was among those
who called upon His name;
They called upon the LORD,
and He answered them.

7 He spoke to them in the
cloudy pillar;
They kept His testimonies and
the ordinance *that* He gave
them.

8 You answered them, O LORD
our God;
You were to them God-Who-
Forgives,
Though You took vengeance
on their deeds.
9 Exalt the LORD our God,
And worship at His holy hill;
For the LORD our God *is* holy.

PSALM 100

A Psalm of Thanksgiving.

MAKE a joyful shout to the
LORD, all you lands!
2 Serve the LORD with gladness;
Come before His presence
with singing.
3 Know that the LORD, He *is*
God;
It is He *who* has made us,
and not we ourselves;
We are His people
and the sheep of His
pasture.

4 Enter into His gates with
thanksgiving,
And into His courts with
praise.
Be thankful to Him,
and bless His name.
5 For the LORD *is* good;
His mercy *is* everlasting,
And His truth *endures* to all
generations.

PSALM 101

A Psalm of David.

I WILL sing of mercy and
justice;
To You, O LORD, I will sing
praises.

2 I will behave wisely in a
perfect way.

STEP
10

690

STEP 10

*Continued to take personal inventory
and when we were wrong promptly admitted it.*

Psalm 101:2–4

As king over Israel, David's position among men was secure. He had come a long way since the days when King Saul had declared him an outlaw. But instead of developing an attitude of overconfident superiority, this psalm shows that David remained humble and determined to obey his heavenly King.

Perhaps David's memories of King Saul prompted this psalm. Saul could appear very righteous and humble in public; but as Saul's personal musician, David knew what the king acted like at home. In private, Saul was moody, vicious, insecure, and insensitive.

David, instead, determined before God that he would be as obedient and godly within his house as he was when he stood before the throngs of Israel. He wanted his heart to be as clean as his public image. This should be our desire, also, but it can only become a reality as we are willing to take honest, careful inventory of our personal lives, admitting our wrongs promptly and moving to correct them.

For further reading on Step 10, turn to page 695.

Daily Encouragement

DAY 301 READING: PSALMS 99:1—101:8

A Thought for the New Day: Nothing so rightly raises our self-awareness as the full realization that *"it is* He *who* has made us."* Loss of self-respect, self-hatred that expresses itself in violent actions, has its roots in denial of our divine origins. That is possibly the greatest human tragedy. Stand on your feet in the presence of God. Answer His call to reflect His honor in the world by becoming all that He designed you to be. *(Turn to page 693.)*

Oh, when will You come to
    me?
I will walk within my house
    with a perfect heart.

3 I will set nothing wicked
    before my eyes;
I hate the work of those who
    fall away;
It shall not cling to me.
4 A perverse heart shall depart
    from me;
I will not know wickedness.

5 Whoever secretly slanders his
    neighbor,
Him I will destroy;
The one who has a haughty
    look and a proud heart,
Him I will not endure.

6 My eyes *shall be* on the
    faithful of the land,
That they may dwell with me;
He who walks in a perfect
    way,
He shall serve me.
7 He who works deceit shall not
    dwell within my house;
He who tells lies shall not
    continue in my presence.
8 Early I will destroy all the
    wicked of the land,
That I may cut off all the
    evildoers from the city of
    the LORD.

PSALM 102

A Prayer of the afflicted, when he is
overwhelmed and pours out his complaint
before the LORD.

 HEAR my prayer, O LORD,
    And let my cry come to You.
2 Do not hide Your face from
    me in the day of my trouble;
Incline Your ear to me;
In the day that I call,
    answer me speedily.

3 For my days are consumed
    like smoke,

And my bones are burned like
    a hearth.
4 My heart is stricken and
    withered like grass,
So that I forget to eat my
    bread.
5 Because of the sound of my
    groaning
My bones cling to my skin.
6 I am like a pelican of the
    wilderness;
I am like an owl of the desert.
7 I lie awake,
And am like a sparrow alone
    on the housetop.

8 My enemies reproach me all
    day long,
And those who deride me
    swear an oath against me.
9 For I have eaten ashes like
    bread,
And mingled my drink with
    weeping,
10 Because of Your indignation
    and Your wrath;
For You have lifted me up
    and cast me away.
11 My days *are* like a shadow
    that lengthens,
And I wither away like grass.

12 But You, O LORD, shall endure
    forever,
And the remembrance of Your
    name to all generations.
13 You will arise *and* have mercy
    on Zion;
For the time to favor her,
Yes, the set time, has come.
14 For Your servants take
    pleasure in her stones,
And show favor to her dust.
15 So the nations shall fear
    the name of the LORD,
And all the kings of the earth
    Your glory.
16 For the LORD shall build up
    Zion;
He shall appear in His glory.
17 He shall regard the prayer of
    the destitute,
And shall not despise their
    prayer.

STEP 1

We admitted we were powerless over our dependencies—
that our lives had become unmanageable.

Psalm 102:1–7

If every day we live feels useless and devoured by forces beyond our control, we might say, "My days are consumed like smoke." If our inner self has ached and accused and questioned until it is almost beyond feeling, we might say, "My heart is stricken and withered like grass." If our food has lost its taste and we can hear nothing but our own inner groaning, we may believe ourselves to be "like a sparrow alone." But the precious Truth is very different indeed. We are not alone. In fact, a kind and loving God hears and has compassion on the groaning of our souls. But we cannot find the peace and security and joy that He offers until we can acknowledge how hopeless our situation has become. We must know beyond a shadow of a doubt that we are powerless to stop the forces that consume our days and wither our hearts. Amazingly, in that very acknowledgment of powerlessness rests the hope we so desperately need.

For further reading on Step 1, turn to page 825.

Daily
Encouragement

DAY 302 READING: PSALM 102:1–28

A Thought for the New Day: One of God's characteristics is that He does not change (vv. 25–27). The visible, created world changes. We change and pass from the scene, but the Lord remains the same forever. This also means that His purposes and promises never alter. We change our minds, but God never does. One lesson we derive from this is to meditate on the plans God has for us. Too many false starts in life lead to a wasted career, but we can line up our lives with God's goals for us. (*Turn to page 695.*)

18 This will be written for the
generation to come,
That a people yet to be
created may praise the
LORD.
19 For He looked down from the
height of His sanctuary;
From heaven the LORD viewed
the earth,
20 To hear the groaning of the
prisoner,
To loose those appointed to
death,
21 To declare the name of the
LORD in Zion,
And His praise in Jerusalem,
22 When the peoples are
gathered together,
And the kingdoms, to serve
the LORD.

23 He weakened my strength in
the way;
He shortened my days.
24 I said, "O my God,
Do not take me away in the
midst of my days;
Your years *are* throughout all
generations.
25 Of old You laid the foundation
of the earth,
And the heavens *are* the work
of Your hands.
26 They will perish, but You will
endure;
Yes, all of them will grow old
like a garment;
Like a cloak You will change
them,
And they will be changed.
27 But You *are* the same,
And Your years will have no
end.
28 The children of Your servants
will continue,
And their descendants will be
established before You."

PSALM 103

A Psalm of David.

BLESS the LORD, O my soul;
And all that is within me,
bless His holy name!

2 Bless the LORD, O my soul,
And forget not all His
benefits:
3 Who forgives all your
iniquities,
Who heals all your diseases,
4 Who redeems your life from
destruction,
Who crowns you with
lovingkindness and tender
mercies,
5 Who satisfies your mouth
with good *things*,
So that your youth is renewed
like the eagle's.

STEP 7

6 The LORD executes
righteousness
And justice for all who are
oppressed.
7 He made known His ways to
Moses,
His acts to the children of
Israel.

8 The LORD *is* merciful and
gracious,
Slow to anger,
and abounding in mercy.
9 He will not always strive *with
us*,
Nor will He keep *His* anger
forever.
10 He has not dealt with us
according to our sins,
Nor punished us according to
our iniquities.

STEP 10

11 For as the heavens are high
above the earth,
So great is His mercy toward
those who fear Him;
12 As far as the east is from the
west,
So far has He removed our
transgressions from us.
13 As a father pities *his* children,
So the LORD pities those who
fear Him.
14 For He knows our frame;
He remembers that we *are*
dust.
15 *As for* man, his days *are* like
grass;

STEP 10

*Continued to take personal inventory
and when we were wrong promptly admitted it.*

Psalm 103:8–18

In Step 10, we are continually reassessing our lives. Are we careful to honor, obey, and serve God with humility? Or have we begun to slip back into our old, codependent patterns? Each day we must honestly, humbly inventory ourselves, admitting our shortcomings to God and asking Him for strength to overcome our problems. As we are careful to maintain this honest and humble frame of mind, God responds to us with His priceless gift of mercy. He does not deal with us "according to our iniquities." Instead, remembering that we are fragile and weak, He has pity on us as a father has pity on his own children.

And since God is merciful and gracious to us, we should be that way toward ourselves, as well. Each day is a chance for growing. If we fail, Jesus is there to pick us up, forgive us, and set us on the right track again. His mercy is "from everlasting to everlasting on those who fear Him."

For further reading on Step 10, turn to page 705.

Daily Encouragement

DAY 303 READING: PSALM 103:1–22

A Thought for the New Day: Among the changeless qualities of God is His mercy, which is "everlasting." David observed that we are very temporary beings, and we soon pass away. But God keeps faith with those who respond to His proposals of love (vv. 17, 18). Although His commands are not really hard, again and again we disobey Him. However, if only we will continue to seek Him with all our hearts, He will forgive us, and He will keep His promises to us. *(Turn to page 697.)*

As a flower of the field,
so he flourishes.
16 For the wind passes over it,
and it is gone,
And its place remembers it no
more.
17 But the mercy of the LORD *is*
from everlasting to
everlasting
On those who fear Him,
And His righteousness to
children's children,
18 To such as keep His covenant,
And to those who remember
His commandments to do
them.

19 The LORD has established His
throne in heaven,
And His kingdom rules over
all.

20 Bless the LORD, you His
angels,
Who excel in strength,
who do His word,
Heeding the voice of His
word.
21 Bless the LORD, all *you* His
hosts,
You ministers of His,
who do His pleasure.
22 Bless the LORD, all His works,
In all places of His dominion.

Bless the LORD, O my soul!

PSALM 104

BLESS the LORD, O my soul!

O LORD my God, You are very
great:
You are clothed with honor
and majesty,
2 Who cover *Yourself* with light
as *with* a garment,
Who stretch out the heavens
like a curtain.

3 He lays the beams of His
upper chambers in the
waters,

Who makes the clouds His
chariot,
Who walks on the wings of
the wind,
4 Who makes His angels spirits,
His ministers a flame of fire.

5 *You who* laid the foundations
of the earth,
So *that* it should not be
moved forever,
6 You covered it with the deep
as *with* a garment;
The waters stood above the
mountains.
7 At Your rebuke they fled;
At the voice of Your thunder
they hastened away.
8 They went up over the
mountains;
They went down into the
valleys,
To the place which You
founded for them.
9 You have set a boundary that
they may not pass over,
That they may not return to
cover the earth.

10 He sends the springs into the
valleys,
Which flow among the hills.
11 They give drink to every beast
of the field;
The wild donkeys quench
their thirst.
12 By them the birds of the
heavens have their
habitation;
They sing among the
branches.
13 He waters the hills from His
upper chambers;
The earth is satisfied with the
fruit of Your works.

14 He causes the grass to grow
for the cattle,
And vegetation for the service
of man,
That he may bring forth food
from the earth,
15 And wine *that* makes glad the
heart of man,

STEP 4

Made a searching and fearless moral inventory of ourselves.

Psalm 104:24

Blaming God for the sin and evil in our world leads to two possibilities: either God is not all-powerful or He is not wise and loving. Of course, such reasoning plays right into Satan's hands. He loves to see us blame God for evil, but the truth is far different. God always has been and always will be all-powerful, totally wise, and loving beyond our ability even to comprehend. None of these attributes, however, negates our free will. As long as human beings inhabit the earth, they will be free to choose whom they will serve. The choice to serve Satan and self results in suffering and injustice. We must move beyond our inclination to blame and instead work to understand the roots of our problems in order to bring about positive change. Romans 8:28 should be a part of our thinking during this process: "And we know that all the things work together for good to those who love God, to those who are the called according to *His* purpose."

For further reading on Step 4, turn to page 701.

Daily Encouragement

DAY 304 READING: PSALM 104:1–35

A Thought for the New Day: A meditation can include a variety of activities, although it usually takes the form of private prayer, praise, and study. In this song, the meditation is directed toward God, and the writer prays that God will be pleased with his thoughts (v. 34). We need to spend time in preparation for good meditation. Although varied, our thoughts need to be fixed on the Lord as their great goal. (*Turn to page 699.*)

Oil to make *his* face shine,
And bread *which* strengthens
man's heart.

16 The trees of the LORD are full
of sap,
The cedars of Lebanon which
He planted,

17 Where the birds make their
nests;
The stork has her home in the
fir trees.

18 The high hills *are* for the wild
goats;
The cliffs are a refuge for the
rock badgers.

19 He appointed the moon for
seasons;
The sun knows its going
down.

20 You make darkness, and it is
night,
In which all the beasts of the
forest creep about.

21 The young lions roar after
their prey,
And seek their food from God.

22 *When* the sun arises, they
gather together
And lie down in their dens.

23 Man goes out to his work
And to his labor until the
evening.

24 O LORD, how manifold are
Your works!
In wisdom You have made
them all.
The earth is full of Your
possessions—

25 This great and wide sea,
In which *are* innumerable
teeming things,
Living things both small and
great.

26 There the ships sail about;
And there is that Leviathan
Which You have made to play
there.

27 These all wait for You,
That You may give *them* their
food in due season.

28 *What* You give them they
gather in;
You open Your hand,
they are filled with good.

29 You hide Your face, they are
troubled;
You take away their breath,
they die and return to their
dust.

30 You send forth Your Spirit,
they are created;
And You renew the face of
the earth.

31 May the glory of the LORD
endure forever;
May the LORD rejoice in His
works.

32 He looks on the earth, and it
trembles;
He touches the hills, and they
smoke.

33 I will sing to the LORD as long
as I live;
I will sing praise to my God
while I have my being.

34 May my meditation be sweet
to Him;
I will be glad in the LORD.

35 May sinners be consumed
from the earth,
And the wicked be no more!

Bless the LORD, O my soul!
Praise the LORD!

PSALM 105

OH, give thanks to the LORD!
Call upon His name;
Make known His deeds among
the peoples.

2 Sing to Him, sing psalms to
Him;
Talk of all His wondrous
works.

3 Glory in His holy name;
Let the hearts of those rejoice
who seek the LORD.

4 Seek the LORD and His
strength;
Seek His face evermore.

*Sought through prayer and meditation to improve our conscious contact with God **as we understood Him,** praying only for knowledge of His will for us and the power to carry that out.*

Psalm 105:1–4

Mostly, we tend to seek God's hand and not His face. When we come before Him, we generally bring a list of needs. And although God has told us that every child of His may petition Him at any time, there is so much more to true fellowship with God. If we really hunger to know our Father deeply, Psalm 105:1–4 can give us tremendous insight. These verses urge us to tell others of God's wonderful deeds and to be able to share what God has done in our lives. Then, too, our hearts should be filled with praise, which bubbles over into joyous song, because such singing glorifies God.

When we make it a habit to keep our minds dwelling on God Himself and all His wonderful attributes and deeds, we will begin to behold His beauty, majesty, and grace. We will begin to see His face.

For further reading on Step 11, turn to page 717.

Daily Encouragement

DAY 305 READING: PSALM 105:1–15

A Thought for the New Day: The covenant, or agreement, described in verses 8–10 was made a thousand years before David's time. God first announced it in fullest form to Abraham. But the promise of the "covenant of grace," as we call it, was as old as Adam and Eve (Gen. 3:15). In that covenant God principally bound Himself to the promise of our salvation in Jesus Christ. So we can see that God's plan to save us predated the New Testament by a very long time. *(Turn to page 701.)*

5 Remember His marvelous
   works which He has done,
   His wonders, and the
   judgments of His mouth,
6 O seed of Abraham His
   servant,
   You children of Jacob,
   His chosen ones!

7 He *is* the Lord our God;
   His judgments *are* in all the
   earth.
8 He has remembered His
   covenant forever,
   The word *which* He
   commanded, for a thousand
   generations,
9 *The covenant* which He made
   with Abraham,
   And His oath to Isaac,
10 And confirmed it to Jacob for
   a statute,
   To Israel *for* an everlasting
   covenant,
11 Saying, "To you I will give the
   land of Canaan
   As the allotment of your
   inheritance,"
12 When they were *but* few in
   number,
   Indeed very few, and
   strangers in it.

13 When they went from one
   nation to another,
   From *one* kingdom to another
   people,
14 He permitted no one to do
   them wrong;
   Yes, He reproved kings for
   their sakes,
15 *Saying,* "Do not touch My
   anointed ones,
   And do My prophets no
   harm."

16 Moreover He called for a
   famine in the land;
   He destroyed all the provision
   of bread.
17 He sent a man before them—
   Joseph—*who* was sold as a
   slave.

18 They hurt his feet with fetters,
   He was laid in irons.
19 Until the time that his word
   came to pass,
   The word of the Lord tested
   him.
20 The king sent and released
   him,
   The ruler of the people let him
   go free.
21 He made him lord of his
   house,
   And ruler of all his
   possessions,
22 To bind his princes at his
   pleasure,
   And teach his elders wisdom.

23 Israel also came into Egypt,
   And Jacob sojourned in the
   land of Ham.
24 And He increased His people
   greatly,
   And made them stronger than
   their enemies.
25 He turned their heart to hate
   His people,
   To deal craftily with His
   servants.

26 He sent Moses His servant,
   And Aaron whom He had
   chosen.
27 They performed His signs
   among them,
   And wonders in the land of
   Ham.
28 He sent darkness, and made *it*
   dark;
   And they did not rebel against
   His word.
29 He turned their waters into
   blood,
   And killed their fish.
30 Their land abounded with
   frogs,
   Even in the chambers of their
   kings.
31 He spoke, and there came
   swarms of flies,
   And lice in all their territory.
32 He gave them hail for rain,
   And flaming fire in their land.

STEP
4

Made a searching and fearless moral inventory of ourselves.

Psalm 105:17–22

Joseph was a man specially chosen by God to become a great and powerful official in Egypt. God planned that he would not only save the Egyptians from famine, but his own family, as well. When we read Genesis 37—47, we learn that the blessings of honor and wealth bestowed upon Joseph were preceded by years of great suffering. Hated by his brothers, sold into slavery, falsely accused of adultery, incarcerated in an Egyptian prison—for a while things seemed to go from bad to worse for Joseph. It seemed that he had every reason to be bitter against his brothers and angry at God.

Many of us have been through similar pain and suffering. Our families have hurt us, and our circumstances in life at times appear hopeless. But if we can move beyond our pain, we may realize as Joseph did, that God can use every part of our past and present suffering to enrich our own lives and the lives of those with whom we come into contact.

For further reading on Step 4, turn to page 769.

Daily Encouragement

DAY 306 READING: PSALM 105:16–45

A Thought for the New Day: This entire psalm is a rehearsal of God's faithfulness to His people. Notice, particularly that the unnamed writer had committed to memory every step of God's dealings with Israel (vv. 16–45). Diaries can be valuable for reminding us of how God has led each of us. Such memories inspire and strengthen our resolve to keep on our way with the Lord. The One who always has been faithful will continue on with us all our days. (*Turn to page 703.*)

33 He struck their vines also,
   and their fig trees,
   And splintered the trees of
   their territory.
34 He spoke, and locusts came,
   Young locusts without
   number,
35 And ate up all the vegetation
   in their land,
   And devoured the fruit of
   their ground.
36 He also destroyed all the
   firstborn in their land,
   The first of all their strength.

37 He also brought them out
   with silver and gold,
   And *there was* none feeble
   among His tribes.
38 Egypt was glad when they
   departed,
   For the fear of them had
   fallen upon them.
39 He spread a cloud for a
   covering,
   And fire to give light in the
   night.
40 *The people* asked, and He
   brought quail,
   And satisfied them with the
   bread of heaven.
41 He opened the rock,
   and water gushed out;
   It ran in the dry places *like* a
   river.

42 For He remembered His holy
   promise,
   And Abraham His servant.
43 He brought out His people
   with joy,
   His chosen ones with
   gladness.
44 He gave them the lands of the
   Gentiles,
   And they inherited the labor
   of the nations,
45 That they might observe His
   statutes
   And keep His laws.

   Praise the LORD!

Joy in Forgiveness

PSALM 106

PRAISE the LORD! **STEP 12**

   Oh, give thanks to the LORD,
   for *He is* good!
   For His mercy *endures*
   forever.

2 Who can utter the mighty
   acts of the LORD?
   Or can declare all His praise?
3 Blessed *are* those who keep
   justice,
   And he who does
   righteousness at all times!

4 Remember me, O LORD, with
   the favor *You have toward*
   Your people;
   Oh, visit me with Your
   salvation,
5 That I may see the benefit of
   Your chosen ones,
   That I may rejoice in the
   gladness of Your nation,
   That I may glory with Your
   inheritance.

6 We have sinned with our
   fathers,
   We have committed iniquity,
   We have done wickedly.
7 Our fathers in Egypt did not
   understand Your wonders;
   They did not remember the
   multitude of Your mercies,
   But rebelled by the sea—the
   Red Sea.

8 Nevertheless He saved them
   for His name's sake,
   That He might make His
   mighty power known.
9 He rebuked the Red Sea also,
   and it dried up;
   So He led them through the
   depths,
   As through the wilderness.
10 He saved them from the hand
   of him who hated *them*,
   And redeemed them from the
   hand of the enemy.

STEP 12

Having had a spiritual awakening as the result of these steps,
we tried to carry this message to others,
and to practice these principles in all our affairs.

Psalm 106:1–3

In Step 12, we are working to develop a mind-set to live by—a pattern of attitudes, responses, and habits that will keep our lives emotionally stable, socially productive, and spiritually growing. We are working to fulfill the instruction given to us in today's meditation.

Our attitude toward life should be one of praise and thankfulness (v. 1). As we continually call to our minds God's mercy on our behalf, His goodness and kindness, His wisdom and love, we will be able to thank and praise Him in all the situations we encounter. This will keep us emotionally stable.

In our daily contact with other people, our response should be a desire to share what He has done for us (v. 2). God will open doors of testimony that will enable us to be socially productive for Him.

And, finally, if we are careful to abide in His Word, obeying His commands and the Holy Spirit's leading, we will be blessed with spiritual growth, which will benefit every area of our life (v. 3).

For further reading on Step 12, turn to page 707.

Daily Encouragement

DAY 307 READING: PSALM 106:1–12

A Thought for the New Day: Very often we meet this phrase, "His name's sake" (v. 8), or something like it, in the Bible. In this expression we are made aware that a person's name can become a symbol for his reputation: "George Smith has a good name." God, too, has a reputation to uphold. He relates Himself to His people, who are known by their association with Him. We need to make sure that we give God a "good name" in everything we do. (*Turn to page 705.*)

11 The waters covered their
      enemies;
      There was not one of them
      left.

STEP
10
12 Then they believed His words;
      They sang His praise.

13 They soon forgot His works;
      They did not wait for His
      counsel,
14 But lusted exceedingly in the
      wilderness,
      And tested God in the desert.
15 And He gave them their
      request,
      But sent leanness into their
      soul.

16 When they envied Moses in
      the camp,
      And Aaron the saint of the
      LORD,
17 The earth opened up and
      swallowed Dathan,
      And covered the faction of
      Abiram.
18 A fire was kindled in their
      company;
      The flame burned up the
      wicked.

19 They made a calf in Horeb,
      And worshiped the molded
      image.
20 Thus they changed their glory
      Into the image of an ox that
      eats grass.
21 They forgot God their Savior,
      Who had done great things in
      Egypt,
22 Wondrous works in the land
      of Ham,
      Awesome things by the Red
      Sea.
23 Therefore He said that He
      would destroy them,
      Had not Moses His chosen
      one stood before Him in the
      breach,
      To turn away His wrath,
      lest He destroy *them*.

24 Then they despised the
      pleasant land;

      They did not believe His word,
25 But murmured in their tents,
      And did not heed the voice of
      the LORD.
26 Therefore He lifted up His
      hand *in an oath* against
      them,
      To overthrow them in the
      wilderness,
27 To overthrow their
      descendants among the
      nations,
      And to scatter them in the
      lands.

28 They joined themselves also
      to Baal of Peor,
      And ate sacrifices made to the
      dead.
29 Thus they provoked *Him* to
      anger with their deeds,
      And the plague broke out
      among them.
30 Then Phinehas stood up and
      intervened,
      And *so* the plague was
      stopped.
31 And that was accounted to
      him for righteousness
      To all generations
      forevermore.

32 They angered *Him* also at the
      waters of strife,
      So that it went ill with Moses
      on account of them;
33 Because they rebelled against
      His Spirit,
      So that he spoke rashly with
      his lips.

34 They did not destroy the
      peoples,
      Concerning whom the LORD
      had commanded them,
35 But they mingled with the
      Gentiles
      And learned their works;
36 They served their idols,
      Which became a snare to
      them.
37 They even sacrificed their
      sons

STEP 10

*Continued to take personal inventory
and when we were wrong promptly admitted it.*

Psalm 106:12–15

The children of Israel had been miraculously delivered from Egyptian bondage. God had saved them and shown them His great power on their behalf. They believed in Him and sang His praises (v. 12).

Unfortunately, that is not the final word in the account of the Israelites in the wilderness. The rest of this psalm is a sad commentary on what it means to forget God. And all believers must be ever watchful and alert for signs of similar backsliding in our own lives.

Our sin, as the Israelites', begins when we allow ourselves to dwell on things other than God and His goodness. Then it progresses to self-determination. Instead of waiting for God to speak and lead, we arrogantly plan our own way. Selfish lusts begin to guide our thinking and our actions (v. 14). Sooner or later we discover that our once healthy souls have shriveled and we are spiritual beggars. The way to avoid this trap is a simple message with profound depths: "Abide in Him."

For further reading on Step 10, turn to page 779.

Daily Encouragement

DAY 308 READING: PSALM 106:13–48

A Thought for the New Day: What is your first thought when trouble comes? It is natural to run as far away as you can at such times. But experience shows that there is no escape from difficulty in the world. Sooner or later we have to stand and face the situation, or else lose everything. It should always come as a relief that you do not need to be alone with your trial. God waits for your cry and will hurry to your aid (v. 44). (*Turn to page 707.*)

And their daughters to
demons,

38 And shed innocent blood,
Even the blood of their sons
and daughters,
Whom they sacrificed to the
idols of Canaan;
And the land was polluted
with blood.

39 Thus they were defiled by
their own works,
And played the harlot by their
own deeds.

40 Therefore the wrath of the
LORD was kindled against
His people,
So that He abhorred His own
inheritance.

41 And He gave them into the
hand of the Gentiles,
And those who hated them
ruled over them.

42 Their enemies also oppressed
them,
And they were brought into
subjection under their hand.

43 Many times He delivered
them;
But they rebelled *against Him*
by their counsel,
And were brought low for
their iniquity.

44 Nevertheless He regarded
their affliction,
When He heard their cry;

45 And for their sake He
remembered His covenant,
And relented according to the
multitude of His mercies.

46 He also made them to be
pitied
By all those who carried them
away captive.

47 Save us, O LORD our God,
And gather us from among
the Gentiles,
To give thanks to Your holy
name,
And to triumph in Your
praise.

48 Blessed *be* the LORD God of
Israel
From everlasting to
everlasting!
And let all the people say,
"Amen!"

Praise the LORD!

BOOK FIVE

Psalms 107–150

PSALM 107

OH, give thanks to the LORD,
for *He is* good!
For His mercy *endures*
forever.

2 Let the redeemed of the LORD
say *so*,
Whom He has redeemed from
the hand of the enemy,

3 And gathered out of the lands,
From the east and from the
west,
From the north and from the
south.

4 They wandered in the
wilderness in a desolate
way;
They found no city to dwell
in.

5 Hungry and thirsty,
Their soul fainted in them.

6 Then they cried out to the
LORD in their trouble,
And He delivered them out of
their distresses.

7 And He led them forth by the
right way,
That they might go to a city
for habitation.

8 Oh, that *men* would give
thanks to the LORD *for* His
goodness,
And *for* His wonderful works
to the children of men!

9 For He satisfies the longing
soul,
And fills the hungry soul with
goodness.

STEP 12

*Having had a spiritual awakening as the result of these steps,
we tried to carry this message to others,
and to practice these principles in all our affairs.*

Psalm 107:1, 2

There was a point in our lives when the bondage of our dependency was a bitter fact of life. We were held hostage by negative thought patterns and powerful habits. But thanks be to God! Our Lord Jesus Christ has changed all that. He has redeemed us from the hand of our enemy. "Redeemed" is a beautiful word that means to "set free by paying the price." Jesus paid the price our addictions sought to extract from us. He suffered and died on the cross so that we would not have to pay that ultimate price. The power by which He conquered death is the same power we can walk in daily because we belong to Him. To meditate on such mercy and grace generates the joyous response of the psalmist himself: "Let the redeemed of the LORD say *so.*"

For further reading on Step 12, turn to page 709.

Daily Encouragement

DAY 309 READING: PSALM 107:1–16

A Thought for the New Day: Readiness to complain produces inner bitterness, and discontent takes its toll on our health and friendships. However, complaining is difficult when we have cultivated a habit of thankfulness. Even in the worst of times, the one who can see beyond outward appearances quickly finds much to be thankful for. God deserves our gratitude just for who He is, and His personal friendship more than compensates for all our misfortunes (v. 15). *(Turn to page 709.)*

10 Those who sat in darkness
        and in the shadow of death,
    Bound in affliction and irons—
11 Because they rebelled against
        the words of God,
    And despised the counsel of
        the Most High,
12 Therefore He brought down
        their heart with labor;
    They fell down,
        and *there was* none to help.
13 Then they cried out to the
        LORD in their trouble,
    And He saved them out of
        their distresses.
14 He brought them out of
        darkness and the shadow of
        death,
    And broke their chains in
        pieces.
15 Oh, that *men* would give
        thanks to the LORD *for* His
        goodness,
    And *for* His wonderful works
        to the children of men!
16 For He has broken the gates
        of bronze,
    And cut the bars of iron in
        two.

17 Fools, because of their
        transgression,
    And because of their
        iniquities, were afflicted.
18 Their soul abhorred all
        manner of food,
    And they drew near to the
        gates of death.
19 Then they cried out to the
        LORD in their trouble,
    And He saved them out of
        their distresses.
20 He sent His word and healed
        them,
    And delivered *them* from their
        destructions.

STEP
12
21 Oh, that *men* would give
        thanks to the LORD *for* His
        goodness,
    And *for* His wonderful works
        to the children of men!
22 Let them sacrifice the
        sacrifices of thanksgiving,

    And declare His works with
        rejoicing.

23 Those who go down to the sea
        in ships,
    Who do business on great
        waters,
24 They see the works of the
        LORD,
    And His wonders in the deep.
25 For He commands and raises
        the stormy wind,
    Which lifts up the waves of
        the sea.
26 They mount up to the
        heavens,
    They go down again to the
        depths;
    Their soul melts because of
        trouble.

STEP
2
27 They reel to and fro, and
        stagger like a drunken man,
    And are at their wits' end.
28 Then they cry out to the LORD
        in their trouble,
    And He brings them out of
        their distresses.
29 He calms the storm,
    So that its waves are still.
30 Then they are glad because
        they are quiet;
    So He guides them to their
        desired haven.
31 Oh, that *men* would give
        thanks to the LORD *for* His
        goodness,
    And *for* His wonderful works
        to the children of men!
32 Let them exalt Him also in the
        congregation of the people,
    And praise Him in the
        assembly of the elders.

33 He turns rivers into a
        wilderness,
    And the watersprings into dry
        ground;
34 A fruitful land into
        barrenness,
    For the wickedness of those
        who dwell in it.
35 He turns a wilderness into
        pools of water,

STEP 12

*Having had a spiritual awakening as the result of these steps,
we tried to carry this message to others,
and to practice these principles in all our affairs.*

Psalm 107:21, 22

A sacrifice costs something, or it is not a sacrifice. When we give a small amount out of our abundance, that may be a good deed but it is not a sacrifice. When we can obey the exhortation given to us in Hebrews 13:15—to "continually offer the sacrifice of praise to God"—we have begun to understand how to offer the sacrifice of thanksgiving. Sometimes we may not feel like rejoicing and giving thanks. Instead, we may be frightened or saddened or confused. But honestly, sincerely giving thanks to God in spite of our circumstances and feelings brings glory to God and also brings a calm and peace to our souls, which greatly affects those around us. We may not understand how or why a particular event could occur, but we can always trust in the kindness and wisdom of our heavenly Father. Our deep trust and ongoing belief in the goodness of God enable us to offer the sacrifice of thanksgiving.

For further reading on Step 12, turn to page 715.

Daily Encouragement

DAY 310 READING: PSALM 107:17–32

A Thought for the New Day: Being caught in a storm at sea is one of life's most terrifying experiences. With no land in sight, all is chaos; and each moment brings impending destruction. Then comes the calm with its blue skies and sunshine. We rejoice because we have been saved from the cold, watery grave. God Himself is in charge of the storms of life; and He gives His own special peace, even as we are being battered by the winds and waves (vv. 29, 30). *(Turn to page 711.)*

And dry land into
watersprings.

36 There He makes the hungry
dwell,
That they may establish a city
for habitation,

37 And sow fields and plant
vineyards,
That they may yield a fruitful
harvest.

38 He also blesses them,
and they multiply greatly;
And He does not let their
cattle decrease.

39 When they are diminished
and brought low
Through oppression, affliction
and sorrow,

40 He pours contempt on princes,
And causes them to wander in
the wilderness *where there
is* no way;

STEP 2

41 Yet He sets the poor on high,
far from affliction,
And makes *their* families like
a flock.

42 The righteous see *it* and
rejoice,
And all iniquity stops its
mouth.

43 Whoever *is* wise will observe
these *things*,
And they will understand the
lovingkindness of the LORD.

PSALM 108

A Song. A Psalm of David.

O GOD, my heart is steadfast;
I will sing and give praise,
even with my glory.

2 Awake, lute and harp!
I will awaken the dawn.

3 I will praise You, O LORD,
among the peoples,
And I will sing praises to You
among the nations.

4 For Your mercy *is* great above
the heavens,
And Your truth *reaches* to the
clouds.

5 Be exalted, O God, above the
heavens,
And Your glory above all the
earth;

6 That Your beloved may be
delivered,
Save *with* Your right hand,
and hear me.

7 God has spoken in His
holiness:
"I will rejoice;
I will divide Shechem
And measure out the Valley of
Succoth.

8 Gilead *is* Mine;
Manasseh *is* Mine;
Ephraim also *is* the helmet for
My head;
Judah *is* My lawgiver.

9 Moab *is* My washpot;
Over Edom I will cast My
shoe;
Over Philistia I will triumph."

10 Who will bring me into the
strong city?
Who will lead me to Edom?

11 *Is it* not You, O God, *who* cast
us off?
And You, O God, *who* did not
go out with our armies?

12 Give us help from trouble,
For vain *is* the help of man.

13 Through God we will do
valiantly,
For *it is* He *who* shall tread
down our enemies.

PSALM 109

To the Chief Musician. A Psalm of David.

D O not keep silent,
O God of my praise!

2 For the mouth of the wicked
and the mouth of the
deceitful
Have opened against me;
They have spoken against me
with a lying tongue.

3 They have also surrounded me
with words of hatred,
And fought against me
without a cause.

*Came to believe that a Power greater than ourselves
could restore us to sanity.*

Psalm 107:41–43

When we come to truly believe and trust in the power of God through Jesus Christ, we will see amazing things happen, especially in our family situations.

In the beginning, God ordained the special place that a family would hold in the life of each individual. God meant for the family to nurture, protect, and fulfill each member. Sadly, not all families follow God's plan. In many instances, families are characterized by indifference, suspicion, frustration, and even emotional and physical harm. But God can change all that. When we come with empty hands and hearts, clinging to nothing and reaching out only for Him, He will fill us with His love and power. When we trust the Lord Jesus to save us, we ourselves will be changed from the inside out. Once we are changed, God can begin to use us to be the catalyst to change our family. And God will act as the Good Shepherd, drawing our family together like a flock.

For further reading on Step 2, turn to page 713.

Daily Encouragement

DAY 311 READING: PSALMS 107:33—108:13

A Thought for the New Day: What a barren prospect the world must be to the atheist, for whom all nature and natural events are the random effects of blind chance. But our psalmist saw otherwise (107:33–43). An intelligent God is in charge of the forces of nature by which we are fed, watered, and clothed. There is no chance event in the regular occurrence of days, months, and seasons. Our benevolent Lord guides all things according to His infinite and wonderful design. (*Turn to page 713.*)

4 In return for my love they are
my accusers,
But I *give myself to* prayer.

5 Thus they have rewarded me
evil for good,
And hatred for my love.

6 Set a wicked man over him,
And let an accuser stand at
his right hand.

7 When he is judged,
let him be found guilty,
And let his prayer become sin.

8 Let his days be few,
And let another take his
office.

9 Let his children be fatherless,
And his wife a widow.

10 Let his children continually be
vagabonds, and beg;
Let them seek *their bread* also
from their desolate places.

11 Let the creditor seize all that
he has,
And let strangers plunder his
labor.

12 Let there be none to extend
mercy to him,
Nor let there be any to favor
his fatherless children.

13 Let his posterity be cut off,
And in the generation
following let their name be
blotted out.

14 Let the iniquity of his fathers
be remembered before the
LORD,
And let not the sin of his
mother be blotted out.

15 Let them be continually
before the LORD,
That He may cut off the
memory of them from the
earth;

16 Because he did not remember
to show mercy,
But persecuted the poor and
needy man,
That he might even slay the
broken in heart.

17 As he loved cursing,
so let it come to him;

As he did not delight in
blessing, so let it be far from
him.

18 As he clothed himself with
cursing as with his garment,
So let it enter his body like
water,
And like oil into his bones.

19 Let it be to him like the
garment which covers him,
And for a belt with which he
girds himself continually.

20 *Let* this *be* the LORD's reward
to my accusers,
And to those who speak evil
against my person.

21 But You, O GOD the Lord,
Deal with me for Your name's
sake;
Because Your mercy *is* good,
deliver me.

22 For I *am* poor and needy,
And my heart is wounded
within me.

23 I am gone like a shadow when
it lengthens;
I am shaken off like a locust.

24 My knees are weak through
fasting,
And my flesh is feeble from
lack of fatness.

25 I also have become a reproach
to them;
When they look at me,
they shake their heads.

26 Help me, O LORD my God!
Oh, save me according to
Your mercy,

27 That they may know that this
is Your hand—
That You, LORD, have done it!

28 Let them curse, but You bless;
When they arise, let them be
ashamed,
But let Your servant rejoice.

29 Let my accusers be clothed
with shame,
And let them cover
themselves with their own
disgrace as with a mantle.

30 I will greatly praise the LORD
with my mouth;

STEP
2

STEP 2

*Came to believe that a Power greater than ourselves
could restore us to sanity.*

Psalm 109:21–27

In Matthew 5, Jesus tells us, "Blessed *are* the poor in spirit, for theirs is the kingdom of heaven" (v. 3). When we are very aware of our own needy and powerless condition, we are in the perfect frame of mind and heart to receive God's blessings. Pride often causes us to be less than honest about who we really are inside. But when our heart is wounded, our flesh feeble, and people shake their heads as they look at us, we have to face the truth about ourselves. Relying on God's mercy instead of our human merit may be a new idea to some of us. But it is the only way in which we can be accepted by God. And because God is a good God, He always receives and helps those who come to Him, depending upon His mercy in Jesus Christ.

For further reading on Step 2, turn to page 729.

Daily Encouragement

DAY 312 READING: PSALM 109:1–31

A Thought for the New Day: Love sometimes goes unreturned. What do we do when friends treat us badly? Do we become bitter? Sink into depression or despair? David made these things a matter of prayer (vv. 4, 5). So doing, he dodged Satan's temptation to be destroyed by unloving acts. May we be inspired and encouraged by his example. (*Turn to page 715.*)

Yes, I will praise Him among the multitude.
31 For He shall stand at the right hand of the poor,
To save *him* from those who condemn him.

PSALM 110

A Psalm of David.

THE LORD said to my Lord,
"Sit at My right hand,
Till I make Your enemies
Your footstool."
2 The LORD shall send the rod of Your strength out of Zion.
Rule in the midst of Your enemies!

3 Your people *shall be* volunteers
In the day of Your power;
In the beauties of holiness,
from the womb of the morning,
You have the dew of Your youth.
4 The LORD has sworn
And will not relent,
"You *are* a priest forever
According to the order of Melchizedek."

5 The Lord *is* at Your right hand;
He shall execute kings in the day of His wrath.
6 He shall judge among the nations,
He shall fill *the places* with dead bodies,
He shall execute the heads of many countries.
7 He shall drink of the brook by the wayside;
Therefore He shall lift up the head.

PSALM 111

PRAISE the LORD!

I will praise the LORD with *my* whole heart,

In the assembly of the upright and *in* the congregation.

2 The works of the LORD *are* great,
Studied by all who have pleasure in them.
3 His work *is* honorable and glorious,
And His righteousness endures forever.
4 He has made His wonderful works to be remembered;
The LORD *is* gracious and full of compassion.
5 He has given food to those who fear Him;
He will ever be mindful of His covenant.
6 He has declared to His people the power of His works,
In giving them the heritage of the nations.

7 The works of His hands *are* verity and justice;
All His precepts *are* sure.
8 They stand fast forever and ever,
And are done in truth and uprightness.
9 He has sent redemption to His people;
He has commanded His covenant forever:
Holy and awesome *is* His name.

10 The fear of the LORD *is* the beginning of wisdom;
A good understanding have all those who do *His commandments.*
His praise endures forever.

PSALM 112

PRAISE the LORD!

Blessed *is* the man *who* fears the LORD,
Who delights greatly in His commandments.

714

STEP 12

Having had a spiritual awakening as the result of these steps,
we tried to carry this message to others,
and to practice these principles in all our affairs.

Psalm 111

There are two kinds of fear—fear that gives weakness and failure, and fear that gives wisdom and success. When our dependencies controlled us, we lived in the shadow of the first kind of fear. We were afraid of our inner urges, afraid of what others would find out about us, afraid of certain situations. This fear limited and defeated us. Now we are no longer enslaved to that first kind of fear. Instead, we are growing daily in a totally different and wonderful fear. This is the fear of the Lord, which fills our hearts with respect, awe, and honor for God. Terror and trembling have been replaced by reverential trust and obedience. Studying His Word and proclaiming His works are becoming an integral part of our lives. We are becoming wise.

For further reading on Step 12, turn to page 755.

Daily Encouragement

DAY 313 READING: PSALMS 110:1—111:10

A Thought for the New Day: You know that the New Testament has much to say about the Savior, but did you realize that the Old Testament also contains a storehouse of references to Him? For this reason Isaiah is called "the Gospel-preaching prophet." David even called Him "my Lord" (110:1), broadening our New Testament view of the Messiah to include His lordship, as well as His servanthood. *(Turn to page 717.)*

God Humbles Himself

2 His descendants will be
mighty on earth;
The generation of the upright
will be blessed.
3 Wealth and riches *will be* in
his house,
And his righteousness endures
forever.
4 Unto the upright there arises
light in the darkness;
He is gracious, and full of
compassion, and righteous.
5 A good man deals graciously
and lends;
He will guide his affairs with
discretion.
6 Surely he will never be
shaken;
The righteous will be in
everlasting remembrance.
7 He will not be afraid of evil
tidings;
His heart is steadfast,
trusting in the LORD.
8 His heart *is* established;
He will not be afraid,
Until he sees *his desire* upon
his enemies.

9 He has dispersed abroad,
He has given to the poor;
His righteousness endures
forever;
His horn will be exalted with
honor.
10 The wicked will see *it* and be
grieved;
He will gnash his teeth and
melt away;
The desire of the wicked shall
perish.

PSALM 113

Praise the LORD!

Praise, O servants of the
LORD,
Praise the name of the LORD!
2 Blessed be the name of the
LORD
From this time forth and
forevermore!

3 From the rising of the sun to
its going down
The LORD'S name *is* to be
praised.

STEP
11

4 The LORD *is* high above all
nations,
And His glory above the
heavens.
5 Who *is* like the LORD our God,
Who dwells on high,
6 Who humbles Himself to
behold
The things that are in the
heavens and in the earth?

7 He raises the poor out of the
dust,
And lifts the needy out of the
ash heap,
8 That He may seat *him* with
princes—
With the princes of His
people.
9 He grants the barren woman a
home,
Like a joyful mother of
children.

Praise the LORD!

PSALM 114

When Israel went out of
Egypt,
The house of Jacob from a
people of strange language,
2 Judah became His sanctuary,
And Israel His dominion.

3 The sea saw *it* and fled;
Jordan turned back.
4 The mountains skipped like
rams,
The little hills like lambs.
5 What ails you, O sea, that you
fled?
O Jordan, *that* you turned
back?
6 O mountains, *that* you
skipped like rams?
O little hills, like lambs?

STEP 11

*Sought through prayer and meditation to improve our conscious contact with God **as we understood Him,** praying only for knowledge of His will for us and the power to carry that out.*

Psalm 113:3

Because we have become children of God through faith in Jesus Christ, we are the earthly representatives of His wonderful name. We are His chosen ambassadors to the world. From the rising of the sun to its going down, we are to praise His name. Of course, it would be impossible for us to verbally praise His name all day long (although singing and quoting Scripture to ourselves is a good habit to get into). But we can praise His name in our conduct and attitudes, as well as in our words. When we allow God's Word to mold our thinking and God's Holy Spirit to direct our conduct, we are very effectively offering praise to Him. Then, too, as those about us observe our actions and the attitude with which they are done, they can offer up praise to God because of us.

For further reading on Step 11, turn to page 725.

Daily Encouragement

DAY 314 READING: PSALMS 112:1—114:8

A Thought for the New Day: What a lovely description of the upright person we read in Psalm 112:4–7! These lines are used as a commentary on the prophet's kindness to a poor widow in Felix Mendelssohn's musical composition, *Elijah.* Notice in verse 7 that the secret of the genuinely righteous is trust. God is for us. That is the philosophy of the Christian! Let us pray to have this constant view in all our circumstances. *(Turn to page 719.)*

7 Tremble, O earth, at the
presence of the Lord,
At the presence of the God of
Jacob,
8 Who turned the rock *into* a
pool of water,
The flint into a fountain of
waters.

PSALM 115

NOT unto us, O LORD, not unto
us,
But to Your name give glory,
Because of Your mercy,
And because of Your truth.
2 Why should the Gentiles say,
Where now *is* their God?"

3 But our God *is* in heaven;
He does whatever He pleases.
4 Their idols *are* silver and gold,
The work of men's hands.
5 They have mouths,
but they do not speak;
Eyes they have, but they do
not see;
6 They have ears, but they do
not hear;
Noses they have,
but they do not smell;
7 They have hands,
but they do not handle;
Feet they have, but they do
not walk;
Nor do they mutter through
their throat.
8 Those who make them are
like them;
So is everyone who trusts in
them.

9 O Israel, trust in the LORD;
He *is* their help and their
shield.
10 O house of Aaron, trust in the
LORD;
He *is* their help and their
shield.
11 You who fear the LORD,
trust in the LORD;
He *is* their help and their
shield.

12 The LORD has been mindful of
us;
He will bless us;
He will bless the house of
Israel;
He will bless the house of
Aaron.
13 He will bless those who fear
the LORD,
Both small and great.

14 May the LORD give you
increase more and more,
You and your children.
15 *May* you *be* blessed by the
LORD,
Who made heaven and earth.

16 The heaven, *even* the heavens,
are the LORD'S;
But the earth He has given to
the children of men.
17 The dead do not praise the
LORD,
Nor any who go down into
silence.
18 But we will bless the LORD
From this time forth and
forevermore.

Praise the LORD!

PSALM 116

I LOVE the LORD, because He
has heard
My voice *and* my
supplications.
2 Because He has inclined His
ear to me,
Therefore I will call *upon Him*
as long as I live.

3 The pains of death
encompassed me,
And the pangs of Sheol laid
hold of me;
I found trouble and sorrow.
4 Then I called upon the name
of the LORD:
"O LORD, I implore You,
deliver my soul!"

STEP
3

STEP 3

*Made a decision to turn our will and our lives
over to the care of God **as we understood Him.***
Psalm 116

Once we have believed in God, our relationship to Him usually is based on a series of natural responses. Some people take longer to move through this series of growth steps, but the pattern is generally the same for all true believers. First John 4:19 tells us that "we love Him because He first loved us." Moving from trust to love takes some people longer than others. But as they get to know God better, they naturally begin to love Him. The more understanding we gain concerning who God is and how much He loves us, the easier it is to love Him. When we really understand His tireless protection, unfathomed wisdom, unconditional acceptance, boundless grace, and merciful kindness, we will move beyond trust and love to devotion. We will joyfully give all that we are and have to Him and know that we have received far more than we have given or could ever give.

For further reading on Step 3, turn to page 765.

Daily Encouragement

DAY 315 READING: PSALMS 115:1—118:29

A Thought for the New Day: What is "precious" (116:15) about the death of the godly? Many things! All their lives and on their last bed God whispers to them intimations of His everlasting love that will never let them go. The death of a Christian is special because, in a real way, it is no death at all, but an entranceway to the life abundant. Thus Jesus' words are true, "Whoever lives and believes in Me shall never die" (John 11:26). *(Turn to page 723.)*

5 Gracious *is* the LORD, and
   righteous;
   Yes, our God *is* merciful.
6 The LORD preserves the
   simple;
   I was brought low, and He
   saved me.
7 Return to your rest, O my
   soul,
   For the LORD has dealt
   bountifully with you.

8 For You have delivered my
   soul from death,
   My eyes from tears,
   And my feet from falling.
9 I will walk before the LORD
   In the land of the living.
10 I believed, therefore I spoke,
   "I am greatly afflicted."
11 I said in my haste,
   "All men *are* liars."

12 What shall I render to the
   LORD
   For all His benefits toward
   me?
13 I will take up the cup of
   salvation,
   And call upon the name of the
   LORD.
14 I will pay my vows to the
   LORD
   Now in the presence of all His
   people.

15 Precious in the sight of the
   LORD
   Is the death of His saints.

16 O LORD, truly I *am* Your
   servant;
   I *am* Your servant, the son of
   Your maidservant;
   You have loosed my bonds.
17 I will offer to You the sacrifice
   of thanksgiving,
   And will call upon the name
   of the LORD.

18 I will pay my vows to the
   LORD

Now in the presence of all His
   people,
19 In the courts of the LORD's
   house,
   In the midst of you, O
   Jerusalem.

Praise the LORD!

PSALM 117

OH, praise the LORD, all you
   Gentiles!
   Laud Him, all you peoples!
2 For His merciful kindness is
   great toward us,
   And the truth of the LORD
   endures forever.

Praise the LORD!

PSALM 118

OH, give thanks to the LORD,
   for *He is* good!
   Because His mercy *endures*
   forever.

2 Let Israel now say,
   "His mercy *endures* forever."
3 Let the house of Aaron now
   say,
   "His mercy *endures* forever."
4 Let those who fear the LORD
   now say,
   "His mercy *endures* forever."

5 I called on the LORD in
   distress;
   The LORD answered me
   and set me in a broad place.
6 The LORD *is* on my side;
   I will not fear.
   What can man do to me?
7 The LORD is for me among
   those who help me;
   Therefore I shall see *my desire*
   on those who hate me.
8 *It is* better to trust in the
   LORD
   Than to put confidence in
   man.
9 *It is* better to trust in the
   LORD

Than to put confidence in
princes.

10 All nations surrounded me,
But in the name of the LORD I
will destroy them.
11 They surrounded me,
Yes, they surrounded me;
But in the name of the LORD I
will destroy them.
12 They surrounded me like bees;
They were quenched like a
fire of thorns;
For in the name of the LORD I
will destroy them.
13 You pushed me violently,
that I might fall,
But the LORD helped me.
14 The LORD is my strength and
song,
And He has become my
salvation.

15 The voice of rejoicing and
salvation
Is in the tents of the
righteous;
The right hand of the LORD
does valiantly.
16 The right hand of the LORD is
exalted;
The right hand of the LORD
does valiantly.
17 I shall not die, but live,
And declare the works of the
LORD.
18 The LORD has chastened me
severely,
But He has not given me over
to death.

19 Open to me the gates of
righteousness;
I will go through them,
And I will praise the LORD.
20 This is the gate of the LORD,
Through which the righteous
shall enter.

21 I will praise You,
For You have answered me,
And have become my
salvation.

22 The stone which the builders
rejected
Has become the chief
cornerstone.
23 This was the LORD's doing;
It is marvelous in our eyes.
24 This is the day which the
LORD has made;
We will rejoice and be glad in
it.

25 Save now, I pray, O LORD;
O LORD, I pray, send now
prosperity.
26 Blessed is he who comes in
the name of the LORD!
We have blessed you from the
house of the LORD.
27 God is the LORD,
And He has given us light;
Bind the sacrifice with cords
to the horns of the altar.
28 You are my God,
and I will praise You;
You are my God, I will exalt
You.

29 Oh, give thanks to the LORD,
for He is good!
For His mercy endures
forever.

PSALM 119

ℵ ALEPH

BLESSED are the undefiled in
the way,
Who walk in the law of the
LORD!
2 Blessed are those who keep
His testimonies,
Who seek Him with the whole
heart!
3 They also do no iniquity;
They walk in His ways.
4 You have commanded us
To keep Your precepts
diligently.
5 Oh, that my ways were
directed
To keep Your statutes!

6 Then I would not be ashamed,
When I look into all Your
commandments.
7 I will praise You with
uprightness of heart,
When I learn Your righteous
judgments.
8 I will keep Your statutes;
Oh, do not forsake me utterly!

ב BETH

9 How can a young man cleanse
his way?
By taking heed according to
Your word.

STEP 6

10 With my whole heart I have
sought You;
Oh, let me not wander from
Your commandments!
11 Your word I have hidden in
my heart,
That I might not sin against
You.
12 Blessed *are* You, O LORD!
Teach me Your statutes.
13 With my lips I have declared
All the judgments of Your
mouth.
14 I have rejoiced in the way of
Your testimonies,
As *much as* in all riches.
15 I will meditate on Your
precepts,
And contemplate Your ways.
16 I will delight myself in Your
statutes;
I will not forget Your word.

ג GIMEL

17 Deal bountifully with Your
servant,
That I may live and keep
Your word.
18 Open my eyes, that I may see
Wondrous things from Your
law.
19 I *am* a stranger in the earth;
Do not hide Your
commandments from me.
20 My soul breaks with longing
For Your judgments at all
times.
21 You rebuke the proud—the
cursed,
Who stray from Your
commandments.
22 Remove from me reproach
and contempt,
For I have kept Your
testimonies.
23 Princes also sit *and* speak
against me,
But Your servant meditates
on Your statutes.
24 Your testimonies also *are* my
delight
And my counselors.

ד DALETH

25 My soul clings to the dust;
Revive me according to Your
word.
26 I have declared my ways,
and You answered me;
Teach me Your statutes.
27 Make me understand the way
of Your precepts;
So shall I meditate on Your
wondrous works.
28 My soul melts from heaviness;
Strengthen me according to
Your word.

29 Remove from me the way of
lying,
And grant me Your law
graciously.
30 I have chosen the way of
truth;
Your judgments I have laid
before me.
31 I cling to Your testimonies;
O LORD, do not put me to
shame!
32 I will run in the way of Your
commandments,
For You shall enlarge my
heart.

ה HE

33 Teach me, O LORD, the way of
Your statutes,

STEP 6

*Were entirely ready to have God
remove all these defects of character.*

Psalm 119:28–40

Psalm 119 is called the wisdom Psalm. As we work through Step 6 of recovery, we will sow in our own lives the seeds of true wisdom, which will eventually yield a harvest of peace and joy.

As the psalmist pours out his heart's longings, we discover that this writer is experiencing feelings and attitudes very similar to our own. Grieved over his shortcomings and longing for God to change him, he asks God to "remove from me the way of lying" (v. 29). Throughout the passage, the psalmist continually acknowledges his need and desire for God to do anything and everything to accomplish this transformation.

This willingness of the writer to place his life squarely in the hands of God shifts the focus away from the insurmountability of the problem and onto the life-changing potential of God's intervention. When we can focus this completely on God's power to accomplish what is necessary in our lives, we will find a total readiness to release our dependencies to Him.

For further reading on Step 6, turn to page 749.

Daily Encouragement

DAY 316 READING: PSALM 119:1–40

A Thought for the New Day: God's Word is an open book to those who approach it prayerfully, but the greatest intellectual who ever lived will miss the point of the message completely if he relies on his own resources (v. 18). God discloses His truth to those who hunger and thirst for Him. "You search the Scriptures . . . but you are not willing to come to Me," Jesus told the scholars (John 5:39, 40). To those who wait at the door of prayer, however, all things will be opened. (*Turn to page 725.*)

And I shall keep it *to* the end.

34 Give me understanding,
and I shall keep Your law;
Indeed, I shall observe it with
my whole heart.

35 Make me walk in the path of
Your commandments,
For I delight in it.

36 Incline my heart to Your
testimonies,
And not to covetousness.

37 Turn away my eyes from
looking at worthless things,
And revive me in Your way.

38 Establish Your word to Your
servant,
Who *is devoted* to fearing
You.

39 Turn away my reproach
which I dread,
For Your judgments *are* good.

40 Behold, I long for Your
precepts;
Revive me in Your
righteousness.

] WAW

41 Let Your mercies come also to
me, O LORD—
Your salvation according to
Your word.

42 So shall I have an answer for
him who reproaches me,
For I trust in Your word.

43 And take not the word of
truth utterly out of my
mouth,
For I have hoped in Your
ordinances.

44 So shall I keep Your law
continually,
Forever and ever.

45 And I will walk at liberty,
For I seek Your precepts.

46 I will speak of Your
testimonies also before
kings,
And will not be ashamed.

47 And I will delight myself in
Your commandments,
Which I love.

48 My hands also I will lift up to
Your commandments,
Which I love,
And I will meditate on Your
statutes.

] ZAYIN

49 Remember the word to Your
servant,
Upon which You have caused
me to hope.

50 This *is* my comfort in my
affliction,
For Your word has given me
life.

51 The proud have me in great
derision,
Yet I do not turn aside from
Your law.

52 I remembered Your
judgments of old, O LORD,
And have comforted myself.

53 Indignation has taken hold of
me
Because of the wicked,
who forsake Your law.

54 Your statutes have been my
songs
In the house of my
pilgrimage.

55 I remember Your name in the
night, O LORD,
And I keep Your law.

56 This has become mine,
Because I kept Your precepts.

ח HETH

57 *You are* my portion, O LORD;
I have said that I would keep
Your words.

58 I entreated Your favor with
my whole heart;
Be merciful to me according
to Your word.

59 I thought about my ways,
And turned my feet to Your
testimonies.

60 I made haste, and did not
delay
To keep Your commandments.

STEP
11

*Sought through prayer and meditation to improve our conscious contact with God **as we understood Him,** praying only for knowledge of His will for us and the power to carry that out.*

Psalm 119:47, 48

Psychologists sometimes describe humankind as a three-faceted entity made up of heart (representing the emotions), body, and mind. If we are to continue to stay on course in our recovery, each of these vital areas must be involved. Psalm 119:47, 48 gives us the guidance we need to keep each part of our lives on track and spiritually growing.

First, our attitudes and emotions must remain positive. If we determine that God and His Word will be first in our lives, then we will find abiding joy and delight in its message, no matter what our circumstances. Our bodies become involved as we put our hands and feet to work for Christ. The good deeds we do for others in the name of Jesus honor and obey His commands. And finally, our minds are renewed by continual meditation (memorization and careful consideration) on God's Word. When all areas of our life are centered in God, His knowledge and power will be increasing in us.

For further reading on Step 11, turn to page 739.

Daily Encouragement

DAY 317 READING: PSALM 119:41–64

A Thought for the New Day: There is no way to answer the curled lip of derision, except to continue patiently in the path God sets before you (v. 51). A greater One than you and I was laughed at as He hung in His deepest agony. So then, shall we be exempt from all social discomfort? God forbid! *Whatever the cup of suffering must be, Lord, give me grace to drink it graciously in remembrance of You.* (Turn to page 727.)

61 The cords of the wicked have
     bound me,
   But I have not forgotten Your
     law.
62 At midnight I will rise to give
     thanks to You,
   Because of Your righteous
     judgments.
63 I *am* a companion of all *those*
     who fear You,
   And of those who keep Your
     precepts.
64 The earth, O LORD, is full of
     Your mercy;
   Teach me Your statutes.

ט TETH

65 You have dealt well with Your
     servant,
   O LORD, according to Your
     word.
66 Teach me good judgment and
     knowledge,
   For I believe Your
     commandments.
67 Before I was afflicted I went
     astray,
   But now I keep Your word.
68 You *are* good, and do good;
   Teach me Your statutes.
69 The proud have forged a lie
     against me,
   But I will keep Your precepts
     with *my* whole heart.
70 Their heart is as fat as grease,
   But I delight in Your law.
71 *It is* good for me that I have
     been afflicted,
   That I may learn Your
     statutes.
72 The law of Your mouth *is*
     better to me
   Than thousands of *shekels of*
     gold and silver.

י YOD

73 Your hands have made me
     and fashioned me;
   Give me understanding, that I
     may learn Your
     commandments.

74 Those who fear You will be
     glad when they see me,
   Because I have hoped in Your
     word.
75 I know, O LORD, that Your
     judgments *are* right,
   And *that* in faithfulness You
     have afflicted me.
76 Let, I pray, Your merciful
     kindness be for my comfort,
   According to Your word to
     Your servant.
77 Let Your tender mercies come
     to me, that I may live;
   For Your law *is* my delight.
78 Let the proud be ashamed,
   For they treated me
     wrongfully with falsehood;
   But I will meditate on Your
     precepts.
79 Let those who fear You turn
     to me,
   Those who know Your
     testimonies.
80 Let my heart be blameless
     regarding Your statutes,
   That I may not be ashamed.

כ KAPH

81 My soul faints for Your
     salvation,
   But I hope in Your word.
82 My eyes fail *from seeking*
     Your word,
   Saying, "When will You
     comfort me?"
83 For I have become like a
     wineskin in smoke,
   Yet I do not forget Your
     statutes.
84 How many *are* the days of
     Your servant?
   When will You execute
     judgment on those who
     persecute me?
85 The proud have dug pits for
     me,
   Which *is* not according to
     Your law.
86 All Your commandments *are*
     faithful;

726

STEP 5

Admitted to God, to ourselves, and to another human being the exact nature of our wrongs.

Psalm 119:66, 67

Perhaps there was a time in your life when the Bible seemed like an outdated book, hardly relevant for the issues of a modern culture. Or maybe it seemed like a book for people who were weak and helpless. Maybe Scripture seemed foreign, mysterious, and confusing to you. But now you have met the Author of the Book and you are beginning to look at all of life very differently.

As we move through the discipline of Step 5, we must acknowledge some negative things about ourselves and possibly about others, as well. But there is an opposite side to the coin of acknowledgment. Even as we are admitting our past wrongs, we are giving mental assent to some "rights." We are acknowledging that God's ways are and always have been good and wise and true. We are confessing our belief in God's judgment, knowledge, and commandments. We are preparing to change.

For further reading on Step 5, turn to page 803.

Daily Encouragement

DAY 318 READING: PSALM 119:65–88

A Thought for the New Day: At times each of us feels unacceptable to God (v. 81). This is not all bad. It is good to doubt ourselves for good reasons. Disobedience is a fact in all of us. At such times, however, the light of hope should not go out: "Heaven and earth will pass away, but My words will by no means pass away," said Jesus (Matt. 24:35). We can hope in Him when self-confidence is gone. (*Turn to page 729.*)

They persecute me
    wrongfully;
Help me!
87 They almost made an end of
    me on earth,
But I did not forsake Your
    precepts.
88 Revive me according to Your
    lovingkindness,
So that I may keep the
    testimony of Your mouth.

ל LAMED

STEP 2

89 Forever, O LORD,
    Your word is settled in
    heaven.
90 Your faithfulness *endures* to
    all generations;
You established the earth,
    and it abides.
91 They continue this day
    according to Your
    ordinances,
For all *are* Your servants.
92 Unless Your law *had been* my
    delight,
I would then have perished in
    my affliction.
93 I will never forget Your
    precepts,
For by them You have given
    me life.
94 I *am* Yours, save me;
    For I have sought Your
    precepts.
95 The wicked wait for me to
    destroy me,
But I will consider Your
    testimonies.
96 I have seen the consummation
    of all perfection,
But Your commandment *is*
    exceedingly broad.

מ MEM

97 Oh, how I love Your law!
It *is* my meditation all the
    day.

98 You, through Your
    commandments, make me
    wiser than my enemies;
For they *are* ever with me.
99 I have more understanding
    than all my teachers,
For Your testimonies *are* my
    meditation.
100 I understand more than the
    ancients,
Because I keep Your precepts.
101 I have restrained my feet from
    every evil way,
That I may keep Your word.
102 I have not departed from
    Your judgments,
For You Yourself have taught
    me.
103 How sweet are Your words to
    my taste,
Sweeter than honey to my
    mouth!
104 Through Your precepts I get
    understanding;
Therefore I hate every false
    way.

נ NUN

105 Your word *is* a lamp to my
    feet
And a light to my path.
106 I have sworn and confirmed
That I will keep Your
    righteous judgments.
107 I am afflicted very much;
Revive me, O LORD, according
    to Your word.
108 Accept, I pray, the freewill
    offerings of my mouth, O
    LORD,
And teach me Your
    judgments.
109 My life *is* continually in my
    hand,
Yet I do not forget Your law.
110 The wicked have laid a snare
    for me,
Yet I have not strayed from
    Your precepts.

STEP 2

Came to believe that a Power greater than ourselves could restore us to sanity.

Psalm 119:89–91

Our God is the Creator of order and faithfulness. Out of the chaos that was eternity past, He established the paths of planets and galaxies. He faithfully keeps our small earth and the vast universe functioning according to His principles and laws. Down through the centuries, those who have understood these things to be true have led productive lives contributing to the welfare of society and even the scientific knowledge of humankind. Just as God was willing to reveal His order and faithfulness to them, He is willing to reveal it to us. The rapid political, social, and economic changes of our shrunken globe may threaten to overwhelm us at times. When we face such distress, we can turn for comfort and peace to these certainties. The truth of God's Word never changes, and God never changes. He will be just as faithful and wise and good for us in our generation as He has been in every preceding one.

For further reading on Step 2, turn to page 733.

Daily Encouragement

DAY 319 READING: PSALM 119:89–120

A Thought for the New Day: No literature in the world has been nearly so badly battered as the Holy Scriptures. Yet, neither has any literature been nearly so well authenticated by many acid tests. This fact makes sense of the words in verse 89. It is God who substantiates His own truth. Thank God, the fickleness of human beings cannot alter that foundation! (*Turn to page 731.*)

111 Your testimonies I have taken
    as a heritage forever,
    For they *are* the rejoicing of
    my heart.
112 I have inclined my heart to
    perform Your statutes
    Forever, to the very end.

ס SAMEK

113 I hate the double-minded,
    But I love Your law.
114 You *are* my hiding place and
    my shield;
    I hope in Your word.
115 Depart from me, you
    evildoers,
    For I will keep the
    commandments of my God!
116 Uphold me according to Your
    word, that I may live;
    And do not let me be ashamed
    of my hope.
117 Hold me up, and I shall be
    safe,
    And I shall observe Your
    statutes continually.
118 You reject all those who stray
    from Your statutes,
    For their deceit *is* falsehood.
119 You put away all the wicked
    of the earth *like* dross;
    Therefore I love Your
    testimonies.
120 My flesh trembles for fear of
    You,
    And I am afraid of Your
    judgments.

ע AYIN

121 I have done justice and
    righteousness;
    Do not leave me to my
    oppressors.
122 Be surety for Your servant for
    good;
    Do not let the proud oppress
    me.

123 My eyes fail *from seeking*
    Your salvation
    And Your righteous word.

124 Deal with Your servant
    according to Your mercy,
    And teach me Your statutes.
125 I *am* Your servant;
    Give me understanding,
    That I may know Your
    testimonies.
126 *It is* time for *You* to act, O
    Lord,
    For they have regarded Your
    law as void.
127 Therefore I love Your
    commandments
    More than gold, yes, than fine
    gold!
128 Therefore all *Your* precepts
    concerning all *things*
    I consider *to be* right;
    I hate every false way.

פ PE

129 Your testimonies are
    wonderful;
    Therefore my soul keeps
    them.
130 The entrance of Your words
    gives light;
    It gives understanding to the
    simple.
131 I opened my mouth and
    panted,
    For I longed for Your
    commandments.
132 Look upon me and be merciful
    to me,
    As Your custom *is* toward
    those who love Your name.
133 Direct my steps by Your word,
    And let no iniquity have
    dominion over me.
134 Redeem me from the
    oppression of man,
    That I may keep Your
    precepts.
135 Make Your face shine upon
    Your servant,
    And teach me Your statutes.
136 Rivers of water run down
    from my eyes,
    Because *men* do not keep
    Your law.

STEP 7

STEP 7

Humbly asked Him to remove our shortcomings.

Psalm 119:133

God's Word carries and generates life because it is the very mind and heart of God Himself. When the power of God's Word connects with a humble and willing spirit, a transformed life is the joyous result.

Each individual life will have its own transformation timetable. For some of us, healing and change will come rapidly. For others, the pace will be slower, perhaps accompanied by peaks of success and valleys of depression. But the outcome is not in doubt. When we are truly submissive to God's work in our lives, the power of His Word is more than sufficient for any trial or obstacle.

Whether we experience God's healing and removal of our shortcomings in a few giant steps or in many smaller ones, the prayer and determination of our hearts should be steadfast: "Direct my steps by Your word."

For further reading on Step 7, Turn to page 797.

Daily Encouragement

DAY 320 READING: PSALM 119:121–152

A Thought for the New Day: In verse 144, the psalmist asked for understanding, that he might live. He was very conscious of his complete dependence on divine wisdom. Whatever native wisdom humankind once enjoyed has been marred by sin. To trust in our own discernment is therefore dangerous. In the New Testament, James the Elder promised wisdom to us if we would seek it from God, who is the fountain of all truth (see James 1:5). *(Turn to page 733.)*

 צ TSADDE

137 Righteous *are* You, O LORD,
And upright *are* Your
judgments.
138 Your testimonies, *which* You
have commanded,
Are righteous and very
faithful.
139 My zeal has consumed me,
Because my enemies have
forgotten Your words.
140 Your word *is* very pure;
Therefore Your servant loves
it.
141 I *am* small and despised,
Yet I do not forget Your
precepts.
142 Your righteousness *is* an
everlasting righteousness,
And Your law *is* truth.
143 Trouble and anguish have
overtaken me,
Yet Your commandments *are*
my delights.
144 The righteousness of Your
testimonies *is* everlasting;
Give me understanding,
and I shall live.

ק QOPH

145 I cry out with *my* whole
heart;
Hear me, O LORD!
I will keep Your statutes.
146 I cry out to You;
Save me, and I will keep Your
testimonies.
147 I rise before the dawning of
the morning,
And cry for help;
I hope in Your word.
148 My eyes are awake through
the *night* watches,
That I may meditate on Your
word.
149 Hear my voice according to
Your lovingkindness;
O LORD, revive me according
to Your justice.
150 They draw near who follow
after wickedness;
They are far from Your law.

151 You *are* near, O LORD,
And all Your commandments
are truth.
152 Concerning Your testimonies,
I have known of old that You
have founded them forever.

ר RESH

153 Consider my affliction and
deliver me,
For I do not forget Your law.
154 Plead my cause and redeem
me;
Revive me according to Your
word.
155 Salvation *is* far from the
wicked,
For they do not seek Your
statutes.
156 Great *are* Your tender
mercies, O LORD;
Revive me according to Your
judgments.
157 Many *are* my persecutors and
my enemies,
Yet I do not turn from Your
testimonies.
158 I see the treacherous,
and am disgusted,
Because they do not keep
Your word.
159 Consider how I love Your
precepts;
Revive me, O LORD, according
to Your lovingkindness.
160 The entirety of Your word *is*
truth,
And every one of Your
righteous judgments
endures forever.

ש SHIN

161 Princes persecute me without
a cause,
But my heart stands in awe of
Your word.
162 I rejoice at Your word
As one who finds great
treasure.

STEP
2

STEP 2

*Came to believe that a Power greater than ourselves
could restore us to sanity.*

Psalm 119:162–166

Almost every culture has legends and stories of treasure hunts. Even today, there are men and women who risk their lives to bring home sunken treasure from decaying ships, or gold nuggets stashed in the deep recesses of the earth. These treasures, however, last only for a short time. They cannot follow us into the realms of eternity. They may purchase us happiness of sorts for a season, but they can never buy true peace and real joy.

Only the Word of God and the Savior revealed in its pages are everlasting treasure for the human soul. If we have tired of the false and transient allurements of the world, and we are beginning to feel the pointlessness of existing for pleasure and self, we need not despair. Eternal treasure, lasting peace, joy, and purpose are available to us through the transforming power of Jesus Christ. Have faith in Him!

For further reading on Step 2, turn to page 735.

Daily Encouragement

DAY 321 READING: PSALM 119:153–176

A Thought for the New Day: In verse 176, we read of a man who was willing to confess his failure. Yes, he had "gone astray," and yet he remembered better things. He recalled the blessing of God's words, and he longed to return to that place of rest and security. That man was not far from God. Already the gap had been closed. God is not deaf to the cry of His lonely, lost ones; and He seeks and finds them, just as the writer prayed. (*Turn to page 735.*)

Plea for Deliverance

163 I hate and abhor lying,
   But I love Your law.
164 Seven times a day I praise
      You,
   Because of Your righteous
      judgments.
165 Great peace have those who
      love Your law,
   And nothing causes them to
      stumble.
166 LORD, I hope for Your
      salvation,
   And I do Your
      commandments.
167 My soul keeps Your
      testimonies,
   And I love them exceedingly.
168 I keep Your precepts and
      Your testimonies,
   For all my ways *are* before
      You.

ת TAU

169 Let my cry come before You,
      O LORD;
   Give me understanding
      according to Your word.
170 Let my supplication come
      before You;
   Deliver me according to Your
      word.
171 My lips shall utter praise,
   For You teach me Your
      statutes.
172 My tongue shall speak of
      Your word,
   For all Your commandments
      are righteousness.
173 Let Your hand become my
      help,
   For I have chosen Your
      precepts.
174 I long for Your salvation, O
      LORD,
   And Your law *is* my delight.
175 Let my soul live,
      and it shall praise You;
   And let Your judgments help
      me.
176 I have gone astray like a lost
      sheep;
   Seek Your servant,

For I do not forget Your
   commandments.

PSALM 120

A Song of Ascents.

IN my distress I cried to the
   LORD,
   And He heard me.
2 Deliver my soul, O LORD, from
      lying lips
   And from a deceitful tongue.

3 What shall be given to you,
   Or what shall be done to you,
      You false tongue?
4 Sharp arrows of the warrior,
   With coals of the broom tree!

5 Woe is me, that I sojourn in
      Meshech,
   That I dwell among the tents
      of Kedar!
6 My soul has dwelt too long
   With one who hates peace.
7 I *am* for peace;
   But when I speak, they *are* for
      war.

PSALM 121

A Song of Ascents.

I WILL lift up my eyes to the
   hills—
   From whence comes my help?
2 My help *comes* from the LORD,
   Who made heaven and earth.

3 He will not allow your foot to
      be moved;
   He who keeps you will not
      slumber.
4 Behold, He who keeps Israel
   Shall neither slumber nor
      sleep.

5 The LORD *is* your keeper;
   The LORD *is* your shade at
      your right hand.
6 The sun shall not strike you
      by day,
   Nor the moon by night.

STEP 2

STEP 2

Came to believe that a Power greater than ourselves could restore us to sanity.

Psalm 121

Because we have chosen the path of Twelve Step recovery, we can assume that our lives have reached a particular juncture. We have begun to question more than we used to. Some of us have done some in-depth soul-searching already. We know that we are not happy or fulfilled with things as they are. But where do we go from here? How can we be delivered from the quagmire of dependency and guilt? Who can help us? The Lord not only can help us, but desires to help us. He created each of us and knows us far better than we know ourselves. He knows where we might stumble and can keep us steady and strong in our time of need. He is always there for us. He never leaves us or forsakes us for any reason. He wants to protect and guide us "from this time forth, and even forevermore." All we need to do is put our trust in His goodness and power.

For further reading on Step 2, turn to page 741.

Daily Encouragement

DAY 322 READING: PSALMS 120:1—121:8

A Thought for the New Day: We admire, and we need, people of strong character—people who are as unchanging as the mountains. But few of us are like that. Indeed the strongest of us would be found wanting if we were weighed in God's scale. God Himself, however, will be the strength and safety of His loved ones (vv. 7, 8). Even in their weakness He does not dismiss them. Rather, He makes them stand in spite of themselves. "He shall preserve your soul." (*Turn to page 737.*)

7 The LORD shall preserve you
from all evil;
He shall preserve your soul.
8 The LORD shall preserve your
going out and your coming
in
From this time forth,
and even forevermore.

PSALM 122

A Song of Ascents. Of David.

I WAS glad when they said to
me,
Let us go into the house of
the LORD."
2 Our feet have been standing
Within your gates, O
Jerusalem!

3 Jerusalem is built
As a city that is compact
together,
4 Where the tribes go up,
The tribes of the LORD,
To the Testimony of Israel,
To give thanks to the name of
the LORD.
5 For thrones are set there for
judgment,
The thrones of the house of
David.

6 Pray for the peace of
Jerusalem:
"May they prosper who love
you.
7 Peace be within your walls,
Prosperity within your
palaces."
8 For the sake of my brethren
and companions,
I will now say, "Peace *be*
within you."
9 Because of the house of the
LORD our God
I will seek your good.

PSALM 123

A Song of Ascents.

U NTO You I lift up my eyes,
O You who dwell in the
heavens.

2 Behold, as the eyes of servants
look to the hand of their
masters,
As the eyes of a maid to the
hand of her mistress,
So our eyes *look* to the LORD
our God,
Until He has mercy on us.

3 Have mercy on us, O LORD,
have mercy on us!
For we are exceedingly filled
with contempt.
4 Our soul is exceedingly filled
With the scorn of those who
are at ease,
With the contempt of the
proud.

PSALM 124

A Song of Ascents. Of David.

" I F it had not been the LORD
who was on our side,"
Let Israel now say—
2 "If it had not been the LORD
who was on our side,
When men rose up against us,
3 Then they would have
swallowed us alive,
When their wrath was kindled
against us;
4 Then the waters would have
overwhelmed us,
The stream would have gone
over our soul;
5 Then the swollen waters
Would have gone over our
soul."

6 Blessed *be* the LORD,
Who has not given us *as* prey
to their teeth.
7 Our soul has escaped as a bird
from the snare of the
fowlers;
The snare is broken,
and we have escaped.
8 Our help *is* in the name of the
LORD,
Who made heaven and earth.

STEP
8

*Made a list of all persons we had harmed,
and became willing to make amends to them all.*

Psalm 124:6–8

The Evil One has a few favorite devices that he uses to ensnare God's children, often quite successfully. The harmless-looking traps of indifference, pride, and bitterness have brought promising spiritual growth to a tragic end for many people. While all believers need to be constantly vigilant against these dangers, those of us in recovery need an extra measure of insight and determination. Because of our backgrounds, the cages of isolation and bitterness may not even feel like cages to us. We may have lived within their confines so long that we have become unaware of their presence. Now in Step 8, we are asking God to make us aware of these attitude sins, which have harmed others or ourselves in some way. We are also asking God to give us the desire to be free of those snares so that we can become open individuals who can sincerely ask forgiveness, as well as sincerely forgive.

For further reading on Step 8, turn to page 743.

Daily Encouragement

DAY 323 READING: PSALMS 122:1—124:8

A Thought for the New Day: God did not intend that we should be orphans. We not only need His fatherly care, but we need the family of His people—the church of God. To grow in understanding and esteem for others besides ourselves we need to be thrown in with people who have needs similar to, yet different from, our own. There we learn to share, sympathize, and be considerate. And we lose our self-importance, too. So let us always be glad to be found in the house of the Lord (122:1). *(Turn to page 739.)*

Joyful Return to Zion

PSALM 125

A Song of Ascents.

THOSE who trust in the LORD
Are like Mount Zion,
Which cannot be moved,
but abides forever.
2 As the mountains surround
Jerusalem,
So the LORD surrounds His
people
From this time forth and
forever.

3 For the scepter of wickedness
shall not rest
On the land allotted to the
righteous,
Lest the righteous reach out
their hands to iniquity.

4 Do good, O LORD, to *those
who are* good,
And to *those who are* upright
in their hearts.

5 As for such as turn aside to
their crooked ways,
The LORD shall lead them
away
With the workers of iniquity.

Peace *be* upon Israel!

PSALM 126

A Song of Ascents.

WHEN the LORD brought back
the captivity of Zion,
We were like those who
dream.
2 Then our mouth was filled
with laughter,
And our tongue with singing.
Then they said among the
nations,
"The LORD has done great
things for them."
3 The LORD has done great
things for us,
Whereof we are glad.

4 Bring back our captivity, O
LORD,

As the streams in the South.

5 Those who sow in tears
Shall reap in joy.
6 He who continually goes forth
weeping,
Bearing seed for sowing,
Shall doubtless come again
with rejoicing,
Bringing his sheaves *with him*.

STEP
9

PSALM 127

A Song of Ascents. Of Solomon.

UNLESS the LORD builds the
house,
They labor in vain who build
it;
Unless the LORD guards the
city,
The watchman stays awake in
vain.
2 *It is* vain for you to rise up
early,
To sit up late,
To eat the bread of sorrows;
For so He gives His beloved
sleep.

STEP
11

3 Behold, children *are* a heritage
from the LORD,
The fruit of the womb *is His*
reward.
4 Like arrows in the hand of a
warrior,
So *are* the children of one's
youth.
5 Happy *is* the man who has his
quiver full of them;
They shall not be ashamed,
But shall speak with their
enemies in the gate.

PSALM 128

A Song of Ascents.

BLESSED *is* every one who
fears the LORD,
Who walks in His ways.

STEP
11

2 When you eat the labor of
your hands,

STEP 11

*Sought through prayer and meditation to improve our conscious contact with God **as we understood Him,** praying only for knowledge of His will for us and the power to carry that out.*

Psalm 127:1, 2

Many of us were brought up to believe that hard work is the measure of a person, and that anyone who wants something badly enough and works hard enough will be a success.

However, we who have walked this program step-by-step know that these thoughts are hollow at best and, indeed, can be considered treacherous lies.

In contrast, this passage from Psalms declares eternal truth to us. First, we must continually acknowledge our utter dependence upon God for any success we hope to have in our lives. Second, He takes special joy in giving good gifts to us who are His beloved. It becomes natural for us to seek such a wonderful God. As we meditate on His Word and speak to Him in prayer, we will discover that this sovereign, powerful God is a loving Father who is pleased to see us resting in Him, looking to Him for direction, and rejoicing in His marvelous gifts.

See page 70 of the introductory material for Step 12.

Daily Encouragement

DAY 324 READING: PSALMS 125:1—127:5

A Thought for the New Day: No people should be happier than God's people (126:1–3). Brought back from the "captivity" of sin, their new-found friendship with the Lord cannot be compared with any other joy. We are like the starving people of the street who are invited to a mansion for an endless banquet. Jesus promised He would be with us forever, "and your joy, no one will take from you" (John 16:22). *(Turn to page 741.)*

You *shall be* happy,
and *it shall be* well with
you.
3 Your wife *shall be* like a
fruitful vine
In the very heart of your
house,
Your children like olive plants
All around your table.
4 Behold, thus shall the man be
blessed
Who fears the LORD.

5 The LORD bless you out of
Zion,
And may you see the good of
Jerusalem
All the days of your life.
6 Yes, may you see your
children's children.

Peace *be* upon Israel!

PSALM 129

A Song of Ascents.

"MANY a time they have
afflicted me from my
youth,"
Let Israel now say—
2 "Many a time they have
afflicted me from my youth;
Yet they have not prevailed
against me.
3 The plowers plowed on my
back;
They made their furrows
long."
4 The LORD *is* righteous;
He has cut in pieces the cords
of the wicked.

5 Let all those who hate Zion
Be put to shame and turned
back.
6 Let them be as the grass *on*
the housetops,
Which withers before it grows
up,
7 With which the reaper does
not fill his hand,
Nor he who binds sheaves, his
arms.

8 Neither let those who pass by
them say,
The blessing of the LORD *be*
upon you;
We bless you in the name of
the LORD!"

PSALM 130

A Song of Ascents.

OUT of the depths I have cried
to You, O LORD;
2 Lord, hear my voice!
Let Your ears be attentive
To the voice of my
supplications.

3 If You, LORD, should mark
iniquities,
O Lord, who could stand?
4 But *there is* forgiveness with
You,
That You may be feared.

5 I wait for the LORD, my soul
waits,
And in His word I do hope.
6 My soul *waits* for the Lord
More than those who watch
for the morning—
I say, more than those who
watch for the morning.

7 O Israel, hope in the LORD;
For with the LORD *there is*
mercy,
And with Him *is* abundant
redemption.
8 And He shall redeem Israel
From all his iniquities.

PSALM 131

A Song of Ascents. Of David.

LORD, my heart is not haughty,
Nor my eyes lofty.
Neither do I concern myself
with great matters,
Nor with things too profound
for me.

2 Surely I have calmed and
quieted my soul,

STEP 2

*Came to believe that a Power greater than ourselves
could restore us to sanity.*

Psalm 130

If somewhere in our background there is the teaching or unspoken principle that we must earn God's kindness and blessing, we may feel unable to approach God. Our separation from God may be very apparent to us, but we do not know how to correct the situation. The good news is that we do not have to. God's requirement for restored fellowship is not self-imposed piety. Instead, it is simple repentance, which acknowledges the fact that we are sinners and then turns in faith to the One whose love forgives. His power can carry us beyond our dependencies, frustrations, and guilt to a life of victory and contentment. "With Him *is* abundant redemption" (v. 7). When we place our hope and trust in His mercy, He will redeem us from all our iniquity.

For further reading on Step 2, turn to page 747.

Daily Encouragement

DAY 325 READING: PSALMS 128:1—130:8

A Thought for the New Day: Thank God for His forgiveness of sins (10:3, 4). There would be no place in the universe for anyone to hide if there were no answer to the real problem of our innate disobedience. But how kind God is! Who can measure His mercy? God became a Man who took our place and bore our sins for us. "If we confess our sins, He is faithful and just to forgive us *our* sins, and to cleanse us from all unrighteousness" (1 John 1:9). (*Turn to page 743.*)

Like a weaned child with his
mother;
Like a weaned child *is* my
soul within me.

3 O Israel, hope in the LORD
From this time forth and
forever.

PSALM 132

A Song of Ascents.

LORD, remember David
And all his afflictions;
2 How he swore to the LORD,
And vowed to the Mighty *God*
of Jacob:
3 "Surely I will not go into the
chamber of my house,
Or go up to the comfort of my
bed;
4 I will not give sleep to my
eyes
Or slumber to my eyelids,
5 Until I find a place for the
LORD,
A dwelling place for the
Mighty *God* of Jacob."

6 Behold, we heard of it in
Ephrathah;
We found it in the fields of
the woods.
7 Let us go into His tabernacle;
Let us worship at His
footstool.
8 Arise, O LORD, to Your resting
place,
You and the ark of Your
strength.
9 Let Your priests be clothed
with righteousness,
And let Your saints shout for
joy.

10 For Your servant David's
sake,
Do not turn away the face of
Your Anointed.

11 The LORD has sworn *in* truth
to David;
He will not turn from it:

"I will set upon your throne
the fruit of your body.
12 If your sons will keep My
covenant
And My testimony which I
shall teach them,
Their sons also shall sit upon
your throne forevermore."

13 For the LORD has chosen
Zion;
He has desired *it* for His
habitation:
14 "This *is* My resting place
forever;
Here I will dwell, for I have
desired it.
15 I will abundantly bless her
provision;
I will satisfy her poor with
bread.
16 I will also clothe her priests
with salvation,
And her saints shall shout
aloud for joy.
17 There I will make the horn of
David grow;
I will prepare a lamp for My
Anointed.
18 His enemies I will clothe with
shame,
But upon Himself His crown
shall flourish."

PSALM 133

A Song of Ascents. Of David.

BEHOLD, how good and how
pleasant *it is*
For brethren to dwell together
in unity!

2 *It is* like the precious oil upon
the head,
Running down on the beard,
The beard of Aaron,
Running down on the edge of
his garments.
3 *It is* like the dew of Hermon,
Descending upon the
mountains of Zion;
For there the LORD
commanded the blessing—
Life forevermore.

STEP
8

STEP 8

*Made a list of all persons we had harmed,
and became willing to make amends to them all.*

Psalm 133

Oil carries symbolic meaning throughout the Bible. Generally, it stands either for healing or for one's receiving the Spirit of Christ. When we become willing and want to make amends and to forgive those who need forgiveness, we experience the spiritual benefits that are represented by the precious oil. The healing balm of God's mercy and blessing flows into our lives. Choosing to obey the many directives in Scripture to forgive and seek forgiveness also opens our hearts to greater control and power from the Holy Spirit who indwells us.

Then our lives can know a freshening and a new vitality, which David compared to the dew coming down on the mountains. Our lives will feel washed and new again.

For further reading on Step 8, turn to page 775.

Daily Encouragement

DAY 326 READING: PSALMS 131:1—134:3

A Thought for the New Day: A great value of family life is the opportunity we have to appreciate others. This sometimes means extending ourselves for the good of brothers and sisters. The same holds true in the family of God. God knows that "unity" is possible only if His children learn to bear one another's burdens (133:1). *(Turn to page 747.)*

PSALM 134

A Song of Ascents.

BEHOLD, bless the LORD,
  All *you* servants of the LORD,
Who by night stand in the
  house of the LORD!
2 Lift up your hands *in* the
  sanctuary,
And bless the LORD.

3 The LORD who made heaven
  and earth
Bless you from Zion!

PSALM 135

PRAISE the LORD!

  Praise the name of the LORD;
  Praise *Him*,
    O you servants of the LORD!
2 You who stand in the house
  of the LORD,
  In the courts of the house of
  our God,
3 Praise the LORD, for the LORD
  is good;
  Sing praises to His name,
  for *it is* pleasant.
4 For the LORD has chosen
  Jacob for Himself,
  Israel for His special treasure.

5 For I know that the LORD *is*
  great,
  And our Lord *is* above all
  gods.
6 Whatever the LORD pleases He
  does,
  In heaven and in earth,
  In the seas and in all deep
  places.
7 He causes the vapors to
  ascend from the ends of the
  earth;
  He makes lightning for the
  rain;
  He brings the wind out of His
  treasuries.

8 He destroyed the firstborn of
  Egypt,
  Both of man and beast.

9 He sent signs and wonders
  into the midst of you, O
  Egypt,
  Upon Pharaoh and all his
  servants.
10 He defeated many nations
  And slew mighty kings—
11 Sihon king of the Amorites,
  Og king of Bashan,
  And all the kingdoms of
  Canaan—
12 And gave their land *as* a
  heritage,
  A heritage to Israel His
  people.

13 Your name, O LORD, *endures*
  forever,
  Your fame, O LORD,
  throughout all generations.
14 For the LORD will judge His
  people,
  And He will have compassion
  on His servants.

15 The idols of the nations *are*
  silver and gold,
  The work of men's hands.
16 They have mouths,
  but they do not speak;
  Eyes they have, but they do
  not see;
17 They have ears, but they do
  not hear;
  Nor is there *any* breath in
  their mouths.
18 Those who make them are
  like them;
  So is everyone who trusts in
  them.

19 Bless the LORD, O house of
  Israel!
  Bless the LORD, O house of
  Aaron!
20 Bless the LORD, O house of
  Levi!
  You who fear the LORD,
  bless the LORD!
21 Blessed be the LORD out of
  Zion,
  Who dwells in Jerusalem!

  Praise the LORD!

PSALM 136

O H, give thanks to the LORD,
   for *He is* good!
   For His mercy *endures*
   forever.
2 Oh, give thanks to the God of
   gods!
   For His mercy *endures*
   forever.
3 Oh, give thanks to the Lord of
   lords!
   For His mercy *endures*
   forever:

4 To Him who alone does great
   wonders,
   For His mercy *endures*
   forever;
5 To Him who by wisdom made
   the heavens,
   For His mercy *endures*
   forever;
6 To Him who laid out the earth
   above the waters,
   For His mercy *endures*
   forever;
7 To Him who made great
   lights,
   For His mercy *endures*
   forever—
8 The sun to rule by day,
   For His mercy *endures*
   forever;
9 The moon and stars to rule by
   night,
   For His mercy *endures*
   forever.

10 To Him who struck Egypt in
   their firstborn,
   For His mercy *endures*
   forever;
11 And brought out Israel from
   among them,
   For His mercy *endures*
   forever;
12 With a strong hand,
   and with an
   outstretched arm,
   For His mercy *endures*
   forever;
13 To Him who divided the Red
   Sea in two,
   For His mercy *endures*
   forever;
14 And made Israel pass through
   the midst of it,
   For His mercy *endures*
   forever;
15 But overthrew Pharaoh and
   his army in the Red
   Sea,
   For His mercy *endures*
   forever;
16 To Him who led His people
   through the wilderness,
   For His mercy *endures*
   forever;
17 To Him who struck down
   great kings,
   For His mercy *endures*
   forever;
18 And slew famous kings,
   For His mercy *endures*
   forever—
19 Sihon king of the Amorites,
   For His mercy *endures*
   forever;
20 And Og king of Bashan,
   For His mercy *endures*
   forever—
21 And gave their land as a
   heritage,
   For His mercy *endures*
   forever;
22 A heritage to Israel His
   servant,
   For His mercy *endures*
   forever.

23 Who remembered us in our
   lowly state,
   For His mercy *endures*
   forever;
24 And rescued us from our
   enemies,
   For His mercy *endures*
   forever;
25 Who gives food to all flesh,
   For His mercy *endures*
   forever.

26 Oh, give thanks to the God of
   heaven!
   For His mercy *endures*
   forever.

God Regards the Lowly

PSALM 137

B Y the rivers of Babylon,
There we sat down, yea, we
wept
When we remembered Zion.
2 We hung our harps
Upon the willows in the midst
of it.
3 For there those who carried
us away captive required of
us a song,
And those who plundered us
required of us mirth,
Saying, "Sing us *one* of the
songs of Zion!"

4 How shall we sing the LORD'S
song
In a foreign land?
5 If I forget you, O Jerusalem,
Let my right hand forget *her*
skill!
6 If I do not remember you,
Let my tongue cling to the
roof of my mouth—
If I do not exalt Jerusalem
Above my chief joy.

7 Remember, O LORD, against
the sons of Edom
The day of Jerusalem,
Who said, "Raze *it*, raze *it*,
To its very foundation!"

8 O daughter of Babylon,
who are to be destroyed,
Happy *shall he be* who repays
you as you have served us!
9 Happy *shall he be* who takes
and dashes
Your little ones against the
rock.

PSALM 138

A Psalm of David.

I WILL praise You with my
whole heart;
Before the gods I will sing
praises to You.
2 I will worship toward Your
holy temple,
And praise Your name

For Your lovingkindness and
Your truth;
For You have magnified Your
word above all Your name.
3 In the day when I cried out,
You answered me,
And made me bold *with*
strength in my soul.

4 All the kings of the earth shall
praise You, O LORD,
When they hear the words of
Your mouth.
5 Yes, they shall sing of the
ways of the LORD,
For great *is* the glory of the
LORD.
6 Though the LORD *is* on high,
Yet He regards the lowly;
But the proud He knows from
afar.

7 Though I walk in the midst of
trouble, You will revive me;
You will stretch out Your
hand
Against the wrath of my
enemies,
And Your right hand will save
me.
8 The LORD will perfect *that
which* concerns me;
Your mercy, O LORD, *endures*
forever;
Do not forsake the works of
Your hands.

PSALM 139

For the Chief Musician. A Psalm of David.

O LORD, You have searched
me and known *me.*
2 You know my sitting down
and my rising up;
You understand my thought
afar off.
3 You comprehend my path
and my lying down,
And are acquainted with all
my ways.
4 For *there is* not a word on my
tongue,

STEP 2

STEP 2

*Came to believe that a Power greater than ourselves
could restore us to sanity.*

Psalm 139:1–16

David wrote in verse 5, "You have hedged me behind and before, and laid Your hand upon me. *Such* knowledge *is* too wonderful for me." We ourselves may have felt "hedged in" at times. We have been aware that an Unseen Force had kept us protected in ways that we did not even want to be protected. We may have felt that somehow the more we tried to run from God, the more we became aware of His Holy Spirit calling to us. Now it is time to stop running. It is time to admit that God knows us better than we know ourselves and that, indeed, we are glad He does. He created us, and He has faithfully loved us and pursued us even when we might have rejected Him. Such love is overwhelming. It brings us to our knees in repentance and trust.

For further reading on Step 2, turn to page 753.

Daily Encouragement

DAY 327 READING: PSALMS 135:1—139:16

A Thought for the New Day: The perfection we usually think about is an unrelenting numerical completeness of one hundred percent. Well, no one is perfect like that. It is right that we hate our sins, but it is divine that God is perfecting us in His time (138:8). God makes our otherwise imperfect days "complete" because He walks with us along the way and whispers, "I know your faults, but I am going to fix them, so do not worry." (*Turn to page 749.*)

But behold, O LORD,
  You know it altogether.
5 You have hedged me behind
  and before,
  And laid Your hand upon me.
6 *Such* knowledge *is* too
  wonderful for me;
  It is high, I cannot *attain* it.

7 Where can I go from Your
  Spirit?
  Or where can I flee from Your
  presence?
8 If I ascend into heaven, You
  are there;
  If I make my bed in hell,
  behold, You *are there*.
9 *If* I take the wings of the
  morning,
  And dwell in the uttermost
  parts of the sea,
10 Even there Your hand shall
  lead me,
  And Your right hand shall
  hold me.
11 If I say, "Surely the darkness
  shall fall on me,"
  Even the night shall be light
  about me;
12 Indeed, the darkness shall not
  hide from You,
  But the night shines as the
  day;
  The darkness and the light *are*
  both alike *to You*.

13 For You have formed my
  inward parts;
  You have covered me in my
  mother's womb.
14 I will praise You, for I am
  fearfully *and* wonderfully
  made;
  Marvelous are Your works,
  And *that* my soul knows very
  well.
15 My frame was not hidden
  from You,
  When I was made in secret,
  And skillfully wrought in the
  lowest parts of the earth.
16 Your eyes saw my substance,
  being yet unformed.

And in Your book they all
  were written,
  The days fashioned for me,
  When *as yet there were* none
  of them.

17 How precious also are Your
  thoughts to me, O God!
  How great is the sum of them!
18 *If* I should count them, they
  would be more in number
  than the sand;
  When I awake, I am still with
  You.

19 Oh, that You would slay the
  wicked, O God!
  Depart from me, therefore,
  you bloodthirsty men.
20 For they speak against You
  wickedly;
  Your enemies take *Your name*
  in vain.
21 Do I not hate them, O LORD,
  who hate You?
  And do I not loathe those who
  rise up against You?
22 I hate them with perfect
  hatred;
  I count them my enemies.

23 Search me, O God,
  and know my heart;
  Try me, and know my
  anxieties;
24 And see if *there is any* wicked
  way in me,
  And lead me in the way
  everlasting.

STEP 6

PSALM 140

To the Chief Musician. A Psalm of David.

DELIVER me, O LORD, from
  evil men;
  Preserve me from violent men,
2 Who plan evil things in *their*
  hearts;
  They continually gather
  together *for* war.
3 They sharpen their tongues
  like a serpent;

STEP 6

*Were entirely ready to have God
remove all these defects of character.*

Psalm 139:23, 24

One of the barriers to success in Step 6 is fear. By now we probably truly want God to work in our lives, but consciously or subconsciously we may also be afraid of that process. Even though we are aware of the negative impact our dependencies have had on our lives, we may still be full of anxiety at the thought of living without these things.

Over the years we have learned to meet such basic human needs as love, acceptance, and comfort in wrong ways. Giving up these wrong and harmful things seems to mean giving up our personal needs. However, just the opposite is true. When God leads us out of dependencies, He does not leave us comfortless and unprotected. His Holy Spirit will be there always to comfort, protect, and strengthen us. And when we take our first steps in the path He has chosen for us, He will meet every need that we have in wonderful and special ways that will surprise and delight us.

For further reading on Step 6, turn to page 751.

Daily Encouragement

DAY 328 READING: PSALMS 139:17—140:13

A Thought for the New Day: When you think your world is falling apart, remember that God is with you. Friendships should be cultivated by as many encounters as possible. Likewise, we need to cultivate God's friendship by repeated special meetings. Morning is a great time for fellowship with God: how perfect it is to awake and know He is there (139:17, 18). God sweetens our lives with the assurance, "I will never leave you" (Heb. 13:8). *(Turn to page 751.)*

The poison of asps *is* under
their lips.   Selah

4 Keep me, O LORD, from the
hands of the wicked;
Preserve me from violent men,
Who have purposed to make
my steps stumble.

5 The proud have hidden a
snare for me, and cords;
They have spread a net by the
wayside;
They have set traps for me.
     Selah

6 I said to the LORD: "You *are*
my God;
Hear the voice of my
supplications, O LORD.

7 O GOD the Lord, the strength
of my salvation,
You have covered my head in
the day of battle.

8 Do not grant, O LORD, the
desires of the wicked;
Do not further his *wicked*
scheme,
Lest they be exalted.   Selah

9 "*As for* the head of those who
surround me,
Let the evil of their lips cover
them;

10 Let burning coals fall upon
them;
Let them be cast into the fire,
Into deep pits, that they rise
not up again.

11 Let not a slanderer be
established in the earth;
Let evil hunt the violent man
to overthrow *him*."

12 I know that the LORD will
maintain
The cause of the afflicted,
And justice for the poor.

13 Surely the righteous shall give
thanks to Your name;
The upright shall dwell in
Your presence.

Prayer for Safekeeping

PSALM 141

A Psalm of David.

LORD, I cry out to You;
Make haste to me!
Give ear to my voice when I
cry out to You.

2 Let my prayer be set before
You *as* incense,
The lifting up of my hands *as*
the evening sacrifice.

3 Set a guard, O LORD, over my
mouth;
Keep watch over the door of
my lips.

4 Do not incline my heart
to any evil thing,
To practice wicked works
With men who work iniquity;
And do not let me eat of their
delicacies.

STEP
6

5 Let the righteous strike me;
It shall be a kindness.
And let him reprove me;
It shall be as excellent oil;
Let my head not refuse it.

For still my prayer *is* against
the deeds of the wicked.

6 Their judges are overthrown
by the sides of the cliff,
And they hear my words,
for they are sweet.

7 Our bones are scattered at the
mouth of the grave,
As when one plows and
breaks up the earth.

8 But my eyes *are* upon You,
O GOD the Lord;
In You I take refuge;
Do not leave my soul
destitute.

9 Keep me from the snares
which they have laid for me,
And from the traps of the
workers of iniquity.

10 Let the wicked fall into their
own nets,
While I escape safely.

STEP 6

*Were entirely ready to have God
remove all these defects of character.*

Psalm 141:3, 4

Addictions and sins of the tongue seem to go hand in hand.
Cursing is often present in those addicted to anger. Lewd speech,
deception, and gossip are part of other dependencies. Sarcasm and
belittling is characteristic of addiction to control. Sometimes these
speech patterns are so ingrained in us that we are not even aware of
how much we use them. When we become ready for God to change
us, He will change not only our actions, but also our attitudes and
words. This is often a bigger surprise and joy to those who know us
than a change in our behavior. Programs and methods may bring
certain behavior changes for a time, but only God can change our
hearts so completely that every aspect of our lives becomes new and
glorifying to Him.

For further reading on Step 6, turn to page 783.

Daily Encouragement

DAY 329 READING: PSALM 141:1–10

A Thought for the New Day: Of course this songwriter could
not see God with his physical eyes, but his thoughts and "inner
sight" were fixed on the Lord (v. 8). In the serene presence of
God we, too, find "refuge" in the storms of life. There is always
the tendency to allow the insistent pressures of time and place
to tune out the Eternal: we need to keep the divine vision in
focus. (*Turn to page 753.*)

PSALM 142

A Contemplation of David. A Prayer when he was in the cave.

STEP 2

I CRY out to the LORD with my
  voice;
With my voice to the LORD I
  make my supplication.
2 I pour out my complaint
  before Him;
I declare before Him my
  trouble.

3 When my spirit was
  overwhelmed within me,
Then You knew my path.
In the way in which I walk
They have secretly set a snare
  for me.
4 Look on *my* right hand and
  see,
For *there is* no one who
  acknowledges me;
Refuge has failed me;
No one cares for my soul.

5 I cried out to You, O LORD:
I said, "You *are* my refuge,
My portion in the land
  of the living.
6 Attend to my cry,
For I am brought very low;
Deliver me from my
  persecutors,
For they are stronger than I.
7 Bring my soul out of prison,
That I may praise Your name;
The righteous shall surround
  me,
For You shall deal bountifully
  with me."

PSALM 143

A Psalm of David.

HEAR my prayer, O LORD,
  Give ear to my
    supplications!
In Your faithfulness answer
  me,
And in Your righteousness.
2 Do not enter into judgment
  with Your servant,

For in Your sight no one
  living is righteous.

3 For the enemy has persecuted
  my soul;
He has crushed my life to the
  ground;
He has made me dwell in
  darkness,
Like those who have long
  been dead.
4 Therefore my spirit is
  overwhelmed within me;
My heart within me is
  distressed.

5 I remember the days of old;
I meditate on all Your works;
I muse on the work of Your
  hands.
6 I spread out my hands to You;
My soul *longs* for You like a
  thirsty land.　　　　Selah

7 Answer me speedily, O LORD;
My spirit fails!
Do not hide Your face from
  me,
Lest I be like those who go
  down into the pit.
8 Cause me to hear Your
  lovingkindness in the
    morning,
For in You do I trust;
Cause me to know the way in
  which I should walk,
For I lift up my soul to You.

STEP 3

9 Deliver me, O LORD, from my
  enemies;
In You I take shelter.
10 Teach me to do Your will,
For You *are* my God;
Your Spirit *is* good.
Lead me in the land of
  uprightness.

11 Revive me, O LORD, for Your
  name's sake!
For Your righteousness' sake
  bring my soul out of
    trouble.

STEP 2

Came to believe that a Power greater than ourselves could restore us to sanity.

Psalm 142

David is surrounded by his enemies, and it appears they will soon destroy him. He has taken refuge in a cave, but he knows the cave cannot save him—the enemy is too strong. David looks to the Lord for safety and deliverance, acknowledging that God alone can bring his "soul out of prison."

When we struggle with addictive behaviors, we feel like our souls are imprisoned. The chaos and confusion in our lives make us prisoners of guilt, fear, frustration, and pain. Our sanity is threatened by the inner forces controlling us.

David knows the cure for such a situation. In verses 5–7, he shifts his focus from his strong enemies to his stronger Lord. He rejoices in his True Refuge and reveals his complete trust and faith in the Lord by declaring confidently, "You shall deal bountifully with me." Likewise, we can turn to God for strength, for comfort, and for restoration to sanity.

For further reading on Step 2, turn to page 759.

Daily Encouragement

DAY 330 READING: PSALMS 142:1—144:15

A Thought for the New Day: "No one cares for my soul" is the piteous cry of one who is desolate and forsaken in the world (142:4). Who could resist such a plea? God surely will not. He hears the sobbing of the orphaned child and the deserted wife, and He will rush to their aid. God is Father to the fatherless and Husband to the widow. Bring your broken heart and pour out your grief. God cares for you. (*Turn to page 755.*)

12 In Your mercy cut off my
    enemies,
And destroy all those who
    afflict my soul;
For I *am* Your servant.

PSALM 144

A Psalm of David.

Blessed *be* the Lord my
    Rock,
Who trains my hands for war,
And my fingers for battle—
2 My lovingkindness and my
    fortress,
My high tower and my
    deliverer,
My shield and *the One* in
    whom I take refuge,
Who subdues my people under
    me.

3 Lord, what *is* man,
    that You take knowledge of
    him?
Or the son of man, that You
    are mindful of him?
4 Man is like a breath;
His days *are* like a passing
    shadow.

5 Bow down Your heavens, O
    Lord, and come down;
Touch the mountains,
    and they shall smoke.
6 Flash forth lightning and
    scatter them;
Shoot out Your arrows
    and destroy them.
7 Stretch out Your hand from
    above;
Rescue me and deliver me out
    of great waters,
From the hand of foreigners,
8 Whose mouth speaks vain
    words,
And whose right hand *is* a
    right hand of falsehood.

9 I will sing a new song to You,
    O God;
On a harp of ten strings I will
    sing praises to You,

10 *The One* who gives salvation
    to kings,
Who delivers David His
    servant
From the deadly sword.

11 Rescue me and deliver me
    from the hand of foreigners,
Whose mouth speaks vain
    words,
And whose right hand *is* a
    right hand of falsehood—
12 That our sons *may be* as
    plants grown up in their
    youth;
That our daughters *may be* as
    pillars,
Sculptured in palace style;
13 *That* our barns *may be* full,
Supplying all kinds of
    produce;
That our sheep may bring
    forth thousands
And ten thousands in our
    fields;
14 *That* our oxen *may be* well-
    laden;
That there be no breaking in
    or going out;
That there be no outcry in our
    streets.
15 Happy *are* the people
    who are in such a state;
Happy *are* the people
    whose God *is* the Lord!

PSALM 145

A Praise of David.

I will extol You, my God, O
    King;
And I will bless Your name
    forever and ever.
2 Every day I will bless You,
And I will praise Your name
    forever and ever.
3 Great *is* the Lord,
    and greatly to be praised;
And His greatness *is*
    unsearchable.

4 One generation shall praise
    Your works to another,

STEP 12

STEP 12

*Having had a spiritual awakening as the result of these steps,
we tried to carry this message to others,
and to practice these principles in all our affairs.*

Psalm 145

When we first meet individuals of great standing, we tend to be awe-struck by their fame or fortune or knowledge. However, if we spend enough time with them, we become aware that they are not much different from the rest of us. Our awe will be diminished by our personal knowledge.

But our response to God is just the opposite. When we first become believers in Jesus Christ, we feel joy, excitement, and awe. Then the deeper we grow in our understanding of God, the deeper and more profound becomes our joyful awe at the love and power of the God who calls us His children. The beauty and majesty of His righteousness, grace, and mercy will constantly be a source of *overwhelming inspiration* and delight.

The more we keep our minds focused on our wonderful Lord, the easier it will be to order our paths according to the principles of His Word and to tell others of His goodness to us.

For further reading on Step 12, turn to page 831.

Daily Encouragement

DAY 331 READING: PSALMS 145:1—147:20

A Thought for the New Day: There is a kind of frustration in genuine worship. It is the frustration we experience in attempting to contemplate and grasp the "unsearchable greatness" of the Lord (145:3). As we lie prostrate on the shore of that infinite Ocean and cry out in wonder, "How great Thou art!" God refreshes us with the living water from His very own Person. Thus renewed, our lives shout forth His praise. (*Turn to page 759.*)

And shall declare Your mighty
    acts.
5 I will meditate on the glorious
    splendor of Your majesty,
    And on Your wondrous
    works.
6 *Men* shall speak of the might
    of Your awesome acts,
    And I will declare Your
    greatness.
7 They shall utter the memory
    of Your great goodness,
    And shall sing of Your
    righteousness.

8 The LORD *is* gracious and full
    of compassion,
    Slow to anger and great in
    mercy.
9 The LORD *is* good to all,
    And His tender mercies *are*
    over all His works.

10 All Your works shall praise
    You, O LORD,
    And Your saints shall bless
    You.
11 They shall speak of the glory
    of Your kingdom,
    And talk of Your power,
12 To make known to the sons of
    men His mighty acts,
    And the glorious majesty of
    His kingdom.
13 Your kingdom *is* an
    everlasting kingdom,
    And Your dominion *endures*
    throughout all generations.

14 The LORD upholds all who fall,
    And raises up all *those who*
    are bowed down.
15 The eyes of all look
    expectantly to You,
    And You give them their food
    in due season.
16 You open Your hand
    And satisfy the desire of every
    living thing.

17 The LORD *is* righteous in all
    His ways,
    Gracious in all His works.

18 The LORD *is* near to all who
    call upon Him,
    To all who call upon Him in
    truth.
19 He will fulfill the desire of
    those who fear Him;
    He also will hear their cry and
    save them.
20 The LORD preserves all who
    love Him,
    But all the wicked He will
    destroy.
21 My mouth shall speak the
    praise of the LORD,
    And all flesh shall bless His
    holy name
    Forever and ever.

PSALM 146

PRAISE the LORD!

Praise the LORD, O my soul!
2 While I live I will praise the
    LORD;
    I will sing praises to my God
    while I have my being.

3 Do not put your trust in
    princes,
    Nor in a son of man,
    in whom *there is* no help.
4 His spirit departs,
    he returns to his earth;
    In that very day his plans
    perish.

5 Happy *is he* who *has* the God
    of Jacob for his help,
    Whose hope *is* in the LORD his
    God,
6 Who made heaven and earth,
    The sea, and all that *is* in
    them;
    Who keeps truth forever,
7 Who executes justice for the
    oppressed,
    Who gives food to the hungry.
    The LORD gives freedom to
    the prisoners.

8 The LORD opens *the eyes of*
    the blind;

The LORD raises those who are bowed down;
The LORD loves the righteous.

9 The LORD watches over the strangers;
He relieves the fatherless and widow;
But the way of the wicked He turns upside down.

10 The LORD shall reign forever—
Your God, O Zion, to all generations.

Praise the LORD!

PSALM 147

PRAISE the LORD!
For *it is* good to sing praises to our God;
For *it is* pleasant, *and* praise is beautiful.

2 The LORD builds up Jerusalem;
He gathers together the outcasts of Israel.

3 He heals the brokenhearted
And binds up their wounds.

4 He counts the number of the stars;
He calls them all by name.

5 Great *is* our Lord,
and mighty in power;
His understanding *is* infinite.

6 The LORD lifts up the humble;
He casts the wicked down to the ground.

7 Sing to the LORD with thanksgiving;
Sing praises on the harp to our God,

8 Who covers the heavens with clouds,
Who prepares rain for the earth,
Who makes grass to grow on the mountains.

9 He gives to the beast its food,
And to the young ravens that cry.

10 He does not delight
in the strength of the horse;
He takes no pleasure
in the legs of a man.

11 The LORD takes pleasure
in those who fear Him,
In those who hope in His mercy.

STEP 3

12 Praise the LORD, O Jerusalem!
Praise your God, O Zion!

13 For He has strengthened the bars of your gates;
He has blessed your children within you.

14 He makes peace *in* your borders,
And fills you with the finest wheat.

15 He sends out His command *to the* earth;
His word runs very swiftly.

16 He gives snow like wool;
He scatters the frost like ashes;

17 He casts out His hail like morsels;
Who can stand before His cold?

18 He sends out His word and melts them;
He causes His wind to blow, *and* the waters flow.

19 He declares His word to Jacob,
His statutes and His judgments to Israel.

20 He has not dealt thus with any nation;
And *as for His* judgments, they have not known them.

Praise the LORD!

PSALM 148

PRAISE the LORD!

Praise the LORD from the heavens;
Praise Him in the heights!

2 Praise Him, all His angels;
   Praise Him, all His hosts!
3 Praise Him, sun and moon;
   Praise Him, all you stars of
   light!
4 Praise Him, you heavens of
   heavens,
   And you waters above the
   heavens!

5 Let them praise the name of
   the LORD,
   For He commanded
   and they were created.
6 He has also established them
   forever and ever;
   He has made a decree which
   shall not pass away.

7 Praise the LORD from the
   earth,
   You great sea creatures and
   all the depths;
8 Fire and hail, snow and
   clouds;
   Stormy wind, fulfilling His
   word;
9 Mountains and all hills;
   Fruitful trees and all cedars;
10 Beasts and all cattle;
   Creeping things and flying
   fowl;
11 Kings of the earth and all
   peoples;
   Princes and all judges of the
   earth;
12 Both young men and maidens;
   Old men and children.

13 Let them praise the name of
   the LORD,
   For His name alone is exalted;
   His glory *is* above the earth
   and heaven.
14 And He has exalted the horn
   of His people,
   The praise of all His saints—
   Of the children of Israel,
   A people near to Him.

Praise the LORD!

PSALM 149

PRAISE the LORD!

Sing to the LORD a new song,
And His praise in the
   congregation of saints.

2 Let Israel rejoice in their
   Maker;
   Let the children of Zion be
   joyful in their King.
3 Let them praise His name
   with the dance;
   Let them sing praises to Him
   with the timbrel and harp.
4 For the LORD takes pleasure in
   His people;
   He will beautify the humble
   with salvation.

5 Let the saints be joyful in
   glory;
   Let them sing aloud on their
   beds.
6 *Let* the high praises of God *be*
   in their mouth,
   And a two-edged sword in
   their hand,
7 To execute vengeance on the
   nations,
   And punishments on the
   peoples;
8 To bind their kings with
   chains,
   And their nobles with fetters
   of iron;
9 To execute on them the
   written judgment—
   This honor have all His saints.

Praise the LORD!

PSALM 150

PRAISE the LORD!

Praise God in His sanctuary;
Praise Him in His mighty
   firmament!

2 Praise Him for His mighty
   acts;
   Praise Him according to His
   excellent greatness!

STEP 2

*Came to believe that a Power greater than ourselves
could restore us to sanity.*

Psalm 149:4

The only people unable to experience God's wonderful grace and mercy are those who choose not to. As long as we are trying to "fix" our circumstances by our power or intellect or determination, we are rejecting the power of God, which is available to us. Step 1 has helped us realize that human effort to free ourselves from dependencies will never succeed. But in admitting our helplessness we have placed ourselves in the path of abundant power and mercy. We have become humble. Now we must reach beyond ourselves— beyond the gimmicks of the world—and place our faith in God through Jesus Christ, who died to free us from the bondage of sin. The moment our hearts respond in faith to God, we become His children, and He beautifies our lives with the greatest gifts imaginable—salvation from the control of sin, and the joy of eternal life with Him.

For further reading on Step 2, turn to page 763.

Daily Encouragement

DAY 332 READING: PSALMS 148:1—150:6

A Thought for the New Day: Praise is the theme of the last three in the collection of psalms. The writer desires that God be praised by all creation and on all instruments of music. The message is clear: Everything we do should be, each in its own way, an act of praise to the One who gives strength and breath to enjoy Him and the life He gives us. (*Turn to page 763.*)

Let All Things Praise God

3 Praise Him with the sound of
the trumpet;
Praise Him with the lute and
harp!
4 Praise Him with the timbrel
and dance;
Praise Him with stringed
instruments and flutes!

5 Praise Him with loud cymbals;
Praise Him with high
sounding cymbals!

6 Let everything that has breath
praise the LORD.

Praise the LORD!

THE BOOK OF
PROVERBS

THE proverbs of Solomon the son of David, king of Israel:

2 To know wisdom and
  instruction,
  To perceive the words of
  understanding,
3 To receive the instruction of
  wisdom,
  Justice, judgment, and equity;
4 To give prudence to the simple,
  To the young man knowledge
  and discretion—
5 A wise *man* will hear
  and increase learning,
  And a man of understanding
  will attain wise counsel,
6 To understand a proverb
  and an enigma,
  The words of the wise
  and their riddles.

STEP 2

7 The fear of the LORD *is* the
  beginning of knowledge,
  But fools despise wisdom and
  instruction.

8 My son, hear the instruction
  of your father,
  And do not forsake the law
  of your mother;
9 For they *will be* graceful
  ornaments on your head,
  And chains about your neck.

10 My son, if sinners entice you,
  Do not consent.
11 If they say, "Come with us,
  Let us lie in wait to *shed* blood;
  Let us lurk secretly for the
  innocent without cause;
12 Let us swallow them alive like
  Sheol,
  And whole, like those who go
  down to the Pit;
13 We shall find all *kinds* of
  precious possessions,
  We shall fill our houses with
  spoil;

14 Cast in your lot among us,
  Let us all have one purse"—
15 My son, do not walk in the
  way with them,
  Keep your foot from their path;
16 For their feet run to evil,
  And they make haste to shed
  blood.
17 Surely, in vain the net is
  spread
  In the sight of any bird;
18 But they lie in wait for their
  own blood,
  They lurk secretly for their
  own lives.
19 So *are* the ways of everyone
  who is greedy for gain;
  It takes away the life of its
  owners.

20 Wisdom calls aloud outside;
  She raises her voice in the
  open squares.
21 She cries out in the chief
  concourses,
  At the openings of the gates in
  the city
  She speaks her words:
22 "How long, you simple ones,
  will you love simplicity?
  For scorners delight in their
  scorning,
  And fools hate knowledge.
23 Turn at my reproof;
  Surely I will pour out my spirit
  on you;
  I will make my words known
  to you.
24 Because I have called and you
  refused,
  I have stretched out my hand
  and no one regarded,
25 Because you disdained all my
  counsel,
  And would have none of my
  reproof,
26 I also will laugh at your
  calamity;
  I will mock when your terror
  comes,

761

27 When your terror comes like a
   storm,
   And your destruction comes
   like a whirlwind,
   When distress and anguish
   come upon you.

28 "Then they will call on me,
   but I will not answer;
   They will seek me diligently,
   but they will not find me.
29 Because they hated knowledge
   And did not choose the fear of
   the LORD,
30 They would have none of my
   counsel
   And despised all my reproof,
31 Therefore they shall eat the
   fruit of their own way,
   And be filled to the full with
   their own fancies.
32 For the turning away of the
   simple will slay them,
   And the complacency of fools
   will destroy them;
33 But whoever listens to me
   will dwell safely,
   And will be secure,
   without fear of evil."

2 My son, if you receive my
   words,
   And treasure my commands
   within you,

STEP
2

2 So that you incline your ear to
   wisdom,
   And apply your heart to
   understanding;
3 Yes, if you cry out for
   discernment,
   And lift up your voice for
   understanding,
4 If you seek her as silver,
   And search for her as *for*
   hidden treasures;
5 Then you will understand the
   fear of the LORD,
   And find the knowledge of
   God.
6 For the LORD gives wisdom;
   From His mouth *come*
   knowledge and under-
   standing;

7 He stores up sound wisdom for
   the upright;
   He is a shield to those who
   walk uprightly;
8 He guards the paths of justice,
   And preserves the way of His
   saints.
9 Then you will understand
   righteousness and justice,
   Equity *and* every good path.

10 When wisdom enters your
   heart,
   And knowledge is pleasant to
   your soul,
11 Discretion will preserve you;
   Understanding will keep you,
12 To deliver you from the way of
   evil,
   From the man who speaks
   perverse things,
13 From those who leave the
   paths of uprightness
   To walk in the ways of
   darkness;
14 Who rejoice in doing evil,
   And delight in the perversity
   of the wicked;
15 Whose ways *are* crooked,
   And *who are* devious in their
   paths;
16 To deliver you from the
   immoral woman,
   From the seductress *who*
   flatters with her words,
17 Who forsakes the companion
   of her youth,
   And forgets the covenant of
   her God.
18 For her house leads down to
   death,
   And her paths to the dead;
19 None who go to her return,
   Nor do they regain the paths of
   life—
20 So you may walk in the way of
   goodness,
   And keep *to* the paths of
   righteousness.
21 For the upright will dwell in
   the land,
   And the blameless will remain
   in it;

STEP 2

Came to believe that a Power greater than ourselves could restore us to sanity.

Proverbs 2:2–12

We have come to a point in our lives when the enticing mirages proffered by our dependencies have given way to the hard, cold facts of reality. Our hearts have become hungry for solid and lasting fulfillment and peace. Proverbs 2 tells us that God honors the sincere seeker of Truth. To come with an open heart and mind is all that is required to truly find God. And when we have come to know Him, we not only receive eternal life in heaven, but the promise of His Holy Spirit's power and wisdom to guide us on earth.

If we are struggling with dependencies, one of our greatest needs is discretion and understanding that will "deliver . . . from the way of evil" (v. 12). To accept Jesus as Savior is to welcome His Spirit's wisdom and power into our lives, giving us all that we need to win the recovery battle.

See page 34 of the introductory material for Step 3.

Daily Encouragement

DAY 333 READING: PROVERBS 1:1—2:9

A Thought for the New Day: Because we often associate the word "fear" (1:7) with simple slavish terror, "awe" or "reverence" may be better word choices for expressing the right attitude toward God. However, reverence includes certain elements of fear that are appropriate, lest we assume a position of flippant disregard for the Lord's majesty as King and Judge. Certainly there can be no practical knowledge without this right regard for the Author of truth and Creator of the realities among which we live and move. (*Turn to page 765.*)

22 But the wicked will be cut off
from the earth,
And the unfaithful will be
uprooted from it.

3 My son, do not forget my law,
But let your heart keep my
commands;
2 For length of days and long life
And peace they will add to
you.

3 Let not mercy and truth
forsake you;
Bind them around your neck,
Write them on the tablet of
your heart,
4 *And* so find favor and high
esteem
In the sight of God and man.

5 Trust in the LORD with all your
heart,
And lean not on your own
understanding;
6 In all your ways acknowledge
Him,
And He shall direct your paths.

7 Do not be wise in your own
eyes;
Fear the LORD and depart from
evil.
8 It will be health to your flesh,
And strength to your bones.

9 Honor the LORD with your
possessions,
And with the firstfruits of all
your increase;
10 So your barns will be filled
with plenty,
And your vats will overflow
with new wine.

11 My son, do not despise the
chastening of the LORD,
Nor detest His correction;
12 For whom the LORD loves He
corrects,
Just as a father the son *in
whom* he delights.

13 Happy *is* the man *who* finds
wisdom,

And the man *who* gains
understanding;
14 For her proceeds *are* better
than the profits of silver,
And her gain than fine gold.
15 She *is* more precious than
rubies,
And all the things you may
desire cannot compare with
her.
16 Length of days *is* in her right
hand,
In her left hand riches and
honor.
17 Her ways *are* ways of
pleasantness,
And all her paths *are* peace.
18 She *is* a tree of life to those
who take hold of her,
And happy *are all* who retain
her.

19 The LORD by wisdom
founded the earth;
By understanding
He established the heavens;
20 By His knowledge
the depths were broken up,
And clouds drop down the
dew.

21 My son, let them not depart
from your eyes—
Keep sound wisdom and
discretion;
22 So they will be life to your soul
And grace to your neck.
23 Then you will walk safely in
your way,
And your foot will not stumble.
24 When you lie down,
you will not be afraid;
Yes, you will lie down
and your sleep will be sweet.
25 Do not be afraid of sudden
terror,
Nor of trouble from the wicked
when it comes;
26 For the LORD will be your
confidence,
And will keep your foot from
being caught.

STEP 3

*Made a decision to turn our will and our lives
over to the care of God **as we understood Him.***
Proverbs 3:5, 6

Recovery literature reminds us that in our dependency illness, "we had been faithful, abjectly faithful to the God of Reason" (*Alcoholics Anonymous*, p. 54). In contrast, wise King Solomon wrote: "Lean not on your own understanding" (v. 5). Although intelligence and reason are precious gifts from God, our most important human relationships and spiritual issues are matters primarily of the heart and not the head.

When we attempt to lean on our own understanding, we encounter numerous recovery barriers. How many times have we tried to think our way out of chronically painful emotions? How many times have we tried to reason our way past the emptiness of spiritual bankruptcy? All to no avail.

Our decision "to turn our will and our lives over to the care of God" involves different forms of surrender. One important surrender is the surrender of an inflated sense of our own intellectual prowess. And so in Step 3 we learn to begin to lean, not on our own understanding, but on the God of our understanding.

See page 38 of the introductory material for Step 4.

Daily Encouragement

DAY 334 READING: PROVERBS 2:10—3:10

A Thought for the New Day: Trust in God is the best part of wisdom (3:5, 6). The alternative is to trust in some finite thing, including oneself, since everybody has to trust in something. However, to trust in what is time-bound is to put faith in what is fallible—and at some point failure will inevitably be the result. On the other hand, success surely awaits when the Lord is directing your ventures. (*Turn to page 767.*)

STEP 9

27 Do not withhold good from
those to whom it is due,
When it is in the power of your
hand to do *so*.

28 Do not say to your neighbor,
"Go, and come back,
And tomorrow I will give *it*,"
When *you have* it with you.

29 Do not devise evil against your
neighbor,
For he dwells by you for
safety's sake.

30 Do not strive with a man
without cause,
If he has done you no harm.

31 Do not envy the oppressor,
And choose none of his ways;

32 For the perverse *person is* an
abomination to the LORD,
But His secret *counsel*
is with the upright.

33 The curse of the LORD *is* on the
house of the wicked,
But He blesses the habitation
of the just.

34 Surely He scorns the scornful,
But gives grace to the humble.

35 The wise shall inherit glory,
But shame shall be the legacy
of fools.

4 Hear, *my* children,
the instruction of a father,
And give attention to know
understanding;

2 For I give you good doctrine:
Do not forsake my law.

3 When I was my father's son,
Tender and the only one in the
sight of my mother,

4 He also taught me, and said to
me:
"Let your heart retain my
words;
Keep my commands, and live.

5 Get wisdom! Get under-
standing!
Do not forget, nor turn away
from the words of my mouth.

6 Do not forsake her,
and she will preserve you;
Love her, and she will keep
you.

7 Wisdom *is* the principal thing;
Therefore get wisdom.
And in all your getting,
get understanding.

8 Exalt her, and she will promote
you;
She will bring you honor,
when you embrace her.

9 She will place on your head an
ornament of grace;
A crown of glory she will
deliver to you."

10 Hear, my son, and receive my
sayings,
And the years of your life will
be many.

11 I have taught you in the way
of wisdom;
I have led you in right paths.

12 When you walk, your steps will
not be hindered,
And when you run,
you will not stumble.

13 Take firm hold of instruction,
do not let go;
Keep her, for she *is* your life.

14 Do not enter the path of the
wicked,
And do not walk in the way of
evil.

15 Avoid it, do not travel on it;
Turn away from it and pass on.

16 For they do not sleep
unless they have done evil;
And their sleep is taken away
unless they make *someone*
fall.

17 For they eat the bread of
wickedness,
And drink the wine of violence.

18 But the path of the just *is* like
the shining sun,
That shines ever brighter unto
the perfect day.

19 The way of the wicked *is* like
darkness;
They do not know what makes
them stumble.

20 My son, give attention to my
words;

STEP 9

Made direct amends to such people wherever possible,
except when to do so would injure them or others.

Proverbs 3:27

Step 9 is a process that requires great wisdom from God and strong reliance on the Holy Spirit. There may be countless people in our lives who come to mind when we begin the process of making amends. We will need God's wisdom to know when and how to go about making necessary amends. We also need to be aware that it may not be "within our power" to make amends to all those we have wronged by our attitudes and actions. If the opening of old relationships may threaten our recovery or another person's emotional stability, we should proceed with utmost caution, if at all. Sincere prayer and time for consideration should be given for each amends to be made so that we can speak and act in the love of Christ. If our amends are received in love and forgiveness, we can rejoice. But even if they are not, we will know that in being obedient to God's commands, we have peace.

For further reading on Step 9, turn to page 781.

Daily Encouragement

DAY 335 READING: PROVERBS 3:11—4:27

A Thought for the New Day: Sometimes you may find yourself in tight spots that are the result of your own folly or mismanagement (3:11, 12). In this way the Lord reminds you how important it is for you to seek His guidance. Be thankful for such correction. You surely would have found yourself in deeper trouble if God had not stopped you where you were. He promises to start you on your way again when you sincerely seek His direction. (*Turn to page 769.*)

Incline your ear to my sayings.

21 Do not let them depart from
your eyes;
Keep them in the midst of your
heart;

22 For they *are* life to those who
find them,
And health to all their flesh.

23 Keep your heart with all
diligence,
For out of it *spring* the issues
of life.

24 Put away from you a deceitful
mouth,
And put perverse lips far from
you.

25 Let your eyes look straight
ahead,
And your eyelids look right
before you.

26 Ponder the path of your feet,
And let all your ways be
established.

27 Do not turn to the right or the
left;
Remove your foot from evil.

5 My son, pay attention to my
wisdom;
Lend your ear to my
understanding,

2 That you may preserve
discretion,
And *that* your lips may keep
knowledge.

STEP 4

3 For the lips of an immoral
woman drip honey,
And her mouth *is* smoother
than oil;

4 But in the end she is bitter as
wormwood,
Sharp as a two-edged sword.

5 Her feet go down to death,
Her steps lay hold of hell.

6 Lest you ponder *her* path of
life—
Her ways are unstable;
You do not know *them.*

7 Therefore hear me now, *my*
children,
And do not depart from the
words of my mouth.

8 Remove your way far from her,

And do not go near the door of
her house,

9 Lest you give your honor to
others,
And your years to the cruel
one;

10 Lest aliens be filled with your
wealth,
And your labors go to the
house of a foreigner;

11 And you mourn at last,
When your flesh and your
body are consumed,

12 And say:
"How I have hated instruction,
And my heart despised reproof!

13 I have not obeyed the voice of
my teachers,
Nor inclined my ear to those
who instructed me!

14 I was on the verge of total
ruin,
In the midst of the
congregation and assembly."

15 Drink water from your own
cistern,
And running water from your
own well.

16 Should your fountains be
dispersed abroad,
Streams of water in the
streets?

17 Let them be only your own,
And not for strangers with
you.

18 Let your fountain be blessed,
And rejoice with the wife of
your youth.

19 *As a* loving deer and a graceful
doe,
Let her breasts satisfy you at
all times;
And always be enraptured with
her love.

20 For why should you, my son,
be enraptured by an immoral
woman,
And be embraced in the arms
of a seductress?

21 For the ways of man *are* before
the eyes of the LORD,

STEP 4

Made a searching and fearless moral inventory of ourselves.

Proverbs 5:3–6

Not all of us have a problem with adultery. But we can all learn from the type of behavior described here.

When we first begin to develop harmful, and perhaps even perverse, dependencies, we do so because it seems pleasant or at least easier than an alternative behavior. Unfortunately, in the end those dependencies become bitter and often even deadly. Only long after the chains are forged can we see how destructive our behavior has become to ourselves and to those around us.

How important it is for us to seriously "ponder [the] path of life"! This is what each of us is attempting in Step 4. We realize that many of our ways and reasons for doing things have been "unstable." But now we determine that with God's help we will begin making an honest personal inventory. We will courageously seek out and identify our weaknesses, knowing that God is with us to impart His wisdom and His unconditional love as we advance through the healing process.

For further reading on Step 4, turn to page 776.

Daily Encouragement

DAY 336 READING: PROVERBS 5:1—7:27

A Thought for the New Day: Nothing so lightens the burden of work as enthusiasm, which is really an indication of the deep personal commitment of the worker. Seek divine guidance for a career that is not boring, but exciting. Then labor becomes enjoyment, the hours pass all too quickly, and your work will be a blessing to those whom you serve. Yes, consider the way of the enthusiastic ant (6:6–8). (*Turn to page 775.*)

And He ponders all his paths.
22 His own iniquities entrap the
wicked man,
And he is caught in the cords
of his sin.
23 He shall die for lack of
instruction,
And in the greatness of his
folly he shall go astray.

6 My son, if you become surety
for your friend,
If you have shaken hands in
pledge for a stranger,
2 You are snared by the words of
your *own* mouth;
You are taken by the words of
your mouth.
3 So do this, my son,
and deliver yourself;
For you have come into the
hand of your friend:
Go and humble yourself;
Plead with your friend.
4 Give no sleep to your eyes,
Nor slumber to your eyelids.
5 Deliver yourself like a gazelle
from the hand *of the hunter*,
And like a bird from the hand
of the fowler.

6 Go to the ant, you sluggard!
Consider her ways and be wise,
7 Which, having no captain,
Overseer or ruler,
8 Provides her supplies in the
summer,
And gathers her food in the
harvest.
9 How long will you slumber,
O sluggard?
When will you rise from your
sleep?
10 A little sleep, a little slumber,
A little folding of the hands to
sleep—
11 So shall your poverty come on
you like a robber,
And your need like an armed
man.

12 A worthless person, a wicked
man,

Walks with a perverse mouth;
13 He winks with his eyes,
He shuffles his feet,
He points with his fingers;
14 Perversity *is* in his heart,
He devises evil continually,
He sows discord.
15 Therefore his calamity shall
come suddenly;
Suddenly he shall be broken
without remedy.

16 These six *things* the LORD
hates,
Yes, seven *are* an abomination
to Him:
17 A proud look,
A lying tongue,
Hands that shed innocent
blood,
18 A heart that devises wicked
plans,
Feet that are swift in running
to evil,
19 A false witness *who* speaks
lies,
And one who sows discord
among brethren.

20 My son, keep your father's
command,
And do not forsake the law of
your mother.
21 Bind them continually upon
your heart;
Tie them around your neck.
22 When you roam, they will lead
you;
When you sleep, they will keep
you;
And *when* you awake, they
will speak with you.
23 For the commandment *is* a
lamp,
And the law *is* light;
Reproofs of instruction *are* the
way of life,
24 To keep you from the evil
woman,
From the flattering tongue of a
seductress.
25 Do not lust after her beauty in
your heart,

Nor let her allure you with her eyelids.

26 For by means of a harlot
A *man is reduced* to a crust of bread;
And an adulteress will prey upon his precious life.

27 Can a man take fire to his bosom,
And his clothes not be burned?

28 Can one walk on hot coals,
And his feet not be seared?

29 So *is* he who goes in to his neighbor's wife;
Whoever touches her shall not be innocent.

30 *People* do not despise a thief
If he steals to satisfy himself when he is starving.

31 Yet *when* he is found, he must restore sevenfold;
He may have to give up all the substance of his house.

32 Whoever commits adultery with a woman lacks understanding;
He *who* does so destroys his own soul.

33 Wounds and dishonor he will get,
And his reproach will not be wiped away.

34 For jealousy *is* a husband's fury;
Therefore he will not spare in the day of vengeance.

35 He will accept no recompense,
Nor will he be appeased though you give many gifts.

7 My son, keep my words,
And treasure my commands within you.

2 Keep my commands and live,
And my law as the apple of your eye.

3 Bind them on your fingers;
Write them on the tablet of your heart.

4 Say to wisdom, "You *are* my sister,"
And call understanding *your* nearest kin,

5 That they may keep you from the immoral woman,
From the seductress
who flatters with her words.

6 For at the window of my house
I looked through my lattice,

7 And saw among the simple,
I perceived among the youths,
A young man devoid of understanding,

8 Passing along the street near her corner;
And he took the path to her house

9 In the twilight, in the evening,
In the black and dark night.

10 And there a woman met him,
With the attire of a harlot,
and a crafty heart.

11 She *was* loud and rebellious,
Her feet would not stay at home.

12 At times *she was* outside,
at times in the open square,
Lurking at every corner.

13 So she caught him and kissed him;
With an impudent face she said to him:

14 "*I have* peace offerings with me;
Today I have paid my vows.

15 So I came out to meet you,
Diligently to seek your face,
And I have found you.

16 I have spread my bed with tapestry,
Colored coverings of Egyptian linen.

17 I have perfumed my bed
With myrrh, aloes, and cinnamon.

18 Come, let us take our fill of love until morning;
Let us delight ourselves with love.

19 For my husband *is* not at home;
He has gone on a long journey;

20 He has taken a bag of money with him,

And will come home on the
appointed day."

21 With her enticing speech
    she caused him to yield,
With her flattering lips
    she seduced him.
22 Immediately he went after her,
    as an ox goes to the
    slaughter,
Or as a fool to the correction
    of the stocks,
23 Till an arrow struck his liver.
As a bird hastens to the snare,
He did not know it *would take*
    his life.

24 Now therefore, listen to me,
    my children;
Pay attention to the words of
    my mouth:
25 Do not let your heart turn
    aside to her ways,
Do not stray into her paths;
26 For she has cast down many
    wounded,
And all who were slain by her
    were strong *men*.
27 Her house *is* the way to hell,
Descending to the chambers of
    death.

8 Does not wisdom cry out,
And understanding lift up her
    voice?
2 She takes her stand on the top
    of the high hill,
Beside the way, where the
    paths meet.
3 She cries out by the gates,
    at the entry of the city,
At the entrance of the doors:
4 "To you, O men, I call,
And my voice *is* to the sons of
    men.
5 O you simple ones,
    understand prudence,
And you fools,
    be of an understanding heart.
6 Listen, for I will speak of
    excellent things,
And from the opening of my
    lips *will come* right things;
7 For my mouth will speak truth;

Wickedness *is* an abomination
    to my lips.
8 All the words of my mouth *are*
    with righteousness;
Nothing crooked or perverse *is*
    in them.
9 They *are* all plain to him
    who understands,
And right to those
    who find knowledge.
10 Receive my instruction, and
    not silver,
And knowledge rather than
    choice gold;
11 For wisdom *is* better than
    rubies,
And all the things one may
    desire cannot be compared
    with her.

12 "I, wisdom, dwell with
    prudence,
And find out knowledge *and*
    discretion.
13 The fear of the LORD *is* to hate
    evil;
Pride and arrogance and the
    evil way
And the perverse mouth I hate.
14 Counsel *is* mine, and sound
    wisdom;
I *am* understanding, I have
    strength.
15 By me kings reign,
And rulers decree justice.
16 By me princes rule, and nobles,
All the judges of the earth.
17 I love those who love me,
And those who seek me
    diligently will find me.
18 Riches and honor *are* with me,
Enduring riches and
    righteousness.
19 My fruit *is* better than gold,
    yes, than fine gold,
And my revenue than choice
    silver.
20 I traverse the way of
    righteousness,
In the midst of the paths of
    justice,
21 That I may cause those who
    love me to inherit wealth,
That I may fill their treasuries.

22"The LORD possessed me at the beginning of His way,
Before His works of old.

23 I have been established from everlasting,
From the beginning, before there was ever an earth.

24 When *there were* no depths I was brought forth,
When *there were* no fountains abounding with water.

25 Before the mountains were settled,
Before the hills, I was brought forth;

26 While as yet He had not made the earth or the fields,
Or the primeval dust of the world.

27 When He prepared the heavens, I *was* there,
When He drew a circle on the face of the deep,

28 When He established the clouds above,
When He strengthened the fountains of the deep,

29 When He assigned to the sea its limit,
So that the waters would not transgress His command,
When He marked out the foundations of the earth,

30 Then I was beside Him,
as a master craftsman;
And I was daily *His* delight,
Rejoicing always before Him,

31 Rejoicing in His inhabited world,
And my delight *was* with the sons of men.

32"Now therefore, listen to me, *my* children,
For blessed *are those who* keep my ways.

33 Hear instruction and be wise,
And do not disdain *it.*

34 Blessed is the man who listens to me,
Watching daily at my gates,
Waiting at the posts of my doors.

35 For whoever finds me finds life,
And obtains favor from the LORD;

36 But he who sins against me wrongs his own soul;
All those who hate me love death."

9 Wisdom has built her house,
She has hewn out her seven pillars;

2 She has slaughtered her meat,
She has mixed her wine,
She has also furnished her table.

3 She has sent out her maidens,
She cries out from the highest places of the city,

4 "Whoever *is* simple,
let him turn in here!"
As for him who lacks understanding, she says to him,

5 "Come, eat of my bread
And drink of the wine *which* I have mixed.

6 Forsake foolishness and live,
And go in the way of understanding.

7 "He who reproves a scoffer gets shame for himself,
And he who rebukes a wicked *man gets* himself a blemish.

8 Do not reprove a scoffer, lest he hate you;
Rebuke a wise man, and he will love you.

9 Give *instruction* to a wise *man,* and he will be still wiser;
Teach a just *man,* and he will increase in learning.

10"The fear of the LORD *is* the beginning of wisdom,
And the knowledge of the Holy One *is* understanding.

11 For by me your days will be multiplied,
And years of life will be added to you.

12 If you are wise,
    you are wise for yourself,
    And *if* you scoff,
    you alone will bear *it*."

13 A foolish woman is clamorous;
    She is simple, and knows
    nothing.
14 For she sits at the door of her
    house,
    On a seat *by* the highest places
    of the city,
15 To call to those who pass by,
    Who go straight on their way:
16 "Whoever *is* simple,
    let him turn in here";
    And *as for* him who lacks
    understanding, she says to
    him,
17 "Stolen water is sweet,
    And bread *eaten* in secret is
    pleasant."
18 But he does not know that the
    dead *are* there,
    That her guests *are* in the
    depths of hell.

10 The proverbs of Solomon:

    A wise son makes a glad father,
    But a foolish son *is* the grief of
    his mother.

2 Treasures of wickedness profit
    nothing,
    But righteousness delivers from
    death.
3 The LORD will not allow the
    righteous soul to famish,
    But He casts away the desire of
    the wicked.

4 He who deals *with* a slack
    hand becomes poor,
    But the hand of the diligent
    makes *one* rich.
5 He who gathers in summer
    is a wise son,
    But he who sleeps in harvest
    is a son who causes shame.

6 Blessings *are* on the head of
    the righteous,

But violence covers the mouth
    of the wicked.
7 The memory of the righteous *is*
    blessed,
    But the name of the wicked
    will rot.

8 The wise in heart will receive
    commands,
    But a prating fool will fall.

9 He who walks with integrity
    walks securely,
    But he who perverts his ways
    will become known.

10 He who winks with the eye
    causes trouble,
    But a prating fool will fall.

11 The mouth of the righteous *is*
    a well of life,
    But violence covers the mouth
    of the wicked.

12 Hatred stirs up strife,
    But love covers all sins.   STEP 8

13 Wisdom is found on the lips of
    him who has understanding,
    But a rod *is* for the back of
    him who is devoid of
    understanding.

14 Wise *people* store up
    knowledge,
    But the mouth of the foolish *is*
    near destruction.

15 The rich man's wealth
    is his strong city;
    The destruction of the poor
    is their poverty.

16 The labor of the righteous
    leads to life,
    The wages of the wicked to
    sin.

17 He who keeps instruction *is in*
    the way of life,   STEP 4

STEP 8

*Made a list of all persons we had harmed,
and became willing to make amends to them all.*

Proverbs 10:12

It is amazing how easy it is to get ourselves into an unpleasant situation and how hard it is to get ourselves out. An impulsive action or thoughtless reply can alienate others quickly and deeply. Once such a cycle of unkind words or actions is established, it feeds upon itself. Strife produces hatred, which produces still more strife. How do we extricate ourselves from such a damaging situation? We do it by choosing to allow God to love others through us. A degree of relinquishment is necessary for this to occur: we must be willing to let go of any desire to prove ourselves right or to retaliate. We must ask God to take bitterness from our hearts. Then as we sincerely seek God's own care and concern for that person, we will discover that the wrongs of the past diminish and disappear beneath the blanket of love.

For further reading on Step 8, turn to page 785.

Daily Encouragement

DAY 337 READING: PROVERBS 8:1—10:12

A Thought for the New Day: So personal is wisdom in Proverbs 8:22 that many have guessed the reference is actually to Christ. In the New Testament Jesus Christ is referred to as the wisdom of His people. In this passage we see wisdom as a personal helper in the whole work of divine creation. Paul wrote that all things were created by Christ (see Col. 1:16). In all our need for daily wisdom, let us habitually resort to Him who is Wisdom personified. (*Turn to page 776.*)

STEP 4

Made a searching and fearless moral inventory of ourselves.

Proverbs 10:17

We have begun to walk in the way of life. We have turned our lives over to God to direct us as He sees fit. As we move into Step 4, God's Holy Spirit will be directing us on a difficult but important journey. We will need to listen closely to His instruction as He brings to our minds certain memories, words of friends and family, as well as our present circumstances. We will have to be willing to be more honest than we have ever been with ourselves. There may be areas of our lives that the Holy Spirit will reprove. How will we accept that reproof? We must ask God to keep us from minimizing or denying issues. We must also ask Him to help us stay on course in our inventory, to refrain from majoring on minor issues, at the expense of truly important ones. Keeping our hearts sincere, open, and willing before God will bring success to our efforts and new understanding to our lives.

For further reading on Step 4, turn to page 789.

Daily Encouragement

DAY 338 READING: PROVERBS 10:13—11:6

A Thought for the New Day: People of integrity are unswervingly devoted to their purpose (11:3). "Upright" individuals must have integrity in order to pursue consistently their goal of righteousness. Otherwise, they would be hot and cold and not very dependable. Single-mindedness is another expression for integrity. Christians are such persons, who have decided to follow Jesus wherever the pathway leads. (*Turn to page 779.*)

But he who refuses reproof
goes astray.

18 Whoever hides hatred *has*
lying lips,
And whoever spreads slander *is*
a fool.

19 In the multitude of words
sin is not lacking,
But he who restrains his lips *is*
wise.
20 The tongue of the righteous
is choice silver;
The heart of the wicked *is*
worth little.
21 The lips of the righteous feed
many,
But fools die for lack of
wisdom.

22 The blessing of the LORD
makes *one* rich,
And He adds no sorrow with it.

23 To do evil *is* like sport to a
fool,
But a man of understanding
has wisdom.
24 The fear of the wicked
will come upon him,
And the desire of the righteous
will be granted.
25 When the whirlwind passes by,
the wicked *is* no *more*,
But the righteous *has* an
everlasting foundation.

26 As vinegar to the teeth
and smoke to the eyes,
So *is* the sluggard to those
who send him.

27 The fear of the LORD prolongs
days,
But the years of the wicked
will be shortened.
28 The hope of the righteous
will be gladness,
But the expectation of the
wicked will perish.
29 The way of the LORD *is*
strength for the upright,

But destruction *will come*
to the workers of iniquity.

30 The righteous will never be
removed,
But the wicked will not inhabit
the earth.
31 The mouth of the righteous
brings forth wisdom,
But the perverse tongue will be
cut out.
32 The lips of the righteous know
what is acceptable,
But the mouth of the wicked
what is perverse.

11 A false balance *is* an
abomination to the LORD,
But a just weight *is* His delight.

2 When pride comes, then comes
shame;
But with the humble *is*
wisdom.

3 The integrity of the upright
will guide them,
But the perversity of the
unfaithful will destroy them.
4 Riches do not profit in the day
of wrath,
But righteousness delivers from
death.
5 The righteousness of the
blameless will direct his way
aright,
But the wicked will fall
by his own wickedness.
6 The righteousness of the
upright will deliver them,
But the unfaithful will be taken
by *their own* lust.

7 When a wicked man dies,
his expectation will perish,
And the hope of the unjust
perishes.
8 The righteous is delivered from
trouble,
And it comes to the wicked
instead.
9 The hypocrite with *his* mouth
destroys his neighbor,

But through knowledge the
righteous will be delivered.

10 When it goes well with the
righteous, the city rejoices;
And when the wicked perish,
there is shouting.

11 By the blessing of the upright
the city is exalted,
But it is overthrown
by the mouth of the wicked.

12 He who is devoid of wisdom
despises his neighbor,
But a man of understanding
holds his peace.

13 A talebearer reveals secrets,
But he who is of a faithful
spirit conceals a matter.

14 Where *there is* no counsel,
the people fall;
But in the multitude of
counselors *there is* safety.

15 He who is surety for a stranger
will suffer *for it,*
But one who hates being
surety is secure.

16 A gracious woman retains
honor,
But ruthless *men* retain riches.

17 The merciful man
does good for his own soul,
But *he who is* cruel
troubles his own flesh.

18 The wicked man does
deceptive work,
But to him who sows
righteousness *will be* a sure
reward.

19 As righteousness *leads* to life,
So he who pursues evil *pursues
it* to his own death.

20 Those who are of a perverse
heart *are* an abomination to
the LORD,
But *such as are* blameless in
their ways *are* His delight.

21 *Though they join* forces,
the wicked will not go
unpunished;

But the posterity of the
righteous will be delivered.

22 *As* a ring of gold in a swine's
snout,
So is a lovely woman who
lacks discretion.

23 The desire of the righteous
is only good,
But the expectation of the
wicked *is* wrath.

24 There is *one* who scatters,
yet increases more;
And there is *one* who
withholds more than is right,
But it *leads* to poverty.

25 The generous soul will be made
rich,
And he who waters will also be
watered himself.

26 The people will curse him who
withholds grain,
But blessing *will be* on the
head of him who sells *it.*

27 He who diligently seeks good
finds favor,
But trouble will come to him
who seeks *evil.*

28 He who trusts in his riches will
fall,
But the righteous will flourish
like foliage.

29 He who troubles his own house
will inherit the wind,
And the fool *will be* servant to
the wise of heart.

30 The fruit of the righteous *is a*
tree of life,
And he who wins souls *is* wise.

31 If the righteous will be
recompensed on the earth,
How much more the wicked
and the sinner.

12 Whoever loves instruction
loves knowledge,

STEP 10

*Continued to take personal inventory
and when we were wrong promptly admitted it.*

Proverbs 12:1

No one enjoys reproof. Even if we are emotionally healthy and
have a perfectly balanced self-image, criticism is not easy to accept
or appreciate. But all of us need people in our lives whom we trust
to tell us the truth, even if it is unpleasant. We should not accept
just anyone's criticism. There are many negative people who get
real enjoyment out of criticizing others. Keep your distance from
such persons. But the words of wise and caring individuals should
always be carefully and prayerfully considered. Each of us has blind
spots in our understanding, which can cause us great harm if
allowed to go unchecked. So if a wise friend has courage and concern enough to confront us about a problem he or she has detected,
we must be humble enough to not only accept the criticism, but to
be thankful for it. When we can respond to constructive criticism
in this way, we insure our emotional and spiritual growth.

For further reading on Step 10, turn to page 813.

Daily Encouragement

DAY 339 READING: PROVERBS 11:7—12:1

A Thought for the New Day: It is easy to see how a merciful
man does good for himself (11:17). Such an individual will be
an object of blessing by those he has served. Also, he will enjoy
the peace and tranquillity that belong to the merciful. "Blessed
are the merciful, for they shall obtain mercy," said Jesus (Matt.
5:7). Not only does God love the merciful, but they are also
generally beloved by their beneficiaries far and near. *(Turn to page 781.)*

But he who hates reproof *is*
stupid.

2 A good *man* obtains favor from
the LORD,
But a man of wicked devices
He will condemn.

3 A man is not established
by wickedness,
But the root of the righteous
cannot be moved.

4 An excellent wife *is* the crown
of her husband,
But she who causes shame *is*
like rottenness in his bones.

5 The thoughts of the righteous
are right,
But the counsels of the wicked
are deceitful.

6 The words of the wicked *are*,
"Lie in wait for blood,"
But the mouth of the upright
will deliver them.

7 The wicked are overthrown
and *are* no more,
But the house of the righteous
will stand.

8 A man will be commended
according to his wisdom,
But he who is of a perverse
heart will be despised.

9 Better *is the one* who is
slighted but has a servant,
Than he who honors himself
but lacks bread.

10 A righteous *man* regards the
life of his animal,
But the tender mercies of the
wicked *are* cruel.

11 He who tills his land will be
satisfied with bread,
But he who follows frivolity *is*
devoid of understanding.

12 The wicked covet the catch of
evil *men*,

But the root of the righteous
yields *fruit*.
13 The wicked is ensnared by the
transgression of *his* lips,
But the righteous will come
through trouble.
14 A man will be satisfied with
good by the fruit of *his*
mouth,
And the recompense of a man's
hands will be rendered to
him.
15 The way of a fool *is* right in his
own eyes,
But he who heeds counsel *is*
wise.
16 A fool's wrath is known at
once,
But a prudent *man* covers
shame.
17 He *who* speaks truth declares
righteousness,
But a false witness, deceit.
18 There is one who speaks like
the piercings of a sword,
But the tongue of the wise
promotes health.
19 The truthful lip shall be
established forever,
But a lying tongue *is* but for a
moment.
20 Deceit is in the heart of those
who devise evil,
But counselors of peace have
joy.
21 No grave trouble will overtake
the righteous,
But the wicked shall be filled
with evil.
22 Lying lips *are* an abomination
to the LORD,
But those who deal truthfully
are His delight.
23 A prudent man conceals
knowledge,
But the heart of fools
proclaims foolishness.
24 The hand of the diligent will
rule,
But the slothful will be put to
forced labor.

STEP 9

Made direct amends to such people wherever possible,
except when to do so would injure them or others.

Proverbs 12:18–20

For many years scientists have researched the interplay between physical health and emotional well-being. They seem to be continually astounded at the physical effects of a joyful and positive state of mind. Christians are not so surprised by such findings because God's Word makes many such connections. While it definitely does not teach that godly living can destroy or dispel all illness, it does indicate that when people have God's peace and wisdom abounding in them, they have fewer physical problems.

This is one of the many positive side-effects of Step 9. When our words and actions reach out to others, bringing emotional healing, there may also be a physical healing of sorts. If bitterness, anger, shame, and guilt are replaced with God's own love and grace flowing from humble hearts, miraculous transformations are possible in our own lives and in the lives of others.

For further reading on Step 9, turn to page 787.

Daily Encouragement

DAY 340 READING: PROVERBS 12:2–24

A Thought for the New Day: Think of all the benefits we would enjoy if everyone would "deal truthfully" (v. 22): the national debt would be reduced because false claims against the government would not exist; divorce would decline drastically because professions of love would not be a mask for greed and other wrong motives; the Christian church would be purer because there would be no hypocrites. Little wonder that the Lord is delighted with truthful people! *(Turn to page 783.)*

25 Anxiety in the heart of man
   causes depression,
   But a good word makes it glad.

26 The righteous should choose
   his friends carefully,
   For the way of the wicked
   leads them astray.

27 The slothful *man* does not
   roast what he took in
   hunting,
   But diligence *is* man's precious
   possession.

28 In the way of righteousness *is*
   life,
   And in *its* pathway *there is* no
   death.

13 A wise son *heeds* his father's
   instruction,
   But a scoffer does not listen to
   rebuke.

2 A man shall eat well
   by the fruit of *his* mouth,
   But the soul of the unfaithful
   feeds on violence.

3 He who guards his mouth
   preserves his life,
   But he who opens wide his lips
   shall have destruction.

4 The soul of a sluggard desires,
   and *has* nothing;
   But the soul of the diligent
   shall be made rich.

5 A righteous *man* hates lying,
   But a wicked *man* is loathsome
   and comes to shame.

6 Righteousness keeps *him*
   whose way is blameless,
   But wickedness overthrows the
   sinner.

7 There is one who makes
   himself rich, yet *has* nothing;
   And one who makes himself
   poor, yet *has* great riches.

8 The ransom of a man's life *is*
   his riches,

But the poor does not hear
   rebuke.

9 The light of the righteous
   rejoices,
   But the lamp of the wicked will
   be put out.

10 By pride comes only
   contention,
   But with the well-advised *is*
   wisdom.

11 Wealth *gained by* dishonesty
   will be diminished,
   But he who gathers by labor
   will increase.

12 Hope deferred makes the heart
   sick,
   But *when* the desire comes,
   it is a tree of life.

13 He who despises the word
   will be destroyed,
   But he who fears the
   commandment will be
   rewarded.   STEP 4

14 The law of the wise *is* a
   fountain of life,
   To turn *one* away from the
   snares of death.

15 Good understanding gains
   favor,
   But the way of the unfaithful *is*
   hard.

16 Every prudent *man* acts with
   knowledge,
   But a fool lays open *his* folly.

17 A wicked messenger falls into
   trouble,
   But a faithful ambassador
   brings health.

18 Poverty and shame *will come*
   to him who disdains
   correction,
   But he who regards reproof
   will be honored.   STEP 6

19 A desire accomplished is sweet
   to the soul,

STEP 6

*Were entirely ready to have God
remove all these defects of character.*

Proverbs 13:18

Shame is a common thread among those of us struggling with addictions. For many, shame was one of the forces that drove us into addiction. Then the dependency itself seemed to bring upon us more shame. But now, step by step, God is turning our lives around and replacing shame with self-respect and honor.

In Steps 4 and 5, we sought God's help and, perhaps, the help of others to come to grips with our shortcomings. We may have uncovered wrong motives, bitterness, pride, or lack of responsibility. Now, in order to truly make these steps worthwhile, we must be willing to "regard" the truths we have discovered about ourselves. We do this by choosing to allow God to work in our lives to remove these faults. To shrink back now means to sentence ourselves to emotional poverty. But to courageously present to God willing hearts will bring honor in ways we cannot yet fully comprehend.

For further reading on Step 6, turn to page 795.

Daily Encouragement

DAY 341 READING: PROVERBS 12:25—13:22

A Thought for the New Day: There is no lack of anxiety in the world and plenty of room for "a good word" in the ear of the discouraged and distressed (v. 25). Do you know someone who needs encouragement? Make an opportunity to speak a word of cheer to that one. You will be surprised at how encouraged you will feel, too. (*Turn to page 785.*)

But *it is* an abomination to
fools to depart from evil.

20 He who walks with wise *men*
will be wise,
But the companion of fools
will be destroyed.

21 Evil pursues sinners,
But to the righteous,
good shall be repaid.

22 A good *man* leaves an
inheritance to his children's
children,
But the wealth of the sinner is
stored up for the righteous.

23 Much food *is in* the fallow
ground of the poor,
And for lack of justice there is
waste.

24 He who spares his rod hates
his son,
But he who loves him
disciplines him promptly.

25 The righteous eats to the
satisfying of his soul,
But the stomach of the wicked
shall be in want.

STEP
8

14 *Every* wise woman builds
her house,
But the foolish pulls it down
with her hands.

2 He who walks in his
uprightness fears the LORD,
But *he who is* perverse in his
ways despises Him.

3 In the mouth of a fool *is* a rod
of pride,
But the lips of the wise will
preserve them.

4 Where no oxen *are*, the trough
is clean;
But much increase *comes* by
the strength of an ox.

5 A faithful witness does not lie,

But a false witness will utter
lies.

6 A scoffer seeks wisdom
and does not *find it*,
But knowledge *is* easy to him
who understands.

7 Go from the presence of a
foolish man,
When you do not perceive *in
him* the lips of knowledge.

8 The wisdom of the prudent
is to understand his way,
But the folly of fools *is* deceit.

9 Fools mock at sin,
But among the upright *there is*
favor.

10 The heart knows its own
bitterness,
And a stranger does not share
its joy.

11 The house of the wicked will
be overthrown,
But the tent of the upright will
flourish.

12 There is a way *that seems*
right to a man,
But its end *is* the way of death.

STEP
1

13 Even in laughter the heart may
sorrow,
And the end of mirth *may be*
grief.

14 The backslider in heart will be
filled with his own ways,
But a good man *will be
satisfied* from above.

STEP
4

15 The simple believes every
word,
But the prudent *man* considers
well his steps.

16 A wise *man* fears
and departs from evil,
But a fool rages and is self-
confident.

17 *He who is* quick-tempered
acts foolishly,

STEP 8

Made a list of all persons we had harmed,
and became willing to make amends to them all.

Proverbs 14:1

What builds a house into a home filled with warmth and genuine comfort? What strips it until it is only a building whose windows stare cold and lonely at passersby? Do warmth and comfort come from fabrics and color choices and modern conveniences? Even though these things may add an air of geniality, coziness, or even plush indulgence, they are not what makes a home warm and comfortable. These special qualities are bestowed by the people who live there, and especially by the wife and mother of the home. When a wife first gives herself to the Lord, amazing things can happen in a household. Nagging is replaced by prayer. Impatience turns to longsuffering. Harsh words are replaced by gentleness and impulsive reaction can become consistent wise love.

Even if only one person in the family is willing to be used by God to restore broken relationships, He can work in wonderful ways.

See page 58 of the introductory material for Step 9.

Daily Encouragement

DAY 342 READING: PROVERBS 13:23—14:19

A Thought for the New Day: A happy life might be defined as one guided by a rarely broken series of right decisions. Many factors influence our judgment for good or evil. We know how true it is that we easily make errors of judgment, and we should have learned by now that it is very possible for us to make fatal judgment calls (14:12). Happily, there is an alternative. If we will surrender our opinions for divine arbitration, God always stands ready to show us the right path, and He will do so. (*Turn to page 787.*)

And a man of wicked
  intentions is hated.
18 The simple inherit folly,
  But the prudent are crowned
  with knowledge.
19 The evil will bow before the
  good,
  And the wicked at the gates of
  the righteous.

20 The poor *man* is hated
  even by his own neighbor,
  But the rich *has* many friends.
21 He who despises his neighbor
  sins;
  But he who has mercy on the
  poor, happy *is* he.

22 Do they not go astray who
  devise evil?
  But mercy and truth *belong* to
  those who devise good.

23 In all labor there is profit,
  But idle chatter *leads* only to
  poverty.

24 The crown of the wise is their
  riches,
  But the foolishness of fools *is*
  folly.

25 A true witness delivers souls,
  But a deceitful *witness* speaks
  lies.

STEP 3
26 In the fear of the LORD
  there is strong confidence,
  And His children will have a
  place of refuge.
27 The fear of the LORD
  is a fountain of life,
  To avoid the snares of death.

28 In a multitude of people
  is a king's honor,
  But in the lack of people
  is the downfall of a prince.

29 *He who is* slow to wrath
  has great understanding,
  But *he who is* impulsive exalts
  folly.

30 A sound heart *is* life to the
  body,
  But envy *is* rottenness to the
  bones.

31 He who oppresses the poor
  reproaches his Maker,
  But he who honors Him
  has mercy on the needy.

32 The wicked is banished
  in his wickedness,
  But the righteous has a refuge
  in his death.

33 Wisdom rests *quietly* in the
  heart of him who has
  understanding,
  But *what is* in the heart of
  fools is made known.

34 Righteousness exalts a nation,
  But sin *is* a reproach to *any*
  people.

35 The king's favor *is* toward a
  wise servant,
  But his wrath *is against* him
  who causes shame.

15 A soft answer turns away
  wrath,
  But a harsh word stirs up
  anger.
2 The tongue of the wise uses
  knowledge rightly,
  But the mouth of fools pours
  forth foolishness.

3 The eyes of the LORD *are* in
  every place,
  Keeping watch on the evil and
  the good.

4 A wholesome tongue *is* a tree
  of life,
  But perverseness in it breaks
  the spirit.

5 A fool despises his father's
  instruction,
  But he who receives reproof is
  prudent.

STEP 8

STEP 9

STEP 9

*Made direct amends to such people wherever possible,
except when to do so would injure them or others.*

Proverbs 15:1–4

Our greatest need at this stage of recovery is not courage.
Courage is necessary to accomplish our goals, but it is not the most
important virtue we need. More than anything else, we should be
asking God to give us "the tongue of the wise," which "uses knowledge rightly." During our recovery, we have gained a great deal of
insight into our own lives and also into the lives of those who are
near to us. Now we must use that knowledge carefully and thought-
fully to make amends, to forgive, and to be forgiven. Some of our
strained or broken relationships may be of such a nature that simple
and straightforward speech and actions are suitable. But others may
require great discernment on our part; we may need to spend time
in prayer and reflection with God before attempting a reconciliation. God has promised to give us all the wisdom we need as we ask
in faith, trusting Him completely.

For further reading on Step 9, turn to page 793.

Daily Encouragement

DAY 343 READING: PROVERBS 14:20—15:4

A Thought for the New Day: If you want to have the whole
world angry with you, just go around arguing with others, toler-
ating no opinions except your own. Even being right does not
give us license to attack those who disagree with us. Patience is
the key here (15:1). Give people time to think things over, and
keep sharp words to yourself. Instead of anger, you will gain the
respect of others. Then you can have something to say they will
want to hear. (*Turn to page 789.*)

6 *In* the house of the righteous
  there is much treasure,
  But in the revenue of the
  wicked is trouble.

7 The lips of the wise disperse
  knowledge,
  But the heart of the fool *does*
  not *do* so.

8 The sacrifice of the wicked
  is an abomination to the
  LORD,
  But the prayer of the upright
  is His delight.

9 The way of the wicked *is* an
  abomination to the LORD,
  But He loves him
  who follows righteousness.

10 Harsh correction *is* for him
   who forsakes the way,
   And he who hates reproof will
   die.

STEP 4
11 Hell and Destruction *are* before
   the LORD;
   So how much more the hearts
   of the sons of men.

12 A scoffer does not love one
   who reproves him,
   Nor will he go to the wise.

13 A merry heart makes a
   cheerful countenance,
   But by sorrow of the heart
   the spirit is broken.

14 The heart of him who has
   understanding seeks
   knowledge,
   But the mouth of fools feeds
   on foolishness.

15 All the days of the afflicted *are*
   evil,
   But he who is of a merry heart
   has a continual feast.

STEP 2
16 Better *is* a little with the fear
   of the LORD,

Than great treasure with
trouble.

17 Better *is* a dinner of herbs
   where love is,
   Than a fatted calf with hatred.

18 A wrathful man stirs up strife,
   But *he who is* slow to anger
   allays contention.

19 The way of the slothful *man*
   is like a hedge of thorns,
   But the way of the upright
   is a highway.

20 A wise son makes a father
   glad,
   But a foolish man despises his
   mother.

21 Folly *is* joy *to him who is*
   destitute of discernment,
   But a man of understanding
   walks uprightly.

22 Without counsel, plans go
   awry,
   But in the multitude of
   counselors they are
   established.

23 A man has joy by the answer
   of his mouth,
   And a word *spoken* in due
   season, how good *it is!*

24 The way of life *winds* upward
   for the wise,
   That he may turn away from
   hell below.

25 The LORD will destroy the
   house of the proud,
   But He will establish the
   boundary of the widow.

26 The thoughts of the wicked
   are an abomination to the
   LORD,
   But *the words* of the pure *are*
   pleasant.

27 He who is greedy for gain
   troubles his own house,

STEP 4

Made a searching and fearless moral inventory of ourselves.

Proverbs 15:11

Cats are fascinating creatures. Their playfulness, curiosity, and changeable moods seem remarkably human at times. One of their most common antics is to hide wherever they can feel protected and unobserved. This behavior corresponds to that of many human beings, and those of us with dependencies play the game so well we can even hide from ourselves. We may have a favorite hiding place—perhaps deception—using lies to hide from our problems. Perhaps we use denial—simply refusing to admit that a problem exists. Some of us may escape into drugs or other addictive agents, while others of us prefer the mask of perfectionism. In these ways we have learned to hide from the world around us, but we can never hide from God. Now we know that He loves us just as we are and forgives us completely as soon as we ask. He longs to cleanse us and transform us by His grace. Facing the reality of who we really are is the first step in that process.

For further reading on Step 4, turn to page 791.

Daily Encouragement

DAY 344 READING: PROVERBS 15:5–27

A Thought for the New Day: There is a right time for everything, and there is always time for speaking words that restore and heal (v. 23). Contrary to a children's rhyme, words can hurt and even destroy, especially remarks made behind the back. There is much need for kind and generous speech. It costs us nothing, but we have the joy of seeing someone helped along an otherwise hard path. Our words can make a difference between death and life for another. *(Turn to page 791.)*

But he who hates bribes will
live.

28 The heart of the righteous
studies how to answer,
But the mouth of the wicked
pours forth evil.

29 The LORD *is* far from the
wicked,
But He hears the prayer of the
righteous.

30 The light of the eyes rejoices
the heart,
And a good report makes the
bones healthy.

 31 The ear that hears the reproof
of life
Will abide among the wise.
32 He who disdains instruction
despises his own soul,
But he who heeds reproof
gets understanding.
33 The fear of the LORD *is* the
instruction of wisdom,
And before honor *is* humility.

16 The preparations of the
heart *belong* to man,
But the answer of the tongue
is from the LORD.

 2 All the ways of a man *are* pure
in his own eyes,
But the LORD weighs the
spirits.

3 Commit your works to the
LORD,
And your thoughts will be
established.

4 The LORD has made all *things*
for Himself,
Yes, even the wicked for the
day of doom.

5 Everyone *who is* proud in heart
is an abomination to the
LORD;

Though *they join* forces,
none will go unpunished.

6 In mercy and truth
Atonement is provided for
iniquity;
And by the fear of the LORD
one departs from evil.

7 When a man's ways please the
LORD,
He makes even his enemies to
be at peace with him.

8 Better *is* a little with
righteousness,
Than vast revenues without
justice.

9 A man's heart plans his way,
But the LORD directs his steps.

10 *Even though* divination *is* on
the lips of the king,
His mouth must not transgress
in judgment.

11 A just weight and balance
are the LORD'S;
All the weights in the bag
are His work.

12 *It is* an abomination for kings
to commit wickedness,
For a throne is established by
righteousness.

13 Righteous lips *are* the delight
of kings,
And they love him who speaks
what is right.

14 As messengers of death *is* the
king's wrath,
But a wise man will appease it.

15 In the light of the king's face *is*
life,
And his favor *is* like a cloud of
the latter rain.

16 How much better *it is* to get
wisdom than gold!
And to get understanding is to
be chosen rather than silver.

17 The highway of the upright *is*
to depart from evil;

STEP 4

Made a searching and fearless moral inventory of ourselves.

Proverbs 16:2, 3

A plane is equipped with an instrument called an artificial horizon indicator. Although our human senses may become confused in the murky thickness of a cloud bank, the horizon indicator is never fooled. Following its guidance, pilots are able to keep their planes positioned exactly as they should be.

How well this illustration relates to our own natural wisdom compared with God's heavenly wisdom! All our ways seem right to us, but only God can really know what path is best for each of us as we go through the storms of life. Trying to run our own lives is like trying to fly a plane through a cloud bank without a horizon indicator.

As we open our lives, completely and honestly, to God's scrutiny and begin to accept His direction, we have taken a major step toward righting them and keeping them off a collision course.

For further reading on Step 4, turn to page 799.

Daily Encouragement

DAY 345 READING: PROVERBS 15:28—16:17

A Thought for the New Day: Proverbs 16:9 is a word of great consolation. It assumes, of course, that we have taken God into our confidence about our plans. So often it happens that our own precious ideas come to nothing, and we may even think we have failed. Then, to our surprise, another door opens, and that alternative turns out to be far better than our own little design. So we say, "Thank you, Lord, for planting our feet in the right path." (*Turn to page 793.*)

He who keeps his way
preserves his soul.

18 Pride *goes* before destruction,
And a haughty spirit before a
fall.
19 Better *to be* of a humble spirit
with the lowly,
Than to divide the spoil
with the proud.

20 He who heeds the word wisely
will find good,
And whoever trusts in the
LORD, happy *is* he.

21 The wise in heart will be called
prudent,
And sweetness of the lips
increases learning.

22 Understanding *is* a wellspring
of life to him who has it.
But the correction of fools *is*
folly.

23 The heart of the wise teaches
his mouth,
And adds learning to his lips.

24 Pleasant words *are like* a
honeycomb,
Sweetness to the soul
and health to the bones.

25 There is a way *that seems*
right to a man,
But its end *is* the way of death.

26 The person who labors,
labors for himself,
For his *hungry* mouth drives
him *on.*

27 An ungodly man digs up evil,
And *it is* on his lips like a
burning fire.
28 A perverse man sows strife,
And a whisperer separates the
best of friends.
29 A violent man entices his
neighbor,
And leads him in a way *that is*
not good.

30 He winks his eye to devise
perverse things;
He purses his lips
and brings about evil.

31 The silver-haired head *is* a
crown of glory,
If it is found in the way of
righteousness.

32 *He who is* slow to anger *is*
better than the mighty,
And he who rules his spirit
than he who takes a city.

33 The lot is cast into the lap,
But its every decision *is* from
the LORD.

17 Better *is* a dry morsel
with quietness,
Than a house full of feasting
with strife.

2 A wise servant will rule over a
son who causes shame,
And will share an inheritance
among the brothers.

3 The refining pot *is* for silver
and the furnace for gold,
But the LORD tests the hearts.

4 An evildoer gives heed to false
lips;
A liar listens eagerly to a
spiteful tongue.

5 He who mocks the poor
reproaches his Maker;
He who is glad at calamity
will not go unpunished.

6 Children's children *are* the
crown of old men,
And the glory of children *is*
their father.

7 Excellent speech is not
becoming to a fool,
Much less lying lips to a prince.

STEP 9

Made direct amends to such people wherever possible,
except when to do so would injure them or others.

Proverbs 16:20–24

One of the great encouragements of recovery is that each day as we conscientiously work through the steps in our recovery program, we are becoming wiser. Our increasing wisdom will begin to show itself in everything we do and say. The way we respond to situations, to other people, and even to our own shortcomings will be healthier and more positive.

Our main desire in Step 9, as Proverbs 16:20 says, is to "[heed] the word wisely" and "find good." When we trust God to give us His wisdom and direction for exactly the right words at the right time, we will find the courage we need to reconcile with others—to ask for, as well as to extend, forgiveness. Verses 22–24 reveal that such understanding is a "wellspring of life" and that the pleasant words we speak will be sweet to our soul and health to our bones. Perhaps that sweetness and health will be extended to those with whom we reconcile, as well.

For further reading on Step 9, turn to page 815.

Daily Encouragement

DAY 346 READING: PROVERBS 16:18—17:6

A Thought for the New Day: What is the real root of happiness? Even sociologists are saying that wealth and possessions do not result in a higher level of contentment than is enjoyed by people of more modest means. There are many routes to temporary happiness: losing weight, changing jobs, a raise in pay, regular exercise, and others. But fixed and permanent happiness can come only with a right relationship to God, the Author of all good (16:20). *(Turn to page 795.)*

8 A present *is* a precious stone in the eyes of its possessor; Wherever he turns, he prospers.

9 He who covers a transgression seeks love, But he who repeats a matter separates *the best of* friends.

STEP 6

10 Reproof is more effective for a wise man Than a hundred blows on a fool.

11 An evil *man* seeks only rebellion; Therefore a cruel messenger will be sent against him.

12 Let a man meet a bear robbed of her cubs, Rather than a fool in his folly.

13 Whoever rewards evil for good, Evil will not depart from his house.

14 The beginning of strife *is like* releasing water; Therefore stop contention before a quarrel starts.

15 He who justifies the wicked, and he who condemns the just, Both of them alike *are* an abomination to the LORD.

16 Why *is there* in the hand of a fool the purchase price of wisdom, Since *he has* no heart *for it?*

17 A friend loves at all times, And a brother is born for adversity.

18 A man devoid of understanding shakes hands in a pledge, *And* becomes surety for his friend.

19 He who loves transgression loves strife, And he who exalts his gate seeks destruction.

20 He who has a deceitful heart finds no good, And he who has a perverse tongue falls into evil.

21 He who begets a scoffer *does so* to his sorrow, And the father of a fool has no joy.

22 A merry heart does good, *like* medicine, But a broken spirit dries the bones.

23 A wicked *man* accepts a bribe behind the back To pervert the ways of justice.

24 Wisdom *is* in the sight of him who has understanding, But the eyes of a fool *are* on the ends of the earth.

25 A foolish son *is* a grief to his father, And bitterness to her who bore him.

26 Also, to punish the righteous *is* not good, *Nor* to strike princes for *their* uprightness.

27 He who has knowledge spares his words, *And* a man of understanding is of a calm spirit.

28 Even a fool is counted wise when he holds his peace; *When* he shuts his lips, *he is considered* perceptive.

18 A man who isolates himself seeks his own desire; He rages against all wise judgment.

STEP 6

*Were entirely ready to have God
remove all these defects of character.*

Proverbs 17:10

Was there a time in your life when you believed the comment "Some people never learn" was coined solely to describe you? Dependencies can make us feel the indescribable frustration of being unable to change our habits. We may have wanted desperately to make a fresh start in life, but we were locked into our destructive life-style.

Now, however, all that is beginning to change for us. We have begun to understand some of the deep reasons for our addictions. We have admitted our shortcomings openly and are aware of the attitudes and actions that are displeasing to God, as well as harmful to ourselves and others. The Holy Spirit is beginning to impress upon us the ways in which God wants us to change. Listening to His loving reproof allows our hearts to become willingly yielded to God's work in us. Listening and readying our hearts reveals us to be wise.

See page 51 of the introductory material for Step 7.

Daily Encouragement

DAY 347 READING: PROVERBS 17:7–28

A Thought for the New Day: A friend is a matchless treasure (v. 17). Jesus' early disciples were not only His pupils, but He even called them His friends. A friend is someone you can count on when everything seems to go wrong. It is great to *have* friends, but even better to *be* a friend. Friendship costs nothing except the sincere desire to help another carry his load along life's road. Ask God for the gift of being a friend. *(Turn to page 797.)*

2 A fool has no delight in
   understanding,
   But in expressing his own
   heart.

3 When the wicked comes,
   contempt comes also;
   And with dishonor *comes*
   reproach.

4 The words of a man's mouth
   are deep waters;
   The wellspring of wisdom
   is a flowing brook.

5 *It is* not good to show
   partiality to the wicked,
   Or to overthrow the righteous
   in judgment.

6 A fool's lips enter into
   contention,
   And his mouth calls for blows.

7 A fool's mouth *is* his
   destruction,
   And his lips *are* the snare of
   his soul.

8 The words of a talebearer *are*
   like tasty trifles,
   And they go down into the
   inmost body.

9 He who is slothful in his work
   Is a brother to him who is a
   great destroyer.

10 The name of the LORD
   is a strong tower;
   The righteous run to it and are
   safe.

11 The rich man's wealth
   is his strong city,
   And like a high wall in his own
   esteem.

STEP 7
12 Before destruction the heart of
   a man is haughty,
   And before honor *is* humility.

13 He who answers a matter
   before he hears *it*,
   It *is* folly and shame to him.

14 The spirit of a man will sustain
   him in sickness,
   But who can bear a broken
   spirit?

15 The heart of the prudent
   acquires knowledge,
   And the ear of the wise
   seeks knowledge.

16 A man's gift makes room for
   him,
   And brings him before great
   men.

17 The first *one* to plead his cause
   seems right,
   Until his neighbor comes and
   examines him.

18 Casting lots causes contentions
   to cease,
   And keeps the mighty apart.

19 A brother offended *is harder to
   win* than a strong city,
   And contentions *are* like the
   bars of a castle.

20 A man's stomach shall be
   satisfied from the fruit of his
   mouth,
   And from the produce of his
   lips he shall be filled.

21 Death and life *are* in the power
   of the tongue,
   And those who love it will eat
   its fruit.

22 *He who* finds a wife finds a
   good *thing*,
   And obtains favor from the
   LORD.

23 The poor *man* uses entreaties,
   But the rich answers roughly.

24 A man *who has* friends must
   himself be friendly,
   But there is a friend *who* sticks
   closer than a brother.

STEP 7

Humbly asked Him to remove our shortcomings.

Proverbs 18:12

Destruction comes in many shapes and sizes. When we have struggled with dependencies, we may have met up with several kinds—financial, emotional, physical, marital, among many others. God, by His mercy, has lifted us from the wasted rubble of our dependencies and has placed us in the green pastures of His grace. But God could not rescue us until we humbled ourselves enough to reach for His saving hands of love.

Now He wants to give us the greener pastures waiting for us on the mountains of victory. He wants us to drink deeply of the clear waters of transformation. Only He can lead us there. Since we cannot find the way by ourselves, we need to humble ourselves again and admit our own inability. Then we must recognize how totally able He is to carry us to the pastures of freedom and peace. Nothing at all is impossible to Him. Let us slip our hand into His and begin the journey.

For further reading on Step 7, turn to page 807.

Daily Encouragement

DAY 348 READING: PROVERBS 18:1–24

A Thought for the New Day: A talented pianist or violinist needs little promotion. The artist's skill precedes all published advertisements about him. If you have a gift from God with which to serve in the world, that gift will speak for itself (v. 16). The apostle Paul wrote that we should seek earnestly the "best gifts" (1 Cor. 12:31), the greatest of which is love (1 Cor. 13). This gift opens the door to many hearts. (*Turn to page 799.*)

19 Better *is* the poor
who walks in his integrity
Than *one who is* perverse in
his lips, and is a fool.

2 Also it is not good *for* a soul *to
be* without knowledge,
And he sins who hastens with
his feet.

3 The foolishness of a man twists
his way,
And his heart frets against the
·LORD.

4 Wealth makes many friends,
But the poor is separated from
his friend.

5 A false witness will not go
unpunished,
And *he who* speaks lies will
not escape.

6 Many entreat the favor of the
nobility,
And every man *is* a friend to
one who gives gifts.

7 All the brothers of the poor
hate him;
How much more do his friends
go far from him!
He may pursue *them with*
words, *yet* they abandon *him*.

8 He who gets wisdom
loves his own soul;
He who keeps understanding
will find good.

9 A false witness will not go
unpunished,
And *he who* speaks lies shall
perish.

10 Luxury is not fitting for a fool,
Much less for a servant to rule
over princes.

11 The discretion of a man makes
him slow to anger,
And *it is to* his glory to
overlook a transgression.

12 The king's wrath *is* like the
roaring of a lion,
But his favor *is* like dew on the
grass.

13 A foolish son *is* the ruin of his
father,
And the contentions of a wife
are a continual dripping.

14 Houses and riches *are* an
inheritance from fathers,
But a prudent wife *is* from the
LORD.

15 Slothfulness casts *one* into a
deep sleep,
And an idle person will suffer
hunger.

16 He who keeps the commandment keeps his soul,
But he who is careless of his
ways will die.

17 He who has pity on the poor
lends to the LORD,
And He will pay back what he
has given.

18 Chasten your son while there
is hope,
And do not set your heart on
his destruction.

19 *A man of* great wrath will
suffer punishment;
For if you deliver *him*,
you will have to do it again.

STEP
4

20 Listen to counsel
and receive instruction,
That you may be wise in your
latter days.

21 There are many plans in a
man's heart,
Nevertheless the LORD's
counsel—that will stand.

22 What is desired in a man is
kindness,
And a poor man is better than
a liar.

STEP
4

Made a searching and fearless moral inventory of ourselves.

Proverbs 19:19

A student teacher must learn one thing very quickly. To get students quiet and attentive, a good teacher lowers his or her voice. Of course, the natural instinct is quite opposite and many new teachers seem to get caught in an escalating spiral of noise as the class becomes more unruly with each boisterous attempt to settle them down.

A life filled with angry outbursts produces very similar and regrettable results. Those who use angry words and tones discover too late that such outbursts have sabotaged the goals toward which they were directed. Anger does not produce efficiency, respect, or true concern. It only produces fear, disloyalty, and alienation. The older we become, the more we realize how terrible this self-inflicted punishment can be.

If we have been addicted to anger, now is the time to understand and admit this problem. If we have been victimized by anger, we need to understand its effects on us and the effects on the victimizer, as well.

For further reading on Step 4, turn to page 801.

Daily Encouragement

DAY 349 READING: PROVERBS 19:1–29

A Thought for the New Day: The word "orthodox" is a compound of two Greek words that mean "right thinking," and, indeed, it is well to think rightly about all things. However, good thinking, by itself, is not enough. We are to show caring and compassion for those around us (v. 17). Reading the Gospel accounts of Jesus' career, we see that He spent much of His time just being kind. Love is what really satisfies the law of God. (*Turn to page 801.*)

23 The fear of the LORD *leads* to
   life,
   And *he who has it* will abide in
   satisfaction;
   He will not be visited with evil.

24 A slothful *man* buries his hand
   in the bowl,
   And will not so much as bring
   it to his mouth again.

25 Strike a scoffer, and the simple
   will become wary;
   Reprove one who has
   understanding, *and* he will
   discern knowledge.

26 He who mistreats *his* father
   and chases away *his* mother
   Is a son who causes shame
   and brings reproach.

27 Cease listening to instruction,
   my son,
   And you will stray from the
   words of knowledge.

28 A disreputable witness scorns
   justice,
   And the mouth of the wicked
   devours iniquity.

29 Judgments are prepared for
   scoffers,
   And beatings for the backs of
   fools.

20 Wine is a mocker,
   Intoxicating drink arouses
      brawling,
   And whoever is led astray by it
   is not wise.

2 The wrath of a king *is* like the
   roaring of a lion;
   Whoever provokes him to
   anger sins *against* his own
   life.

3 *It is* honorable for a man to
   stop striving,

Since any fool can start a
   quarrel.

4 The sluggard will not plow
   because of winter;
   Therefore he will beg during
   the harvest
   And *have* nothing.

5 Counsel in the heart of man *is
   like* deep water,
   But a man of understanding
   will draw it out.

6 Most men will proclaim each
   his own goodness,
   But who can find a faithful
   man?

7 The righteous *man* walks in his
   integrity;
   His children *are* blessed after
   him.

8 A king who sits on the throne
   of judgment
   Scatters all evil with his eyes.

9 Who can say, "I have made my
   heart clean,
   I am pure from my sin"?

10 Diverse weights *and* diverse
   measures,
   They *are* both alike,
   an abomination to the LORD.

11 Even a child is known by his
   deeds,
   By whether what he does *is*
   pure and right.

12 The hearing ear and the seeing
   eye,
   The LORD has made both of
   them.

13 Do not love sleep,
   lest you come to poverty;
   Open your eyes, *and* you will
   be satisfied with bread.

14 "*It is* good for nothing,"
   cries the buyer;

STEP 4

Made a searching and fearless moral inventory of ourselves.

Proverbs 20:1

Of all the childhood hurts we must endure, mocking may be the worst. When our peers scoff, jeer at, and ridicule us, the emotional pain can leave lifelong scars. Who then would seek to be mocked continually? Although it is hard to understand, those who allow substance abuse to control their lives are actually inviting scorn and ridicule. That in which they seek solace and comfort becomes the very thing that unfeelingly destroys them.

In Step 4, those of us who have suffered the shame and ridicule that substance abuse brings are seeking to understand the origins of our suffering. Why have we chosen wrong ways to comfort ourselves? What patterns of personality and life-style are contributors to this problem? As we prayerfully and sincerely seek to face the truth concerning who and why we are what we are, let us be encouraged. We are taking the steps we need to insure that we will no longer be deceived and led astray. We are taking steps toward wisdom.

For further reading on Step 4, turn to page 805.

Daily Encouragement

DAY 350 READING: PROVERBS 20:1–20

A Thought for the New Day: The warning in verse 20 makes us thoughtful about the importance God places on family unity and mutual respect. The fifth commandment (Ex. 20:12) promises long life to those who honor their parents, and one of the early signs of a declining society is the failure of the family. See a family circle where aging parents are held in high regard, and you will also see children who are happy, prosperous, and lovers of the truth. (*Turn to page 803.*)

But when he has gone his way,
then he boasts.

15 There is gold and a multitude
of rubies,
But the lips of knowledge *are* a
precious jewel.

16 Take the garment of one who
is surety *for* a stranger,
And hold it as a pledge *when it*
is for a seductress.

17 Bread gained by deceit *is* sweet
to a man,
But afterward his mouth will
be filled with gravel.

18 *Every* purpose is established by
counsel;
By wise counsel wage war.

19 He who goes about *as* a
talebearer reveals secrets;
Therefore do not associate with
one who flatters with his lips.

20 Whoever curses his father or
his mother,
His lamp will be put out in
deep darkness.

21 An inheritance gained hastily
at the beginning
Will not be blessed at the end.

22 Do not say, "I will recompense
evil";
Wait for the LORD,
and He will save you.

23 Diverse weights *are* an
abomination to the LORD,
And a false balance *is* not
good.

24 A man's steps *are* of the LORD;
How then can a man
understand his own way?

25 *It is* a snare for a man to
devote rashly *something as*
holy,

And afterward to reconsider
his vows.

26 A wise king sifts out the
wicked,
And brings the threshing wheel
over them.

27 The spirit of a man *is* the lamp
of the LORD,
Searching all the inner depths
of his heart.

28 Mercy and truth preserve the
king,
And by lovingkindness he
upholds his throne.

29 The glory of young men
is their strength,
And the splendor of old men
is their gray head.

30 Blows that hurt cleanse away
evil,
As *do* stripes the inner depths
of the heart.

21 The king's heart *is* in the
hand of the LORD,
Like the rivers of water;
He turns it wherever He
wishes.

2 Every way of a man *is* right
in his own eyes,
But the LORD weighs the
hearts.

3 To do righteousness and justice
Is more acceptable to the LORD
than sacrifice.

4 A haughty look, a proud heart,
And the plowing of the wicked
are sin.

5 The plans of the diligent *lead*
surely to plenty,
But *those of* everyone *who is*
hasty, surely to poverty.

6 Getting treasures by a lying
tongue

Admitted to God, to ourselves, and to another human being the exact nature of our wrongs.

Proverbs 21:2

What is the difference between reasons and excuses? More often than not, it depends on which side of the fence we are on. If we are confronted about a problem concerning ourselves, we have *reasons* for the situation. But if we are confronting someone else, we are often quick to declare the response given to be *excuses*.

So how can we move from seeing things strictly from our own point of view to being able to see them from God's perspective? We are only able to see God's truth about a situation when we become totally willing to yield every attitude and preconceived notion to Him. If we come to Him willing to see and admit truth—whatever that truth might be—then God will honor us. He will not only reveal the truth to us through the Holy Spirit and His Word, but He will enable us to respond in the light of that truth.

For further reading on Step 5, turn to page 821.

Daily Encouragement

DAY 351 READING: PROVERBS 20:21—21:6

A Thought for the New Day: Whether they have kings or not, all kinds of governments are in view in Proverbs 21:1. In this time when society properly fears the abuse of bureaucratic power, the Christian can take comfort in knowing that governing authorities are in the hands of a still greater Power. We are not at the mercy of capricious men and women. (*Turn to page 805.*)

Is the fleeting fantasy of those
who seek death.

7 The violence of the wicked will
destroy them,
Because they refuse to do
justice.

8 The way of a guilty man *is*
perverse;
But *as for* the pure, his work *is*
right.

 9 *It is* better to dwell in a corner
of a housetop,
Than in a house shared with a
contentious woman.

10 The soul of the wicked desires
evil;
His neighbor finds no favor in
his eyes.

11 When the scoffer is punished,
the simple is made wise;
But when the wise is
instructed, he receives
knowledge.

12 The righteous *God* wisely
considers the house of the
wicked,
Overthrowing the wicked for
their wickedness.

13 Whoever shuts his ears to the
cry of the poor
Will also cry himself and not
be heard.

14 A gift in secret pacifies anger,
And a bribe behind the back,
strong wrath.

15 *It is* a joy for the just to do
justice,
But destruction *will come* to
the workers of iniquity.

16 A man who wanders from the
way of understanding
Will rest in the congregation of
the dead.

17 He who loves pleasure
will be a poor man;
He who loves wine and oil
will not be rich.

18 The wicked *shall be* a ransom
for the righteous,
And the unfaithful for the
upright.

19 *It is* better to dwell in the
wilderness,
Than with a contentious and
angry woman.

20 *There is* desirable treasure,
And oil in the dwelling of the
wise,
But a foolish man squanders it.

21 He who follows righteousness
and mercy
Finds life, righteousness and
honor.

22 A wise *man* scales the city of
the mighty,
And brings down the trusted
stronghold.

23 Whoever guards his mouth and
tongue
Keeps his soul from troubles.

24 A proud *and* haughty *man*—
"Scoffer" *is* his name;
He acts with arrogant pride.

25 The desire of the slothful kills
him,
For his hands refuse to labor.
26 He covets greedily all day long,
But the righteous gives
and does not spare.

27 The sacrifice of the wicked *is*
an abomination;
How much more *when* he
brings it with wicked intent!

28 A false witness shall perish,
But the man who hears *him*
will speak endlessly.

STEP 4

Made a searching and fearless moral inventory of ourselves.

Proverbs 21:9

As we take our Step 4 inventory, we look deep within ourselves to uncover who we are, why we are the way we are, how we respond to who we are, and how we relate to God and to those around us. As we question ourselves, some of us may find within our makeup the personality of the contentious woman. Are we overbearing, demanding, argumentative? Do others seek out our company, or do they avoid us whenever possible?

For some of us, a contentious spirit may reflect our own feelings of low esteem. We may hide behind negative attitudes in order to hold others at a distance. For others of us, an inflated view of our own self-importance or a demand for perfectionism may be at the root of our belligerence.

Identifying why we are quarrelsome is essential if we are to know how to ask God to help us turn around this unattractive and destructive behavior.

For further reading on Step 4, turn to page 809.

Daily Encouragement

DAY 352 READING: PROVERBS 21:7–31

A Thought for the New Day: It is easy to get the impression that expediency, not righteousness or mercy, is the order of the time in which we live. For many this seems unhappily true, but such a view is shortsighted. Those who live by "the law of the jungle" will usually end up being the prey themselves, and all their days they must live in fear of becoming the victim. But the truly righteous and merciful, though often suffering, have the reward of divine approval (v. 21). (*Turn to page 807.*)

29 A wicked man hardens his
    face,
  But *as for* the upright,
    he establishes his way.

30 *There is* no wisdom or
    understanding
  Or counsel against the LORD.

31 The horse *is* prepared for the
    day of battle,
  But deliverance *is* of the LORD.

22 A *good* name is to be chosen
    rather than great riches,
  Loving favor rather than silver
    and gold.

2 The rich and the poor have this
    in common,
  The LORD *is* the maker of them
    all.

3 A prudent *man* foresees evil
    and hides himself,
  But the simple pass on
    and are punished.

4 By humility *and* the fear of the
  LORD
  Are riches and honor and life.

5 Thorns *and* snares *are* in the
    way of the perverse;
  He who guards his soul will be
    far from them.

6 Train up a child
    in the way he should go,
  And when he is old
    he will not depart from it.

7 The rich rules over the poor,
  And the borrower *is* servant to
    the lender.

8 He who sows iniquity will reap
    sorrow,
  And the rod of his anger will
    fail.

9 He who has a bountiful eye
    will be blessed,

For he gives of his bread to the
  poor.

10 Cast out the scoffer,
    and contention will leave;
  Yes, strife and reproach will
    cease.

11 He who loves purity of heart
  And has grace on his lips,
  The king *will be* his friend.

12 The eyes of the LORD preserve
    knowledge,
  But He overthrows the words
    of the faithless.

13 The slothful *man* says,
  "*There is* a lion outside!
  I shall be slain in the streets!"

14 The mouth of an immoral
    woman *is* a deep pit;
  He who is abhorred of the
    LORD will fall there.

15 Foolishness *is* bound up in the
    heart of a child,
  But the rod of correction will
    drive it far from him.

16 He who oppresses the poor to
    increase his *riches*,
  And he who gives to the rich,
    will surely *come* to poverty.

17 Incline your ear and hear the
    words of the wise,
  And apply your heart to my
    knowledge;

18 For *it is* a pleasant thing if you
    keep them within you;
  Let them all be fixed upon your
    lips,

19 So that your trust may be in
    the LORD;
  I have instructed you today,
    even you.

20 Have I not written to you
    excellent things
  Of counsels and knowledge,

STEP 7

Humbly asked Him to remove our shortcomings.

Proverbs 22:4

Humility and the fear of the Lord are themes we deal with repeatedly in our recovery process. We needed humility to admit our helplessness and to trust in His power alone. We needed humility to see and admit our faults. And now we again must humble ourselves before God as we acknowledge how much we need deliverance and look to the total sufficiency of Jesus to remove every barrier.

We must also be willing to do the things God directs us to do through His Word. This is the essence of having the fear of the Lord in our lives. It means we are eager to obey Him.

When these two qualities are the foundation for each day that we live, God can accomplish for us all that we need to overcome our problems. But there is more! Proverbs 22:4 is a principle with promise. Trust and obedience in God will bring to our lives spiritual and emotional and eternal riches that are abundant and fulfilling.

See page 55 of the introductory material for Step 8.

Daily Encouragement

DAY 353 READING: PROVERBS 22:1–21

A Thought for the New Day: Unfortunately, some views of education fail to recognize the value of teaching that will preserve the child from self-destructive ways in later life. Sound principles of morality are needed before learning self-expression, for even creativity needs discipline; otherwise, decency becomes in short supply. Parents who patiently train youth in divine things will enjoy the reward of seeing their children grow up in honor (v. 6). (*Turn to page 809.*)

21 That I may make you know
the certainty of the words of
truth,
That you may answer
words of truth
To those who send to you?

22 Do not rob the poor because he
is poor,
Nor oppress the afflicted at the
gate;
23 For the LORD will plead their
cause,
And plunder the soul of those
who plunder them.

24 Make no friendship with an
angry man,
And with a furious man do not
go,
25 Lest you learn his ways
And set a snare for your soul.

26 Do not be one of those
who shakes hands in a
pledge,
One of those who is surety for
debts;
27 If you have nothing *with
which* to pay,
Why should he take away your
bed from under you?

28 Do not remove the ancient
landmark
Which your fathers have set.

29 Do you see a man *who* excels
in his work?
He will stand before kings;
He will not stand before
unknown *men.*

23 When you sit down to eat
with a ruler,
Consider carefully what *is*
before you;
2 And put a knife to your throat
If you *are* a man given to
appetite.
3 Do not desire his delicacies,
For they *are* deceptive food.

4 Do not overwork to be rich;
Because of your own
understanding, cease!
5 Will you set your eyes on that
which is not?
For *riches* certainly make
themselves wings;
They fly away like an eagle
toward heaven.

6 Do not eat the bread of a
miser,
Nor desire his delicacies;
7 For as he thinks in his heart,
so *is* he.
"Eat and drink!" he says to you,
But his heart is not with you.
8 The morsel you have eaten,
you will vomit up,
And waste your pleasant
words.

9 Do not speak in the hearing of
a fool,
For he will despise the wisdom
of your words.

10 Do not remove the ancient
landmark,
Nor enter the fields of the
fatherless;
11 For their Redeemer *is* mighty;
He will plead their cause
against you.

12 Apply your heart to
instruction,
And your ears to words of
knowledge.

13 Do not withhold correction
from a child,
For *if* you beat him with a rod,
he will not die.
14 You shall beat him with a rod,
And deliver his soul from hell.

15 My son, if your heart is wise,
My heart will rejoice—indeed, I
myself;
16 Yes, my inmost being will
rejoice
When your lips speak right
things.

STEP 4

Made a searching and fearless moral inventory of ourselves.

Proverbs 22:24, 25

"But everybody's doing it!" has been the cry of many a child who feels his parents have conspired to make him an oddity among his peer group. Often the need for acceptance is so strong, however, that it can drive us to do things we know are not wise or right. If we have a dependent personality, we are at high risk for poor judgment in this area. We should keep this in mind during our Step 4 inventory. If succumbing to this kind of temptation has been our undoing, we not only need to ask ourselves why, but we also need to determine what attitudes must be changed and how they can be changed. We need to learn to use the strength the Holy Spirit can give us to keep from falling under the negative influences of others. We need His peace and security to surround us when we must take a stand that may bring ridicule. In Christ's power we can know freedom from life's snares.

For further reading on Step 4, turn to page 811.

Daily Encouragement

DAY 354 READING: PROVERBS 22:22—23:18

A Thought for the New Day: There is no need to be driven by desire for the positions or possessions of others (23:17, 18). Envy never gets enough, and perpetual misery is the result. *"Be content with such things as you have"* (Heb. 13:5) may be a joke to some, but there is a promise added: "I will never leave you." If you really have Jesus as your Friend, what else do you need? But God does provide for our necessities, and usually more. *(Turn to page 811.)*

17 Do not let your heart envy
  sinners,
 But in the fear of the LORD
  continue all day *long;*
18 For surely there is a hereafter,
 And your hope will not be cut
  off.

19 Hear, my son, and be wise;
 And guide your heart in the
  way.
20 Do not mix with winebibbers,
 Or with gluttonous eaters of
  meat;
21 For the drunkard and the
  glutton will come to poverty,
 And drowsiness will clothe *a*
  man with rags.

22 Listen to your father who
  begot you,
 And do not despise your
  mother when she is old.

23 Buy the truth, and do not sell
  it,
 Also wisdom and instruction
  and understanding.

24 The father of the righteous
  will greatly rejoice,
 And he who begets a wise *child*
  will delight in him.
25 Let your father and your
  mother be glad,
 And let her who bore you
  rejoice.

26 My son, give me your heart,
 And let your eyes observe my
  ways.

27 For a harlot *is* a deep pit,
 And a seductress *is* a narrow
  well.
28 She also lies in wait as *for* a
  victim,
 And increases the unfaithful
  among men.

29 Who has woe?
 Who has sorrow?
 Who has contentions?
 Who has complaints?

Who has wounds without
  cause?
 Who has redness of eyes?
30 Those who linger long at the
  wine,
 Those who go in search of
  mixed wine.
31 Do not look on the wine when
  it is red,
 When it sparkles in the cup,
 When it swirls around
  smoothly;
32 At the last it bites like a
  serpent,
 And stings like a viper.
33 Your eyes will see strange
  things,
 And your heart will utter
  perverse things.
34 Yes, you will be like one who
  lies down in the midst of the
  sea,
 Or like one who lies at the top
  of the mast, *saying:*
35 "They have struck me,
  but I was not hurt;
 They have beaten me,
  but I did not feel *it.*
 When shall I awake, that I
  may seek another *drink?"*

24 Do not be envious of evil
  men,
 Nor desire to be with them;
2 For their heart devises
  violence,
 And their lips talk of
  troublemaking.

3 Through wisdom a house is
  built,
 And by understanding it is
  established;
4 By knowledge the rooms are
  filled
 With all precious and pleasant
  riches.

5 A wise man *is* strong,
 Yes, a man of knowledge
  increases strength;

STEP 4

Made a searching and fearless moral inventory of ourselves.

Proverbs 23:29–35

The six questions of Proverbs 23:29 denote three kinds of suffering that substance abuse brings to our lives. Substance abuse causes woe and sorrow (emotional pain). It brings us social problems as we experience contention and complaint within our families, at school, or at work. And, finally, we suffer physical problems—"wounds without cause" and "redness of eyes."

Verse 31 speaks eloquently of the allure of alcohol, and anyone who has watched beer commercials can understand the warning. It looks so good in the glass, frothy and bubbly. Then, too, everyone in the commercials seems to be having such a good time. Advertisers are not eager to show the bite of the serpent alcohol, however. They do not show the hangover, the broken home, or the horrible accident. The drunken swaying, the brawling, and the constant need for another drink complete the picture in verses 34 and 35. It is not a pretty painting, but many of us need to assess our lives in the light of these verses and accept the truth about our lives.

For further reading on Step 4, turn to page 817.

Daily Encouragement

DAY 355 READING: PROVERBS 23:19–35

A Thought for the New Day: Truth is a commodity that is bought with attentive effort (v. 23), but it can be sold cheaply in exchange for destructive error. Truth is like gold because there is nothing to compare with its value. It should be treasured until the day when paper money will be worthless. Thus false philosophy will bring great spiritual poverty in the day when we must stand before God. On the other hand, the truth will assure us of life when the worlds are aflame. (*Turn to page 813.*)

wise counsel
ou will wage your own war,
nd in a multitude of
counselors *there is* safety.

7 Wisdom *is* too lofty for a fool;
He does not open his mouth in
the gate.

8 He who plots to do evil
Will be called a schemer.
9 The devising of foolishness *is*
sin,
And the scoffer *is* an
abomination to men.

10 *If* you faint in the day of
adversity,
Your strength *is* small.

11 Deliver *those who* are drawn
toward death,
And hold back *those* stumbling
to the slaughter.
12 If you say, "Surely we did not
know this,"
Does not He who weighs the
hearts consider *it?*
He who keeps your soul,
does He *not* know *it?*
And will He *not* render to *each*
man according to his deeds?

13 My son, eat honey because *it is*
good,
And the honeycomb *which is*
sweet to your taste;
14 So *shall* the knowledge of
wisdom *be* to your soul;
If you have found *it,*
there is a prospect,
And your hope will not be cut
off.

15 Do not lie in wait, O wicked
man, against the dwelling of
the righteous;
Do not plunder his resting
place;
16 For a righteous *man* may fall
seven times
And rise again,

But the wicked shall fall by
calamity.

17 Do not rejoice when your
enemy falls,
And do not let your heart be
glad when he stumbles;
18 Lest the LORD see *it,*
and it displease Him,
And He turn away His wrath
from him.

19 Do not fret because of
evildoers,
Nor be envious of the wicked;
20 For there will be no prospect
for the evil *man;*
The lamp of the wicked
will be put out.

21 My son, fear the LORD and the
king;
Do not associate with those
given to change;
22 For their calamity will rise
suddenly,
And who knows the ruin those
two can bring?

23 These *things* also *belong* to the
wise:

It is not good to show
partiality in judgment.
24 He who says to the wicked,
"You *are* righteous,"
Him the people will curse;
Nations will abhor him.
25 But those who rebuke *the
wicked* will have delight,
And a good blessing will come
upon them.

26 He who gives a right answer
kisses the lips.

27 Prepare your outside work,
Make it fit for yourself in the
field;
And afterward build your
house.

28 Do not be a witness against
your neighbor without cause,

STEP 10

*Continued to take personal inventory
and when we were wrong promptly admitted it.*

Proverbs 24:30–34

This passage could be considered an allegory (an earthly picture with a deeper, spiritual meaning) of Step 10. Our new life is like a field that needs careful attention and cultivation in order to stay fruitful. If we become negligent (slothful) and fail to appreciate the importance of a consistent walk with God, before we know it the beautiful vineyard of recovery will be overgrown with the thorns of wrong attitudes. The strong walls of God's power and our trust will begin to crumble a stone at a time. If we do not rouse ourselves from this spiritual lethargy, asking God to give us the faithfulness we need, we may be attacked and plundered by temptation.

The warning is a good one. But there is also a positive side to this exhortation: the sincere, abiding heart produces the fruit of the Spirit and reaps a harvest of contentment and blessing.

See page 66 of the introductory material for Step 11.

Daily Encouragement

DAY 356 READING: PROVERBS 24:1–34

A Thought for the New Day: A wise person is not headstrong and arrogant. We must realize that we often have tunnel vision; and in order to see the larger picture, we need the input of others (v. 6). We are constantly making decisions, and some of them may be for life or death. So let us cultivate the habit of consulting trusted friends, especially in those matters we are inclined to feel most strongly about. It is when emotions are high that we most need advice. (*Turn to page 815.*)

For would you deceive with
your lips?

29 Do not say, "I will do to him
just as he has done to me;
I will render to the man
according to his work."

30 I went by the field of the
slothful,
And by the vineyard of the
man devoid of understanding;

31 And there it was,
all overgrown with thorns;
Its surface was covered with
nettles;
Its stone wall was broken
down.

32 When I saw *it*, I considered *it*
well;
I looked on *it and* received
instruction:

33 A little sleep, a little slumber,
A little folding of the hands to
rest;

34 So your poverty will come *like*
a prowler,
And your want like an armed
man.

25 These also *are* proverbs of
Solomon which the men of
Hezekiah king of Judah copied:

2 *It is* the glory of God
to conceal a matter,
But the glory of kings
is to search out a matter.

3 *As* the heavens for height
and the earth for depth,
So the heart of kings *is*
unsearchable.

4 Take away the dross from
silver,
And it will go to the
silversmith *for* jewelry.

5 Take away the wicked from
before the king,
And his throne will be
established in righteousness.

6 Do not exalt yourself in the
presence of the king,

And do not stand in the place
of great *men;*

7 For *it is* better that he say to
you,
"Come up here,"
Than that you should be put
lower in the presence of the
prince,
Whom your eyes have seen.

8 Do not go hastily to court;
For what will you do in the
end,
When your neighbor has put
you to shame?

9 Debate your case with your
neighbor *himself*,
And do not disclose the secret
to another;

10 Lest he who hears *it* expose
your shame,
And your reputation be ruined.

11 A word fitly spoken
is like apples of gold
In settings of silver.

STE
9

12 *Like* an earring of gold
and an ornament of fine gold
Is a wise reprover to an
obedient ear.

13 Like the cold of snow in time
of harvest
Is a faithful messenger to those
who send him,
For he refreshes the soul of his
masters.

14 Whoever falsely boasts of
giving
Is like clouds and wind without
rain.

15 By long forbearance a ruler is
persuaded,
And a gentle tongue breaks a
bone.

16 Have you found honey?
Eat only as much as you need,
Lest you be filled with it and
vomit.

STEP 9

*Made direct amends to such people wherever possible,
except when to do so would injure them or others.*

Proverbs 25:11

The currencies of the world are in a constant state of flux. The pound, dollar, yen, franc, and others do not carry inherent value. Their worth is only as strong as the economy of the government that generates them. But silver and gold have a standard all their own that is less dependent on a particular country's economy. They are considered a timeless treasure. However, Solomon, who was the richest man who ever lived, considered something else to be just as timeless a treasure. He declared that wise words, spoken at the right time and in the right way were like elegant artworks of silver and gold. As we approach Step 9, we should be asking the Holy Spirit to fill our minds with understanding and our hearts with true love and concern for those to whom we make amends. Then our sincere, wise, and well-timed words will become a lasting treasure of reconciliation.

See page 62 of the introductory material for Step 10.

Daily Encouragement

DAY 357 READING: PROVERBS 25:1–15

A Thought for the New Day: It makes a lot of sense to discuss our problems with the one who is immediately concerned, not with others (vv. 9, 10). That is good communication. True, you may lose a friend by your honesty. But if you speak to others about that person you are in danger of destructive talk, while the person concerned will now have much more to complain about because of your breach of confidence. *(Turn to page 817.)*

17 Seldom set foot in your
    neighbor's house,
    Lest he become weary of you
    and hate you.

18 A man who bears false witness
    against his neighbor
    Is like a club, a sword,
    and a sharp arrow.

19 Confidence in an unfaithful
    man in time of trouble
    Is like a bad tooth
    and a foot out of joint.

20 *Like* one who takes away a
    garment in cold weather,
    And like vinegar on soda,
    Is one who sings songs to a
    heavy heart.

21 If your enemy is hungry,
    give him bread to eat;
    And if he is thirsty,
    give him water to drink;
22 For *so* you will heap coals of
    fire on his head,
    And the Lord will reward you.

23 The north wind brings forth
    rain,
    And a backbiting tongue an
    angry countenance.

24 *It is* better to dwell in a corner
    of a housetop,
    Than in a house shared with a
    contentious woman.

25 *As* cold water to a weary soul,
    So *is* good news from a far
    country.

26 A righteous man who falters
    before the wicked
    Is like a murky spring
    and a polluted well.

27 *It is* not good to eat much
    honey;
    So to seek one's own glory *is*
    not glory.

28 Whoever *has* no rule over his
    own spirit
    Is like a city broken down,
    without walls.

STE 4

26 As snow in summer
    and rain in harvest,
    So honor is not fitting for a
    fool.

2 Like a flitting sparrow,
    like a flying swallow,
    So a curse without cause shall
    not alight.

3 A whip for the horse,
    A bridle for the donkey,
    And a rod for the fool's back.
4 Do not answer a fool according
    to his folly,
    Lest you also be like him.
5 Answer a fool according to his
    folly,
    Lest he be wise in his own
    eyes.
6 He who sends a message by
    the hand of a fool
    Cuts off *his own* feet
    and drinks violence.
7 *Like* the legs of the lame that
    hang limp
    Is a proverb in the mouth of
    fools.
8 Like one who binds a stone in
    a sling
    Is he who gives honor to a
    fool.
9 *Like* a thorn *that* goes into the
    hand of a drunkard
    Is a proverb in the mouth of
    fools.
10 The great *God* who formed all
    things
    Gives the fool *his* hire and the
    transgressor *his* wages.
11 As a dog returns to his own
    vomit,
    So a fool repeats his folly.
12 Do you see a man wise in his
    own eyes?
    There is more hope for a fool
    than for him.

STE 1

STEP 4

Made a searching and fearless moral inventory of ourselves.

Proverbs 25:28

In ancient times, building a city without erecting strong walls was unthinkable. Such a city would have been vulnerable to attacks from wild animals, roaming bands of thieves, and enemy armies. And when King Solomon saw an undisciplined man or a man who did not keep his emotions properly controlled, the city without walls came to mind. This is because such a person is so vulnerable to the circumstances of life, as well as to the ravages of his or her own appetite. An undisciplined individual has difficulty standing up against adversity or remaining committed to a desired course of action. One who does not rule the emotions may be swept to ruin by impulsive sexual desires, outbursts of anger, the need to gamble, and so on.

However, when we realize the extent of our problem, we can do so with courage and optimism. God can rebuild our broken walls and make our city clean and beautiful again.

For further reading on Step 4, turn to page 819.

Daily Encouragement

DAY 358 READING: PROVERBS 25:16—26:16

A Thought for the New Day: Several times in Proverbs the writer praises the virtue of silence. There is a time for talking and a time for quiet reflection. Many words are lost on the sick person in pain. Sit by quietly and pray. The sufferer may be waiting for an opportunity to share something with you. In any case, your quiet presence and prayer will be treasured more than your words (25:20). *(Turn to page 819.)*

13 The slothful *man* says,
"*There is* a lion in the road!
A fierce lion *is* in the streets!"

14 *As* a door turns on its hinges,
So *does* the slothful *turn* on his
bed.

15 The slothful *man* buries his
hand in the bowl;
It wearies him to bring it back
to his mouth.

16 The sluggard *is* wiser in his
own eyes
Than seven men who can
answer sensibly.

17 He who passes by *and* meddles
in a quarrel not his own
Is like one who takes a dog by
the ears.

18 Like a madman who throws
firebrands, arrows, and death,

19 *Is* the man *who* deceives his
neighbor,
And says, "I was only joking!"

20 Where *there is* no wood,
the fire goes out;
And where *there is* no
talebearer, strife ceases.

21 *As* charcoal *is* to burning coals,
and wood to fire,
So *is* a contentious man
to kindle strife.

22 The words of a talebearer *are*
like tasty trifles,
And they go down into the
inmost body.

23 Fervent lips with a wicked
heart
Are like earthenware covered
with silver dross.

24 He who hates, disguises *it* with
his lips,
And lays up deceit within
himself;

25 When he speaks kindly,
do not believe him,
For *there are* seven
abominations in his heart;

26 *Though his* hatred is covered
by deceit,
His wickedness will be revealed
before the *whole* congregation.

27 Whoever digs a pit will fall into
it,
And he who rolls a stone
will have it roll back on him.

28 A lying tongue hates *those*
who are crushed by it,
And a flattering mouth works
ruin.

27 Do not boast about
tomorrow,
For you do not know what a
day may bring forth.

2 Let another man praise you,
and not your own mouth;
A stranger, and not your own
lips.

3 A stone *is* heavy and sand *is*
weighty,
But a fool's wrath *is* heavier
than both of them.

4 Wrath *is* cruel and anger a
torrent,
But who *is* able to stand before
jealousy?

5 Open rebuke *is* better
Than love carefully concealed.

6 Faithful *are* the wounds of a
friend,
But the kisses of an enemy *are*
deceitful.

7 A satisfied soul loathes the
honeycomb,
But to a hungry soul every
bitter thing *is* sweet.

8 Like a bird that wanders from
its nest
Is a man who wanders from his
place.

STEP
4

STEP
4

Made a searching and fearless moral inventory of ourselves.
Proverbs 26:20–22

Gossip and a contentious spirit are the two edges on the knife of a critical spirit. Gossip is more covert in its methods, while contention is overt. Yet, both are extremely harmful to ourselves and others. Strife, bitterness, mistrust, and isolation follow in their wakes. If we have felt that others have hurt us by the distance we perceive in our relationships, perhaps we should stop and consider what and how we are communicating. And if we must conclude that gossip and/or contention is a part of our personalities, we must ask ourselves three questions. First, what in our backgrounds makes this type of communication seem normal? Second, what need are we attempting to meet by this behavior? Third, specifically how have we harmed ourselves and others by our words? Understanding is the first step toward healthier and kinder ways of relating.

For further reading on Step 4, turn to page 827.

Daily Encouragement

DAY 359 READING: PROVERBS 26:17—27:9

A Thought for the New Day: Gossip destroys people's lives. When we hear bad news about someone's character, it is a mark of virtue to keep it to ourselves. Talk to God about it, and pray for the individual concerned. If it seems wise, go and speak to that person yourself. But go as a healer and certainly not as a faultfinder. Seek every opportunity to put a stop to the rumor when you hear it (26:20). (*Turn to page 821.*)

9 Ointment and perfume
  delight the heart,
  And the sweetness of a man's
  friend *does so* by hearty
  counsel.

10 Do not forsake your own
   friend or your father's friend,
   Nor go to your brother's house
   in the day of your calamity;
   For better is a neighbor nearby
   than a brother far away.

11 My son, be wise,
   and make my heart glad,
   That I may answer him who
   reproaches me.

12 A prudent *man* foresees evil
   and hides himself;
   The simple pass on *and* are
   punished.

13 Take the garment of him who
   is surety for a stranger,
   And hold it in pledge *when* he
   is surety for a seductress.

14 He who blesses his friend with
   a loud voice, rising early in
   the morning,
   It will be counted a curse to
   him.

15 A continual dripping on a very
   rainy day
   And a contentious woman are
   alike;

16 Whoever restrains her
   restrains the wind,
   And grasps oil with his right
   hand.

STEP 5
17 *As iron sharpens iron,*
   So a man sharpens the
   countenance of his friend.

18 Whoever keeps the fig tree
   will eat its fruit;
   So he who waits on his master
   will be honored.

19 As in water face *reveals* face,

So a man's heart *reveals* the
man.

20 Hell and Destruction are never
   full;
   So the eyes of man are never
   satisfied.

21 The refining pot *is* for silver
   and the furnace for gold,
   And a man *is valued* by what
   others say of him.

22 Though you grind a fool in a
   mortar with a pestle along
   with crushed grain,
   Yet his foolishness will not
   depart from him.

23 Be diligent to know the state
   of your flocks,
   And attend to your herds;

24 For riches *are* not forever,
   Nor does a crown *endure* to all
   generations.

25 *When* the hay is removed,
   and the tender grass shows
   itself,
   And the herbs of the
   mountains are gathered in,

26 The lambs *will provide* your
   clothing,
   And the goats the price of a
   field;

27 *You shall have* enough goats'
   milk for your food,
   For the food of your
   household,
   And the nourishment of your
   maidservants.

28 The wicked flee when no
   one pursues,
   But the righteous are bold as a
   lion.

2 Because of the transgression of
  a land, many *are* its princes;
  But by a man of understanding
  and knowledge
  Right will be prolonged.

3 A poor man who oppresses the
  poor

STEP 5

Admitted to God, to ourselves, and to another human being the exact nature of our wrongs.

Proverbs 27:17

"Confess *your* trespasses to one another, and pray for one another, that you may be healed," we read in James 5:16. These verses in Proverbs help us understand how confession aids healing. When we have a trusted friend who is able to listen to our admissions with wisdom and sympathy, we have found much more than a shoulder to "unload" on. We have found someone who can also deepen us spiritually and encourage us emotionally and intellectually. And even if we feel we are novices yet in our own understanding, we can still be encouragers by sharing what God is doing in our lives. Each of us then becomes a tool God can use to sharpen each other's virtues and abilities.

For further reading on Step 5, turn to page 823.

Daily Encouragement

DAY 360 READING: PROVERBS 27:10–27

A Thought for the New Day: Good intentions are all very well, but good intentions and the actions that result from them must be guided by mature caution. We ought to learn by experience, as well as from verse 12, that the possibility of even tragic error is always just at hand, except for the grace of God. Let us be ready to recognize danger when it is present and know how to take evasive action. God gives wisdom to those who ask Him. (*Turn to page 823.*)

Is *like* a driving rain which
　leaves no food.

4 Those who forsake the law
　　praise the wicked,
　But such as keep the law
　　contend with them.

5 Evil men do not understand
　　justice,
　But those who seek the LORD
　　understand all.

6 Better *is* the poor who walks
　　in his integrity
　Than one perverse *in his* ways,
　　though he *be* rich.

7 Whoever keeps the law
　　is a discerning son,
　But a companion of gluttons
　　shames his father.

8 One who increases his
　　possessions by usury and
　　extortion
　Gathers it for him who will
　　pity the poor.

9 One who turns away his ear
　　from hearing the law,
　Even his prayer *shall be* an
　　abomination.

10 Whoever causes the upright to
　　go astray in an evil way,
　He himself will fall into his
　　own pit;
　But the blameless will inherit
　　good *things*.

11 The rich man *is* wise in his
　　own eyes,
　But the poor who has
　　understanding searches him
　　out.

12 When the righteous rejoice,
　　there is great glory;
　But when the wicked arise,
　　men hide themselves.

13 He who covers his sins will not
　　prosper,

But whoever confesses and
　forsakes *them* will have
　mercy.

14 Happy *is* the man
　　who is always reverent,
　But he who hardens his heart
　　will fall into calamity.

15 *Like* a roaring lion and a
　　charging bear
　Is a wicked ruler over poor
　　people.

16 A ruler who lacks under-
　　standing *is* a great oppressor,
　But he who hates covetousness
　　will prolong *his* days.

17 A man burdened with
　　bloodshed will flee into a pit;
　Let no one help him.

18 Whoever walks blamelessly
　　will be saved,
　But *he who is* perverse *in his*
　　ways will fall at once.

19 He who tills his land
　　will have plenty of bread,
　But he who follows frivolity
　　will have poverty enough!

20 A faithful man
　　will abound with blessings,
　But he who hastens to be rich
　　will not go unpunished.

21 To show partiality *is* not good,
　Because for a piece of bread a
　　man will transgress.

22 A man with an evil eye hastens
　　after riches,
　And does not consider that
　　poverty will come upon him.

23 He who rebukes a man will
　　find more favor afterward
　Than he who flatters with the
　　tongue.

STEP 5

*Admitted to God, to ourselves, and to another human being
the exact nature of our wrongs.*

Proverbs 28:13, 14

The practice of confession is an ancient tradition of our Judeo-Christian faith. Without confession, our deepest emotional pains, including fear, anger, and resentment, remain buried within us like corrosive agents. Similar to toxic environmental wastes, these buried toxic emotions eventually leak out to contaminate all of the vital relationships of our lives. For example, deeply buried resentments toward an authoritarian father may fester for three or four decades and then erupt as an irrational anger toward all authority figures in our contemporary adult life. Fear of an emotionally suffocating mother may linger for years and prevent our creating healthy intimacy in any of our adult relationships.

If we cling to these old poisons, we also run the grave risk of excluding God's healing mercy. The words of Proverbs are explicit in this warning: "He who covers his sins will not prosper, but whoever confesses and forsakes *them* will have mercy" (v. 13). Step 5 is the active step of breaking our hardened hearts to expose them to God's tender mercies.

See page 47 of the introductory material for Step 6.

Daily Encouragement

DAY 361 READING: PROVERBS 28:1–23

A Thought for the New Day: Why should I be reverent? The person who lacks respect for others—even for God—is headed for a lot of trouble (v. 14). In the absence of regard for others comes self-disrespect, also, followed by self-indulgence and immorality with all their destructive effects. Reverence becomes us just because we are human and made in God's likeness. Reverence is the primary ingredient of real love toward God and others. (*Turn to page 825.*)

24 Whoever robs his father or his
    mother,
And says, "*It is* no
    transgression,"
The same *is* companion to a
    destroyer.

25 He who is of a proud heart
    stirs up strife,
But he who trusts in the LORD
    will be prospered.

26 He who trusts in his own heart
    is a fool,
But whoever walks wisely
    will be delivered.

27 He who gives to the poor will
    not lack,
But he who hides his eyes will
    have many curses.

28 When the wicked arise,
    men hide themselves;
But when they perish,
    the righteous increase.

29 He who is often reproved,
    and hardens *his* neck,
Will suddenly be destroyed,
    and that without remedy.

2 When the righteous are in
    authority, the people rejoice;
But when a wicked *man* rules,
    the people groan.

3 Whoever loves wisdom makes
    his father rejoice,
But a companion of harlots
    wastes *his* wealth.

4 The king establishes the land
    by justice,
But he who receives bribes
    overthrows it.

5 A man who flatters his
    neighbor
Spreads a net for his feet.

6 By transgression an evil man is
    snared,

But the righteous sings and
    rejoices.

7 The righteous considers the
    cause of the poor,
But the wicked does not
    understand *such* knowledge.

8 Scoffers ensnare a city,
But wise *men* turn away wrath.

9 *If* a wise man contends with a
    foolish man,
Whether the fool rages or
    laughs, *there is* no peace.

10 The bloodthirsty hate the
    blameless,
But the just seek his well-
    being.

11 A fool vents all his feelings,
But a wise *man* holds them
    back.

12 If a ruler pays attention to lies,
All his servants *become*
    wicked.

13 The poor *man* and the
    oppressor have this in
    common:
The LORD gives light to the
    eyes of both.

14 The king who judges the poor
    with truth,
His throne will be established
    forever.

15 The rod and reproof give
    wisdom,
But a child left *to himself*
    brings shame to his mother.

16 When the wicked are
    multiplied, transgression
    increases;
But the righteous will see their
    fall.

17 Correct your son,
    and he will give you rest;

STEP 1

*We admitted we were powerless over our dependencies—
that our lives had become unmanageable.*

Proverbs 28:26

Early in the opening verses of Proverbs we are given the foundation for all that follows when Solomon declares, "The fear of the LORD *is* the beginning of knowledge." A good description of "fearing God" is simply believing that God is who He says He is. The Bible tells us in many passages that God is omnipotent and omniscient. This means that He alone is all-powerful and all-wise. To know only those two things about Him would impress us, but we still might find it difficult to trust our lives to Him. That is why God became a Man who willingly died for each of us, no matter how sinful we are: "In this is love, not that we loved God, but that He loved us and sent His Son *to be* the propitiation [appeasement and reconciliation] for our sins" (1 John 4:10).

Only foolish people continue to trust in themselves once they know the power, wisdom, and love God freely offers to them in Jesus.

See page 30 of the introductory material for Step 2.

Daily Encouragement

DAY 362 READING: PROVERBS 28:24—29:16

A Thought for the New Day: "Nice guys finish last!" is the cynic's proverb. The corollary is that arrogance is a desirable virtue if you want to "make it" in the world. However, if you follow the career of the proud man over the long term, at the end of that road you will find a disappointed and disillusioned person. Self-love sours the soul at last, but gladness in serving, using the gifts of God, yields a beautiful spirit and results in the blessing of many (28:25). (*Turn to page 827.*)

Yes, he will give delight to
your soul.

18 Where *there is* no revelation,
the people cast off restraint;
But happy *is* he who keeps the
law.

19 A servant will not be corrected
by mere words;
For though he understands,
he will not respond.

20 Do you see a man hasty in his
words?
There is more hope for a fool
than for him.

21 He who pampers his servant
from childhood
Will have him as a son in the
end.

22 An angry man stirs up strife,
And a furious man abounds in
transgression.

23 A man's pride will bring him
low,
But the humble in spirit will
retain honor.

24 Whoever is a partner with a
thief hates his own life;
He swears to tell the truth,
but reveals nothing.

25 The fear of man brings a snare,
But whoever trusts in the LORD
shall be safe.

26 Many seek the ruler's favor,
But justice for man *comes*
from the LORD.

27 An unjust man *is* an
abomination to the righteous,
And *he who is* upright in the
way *is* an abomination to the
wicked.

30 The words of Agur the son of
Jakeh, *his* utterance. This

man declared to Ithiel—to Ithiel
and Ucal:

2 Surely I *am* more stupid than
any man,
And do not have the
understanding of a man.
3 I neither learned wisdom
Nor have knowledge of the
Holy One.

4 Who has ascended into heaven,
or descended?
Who has gathered the wind in
His fists?
Who has bound the waters in a
garment?
Who has established all the
ends of the earth?
What *is* His name,
and what *is* His Son's name,
If you know?

5 Every word of God *is* pure;
He *is* a shield to those who put
their trust in Him.
6 Do not add to His words,
Lest He reprove you,
and you be found a liar.

7 Two *things* I request of You
(Deprive me not before I die):
8 Remove falsehood and lies far
from me;
Give me neither poverty nor
riches—
Feed me with the food *You*
prescribe for me;
9 Lest I be full and deny *You,*
And say, "Who *is* the LORD?"
Or lest I be poor and steal,
And profane the name of my
God.

10 Do not malign a servant to his
master,
Lest he curse you,
and you be found guilty.

11 *There is* a generation
that curses its father,
And does not bless its mother.
12 *There is* a generation
that is pure in its own eyes,

STEP
4

Made a searching and fearless moral inventory of ourselves.
Proverbs 29:22, 23

Those of us who have trouble with anger may also have trouble admitting the root causes of that anger. We may be used to excusing our pouting or outbursts by blaming other people or circumstances—"If my son would just obey, I wouldn't need to get angry." "If my wife would be more careful with our money, I wouldn't be so upset all the time." The angry person, Proverbs says, "abounds in transgression." Cursing, insulting others, being rude, lacking kindness, being domineering, being bitter—emotional and physical cruelty of all sorts grow from an angry spirit. And anger is the child of pride and control. Eventually, an angry person loses the very things he or she attempted to gain through anger—the respect and compliance of others. Anger breeds only rebellion and disgust. The path to freedom from the habit of anger is to humbly accept the fact that we are the ones with the problems; then God can begin to show us better ways of relating.

For further reading on Step 4, turn to page 829.

Daily
Encouragement

DAY 363 READING: PROVERBS 29:17—30:9

A Thought for the New Day: The Word of God is not merely a set of general principles to live by: its "every word" is important (30:5, 6). To neglect that fact is to forget the Bible's Author. In all our devotion and meditation, let us carefully consider the treasury that resides in every detail of what God is speaking to us. Our reward will be that our thoughts will become captive to the mind of Christ Himself. *(Turn to page 829.)*

Yet is not washed from its
filthiness.

13 *There is* a generation—
   oh, how lofty are their eyes!
   And their eyelids are lifted up.
14 *There is* a generation whose
   teeth *are like* swords,
   And whose fangs *are like*
   knives,
   To devour the poor from off
   the earth,
   And the needy from *among*
   men.

15 The leech has two daughters,
   Crying, "Give! Give!"

   There are three *things that* are
   never satisfied,
   Four *things* never say, "It is
   enough":
16 The grave,
   The barren womb,
   The earth *that* is not satisfied
   with water,
   And the fire *that* never says,
   "It is enough."

17 The eye *that* mocks *his* father,
   And scorns obedience to *his*
   mother,
   The ravens of the valley will
   pick it out,
   And the young eagles will eat
   it.

18 There are three *things which*
   are too wonderful for me,
   Yes, four *which* I do not
   understand:
19 The way of an eagle in the air,
   The way of a serpent on a
   rock,
   The way of a ship in the midst
   of the sea,
   And the way of a man with a
   virgin.

20 This *is* the way of an
   adulterous woman:
   She eats and wipes her mouth,
   And says, "I have done no
   wickedness."

21 For three *things* the earth is
   perturbed,
   Yes, for four it cannot bear up:
22 For a servant when he reigns,
   A fool when he is filled with
   food,
23 A hateful *woman* when she is
   married,
   And a maidservant who
   succeeds her mistress.

24 There are four *things which*
   are little on the earth,
   But they *are* exceedingly wise:
25 The ants *are* a people not
   strong,
   Yet they prepare their food in
   the summer;
26 The rock badgers are a feeble
   folk,
   Yet they make their homes in
   the crags;
27 The locusts have no king,
   Yet they all advance in ranks;
28 The spider skillfully grasps
   with its hands,
   And it is in kings' palaces.

29 There are three *things which*
   are majestic in pace,
   Yes, four *which* are stately in
   walk:
30 A lion, *which is* mighty among
   beasts
   And does not turn away from
   any;
31 A greyhound,
   A male goat also,
   And a king *whose* troops *are*
   with him.

32 If you have been foolish in
   exalting yourself,
   Or if you have devised evil,
   put your hand on *your*
   mouth.

STEP 4

33 For *as* the churning of milk
   produces butter,
   And *as* wringing the nose
   produces blood,
   So the forcing of wrath
   produces strife.

STEP 4

Made a searching and fearless moral inventory of ourselves.

Proverbs 30:11, 12

While it is very difficult for some people to accept the role parents have played in contributing to their dependencies, others of us need to take the words of Proverbs 30:11, 12 seriously to heart. If we have trouble accepting responsibility for our actions and attitudes, we may tend to see ourselves only as innocent victims forced into wrong choices and habits by the circumstances of our childhoods. We may believe we are simply prisoners of dysfunctional homes and an unfeeling society. If this seems to sum up your attitude about life, beware! Such a mind-set leads to hopelessness, bitterness, and despair. The scripture strongly emphasizes that every person has the ability to make moral choices and that the power of God in any life can overcome even the most deeply ingrained patterns of wrong.

It also teaches us to give to God hearts of thankfulness. We may wonder what in our backgrounds is worthy of blessing and thankfulness; but if our hearts are *willing* to give thanks, God will show us.

See page 44 of the introductory material for Step 5.

Daily Encouragement

DAY 364 READING: PROVERBS 30:10–33

A Thought for the New Day: Uncontrolled anger never solved anything, but it has aggravated many a problem (v. 33). We may frighten people with our wrath for the time being, but they certainly will not love us in return. We may force people to do our will, but their hearts will remain unchanged toward us or toward righteousness. Only God can change hearts. (*Turn to page 831.*)

Words from a King's Mother

31 The words of King Lemuel, the utterance which his mother taught him:

2 What, my son?
And what, son of my womb?
And what, son of my vows?

3 Do not give your strength to women,
Nor your ways to that which destroys kings.

4 *It is* not for kings, O Lemuel,
It is not for kings to drink wine,
Nor for princes intoxicating drink;

5 Lest they drink and forget the law,
And pervert the justice of all the afflicted.

6 Give strong drink to him who is perishing,
And wine to those who are bitter of heart.

7 Let him drink and forget his poverty,
And remember his misery no more.

8 Open your mouth for the speechless,
In the cause of all *who are* appointed to die.

9 Open your mouth, judge righteously,
And plead the cause of the poor and needy.

10 Who can find a virtuous woman?
For her worth *is* far above rubies.

11 The heart of her husband safely trusts her;
So he will have no lack of gain.

12 She does him good and not evil
All the days of her life.

13 She seeks wool and flax,
And willingly works with her hands.

14 She is like the merchant ships,
She brings her food from afar.

15 She also rises while it is yet night,
And provides food for her household,
And a portion for her maidservants.

16 She considers a field and buys it;
From her profits she plants a vineyard.

17 She girds herself with strength,
And strengthens her arms.

18 She perceives that her merchandise *is* good,
And her lamp does not go out by night.

19 She stretches out her hands to the distaff,
And her hand holds the spindle.

20 She extends her hand to the poor,
Yes, she reaches out her hands to the needy.

21 She is not afraid of snow for her household,
For all her household *is* clothed with scarlet.

22 She makes tapestry for herself;
Her clothing *is* fine linen and purple.

23 Her husband is known in the gates,
When he sits among the elders of the land.

24 She makes linen garments and sells *them*,
And supplies sashes for the merchants.

25 Strength and honor *are* her clothing;
She shall rejoice in time to come.

26 She opens her mouth with wisdom,
And on her tongue *is* the law of kindness.

27 She watches over the ways of her household,
And does not eat the bread of idleness.

28 Her children rise up and call her blessed;

STEP
12

STEP 12

*Having had a spiritual awakening as the result of these steps,
we tried to carry this message to others,
and to practice these principles in all our affairs.*

Proverbs 31:26–31

As Proverbs 31:26–31 points out, parental influence is projected in three ways: by words, by actions, and by attitudes.

When we are fully surrendered to God and His will for us, those means will communicate a godly life-style: Our words will be filled with the wisdom and kindness described in verse 26, because we are daily meditating on God's Word and seeking Him in prayer. Our actions will reflect caring and the inclination to do what needs to be done (vv. 27, 28) as we seek to bring honor to the Lord and security to those around us. Our attitude of fearing the Lord (that is, trusting, loving, and honoring Him, v. 30) will have the greatest impact of all in changing lives. In fact, our attitude becomes the message we carry to others by our words and our deeds.

As we practice Step 12 as a regular part of our lives, we can, with God's help, embody the ideal given us in Proverbs 31.

This is your last Step 12 meditation.

Daily Encouragement

DAY 365 READING: PROVERBS 31:1–31

A Thought for the New Day: The words of verse 9 were given to a king, but they apply just as well to you and me. We each have a charge from the Lord to make fair decisions ("judge righteously") and not to serve our own whims or personal interest. Self-vindication and self-promotion are natural instincts; but as Christians we have no need to justify ourselves, because God has promised to be our Justifier. He watches over all our ways for our good.

Her husband *also*, and he praises her:

29 "Many daughters have done well,
But you excel them all."

30 Charm *is* deceitful and beauty *is* vain,
But a woman *who* fears the LORD, she shall be praised.

31 Give her of the fruit of her hands,
And let her own works praise her in the gates.

About the New King James Version

Purpose

In the Preface to the 1611 edition, the translators of the Authorized King James Version state that it was not their purpose "to make a new translation . . . but to make a good one better." Indebted to the earlier work of William Tyndale and others, they saw their best contribution to consist in revising and enhancing the excellence of the English versions which had sprung from the Reformation of the sixteenth century.

After nearly four hundred years, the King James is still deeply revered among English-speaking peoples throughout the world. This is in part due to the majesty of the form of the work, but also because it has been the mainspring of the religion, language, and legal foundations of our civilization. For these reasons the publishers have followed the method of the original translators, thus unlocking for today's readers the spiritual treasures found especially in the Authorized Version of the Holy Scriptures.

The 1611 scholars understood that a genuinely worshipful form is appropriate to the expression of divine matters. They accordingly disciplined their talents to render not only well-chosen English words appropriate to their time, but also a graceful, often musical arrangement of language which has stirred the hearts of Bible readers through the years. The translators and editors of the present edition, while sensitive to the late twentieth-century English idiom, and while making precise comparisons with the Hebrew and Greek texts, have similarly exercised special care to maintain the lyrical quality which is a notable characteristic of the Authorized Version.

English usage has undergone profound change since the first publication of the King James edition. This has created a growing difficulty for readers of our time, although students of the Bible still applaud the reverence of attitude which is timeless in the Authorized Version. In 1786 the Catholic scholar, Alexander Geddes, said of the King James, "If accuracy and strictest attention to the letter of the text be supposed to constitute an excellent version, this is of all versions the most excellent." George Bernard Shaw became a literary legend in our century because of his severe and often humorous criticisms of our most cherished values. Surprisingly, however, Shaw pays the following tribute to the scholars commissioned by King James: "The translation was extraordinarily well done because to the translators what they were translating was not merely a curious collection of ancient books written by different authors in different stages of culture, but the Word of God divinely revealed through His chosen and expressly inspired scribes. In this conviction they carried out their work with boundless reverence and care and achieved a beautifully artistic result." History agrees with these estimates. Therefore, in unveiling the treasured sublimity of form in the traditional English Bible, scrupulous care has been taken in the present edition to honor and preserve the work of precision which is also the legacy of the original translators. This purpose is achieved largely by careful integration of present-day vocabulary, punctuation, and syntax wherever obscurity exists. Words representing ancient objects, such as *chariot* and *phylacteries*, have no modern substitutes and are necessarily retained.

Paraphrasing has been avoided as a common method of solution to difficulties of translation in the New King James Version. Where new translation has been appropriate, the most precise reproduction of the original has been sought by considering the history, usage, and etymology relating to each text. In these cases, to maintain the integrity of King James diction, words are employed which are already part of the general vocabulary of the 1611 version, when they are agreeable to the context under consideration.

The Style

A special feature of the New King James Version is its conformity to the thought-flow of the 1611 version. The reader discovers that the sequence and identity of words, phrases, and clauses of the new edition, while much clearer, are so close to the traditional that there is remarkable ease in listening to the public reading of either edition while following with the other.

King James doctrinal and theological terms are generally familiar to English-speaking peoples. Such terms have been retained except where the original language indicates the need for clarification.

Readers of the Authorized Version will immediately be struck by the absence of several pronouns: *thee, thou,* and *ye* are replaced by the simple *you,* while *your* and *yours* are substituted for *thy* and *thine* as applicable. *Thee, thou, thy,* and *thine* were once forms of address to express a special relationship to human as well as divine persons. These pronouns are no longer part of our language. However, reverence for God in the present work is preserved by capitalizing pronouns, including *You, Your,* and *Yours,* which refer to Him.

In addition to the pronoun usages of the seventeenth century, the *-eth* and *-est* verb endings so familiar in the earlier King James editions are now obsolete. Unless a speaker is schooled in the peculiar verb endings, there is common difficulty in selecting the correct form to be used with a given subject of the verb in vocal prayer. For example, should we use *love, loveth,* or *lovest? do, doeth, doest,* or *dost? have, hath,* or *hast?* Because of such problems, contemporary English usage has been substituted for the previous verb endings.

Throughout their investigations, the publishers have observed that the real character of the Authorized Version does not reside in its archaic pronouns or verbs or other grammatical forms of the seventeenth century but rather in the care taken by its scholars to impart the letter and spirit of the original text in a stately and reverent cadence.

The Format

The format of the New King James Version is designed to enhance the intrinsic characteristics of vividness and devotion in the Holy Scriptures:

- Page headings assist the reader to identify topics and transitions in the biblical content.
- Oblique typeface in the New Testament indicates a quotation from the Old Testament.
- Verse numbers in bold type indicate the beginning of a paragraph.
- Poetry is structured as contemporary verse to enhance the original poetic beauty of the passage.
- The covenant name of God was usually translated from the Hebrew as "Lord" (using capital letters as shown) in the King James Old Testament. This excellent tradition is maintained. Wherever this name is quoted in the New Testament, the name is likewise capitalized.
- Words in *italics* indicate the use of additional English words where expressions in the original language require clarification, the same method practiced throughout the history of the King James Version.

In faithfulness to our readers, it has seemed consistent with our task to cooperate with competent scholars who are governed by the first principle of divine authorship of the Holy Scriptures, as the Bible itself attests. Therefore, all participating scholars have signed a document of subscription to the plenary and verbal inspiration of the original autographs of the Bible.

New Testament

There is more manuscript support for the New Testament than for any other body of ancient literature. Over five thousand Greek, eight thousand Latin, and many more manuscripts in other languages attest to the integrity of the New Testament.

There is only one basic New Testament used by Protestants, Roman Catholics, and Orthodox, by conservatives and liberals. Minor variations in hand copying have appeared through the centuries, before mechanical printing began in A.D. 1450.

Some variations exist in the spelling of Greek words, in word order, and in similar details. These ordinarily do not show up in translation and do not affect the sense of the text.

Other manuscript differences, regarding the omission or inclusion of a word or clause, and two paragraphs in the Gospels, should not overshadow the overwhelming degree of *agreement* which exists among the ancient records. Bible readers may be assured that the most important differences in the English New Testament of today are due, not to manuscript divergence, but to the way in which translators view the task of translation: How literally should the text be rendered? How does the translator view the matter of biblical inspiration? Does the translator adopt a paraphrase when a literal rendering would be quite clear and more to the point?

The New King James Version, following the historic precedent of the Authorized Version, maintains a literal approach to translation, except where the idiom of the original language is not readily understood in our tongue. The manuscript preferences cited in many contemporary translations of the New Testament are due to recent reliance on a relatively few manuscripts discovered in the late nineteenth and early twentieth centuries. Dependence on these manuscripts, especially two, the Sinaitic and Vatican manuscripts, is due to the greater age of these documents. However, in spite of their age, some scholars have reasons to doubt their faithfulness to the autographs, since they often disagree with one another and show other signs of unreliability. The Greek text obtained by using these sources and related papyri is known as the Alexandrian text.

On the other hand, the great majority of existing manuscripts are in substantial agreement. Even though many are late, and none are earlier than the fifth century, most of their readings are verified by ancient papyri, ancient versions, and quotations in the writings of the early church fathers. This large body of manuscripts is the source of the Greek text underlying the King James Bible. It is the Greek text used by Greek-speaking churches for many centuries, presently known as the Textus Receptus, or Received Text, of the New Testament.

Since the latter part of the nineteenth century the theory has been held by some scholars that this traditional text of the New Testament had been officially edited by the fourth-century church. Recent studies have caused significant changes in this view, and a growing number of scholars now regard the Received Text as far more reliable than previously thought. In light of these developments, and with the knowledge that most textual variants have no practical effect on translation, the New King James New Testament has been based on this Received Text, thus perpetuating the tradition begun by William Tyndale in 1525 and continued by the 1611 translators in rendering the Authorized Version.

Readers may be assured that textual debate does not affect one in a thousand words of the Greek New Testament. Furthermore, no established doctrine is called into question by any doubts about this or that text. The Christian can approach the New Testament with confidence.

Psalms and Proverbs

The devotional quality imparted to the Scriptures by the 1611 scholars is especially apparent in the poetic and prophetic books. As an aid to devotional reading, *Serenity for Every Day* includes Psalms and Proverbs cast in the form of modern English verse. These treasured volumes of poetry and wisdom are presented in contemporary English while preserving the literary qualities and precise sense of the original Hebrew.

Like their 1611 predecessors, these editions of Psalms and Proverbs are translated from the Masoretic text. This is the traditional text used for over a thousand years in Hebrew congregations.

In closing, let readers be encouraged to approach the Scriptures "not as the word of men, but as it is in truth, the word of God, which also effectively works in you who believe" (1 Thess. 2:13). The same Holy Spirit who originated the Scriptures must also make them clear to the reader, for the truths they contain "are spiritually discerned" (1 Cor. 2:14). It is through the work of the Spirit of life that the Word of life accomplishes its purpose in human hearts and minds. May God teach us His life-giving truth as we submit to Him, that He alone may be glorified.

—The Publishers